INTERNATIONAL TRADE LAW

In today's globalised world, an understanding of international trade is essential for those studying and practising law, business, banking and finance. *International Trade Law* offers a comprehensive and informed analysis of the complexities of an international sale transaction through case law, policy documents, legislation, international conventions and rules adopted by international organisations such as the ICC. Focusing on international sales of goods and the various contractual relations that arise as a result of the sale transaction, this book considers and discusses:

- Standard trade terms, the Convention on International Sales of Goods 1980 and the UNIDROIT Principles for International Commercial Contracts 2004;
- Issues relating to E-Commerce including electronic transport documents, especially electronic bills of lading;
- International transportation of cargo, both unimodal (sea, air, land and rail) and multimodal, the various conventions affecting such transportation and the new convention (Rotterdam Rules) drafted by the UNCITRAL and CMI;
- Insurance and payment mechanisms, in particular letters of credit and the recently adopted UCP 600;
- Dispute resolution including issues of jurisdiction, applicable law, arbitration and mediation;
- Corruption as a major challenge to conducting business and the various anti-corruption conventions, in particular the OECD Anti-Bribery Convention 1997 and the UN Convention Against Corruption 2003.

Accessible to students encountering this often challenging area of the law for the first time, *International Trade Law* clarifies a range of topics through tables and diagrams, and directs the reader to relevant further reading, online resources, and journal articles throughout.

Indira Carr is Professor of Law at the University of Surrey.

INTERNATIONAL TRADE LAW

Fourth Edition

Indira Carr
MA (Delhi), BPhil (Liverpool), LLM, PhD (Exeter)
Professor of Law
University of Surrey

with contributions on Private
International Law by
Peter Stone
MA, LLB (Cantab), Barrister (Middle Temple)
Professor of Law
University of Essex

 Routledge·Cavendish
Taylor & Francis Group
LONDON AND NEW YORK

Fourth edition published 2010
by Routledge-Cavendish
2 Park Square, Milton Park, Abingdon, Oxon OX14 4RN

Simultaneously published in the USA and Canada
by Routledge-Cavendish
711 Third Avenue, New York, NY 10017 (8th Floor)

Routledge-Cavendish is an imprint of the Taylor & Francis Group, an informa business

© 1995, 2010 Indira Carr

Previous editions published by Cavendish Publishing Limited
First edition 1995
Second edition 1999
Third edition 2005

Typeset in Palatino by
RefineCatch Limited, Bungay, Suffolk
Printed and bound in Great Britain by
TJ International, Padstow, Cornwall

British Library Cataloguing in Publication Data
A catalogue record for this book is available from the British Library

Library of Congress Cataloging in Publication Data
Carr, Indira
International trade law / Indira Carr; with contributions on private international law
by Peter Stone – 4th ed.
p. cm.
Foreign trade regulation–Great Britain.   I. Stone, Peter, 1947–   II. Title.
KD2460.C37 2010
343.41'087–dc22
2009011535

ISBN10: 0–415–45842–0 (hbk)
ISBN10: 0–415–45843–9 (pbk)
ISBN10: 0–203–87254–1 (eBook)

ISBN13: 978–0–415–45842–9 (hbk)
ISBN13: 978–0–415–45843–6 (pbk)
ISBN13: 978–0–203–87254–3 (eBook)

In fond memory of my parents

Rajeswari Mahalingam
(10 October 1931 to 21 December 2000)

Gopal Mahalingam
(16 June 1925 to 1 December 2002)

PREFACE

This new fourth edition of the book consists of six Parts (Part I: International Sales of Goods, Part II: Regulating the Electronic Commerce Environment, Part III: Transportation of Cargo, Part IV: Financing and Insurance, Part V: Dispute Resolution, and Part VI: Corruption). It aims to provide a comprehensive and informed appreciation of the complexities of an international sale transaction. As with the earlier editions, this revised edition focuses on CIF and FOB contracts for the international sale of goods, and the various contractual relationships that arise as a result of meeting those obligations from transportation through to insurance.

Part I, besides examining standard trade terms, includes a chapter on the Convention on the International Sale of Goods 1980 (popularly known as the 'Vienna Convention') due to its worldwide impact. Since electronic communications are an inevitable part of modern day commerce, Part II focuses on the regulation of the electronic commerce environment by examining the various European and legal instruments relating to electronic commerce and electronic signatures. Part III on transportation covers all the different modes of international carriage of goods including multimodal transportation. One of its chapters is devoted to the Hamburg Rules and the recently adopted Rotterdam Rules. Part IV examines insurance and financial aspects of an international sale transaction. Part IV on dispute resolution covers issues of jurisdiction and applicable law along with arbitration and mediation as a form of dispute resolution. I would like to particularly thank Professor Peter Stone of the University of Essex for writing Chapters 16, 17 and 18 of Part V. Part VI on corruption is new to this edition. Payment of bribes to foreign public officials to secure licences and contracts is a common problem in the world of international business, but it is only in the last ten years or so that the international community has taken concerted action to combat corruption through the adoption of regional and international conventions. This Part concentrates on the anti-bribery convention drafted by the Organisation for Economic Co-operation and Development and the anti-corruption convention drafted by the United Nations. Throughout the book references are made to cases, international developments in the form of conventions, model laws and rules. Each Chapter also includes a suggested reading list. Wherever possible, tables and diagrams are included to aid understanding.

This book does not include any legislative or other materials since these are readily available in Carr, I and Kidner, R, *International Trade Law Statutes and Conventions* (6th edn, 2010), published by Routledge. The reader is also referred throughout to website addresses where they can access the relevant legislation. The appendices section in this book is therefore limited and includes those standard forms (e.g., the FIATA Multimodal Bill of Lading, and the GENCON charterparty form) which are not included in *International Trade Law Statutes and Conventions*.

It is hoped that this book will be used by undergraduate and postgraduate law students following international trade law or international commercial law courses and students from other disciplines such as business studies, export management, banking and finance.

The writing of an academic book involves the support of a great many – colleagues, friends, family, students, well-wishers and the publication team. I am thankful to all for their contributions. I am greatly indebted to Brian Carr for his constant support and encouragement.

The law is stated on the basis of material available to me on 1 February 2009.

Indira Carr
Oxshott
March 2009

CONTENTS

PART II REGULATING THE ELECTRONIC COMMERCE ENVIRONMENT

PART V DISPUTE RESOLUTION

16 CIVIL JURISDICTION — 517

17 CHOICE OF LAW — 563

APPENDICES

TABLE OF CASES

TABLE OF STATUTES

TABLE OF STATUTORY INSTRUMENTS

TABLE OF EUROPEAN LEGISLATION

TABLE OF OTHER LEGISLATION AND
OTHER MATERIALS

TABLE OF ABBREVIATIONS

AAA	American Arbitration Association
ACDC	Australian Commercial Disputes Centre
ACICA	Australian Centre for International Commercial Arbitration
ADR	alternative dispute resolution
ADR Rules	ICC ADR Rules, ICC Publication 809
Amended version	Warsaw Convention as amended by the Hague Protocol 1955
BALTIME	Baltic and International Maritime Conference Uniform Time Charter
BEA	Bills of Exchange Act 1882
BIFA	British International Freight Association
BIMCO	Baltic and International Maritime Council
C&F	cost and freight
CBI	Confederation of British Industries
CEDR	Centre for Dispute Resolution
CEFIC	Conseil Européen des Fédérations l'Industrie Chimique
CIF	cost, insurance, freight
cif & c&t	cost, insurance, freight and commission and interest
cif & e	cost, insurance, freight and exchange
cif & c	cost, insurance, freight and commission
CIM Rules	Uniform Rules Concerning the Contract for the International Carriage of Goods by Rail
CIP	carriage and insurance paid to
CISG	Convention on International Sales of Goods 1980
CMA	Computer Misuse Act 1990
CMI	Comité Maritime International
CMI Rules	CMI Rules for Electronic Bills of Lading 1990
CMR	Convention on the International Carriage of Goods by Road 1956
COD	cash on delivery
COE Convention	Convention on Cybercrime 2003
Conditions	Standard Trading Conditions 2000b
COTIF	Convention Internationale sur le Transport de Marchandises par chemin de fer
CPT	carriage paid to
DAF	delivered at frontier
DDP	delivered duty paid
DDU	delivered duty unpaid
DEQ	delivered ex quay

DES	delivered ex ship
DTI	Department of Trade and Industry
EC Model Law	UNCITRAL Model Law on Electronic Commerce 1996
ECE	United Nations Economic Commission for Europe
ECHR	European Convention on Human Rights 1950
E-commerce	electronic commerce
E-Commerce Directive	Directive 2000/31/EC on Certain Legal Aspects of Information Society Services in Particular Electronic Commerce in the Internal Market
EDI	electronic data interchange
EDIFACT	United Nations Electronic Data Interchange for Administration, Commerce and Transport
ES Directive	Directive 1999/93/EC on a Community Framework for Electronic Signatures
ES Model Law	UNCITRAL Model Law on Electronic Signatures 2001
eUCP	Electronic Transmission Supplement Uniform Customs and Practices for Documents Credits
Factoring Convention	UNIDROIT Convention on International Factoring 1988
FAS	free alongside ship
FATF	Financial Action Task Force
FCA	free carrier
FCPA	Foreign Corrupt Practices Act
FERTICON	Chamber of Shipping Fertilisers Charter
FIATA	International Federation of Freight Forwarders Associations
FIATA Bill	FIATA Negotiable Multimodal Transport Bill of Lading
FOB	free on board
FOBs	FOB stowed
FOBST	FOB stowed and trimmed
FOBT	FOB trimmed
FOR	free on rail
FOSFA	Federation of Oils, Seeds and Fats Associations
FOT	free on truck
GAFTA	Grain and Feed Association
GAMA	Global Arbitration and Mediation Association
GATT	General Agreement on Tariffs and Trade
Guide	Guide to Enactment of the UNCITRAL Model Law on Electronic Commerce
GUIDEC	General Usage for International Digitally Ensured Commerce
Hague Rules	Brussels International Convention for the Unification of Certain Rules Relating to Bills of Lading, Brussels, 1924

Hamburg Rules	Convention on the International Carriage of Goods by Sea, Hamburg, 1978
ICAO	International Civil Aviation Organization
ICC	International Chamber of Commerce
ICSID	International Centre for Settlement of Investment Disputes
IETF	Internet Engineering Task Force
IFF 1984	Institute of Freight Forwarders Conditions 1984
ILA	International Law Association
INCOTERMS	International Rules for the Interpretation of Trade Terms
Instrument	Preliminary Draft Instrument on the Carriage of Goods by Sea
INTERTANKO	International Association of Independent Tanker Owners
ISBP	International Standard Banking Practice
ISO	International Standards Organisation
ISP 98	International Standby Practices 1998
ISPs	Internet Service Providers
IT	information technology
LCIA	London Court of International Arbitration
Legislative Provisions	UNCITRAL Model Law on International Commercial Conciliation 2002
LJ	Law Journal
LR	Law Review
Montreal Convention	Montreal Convention 1999
Montreal4	Montreal Additional Protocol No 4, 1995
MT Convention	United Nations Convention on International Multimodal Transport of Goods 1980
NAI	Nederland Arbitrage Instituut
New York Convention	New York Convention on the Recognition and Enforcement of Foreign Arbitral Awards 1958
NORGRAIN 89	North American grain charterparty issued by the Association of Shipbrokers and Agents (USA) Inc
NYPE	New York Produce Exchange
ODETTE	Organisation for Data Exchange by Teletransmission in Europe
OECD	Organisation for Economic Co-operation and Development
OREVOY	Baltic and International Maritime Conference standard ore charterparty
OTIF	Inter-governmental Organisation for International Carriage by Rail
Ottawa Convention	UNIDROIT Convention on International Factoring
PACE	Police and Criminal Evidence Act 1984

PGP	Pretty Good Privacy
PIN	Personal Identification Numbers
ppi	policy proof of interest
R89(9)	Recommendation 89(9) on Computer Related Crime
RCCEB	Rules of Conduct to Combat Extortion and Bribery
Receivables Convention	UN Convention on the Assignment of Receivables in International Trade 2001
Regulation	EC Regulation 44/2001 on Jurisdiction and the Recognition and Enforcement of Judgments in Civil and Commercial Matters
RIP	Regulation of Investigatory Powers Act 2000
Rome Convention	EC Convention on the Law Applicable to Contractual Obligations
ro-ro	roll on, roll off
Rotterdam Rules	UN Convention on Contracts for the International Carriage of Goods Wholly or Partly by Sea
SDR	Special Drawing Right
SEC	Securities and Exchange Commission
SFO	British Serious Fraud Office
SG policy	Ships and goods policy
SITPRO	Simplification of International Trade Procedures
SPs	States Parties
SSL	Secure Sockets Layer
Standby Convention	United Nations Convention on Independent Guarantees and Standby Letters of Credit 1995
TANKERVOY 87	Tanker voyage charterparty 1987
TI	Transparency International
UCP	Uniform Customs and Practice for Documentary Credits 500
ULFIS	Uniform Law on the Formation of International Sales
ULIS	Uniform Law on International Sales
UN	United Nations
UN/EDIFACT	United Nations Electronic Data Interchange for Administration, Commerce and Transport
Unamended version	Warsaw Convention 1929
UNCID	Uniform Rules of Conduct for Interchange of Trade Data by Teletransmission 1987
UNCITRAL	United Nations Commission on International Trade Law
UNCITRAL Convention	UN Convention on International Bills of Exchange and International Promissory Notes 1988
UNCITRAL Rules	UNCITRAL Conciliation Rules 1980
UNCTAD	United Nations Conference on Trade and Development

UNCTAD/ICC	Rules for Multimodal Transport Documents 1992
UNECE	United Nations Economic Commission for Europe
UNESCO	United Nations Educational, Scientific and Cultural Organization
UNIDROIT	International Institute for the Unification of Private Law
UNODC	United Nations Office on Drugs and Crime
URC	ICC's Uniform Rules for Collections
URDG	Uniform Rules for Demand Guarantees
Vienna Convention	Convention on International Sales of Goods 1980
WIPO	World Intellectual Property Organisation
WTO	World Trade Organization

INTRODUCTION

Free trade among nations is largely seen as the key to economic growth,[1] peace and better standards of living, leading to a happier state of human existence at a global level.[2] The General Agreement on Tariffs and Trade (GATT) 1947, borne out of the cornucopia of horrors that the world witnessed in the 1930s and 1940s, enshrined the philosophy of free trade using the principles of non-discrimination[3] (also known as Most Favoured Nation obligation) and the elimination of quantitative restrictions.[4] This philosophy of free trade continues to this day in the form of GATT 1994.[5] The gradual growth in international trade since the 1950s is largely due to the influence of GATT on the world stage, and it seems that this growth is set to continue. Developing countries like Brazil, China and India have emerged as key players in the provision of manufactured goods and services on the international scene and are setting a trend for other developing nations to follow. The philosophy of free trade, however, has not gone unchallenged. Over time, the world has become more aware of the global effects of environmental degradation, and the exploitation of the economically disadvantaged and the young by commercial enterprises. Social and ethical issues in the context of trade have taken on a new meaning and non-governmental organisations have successfully harnessed citizens to question the role of the World Trade Organization (WTO) and the philosophy of free trade as enshrined in GATT 1994, so much so that there is widespread agreement that trade needs to acquire a human face.[6]

Of course, of itself, a regulatory framework that promotes free trade is insufficient to promote growth in trade. It needs to be backed by adequate infrastructures in sectors that affect trade such as transportation, banking, marketing and communication. Equally, the legal framework, which affects the rights and obligations of the parties entering into business transactions at the international level, needs to be clear and certain. Lack of legal certainty has the potential to act as an impediment to trade. After all, the parties would wish to know the nature and extent of the obligations they undertake and the remedies available to them should they breach the contractual terms. Given the plurality of legal systems and the variations in liability schemes, harmonisation through international conventions is widely seen as the best option of imparting certainty to the legal questions that arise in the context of international commercial transactions. International organisations such as the United Nations

---

1   This view owes much to the work of Adam Smith (*An Inquiry Into the Nature and Causes of the Wealth of Nations*, 1776, Stahn and Caldwell) and David Ricardo (*On the Principle of Political Economy and Taxation*, 1817, John Murray).

2   There are trade theorists who think that free trade does not provide the best solution in economic terms. Protectionism and unfair trade practice are seen as providing greater economic benefit to a country (see Krugman, 'Increasing returns, monopolistic competition and international trade' (1979) 9(4) Journal of International Economics 467).

3   The principle of non-discrimination requires that a contracting party should treat all contracting states alike so that where a trade advantage has been contracted by one contracting party to another, that advantage should be granted equally to all other contracting parties. Also, no discrimination should be made between imported products and domestically produced like products.

4   Refers to quotas, import/export licences or other measures.

5   Set out in Annex 1A to the World Trade Organization Agreement, it contains many of the key provisions of the GATT 1947.

6   See Bhagwati, *In Defense of Globalization*, 2004, OUP; Held and McGrew, *Globalization/Anti-Globalization*, 2002, Polity; Carr, 'Towards reconciling free trade and environment', in Eonomides, Betten, Bridge *et al* (eds), *Fundamental Values*, 2000, Hart Publishing.

Commission on International Trade Law (UNCITRAL) and the United Nations Conference on Trade and Development (UNCTAD) took on the task of addressing various legal aspects affecting an international commercial contract, such as carriage of goods, sales of goods, agency, factoring and standby letters of credit using international conventions as the preferred method for achieving the desired harmonisation. The passage of international conventions, however, is not always that smooth. Dogged by delays, diplomatic tensions, and bureaucratic measures right from the drafting and adoption stages through to the ratification and implementation stages, many international conventions, where ratified, are ratified by only a handful of states. If success is to be measured by the number of ratifications, there are only a few successful conventions. Two of these, the Convention on International Sale of Goods 1980 and the Hague-Visby Rules are examined in Chapters 2 and 8 of this book. As a response to the limited usefulness of international conventions, UNCITRAL has moved towards formulating model laws which provide a legal framework for states to adopt and adapt to suit their own needs. The Model Law on Electronic Commerce adopted by UNCITRAL is an illustration of a successful model law and is examined in Chapter 3. While doing away with the negative features of an international convention, a model law does not achieve the same level of harmonisation, thus affecting the level of legal certainty that commercial actors seek. Nevertheless, model laws do play a useful role in bringing about some degree of uniformity. While this mode seems to be the currency of the day it must be said that international conventions have not entirely lost their appeal. For instance, the recent Preliminary Draft Transport Instrument on Carriage of Goods by Sea under consideration by the Comité Maritime International (CMI) and UNCITRAL, considered in Chapter 9, is expected to be in the form of an international convention.

Alongside these organisations, the International Chamber of Commerce (ICC) also plays a dominant role in ensuring a level of harmonisation through the formulation of rules for incorporation by those engaged in international business transactions. Many of these rules are based on what the merchants or specific sectors may have adopted as standard practices over time for their own convenience.[7] The Uniform Customs and Practice for Documentary Credits (UCP), International Standard Banking Practice (ISBP) and International Rules for the Interpretation of Trade Terms (INCOTERMS) are well-known formulations emanating from the ICC. Alongside the ICC there are also other organisations, such as the International Federation of Freight Forwarders Association (FIATA), that play an important role in the harmonisation of international commercial law through the promotion and use of standard forms such as the FIATA Multimodal Transport Bill of Lading. References to rules and standard forms are to be found in many of the chapters in this book (eg, Chapters 1, 13, 14, 15, 19 and 20).

The subject of international trade can be approached from different perspectives. For instance, a study of the regulatory framework provided by the WTO and GATT 1994 and other regional agreements such as the North American Free Trade Agreement (NAFTA) or Common Market of the Southern Cone (MERCOSUR)[8] would qualify as a study of international trade. Equally, the legal incidents surrounding an international business transaction, be it sale of goods, distribution agreements or

---

7 This is frequently referred to as 'law merchant' or *lex mercatoria*.
8 Texts of both these agreements are available at www.sice.oas.org.

transfer of know-how, also form part of international trade law. In writing a book of this modest length it has been necessary to be highly selective. This book focuses on international sale of goods, use of electronic data interchange for commercial transactions, transportation of goods using different modes of transport, payment of the price and the law affecting the different methods of resolving disputes from litigation through to mediation. This book is unique in including a chapter on the international efforts to fight corruption which is a constant problem faced whilst conducting international business. The emphasis of this book is on the international. However, reference to domestic legislation is made as and where relevant. The book, divided into six parts, is comprised of 21 chapters and it would not be an exaggeration to say that each chapter in this book could easily be converted into a book of around 500 pages, at the very least.

Chapter 1 starts with an examination of the obligations of the buyer and seller under two of the most popular standard terms used in international sale contracts: CIF and FOB. Devised by merchants for their own convenience, the ICC has done a great deal in standardising and popularising trade terms through its INCOTERMS. The chapter concludes with a brief overview of other standard terms recommended for use with modes of transport other than sea. Chapter 2 focuses on the Convention on the International Sale of Goods 1980. Its wide ratification by the member states of the European Union (EU) and the United States means that it plays an important role in determining the obligations and liabilities of the seller and the buyer to an international sale of goods contract. This factor cannot be lightly dismissed and it will not be that long before the courts in the United Kingdom are called upon to interpret this convention. It also seems that the United Kingdom is likely to ratify it in the very near future.

Part II, consisting of Chapters 3 and 4, addresses the legal issues surrounding the use of electronic communication for the purposes of contracting. It considers the legislation adopted by UNCITRAL, both in relation to electronic contracting and the use of digital signatures for securing the electronic transaction. Where relevant, developments within the EU and proposals from organisations such as the ICC are also highlighted. An interesting exploration in this part is the threat posed to e-commerce by cybercrime and the attempts to combat the problem both at the domestic and international levels. Part III, consisting of nine chapters, is the longest section in this book. It deals with the different types of international transportation of cargo ranging from the unimodal (sea, air, rail and road) to a combination of modes, besides examining transport documentation, especially the bill of lading. Undoubtedly there is a surfeit of conventions affecting unimodal transportation of cargo. Part III, besides examining these conventions, also considers the initiatives by organisations such as FIATA and the ICC in harmonising rules in respect of multimodal transportation of cargo which, as yet, is not subject to the mandatory application of an international convention.

The goods sold are often subject to an insurance contract. Chapter 14 in Part IV, using marine insurance as an illustration, highlights the general principles underlying insurance contracts. Since payment for the goods is a major feature of the sale contract, Chapter 15 considers the various payment mechanisms that are available but focuses on letters of credit, described often as the life blood of commerce.

Harmonisation of international commercial law has, to some extent, been achieved through international conventions, adoption of standard forms formulated by trade associations and incorporation of rules formulated by organisations such as the ICC. Where such conventions and other legal materials exist, they are not comprehensive. Furthermore, the harmonisation is far from complete. In these circumstances, it is common for sale contracts and other associated contracts, such as the carriage contract or the letter of credit arrangement, to contain clauses in respect of the law that is to be applied to the contract and jurisdiction. They may also contain arbitration and alternative dispute resolution clauses, thus giving the opportunity for the parties to settle the dispute using mechanisms other than litigation. Chapters 16 and 17 of Part V deal respectively with the civil jurisdiction of English courts and the rules applicable by English law for determining the substantive law applicable to a contract. Chapter 18 considers the recognition in England of foreign judgments. Chapter 19 deals with arbitration as an alternative to litigation and examines arbitration in the context of the Arbitration Act 1996. The penultimate chapter deals with mediation and international development in the form of a model law from UNCITRAL.

Bribery is a constant issue faced by businesses when doing business abroad. Whilst the ICC had drawn up Rules of Conduct on Extortion and Bribery in International Business Transactions as far back as 1977, it is only since the mid 1990s that there has been a conscious shift on the part of the international community to fighting corruption through conventions aimed at harmonisation of anti-corruption laws across jurisdictions. The two conventions that have taken off in terms of the number of ratifications received are the OECD Anti-Bribery Convention and the UN Convention against Corruption and these are examined in Chapter 21.

PART I

INTERNATIONAL SALES OF GOODS

OVERVIEW

Merchants, driven by economic goals, have always spoken in a common language. A manifestation of this common language is the use of standard trade terms in cross-border trade. Chapter 1 of Part I starts off by concentrating on frequently used terms such as CIF (cost, insurance, freight) and FOB (free on board), and examines their interpretation in English law. As and where relevant, reference is made to the Sale of Goods Act 1979. The chapter then moves on to trade terms under the INCOTERMS 2000 drafted by the International Chamber of Commerce (ICC). Chapter 1 also contains useful tables listing the responsibilities of the seller and the buyer under the different trade terms.

As part of the drive towards harmonising the law relating to international sales, the 1970s witnessed the drafting of the Convention on the International Sale of Goods by the United Nations Commission of International Trade Law (UNCITRAL) which has proved, despite the compromises, to be an extremely popular convention with a growing databank of cases decided in different jurisdictions. Even though the UK is yet to ratify this convention, Chapter 2 provides a comprehensive account of this instrument adopted in 1980 for a number of reasons. First, the UK is intending to ratify this convention shortly. Secondly, given its wide ratification by important trading nations such as the US, and member states of the European Union, at some stage courts in England will be interpreting this convention – for instance, where the parties have agreed to apply the convention to their sale contract. Finally, a study of international sales law will be incomplete, regardless of whether a country has ratified the Convention on the International Sale of Goods 1980 (ie, the 'Vienna Convention') or not, due to its dominant position on the international sales law scene. It has been in force since 1988. Its wide acceptance and the resulting database of cases make the study of the Vienna Convention not only academically interesting, but practically relevant.

CHAPTER 1

STANDARD TRADE TERMS

INTRODUCTION

International sale contracts commonly contain abbreviations such as CIF (cost, insurance, freight), C&F (cost and freight), FOB (free on board) and FAS (free alongside ship). These abbreviations are trade terms which define the obligations of the seller and the buyer as regards the point of delivery, procurement of transport documents, contract of insurance, and other documents necessary for the export and import of cargo. Trade terms are largely a product of mercantile custom which have now been assimilated into English law.

Trade terms, primarily devised for mercantile convenience, over time came to be variously interpreted. CIF contracts, for instance, were often misconstrued as contracts for the delivery of goods at the port of arrival since they named the port of destination. In order to reduce misunderstandings, international organisations, such as the International Chamber of Commerce (ICC), set out to standardise the rules of interpretation of these terms. The first set of rules, known as INCOTERMS (International Rules for the Interpretation of Trade Terms), was published in 1936. Since then, the ICC has periodically introduced new terms and revised existing trade terms to accommodate new modes of transport and emerging trade practices such as electronic transmission of transport documents. The latest version was published in 2000.[1] It is understood that the ICC is currently working on a version of INCOTERMS to handle electronic presentation of documents.[2] INCOTERMS have to be specifically incorporated in the contract by the parties. Where the parties have failed to do this and the contract is governed by English law, interpretation of these trade terms in English law is relevant.

Though there are a variety of terms in common use, it is beyond the scope of this chapter to provide a full examination of them all. Instead, a lengthy discussion of CIF and FOB terms is provided since these terms are commonly used in contracts involving sea carriage and most export cargo is transported by sea. The chapter focuses largely on the interpretation of CIF and FOB terms and their variants, such as FOB with additional services, FAS and C&F, under English law,[3] before providing an outline of the rules of interpretation under INCOTERMS 2000. The chapter concludes with an overview of other trade terms contained in INCOTERMS 2000.

---

1   As the ICC itself admits, compared with the 1990 version of INCOTERMS, the 2000 version effects few changes (see Introduction to INCOTERMS). The changes are to reflect trade practice. Substantial changes are made in relation to three terms – FAS, DEQ (delivered ex quay) and FCA (free carrier). Under FAS and DEQ, customs clearance and payment of duty obligations have been changed; and in relation to FCA loading and unloading obligations. (Note that the 1990 INCOTERMS instituted important changes – firstly, the replacing of C&F with CFR (cost and freight) and the acceptability of electronic documentation.)

2   Note that the ICC has produced a supplement to the Uniform Customs and Practices for Documentary Credit which addresses electronic presentation of documents. See Chapter 15 (pp 502–3) for further on this. Attention must also be drawn to INCOTERMS 1990 which enables parties, if they agree, to use electronic equivalents of paper documents such as invoices.

3   As and where relevant reference is made to the Sale of Goods Act 1979. What is said in relation to CIF and FOB contracts under English law equally applies to most Commonwealth countries – eg, India, Australia, and Malaysia. See also Sassoon, 'Application of FOB and CIF sales in common law countries' [1981] ETL 50.

EX WORKS

Ex works is the most convenient trade term for the seller. Under an ex works sale contract, the seller undertakes to have the goods available for collection by the buyer at the seller's premises – for instance, factory, warehouse or mine. As to whether the seller is obliged to pack the goods for export or for taking delivery of the goods, this has to be determined from the terms of agreement. It is likely that the contract stipulates that the seller is to pack the goods for export at the buyer's expense.[4]

Where the parties have incorporated Ex Works INCOTERMS 2000, the seller is required to provide 'at his expense packaging ... required for the transport of the goods, to the extent that the circumstances relating to the transport (for example, modalities, destination) are made known to the seller before the contract of sale is concluded' (A9 Ex Works). This undertaking is imposed on the seller only where it is not usual for the particular trade to make the goods available unpacked.

As for carriage of cargo, insurance cover, obtaining export licences and import licences, the arrangements have to be made by the buyer. Under INCOTERMS 2000, the seller will be required to render any assistance in obtaining an export licence at the buyer's request, risk and expense. The buyer is likely to ask the seller's help where, for instance, he is unfamiliar with the bureaucratic procedures in the seller's country, or the seller is registered with the relevant authorities for obtaining an export licence.

CIF CONTRACTS

CIF is, perhaps, one of the most popular of the trade terms used in international sale contracts where sea carriage is envisaged. 'It is,' as Lord Wright observed in *Ross T Smyth and Co Ltd v TD Bailey, Son and Co*,[5] 'a type of contract which is more widely and more frequently in use than any other contract used for purposes of sea-borne commerce. An enormous number of transactions, in value amounting to untold sums, are carried out under CIF contracts' (at p 67).

What is a CIF contract?

CIF stands for cost, insurance, freight. The price of goods in CIF contracts is inclusive of freight (consideration, reward payable in respect of carriage of cargo from loading point to point of discharge) and insurance costs to the destination specified by the contract. A CIF contract, as Scrutton J said in *Arnhold Karberg v Blythe, Green, Jourdain and Co*,[6] is not a contract that goods shall arrive, but a contract to supply goods that comply with the contract of sale, and to obtain a contract for carriage and contract of insurance (at p 388).

CIF contracts are generally attractive to both seller and buyer. As far as the seller is concerned, he can charge a higher price taking into account the extra services – that is, obtaining shipping space and insurance – he provides. His margin of profit in a CIF contract could be substantially higher than in an FOB contract since he may be able to

---

4   *Commercial Fibres (Ireland) Ltd v Zabaida* [1975] 1 Lloyd's Rep 27.
5   [1940] 3 All ER 60.
6   [1915] 2 KB 379.

obtain reasonable rates for freight and insurance depending on the prevailing economic conditions. The seller usually gets paid for the goods before their arrival at destination, since payment for goods in CIF contracts often takes place when the documents (that is, invoice, insurance policy and bill of lading) are tendered to the buyer, or to the bank in the event of a documentary credit arrangement between the seller and the buyer. However, it must be noted that payment does not always take place against tender of documents. The parties may have agreed to deferred payment credit – for example, providing for payment 30 days from the date of bill of lading.[7] The attractiveness of a CIF contract, as far as the buyer is concerned, is that he does not have to undertake the task of finding shipping space or insurance, which may be all the more difficult in a foreign country due to unfamiliarity with local business practices. Of course, the buyer could appoint an agent in the country of export to undertake the tasks of obtaining shipping space and insurance cover, but this assumes that the costs of an agent can be covered, or a reliable and trustworthy agent can be found for a reasonable remuneration. The risk of any increases in transportation and insurance costs also remains with the seller. Further, the goods do not have to be paid for until the relevant documents are tendered. Once the necessary documents are acquired, he is able to sell the goods to a third party on the strength of the documents. The buyer also acquires the right to sue the carrier, under the Carriage of Goods by Sea Act 1992, with the transfer of the bill of lading.[8]

Interestingly, the use of CIF and FOB terms is closely linked to the economic climate of a country – in particular, developing countries. Where foreign currency (that is, hard currency such as US dollars, German Euros) reserve is healthy in a developing country, importing merchants do not hesitate to contract on CIF terms. Where this is not the case, they prefer FOB terms, since it will result in a saving of freight and insurance payable to the seller in hard currency under a CIF contract. Some countries, such as Colombia, Algeria, Pakistan and Iran, prohibit imports on CIF terms.[9]

Judicial definition of a CIF contract

CIF contracts have been judicially defined in a number of cases.[10] The best definition provided in modern times is perhaps that of Lord Atkinson in *Johnson v Taylor Bros*[11] who described a CIF contract as follows:

> . . . when a vendor and purchaser of goods . . . enter into a CIF contract . . . the vendor in the absence of any special provision to the contrary is bound by his contract to do [the following]. First, to make out an invoice of the goods sold. Secondly, to ship at the port of shipment goods of the description contained in the contract. Thirdly, to procure a contract of affreightment under which the goods will be delivered at the destination contemplated by the contract. Fourthly, to arrange for an insurance upon the terms current in the trade which will be available for the benefit of the buyer. Fifthly, with all reasonable despatch to send forward and tender to the buyer these shipping

---

7   See Chapter 15. See also *Vitol SA v Norelf Ltd* [1993] 2 Lloyd's Rep 301.
8   See Chapter 6, pp 190–3 below.
9   See International Union of Marine Insurance (IUMI) 1994 list. Website www.iumi.com.
10 See *Ireland v Livingstone* (1872) LR 5 HL 395; *Biddell Brothers v E Clemens Horst Co* [1911] 1 KB 934; *Ross T Smyth and Co Ltd v TD Bailey, Son and Co* [1940] All ER 60.
11 (1920) 122 LT 130.

documents, namely, the invoice, bill of lading and policy of assurance, delivery of which to the buyer is symbolic delivery of the goods purchased, placing the same at the buyer's risk and entitling the seller to payment of their price . . . if no place be named in the CIF contract for the tender of the shipping documents they must *prima facie* be tendered at the residence or the place of business of the buyer [at p 155].

The above definition is what may be called a standard CIF contract. According to Lord Atkinson's definition, the seller is required to ship goods at the port of shipment in a CIF contract. However, this is not always the case. It is possible for the seller to contract on CIF terms for goods that are already afloat.[12] This may be achieved in a number of ways. For instance:

(a) the seller may have shipped the goods prior to the sale hoping to find purchasers while the cargo is on the high seas. In other words, the ship is a floating warehouse. This is not uncommon in the oil and grain trade. Sellers prefer this mode of dealing with goods since they can take advantage of price fluctuations. It is likely that the seller in such cases has chartered a ship to transport his cargo (that is, hired the use of a vessel for named voyages or for a period of time) and obtained a number of bills of lading from the shipowner with the intention of transferring them to the purchasers;[13]

(b) the seller may have purchased the goods from a third party.[14]

The parties who have contracted on CIF terms may have varied some of the obligations undertaken by them. There may be a clause in the contract stating that the seller is to retain the risk in the goods even after payment for the goods. The general rule seems to be that where a contract is expressed to be on CIF terms, it should be construed as a CIF contract, and clauses that are repugnant to the central obligations of a CIF contract are to be disregarded. *Law and Bonar Ltd v British American Tobacco Ltd*[15] is an illustration of this approach. The contract of sale in this case was on CIF terms, but it also contained a clause stating that the risk was to remain with the sellers until actual delivery to the buyers. The clause was held to be inapplicable.

It is also possible that a contract expressed to be on CIF terms may contain clauses that suggest that the parties never intended to contract on CIF terms. In this case, the nature of the contract would change.[16] In *Comptoir d'Achat et de Vente Boerenbond Belge SA v Luis Ridder Limitada (The Julia)*,[17] the sellers (in the Argentine) sold 500 tons of rye CIF Antwerp to the buyers (in Belgium). The contract contained, amongst others, the following terms:

(a) payment was to be made in exchange for bills of lading and/or delivery order and policies and/or certificates of insurance;

---

12 *Hindley and Co Ltd v East Indian Produce Co Ltd* [1973] 2 Lloyd's Rep 515.

13 See Chapters 5 and 6.

14 *Hindley and Co Ltd v East Indian Produce Co Ltd* [1973] 2 Lloyd's Rep 515.

15 (1916) 115 LT 612.

16 This applies equally to cases where other standard terms are used. Clauses in the contract may indicate a contrary intention thus displacing the trade term expressed in the contract. See *Scottish & Newcastle International Ltd v Othon Ghalanos Ltd* [2008] 1 Lloyd's Rep 462 (a contract stating that delivery was to be 'CFR Limassol') where the Court found that all the indicia of an FOB contract were present since the contract stated that the proforma invoice and the final invoices were to show the FOB price and the buyers had agreed the freight rate with the shipping line's agents in Cyprus. See 'FOB Contracts' below.

17 [1949] 1 All ER 269.

(b) condition of the grain was to be guaranteed on arrival; and

(c) any deficiency in the weight of the arrived cargo below that stated in the bill of lading was to be paid for by the sellers.

A cargo of 1,120 tons of rye was shipped and a delivery order addressed to M/s Van Bree of Antwerp (cargo superintendents for the sellers) was sent to the buyers. Delivery orders are generally used where cargo has been shipped under one bill of lading and the buyer has bought only a part of the cargo. The delivery order requested Van Bree to release 500 tons of the cargo on arrival. The delivery order contained an endorsement by Van Bree, who undertook to honour the request. The buyers paid the price against the delivery order. The buyers, however, did not receive the cargo. While the cargo was at sea, Belgium was invaded by the Germans and the cargo re-routed to Lisbon, where it was sold. The buyers demanded the return of the money they had paid for the cargo, on the basis that there had been a total failure of performance. At first instance, it was held that there was no failure of performance, since the buyers had obtained something of commercial value – namely, the delivery order. The judgment was affirmed by the Court of Appeal with three of the judges dissenting. In the House of Lords, judgment was given for the buyers on the basis that even though the contract was expressed to be on CIF terms, it could not be construed as a CIF contract on reading all the terms of the contract, since the sellers never intended to part with property to the goods until the moment of delivery. As Lord Porter said:

> The strict form of a CIF contract may, however, be modified: a provision that a delivery order may be substituted for a bill of lading or a certificate of insurance for a policy, would not . . . make the contract concluded upon something other than on CIF terms, but in deciding whether it comes within that category or not, all the permutations and combinations of provision and circumstances must be taken into consideration. Not every contract which is expressed to be a CIF contract is such . . . The true effect of all its terms must be taken into account, though, of course, the term CIF must not be neglected . . .
>
> The object and the result of a CIF contract is to enable sellers and buyers to deal with cargoes or parcels afloat and to transfer them freely from hand to hand by giving constructive possession of the goods which are being dealt with. Undoubtedly, the practice of shipping and insuring produce in bulk is to make the process more difficult, but a ship's delivery order and a certificate of insurance transferred to or held for a buyer still leaves it possible for some, though less satisfactory, dealing with the goods whilst at sea to take place. The practice adopted between buyers and sellers in the present case renders such dealing well nigh impossible. The buyer gets neither property nor possession until the goods are delivered to him at Antwerp, and the certificate of insurance, if it endures to his benefit at all except on the journey from ship to warehouse, has never been held for or delivered to him. Indeed, it is difficult to see how a parcel is at the buyer's risk when he has neither property nor possession except in such cases . . . obtained by attornment of the bailee to him.
>
> The vital question . . . is whether the buyers paid for the documents as representing the goods or for the delivery of the goods themselves. The time and place of payment are elements to be considered but by no means conclusive of the question: such considerations may . . . indicate a payment in advance, or . . . payment postponed until the arrival of the ship, though property . . . or risk have passed to the buyer whilst the goods are still at sea . . . the whole circumstances have to be looked at and where . . . no further security beyond that contained in the original contract passed to the buyers as a result of payment, where the property and the possession remained in the sellers at Antwerp, where the sellers were to pay for the deficiency in bill of lading weight, guaranteed

condition on arrival and made themselves responsible for all averages, the true view . . .
is that it is not a CIF contract even in a modified form but a contract to deliver at
Antwerp [at pp 275–6].

The crucial question in *The Julia*[18] was whether the delivery order had imparted any
rights of control over the cargo to the buyers. In the circumstances, the delivery order
was a merchant's delivery order (an order from the merchant to his agent to release
the cargo on arrival) which did not give any property rights to the goods. Had the
delivery been a ship's delivery order, the conclusion may have been different.[19]

Further, in this case, the seller undertook to guarantee the quantity as well as the
condition of the cargo on arrival, suggesting thereby it was an arrival contract (often
called 'ex ship').[20] In other words, the contract was one for delivery of goods at the
named port. Symbolic delivery of the goods[21] had not taken place when the delivery
order was tendered to the buyers. The sellers had to refund the money paid by the
buyers.

Is a CIF contract simply a sale of documents?

Since the goods can be paid for and sold on the strength of the documents, it is
commonly said that a CIF contract is nothing more than a sale of documents. Judicial
support for this is to be found in the statement of Scrutton J in *Arnhold Karberg
v Blythe, Green, Jourdain and Co:*[22]

> . . . the key to many of the difficulties arising in CIF contracts is to keep firmly in mind
> the cardinal distinction that a CIF sale is not a sale of goods but a sale of documents
> relating to goods. It is not a contract that goods shall arrive, but a contract to ship goods
> complying with the contract of sale, to obtain, unless the contract otherwise provides,
> the ordinary contract of carriage to the place of destination, and the ordinary contract of
> insurance of the goods on that voyage, and to tender these documents against payment
> of the contract price. The buyer then has the right to claim the fulfilment of the contract
> of carriage, or, if the goods are lost or damaged, such indemnity for the loss as he
> can claim under the contract of insurance. He buys the documents, not the goods,
> and it may be that under the terms of the contracts of insurance and affreightment he
> buys no indemnity for the damage that has happened to the goods. This depends on
> what documents he is entitled to under the contract of sale. In my view, therefore, the
> relevant question will generally be not 'what at the time of declaration or tender of
> documents is the condition of the goods?' . . . but 'what at the time of tender of the
> documents, was the condition of those documents as to compliance with the contract of
> sale?' [at p 388].

The above statement, however, was expressly rejected by Bankes and Warrington LJJ
in the Court of Appeal, who said that the correct description of a CIF contract is that it
is a contract for the sale of goods to be performed by the delivery of documents (at
p 495). It may, however, be possible to find some support for Scrutton J's statement
that a CIF contract is nothing more than a sale of documents, since a number of legal
rights and liabilities attach to the documents. For instance, the buyer's obligation to

---

18   *Ibid.*
19   See 'Delivery order – a good substitution?', pp 16–17 below.
20   See 'CIF and arrival contracts', pp 31–2 below.
21   *Johnson v Taylor Bros* (1920) 122 LT 130.
22   *Arnhold Karberg and Co v Blythe, Green, Jourdain and Co* [1916] 2 KB 379.

pay against the tender of documents,[23] and the right to reject a bad tender of documents,[24] suggest that documents do play an important role in CIF contracts. Though the importance of documents cannot be denied, it should be emphasised that they assume their importance by virtue of the contract of sale. As stated by the Court of Appeal in *Arnhold Karberg*,[25] a CIF contract is a sale of goods that is performed by the delivery of the documents.

The duality of obligations of a seller in a CIF contract – namely obligations in respect of goods which are the subject matter of the contract and tender of documents covering the goods – was reiterated in *Hindley and Co Ltd v East Indian Produce Co Ltd*.[26] In this case, the sellers sold to the buyers a cargo of jute on C&F terms. The sellers bought the goods from a third party and tendered the bill of lading (obtained from the third party) to the buyers. On arrival, it was found that no goods had been shipped. The sellers submitted that they were not liable to the buyers, since a contract of sale on C&F and CIF terms was a sale of documents and performance took place with delivery of the documents. The bill of lading they had tendered appeared, on the face of it, to be regular, and on this they had also relied. Further, they did not ship the goods – they were merely parties in a string of sales and were in no way connected to events that led to the issue of a bill of lading in the absence of goods on board the ship. Kerr J, referring to passages in *Arnhold Karberg and Co v Blythe, Green, Jourdain and Co*[27] and *Biddell Brothers v E Clemens Horst Co*,[28] found for the buyers and said it is an oversimplification to perceive a CIF contract as a sale of documents. It is instead a contract for the sale of goods to be performed by the delivery of documents. He also could not see any grounds in the face of clear statements found in cases as well as textbooks for distinguishing a seller who is the shipper from one who is not. In the words of Kerr J:

> . . . it follows from all these passages – and is indeed a matter of elementary law – that a C&F or CIF contract is to be performed by the tender of documents covering goods which have been shipped either by the seller or by someone else in accordance with the terms of the contract. If no goods have in fact been shipped the sellers have not performed their obligation. I cannot see any basis for the distinction which the sellers here seek to draw between a seller who is the shipper and a seller who is not the shipper. At the date of the contract it may well be unknown which means of performance the particular seller will employ, and in an ordinary CIF or C&F contract, as in the present case, there will be nothing in the contract which restricts his choice between the alternative methods of performance [at p 518].

Duties of the seller under a CIF contract

The seller is under an obligation to ship goods that correspond to the contract description at the port of shipment. Under s 13 of the Sale of Goods Act 1979, where a sale took place by description, it was an implied condition that the goods would correspond

---

23   See *Manbre Saccharine v Corn Products Co* [1919] 1 KB 189.
24   See *Kwei Tek Chao v British Traders and Shippers Ltd* [1954] 1 All ER 779.
25   *Arnhold Karberg and Co v Blythe, Green, Jourdain and Co* [1916] 1 KB 495. See also Odeke, 'The nature of a CIF contract – is it a sale of documents or a sale of goods?' [1993] Journal of Contract Law 158.
26   [1973] 2 Lloyd's Rep 515.
27   [1916] 1 KB 495, at pp 513–14.
28   [1911] 1 KB 214, at p 220.

to that description. So, where the goods did not match the description, the buyer (regardless of whether he was dealing as a consumer or a non-consumer) could reject the goods and obtain damages.[29]

Terms relating to packaging or the date of shipment are generally regarded as part of the description of the goods. In *Manbre Saccharine Co v Corn Products*,[30] the contract was for the sale of starch in 280 lb bags. The cargo was shipped partly in 280 lb bags, and partly in 140 lb bags. The sellers argued that the packing of the goods was not a material part of the bargain. However, the court held that the packaging was a part of the description of the goods, and the sellers were in breach of shipping goods that did not correspond to the contract description:

> It is clear that such words were an essential part of the contract requirement. They constitute a portion of the description of the goods. The size of bags may be important to a purchaser in view of sub-contracts or otherwise. If the size of the bags was immaterial, I fail to see why it should have been so clearly specified in the contract. A vendor must supply goods in accordance with the contract description, and he is not entitled to say that another description will suffice for the purposes of the purchaser [at p 207].

As for time of shipment, it is regarded as part of the description of the goods. Since it is a condition, the buyer cannot only repudiate the contract, but also obtain damages. In *Bowes v Shand*,[31] the contract was for a shipment of rice from Madras, shipment to take place during March and/or April 1874. Part of the cargo was shipped in February and the rest in March. The court held that the parties had contracted to buy rice shipped during March/April and the buyers were not bound to take rice shipped during February since it was not the same article for which they had bargained. As Lord Blackburn said:

> . . . to adopt an illustration which was used a long time ago by Lord Abinger, and which always struck me as being a right one, that it is an utter fallacy, when an article is described, to say that it is anything but a warranty or a condition precedent that it should be an article of that kind, and that another article might be substituted for it. As he said, if you contract to sell peas, you cannot oblige a party to take beans. If the description of the article tendered is different in any respect it is not the article bargained for, and the other party is not bound to take it. I think in this case what the parties bargained for was rice, shipped at Madras or the coast of Madras. Equally good rice might have been shipped a little to the north or a little to the south of the coast of Madras . . . and probably equally good rice might have been shipped in February as was shipped in March, or equally good rice might have been shipped in May as was shipped in April, and I dare say equally good rice might have been put board another ship as that was put on board the *Rajah of Cochin*. But the parties have chosen, for reasons best known to themselves, to say: We bargain for rice, shipped in this particular region, at that particular time, on board that particular ship, and before the defendants can be compelled to take anything in fulfilment of that contract it must be shown not merely that it is equally good, but that it is the same article as they have bargained for – otherwise they are not bound to take it [at p 480].

The reason for regarding time of shipment as a part of the description of the goods can be explained in terms of the crucial role that time plays in mercantile contracts.

---

29 The position has changed in relation to non-consumer sales due to amendments to s 13 introduced by s 15A of the Sale and Supply of Goods Acts 1994, on which, see 'Right of rejection', pp 28–9 below.

30 [1919] 1 KB 189.

31 [1877] 2 AC 433.

Generally speaking, time, for both the seller and the buyer, is important for sorting out payment arrangements. It is also possible that time may be important for the buyer who may wish to fulfil his contractual obligations with other parties. To quote Lord Cairns:

> ... merchants are not in the habit of placing upon their contracts stipulations to which they do not attach some value and importance, and that alone might be a sufficient answer. But, if necessary, a further answer is obtained from two other considerations. It is quite obvious that merchants making contracts for the purchase of rice, contracts that oblige them to pay in a certain manner for the rice purchased, and to be ready with the funds for making that payment, may well be desirous both that the rice should be forthcoming to them not later than a certain time, and also that the rice shall not be forthcoming to them at a time earlier than it suits them to be ready with the funds for its payment ... There is still another explanation ... these contracts were made for the purpose of satisfying and fulfiling other contracts ... made with other persons, and it is at least doubtful whether ... made in another form, or a contract made without this stipulation as to the shipment during these months, would have been a fulfilment of those other contracts which they desired to be in a position to fulfil [at p 463].

Though *Bowes v Shand*[32] was decided before the Sale of Goods Act 1893, subsequent cases have acknowledged that the time of shipment is a part of the description of the goods and is within s 32 of the Sale of Goods Act.[33]

Section 13, as stated earlier, is affected by the new s 15A introduced by the Sale and Supply of Goods Act 1994. According to s 15A, where the breach is so slight that it would be unreasonable for the buyer to reject the goods, and the buyer does not deal as a consumer, the breach is not to be treated as a breach of condition, but may be treated as a breach of warranty.

As regards packaging, in some circumstances, it is possible that the breach may be trivial enough to be treated as a breach of warranty – for instance, where goods are packed in polyethylene bags of adequate strength instead of the hessian bags stipulated in the contract. As for time of shipment, it is difficult to see when a breach will be regarded as slight given that time is of the essence in most commercial contracts.

The seller may meet his obligation of shipping goods at the port of shipment in one of a number of ways. The most obvious is where he actually loads such goods at the port of shipment. Alternatively, he may allocate to the contract goods from a bulk that he has already shipped, or he may buy goods that are already afloat from a third party and allocate them to the contract.[34] It is not uncommon to find the second and third methods of allocation of cargo in the sale of commodities, such as coffee and oil, which are subject to rapid price fluctuations.

It is quite common in international sales contracts for the buyer to ask the seller to provide a notice of appropriation. Appropriation attaches the goods to the contract. The notice of appropriation, which normally identifies the goods, the quantity and name of the ship, serves a number of purposes: for example, the buyer can calculate the date of the arrival of the goods and arrange for their collection, or sub-sell them should he wish to. Since the buyer uses the notice of appropriation to perform his obligations in respect of others, the law requires that the seller comply with the terms of the notice of appropriation. The buyer is entitled to reject where there is a breach of

32 (1877) 36 LT 857; [1877] 2 AC 433.
33 See *Aron (J) and Co v Comptoir Weigmont* (1921) 37 TLR 879.
34 See *PJ van der Zijden Wildhandel NV v Tucker and Cross Ltd* [1975] 2 Lloyd's Rep 240.

the notice of appropriation requirements. In *Société Italo-Belge pour le Commerce et l'Industrie v Palm and Vegetable Oils (Malaysia) Sdn Bhd (The Post Chaser)*,[35] the contract provided that 'Declaration of ship to be made to buyers in writing as soon as possible after vessel's sailing'. The bill of lading was dated 6 December 1974 but the declaration was sent in January 1975. No protest was made by the buyer, who sold the goods to Conti. Conti sold the cargo to Lewis and Peat, Lewis and Peat to ICC and ICC to NOGA. The notice of appropriation was passed up the string to NOGA who, on 14 January, rejected it. According to Goff J, the declaration of ship:

> ... constituted an essential step in the seller's performance of his contractual obligations. It is, moreover, an important step; because, once such a declaration is made, the buyer can then appropriate goods from the ship so declared in performance of his obligations to a particular sub-buyer to whom he has already agreed to sell goods of the same contractual description. In these circumstances, since traders must wish to balance their books, it is not surprising to find the Board of Appeal stating that 'traders attach great importance to the necessity of passing on all such notices without delay', that is, normally on the day when such notice is received [at p 699].

The phrase 'as soon as possible' also indicated that speedy declaration was important. As for the lack of protest from the buyer, this was not seen by the court as giving rise to an unequivocal representation that they had waived their rights.

Once given, the seller cannot revoke the appropriation, unless the contract provides for this possibility. So, where the seller erroneously made a wrong declaration of ship, the buyer will be well within his rights to reject the cargo; for instance, where the buyer rejected the goods since the notice of appropriation declared the *Iris*, whereas the cargo was on the *Triton*.[36] The contract may provide for correction of errors on the notice of appropriation. The wording of the clause will determine the corrections allowed.[37]

The seller would fulfil his obligation to ship the goods only where they have actually been placed on board the ship. It is not sufficient if he shows that he has left the goods with the shipowner to be loaded at a later time.[38]

Duty to procure and prepare documents

The seller is under a duty to procure and prepare proper shipment documents. In the absence of express provisions regarding documents, the seller must prepare an invoice, and obtain bill(s) of lading and an insurance policy or policies. Where the contract requires documents such as pre-shipment inspection certificates, certificates of quality, or certificates of origin, the seller must obtain these.

Invoice

The seller in a CIF contract is under an obligation to tender to the buyer an invoice 'debiting the consignee with the agreed price (or the actual cost and commission, with

---

35 [1981] 2 Lloyd's Rep 695.
36 See *Grain Union SA Antwerp v Hans Larsen A/S Aalborg* (1933) 38 Com Cas 260.
37 See *Warren Import Gesellschaft, Krohn and Co v Alfred C Toepfer* [1975] 1 Lloyd's Rep 322 and *Kleinjan and Holst NV v Bremer Handelsgesellschaft MbH* [1972] 2 Lloyd's Rep 11.
38 See 'Bill of lading', pp 15–16 below.

the premiums of insurance, and freight, as the case may be), and giving him credit for the amount of the freight which he will have to pay the shipowner on actual delivery'.[39] The seller will give credit on freight to the buyer where freight is to be paid on delivery, as opposed to advance (or prepaid) freight, under the terms of the contract of carriage.[40]

Bill of lading

As for the bill of lading,[41] the seller must ensure that it is transferable so that the buyer can sell the goods during transit. He must also obtain a shipped bill of lading. A 'received for shipment' bill of lading will be insufficient, since the buyer will not know whether or not the goods are on board ship. In *Diamond Alkali v Bourgeois*,[42] the bill of lading said that the goods had been received for shipment. The court held that this was not a proper bill of lading for the purposes of a CIF contract. It was a mere receipt.

The bill of lading must be clean[43] – that is, it must not contain any reservations entered by the carrier as to the apparent condition of the goods, or packing of the goods. The reason for the insistence on a clean bill of lading is because the buyer in a CIF contract pays for the goods against the strength of the documents. A clean bill of lading strongly indicates that the goods have been received in good order by the shipowner. The shipowner does not examine the contents of the package, and it is possible that the buyer, on arrival, discovers that the goods do not answer the contract description, or are not of satisfactory quality. In this event, the buyer can always bring an action against the seller for breach of s 13 or s 14 of the Sale of Goods Act 1979. Also, where the contract is financed by documentary credit, the banks would normally insist on a clean bill.[44]

The bill of lading must cover the entire voyage – that is, from the port of shipment to the port of destination. In *Landauer and Co v Craven and Speeding Bros*,[45] 400 bales of hemp were sold CIF. The seller had the option of shipping the goods from either the Philippines or Hong Kong. The goods were shipped from the Philippines to Hong Kong where they were transferred to a new ship bound for London. The bill of lading was from Hong Kong to London, and the insurance policy from the Philippines to London. It was held that the bill of lading was not a proper bill, since the buyer could not sue for damage to the goods without a bill of lading covering the voyage from the Philippines to Hong Kong. It was argued that the insurance policy that covered the entire voyage from the Philippines to London could supplement the bill of lading. It was held that an insurance policy was insufficient, since the damage to the goods could be of a kind that was not covered by insurance.

The shipment date must be correct on the bill of lading. This is regarded as a term of major importance – that is, a condition of the contract. So, where a bill of lading

---

39   See *Ireland v Livingstone* (1872) LR 5 HL 395, at p 406.
40   See Chapters 7 and 8.
41   See Chapter 6.
42   [1921] 3 KB 443.
43   For an interesting case, see *The Galatia* [1980] 1 All ER 501.
44   See Chapters 6 and 15.
45   [1912] 2 KB 94. See also *Hansson v Hamel and Horley Ltd* [1922] 2 AC 36.

shows a wrong date through genuine error, the buyer will be able to reject the documents.[46]

Delivery order – a good substitution?

The parties may agree to substitute the bill of lading with a delivery order. Delivery orders are generally used where cargo has been shipped under one bill of lading, and the buyer has bought only part of the cargo. The question of whether the delivery order is a good substitution for a bill of lading depends on the nature of the delivery order. A delivery order that is addressed to a person in possession of the goods (generally, the shipowner) who undertakes to deliver to the buyer or order, will be regarded as a valid substitution. It is regarded as an acceptable substitute since it gives the buyer control over the goods. Where the delivery order does not enable the buyer to exercise control over the goods, it is not recognised as a good replacement for a bill of lading. So, an order addressed to a party not yet in possession of the goods is not a good substitution, since it is possible that the party to whom the order is addressed might never obtain possession of the goods – for instance, where the goods are lost. Similarly, an order to the seller's agent instructing the agent to deliver to the seller's order is not a good substitution, since the seller still retains control over the goods. In *Warren Import Gesellschaft, Krohn and Co v Internationale Graanhandel Thegra NV*,[47] the delivery order was addressed to the agents of the charterers, who were an associate company of the sellers. The buyers refused to accept the delivery orders on the basis that they were addressed to the sellers' agent, and were, therefore, not ship's delivery orders. The court held that the delivery orders were insufficient substitutions for two reasons: first, they were addressed to persons who were not yet in possession of the goods, and secondly, there was no undertaking on the part of anyone that the goods would be delivered to the buyers. In other words, there was no indication in the delivery orders that the buyers were to be placed in a position of control over the goods.

Kerr J also explained the role of delivery orders in CIF sales and the qualities they must possess in order to be effective replacements for bills of lading as follows:

> It is trite law that it is a fundamental feature of [CIF] contract, since it required the buyer to pay the price against documents . . . that he should so far as possible obtain control over the goods by means of the documents . . . where a CIF contract entitles the seller to tender delivery orders instead of bills of lading, so as to enable him to split cargoes . . . the contract should *prima facie* be so construed that these objects, although they cannot be attained in full, are nevertheless attained as far as possible. I therefore consider that an option to tender delivery orders instead of bills of lading in a CIF contract should *prima facie* be interpreted as intended to confer upon the buyer control over the goods covered by the delivery order, even though falling short of ownership, and also some rights against the person in possession of the goods, even though falling short of the rights conferred by the transfer of bills of lading. These objects can in practice be achieved in two main ways so as to overcome, so far as possible, the shortcomings of delivery orders in comparison with bills of lading, viz, they are non-transferable documents of title and that they are a mere transfer of the goods and will not transfer

---

46   See *James Finlay and Co v Kwik Hoo Tong HM* [1929] 1 KB 400. See also *Proctor & Gamble Philippine Manufacturing Corp v Becker* [1988] 2 Lloyd's Rep 21.
47   [1975] 1 Lloyd's Rep 146.

contractual rights against the carrier. First, these objects can be achieved by the person in possession being ordered by the sellers to deliver the goods to the buyer and the latter thereupon attorning to the buyer. Secondly, they can be achieved by a direct undertaking by the person in possession to deliver the goods to the buyer or to his order. In either event, the person in possession could of course effect the attornment or give the undertaking through a duly authorised agent. Both these objects can be achieved by means of documents which are loosely described as 'delivery orders', albeit in some cases loosely. On the other hand, a document which is not addressed to or issued to a person who is then in possession of the goods, or which does not contain an undertaking by the person in possession of the goods to hold the goods for, or to deliver them to, the buyer or his order, would fail to achieve an essential object of a CIF contract, even though it can also be described as a 'delivery order'. *Prima facie*, therefore, in the absence of language evidencing a contrary intention, the latter class of documents should be held to be an insufficient tender under a CIF contract [at pp 153–54].

It must be emphasised that a delivery order of the right kind will be a good substitution only where the parties have agreed to such a substitution. Where there is no agreement between the parties, the tender of a delivery order for a bill of lading, even if it imparts control over the goods to the buyer, is not a good tender, and the buyer will be able to reject the documents.

Insurance

The seller under a CIF contract must obtain insurance cover and tender the insurance documents to the buyer. In the absence of express contractual provisions, the seller must obtain a valid policy on terms that are current in the trade for the benefit of the buyer from reputable insurers for the transit contemplated by the contract, and the particular cargo. Where the seller fails to obtain insurance cover, or does not obtain adequate insurance cover, the goods will be at the risk of the seller. For instance, in *Lindon Tricotagefabrik v White and Meacham*,[48] the seller who did not obtain insurance cover for the entire transit was unsuccessful in obtaining the price of the goods when they were stolen while awaiting delivery to the buyer's correct address.

Kind of cover and amount of cover

The contract of sale might stipulate the kind of cover that the seller is to obtain. Where there are no express stipulations, the seller must obtain insurance on terms that are current in the trade. So, the question of whether he should obtain, for instance, a policy covering 'all risks' (known as 'all risks' cover) or a policy covering risks other than 'capture, seizure and detention' (known as 'free of capture, seizure and detention' cover) is a question of fact to be determined by taking into account the kind of cargo, the route of the voyage, and the practices that are accepted as usual in that particular trade. If it is usual to obtain 'all risks' cover in the trade, the seller would be in breach for not obtaining such cover[49] and the buyer would be able to reject the documents when tendered by the seller.[50]

---

48 [1975] 1 Lloyd's Rep 384.
49 See *Borthwick v Bank of New Zealand* (1900) 17 TLR 2; (1900) 6 Com Cas 1.
50 See 'Right of rejection', pp 28–9 below.

As for the amount of cover, it must be for a reasonable value of the goods. The question of what constitutes reasonable value is very much a question of fact to be calculated in terms of the value of the goods at the time of shipment. However, it is possible to stipulate that the amount of cover must include freight charges and a percentage of the expected profits.[51]

Insurance to cover subject matter of sale and entire transit

The insurance obtained by the seller must cover only those goods that have been sold by him to the buyer. In other words, the insurance must cover only those goods mentioned in the shipping documents – that is, the bills of lading. Where the seller obtains an insurance policy that covers not only the buyer's goods, but also goods belonging to others, the seller will be in breach of his obligations under a CIF contract.[52] The reason why this is regarded as a breach is that, in the event of a claim, the many rights flowing from the insurance policy could assume a complexity that may be difficult to deal with.[53]

The insurance must cover the entire transit that is envisaged by the contract of sale. Where the insurance covers only part of the voyage, the buyer will be able to reject the documents upon tender.[54]

Policy

The seller is under an obligation to tender an insurance policy under a CIF contract. Anything short of an insurance policy is insufficient to discharge the seller's obligation to tender a policy. In other words, a substitution of an insurance policy by documents containing a written statement of the existence of a policy will not be regarded as a good substitution. The reason for this strict requirement is to protect the buyer. Only insurance policies are transferable, which means that the buyer can sue the underwriter on the policy. Moreover, where there is a documentary credit arrangement, the banks would prefer an insurance policy, rather than a broker's note, or a letter indicating the existence of an insurance policy, since the policy is security if the goods are lost. So, where the goods are damaged during transit, the buyer will be able to claim from the insurer directly on the basis of the insurance policy. In *Manbre Saccharine Co Ltd v Corn Products Co Ltd*,[55] the sellers informed the buyers by letter that the cargo was covered by insurance 'in accordance with the terms of policy of insurance in our possession re shipment ex *SS Algonquin*'. The policy covered cargo other than the cargo that was the subject of the sale. The sellers argued that the letter sent to the buyers amounted to either an equitable assignment of the insurance moneys to the extent of the value of the goods sold to the buyers, or a declaration of trust to such amount in respect of these moneys. Accordingly, the letter was as good as a tender of an insurance policy. They also stated that such letters were a common practice

---

51   See *Tomvaco v Lucas; Harland and Wolff v Burstall* (1901) 84 LT 324; *Loders and Nucoline Ltd v The Bank of New Zealand* (1929) 45 TLR 203.
52   See *Hickox v Adams* (1876) 34 LT 404.
53   See *Manbre Saccharine v Corn Products Co* [1919] 1 KB 189.
54   See *Landauer and Co v Craven and Speeding Bros* [1912] 2 KB 94; *Belgian Grain and Produce v Co* (1919) 1 LIL Rep 256.
55   [1919] 1 KB 189.

amongst businessmen. The court, however, came to the conclusion that there was a vast difference between the letter and an insurance policy that was transferable under s 50(3) of the Marine Insurance Act 1906; the letter, therefore, was not an acceptable substitution.

Similarly, a certificate of insurance is not a good substitution for an insurance policy for the following reasons. First, a certificate of insurance is generally subject to the terms of the policy, which means that the buyer will not know the terms of insurance in case the goods are lost or arrive damaged. Secondly, a certificate cannot be transferred like a policy to the buyer by endorsement which means that the buyer will not have a right of action against the insurers.

The question of substituting a certificate of insurance for an insurance policy was considered in *Diamond Alkali Export Corp v Fl Bourgeois*[56] and the court came to the conclusion that it was not a good substitution. MacCardie J, without any hesitation, said:

> ... I feel that a certificate of insurance falls within a legal classification, if any, different to that of a policy of insurance. The latter is a well known document with clearly defined features. It comes within definite, established and statutory legal rights. A certificate, however, is an ambiguous thing ... No rules have been laid on it. Would the buyer sue upon the certificate or upon the original policy plus a certificate ... before the buyer can sue at all he would have to show that he is an assignee of the certificate ... In what way can he become assignee? It is vital to remember the provisions of the Marine Insurance Act 1906. Now the relevant statutory provision is s 50(3) ... In my view, the Act of 1906 deals with marine policies only. It does not, I think, cover other documents, although they may be said to be the 'business equivalent' of policies ... a document of insurance is not a good tender in England under an ordinary CIF contract unless it be an actual policy and unless it falls within the provisions of the Marine Insurance Act 1906, as to assignment [at pp 455–56].

However, it may be possible to substitute the insurance policy with a certificate of insurance, where the contract of sale expressly provides for the tender of a certificate of insurance instead of a policy, in which case the substitution would be acceptable.[57]

A related question that arises is whether the tendering of a foreign insurance policy will be regarded as a good tender. In *Malmberg v HJ Evans and Co*,[58] the sellers tendered a policy of a Swedish company which the buyers rejected on the grounds that it was a foreign insurance policy. The court held that a foreign policy valid in every respect was a good tender:

> I do not think it is the law that any objection can be taken to this policy on the ground that it is the policy of a Swedish company. It seems to me that in as much as we under our CIF contracts as sellers always provide an English policy, we are bound when we are buyers to accept as a policy to which no objection can be taken a policy issued by a company or underwriters in the country from which the goods come and in which the sellers carry on business [at p 238].

Of course, if the sellers had obtained insurance from a non-reputable Swedish insurance company, the situation would be different. It is, however, not unusual for

---

56   [1921] 3 KB 443.
57   See *Burstall v Grimsdale* (1906) 11 Com Cas 280.
58   (1924) 41 TLR 38.

contracts to include stipulations that require the sellers to obtain insurance from companies or underwriters domiciled in the UK.[59]

Licences

Depending on the laws pertaining to export and import in the exporting and importing countries respectively, it may be necessary to obtain export and import licences. The question of who is responsible for obtaining these licences may be dealt with in the contract but, in the absence of any agreement, the export licence must be obtained by the exporting party – that is, the seller – and the import licence by the importing party – that is, the buyer. In *Mitchell Cotts and Co (Middle East Ltd) v Hairco Ltd*,[60] the contract was for the purchase of goat hair. The contract was on CIF terms, payment to be made after approval of the goods at the port of arrival. The contract did not contain a term about responsibility for obtaining an import licence. On arrival, the customs authorities seized the goods. The buyers, who had already accepted the shipping documents, refused to pay for the goods. They contended that the approval was a condition precedent to the obligation to pay, and it was the sellers' duty to obtain the necessary import licence. The court held that the duty of obtaining the licence for importing goat hair was that of the buyers.

The question that naturally arises in this context is the extent of responsibility that each party has in relation to these obligations. In other words, is the obligation to obtain the licence an absolute one, or is it one of reasonable diligence? The level of responsibility depends on what the parties have agreed to. Where there is no agreement, it seems the parties must exercise reasonable care. In *Anglo-Russian Merchant Traders Ltd v Batt*,[61] the seller and buyer were both resident in England. They contracted, fully aware there was a prohibition against the export of aluminium and that a licence was required from the Russian authorities for its export. The seller was unable to obtain a licence. The court held that the seller was not liable for damages for failure to ship the cargo. He had not expressly undertaken to get the licence. There was an implied undertaking to take all reasonable steps to obtain the licence.

However, in *KC Sethia (1944) Ltd v Partabmull Rameshwar*,[62] the court found that there was no room for implying a provision that the sellers undertook to use their best endeavours in obtaining a quota. The contract was for the sale of Indian jute CIF Genoa by October 1948. The Indian Government introduced a quota system for the export of jute and the quota was to be calculated in terms of the basic year chosen by the sellers. The sellers chose 1946 as their basic year. During that year, they had not sold any jute to Italy and, therefore, could not get a quota allowing them to export jute to Italy. The sellers were unable to ship the goods. They contended that there was an implied term in the contract which placed them under an obligation of exercising due diligence to obtain the permit, which they had satisfied, and the contract should therefore be cancelled. The court held that the sellers had undertaken to get the licences, on the reasoning that, even though both parties knew that the export of jute was subject to a quota system, only the sellers knew which year they could choose for

---

59   See *Promos SA v European Grain and Shipping Ltd* [1979] 1 Lloyd's Rep 375.
60   [1943] 2 All ER 552.
61   [1917] 2 KB 679.
62   [1951] 2 Lloyd's Rep 89.

the calculation of the quota, and whether they could fulfil their contracts on the basis of the quota allowed to them. They had given the impression to the buyers that they would get the licence. Their obligation was therefore an absolute one.

Where a party undertakes to sell goods subject to the obtaining of a licence, the expectation would be one of exercising reasonable diligence to obtain a licence. The reason for this is that the use of the phrase 'subject to' indicates an element of risk.[63]

Where the seller (who has not undertaken an absolute obligation) is unable to obtain a licence despite the exercise of reasonable diligence, he will not be liable for failure to ship the goods. Of course, where the seller has not exercised reasonable care to obtain the licence, he will be liable for failure of performance.[64]

Tender of documents

As stated earlier, the seller under a CIF contract is under an obligation to tender the documents specified in the contract of sale. For instance, the contract might stipulate the tender of documents, such as a certificate of quality, and a certificate of origin. Where the documents called for in the contract are not tendered by the seller, the buyer can reject the documents. In the absence of express stipulation, the seller must tender the following documents:

(a) a bill of lading;
(b) an insurance policy;
(c) documents required by the custom; and
(d) an invoice.

Where the seller's tender is a bad tender, it may be possible for him to retender provided it is within the time limit set. In *Borrowman, Phillips and Co v Free and Hollis*,[65] the seller offered maize on board *The Charles Platt* to the buyer without shipping documents. The buyer rejected the offer on the grounds that the shipping documents were not tendered with it. The seller subsequently offered maize on board *The Maria D* with shipping documents. The buyer rejected this offer. It was argued for the buyer that, once the seller appropriated certain goods to the contract of sale, his election was irrevocable. The Court of Appeal concluded that the doctrine of election did not apply in the circumstances, since the buyer's contention was that the cargo of *The Charles Platt* was not in accordance with the contract. The subsequent tender was, therefore, good. *Borrowman v Free* is not a case that deals with retender of documents, but it is difficult to see why it cannot be applied by analogy to a case of a retender of documents as long as the seller can do so within the time limit.

When must the documents be tendered?

In the absence of express stipulation regarding the time for tender of documents to the buyer, the courts will imply that the seller must take all reasonable measures to tender

63 *KC Sethia (1944) Ltd v Partabmull Rameshwar* [1951] 2 Lloyd's Rep 89, at pp 97–8; *Peter Cassidy Seed Co Ltd v Osuustukkukauppa* IL [1957] 1 WLR 273.
64 See *Ross T Smyth and Co Ltd (Liverpool) v WN Lindsay Ltd (Leith)* [1953] 2 Lloyd's Rep 378.
65 (1878) 48 LJ QB 65. See also *Motor Oil Hellas (Corinth) Refineries SA v Shipping Corp of India (The Kanchenjunga)* [1990] 1 Lloyd's Rep 391.

them to the buyer. What is reasonable will, of course, depend on the circumstances. If the seller has received documents such as bills of lading, then he must tender these soon after as he has received them, since the bill of lading is after all the 'key to the warehouse'. Without a bill of lading, the buyer will be unable to sell the goods on to a third party, or take delivery of them himself. If the seller holds onto these documents for a length of time after their receipt, then his behaviour will be deemed unreasonable. As Brett MR stated in *Sanders v Maclean*:[66]

> ... stipulations which are inferred in mercantile contracts are always that the party will do what is mercantilely reasonable. What, then, is the contract duty which is to be imposed by implication on the seller of goods at sea with regard to the bill of lading? I quite agree that he has no right to keep the bill of lading in his pocket, and when it is said that he should do what is reasonable, it is obvious that the reasonable thing is he should make every reasonable exertion to send forward the bill of lading as soon as possible after he has destined the cargo to the particular vendee or consignee. If that be so, the question whether he has used such reasonable exertion will depend upon the particular circumstances of each case. If there is perishable cargo or one upon which heavy charges must surely be incurred, the reasonable thing for him is to make even a greater exertion than he would in the case of another cargo. That is one of the circumstances to be considered. Another circumstance would be from whence is the shipment? How near is the consignor to the ship so as to enable him to get possession of the bill of lading? (At p 337.)

Where there is express provision regarding tender of documents, then the seller must comply with the stipulation. In the event of delay in tendering the documents, the buyer will be entitled to reject them.[67]

Place of tender

The documents must be tendered, in the absence of express provision, at the buyer's place of business or residence.[68]

Seller's remedies[69]

(a) Action for price

Under s 49(1) of the Sale of Goods Act 1979, the seller can sue the buyer for the price where property in the goods has passed to the buyer and he wrongfully neglects or refuses to pay for the goods.

Other than this, the seller has a lien over the goods even if property has passed to the buyer. That is, he can retain the goods till he is paid for them. But this is possible only where he is in possession of the goods.

(b) Damages for non-acceptance

Under s 50(1) of the Sale of Goods Act 1979, the seller can sue the buyer for damages for non-acceptance where he wrongfully neglects, or refuses to pay for the goods. The measure of damages *prima facie* is the difference between the

---

66   (1883) 11 QBD 327.
67   See *Toepfer v Verheijdens Veervoeder Commissieurhandel* [1980] 1 Lloyd's Rep 143.
68   See *The Albazero* [1976] 2 Lloyd's Rep 467.
69   See also remedies under the Convention on International Sale of Goods 1980, pp 83–91.

market price and the contract price at the time the cargo ought to have been accepted. Where no time is fixed, the contract price at the time of refusal to accept the goods will be used for the purposes of calculating the damages (see s 50(3) of the Sale of Goods Act 1979).

In CIF contracts, the time for acceptance would be the time when the documents ought to have been accepted by the buyer.

(c) Other remedies

The Sale of Goods Act 1979 also provides other remedies even where property in the goods has passed. Not all are suitable in the context of international sale. First, an unpaid seller (s 38(1)) has a lien on the goods provided he is in actual possession of them (s 39(1)). In other words, he can retain the goods until the buyer pays for the goods. Section 41 lists the circumstances in which the seller can retain possession of the goods until payment. These are:

(a) where the goods have been sold without any stipulation as to credit;[70]

(b) where the goods have been sold on credit but the term of the credit has expired; or

(c) where the seller has become insolvent.

The unpaid seller loses his right of lien in the following circumstances:

(a) when he delivers the goods to a carrier or other bailee or custodier for the purposes of transmission to the buyer without reserving the right of disposal (s 19)[71] of the goods;

(b) when the buyer or his agent lawfully obtains possession of the goods;

(c) by waiver of the lien or the right of retention (s 48(1)).

In an international sale context, the right of lien is likely to be of limited use since in cases where he has contracted on terms other than 'ex works' he is likely to have handed over the goods to the carrier as required by the terms of the contract.

Section 39(1)(b) gives a further remedy to the seller to stop the goods in transit after he has parted possession with them. But this is subject to certain conditions. First, it is available only where the buyer is insolvent (s 39(1)(b)) and while they are in transit (s 44).[72] Transit for the purposes of this remedy is when the goods are delivered to the carrier, bailee or custodier for transmission to the buyer until the buyer, or his agent, takes delivery of them from the carrier, bailee or custodier (s 45(1)). Acknowledgment by the carrier that he is holding the goods for the buyer will bring the transit to an end (s 45(3)). It is possible that the buyer may have chartered a ship to carry the goods.[73] The question of whether the goods are in the possession of the master as carrier or agent will depend on the circumstances (s 45(5)).[74] Stoppage in transit is effected by seller by either taking actual possession of the goods or by giving notice (s 46(2), (3)) to the carrier, bailee or custodier who is in possession of the goods (s 46(1)).

---

70 Most international sales include some credit stipulation. See also Chapter 15.

71 Sale contracts normally include reservation of title clauses. See *Aluminium Industrie Vassen BV v Romalpa Aluminium Ltd* [1976] 1 Lloyd's Rep 443 and subsequent cases. See also Davies, *Effective Retention of Title*, 1991, Fourmat; Davies (ed), *Retention of Title Clause in Sale of Goods Contracts in Europe*, 1999, Ashgate; Wheeler, *Retention of Title Clauses: Impact and Implication*, 1988, OUP; Guest *et al* (eds), *Benjamin's Sale of Goods*, 2002, Sweet & Maxwell.

72 See also *The Tigress* (1863) 32 LJPM & A 97.

73 See Chapter 5.

74 See also s 45(2)–(4); 45(6)–(7) on duration of transit.

It must also be added that the buyer may have sold the goods on to third parties. In these circumstances, the seller will still have the right to exercise lien or stoppage in transit unless the seller has assented to that sale (s 47(1)),[75] or the document of title (for example, bill of lading) has been lawfully transferred to a third party taking in good faith and for valuable consideration (s 47(2)).[76]

Right of resale is another remedy provided by the Sale of Goods Act 1979 in s 48(2) and is available to an unpaid seller where the goods are of a perishable nature, or where he gives notice to the buyer of his intention to resell and the buyer does not pay or tender the price within a reasonable time. In the event of resale, the seller also has the right to recover from the original buyer damages for any loss occasioned by his breach of contract.

Passing of property

Under English law, in a contract for the sale of goods 'the seller agrees to transfer property in the goods to the buyer for a money consideration called the price' (s 2(1)). What is transferred is ownership or the absolute legal interest in the goods. Passing of property is the central event in a sales contract. Such a buyer who acquires goods from a 'seller' who is not an owner can recover the moneys paid on grounds of a total failure of consideration.[77]

Passing of property is not related to delivery or possession in English law such that the goods, for instance, could be on the seller's premises and property is with the buyer; or the goods could be delivered to the buyer even though the seller retains property in the goods. Due to the fragmentation of property, delivery and possession, the issue of who has property in the goods is of practical importance in the event of:

(a) insolvency. For instance, where property remains with the seller, the goods will not become part of the pool to be distributed to the buyer's creditors (according to their standing) were the buyer to become insolvent. The seller will be able to repossess the goods;

(b) loss or damage to the goods. Risk generally passes with property, unless otherwise agreed (s 20(1)), and therefore risk of loss or damage will be borne by the person who has property in the goods. However, the situation in a CIF contract is different where risk and property are not linked;[78] and

(c) claim for payment of price. If property has passed to the buyer, who refuses to take delivery of goods, the seller will be able to sue for the price (s 49(1)).[79]

The question of when property passes is to be established from ss 17–19 of the Sale of Goods Act 1979. According to s 17(1), property passes when the parties intend it to. The intention of the parties is to be gathered from the terms of the contract, the conduct of the parties and the circumstances. In an ideal world, the parties would include an express clause in respect of the passage of property. However, this is rarely the case. In the absence of an agreement between the parties, the passing of property is determined by looking to s 18, which lays down specific rules covering specific

---

75   See also *DF Mount v Jay and Jay Provisions* [1960] 1 QB 159.
76   See also *Leask v Scot Bros* (1877) 2 QBD 376.
77   *Rowland v Divall* [1923] 2 KB 500.
78   See 'Passing of risk', pp 20–7 below.
79   See 'Seller's remedies', pp 22–5 above.

situations. For example, in the case of unascertained goods, property cannot pass until there is unconditional appropriation of the goods to the contract (s 18 r 5).[80] The seller has a right to retain property in the goods till certain conditions are fulfilled, according to s 19, which states:

> Where there is a contract for the sale of specific goods, or where goods are subsequently appropriated to the contract, the seller may, by the terms of the contract or appropriation, reserve the right of disposal of the goods until certain conditions are met.

When it comes to CIF sales, there are a number of possibilities for passing property:

(a) Property could pass when goods are placed on board the ship, that is, on shipment (though this is highly unusual in CIF sales). This is possible only as long as the seller has not reserved the right of disposal. Where the seller retains the shipping documents, this may indicate that he has reserved the right of disposal. Section 19(2) gives a statutory presumption in favour of the seller. According to this provision, the seller, were he to make out the bill of lading in his name or to his order, is presumed to retain property in the goods. Being a presumption, it can be defeated. The seller is likely to retain the bill of lading as security for payment. Alternatively, he may wish to retain it in order to obtain bridging finance for the period from the time of shipment to the time of payment on delivery of documents to the buyer.[81] A seller may obtain the bill of lading to the order of the buyer. This leads to the inference that property was to pass on shipment. However, retention of the bill of lading by the seller is likely to suggest the seller intended to reserve the right of disposal.[82]

(b) Property could pass upon the transfer of documents to the buyer, and payment of the price by the buyer to the seller. In most CIF contracts, property generally passes this way.[83] The property that the buyer gets, however, is conditional property. That is, if the goods are not in conformity with the contract of sale, the property would revest in the seller.[84]

(c) Property could pass on tender of bill of lading even though the buyer has not paid for the goods since the seller has agreed to give credit to the buyer.

(d) However, where the goods form part of a bulk, under s 16, property can pass only when the goods are ascertained. So, where the buyer has paid for the goods against documents, property will not pass upon payment, but upon ascertainment of the goods. Normally, in CIF sales, this will take place at a date later than the date of payment. An unfortunate consequence of this rule is that the buyer could suffer heavy losses were the seller to become bankrupt or insolvent after payment, but before ascertainment of the goods. In *Re Wait*,[85] the buyer bought 500 tons of wheat out of a bulk of 1,000 tons of wheat on board the *SS Challenger*. The buyer paid the seller for the goods but, before the goods could be ascertained, the seller went bankrupt. The trustees in bankruptcy claimed the entire cargo on the basis of s 16. The buyer argued that property had passed in equity, even

---

80   See 'Duties of the seller under a CIF contract', pp 11–14 above.
81   *Ross T Smyth and Co Ltd v TD Bailey, Son and Co* [1940] 3 All ER 60, at p 68.
82   *The Kronprinsessan Margareta* [1921] 1 AC 486.
83   *The Glenroy* (1945) 170 LT 273; *The Miramichi* (1915) 112 LT 349; see also *The Albazero* [1977] AC 774.
84   See *Kwei Tek Chao v British Traders and Shippers Ltd* [1954] 1 All ER 779.
85   (1927) 136 LT 552.

though it may not have under the Sale of Goods Act. The court held that the question of passage of property had to be determined entirely on the basis of the statute, according to which, property had not passed to the buyer. To quote Atkin LJ:

> Without deciding the point, I think that much may be said for the proposition that an agreement for the sale of goods does not import any agreement to transfer property other than in accordance with the terms of the Code, that is, the intention of the parties to be derived from the terms of the contract, the conduct of the parties and the circumstances of the case, and unless a different intention appears from the rules set out in s 18. The Code was passed at a time when the principles of equity and equitable remedies were recognised and given effect in all our courts ... The total sum of legal relations (meaning by the word 'legal' existing in equity as well as in common law) arising out of the contract for the sale of goods may well be regarded as defined by the Code. It would have been futile in a code intended for commercial men to have created an elaborate structure of rules dealing with rights at law, if at the same time it was intended to leave, subsisting with the legal rights, equitable rights inconsistent with, more extensive, and coming into existence earlier than the rights so carefully set out in the various sections to the Code [at p 635].

The effect of s 16 in situations like *Re Wait* is extremely unjust as far as the buyer is concerned, since he is left without any remedy against the seller. One way to circumvent this inequity would be to contract out of s 16 – that is to say, the parties could agree to transfer property upon payment. This, however, is not possible, since s 16 is mandatory. In other words, the parties cannot contract out of it.

The Law Commission Report, *Sale of Goods Forming Part of a Bulk*,[86] recommended that the inequity caused by s 16 could be resolved by introducing a new rule which would allow a prepaying buyer of a specified quantity of an identified bulk to be a tenant in common of the whole.[87] The recommendations are reflected in the new ss 20A and 20B of the Sale of Goods Act 1979, introduced by the Sale of Goods Amendment Act 1995.

Passing of risk[88]

Under s 20 of the Sale of Goods Act 1979, risk passes along with property. This, however, is not true of CIF contracts. The passing of risk and the passing of property are not simultaneous. In CIF contracts, risk passes on shipment,[89] whereas property normally passes much later, when the documents are tendered to the buyer.[90] Since risk passes upon shipment, this places the buyer under an obligation to pay for the goods against a valid tender of documents. This is the case even when the goods have been lost or damaged before the tender of documents. This rule, in normal circumstances, would not be to the buyer's detriment, since the buyer can always claim for the loss from the carrier or the insurer. As stated in *Manbre Saccharine Co Ltd v Corn*

---

86 Law Com No 215 HC 807, 1993, HMSO.
87 See paras 4.1, 4.2 and 5.2.
88 See also Chapter 2, pp 81–3, for passing of risk under the Convention on International Sale of Goods 1980.
89 See 'Judicial definition of a CIF contract' above; *Law and Bonar Ltd v British American Tobacco Ltd* [1916] 2 KB 605.
90 See 'Passing of property', pp 24–6 above.

Products Co Ltd,[91] 'the purchaser in case of loss will get the documents he bargained for; and if the policy be that required by the contract, and if the loss be covered thereby, he will secure the insurance moneys. The contingency of loss is within and not outside the contemplation of the parties to a CIF contract' (at p 204).

However, where the loss or damage is due to events not covered by insurance, or is subject to exclusion clauses in the contract of carriage, the buyer will bear the loss. In *C Groom Ltd v Barber*,[92] the goods were lost before appropriation to the contract due to war. The insurance policy did not cover loss or damage due to war. There was no right of action against the carrier. The buyer, nonetheless, had to pay for the goods against the tender of documents.

Duties of the buyer

Payment against documents

As stated earlier, the tender of documents is an important event in CIF contracts. The documents represent the goods. The buyer must accept a good tender of documents, and pay for the goods upon tender of the documents. He cannot postpone payment until the arrival of the goods.[93] This is the case even where the goods are lost, or damaged prior to the tender of the documents, and the seller is aware of the loss or damage to the cargo. In *Manbre Saccharine v Corn Products*,[94] the documents were tendered to the buyers two days after a submarine sank the ship carrying the cargo. The sellers were aware of this but, nevertheless, tendered the documents. The court held that, since all the documents were in order, the sellers could tender them to the buyers, even though the goods were no longer in existence. The buyers, in this event, will look to their insurers to recoup their losses, assuming that the loss is caused by an event provided for in the cover. As McCardie J said:

> If the vendor fulfils his contract by shipping the appropriate goods in the appropriate manner, under a proper contract of carriage, and if he also obtains the proper documents for tender to the purchaser, I am unable to see how the rights or duties of either parties are affected by the loss of the ship or goods, or by knowledge of such loss by the vendor, prior to the actual tender of the documents . . . For the purchaser in case of loss will get the documents he bargained for; and if the policy be that required by the contract and, if the loss be covered thereby, he will secure the insurance moneys. The contingency of loss is within and not outside the contemplation of the parties to the CIF contract [at pp 203–04].

The payment to the seller must be in the currency agreed by the contract of sale, and any fluctuations in the currency between the conclusion of the contract and tender of the documents is at the seller's risk. The seller, however, can protect himself against currency fluctuations through express and unambiguous clauses in the contract.[95]

---

91   [1919] 1 KB 189.
92   [1915] 1 KB 316.
93   [1911] 1 KB 934, at p 955.
94   [1919] 1 KB 189.
95   *Alan (WJ) and Co Ltd v El Nasr Export and Import Co* [1972] 2 QB 189.

Buyer to name port of destination

Where several ports of destination are specified in the contract, the buyer must inform the seller of the choice of destination before the shipment is due.

Buyer to take delivery

The buyer must take delivery at the port of destination, and is responsible for the unloading charges, unless the unloading charges are included in the contract of carriage. Normally, shipping lines include the cost of unloading in the freight charges.

Import licences

The buyer is responsible for obtaining any licences required for importing the cargo, unless the parties have agreed otherwise in the contract.[96]

Buyer's remedies

Right of rejection

The buyer in a CIF contract has two distinct rights of rejection:

(a) He can reject the documents upon tender, where the seller does not tender the right documents or where the documents are incorrect. For instance, where the seller tenders a mate's receipt instead of a bill of lading, the buyer will be able to reject the documents. Likewise, where a shipment period is stipulated by the contract, and the bill of lading shows that the goods were not shipped during the period specified in the contract, the buyer will be able to reject the documents.

An inspection of the documents should be sufficient for the buyer to decide whether the statements relating to date of shipment, quantity of goods shipped, etc, are genuine or not. It may not be possible to tell on a reasonable inspection that the documents tendered are forged, but the buyer may discover that the documents are forged or contain inaccuracies subsequent to the acceptance of the goods on arrival. In these circumstances, his failure to reject the goods will not extinguish his rights in relation to the documents. In *Kwei Tek Chao v British Traders and Shippers Ltd*,[97] the sellers sold Rongalite C (a chemical) to the buyers CIF Hong Kong. The date of shipment was to be on or before 31 October. The goods were not loaded until 3 November. The bills of lading signed by the shipowners stated 'received for shipment and since shipped 31 October'. However, with the knowledge of the shipping agents, the words 'received for shipment and since' had been erased, but the sellers were unaware of this. On presentation, the documents were accepted by the buyers, who sold the goods on to the sub-purchasers. The

---

96 See 'Licences', pp 20–1 above.
97 [1954] 2 QB 459. See *Panchaud Frères SA v Establissements General Grain Co* [1970] 1 Lloyd's Rep 53 on the operation of estoppel where the buyer acts in a manner that indicates that he is not going to exercise his right to reject the documents. See also *Procter and Gamble Philippine Manufacturing Corp v Peter Cremer Gmbh & Co (The Manila)* [1988] 3 All ER 843; *Soules Caf v PT Transap of Indonesia* [1999] 1 Lloyd's Rep 917.

sub-purchasers discovered that the goods had not been shipped on 31 October, and requested cancellation of the sub-sale. The buyers, who took delivery of the goods, brought an action against the sellers for tendering inaccurate documents, and claimed return of the price or damages. Unfortunately for the buyers, the price of the chemical had fallen dramatically in the Hong Kong market. The sellers argued that, in accepting the goods, the buyers had waived the breach of contract relating to the date of shipment on the bill of lading. The court held that there were two rights of rejection. The failure to reject the goods on arrival, since they did not match the contract description, did not extinguish their right to claim damages for their loss of the right to reject the documents. As Devlin J said:

> There is not, in my judgment, one right to reject; there are two rights to reject. A right to reject is, after all, only a particular form of right to rescind the contract. Wherever there is a breach of condition, there is a right to rescind the contract and, if there are successive breaches of different conditions one after the other, each time there is a breach, there is a right to rescind ... If there is a late shipment, as there was in this case, the date of the shipment being part of the description of the goods, the seller has not put on board goods which conform to the contract description, and therefore he has broken that obligation. He has also made it impossible to send forward a bill of lading which at once conforms with the contract and states accurately the date of the shipment. Thus the same act can cause two breaches to two independent obligations [at p 480].

(b) The buyer can reject the goods on arrival if the goods do not correspond to the contract description (s 13), or are not of a satisfactory quality (s 14). However, where the breach is slight, it may be treated as a breach of warranty, according to s 15A(1) (introduced by s 4(1) of the Sale and Supply of Goods Act 1994), which means that the buyer will be unable to reject. Section 15A states:

15A(1) Where in the case of a contract of sale:

(a) the buyer would, apart from this sub-section, have the right to reject goods by reason of a breach on the part of the seller of a term implied by s 13, 14 or 15 above; but

(b) the breach is so slight that it would be unreasonable for him to reject them, then, if the buyer does not deal as a consumer, the breach is not to be treated as a breach of condition but may be treated as a breach of warranty.

The buyer must exercise his right to reject within a reasonable time, to be determined by taking into account existing circumstances. If he does not do so, he would be deemed to have accepted the tender and his remedy will lie only in damages.

Damages for failure to tender valid documents or deliver goods

Where the seller fails, or refuses, to tender valid documents or deliver goods, the buyer has the right to sue for damages for non-delivery. Under s 51(3), the measure of damages is '*prima facie* to be ascertained by the difference between the contract price and the market or current price of the goods at the time or times when they ought to have been delivered, or (if no time was fixed) then at the time of the refusal to deliver'.[98] In CIF contracts, the time when delivery is due is the time when documents

---

98 It is not unusual for the parties to a contract to include detailed clauses on calculation of damages in the event of default. For an illustration, see *Fleming and Wendeln GmbH and Co v Sanofi SA/AG* [2003] 2 Lloyd's Rep 473.

are due. After all, in CIF contracts, the documents represent the goods. In *Sharpe (C) and Co v Nosawa and Co*,[99] a cargo of peas sold CIF London, shipment in June, were not shipped. Had documents (obtained on shipment) been posted, they would have arrived in the third week of July. The cargo itself would have arrived in August. The price of Japanese peas in August was substantially higher than the price in July. The seller, who agreed there was a breach of contract, said that damages should be calculated on the basis of the difference between the contract price and the market price in July, while the buyer argued that the price in the month of August was the market price. The court came to the conclusion that, in a CIF contract, performance takes place when documents are tendered and, hence, July was the relevant month for the purposes of calculating damages. The onus is on the buyer to mitigate the damage. He would be acting reasonably were he to buy goods on the spot on the day (or during the period) he would have had delivery. Atkin J explained the issue thus:

> [The buyer's] remedies are specified in s 51 of the Sale of Goods Act 1893. His right is to place himself as nearly as possible in that position in which he would have been if the contract had been fulfilled ... could the buyers have gone into the market at the time when the contract ought to have been performed and have bought goods cif June shipment? If so, the difference of price would be the measure of damages. I am not satisfied that they could have bought 93 tons of Japanese peas CIF June shipment, although there was some evidence that they could have bought smaller parcels. The damages are to be assessed on the basis of reasonable conduct on the part of the purchaser. In the circumstances of this case, the reasonable thing for a merchant to do who could not buy the goods coming forward would be to go home into the market and buy the goods on the spot. In that way he would put himself as nearly as may be in the position as if the contract had been fulfilled, and would have got control of an equivalent amount of goods. It is true that he may incur further expense by reason of having to take up the goods at once, the cost of warehousing, insuring, etc, but that would be part of his damages. It has been suggested that he might and ought to wait until the goods would have arrived. That, in my view, puts him into a different position. If the contract had been performed he would have had control of the goods at the time when the documents would have arrived. If he awaits the arrival of the goods, in as much as that may not happen for weeks or months, he is in the meantime subjecting the vendor to the risk of fluctuations in the market not contemplated by the parties and not reasonable. The reasonable course for the plaintiffs is to go into the market and buy goods. There is no doubt that they could have bought the Japanese peas on the spot in July [at pp 819–20].

The principle enunciated in the above case was affirmed in *Garnac Grain Inc v HMF Faure and Fairclough Ltd*.[100]

Damages for late shipment and late tender

Generally, in CIF contracts, the shipment period is specified in the contract. A breach of this term is regarded as a breach of a condition. It will be possible for the buyer to be aware of the late shipment date from the shipment documents and he will, therefore, be able to reject the documents upon tender. However, if he elects to accept the documents, he can still obtain damages. *Prima facie*, the measure of damages is the

---

99   [1917] 2 KB 814.
100 [1967] 2 All ER 353.

difference between the CIF value of the goods at the time when the documents would have been tendered had the cargo been shipped on the specified date, and the CIF value of the goods when the documents were actually tendered.

Where the goods are sent within the shipment period, but there is a delay in the tender of documents, the buyer will be able to claim damages. *Prima facie*, the damages would be the difference between the CIF values of the goods at the actual time of tender of the documents and at the time when the documents should have been tendered.

Damages for defective goods

The buyer may also claim damages for defective goods. The measure of damages is to be calculated in terms of s 53(3). It is *prima facie* the difference between the value of the goods at the time of delivery to the buyer and the value they would have had if they had answered to the warranty.

Variants of a CIF contract

Merchants frequently vary the cif terms. Terms such as cif&c (cost, insurance, freight and commission), cif&e (cost, insurance, freight and exchange) and cif&c&i (cost, insurance, freight and commission and interest) are commonly found in sale contracts. No established practices exist in respect of these terms and it is very much a matter for the parties to agree on what the variations to the cif theme are meant to cover. For instance, exchange could refer to fluctuations in the exchange rate, or it may refer to the commissions that may be charged by banks in the process of conversion. Similarly, the reference to commission may mean a number of things – it could be the commission charged by export houses (in the exporting country) acting as purchasing agents for the buyers, or commission charged by the bank when the seller negotiates the bill of exchange accepted by the buyer.[101]

CIF and arrival contracts

Frequently, arrival contracts tend to be confused with CIF, as illustrated by *Comptoir d'Achat et de Vente SA Luis de Ridder Limitada (The Julia)*.[102] The important point to remember about a CIF contract is that the documents are symbolic of the goods, so that delivery of the documents (bill of lading) is constructive delivery of the goods. In the case of arrival (also known as ex ship port of arrival) contracts, the seller undertakes to deliver the goods on arrival of the goods at the destination. In other words, 'the seller has to cause delivery to be made to the buyer from a ship which has arrived at the port of delivery and has reached a place therein, which is usual for delivery of goods of the kind in question'.[103] Risk in these types of contracts will pass on delivery of the goods to the buyer.

Under INCOTERMS 2000, where the contract is on DES (delivered ex ship) terms, the seller delivers the goods when they are placed at the disposal of the buyer at the

---

101 See Chapter 15.
102 [1949] 1 All ER 269. See also 'Judicial definition of a CIF contract', pp 7–10 above.
103 *Per* Lord Sumner in *Yangtsze Insurance Association v Lukmanjee* [1918] AC 585, at p 589.

usual unloading point at the port of destination (A4 DES). The seller bears the risk of loss or damage to the goods until delivery at the destination (A5 DES).

CIF CONTRACTS UNDER INCOTERMS 2000

Under INCOTERMS 2000, the obligations of the parties to a CIF contract are, to a large extent, similar to those found in English law. The important difference, however, is that INCOTERMS 2000[104] have adapted the term to accommodate the increasing use of electronic documents in commercial transactions. So, where the parties have agreed to communicate electronically, they can agree to substitute an invoice or a bill of lading with their electronic equivalent. Though INCOTERMS allow for the use of an electronic bill of lading, it must be stressed that the Carriage of Goods by Sea Act 1971 (legislation implementing the Hague-Visby Rules which unifies the law relating to bills of lading) will not automatically govern the electronic bill, unless incorporated expressly.[105] There may also be problems on the admissibility of computer-generated documents in legal proceedings, in the event of litigation in some jurisdictions, though this question seems to be adequately addressed in England.[106]

Obligations of the seller

(a) Ship goods answering to contract description

The seller, under the rules, must ship goods that are in conformity with the contract of sale (A1 CIF).

(b) To procure and prepare documents

Invoice and pre-shipment inspection certificates

The seller must provide a commercial invoice, or its equivalent in electronic form, and obtain any pre-shipment inspection certificates, certificates of quality, etc, if required by the contract of sale (A1 CIF).

Contract of carriage

The seller must contract for the carriage of the goods to the named port of destination by the usual route at his own expense (A3(a) CIF). The contract of carriage must:

- be dated within the shipment period agreed by the contract;
- cover the contract goods;
- allow the buyer to take delivery of the goods at the port of destination; and
- unless otherwise agreed, enable the buyer to sell the goods during transit through transfer of the document, or by notice to the carrier (A8 CIF).

The transport document normally obtained by the seller would be a bill of lading. However, under the rules, the parties are free to agree to a non-negotiable sea waybill, or an inland waterway document, and, where the parties have agreed to

---

104   The recognition of electronic documentation was first introduced by INCOTERMS 1990.
105   See Chapter 8, pp 268–73.
106   See Chapter 6, pp 197–202. See also Civil Evidence Act 1995 and Abeyratne, 'Some recent trends in evidential issues on electronic data interchange – the Anglo American response' [1994] Trading Law 103.

communicate electronically, they may agree to replace t̶
with their electronic equivalents (A8 CIF).

Where the bill of lading is issued in several originals, the
set of originals – that is, all the originals – to the buyer
makes reference to charterparty terms, the seller mu̶
charterparty, so that the buyer will have notice of the terms of ca̶..̶. ̶

Contract of insurance

The buyer must procure at his expense, in the absence of express agreement, minimum insurance cover, in accordance with the Institute of Cargo Clauses (or another similar set of clauses), from a reputable insurance company. The insurance cover must enable the buyer, or any other person with insurable interest in the cargo, to claim directly from the insurer. The seller must provide the buyer with the insurance policy, or other evidence of insurance cover. The minimum insurance obtained must cover the contract price plus 10%, to be provided in the currency of the contract (A3(b) CIF).

Where the buyer requires insurance cover for risks such as wars, strikes, riots and civil commotions, the seller must arrange such cover at the buyer's expense (A3(b) CIF).

(c) To check, pack, mark and deliver the goods

The seller is under an obligation to deliver the goods on board ship at the port of shipment on the date, or within the period, stipulated by the contract (A4 CIF). The seller must pack the goods and mark the goods at his expense. He is also responsible for the costs of checking operations, such as quality checking, weighing, measuring and counting, that take place prior to delivery (A9 CIF).

(d) Loading costs and freight

The seller is responsible for carriage charges to the agreed destination. He has also to bear the costs of transporting the goods to the port of loading, and loading the goods on board ship, as well as for any costs for unloading the goods at the port of discharge levied by the shipping line when contracting for carriage (A6 CIF).

(e) Notice to buyer

The seller must inform the buyer of delivery of the cargo on board the ship, and provide any other information he may require to make necessary arrangements to take delivery (A7 CIF).

(f) Export licences and customs formalities

The party responsible for obtaining export licences, or the required official authorisation for the export of the goods, is the seller. He must do so at his own risk and expense. He is also obliged to carry out all the customs formalities (A2 CIF) and bear all the costs of customs formalities as well as any duties, taxes, and other official charges payable upon exportation (A6 CIF).

(g) Risk

The seller bears all risks of loss or damage until the moment the goods have passed the ship's rail at the port of shipment (A5 CIF).

(h) Other obligations

The buyer may require documents (or their electronic equivalents) from the country of origin and/or shipment for the import of goods, or their transit through another country. Where the buyer requests the seller to obtain these documents, he must provide every assistance at the buyer's risk and expense (A10 CIF).

ions of the buyer

Notice to seller

Where the buyer has the right to determine the time of shipping or the port of shipment, he must inform the seller when and where he wants the goods in good time, so that the seller can make suitable arrangements (B7 CIF). If he fails to give notice, and the goods have been duly appropriated to the contract, he is responsible for additional costs (for instance, storage charges) from the agreed date or the expiry date of the period fixed for shipment (B6 CIF).

(b) Insurance

The buyer must provide the seller with any information he may require for obtaining cargo insurance (B10 CIF).

(c) Acceptance of transport documents

The buyer must accept the transport documents if they are in accordance with the rules set out in INCOTERMS 2000 and conform to the contract (B8 CIF).

(d) Payment of price

The buyer must pay the agreed price to the seller (B1 CIF).

(e) Risk

The buyer bears all risk of loss or damage from the time the goods have passed the ship's rail. If the buyer fails to notify the seller when and where to send the goods in accordance with B7,[107] the buyer will bear the risk from the agreed date of shipment or the last date of the shipment period. The buyer will be placed under this risk only if the goods have been clearly set aside, or identified in some other manner as the contract goods (B5 CIF).

(f) Payment of other costs, duties, taxes

The buyer is responsible for the costs of any pre-shipment inspection, unless mandated by the authorities in the country of export (B9 CIF). Where the buyer has requested documents or equivalent electronic messages from the seller for the importation of the cargo or for their transit through another country, he must reimburse the seller for the costs (B10 CIF).

The buyer is also responsible for any duties, taxes, official charges, and other costs for carrying out customs formalities during transit and at the port of destination (B6 CIF).

(g) Import licence and customs formalities

It is the duty of the buyer to obtain, at his own risk and expense, any import licence, or other official authorisation, that may be required for importing the cargo. He is also responsible for carrying out all customs formalities where the goods pass through another country in transit and at the port of arrival (B2 CIF).

(h) Taking delivery

The buyer must accept delivery when the goods have been delivered in accordance with A4 – that is, where the seller has delivered the goods on board the vessel at the port of shipment within the shipment period stipulated by the contract. He must receive the goods from the carrier at the port of destination (B4 CIF). The

---

107   See 'Notice to seller', above.

buyer is responsible for all costs from the time they have been delivered over the ship's rail. This includes all costs incurred during transit and all unloading charges, which may include lighterage and wharfage charges (B6 CIF). It is possible that the costs of unloading, etc, at the port of destination may already be included in the freight charges.

C&F CONTRACTS

It is often the case that sellers and buyers contract on C&F terms instead of CIF terms. The seller under C&F (cost and freight) terms undertakes to contract for the carriage of goods but does not undertake to obtain insurance. As Brandon J said, in *The Pantanassa*,[108] 'C&F contracts only differ from CIF contracts in that the sellers are not required to insure the goods for the buyer' (at p 855). The undertakings in respect of transport arrangements and export licences in a C&F contract are the same as those expected of the seller in a CIF contract. 'C&F terms are commonly used where the importing country prohibits insurance of cargo by the buyer abroad – a step frequently resorted to in developing countries to protect the local insurance industry. According to the list issued by the International Union of Marine Insurance (IUMI)[109] in 2008, developing nations, such as Nigeria, Pakistan, Bangladesh, Venezuela, Ghana and Ecuador prohibit insurance of imports abroad. It would theoretically be possible for the seller to quote CIF prices and obtain insurance from an insurer in the country of import. In practice, however, the buyer is likely to have a better understanding of local insurance customs and may well be better placed to obtain cover at lower premiums.

It goes without saying that the seller needs to inform the buyer of shipment to enable the latter to take out insurance. Failure to notify would mean that the seller bears the risk of loss during transit under s 32(3) of the Sale of Goods Act 1979.[110]

C&F AND INCOTERMS

The 1990 version of INCOTERMS replaced C&F with the acronym CFR, which also stands for cost and freight. It is unclear why the ICC felt the need to replace C&F with CFR, given that the former is still in wide use and well understood in the mercantile community. There is nothing in the introduction to indicate the reason for the change. It could not be that CFR is meant for use with all modes of transport – for example, air transport, road transport – since it is specifically reserved for use with sea and inland waterway transport. (The term CPT – carriage paid to – is recommended for use with other modes of transport.) Interestingly, Sassoon observes that the substitution of the term C&F by the term CFR is 'undesirable . . . in light of the long and continued use of the more familiar term'.[111] INCOTERMS 2000 retains CFR introduced by INCOTERMS 1990.

---

108 [1970] 1 All ER 848.
109 See FFSA/DMAT – Freedom of Insurance – 03/2008 available at www.iumi.com. The list also provides references to relevant legislative provisions.
110 See 'Duties of seller under classic FOB contract', pp 38–41 below.
111 Sassoon, *CIF and FOB Contracts*, 1995, Sweet & Maxwell, p 29, para 25.

Where CFR INCOTERMS 2000 is incorporated into the contract, the seller is responsible for obtaining the contract of carriage (A3 CFR) and export licences (A2 CFR). He is also required to carry out all customs formalities required for the exportation of the goods.[112] The transfer of risk occurs, as in CIF INCOTERMS 2000, when the goods pass the ship's rail (A5 CFR). As for obligations in respect of packaging, marking and notice to the buyer, they are identical to the obligations required of the seller under CIF INCOTERMS 2000.[113] The buyer's obligations also are no different from those required under a CIF contract. The buyer is not required to obtain a contract of insurance under CFR, though it would be in his best interests to obtain one from the moment risk passes to him.

As stated earlier, INCOTERMS 2000 have to be specifically incorporated. It is possible that the parties have also inserted terms in relation to obligations such as loading that conflict with the loading obligations as outlined by INCOTERMS. In such a case, the contractual terms as agreed between the parties will override INCOTERMS, thus ensuring the reduction of any conflict.[114]

FOB CONTRACTS

Unlike CIF contracts where definitions abound, there are no definitions concerning free on board (FOB) contracts – a consequence of the variety of uses to which the term was put during its 200-year history. It was used in domestic, as well as in export, contracts. In domestic contracts, the manufacturer or wholesale trader would often quote a price on FOB terms to the exporter. And, in export contracts, the use of the term was not restricted to sea carriage. It came to be associated with rail (FOR – free on rail), road (FOT – free on truck) and air transport (FOB airport). The 1980 version of INCOTERMS listed FOR, FOT[115] and FOB airport for use with rail, road and air transport respectively, but INCOTERMS 1990 replaced these with a single term, FCA (free carrier), which is to be used in relation to all modes of transport. INCOTERMS 2000 continues to use FCA. The change was necessitated by the growth in the use of containers and the increased employment of a number of modes of transport (multi-modal transport). The lack of definitions could, therefore, be attributed to its 'flexibility'. Nonetheless, the gist of an FOB contract can be gathered from *Wimble and Sons v Rosenberg and Sons*,[116] where it was described as a contract for the sale of goods where the seller agrees to deliver the goods over the ship's rail, and the buyer agrees to convey it overseas.

It was in *Pyrene and Co v Scindia Navigation Co Ltd*[117] that Devlin J categorised the

---

112 *Ibid*. It is possible that customs authorities in some countries may require the value to be declared as a CIF or FOB value for the purposes of calculating duty. While this is not a bar to using other standard trade terms found in INCOTERMS, the value of the goods will have to be translated into CIF or FOB value. See Q1 in Jiménez (ed), *Incoterms Q&A*, 1998, ICC.

113 See 'CIF contracts under INCOTERMS 2000', pp 32–5 above.

114 See Jiménez (ed), *Incoterms Q&A*, 1998, ICC.

115 While the INCOTERMS 1990 removed terms such as FOB (airport) and FOT, they are nonetheless used widely. In a recent case involving FOT, see *Bulk Trading Corp Ltd v Zenziper Grains and Foodstuffs* [2001] 1 Lloyd's Rep 357, the Court of Appeal held that an FOT contract that provided delivery to be made at a number of destinations was not analogous to an FOB contract that so similarly provided.

116 [1913] 3 KB 743.

117 [1954] 1 Lloyd's Rep 321.

different varieties of FOB contracts. This classification was approved and neatly summarised in the subsequent case of *The El Amria and The El Minia*,[118] as follows:

> In the first, or classic type, the buyer nominated the ship and the seller put the goods on board for the account of the buyer, procuring a bill of lading. The seller was a party to the contract of carriage and if he had taken the bill of lading to his order, the only contract of carriage to which the buyer could become a party was that contained in or evidenced by the bill of lading which was endorsed to him by the seller.
>
> The second is a variant of the first, in that the seller arranges for the ship to come on berth, but the legal incidents are the same.
>
> The third is where the seller puts the goods on board, takes a mate's receipt and gives this to the buyer or his agent who then takes a bill of lading. The buyer was a party to the contract *ab initio* [at p 32].

In the first (classic FOB) and the second (FOB with additional services) types of FOB contracts, the fact that the bill of lading is in the seller's name is likely to raise the presumption that he is reserving the right of disposal, since s 19(2) of the Sale of Goods Act 1979 states 'where goods are shipped and by the bill of lading the goods are deliverable to the order of the seller or his agent, the seller is *prima facie* to be taken to reserve the right of disposal'. However, this presumption is displaceable.[119]

In the third type, the bill of lading is obtained by the buyer's nominated agent or the buyer himself. However, it is the seller who obtains the mate's receipt, since he still has the responsibility of putting the goods on board ship. The mate's receipt, consisting of statements about quantity and condition, is given when the goods are received by the carrier and it is on the basis of the mate's receipt that the master of the ship issues the bill of lading. A mate's receipt is not negotiable although, in some countries (for example, Malaysia), it may acquire the status of a document of title by virtue of custom.[120] In England, no such custom is found. The nature of a mate's receipt was succinctly described by Lord Wright in *Nippon Yusen Kaisha v Ramjiban Serowgee*[121] as follows:

> The mate's receipt is not a document of title to the goods shipped. Its transfer does not transfer property in the goods, nor is its possession equivalent to possession of the goods. It is not conclusive, and its statements do not bind the shipowner as to statements in a bill of lading signed with the master's authority. It is, however, *prima facie* evidence of the quantity and condition of the goods received and, *prima facie*, it is the recipient or possessor who is entitled to have the bill of lading issued to him. But, if the mate's receipt acknowledges receipt from a shipper other than a person who actually receives the mate's receipt, and, in particular, if the property is in that shipper, and the shipper has contracted for the freight, the shipowner will *prima facie* be entitled, and indeed bound, to deliver the bill of lading to that person [at pp 445–46].

From the above, where the seller obtains a mate's receipt in his own name, he could perhaps hold on to it until he gets paid, since the bill of lading is normally issued on production of a mate's receipt. It is not unknown for a bill of lading to be issued without a mate's receipt.[122]

---

118   [1982] 2 Lloyd's Rep 28.
119   (1918) 117 LT 738. See also *Evergreen Marine Corp v Aldgate Warehouse (Wholesale) Ltd* [2003] 2 Lloyd's Rep 596.
120   *Wah Tat Bank v Chan Cheng Kum* [1967] 2 Lloyd's Rep 437.
121   [1938] AC 429.
122   See *Schuster v McKellar* (1857) 7 E&B 704.

In a recent case, *Scottish & Newcastle International Ltd v Othon Ghalanos Ltd,*[123] the House of Lords took the opportunity to enunciate the characteristics of an FOB contract whilst contrasting it with C&F contracts. According to Lord Mance:

[T]here are three general differences between fob and c&f contracts:

(i) First, an fob contract specifies a port or range of ports for shipment of the goods. A c&f contract specifies a port or ports to which the goods are consigned.

(ii) Secondly, an fob contract requires shipment (whether by or on behalf of the seller or the buyer) of the goods at the port (or a port within the range) so specified; ie the seller cannot buy afloat . . . In contrast, under a c&f contract responsibility for shipment rests on the seller, and this can be fulfilled by the seller either shipping goods or acquiring goods already afloat after shipment, and moreover shipment can be at *any* port (unless the contract otherwise provides).

(iii) Thirdly, and as a result, a c&f contract involves (subject to any special terms) an all-in-quote by the seller, who carries the risk of any increase (and has the benefit of the reduction) in the cost of carriage. In contrast, under an fob contract, although the seller may contract for and pay the freight, the buyer carries the risk (and has the benefit) of any such fluctuation.[124]

Duties of the seller under a classic FOB contract

(a) Ship goods of contract description at port of shipment

The seller must ship goods that answer to the contract description. As already stated, s 13 of the Sale of Goods Act 1979 implies that, where the contract is for sale of goods by description, the goods will correspond to that description.[125] In the event of a breach where the buyer is not a consumer, but the breach is so slight that it would be unreasonable for the buyer to reject the goods, the breach may be treated as breach of a warranty rather than breach of a condition (s 15A).

The seller must deliver the goods at the specified place of shipment. This is regarded as a condition of the contract; in the event of a breach, the buyer will be able to repudiate the contract and obtain damages. As Colman J said in *Petrograde Inc v Stinnes Handel Gmbh,*[126] to classify this term as an innominate term would only result in frequent disputes over whether the buyer could reject the goods at the destination. For the sake of certainty, the term is held to be a condition.

(b) Pay handling and transportation costs

The seller is responsible for all the handling and transportation costs up to the moment the goods cross the ship's rail. This would include the costs of loading and stevedoring, unless port custom (that is, what is usually done at the port) indicates otherwise.

(c) Ship goods on time at port of shipment

Under an FOB sale, the buyer is responsible for making the arrangements for shipping the goods to their destination. The seller, therefore, is not under a duty to ship the goods until he has received shipment instructions from the buyer. Once

---

123 [2008] 1 Lloyd's Rep 462.
124 At 468. See also 'CIF Contracts', pp 6–32 above and 'Duties of the seller under a classic FOB contract' and 'Duties of the buyer', (pp 38–41 and pp 42–3) below.
125 See 'Duties of seller under a CIF contract', pp 11–14 above.
126 [1995] 1 Lloyd's Rep 142, at p 150.

the seller is instructed by the buyer, the seller is bound to ship the goods within the shipping period stated.

In a traditional FOB contract, time of shipment is of the essence of the contract and is regarded as a condition of the contract.[127]

The buyer is under an obligation to name the port of shipment in an FOB contract. There is no requirement that this be expressly agreed in the contract of sale.[128]

The contract of sale might fix the shipping period and give the buyer the option to fix the time of shipment. Where such an option exists, the buyer must notify the seller in good time of the arrival of the ship so that he can meet his contractual obligations.

In some cases, the contract of sale might give the seller the option to fix the time of shipment. Where such an arrangement exists, the seller must notify the buyer of the date so that he can arrange for a ship to arrive and load the goods. In the absence of an express provision regarding notification by the seller, the courts will imply such a term in the contract. In *Harlow and Jones Ltd v Panex (International) Ltd*,[129] the contract stipulated that the cargo was 'to be delivered during August/ September at supplier's option'. The seller notified the buyer that half of the cargo was ready for an August shipment and the buyer should therefore arrange a vessel for August. The buyer did not respond to the seller's request. On 1 August, the buyer informed the seller that he would be calling for loading of the first instalment between 12 and 22 August, and of the remainder at the end of August. On 3 August, the buyer informed the seller that he would not be able to load between 12 and 22 August, since he had received no confirmation to his communication of 1 August. On 11 August, the buyer wanted the seller to give a guarantee that he would be able to load the entire cargo between 24 and 27 August. On 22 August, the buyer cancelled the contract on the basis that the seller had repudiated the contract. The seller's claim for damages for breach succeeded. The court held that the seller had the option to decide when to ship and in these circumstances 'it is necessary to make ... an implication that before the buyers need nominate the ship the sellers will notify them when, or approximately when, the sellers expect to load' (at p 526).

It is not unusual for contracts to include express clauses or incorporate rules formulated by trade associations in respect of delivery, stipulating for instance, that goods should be ready to be delivered at any time within the contract period. Does this mean that the buyer will have to have the cargo ready by the quayside at all times or does it mean that it has to be available for loading when the vessel is ready for loading? And, how are such clauses or incorporation of rules to be treated – as condition or warranties?

In interpreting such clauses it seems that the courts will examine the clause against its contractual background and mercantile context. The difficulties surrounding the interpretation of a 'ready to be delivered' clause is well illustrated in the different views that emerged in *Compagnie Commerciale Sucres et Denrées v C. Czarnikow Ltd (The Naxos)*[130] during its passage through the courts. Here the

---

127 *Bunge Corporation v Tradax Export SA* [1981] 2 Lloyd's Rep 1.
128 See *David T Boyd and Co Ltd v Luis Louca* [1973] 1 Lloyd's Rep 209.
129 [1967] 2 Lloyd's Rep 509.
130 [1991] 1 Lloyd's Rep 29.

parties contracted on ASSUC[131] Sugar Contract No 2 (for EEC FOB Stowed Trade 1984) for the sale of 12,000 tonnes of white crystal sugar, FOB and stowed one nominated EEC port per vessel, seller's quay. The contract stated that shipment was to be in May/June 1986 and the buyer was to give not less than 14 days' notice of the vessel's expected readiness to load and also provided that the contract was subject to the rules of the Refined Sugar Association. Rule 14(1) specifically provided: 'In cases of f.a.s., f.o.b. and free stowed in hold (f.o.b. stowed) the Seller shall have the sugar ready to be delivered to the Buyer at any time within the contract period'.[132] The ETA (estimated time of arrival) of the nominated vessel (The Naxos) was 29/31 May and the buyers notified the sellers that if they did not commence loading on May 29 they would be in breach of contract. In response, on May 29, the sellers sent a telex informing the buyers that due to a long string of contracts it had not been possible to pass on 14 days' notice all the way down the chain in order to enable commencement of loading. On June 3, in the absence of loading on the part of the seller, the buyers informed the seller that the contract had been terminated and claimed for damages (the difference between the contract price and the higher price paid by the buyers for substitute cargo). The sellers stated they were not liable.

The arbitrators found that there was a breach of a condition and hence the buyers could terminate the contract. On appeal by the sellers the court held no separate duty was imposed on the sellers by Rule 14(1) and it could not be regarded as a condition. The buyers appealed. The Court of Appeal found that though an additional express obligation had been imposed by Rule 14 and Rule 14(1)[133], lacking a precise time for the performance of the obligation, was not a time clause. In the absence of any other indications it was not a condition.[134] The buyers appealed.

Allowing the appeal the House of Lords interpreted 'ready to be delivered' against its context to mean that 'the seller shall have the sugar called forward available for loading without delay or interruption as soon as the vessel is ready to load the cargo in question'.[135] And as for the issue of whether Rule 14(1) was a condition the House of Lords held (with Lord Brandon dissenting)[136] that it was, relying on the view of the arbitration panel. For Lord Ackner Rule 14(1) was:

---

131 Professional Association of Sugar Traders of the European Union.
132 The other paragraphs of Rule 14 read as follows:
　　(2) The Buyer, having given reasonable notice, shall be entitled to call for delivery of the sugar between the first and last working day inclusive of the period of delivery.
　　(3) If the vessel (or vessels) has presented herself in readiness to load within the contract period but has failed to be presented within 5 calendar days of the date contained in the notice above calling for delivery of the sugar, the Buyer shall be responsible for any costs incurred by the Seller by reason of such delay exceeding the 5 calendar days.
　　(4) If the vessel (or vessels) has presented herself in readiness to load within the contract period, but loading has not been completed by the last working day of the period, the Seller shall be bound to deliver and the Buyer bound to accept delivery of the balance of the cargo or parcel up to the contract quantity.
133 Lloyd L J dissenting.
134 Sir Michael Kerr dissenting.
135 At 35.
136 In Lord Brandon's view too much reliance had been placed by Lord Ackner on the views of the arbitrators. While recognising that 'the view of arbitrators is important and should be accorded proper respect' he felt that the arbitrators had focused on a single obligation and 'not enough on the general scheme and tenor of the contract as a whole' [at 31].

crucially important to the buyers since it removed the risk that the absence of insuf-ficiency of cargo would be an absence of delay . . . the rule ensures to a very large extent that loading will be promptly commenced and speedily carried out and thus enable the buyers punctually to perform their own obligations to their customers. The rule tends to provide certainty which is such an indispensable ingredient of mercantile contracts[137].

(d) Deliver goods on specified date

As for date of delivery, this is related to the date of shipment. The seller is deemed to have delivered the goods to the buyer when the goods pass the ship's rail on the date of shipment. The time of arrival at the port of destination is irrelevant.[138]

(e) Notify buyer of shipment

According to s 32(3) of the Sale of Goods Act 1979, 'where goods are sent by the seller to the buyer by a route involving sea transit, under circumstances in which it is usual to insure, the seller must give such notice to the buyer as may enable him to insure them during their sea transit and, if the seller fails to do so, the goods are at his risk during such sea transit'. Section 32(3) does not, however, impose any liability on the seller for his failure to notify the buyer.

Though s 32(3) applies to FOB contracts, its effect seems somewhat minimal. In *Wimble, Sons and Co Ltd v Rosenberg and Sons*,[139] goods were sold FOB Antwerp to be shipped as required by the buyer. The buyer instructed the seller to send the goods to Odessa, and asked him to arrange the ship and advance the freight to his account. The cargo became a total loss two days after shipment. The buyer became aware of the shipment when he received the bill of lading three days after the goods were lost. The seller sued the buyer for the price. The buyer argued that the goods were at the seller's risk, since he had not been given notice of the shipment.

The court came to the conclusion that s 32(3) applied to FOB contracts. However, in the present case, the buyer had sufficient information to insure the goods even though he may not have had the name of the ship or the exact date of sailing. According to Buckley LJ:

> . . . [the contract of sale] gave the buyer knowledge of all the necessary particulars other than knowledge which rested with himself or was determinate by himself, namely, first, the port of discharge, and, secondly, the name of the ship. The former was within his own knowledge and was supplied by him . . . The latter was not necessary to enable him to insure, and in fact he waived knowledge of it by leaving it to the seller to select the ship [at pp 754–55].

It is unclear under which circumstances s 32(3) could be successfully invoked. If the statement made by Buckley LJ is correct, in most FOB contracts, the buyer will have sufficient information about the period of shipment, the ports of shipment and des-tination to take out insurance, in which case s 32(3) would never apply to FOB sales.

Seller's remedies

The seller can sue the buyer in the event of non-payment where property in the goods have passed. He can also sue the buyer for damages for non-acceptance. Further, he

---

137 At 37.
138 *Frebold and Sturznickel (trading as Panda OHG) v Circle Products Ltd* [1970] 1 Lloyd's Rep 499.
139 [1913] 3 KB 743.

also has other rights provided by the Sale of Goods Act 1979 – lien, stoppage in transit and the right of resale.[140]

Duties of the buyer

(a) Secure shipping space

As already stated, the buyer in an FOB contract is responsible for arranging the shipment of the goods to their destination. This means that the first duty of the buyer is to secure shipping space, and inform the seller in good time, so that he can fulfil his side of the bargain. In other words, the buyer must inform the seller of the name of the ship and the time of its availability for loading, so that the seller can bring the goods to the port of loading and ship the goods in accordance with the contract of sale.

The buyer must ensure that the shipping space he has acquired will enable the seller to load the goods on to the ship within the shipping period specified in the contract of sale. In *Cunningham v Munro*,[141] the contract of sale for bran FOB Rotterdam specified October as the shipment period. The sellers obtained the goods from their suppliers on 13 October. The buyers were unable to get a ship to load the bran until 28 October. The sellers claimed that the buyers were in breach of nominating a ship within the shipment period, and were liable to pay the warehousing costs. The court held that the shipment period of October specified in the contract placed the buyers under an obligation to nominate a ship that would load the goods before the end of October. They had provided a ship which would enable the sellers to load the goods over the ship's rail within October, and the buyers were therefore not in breach.

Where the buyer is unsuccessful in obtaining shipping space to allow the seller to fulfil his obligation to load within the specified period, the buyer may be liable for paying extra warehousing costs.

Where the nomination of the ship is ineffective, the buyer will be able to withdraw the nomination and renominate another vessel provided the loading operation can be completed within the contract period. In *Agricultores Federados Argentinos v Ampro SA*,[142] the shipment was to be between 20 and 29 September. The buyer nominated *The Oswestry Grange* but, due to heavy weather, she was delayed and could not load until 30 September. On 20 September, the buyer found another vessel, *The Austral*, which was already at the port of loading. Had the seller co-operated, the loading could have been completed on time. The court held the renomination to be valid. According to Widgery J:

> ... the rights of the parties are to be regulated by the general law as it applies to an FOB contract. As I understand it, the general law applying in such a contract merely is that the buyers shall provide a vessel which is capable of loading within the stipulated time, and if, as a matter of courtesy or convenience, the buyers inform the sellers that they propose to provide vessel A, I can see no reason in principle why they should not change their minds and provide vessel B at a later stage, always assuming that vessel B is provided within such a time as to make it possible for her

140   See 'Seller's remedies', pp 41–2 above.
141   (1922) 28 Com Cas 42.
        [1965] 2 Lloyd's Rep 157.

> to fulfil the buyers' obligations under the contract. I can see no principle at all to indicate in a case of this kind that when the buyers had nominated *The Oswestry Grange* they were in any way inhibited at any time from changing their minds and substituting *The Austral*, provided always, as the fact here, that *The Austral* was capable of accepting the cargo within the time for shipment stipulated in the contract [at p 167].

In the circumstances, the buyer was correct to treat the seller's behaviour as an anticipatory breach and a repudiation of the contract.

Where the seller incurs extra expenses as a result of renomination, these will be to the account of the buyer. Since the right of substitution imports an element of uncertainty to the transaction, the parties are free to exclude the right of substitution with suitable clauses, such as 'nomination, once given, cannot be withdrawn'.

The contract may provide that the seller receives notification of nomination of ship and its readiness to load in advance of delivery – for example, 10 days before delivery. In these circumstances, a nomination of a substitute vessel that takes place within the shipping period, but does not satisfy the notification period, will be ineffective. If the buyer fails to nominate an effective ship, or give instructions to the seller on time to enable him to make suitable arrangements for loading of the cargo, the buyer will be liable in damages for non-acceptance. He will, however, not be liable for the price of the goods. This is because property would not have passed to the buyer until the cargo is placed on board the ship. In *Colley v Overseas Exporters*,[143] the vessel nominated by the buyer was withdrawn by the shipowner. The buyer was unable to find a substitute vessel. The seller argued that the buyer was liable for the contract price. The court held that, since property had not passed to the buyer, the seller could not sue for the price.

(b) Payment of price

The buyer is under an obligation to pay for the goods in accordance with the contract. Generally, the contract would make express provisions as to how and when payment is to be effected. For instance, the contract may state 'payment cash against documents' or 'payment by banker's documentary credit'.

Where there are no specific provisions in the contract, the price will be due on delivery to the buyer. This, in the case of FOB sales, will be when the goods pass the ship's rail. However, where the bill of lading is made out in the seller's name, this raises the inference that payment is to be made when the bill of lading is tendered.[144]

Buyer's remedies

The buyer may be able to reject the goods on arrival if they do not correspond to the contract description. He may also be able to reject the goods if they are not of satisfactory quality, or obtain damages for defective goods.[145] Where the seller fails to deliver the goods, the buyer has the right to sue for damages for non-delivery.[146]

---

143   (1921) 126 LT 58; [1921] 3 KB 302
144   See 'Passing of property', p 45 below.
145   See as 13, 14 and s 15A(1) of the Sale of Goods Act 1979. See also 'Right of rejection', pp 28–9 above.
146   See s 51(3) of the Sale of Goods Act 1979. See also and 'Damages For failure to tender valid documents or deliver goods' under CIF contracts, pp 29–30 above.

Export and import licences

It is not possible to state a clear general rule with regard to the party responsible for obtaining export licences, since conflicting views emerge from the case law in this area. In *HO Brandt and Co v HN Morris and Co Ltd*,[147] the buyer, an American firm, appointed Brandt and Co in Manchester as the agent to purchase 60 tons of aniline oil FOB Manchester. The agent placed an order for this amount with the defendants. Subsequent to the signing of the contract of sale, the government issued an order prohibiting the export of the oil without a licence. The seller was unable to obtain a licence. The buyer sued for non-delivery. The Court of Appeal held that the duty of obtaining the licence was that of the buyer, since the buyer's obligation in an FOB contract was to provide an effective ship which could legally carry the goods. Scrutton LJ said:

> The buyers must provide an effective ship, that is to say, a ship which can legally carry the goods. When the buyers have done that, the sellers have to put the goods on board the ship. If that is so, the obtaining of a licence to export is the buyer's concern. It is their concern to have the ship sent out of the country after the goods have been put on board and the fact that ... a prohibition against export includes a prohibition against bringing the goods on to any quay or other place to be shipped for exportation does not cast a duty of obtaining the licence on the sellers. Bringing the goods on to the quay is merely subsidiary to the export which is the gist of the licence [at p 798].

However, in *AV Pound and Co Ltd v MW Hardy and Co*,[148] the House of Lords came to a different conclusion. In this case, the contract was for the sale of 300 tons of turpentine FAS (free alongside ship) Lisbon. The seller knew East Germany as the intended destination. Under Portuguese law, the export of turpentine required an export licence. Neither the seller nor the buyer was registered with the Portuguese authorities for licence purposes. The seller's supplier, however, was. The seller, through his supplier, was unable to obtain a licence due to the destination. The buyer refused to nominate a substitute port. The court concluded that the duty was the seller's since, in the circumstances, he was in a better position to obtain the licence – after all, his supplier was registered with the authorities. The court distinguished *HO Brandt and Co v HN Morris and Co Ltd*[149] on the basis that both parties to the contract there were in Britain. To quote Viscount Kilmuir:

> In my opinion, the decision in *HO Brandt and Co v HN Morris and Co Ltd* is authority only for the proposition that where a British buyer has bought goods for export from Britain, and a British prohibition on export except with a licence supervenes, then there is a duty on such a buyer to apply for a licence, because not only is he entitled to apply to the relevant British authority, but he alone knows the full facts regarding the destination of the goods.
>
> I cannot extract from *HO Brandt and Co v HN Morris and Co Ltd* a general rule that, on every FOB or FAS contract, the buyer must supply a ship into which, or alongside which, the goods can legally be placed where there exists a prohibition on export except with a licence [at pp 643–44].

The court was reluctant to lay down any general rules about the duty of obtaining export licences, and it seems that the question is one that has to be decided in the light

---

147 [1917] 2 KB 784.
148 [1956] 1 All ER 639.
    [1917] 2 KB 784.

of surrounding circumstances. Nonetheless, it is generally presumed that the seller has the obligation to obtain the export licence. The level of responsibility to be exercised by the seller in obtaining an export licence will depend on the parties' agreement.[150]

In contrast, the rules relating to obtaining export licences are clear under INCOTERMS.[151]

Passing of property

According to s 17 of the Sale of Goods Act 1979, property passes when the parties so intend. The intention of the parties is to be gathered from the circumstances. In FOB sales, property generally passes when the goods cross the ship's rail.[152] This is not always the case, however.

Where the seller obtains the bill of lading in his own name, according to s 19(2), the seller is *prima facie* to be taken to have reserved the right of disposal. Section 19(2) only raises a presumption, and it is possible to rebut this presumption.[153]

Where goods form part of a bulk, then property will pass upon their ascertainment. For ascertainment to take place, there must be an irrevocable act on the part of the seller. In *Carlos Federspiel and Co SA v Charles Twigg and Co Ltd*,[154] the buyer bought 85 bicycles and paid for them in advance. The bicycles were packed, the buyer's name was attached to the package, and the shipment was also registered. However, the bicycles had not been sent to the port of loading. The receiver claimed the bicycles were part of the assets charged to the debenture holders. The court came to the conclusion that the buyer had not acquired property, since the intention was to pass property upon shipment. The packing, marking and other acts of the seller did not constitute irrevocable earmarking.[155]

Passing of risk[156]

According to s 20 of the Sale of Goods Act 1979, risk passes with property. In FOB sales, risk passes along with property upon shipment – that is, when the goods pass the ship's rail.[157]

The postponement of passing of property to a time later than that of shipment, however, will not affect the time of passing of risk.[158] So, where the goods have not been ascertained, or where the seller retains the bill of lading, risk will, nevertheless, pass when the goods cross the ship's rail.[159]

---

150 See 'Licences' under CIF contracts, pp 20–1 above.
151 See 'FOB contracts under INCOTERMS 2000', pp 47–9 below.
152 *Pyrene and Co v Scindia Navigation Co Ltd* [1954] 1 Lloyd's Rep 321. See also *Colonial Insurance Co of New Zealand v Adelaide Marine Insurance* (1886) 12 App Cas 128.
153 *The Parchim* (1918) 117 LT 738. See also *Mitsui and Co Ltd v Flota Mercante Grancolumbiana SA (The Ciudad de Patso)* [1989] 1 All ER 951; 'Passing of property' under CIF contracts above.
154 [1957] 1 Lloyd's Rep 240.
155 See 'Passing of property' under CIF contracts, pp 24–6 above.
156 See also 'Passing of risk' in Chapter 2, pp 81–4 below.
157 *Pyrene and Co v Scindia Navigation Co Ltd* [1954] 1 Lloyd's Rep 321. See also 'Passing of Risk' under a CIF contract.
158 See *Stock v Inglis* (1885) 10 App Cas 263.
159 See also Chapter 2 on the passing of risk under the Convention on the International Sale of Goods 1980.

VARIANTS OF AN FOB CONTRACT

Merchants, in response to their needs, have tended to add extra obligations to be undertaken by the seller with terms such as FOB stowed (FOBS), FOB trimmed (FOBT), FOB stowed and trimmed (FOBST).[160] Where such terms are used, the seller is required to stow the goods on board the ship, so that space on the ship is utilised in the most efficient manner without affecting stability of the ship, or trim (levelling of dry bulk cargo) the cargo. It is likely that, in these cases, risk does not pass when the goods pass the ship's rail. However, no precise rules can be formulated, since it is dependent on a number of factors – for example, custom at port, terms of the contract, and whether the seller in fact has a say in how the goods are trimmed or stowed.

FOB with additional services

In an FOB with additional services contract, the seller takes on further duties, such as the arrangement of shipping and insurance. The seller procures the bill of lading in his name and tenders it to the buyer for payment. The incidents in this type of contract are comparable to that of a CIF contract.[161] The freight and insurance costs in an FOB with additional services contract are to the buyer's account. Freight charges and insurance premiums are not included in the price quoted by the seller, as in a CIF contract, and any increases in freight or insurance will have to be borne by the buyer, not the seller. By contrast, in a CIF contract, it is the seller who bears the costs. The seller may also charge a commission for the services he has rendered the buyer in obtaining the contract of carriage and the contract of insurance in an FOB with additional services contract. The buyer is likely to require these additional services of the seller when he is ill placed to obtain them in the seller's country. It is also possible that the buyer may prefer this term to lower his liability in respect of import duties calculated on the price of goods, since the CIF price is an all-inclusive price.

FAS CONTRACTS

FAS stands for free alongside ship. Apart from delivery of goods, the obligations of the seller and the buyer are the same as those found under a classic FOB contract. The seller in an FAS contract is to bring the goods alongside the ship and is responsible for all costs incurred, including dock dues and port charges. It falls on the buyer to load the goods on board the ship and to pay all charges incurred in the loading of the goods. It is possible that the loading may be undertaken by the carrier, in which case the charges are likely to be part of the freight payable. Risk passes to the buyer when the goods are placed at the disposal of the buyer alongside the ship at the port of shipment. The buyer has the duty, as under a classic FOB term, to nominate a suitable ship. As for the export licence, normally the seller will be expected to obtain it, though in some cases circumstances may indicate otherwise.[162]

---

160 See Reynold, 'Stowing, trimming and their effects in delivery, risk, property in sales "FOBS", "FOBT" and "FOBST" ' [1994] LMCLQ 119.

161 See 'CIF Contracts', pp 6–32 above.

162 See 'Export and import licences' under FOB contracts, pp 44–5 above.

As stated earlier, INCOTERMS 2000 introduced substantive changes to the obtaining of licences in respect of FAS.[163] Where INCOTERMS 2000 are incorporated, it is the seller's duty to obtain at his expense export licence, authorisation and other customs formalities for the exportation of the goods (A2 FAS). Equally, he has to pay duties, taxes and other charges that are payable on export (A6 FAS).

FOB contracts under INCOTERMS 2000

The obligations of the parties to an FOB contract governed by INCOTERMS 2000 are largely similar to those found in English law, except for one important difference. INCOTERMS have clear rules about the party responsible for obtaining an export licence, thereby introducing a much desired element of certainty.

Obligations of the seller

(a) Ship goods of contract description

The seller must provide goods that are in conformity with the contract of sale (A1 FOB).

(b) To prepare the invoice and other documents

The seller must provide a commercial invoice for the goods. This may be replaced by its electronic equivalent where the parties agree. The seller will also be required to furnish other evidence of conformity of goods. The sale contract would normally stipulate these. They are likely to be certificates of quality or certificates of inspection.[164]

(c) To check, pack, mark and deliver the goods

The seller must deliver the goods on board the ship at the named port of shipment on the specified date. Where no date is specified, then he must deliver within the period stipulated in the contract of sale, and in the manner customary at the port.[165] The seller must, at his expense, mark and pack the goods as necessary to meet his obligation of delivery. He is also responsible for the costs of checking operations, such as quality checking, weighing, measuring, and counting, that take place prior to delivery (A4 and A9 FOB).

(d) Loading costs and freight

Since the seller meets his obligation of delivery only when he places the goods on board the ship at the port of shipment, he is responsible for all loading charges until the moment the goods pass the ship's rail (A6 FOB).

---

163 Under the 1990 version of INCOTERMS, the duty for obtaining an export licence did not rest on the seller, though he was placed under an obligation to 'render the buyer, at the latter's request, risk and expense, every assistance in obtaining any export licence or other official authorisation necessary for the exportation of the goods' (A2 FAS INCOTERMS 1990). It was the buyer who had to obtain the export licence (B2 FAS INCOTERMS 1990). Equally, the buyer was responsible for duties and other charges for exportation (B6 FAS INCOTERMS 1990).

164 A1 FOB.

165 Custom at a port, for instance, might require the seller to stow the goods on board the ship.

(e) Notice to buyer

The seller must give sufficient notice to the buyer that the goods have been placed on board the ship (A7 FOB).

(f) Export licences and customs formalities

Under the rules, the seller is responsible for obtaining the export licence and other official authorisation. He must do so at his own risk and expense. He is also obliged to carry out all the customs formalities at his expense and pay any duties, taxes and other official charges (A2 and A6 FOB).

(g) Proof of delivery

The seller must provide the buyer with any proof of delivery of the goods. This normally would be a mate's receipt. Where the buyer requires transport documents such as a negotiable bill of lading, a non-negotiable sea waybill, an inland waterway document, or a multimodal transport document, the seller must assist the buyer to obtain such a document at the latter's risk and expense. Where the parties have agreed to electronic data interchange, then the transport document can be replaced with an electronic equivalent (A8 FOB). Note that there is no obligation on the part of the seller to obtain a contract of carriage (A3 FOB).

(h) Insurance

There is no obligation on the part of the seller to obtain insurance (A3 FOB). The seller must provide the buyer, upon his request, with any information necessary for obtaining insurance (A10 FOB).

(i) Risk

The seller must bear the risk of any loss or damage to the goods until such time as the goods have passed the ship's rail at the port of shipment (A5 FOB).

(j) Other obligations

Where the buyer requests documents (or their electronic equivalents), other than transport documents, for the import of the goods or their transit through another country, the seller must render every assistance in obtaining these, but at the buyer's risk and expense (A10 FOB).

Obligations of the buyer

(a) Notice to seller

The buyer must give the seller sufficient notice of the name of the ship, the port of loading and the required delivery time (B7 FOB).

(b) Contract of carriage

The buyer must contract for the carriage of goods from the named port of shipment to the port of destination at his expense (B3 FOB). Delays in berthing of the vessel may result in demurrage charges. Under INCOTERMS, these costs lie with the buyer since he is responsible for arranging the contract of carriage. Equally, the responsibility of obtaining a berth lies with the buyer.[166] This of course means

---

166 See answer to Q17, 'FOB berthing and demurrage charges', in Jiménez (ed), *Q&A INCOTERMS*, 1998, ICC. Though the answer has been given in the context of the 1990 version of INCOTERMS, there is no difference between FOB INCOTERMS 1990 and FOB INCOTERMS 2000.

that any incidental expenses and arrangements to enable the seller to meet his obligation to deliver on board the vessel is with the buyer.[167] In other words, the buyer takes on the risk of transport-related responsibilities.

(c) Accept proof of delivery

The buyer must accept the transport document provided by the seller as proof of delivery (B8 FOB).

(d) Payment of price

The buyer must pay the price agreed by him in the contract of sale (B1 FOB).

(e) Risk

The goods are at the buyer's risk from the moment they have passed the ship's rail at the port of shipment. However, where the buyer fails to inform the seller about the name of the ship, the port of shipment, and the required delivery date, or if the named vessel fails to arrive on time, or is unable to take the cargo, or closes for cargo earlier than the stipulated date, the buyer bears the risk from the agreed date or the expiry date of the period fixed for delivery. He is placed under this risk only if the goods have been clearly set aside, or otherwise identified as the contract goods (B5 FOB).

(f) Payment of other costs, duties and taxes

The buyer is responsible for the costs incurred in pre-shipment inspection, unless mandated by the exporting country's authorities (B9 FOB). Where the buyer has requested the seller to obtain documents (or their electronic equivalents) for importation of the cargo, or for their transit through third countries, the seller must be reimbursed for the costs incurred (B10 FOB). The buyer is also responsible for any duties, taxes and other charges that may be levied on the goods, and for carrying out all customs formalities during transit, and at the port of destination (B10 FOB).

(g) Import licences and customs formalities

The buyer must, at his own risk and expense, obtain an import licence, or official authorisation necessary for importing the cargo. He is also responsible for carrying out all customs formalities in the country of import and, where required, in the countries through which the goods are passing (B2 FOB).

(h) Taking delivery

Delivery to the buyer takes place when the cargo is placed on board the named ship on the date or at the stipulated time (B4 FOB). From the moment the goods cross the ship's rail, the buyer bears all the costs. Where additional costs are incurred due to the buyer's failure to nominate a ship, or where a nominated ship arrives late or is unable to carry the cargo, these will be to the buyer's account, provided the goods have been clearly set aside or otherwise identified (B6 FOB).

INCOTERMS 2000 – a brief overview

As stated earlier, INCOTERMS, first formulated in 1936 by the International Chamber of Commerce, have undergone various modifications to introduce new terms for

---

167   As Jiménez notes in relation to the answer to Q17, 'The panel of experts firmly closed the door on the possibility for an FOB buyer to escape his contractual obligations by claiming that berthing was difficult to obtain in a timely manner'. Jiminez (ed), *Q&A INCOTERMS*, 1998, ICC, p 85.

emerging modes of transport, such as air and road transport. The current version – the 2000 version – does not introduce that many changes to the 1990 version. While retaining the arrangement of terms as adopted in INCOTERMS 1990, it ensures that the wording used in INCOTERMS 2000 reflects accurately trade practice and introduces substantive changes in relation to FAS, DEQ and FCA terms. In relation to FCA, changes to loading and unloading obligations have been amended; and in relation to FAS and DEQ, customs clearance and payment of duty obligations have been amended.[168]

The move away from terms related to transport modes was felt necessary in order to meet the growing use of multimodal transport (that is, use of more than two modes of transport – for example, sea/road/sea) brought about as result of containerisation. As a result, mode-specific terms found in the 1980 version of INCOTERMS, such as FOR (free on rail) and FOT (free on truck), are dropped.

A point to note about INCOTERMS is that they apply to a contract only where the parties agree to be governed by their provisions. Of course, it is possible that some states may have given statutory effect to INCOTERMS, in which case they would apply if the contract attracts the application of the law of that state. The UK has not given statutory effect to INCOTERMS. It is, however, possible that a contract may not specifically provide for INCOTERMS since it is customary in that particular trade to use INCOTERMS. Were this the case, English courts will take on board prevalent mercantile custom to determine the responsibilities of the parties.[169]

It must be noted that, in spite of extensive rules, ranging from providing goods in conformity with the sale contract, obtaining licences, authorisations, contract of carriage, contract of insurance to delivery, passing of risk, checking, packaging and marking, division of costs and giving notice to buyer, INCOTERMS are not comprehensive. Issues such as what constitutes conformity of goods with the contract of sale, remedies for breach of obligations set by INCOTERMS, and passing of property, still need to be resolved by looking to the law that governs the contract.[170]

INCOTERMS 2000, like its predecessor, arranges trade terms into four groups: (a) E term; (b) F terms; (c) C terms; and (d) D terms. Each group reflects the level of risk undertaken by the seller. The level of risk is at its minimum in an E term and its highest in a D term. An increase in the seller's level of risk results in a corresponding decrease in the level of risk assumed by the buyer.

(a) E term

This group consists of one term – ex works (ExW). The level of risk is at its lowest, as far as the seller is concerned. His obligation to deliver under the contract is fulfilled as soon as he makes the goods available at his premises for collection by the buyer.

(b) F terms

This group consists of three terms – free carrier (FCA), free alongside ship (FAS) and free on board (FOB). FCA is recommended for use where rail, road, air or

---

168   See Tables 1(a), 1(b) and 1(c).
169   See also Chapter 2 on the attitude of the Convention on the International Sale of Goods 1980 to trade usage and mercantile customs.
170   Given that many states have ratified the Convention on the International Sale of Goods 1980, it is likely that this convention may decide issues relating to conformity of goods, remedies, etc. Note, however, that passing of property is not dealt with by this convention.

multimodal transport is envisaged. FCA can also be used for sea or inland water-way transport where the ship's rail is not the convenient point for passing of risk, as, for instance, in ro-ro (roll on, roll off) traffic – that is, where trucks or trailers are driven straight on and straight off a ship. FOB and FAS are to be used for inland waterway or sea transport. In an F term, the seller agrees to deliver the goods to the carrier (FCA), alongside the ship (FAS), or on board the vessel (FOB), and also undertakes to obtain the export licence or other official authorisation.

(c) C terms

This group contains four terms – cost and freight (CFR), cost, insurance, freight (CIF), carriage paid to (CPT) and carriage and insurance paid to (CIP). CFR and CIF are to be used for sea or inland waterway transport, whereas CPT and CIP are to be used where rail, road, air or multimodal transport is envisaged. Once again, CPT and CIP can also be used for sea and inland waterway transport where the ship's rail is not the point at which risk is to pass from the seller to the buyer (see above, 'F terms'). Under C terms, the seller is obliged not only to hand over the goods to the carrier and obtain export licences, but has to obtain the contract of carriage (CFR and CPT) and insurance (CIF and CIP).

(d) D terms

This group consists of delivered at frontier (DAF), delivered ex ship (DES), delivered ex quay (DEQ), delivered duty unpaid (DDU), and delivered duty paid (DDP). DAF is intended for use with air, rail, road or multimodal transport. DES and DEQ are to be used with inland waterway or sea transport, and DDU and DDP are recommended for use with any form of transport. The seller's obligations are at their maximum in D terms. He undertakes to make the goods available for collection at a named frontier (DAF), or on board a ship (DES), or on the quay (DEQ), or at the named place of destination in the country of importation, not having paid the duties (DDU), or having paid the duties (DDP). In the case of DEQ, DDU and DDP, the seller has to obtain the import licences and other official authorisation.

It is quite common for parties to use INCOTERMS 2000 but also add extra qualifying words. A frequently found variant of CIF INCOTERMS 2000 is 'CIF landed port of destination'. Where variants are used, it is not possible precisely to state the extent of obligations undertaken by the parties. The meaning of the term will have to be gathered by looking to the intention of the parties or the custom in the trade, if relevant.

The International Chamber of Commerce, in the 'Introduction' to INCOTERMS 1990, recommends that it is not advisable to use abbreviations added to the C terms unless the meaning of the abbreviations is clearly understood and accepted by the contracting parties or under any applicable law or custom of the trade[171] – a view repeated in *INCOTERMS in Practice*,[172] published by the ICC.

CONCLUSION

It is apparent from the discussion of CIF and FOB that the contract of carriage in the form of a bill of lading plays an extremely important role in international trade. Part

---

171   See para 11, 'Introduction', INCOTERMS 2000.
172   1995, ICC.

e 1a: Seller's responsibilities in respect of contract of carriage, insurance, export/import licences under INCOTERMS 2000

JUP	Specific terms	Mode of transport	Seller's responsibility in respect of contract of carriage	Seller's responsibility in respect of Cargo Insurance	Seller's Responsibility in respect of export licence	Seller's responsibility in respect of import licence
E	Ex works (eg, seller's warehouse, factory)		None	None	None (However, render assistance with obtaining export licence, at buyer's request. Expense and risk buyer's)	None
F	FCA (free carrier – named place)	Rail, road, air, sea, inland waterway, multimodal*	None. (However, if commercial practice or at buyer's request, seller may contract for carriage on usual terms. Risk and expense buyer's)	None	Obtain at own expense export licence and carry out all customs formalities for export	None
	FAS (free alongside ship – named port of shipment)	Sea, inland waterway	None	None	Same as FCA (above)	None
	FOB (free on board – named port of shipment)	Sea, inland waterway	None	None	Same as FCA (above)	None
C	CFR (cost and freight – named port of shipment)	Sea, inland waterway	Contract at own expense on usual terms for carriage of goods by sea to port of destination on usual route	None	Obtain at own expense any export licence and carry out all customs formalities for export	None
	CIF (cost, insurance, freight – named port of shipment)	Sea, inland waterway	Same as CFR (above)	Obtain cargo insurance as per contractual agreement at own expense. To use reputable insurance company	Same as CFR (above)	None
	CPT (carriage paid to – named port of shipment)	Rail, road, air, sea, inland waterway, multimodal*	Contract at own expense for carriage on usual terms and usual route to destination	None	Obtain at own expense any export licence and carry out all formalities for export	None
	CIP (carriage and insurance paid to – named port of destination)	Rail, road, air, sea, inland waterway, multimodal*	Same as CPT (above)	Same as CIF (above)	Same as CPT (above)	None
D	DAF (delivered at frontier – named place)	Rail, road, air, sea, inland waterway, multimodal*	Contract at own expense for carriage by usual route and in a customary manner to destination	None	Obtain at own risk and expense export licence, customs formalities for exportation and transit through countries en route	None
	DES (delivered ex ship – named port of destination)	Sea, inland waterway	Contract at own expense for carriage by usual route and in a customary manner to destination	None	Same as DAF (above)	None
	DEQ (delivered ex quay duty paid – named port of destination)	Sea, inland waterway	Same as DES (above) (except carriage to quay at destination)	None	Same as DAF (above)	None
	DDU (delivered duty unpaid – named port of destination)	Rail, road, air, sea, inland waterway, multimodal*	Same as DES (above) (except carriage to agreed destination)	None	Same as DAF (above)	None
	DDP (delivered duty paid – named place of destination)	Rail, road, air, sea, inland waterway, multimodal*	Same as DES (above) (except carriage to agreed destination)	None	Same as DAF (above)	Obtain at own risk and expense import licence and carry out customs formalities for import

* Multimodal (also called combined or inter-modal transport) is carriage involving two or more modes of transport (eg, road/sea/road/rail/sea/road).

Table 1b: Buyer's responsibilities in respect of contract of carriage, insurance, export/import licences under INCOTERMS 2000

Group	Specific terms	Mode of transport	Buyer's responsibility in respect of contract of carriage	Buyer's responsibility in respect of cargo insurance	Buyer's responsibility in respect of export licence	Buyer's responsibility in respect of import licence
E	Ex works (eg, seller's warehouse, factory)		None under INCOTERMS (it will be up to buyer to sort out transport arrangements)	None under INCOTERMS (it will be in buyer's interest to take out insurance on passing of risk)	To obtain at own risk and expense export licence, and carry out all customs formalities, including transit	To obtain at own risk and expense import licence. Carry out all customs formalities including transit
F	FCA (free carrier – named place)	Rail, road, air, sea, inland waterway, multimodal*	Contract at own expense for carriage from named place	None (see works, above)	None	Same as ex works (above)
	FAS (free alongside ship – named port of shipment)	Sea, inland waterway	Contract at own expense for carriage from named port of shipment	None (see ex works, above)	None	Same as ex works (above)
	FOB (free on board – named port of shipment)	Sea, inland waterway	Same as above	None (see ex works, above)	None	Same as ex works (above)
C	CFR (cost and freight – named port of shipment)	Sea, inland waterway	None	None (see ex works, above)	None	Same as ex works (above)
	CIF (cost, insurance, freight – named port of shipment)	Sea, inland waterway	None	None (see under seller's obligation, Table 1.1a)	None	Same as ex works (above)
	CPT (carriage paid to – named port of shipment)	Rail, road, air, sea, inland waterway, multimodal*	None	None (see ex works, above)	None	Same as ex works (above)
	CIP (carriage and insurance paid to – named port of destination)	Rail, road, air, sea, inland waterway, multimodal*	None	See CIF above	None	Same as ex works (above)
D	DAF (delivered at frontier – named place)	Rail, road, air, sea, inland waterway, multimodal*	None	None (see ex works, above)	None	To obtain at own risk and expense licence, and carry out customs formalities at frontier and transit as required
	DES (delivered ex ship – named port of destination)	Sea, inland waterway	None	None (see ex works, above)	None	To obtain at own risk and expense import licence and carry out customs formalities
	DEQ (delivered ex quay duty paid – named port of destination)	Sea, inland waterway	None	None (see ex works, above)	None	Same as DES (above)
	DDU (delivered duty unpaid – named port of destination)	Rail, road, sea, inland waterway, multimodal*	Same as DES (except carriage to agreed destination)	None	None	Same as DES (above)
	DDP (delivered duty paid – named place of destination)	Rail, road, air, sea, inland waterway, multimodal*	Same as DES (except carriage to agreed destination)	None	None	None (However, render assistance with obtaining licence at seller's request, risk and expense)

* Multimodal (also called combined or inter-modal transport) is carriage involving two or more modes of transport (eg. road/sea/road/rail/sea/road).

Table 1c: Passing of risk under INCOTERMS 2000

GROUP	SPECIFIC TERMS	MODE OF TRANSPORT	PASSING OF RISK
E	Ex works (eg, seller's warehouse, factory)		Buyer assumes risk when goods placed at his disposal at agreed delivery point
F	FCA (free carrier – named place)	Rail, road, air, sea, inland waterway, multimodal*	Buyer assumes risk on delivery – ie, placed in custody of carrier at agreed place
	FAS (free alongside ship – named port of shipment)	Sea, inland waterway	Buyer assumes risk on delivery – placing of goods alongside ship on date/within time stipulated
	FOB (free on board – named port of shipment)	Sea, inland waterway	Buyer assumes risk when goods pass ship's rail at port of shipment
C	CFR (cost and freight – named port of shipment)	Sea, inland waterway	Same as FOB (above)
	CIF (cost, insurance, freight – named port of shipment)	Sea, inland waterway	Same as FOB (above)
	CPT (carriage paid to – named port of shipment)	Rail, road, air, sea, inland waterway, multimodal*	Buyer assumes risk on delivery – ie, placed in custody of carrier at agreed place
	CIP (carriage and insurance paid to – named port of destination)	Rail, road, air, sea, inland waterway, multimodal*	Same as CPT (above)
D	DAF (delivered at frontier – named place)	Rail, road, air, sea, inland waterway, multimodal*	Buyer assumes risk on delivery at frontier
	DES (delivered ex ship – named port of destination)	Sea, inland waterway	Buyer assumes risk when goods placed at disposal of buyer on board ship
	DEQ (delivered ex quay duty paid – named port of destination)	Sea, inland waterway	Buyer assumes risk when goods placed at disposal of buyer on quay/wharf
	DDU (delivered duty unpaid – named port of destination)	Rail, road, air, sea, inland waterway, multimodal*	Buyer assumes risk when goods placed at disposal of buyer
	DDP (delivered duty paid – named place of destination)	Rail, road, air, sea, inland waterway, multimodal*	Buyer assumes risk when goods placed at disposal of buyer

* Multimodal (also called combined or inter-modal transport) is carriage involving two or more modes of transport (eg, road/sea/road/rail/sea/road).

III on the transportation of goods will examine the rights and liabilities associated with bills of lading along with the two international conventions – the Hague-Visby Rules and the Hamburg Rules – which set out the responsibilities and liabilities of the parties to a bill of lading. Before proceeding to transport documentation, the next chapter will examine the Convention on the International Sale of Goods 1980 drafted by UNCITRAL to see how it addresses the obligations of the seller and the buyer and remedies available to the parties to the sale contract in the case of breach by either of the parties.

FURTHER READING

Atiyah, Adams & MacQueen, *The Sale of Goods*, 2005, Pearson.

Bennett, 'FOB contracts: substitution of vessels' [1990] LMCLQ 466.

Bridge, *The International Sale of Goods*, 2007, OUP.

Crawford, 'Analysis and operation of a CIF contract' [1955] Tulane LR 396.

Debattista (ed), *Incoterms in Practice*, 1995, ICC.

Eckersley, 'International sale of goods – licences and export prohibitions' [1975] LMCLQ 265.

Elliott, 'The changing face of documentation in the carriage of goods', in Sharpe and Spicer (eds), *New Directions in Maritime Law*, 1984, Carswell.

Evans, 'FOB and CIF contracts' [1993] ALJ 844.

Feltham, 'The appropriation in a CIF contract of goods lost or damaged at sea' [1975] JBL 273.

Gillies and Moens (eds), *International Trade and Business Law, Policy and Ethics*, 2nd edn, 2005, Cavendish Publishing.

Gower, 'FOB contracts' (1956) 19 MLR 417.

Hermann, *International Trade Terms: Standard Terms for Contracts for International Sale of Goods*, 1993, Graham and Trotman/M Nijhoff.

Horn, *Adaptation and Renegotiation of Contracts in International Trade and Finance*, 1985, Kluwer.

Murray, 'Risk at loss of goods in transit: a comparison of the 1990 Incoterms with terms from other voices' (1991) 23 University of Miami Inter-American LR 93.

Murray *et al.*, *Schmithoff's Export Trade*, 2007, Stevens.

New York County Lawyers' Association, *Handbook on Customs and International Trade Law*, 1996, Oceana.

Odeke, 'The nature of cif contract – is it a sale of documents or a sale of goods?' [1993] Journal of Contract Law 158.

Ramberg, *Guide to Incoterms 1990*, 1991, ICC.

Reynolds, 'Stowing, trimming and their effects on delivery, risk, property in sales "FOBS", "FOBT" and "FOBST" ' [1994] LMCLQ 119.

Sassoon, *CIF and FOB Contracts*, 1995, Sweet & Maxwell. (New edition expected)

Sassoon, 'Application of FOB and CIF sales in common law countries' [1981] ETL 50.

Schmithoff, *International Trade Usages*, 1987, Institute of International Business Law.

Treitel, 'Time of shipment in fob contracts' [1991] LMCLQ 147.

Treitel, 'Damages for breach of a cif contract' [1988] LMCLQ 457.

Treitel, 'Rights of rejection under CIF sales' [1984] LMCLQ 565.

CHAPTER 2

THE VIENNA CONVENTION ON THE INTERNATIONAL SALE OF GOODS 1980

INTRODUCTION

Ideally, any international sale contract should include a choice of law clause – a clause stipulating the law applicable to the contract, such as English law.[1] Parties often, through oversight or ignorance, omit to include a choice of law clause. It is also possible that the parties have found it difficult to agree on such a clause. In the event of a dispute, the forum applies its private international rules[2] to determine the law applicable to the contract. The law relating to sale contracts varies from state to state and any uncertainty with regard to applicable law means uncertainty also in respect of the rights and obligations of the parties to the contract and the available remedies in the event of a dispute. One way to tackle this uncertainty is to harmonise the law relating to international sales in the form of an international convention for worldwide adoption, thus enabling the application of a uniform set of rules to such transactions. This task of harmonising the law relating to international sales of goods at an international level started in 1930 under the auspices of the International Institute for the Unification of Private Law (UNIDROIT).[3] Interrupted by the Second World War, work resumed in the early 1950s, and in 1964 two conventions were adopted: Uniform Law on International Sales (ULIS) and Uniform Law on the Formation of International Sales (ULFIS). Ratified only by a handful of states, including the United Kingdom,[4] they were criticised on both political and legal grounds.[5] Unpopularity of the ULIS and ULFIS meant a return to the drawing board.[6] The United Nations Commission on International Trade Law (UNCITRAL)[7] was seen as the ideal organisation to undertake the task of drafting such an international convention, since its membership consisting of developing (Third World) and developed nations, and socialist countries, would counter any political objections that might be levelled by the socialist or Third World quarters. The Working Group set to work in 1969 with ULIS and ULFIS as springboards and submitted two draft conventions in 1976 and 1977 to the Commission. On review, the Commission combined the two draft

---

1   If English law applies to a sale, the Sale of Goods Act 1979 will apply to the contract. Reference to provisions as and where relevant in the context of cost, insurance, freight (CIF) and free on board (FOB) contracts was made in Chapter 1. For an excellent comprehensive account of the Sale of Goods Act, see Furmston, *Sale and Supply of Goods*, 2000, Cavendish Publishing.
2   See Chapters 16 and 17 for further on the Brussels Regulation I, the Rome Convention 1980 and Rome I.
3   It was set up as an auxiliary organ of the League of Nations in 1926. Subsequent to the demise of the League of Nations, the UNIDROIT was re-established on the basis of the UNIDROIT statute.
4   These conventions, implemented by the United Kingdom with the Uniform Laws on International Sales Act 1967, entered into force in 1972. The text is available in Carr and Kidner, *International Trade Law Statutes and Conventions*, 5th edn, 2008, Routledge-Cavendish Publishing.
5   For an interesting comparison of some of the provisions of ULFIS and the UNCITRAL Convention on the International Sale of Goods 1980, see Barbić, in Voskuil and Wade (eds), *Hague-Zagreb Essays on the Law of International Trade*, Vol 4, 1983, TMC Asser Institute.
6   See Magnus, 'European experience with the Hague sales law' [1979] Comparative Law Yearbook 105.
7   See Farnsworth, 'UNCITRAL Why? What? How? When?' (1972) 20 American Journal of Comparative Law 314.

conventions into one – the Convention on the International Sale of Goods – and submitted it to the Diplomatic Conference held at Vienna.[8] The Convention on International Sales of Goods 1980 ('CISG' or popularly known as the 'Vienna Convention') came into force in 1988 with the required 10 ratifications.[9] Since then, there has been a steady stream of ratifications.[10] Popularity of the Convention on International Sales of Goods 1980 (hereinafter 'Vienna Convention') has brought it to prominence in the field of international commercial law.

As for the United Kingdom, it has not yet ratified the Convention. The reception of the Convention is less than enthusiastic for a variety of reasons. Among them:

(1) unfamiliarity with some of the concepts and rights introduced by the Vienna Convention such as fundamental breach,[11] right to cure after the time fixed for performance, and the self-help remedy of reducing the price where non-conforming goods are delivered;

(2) popularity of the well-established Sales of Goods Act 1979 in the international commercial sector as evidenced by the use of choice of English courts as a forum for dispute resolution, and the choice of English law clauses in contracts even where the contracting parties do not have any connection with the United Kingdom and the movement of goods does not involve the United Kingdom;

(3) doubts about producing uniformity since it is likely to be interpreted variously;

(4) minimum effectiveness since most commercial traders are likely to opt out of the Convention;[12] and

(5) incomprehensiveness, since the Vienna Convention does not address issues such as the validity of the contract and passing of property.[13]

Reluctance to ratify on the part of the United Kingdom has come under criticism. For instance, Barry Nicholas, a prominent academic and member of the UNCITRAL Group, while sympathetic to the hesitation of British lawyers to embrace the Vienna Convention, correctly observes:

> There are indeed grounds for an English lawyer to feel disquiet about the convention and the way in which it is developing. But this is no longer a ground, if it ever was one, for refusing to ratify the convention. On the contrary, it is a ground for ratifying quickly,

---

8 For more on the historical background, see Farnsworth 'The Vienna Convention: history and scope' (1984) 12 International Lawyer 17.

9 The text of this Convention is reproduced in Carr and Kidner, *International Trade Law Statutes and Conventions*, 5th edn, 2008, Routledge-Cavendish. The full text is also available on www.uncitral.org. They also maintain a database of reported cases relating to this convention. Another useful database of cases and other bibliographic materials is maintained by http:// cisgw3.law.pace.edu.

10 Visit www.uncitral.org for an up-to-date list of ratifications along with details of reservations.

11 This is not be confused with the notion of fundamental breach as developed in English law. See *Photo Productions v Securicor* [1980] AC 827 and Chapters 7 and 8, pp 213–16, 243–6 below. The problem with the Vienna Convention in the UK has largely been due to compromises between civil law and common law approaches in order to produce a convention that would be adopted. See Merryman, 'In the convergence (and divergence) of the civil law and the common law' (1981) 17 Stanford Journal of International Law 357; Rossett, 'The international sales convention: a dissenting view' (1984) 18 International Lawyer 445.

12 See 'Party autonomy and the Vienna Convention', pp 68–9 below.

13 Some of these objections can be found in Law Reform Committee of the Council, *1980 Convention on Contracts for the International Sale of Goods*, 1981, Law Society of England and Wales.

so that the experience of English lawyers and the English Commercial Court may influence the way in which the convention is applied.[14]

In October 1997, the Department of Trade and Industry (DTI) published a consultation document with a view to inviting views since it felt the time was right to reconsider the issue of ratification of the Vienna Convention in the interests of the UK traders due to its popular acceptance worldwide. As the DTI observed:

> Since 1989, the number of countries ratifying the Convention has more than doubled to 48 . . .
>
> This evidence suggests the UK is becoming increasingly isolated within the international trading community in not having ratified the convention. We judge the time is right therefore to consider again whether our international traders are at a disadvantage because the UK is not a party to the convention and therefore does not have access to a law which was drafted specifically for international sales in the modern world. Ratification would also enable our courts to contribute towards the interpretation and development of the convention, which is taking place at the moment without our participation.[15]

Of the 450 consultation documents sent out, the DTI received only 36 responses. Twenty-eight of the responses supported ratification on the grounds that use of a neutral and uniform law would be beneficial in an increasingly globalised marketplace. Seven responses were against ratification on the grounds listed above.[16] Three responses did not take any clear view on the matter.[17] The poor response rate is indeed surprising, if not alarming, given the involvement of a government department in canvassing opinions on the suitability of ratifying the convention. This could be an indication of ignorance or apathy on the part of interested parties towards the Vienna Convention.

According to a communication from the DTI dated February 1999, the Government is expected to bring the Vienna Convention into 'national law when there is time available in the legislative programme'. At the time of writing the previous edition, the author was informed by the DTI that the Government intended to ratify the Convention as soon as a convenient slot in Parliament's legislative timetable was available. This is yet to happen. Regardless of this apparent apathy, it is important to include a discussion of this convention since it is likely to affect a great many international sales contracts. Most member states of the European Union are parties to the convention; so are the world's biggest traders such as the US and China. It is also likely that the British courts will be called upon to interpret the convention either because the parties have chosen the Vienna Convention to apply to their sales contract or the application of private international law rules lead to the law of state that is a party to the Vienna Convention.

---

14   Nicholas, 'The United Kingdom and the Vienna Sales Convention: another case of splendid isolation?', available at www.cnir.it.

15   DTI, *United National Convention on Contracts for the International Sale of Goods (the Vienna Convention): A Consultation Document*, 1997, DTI (available at www.dti.gov.uk), paras 22 and 23. The DTI also produced a consultation document in 1989, *United Nations Convention on Contracts for the International Sale of Goods*, DTI. See also Azzouni, 'The adoption of the 1980 Convention on the International Sale of Goods by the United Kingdom', available at www.cisg.law.pace.edu/cisg/biblio/azzouni.html.

16   Based on the information obtained from the DTI.

17   I would like to thank Mr Fraser Murrey, Business Law Unit, Department of Trade and Industry, for providing me with information on the responses to the consultation document.

The United Kingdom is by no means alone in voicing its dissatisfaction with the Vienna Convention. Criticisms have come from a variety of quarters including practitioners and academics. Arthur Rossett expresses the dissatisfaction constructively and lucidly in the following manner:

> We should not fault the drafters of the [Vienna Convention] for their inability to arrive at a Continental style code that concisely and clearly states universal principles of sales law. The 68 nations that participate in UNCITRAL are incapable of any such agreement. I fault the pretense that there are grand principles at work and transcendent values being vindicated. In fact, the convention is largely a cut-and-paste job, and the primary operative drafting principle was to produce a document that all could agree to and none would reject. I do wish that the drafters had seen their task more realistically as one of building from transaction and practice to principle ... I wish they had shown greater realization that the process upon which they had embarked is an organic, continuing one ... What we need are conventions more sensitive to the need to incorporate the capacity for change, growth and discovery into the process of harmonization.[18]

While the focus of this chapter is the Vienna Convention, reference to the ULIS and the ULFIS conventions will be made as and where relevant.[19] There is also reference to case law relating to various provisions of the Vienna Convention. The reference is however limited by the availability of English translations of judgments. A brief section on developments[20] that may impinge on international sales transactions since the Vienna Convention is also included.

Briefly, the reason for the lack of interest in the ULIS and ULFIS conventions is by and large political, though legal uncertainties also played a role. They were seen as a European convention since 19 of the 28 states represented at the conference were from Western Europe. Socialist countries and developing countries from Asia and Africa were largely unrepresented, so were many of the Commonwealth countries. The US, which took part very late in the day (when it joined UNIDROIT in 1963), saw no reason in ratifying it. According to Bainbridge:

Objections of the US delegation to ULIS centred on four basic points:

(1) ULIS was conceived primarily in the light of external trade between common boundary nations geographically near to each other;

(2) ULIS devoted insufficient attention to international trade problems involving overseas shipments;

(3) ULIS did not balance the reciprocal rights and obligations of sellers and buyers viewed in the light of practical realities of trade practices; and

(4) ULIS would not be understood by individuals in the commercial field.[21]

While the ULIS and ULFIS have been ratified by the United Kingdom, they are hardly used by parties to an international sales contract.[22] It seems the situation is

---

18 Rossett, 'CISG laid bare: a lucid guide to a muddy code' (1988) 12(3) Cornell International LJ 575, at p 589.

19 For further on these conventions, see Sutton, 'The Hague Conventions of 1964 and the unification of the law of international sale of goods' (1971) 7 University of Queensland LJ 145.

20 The UNIDROIT Principles of International Commercial Contracts and the Principles of European Contract Law. The texts of these instruments are available at www.jus.uio.no.

21 'Trade usages in international sales of goods: an analysis of the 1964 and 1980 Sales Convention' (1984) 24 Virginia Journal of International Law 619, at p 625.

22 See Feltham, 'The United Nations Convention on Contracts for the International Sale of Goods' (1981) JBL 346.

no different in other countries which have ratified them. Regardless of their limited use, it must be said that these conventions have provided the foundations for, if not influenced, many of the provisions of the Vienna Convention.

THE VIENNA CONVENTION

Structure and features

The drafters intended to offer the Vienna Convention as a truly international instrument in the interests of wide acceptance, thus furthering the fundamental objectives of harmonisation and certainty. As such, it does not promote or adopt principles found in any one legal system in preference to another but strives towards a compromise that would be acceptable to all regardless of their legal or economic background. As one writer points out, it is 'a marriage between socialist, third world, common, and civil law principles'.[23] As to whether the marriage is a successful one or not will become clearer over time with an analysis of the fast growing case law database from different jurisdictions (currently, mostly European) collected by UNCITRAL.[24] As part of the harmonisation drive and to endorse the international nature of the convention, it has, unlike many of the other international conventions, such as the Warsaw Convention and the Hague Rules on air and sea carriage respectively,[25] a provision on its interpretation. The desire for global acceptance was pursued at the cost of leaving out legal issues central to a sales transaction. Passing of property, validity of contract, product liability, and consumer sales are some of the areas that have not been tackled in the Vienna Convention. In these matters, one must resort to the relevant domestic law applicable to the contract. Other features are party autonomy (freedom of the parties to a transaction to opt out of the convention) and use of language exhibiting a pragmatism that would appeal to the mercantile community. In order to avoid the perceived difficulties associated with legal technical language by non-lawyers and lawyers (from different jurisdictions) alike, the provisions avoid, for the most part, technical legal jargon thus making it more accessible. As Kazuaki Sono observes:

> [The Vienna Convention] avoids using the shorthand of legal rules that might be interpreted differently in different legal systems. Instead it speaks directly to the business community by providing the results that would meet the ordinary expectations of a business person.[26]

The Vienna Convention is comprised of four parts: Part I (Arts 1–13) on sphere of application and general provisions; Part II (Arts 14–24) on formation of contract; Part III (Arts 25–88) on obligations of the seller, the buyer, remedies for breach of contract by seller and buyer, passing of risk and damages; and Part IV (Arts 89–101)

---

23 Zwart, 'The new international law of sales: a marriage between socialist, third world, common, and civil law principles' (1988) 13 North Carolina Journal of International Law and Commercial Regulation 109.

24 It is inevitable that during the settling-down period there will be teething problems. The collection of cases show different approaches to interpretation and a reluctance to refer to decisions from other jurisdictions.

25 See Chapters 8 and 10.

26 'Restoration of the rule of reason in contract formation: has there been civil and common law disparity?' (1988) 21(3) Cornell International LJ 477.

on final provisions dealing with matters such as depositary, reservations and entry into force.

Sphere of application

Article 1 of the convention starts off by saying that it applies to 'contracts of sale of goods'. Predictably, the first question that is likely to come to mind is 'What constitutes a sale for the purposes of the Vienna Convention?'[27] No definition is provided.[28] Nevertheless, an understanding of a contract of sale can be gathered from the rights and obligations of the seller and the buyer. Derived from the convention's provisions and widely accepted, the sale contract is defined as 'the contract by virtue of which the seller has to deliver the goods, hand over any documents relating to them and transfer any property in the goods, whereas the buyer is bound to pay the price for the goods, and take delivery of them'.[29] Since payment of a price is central to a sale contract, the generally held view[30] is that the convention does not apply to barters where goods are exchanged for goods or services[31] and both parties take on the role of seller and buyer.[32] The same goes for distribution agreements,[33] though it seems that sales concluded under a distribution agreement will attract the application of the Vienna Convention.[34] Also agency agreements are outside its scope.[35]

Unlike ULIS, the Vienna Convention does not look to factors associated with the transaction such as the movement of goods from one state to another or the places of offer and acceptance to determine the applicability of the convention (Art 1 of ULIS). Focus instead is on the contracting parties' place of business and knowledge on the contracting parties' part of the international character of the transaction. A contract for the sale of goods will come within the ambit of the Vienna Convention if:

- the places of business are in different states (Art 1); and
- both these states are contracting states to the Vienna Convention (Art 1(1)(a));[36] and
- both parties know that they have places of business in different states on the basis

---

27 Section 2(1) of the Sale of Goods Act 1979 defines a contract of sale thus:
      ... is a contract by which the seller transfers or agrees to transfer the property in the
      goods to the buyer for a money consideration, called the price.
28 ULIS also does not provide a definition.
29 Ferrari, 'Specific topics of the CISG in the light of judicial application and scholarly writing' (1995) 15 Journal of Law and Commerce 1.
30 See Honnold, *Uniform Law of International Sales*, 1991, Kluwer.
31 *Re Westminster Property Group plc* [1985] 1 WLR 676.
32 For further details on barters and other types of counter-trade such as buy-back agreement, see UNCITRAL, *Legal Guide on International Countertrade Transaction*, 1992 (available at www.uncitral.org) and Countertrade, Publication No 944, ICC. However, it could be argued that if a price is assigned to the goods it may come within the scope of the Convention.
33 See *Decision of Metropolitan Court Budapest, 19 March 1996* (Case 126), CLOUT Database at www.uncitral.org.
34 See *Oberlandesgericht Düsseldorf*, 11 July 1996, n 6U 152/9S, available at www.unilex.info.
35 See *Amtsgericht Alsfield*, 12 May 1995, 31C 534/94, available at www.unilex.info.
36 See *Interag Co Ltd v Stafford Phase Corp*, 2d instance 983 F 2d 1047 (2nd Cir 1992) where the Vienna Convention was applied on the basis that both parties had places of business in contracting states (the US and Hungary); See also *Oberlandesgericht München, 8 March 1995, Case No 7 U 5460/94* (Case 134), available CLOUT Database.

of the contract, or dealings or information disclosed before or at the conclusion of the contract (Art 1(2)).

Nationality of the parties is an irrelevant factor for the application of the convention (Art 1(3)).

By way of illustration, a contract between a seller with a place of business in Hungary and a buyer with a place of business in Germany will be subject to the Vienna Convention since both are contracting states, provided that the parties to the contract are aware of the international character of the transaction and have not agreed to opt out of the Vienna Convention.[37] This focus on places of business is prone to produce results that may strike as odd. For instance, a contract between parties with places of business in France and the US where goods are transported from Marseilles to Paris will trigger the Vienna Convention while a contract between two parties with places of business in the US with goods to be transported from New York to Florence will not. Suggestions were made during discussions that transportation of goods should be included as a factor for establishing the internationality of the sale transaction but rejected on the grounds that details of transportation of goods are not always determined at the conclusion stage.

In spite of the importance of place of business for the applicability of the Vienna Convention, it is left undefined. Article 10 addresses the situation where a party has more than one place of business. Is the place of business the place where the business organisation is registered? Or, is it the place where important decisions regarding the organisation's running are taken? Permanency may be one contributory factor. And the place where the transaction is to be performed may also be a relevant factor on the basis of Art 10. This lack of clarity leaves room for a variety of interpretations. As Grigera Naon, writing from an Argentinian perspective, highlights:

> The notion of 'place of business' and its Spanish translation *establecimiento* are highly ambiguous terms. The representative from Czechoslovakia has previously observed with respect to the preliminary draft . . . that a definition of this concept in the final text would be indispensable if problems of interpretation – which could lead to unpredictable and irregular application by national courts – were to be avoided. That this remark is fully justified is confirmed by the fact that while the representative of the International Chamber of Commerce interpreted 'place of business' as a permanent commercial organisation, including an office and the presence of employees devoted to the sale of goods or services, the Secretariat of the United Nations, in commenting upon the draft convention, believed that 'place of business' was either the place where the party (if not a physical person) has been incorporated or duly organised, or where the controlling bodies of the company are based. Latin American legal literature distinguishes in turn between the 'seat', 'domicile' and '*establecimiento*' of a '*sociedad*'. The seat coincides with the actual, effective and intended place from which the *sociedad* is managed, the domicile is the place where the formalities of incorporation of the *sociedad* were fulfilled, while the *establecimiento* is the place where the manufacturing and productive activity of the *sociedad* is carried out.[38]

Applicability is extended on the basis of private international law principles even where the parties do not have their places of business in contracting states. Article 1(1)(b) provides for the application of the Vienna Convention when rules of private

---

37   See 'Party autonomy and the Vienna Convention', pp 68–9 below.
38   'The UN Convention on Contracts for the International Sale of Goods', in Horn and Schmithoff (eds), *The International Law of Commercial Transactions*, 1982, Kluwer, at p 97.

international law lead to the application of the law of a contracting state. This rule is obviously intended to widen the impact of the Vienna Convention to apply to transactions entered into by parties who are not located in contracting states. To illustrate: a sale transaction entered into by parties located in England and France might attract the application of Vienna Convention on the basis of Art 1(1)(b). Since Art 1(1)(b) introduces an element of surprise on an unsuspecting party, many delegations objected to the widening of the application of the Vienna Convention.[39] A compromise was reached at the last minute and countries that did not desire to be bound by Art 1(1)(b) could make a reservation to exclude the provision under Art 95.

As Winship notes:

> At the 1980 Vienna Conference . . . sub-para 1(b) came under renewed attack . . . Interested in observing their domestically-adopted international trade laws, Czechoslovakia and the German Democratic Republic supported the Federal Republic of Germany's previous proposal . . . The Czechoslovak representative again explained that his government submitted this proposal so that its special law governing international trade would continue to be applicable in situations where one of the parties to an international sales contract did not have its place of business in a contracting state. To the surprise of some observers, the conference accepted this proposal . . . with little debate or opposition [at p 508].

Many countries, including the US, have done so.[40]

Interestingly, it seems that the Vienna Convention is coming to be perceived as part of trade usage or *lex mercatoria*[41] by arbitration tribunals and (arguably) applied even in the absence of criteria triggering their applicability. Award 5713[42] of 1989 of the International Chamber of Commerce Tribunal provides an interesting illustration. The seller located in Turkey and the buyer in Switzerland entered into a contract in 1979 (a year before the Vienna Convention was adopted) for sale of goods on FOB terms. The goods did not conform to the specifications agreed by the parties with the result that the buyer treated the goods to make them saleable. He sold them at a loss. The seller demanded payment in full. The buyer counterclaimed compensation for direct losses, lost profits and interest. The contract did not include a choice of law clause. In the absence of choice of law, the tribunal, applying cll 13(3) and 13(5) of the International Chamber of Commerce Arbitration Rules 1975, took into account the Vienna Convention as the best source of prevailing trade usages. It is indeed an odd decision given that the Vienna Convention had not even been adopted at the time of conclusion of the contract and it is highly doubtful whether the parties

---

39   *Report of Working Group on the International Sale of Goods* (First Session), UN Doc A/CN 9/35 paras 24 and 25. See also Winship, 'Private international law and the UN Sales Convention' (1988) 12 Cornell International LJ 487.

40   It is possible that parties may not have agreed on a choice of law clause at the time of conclusion of the contract but may do so upon dispute. See *Russia 30 December 1998 Arbitration Proceeding 62/1998* (available at http://cisgw3.law.pace.edu/cases/981230r1.html), where there was no applicable law provision but the buyer from India (claimant) offered that the substantive rules of Russian law be applied. This meant the application of the Vienna Convention had precedence over domestic civil law by virtue of Art 15(4) of the Russian Federation Constitution.

41   There is no clear definition of *lex mercatoria*. In some quarters, it is seen as comprising of trade usages that have become embodied in legislation or model laws and for some it also includes transnational law.

42   Case 45, abstract available CLOUT Database www.uncitral.org. See also Petrochilos, 'Arbitration conflict of law rules and the 1980 International Sales Convention' (1999) 52 Revue Hellenique de Droit International 191.

had the convention (still at the deliberation stage at the time in question) in mind. And, justification on the basis that the Vienna Convention is a codification of existing usages is near impossible since it is an instrument derived through diplomatic endeavour and compromise of differing legal principles.[43]

The approach of the Vienna Convention to leave areas of controversy and areas adequately addressed by internationally recognised rules well alone affects certain types of transactions and the sale of certain types of goods.[44] First in the list are consumer transactions – goods bought for personal, family or household use, provided the seller is aware, are excluded.[45] Predictably, these are excluded since consumer transactions are normally protected to varying degrees by the mandatory laws of a state. It would be difficult to achieve a common framework for consumer sales in the absence of a common policy amongst states. Of course, the provision leaves a penumbra of uncertainty. For instance, will the purchase of a laptop by a doctor which he intends to use mostly for personal use and occasionally for professional purposes fall within or outside the convention? Further, who bears the burden of proving the seller's knowledge of the intended use of the goods for personal, family or household use? The Vienna Convention does not tackle procedural issues such as burden of proof and the suggestion often made is that such matters are to be decided by the law of the forum.[46]

Auction sales are excluded by the Convention since auction contracts are normally concluded at the fall of the hammer and it would be impracticable to determine the place of business of the buyer at the conclusion of the contract (Art 2(b)).[47] Moreover, sales by auction are unusual in international trade. Sales on execution or by authority of law are also subject to domestic law (Art 2(c)). Sale of stocks, shares, investment securities, negotiable instruments also fall outside the Vienna Convention since these are subject to their own rules (Art 2(d)). However, it does not exclude sales of goods which involve documents (documentary sales) such as a sale of goods on CIF terms. Article 2(e) excludes the sale of ships, vessels, hovercraft or aircraft,[48] the reason being that sea- and airborne vessels are viewed as real estate by many jurisdictions and therefore subject to special rules. In the absence of definition of ships and aircraft, it is unclear whether the sale of luxury yachts, small boats and gliders come within the exclusion. Inevitably, in the absence of any clear view in the *travaux*

---

43 Eg, *Award No 370 (429-370-1) (1989) of the Iran-US Claims Tribunal (Watkins-Johnson Co, Watkins-Johnson Ltd v The Islamic Republic of Iran and Bank Saderal Iran)* available at http://cisgw3.law. pace.edu/cases/890728i2.html. See also Hyland, 'Note on ICC Arbitration Case No 5713 of 1989', in Kritzer (ed), *Guide to the Practical Applications of the United Nations Convention on Contracts for the International Sale of Goods*, Vol 2 (loose-leaf publication), 1994, Kluwer.

44 The sale of software is not specifically excluded. See *Landgericht München, 8 February 1995 n 8 HK 24667/93* (Case 131) available from CLOUT Database at www.uncitral.org. However, it seems that only off-the-peg software (standard software) will come within the Vienna Convention. Custom made software would be regarded as sale of services and thus would be excluded under Art 3(2).

45 Article 2(a) states:
    The convention does not apply to sales:
    (a) of goods bought for personal, family or household use, unless the seller, at any time before or at the conclusion of the contract, neither knew, nor ought to have known that the goods were bought for any such use.

46 See 'Exclusion of issues', pp 66–8 below.

47 Article 2, for the most part, is based on Art 5 of ULIS, though it excluded sales by instalments in Art 5(2).

48 Unlike ULIS, there is no requirement for the ships to be registered (see Art 5(1)(b)).

preparatoires, a number of opinions have emerged. Honnold believes that it is to be construed in functional terms so that a vessel which is not used for transportation of goods or persons would come within the Art 2(e), while others suggest that 'ship' should be restricted to large vessels or leave it to domestic law to determine whether a boat is or is not a ship.[49] Views also differ on whether the exclusion applies equally to the components – that is, essential components such as engines, propellers – of the vessels. Case law however seems to suggest otherwise. In *United Technologies (Pratt and Whitney) v Malev Hungarian Airlines*,[50] the contract was for the sale of aircraft engines – an essential component of the aircraft. The court held that the convention was applicable to the transaction. Sale of electricity (Art 2(f)) is also excluded since this is subject to detailed bilateral agreements.

Another important exception is in respect of goods that are ordered (made-to-order goods). While goods to be manufactured or produced fall within its scope,[51] if a substantial part of the material used in the manufacture of production of goods is provided by the person who orders, the sale transaction, according to Art 3(1), falls outside the Vienna Convention. A number of decided cases illustrate its application. Contracts where the preponderant part of the party who supplies goods consists of supply of labour or other services are also outside the ambit of the Vienna Convention.[52]

Exclusion of issues

A number of areas of an international sales transaction are specifically excluded by Art 4. Validity of the contract is excluded from the Vienna Convention. This means that issues such as legal capacity, illegality, mistake and agency contracts are left untouched.[53] Applicable law will therefore be relevant where validity[54] of the contract is at issue. In spite of its importance, the issue of property[55] is also excluded, since it was felt that due to the divergent approaches it would be difficult to reach a consensus. The exclusion does not mean that the Vienna Convention does not broach the matter at all; it does in so far as placing the seller under an obligation to transfer property in the goods to the buyer. As to when, where and how, they are matters to be

---

49 See Honnold, *Uniform Law of International Sales*, 1991, Kluwer; Schlechtriem, *Uniform Sales Law*, 1986, Manzsche Verlags- und Universitätsbuchhandlung.

50 *Supreme Court (Legfelsobb Bíróság) 25 September 1992* – translation available in (1993) 13 Journal of Law and Commerce 31.

51 See Commercial Court des Kantons OR 2001.00029, 5 November 2002 at http://cisgw3.law/pace/edu.cases/021105s1.html, where a contract for the manufacture of three triumphal arches held to be at par with a sales contract under Art 3(1) of the Vienna Convention.

52 Article 3(2). See *Corte Suprema di Cassazione, Sez Un, 9 June 1995 n 6499* available at www.unilex.info where the seller manufactured leather goods and also marked them with the buyer's brand. However, academic opinion seems to place the emphasis on the value of the goods for determining whether the contract is one for services or for goods – see Honnold, *Uniform Law of International Sales*, 1991, Kluwer.

53 The set-off of claims is also excluded. In *Amtsgericht Duisburg, 13 April 2000 49C 502/00* available at http://cisgw3.law.pace.edu/cases/000413g1.html, the court in relation to a set-off claim applied the private international law to determine the applicable law.

54 See *Landgericht Aachen, 14 May 1993*, available at http://cisgw3.alw.pace.edu/cases/930524g1.html on the issue of challenge to a validity of contract where the contract is contingent upon certain circumstances. See also Karollus, 'Judicial interpretation and application of the CISG in Germany 1988–94' (1995) Cornell Review of the Convention on Contracts for the International Sale of Goods 51.

55 See Arts 41 and 42.

resolved by the applicable law. Article 5 extends the exclusion to include liability for personal injury or death;[56] it is silent, however, on the issue of liability for damage to property. While there are proponents for the view that this is a matter for tort, the widely held opinion is that the Vienna Convention displaces tort liability, and compensation is to be calculated on the basis provided by Art 74.[57] Case law tends to support the majority view. For instance, a Swiss court held that damage caused to the buyer's premises due to a leak was within the ambit of the Vienna Convention.[58]

An issue that has been discussed at both judicial and scholarly level is burden of proof under the Vienna Convention. Apart from Art 79,[59] the Vienna Convention does not mention burden of proof. Whether this silence means that the issue is to be decided by resorting to domestic law has been addressed both by the courts and scholarly writing. A number of cases have resorted to domestic law;[60] at the same time, there are cases that have not. The latter is the better approach since it promotes uniformity. As Ferrari observes in the interests of uniformity, the gap in respect of burden of proof should be filled by resorting to the general principles underlying the Vienna Convention. Citing Swiss and Italian cases in support, he formulates the following three general principles:

(1) any party which wants to derive beneficial legal consequences from a legal provision has to prove the existence of the factual prerequisites of that provision;

(2) any party claiming an exception has to prove the existence of the factual prerequisites of that exception; and

(3) those facts that are exclusively in a party's sphere of responsibility and which therefore are, at least theoretically, better known to that party have to be proven by that party, since it is that party who exercises the control over that sphere.[61]

At this juncture, it makes sense to raise the issue of parol evidence (often perceived as a procedural evidentiary matter) that has seen some discussion.[62] Two US cases involving the Vienna Convention – *MCC-Marble Ceramic Center v Ceramica Nuova d'Agostin, SpA*[63] and *Beijing Metals and Mineral Import/Export Corp v American Business Center Inc*[64] – are relevant. The MCC case revolved round the issue of whether the parol evidence rule precluded the plaintiff from relying on an oral understanding that terms on the pre-printed form would not be used. At the lower judicial level, it was

---

56   See however *Oberlandesgericht Düsseldorf, 2 July 1993*, available from the CLOUT Database www.uncitral.org.

57   See Schlectriem, 'Border of tort and contract' (1988) 21(3) Cornell International LJ 467.

58   *Handelsgericht Zürich, HG 920670, 26 April 1995* available at www.unilex.info.

59   Article 79(1) states:
       A party in not liable for a failure to perform any of his obligations if he proves that the failure was due to an impediment beyond his control and that he could not reasonably be expected to have taken the impediment into account at the time of the conclusion of the contract or to have avoided or overcome it or its consequences.

60   See *ICC Arbitration Case No 6653 of 1993* available at http://cisgw3.law.pace.edu/cases/936653i1.htm in respect of burden of proof and non-conforming goods.

61   'Burden of Proof under the CISG' (2000) 5 Revue de Droit des Affaires Internationales 665 (available at www.cisg.law.pace.edu). See also *District Court Rimini 26 November 2002* – translation of case available at http://cisgw3.law.pace.edu.cases/021126i3.html.

62   The rule that if a contract is put in writing, then evidence of prior agreements and negotiations will not be included.

63   144 F 3d 1384 (11th Cir 1998).

64   993 F 2d 1178 (5th Cir 1993).

held that the affidavits submitted by MCC-Marble were barred by the parol evidence rule. On appeal, the court considered *Beijing Metals* where the parol evidence rule was held to apply but concluded it was not persuasive. It concluded that statements made by the party had to be considered in the light of Art 8 of the Vienna Convention. Article 8(3) gave the most important clue about the issue of the non-applicability of the parol evidence rule in the context of the Vienna Convention since it clearly states that 'in determining the intent of a party or the understanding a reasonable person would have had, due consideration is to be given to all relevant circumstances of the case including the negotiations, any practices which the parties have established between themselves, usages and any subsequent conduct of the parties'. Since all relevant circumstances have to be given due consideration, the court held that the parol evidence rule[65] was of no relevance in the Vienna Convention. The *MCC-Marble* approach to the parol evidence rule in the context of the Vienna Convention seems to be the correct one and the court has to be commended for its efforts to consider the Vienna Convention instead of looking to domestic law.[66]

Party autonomy and the Vienna Convention

The Vienna Convention endorses the principle of party autonomy recognised as fundamental to international commercial transactions by private international law rules in most legal systems. The Vienna Convention is not mandatory in character and Art 6 provides that parties may exclude its application altogether. There is no indication in Art 6 whether this agreement should be express or implied.[67] The best method obviously is clear in express words such as 'This contract is not subject to the Vienna Convention'. It could also be excluded with a choice of law clause, or agreeing to terms that are inconsistent with the Vienna Convention provisions. For instance, parties (with places of business in contracting states) to a sale contract may choose English law as the governing law of their contract, or they may use standard terms that are derived from English sales law. Since England is not a contracting party, the courts are likely to look to the Sale of Goods Act 1979 to resolve the issues in the sale contract. But what if the parties have chosen the law of a country that is a party to the Convention?[68] Is the contract subject to the Vienna Convention or the domestic law? This issue was considered in one of the early cases in Italy. In *Nuovo Fucinati SpA v Fondemental International AB*,[69] the contract

---

65 Note that the MCC-Marble case said that the parol evidence rule is based on substantive law.
66 See Andreason, '*MCC-Marble Ceramic Center*: the parol evidence rule and other domestic law under the Convention on Contracts for the International Sale of Goods' (1999) Brigham Young University LR 351. See also Moore, 'The parol evidence rules and the United Nations Convention on Contracts for the International Sale of Goods: justifying *Beijing Metals* and *Minerals Import/Export Corp v American Business Center Inc*' (1995) Brigham Young University LR 1347.
67 Article 3 of ULIS, by contrast, provides that the exclusion could be express or implied.
68 Even a choice of jurisdiction might attract the application of the Vienna Convention as *SARL Sodime-La Rosa v Softlife Design Ltd et al* ((Case 223), available CLOUT Database – www.uncitral.org) indicates. The contracting parties were from France and England. The general condition of sale included a French jurisdiction clause. On a plea of lack of jurisdiction by the English buyer, the court held that the French courts had jurisdiction and the applicable law was that of France and hence the Vienna Convention governed the contract. The dispute concerned the place of payment of price and, applying Art 57 of the Vienna Convention, the court concluded that it was the seller's place of business.
69 Case No RG 4267/88, 29 March 1993 available at http://csgw3.law.pace.edu/cases/930329i3.html.

was for the sale of iron chrome between an Italian seller and a Swedish buyer. Italy was a party to the Vienna Convention and Sweden was not at the time of the conclusion of the contract, which meant that Art 1(1)(a) did not apply. The parties, however, had chosen Italian law as the law governing the contract. The choice, according to the Tribunale Civile di Monza, rendered Art 1(1)(b) inapplicable and the contract was governed by Italian domestic law. The decision is indeed surprising since choice of Italian law would obviously include the Vienna Convention to which Italy was a party. It has been criticised in legal writings. For instance, according to Ferrari:

> . . . the effect of the parties designating the law of a contracting state as occurred in the transaction before the Tribunal of Monza remains very debatable. According to some, such a designation excludes the application of the convention – at least where absent the parties' agreement concerning choice of law, the law of a contracting state (and therefore, the Vienna Convention [pursuant to Art 1(1)(b)]) would be applicable. To apply the convention in these circumstances, it is argued, would deprive the parties' choice of law of any practical effect. This analysis should be rejected. A choice of law agreement designating the law of a contracting state, when made without clear reference to the purely domestic law of the designated jurisdiction, does not exclude the applicability of the Vienna Convention. On the contrary, such an agreement makes it certain that the convention applies. In addition, an agreement to apply the law of a contracting state has the effect of designating the law applicable to questions outside the scope of the convention. This avoids problems in using conflict rules to determine the law applicable to such questions. It follows, therefore, that the refusal of the Tribunal of Monza to apply the Vienna Convention was not justified, even taking into consideration the parties' agreement – provided for by the convention itself – to exclude its application.[70]

Ferrari's forceful argument, it seems, is the correct one. Decisions in other jurisdictions[71] also support it. In Case Number SCH-4318,[72] an arbitration tribunal had to decide whether the Vienna Convention applied to a sale transaction where the parties – one from a contracting state (Austria) and the other from a non-contracting state (Germany) – had stated Austrian law to be the applicable law. The tribunal, on the basis of the predominant view in commentaries on the Vienna Convention,[73] concluded that the choice of Austrian law was to be understood as the national law of Austria including the Vienna Convention as its international sales law, and not merely to domestic sales law.

Other than exclusion in whole, parties may exclude the Vienna Convention in parts or vary the effect of any of the provisions subject to the limitations laid down in Art 12. According to Art 12, the Vienna Convention's dispensation with writing does not apply if a party is located in a country that ratified the convention with a reservation permitted by Art 96.

---

70 Ferrari, 'Uniform Law of International Sales: issues of applicability and private international law' (1995) 15 Journal of Law and Commerce 159, at p 173, available at http://cisgw3.law.pace.edu.

71 See *ICC Arbitration Case No 6653* of 1993 (Abstract No 103, available CLOUT Database, www.uncitral.org). Parties' choice of French law led to the application of the Vienna Convention.

72 *Internationales Schedisgericht der Bundeskammer der gewerblichen Wirtschaft*, available at http//cisgw3.law.pace.edu.

73 Citing Bonnell, in Bianca and Bonnell (eds), *Commentary on International Sales Law*, 1987, Giuffrè.

Trade usage and the Vienna Convention

As seen in Chapter 1, trade usages and trade terms play an important role in international commercial law, and for a convention to be successful it needs to be sympathetic to them. How does the Vienna Convention tackle the issue of trade usages? Like every other provision, the provision on trade usage, Art 9, is the result of a compromise. It was fiercely debated, since the attitude to trade usages varied amongst the delegates. Socialist countries were wary of trade usages[74] since they preferred the contract to be secure and certain so that the parties are not taken by surprise, especially where local usages are adopted.[75] They also perceived trade usage as the product of a limited group of countries (Western nations) and did not reflect an opinion shared globally – a view equally shared by third world countries. This does not mean that Socialist countries did not recognise trade usages. By and large they do, provided they are widely recognised – that is, internationally well known – clear and certain.[76] By contrast, Western nations felt comfortable with the recognition of trade usage by the Vienna Convention and in giving primacy to them.

The recognition of trade usage in the convention is nothing new. Trade usage was recognised in ULIS (Art 9), but was criticised for allowing a number of permutations.[77] What is novel, however, are some of requirements for trade usage to take effect. The Vienna Convention recognises both express and implied usages. Knowledge plays a vital role in incorporating usages impliedly: that is, whether the parties knew or ought to have known of the usage, that the usage is widely known in international trade,[78] and the usage is regularly observed by the parties in contracts of the type involved in the particular trade concerned. It seems that trade usage as perceived by the Vienna Convention will not include custom.[79] Article 9 also covers practices that the parties have established between themselves. It seems from decided

---

74   For a comparison with trade usage in ULIS, see Bainbridge, 'Trade usages in international sales of goods: an analysis of the 1964 and 1980 Sales Conventions' (1984) 24 Virginia Journal of International Law 619. For further on foreign trade in planned economies, see Dore, 'Plan and contract in the domestic and foreign trade of the USSR' (1980) 8 Syracuse Journal of International Law and Commerce 29.

75   Eörsi, 'A propos the 1980 Vienna Convention on Contracts for the International Sale of Goods' (1983) 31 American Journal of Comparative Law 333.

76   Report of the Secretary General (1970) 1 Yearbook UNCITRAL UN Doc A/CN 9/Ser A 1970, at pp 549–50.

77   See Jokela, 'The role of usages in the Uniform Law on International Sales' (1966) 10 Scandinavian Studies in Law 81.

78   In *BP International Ltd and BP Exploration & Oil Inc, Plaintiffs-Appellants v Empresa Estatal Petroleos Ecuador et al Defendants, Empresa Estatal Petroleos de Ecuador and Saybolt Inc, Defendants-Appelles*, US Court of Appeals 5th Cir 02-21066, 11 June 2003 (available at http://cisgw3.law.pace.edu/cases/03611u1.html), it was acknowledged that the Vienna Convention incorporates INCOTERMS. Even if they are not global, the fact that they are well known in international trade means that they are incorporated through Art 9(2) according to the judgment. Since the parties had contracted on CFR terms, risk was seen as passing when the goods passed the ship's rail. See Chapter 1, pp 35–36 above, for further on CFR INCOTERMS and C&F.

79   See Honnold, *Uniform Law for International Sales under the 1980 United Nations Convention*, 1999, Kluwer; Karlgren, 'Usages and statute law' (1961) 5 Scandinavian Studies in Law 39; Wortley, 'The relevance of course of dealing, usages and customs in the interpretation of international commercial contracts' (1977) 1 New Directions in International Trade Law 139; Bainbridge, 'Trade usages in international sale of goods: an analysis of the 1964 and 1980 Sales Conventions' (1984) 24 Virginia Journal of International Law 619.

cases that regularity of behaviour on a couple of occasions will be insufficient for the purpose of establishing a practice.[80]

Interpretation of the Vienna Convention

While adoption of an international convention introduces harmonisation and certainty, there is no surety that the degree of harmonisation and certainty achieved will be high since different jurisdictions are likely to interpret the provisions variously given the richness of language. One way to counter disharmony is to include an interpretation provision within the convention itself. The Vienna Convention has just such a provision in its Art 7, which states:

(1) In the interpretation of this convention, regard is to be had to its international character and to the need to promote uniformity on its application and the observance of good faith in international trade.

(2) Questions concerning matters governed by this convention which are not expressly settled in it are to be settled in conformity with the general principles on which it is based or, in the absence of such principles, in conformity with the law applicable by virtue of the rules of private international law.

There is, however, a gap between theory and practice as experience with the Vienna Convention illustrates. In spite of the extensive case database maintained by UNCITRAL on the Vienna Convention (and available on their website), there is reluctance on the part of courts to refer to opinions from other jurisdictions as an aid to interpretation. According to Murray,[81] judges tend to interpret the Vienna Convention, in spite of Art 7, with a 'domestic legal lens'. This view is equally backed by scholars with a civil law background. For instance, Bonnell and Liguori state that 'very rarely do decisions take into account the solutions adopted on the same point by courts in other countries'.[82] Having said this, reference must be made to recognition of the international nature of conventions and the need to refer to foreign judgments on the part of British judges. For instance, even in the absence of an interpretation provision in the Hague Rules,[83] the House of Lords in *Stag Line Ltd v Foscola, Mango and Co*[84] took the view that the interpretation of international conventions should not be rigidly controlled by domestic precedents of antecedent date but that the language should be construed on broad principles of general acceptance. Similar sentiments have been expressed in the interpretation of other international transport conventions. In *Corocraft Ltd v Pan American Airways Inc*, Lord Denning said 'even if I disagreed, I would follow [decisions of other courts] in a manner which is of international concern. The courts of all countries should interpret [the Warsaw Convention][85] in the same way'.[86]

---

80 See *AG Duisburg, 13 April 2000 49 C 502/00*, available at http://cisgw3.law.pace.edu/cases/000413g1.html.

81 Murray, 'The neglect of CISG: a workable solution' (1998) 17 Journal of Law and Commerce 365.

82 Bonnell and Liguori, 'The UN Convention on the International Sale of Goods; a critical analysis of current international case law' (1997) 2 Revue de Droit Uniforme 385.

83 International Convention for the Unification of Certain Rules Relating to Bills of Lading, Brussels 1924. See also Chapter 8.

84 [1932] AC 328.

85 Convention for the Unification of Certain Rules relating to International Carriage by Air 1929. See also Chapter 10.

86 [1969] 1 QB 616, at p 655.

There is controversy and debate still raging around the good faith part of Art 7. Honnold,[87] on the basis of its drafting history, is of the view that good faith relates only to the interpretation of the convention, while Schlechtriem[88] is of the opinion that it is a general principle. The developing interpretation in case law seemingly favouring good faith in contract performance has not been widely followed to give a decisive answer on this matter, though it seems that following the view that good faith is an underlying principle may help fill in some of the gaps that emerge in the Vienna Convention.

Formation of a contract

The Vienna Convention adopts the traditional offer-acceptance framework for determining the existence of a contract. Consideration, a concept found in common law, plays no role. However, the common lawyer will find much that is familiar and unfamiliar in the formation of contract under the Vienna Convention. No specific formal requirements are imposed and a contract can be concluded in any form, oral exchange or otherwise.[89] Article 11, however, was the subject of some debate since socialist countries such as Russia, used to strict formal requirements for international trade transactions,[90] were unhappy with contracts coming into existence on the basis of oral communication; similarly, with modification and termination. It was therefore agreed[91] that states requiring written communication could make a reservation under Art 96. Once a reservation is made under Art 96, it is mandatory and the contracting parties cannot agree to depart from the writing requirement. To illustrate, a contract of sale between two parties with places of business in contracting states, one of whom has an Art 96 reservation, will not be able to opt out of the formal requirement that the contract be in writing.

An offer, under the Vienna Convention (Art 14):

- must be addressed to a specific person;
- must be sufficiently definite (that is, the offer must indicate the goods and fix the quantity and price explicitly or implicitly); and

---

87 Honnold, *Uniform Law for International Sales under the 1980 United Nations Convention*, 1999, Kluwer.

88 Schlechtriem (ed), *Commentary on the UN Convention on the International Sale of Goods* (Thomas (trans)), 1998, Clarendon Press. See Kastely, 'Unification and community: a rhetorical analysis of the United Nations Sales Convention' (1988) 8 Northwestern Journal of International Law and Business 574; Koneru, 'The international interpretation of the UN Convention on the Contracts for the International Sale of Goods: an approach based on general principles' (1997) 6 Minnesota Journal of Global Trade 105; Schlechtriem, 'Good faith in German law and International Uniform Laws', available at www.cnr.it/CRDCS/schlechtriem.htm. The text of the Vienna Convention, case law and various articles are available on this excellent website: www.cisg.law.pace.edu.

89 See Art 15 of ULIS and Art 3 of ULFIS for a similar provision. Note that the UNIDROIT Principles for International Commercial Contracts in Art 1.7 specifically adopts the notion of good faith as a founding principle. On whether the Vienna Convention allows electronic communications see *CISG – Advisory Council Opinion no 1*, available at www.cisg.law.pace.edu. See also Chapter 3.

90 Eg, General Conditions of Delivery of Goods between Enterprises of the Member States of the Council for Mutual Economic Assistance. For more on the Council for Mutual Economic Assistance and trading system, see Metcalf, *The Council for Mutual Economic Assistance*, 1997, Columbia UP. This organisation was an economic one of Communist countries. Formed in 1949, it was dissolved in 1991.

91 See Art 12.

- must indicate the intention on the offeror's part to be bound in the event of acceptance.

While Art 14 states that the price must be fixed either explicitly or implicitly, Art 55 of the Vienna Convention goes on to state:

> Where a contract has been validly concluded but does not expressly or implicitly fix or make provision for determining the price, the parties are considered in the absence of any indication to the contrary to have impliedly made reference to the price generally charged at the time of the conclusion of the contract or such goods sold under comparable circumstances in the trade concerned.

It seems there is a conflict between Art 14 and Art 55. Article 14 seems to suggest there is no offer if the price is not fixed, either implicitly or explicitly, whereas Art 55 suggests there is a contract even in the absence of explicit/implicit agreement of price. Unsurprisingly, there are disparate opinions among scholars in respect of the interplay between Arts 14 and 55. Honnold is of the opinion there is no contradiction – Art 14 is concerned with offers and the emphasis of Art 55 is on contracts that are validly concluded but have not made express or implied provision for determining the price. There is support for this view from other scholars as well.[92] The alternative view is that Art 55 is of relevance to those contracting states to the Vienna Convention who have made a reservation that they will not be bound by Part II.[93] As for case law, Art 55 has been cited in a number of judgments. The earliest cases relating to undetermined price emanated from Hungary. In the first case, *Adamfi Video Production Gmbh v Alktok Studisa Kisszovetkezet*,[94] the price, using Art 9(1), was determined on the basis of past course of dealings between the parties and no reference was made to Art 55. The next case, *United Technologies (Pratt and Whitney) v Malev Hungarian Airlines*,[95] involved sale of engines by the plaintiffs for Boeings that Hungarian Airlines were planning to buy. The offer did not quote an exact price but the court at first instance held that a contract was concluded since the offer made provision for the quantity and price. On appeal, the Supreme Court overturned the decision holding that for the purposes of Art 14(1) a bid is properly defined if it indicates the products, the quantity and the price, or contains directions as to how these terms can be defined. Article 55 could not be used to determine the price for a product like a jet engine which has no market price. A rather surprising interpretation of Art 55, given that it does not differentiate between products for the purposes of determining price.

Flechtner is critical of the decision in this case and it is difficult not to agree with him. He says:

---

92 Schlechtriem, *Uniform Sales Law*, 1986, Manzsche Verlags-und Universitätsbuchhandlung; see also Eörsi in Bianca and Bonnell, *Commentary on International Sales Law: The 1980 Vienna Convention, 1987*, Giuffrè; Hartnell, 'Rousing the sleeping dog: the validity of the exception to the Convention on Contracts for the International Sale of Goods' (1993) 18 Yale Journal of International Law 1; Garro, 'Reconciliation of legal traditions in the UN Convention on Contracts for the International Sale of Goods' (1989) 23 International Lawyer 443.

93 See *United Nations Conference on Contracts for the International Sale of Goods (Vienna 10 March-11 April 1980)*, Official Records 1, 45, 1981, New York; Murray Jr, 'An essay on the formation of contracts and related matters under the United Nations Convention on Contracts for the International Sale of Goods' (1988) 8 Journal of Law and Commerce 11.

94 *Municipal Court, Budapest AZ 12.G.41.471/1991/21, 24 March 1992* – abstract available from CLOUT Database at www.uncitral.org.

95 *Supreme Court GF.I.31.349/1992/9, 24 September 1992*, translation available in (1992) 13 Journal of Law and Commerce 31.

The decision is subject to several criticisms. First, it rewards Malev's bad faith in repudiating an agreement that, when made, the buyer almost certainly assumed was binding. Imagine if the tables were turned, and it was Pratt and Whitney who refused to sell the engines after Malev had committed to purchase the Boeing aircraft. Secondly, the decision ignores the international character of the convention by straining for an interpretation favourable to the party of the same nationality as the court.[96]

However, not all decisions are as extreme nor preclude the view that there is a valid contract where no price has been fixed. In *Arbitration Case of Bulgarian Chamber of Commerce and Industry 14/98 Bulgaria, 30 November 1998*,[97] the tribunal concluded that in situations where the price is only tentatively defined it does not follow that there is no valid contract for sale. The issue was to be determined as provided for by Art 55 – that is, in terms of the price generally charged at the time of the conclusion of the contract for such goods sold under comparable circumstances in the trade concerned. It is not absolutely clear from the case as translated whether the parties had indicated a price range. Cases from other jurisdictions also indicate that Art 55 is relevant where no price is agreed,[98] lending support to the view taken by Honnold.

An offer, not unlike the rule in common law, is effective upon receipt. Unlike common law, the Vienna Convention makes room for a firm offer. As for revocation of an offer, rules differ among civil law and common law traditions. At common law, an offer can be revoked any time before acceptance even where the offeror agrees to keep the offer open until a fixed date. One way for the offeree to protect himself against revocation is to provide consideration. In the civil law tradition on the other hand, where a period of time is fixed, the offeror cannot revoke the offer during that period. The issue of revocability of offer is addressed in Art 16. It is a peculiar provision prone to either a common law biased or a civil law biased interpretation. According to Art 16(1), 'until a contract is concluded, an offer may be revoked if the revocation reaches the offeree before he has dispatched the acceptance'. There is much that is familiar to the common law system in this provision. Article 16(2) then goes on to say that 'an offer cannot be revoked (a) if it indicates, whether by stating a fixed time for acceptance or otherwise, that it is irrevocable, or (b) if it was reasonable for the offeree to rely on the offer as being irrevocable and the offeree has acted in reliance on the offer'. Equally, there is much that is familiar to the civil law system in para 2. Given that Art 16 reflects rules that are familiar to both sides, there is a real danger that in interpreting this provision emphasis will be put on the part that is most familiar. To illustrate: if an offer states 'Please reply by 29 January', it is likely to be interpreted as giving a fixed time for acceptance by the civil law tradition, whereas the common law tradition will see it as simply indicating when the offer is to lapse, not irrevocability. It has been suggested by various commentators that the provision should be interpreted independently of any legal doctrine the lawyers may bring with them.

---

96 'The several texts of the CISG in a decentralized system: observations on translations, reservations and other challenges to the uniformity principles in Art 7(1)' (1998) 17 Journal of Law and Commerce 187, at p 205.

97 Available at http://cisgw3.law.pace.edu/cases/981130bu.html.

98 See *Supreme Court 2 Ob 547/93, 10 November 1993* (1995) Zeitschrift für Rechtsvergleichung 79; *Bezirksgericht St Gallen 3PZ97/18, 3 July 1997* – abstract available from CLOUT Database www.uncitral.org where the court did not rule out the applicability of Art 55 though, in the case under consideration, they said there was a sufficiently definite price on the basis of what was said in the offer and the subsequent behaviour of the buyer; *Oberlandesgericht Rostock 6U126/00, 10 October 2001*, abstract available at www.unilex.info, where the court held that reasonable price has to be determined by using price list.

To superimpose a received doctrine in its interpretation, as Sono states, would 'distort the convention's rules, which are in fact tailored to meet the reasonable expectations of the business community'.[99] According to Schlectriem, the stating of a period of acceptance by the offer simply creates a rebuttable presumption of irrevocability and Art 8 should be used to establish the intention of the parties.

In order to accept, the offeree needs to indicate his assent either with a statement or other conduct. Mere silence on his part will not constitute an acceptance (Art 18(1)). Acceptance of the offer becomes effective when it is received by the offeror (Art 18(2)),[100] though it can be withdrawn before the acceptance reaches the offeror or at the same time as the acceptance would have become effective (Art 22). As indicated earlier, it is possible under the Vienna Convention to conclude a contract orally. If the offer is an oral offer, then acceptance to an oral offer must be immediate according to Art 18(2).[101] Presumably, it will not be possible to withdraw an oral acceptance to an oral offer since Art 22 envisages that the acceptance is not immediate but will take time to reach the offeror.

In international trade, it is not uncommon for merchants to use their standard forms reflecting terms that are beneficial to the merchant who has drafted the form. Often the acceptance sent on a standard form is likely to be on terms different from those found in the offer. In these circumstances, the issue is to establish the terms on which the contract is concluded. Common law follows what is often called the mirror image rule – that is, the offer and acceptance must match.[102] Where the terms of the purported acceptance are different from that of the offer, it is a counter-offer. So, even a slight variation would constitute a counter-offer.

The Vienna Convention, while adopting the mirror image rule, allows for some distortion. While Art 19(1) unambiguously states that 'a reply to an offer that purports to be an acceptance but contains additions, limitations or other modifications is a rejection of the offer and constitutes a counter-offer', Art 19(2) states that a reply which contains additional or different terms which do not materially alter the terms of the offer will constitute an acceptance, and the contract terms will consist of those in the offer along with the modifications in the acceptance unless the offeror objects. However, where the acceptance contains terms that materially alter the terms of the offer, then the purported acceptance will be a counter-offer. The Vienna Convention provides an inexhaustive list of terms that are likely to be regarded as material alterations. These according to Art 19(3) are terms relating to price,[103] payment, quantity,

---

99   Sono, 'Restoration of the rule of reason in contract formation: has there been civil and common law disparity?' (1988) 21 Cornell International LJ 474, at p 479.

100   See *Cour de Justice, Genève C/11185/2001, 13 September 2002*, available at http://cisgw3.law.pace.edu/cases/020913s1.html.

101   Of course, an oral offer can fix a time for acceptance.

102   See *Hyde v Wrench* (1840) 49 ER 132; *Butler Machine Tool Co Ltd v Ex-Cell-O Corp (England) Ltd* [1979] 1 All ER 965. See also Shanker, ' "Battle of the forms": a comparison and critique of Canadian, American and historical common law perspectives' (1979–80) 4 Canadian Business LJ 263; Winship, 'Formation of international sales contracts under the 1980 Vienna Convention' (1983) International Lawyer 1; Cigoj, 'International sale of goods: formation of contracts' (1976) Netherlands International LR 257; Kelso, 'The United Nations Convention on Contracts for the International Sale of Goods: contract formation and the battle of forms' (1983) Columbia Journal of Transnational Law 528; Thatcher, 'Battle of the forms: solution by revision of section 2–207' (1984) 16 Uniform Commercial Code LJ 237; Murray Jr, 'The chaos of the "battle of the forms" solution' (1986) 39 Vanderbilt LR 1307.

103   See *Magellan International Corporation v Salzgitter Handel Gmbh*, US District Court, Northern District of Illinois, 99 C 153, 7 December 1999 (available at http://cisgw3.law.pace.edu/cases/991207u1.html) where a price change proposal was regarded as counter-offer.

place and time of delivery, extent of one party's liability to the other and settlement of disputes. It seems therefore that only minor changes are likely to be treated as immaterial – for instance, where an offer quotes the price FOB Singapore and the acceptance states Free on Board Singapore.

Obligations of the seller

According to Art 30, the seller is under an obligation to:

- deliver goods;
- hand over the documents; and
- transfer property in the goods.[104]

The Vienna Convention does not list the kind of documents the seller is required to hand over to the buyer. In international sales, it is usual for the seller to require certificates of origin, quality, transport documents and other documents required for customs clearance. The sale contract would stipulate the documents required. Use of trade terms would also indicate the minimum requirements in respect of documents to be tendered to the buyer.[105]

The obligation to deliver is dealt with in Art 31. The sale contract is likely to stipulate the particular place where delivery is to take place. In the absence of such a stipulation, according to Art 31, delivery is dependent on the circumstances. So, where the contract of sale involves carriage of goods, then delivery will take place when the goods are handed over to the first carrier for transmission to the buyer.[106] If the contract of sale does not involve carriage of goods, and where the contract relates to specific goods, or unidentified goods to be drawn from a specific stock or to be manufactured or produced, and the parties knew that the goods were at a particular place or to be manufactured at a particular place, delivery takes place when the goods are placed at the buyer's disposal at that place according to Art 31(b). In all other cases, delivery takes place when the goods are placed at the buyer's disposal at the seller's place of business at the conclusion of the contract according to Art 31(c). The Vienna Convention is silent as to whether the seller needs to satisfy any formalities in placing the goods at the buyer's disposal. Presumably, he will have to notify the buyer that the goods are at his disposal so that he can take over the goods thus enabling the passing of risk from the seller to the buyer.[107] It is more than likely, as Lando says, that Art 31 will be of limited use since it is likely that parties have used trade terms in their contract of sale. However, use of trade terms may itself cause problems.[108] If INCOTERMS are used, then no doubt it embodies a uniform approach to a number of obligations from delivery, passing of risk to obtaining of export and

---

104 There are no provisions in the Vienna Convention in respect of transfer of property and the issue will be decided according to the law applicable to the contract. In *Oberlandsgericht Koblenz 5 U 534/91, 16 January 1992*, available at www.unilex.info, it was held that the validity of retention of title clauses fell outside the ambit of the Vienna Convention.

105 See Chapter 1 for further on trade terms and documentation.

106 Parties may derogate from the provisions of the Vienna Convention. Where this is the case, the onus is on the party raising derogation. See *AG Duisburg, 13 April 2000, 49 C 502/00* available at http://cisgw3.law.pace.edu/cases/00413g1.html.

107 See Art 69; see also 'Passing of risk', pp 81–3 below.

108 See Bianca and Bonnell, *Commentary on International Sales Law: The 1980 Vienna Convention*, 1987, Giuffrè.

import licences. Where parties have not referred to INCOTERMS specifically, then it may cause problems since trade terms may be interpreted differently in different jurisdictions. The situation gets more complicated where the parties agree on terms not widely used such as 'CIF landed port of destination'.

The matter will presumably be resolved by looking to Arts 8, 9 and choice of law. As for the date of delivery, the sale contract would normally stipulate this – it could be a fixed date or within a fixed period or on the happening of an event such as the buyer opening a letter of credit. According to Art 33, delivery should take place if the date is fixed on that date. Where the parties agree on a period of time, then within that period. The choice of when to deliver within that period will be the seller's unless circumstances indicate that the buyer is to choose the date. Resort to Art 8 may be required to establish the parties' intention. Where the agreement does not indicate a fixed period or a fixed time, goods are to be delivered within a reasonable time after conclusion of the contract. What is reasonable will inevitably depend on the circumstances of each case. Equally, where the seller is required under the contract to hand over documents, he is required to do so at the time and place agreed by them.[109]

As for goods that are delivered, Art 35(1) requires that they are of the quantity, quality and description required by the contract, and are contained or packaged in the manner required by the contract. Goods will not conform[110] if they are not fit for the purpose for which goods of the same description would ordinarily be used (Art 35(2)(a)), are not fit for the particular purpose made known to the seller expressly or impliedly (Art 35(2)(b)),[111] do not possess the qualities of goods which the seller has held out to the buyer as sample or model (Art 35(2)(c)), are not packaged in the usual manner, or adequately to preserve and protect the goods (Art 35(2)(d)).

Obligations of the buyer

The buyer is obliged to take delivery of the goods under Art 53, and Art 60 obliges the buyer to doing all acts which could reasonably be expected of him in order to enable the seller to make delivery and in taking over the goods. He is also placed under a duty to examine the goods once the goods have been delivered and give timely notice in the event of non-conformity of goods. Unlike ULIS, which requires the buyer to examine the goods promptly,[112] under Art 38(1) of the Vienna Convention the examination of the goods must take place within as short a time as is practicable in the circumstances. Under Art 38(1), it is not a requirement that the buyer personally examines the goods. The goods may be examined by his employees or through others

---

109 If he delivers documents before the date agreed, he could cure any defects in the documents until the agreed time according to Art 34. See 'Fixing additional time for performance and curing the breach', pp 85–6 below.

110 See *Oberlandsgericht Schleswig 11 U40/01, 22 August 2002* (available at www.unilex.info) on the issue of non-conforming goods. The contract involved the sale of sheep and the buyer said that he had indicated that he wanted sheep ready for slaughter, not raw-boned sheep. The court said that the onus was on the buyer to show that he had informed the seller of his intention to slaughter the sheep immediately. In the circumstances, sufficient evidence had not been produced to convince the court.

111 Parties may agree otherwise through express disclaimers. Presumably, the wording will have to be clear. See *Ajax Tool Works Inc v Can-Eng Manufacturing Ltd*, US District Court, North District Court of Illinois 01 C 5938, 29 January 2003 (available at http://cisgw3/law. pace.edu/cases/0130129ul.html) for an illustration.

112 See Art 39 of ULIS.

appointed by him for that task. It could also be a third party, such as the second buyer, who has bought the goods during transit from the first buyer.

Most international sales are likely to involve the carriage of goods where the seller might be involved in arranging the shipment of goods as in CIF sales or loads the goods on the vessel nominated by the buyer as in FOB sales.[113] It may not be practicable to inspect the goods at the point of departure. The same applies to the case where the goods are sold during transit.[114] The buyer might not have the time to examine the goods or it may be difficult to remove all the packaging to examine the goods. Article 38 is sympathetic to the various practices found in international sales and the contingencies that may arise. Article 38(2) provides that, where the contract involves carriage of goods, examination may be deferred until the goods have arrived at the destination. Where the goods are redirected or redispatched by the buyer without a reasonable opportunity to examine them and where the seller knows or ought to have known of the possibility that goods are likely to be redispatched or redirected at the conclusion of the contract, examination may be deferred until after the goods have arrived at the new destination. The seller is likely to know of such a possibility, for instance, where the buyer requests the seller to give him a transferable bill of lading.[115] Of course, the extension allowed for the purposes of examination of goods places the seller in a difficult situation but, according to Art 38(3), it seems that the buyer has to establish that the seller knew or ought to have known of the redirection at the time of conclusion of the contract. It is often said that Art 38(3) is incomplete since it does not address resale by the buyer. As Bianca and Bonnell[116] observe, however, resale in most cases is likely to involve redispatch or redirection in transit. Where the goods are packed in a manner for resale to consumers, then Art 38(1) is relevant.

It is not clear from Art 38 whether the examination has to be thorough or whether examination of a random sample is sufficient. It seems from the Commentary,[117] the method of examination is to be determined on the basis of what is acceptable in international usage. Past practices between the parties may also be a relevant factor. Of course, it is always open to the parties to specify the level and kind of examination in their agreement. Interestingly, ULIS in Art 38(4) in relation to examination states that 'the methods of examination shall be governed by agreement of the parties or, in the absence of such agreement, by the law or usage of the place where the examination is to be effected'. It is inevitable that reliance on the law or usage of the place will introduce a considerable degree of uncertainty and the drafters of the Vienna Convention decided not to include a similar provision but instead indicating in the *travaux preparatoire* that international usage would be relevant. In the absence of a widely adopted international usage, the best course would be to consider the issue on the basis of what would be reasonable in the circumstances.

---

113 See Chapter 1, for further on transport arrangements under the various trade terms.
114 Note that under ULIS where goods were sold during transit the examination of the goods could be deferred only if they had not been transhipped. Transhipment, however, is a common occurrence and the ULIS provision was often criticised for being unduly favourable to the seller. The Vienna Convention, however, does not place this condition in the event of goods being redirected or redispatched by the buyer.
115 See Chapter 6 for further on transferability of a bill of lading and the associated rights.
116 In Bianca and Bonnell (eds), *Commentary on International Sales Law: The 1980 Vienna Convention*, 1987, Giuffrè.
117 See *United Nations Conference on Contracts for the International Sale of Goods (Vienna 10 March–11 April 1980)*, Official Records I, 34, 1981, New York.

In the event the buyer has discovered or ought to have discovered a lack of conformity, Art 39(1) places the buyer under an obligation to notify the seller of the defect within a reasonable time. If he fails to do so, he loses the right to rely on lack of conformity. In any event, the buyer loses the right to rely on a lack of conformity if he does not give the seller notice of non-conformity within two years from the date on which the goods were handed over (Art 39(2)).[118]

Reasonable time is a flexible notion to be construed according to surrounding circumstances. What is reasonable time for a piece of machinery[119] will not be reasonable for perishable items. It also seems that timely notice is to be determined on the basis of usage.[120] Emerging case law from various jurisdictions also indicates that that is how the phrase 'reasonable time' is being construed. In *Al Palazzo Srl v Bernardaud di Limoges SA*,[121] the buyer who ordered porcelain plates for use at his restaurant failed to pay the second instalment of the price, alleging that the goods were affected by defects such as chips and cracks. The seller argued that buyer had lost his right to rely on lack of conformity due to failure to give notice within a reasonable time[122] as required under Art 39(1). While taking into account the construction of reasonable time in other jurisdictions, the court concluded that a six-month period was too extended due to the nature, use and purpose for which the goods were bought – namely, their use in the buyer's business. Past course of dealings may also be a relevant factor. The burden of proof is on the buyer to show that timely notice was given. As the Italian court said '. . . it must be reiterated that the principle "*onus probandi incumbit et qui dicit*" . . . is a general principle on which the CISG is based'.[123]

If reasonable time[124] is construed on the basis of surrounding circumstances, nature of the goods and usage, then without doubt Art 39 can be said to affect certainty, uniformity and predictability – the aims the Vienna Convention promotes. Of course, if the parties so wish, they can set their own time limits in respect of notification. This is the step that parties to a contract for the sale of cold rolled metal in coils took in *Internationales Schiedsgericht der Bundeskammer der gewerblichen Wirtschaft SCH 4318, 15 June 1994*.[125] They included the following clauses:

> Seller's warranty against defects in the goods is subject to the condition that buyer examine the goods immediately after taking delivery and give without delay written

---

118　It must be noted that the time limit set by this provision is subject to any time limits set by the contractual period of guarantee.

119　In *Shuttle Packaging Systems LLC v Tsonakis 01 C 691 (WD Mich, 17 Dec 2001)* available on Westlaw Reference WL 34046276 in relation to machinery for producing plastic pots the court said that 'it is also clear from statute that on occasion it will not be practicable to require notification in a matter of few weeks. For this reason, the outer limit of two years was set for the purpose of barring late notices'. See also *Chicago Prime Packers Inc v Northam Food Trading Co 01 C 4447* available at http://cisgw3.law.pace.edu/cases/030529u1.html.

120　See Art 9 of the Vienna Convention.

121　Italy 26 November 2002 District Court Rimini – translation of case available at http://cisgw3.law.pace.edu/cases/021126i3.html.

122　The items were examined two months after delivery and notice given six months after delivery.

123　See para 4 of *Al Palazzo Srl v Bernardaud di Limoges SA*. See also *Handelsgericht Zürich, 9 September 1993 [HG 930138 U/H 93]* available at http://cisgw3.law.pace.edu/cases/9300909s1.html.

124　For an exhaustive article on reasonable time and Art 39(1) of the Vienna Convention, see Andersen, 'Reasonable time in Article 39(1) of the CISG – is Article 39(1) truly a uniform provision?' at http://www.cisgw3.law.pace.edu/cisg/biblio/andersen.html.

125　At http://cisgw3.law.pace.edu/cases/940615a4.html.

> notice of any defects discovered and substantiate its findings with an expert statement by an internationally recognised testing company.
>
> Complaints as to defects not recognizable immediately must be made no later than two months after the goods have been handed over.

Despite these clauses, the buyer took well over two months to give notice, but the buyer alleged that seller could not set up the defence of late notice since the parties had derogated from the time limit as established by the contract on the basis that the seller had recognised the complaints and they had talked about legal settlement. Referring to the concept of reliance found in Arts 16(2)(b) and of 29(2) alongside citing Arts 7(1) and (2), the tribunal raised estoppel to find in favour of the buyer. In the words of the tribunal:[126]

> ... at least the principle of estoppel or, to use another expression, the prohibition of venire contra factum proprium, which represents a special application of the general principle of good faith, may without doubt be seen as one of the 'general principles on which the convention is based', which according to Art 7(2) of the CISG may be settled in the convention ...
>
> In the case in point, the requirements for forfeiture are met. The [seller] may never have had the intention of waiving the defence of late notice; however, objectively, its conduct after receiving the first complaint from the [buyer] was such as to give the latter the justifiable impression that it recognised the lawfulness of the complaint despite the lateness of the transmission ... What is even more important is the fact that the [seller] repeatedly made statements ... from which the latter could reasonably infer that the [seller] would not set up the defence of late notice.

The above decision reveals a mature approach by the arbitration tribunal which, instead of resorting to domestic law on the basis of silence on the part of the Vienna Convention, studied the convention closely to reveal the principle of estoppel.

While Art 39 unambiguously states the right to claim non-conformity is lost if the notice requirements are not met, the harshness of the rule is somewhat tempered by Art 44 which states:

> Notwithstanding the provisions of paragraph (1) of Art 39 and paragraph (1) of Art 43, the buyer may reduce the price in accordance with Art 50 or claim damages, except for loss of profit, if he has reasonable excuse for his failure to give the required notice.[127]

It is difficult to see how effective this position will be in practice since the onus will be on the buyer to show that he had a reasonable excuse for failure of notification, a point also made by Bianca and Bonnell. It is, however, possible that the buyer may have a reasonable excuse for failure where the merchandise bought is equipment and faults become apparent over time with use.

The seller's right to rely on late notice as a defence is lost where the lack of conformity relates to facts which the seller knew or could not have been unaware of and which he did not disclose to the buyer according to Art 40. *Landsgericht Trier 7 HO*

---

126 As translated. See paras 5.6 and 5.7 of translated text available at www.unilex.info.

127 Note there is no similar provision in ULIS. Article 44 was a last-minute compromise to appease those who thought that Art 39 was too harsh on the buyer. The problems of traders from developing countries were another reason that was highlighted during the course of negotiations. See Date-Bah, 'Vienna Sales Convention 1980 – developing countries' perspectives', in Penna (ed), *Current Developments in International Transfers of Goods and Services (6th Singapore Conference on International Business Law, September 1992)*, 1994, Butterworths Asia.

78/95, 12 October 1995[128] provides an interesting illustration. A consignment of wine was sold by the Italian seller to a German buyer. The German authorities seized the wine and destroyed it since it contained 9% water with which the wine had been mixed. The buyer refused payment. The seller said that the buyer could not rely on non-conformity since he had not examined the wine. The court held that he could since the seller could not have been unaware of the non-conformity. It also went on to add that the delivery of wine with water additions which is not fit for circulation constitutes wilful deceit.[129]

The buyer is also obliged to pay the price for the goods on the date fixed and take the formalities required to effect payment.[130] So if the sale agreement requires the opening of a letter of credit, then the buyer must take the necessary steps. In the absence of agreement, the place of payment according to Art 57 is the seller's place of business. If payment is against handing over of goods or documents, then at the place where the goods or documents are handed over.

Passing of risk

As indicated in Chapter 1, passing of risk is an important event in the sale of goods. Once the buyer acquires risk, he becomes liable for the price even if the goods are lost or damaged. Under English law – that is, the Sales of Goods Act 1979 – the general rule is that risk passes along with property though there are exceptions to this.[131]

The Vienna Convention also contains provisions relating to passing of risk. The consequences of the passing of risk from seller to buyer are no different from those found in English domestic law. Article 66[132] states that:

> . . . loss of or damage to the goods after the risk has passed to the buyer does not discharge him from his obligation to pay the price, unless the loss or damage is due to an act or omission of the seller.[133]

It is likely that most contracts will contain terms stating when risk is to pass, or the use of trade terms will also determine the passing of risk. In their absence, the Vienna Convention's rules relating to passing of risk will come into play. Instead of providing

---

128 Available http://cisgw3.law.pace.edu/cases/951012g.html. See also *Oberlandsgericht Schleswig 11U 40/01, 22 August 2002*, available at http://cisgw3.law.pace.edu/cases/020822g2.html.

129 See also *LG Darmstadt 10 O 72 00, 9 May 2000*, available at http://www.cisgw3.law.pace.edu/cases/000509g1.html.

130 See Arts 53, 54 and 59.

131 See sections on 'Passing of risk' in Chapter 1, pp 26–7 and 45.

132 See Art 96 of ULIS which is substantively similar.

133 The burden of showing the seller's act or omission is on the buyer: *Tribunal of International Commercial Arbitration at the Russian Federation Chamber of Commerce and Industry 342/1998, 17 May 1999*, available at http://cisgw3.law.pace.edu/cases/990517r1.html. In *CIETAC 1995* (available at www.unilex.info), the contract was on CIF terms. The buyer had given explicit instructions to the seller to tell the carrier that the cargo was subject to deterioration at high temperatures and that it must be stored in a relatively cool place, and must be transported on a direct line. Appropriate instructions were not given by the seller and the goods arrived damaged. Notwithstanding the rule that risk passes on crossing ship's rail, the Chinese International Economic and Trade Arbitration Commission applying Art 66 said that the damage was caused by an act or omission of the seller. The reason for this deviation from the CIF rule was that the parties had entered into a separate contractual agreement on temperature and storage conditions during transport.

a general rule on passing of risk, the Vienna Convention ties risk to particular situations – that is, whether the sale contract involves carriage or not.

Most international sales contracts are likely to involve transportation of goods, be it by road, air, or a combination of different modes. So, where transportation is involved, risk, according to Art 67, will pass when the goods are handed over to the first carrier.[134] And, if the contracting parties have agreed to hand the goods over to the transporter at a particular place (for example, *ss Lakshmee* at the port of Singapore), then risk will pass once the goods are handed to the carrier at the stipulated place. It seems according to the commentaries that the carrier has to be an independent carrier for these purposes.[135] Where the seller uses his own transportation, Art 69 rather than Art 67 is relevant.

Use of trade terms however would result in rules relating to passing of risk embedded in trade terms[136] to supersede those of the Vienna Convention due to Art 9. However, courts may not always follow this view as *Cámara Nacional de Apelacioned en lo Comercial*[137] indicates. The contract in this case was concluded on C&F terms. The court said that the C&F clause obliged the seller to hand over the goods to the carrier and pay the freight but did not affect the passing of risk. They turned to Art 67 to resolve the passing of risk and concluded it did when it was handed over to the first carrier for transmission. It is indeed odd that the court did not refer to Art 9 to establish passing of risk in C&F contracts.[138] It is unclear from the case abstract whether the court was referring to Argentinian law when listing the obligations in respect of C&F contracts.

It must be added that the retention of documents by the seller does not affect the passing of risk under Art 67 though the goods need to be clearly identified to the contract by markings, shipping documents, notice or otherwise to enable risk to pass (Art 67(2)).

Since it is common practice in international sales to sell goods while they are in transit, Art 68 addresses the issue of passing of risk of goods sold during transit. Risk will normally pass when the contract is concluded. In some circumstances, it is possible for it to pass before the conclusion of the contract, that is, at the time when the goods were handed over to the carrier. The circumstances most likely to indicate this are insurance documents.[139] The seller however in Art 68 is subject to the principle of good faith. So, if the seller at the conclusion of contract of sale knew or ought to have known that the goods had been lost or damaged and did not disclose this to the buyer, the loss or damage is at the risk of the seller. The retroactive passing of risk is to the

---

134 See *OLG Schleswig 11 U 40/01, 22 August 2002*, available http://cisgw3.law.pace.edu/cases/020822g2.html.

135 See Schlechtriem, *Uniform Sales Law*, 1986, Manzsche Verlags-und Universitätsbuchhandlung, at p 88.

136 See Chapter 1 for passing of risk and trade terms. Note however that INCOTERMS 2000 do not address the consequences once risk passes, or for that matter the effect of the seller's act or omission and risk.

137 31 October 1995, abstract available from CLOUT Database (Abstract No 191), at www.uncitral.org.

138 Risk generally passes when the goods pass the ship's rail. Note that INCOTERMS 2000 uses CFR not C&F.

139 See Schlechtriem, *Uniform Sales Law*, 1986, Manzsche Verlags-und Universitätsbuchhandlung, at p 91. See also Goodfriend, 'After the damage is done: risk of loss under the United National Convention on International Sale of Goods' (1984) 22 Columbia Journal of Transnational Law 575.

benefit of the buyer since it may not always be possible to ascertain when the damage took place, thus creating uncertainties. The buyer in these circumstances can claim the benefit of the insurance instead of facing the uncertainties caused by splitting the risk during transit. Where goods are to be sold on CIF terms during transit, it is normal for the seller to obtain floating policies or open cover.[140]

Situations that do not fall within Arts 67 or 68 are covered by Art 69. According to Art 69, risk passes when goods are taken over by the buyer. So, where the goods are to be delivered at a particular place other than the seller's place of business, such as a warehouse of a third party, risk will pass when delivery is due and the buyer is aware of the fact that the goods are placed at his disposal. Obviously, the seller will need to notify the buyer.[141]

Remedies

In the event of a breach either by the seller or the buyer, the Vienna Convention makes available a number of remedies. While most of the available remedies are common to the seller and buyer, specific attention will be drawn when they are not.

Avoidance, fundamental breach and restitution

Avoidance, arguably, is one of the harshest remedies in the event of a breach. The Vienna Convention is primarily interested in ensuring the fulfilment of the contract and introduces remedies, as discussed below, that may strike as novel and a departure from remedies available at common law. Nevertheless, the Vienna Convention does make room for avoidance in some extreme circumstances.[142] For avoidance, the breach must be a fundamental breach which is defined in Art 25:

> A breach of contract committed by one of the parties is fundamental if it results in such detriment to the other party as substantially to deprive him of what he is entitled to expect under the contract, unless the party in breach did not foresee and a reasonable person of the same kind would not have foreseen such a result.

For there to be fundamental breach, the following criteria need to be met:

(1) There is a detriment. This should not normally be difficult to establish since most breaches such as late delivery, non-payment for goods, lack of conformity of goods with the specifications are likely to produce some detriment of an economic kind.

(2) The detriment must substantially deprive the other party of what he is entitled to expect under the contract.[143] This will depend on the circumstances though it may be possible to say that where the seller does not deliver goods, or delivers goods

---

140   See Chapter 14.
141   See *Oberlandsgericht Hamm 19 U 127/97, 23 June 1998*, available at http://cisgw3.law.pace. edu/cases/980263g1.html.
142   See Art 49. See also 'Fixing additional time for performance and "curing" the breach', pp 85–6 below.
143   See *Shuttle Packaging System LLC v Jacob Tsonakis INA SA and INA Plastics Corporation*, US District Court, Western District of Michigan, 1:01-CV-691, 17 December 2001, available at http://www.cisgw3.law.pace.edu/cases/011217u1.html.

other than those contracted for, or the buyer does not accept delivery,[144] the detriment could be substantial.

(3) Forseeability of the result. It is however unclear from the Vienna Convention as to when the detriment is foreseeable – at the time of conclusion of the contract or at the time of the breach.[145]

The antecedent to Art 25 is Art 10 of ULIS which defined it in the following manner:

> ... a breach of contract shall be regarded as fundamental wherever the party in breach knew, or ought to have known, at the time of the conclusion of the contract, that a reasonable person in the same situation as the person would not have entered into the contract if he had foreseen the breach and its effects.

Article 10 of ULIS was subjected to much criticism since it introduced a subjective element.

There are certain formalities to be met by the party electing avoidance. His declaration of avoidance is effective only upon notification to the other party. The party in breach however bears the risk of the notification not reaching him since Art 27 provides as follows:

> Unless otherwise expressly provided in this Part of the convention, if any notice, request or other communication is given or made by a party in accordance with this Part and by means appropriate in the circumstances, a delay or error in the transmission of the communication or its failure to arrive does not deprive that party of the right to rely on the communication.

The issue of whether there is a fundamental breach giving rise to avoidance will depend on the circumstances. The parties may have indicated the importance of the term in the contract – for instance, packaging requirements or the precise date of delivery to meet the subsequent obligations (such as resale or re-export) a buyer may have in relation to those goods.[146]

It however seems that the courts are not always that keen to promote avoidance as a remedy for fundamental breach and prefer to reserve it only for exceptional circumstances. In *HG Aargau OR 2001.00029, 5 November 2002*,[147] the Swiss Commercial Court said:

> The UN Sales Convention proceeds from the fundamental precedence of preservation of the contract, even in case of an objective fundamental defect. When in doubt, the

---

144 See *R Gmbh v O Ag (Kantonsgercht Schaffhausanug) 1 A 3 2001 34*, 12 December 2002, available at http://cisgw3.law.pace.edu/cases/021212s1.html, where non-acceptance of delivery by the buyer constituted fundamental breach.

145 Schlectriem is of the view that it is the conclusion of the contract since the party's interest is fixed by the terms of the contract which also fixes the conclusion of the contract as the relevant time for knowledge or foreseeability. As he illustrates, 'a contract in which delivery is not binding cannot be turned into a transaction where time is of the essence merely because the seller later learns that the buyer has obligated himself to sell the goods at a particular time', *Uniform Sales Law*, 1986, Manzsche Verlags-und Universitätsbuchhandlung, at p 60.

146 According to Honnold, the question of whether a breach is fundamental should be decided by taking into account all the circumstances including the effect of a rightful offer to cure (see *Uniform Law for International Sales under the 1980 United Nations Convention*, 1999, Kluwer). See on drafting guidance, McMahon, 'Guide for managers and counsel – drafting CISG contracts and documents and compliance tips for traders', August 2003, available at http://www.cisg.law.pace.edu/cisg/contracts.html.

147 Available at http://cisgw3.law.pace.edu/cases/021105s1.html.

contract is to be maintained even in case of fundamental defects, and an immediate contract avoidance should stay exceptional, because, as long and so far as (even) a fundamental defect can still be removed by remedy or replacement, the fulfilment of the contract by the seller is still possible and the buyer's essential interest in the performance is not yet definitively at risk ... That the buyer is obliged to accept a remedy (subsequent cure of the defect) offered by the seller results from Art 48(2) CISG ... For this reason, the buyer does not have the right to reject the contract even in case of an objective fundamental defect as long as and as far as the seller comes up with a remedy (subsequent cure of the defect) and such is still possible [at para 4(b)(aa)].

Fixing additional time for performance and 'curing' the breach

Not all breaches are going to be fundamental to enable a party to avoid the contract. And, even if they are, the party might not wish to avoid the contract. Given that the philosophy behind the Vienna Convention is to enable performance by the parties, it introduces a remedy that is unusual in common law systems – that is, the fixing of an additional period of time for performance by the other party.[148] This possibility is available to both the buyer and the seller. Article 47 enables the buyer to fix an additional period of time of reasonable length for performance by the party in breach. During this period, he cannot avail himself of any other remedy for breach available to him unless he receives notice from the seller that he will not be able to perform. Article 63 provides a parallel provision in favour of the seller. In the event an additional time is fixed, both Arts 47 and 63 state that the right to claim in damages for delay in performance is not lost.

Article 37 also gives the seller the right to cure any defects, partial delivery or replace non-conforming goods up to the date for delivery provided it does not cause the buyer unreasonable inconvenience or unreasonable expenses. Article 48 provides a further remedy for the seller to cure after the date of delivery is past. He may, after the date of delivery, at his own expense, perform his obligation as long as he can do this without causing unreasonable delay and uncertainty to the buyer according to Art 48 as long as the contract has not been avoided under Art 49.[149] It seems from a reading of Arts 48 and 49 that the seller is placed under a difficult situation of whether to carry on with curing the breach since it is endangered by the buyer's right to avoid.[150] Schlectriem[151] is of the view that this is not a major problem since the failure to meet the delivery deadline is not of itself a fundamental breach unless the contractual terms indicate that time is of the essence. So a cure within a reasonable time would not constitute a fundamental breach giving rise to avoidance. Given that the Vienna Convention's purpose is to ensure that the parties are given the

---

148 This fixing of an additional period for performance is often compared to the German remedy of *Nachfrist*.

149 The buyer can avoid the contract under Art 49 where there is a fundamental breach of contract or in the cases of non-delivery where the seller does not deliver within the additional period fixed by the buyer in accordance with Art 47(1). In *Giustina International SpA v Perfect Circle Europe (formerly Floquet Monopole (SARL))* (Case 225), 29 January 1998, available from CLOUT Database at www.uncitral.org, the court held that buyer could avoid the contract for non-conformity of goods since the buyer had reasonably endeavoured to maintain the contract in force by meeting the requirements of notice (Art 39), in seeking rectification (Art 46), and granting additional periods for rectification sought by the seller (Art 47).

150 See Will, in Bianca and Bonnell, *Commentary on International Sales Law: The 1980 Vienna Convention*, 1987, Giuffrè.

151 See *Uniform Sales Law*, 1986, Manzsche Verlags-und Universitätsbuchhandlung, at pp 77–8.

opportunities to perform the contract, Schlectriem's solution to the apparent problem is attractive.

In the event of avoidance, both parties are released from their obligations subject to any damages that may be due. Where there has been partial or total performance, the party who has performed may claim restitution from the other party (Art 81).

The Vienna Convention also provides for the preservation of goods received by the buyer in the event he intends to exercise any rights under the Vienna Convention or intends to reject them (Arts 85–88).

Specific performance

Under the Vienna Convention, the buyer or the seller may require specific performance of the contract from the party in breach. Article 46(1) provides that 'the buyer may require performance by the seller of his obligations unless the buyer has resorted to a remedy which is inconsistent with this requirement'. Where the goods do not conform and the non-conformity constitutes a fundamental breach, the buyer may request for substitute goods provided the request for substitute goods is made along with the notice of non-conformity (Art 39)[152] or within a reasonable time after notice (Art 46(2)). The buyer has also the right to require the seller to remedy any lack of conformity by repair unless it would be unreasonable in the circumstances provided the request is made in conjunction with the notice of non-conformity or within a reasonable time after notice (Art 46(3)). It must be added that in seeking specific performance the claimant does not lose any right to claim damages since Art 45(2) states that 'the buyer is not deprived of any right he may have to claim damages by exercising his right to other remedies'.

Equally, the seller may require the buyer to pay the price, take delivery or perform his other obligations, unless the seller has resorted to a remedy which is inconsistent with this requirement under Art 62. The seller like the buyer also does not lose the right to claim damages under Art 61(2).

The remedy of specific performance is not unknown in common law jurisdictions but is available only in limited circumstances, for instance, where monetary damages are not regarded as adequate.[153] It must be noted that under the Vienna Convention specific performance is not conditional on damages being inadequate. In the context of sale of goods, it is unlikely to be awarded that often since it would be possible to source similar goods from another merchant. Courts in England are reluctant to order specific performance even where acquiring goods from another source could take

---

152   See also 'Obligations of the buyer', pp 77–81 above.
153   Section 52(1) of the Sale of Goods 1979 states:

> In any action for breach of contract to deliver specific or ascertained goods, the court may, if it thinks fit, on the plaintiff's application, by its judgment or decree direct that the contract shall be performed specifically, without giving the defendant the option of retaining the goods on payment of damages.

> See also Treitel, 'Specific performance in the sale of goods' [1966] Business Lawyer 211; Farnsworth, 'Damages and specific relief' (1979) 27 American Journal of Comparative Law 247; Schwartz, 'The case for specific performance' (1979) 89 Yale LJ 271; Ullen, 'The efficiency of specific performance: towards a unified theory of contract remedies' (1984) 83 Michigan LR 341; Szladits, 'The concept of specific performance in civil law' (1955) 4 American Journal of Comparative Law 208.

well over nine months as *Société des Industries Métallargiques SA v Bronx Engineering Co Ltd*[154] suggests. This reluctance can cause problems for the buyer. The Vienna Convention follows the civil law tradition in respect of specific performance and this is no bad thing given the grief that hunting for goods on the open market can cause. However, Art 28 of the Vienna Convention curtails the uniform availability of specific performance since it states that a 'court is not bound to enter a judgment for specific performance unless the court would do so under its own law in respect of similar contracts of sale not governed by this convention'. This means that an English forum, given the approach to specific performance in domestic law, may well curtail the availability of specific performance where the Vienna Convention applies to the contract of sale.[155] However, they might not, since English courts are sympathetic towards achieving uniform interpretation of international conventions. By including Art 28,[156] the drafters of the Vienna Convention have eroded the level of uniformity they intended to achieve. As to whether this was a compromise in favour of the common law countries is debatable since the common law countries do not seem to have raised vociferous objections to Art 46 or 62.

Reduction of price

Reduction of price where the goods do not conform is another remedy available to the buyer. This remedy is open to him provided the seller does not remedy the failure to perform his obligations and the buyer does not refuse the seller's offer of remedy. Article 50 states:

> If the goods do not conform with the contract and whether or not the price has already been paid, the buyer may reduce the price in the same proportion as the value that the goods actually delivered had at the time of the delivery bears to the value that conforming goods would have had at that time. However, if the seller remedies any failure to perform his obligations in accordance with Article 37 or 48[157] or if the buyer refuses to

---

154   [1975] 1 Lloyd's Rep 465. See also *Sky Petroleum Ltd v VSP Petroleum Ltd* [1974] 1 WLR 576.

155   In *Magellan International v Salzgitter Handel*, 99 C 5153, US District Court, Northern District of Illinois Eastern Division (available at http://cisgw3.law.pace.edu/cases/991207u1.html), the court in dealing with specific performance in the Vienna Convention said that reference is to be made to the UCC (Uniform Commercial Code). It said:

> But convention Art 28 conditions the availability of specific performance:
> . . .
> Simply put, that looks to the availability of such relief under the UCC . . .
> Under UCC §2-716(1) a court may decree specific performance 'where the goods are unique or in other proper circumstances'.

156   Lando suggests that this article may also work to the benefit of civil law countries. He writes:

> They may invoke Art 28 to remedy one of the flaws of Art 79. It provides that certain impediments (*force majeure*) will excuse a party from liability in damages for non-performance. It also provides in para (5) that 'nothing in this article prevents either party from exercising any right other than to claim damages . . .' However, in cases of exemption from liability because of a lasting impediment, it would be inconsistent to require a party to perform specifically when he is free from paying damages for non-performance. Courts in countries which in these cases would not enter a judgment for specific performance may take advantage of the freedom not to do so provided in Art 28 Bianca and Bonnell, *Commentary on International Sales Law: The 1980 Vienna Convention*, 1987, Giuffrè at 237. See also *Zürich Arbitration Proceeding, 19960531, 31 May 1996* (available at http://cisgw3.law.pace.edu/cases/960531s1.html), where specific performance was claimed as an alternative.

157   See 'Fixing additional time for performance and "curing" the breach', pp 85–6, above.

accept performance by the seller in accordance with those Articles, the buyer may not reduce the price.[158]

Interest on arrears

The Vienna Convention provides for payment of interest in the event of failure to pay or refund the price. Article 78 provides that 'if a party fails to pay the price or any other sum that is in arrears, the other party is entitled to interest on it, without prejudice to any claim for damages recoverable under Art 74'. Equally, Art 84(1) states that 'if the seller is bound to refund the price, he must also pay interest on it, from the date on which the price was paid'. While these rules may be clear in themselves, there is no indication in the Vienna Convention as to how the rate of interest is to be determined.[159] The answer depends on whether the omission in respect of interest rate is seen as a gap[160] or whether it is seen as falling outside the scope of the Vienna Convention. Scholarly opinions vary but by and large the favoured view is that it is outside the scope of the Vienna Convention and is to be resolved by looking to domestic law.[161] And case law from many jurisdictions supports this interpretation. There is also support for the view that the issue should be determined on the basis of the principles found in the Vienna Convention. While the Vienna Convention does not enunciate the principles, they can be created from a reading of the provisions. Article 74, for instance,[162] is founded on the principle of full compensation – a principle recognised and applied by some tribunals in the context of determining interest.[163] An interesting decision is that of International Chamber of Commerce in

---

158   See *Interrag Co Ltd v Stafford Phase Corp*, 2d instance 983 F 2d 1047 (2nd Cir 1992) where defective goods were sold by the US buyer. The court whilst referring to § 2-724(212) of UCC (Sales) and Art 50 of the Vienna Convention said that it was well settled that the price obtained for defective goods on resale is probative of the value of the goods as actually received.

159   ULIS took a different approach. Art 83 states:

   Where the breach of contract consists of delay in the payment of the price, the seller shall in any event be entitled to interest on such sum as is in arrears at a rate equal to the official discount rate in the country where he has his place of business or, if he has no place of business, his habitual residence, plus 1%.

   There were a lot of objections to adopting this formula during the deliberations of the UNCITRAL Working Group, specially the rate of interest. And Islamic legal systems based on Shari'a law forbid charging of interest (*riba*). For more on the debate, see Honnold, *Documentary History of the Uniform Law for International Sale*, 1989, Kluwer. See also Gotanda, 'Awarding interest in international arbitration' (1996) 90 American Journal of International Law 40.

160   See Art 7(2) of the Vienna Convention.

161   Nicholas, in Bianca and Bonnell, *Commentary on International Sales Law: The 1980 Vienna Convention*, 1987, Giuffrè; Schlechtriem, 'Recent developments in international sales law' (1983) 18 Israel LR 309; Sutton, 'Damages under the United Nations Convention' (1989) 50 Ohio State LJ 737.

162   Other relevant provisions that provide principles to fill in the interest rate gap are Art 84 (see Koneru, 'The International interpretation of the UN Convention on Contracts for the International Sale of Goods – an approach based on general principles' (1997) 6 Minnesota Journal of Global Trade 195) and Arts 55 and 57 (see Zoccolillo Jr, 'Determination of the interest rate under the 1980 United Nations Convention on Contracts for the International Sale of Goods: general principle vs national law', available at http://cisgw3.law.pace.edu/cisg/biblio/zoccolillo.html).

163   See *Internationales Schiedsgericht der Bundeskammer der gewerblichen Wirtschaft-Wien 15 June 1994 (SCH 4366), (SCH 4318)*, English translation available at www.unilex.info. In *Landgericht (hereinafter LG) Hamburg 26, September 1990 (5 O 543/88)*, interest was awarded at the loan rate. Available at www.unilex.info.

Basel.[164] The tribunal, acknowledging that the issue of interest is a gap to be filled by referring to principles, resolved the matter by looking at the UNIDROIT Principles of International Commercial Contracts and Principles of European Contract Law.[165] Reference was made to Art 7.4.9[166] of the UNIDROIT Principles of International Commercial Contracts and Art 4.507[167] of the Principles of European Contract Law. As to whether this is a satisfactory solution is debatable. On the one hand, neither the UNIDROIT Principles nor the Principles of European Contract Law were in existence when the Vienna Convention was being drafted to say that drafters had these other instruments in mind at the time of drafting. Further, not all jurisdictions are likely to view these later instruments favourably[168] which means that there is going to be a multitude of opinions emerging, thus creating uncertainty that the Vienna Convention is meant to dissipate.[169] Of course, it is possible to support the opinion expressed by the ICC Tribunal on the basis that the Principles are a reflection of mercantile practice and thus a part of *lex mercatoria*, and that the UNIDROIT Principles were built upon the provisions of the Vienna Convention with the intention of filling in the gaps and for providing a more comprehensive set of rules to govern international commercial contracts.

The current state of affairs in interpreting Art 78 is far from satisfactory and as Zocolillo Jr colourfully expresses:

> Article 78 of the CISG, although facially simplistic, has proven to be one of the most complex and enigmatic provisions of the convention. Religious, political, and economic disparity among the nations whose delegates participated in the creation of the CISG created friction as to what interests would be reflected in the convention's explicit references to interest. Although the general principles these parties devised can speak volumes, the parties did not devise specific language on rate of interest. This has left the international commercial community with a significant 'pothole' on the road to uniformity. In repairing potholes, it is desirable that the material used to fill the pothole match the material used to construct the road . . . To fill the 'rate' gap

---

164 *ICC Arbitral Award 8128/1995*, available UNILEX database at www.unilex.info.

165 For further on these, see 'Conclusion: Recent International Initiatives', pp 92–5 below.

166 It states:

    (1) If a party does not pay a sum of money when it falls due, the aggrieved party is entitled to interest upon that sum from the time when payment is due to the time of payment whether or not the payment is excused.

    (2) The rate of interest shall be the average short-term lending rate to prime borrowers prevailing for the currency of payment at the place of payment, or where no such rate exists at that place, then the same rate in the state of the currency of payment. In the absence of such a rate at either place, the rate of interest shall be the appropriate rate fixed by law of the state of the currency of payment.

    (3) The aggrieved party is entitled to additional damages if the non-payment caused it greater harm

167 It states:

    (1) If payment of a sum is delayed, the aggrieved party is entitled to interest on that sum from the time when payment is due to the time of payment at the average commercial bank short-term lending rate to prime borrowers prevailing for the contractual currency of payment at the place where the payment is due.

    (2) The aggrieved party may in addition recover damages for any further loss, so far as these are recoverable under this section.

168 It is difficult to see why non-European states should subscribe to the Principles of European Contract devised by a team largely drawn from the European Union.

169 See Viscasillas, 'UNIDROIT Principles of International Commercial Contracts' (1996) 13 Arizona Journal of International and Comparative Law 381; Garro, 'The gap-filling roles of the UNIDROIT Principles in International Sales Law: some comments in the interplay between the Principles and the CISG' (1995) 69 Tulane LR 1149.

of Art 78 with national laws is equivalent to filling the pothole with different materials.[170]

Damages

In addition to the above remedies, the seller and the buyer are entitled to damages from the party in breach and according to Art 74:[171] '... damages for breach of contract by one party consist of a sum equal to the loss, including loss of profit, suffered by the other party as a consequence of the breach. Such damages may not exceed the loss which the party in breach foresaw or ought to have foreseen at the time of the conclusion of the contract in the light of the facts and matters of which he then knew or ought to have known as a possible consequence of the breach of contract'.[172] However, this is subject to whether the party claiming damages has taken reasonable steps to mitigate his loss including loss of profit. Failure to do so would allow the party in breach to claim a reduction in the damages in the amount by which the loss should have been mitigated according to Art 77 of the Vienna Convention. The measure of damages is the difference between the contract price and the current price,[173] and contract price is defined in Art 76(2) as 'the price prevailing at the place where delivery of the goods should have been made or, if there is no current price at that place, the price at such other place as serves as reasonable substitute, making due allowances for the differences in the cost of transporting the goods'.

A number of cases have considered damages[174] under the Vienna Convention provisions but it is difficult to state precisely how Art 74 is likely to be construed. For instance, in *Delchi Carrier SpA v Rotorex Corp*,[175] while dealing with consequential damages, the court (despite stating that the Vienna Convention governed the contract) seems to have fallen back on New York law[176] rather than focusing on the forseeability requirement in Art 74.[177]

It is common in sales contracts for the parties to agree the amount of damages

---

170   See Part IV (Conclusion), 'Determination of the interest rate under the 1980 United Nations Convention on Contracts for the International Sale of Goods: general principle vs national law', available at http://cisgw3.law.pace.edu/cisg/biblio/zoccolillo.html.

171   On claiming cost of proceedings, see *Schiedgericht der Handelskammer [Arbitration Tribunal] Hamburg, 21 March 1996*, available at http://cisgw3.law.pace.edu/cases/960321g1.html.

172   In English law, the remoteness rule is to be found in *Hadley v Baxendale* (1854) 23 LJ Ex 179 according to which the defendant is liable for loss as may fairly and reasonably be considered as arising naturally and for loss as may reasonably be supposed to have been in the contemplation of both parties at the time they made the contract, as the probable result of the breach of it.

173   See Art 76. If substitute goods have been bought, then it is the difference between the contract price and the substitute transaction – see Art 75.

174   Damages could include attorney's fees – see *LG Berlin, 21 March 2003*, available at http://cisgw3.law.pace.edu/cases/1030321g1.html.

175   71 f.3d 1024 (2d Cir 1995).

176   It seems that according to New York law 'as a matter of law, a plaintiff cannot recover consequential damages without evidence demonstrating a defendant's tacit agreement at the time of contracting to accepting responsibility for such damages'. See Schneider, 'Consequential damages in the international sale of goods: analysis of two decisions' (1995) 16 Journal of International Business Law 615.

177   The reasoning process and the decision has been heavily criticised – see Darkey, 'A US court's interpretation of damage provisions under the UN Convention on Contracts for the International Sale of Goods: a preliminary step towards an international jurisprudence of CISG or a missed opportunity?' (1995) 15 Journal of Law and Commerce 139.

payable by the party in breach.[178] Such clauses – known as liquidated damages clauses – are not addressed by the Vienna Convention and the issue has come up for consideration in a number of cases. In *ICC Arbitration Case 7197 of 1992*,[179] the dispute concerned the failure of the Bulgarian buyer to pay the Austrian seller within the payment period agreed between the parties. They had included a clause limiting the damages to an agreed percentage of the contract price. Noting that the Vienna Convention did not address liquidated damages, the tribunal turned to domestic law to determine the validity of the clause. The conclusion reached has been criticised by Koneru who says that there was no need for the tribunal to enquire whether the clause was valid or not; the issue should have been decided on the basis of freedom of contract and good faith as expressed by Arts 6 and 7.[180] While the suggestion put forward has its attractions, it is arguable, given the debate surrounding good faith in Art 7, whether it would be used uniformly in the manner suggested by Koneru. It is more than likely that liquidated damages issue will be decided by turning to domestic law. Support for this approach can be sought from the deliberations leading to the Vienna Convention where delegates felt that liquidated damages should be left to be addressed by another instrument.

Exemption

The Vienna Convention, in some circumstances, exempts a party from liability. According to Art 79(1), 'a party is not liable for failure to perform any of his obligations if he proves that the failure was due to an impediment beyond his control and that he could not reasonably be expected to have taken the impediment into account at the time of the conclusion of the contract or to have avoided or overcome its consequences'. Relief from liability for damages will depend on the circumstances. Incidents such as the refusal on the part of the manufacturer to supply the goods to the seller,[181] or increase in prices on the open market,[182] will be insufficient to trigger this provision. One of the downsides of this provision is that the party who fails to perform due to impediments (obligor) is not liable in damages. This means that other remedies are still available to the other party (obligee) including specific performance. The obligee may elect avoidance provided there is a fundamental breach. This option of avoidance is however not available to the obligor. This is different from the English doctrine of frustration[183] where the contract comes to an end in the event of frustration.

---

178 For an analysis on the English approach, see Goode, *Hire Purchase Law and Practice*, 1970, Butterworths.

179 Available at http://cisgw3/law.pace.edu/cases/927197i1.html.

180 See Koneru, 'The international interpretation of the UN Convention on Contracts for the International Sale of Goods: an approach based on general principle' (1997) 6 Minnesota Journal of Global Trade 105.

181 *Tribunal of International Commerce Arbitration at the Russian Federation Chamber of Commerce and Industry 155/1994, 16 March 1995*, available at www.cisgw3.law.pace.edu/cases/950316r1.html.

182 *Court of Arbitration of the International Chamber of Commerce 6281 of 1989, 26 August 1989*, available at http://cisgw3.law.pace.edu/cases/896281i1.html.

183 Frustration in common law occurs:

> . . . whenever the law recognises that without default of either party a contractual obligation has become incapable of being performed because the circumstances in which performance is called for would render it a thing radically different from that which was undertaken by the contract. *Non haec in foedera a veni.* It was not this that I promised to do [*per* Lord Radcliffe, *David Contractors Ltd v Fareham UDC* [1956] AC 696, at p 729].

Article 79 has come under repeated criticism[184] and parties might prefer to include suitable clauses to address the consequences flowing from impediments, including supervening onerousness, beyond the control of the obligor.[185]

CONCLUSION: RECENT INTERNATIONAL INITIATIVES

UNIDROIT Principles of International Commercial Contracts

UNIDROIT, the organisation that drafted ULIS and ULFIS, set about in 1972 to codify international trade law. Shelved for a number of years, a Working Group consisting of academics, judges and civil servants was set up in 1980 to resume work on the shelved project now titled Principles for International Commercial Contracts (hereinafter 'UNIDROIT Principles').[186] For the purposes of the UNIDROIT Principles, they studied the commercial law of a number of states. In particular, they concentrated on the Algerian Civil Code, 1975, the People's Republic of China's Foreign Economic Contract Law, 1985, the ubiquitous US Uniform Commercial Code, and the Dutch Civil Code and Civil Code of Quebec both of which were undergoing amendments. Legislative products in related areas of other international organisations such as the UNCITRAL and the ICC were also studied closely. In 1994, UNIDROIT[187] published the Principles of International Commercial Contracts.[188]

The UNIDROIT Principles are neither a convention nor a model law.[189] They are to be regarded as general rules that aim to achieve a balance between competing interests. The Preamble sets out the circumstance where the UNIDROIT Principles will play a role. The most obvious is where the parties have agreed that their contract is to be governed by them.[190] It is also expected that they will be applied when the

---

For further on frustration, see McKendrick (ed), *Force Majeure and Frustration of Contract*, 1991 LLP.

184   See, eg, Nicholas, 'Impracticability and impossibility in the UN Convention on Contracts for the International Sale of Goods', in Galston and Smit (eds), *International Sales*, 1984, Matthew Bender.

185   See McMahon, 'Drafting CISG contracts and documents and compliance tips for traders', available at www.cisg.law.pace.edu/cisg/contracts.html.

186   The text of this instrument is available at www.unidroit.org. It is also reproduced in Carr and Kidner, *International Trade Law Statutes and Conventions*, 2008, Routledge-Cavendish.

187   UNIDROIT has 59 member states comprising of countries from both the developing and developed worlds – eg: Australia, Canada, Austria, UK, India, Iran, China, and Bolivia. For a complete list see www.unidroit.org.

188   The text of the UNIDROIT Principles is available at www.unidroit.org. The work is ongoing and the working group of recent has addressed various topics such as agency, assignment of contractual rights, and contracts for the benefit of third parties. In April 2004, the UNIDROIT adopted the 2004 version of the UNIDROIT Principles. It now contains sections on authority of agent, third party rights, set-off, assignment of rights, transfer of obligation and assignment of contracts, and limitation periods. The text of the UNIDROIT 1994 is also suitably adapted to meet the needs of electronic contracting. For further details, visit www.unidroit.org.

189   For instance, the Model Law on Electronic Commerce and the Model Law on Electronic Signatures drafted by the UNCITRAL. See Chapters 3 and 4 below for an examination of these model laws.

190   UNIDROIT recommends the following model clauses for parties wishing to incorporate the UNIDROIT Principles:
      'This contract shall be governed by the UNIDROIT Principles (2004) [except as to Articles . . .]';
      'This contract shall be governed by the UNIDROIT Principles (2004) [except as to

parties have agreed for *lex mercatoria*[191] to apply to their contract, or used in interpreting or supplementing international uniform law instruments such as the Vienna Convention. The drafters also hope that legislators, both at a national or international level, will use the UNIDROIT Principles to draft their legislation. Indeed, it is strange that the UNIDROIT opted to go down the route of producing a non-binding instrument that is unlikely to achieve the expressed objective of the UNIDROIT Principles to establish 'a balanced set of rules designed for use throughout the world irrespective of the legal traditions and the economic and political conditions of the countries in which they are to be applied'.[192] Part of the reason is probably time and flexibility – the time taken to agree to the text of a convention and the delays faced in its implementation.

The UNIDROIT principles are comprehensive and go beyond the Vienna Convention in addressing a number of issues not found in the Vienna Convention. These range from validity of contracts (mistake, threat and misrepresentation but excluding illegality or capacity) to agency and limitation periods. In a book of this length it is not possible to examine all of the aspects of the UNIDROIT Principles in detail. A few pertinent observations of the commonalities and some of the differences are made below.

The provisions on formation of contract are, by and large, similar to the Vienna Convention though there are some differences. The two instruments take different approaches to battle of forms. While the Vienna Convention focused on material alterations the UNIDROIT Principles' focus is on substance. According to Art 2.1.22 a contract will be concluded on the basis of the agreed terms and any standard terms which are common in substance unless the other party indicates in advance or later without undue delay informs the other party that it does not intend to be bound by such a contract. It is debatable whether this focus on finding common terms by examining the substance of the clauses offers a better solution since it is assumed it will be easy to agree on the substance from the wording of the terms.

What does stand out in the Principles is the expectation that both parties will act in accordance with good faith and fair dealing.[193] This is a fundamental principle and where the UNIDROIT Principles are applicable to a contract then the parties cannot contract out of this fundamental principle even though party autonomy is recognised.[194] Good faith however is undefined. Inconsistent behaviour can be said to be one aspect of lack of good faith and Art 1.8 specifically prohibits a party from behaving inconsistently where it has caused the other party to have an understanding and that other party reasonably acted in reliance on that, to its detriment. Equally the inclusion of unexpected or surprising terms in contracts shows lack of good faith and fair dealing. Article 2.1.20 deals with this by providing that if standard terms contain a

---

Articles . . .], supplemented when necessary by the law [jurisdiction X]', if parties wish to apply the law of a particular jurisdiction along with the UNIDROIT Principles [www.unidroit.org/English/principles/model.htm].

191   Surprisingly, the mercantile community does not seem to have taken part in the deliberations leading to the drafting of the principles.

192   'Introduction' to the UNIDROIT Principles.

193   Art 1.7. Good faith is also referred to in Arts 4.8 and 5.1.2. See Farnsworth, 'Duties of Good Faith and Fair Dealing under the UNIDROIT Principles: Relevant International Conventions and National Law' 3 (1995) 3 Tulane Journal of International Comparative Law 47.

194   Art 1.5.

term which the party would 'not reasonably have expected it, that term will be ineffective, unless it has been expressly accepted by that party'.

Unlike the Vienna Convention, the Principles do recognise that parties enter into pre-agreement and therefore include special provisions on this issue. Article 2.1.15 preserves the parties' freedom to negotiate and failure to agree. However, negotiations carried out in bad faith or negotiations broken in bad faith attracts liability and the affected party can sue for losses caused. As opposed to good faith, some indication of what constitutes bad faith is provided in Art 2.1.15. In particular it will include situations where a party enters into negotiation or continues negotiations never intending to reach agreement, as for instance where a trader about to set up a factory for manufacturing widgets enters into negotiations with another for the purchase of widgets simply to find out the pricing policy without ever intending to enter into a contract for the purchase of widgets. The commercial world is full of duplicitous behaviour and it is good to see the inclusion of a special provision relating to bad faith in negotiations.

One of the features that stands out with the UNIDROIT Principles is Chapter 4 on Interpretation. While some aspects for the interpretation of contracts, such as intention of the parties and trade usages, are to be found in the Vienna Convention,[195] Chapter 4 of the Principles highlights the various well-established techniques for interpretation of contracts, such as the use of the reasonable person standard where the common intention of the parties cannot be established (Art 4.1) and the *contra proferentum* rule (Art 4.6).

In relation to performance of the obligations under the contract, the expectation is that both parties will meet their obligations. Nevertheless, the UNIDROIT Principles take a pragmatic approach in the event of hardship where the equilibrium of the contract has been altered due to a number of reasons – eg, where the risk of the events was not assumed by the disadvantaged party, or the events become known to the disadvantaged party after the conclusion of the contract. In these circumstances the parties can renegotiate, but if they fail to reach agreement they are free to resort to the courts who may, if they find hardship, terminate the contract or restore the equilibrium.[196] In relation to non-performance, in general, the remedies found in the Vienna Convention, such as cure, repair and replacement of defective performance and additional period for performance, are included in the Principles. Article 7.3.1 addresses the issue of the right to terminate the contract but does not use the phrase 'fundamental breach'. Instead it talks of fundamental non-performance, and to decide whether a failure to perform an obligation amounts to a fundamental non-performance it lists a number of relevant factors. These include: whether the non-performance is intentional or reckless; whether strict compliance with the obligations which has not been performed is of the essence under the contract; and whether the non-performance gives the aggrieved party reason to believe that it cannot rely on the other party's future performance.

As stated above the UNIDROIT Principles are innovative and undergo periodic revisions. The 2004 version includes provisions on set-off (Chapter 8), assignment of rights, transfer of obligations and assignment of contracts[197] (Chapter 9) and

---

195   See Art 8, Vienna Convention.
196   Arts 6.2.1, 6.2.2 and 6.2.3.
197   There are two international conventions in this field: the UNIDROIT Convention on International Factoring, 1998 and the UN Convention on the Assignment of Receivables in International Trade, 2001. These conventions have not had a wide impact.

limitations periods (Chapter 10)[198]. All in all the Principles provide a well-rounded set of rules to govern international commercial contracts.

UNIDROIT has been following the progress of this instrument and, based on questionnaires sent out by the organisation, it seems they have been well received. The UNIDROIT Principles have served as a source of inspiration for legislators revisiting their civil codes, and inspired parties to choose the principles to govern their contract.[199] There is also evidence that arbitration tribunals are applying the UNIDROIT Principles besides referring to them as part of *lex mercatoria*.[200] This positive report suggests that this instrument may have wider impact than initially thought.

Principles of European Contract Law

While the political, social and economic objectives of the member states of the European Union are broadly similar, it is well known that the legal systems of the member states vary from the common law system of Britain to the civil law tradition of the continent. Since differences in legal approaches can form a barrier to trade,[201] in 1982 the Commission on European Contract Law,[202] consisting of practitioners and academics from the member states of the European Union, began work on the Principles of European Contract Law (PECL).[203] Other than referring to the domestic law of the European states, the drafters also referred to the US Restatements on Contract and Restitution and the Vienna Convention for formulating principles. They were also influenced by the work at UNIDROIT since some of the members of the Working Group were also members of the group drafting the UNIDROIT Principles. The PECL addresses a wide variety of issues such as agency along with contractual issues such as validity, formation of contract, breach and remedies. The drafters expect PECL to be of relevance where parties agree their contract is to be governed by general principles of law or *lex mercatoria*. It is difficult to predict whether this instrument will be popularly received internationally since it may be perceived as embodying an European bias.

---

198   This seems to be largely modelled on the UN Convention on the Limitation Period in the International Sale of Goods 1974 with some significant departures on issues such as when the limitation period starts to run.

199   See Bonnell, 'The UNIDROIT Principles in practice – the experience of the first two years', available at http://cisgw3.law.pace.edu/cisg/biblio/pr_expr.html. See also Baron, 'Do the UNIDROIT Principles of International Commercial Contracts form a new *lex mercatoria*?', available at http://cisgw3.law.pace.edu/cisg/biblit/baron.html.

200   *Ibid.*

201   As Lando observes:

   . . . many businessmen are afraid. Fear of the unknown and incomprehension keep many potential exporters and importers away from the European market. The existing variety of laws hampers the mobility of the European businessman. It is a non-tariff barrier to trade ['Principles of European Contract Law', available at www.kclc.or.jp/english/ sympo. EUDialogue/lando.html].

202   The Commission is a non-governmental organisation and is not an European Community institution though it has received subsidies from the Community.

203   The text of this instrument is available at www.jus.uio.no. See also Lando and Beale (eds), *The Principles of European Contract Law*, Pts I and II, 1999, Kluwer; Hesselink, 'The Principles of European Contract Law: some choices made by the Lando Commission' (2001) Global Jurist Frontiers Article 4, available at www.bepress.com.

FURTHER READING

Audit, 'The Vienna Sales Convention and the *lex mercatoria*', available at http://cisgw3.law.pace.edu/cisg/biblio/audit.html.

Babiak, 'Defining "fundamental breach" under the United Nations Convention on Contracts for the International Sale of Goods' (1993) 6 Temple International and Comparative LJ 113.

Berman and Ladd, 'Risk of loss or damage in documentary transactions under the Convention on the International Sale of Goods' (1988) 21(3) Cornell International LJ 423.

Bianca and Bonnell (eds), *Commentary on International Sales Law: The 1980 Vienna Convention*, 1987, Giuffrè.

Boele-Woeki *et al*, *Comparability and Evaluation: Essays on Comparative Law, Private International Law and International Commercial Arbitration*, 1994, TMC Asser Institute.

Bonnell, 'The UNIDROIT Principles of International Commercial Contracts and the Principles of European Contract Law: similar rules for the same purpose?' [1996] Uniform LR 229.

Bonnell, 'UNIDROIT Principles 2004 – the new edition of the Principles of International Commercial Contracts adopted by the International Institute for the Unification of Private Law' [2004] Uniform LR 5.

Bridge, *The International Sale of Goods*, 2007, OUP.

Cook, 'The UN Convention on Contracts for the International Sale of Goods: a mandate to abandon legal ethnocentricity' (1997) 16 Journal of Law and Commerce 257.

Eörsi, 'A propos the 1980 Vienna Convention on Contracts for the International Sale of Goods' (1983) 31 The American Journal of Comparative Law 333.

Ferrari, 'Uniform application and interest rates under the Vienna Sales Convention' (1995) Georgia Journal of International and Comparative Law 467.

Garro, 'Contribution of the UNIDROIT Principles to the advancement of international commercial arbitration' (1994) 3 Tulane Journal of International and Comparative Law 94.

Gordley, 'An American perspective on the UNIDROIT Principles', available at http://servizi.iit/cnr.it/~crdcs/Gordley.htm.

Grewal, 'Risk of loss in goods sold during transit: a comparative study of the United Nations Convention on Contracts for the International Sale of Goods, the Uniform Commercial Code, and the British Sale of Goods Act' (1991) 14 Loyola Los Angeles International and Comparative LR 93.

Honnold, *On the Road to Unification for the Law Sales*, 1983, Kluwer.

Honnold, *Uniform Law of International Sales*, 1999, Kluwer.

Komarov, 'The UNIDROIT Principles of International Commercial Contracts: a Russian view' [1996] Uniform LR 247.

Lee, 'The UN Convention on Contracts for the International Sale of Goods: OK for the UK?' [1993] JBL 131.

Lookofsky, 'The limits of commercial contract freedom: under the UNIDROIT "Restatement" and Danish law' (1998) 46 American Journal of Comparative Law 485.

Lookofsky, 'In *dubio pro conventione*? Some thoughts about opt-outs, computer programs and pre-emption under the 1980 Vienna Sales Convention CISG' (2003) 13 Duke Journal of International and Comparative Law 263.

Maskow, 'Hardship and *force majeure*' (1992) 40 American Journal of Comparative Law 657.

Maurer, 'The United Nations Convention on Contracts for the International Sale of Goods' (1989) 15 Syracuse Journal of International Law and Commerce 306.

Murray Jr, 'An essay on the formation of contracts and related matters under the United Nations Convention on Contracts for the International Sale of Goods' (1988) 8 Journal of Law and Commerce 11.

Nicholas, 'The Vienna Convention on International Sales' (1989) 105 LQR 201.

Rossett, 'Critical reflections on the United Nations Convention on Contracts for the International Sale of Goods' (1984) 45 Ohio State LJ 265.

Tuggey, 'The 1980 United Nations Convention on Contracts for the International Sale of Goods: will a homeward trend emerge?' (1986) 21 Texas International LJ 541.

Van Houtte, 'The principles of international commercial contracts' (1995) 11 Arbitration Journal 373.

Veythia, 'The requirement of justice and equity in contracts' (1995) 69 Tulane LR 1191.

Walsh, 'Harmonisation and standardisation of legal aspects of international trade' (1977) 52 The Australian LJ 608.

Ziontz, 'A new Uniform Law for the International Sale of Goods: is it compatible with American interests?' (1980) 94 Northwestern Journal of International Law and Business 129.

PART II

REGULATING THE ELECTRONIC COMMERCE ENVIRONMENT

OVERVIEW

The information technology (IT) revolution in the form of the Internet had an enormous impact on the means of conducting international commerce in the last decade of the last century. The use of electronic means for conducting sales was heralded as an economic boon to developed and developing nations alike. Suddenly, the commercial world had direct access to a global marketplace and they could exploit it in an efficient and economically advantageous manner. Politicians, policy makers and non-governmental organisations welcomed the Internet with open arms as providing an opportunity for raising the standards of living and providing a means of reducing the levels of poverty worldwide. Of course, the use of IT for conducting business and concluding contracts raises a number of legal issues – among them the formation of contracts. A number of international organisations set out to iron out the legal uncertainties and difficulties with the intention to promote electronic commerce.

Chapter 3 highlights the policies of major trading partners – the US and the European Union (EU) – in respect of electronic commerce and the legal harmonisation brought about through the Model Law on Electronic Commerce formulated by the well-known international organisation UNCITRAL (United Nations Commission on International Trade Law). This chapter also considers in brief the EU Directive on E-Commerce and initiatives from other organisations such as the ICC (International Chamber of Commerce) and the UN Convention on the Use of Electronic Communications in International Contracts.

Chapter 4 concerns itself with security issues relating to electronic transactions – the securing of an electronic transaction through the use of digital/electronic signatures and securing the electronic environment from external threats. The first half of this chapter examines digital signatures and UNCITRAL's Model Law on Electronic Signatures. The second half considers international legislative developments in relation to computer crime.

CHAPTER 3

ELECTRONIC COMMERCE – LEGAL ISSUES AND HARMONISATION

INTRODUCTION

The mid-1990s was heralded by politicians, economists, law makers and commercial entities as groundbreaking for worldwide economic development. The reason – the opening of the Internet[1] for public use. Information could now be freely circulated globally through computer networks provided people had the necessary skills and access to computer hardware and software to tap into information available on these networks. Creation of this open network imparted a new sense of living within a global community or a global village where people could be in constant touch regardless of spatial and temporal differences. The Internet provided a ready platform for commerce to flourish – sellers could advertise their wares and services globally and buyers, businesses and consumers alike[2] had access to products at competitive prices. Sellers could provide product information, prices, delivery terms, and interested parties could negotiate terms and conclude contracts electronically. Direct access to a potentially large customer base meant that sellers did not have to opt for the traditional methods for selling their products – for example, use of agents to market their products in distant lands. Equally, buyers did not have to go through agents to find suitable manufacturers of products they required. The information and communications technology revolution was creating a new means of conducting business, namely, conducting commerce electronically or e-commerce.[3]

Emergence of any new technology raises interesting issues for policy makers, law makers and other stakeholders. And more so where the technology is expected to have a wide economic impact and is readily embraced. The likely effects – social, moral and economic, amongst others – of the new technology have to be assessed and decisions need to be taken on the extent to which its use has to be regulated. It is a matter of striking a fine balance between the expected risks of the new technology and the opportunities created by it. The history of mankind is replete with instances of new technologies that have had enormous impact on society and policy makers and law makers have stepped in to regulate the behaviour of those using the technology. The aviation industry is a good illustration where regulations were put in place early on to promote the development of the aviation industry and to provide a minimum level of protection for air passengers.[4]

---

1   The Internet is a vast collection of interconnected computer networks that use a protocol known as TCP/IP. The Internet evolved from ARPANET (Advanced Research Projects Network) – established by the US Department of Defense. It is a wide area networking system that would survive nuclear attacks. See http://1001.resources.com for further definitions.

2   Of course, it must be stressed that online sales are equally affected by the export/import restrictions that affect offline sales.

3   Defined by the OECD (Organisation for European Co-operation and Development) thus:
    . . . [it] refers generally to all forms of commercial transactions involving both organisations and individuals, that are based upon the electronic processing and transmission of data, including text, sound and visual images. It also refers to the effects that the electronic exchange of commercial information may have on the institution and processes that support and govern commercial activities [*Electronic Commerce: Opportunities and Challenges for Governments*, 1997, available at www.oecd.org].

4   See Chapter 10 for an international regulatory measure adopted widely in respect of carriage by air.

The Internet's radical character is a challenge for policy makers and legislators. Lacking geographic containment, it knows no national boundaries. Information posted on a website in Borneo can be accessed within seconds from the UK. As a truly global medium, it is a significant contributor to globalisation. As with globalisation, the logic of the Internet is economic.

This chapter highlights some of the US and EU policies in respect of electronic commerce (hereinafter 'e-commerce') and the legal harmonisation of specific issues relating to e-commerce at the UNCITRAL and EU levels alongside the initiatives from international organisations such as the ICC. It must be noted that the Internet raises a whole host of legal issues – for instance, the posting of pornographic and racist materials, data protection and intellectual property-related issues.[5] These are not considered here since they are outside the scope of this book.

POLICY CONSIDERATIONS, E-COMMERCE AND INTERNATIONAL REGULATORY MEASURES

New technological developments always raise important issues: among them, economic, moral and social impact of the technology, and the legal framework to establish the rights and liabilities of the various actors involved in the use of that technology. The extent to which a state should intervene in the affairs of those affected by the technology is dependent on a number of factors: the level of the perceived risk, both in the short and in the long term, to a given society by the various actors, groups, interests and individuals within that society; the flexibility of the existing legal framework to cope with legal issues that arise in the context of the new technology and its use; the abilities of those within a given society to regulate their affairs in a manner that ensures that legal rights of individuals (or, for that matter, the moral fabric of that society) are not undermined; and the nature of the actors involved in the use of the technology. Policy makers, legislators and other stakeholders such as non-governmental entities face tough issues and choices. Philosophical convictions, cultural beliefs and social norms also contribute to the choices they make. For instance, stakeholders involved with the protection of weaker parties, such as consumers or the mercantile interests of least developed countries, may prefer more interference from the state as opposed to self-regulatory schemes imposed by trade associations, whereas policy makers motivated by economic arguments may wish to impose the least amount of restriction to enable competition, and the resulting benefits from that competition, such as economic growth, investment in product development, and greater consumer choice.

A reason commonly advanced for regulation[6] at the national level through state intervention in the affairs of men and markets is the public good. As a noble aim, it is attractive and has the potential to gain wide acceptance even though it is difficult to state with clarity what public good embodies, or from where it derives its content. Is its content derived from social norms, or moral standards, or purely altruistic

---

5   For further on this, see Lloyd, *Information Technology Law*, 5th edn 2008, OUP.

6   In the context of information and communications technology, it may also be possible to use technology to reach the social/public policy goals – eg, filters, and privacy enhancing techniques. See Reidenberg, '*Lex informatica*: the formulation of information policy rules through technology' (1998) 3 Texas LR 553.

concerns devoid of any self-interests? Are moral standards universal? Are they the same across cultures? Do they change over time? Even if these questions are answerable, it is questionable whether all state intervention measures are driven by this noble ideal of the public good. It is not unknown for governments (driven by political ambitions) to introduce regulation that promotes the interests of the few – for instance, economically strong commercial interests. The issue of benefit to the public at large in these circumstances is a purely contingent matter.

Even where the motivation behind regulation is the public good, it tends to veer towards 'unproductive activities'.[7] Amongst others, there may be the tendency to introduce burdensome bureaucratic procedures, greater attention may be paid to lobbying with the intention of introducing further regulation favouring commercial interests, it may result in greater litigation, and in extreme circumstances provide a fertile bed for corruption.[8] Monies that could have been usefully spent towards further investment and product development and improvement are likely to be spent elsewhere resulting, in the long run, in technical as well as economic inefficiency.

Self-regulation is often offered as an alternative to regulation. Industries under this scheme regulate themselves through specific industry-related associations whose members follow codes of conduct.[9] Normally, the industry, the government and consumer associations are involved in the drawing up of the codes. The industry benefits in a number of ways – in return for following a code of conduct, it is assured that it does not have to waste valuable resources in tackling bureaucratic hurdles. In marketing terms, it also makes sense since it contributes to consumer confidence thus boosting sales. It also exhibits that the industry is a willing contributor to meeting the social/policy objectives thus reducing the risk of alienation. The government benefits since the costs of regulation and enforcement are passed on to the industry without losing sight of the social and policy objectives. Minimum intervention in the form of regulation is also likely to fuel economic growth. The extent to which the government is actively involved in the drafting of the code or in monitoring that the industry seriously follows the code will vary from state to state. It might also depend on the sector that is the subject of self-regulation. It may be that in some areas the government may wish to adopt a hands-on approach while in others it might wish to adopt a minimalist approach. Government involvement, regardless of the level, helps in facilitation of the self-regulatory scheme and ensuring that the self-regulatory scheme co-exists comfortably with existing regulation. And in the context of globalisation, governments can play an important role in promoting self-regulation at an international level.[10] Consumers also benefit in contributing to the code of conduct since it gives them an opportunity to voice and address their concerns thus contributing to consumer confidence and assurance. And in a global community, consumers

---

7   Phrase used by Bhagwati and Srinivasan in 'Revenue seeking: a generalisation of the theory of tariffs' (1980) 80 Journal of Political Economy 1069. See also Buchanan, Tollosin and Tullock (eds), *Toward a Theory of the Rent-Seeking Society*, 1980, A and M Press.

8   See Salbu, 'Extraterritorial restriction of bribery: a premature evocation of the normative global village' (1999) 24 Yale Journal of International Law 223; Nichols, 'Regulating transnational bribery in times of globalisation and fragmentation' (1999) 24 Yale Journal of International Law 257; Carr 'Fighting corruption through the UN Convention on Corruption 2003: a global solution to a global problem' (2005) 11 ITLR 24.

9   Codes of conduct (also called codes of practice, codes of ethics) are normally voluntary. They usually list practices relating to the business set as a minimum standard.

10 International self-regulatory schemes are not unknown. One example is the ISO (International Standards Organisation), a federation of national standards bodies from well over 100 countries. It is responsible for formulating agreed standards for goods and services.

also play a role in alerting the industry to best practices followed in other states. Where codes of conduct are breached, the codes may provide for forum, mode of dispute resolution, and appropriate remedies.

A word of warning however must be added in respect of self-regulation. It might not suit all industries. The industry, as stated earlier, bears the costs of participating in a self-regulatory scheme. Where the industry consists of small-scale units, they might be unwilling to participate in such schemes.[11] They might feel compelled to pass on these costs to the consumer, which in the long term may stunt economic growth. Further self-regulation may not suit all countries since it requires the necessary infrastructure – an ethos of consumer awareness and consumer participation (at a group level), willingness on the part of industry to seriously participate in the self-regulatory scheme alongside absorbing the costs of self-regulation. Developing countries, for instance, may not always provide a conducive environment for the effective operation of self-regulation due to unwillingness on the part of the industry to participate in a self-regulatory scheme. To some extent, co-regulation where the government takes on a more active role (for example, by requiring a mandatory code or enforcing compliance with the code) may be seen as a viable alternative. Self-regulation may not also suit certain sectors – such as protection of intellectual property rights, public health, and privacy and data protection.

The Internet as an information and communications medium can be used for a variety of purposes other than conducting electronic commerce. As such, it may be necessary to use a mix of regulation and self-regulation for its efficient use. One of the earliest documents that substantially influenced the regulatory aspects of the Internet is *A Framework for Electronic Commerce* formulated by the Clinton administration in 1997.[12] As this document highlights, while self-regulation should be the guiding force in the e-commerce arena, regulation may be necessary to support a predictable and simple legal environment for electronic commerce. It states:

> In some areas, government agreements may prove necessary to facilitate electronic commerce and protect consumers . . . Where government intervention is necessary to facilitate electronic commerce, its goal should be to ensure competition, protect intellectual property and privacy, prevent fraud, foster transparency, support commercial transactions, and facilitate dispute resolution [Principle 13].

This document also sees itself as formulating an international policy in respect of e-commerce and urges international organisations such as the UNCITRAL and ICC to work towards modifying existing rules and creating new rules to support the use of the new technology alongside working towards harmonisation. As the following sections and Chapter 4 indicate, international organisations have responded favourably to this call, resulting in some level of harmonisation across jurisdictions in respect of the legal recognition of electronic transactions.

Before moving on, a brief reference to the EU response to the challenges posed by e-commerce is in order. The European policies are outlined in *A European Initiative on Electronic Commerce*.[13] Like the US policy document, it recognises the need for global consensus given the transnational character of electronic commerce. However,

---

11 See Consumer Affairs Division, *Codes of Conduct*, 1998, Department of Industry, Science and Tourism.

12 Available at http://uazone.org/gis/ecomm.htm.

13 COM 97(157) 15.04.97.

predictably, the document exhibits sensitivity to an essential characteristic of the Union – the Single Market – and the need to enable e-commerce participants to realise the potential of this Internal Market. It states:

> In order to allow for electronic commerce to reap the full benefits of the Single Market, it is essential to avoid regulatory inconsistencies and to ensure a coherent legal and regulatory framework for electronic commerce at EU level. This should be based on the application of key Internal Market principles.

The two directives – one on e-commerce[14] and the other on electronic signatures[15] – realise the objective of ensuring a minimum level of legal coherence.

ELECTRONIC DATA INTERCHANGE (EDI) AND INTERCHANGE AGREEMENTS

The potential for conducting business using computer technology was not a novel idea introduced by the Internet revolution. EDI was in common use as far back as the 1980s and still continues to be used today. The difference between the Internet and EDI is that, in the latter, the communications take place within a closed network. EDI is often defined as 'the inter-company computer-to-computer communication of standard transactions in a standard format that permits the receiver to perform the intended transaction'.[16]

The move to EDI was largely driven by economic factors and efficiency arguments. EDI provides numerous advantages. Foremost is the lowering of transaction costs from the stage of acquiring information to producing relevant documents such as invoice and export/import documentation. There is substantial lowering of personnel costs since much of the work done by clerks – in the form of mailing of documents, filling of forms – would be done by computers. There is also the added advantage of fewer errors since information received does not have to be manually re-keyed into another computer system. Response time to purchase orders is also speeded up. All in all, EDI increases the efficiency of an organisation.

The aim of EDI is to perform certain business functions automatically without human intervention – for instance, the processing of a purchase order or sending of an invoice to a customer. Since computers, unlike humans, are unable to arrange information sent in free text into an intelligible format, it was necessary to adopt standards in relation to pertinent information such as mailing/shipping information,[17] order number, price, quantity that would enable a computer to recognise and process the incoming data. Industries such as the motor industry in Europe set about creating their own standard in ODETTE,[18] and the chemical industry in CEFIC.[19] These standards normally would specify the type of documents (for example, invoice) that can be transmitted electronically, the order of the data, their sequence and their

---

14   See pp 117–20 below.
15   See Chapter 4.
16   See Sokol, *Electronic Data Interchange: The Competitive Edge*, 1989, McGraw-Hill.
17   In computing language known as data segments. The mailing address is a data segment and the detail such as street name within the data segment is known as a data element.
18   Organisation for Data Exchange by Teletransmission in Europe; www.odette.org.
19   Conseil Européen des Fédérations l'Industrie Chimique; www.cefic.be.

interpretation. It was however felt that there was a need to adopt an international standard if EDI was to prove effective. One of the organisations in Europe to work on standardisation of message structure was the UNECE.[20] Its work, along with that of the ISO,[21] resulted in the UN/EDIFACT.[22] The work on EDIFACT is ongoing and new standards are continually adopted, and existing standards modified to accommodate trade practices and to reflect industry requests.

Unsurprisingly, the ICC also responded rapidly to the developing commercial interest in the use of EDI. It formulated a code of conduct known as UNCID[23] to facilitate the use of EDI in international trade. It aims to make the electronic interchange secure by ensuring that common messaging structures are used,[24] and acceptable systems are in place to deal with authentication of messages, verification of messages[25] and maintenance of communication logs.[26] It must be noted that the focus of the UNCID is the interchange of data and not the content of the data. Many of the provisions in the UNCITRAL Model Law on Electronic Commerce are traceable to the ideas enshrined in the UNCID.

UNCITRAL MODEL LAW ON E-COMMERCE

Background, guiding principles and harmonisation

The text of the UNCITRAL Model Law on Electronic Commerce was adopted in 1996. Its origin however is traceable to 1985 when the Commission considered a report[27] highlighting the legal problems associated with the use of computer-to-computer communications. The report focused on the writing requirement and signatures for the purposes of validity and enforceability of contract and recommended that governments review existing legal rules that required paper documentation or signatures as conditions for the validity or enforceability of a transaction with a view to amending them suitably to permit documents in a computer-readable form. Work on electronic contract formation continued within UNCITRAL and it was felt that a common legal framework facilitating electronic data interchange was required to impart legal certainty while mindful of the retention of a flexible approach where legislative action may be regarded as premature.[28] In 1992, a Working Group on Electronic Data Interchange was set up. The emergence of the Internet widened the focus of the Working Group to include more modern methods of communication alongside EDI. Their work resulted in what we now know as the Model Law on

---

20   United Nations Economic Commission for Europe. See also Troye, 'The development of legal issues of EDI under the European Union TEDIS Programme' (1994) The EDI LR 195; European Parliament, 'European information highways: which standards?' (1995), European Communities/Union EUR-OP/OOPEC/OPOCE.
21   International Standards Organisation.
22   United Nations Electronic Data Interchange for Administration, Commerce and Transport.
23   Uniform Rules of Conduct for Interchange of Trade Data by Teletransmission. The text of this document is available at www.unece.org. Also reproduced in Walden (ed), *EDI and the Law*, 1989, Blenheim Online.
24   See Art 4 of UNCID.
25   See *ibid*, Arts 6 and 7.
26   See *ibid*, Art 10.
27   'Legal value of computer records', UN Doc A/CN 9/265.
28   Paragraph 130, UN Doc A/CN 9/360.

Electronic Commerce (hereinafter 'EC Model Law'). The EC Model Law is published along with a Guide to the Enactment (hereinafter 'Guide') to be used as an aid to interpretation.

It must be noted that a model law does not have the same legislative weight as a convention and perhaps does not bring the same level of unification. But it does away with many of the delays and bureaucratic measures associated with conventions. States are free to adopt the model law as it stands or base their law using the model law as a starting point.[29] There is also scope for manoeuvrability within the EC Model Law. For instance, Arts 5, 6, 7, 8, 11 and 12 allow the states to limit the application of those provisions to specific areas.[30] It must be added that the EC Model Law has had worldwide impact and many legislations have either adopted it or drawn inspiration for their own law from it.[31]

The EC Model Law consists of two parts – Part I on electronic commerce in general and Part II on Electronic Commerce in Specific Areas. Part I consists of three chapters – Chapter I (Arts 1–4) on general provisions such as definitions, interpretation and party autonomy, Chapter II (Arts 5–10) on application of legal requirements such as writing, signature and originals to data messages, and Chapter III (Arts 11–15) on communication of data messages such as validity of messages. Part II consists of one chapter (Arts 16–17) and deals with carriage of goods.

The aim of the EC Model Law is to facilitate electronic commerce by removing the legal uncertainties that may surround data sent through electronic means. But before moving onto substantive provisions, a few words must be said about the guiding principles of this model law: functional equivalence, party autonomy and uniformity.

As indicated earlier, the requirements of form – writing, signature, original – are the stumbling blocks to electronic contracting. The Working Group could have addressed this problem by redrawing the contours of the law relating to validity of contracts. In pragmatic/political terms, such a step may not have found many supporters. Instead, the Working Group adopted a different method. Termed the 'functional equivalence approach', they looked at the functions performed by writing, signature and original with a view to seeing whether these functions could be fulfilled through e-commerce techniques. The functions performed by writing, as is well known, are accessibility to all and a high degree of permanence besides providing evidence to courts and administrative authorities. A signature is usually used for authentication purposes. The Working Group was equally mindful in adopting this approach that users of e-commerce were not discriminated against by the imposition of stringent standards on the e-commerce user (paras 15–18). The functional equivalence approach is adopted in relation to Arts 6–8.

The principle of party autonomy is enshrined in Art 4. It is no secret that businesses prefer to agree to their own terms, and legislation that allows them this possibility is likely to find favour with them. There is only limited party autonomy in the EC Model Law. According to Art 4(2), provisions contained in Chapter II of Part I cannot be varied by agreement since requirements relating to form such as writing, signature and presentation/retention of originals, and admissibility of evidence are

---

29   See, eg, the Indian Information Technology Act 2000.
30   Eg, Art 11(2) reads: 'The provisions of this Article do not apply to the following . . .'.
31   To name a few, Australia, Singapore and New Zealand.

mandatory in most jurisdictions and may 'reflect decisions of public policy'. As the Guide states:

> The reason for such a limitation is that the provisions of the Model Law contained in Chapter II of Part I may, to some extent, be regarded as a collection of exceptions to well-established rules regarding the form of legal transactions. Such well-established rules are normally of a mandatory nature since they generally reflect decisions of public policy. An unqualified statement regarding the freedom of parties might be misinterpreted as allowing the parties, through a derogation to the Model Law, to derogate from mandatory rules adopted for reasons of public policy [para 44].

In order to achieve the stated objective of legal certainty, it is important that the EC Model Law is interpreted in a uniform fashion across jurisdictions. Inspired by Art 7 of the Convention on the International Sale of Goods 1980,[32] Art 3(1) of the EC Model Law provides that in its interpretation regard is to be had to its international origin and to the need to promote uniformity in its application and the observance of good faith. Other than referring to the *travaux préparatoires* (including the Guide), courts will be expected to refer to interpretation of the EC Model Law in other jurisdictions. Theoretically reasonable, it is questionable whether this will be followed in practice.[33] Standardisation is more likely to be introduced through mercantile usage rather than cross-jurisdiction judicial reference.

Where questions concerning matters governed by the EC Model Law but not expressly settled by it arise, according to Art 3(2), they are to be settled in conformity with the general principles on which it is based. While the principles are not outlined in a specific provision,[34] the Guide helpfully provides a non-exhaustive list. These are to: (1) facilitate e-commerce among and within nations; (2) validate transactions entered into by means of new information technologies; (3) promote and encourage the implementation of new information technologies; (4) promote the uniformity of law; and (5) support commercial practice.

Part I – e-commerce

Scope, requirements of form and evidential issues

The scope of application is laid out in Art 1 which states that the EC Model Law is to apply to commercial activities. Commercial activities include not just sales but other commercial relationships, such as factoring, agency agreements, distribution agreements, leases, industrial co-operation and transportation of goods by air, sea, rail or road. Consumers are not specifically addressed since different jurisdictions have different consumer protection regulations guided by their national policies. The Guide, however, indicates that national legislators adopting the EC Model Law are free to extend its applicability to consumer contracts. It must also be noted that the footnote defining commercial activities includes carriage of passengers by rail, road, air and sea. To this extent, consumers do fall within the ambit of Art 1.

There is also no mention in Art 1 as to whether the EC Model Law is intended to

---

32 See Chapter 2, pp 71–2 above. Also see Chapter 4, pp 130–1 below.
33 See pp 71–3 on the interpretation of the Convention on the International Sale of Goods 1980.
34 The principle of uniformity and legal certainty can however be gathered from Art 3 on interpretation.

apply to e-commerce transactions with an international element. It is meant to apply to both domestic and international commercial transactions conducted electronically. States wishing to adopt the EC Model Law, however, may restrict its applicability to international transactions. The wording suggested by the EC Model Law for these purposes is 'This law applies to a data message as defined in para (1) of Art 2 where the data message relates to international commerce'. While states have the flexibility to restrict its applicability to international commerce, the Guide, however, recommends that the EC Model Law should be applied as widely as possible since its objective is to promote legal certainty (para 29). States desirous of limiting the recognition of data messages in specific cases still have the freedom to do so under various provisions allowing some degree of flexibility – for instance, Art 6 on writing and Art 7 on signature. They might wish to do so in the case of leasing commercial property or contracts relating to intellectual property rights.

Applying the principle of functional equivalence, Art 5 imparts legal recognition to data messages thus indicating that data messages are not to be discriminated against on the basis of their nature. 'Data message' is defined in Art 2(a) as information generated, sent, received or stored by electronic optical or similar means including, but not limited to, EDI, electronic mail, telegram, telex or telecopy. Any drafter of a provision addressing information and communication technology has a difficult task – to ensure that it can embrace new and rapid developments in the technology. Use of the phrase 'similar means' is intended to do just that. But what comes as a surprise are the inclusion of telex, telegram and telecopy. Why include communication techniques that have been around for well over 50 years within the definition? Since uncertainties surround the legal status of telex messages and telegrams in some jurisdictions, the drafting of the EC Model Law was seen as an opportunity to settle the ambiguities. Also given that a telecopy could be generated by a computer, it was felt that specific mention of these communication techniques would be appropriate. The EC Model Law does not provide a definition of electronic commerce.[35] However, EDI is defined in Art 2(b) as the electronic transfer from computer to computer of information using an agreed standard to structure the information. It is unclear whether this definition covers situations where data is not transferred through a telecommunications system but with disks containing EDI messages that are posted to the recipient for downloading on to the computer. According to the Guide, this should cause no great concern since messages using such communication techniques would fall within Art 2(a) (para 34).

Article 6(1) addresses the requirement of writing found in non-electronic (paper-based environment) by focusing on the notion of information capable of being reproduced and read. It provides that a data message where the information is accessible so as to be usable for subsequent reference would meet the requirement of writing.

Signature, another common legal requirement, is dealt with in Art 7 which

---

35   The Guide notes that the EC Model Law does not provide a definition of e-commerce but considers it as a notion encompassing a variety of means of communication. It states in para 7 that: 'among the means of communication encompassed in the notion of "electronic commerce" are the following modes of transmission based on the use of electronic techniques: communication by means of EDI defined narrowly as the computer-to-computer transmission of data in standardised format, transmission of electronic messages involving the use of either publicly available standards or proprietary standards; transmission of free-formatted text by electronic means, for example, through the Internet. It was also noted that, in certain circumstances, the notion of "electronic commerce" might cover the use of techniques such as telex and telecopy'.

provides that it is met in relation to a data message if: (a) a method is used to identify that person and to indicate that person's approval of the information contained in the data message; and (b) that method is as reliable as was appropriate for the purpose for which the data message was generated or communicated, in the light of all the circumstances, including any relevant agreement. The Guide indicates factors such as the kind and size of the transaction, the nature of the trade activity, trade customs and practices, and the degree of acceptance of the method of identification in the industry. It must be noted that since the adoption of this model law, UNCITRAL has also adopted a model law devoted to electronic signatures.[36] Some guidance may also be sought from that model law to establish the appropriateness of the method used to identify the person.

The call for 'originals' in the paper-based environment (for example, presentation of an original bill of lading) is dealt with in Art 8(1), which states:

> Where the law requires information to be presented or retained in its original form, that requirement is met by a data message if:
>
> (a) there exists a reliable assurance as the integrity of the information from the time when it was first generated in its final form, as a data message or otherwise; and
>
> (b) where it is required that information be presented, that information is capable of being displayed to the person to whom it is presented.

Integrity and reliability are pertinent to establishing the originalness of the data message and these are addressed in Art 8(3). The criteria for assessing integrity are whether the information has remained complete and unaltered. This means that there must be secure systems in place that can detect alterations to the message. As for reliability, that is to be decided on the basis of the purpose for which the information was generated and in light of all the relevant circumstances.

Admissibility of computer evidence is often cited in scholarly writings as a reason for the uncertainty surrounding electronic transactions.[37] This issue along with evidential weight of data message is dealt with in Art 9. Article 9(1) provides that data messages should not be denied admissibility on the grounds it is a data message or that it is not in its original form. As for evidential weight, that is to be determined on the basis of the reliability and integrity of the system, the manner in which the originator was identified and other relevant factors according to Art 9(2).

In some circumstances (for example, auditing purposes, tax purposes), law may require the retention of records. Article 10 addresses the issue of storage of data message using accessibility, integrity and accurate log information for the purposes of imparting legal recognition to records held as data messages.

Formation of contract, validity, attribution and time and place of dispatch/receipt of data messages

Recognition of formation of contract by electronic means and its validity is addressed by Art 11. The constituent elements of a contract – offer and acceptance – can be expressed according to Art 11(1) by means of a data message. It also goes on to state

---

36 Electronic signatures can be used not only for identification purposes but also for encryption of a document. See Chapter 4; pp 126–8.

37 See Abeyratne, 'Some recent trends in evidential issues on electronic data interchange – the Anglo-American response' (1994) 10(2) Computer Law and Practice 41.

that contracts formed using data messages shall not be denied validity or enforceability. Further, as between the originator and addressee of a data message, a declaration of will or other statement is not to be denied legal effect, validity or enforceability on the grounds that it is in the form of a data message according to Art 12(1). So, where a buyer sends notification of defective goods to the seller by electronic means, Art 12(1) would enable these messages to be treated in the same manner as other conventional means of communication. It is obvious that these provisions are geared to promote legal certainty in the use of electronic means of communication. In other words, parties can transact electronically with the certain belief that the transaction will not be denied legal effect or validity purely on the basis of the nature of communication medium used. It must, however, be noted that the EC Model Law is not concerned with the law on formation of contracts, or the precise moment when a contract is concluded. These are to be dealt with under the law applicable to the contract.[38] And where the contract is for the international sale of goods, it might attract the application of the Convention on the International Sale of Goods 1980, which has its own provisions on contract formation. Further, the UNIDROIT Principles for International Commercial Contracts may also be relevant.[39] It must also be noted that the EC Model Law gives freedom to the parties to agree otherwise in respect of Arts 11 and 12.

A problem normally voiced about electronic messages is the uncertainty in attributing messages to those who are supposed to have sent them. What guarantee is there that the electronic message is really sent by the person who is indicated as being the originator?[40] One way of resolving this uncertainty would be to follow up the electronic message with a paper document. This defeats the advantages – speed, efficiency and economic benefits – normally advanced in favour of electronic communication. The EC Model Law handles this uncertainty by presuming that a data message under certain conditions would be regarded as that of the originator. So, where the originator and the addressee agree upon an authentication procedure and that procedure is applied by the addressee, the message will be attributed to the originator according to Art 13(3)(a). It is possible that an agent or other person may also have access to the authentication procedure. In circumstances where such parties by virtue of their relationship with the originator apply the agreed procedure to the message, it will be presumed to have come from the originator under Art 13(3)(b). This presumption, however, is displaceable under certain circumstances. In the case of situations falling within Art 13(3), according to Art 13(4)(a), the presumption is displaced as of the time when the addressee has both received notice from the originator that the data message is not that of the originator and had reasonable time to act accordingly. Article 13(4)(a), however, should not be perceived as an easy option for an originator to retract his message by sending a notice, since Art 13(1) clearly states that a data message is that of the originator if it was sent by the originator itself. In other words, the originator is bound by the data message sent to the addressee, unless of course it can be shown that the agreed authentication procedures had not been applied by the addressee, in which case the notice becomes effective. However, the notice does not have retroactive effect. It will release the originator from the binding effect of the data message only from the time of receipt of notice. He is still bound by

---

38   See Chapters 16 and 17.
39   For further on these instruments, see Chapter 2.
40   See paras 83–92.

the data message before the time of receipt. The presumption in cases that fall within Art 13(3)(b) is displaced at any time when the addressee knew or should have known had it exercised reasonable care or used any agreed procedure that the data message was not that of the originator (Art 13(4)(b)).

A frequent business practice is the request for a return receipt – an acknowledgment by the recipient of the paper document to the sender stating that the recipient has received the sender's communication. Sometimes, the return receipt might also request the recipient to confirm that the contents of the letter/document have been read and agreed with. The practice obviously is intended to enhance the level of certainty in relation to what the parties have agreed to as between themselves. Further, in the event of a subsequent dispute, these documents could be used effectively to show that the purported document was received by the other party or, where circumstances permit, to ascertain the extent of their agreement. The EC Model Law replicates this business practice in relation to data messages in Art 14 which deals with acknowledgment of receipt. Where the originator and addressee have agreed that messages will be acknowledged, then Art 14(2)–(4) covers a variety of situations ranging from lack of agreement between the parties about the form or method of agreement, to the period of time tolerated for receiving a receipt where a data message is not conditional upon receipt. Of course, data messages sent between the originator and addressee are likely to contain important information that will have legal consequences. It is made clear in Art 14(7) that Art 14 is not intended to deal with the legal consequences that may flow either from that data message or from the acknowledgment of its receipt, except in so far as it relates to the sending or receipt of the data message.

Important legal questions are determined on the basis of time and place of dispatch/receipt of messages. For instance, a postal acceptance of a postal offer under English law takes place at the time of dispatch with the result that the contract is concluded at the time of dispatch.[41] Article 15 addresses the issue of time and place of dispatch/receipt of data messages and provides default rules in the event parties have not agreed otherwise. Dispatch of a data message occurs, according to Art 15(1), when it enters an information system outside the control of the originator. Information system is defined widely as a system for generating, sending, receiving, storing or otherwise processing data messages (Art 2(f)). From the Guide, it is apparent that it could include not only the communications network but also a mailbox or a telecopier. So, where the message enters a server for onward transmission and the server is not under the originator's control, the dispatch would have taken place. The question of receipt is dealt with on the basis of whether the addressee has designated a particular information system for the purposes of receipt of the data message. So, where the addressee has designated an information system for receiving purposes, then receipt occurs when the data message enters the designated system. For example, if i.m.carr@kent.ac.uk is designated as the information system for receipt purposes, receipt will take place at the time the data message enters that system. Where the data message is sent to the addressee's information system, that is not the designated information system for the purposes of receipt so then receipt occurs at the time of retrieval. To illustrate, if the message is sent to imcarr@btinternet.com which is not the designated information system, then receipt will occur when the

---

41   *Dunlop v Higgins* (1848) 1 HLC 381; *Stevenson, Jacques and Co v Maclean* (1880) 5 QBD 346.

message is retrieved from imcarr@btinternet.com. In the absence of designation of an information system for purposes of receipt, receipt occurs when the data message enters an information system of the addressee.

As for place of dispatch and receipt, it is tied to the place of business of the originator and the addressee. It is likely that the parties have more than one place of business. In this case, the place of business is that which has the closest relationship with the underlying transaction. Where there is no underlying transaction, then the principal place of business. Where there is no place of business, then reference is to be made to its habitual residence (Art 15(4)).[42]

Part II – carriage of goods

The focus of this part is e-commerce in specific areas – more particularly, carriage of goods. Transportation of goods is central to international sale of goods and as indicated in Part III of this book, transport documents in the form of bills of lading play a central role in the sale/purchase chain. The issue of using paperless transport documents has been discussed since the 1980s.[43] While the move to electronic documentation where transport documents simply act as receipts or notify parties of the terms and conditions of carriage is seen as unproblematic, the paperless medium poses problems where transferability is required. In the offline world, a bill of lading is normally transferred by endorsement along with a physical transfer of the document. The transferability issue can however be addressed satisfactorily in the online world as a result of recent technological developments in the form of electronic signatures for authentication. The Bolero Rules illustrate how an electronic bill of lading can be transferred using a combination of digital signatures and trusted third parties.[44]

The EC Model Law facilitates the use of electronic transport documentation by providing a legal framework. The provisions are meant to apply not only to transport documents found in the maritime sector but also those used in the context of road, rail, air and multimodal transport. Article 16, which outlines the scope of Part II, is drafted in a manner to include a variety of transport documents including air way-bills, bills of lading, multimodal transport documents and charterparties. Following the general principles of functional equivalence, Arts 17(1) and (2) enable the replacement of a paper document with a paperless document and endorsement or transference of the paperless document through electronic means. While Arts 17(1) and (2) enable the replacement of a paper document with an electronic one, there is still the problem of establishing that the rights/obligations associated with a transport document are those of the intended person. For instance, where a paper bill of lading is used, the right to claim delivery of the goods is acquired and established as a result of the transfer of the paper document. The right to claim belongs to a particular person (or persons in the case of joint title) and no other. This 'guarantee of singularity', namely, that one person and no other[45] can lay claim to the rights in the electronic

---

42 Note that this provision is based on Art 10 of the Convention on the International Sale of Goods 1980. See Chapter 2, pp 62–3 above.

43 See Chapter 6, pp 197–204 below.

44 See Chapter 6, pp 203–4 below.

45 According to the explanatory memorandum, the use of the word 'one person and no other person' in Art 17 is not intended to exclude the situation where more than one person might jointly hold title to the goods. See para 116.

environment is established by the use of a reliable method[46] that renders these data messages unique. Article 17(3) provides that where the 'right is to be granted to, or an obligation is to be acquired by, one person and no other person, and the law requires that in order to effect this, the right or obligation must be conveyed to that person by the transfer, or use, of a paper document, that requirement is met if the right or obligation is conveyed by using one or more data messages, provided a reliable method is used to render such data message or messages unique'. The Guide interprets 'a reliable method' as 'referring to the use of a reliable method to secure that data message purporting to convey any right or obligation of a person might not be used by, or on behalf of, that person inconsistently with any other data messages by which the right or obligation was conveyed by or on behalf of that person'.[47] The standard of reliability, according to Art 17(4), is to be gauged on the basis of the purposes for which the right/obligation was conveyed, and other circumstances including any relevant agreement.

Mention must be made at this juncture of the numerable international conventions that govern the rights and liabilities of the parties to a carriage of goods contract. In the maritime context, where bills of lading are widely used, the Hague and Hague-Visby Rules are widely ratified conventions. These Rules, mandatorily applicable to bills of lading that meet the stipulated conditions, do not make any provision for electronic bills of lading. In order to attract applicability of carriage conventions that would mandatorily apply to paper documents to their electronic versions, Art 17(6) provides that '. . . if a rule of law is compulsorily applicable to a contract of carriage of goods which is in, or is evidenced by, a paper document, that rule shall not be inapplicable to such a contract of carriage of goods which is evidenced by one or more data messages by reason of the fact that the contract is evidenced by such data message or messages instead of by a paper document'. It is odd that the drafters, instead of simply stating that the rules applicable to paper documents apply also to electronic documents, have used the phrase 'shall not be inapplicable' to extend the applicability of the international conventions to electronic documents. The Guide advances a reason for this. It seems the drafters did not wish, given the wide scope of Art 17, to extend the applicability of international conventions such as the Hague-Visby Rules to contracts to which such rules were not meant to apply, that is, to other types of contracts. It is questionable whether the drafters were adopting too overcautious an approach since conditions other than documentary requirements have also to be met for the applicability of these international conventions.[48]

OTHER INTERNATIONAL INITIATIVES – THE INTERNATIONAL CHAMBER OF COMMERCE

The ICC is also a keen participator in the promotion of e-commerce. Their engagement with EDI, as we saw earlier, resulted in the widely accepted Uniform Rules on Conduct for Interchange of Trade Data by Teletransmission (UNCID) published in 1987. UNCID however was specifically designed for closed networks and was

---

46   Use of digital signatures may be one way of achieving this. See, for instance, the CMI Rules on Electronic Bills of Lading and the Bolero Rules – Chapter 6, pp 197–204 below.
47   See para 117.
48   See Chapter 8, pp 268–73 below.

insufficient for establishing trust and reliability in open networks. The ICC therefore set out to work on international guidelines for e-commerce on the open network. This resulted in the publication of General Usage for International Digitally Ensured Commerce[49] (GUIDEC) in 1997 and a subsequent document GUIDEC II in 2001. It provides a statement of best practices for adoption by businesses to promote trust in e-commerce by focusing on issues such as authentication devices, certification policies, public key certificates and record keeping.[50]

THE EU DIRECTIVE ON E-COMMERCE

Directive 2000/31/EC on Certain Legal Aspects of Information Society Services, in particular Electronic Commerce, in the Internal Market (Directive on Electronic Commerce)[51] was adopted on 8 June 2000.[52] It would be a mistake to assume from the short title that this directive covers much the same ground as the EC Model Law. While there are a couple of provisions dealing with contractual matters, its major focus is the free movement of information society services amongst member states and the protection of the online consumer. This is in keeping with the principles outlined in *A European Initiative in Electronic Commerce*.[53] It states '. . . the first objective is to build trust and confidence . . . both consumers and businesses must be confident that their transaction will not be intercepted or modified, that the seller and buyer are who they say they are and that transaction mechanisms are available, legal and secure . . . The second objective is to ensure full access for electronic commerce to the single marketplace' (at paras 35–38). What follows is a brief summary of the main provisions of this directive (hereinafter E-Commerce Directive).

E-commerce, free movement of services and transparency provisions

As with the EC Model Law, the E-Commerce Directive does not provide a definition of e-commerce. The reason is that e-commerce uses a variety of communicative techniques. As *A European Initiative in Electronic Commerce* states:

> It includes a wide number of applications in the narrowband (videotext), broadcast (teleshopping), and offline environment (catalogue sales on CD-ROM), as well as proprietary corporate networks (banking) . . . the Internet is generating many innovative hybrid forms of electronic commerce – combining, for example, digital television infomercials with Internet response mechanisms (for immediate ordering), CD-ROM catalogues with Internet connections (for content or price updates) and commercial Web sites with local CD-ROM extension (for memory-intensive multimedia demonstrations) [at para 8].

In these circumstances, it was felt best not to provide a definition, since it is unlikely to

---

49   These documents are available at www.iccwbo.org.
50   For more on the use of digital signatures for authentication purposes and the role of certification service providers, see Chapter 4. See also ICC Document ECP WG 1/13 of 12 October 1998.
51   The majority of the provisions has been transposed into UK law by the Electronic Commerce (EC Directive) Regulations 2002 (SI 2002/2013).
52   OJL 178, 17.7.2000 p1.
53   COM (97) 157, 15.04.97.

be sufficiently progressive to accommodate new developments relating to the electronic marketplace.

Article 1(5) of the E-Commerce Directive, however, does indicate the kind of information society services[54] that would fall outside its scope. These are:

- the activities of notaries or equivalent professions to the extent that they involve a direct and specific connection with the exercise of public authority;
- the representation of a client and defence of his interests before the courts;
- gambling activities which involve wagering a stake with monetary value in games of chance, including lotteries and betting transactions.

It is clear from the above exclusions that the E-Commerce Directive includes a wide range of activities – from sale of goods, accountancy services, medical services to legal services – that would be on offer, for instance, on the Internet.

As stated earlier, one the objectives of the E-Commerce Directive is to ensure the free movement of information society services between member states. This is promoted in Art 4 which provides that the taking up and the pursuit of the activity of an information society services provider is not to be made subject to prior authorisation or any other requirement having equivalent effect. This means that a broker, for instance, wishing to offer his insurance products through a website need not obtain prior authorisation for doing so. However, the information society service provider is required to meet certain transparency requirements indicated in the E-Commerce Directive. These transparency provisions operate to a large extent to assure the consumer that the online provider possesses an offline identity and this offline identity is traceable. According to Art 5(1), an information society service provider has to provide in an easy, directly and permanently accessible manner at the very least the following information:

- the name of the service provider;
- the geographic address at which the service provider is established;
- the details of the service provider, including his electronic mail address, which allow him to be contacted rapidly and communicated with in a direct and effective manner;
- where the service provider is registered in a trade or similar public register, the trade register in which the service provider is entered and his registration number, or equivalent means of identification in that register;
- where the activity is subject to an authorisation scheme, the particulars of the relevant supervisory authority.

Where the service is that of a regulated profession, then information as listed in Art 5(1)(f) has to be provided.

Since the information service provider is likely to market his services or goods on the Internet in a variety of ways – for example, advertisements – the provider is required to meet certain transparency requirements set out in Art 6. The commercial communication[55] has to be clearly identifiable as such and the natural or legal person

---

54 A definition of information society services is not provided in the EU Directive. But Art 2 refers to Directive 98/34/EC as amended by Directive 98/48/EC for the purposes of defining information society services. Article 1(2) of Directive 98/34/EC as amended defines information society service as:

     ... any service normally provided for remuneration, at a distance, by electronic means and at the individual request of a recipient of services.

55 Defined in Art 2(f) as:

     ... any form of communication designed to promote, directly or indirectly, the goods, services or image of a company, organisation or pursuing a commercial, industrial or craft activity or exercising a regulated profession.

on whose behalf the commercial communication is made shall be clearly identifiable as such. Where promotional offers or promotional competitions are the subject matter of the communication, then they should be clearly identifiable as such and the conditions must be easily accessible, and presented clearly and unambiguously.

Contractual matters

Article 9 addresses the issue of legal recognition of electronic transactions. It requires member states to ensure that 'legal requirements applicable to the contractual process neither create obstacles for the use of electronic contracts nor result in such contracts being deprived of legal effectiveness and validity on account of their being made by electronic means' (Art 9(1)). Member states, however, have limited autonomy to exclude certain contracts from the scope of Art 9(1). These according to Art 9(2) are:

- contracts that create or transfer rights in real estate, except for rental rights;
- contracts requiring by law the involvement of courts, public authorities or professions exercising public authority;
- contracts of suretyship granted and on collateral securities furnished by persons acting for purposes outside their trade, business or profession;
- contracts governed by family law or by the law of succession.

Prior to the placing of an order, the information society service provider has to also provide information relating to the different technical steps to follow to conclude the contract, the technical means of identifying and correcting input errors prior to placing the order, the accessibility of the concluded order, and the languages offered for the conclusion of the contract (Art 10).

The E-Commerce Directive addresses the time of conclusion of contract where technological means are used. While parties other than consumers are free to agree otherwise, in the case of contracts involving consumers where the order is placed using technological means, the service provider has to acknowledge receipt of the recipient's order without delay electronically. The order and the acknowledgment will be deemed to be received when the parties to whom they are addressed are able to access them.[56]

Liability of third party service providers

The Internet Service Providers (ISPs) play an important role by providing access to communication networks and also in hosting of web pages. A question likely to concern ISPs is their liability for the content of the messages that travels through their networks or are hosted on their website. Making ISPs liable for the illegal content of the information would be a backward step if the intention is to ensure the growth of e-commerce. The E-Commerce Directive is mindful of this and approaches the issue sensitively. Article 12 of the E-Commerce Directive makes clear that mere conduits are not liable for the information transmitted as long as the provider does not initiate the transmission, does not select the receiver of the transmission or does not select or modify the information contained in the transmission. Article 15 states clearly that a

---

56   On the issue of jurisdiction, see Chapter 16.

provider is not under a general obligation to monitor information that is transmitted or stored by them. Neither is there an obligation to positively seek facts or circumstances indicating illegal activity.[57] Article 14 makes the position in respect of hosting clear. The ISP is exempted from liability where '(a) the provider does not have actual knowledge of the illegal activity or information and, as regards claims for damages, is not aware of facts or circumstances from which the illegal activity or information is apparent; or (b) the provider upon obtaining such knowledge or awareness, acts expeditiously to remove or to disable access to the information'. The provider, under Art 14(3), however, is subject to injunctive relief that may be ordered by a court or administrative authority. 'Caching' (temporary storage of information for speedier access)[58] is also dealt with in a similar way in Art 13.

Implementation

The E-Commerce Directive encourages the drawing up of codes of conduct by trade, professional and consumer associations in the proper implementation of Arts 5–15, thus encouraging self-regulation to some extent. As to whether this will prove effective in attaining the intended level of consumer protection in a large marketplace is debatable.[59] The electronic shopping mall is certainly that. However, it seems from Art 16(1)(b) that the Commission expects the adoption of voluntary codes not only at the national but also at Community level and encourages these to be transmitted to the Commission. The issue of enforcement is also addressed in the E-Commerce Directive and, according to Art 20, member states are free to determine the sanctions applicable to infringements of national provisions adopted on the basis of the E-Commerce Directive. As for the sanctions, they are to be effective, proportionate and dissuasive.

THE UNITED NATIONS CONVENTION ON THE USE OF ELECTRONIC COMMUNICATIONS IN ELECTRONIC CONTRACTS

This chapter will not be complete without a brief overview of United Nations Convention on the Use of Electronic Communications in International Contracts (hereinafter 'EC Convention'). This Convention was adopted in November 2005 but it is not yet in force.[60] The purpose of the EC Convention is to provide a practical framework for dealing effectively with electronic communications in international contracts. It adopts the functional equivalence approach adopted by the EC Model Law and includes a few substantive rules to ensure that electronic communications are effective.

---

57   Txt available at www.uncitral.org. The text is also reproduced in Carr and Kidner, *International Trade Law Statutes and Conventions*, 5th edn, 2008, Routledge-Cavendish.
58   It requires three signatures to come into force.
59   See Explanatory Memorandum, para 56. The Explanatory Note is attached to the text of the Convention and is accessible on www.uncitral.org.
60   For more on applicable law see Chapter 17.

Scope of application

The EC Convention is meant to apply to electronic communications where they are used in the formation stages of a contract (for example, requests, offers, acceptances) or in the performance of the contract (for example, notice of termination, notice of delivery). The word 'contract' for the purposes of the Convention is construed broadly and according to the Explanatory Note it includes arbitration agreements.[61] To bring the electronic communications within the ambit of this Convention the parties' places of business must be in two different states (Art 1). It is not however essential that both states are contracting states to the EC Convention, unlike the Vienna Convention.[62] The reason for not requiring both states to be contracting states gives the EC Convention greater reach. As long as the electronic communications attract the application of the law of a contracting state it will be subject to the EC Convention. Contracting states however are free to enter a reservation and declare that the EC Convention is to apply only to an electronic communication where both states are contracting states (Art 19 (1)(a)).

The meaning of electronic communications is to be gathered from Arts 4(a) and (b) and refers to data messages where the 'information is generated, sent, received or stored by electronic, magnetic, optical or similar means, but is not limited to electronic data interchange, electronic mail, telex or telecopy'.

One of the core elements of the EC Convention is the 'place of business' (a phrase also used in the Vienna Convention but left undefined). The EC Convention is not silent on this matter and a definition is provided in Art 4(h), according to which it refers to a non-transitory establishment from where the economic activity is pursued. The specific location of temporary provision of goods or services is irrelevant. So use of warehouses on the dockside would not be relevant because it is a transitory establishment. The EC Convention does not oblige the parties to reveal their places of business. However, Art 6 does contain some default rules for determining the location of a party. According to Art 6(1) it will be presumed that the location indicated by the party will be its place of business. And where the parties have more than one place of business, then the place of business which has the closest relationship to the relevant contract will be the place of business for the purposes of the Convention (Art 6 (2)).[63] Location of the equipment or information system is irrelevant for the purposes of place of business (Art 6(4)). Domain names and e-mail addresses connected to a particular country also do not raise a presumption that the place of business is located in that country.

While there is no positive duty on the parties to disclose their identities or places of business, this is however subject to the rule of law. So, if the law of a contracting state requires such information to be disclosed then that takes precedence and the parties will be subject to any legal consequences flowing from there (Art 7).

To determine the applicability of the EC Convention it is also necessary to determine whether the contract to which the electronic communications relate falls within

---

61 The text of the new convention has been adopted and is to be known as the Rotterdam Rules. See Chapter 9 for further on this.

62 See *An Action Plan on Promoting Safe Use of the Internet*, COM (97) 582.

63 For instance, when I access the UNCITRAL Model Law on Electronic Commerce using the university's web server, the server stores the data for a couple of days, so that it can be accessed quickly on a subsequent occasion.

the exclusions listed in Art 2. The excluded contracts include consumer contracts and various types of financial transactions. Unlike the EC Model Law, which in Part II facilitated the use of electronic transport documentation, Art 2 (c) states that the EC Convention is not to apply to bills of exchange, promissory notes, bills of lading, warehouse receipts or any transferable document or instrument that entitles the bearer or beneficiary to claim the delivery of the goods or the payment of a sum on money. The reason for their exclusion, according to the Explanatory Note (para 81) is:

> The issues raised by negotiable instruments and similar documents, in particular the need for ensuring their uniqueness, go beyond simply ensuring the equivalence between paper and electronic forms, which is the main aim of the Electronic Communications Convention and justifies the exclusion ... UNCITRAL was of the view that finding a solution for this problem required a combination of legal, technological and business solutions, which had not yet been fully developed and tested (see A/CN.9.571/para. 136).

It is also possible that at the time of the negotiations of this Convention UNCITRAL was mindful that both UNCITRAL and CMI were working on a new convention that was to contain a specific provision on electronic transport documents.[64]

Party autonomy is recognised by the EC Convention, thus giving the parties the right to exclude the application of the Convention altogether, or vary the effect of any of its provisions (Art 7). As for interpretation, it is dealt with in Art 5 and its wording is no different from that of the Vienna Convention (see pp 70–1 above).

Functional equivalence

As stated in the introduction to this section, the functional equivalence approach is adopted by the EC Convention and in this it is no different from the EC Model Law (see pp 109–110 above). So contracts cannot be denied validity or enforceability on the basis that electronic communications were used (Art 8). Equally form requirements are dealt with in Art 9.

The EC Convention allows for the possibility of electronic communications carried out by electronic agents (automated message systems). Where such systems are used for electronic communications they are not to be denied validity or enforceability on the basis that no natural person reviewed them (Art 12). However where such systems are used for interactive order placing the presumption is that they are invitations to treat, unless the party using such an interactive system indicates a willingness to be bound by the acceptance (Art 11).

The EC Convention does recognise that there is room for error. Error or mistake is not an issue which is addressed in the EC Model Law. The Explanatory Note in para 232 makes it clear that the drafters were sensitive to the difficulties of dealing with error in general but preferred to deal with the issue of error in only one specific situation, that is, where a natural person makes errors when dealing with automated messages and no opportunities are provided to make corrections. In these circumstances Art 14(1) allows the party to withdraw the relevant part of the communication, provided that the other party is notified of the error as soon as possible

---

64 See also European Consumer Law Group, 'Non-legislative means of consumer protection' (1983) 6 Journal of Consumer Policy 203; Rickett (ed), *International Perspectives on Consumers' Access to Justice*, 2003, CUP.

and no material benefit or value from the goods or services has been received from the other party.

Time and place of dispatch and receipt

The EC Convention deals with these issues in Art 10 and follows the EC Model Law, although the wording is slightly different. But according to the Explanatory Note (para 15) it is not intended to produce a difference in practice. The difference in wording simply reflects the 'general elements commonly used to define dispatch and receipt under domestic law'.

Relationship to other instruments

The EC Convention tries to remedy, in Art 20, the lack of specific provisions on electronic communications in contract formation or contract performance in other international conventions and lists a number of conventions for these purposes. Among those listed are the Convention on the Recognition and Enforcement of Arbitral Awards, 1958 and the United Nations Convention on Contracts for the International Sale of Goods, 1980. Where a state has ratified the EC Convention and is a contracting state, or is to become a contracting state to the listed conventions, the expectation is that the courts of the state will apply the EC Convention in relation to the electronic communications used in dealings that attract the application of the listed conventions. For instance, if two parties have entered an agreement to which the Vienna Convention applies and they enter into electronic communications in respect of, let's say, failure to deliver, and the forum state is also a party to the EC Convention, then Art 20 enables its application to those electronic communications. According to the Explanatory Note (para 290)

> These provisions aim at providing a domestic solution for a problem originating in international instruments. They are based on the recognition that domestic courts already interpret commercial law instruments. Paragraphs 1 and 2 of article 20 of the Electronic Communications Convention ensure that a Contracting State would incorporate into its legal system a provision that directs its judicial bodies to use the provisions of the Convention to address legal issues relating to the use of data messages in the context of other international conventions (see A/CN.9.548 para 49).

CONCLUSION

The initiatives considered in this chapter address only part of the issues relating to the facilitation of electronic transactions. Electronic signatures have emerged as an important tool in boosting the authenticity and authentication of a message with the result that UNCITRAL as well as the EU have drafted instruments to bring about harmonisation in their use in electronic transactions. The following chapter focuses on the legislative initiatives alongside developments in respect of protecting the electronic medium from external threats.

FURTHER READING

Abbott and Snidal, 'Hard and soft law in international governance' (2000) 54 International Organisation 421.

Bennett and Raab, *The Governance of Privacy: Policy Implication in Global Perspective*, 2003, Ashgate.

Braithwaite and Drahos, *Global Business Regulation*, 2000, CUP.

Dickie, *Internet and Electronic Commerce Law in the European Union*, 1999, Hart Publishing.

Froomkin, 'Of government and governance' (1999) 14 Berkeley Technology LJ 32.

Froomkin, 'Habermas@discourse.net: toward a critical theory in cyberspace' (2003) 3 Harvard LR 751.

Koops, Prins and Hijmans (eds), *ICT Law and Internationalisation: A Survey of Government Views*, 2000, Kluwer.

Kralingen and Prins, 'To regulate or not to regulate: prevalence and impact of a virtual law society' (1997) 4(2) The EDI LR 91.

Krcmar, Bjørn-Andersen and Callaghan (eds), *EDI in Europe*, 1995, John Wiley.

Lessig, 'The zones of cyberspace' (1996) 48 Stanford LR 1408.

Mayer, 'Europe and the Internet: the old world and the new medium' (2000) 11 European Journal of International Law 149.

Ogus, 'Rethinking self-regulation' (1995) 15 Oxford Journal of Legal Studies 97.

Perritt, 'Economic and other barriers to electronic commerce' (2000) 21 University of Pennsylvania Journal of International Economic Law 563.

Reams, Kutten and Strehler, *Electronic Contracting Law*, 1992–93, Clark Boardman Callaghan.

Reich and Smith (eds), 'Special issue: implementing the consumer-supplier dialogue through soft law?' [1984] Journal of Consumer Policy, at pp 111–321.

Reidenberg, 'Governing networks and cyberspace rule making' (1996) 45 Emory LJ 912.

Shapiro, *The Control Revolution*, 1999, Public Affairs.

Stephan, 'The futility of unification and harmonisation in international commercial law' (1999) 39 Virginia Journal of International Law 743.

Van Klink and Prins, *Law and Regulation: Scenarios for the Information Age*, 2002, IOS.

Walden (ed), *EDI and the Law*, 1989, Blenheim Online.

Walden, 'Proving the electronic trade instrument' [1994] The EDI LR 239.

CHAPTER 4

THE ELECTRONIC TRANSACTION AND SECURITY ISSUES

INTRODUCTION

It is trite to extol the virtues of the IT (information technology) revolution, its ability to shrink space and time, to bring people together without traversing long distances, to create new marketplaces and to contribute to global economic growth. The positive effects of electronic commerce (e-commerce) for the economy have been rehearsed and voiced in the policy documents of states[1] and regional groupings,[2] eagerly welcomed by the commercial community and enthusiastically celebrated by the media. Peculiarities of the digital medium (for example, its intangibility) pose problems. Authenticity, integrity and authentication of electronic messages are open to doubt. Numerous questions arise in relation to electronic messages. Among them: can the electronic message be trusted? Does it originate from the person claiming to send it? Can the message be relied upon? How secure is the message, given that electronic documents can be easily manipulated? Is the received message the same as the message sent? What legal status does an electronically signed message have? Can a sender be held to his electronically communicated message should a dispute arise? Is it enforceable? Do electronic messages and electronic signatures meet the legal requirements of writing and signature?

Vulnerability of the electronic medium from external threats such as hacking,[3] the introduction of viruses[4] and worms,[5] the use of computers for committing fraud and blackmail, and manipulation of computer-held material causes untold economic harm[6] and adds a further layer of uncertainty. It has the potential to undermine the effectiveness and reliability of the medium. There is no doubt that commercial transactions are fraught with risks, more so when they involve an international element. While businesses are mindful of these dangers and take steps to reduce their level of risk, it would be foolhardy to use a medium, regardless of its advantages, that greatly increases the level of risk – legal or otherwise. These vulnerabilities and legal uncertainties are sufficiently potent to act as a barrier to e-commerce[7] with the result

---

1   *A Framework for Global Electronic Commerce* (President William J Clinton and Vice President Albert Gore Jr, Washington DC).

2   See *A European Initiative in Electronic Commerce*, COM (97) 157 final, 16 April 1997, available at www.cordis.lu/esprit/src/ecomcom.htm.

3   Unauthorised entry into a computer site. It often also involves unauthorised obtaining of information from that site. For instances of hacking and computer fraud, visit www.usdoj.gov.

4   Literally, it is nothing more than a program that copies itself but is usually a malicious code that prevents or slows down the operation of a computer system. Note that this is a device which is intended to cause harm and should not be confused with a bug which may cause many problems but is an unintentional fault in a computer program, a result of a human error on the part of the programming team.

5   A 'chain letter' that propagates through a network. It may cause enormous problems and often carries with it a virus.

6   See *Hi-Tech Crime: The Impact on UK Business*, 2003, National Hi-Tech Crime Unit. Also see 'The risk of computer crime to small and medium sized enterprises', available at www.nhtcu.org.

7   E-commerce is commonly defined as trade that takes place over the Internet with a buyer visiting the seller's website and includes business-to-business (B2B); business-to-customer (B2C), consumer-to-business (C2B) and customer-to-customer (C2C) trade. Many of the events and factors associated with a contract such as pre-contractual negotiations, offer, acceptance, terms of the

that policy makers both at the regional and international level have tried to address the problems through legislation. Whether the legislative steps are adequate to cope with the vulnerabilities of the medium is debatable.

This chapter focuses on security aspects from two angles. First, making an electronic transaction secure through the legal recognition of emerging technology that boosts the integrity and reliability of electronic messages and, secondly, the increased protection of the electronic medium from external threats through criminal legislation. The first half concentrates on electronic signatures used both for establishing the authenticity of the message and authentication of a message, and considers for the most part the Model Law on Electronic Signatures drafted by the United Nations Commission on International Trade Law (UNCITRAL).[8] A brief account is also provided of the EU Directive on Electronic Signatures and the United Kingdom legislation relating to electronic signatures: Electronic Communications Act 2000 and Electronic Signatures Regulation 2002. The second half of the chapter focuses on how policy makers have responded to the vulnerability of the medium from external threats in the form of computer misuse legislation. Once again, the focus is from an international perspective in the form of recommendations and the international convention from the Council of Europe, though references are made to legislation adopted by various countries.

ELECTRONIC SIGNATURES AND UNCITRAL

On 5 July 2001, UNCITRAL approved the Model Law on Electronic Signatures (hereinafter 'ES Model Law'), thus completing Phase I of its programme for the facilitation of e-commerce.[9] By no means the first, it owes much to the American Bar Association Guidelines on Digital Signatures,[10] the variety of legislation validating electronic signatures passed at the state level in the United States,[11] and the European Directive on Electronic Signatures.[12]

---

contract are conveyed and stored electronically. See 'E-commerce survey' (2000) *The Economist*, 26 February, at p 6.

8 United Nations Commission on International Trade Law, at www.uncitral.org.

9 The Model Law on Electronic Commerce 1996 as amended in 1998 is the other document that has received worldwide success. Countries such as Australia, Bermuda, Colombia, France, Hong Kong Special Administrative Region of China, India, Ireland, Philippines, Republic of Korea, Singapore, Slovenia have based their legislation on the Model Law. The issue of signatures was addressed by the Model Law on Electronic Commerce and Art 7, founded on the functions of a signature, and provides:

   (1) Where the law requires a signature of a person, that requirement is met in relation to a data message if:

      (a) a method is used to identify that person and to indicate that person's approval of the information contained in the data message; and

      (b) that method is as reliable as was appropriate for the purpose for which the data message was generated or communicated, in the light of all the circumstances, including any relevant agreement.

   (2) ...

The Model Law on Electronic Commerce however did not deal with issues such as reliability, certification processes, nor the liability issues of the various parties involved in the creation and use of electronic signatures. Hence the drafting of the ES Model Law. See Chapter 3, above, for further on the Model Law on Electronic Commerce.

10 Available www.abanet.org.

11 For details of legislation on electronic signatures, visit the excellent website of McBride Baker and Coles at www.mbc.com/ecommerce/ecommerce.asp.

12 Directive 1999/93/EC of the European Parliament and of the Council of 13 December 1999 on a Community Framework for Electronic Signatures OJEC L13/12 (19.1.2000).

IT professionals, as far back as the 1970s, were working on the confidentiality/integrity problems associated with electronic communications. Asymmetric cryptography was seen as providing the required level of security and systems such as Pretty Good Privacy (PGP) and Secure Sockets Layer (SSL) before encrypting data came to the fore. As opposed to symmetric cryptography, which uses the same key to encrypt and decrypt a message, asymmetric cryptography uses a pair of keys – a private key and public key – that are related mathematically.[13] The private key kept by the owner is used to encrypt the data and the public key, available to those with whom he wishes to communicate, is used to decode the data. Associated with certificates issued by trusted third parties/certification service providers, this technology could be used for establishing the identity of the sender and for authentication. Hailed as a digital signature[14] (a digital answer to a handwritten signature) and expecting widespread adoption,[15] legislators rushed to pass legislation authorising the use of this technology to meet the signature requirements prescribed by law. For instance, the Utah Digital Signature Act[16] defines a digital signature by reference to this technology as a 'transformation of a message using an asymmetric cryptosystem such that a person having the initial message and the signer's public key can accurately determine whether (a) the transformation was created using the private key that corresponds to the signer's public key; and (b) the message has been altered since the transformation was made'.[17] While digital signature is a type of electronic signature,[18] confusion reigned, with some using 'digital signature' in a wider sense to mean electronic signature.[19] It was against this backdrop that UNCITRAL set out to work on its ES Model Law with the intention of harmonising the law without resorting to the promotion of a specific technology.

The following sections set out the founding principles of the ES Model Law and examine the various provisions. The ES Model Law, while providing a workable framework, however, is by no means comprehensive and leaves a lot for the state adopting the ES Model Law to work out what may be core legal issues – for instance, the type and levels of liability.

---

13   Note that CMI Rules on Electronic Bills of Lading also uses public/private key technology for the purposes of transferring a bill of lading. See Chapter 6, pp 197–204 below, for further on electronic bills of lading.

14   For a detailed account of digital signature technology, see Baum and Ford, *Secure Electronic Commerce: Building the Infrastructure for Digital Signatures and Encryption*, 1997, Prentice Hall.

15   Doubts have been cast on whether digital signatures have caught on. See Aalberts and van der Hof, *Digital Signature Blindness* (1999), available at http://rechten.uvt.nl/simone/Ds-art.htm. See also Winn, 'The emperor's new clothes: the shocking truth about digital signatures and Internet commerce', available at http://faculty.smu.edu/jwinn/shocking-truth.htm.

16   Utah Code Annotated §§ 46–3–101 to 504.

17   Also see Oregon Electronic Signature Act, Oregon Revised Statutes § 192.825; Nevada Revised Statutes: Chapters 720, Title 59. The various definitions of digital signatures are available on www.mbc.com/ecommerce.

18   It also includes PIN (Personal Identification Numbers) and biometrics-based identifier such as a fingerprint.

19   See Texas Business and Commerce Code § 2.108. Available at www.mbc.com/ecommerce.

Founding principles

Harmonisation and certainty

Harmonisation at a global level, which also has the added advantage of imparting certainty, is at the heart of the ES Model Law. International conventions,[20] the most effective way to achieve harmonisation, have their shortcomings. Fuelled by politics, differences in legal systems and legal understanding and intranslatability of concepts at the linguistic level, international conventions face interminable delays at the drafting stage. Once the text is agreed, it may take years for it to go through the various bureaucratic processes at the state level for it to be ratified, and the required numbers of ratification for it to come into force.[21] Further, conventions may not attract widespread ratification due to their inflexibility. States may wish to opt out of certain provisions, which might not be possible under the convention. Of late, UNCITRAL (perhaps as a political move to maintain its status in the international arena as a major law-making organisation in international trade matters) has been moving more towards drafting model laws[22] – that is, recommendations made by a body composed of government representatives and experts such as practitioners, and academics. While the differences in legal understanding cannot be totally cured, model laws by comparison do not share bureaucratic nightmares or rigidity to the same extent.[23] They do not require the requisite numbers of ratification to come into force and states, while free to adopt the model law verbatim, may amend it to suit their needs, or use it as a framework for drafting their legislation. This level of flexibility increases the chance for widespread adoption, albeit at the cost of a high degree of harmonisation (paras 26–28). Widespread adoption should also contribute to certainty about the legal force of electronic signatures.

Party autonomy

In the absence of legal solutions to uncertainties, it is not unknown for parties to a business transaction to agree to solutions in the contract. The ES Model Law preserves party autonomy. It is not mandatory in character and provides for variation by agreement subject to any limitations that may be imposed by the applicable law – for instance, on grounds of public policy. This principle is embodied in Art 5 which states that '. . . the provisions of this law may be derogated from or their effect may be varied by agreement, unless that agreement would not be valid or effective under applicable law'. Articles 3, 6 and 12 specifically further reinforce the principle of party autonomy expressed by Art 5. While Art 5 does not indicate whether the agreement should be

---

20 International conventions and model laws are often regarded as part of the 'new *lex mercatoria*' because of their transnational character. See Goldstajn, 'The new law merchant' [1961] JBL 12; Lando, 'The *lex mercatoria* and international commercial arbitration' [1961] ICLQ 747. For a different viewpoint, see Highet, 'The enigma of the *lex mercatoria*' (1989) 63 Tulane LR 613.

21 Eg, the text of the United Nations Convention on the Carriage of Goods by Sea (aka the Hamburg Rules) drafted by the UNCITRAL and adopted in 1978 took 14 years to come into force.

22 Eg, the Model Law on International Commercial Arbitration 1985, Model Law on International Credit Transfer 1992, and the Model Law on Cross Border Insolvency 1997.

23 See Andersen, 'The UNCITRAL draft Model Law on EDI – its history and its fate', available at www.lex-electronica.org/articles/vl-1/andersen.html.

express or implied, the explanatory memorandum makes clear that variation by agreement may be express or implied (para 112). Factors such as behaviour of the parties and past course of dealings would therefore be relevant to determine whether there is variation by agreement.

Technology neutrality and non-discrimination

From the start, the issue of whether the electronic authentication legislation should be technology specific – referring to a particular type of technology such as asymmetric cryptosystem that uses private-public key pair – or technology neutral has been scrutinised closely by legislators. Technology specific legislation has the advantage of promoting legal certainty but is inflexible to accommodate new technology and legislation is likely to become quickly outdated if new technologies are adopted by the marketplace. Technology neutral legislation that is open textured, on the other hand, has the flexibility to adapt itself to new developments. Further, it does not stifle competition or innovation by giving preference to a specific technology.[24] The ES Model Law is founded on the principle of technology neutrality as indicated by Art 3 which states that '. . . nothing in this law . . . shall be applied so as to exclude, restrict or deprive of legal effect any method of creating an electronic signature that satisfies the requirements referred to in Art 6(1) or otherwise meets the requirements of applicable law'. The explanatory memorandum also makes clear that Art 3 'embodies the fundamental principle that no method of electronic signature should be discriminated against . . . [and] . . . the fundamental principle of non-discrimination is of general application'[25] subject of course to the principle of party autonomy.

The principle of non-discrimination also encompasses cross-border recognition of electronic signatures and certificates for legal purposes. The place of origin of electronic signatures and certificates is not to contribute to determining the legal effectiveness of an electronic signature or certificate.[26]

Functional equivalence

The UNCITRAL adopts a 'functional equivalence approach' in drafting its legislation – an approach that extrapolates the functions of a paper document[27] to create the criteria that need to be met by the paperless document for attaining a status equivalent to that of the paper document.[28]

---

24 See Beary, 'The digital signature debate: technology neutral or specific?', available at http://raven.cc.ukans.edu/~cybermom/CLJ/beary.htm who argues for technology specific legislation.

25 UN Doc A/CN 9/WG IV/WP 88, para 106, available at www.uncitral.org.

26 See pp 135–6 below.

27 See section E, paras 15–18 of the Guide. It describes the functional equivalence approach as 'based on analysis of the purposes and functions of the traditional paper-based requirement with a view to determining how those purposes and functions could be fulfilled through electronic techniques'. A paper document is legible, unalterable, reproducible, capable of authentication and acceptable as evidence to public authorities and courts. As UNCITRAL notes, however, in adopting a functional equivalence approach, one must not impose more stringent standards of security on electronic commerce users than in a paper-based environment (para 16).

28 See 'Nature and reliability of an electronic signature', pp 131–3 below for the functions identified for a handwritten signature.

The Model Law on Electronic Signatures

Interpretation

Before proceeding with an assessment of the ES Model Law a few words must be said about its interpretation. As part of the drive towards harmonisation and certainty, it includes an interpretation provision inspired by Art 7[29] of the Convention on the International Sale of Goods 1980 (the 'Vienna Convention') (also drafted by UNCITRAL). According to Art 4, in interpreting the ES Model Law 'regard is to be had to its international character and to the need to promote uniformity in its application and the observance of good faith'. While the provision is rational in a global world promoting transnational law, it is difficult to assess what exactly is expected of a court or tribunal under Art 4. If legislation based on the ES Model Law becomes part of domestic law, are the courts expected to disregard rules of interpretation formulated and developed in their legal system? Are they to disregard the interpretation of identical words in other domestic legislation? Are they to explore how courts in other jurisdictions interpret the provisions? Are the judges expected to rid themselves of the conceptual framework derived from their own domestic law? In an ideal world, in aiming towards harmonisation, it makes sense to leave the shackles created by sovereignty. There is however a gap between theory and practice as experience with the Vienna Convention illustrates. In spite of the extensive case database maintained by UNCITRAL on the Vienna Convention (and available on their website), there is a reluctance on the part of courts, regardless of the legal background, to refer to opinions from other jurisdictions as an aid to interpretation.[30] If the response to Art 7 of an international treaty is so negative, what hope is there for an interpretation provision in a model law? Having said this, it must also be acknowledged that, in the United Kingdom, judges are willing to consider foreign judgments as cases such as *Stag Line Ltd v Foscola, Mango and Co*[31] and *Corocraft Ltd v Pan American Airways Inc*[32] indicate.

The latter part of Art 4 of the ES Model Law makes reference to the observance of good faith. Good faith in what, by whom and at what stage? Are the parties to observe good faith in the use of electronic signatures? Where parties vary the terms by agreement, are they bound by the principle of good faith? Are the parties to observe good faith in the performance of contracts that use electronic signatures? Are they to observe good faith during pre-contractual negotiations? Or, does it mean that the judiciary must take in good faith the interpretation of the ES Model Law in other jurisdictions? Is acting in good faith the same as acting reasonably? Impregnated with a moral flavour, good faith is a vague term that everyone comprehends and does not comprehend at the same time. The explanatory memorandum is of no help. In importing Art 7 of the Vienna Convention with a few changes, the drafters have

---

29 See 'Interpretation of the Vienna Convention', pp 71–2 above.
30 See Chapter 2, pp 71–2 above, for further on this issue. See also Murray, 'The neglect of CISG: a workable solution' (1998) 17 Journal of Law and Commerce 365; Bonnell and Liguori, 'The UN Convention on the International Sale of Goods: a critical analysis of current international case law' (1997) 2 Revue de Droit Uniforme 385.
31 [1932] AC 328. See Chapter 8, pp 231–3 below, for further on the interpretation of the Hague Rules and Hague-Visby Rules in respect of bills of lading.
32 [1969] 1 QB 616, at p 655. See Chapter 10, p 335 below, for further on the interpretation of the Warsaw regime on international carriage by air.

unwittingly brought into the ES Model Law the controversy and debate that is still raging around the good faith part of Art 7.[33]

Applicability

The ES Model Law applies to electronic signatures that are used in the commercial sphere (Art 1). Following the definition adopted in the ES Model Law, the word 'commercial' is defined in a footnote to Art 1, and is interpreted widely to cover matters that arise from commercial relationship, be it contractual or not. Commercial relationships include 'any trade transaction for the supply or exchange of goods or services; distribution agreement; commercial representation or agency; factoring; leasing; construction of works; consulting; engineering; licensing; investment; financing; banking; insurance; exploitation agreement or concession; joint ventures and other forms of industrial or business co-operation; carriage of goods or passengers by air, sea, rail or road'. Though doubts may be raised in the absence of specific mention about its applicability to consumers, the second sentence of Art 1 states that it is not meant to override any consumer protection law, thus suggesting that the ES Model Law is not meant to exclude consumer transactions. The explanatory memorandum endorses this view by stating that the provisions of the ES Model Law may be beneficial for consumer protection but goes on to state that dependent on existing consumer protection policies, legislators may wish to exclude consumers from the sphere of application.[34] The ES Model Law does not define 'consumer' and leaves that to be determined by the applicable law.

Nature and reliability of an electronic signature

As stated earlier, the UNCITRAL followed a 'functional equivalence'[35] approach for formulating both the Model Law for Electronic Commerce and ES Model Law. Among the functions for a handwritten signature identified by the Working Group are: '. . . to identify a person; to provide certainty as to the personal involvement of that person in the act of signing; to associate that person with the content of a document'. Depending on the nature of the document signature, they also identified other uses: '. . . to attest to the intent of a party to be bound by the content of signed contract; the intent of a person to endorse authorship; the intent of a person to associate itself with the content of a document written by someone else; the fact that, and the time when, a person had been at a given place'.[36] However, in order to define electronic signature for the purposes of the ES Model Law, the drafters took the smallest common denominators, these being the identification and the intent to sign. Article 2(a) defines electronic signature as 'data in an electronic form in, affixed to or logically associated with, a data message, which may be used to identify the signatory in relation to the data message and indicate the signatory's approval of information contained in the data message'. Data message refers to information that is sent, generated, received or stored by electronic, optical or similar means. It includes, but is not

---

33   See Chapter 2, pp 71–2 above.
34   A/CN 9/WG IV/WP 88, para 90.
35   See p 130 above.
36   A/CN 9/WG IV/WP 88, para 29.

limited to, electronic data interchange (EDI), electronic mail, telegram, telex or telecopy.

The definition of electronic signature is open ended and does not promote any specific technology. The electronic signature could be a digital signature, a digitised image of a handwritten signature or based on biometrics such as a fingerprint or iris scan. The level of security will vary depending on the type of electronic signature. For an electronic signature to be legally effective, the ES Model Law requires that electronic signatures meet the requirements of reliability in the light of all the circumstances including any agreement there might be between the parties. Similarly, the definition of data message with its reference to 'similar means' is sufficiently flexible to encompass new technological developments. Reliability requirements for a legally effective electronic signature are stated in Art 6(3). First, the signature creation data must be linked to a signatory and no other person. Secondly, the signature creation data[37] at the time of signing must be under the control of the signatory and of no other person, any alteration to the electronic signature after the time of signing is detectable, and where the legal requirement for a signature is for ensuring the integrity of the information to which it relates, any alteration made after signing is detectable. Issues such as whether the signature creation data is uniquely linked to or under the control of the signatory, or for that matter, the question of whether any alteration is detectable after signing are technical issues and will depend on the technology and the mechanisms that have been put in place by the signatory and the certification service provider. For instance, whether the signatory has sole control of the signature creation data will depend on the specific circumstances. To illustrate, where signature creation data is available on a network and is capable of being used by any number of people, for the ES Model Law to be applicable it is essential that there is one signatory who maintains control over the signature creation data.[38]

Without intending to affect the principle of party autonomy, the ES Model Law makes room, in its Art 7, for the enacting state to designate a public or private authority to specify the types of electronic signatures that would meet the reliability criteria set out in Art 6, subject to the proviso that the recommended technology meet recognised international standards. The explanatory memorandum makes clear that the standard is not to be interpreted restrictively and is not confined to standards set by the ISO or IETF.[39] It includes trade usages, industry practices, recommendations from international organisations such as the International Chamber of Commerce (ICC) and UNCITRAL.[40] While trade usages are unlikely to raise eyebrows among Western commercial interests, inclusion of trade usages, for instance, in Art 9[41] of the Vienna Convention, was fully debated during the preparatory stages. Developing countries feared that trade usages, which could include locally adopted usages, would be to the detriment of their traders since they introduce a surprise element into the contract.[42] Hence, Art 9(2) makes reference to internationally known usages thus minimising the risk of uncertainty associated with trade usages. The explanatory memorandum to

---

37 Refers to codes that are used to link the electronic signature to the signatory.
38 See A/CN 9/WG IV/WP 88, paras 119–23.
39 Internet Engineering Task Force.
40 A/CN 9/WG IV/WP 88, para 130.
41 See Chapter 2, pp 70–1 above.
42 They also perceived trade usages largely as a product of a limited number of countries from the Western world, a view shared by the socialist countries.

the ES Model Law does not state that trade usages have to be internationally known. The requirement in Art 7 that the recommended technology meets international standards however seems to suggest that trade usages also need to have an international status.

Responsibilities of the parties

The UNCITRAL envisages three parties taking part in the use and creation of an electronic signature:

- the signatory, who is the holder of the signature creation device;
- the third party (known as the certificate service provider) who plays a central role in adding integrity to the electronic signature by issuing certificates that confirm the link between the signatory and the signature creation data; and
- the party who relies on the electronic signature.[43]

Unlike other recent legislation on electronic signatures – for instance, the EU Directive on Electronic Signatures[44] – the ES Model Law imposes responsibilities on all three actors engaged in the use and creation of an electronic signature that has legal effect.

The signatory, as the holder of signature creation data that creates signatures that have legal effect, is expected to keep it under his control and take reasonable care to avoid its unauthorised use. The issue of whether he has exercised reasonable care or not will presumably be determined on an objective basis. The signatory is placed under an obligation to use the means provided by the certification service provider or use reasonable efforts to inform those who are likely to rely on the electronic signature where he knows that the signature creation data has been compromised, or his knowledge of circumstances that raise a substantial risk that the signature creation data may have been compromised. He is also to ensure that material representations made by him that are relevant to acquiring a certificate are accurate and complete during the life cycle of certificate. From the explanatory memorandum, it appears that the life cycle of a certificate runs from the application to the revocation or expiry of a certificate.[45] Applying the interpretation provision, it could be said that the signatory is expected to exercise good faith in making his material representations on the basis of which the certificate is issued.

Similarly, the certification service provider has to meet a list of obligations under the provisions of Art 9(1) where the electronic signature used has a legal effect. In brief, the list can be grouped broadly into the following obligations: to adhere to representations made in its policy statements; to exercise reasonable care to ensure accuracy of information included in the certificate during its life cycle; to include information (such as the identity of the certification service provider, limitation on the value for which the signature creation data may be used); to make available to the relying party information that would be relevant to a particular certificate; to ensure availability of a notification system to the signatory which the signatory can use where the signature creation data has been compromised; and to utilise trustworthy systems and human resources in conducting its services. Article 10 deals with the issue of trustworthiness raised in Art 9(1). It is broad in its interpretation and,

---

43 See Art 2 for definitions.
44 See Art 6 of the Directive which imposes liability on the certification service provider in relation to a qualified certificate.
45 A/CN 9/WG IV/WP 88, para 135.

among other factors, financial resources, quality of hardware and software, extent of audit by an independent body, and accreditation of the certification service provider are be taken into consideration in establishing whether the requirement of trustworthiness is met.

As for the relying party, Art 11(a) places him under an obligation to verify the reliability of an electronic signature. Where it is supported by a certificate, he is to take 'reasonable steps to verify the validity, suspension or revocation of the certificate, and to observe any limitation with respect to the certificate' (Art 11(b)).

What happens if the actors do not meet the obligations set out in the ES Model Law? In Arts 8(2), 9(2) and 11, the ES Model Law provides that they will bear the legal consequences of their failure to exercise their respective obligations. While it is reasonable to impose obligations on the signatory and the certification service provider and expect them to bear the legal consequences, it is debatable whether this should extend to all members who fall within the class termed 'relying party'. Relying party could include not only big businesses (including IT service providers) but also small to medium sized enterprises and consumers. It is questionable whether small to medium sized enterprises, especially in developing countries, will have the expertise and personnel to take the necessary steps to verify the signatures. Given the ES Model Law is designed for global adoption, it is a pity that it has been drafted taking into account circumstances prevailing in developed countries. The same can be said for consumers. It is unclear whether the Working Group considered the possibility of varying the nature of the obligations by differentiating the 'relying party' into different types such as IT service providers (who, for instance, endorse certificates issued by foreign certification services), large businesses, small to medium sized enterprises, and consumers. Of course, parties who are unhappy with the obligations imposed by the ES Model Law are free to agree to their own terms. And, it is always open for a state to derogate from the provisions of the ES Model Law when legislating for electronic signatures.

What kind of legal consequences does the ES Model Law envisage in the event of a breach? Unfortunately, this is left open to be determined by the national law. Legal consequences could be criminal or civil liability, and the nature of liability could, for instance, be fines or damages. This open-ended attitude towards legal consequences introduces an element of surprise and uncertainty given the promotion of cross-border recognition of certificates and electronic signatures by the ES Model Law. A certification service provider might find that he is suddenly subject to unexpected liabilities of a foreign jurisdiction. While it is open to a certification service provider to protect himself with insurance cover, uncertainties in respect of type and level of liability are likely to increase insurance premiums. It may even contribute to stifling not only competition but the development of certification service industry in developing countries.

It appears from the explanatory memorandum that the working group had initially planned to draft detailed rules in respect of the obligations of the various parties involved in an electronic signature. They could not however agree on the content of the rules due to the emerging and significant role of self-regulation in various countries. In the end, they opted for a minimal code of conduct as embodied in Arts 8, 9 and 11.[46] It is a pity they did not persist in arriving at detailed rules since

46   A/CN 9/WG IV/WP 88, para 132.

not all countries, especially the developing, have the infrastructure or the capacity in the IT industry for adopting a self-regulatory scheme. At the end of the day, they will have to draft supplemental rules to achieve a comprehensive framework for the facilitation of electronic signatures. Some might find this difficult, lacking knowledge and experience of the consequences that flow from the use of electronic signatures. In a world where international commerce is dependent on information technology, a legal framework to facilitate e-commerce is essential if they wish to maintain their market share.

Cross-border recognition of certificates and electronic signatures

In keeping with the principle of non-discrimination, the geographic location where the electronic signature was created or the certificate issued will not determine whether the certificate or electronic signature is legally effective (Art 12(1)(a)). What will affect its effectiveness is the level of reliability. Realising that reliability require-ments may vary from jurisdiction to jurisdiction, the drafters of the ES Model Law use 'equivalence' rather than 'identical' as a measure. According to Arts 12(2) and (3), a certificate or an electronic signature issued outside the domestic jurisdiction will be legally effective if it offers a 'substantial equivalent level of reliability'. The courts will consider each case on its merits and look for equivalence using the requirements for domestic certificates and electronic signatures as a yardstick. The factors that are likely to make an impact are already set out in Arts 6, 9 and 10. Article 12(4) further adds that, for the purposes of Arts 12(2) and (3), regard shall be had to 'recognised international standards'. The explanatory memorandum makes clear that this is to be interpreted as international technical and commercial standards and standards and norms adopted by governmental and intergovernmental bodies. These standards may be laid down as codes of conducts, statements of best practice, recommendations or guidelines.[47]

The flexibility shown by the ES Model Law towards certificates and electronic signatures originating from foreign jurisdiction recognises the global nature of e-commerce and aims to ease the entry of businesses into the electronic marketplace. It is guided by the spirit of free trade. A framework based on licensing and registra-tion in the jurisdiction where recognition is sought could have been used to ensure that foreign certificates and electronic signatures meet the requirements laid down in that jurisdiction. This would have proved costly and burdensome on those providing certification and electronic signature services and could have acted as a barrier in some circumstances. For instance, small to medium sized traders in developing coun-tries could have found themselves unable to transact electronically if their electronic signature providers did not have the facilities to obtain licences in multiple jurisdic-tions and the trader did not have the financial strength to obtain the services of a provider from another jurisdiction (where allowed under the law of the trader's state) who did have multiple jurisdiction licences.

Following the principle of party autonomy, Art 12(5) provides that parties as between themselves are free to agree on the use of certain types of certificates and electronic signatures as sufficient for cross-border recognition. However, once again, this freedom is curtailed by relevant mandatory provisions of the applicable law.

---

47   A/CN 9/WG IV/WP 88, para 154.

In conclusion, the global significance of e-commerce is a fact, and it is important that divergent approaches to legislation and the resulting uncertainties do not curtail the growth of e-commerce. One way to achieve legal certainty and predictability is to harmonise the laws, and undoubtedly UNCITRAL has played a central role in formulating model laws for both electronic commerce and electronic signatures. While the ES Model Law addresses the various legal issues including cross-border recognition raised by electronic signatures sympathetically, it is not sufficiently comprehensive to achieve the desired level of harmonisation. What may be core provisions are left to be addressed by national law. For instance, the issue of liability where obligations by the signatory, certification service provider and the relying party are not met provides a good illustration. Matters of procedure (such as the burden of proof) are also ignored. In a framework that promotes cross-border recognition of certificates and signatures, the omission of liability and procedural issues is odd and it would not be unfair to say that the ES Model Law is a half-hearted attempt at harmonisation.

THE EU DIRECTIVE ON ELECTRONIC SIGNATURES AND THE UK LEGISLATION: ELECTRONIC COMMUNICATIONS ACT 2000 AND THE ELECTRONIC SIGNATURES REGULATION 2002

Directive 1999/93/EC on a Community Framework for Electronic Signatures[48] (hereinafter 'ES Directive') was published on 19 January 2000. There is some similarity between the ES Directive and the ES Model Law since UNCITRAL used the ES Directive, alongside others, to draft its provisions. However, the ES Directive was drafted to promote the internal market and therefore addresses various aspects of the internal market including consumer needs. Article 3 ensures free movement of services and member states cannot make the provision of certification services subject to prior authorisation, but it allows member states to 'introduce or maintain voluntary accreditation schemes aimed at enhanced levels of certification-service provision'. The conditions for such schemes must, however, be 'objective, transparent, proportionate and non-discriminatory'.

The ES Directive makes distinction between a 'certificate' and a 'qualified certificate'. The latter needs to meet the benchmarks set out in the Annexes. This is to ensure trust and confidence. Annex II of the ES Directive lists the requirements that certification service providers who issue 'qualified certificates'[49] have to meet. Annex II lists criteria that ensure the integrity of the certificate and thus requires the certificate service provider to demonstrate the reliability of the certificate, starting from the identification of the certificate holder through to security and trustworthiness of the systems and products used, and the management of the systems, competence of personnel, and services provided. Annex I sets out the requirements of qualified certificate and lists, amongst others, identity of both the certification service provider, the name of the signatory, validity of the certificate, limits on the value of the transaction and limitations on the scope of use of the certificate. Inevitably, to ensure that the requirements set out in respect of the qualified certificate are met, there needs to be some degree of supervision of the certification service providers. The ES Directive

---

48 OJ L13 (19.1.2000), p 12. The text is also available in Carr and Kidner, *International Trade Law Statutes and Conventions* 5th edn, 2008, Routledge-Cavendish.

49 Defined in Art 2(10).

leaves the member states free to choose the means of supervision in Art 3(3). The United Kingdom opted to adopt a *de minimis* scheme since the extent of use of qualified certificates is unknown. The supervisory function lies with the Secretary of State and it is expected the private sector led tScheme[50] – a scheme established by the Alliance for Electronic Business[51] which grants approval or a trust mark to those certification service providers who meet their assessment criteria – will provide assistance. Regulation 3 of the Electronic Signatures Regulation 2002[52] (implementing the ES Directive) which came into force on 8 March 2002 provides that the Secretary of State will establish and maintain a register of certification service providers established in the UK who issue qualified certificates, and keep under review the carrying on of their activities. The Secretary of State is also imparted with the power to make evidence of practices adopted by certification service providers that are likely to prove detrimental to interests of those who rely on or use the certificates available to the public.

The ES Directive also imposes a minimum level of liability on providers who issue qualified certificates to the public. According to Art 6(1), where an entity or person[53] who reasonably relies on the qualified certificate for the accuracy of information on the certificate and that it contains all the details prescribed for a qualified certificate, and for assurance that at the time of issuance of the certificate the signatory identified held the signature creation data corresponding to the signature verification data given in the certificate suffers loss, the certificate service provider is liable in damages unless he can prove that he has not acted negligently. The onus is cast on the service provider to show lack of negligence. Equally, Art 6(2) makes the certification service provider liable for failure to register the revocation of a qualified certificate unless he can show that he has not acted negligently. Both these provisions have been implemented by reg 4 of the Electronic Signatures Regulation 2002.

It must also be noted that the ES Directive makes a distinction between an electronic signature[54] and an advanced signature.[55] Though the ES Model Law does not draw distinction between a signature and an advanced signature, the definition of advanced signature in the ES Directive is comparable to that of the criteria that need to be met by the electronic signature for it to be reliable.[56]

---

50 This development was in response to Pt I of the Electronic Communications Act 2000 where the government took powers to establish a statutory voluntary approvals regime. Under the tScheme, certification service providers who apply are independently assessed and allowed to use an approval (trust) mark. The members are regularly monitored. This is an instance of government and the private sector working in partnership.

51 Consisting of industry bodies interested in e-commerce. Visit www.tscheme.org for further information.

52 The text of this statutory instrument is available at www.opsi.gov.uk.

53 This includes legal or natural persons.

54 Defined in Art 2(1) as:

. . . data in electronic form which are attached to or logically associated with other electronic data and which serve as a method of authentication.

55 Defined in Art 2(2) as:

. . . an electronic signature that meets the following requirements:

(a) it is uniquely linked to the signatory;
(b) it is capable of identifying the signatory;
(c) it is created using means that the signatory can maintain under his sole control; and
(d) it is linked to the data to which it relates in such a manner that any subsequent change of the data is detectable.

56 See Art 6 of the ES Model Law.

The ES Directive also addresses the legal status of electronic signatures and provides in Art 5(1) that they are treated as equivalent to handwritten signatures and also admissible as evidence in legal proceedings. The UK had addressed this issue at an early stage of its legislative programme in respect of electronic communications. The Electronic Communications Act 2000 in s 7 recognises the legal admissibility of electronic signatures.

A provision that perhaps stands out in the ES Directive is that relating to data protection. Since Directive 95/46 on the protection of individuals with regard to the processing of personal data and on the free movement of such data[57] imposes certain restrictions on the processing and circulation of personal data relating to individuals, Art 8 requires member states to ensure that certification service providers comply with the directive. Certification service providers can collect data only directly from the data subject or after the explicit consent of the data subject according to Art 8(2).[58]

ELECTRONIC MEDIUM AND COMPUTER MISUSE

As stated previously, the electronic medium is prone to external attacks from a variety of sources – for example, hackers keen to test the vulnerability of security systems to deter hacker attacks, criminals interested in obtaining commercial/industrial/ confidential information for the purposes of blackmail and engaging in other illegal activities such as fraud. Many countries, realising the opportunities that IT provides for criminal activities, have passed legislation on computer crime or computer misuse.

The phrase 'computer crime' or 'computer misuse' (IT crime, cybercrime) has no precise definition and is largely perceived as covering a multitude of computer-related offences ranging from unauthorised access to computers and computer-held material, causing damage to computer-held information, trafficking in computer passwords and 'hacking-friendly technology', computer fraud, manufacturing/selling pirated copies of software through to production and distribution of computer-generated information/sexual images of minors and hate speech. Few countries, however, have legislation broad enough to criminalise all types of computer crime. The recent Council of Europe Convention on Cybercrime, however, adopts a comprehensive approach to computer crime and is examined in the following sections.

Legislative developments in different jurisdictions

The United Kingdom was one of the first countries to pass legislation relating to computer misuse in its Computer Misuse Act 1990.[59] It created three offences: unauthorised access of computers (s 1), unauthorised access with the intention of committing further offences (s 2), and unauthorised modification of computer material (s 3). The drive in the United Kingdom to criminalise the activities of hackers and other mischief mongers was economic in character. The parliamentary debates recorded in *Hansard* clearly indicate that the impetus behind criminalising computer

---

57 Implemented in the United Kingdom by the Data Protection Act 1998.
58 Implemented in the United Kingdom by reg 5 of the Electronic Signatures Regulation 2002.
59 The text of this statute is available at www.hmso.gov.uk. Also reproduced in Carr and Kidner *International Trade Law Statutes and Conventions*, 5th edn, 2008, Routledge-Cavendish.

misuse was largely economic and commercial. The motivation was heightened by a fear that, in a world where trade and employment are becoming increasingly global, Britain needed to offer firms such protection to encourage inward investment in a fiercely competitive market. As Mitchell states 'capital is able to behave . . . like a plague of locusts circling the globe, touching down hither and yon, devouring whole places as it seeks even better comparative advantage'.[60] This has intensified competition between places at an international level; countries are looking for any advantage, or the elimination of any disadvantage, to attract businesses to locate within their territory. It seems that making computer misuse criminal was one of these factors.

In introducing the Computer Misuse Bill, Michael Colvin MP made this the main tenet of his reasoning. He asserted (in 1990) that '. . . computer misuse probably costs the United Kingdom between £400 million – the CBI's[61] figure – and perhaps as much as £2 billion a year'.[62] He went on to explain that 'we are in the vanguard of countries seeking to encourage greater use of information technology to create wealth and . . . we are doing our best to attract inward investment to the United Kingdom . . . There is a real risk that, if nothing is done, the United Kingdom could become an international hackers' haven'.[63] Other Members of Parliament expressed similar sentiments,[64] as did some in the Lords.[65] Some noted the importance given to the protection of the criminal law by the CBI, or by industries that they represented or which had made representations to them.[66] Support from the computer industry was also noted,[67] or assumed through such statements as 'the computer industry will welcome the Bill because it cannot build into its technology the necessary safeguards to prevent hacking or other offences. At the moment, such safeguards are technically impossible and therefore the law must fill the gap'.[68]

Criminalisation of computer misuse was thus widely seen as reducing commercial risks or dangers. One result was a general trend for nations to use criminal laws to curb these activities. This was a process with an inherent tendency towards an escalation in both the nature and punishment for breach of computer misuse.[69] Perceived business pressure together with a national wish to stimulate or encourage economic investment were, certainly on the basis of the parliamentary debates,[70] the major motives leading to legislation.

Many of the Commonwealth countries followed the trend set by the UK and now have some form of legislation against computer misuse, and there has been some tendency for these laws to become more prohibitive. For example, the Malaysia

---

60   Mitchell, 'The annihilation of space by law: the roots and implications of anti-homeless laws in the United States' (1997) 29(3) Antipode 303, at p 303.

61   Confederation of British Industries.

62   HC Deb vol 166 col 1134, 9 February 1990.

63   HC Deb vol 166 col 1135, 9 February 1990.

64   HC Deb vol 166, 9 February 1990.

65   HL Deb vol 519, 15 May 1990.

66   HC Deb vol 166 cols 1152, 1154, 9 February 1990.

67   HL Deb vol 519 col 235, 15 May 1990.

68   HC Deb vol 166 col 1143, 9 February 1990. Speech by Mr Norman Hogg MP.

69   See Carr and Williams, 'Regulating the e-commerce environment: enforcement measures and penalty levels in the computer misuse legislation of Britain, Malaysia and Singapore' (2000) 16(5) Computer Law and Security Report 295. In HL Deb vol 519 col 240, 15 May 1990, Lord Milne noted that they had to pass legislation quickly because they were behind other countries in this respect.

70   HC Deb vol 166 cols 1155, 1162, 1163, 9 February 1990.

Computer Crimes Act 1997 contains similar offences to the three[71] set out in the British legislation but adds to the list unauthorised disclosure of access codes (s 6); attempts, aiding and abetting (s 7);[72] and obstruction of a lawful search or failure to comply with a lawful search (s 11). Penalties are considerably higher than in the United Kingdom and the powers of investigation are invasive.[73] More recently, the Indian Information Technology Act 2000 contains similar criminal provisions although simple access to another computer is not made a crime. The protection is essentially for unauthorised access to a secure system (one officially listed as secure rather than one with a protected code) but digital signature offences, computer misuse or hacking source code and publication of obscene material are all included. Another interesting example is the Singapore Computer Misuse Act 1993 as amended in 1998 which includes all the offences found in the British Computer Misuse Act[74] plus unauthorised use or interception of computer services (s 6), unauthorised obstruction of the use of computers (s 6A), and accessing protected computers (s 6C).[75] The penalties are set especially high following the 1998 amendments.

Nonetheless, despite a wider collection of possible offences, wide powers of investigation and stringent and recently increased maxima for offenders, there have been relatively few prosecutions under the Singapore Act. The same can be said in relation to the United Kingdom Computer Misuse Act 1990 (hereinafter 'CMA').

Lack of prosecutions is attributable to a number of reasons. First, it is essentially a hidden activity. Victims are usually unaware that any offence has occurred since there is no breach of physical integrity. One consequence is that the elements of computer crime which have been taken seriously by the police have tended to mirror offences committed in other mediums. Secondly, lack of sufficient police powers is often cited as another reason. Certainly, investigation of crimes involving computers pose particular problems: computer-held information is intangible, prone to easy manipulation and corruption, and may be encrypted; and computers may be networked to information databases and other computers spread over many locations, national and international. Traditional policing methods may therefore be ill-suited to investigations in this area. Despite this, the only extra power to investigate provided by s 14 of the CMA enables a circuit judge to issue a search warrant where there are reasonable grounds for believing that a basic hacking offence (s 1 offence) has been or is about to be committed on the specified premises. Grant of search warrants for ss 2 and 3 offences fall under the normal powers already set out in s 8 of the Police and Criminal Evidence Act 1984 (hereinafter 'PACE').[76] Similarly, powers to seize materials already

---

71 Sections 3, 4 and 5 respectively.

72 This is not truly an addition to the powers in England and Wales as, although there is no provision in the Act, the standard rules on attempts and aiding and abetting in England and Wales apply. Therefore, attempt falls under the Criminal Attempts Act 1981 and aiding and abetting, which is now usually constructed merely as aiding, falls under the general common law rules.

73 The powers of investigation set out in the Regulation of Investigatory Powers Act 2000 take the powers in Britain to a similar level.

74 Sections 3, 4 and 5.

75 Note that this offence can only be committed if the access is done in the course of committing an offence under s 3, 5, 6 or 6A.

76 A search warrant can be issued when a Justice of the Peace is satisfied that a serious arrestable offence has been committed on the premises and that relevant evidence is likely to be found on the specified premises.

existed in s 19 of PACE[77] and intercepting communications was set out in s 2 of the Interception of Communications Act 1985.[78] This is now regulated under Part I of the Regulation of Investigatory Powers Act 2000 (hereinafter 'RIP').

The RIP,[79] which renders most interceptions of communications illegal (even within private systems),[80] empowers the Secretary of State to issue warrants (s 5).[81] But more importantly, Part III of RIP brings new, invasive search powers that are particular to the electronic arena and deals with the issue of encrypted data. It had been asserted that the inability to access codes to allow encrypted data to be read was hampering investigation of computer crime[82] and would certainly prove to be a major problem in the future.[83] This claim is at the very least debatable and not all experts would view it as an impediment to investigations.[84] More pertinently, encryption is absolutely essential to business to ensure integrity and privacy and avoid legal problems.[85] Despite its questionable necessity, s 49 of the RIP empowers police officers to demand a code key for decryption of computer files in situations where the authorities have 'reasonable grounds to believe' that someone has a key; where disclosure is necessary to protect certain defined interests;[86] where the requirement is proportionate to what is sought; and where the code cannot be obtained by other means. All that the prosecution needs to prove is that an individual has or had a key. Then, under s 53, any refusal will be an offence punishable with imprisonment – one is guilty until proved innocent. Loss of the key would be no defence. This certainly seems to be a breach of fundamental rights and there has been, on this and other

---

77 Anything on the premises may be seized to prevent concealment or alteration at a later date. Where information is contained in a computer and is accessible from the premises, the authorities can require that it is produced in a form that can be taken away and is visible and legible in order to prevent the evidence being destroyed (s 19(4)).

78 A warrant can be obtained from the Secretary of State only if necessary for national security; or for the economic well-being of the country; or for preventing or detecting serious crime (defined as crime which could reasonably be expected to lead to three years' imprisonment for a person with no previous criminal record). See also s 10(3)(b) of the Interception of Communications Act 1985.

79 The text can be found at www.parliament.the-stationery-office.co.uk/pa/ld199900/ ldbills/ 061/2000061.htm.

80 Section 1 of the RIP creates a new tort of unlawful interception.

81 These can be issued where it is *necessary* in the interests of 'national security'; 'preventing or detecting serious crime'; 'safeguarding the economic well-being of the United Kingdom' (this last is only possible if it covers the acts of someone outside the United Kingdom).

82 Offenders were using this technology to hide obscene data or other unacceptable data, to hide their identity when performing illegal functions, to facilitate money laundering in a more secure environment, etc.

83 According to the National Criminal Intelligence Service, encryption poses special problems for enforcement authorities and the Director General is quoted in *The Times* (7 May 1999, p 31, 'Bill holds the key to policing commerce on the Internet') as saying 'We must ensure that the needs of law enforcement are balanced against those of commerce and industry, and that we have the capability to pursue investigations effectively when criminals use encryption'. Criminal investigators estimate that computer crime is costing the UK economy at least £50 billion a year and that access to decryption codes would help to counter this.

84 Interestingly, according to RJ Anderson, encryption is not a problem faced by enforcement authorities (see 'Response of Ross Anderson to the DTI consultation paper "Trusted third parties and the protection of encryption services"', 21 October 1997, available at www.cl.cam.ac.uk/users/rja14/dtiresponse/dtiresponse.html).

85 See Price, 'Understanding contemporary cryptography and its wider impact upon the general law' (1999) 12(2) International Review of Law Computers and Technology 95 who argues that cryptography is of legal and commercial necessity to avoid indeterminate liability.

86 Those provided for under Art 8(2) of the European Convention on Human Rights and Fundamental Freedoms.

grounds, strong advice from both the net community[87] and the British Chambers of Commerce[88] against the wisdom of enacting such provisions.

With these new powers, investigation of computer crime should be rendered simpler. In theory, this should lead to more cases but this leads to the third impairment to prosecution of these cases – there is a dearth of IT crime control personnel available.[89] Recently, some officers have been trained and specialist units have been formed[90] which should address issues relating to availability of personnel and their expertise.

The international nature also complicates the investigative process. Locating the suspect is problematic given the complex communication process normally involved. Although the 'terminal' computer may have electronic 'fingerprints' from the sites visited, a knowledgeable offender may have manipulated, blocked or permanently erased any such clues (though experts claim that these fingerprints can never be fully erased). In any event, using clues obtained from the offenders' computer assumes that the offender, or suspect, has been located. This involves further complications. The individual may live in another state and although, technically, searches for offenders can take place globally by using powerful programs and interception of communications, most states present legal barriers on grounds of breach of territorial sovereignty. The capability of tracing the offender can be nullified by the lack of international agreement on the power to do so. And even where a state does successfully carry out the necessary search, legal authority will still be required both to extradite the individual and to seize and preserve as evidence the computer and its information. The recently adopted Council of Europe Convention on Cybercrime 2001 which deals with procedural aspects of computer crime investigation,[91] were it to be widely ratified, would ease many of the procedural hurdles faced by investigating authorities in an international context.

---

87 It could cause innocent people to put their privacy in jeopardy by failing to encrypt data for fear of later being unable to decrypt it and so being criminalised. See comments on earlier legislation in *The Guardian*, 25 November 1999, online p 7. Also see Bowden, 'Decrypt with care' (1999) *Financial Times*, 21 December. 'Surveillance Bill under fire', from BBC News service found at http://news.bbc.co.uk/hi/english/sci/tech/newsid_638000/638041.stm. Jean Eaglesham, 'Big brother: government unveils e-mail surveillance law' (2000) *Financial Times*, 11 February. Doward, 'Father of the Web lashes snooping Bill' (2000) *Observer*, 11 June. Other references can be found at www.fipr.org/policywatch.html.

88 See Brown, Davies and Hosein (eds), *The Economic Impact of the Regulation of Investigatory Powers Bill*, published 12 June 2000, available at www.britishchambers.org.uk/newsandpolicy/downloads/lsereport.doc. On p 1, they state that 'As it stands, RIP is likely to create a legal environment which will inhibit investment, impede the evolution of e-commerce, impose direct and indirect costs on business and the consumer, diminish overall trust in e-commerce, disrupt business-to-business relationships, place UK companies at a competitive disadvantage, and create a range of legal uncertainties which will place a growing number of businesses in a precarious position.'

89 In 1996, Thackeray of the Police Research Group noted that the police lose interest in cases involving computers and that the approach in Britain lacks sophistication; see McCormack (1996) *Daily Telegraph*, 5 November.

90 Both Manchester and London have Computer Crime Units and other forces often have specially trained officers. The National Crime Squad is also available to look at crimes which cross either force boundaries or national boundaries. Also, the National Hi-Tech Crime Unit. Visit www.nhtcu.org for further on the role of this unit.

91 See pp 143–9 below for further on the Council of Europe Convention on Cybercrime.

Council of Europe and computer crime

The Council of Europe was a prime mover in the area of computer crime in Europe. Its Recommendation 89(9) on Computer Related Crime[92] (hereinafter 'R89(9)') was a starting point for many of its member states for formulating their legislation.[93] R89(9) suggested eight specific types of conduct that should be incorporated into the criminal laws of member states: computer-related fraud; computer forgery; damage to computer data or programs; computer sabotage; unauthorised access; unauthorised interception of data transmission; unauthorised reproduction of a protected computer program; and unauthorised reproduction of a topography. R89(9) also suggests four other activities that should be discouraged: alteration of computer data or computer programs; computer espionage; unauthorised use of a computer; and unauthorised use of a computer program.

R89(9), however, did not address procedural issues surrounding computer crime investigation. The Council of Europe subsequently dealt with procedural matters in Recommendation 95(13).[94] Regardless of these recommendations, there was wide divergence in computer crime legislation across member states and it was felt that it would be best to draft a convention with the intention that it would have a wider impact internationally – not only within Europe but outside of Europe. A number of non-European countries were also invited to take part and this resulted in the Council of Europe Convention on Cybercrime.

Council of Europe's Cybercrime Convention

The Council of Europe in 1997 took on the task of drafting the first multilateral or international instrument to fight criminal activity on computer networks. This resulted in the Convention on Cybercrime[95] (hereinafter 'COE Convention'). It requires signatures from five countries, three of whom must be member states, before it comes into operation (Art 36). From the beginning, observer nations such as Canada, Japan, South Africa and most importantly the US have participated fully in the negotiations and this inevitably has had marked effects on the shape of the final document.

The COE Convention consists of four chapters: Chapter I (Art 1) deals with definition of terms; Chapter II (Arts 2–22) with measures to be taken at the national level; Chapter III (Arts 23–35) with international co-operation; and Chapter IV (Arts 36–48) with final provisions. Chapters II and III are divided further into sections. Section 1 of Chapter II deals with substantive criminal law, s 2 with procedural law

---

92 1989, Strasbourg: Council of Europe. Summary of text available at www.coe.int.

93 Eg, Germany and Italy.

94 *Recommendation No R95(13) Concerning Problems of Criminal Procedural Law Connected to Information Technology and Explanatory Memorandum*, 1995, Council of Europe; electronic version available at www.coe.int.

95 Adopted 23 November 2001. The convention came into force on 1 July 2004. The text of this convention is available at www.coe.int. It is also reproduced in Carr and Kidner, *International Trade Law Statutes and Conventions*, 5th edn, 2008 Routledge-Cavendish. There is also an Additional Protocol to the Convention on Cybercrime concerning Criminalisation of Acts of a Racist and Xenophobic Nature Committed through Computer Systems. This was adopted on 28 January 2003 and entered into force on 1 March 2006. The text of this Protocol is available at www.coe.int.

and s 3 with jurisdiction. Section 1 of Chapter III deals with general principles, and s 2 with specific provisions.

Offences criminalised

Ambitious in casting its net wide, the COE Convention requires signatory states to criminalise a host of activities that, in one way or another, are connected to a computer, computer material, computer operation or computer system. Offences are categorised into four groups:

Group 1:   Offences against confidentiality, integrity and availability of computer
              data and systems;

Group 2:   Computer-related offences;

Group 3:   Content-related offences;

Group 4:   Copyright-related offences.

Prior to examining these offences, it makes sense to highlight the common elements that run through them. Other than intent, criminality under the COE Convention will follow only if the act is done 'without right'. While the phrase 'without right' is left undefined in the COE Convention, there are indications of its intended meaning in the explanatory memorandum. It certainly leaves open the possibility of allowing usual legal defences such as consent and necessity, activities backed by government authority or required for other legitimate purposes such as the maintenance of a network. It would also allow defences based on fundamental human rights.

Group I

Offences created under Group 1 are intended to control activities that compromise confidentiality, integrity and availability of computer-held data and systems. Article 2 makes unauthorised access of a computer system with the requisite intention an offence. A computer system is defined as any device or a group of interconnected or related devices, one or more of which, pursuant to a program, performs an automatic processing of data. It is aimed at activities such as hacking, cracking and computer trespass.[96] Making illegal mere unauthorised intrusion is justified on economic grounds. Breach in secure perimeters of a system inevitably results in time and money spent on locating the breach, assessing the resulting damage (financial or otherwise) and improvements in security measures be it in the form of installation of a better system or the re-education of personnel. Persuasive though the economic arguments are, the sagacity of making unauthorised access of computer systems per se an offence is questionable. Drawing a parallel with trespass, individuals and commercial entities incur costs in re-installing security systems, checking of belongings and files, yet pure trespass is not often an offence. Is there then a need to treat unauthorised intrusion of computer systems as illegal? The COE Convention is not the first instrument to include this in the list of offences. Other jurisdictions have a similar provision in computer crime statutes.[97] Mention, however, must be made of its limited success in

---

96   Each of these terms basically involves unauthorised access of a computer, a computer system
     or a computer site.
97   Eg, Singapore, Malaysia and Britain.

terms of the rate of detection and prosecutions in other jurisdictions.[98] Would it have been more effective to cast the onus on the computer owners by requiring them to follow minimum security measures before making people criminally liable for simple access? Or, could the COE Convention have followed an alternative adopted in a number of other jurisdictions with legislation on computer crime? For instance, under s 70 of the Indian Information Technology Act 2000, simple access is made an offence only if it involves a protected system – a system that the state has declared to be protected.

Article 3 makes unauthorised interception of non-public transmissions of computer data with the requisite intention an offence. Aimed at protecting the right to privacy embodied in Art 8[99] of the European Convention on Human Rights (ECHR), this provision makes eavesdropping of electronic data transfer, whether by telephone, fax, email or file transfer, and tapping, intercepting or recording electromagnetic emissions,[100] an offence. The interception must be of a non-public transmission. According to the explanatory memorandum (para 54), 'non-public' qualifies the nature of the communication and not the data. In other words, data may be something that is publicly available but the parties wish to communicate confidentially. Alternatively, the service, though available to all on a public network, is permitted only upon payment of a fee (for example, Pay TV). Article 3 is also intended to protect the communication between employees, be it for business purposes or otherwise as long as they are 'non-public transmissions of computer data'.[101]

Article 4 makes unauthorised and intentional damaging, deletion, deterioration, alteration or suppression of computer data an offence. Introduction of malicious codes such as viruses, Trojan horses[102] as well as the resulting modification will be caught by this provision. Article 4 also allows states to enter a reservation in respect of the Art 4 offence – that is, they may require that the conduct results in serious harm. No explanation of what constitutes serious harm for the purposes of this article is provided; it is left to the state to interpret the phrase. In most states, it is likely that 'serious harm' would be defined in economic terms (loss of time or money) and it would therefore protect mostly business interests.

Unauthorised and intentional hindering (interference with the proper functioning) of a computer system by inputting, transmitting, damaging, deleting, deteriorating,

---

98   See Carr and Williams, 'Securing the e-commerce environment' (2000) 16(5) Computer Law and Security Report 295.

99   It states:
   Everyone has the right to respect for his private and family life, his home and his correspondence.
   There shall be no interference by a public authority with the exercise of this right except as is in accordance with the law and is necessary in a democratic society in the interests of national security, public safety or the economic well-being of the country, for the protection of health or morals, or for the protection of the rights and freedoms of others.

100 Electromagnetic emissions are emissions emitted by a computer during its operation. With the right tools, it is possible for data to be reconstructed from the emissions even though the emissions in themselves are not considered to be data by the convention. Computer data is defined in Art I(b) as 'any representation of facts, information or concepts in a form suitable for processing in a computer system, including a program suitable to cause a computer system to perform a function'.

101 This falls in line with the judgment of the European Court of Human Rights in *Halford v UK* (1997) 24 EHRR 523 (25 June 1997, Case 20605/92).

102 A program which deliberately does something, often harmful, in addition to what is expected. Eg, a program may contain a type of time bomb which will release a virus if an illegal copy is used.

altering or suppressing computer data is made an offence under Art 5. This provision is aimed at blocking, denial of service,[103] mail bombing[104] or interference with the use of a system through the use of malicious codes. However, according to the provision, the hindering must be serious. The COE Convention fails to clarify the term; neither does it state whether the hindrance needs to be temporary or permanent, partial or total. The explanatory memorandum leaves the parties to decide the level of hindrance required for it to be considered serious (para 67). Nonetheless, there is some indication in the explanatory memorandum that the drafters would consider sending of data that has a significant detrimental effect on the ability of the user to use the system or communicate with other systems as serious. Presumably, detrimental effect is measured in economic terms (loss of time, money, man-hours, etc). This provision does not outlaw spamming (sending of unsolicited mailing for commercial or other purposes to multiple addresses)[105] as such. However, according to the explanatory memorandum, such behaviour should be criminalised where there is intentional and serious hindering of communication. Yet again, the emphasis is on economic consequences. Admittedly, economic detriment caused by spamming for small Internet service providers may be far reaching, since it could affect the capacity/reliability of their communication systems and force them out of the market. Small businesses may also be dissuaded from using computers for communication to avoid the nuisance caused by unsolicited mailings, thus losing the opportunity to expand their commercial activities worldwide. Spamming, however, could also include unsolicited but distressing mailings (for example, homophobic messages, racist material). The impact of such mailings on individuals may be extreme, but there is nothing in the explanatory memorandum to suggest that psychological detriment caused to individuals is relevant.

Production, sale, procurement for use, import, distribution or otherwise making available a device designed to commit Arts 2–5 offences, or a password, access code or similar data that is capable of enabling access of a computer system when accompanied with the requisite intention are made offences under Arts 6(1)(1) and 6(1)(2). Hackers' bulletin boards, software programs facilitating access, creation/compilation of hyperlinks to facilitate access hacking devices will be caught by this provision. The production, sale, etc, of such devices is not criminalised where it is for the purposes of testing or protection of a computer. In other words, the devices must be objectively designed, or adapted, primarily for the purposes of committing an offence. While this makes sense in the abstract, it is debatable whether in practice it will be easy to establish clearly that a tool has been made purely for a criminal purpose. So-called hackers' tools have a dual use in that they can be used effectively to assess the vulnerability of a system, and no producer or seller of such devices would be willing to admit that he produced or sold the device for criminal purposes. The exclusion of dual-use devices leaves the area wide open; all one needs to show is that criminal use is not the primary purpose or function for the device and there is a defence. It may be that states desirous of controlling the criminal use of hackers' tools may introduce registers and licensing schemes as in the case of sale of firearms. As to whether this is

---

103 Attack on a website with spoof traffic until there is overloading of the computer system, effectively blocking legitimate use.

104 Sending large quantities of mail to a recipient in order to block their communications.

105 Most email users at some stage receive mailings for dubious products, get-rich-quick schemes, or quasi-legal services.

financially and administratively feasible is doubtful; serious hackers will make their purchases abroad in any event.

Group 2

This group creates two offences: computer-related forgery (Art 7) and computer-related fraud (Art 8). Article 7 creates the offence of forgery in respect of electronic documents. An Art 7 offence is committed where without authority and with intention computer data is deleted, suppressed or altered which results in inauthentic data with the intention that it is considered or acted upon for legal purposes as authentic. Article 7 is aimed at protecting the reliability and thus the evidentiary value of the electronic document. Manipulation of digital signatures, or contents of an electronic stored message, with the intent they considered or acted upon as if they were authentic for legal purposes will be caught by this provision. The state may require an intention to defraud for criminal liability to attach.

Aimed at activities such as credit card fraud and illegal transfer of electronic funds, Art 8 makes alteration, input, deletion or suppression of computer data or any interference with the functioning of a computer system with the dishonest or fraudulent intent of procuring economic benefit for oneself or another an offence.

Group 3

Offences listed in Groups 1, 2 and 4 are to be found in R89(9) on computer-related crime.[106] Group 3 is an important development in the light of the use of the Internet for distribution of offensive material and contains the potential to protect human dignity. It focuses on child pornography and makes the production, offering, distribution, transmission, procuring and possession of child pornography (committed intentionally and without right) in a computer system an offence (Art 9).

Group 4

Sale of pirated software, entertainment disks, etc, at a commercial level continues to be an endemic problem and costs the IT industry and the exchequer billions of pounds annually. The COE Convention in Art 10 makes infringement of copyright[107] and related rights[108] where such acts are committed intentionally on a commercial scale by means of computer system an offence.

---

106 The minimum list includes computer-related fraud, computer forgery, damage to computer data or programs, computer sabotage (intentionally hindering the lawful use of a computer system (includes a telecommunications facility)), unauthorised access, unauthorised interception, unauthorised reproduction of computer program and unauthorised reproduction of a topography. The optional list includes alteration of computer data, computer programs, computer espionage, unauthorised use of a computer and unauthorised use of a protected computer program.

107 Infringement of copyright as defined in the Berne Convention for the Protection of Literary and Artistic Works 1886, the WIPO Copyright Treaty 1996, and the 1993 TRIPS Agreement. The texts of all these instruments are available at www.wipo.org.

108 As defined pursuant to the obligations undertaken under the International Convention for the Protection of Performers, Producers of Phonograms and Broadcasting Organisations, TRIPS Agreement and the WIPO Performances and Phonograms Treaty.

Aiding, abetting and attempt

Article 11(1) introduces additional offences of aiding or abetting of the offences contained in Arts 2–10, provided it is accompanied by the intent to commit such an offence. Harmful material is communicated via conduits that are provided by Internet Service Provider (ISPs).[109] The relevant issue is whether the ISPs are answerable in criminal law for the information that is sent through their network. Are they placed under an obligation to monitor the data flowing through their system? The explanatory memorandum makes clear that the ISP needs to have the necessary criminal intent in order to be caught by Art 11, and the provision does not place the ISP under an obligation to monitor content to avoid criminal liability. Article 11(2) makes attempt to commit offences covered by Arts 3–5, 7, 8, 9(1)(a) and 9(1)(c) when committed intentionally an offence. The convention, however, allows a state to reserve the right not to apply, in whole or in part (Art 11(2)).

Corporate liability

The COE Convention, in Art 12, recommends that legal persons are also to be made liable for any of the above criminal offences committed for their benefit (even if they do not actually benefit) by a natural person who has a leading position within the legal person. Powers of representation, authority to take decisions on behalf of the legal person, and authority to exercise control within the legal person are the factors that determine whether a natural person has a leading position or not. Legal persons can also be made liable where the lack of supervision or control by the natural person in a leading position has resulted in commission of criminal offences under the COE Convention. This provision imposes a burden on legal persons to ensure that effective security systems in respect of computer systems are put in place. It must be pointed out that lack of security is a major contributory factor of cybercrime.

Of course, there may be problems with the provisions concerning enforcement and co-operation between states where one state is asked for search powers against a large and economically strategic company situated within its territory. This is likely to be exacerbated where the request comes from another state where the supposed victim is a direct competitor of the first company. Inclusion of this may therefore limit the lengths to which states are willing to agree to broad powers of co-operation on matters involving investigation that are dealt with in Chapter III of the COE Convention.

Penalties

Article 13 of the COE Convention addresses the issue of sanctions in respect of the offences created by Arts 2–12. While advancing the recommendation that the parties signing the COE Convention should take steps to adopt a penalty scheme that is effective, proportionate and dissuasive, including deprivation of liberty, no specific scheme or scale is expressed. Each state is free to adopt a scheme that best fits with its

---

109   Defined as 'any public or private entity that provides to users of its service the ability to communicate by means of a computer system, and any other entity that processes or stores computer data on behalf of such communication service or users of such service'.

policies and principles of criminal justice. There is no suggestion there should be proportionality of penalties as between member states; presumably, proportionality advocated by the COE Convention refers purely to scales adopted within each state. This may prove to be a weakness of the COE Convention.[110] States wishing to attract economic inward investment may be tempted to compete with each other by toughening their criminal law through sanction levels indicating, thus, their attractiveness as a safe haven for locating a business. There are already signs of this trend as indicated by the computer misuse legislation of Singapore, India and Malaysia. Such an approach is illogical since IT does not respect international boundaries. Some harmonisation of penalty levels might have proved useful since it would have stopped an eager embrace of high punitive measures by states in the name of providing a safe environment for inward investment. Moving to corporate liability, the COE Convention recommends that the sanctions may be criminal or non-criminal including monetary sanctions. It is likely that fines will be used widely. The convention once again does not provide an indication of scales and it is likely that there will be wide variance among states.

It may also be that failure to tackle this issue might lead to the failure of the COE Convention. Just as states are unwilling to co-operate where their criminal laws differ, they may also drag their feet where the penalties are outwith their own. Developing nations who wish to ratify might therefore set very low, almost non-existent, penalties for copyright infringement and may be unwilling or slow to co-operate when it is a question of their economic well-being due to a more punitive regime in respect of intellectual property rights infringements elsewhere. It might have been sensible to set penalties, at least in this area. A scheme of injunctions and low level fines for most infringements could be a compromise solution.

Council of Europe and procedural aspects of cybercrime investigation

Investigation of crime involving information technology poses special problems for enforcement authorities. The Council of Europe started work on this aspect in the early 1990s which resulted in Recommendation 95(13) (hereinafter 'R95(13)'). This was followed by the Council of Europe Cybercrime Convention in 2001,[111] which addresses procedural aspects of computer crime investigation. The purpose of this section is to examine these provisions to see how far they will assist in the investigation of IT-related crime. However, before proceeding to do this, by way of background, R95(13) will be considered since many of the provisions found in the COE Convention are based on this document.

---

110   See Carr and Williams, 'A step too far in controlling computers?: the Singapore Computer Misuse (Amendment) Act 1998' (2000) 8(1) The International Journal of Law and Information Technology 48.

111   See Carr and Williams, 'Draft cybercrime convention' (2002) 18 Computer Law and Security Report 83. The material included under R95(13) below is derived from Carr and Williams, 'Council of Europe on the Harmonisation of Criminal Procedural Law Relating to Information Technology (Recommendation No R95(13)) – some comments' [1998] JBL 469.

R95(13)

The recommendations in R95(13) are extensive and include not only search, seizure, surveillance and cryptography but also other aspects such as collection of statistics, training of personnel and co-operation between enforcement authorities. Only the pertinent recommendations are considered here.

Search, seizure and technical surveillance

Traditional search and seizure methods[112] are by and large inadequate when it comes to investigating computer-held information. Computer-held information is intangible, and prone to easy manipulation and corruption. Use of networks brings with it its own challenges. For instance, information may be stored in computer systems spread over many locations (sometimes foreign locations) and the suspect's computer merely used as a terminal. During the course of the search, the suspect may move data to another computer since information can be transferred from one system to another at great speed. The search, where successful, may reveal the information to be encrypted, making evidence gathering a difficult task, if not an impossible one, for the authorities. Due to the technological permutations, enforcement authorities need to have sufficient powers to: (a) search computers located both on the suspect's premises and elsewhere; (b) seize information and fix it in a manner so that it cannot be tampered with; (c) intercept data traffic; and (d) obtain co-operation from third parties such as network providers to enable decryption.

The Council of Europe makes the following four recommendations with regard to provisions on search and seizure:

> *Principle No 1*: the legal distinctions between searching computer systems and seizing data stored therein, and intercepting data in the course of transmission, should be clearly delineated and applied (R95(13), at p 18).
>
> *Principle No 2*: criminal procedural laws should permit investigating authorities to search computer systems and seize data under similar conditions as under traditional powers of search and seizure. The person in charge of the system should be informed that the system has been searched and of the kind of data that has been seized. The legal remedies that are provided for in general against search and seizure should be equally applicable in case of search in computer systems and in case of seizure of data therein (R95(13), at p 20).
>
> *Principle No 3*: during the execution of a search, investigating authorities should have the power, subject to appropriate safeguards, to extend the search to other computer systems within their jurisdiction which are connected by means of a network and to seize the data therein, provided that immediate action is required (R95(13), at p 23).
>
> *Principle No 4*: where automatically processed data is functionally equivalent to the notion of a traditional document, provisions in the criminal procedural law relating to search and seizure of documents should apply equally to it (R95(13), at p 25).

As noted earlier, search generally involves physical presence of the investigator in the place where the search is conducted, making the investigation open and apparent to

---

112 In traditional search and seizure, investigating authorities are normally present at the location where the search is conducted and the objects seized, be they documents, tools, clothing, are tangible (visible to the eye, capable of being touched and so on).

the occupier of the premises or owner of the goods. This is in contrast to interception of communication where the investigator's presence is not generally known. The demarcation between search and interception when it comes to IT is fuzzy since it is possible to search a computer, where networked, from a remote terminal. It therefore becomes important to decide which type of activity is covered by procedures relating to search and which by procedures relating to interception. The Council of Europe suggests a possible solution for the purposes of separation: where information is inert (static and stored in one machine or in one file), search and seizure procedures are recommended, and where data are moving between computers or storage files, interception procedures. While acknowledging that this is not the only solution, the Council of Europe emphasises clarity whichever method is adopted.[113]

As for technical surveillance, developments in communications technology have eroded the distinctions between computer communication, telecommunication, radio, television and cable communication. By and large, the difference between public and private communications is also breaking down. So, for the purposes of gathering evidence, investigating authorities require access to traffic data. R95(13) therefore makes the following recommendations to supplement existing rules on interception:

> *Principle No 5*: in view of the convergence of information technology and telecommunications, laws pertaining to technical surveillance for the purposes of criminal investigations, such as interception of telecommunications, should be reviewed and amended where necessary to ensure their applicability (R95(13), at p 26).

> *Principle No 6*: the law should permit investigating authorities to avail themselves of all necessary technical measures that make possible the collection of traffic data in investigation of crimes (R95(13), at p 31).

> *Principle No 7*: when collected in the course of a criminal investigation and in particular when obtained by means of intercepting telecommunications, data which is the object of legal protection and processed by a computer system should be secured in an appropriate manner (R95(13), at p 33).

> *Principle No 8*: criminal procedural laws should be reviewed with the view of making possible interception of telecommunications and the collection of traffic data[114] in respect of the investigation of serious offences against confidentiality, integrity and availability of telecommunication or computer systems (R95(13), at p 34).[115]

Principle 6 deals with what may be seen as the less intrusive measure of discovering the source of a communication and its destination. As this does not involve knowledge

---

113   Whilst accepting that there is a conceptual difference between search and interception, any application of this theoretical distinction to IT is likely to prove problematic. The suggestion of the Council of Europe is that the distinction be based on the state the information is in, ie, in terms of whether the information is inert or in transit. This demarcation is likely to work if one assumes that it applies to the state of the information when held by the user, not when accessed by enforcement officers, since in the latter information may well be transmitted from one terminal to another as part of the search. Furthermore, choosing this delineation may require greater controls in cases where information on remote computers is accessed to protect the rights of those users of remote computers.

114   The FBI introduced a system called the Carnivore in July 2000. It is a monitoring system that allows them to collect a suspect's e-mail without their knowledge or consent. It seems that before its use they must assess the appropriateness of its use and obtain the Department of Justice approval. See Dunham, 'Carnivore, the FBI's e-mail surveillance system: devouring criminals, not privacy' (2002) 54 Fed Comm LJ 543.

115   Any talk of interception of communications raises the sensitive issue of privacy. In the context of the ECHR, interception of communications is prohibited unless certain minimum standards are met. See for example *Malone v UK (A/82)* (1984) 7 EHRR 14; *Klass v Federal Republic of Germany* (A28) (1979–80) 2 EHRR 214.

of the contents of the communication, most individuals consider this to be less intrusive than interception. Nonetheless, the methods of obtaining the information may involve techniques which resemble those of interception and would need to be regulated by the same rules as for interception of communications. In Britain, police authorities have no specific powers to obtain details concerning the use of telephone or other telecommunication lines. The matter of passing relevant information is left entirely to the discretion of the companies operating the lines. The only means by which the information may be accessed is either if the companies who run the lines agree to co-operate, or if the authorities obtain a search warrant which allows them to obtain documents which contain the evidence or require a computer printout of anything contained in a computer. This assumes that such information is held by the telecommunications companies. The use of search and seizure powers to obtain such information may seem over-intrusive, an over-burdensome use of power but as it carries with it safeguards it may be the best method. There is one major problem, however. If the telecommunications company does not keep records of the type for which a search warrant is issued, there is no power to require them to generate records of this type, and a warrant allowing a very wide retrieval of information would be excessively intrusive into the privacy of third parties.[116]

Inevitably, some of the information gathered during interception of communication – be it in relation to the source or destination of communications or the contents of communication – is likely to be of a sensitive nature and may have economic or political value. It is therefore essential that in creating legislation allowing interception, sufficient guards are placed to ensure protection of data. Where a person suffers losses as a result of mismanagement of data by the investigating authorities, there must be some means of compensating the losses. R95(13) gives due consideration to these issues in the explanatory memorandum to Principle 7.

Co-operation with investigating authorities, cryptography[117]

The gathering of evidence in a computer environment is difficult, since: (a) the evidence is intangible; (b) information of evidential value may be fragmented over different systems and in a number of locations; and (c) knowledge of sophisticated computer systems and encryption techniques may be needed.[118] In light of these difficulties, R95(13) makes the following recommendations regarding co-operation by the suspect and third parties (innocent witnesses, operators and service providers):

> *Principle No 9:* subject to legal privileges or protection, most legal systems permit investigating authorities to order persons to hand over objects under their control that are required to serve as evidence. In a parallel fashion, provisions should be made for

---

116   Since monitoring or intercepting telecommunications lines normally generates information much wider than that sought by the original interception, adequate protective steps to ensure that investigating authorities have access only to the required information are required. The German provisions relating to surveillance may provide a possible model, where the judiciary control material obtained during surveillance and the police have access only to material regarded as relevant to their investigation by the judiciary.

117   The Organisation for Economic Co-operation and Development (OECD) and the European Commission also examined the extent to which a state should intervene in the use of cryptography. Guidelines were issued in late 1997. Visit www.oecd.org.

118   Note that the recommendation does make suggestions about the training of investigating personnel and the creation of a special unit to deal with computer-related offences.

the power to order persons to submit any specified data under their control in a computer system in the form required by the investigating authority (R95(13), at p 35).

Principle No 10: subject to legal privileges or protection, investigating authorities should have the power to order persons who have data in a computer system under their control to provide all necessary information to enable access to a computer system and the data therein. Criminal procedural law should ensure that a similar order can be given to other persons who have knowledge about the functioning of the computer system or measures applied to secure the data therein (R95(13), at pp 36–37).

Principle No 11: specific obligations should be imposed on operators of public and private networks that offer telecommunication services to the public to avail themselves of all necessary technical measures that make possible the interception of telecommunications by the investigating authorities (R95(13), at p 39).

Principle No 12: specific obligations should be imposed on service providers who offer telecommunication services to the public, either through public or private networks, to provide information to identify the user, when so ordered by the competent investigating authorities (R95(13), at p 40).

The explanatory memorandum makes clear that the powers in relation to third parties should be extensive enough to require their active participation in providing access to files and, if need be, provide passwords and other details about encryption techniques to enable such access (p 38), subject to any legal privileges such as attorney-client confidentiality (p 36). As for private and public network operators, they are not only required to assist the authorities in the interception but put in place adequate technical devices that allow interception. Where there is an inbuilt encryption mechanism in the system, the operator should be placed under an obligation to decrypt the message for the authorities (p 39). Principle 12 takes this obligation further by suggesting that service providers should be required to identify users when required. It goes without saying that imparting such open-ended powers to enable intrusion is likely to create a society that lives in constant fear of enforcement authorities. Any attempt to introduce such far-ranging measures should be balanced by stringent safeguards. R95(13) does not suggest the type of sanction in the event of non-compliance. Presumably, in most jurisdictions, this would take the form of imprisonment or fine since the recommendations apply to both natural and legal persons (p 38).[119]

As is well known, cryptography greatly enhances the security of information since it protects information from the prying eyes of unauthorised third parties.[120] Given its usefulness to those engaged in illegal activities such as child pornography, corruption, drug trafficking, money laundering and terrorism, it inevitably raises the important policy issue of whether steps should be taken to protect society from the harmful effects of such a technology. Principle 14 of R95(13) recognises the harmful potential of cryptography and suggests that 'measures should be considered to

---

119 On the human rights front, the recommendation that the person under investigation be ordered to provide all information necessary to access a computer and computer data in a form required – ie, computer printout, decrypted, etc – is likely to cause concern since, under Art 6(1) and (2) of the ECHR, there is an obligation on states to guarantee individuals the right of a fair trial, and to preserve and respect the right of individuals to be 'presumed innocent until proved guilty according to law'. These rights have been interpreted as covering the right against self-incrimination. See Carr and Williams, 'Council of Europe on the Harmonisation of Criminal Procedural Law Relating to Information Technology (Recommendation No R95(13)) – some comments' [1998] JBL 469.

120 Encryption through digital signatures also contributes to a message's integrity and the sender's identity.

minimise the negative effects of the use of cryptography on the investigation of criminal offences, without affecting its legitimate use more than is strictly necessary'. However, R95(13) does not provide a list of specific measures that could be taken apart from a brief allusion in the explanatory memorandum to place restrictions on the possession, distribution or use of cryptography, thus leaving it to states to arrive at an acceptable solution that ensures the interests of the public at large without affecting the rights of genuine users. An obvious option is to give extensive powers to enforcement authorities to intercept communications. Interception without the cryptographic key would prove inadequate and code breaking would not be cost effective.[121]

Handling of electronic evidence and admissibility

Other than the above, R95(13) also covers issues of handling of electronic evidence and its admissibility, collection of statistics, training of officers and international co-operation in the search and seizure of evidence.

As for the collection, preservation and presentation of electronic evidence, the Council of Europe suggests that special procedures must be in place since electronic evidence is prone to corruption and manipulation which is not visible to the eye. Providing for special procedures for electronic evidence will therefore establish its integrity and authenticity. As regards admissibility of electronic evidence, it is correct to say that this is provided for in a country's procedural laws since much of the evidence in computer-related criminal activities is likely to be of an electronic nature. England and Wales have legislation in place that will allow this.

Due to the cross-border nature of computer-related crime, evidence relating to an offence is likely to be spread over many countries. This means that network searches may need to be executed at transborder level which may be done in a number of ways – by conducting the search from the country where the entity under criminal investigation is present or requesting enforcement authorities of the country where the evidence is situated to obtain the evidence. Of course, searches, albeit via a net-work of a system that is physically located in another state, will raise sovereignty issues, and the co-operation of enforcement authorities of another country cannot always be expected. R95(13)'s special reference to the need for international cooper-ation through international agreements and mutual assistance is embodied in Principles 17 and 18.

Procedural aspects in the Council of Europe Convention on Cybercrime

The drafters of the COE Convention seem to have taken R95(13) fully on board, while expecting parties to ensure that in the implementation and application of the COE Convention there will be safeguards in place for the adequate protection of human rights and liberties (Art 15). The COE Convention imparts enforcement authorities to search computer systems and seize information (Art 19); order service providers

---

121 Of course, human rights provisions must be taken into account when passing legislation in respect of encryption. Were a similar proposal to be put forward in European states, it will have to take into account Art 8 of the ECHR. See Carr and Williams, 'Council of Europe on the Harmonisation of Criminal Procedural Law Relating to Information Technology (Recommendation No R95(13)) – some comments' [1998] JBL 469.

(within their jurisdiction) to provide information in respect of the subscriber, such as identity, postal address, billing and payment information (Art 18); collect traffic data in real time and ask others such as service providers to assist in its collection (Art 20); and intercept content data (Art 21).[122]

As stated earlier, the borderless nature of IT means that investigation authorities will need to obtain information and evidence from computer systems located in other jurisdictions. They may also need to monitor traffic data across borders. Effective investigation therefore requires international co-operation and mutual assistance. There are a number of mutual assistance treaties – for instance, the Council of Europe Convention on Mutual Assistance in Criminal Matters 1959. The COE Convention does not intend to displace any of the existing conventions and bilateral treaties but supplements/enhances the available framework by addressing the particular needs of detecting computer crime. Article 23 formulates the general principles and expects mutual assistance to the greatest extent possible for the purpose of investigation or proceedings concerning criminal offences related to computer systems and data, or for the collection of evidence in electronic form of a criminal offence. Since speed is an essential component for successful investigation, in urgent cases, the COE Convention does away with rigid formalities for requesting mutual assistance and enables parties to request assistance using e-mails and other forms of instantaneous communication. Also, request for expeditious preservation of stored data is allowed under Art 29 and expeditious disclosure of preserved data under Art 30. Refusal for preservation of data is allowed in limited circumstances: where the condition of dual criminality[123] is not fulfilled; where the request concerns a political offence or an offence related to a political offence; and in the interests of sovereignty, security or public order. Request for mutual assistance relates not only to the access of stored data but also to real-time collection of traffic data. Another ground-breaking provision is Art 35 which requires each party to designate a 24/7 point of contact for providing immediate assistance.

Where states are not parties to mutual assistance agreements, Arts 27 and 28 make provisions for procedures such as establishing central authorities to aid cooperation and regulating confidentiality of requests and information.

From the above, it is clear that the problems in investigation posed by anonymity and encryption can be addressed if the framework suggested by the Council of Europe is adopted. Inevitably, the costs of keeping logs and other subscriber information will fall on the service provider which might increase the overall costs. If the consequence of this is a safer net environment, then it may, according to some, be a price worth paying.[124]

---

122 The United Kingdom's RIP includes provisions that gives enforcement authorities the right to obtain the relevant key from service providers for accessing encrypted information. The Anti-Terrorism Security and Crime Act 2001 allows the Secretary of State to issue, and revise, a code of practice relating to the retention by communications providers of communications data obtained by or held by them. This is justified on grounds of national security and crime prevention.

123 The convention also addresses extradition in Art 24 and parties are required to extradite individuals for offences criminalised under Arts 2–11 of the Convention, provided the offence is punishable under the laws of both countries by a maximum of one year imprisonment or a more severe penalty. This meets the minimum threshold set by the Council of Europe Convention on Extradition 1957.

124 For an interesting economic analysis, see Hamdani, 'Who's liable for cyberwrongs?' (2002) 87 Cornell LR 901.

CONCLUSION: A BRIGHT FUTURE FOR E-COMMERCE?

It seems that international organisations, governments and governmental organisations have been driven by the need to ensure there are sufficient safeguards in place that would reduce the economic risks posed by legal uncertainties and that the vulnerabilities of the system are reduced to a tolerable level. While the work of the UNCITRAL in relation to legal effectiveness of electronic communications may have brought about some harmonisation, it is uncertain whether the legislative steps in the form of creating specific computer related offences have created a desirable level of safety in the electronic environment. Despite well publicised losses to the industry due to vulnerability of the electronic medium, paucity of prosecutions comes as a surprise and is a strong indicator that the creation of computer specific offences is inadequate. It might be best for businesses to protect themselves against the peculiar susceptibilities of the medium through adequate security management and security devices. For instance, a survey of information security breaches conducted by Price-Waterhouse Coopers and the Department of Trade and Industry (DTI)[125] in 2002 indicated that investment in information security in the United Kingdom was low despite security incidents that cost the United Kingdom billions of pounds in 2001. The report recommended that businesses create a security aware culture and put in place appropriate steps in security management such as use of adequate technical security devices, qualified personnel, penetration testing of its web sites and security audits. While these suggestions are of a practical nature, it must be emphasised that a legal framework promoting the use of the electronic medium of itself is insufficient to reduce the vulnerabilities of the medium or protect the electronic environment from external threats. Policy makers, governments and international organisations have done their best to provide a legal framework for electronic commerce – its full utilisation and success are now in the hands of businesses.

FURTHER READING

DTI, *Licensing of Trusted Third Parties for the Provision of Encryption Services: Public Consultation Paper on Detailed Proposals for Legislation*, March 1997, DTI.

Fafinski, *Computer Misuse: Response, Regulation and the Law*, 2009, Willan.

OECD, 'Gateways to global market: consumers and electronic commerce', 1997, available at www.oecd.org.

Perritt Jr, *Law and the Information Superhighway*, 1996, John Wiley.

Thomas and Loader (eds), *Cybercrime*, 2000, Routledge.

Wall (ed), *Crime and the Internet*, 2001, Routledge.

Weiss, 'Security requirements and evidentiary issues in the interchange of electronic documents' (1993) 12 John Marshall Journal of Computer and Information Law 425.

Williams and Carr, 'Crime, risk and computers' [2002] Electronic Communications LR 23.

---

125 'Information Security Breaches Survey 2002'. See also 'BERR Information Security Breaches Survey 2008' available at www.security-survey.gov.uk.

PART III

TRANSPORTATION OF CARGO

OVERVIEW

Transportation of goods from the seller's country to the buyer's country is an important part of any international sale contract. This applies equally to contracts concluded offline and those online, unless of course the sale is for software, electronic books and other electronically stored information that can be transferred online.

Much of the cargo in international trade is still transported by sea, and bills of lading continue to play an important role as a transport document. Among its many characteristics is its role as a transferable document of title which contributes to its popularity. International developments in relation to the carriage of goods by sea are significant. The number of conventions in force – the Hague Rules, the Hague-Visby Rules and the Hamburg Rules – affecting sea transportation, in particular, bills of lading, and the new transport convention (the Rotterdam Rules) indicate the commercial and political interest vested in sea carriage by both the developed and developing countries. The Hague Rules and the Hague-Visby Rules, products of shipowning interests are influential and widely accepted, determine the responsibilities and liabilities of the carrier where goods are transported using bills of lading or documents of title. On the contrary, the Hamburg Rules, which casts its net wider as a result of a strong political agenda on the part of developing nations, when measured against the numbers of ratification, are of limited application. The current regime of three conventions is, to say the least, undesirable. Emerging new practices in relation to transport documents in the form of electronic bills of lading and electronic waybills as a result of developments in information technology also compound the uncertainties. Hence, the drafting of a new convention which was adopted in 2008.

Chapters 5 and 6 start off with the different guises of a contract of carriage of goods by sea. Chapter 5 deals with voyage charterparties in brief and Chapter 6 with bills of lading, a multipurpose transport document that plays a dominant role in international sales involving sea transportation. Chapter 7 deals with obligations of the carrier and the shipper in respect of a bill of lading under common law and Chapter 8 with the Hague Rules and the Hague-Visby Rules (implemented in the United Kingdom by the Carriage of Goods by Sea Act 1971). Chapter 9, while considering and highlighting the merits of the Hamburg Rules, concludes with a brief account of the new transport convention, known as the Rotterdam Rules which will be open for signature in November 2009.

While sea carriage is the predominant mode of transporting worldwide, other forms of unimodal transport – air, rail and road – also play an important role on the international cargo transportation scene. The responsibilities and liabilities of the parties to transport contracts involving these different modes of transportation have been regulated by various international conventions. Chapter 10 deals with the Warsaw regime that affects international transportation of cargo by air and concludes with a section on the Montreal Convention 1999. Chapter 11 considers the CIM 1999, the international convention affecting transportation by rail and Chapter 12 devotes itself to the Convention on the International Carriage of Goods by Road 1956 (CMR), an international convention affecting international road transportation of cargo.

Containerisation brought its own exciting developments in the form of door-to-door transport using a combination of modes of transportation and the use of a multimodal (combined) transport document. Attempts to harmonise the law through an international convention surprisingly have been unsuccessful. The final chapter in this part therefore looks at the current legal framework against the backdrop of standard forms used by trade associations such as British International Freight Association (BIFA) (in the United Kingdom) and the International Federation of Freight Forwarders Associations (FIATA) which draws upon the United Nations Conference on Trade and Development (UNCTAD)/International Chamber of Commerce (ICC) Rules on Multimodal Transport. As and where relevant, the reader's attention is drawn to recent studies and proposals emanating from international organisations such as the United Nations Economic Commission for Europe (UNECE) and UNCTAD.

CHAPTER 5

TRANSPORTATION OF GOODS BY
SEA – CHARTERPARTIES

INTRODUCTION

As seen in Chapter 1, under a contract for sale on cost, insurance, freight (CIF) terms, the seller is responsible for arranging transport of cargo from his country to the buyer's. Even where the sale is not on CIF terms, transport is still an integral part of an international sale transaction. For instance, in a free on board (FOB) contract, the buyer may arrange transport, or he may ask the seller to arrange transport on his behalf. Depending on the amount of cargo, a number of options are open to the shipper (seller or buyer) where sea carriage is envisaged. Where the cargo is insufficient to fill the entire cargo space of a ship, it is normal for the shipper to find space on a liner service[1] and obtain a bill of lading – a document that the seller is obliged to tender to the buyer in a CIF contract.[2] Where the shipper is the buyer, he is also likely to obtain a bill of lading which, due to its versatility, can be used to sell the goods on to a third party or used as security for raising money to finance the sale.[3] Where the amount of cargo is sufficient to take up a vessel's full cargo carrying capacity, it is commonplace to charter a ship. Under this type of arrangement, the shipowner agrees to make the ship available to the charterer for a specified voyage(s) – for example, from Southampton to Singapore – or a specified period of time – from 1 January 2008 to 1 January 2009. However, not all charterparties fall neatly into these two classifications. A number of variations are found in practice – trip charter, consecutive voyage charter and long term freighting contracts. In a trip charter, the contract is for a voyage on time charter terms thereby providing a minimum/maximum period for the voyage.[4] In a consecutive voyage charter, the contract is for a number of consecutive voyages within an agreed period, and in a long term freighting contract, the agreement is to carry quantities of cargo on particular routes over an agreed period of time with the shipowner choosing the ships.

The contract between the charterer (one who charters the ship) and the shipowner is known as a charterparty.[5] In English law, there is no requirement that it be in a written form. However, it is usual for the charterparty to be in writing. The charterparty will identify the vessel, the cargo it is to carry, the voyage(s) or time for which the ship is made available, and contain terms in respect of the various responsibilities

---

1   In liner service, there is a regular schedule of sailings to particular ports. This is different from tramp shipping where sailings are dependent on cargo and there is no regular schedule. A tramp shipping service is normally used for sending bulk cargo in shiploads. Note that tramps are not common carriers – they are contract carriers. See Buckley, *The Business of Shipping*, 8th edn, 2008 Cornell Maritime.

2   See Chapter 1, pp 15–16.

3   See Chapters 6, 7, 8 and 15. Note that the bill of lading is also a document called for under a documentary credit (letter of credit) arrangement. See Chapter 15 for further on documentary credit arrangements.

4   These are classified however as time charters for the purposes of Law Reform (Frustrated) Contracts Act 1943 which does not apply to voyage charters (s 2(5)). See also *The Eugenia* [1964] 2 QB 226. Note that in a trip charter the charterer pays hire, not freight.

5   The chartering arrangements are not always that simple. It is not unknown for a time charterer to subsequently sub-charter the vessel to another party on a voyage charterparty, as in *The Torepo* [2002] 2 Lloyd's Rep 535.

and liabilities of the shipowner and the charterer. Charterparties have been standard-ised since the beginning of the 20th century by organisations such as the Baltic and International Maritime Conference – now known as the Baltic and International Maritime Council (BIMCO) – and the Chamber of Shipping. A number of standard charter forms are available – some for use with all cargoes, and some for special cargoes, such as grain. Of course, the parties may vary the charterparty clauses, should they wish to. It is not unusual to find amendments or additional clauses, since some of the standard charterparties drafted in the early part of the 20th century do not reflect the current trade practice.[6] Other than standard form charterparties, charterers who charter vessels on a frequent basis (for example, oil companies) have their own charterparty forms – for example, British Petroleum's Beepeevoy and Shell's Shellvoy. Terms expressed in the charterparty, provided it is governed by English law, are subject to rules of interpretation of contract terms and general principles of English contract law.[7] However, English common law implies a few obligations on the part of the shipowner and the charterer, and these are considered in this chapter. Before going on to the common law implied undertakings, a brief description of the different types of charterparties is provided.

TYPES OF CHARTERPARTIES

Charterparties are classified into three (basic) types: voyage charterparties, time charterparties and demise charterparties. A brief description of these three types is given below. However, only the voyage charterparty is examined in this chapter. The others are outside the scope of this book, since they are concerned with the hire, employment or lease of the vessel.

Voyage charterparty

Under a voyage charterparty, the shipowner agrees to charter the vessel to the charterer for one or more specified voyages. The vessel remains under the control of the shipowner who is responsible for equipping and manning the vessel. The crew and master are employees of the shipowner, and he is responsible for their wages. The shipowner in a voyage charterparty undertakes to transport the goods to the port(s) specified in the charterparty. The charterer undertakes to provide the specified cargo and pay for the services either as a lump sum for the voyage, or in terms of the amount and type of cargo carried.

A number of standard forms are in use. The most well known standard form for use with general cargo is GENCON charterparty, approved by BIMCO. The form, despite revisions (in 1922 and 1976), was not comprehensive with the result that parties using GENCON regularly inserted additional clauses.[8] BIMCO therefore produced an amended version of GENCON known as GENCON 1994.[9] The 1994

---

6 *Carras (JC) and Sons (Shipbrokers) Ltd v President of India (The Argobeam)* [1970] 1 Lloyd's Rep 282, at p 287.

7 See *Louis Dreyfus et Cie v Parnaso Cia Naviera SA (The Dominator)* [1959] QB 514 *Salamis Shipping (Panama) Sa v Edm van Meerbeeck and Co SA (The Onsilos)* [1971] 2 Lloyd's Rep 29.

8 See *Overseas Transportation Co v Mineralimportexport (The Sinoe)* [1971] 1 Lloyd's Rep 514.

9 Specimen copy reproduced in Appendix 2.

version has introduced new clauses, such as cl 19, on law and arbitration, and has modified a number of clauses to reflect modern practice – for instance, cl 8 (lien)[10] clause and cl 10 (bills of lading). There are also other standard forms for use with specific cargo – for example, NORGRAIN 89 (North American grain charterparty issued by the Association of Shipbrokers and Agents (USA) Inc) for use in the carriage of grain, OREVOY (the Baltic and International Maritime Conference standard ore charterparty) for use in the carriage of ore, and FERTICON (Chamber of Shipping fertilisers charter) for use in the carriage of fertilisers.[11]

Time charterparty

Under a time charterparty, the charterer hires the vessel for a specified period of time. As in a voyage charter, the shipowner retains control of the ship and the employees on board the ship. However, the charterer is responsible for its deployment, the number of voyages it undertakes, and the destination of the voyages. The shipowner in a time charterparty does not undertake to transport the goods to a specified port(s) as in a voyage charterparty. There are also a number of standard time charter forms – the most well known of these are BALTIME (Baltic and International Maritime Conference uniform time charter) and the NYPE (New York Produce Exchange time charter).[12] Due to the nature of time charterparties, their terms concentrate on employment of vessel, speed of vessel, maintenance of vessel, hire period, return of vessel, payment of hire, etc. Since the emphasis of time charterparties relates to the vessel, they are beyond the scope of this book and therefore not examined in this chapter.[13]

Demise charterparty

Also known as a bareboat charterparty, in this type of charterparty, the shipowner passes possession and control of ship to the charterer. The shipowner is no longer responsible for equipping the ship or employing the crew as in a voyage or time charterparty. For the duration of the charter, the charterer is responsible for manning, equipping and insuring it. Mackinnon LJ, in *Sea and Land Securities v Dickinson and Co*,[14] formulated the difference thus:

> ... the distinction between the demise and other forms of charter contract is as clear as the difference between the agreement a man makes when he hires a boat in which to row himself and the contract he makes with a boatman to take him for a row [at pp 69–70].

Once again, due to its nature, a demise charterparty is beyond the scope of this book.

---

10   For further information, see 'Lien', pp 225–6 below.
11   For specimen copies of these other forms, see Glass, Todd and Clarke, *Standard Form Contracts for the Carriage of Goods*, 2000, LLP.
12   See Appendix 3 for a specimen copy of NYPE 93.
13   See Wilson, *Carriage of Goods by Sea*, 6th edn, 2008, Pearson Longman for an excellent account of time charterparties.
14   [1942] 2 KB 65.

COMMON LAW IMPLIED OBLIGATIONS IN A VOYAGE CHARTERPARTY

As stated earlier, common law implies a number of undertakings on the part of the shipowner and the charterer. On the part of the shipowner, common law implies that he will:

(a) provide a seaworthy ship;

(b) proceed with due dispatch;

(c) carry the cargo to the agreed destination without deviation; and

(d) use due care and skill in navigating the vessel and carrying the goods.

These obligations on the part of the shipowner are also implied in a bill of lading governed by common law. The scope of these undertakings and the effect of the breach of these terms are considered in Chapter 7 below.

For the charterer's part, common law implies that he will:

(a) nominate a safe port; and

(b) not ship dangerous goods without disclosure.

Nomination of a safe port

'Safe port' was defined in *Leeds Shipping v Société Française Bunge (The Eastern City)* [15] in the following manner:

> . . . a port will not be safe unless, in the relevant period of time, the particular ship can reach it, use it and return from it without, in the absence of some abnormal occurrence, being exposed to danger which cannot be avoided by good navigation and seamanship [at p 131].

It is difficult to construct *a priori* an exhaustive list of situations likely to fall within the definition provided in *The Eastern City*. The matter is one of fact and has to be decided in the light of factors such as the vessel's manoeuvrability and availability of weather reports. Most obvious incidents likely to render a port unsafe are meteorological events which cannot be avoided through good navigation. For instance, unpredictable weather and absence of weather reports may render a port unsafe. *The Dagmar* [16] illustrates this well. The defendants in this case ordered the vessel to Cape Chat, where there was a sudden swell and the moorings of the ship came apart, as a result of which she went aground. The master had asked for weather reports, but these were not provided. In the circumstances, the court held that there was no negligence on the master's part, and the port was unsafe.

Disturbances of a political nature may also render a port unsafe. In *Ogden v Graham,* [17] under the voyage charterparty, the vessel was to go to a safe port in Chile, with leave to call at Valparaiso. At Valparaiso, she was ordered to Carrisal Boju. The port was closed by government order, and the vessel was likely to be confiscated on entry. The ship waited for the port to open and discharged the goods. Shipowners claimed

---

15   [1958] 2 Lloyd's Rep 127.

16   [1968] 2 Lloyd's Rep 563. For a recent example, see *The Marinicki* [2003] 2 Lloyd's Rep 655.

17   (1861) 31 LJQB 26.

damages for the delay. The issue was whether political safety came within the safe port obligation. Blackburn J had no hesitation in finding that it did. According to him:

> In the absence of all authority bearing on this matter, I am of the opinion that under the terms of the charterparty like the present the charterer is bound to name a place which at the time he names it is one into which the ship can get; and that although the ship can physically get into it as far as navigation and what may be called the natural incidents are concerned, yet if that would be at the certain risk of confiscation then the place is not a 'safe port' [at p 29].

Obstacles of a temporary nature, however, will not render a port unsafe. In the event of a temporary obstacle, the master will be expected to wait for a reasonable time until it is removed or has abated.[18] Only where the delay is such as to frustrate the object of the contract will there be a breach of the safe port undertaking. In *Grace v General Steam Navigation Co Ltd (The Sussex Oak)*,[19] it was held that an icebound port did not render the port unsafe unless it was icebound for a period which would frustrate the object of the charterparty.

The shipowner is not under an obligation to ensure that the port nominated is safe. On arrival, in the face of obvious danger, if the master enters the port, the safe port undertaking in the charter will not benefit the shipowner since the negligence would have broken the chain of causation.[20] The master can refuse to enter the port nominated if he thinks it is dangerous to enter it. Whether the voyage charter allows the charterer to nominate another port, in the absence of an express term,[21] is open to doubt. The GENCON 1994 charterparty, in cl 1, provides that 'the vessel is to proceed to the discharging port(s) . . . or so near thereto as she may safely get and lie always afloat, and there deliver the cargo' which imparts the right to the shipowner to discharge the goods at another port. The distance of the alternative port from port of discharge that will be tolerated will depend on the availability of alternative safe ports in the immediate vicinity of the discharging port. Where ports are sparse (as is in certain parts of the world), the shipowner will be able to discharge the goods at a port that is a fair distance from the port originally nominated.[22]

A question that vexed shipping lawyers until recently is the scope of the safe port undertaking, that is, when should the port be safe and for what length of time? In other words, is safety of the port an absolute continuing obligation, that is, from the moment of its nomination to the moment of damage,[23] or is it limited to the safety of the port at the time of nomination and its expected safety from the moment of its arrival to its departure? Clarification about the scope was provided by the House of Lords in *Kodros Shipping Corp v Empresa Cubana de Fletes (The Evia) (No 2)*.[24] The vessel

---

18   See *Independent Petroleum Group v Seacarriers* [2006] EWHC 3173 where the port of Beira held to be unsafe, due to failure of port authorities to monitor a navigation channel prone to shifting sands. Damages for detention awarded. For some more recent cases on the safe port obligation see *The Livanita* [2007] EWHC 1317 (Comm); *The Archinidis* [2008] EWCA Civ 175.

19   [1950] 2 KB 383.

20   See *The Kanchenjunga* [1990] 1 Lloyd's Rep 391; *Compania Naviera Maropan SA v Bowaters Lloyd Pulp and Paper Mills Ltd (The Stork)* [1955] 2 QB 68.

21   Where a right to decline a nomination is given, the master is expected to act honestly and in good faith. See *Abu Dhabi National Timber Co v Products Star Shipping Ltd (The Product Star) (No 2)* [1993] 1 Lloyd's Rep 397.

22   See *The Athamas* [1963] 1 Lloyd's Rep 287.

23   See *NV Stoomv Maats 'De Maas' v Nippon Yusen Kaisha (The Pendrecht)* [1980] 2 Lloyd's Rep 56.

24   [1982] 2 Lloyd's Rep 307.

was chartered under the BALTIME form (a time charterparty). The form, expressly in cl 2, provided that the ship was to be employed between safe ports which reflects the undertaking implied at common law. The charterers nominated Basrah (Iraq) as the port of unloading. At the time of nomination, there was no reason to believe that Basrah could be rendered unsafe due to hostilities. The ship arrived in Shatt al Arab on 1 July, but had to wait till 20 August for a berth in Basrah. Unloading was completed on 22 September. However, on that day, all sea traffic in Shatt al Arab ceased, due to war between Iran and Iraq. The arbitration tribunal held the charterparty was frustrated, and the shipowner appealed on the grounds that the frustration was self-induced due to the breach of the safe port undertaking embodied in cl 2 of the charterparty. After careful examination of existing case law on the safe port undertaking, the House of Lords concluded that the undertaking was not a continuing contractual promise, but referred only to the prospective safety of the port. According to Lord Roskill:

> ... the charterer's contractual promise ... relate[s] to the characteristics of the port or place in question and in my view means that, when the order is given, that port or place is prospectively safe for the ship to get to, stay at, so far as necessary, and in due course, leave [at p 315].

The responsibility of the charterer, however, does not extend to abnormal or unexpected events. As Lord Roskill reasoned:

> ... if those characteristics are such as to make that port or place prospectively safe in this way, I cannot think that if, in spite of them, some unexpected and abnormal event thereafter suddenly occurs which creates conditions of unsafety where conditions of safety had previously existed and as a result the ship is delayed, damaged or destroyed, that contractual promise extends to making the charterer liable for any resulting loss or damage, financial or physical. So to hold would make the charterer the insurer of such unexpected and abnormal risks which in my view should fall upon the ship's insurers ... unless ... the owner chooses to be his own insurer in these respects [at p 315].

However, the charterer's obligation is not fulfilled upon nomination of a prospectively safe port. Should a port become unsafe while the vessel is approaching the destination, the charterer is obliged to renominate another port and, should it be already in the port, it should be asked to leave the port forthwith, provided it can. In other words, the charterer is placed under a further and secondary obligation. As expressed by Lord Roskill:

> ... while the primary obligation is ... to order the ship to go only to a port which, at the time when the order is given, is prospectively safe for her, there may be circumstances in which, by reason of a port, which was prospectively safe when the order to go to it was given, subsequently became unsafe ... imposes a further and secondary obligation.
>
> In this connection, two possible situations require to be considered. The first situation is where, after the time charterer has performed his primary obligation by ordering the ship to go to a port which, at the time of such order, was prospectively safe for her, and while she is still proceeding towards such port in compliance with such order, new circumstances arise which render the port unsafe. The second situation is where, after the time charterer has performed his primary obligation by ordering the ship to go to a port which was, at the time of such order, prospectively safe for her, and she has proceeded to and entered such port in compliance with such order, new circumstances arise which render the port unsafe.
>
> In the first situation ... the time charterer ... [is] to order her to go to another port which, at the time when such fresh order is given, is prospectively safe for her. This is

because . . . the charterer . . . [is] to do all that he can effectively do to protect the ship from the new danger in the port which has arisen since his original order for her to go to it was given.

In the second situation . . . [if] it is not possible for the ship so to leave, then no further and secondary obligation is imposed . . . [If] it is possible for the ship to avoid the new danger in the port which has arisen by leaving, then a further and secondary obligation is imposed . . . to order the ship to leave the port forthwith, whether she has completed loading or discharging or not . . . to order her to go to another port which, at the time when such fresh order is given, is prospectively safe for her [at pp 319–20].

On the facts of the case, the court held that there was no breach of the safe port obligation. Basrah was a prospectively safe port at the time of nomination and she was trapped in Basrah due to an abnormal occurrence.

In a case decided in 1983,[25] the vessel was unable to enter Basrah until 20 September. Likelihood of war was imminent, but the charterer did not order the ship to leave, which she could have done. The court found that the charterer was in breach of the safe port obligation.

The secondary obligation, however, raises a number of questions. Does the further obligation require the charterer to be vigilant at all times continuously – that is, to check there are no abnormal or unusual occurrences, or likelihood of abnormal or unusual occurrences in the nominated port or on the way to the nominated port? What standard of care must he exercise? Is it one of due diligence or is it absolute? Is the secondary obligation personal to the charterer? In other words, is he liable for the negligence on the part of expert third parties from whom he has taken advice?

The standard for establishing whether a 'political risk' renders a port unsafe seems to be that of the reasonable shipowner or master as indicated by *K/S Penta Shipping A/S v Ethiopian Shipping Lines Corp (The Saga Cob).*[26] In other words, if a reasonable shipowner or master would decline to send or sail his vessel in the face of a political risk, the port would be unsafe (at p 551).[27]

The meaning of safe port expounded in *The Evia (No 2)* applies equally to voyage charterparties, as was pointed out by Lord Roskill. However, unlike in a time charter, the voyage charterer has no control over employment of the ship. The voyage charter may provide for a range of ports but, once nominated, there is no right to renominate unless there is a clause to that effect. Similarly, in a charterparty naming a specific port. No guidance is provided on how the secondary obligation will be construed in these cases. Their Lordships preferred silence in *The Evia (No 2)*. In the words of Lord Roskill:

. . . What is a voyage charterer to do . . .? My Lords, this problem seems never to have been judicially considered in any detail: indeed . . . in *The Houston City* [1956] AC 266, the Privy Council expressly denied to consider it.

. . . I find it much more difficult to say what are the comparable obligations under a voyage charterparty at any rate where there is no express right to renominate. The well-known decision in *Duncan v Köster (The Teutonia)* (1872) LRPC 171 – a case decided long

---

25   *The Lucille* [1983] 1 Lloyd's Rep 387.

26   [1992] 2 Lloyd's Rep 545. This case considered the safety of the port of Massawa in the light of guerrilla activities of rebel Eritrean forces in and around the coastal waters. Note that this was in the context of a time charterparty. See also *Dow-Europe v Novokia Inc* [1998] 1 Lloyd's Rep 306.

27   See also *Pearl Carriers Inc v Japan Line Ltd (The Chemical Venture)* [1993] 1 Lloyd's Rep 508, at p 520; *The Kanchenjunga* [1990] 1 Lloyd's Rep 391, at pp 397–400.

before the doctrine of frustration assumed its present form – has always presented difficulties and voyage charterparties today almost invariably contain war and strike clauses which give the shipowner and their masters the right sometimes to require another nomination and sometimes an unfettered right to proceed elsewhere. I think, therefore, in a case where only a time charterparty is involved, that it would be unwise ... to give further consideration to the problems of which might arise in the case of voyage charterparty ... I would leave these problems for later consideration if and when they arise [at pp 318–20].

One possible solution is to construe the secondary obligation as giving rise to an implied obligation to renominate in a voyage charterparty. This could be justified on the grounds that to hold a voyage charterer liable in the absence of an express renomination clause would make the charterer the insurer for an emerging imminent danger, the effects of which could be avoided by taking evasive action. This implied obligation to renominate should, however, be used sparingly, that is, only where the voyage charterparty does not have an express renomination clause, and where the circumstances indicate imminent danger. Interestingly, some of the voyage charter-parties do have a renomination clause. For instance, cl 2 of TANKERVOY 87 (Tanker voyage charterparty 1987) provides for nominations and renominations as follows:

Charters shall nominate loading and discharging ports or places and shall have the option of ordering the vessel to a safe port or place en route ...

If after loading or discharging ports or places are nominated, charterers desire to vary them, owners agree to issue such revised instructions as are necessary to give effect to charterer's revised orders ...

In the event of breach of the safe port obligation, the charterer becomes liable for damages incurred by the shipowner – both for physical loss (for example, damage to the fabric of the ship) and economic loss (for example, hire). This right to damages is not affected where a shipowner does not refuse nomination of an unsafe port. However, the shipowner will not be successful with his claim for damages where the charterer is able to show that the acceptance on the part of the shipowner of the nomination amounted to a waiver,[28] or where the behaviour on the part of the shipowner is of a character (that is, unreasonable) that breaks the chain of causation. As Morris LJ indicated in *Compania Naviera Maropan SA v Bowaters Lloyd Pulp and Paper Mills Ltd (The Stork)*:[29]

The owners must not throw their ship away. If, having the opportunity to refrain from obeying the order, and having the knowledge that the ship had been wrongly directed to run into danger, those responsible for the ship allow her to be damaged, when they could have saved her, it would be contrary to reason if damages could be recovered ... they would not be the result of the breach of contract, but of the deliberate and unneces-sary act of those in control of the ship [at p 104].[30]

Not to ship dangerous goods

The obligation on the part of the charterer not to ship dangerous goods without disclosure is also implied by common law in bills of lading. The meaning of

---

28   See *Pearl Carriers Inc v Japan Line Ltd (The Chemical Venture)* [1993] 1 Lloyd's Rep 508.
29   [1955] 2 QB 68.
30   See also *The Kanchenjunga* [1990] 1 Lloyd's Rep 391.

dangerous goods and the scope of the undertaking are examined in detail in Chapter 7, p 217 below.

COMMON LAW IMMUNITIES

Common law implies a number of immunities that operate in favour of the shipowner in charterparties. The shipowner is not liable for loss or damage to cargo that is caused by:

(a) an act of God;

(b) an act of the Queen's enemies; and

(c) inherent vice.

These immunities are also implied in bills of lading governed by common law. The scope of these immunities is examined in Chapter 7.

USUAL EXPRESS TERMS

A voyage charterparty usually contains a number of express terms. It is not possible to examine all the terms, since the wording of these terms varies from charterparty to charterparty. What is provided here is a list of terms which are likely to be found in most standard form charterparties.

The charterparty will contain a number of clauses, including introductory clauses identifying the vessel's identity, its cargo capacity, the time from when performance of the charter is to start and cancellation clause.[31] Where the vessel is in the port of loading, it would be easy to fix the start date precisely. Since, the vessel, in most cases, is unlikely to be at the port of loading, it is common practice to indicate where the vessel is on the date of the charter or when it can be expected to be ready to load. Express terms relating to the position of a ship on the date of the charter has import-ant consequences. In *Behn v Burness*,[32] the charter stated that the vessel was described as 'now in the port of Amsterdam'. At the time of the charter, the vessel was 62 miles away and arrived at Amsterdam four days later. The charterer refused to load the cargo onto the ship. The clause was held to be a condition, since charterers use the position of the ship on the date of the charter to calculate the time of the ship's arrival at the port of loading and inaccurate statements in respect of position would under-mine the foundation of the contract. Similarly, 'expected ready to load'[33] clauses, it seems, will be construed as conditions. For instance, in *Maredelanto Compañia Naviera SA v Bergbau-Handel Gmbh (The Mihalis Angelos)*,[34] the ship was chartered for a voyage from Haiphong to Hamburg or other European ports. The charter described the vessel as 'now trading and expected ready to load under this charter about 1 July 1965'. On

---

31   See, for instance, *The Democritos* [1976] 2 Lloyd's Rep 149.

32   (1863) 3 B&S 1; (1863) Ex Ch 751.

33   These clauses should not be confused with NOR (notice of readiness). 'Notice of readiness' (to load) by custom is given by the shipowner to the charterer thus triggering the running of laytime (time agreed for loading/discharging of cargo). See *The Mexico 1* [1990] 1 Lloyd's Rep 507 on the effect of failure to give NOR on laytime. See also *The Happy Day* [2002] 2 Lloyd's Rep 487 on notice of readiness to discharge.

34   [1971] 1 QB 164.

17 July, the charterers repudiated their contract. There was evidence on the date of the charter (25 May 1965) that the owners could not have reasonably estimated the vessel to be at Haiphong on 1 July. The court held that the 'expected ready to load' was a condition and the repudiation effective. According to Megaw LJ:

> [The owner] is undertaking that he honestly and on reasonable grounds believes at the time of the contract that the date named is the date when the vessel will be ready to load. Therefore, in order to establish a breach of that obligation, the charterer has the burden of showing that the owner's contractually expressed expectation was not his honest expectation, or at least that the owner did not have reasonable grounds for it.
>
> In my judgment, such a term in a charterparty ought to be regarded as being a condition of the contract . . . that is, that when it has been broken, the other party can, if he wishes, by intimation to the party in breach, elect to be released from performance of his further obligations under the contract; and he can validly do so without having to establish that on the facts of the particular case the breach has produced serious consequences which can be treated as 'going to the root of the contract' . . . [at p 204].

Clauses on specific cargo or cargoes and the quantity to be carried, agreed rate of freight, time allowed for loading and unloading of the cargo (called laydays) are also found in the charter. Where the charterer does not load the cargo specified, he is in breach of the charterparty. In these circumstnaces, the shipowner can repudiate the contract. As to whether the shipowner exercises this right, or agrees to load cargo of another type, is dependent on the circumstances. Where the market conditions do not favour shipping interests – that is, in lean times – the shipowner may decide to waive the breach and agree to carry other cargo provided by the charterer. As stated earlier, freight charges are calculated on the kind of cargo carried. Change in cargo will mean change in freight rates, and the charterer will be required to pay the market rate of freight for that cargo.[35] Where the charterer does not provide the amount of cargo agreed he will be required to pay damages for the amount of freight lost (also known as dead freight).

The charterparty, as stated earlier, usually specifies the laydays/laytime,[36] that is, a period of time agreed for the purposes of loading or discharging of cargo from the ship. In the absence of a term on laydays in the charterparty, it will be implied that the operations of loading and discharge are carried out within a reasonable time, taking into account the circumstances of the case such as facilities available at the port, the custom of the port, etc.[37] Where the charterer is unable to load/discharge cargo within the days agreed in the charterparty, the charterer is in breach of the contract and will be liable to the shipowner in damages for detaining the vessel to complete loading/discharging. It is therefore common practice to insert a demurrage clause in the charter, a clause that fixes the amount of damages payable for exceeding the laydays.[38] The courts will normally respect the sum stipulated in the demurrage clause, unless it is so high as to be unconscionable in keeping with the general approach in English law to liquidated damages and penalties.[39] Demurrage runs continuously. It will accrue despite strikes, bad weather, etc, unless the demurrage clause is worded to

---

35   *Steven v Bromley* [1919] 2 KB 722.
36   See cl 6 of GENCON 1994, 1976.
37   *Van Liewen v Hollis* [1920] AC 239.
38   See cl 7 of GENCON 1994, 1976.
39   *Dunlop Pneumatic Tyre Co Ltd v New Garage and Motor Co Ltd* [1915] AC 79, at p 86ff.

take account of these events.[40] There may be exceptions in the charter in relation to laytime provisions, but these will not be effective in respect of demurrage unless they are suitably worded.

It is possible that a charterer completes the loading/discharging operation before the expiry of the laydays. Where this is the case, the charterer cannot detain the ship on the basis that the laydays have not been exhausted – the reason being that laydays are for the sole purpose of loading/discharging operations. So where, after completion of loading and within the laytime, the charterer detains the vessel for the purposes of documentation, he will be liable for detention.[41]

Other than the above terms, the charterparty may contain terms about seaworthiness of the ship and deviation, which may displace the common law implied obligations where clearly worded.[42] For instance, cl 3 of GENCON 1994 provides in respect of deviation that 'the vessel has liberty to call at any port or ports in any order, for the purpose to sail without, to tow and/or assist vessels in all situations, and also to deviate for the purpose of saving life and/or property'. In respect of seaworthiness, for example, cl 1(a) of TANKERVOY 87 states that 'the owners shall before and at the beginning of the loaded voyage exercise due diligence to make the vessel seaworthy and in every way fit for the voyage, with her tanks, valves, pumps and pipelines tight, staunch, strong and in good order and condition with a full and efficient complement of master, officers and crew for a vessel of her type, tonnage and flag'.

Clauses exempting the carrier from liability for loss or damage to goods due to events such as the negligence of the master of crew, storms, strikes, wars and ice are also commonly found in charterparties.[43] Some of the express exemption clauses frequently found in charterparties are also found in bills of lading and are therefore examined in Chapter 7.

Jurisdiction, arbitration and applicable law clauses[44] are also not uncommon. Where the standard form does not provide for these, it may well be in the parties' interests to come to an agreement on choice of law and choice of jurisdiction to avoid nasty surprises in the course of resolving disputes. Interestingly, many charterparties choose England as the venue and English law as the applicable law – perhaps due to England's historical past in shipping and commerce.

As stated earlier, in a voyage charter, the master may be asked to issue bills of lading by the charterer. Bills of lading issued under charterparties frequently incorporate terms contained in the charterparty. The extent to which these terms bind the bill of lading holder (who is not the charterer as in the case of a buyer in a CIF contract) are examined in the following chapter.

CONCLUSION

As stated in the introduction to this chapter, even where goods are transported under a voyage charter, it is commonplace for the charterer to obtain bills of lading from the

---

40   *The John Michalos* [1987] 2 Lloyd's Rep 18; *The Nordic Navigator* [1984] 2 Lloyd's Rep 182.
41   *Nolisement (Owners) v Bunge y Born* [1971] 1 KB 160.
42   See Chapter 7, pp 213–16 below.
43   See, eg, cll 2, 16, 17 and 18 of GENCON 1994; cl 26 of TANKERVOY 87.
44   See Chapters 16 and 17 on jurisdiction and applicable law issues and Chapter 19 for arbitration.

master regardless of whether or not the sale is on CIF terms. The bill of lading's pivotal role in international commerce is due to characteristics peculiar to it. The next four chapters therefore concentrate on the characteristics of a bill of lading, common law as it affects bills of lading and the international conventions that determine the responsibilities and liabilities arising under a bill of lading.

FURTHER READING

Baker, 'The safe port obligation and employment and indemnity clauses' [1988] LMCLQ 43.

Baker and David, 'The politically unsafe port' [1986] LMCLQ 112.

Baughen, *Shipping Law*, 3rd edn, 2004, Cavendish Publishing.

Boyd, Burrows, and Foxton (eds), *Scrutton on Charterparties and Bills of Lading*, 20th edn, 1996, Sweet & Maxwell.

Colinvaux *et al*, *Carver's Carriage by Sea*, 2 vols, 13th edn, 1982, Stevens.

Cooke *et al*, *Voyage Charters*, 3rd edn, 2007, LLP.

Davenport, 'Unsafe ports, again' [1993] LMCLQ 150.

Herman, and Goldman, 'The master's negligence and charterer's warranty of safe port/berth' [1983] LMCLQ 615.

Hibbits, 'The impact of the Iran-Iraq cases on the law of frustration of charterparties' [1985] JMLC 441.

Powles, 'Sea ports and voyage charterparties' [1987] JBL 491.

Reynolds, 'The concept of safe ports' [1974] LMCLQ 179.

Tetley, *Marine Cargo Claims*, 4th edn, 2008, Blais.

United Nations Conference on Trade and Development, *Charterparties: A Comparative Analysis (Report by UNCTAD Secretariat)*, TD/B/C4/ISL/55, 27 June 1990.

Wilson, *Carriage of Goods by Sea*, 6th edn, 2008, Longman.

CHAPTER 6

BILLS OF LADING

INTRODUCTION

The bill of lading, as indicated in Chapter 1, plays a vital role in international commerce where sea carriage is envisaged. Its use is traceable to the 14th century.[1] In its primitive form, it was a receipt indicating the nature of the cargo and the quantity. Time, convenience and mercantile practice saw the incorporation of terms of carriage in the bill of lading and its elevation to a document of title, such that possession of the bill of lading was deemed constructive possession of the goods. Recognition of the bill of lading as a symbol for the goods made way for the sale of goods to a third party during transit (that is, while they were on the high seas). Goods were symbolically delivered by endorsement and transfer of the bill of lading.[2] Transfer of the bill of lading to the third party did not, however, operate to transfer rights under the bill of lading to the third party, due to the doctrine of privity.[3] In order to effect an automatic transfer of contractual rights to the endorsee, the Bills of Lading Act was enacted in 1855. Due to problems caused largely by poor drafting,[4] this statute was repealed in 1992, and replaced with the Carriage of Goods by Sea Act 1992.[5]

This chapter considers the nature of a bill of lading, the evidentiary effect of statements made on a bill of lading, and the rights and liabilities of the holder of a bill under both the Bills of Lading Act 1855 and the Carriage of Goods by Sea Act 1992. The latter part of this chapter focuses on the problems created by the Bills of Lading Act 1855, since it provides the necessary backdrop to assess and appreciate the changes instituted by the Carriage of Goods by Sea Act 1992. The concluding part addresses electronic bills of lading, the CMI[6] Rules on Electronic Bills of Lading and the BOLERO (Bills of Lading in Europe)[7] Rules.

---

1   See Bennett, *The History and Present Position of the Bill of Lading as a Document of Title to Goods,* 1914, CUP for an excellent historical account. Also see McLaughlin, 'The evolution of the ocean bill of lading' (1926) 35 Yale LJ 548; Section II of Kozolchyk, 'Evolution and present state of the ocean bill of lading from a banking law perspective' [1992] JMLC 161.

2   See *Sanders v Maclean* (1883) 11 QBD 327, at p 341.

3   Note, however, that the Contract (Rights of Third Parties) Act 1999 enables a third party to sue on the contract provided the conditions laid down in the Act are met. However, by virtue of s 6(5), contracts of carriage by sea are excluded. See s 6(6)(b) for the definition of contracts for carriage of goods by sea. See also 'Liability in contract and in tort and availability of limitation', Chapter 8, pp 254–9 below.

4   See for instance, Trietel, 'Bills of lading and third parties' [1982] LMCLQ 294.

5   The text of this Act is available in Carr and Kidner, *International Trade Law Statutes and Conventions,* 5th edn, 2008, Routledge-Cavendish.

6   Comité Maritime International.

7   Bolero International Ltd, London, UK.

NATURE OF A BILL OF LADING

Neither common law nor existing legislation affecting bills of lading[8] or the terms of carriage where a bill of lading is used[9] provide a definition of a bill of lading. Its essence is to be gathered from the various functions it assumes. It is a receipt, evidence of the contract of carriage, a contract of carriage and a document of title, depending on whether the holder of the bill of lading is the shipper, consignee, or endorsee. The many roles are examined below.

Bill of lading as a receipt

In the hands of the shipper, the bill of lading is a receipt for:

(a) the quantity of goods received;

(b) the condition of goods received; and

(c) leading marks.

The evidentiary weight of representations relating to quantity and condition of the goods, and leading marks, is not uniform. It is dependent on factors such as whether the bill of lading is held by the shipper or an endorsee, and whether it falls within the Carriage of Goods by Sea Act 1971, or outside of it.

Bills within the Carriage of Goods by Sea Act 1971

Under Art III(3) of the Carriage of Goods by Sea Act 1971, the carrier is obliged, on demand by the shipper, to issue a bill of lading which contains, among other things, the leading marks (marks on packaging necessary for identification of the goods), the number of packages or pieces, or the quantity or weight of the goods, and the apparent order and condition of the goods. Statements made on the bill of lading are regarded as *prima facie* evidence of the receipt of the goods as described under Art III(4). Proof to the contrary may therefore be provided by the carrier. Once transferred to a third party acting in good faith, however, the carrier cannot submit proof to the contrary. This change in the evidentiary weight of the statements is obviously to protect the transferee, who purchases the goods relying on information contained in the bill of lading.[10]

---

8   Section 1(2) of the Carriage of Goods by Sea Act 1992 refers only to transferable bills for the purposes of the Act. This reference only to a transferable bill has raised doubts as to whether a non-transferable bill of lading (also known as a straight bill of lading) can be regarded as a document. Eg, in *Voss v APL Co Pte Ltd* [2002] 2 Lloyd's Rep 707, at p 720, the Singapore Court of Appeal said that confusion in respect of whether a straight bill of lading was a document of title (that is, presentation of document for the purposes of taking delivery) was caused by the Carriage of Goods by Sea Act 1992 which requires the bill of lading to be transferable before it is a bill of lading for the purposes of the Act. See *The Rafaela S* [2003] EWCA Civ 556 for the approach in the English courts. See also Chapter 8, pp 269–73 below.

9   Carriage of Goods by Sea Act 1971 – legislation implementing the Hague-Visby Rules. See Chapter 8 for further on the Hague-Visby Rules. Note, however, the UN Convention on the Carriage of Goods by Sea Act 1978 provides a definition in its Art 1(7). See Chapter 9.

10 See Chapter 8, pp 242–3 below, for further discussion.

Bills outside the Carriage of Goods by Sea Act 1971

Statements as to quantity

Common law regards a statement specifying quantity received in a bill of lading as *prima facie* evidence of the quantity shipped. The burden of proving that the cargo as specified has not been shipped falls on the carrier. This burden is an absolute one in that the carrier must show that the goods were in fact not shipped. In *Smith v Bedouin Steam Navigation Co*,[11] the bill of lading stated that 1,000 bales of jute had been shipped, whereas only 988 bales were delivered. It was held that the carrier could successfully discharge the burden of proof only if he could show that, in point of fact, the goods were not shipped, not merely that the goods may not possibly have been shipped (at p 79).

Where it is established that the goods were not in fact shipped, the carrier, at common law, is not liable even against a bona fide transferee of the bill for value. In *Grant v Norway*,[12] the master of the ship signed a bill of lading which stated that 12 bales of silk had been shipped. The cargo, in fact, had not been loaded. The endorsees had no remedy once the carrier had established that the cargo had not been loaded, on the grounds that the master had no authority to sign bills of lading for goods that had not been put on board the ship. The *Grant v Norway* decision does not favour the consignee or endorsee who normally relies on statements made on the bill of lading, thus undermining the purpose of a bill of lading in international commerce.

The *Grant v Norway* problem was addressed by s 3 of the Bills of Lading Act 1855, according to which:

> . . . every bill of lading in the hands of a consignee or endorsee for valuable consideration representing goods to have been shipped on board a vessel shall be conclusive evidence of such shipment as against the master or other person signing the same, notwithstanding that such or some part thereof may not have been so shipped, unless such holder of the bill of lading shall have had actual notice at the time of receiving the same that the goods had not in fact been laden on board.
>
> Provided that the master or other person so signing may exonerate himself in respect of such misrepresentation by showing that it was caused without any default on his part, and wholly by the fraud of the shipper, or of the holder, or some person under whom the holder claims.

The solution offered in this provision was of limited use since it raised an estoppel only where the holder has an independent cause of action against the party signing the bill. It did not create a cause of action in favour of the party holding the bill. Further, the statement was conclusive evidence only against the master or other person signing the bill, and did not extend to the carrier!

The Bills of Lading Act 1855 was repealed[13] and replaced by the Carriage of Goods by Sea Act 1992. According to s 4 of this legislation (which replaces s 3 of the Bills of Lading Act 1855), statements in bills of lading representing goods to have been shipped on board a vessel, or as received for shipment on board a vessel signed by the master of the vessel or by a person who has express, implied or apparent authority of

---

11   [1896] AC 70.
12   (1851) 10 CB 665.
13   See s 6(2) of the Carriage of Goods by Sea Act 1992.

the carrier to sign bills of lading will, in the hands of the lawful holder of the bill of lading, be regarded as conclusive evidence against the carrier of the shipment of the goods or the receipt of the goods for shipment. The focus of s 4 is bills of lading, which means that the *Grant v Norway* doctrine applies to straight bills of lading or waybills (that is, bills of lading made out to a named consignee that are not transferable).

It would be open to the parties to agree that the statements on waybills are to be regarded as conclusive evidence in the hands of the consignee who takes it in good faith. The CMR Rules on Waybills[14] provides for such a possibility in Rule 5(a)(ii) as follows:

> In the absence of reservation by the carrier, any statement in a sea waybill or similar document as to the quantity or condition of the goods shall:
> (a) as between the carrier and shipper be *prima facie* evidence of receipt of the goods as so stated;
> (b) as between the carrier and the consignee be conclusive evidence of receipt of the goods as for stated, and proof to the contrary shall not be permitted, provided always that the consignee has acted in good faith.

However, for these Rules to apply they must be incorporated into the waybill. But if these Rules are in common use it may be possible to argue that they have become part of mercantile custom, even in the absence of incorporation.

Endorsement of the bill of lading with statements such as 'weight and quantity unknown', and 'said to weigh 10 tons', is open to the carrier. Such endorsements are recognised by the courts, since information on quantity entered on a bill of lading is based on statements made by the shipper and which are not normally verified by the carrier. Where the bill of lading contains statements such as 'quantity unknown' alongside the gross weight entered by the shippers for the purposes of s 4, the weight entered is not a representation that the quantity was shipped.[15]

Statements as to condition

In the hands of a shipper, statements as to condition of the goods shipped are regarded as *prima facie* evidence. However, in the hands of the bona fide transferee for value, the statements provide conclusive evidence. In *Compania Naviera Vascongada v Churchill*,[16] timber awaiting shipment was stained by petroleum. The master issued a bill of lading which stated that the goods were shipped in apparent good order and condition. There was no reference to the bad condition of the goods. As against the transferee, the carriers were estopped from denying the veracity of their statement in the bill of lading.

---

14 Text available in Carr and Kidner, *International Trade Law Statutes and Conventions*, 5th edn, 2008, Routledge-Cavendish.
15 See *The Mata K* [1998] 2 Lloyd's Rep 614, where Clarke J said:
      . . . a bill of lading which states that 11,000 tones of cargo were shipped 'quantity unknown' is not a representation that 11,000 tonnes were shipped. Any other conclusion would give no meaning to the expression 'quantity unknown' [at p 616].
    See also *Noble Resources Ltd v Cavalier Shipping Corp (The Atlas)* [1996] 1 Lloyd's Rep 642, at p 646; *River Gurara (Cargo Owner) v Nigerian National Shipping Line Ltd* [1998] 1 Lloyd's Law Rep 225, at p 234. See also Chapter 8, pp 242–3 below.
16 [1906] 1 KB 237.

This estoppel is effective only where the defects would be apparent to the carrier on a reasonable inspection of the cargo. In *Silver v Ocean Steamship Co*,[17] a cargo of Chinese eggs packed in tins were not covered with cloth or any other form of packing. No mention of the defective packing was made on the bills. On arrival, the goods were found to be damaged. It was also found that the tins had pinhole perforations. The carrier was estopped from denying the insufficient packing of the tins but could not be estopped from alleging the presence of the pinhole perforations, since these would not have been apparent on a reasonable inspection. This suggests that the standard of care required of a carrier is no more than that of reasonable diligence.

The carrier can make reservations on the bill of lading with statements such as 'condition unknown'. Such phrases are construed strictly, since statements as to condition are presumed to be made by the carrier only after a reasonable inspection of the cargo.[18]

It may not, however, be possible for the master to include a statement regarding the apparent order or condition of the goods if the description of the goods in the bill of lading makes reference to the less than perfect condition of the goods, as for instance, where the goods are described as damaged vehicles. In *Sea Success Maritime v African Maritime Carriers*[19] the cargo of steel was rusty. The charterer intended to incorporate in the bill of lading the apparent order and description of the cargo as found by the surveyors. In these circumstances, according to Aikens J 'there would be no need to qualify the statement of the apparent order and condition of the cargo as described in the bill of lading presented for signature by the master or his agent' (at para 35).

Statements as to leading marks

Where the carrier records leading marks on the bill of lading, he will not be estopped at common law from denying that the goods were shipped under the marks as described in the bill. However, where the marks are essential to the identification or description of the cargo, the *prima facie* evidence rule is applied. In *Parsons v New Zealand Shipping Co*,[20] frozen lambs, shipped under a bill of lading, stated that 608 carcasses had been shipped bearing the mark 622X. On arrival, endorsees found that 101 of the 608 carcasses carried a different mark, 522X. The endorsees refused to accept delivery of the carcasses bearing 522X. The issue turned on whether the marks were material to the identity of the goods – that is, whether they indicated characteristics essential to the nature and identity of the goods, or whether they were placed purely for easy tracing. On the particular facts, the marks were not found material to the identity of the goods and the carrier was not estopped from denying that all the carcasses shipped bore the mark 622X. As Collins J explained:

> ... if mere identification marks are within the estoppel, any discrepancy between the mark on the goods and the marks in the margin would equally destroy the identity. Every difference would be equally material, whether the result of accident or clerical error. To hold this would impose an enormous and, indeed, having regard to the

---

17   [1930] 1 KB 416; (1930) 142 LT 244.
18   Such statements are to be based on a reasonable assessment of the apparent order or condition of the goods. See Colman, J, *The David Agmashenebeli* [2003] 1 Lloyd's Rep 92.
19   [2005] EWHC 1542 (Comm).
20   [1901] 1 QB 548.

practice of tallying, an impossible task on the shipowners. Marks which convey a meaning as to the character of the goods stand on a totally different footing. These, it seems to me, would be embraced in the estoppel, because the characteristics which they indicate are essential to the identity of the goods, and an article so marked is a different article in the market from one not so marked. They are material factors in the identity as distinguished from identification of the goods sold, and therefore a discrepancy between the goods described and the goods shipped would mean a difference of identity . . .

But, as it is found as a fact that these figures conveyed nothing whatever to the dealers in these goods, and, further, that the first figure indicated in fact nothing which had any bearing on the quality of the goods, was merely a private mark helping the manufacturers to trace them through their books, it seems to me that any considerations based on them can have no place in the discussion [at pp 565–67].

It seems from the above judgment that the distinction between a public and a private mark is an important factor in establishing whether a mark is, or is not, material to the identity of the goods. A mark is public if it is so recognised by those dealing in goods – that is, to be established by the response of businesses dealing in the goods. If the mark means, is associated with, or indicates in some way the nature of the goods, the *prima facie* evidence rule will come into play.

Enforceability of indemnity agreements for issuing clean bills of lading

It is apt, at this juncture, to say something about indemnity agreements that the shipper and the carrier may enter into for producing a clean bill of lading – that is, a bill of lading with no reservations on it. Reservations on a bill of lading affect its commercial value in a number of ways:

(a) the consignee normally relies on the bill of lading to establish whether the goods as agreed in the contract of sale have been shipped, and where the bill of lading is claused (that is, contains reservations) he may refuse payment;

(b) should the consignee or the shipper (that is, where he still has not got a buyer) want to sell the cargo during transit, it is unlikely to be sold on the basis of a claused bill of lading; and

(c) as a document of title,[21] the bill of lading is often used to raise money from banks and finance houses. These institutions normally prefer to lend money against a clean bill of lading.[22]

Given the commercial importance of a clean bill of lading, it is not unusual for the shipper to ask the carrier to issue one on the understanding that he will indemnify the carrier for any losses incurred by him as a result of issuing such a bill. Enforceability of such agreements really depends on the circumstances of each case. Where the carrier, despite his knowledge of the unsatisfactory condition of the goods, issues an unclaused bill, the indemnity agreement with the shipper will be unenforceable should the shipper fail to pay. *Brown, Jenkinson and Co Ltd v Percy Dalton (London) Ltd*[23] provides a good illustration. In this case, the plaintiffs issued a clean bill of lading even though they knew that the barrels containing

---

21   See 'Bill of lading as document of title', pp 181–3 below.
22   See Chapter 15.
23   [1957] 2 Lloyd's Rep 1.

orange juice were old and leaking, against an indemnity from the defendants, which read:

1   We the undersigned hereby certify that we are aware that in connection with the undermentioned goods . . . the following have been noted at the time of shipment: old and frail containers in leaking condition . . . to avoid any misunderstanding with third parties, we request no mention be made of the above in the bills of lading.

2   . . .we herewith undertake to indemnify the master, vessels, the owners or their representatives against all losses or damage of any nature whatsoever which might arise from the issuance of clean bill of lading for the said goods.

The plaintiffs sued the defendants on the indemnity agreement for the loss suffered. Since the plaintiffs made a representation on the bill of lading which they knew to be false, the court held that the agreement was unenforceable for fraud. According to Morris LJ:

. . . on the facts which are not in dispute, the position was, therefore, that at the request of the defendants the plaintiffs made a representation which they knew to be false and which they intended should be relied on by persons who received the bill of lading, including any banker who might be concerned. In these circumstances, all the elements of the tort of deceit were present. Someone who could prove that he suffered damage by relying on the representation could sue for damages. I feel impelled to the conclusion that a promise to indemnify the plaintiffs against any loss resulting to them from making the representation is unenforceable. The claim cannot be put forward without basing it in an unlawful transaction. The promise on which the plaintiffs rely is, in effect, this: If you make a false representation which will deceive indorsees or bankers, we will indemnify you against any loss that may result to you. I cannot think that a court should lend its aid to enforce such a bargain [p 9].

Besides public policy, it goes without saying that the court was preserving the integrity of the bill of lading in international commerce. Pearce LJ makes this point lucidly:

. . . in the last 20 years, it has become customary, in the short-sea trade in particular, for shipowners to give a clean bill of lading against an indemnity from the shipper in certain cases where there is a *bona fide* dispute as to the condition or packing of the goods. This avoids the necessity of rearranging any letter of credit, a matter which can create difficulty where time is short. If the goods turn out to be faulty, the purchaser will have recourse against the shipping owner, who will in turn recover under his indemnity from the shippers. Thus, no one will ultimately be wronged.

This practice is convenient where it is used with conscience and circumspection, but it has its perils if it is used with laxity and recklessness. It is not enough that the banks or the purchasers who have been misled by clean bills of lading may have recourse at law against the shipping owner. They are intending to buy goods, not law suits . . . trust is the foundation of trade; and bills of lading are important documents. If the banks and purchasers felt that they could no longer trust bills of lading, the disadvantage to the commercial community would far outweigh any conveniences provided by the giving of clean bills of lading against indemnities [p13].

Of course, indemnities given in genuine circumstances – for example, where there is a dispute about the condition of the goods, or adequacy of packaging, between the shipowner and the shipper – are enforceable.[24]

---

24   See 'Bills of Lading and Fraud', pp 195–7 below.

Bill of lading as evidence of contract of carriage

A bill of lading, even though it normally contains the terms of carriage, is regarded *in the hands of the shipper* as evidence of the contract of carriage, since the contract with the shipper is likely to have been concluded orally long before the issue of the bill of lading, and it is possible that the document varies some of the agreed terms or contains terms that have not been agreed to by the parties. According to Lush J in *Crooks v Allan:*[25]

> . . . a bill of lading is not the contract, but only evidence of the contract; and it does not follow that a person who accepts the bill of lading which the shipowner hands him necessarily, and without regard to circumstances, binds himself to abide by all its stipulations. If a shipper of goods is not aware when he ships them, or is not informed in the course of the shipment, that the bill of lading which will be tendered to him will contain such a clause, he has a right to suppose that his goods are received on the usual terms, and to require a bill of lading which shall express those terms [pp 40–41].

Where the terms contained in the bill of lading do not reflect the terms agreed orally, evidence regarding the oral agreement may be submitted by the shipper. In *The Ardennes,*[26] the shipper of a consignment of oranges was assured by the ship's agent that the vessel would sail directly to London and arrive there before 1 December. The ship, however, stopped at Antwerp on her way to London and arrived at London on 4 December. When sued for breach of contract by the shipper, the shipowner relied on the bill of lading which contained a clause giving the ship liberty to deviate during the course of her voyage. The court, however, came to the conclusion that the oral evidence put forward by the shipper was admissible. Lord Goddard CJ clearly acknowledged in his judgment that 'a bill of lading is not, in itself, the contract between the shipowner and the shipper of the goods, though it has been said to be excellent evidence of its terms . . . the contract has come into existence long before the bill of lading is signed' (p 59).

The judgment from the Court of Appeal in *Cho Yang Shipping Co Ltd v Coral (UK) Ltd*[27] affirms the above view:

> . . . in English law, the bill of lading is not the contract between the original parties but is simply evidence of it (for example, *The Ardennes* (1950)).[28] Indeed, though contractual in form, it may in the hands of a person already in contractual relation with the carrier (for example, a character) be no more than a receipt (*Rodocanachi v Milburn* (1886)).[29] Therefore, as between shipper and carrier, it may be necessary to inquire what the actual contract between them was; merely to look at the bill of lading may not in all cases suffice. It remains necessary to look at and take into account the other evidence bearing upon the relationship between the shipper and the carrier and the terms of contract between them . . . The terms upon which the goods have been shipped may not be in all respects the same as those actually set in the bill of lading . . . [at p 643].

---

25   (1879) 5 QBD 38.
26   [1951] 1 KB 55.
27   [1997] 2 Lloyd's Rep 641.
28   [1950] 2 All ER 517; [1951] 1 KB 55.
29   (1886) 18 QBD 67.

Bill of lading as contract of carriage

The view that the bill of lading is evidence of the contract of carriage is correct only in so far as the holder of the bill is the shipper. Upon endorsement to a third party (that is, the consignee or endorsee) *in the hands of that third party*, the bill of lading is the contract of carriage. Any oral or written agreement between the shipper and the shipowner not expressed on the bill of lading will not affect the third party on grounds of lack of notice. In *Leduc v Ward*,[30] the endorsee of a bill of lading sued the shipowner for loss to cargo as a result of deviation. The shipowner contended that they were not liable, since the shipper was aware, at the time of shipment, that the ship would deviate. The court held that anything that took place between the shipper and the shipowner not embodied in the bill of lading could not affect the endorsee. The endorsee acquired his rights of suit and liability in respect of the goods by virtue of s 1 of the Bills of Lading Act 1855, which provides that 'every consignee . . . every endorsee . . . shall have transferred to and vested in him all rights of suit, and be subject to the same liability in respect of such goods, as if the contract contained in the bill of lading had been made with himself'. According to Lord Esher MR:

> . . . it has been suggested that the bill of lading is merely in the nature of a receipt for the goods, and that it contains no contract for anything but the delivery of the goods at the place named therein. It is true that, where there is a charterparty, as between the shipowner and the charterer, the bill of lading may be merely in the nature of a receipt for the goods, because all the other terms of the contract of carriage are contained in the charterparty; and the bill of lading is merely given as between them to enable the charterer to deal with the goods while in the course of transit; but, where the bill of lading is indorsed over, as between the shipowner and the indorsee, the bill of lading must be considered to contain the contract, because the former has given it for the purpose of enabling the charterer to pass it on as the contract of carriage for the goods [at p 479].

Bill of lading as document of title

Physical inability of the merchant to deliver the cargo (due to long transit periods) may have triggered the custom amongst merchants to treat the bill of lading as a symbol for the goods. Until goods are physically delivered, possession of the bill of lading is deemed to be constructive possession of the goods. Transfer of the bill of lading by the seller to the buyer is deemed to be a symbolic delivery of the goods to the buyer, and the buyer, on the ship's arrival, could demand delivery of the goods. As Bowen LJ said, in *Sanders v Maclean*:[31]

> . . . a cargo at sea, while in the hands of the carrier, is necessarily incapable of physical delivery. During this period of transit and voyage, the bill of lading by the law merchant is universally recognised as its symbol; and the endorsement and delivery of the bill of lading operates as a symbolical delivery of the cargo . . . It is a key which in the hands of the rightful owner is intended to unlock the door of the warehouse, floating or fixed, in which the goods may chance to be [p 341].

Since possession of the bill of lading is regarded as good as possessing the goods, the buyer can sell the goods on while they are at sea to a third party by simply endorsing

---

30 (1888) 20 QBD 475.
31 (1883) 11 QBD 327.

the bill of lading and delivering it to the third party. The third party, by becoming the holder, can demand delivery of the goods on arrival.

Not all bills of lading, however, are transferable. To impart transferability to a bill of lading, it must be drafted as an *order* bill – that is, where the carrier is to deliver the goods to a *named consignee or to his order or assigns*. It must be noted that bills of lading made out to named consignees, known as straight bills of lading, are not documents of title.[32]

Upon endorsement, the endorsee takes the place of the original party to the bill of lading, and will be able to sue and be sued on all the terms, express and implied, in the bill of lading despite privity of contract. This is achieved by the combined operation of ss 2 and 3 of the Carriage of Goods by Sea Act 1992.[33] The consignee or endorsee under the Bills of Lading Act 1855 acquired their rights and liabilities by virtue of s 1 which provides:

> Every consignee of goods named in a bill of lading, and every endorsee of a bill of lading, to whom property in the goods therein mentioned shall pass upon or by reason of such consignment or endorsement, *shall have transferred to and vested in him all rights of suit, and be subject to the same liabilities in respect of such goods as if the contract contained in the bill of lading had been made with himself* [emphasis added].

Quality of title acquired by transferee

Commonly said to be a negotiable document in commercial circles, a bill of lading is not to be equated with a bill of exchange, which is a negotiable instrument in the strict (legal) sense of the term.[34] The holder of an endorsed bill of lading does not obtain a bill of lading free of defects. That is, a holder who endorses a bill of lading cannot give a better title than the one he has. So, if he has no title, he cannot pass one. In other words, the bona fide transferee for valuable consideration of a bill of lading acquires as good a title as the transferor possesses. As Lord Campbell in *Gurney v Behrend*[35] observed:

> ... a bill of lading is not, like a bill of exchange or a promissory note, a negotiable instrument which passes by mere delivery to a bona fide transferee for valuable consideration, without regard to the title of the parties who make the transfer. Although the shipper may have endorsed in blank a bill of lading deliverable to his assigns, his rights are not affected by an appropriation of it without his authority. If it be stolen from him, or transferred without his authority, a subsequent bona fide transferee for value cannot make title under it against the shipper of the goods. The bill of lading only represents the goods, and, in this instance, the transfer of the symbol does not operate more than a transfer of what is represented [at p 271].

---

32 However, in *The Rafaela S* [2003] EWCA Civ 556, where the straight bill of lading required the bill of lading to be presented for delivery, it was held to be a document of title for the purposes of the Hague-Visby Rules (see Chapter 8, pp 269–70 (below). See also Tiberg, 'Legal qualities of transport documents' [1998] Tulane Maritime LJ 1; *Voss v APLC Co Pte Ltd* [2002] 2 Lloyd's Rep 707 (Singapore, CA).

33 See 'The Carriage of Goods by Sea Act 1992', pp 189–93 below for further on these sections and the developing case law in this area.

34 See 'Bills of Exchange', Chapter 15.

35 (1854) 3 E&B 262.

It therefore makes more sense in legal terms to talk of the bill of lading as a transferable document[36] rather than a negotiable document.

Delivery against bills of lading

Since the bill of lading is a document of title, the carrier is under an obligation to deliver the cargo only against an original bill of lading. If the carrier delivers goods without the production of a bill of lading, he will be liable in contract and in tort (for conversion) to the bill of lading holder.[37] Where a person seeks to take delivery of goods in the absence of an original bill of lading, he must prove to the carrier's reasonable satisfaction that he is entitled to possession of the goods and there is a reasonable explanation for the absence of the bills of lading – for instance, where it can be shown that the bills of lading are lost.[38] Frequently, the carrier may be asked to notify a customs broker, banker or warehouseman of the arrival of the goods. Such clauses are known as 'notify party' clauses. 'Notify party' clauses do not curtail the operation of the rule that delivery must take place against the original bill of lading. It is, however, possible that the law of the country or custom of the port requires that goods be delivered to an agent (of the bill of lading holder) without the production of a bill of lading. In these circumstances, it seems, from *The Sormovskiy 3068*, that the carrier will not be liable for breach of contract were he to deliver the goods without presentation. Custom, however, according to Clarke J, must be construed strictly, and must be distinguished from practice. He drew the distinction between law, custom and practice thus:

Law

If it were a requirement of the law of the place of performance that the cargo must be delivered to the CSP as the agent of the plaintiffs without the presentation of an original bill of lading, the defendants would, in my judgment, have performed their obligations under the contract of carriage. Any other conclusion would mean that the contract could not be lawfully performed, which could not have been intended by the parties.

Custom

Equally, if there were a custom of the port . . . that cargo was always delivered to . . . the agent of the person entitled to possession without the production of an original bill of lading, delivery to the [agent] would probably amount to performance of the defendants' obligations under the contract of carriage. However, custom in this context means custom in its strict sense: that it must be reasonable, certain, consistent with the contract, universally acquiesced in and not contrary to law: see *Scrutton on Charterparties*, p 1416.

Practice

Practice must, in my judgment, be distinguished from custom. A vessel may be discharged by any method which is consistent with the practice in the port: see *Carver's Carriage by Sea*, 13th edn, vol 2, para 1542. It would not, however, in my judgment be good performance of the defendants' obligations under the contract if it were merely the practice for vessels to deliver goods to the CSP without presentation of a bill of lading in circumstances where neither the law nor custom (in its strict sense) required it [p 275].[39]

---

36 In some jurisdictions however the bill of lading is regarded as a negotiable document. See Yiannapoulos (ed), *Ocean Bills of Lading: Traditional Forms, Substitutes and EDI Systems*, 1995, Kluwer.

37 See *Sze Hai Tong Bank Ltd v Rambler Cycle Co Ltd* [1959] 2 Lloyd's Rep 114, at p 120.

38 See *Sucre Export SA v Northern Shipping Ltd (The Sormovsky 3068)* [1994] 2 Lloyd's Rep 266.

39 See also *East West Corp v DKBS 1912 and AKTS Svendborg Utaniko Ltd, P&O Nedlloyd BV* [2002] 2 Lloyd's Rep 182, at pp 202–7.

It is common for bills of lading to contain a clause that allows the carrier to discharge goods without production of a bill of lading against a warranty of title, and an indemnity clause in favour of the carrier for any loss he suffers as a result of discharging the goods in the absence of a bill of lading. Clause 46 of the charter in *The Sormovskiy 3068* provided that the shipowners could discharge the cargo against production of a bank guarantee if the original bills of lading were not in the discharge port in time for the vessel's discharge. This clause had been incorporated into the bill of lading. However, according to Clarke J, 'the purpose of the clause was to ensure the [shipowners] would discharge even if the bill of lading was not available for presentation, but on terms they would be protected by a letter of indemnity. It thus contemplated that they would be liable to the holder of the bill of lading if they delivered otherwise than in return for an original bill of lading' (p 274). Put another way, the indemnity clause did not make the delivery of the goods without presentation of the bill of lading lawful. Its purpose was to protect the shipowner if he did do what he was not contractually obliged to do: 'A shipowner who delivers goods without production of a bill of lading does so at his own peril', as Lord Denning said in *Sze Hai Tong Bank Ltd v Rambler Cycle Co Ltd*.[40] Where a bill of lading is lost, according to *The Houda*,[41] the best course of action would be to obtain a court order to the effect that 'on tendering a sufficient indemnity the loss of the bill of lading is not to be set up as a defence'.[42]

Forgery of documents is a common phenomenon in international trade. It is not unknown for forged documents to be presented for delivery purposes. What is the position of the innocent carrier were he to deliver against a forged bill of lading? This issue was examined in *Motis Exports Ltd v Dampskibsselskabet AF 1912 Aktieselskab, Akteiselskabet Dampskibsselskabet Svendborg*.[43] The cargo was carried under Maersk Line bills of lading which included cl 5(3)(b) that stated:

> Where the carriage called for commencement at the port of loading and/or finishes at the port of discharge, the carrier shall have no liability whatsoever for any loss or damage to the goods while in its actual or constructive possession before loading or after discharge over ship's rail, or if applicable, on the ship's ramp, howsoever caused.

The carriers released the goods against forged bills of lading. Rix J in the Queen's Bench concluded that it was a case of misdelivery.[44] The carrier in the Court of Appeal submitted that Rix J was wrong in categorising the event as misdelivery rather than theft and that cl 5(3)(b) excluded liability for theft. On appeal, the court without hesitation agreed that what took place was a misdelivery and that a forged bill of lading is a nullity. In these circumstances, cl 5(3)(b) was ineffective in protecting the carrier. According to Stuart-Smith LJ:

> In my judgment, Mr Justice Rix was correct to characterise what occurred as misdelivery. A forged bill of lading is in the eyes of the law a nullity; it is simply a piece of paper with writing on it, which has no effect whatever. That being so, delivery of the goods was not in exchange for the original bill of lading but for a worthless piece of paper. No doubt so far as the owner of the goods is concerned there is little difference between theft of the goods by taking them without consent of the bailee and delivery with his consent where the consent is obtained by fraud. Mr Dunning, adopting the colourful

---

40 [1959] 2 Lloyd's Rep 11, at p 120.
41 [1994] 2 Lloyd's Rep 541.
42 See Leggatt LJ at p 558.
43 [2000] 1 Lloyd's Rep 211.
44 [1999] 1 Lloyd's Rep 837.

phrase sometimes used of a bill of lading, that it is the key to the floating warehouse ... said that it made no difference whether the thief used a duplicate key to break in and steal or a forged metaphorical key. But one cannot take the metaphor too far. In my judgment, cl 5(3)(b) is not apt on its natural meaning to cover delivery by the carrier or his agent, albeit the delivery was obtained by fraud. I also agree with the judge even if the language was apt to cover such a case; it is not a construction which should be adopted, involving as it does excuse from performing an obligation of such fundamental importance. As a matter of construction, the courts lean against such a result if adequate content can be given to the clause. In my view ... it is wide enough also to cover loss caused by negligence, provided the loss is of the appropriate kind [at p 216].

It seems from the above that a clause absolving the carrier of liability in the event of delivery against a forged bill of lading will not be construed in his favour on the grounds that delivery against an original bill of lading is a fundamental obligation.[45]

It must be noted that, where the bill of lading is made out to a named consignee – that is, where it is not a transferable bill of lading[46] – there is no requirement that delivery take place against its production unless of course the bill of lading expressly states that delivery is to be against presentation.[47] In these circumstances, the straight bill of lading will be regarded as a document of title for the purposes of the Hague-Visby Rules.[48]

RIGHTS AND LIABILITIES OF CONSIGNEE/ENDORSEE

Parties to a bill of lading are normally the shipper (consignor) and the carrier. The English law doctrine of privity prevented a consignee or endorsee of a bill of lading from suing the carrier on the bill of lading. The Bills of Lading Act, enacted in 1855, operated to transfer the rights and liabilities under a contract of carriage to a third party, but was not always effective in transferring them due to:

(a) poor drafting;

(b) restrictive reading of the legislation;

---

45 Mance LJ, however, seems to be suggesting that a clause suitably worded may help the carrier when he says:

There is no dispute that an appropriately worded clause could achieve the result for which the shipowner contends [at p 217].

However, further down the page, he could be construed as saying that the ship's obligation to deliver against presentation of original bills of lading is of central importance when he says:

A shipowner issues bills of lading to serve as the key to the goods and ought usually to be well placed to recognise its own bills of lading ... the bill of lading serves ... an important general role in representing and securing both title to and physical possession of the goods ...

For a more recent case see *Transfigura Beheer BV v Mediterranean Shipping Co (The Amsterdam)* [2007] 1 Lloyd's Rep 88 which treated forged bills of lading as void and as of no effect. *Sze Hai Tong Bank v Rambler Cycle Co Ltd* [1959] 2 Lloyd's Rep 11 cited with approval.

46 Also known as a straight bill of lading.

47 See *The Rafaela S* [2003] EWCA Civ 556. Of course, this raises the important question of whether a non-transferable bill of lading is a document of title. This is an important issue when it comes to the applicability of the Carriage of Goods by Sea Act 1971. See Chapter 8, pp 269–70 below. See also Tetley, 'Waybills: the modern contract for carriage of goods by sea', Pts I and II [1983] JMLC 465; [1984] JMLC 41.

48 See Chapter 8 for further on the Hague-Visby Rules.

(c) concurrent operation of s 1 of the Bills of Lading Act 1855 and s 16[49] of the Sale of Goods Act 1979 (on passing of property); and

(d) inflexibility of the Act to respond adequately to emerging commercial practices brought about by advances in transport technology.

Inadequacies of the Bills of Lading Act 1855 are considered in the following paragraphs, to highlight the improvements introduced by the Carriage of Goods by Sea Act 1992, which replaced the earlier legislation.

Problems caused by the Bills of Lading Act 1855

The problematic s 1 of the Bills of Lading Act 1855 states that:

> ... every consignee of goods named in a bill of lading, and every endorsee of a bill of lading, *to whom property in the goods therein mentioned shall pass* upon or by reason of such consignment or endorsement, shall have transferred to and vested in him all rights of suit, and be subject to the same liabilities in respect of such goods as if the contract contained in the bill of lading had been made with himself [emphasis added].

Under this provision, the consignee or endorsee of a bill of lading acquires the right to sue on the contract only where property has passed to the consignee or endorsee. A consignee or endorsee caught in the following situations cannot sue on the bill of lading:

(a) where no intention to pass property is present – for example, where a pledgee lends money against the bill of lading;[50]

(b) where property passes post-endorsement – where the sale is of goods forming part of a bulk and the goods are ascertained subsequent to endorsement;[51]

(c) where property passes independently of endorsement – for example, where goods are delivered to the buyer against a letter of indemnity due to the late arrival of the bill of lading;[52] and

(d) where no property passes – for example, where goods are lost or the seller reserves title in the goods.

The courts (driven by common sense) veered in favour of the consignee/endorsee by finding an implied contract, or finding liability in tort as the following sections show. The reasoning, largely developed to combat the injustice of a particular case, was not always intellectually tidy.

Position of pledgees

Intention to transfer property, as stated earlier, is essential for acquiring rights and liabilities under the Bills of Lading Act 1855. Transfer of a bill to a third party for raising finance did not impart rights or liabilities to the third party. *Sewell v Burdick*[53]

---

49   This section was amended as a result of the Law Commission Report, *Sale of Goods Forming Part of a Bulk*, Law No 215 HC 807, 1993, HMSO, which are reflected in ss 20A and 20B of the Sale of Goods Act 1979.

50   See 'Position of pledgees', pp 186–7 below.

51   See 'Right to sue and bulk goods', p 187 below.

52   See 'Endorsement of bill of lading after delivery', p 189 below.

53   [1884] 10 AC 74.

illustrates this well. In this case, a cargo of machinery was shipped to Russia. The shipper, who endorsed the bills in blank to the banker in order to obtain a loan, failed to collect the goods at the port of destination. The carrier, unable to recover full freight from the sale of the goods, brought an action for the balance owing against the banker as endorsee. The House of Lords held that the banker was not liable for the balance of freight as he was not a party to the contract of carriage. No intention to transfer ownership in the goods to the bankers was present. This decision is justifiable on policy grounds. To make banks and other pledgees liable to the shipowner for freight and other charges due to the mere fact of endorsement could affect international commerce. Banks and other lenders would refuse to lend money to merchants under such onerous conditions. Of course, in some circumstances, the ruling in *Sewell v Burdick* could act to the detriment of the pledgee – that is, where the pledgee realises his security by taking delivery of the goods. Unable to sue on the bill of lading, he may be able to rely on the existence of an implied contract.[54]

Right to sue and bulk goods

Where goods shipped in bulk are covered by several bills of lading, endorsements of these bills to various third parties are not effective in transferring the rights under the Bills of Lading Act 1855. The right to sue arises only when property in the goods has passed and this, in the sale of part of a bulk, happens only when the goods are ascertained under s 16 of the Sale of Goods Act 1979. The injustice caused by the concurrent operation of s 1 of the Bills of Lading Act and s 16 of the Sale of Goods Act 1979 was corrected by finding either: (a) an implied contract; (b) a special contract; or (c) liability in tort.[55]

The implied contract approach

A contract on the terms contained in the bill of lading between the carrier and the endorsee was implied, provided some consideration from the endorsee to the carrier was present. Taking delivery of goods against freight by the endorsee was deemed sufficient to find an implied contract – the payment of freight being the consideration. *Brandt v Liverpool, Brazil and River Plate Steam Navigation Co Ltd*[56] illustrates this approach. The pledgee of the bill of lading took delivery of the goods from the shipowner after paying freight. The Court of Appeal implied a contract on terms contained in the bill of lading between the pledgee and the shipowner. To imply a contract, an element of consideration must be present. In its absence, there is no remedy for the bill of lading holder. In *The Aramis*,[57] cargo was shipped in bulk, for which several bills of lading were issued. By the time the plaintiff presented his bill of lading, the cargo had been exhausted. The freight had been prepaid by the shipper. A contract on the terms set out in the bill of lading between the endorsee and the carrier could not therefore be implied.

Some degree of co-operation between the cargo receiver and the carrier may also

---

54   See 'The implied contract approach', pp 187–8 below.
55   See pp 187–9 below for all three approaches.
56   [1924] 1 KB 575.
57   [1989] 1 Lloyd's Rep 213.

result in the finding of an implied contract. In *The Captain Gregos (No 2)*,[58] the court found an implied contract between the carrier and the ultimate purchaser, who took delivery against a letter of indemnity on the basis that the cargo of oil could not have been delivered without the active co-operation of the purchaser and the crew of the vessel. The question of co-operation is a matter of fact. For instance, in *The Gudermes*,[59] on the facts, the courts were unwilling to find an implied contract between the purchaser and the carrier.

The special contract approach

The existence of a 'special contract' – a contract made by the consignor on behalf of the consignee with the shipowner which the consignor can enforce even after property in the goods has passed to the consignee – is an alternative. It was successfully invoked in *Dunlop v Lambert*[60] to circumvent the doctrine of privity[61] at a time when the Bills of Lading Act 1855 had not been enacted. The 'special contract' approach was argued by the plaintiff (charterer) in *The Albazero*.[62] The endorsee had the right to sue the carrier on the bill of lading since property had passed to him but could not do so since he had failed to institute proceedings within the time limit set by the terms on the bill of lading. The charterers therefore sued on behalf of the endorsees. The court concluded it did not apply to situations where the consignee/endorsee had the necessary contractual rights flowing from the contract of carriage.

Liability in tort

Where the claim for damage to cargo is based on negligence on the part of the carrier, his servants or agents, the courts, at times, found liability in tort in the absence of a contractual relationship. Until 1986, judicial opinion swung between liberal and restrictive approaches. The former did not insist on a contractual relationship to find tortious liability. For instance, in *The Irene's Success*,[63] coal (purchased on cif terms) was damaged by sea water during the voyage. The plaintiffs were not the legal owners (not being holders of the bill of lading) at the time of the damage. An action in negligence was brought against the carriers, on the reasoning that they were at risk at the time the cargo was damaged. Lloyd J had no hesitation in saying that the plaintiff could sue in tort on the grounds that the incidence of risk in cif sales was well known to shipowners. The restrictive approach, on the other hand, required that, for an action in negligence to succeed, the plaintiff must, at the commission of the tort, be the owner of the goods, as *Margarine Union v Cambay Prince*[64] illustrates. In this case, a cargo of dried coconuts was damaged due to the shipowner's failure to fumigate the

---

58   [1990] 2 Lloyd's Rep 395.

59   [1993] 1 Lloyd's Rep 311 (CA).

60   (1839) 7 ER 825.

61   Note, however, that many of the problems created by privity are resolved by the Contracts (Rights of Third Parties) Act 1999. See MacMillan, 'A birthday present for Lord Denning: the Contracts (Rights of Third Parties) Act 1999' (2000) 63 MLR 721.

62   [1976] 2 Lloyd's Rep 467. See *McAlpine v Panatown* [2000] 3 WLR 946 on the applicability of the special contract approach to building contracts. See also MacMillan, 'The end of the exception in *Dunlop v Lambert?*' [2001] LMCLQ 338.

63   [1981] 2 Lloyd's Rep 635.

64   [1969] 1 QB 219.

holds of the ship. The plaintiff (not the legal owner of the goods) obtained delivery against a delivery order. Roskill J had no hesitation in holding that the plaintiff could not succeed, since he was not the legal owner of the goods when the damage occurred.

This sharp division in judicial opinion was ultimately resolved by the House of Lords in *The Aliakmon*,[65] when it held that for an action in negligence to succeed, the plaintiff must, at the time of the commission of the tort, be the owner[66] of the goods that suffered damage.

Endorsement of bill of lading after delivery

Where endorsement of a bill of lading takes place after the passage of property, the bill of lading does not impart rights to a third party. In *The Delfini*,[67] the plaintiffs bought part of a cargo carried in bulk. Under the contract, payment was to be made either against shipping documents or a letter of indemnity in the event that the bills of lading were unavailable at the date of payment. The sellers also wanted a bank guarantee not later than the nomination of the vessel. The plaintiffs took delivery of the goods against a letter of indemnity, which the sellers had issued to the ship with instructions to deliver without a bill of lading. They also paid for the goods against a letter of indemnity issued to them by the sellers. Subsequent to delivery and payment, the plaintiffs received the bill of lading. They sued the shipowner on the bill for short delivery.

The court held that the plaintiffs had no rights of action under the Bills of Lading Act 1855, since endorsement of the bill did not play a causal role in the passing of property. Property passed when the plaintiffs paid for the goods against the letter of indemnity furnished by the sellers.

THE CARRIAGE OF GOODS BY SEA ACT 1992

Rights of suit

The Carriage of Goods by Sea Act 1992, unlike the Bills of Lading Act 1855, separates contractual rights from the passing of property. This legislation enables the lawful holder of a bill of lading to sue the carrier in contract irrespective of the question of passage of property by reason of consignment or endorsement bringing British law into line with the laws of several member states of the European Union (Holland, France, Germany, Sweden and Greece), and the US. The Carriage of Goods by Sea Act 1992 reflects the recommendations made by the Law Commission in their report *Rights of Suit in Respect of Carriage of Goods by Sea* (hereinafter 'Report').[68]

Two other options were open to the Law Commission. The first, an administratively simple option, was to take a wide view of s 1 of the Bills of Lading Act 1855,

---

65   [1986] 2 All ER 145; [1986] 1 Lloyd's Rep 1.

66   Physical possession of bills of lading may not always give a sufficient possessory title to sue in tort – see *East West Corp v DKBS 1912 and Akts Svendborg Utaniko Ltd v P&O Nedlloyd BV* [2003] 1 Lloyd's Rep 239.

67   [1990] 1 Lloyd's Rep 252.

68   Law Com No 196, 1991, HMSO.

such that any lawful holder of the bill of lading would be allowed to sue the carrier if, at some stage, property passed to him under a contract in pursuance of which he became the lawful holder. While resolving *The Delfini*[69] problem, it would not impart rights of suit to those bill of lading holders who had not obtained property in the goods, for example, where they were lost before they could be ascertained.

The second option was the replacement of references to property in s 1 with risk. This would have permitted a lawful bill of lading holder to sue and be sued if he was at risk in respect of the loss which occurred. It would, however, exclude bill of lading holders such as pledgees who wished to realise their security. Unfamiliarity with the concept of risk was also a strong detracting factor.[70]

Transfer of rights and transfer of liabilities are, unlike the Bills of Lading Act 1855, dealt with in two separate sections in the Carriage of Goods by Sea Act 1992. Section 2 deals with the transfer of rights and s 3 with transfer of liabilities.

Transfer of rights

Since 16 September 1992, any lawful holder of a bill of lading, a sea waybill or a delivery order acquires the right to sue the carrier in contract for loss or damage to the goods, regardless of whether property in the goods has passed or not, under s 2 of the Act, which states:

Subject to the following provisions of this section, a person who becomes:

(a) the lawful holder[71] of a bill of lading;

(b) the person who (without being an original party to the contract of carriage) is the person to whom delivery of the goods to which a seawaybill relates is to be made by the carrier in accordance with that contract; or

(c) the person to whom delivery of the goods to which a ship's delivery order relates is to be made in accordance with the undertaking contained in the order shall (by virtue of becoming the holder of the bill or, as the case may be, the person to whom delivery is made) have transferred to and vested in him all rights of suit under the contract of carriage as if he had been a party to the contract.

It must be noted that the Act also imparts rights of suit to holders of sea waybills and delivery orders, which reflects the realities of commercial practice.

Problems highlighted earlier (*The Aliakmon*,[72] *The Aramis*,[73] and *The Delfini*[74]) should no longer arise. Attachment of rights of suit to bills of lading which can be

---

69 [1990] 1 Lloyd's Rep 252. See 'Endorsement of bill of lading after delivery', p 189 above.

70 See paras 2.18–2.23 of the Report.

71 See s 5(2) on the interpretation of bill of lading holder. The lawful holder also includes a pledgee. In *Motis Exports Limited v Dampskibsselskabet AF 1912 v Aktieselskab, Aktieselskabet Dampskibsselskabet Svendborg* (2001) available on Westlaw database (2001 WL 239695), in an application for a summary judgment, Moore-Bick J said that 'the deposit of a generally indorsed bill of lading with the intention of creating a pledge over the goods operates to render the pledgee the holder the bill of lading under the Carriage of Goods by Sea Act 1992 ... Sub-section 5(2)(b) refers to the completion of *any other transfer* of the bill; these are wide words which in my view are capable of embracing a transfer by way of pledge' (para 17). This also includes holder of a bearer bill. See *Keppel Tatlee Bank v Bandung Shipping* [2003] 1 Lloyd's Rep 619.

72 [1986] 2 All ER 145; [1986] 1 Lloyd's Rep 1.

73 [1989] 1 Lloyd's Rep 213 (CA).

74 [1990] 1 Lloyd's Rep 252.

acquired after delivery creates the possibility of improper trading in bills of lading (that is, where bills could be negotiated for cash in the open market purely as causes of action against the carriers subsequent to delivery).[75] This is addressed by s 2(2)(a), which operates to prevent the transfer of rights to a holder unless that party has become a holder of the bill 'by virtue of a transaction effected in pursuance of any contractual or other arrangements made before the time when such a right to possession ceased to attach to possession of the bill'.[76]

Upon transfer, as provided for in s 2(1), the rights to enforce the contract previously vested in any other person are extinguished under s 2(5), which states:

> Where rights are transferred by virtue of the operation of sub-s (1) above in relation to any document, the transfer for which that sub-section provides shall extinguish any entitlement to those rights which derives:
>
> (a) where that document is a bill of lading, from a person's having been an original party to the contract of carriage; or
>
> (b) in the case of any document to which the Act applies, from the previous operation of that sub-section in relation to that document;
>
> but the operation of that sub-section will be without prejudice to any rights which derive from a person's having been an original party to the contract contained in, or evidenced by, a sea waybill and, in relation to a ship's delivery order, shall be without prejudice to any rights deriving otherwise than from the previous operation of that sub-section in relation to that order.

The shipper's rights are extinguished upon endorsement. The category of parties with rights to sue on the bill of lading are restricted to avoid multiplicity of actions. Giving the right to sue to the seller would entail giving intermediate sellers on risk the right to sue.[77]

In *Motis Exports Ltd v Dampskibsselskabet AF 1912 v Aktieselskab, Aktieselskabet Dampskibsselskabet Svendborg*,[78] the banks held the bills of lading for advances that had been given to the claimants (shippers). There was misdelivery of the goods. The buyers had no intention of taking up the bills of lading when the bill of lading was forwarded by the bank to its correspondent bank for collection. The bank debited the claimants' account and returned the bills of lading to the claimants. On the return of the original bills of lading indorsed in blank, the claimants, it was held, became the holders of the bill of lading for the purposes of the Carriage of Goods by Sea Act 1992 and could exercise their rights under s 2.[79]

It was suggested by the defendants that before the receipt of the bills of lading the claimants were aware that the goods had been misdelivered against forged

---

75 See para 2.43 of the Report.

76 *Ibid*, para 2.44. See *The Ythan* [2006] 1 Lloyd's Rep 457 where bill transferred after insurance settlement.

77 *Ibid*, para 2.34.

78 Available on Westlaw under ID tag 2001 WL 239695.

79 In *East West Corp v DKBS 1912* [2002] 2 Lloyd's Rep 182, the sellers named the bank as consignees. The bank obtained rights under s 2(1) of the Carriage of Goods by Sea Act 1992. The bank subsequently transferred the bills of lading to the seller but did not indorse them. The sellers argued they had become holders by virtue of the operation of ss 2(2) and 5(2)(c). It was held that these sections are relevant only where the bills of lading were spent. This was not the situation here – the bills had not ceased to be a transferable document of title since they gave a right of possession against the carrier (at pp 191–2). See also *The David Agmashenebeli* on the operation of s 2(2)(a).

documents; they did not thereafter become holders in good faith as required by s 5(2). However, since the claimants became holder as a result of pre-existing commercial arrangement (security for credit) the court did not address the question of whether a person who becomes the holder of a bill of lading in the knowledge that the goods have been lost or destroyed while in the hands of the carrier is a holder in good faith.

The seller has a limited right of suit and this is where he wishes to sue on the contract of carriage – for example, where the buyer rejects the goods on arrival. This right is imparted by s 2(2)(b) which states:

> 2(2) Where, when a person becomes the lawful holder of a bill of lading, possession of the bill no longer gives a right (as against the carrier) to possession of the goods to which the bill relates, that person shall not have any rights transferred to him by virtue of sub-s (1) above unless he becomes the holder of the bill:
>
> (a) ...
>
> (b) as a result of the rejection to that person by another person of goods or documents delivered to the other person in pursuance of any such arrangements.

Section 2(2)(b) does not operate to give rights of suit to the seller in other situations, where he remains on risk.

As for intermediate holders, their rights are extinguished upon transfer.[80] An intermediate owner is left to his own devices should he remain on risk upon endorsement. One solution would be to arrange an assignment of the buyer's rights against the carrier.[81]

Questions do arise whether the Carriage of Goods by Sea Act 1992 has done away with the right to claim in bailment.[82] In *DKBS v East West Corp*,[83] goods were shipped at Hong Kong for delivery at Chile, cash on delivery terms. The bills of lading named Chilean banks as consignees. On arrival, the goods were placed in a licensed customs house since no duty had been paid in advance. Once the duty was paid, they were released to Gold Crown (the buyer) without the production of bills of lading. No payment was made by the buyer and the carriers were sued for misdelivery. The carriers contended that the claimants did not have any title to sue under the Carriage of Goods by Sea Act 1992. The claimants, among others, contended that they had retained their rights as shippers, and they had in any event title to claim in bailment. Thomas J concluded on the basis of ss 2 and 5 of the Carriage of Goods by Sea Act 1992 that the claimants had parted with all rights of suit to the Chilean banks. And more importantly, he concluded that, as a result of the transfer of the bills of lading to the Chilean banks, the claimants had lost their right to immediate possession. This meant they had no rights in bailment upon transfer,[84] although he concluded that they could as proprietors of the goods claim for the permanent

---

80   *Borealis AB v Stargas Ltd (The Berge Sisar)* [1988] 4 All ER 821.

81   See para 2.40 of the Report.

82   Bailment is peculiar to common law; it is *sui generis* and exists independently of contract or tort. The law of bailment allows the owner of the goods or a person who has a right to possession to bring an action in bailment against third parties with whom no contractual relationship exists. Bailment comes into existence when X is knowingly and willingly in possession of goods belonging to Y. X is the bailee and Y the bailor – ie, one who leaves the goods in possession of X. It is likely that bailment will be for reward, though gratuitous bailment is recognised. See also Chapter 13.

83   [2003] 1 Lloyd's Rep 239.

84   See *East West Corp v DKBS 1912 and AKTS Svendborg Utaniko Ltd, P&O Nedlloyd BV* [2002] 2 Lloyd's Rep 182, at pp 191–3.

deprivation of their proprietary interest resulting as a consequence of the delivery to the buyers. On appeal, the respondents challenged the judge's reasoning on a number of grounds: '(i) that they were the original bailors; (ii) that whether or not their delivery of the bills to the Chilean banks transferred any right to immediate possession of the goods depended at common law upon their and the bank's intention and that there was no such intention to transfer any such right; (iii) that there is nothing in the 1992 Act to alter this position or to transfer their rights in bailment to the Chilean banks; and (iv) that the fact that the banks at all times held the bills for the respondents enabled the respondents to sue in bailment as the bank's principals.'[85] After a review of authorities such as *The Pioneer Container*,[86] Mance LJ concluded that the case under consideration 'was not one of bailment and sub-bailment of the container load of goods', though

> ... in respect of the shipping documents themselves, the Chilean banks were, on the face of it, bailees, but even assuming that the delivery to them of the bills of lading passes to them a constructive or symbolic possessory interest in the goods, the Chilean banks cannot be realistically viewed as bailees of goods *vis à vis* the respondents ... a relationship of bailment continued in existence between the respondents and the shipping line despite the respondent's transfer.[87]

Imposition of liabilities

The carrier acquires enhanced rights of claim against the bill of lading holder. Section 3(1) of the Carriage of Goods by Sea Act 1992 states that any person in whom rights are vested by virtue of s 2(1) 'takes or demands delivery from the carrier of any of the goods to which the document relates; makes a claim under the contract of carriage against the carrier in respect of those goods; or is a person who, at a time before the rights were vested in him, took or demanded delivery from the carrier of any of those goods', and is subject to the same liabilities under that contract as if he were a party to the contract.

This provision does not state whether the bill of lading holder is only liable for those events that occur post-endorsement, or whether he is liable for events pre-endorsement. For instance, is the bill of lading holder liable for damage caused due to dangerous goods at the time of shipment, or freight and demurrage on loading? Also, under s 3(1), the bill of lading holder who has received no goods at all is liable.

As for liability incurred before endorsement, s 3(3) may provide a possible solution since this section retains the liability of the original parties to the contract of carriage. Where the shipper has the contractual obligation to pay freight or demurrage on loading, he will remain liable to the carrier. This view finds support in the *obiter* statement found in *Effort Shipping Co Ltd v Linden Management SA and Others*.[88] The issue before the court in this case was whether the liability of the shipper for the damage caused due to shipment of the dangerous goods was transferred to endorsees (purchasers) under s 1 of the Bills of Lading Act 1855. The court held that the purpose of the Bills of Lading Act 1855 was to create an exception to the doctrine of privity

---

85 [2003] 1 Lloyd's Rep 239, at p 248.
86 [1994] 2 AC 324. See also Chapter 13.
87 At p 252. See also para 49, p 255.
88 [1998] 2 WLR 206.

and that the endorsee became subject to the same liabilities as the shipper by way of addition, and not substitution, which meant that the shipper remained liable. Lord Lloyd went on to observe that 'the result would have been the same under s 3(3) of the Carriage of Goods by Sea Act 1992' (pp 214–15).

As for those who hold bills of lading for security purposes, they will not be liable unless they take or demand delivery of the goods, under s 3(1). This preserves the position developed in *Sewell v Burdick*,[89] where the bank was not liable for the freight owed to the carrier.

The question of what constitutes demand was considered in *Borealis AB Stargas Ltd and Another (Bergesen DY a/s Third Party), Borealis AB v Stargas Ltd and Others.*[90] Since the nature of the consequences flowing from s 3 were important, it was construed as not including taking of samples by the endorsee but as meaning a formal demand. According to Lord Hobhouse:

> A 'demand' might be an invitation or request, or, perhaps, even implied from making arrangements; or it might be a more formal express communication . . . From the context of the Act and the purpose underlying s 3(1), it is clear that s 3 must be understood in a way which reflects the potentially important consequences of the choice or election which the bill of lading holder is making. The liabilities, particularly when alleged dangerous goods are involved, may be disproportionate to the value of the goods; the liabilities may not be covered by insurance, the endorsee may not be fully aware of what the liabilities are. I would therefore read the phrase 'demands delivery' as referring to a formal demand made to the carrier or his agent asserting the contractual right as endorsee of the bill of lading to have the carrier deliver goods to him. And I would read the phrase 'makes a claim under the contract of carriage' as referring to a formal claim against asserting a legal liability of the carrier under the contract of carriage to the holder of the bill of lading [at p 228].

But what about the liability of an intermediate holder who subsequently endorses the bill of lading to another? In *Borealis AB Stargas Ltd and Another (Bergesen DY a/s Third Party), Borealis AB v Stargas Ltd and Others*, the intermediate holder on rejecting the cargo after taking samples subsequently endorsed the bill of lading to another purchaser. Does he remain liable post-endorsement? Unlike s 2 which has an express specific provision in s 2(5) about the rights of intermediate holders, s 3 is silent. Lord Hobhouse concluded that, on transfer, the liabilities of the intermediate holder are extinguished on two grounds. First, on the basis that ss 2 and 3 had adopted the wording of the Bills of Lading Act 1855, thus indicating the intention to preserve their interpretation in cases such as *Smurthwaite v Wilkins*.[91] Secondly, there is the principle of mutuality, embedded in s 3(1), since liabilities attach only when the rights are acquired. In the words of Lord Hobhouse:

> . . . it makes it fundamental that, for a person to be caught by s 3(1), he must be the person in whom the rights of suit under the contract of carriage are vested pursuant to s 2(1). The liability is dependent upon the possession of the rights. It follows that, as there is no provision to the contrary, the Act should be construed as providing that, if the person should cease to have the rights vested in him, he should no longer be subject to the liabilities. The mutuality which is the rationale for imposing the liability has gone. There is no longer the link between benefits and burdens [at p 233].

---

89 [1884] 10 AC.
90 [2002] 2 AC 205.
91 (1862) 11 CBNS 842. See Erle CJ at p 848.

BILLS OF LADING AND FRAUD

Before going on to consider the impact of information technology, attention must be drawn to fraud in bills of lading. Bills of lading are normally issued in sets of three or six originals. This mercantile practice enables the bill to be sent to the consignee by different modes of dispatch and ensures that the consignee gets at least one of the originals on time to take delivery of the goods at the destination. Treating each bill of lading as an original leaves it open to misuse. The carrier, as stated earlier, delivers the cargo against presentation of the bill of lading and it is not necessary for the holder of a bill of lading to present the entire set to the carrier. Presentation of part of a set is enough. Delivery of the cargo against one of a set would cause no problems if the consignee/endorsee had the entire set. However, it is normal for the endorser to transfer only part of a set to the endorsee, which means that both the endorsee and endorser possess part of a set, where part of the set is endorsed to the endorsee, and the others remain unendorsed (or may be endorsed, in cases of fraud, to other third parties). Since each bill in the set is treated as an original, the endorser (or other third parties), as well as the endorsee, can demand delivery. The dangers inherent in issuing bills of lading in sets of three or six originals were spotted by Lord Blackburn in *Glyn Mills v East and West India Dock Co*,[92] when he said:

> ... the very object of making a bill of lading in parts would be baffled unless the delivery of one part of the bill of lading, duly assigned, had the same effect as the delivery of all the parts would have had. And the consequence of making a document of title in parts is that it is possible that one part may come into the hands of one person who *bona fide* gave value for it under the belief that he thereby acquired an interest in the goods, either as purchaser, mortgagee or pawnee, and another may come into the hands of another person, who, with equal *bona fides*, gave value for it under the belief that he thereby acquired a similar interest. This cannot well happen unless there is fraud on the part of those who pass the two parts to different persons [at p 604].

Despite their proneness to fraud and developments in communications technology, merchants continue to issue bills of lading in sets. Why this practice continues to this day in unclear. Lord Blackburn found this mercantile custom equally perplexing:

> I have never been able to learn why merchants and shipowners continue the practice of making out a bill of lading in parts. I would have thought that, at least since the introduction of quick and regular communications by steamers, and still more since the establishment of electric telegraph, every purpose would be answered by making one bill of lading only which should be the sole document of title, and taking as many copies, certified by the master to be true copies, as it is thought convenient: those copies would suffice for every legitimate purpose for which the other parts of the bill can now be applied, but could not be used for the purpose of pretending to be holder of a bill already parted with. However, whether because there is some practical benefit of which I am not aware, or because, as I suspect, merchants dislike to depart from an old custom for fear that the novelty may produce some unforeseen effect, bills of lading are still made out in parts, and probably will continue to be so made out [at p 605].

Bills of lading drawn in sets normally provide that 'one being accomplished, the others are to stand void'. This is to protect the carrier, were he to deliver against an unendorsed or a validly endorsed bill of lading. In the event of misdelivery, the

---

92   (1882) 7 App Cas 591.

carrier will not be liable if he has no notice of other endorsements. There is no duty on the carrier to make inquiries of the unendorsed bill of lading holder whether any assignments have taken place. Of course, it is always open for the assignee to protect against misdelivery by contacting the shipowner as soon as the assignment has taken place and inform him of his acquired rights. This does not happen often in practice. In *Glyn Mills v East and West India Dock Co*,[93] a set of three bills of lading was issued, naming Cottam and Co as the consignees. Freight was to be payable on arrival of the goods at London. Cottam and Co endorsed one bill of lading as security to Glyn Mills and retained the other two bills in the set. When the goods arrived in London, they were warehoused, and Cottam and Co obtained delivery of the goods from the warehouse on presentation of the unendorsed bill of lading and upon payment of freight due. Glyn Mills brought an action against the warehouseman for misdelivery. The House of Lords held that the warehouseman was not liable for misdelivery, since:

> ... it would be neither reasonable nor equitable, nor in accordance with the terms of such a contract, that an assignment of which the shipowner has no notice should prevent a *bona fide* delivery under one of the bills of lading, produced to him by the person named on the face of it as entitled to delivery (in the absence of assignment), from being a discharge to the shipowner. Assignment, being a change of title since the contract, is not to be presumed by the shipowner in the absence of notice, any more than a change of title is to be presumed in any other case when the original party to a contract comes forward and claims its performance, the party having no notice of anything to displace his right ... it is for the assignee to give notice of his title to the shipowner if he desires to make it secure and not for the shipowner to make such inquiry [at p 596].

Where a carrier delivers cargo in the absence of a bill of lading, the carrier will be in breach of contract. The breach is regarded as a fundamental breach, such that he will lose the benefit of the exception clauses in the contract of carriage. In *Sze Hai Tong Bank Ltd v Ramber Cycle Co Ltd*,[94] the carrier discharged the goods to their agents, who delivered the goods against an indemnity from the bank. No bill of lading was presented. The bill of lading contained a clause, which read:

> During the period before the goods are loaded on or after they are discharged from the ship on which they are carried by sea, the following terms and conditions shall apply to the exclusion of any other provisions in this bill of lading that it may be inconsistent therewith, *viz*, (a) so long as the goods remain in the actual custody of the carrier or his servants ... (b) whilst the goods are being transported to or from the ship ... (c) in all other cases the responsibility of the carrier, whether as a carrier or as a custodian or as a bailee of the goods, shall be deemed to commence only when the goods are loaded on the ship and to cease absolutely after they are discharged therefrom.

The issue was whether the carrier could rely on this clause to absolve him from liability for delivering the goods without production of a bill of lading. The court held that the clause could not protect the carrier, for:

> ... if such an extreme width were given to the exemption clause, it would run counter to the main object and intent of the contract. For the contract, as it seems to their Lordships, has, as one of its main objects, the proper delivery of the goods by the shipping company 'unto order or his or their assigns' against production of the bill of lading. It would defeat this object entirely if the shipping company was at liberty, at its own will and pleasure, to deliver the goods to somebody else, to someone not entitled at

---

93   (1882) 7 App Cas 591.
94   [1959] 2 Lloyd's Rep 114.

all, without being liable for the consequences . . . they deliberately disregarded one of the prime obligations of the contract. No court can allow so fundamental a breach to pass unnoticed under the cloak of a general exemption clause [at pp 120–21].

Lord Denning's reference to fundamental breach, however, has to be interpreted in the light of *Photo Productions Ltd v Securicor Transport Ltd*.[95] Were a case similar in facts to *Sze Hai Tong*[96] to come before the courts again, no doubt they would hold the clause ineffective, on the grounds that it defeats the main purpose of the contract. After all, as Lord Denning said,' . . . if the exemption clause upon its true constructions absolved the shipping company from an act such as that, it seems that, by parity of reasoning, they would have been absolved if they had given the goods away to some passerby or had burnt them or thrown them into the sea . . . there is, therefore, an implied limitation in the clause'.[97] The case of *The Ines*,[98] where goods were delivered without production of a bill of lading, lends support. In holding that cl 3, which provided:

> . . . after discharge, the goods are to be at the sole risk of the owners of the goods and thus the carrier has no responsibility whatsoever . . . for the goods . . . subsequent to the discharge from the ocean vessel . . .

was insufficient to excuse misdelivery, Clarke J clearly stated that:

> . . . one of the key provisions, so far as the shipper is concerned, is the promise not to deliver the cargo other than in return for an original bill of lading . . . The parties would not . . . be likely to have contracted out of it. Thus, clear words would be required for them to have done so. The clause should be construed so as to enable effect to be given to one of the main objects and intents of the contract, namely, that the goods would only be delivered to the holder of an original bill of lading [at p 152].[99]

ELECTRONIC DATA INTERCHANGE (EDI) AND THE CARRIAGE OF GOODS BY SEA ACT 1992

As stated in Chapter 1, INCOTERMS 2000, expecting an increase in the use of electronic means of communication, have made suitable amendments in trade terms to accommodate the use of electronic bills of lading. Developments relating to paperless trading have also been anticipated by the Carriage of Goods by Sea Act 1992, even though the Commission's consultation document did not consider electronic transmission of transport documents. Section 1(5) of this legislation empowers the Secretary of State to make provisions for the application of the Act to cases where a telecommunications system or any other information technology is used for effecting transactions corresponding to:

(a) the issue of a document to which the Act applies;

(b) the endorsement, delivery or other transfer of such a document; or

(c) the doing of anything else to such a document.

---

95 [1980] AC 827; [1980] 1 All ER 556.
96 See 'Duty to pursue the contract voyage' in Chapter 8, pp 243–6.
97 [1959] 2 Lloyd's Rep 114, at p 120.
98 [1995] 2 Lloyd's Rep 144.
99 See also 'Delivery Against Bills of Lading', pp 183–4.

'Information technology' is defined in s 5(1) to include any computer or other technology by means of which information or other matter may be recorded or communicated, without being reduced to documentary form. This definition appears to be sufficiently wide to include other means of information transfer through intangible means that may be developed in the future.

So far, the Secretary of State has not exercised his powers under s 1(5), since electronic bills of lading are not yet in common use.

However, since the passing of the Carriage of Goods by Sea Act 1992, many developments have taken place both technologically and legislation wise at the domestic as well as at the international level. Contracts concluded electronically are now recognised widely in many juridisctions[100] largely as a result of the United Nations Commission on International Trade Law (UNCITRAL) Model Law on Electronic Commerce.[101] Equally, formal requirements for a contractual document such as signatures have been made possible as a result of legislation modelled on the UNCITRAL Model Law on Electronic Signatures.[102] Further, the CMI Rules on Electronic Bills of Lading and the BOLERO Rules have made the use of electronic bills of lading a reality. But before considering these developments, a few words on the advantages and disadvantages of using paperless documents.

Advantages and disadvantages of using electronic documents

Electronic bills of lading are regarded by some traders and practitioners as a vast improvement on paper bills of lading, since they will see a reduction in:

(a) problems created by late arrival of documents at the port of discharge; and

(b) fraud, since bills of lading will no longer be sent in sets of three or six originals.

There is some truth in the view that problems, legal and logistical, associated with the late arrival of mailed transport documents, will be solved by their electronic transmission. Whether this will reduce the incidence of fraud in bills of lading is debatable. The incidence of fraud may well increase due to the likelihood of computer misuse – more so, where an open network, such as the Internet, is used. The successful implementation of paperless documents in the shipping industry is possible only if:

(a) there are reliable security devices that would make it near impossible for the fraudster or hacker to gain access;

(b) there are adequate mechanisms in the available law or new laws are enacted at both national and international levels, that would deter the would-be hacker or fraudster;

(c) there is greater co-operation between countries to exchange information about cross-border data flow and access to evidence; and

(d) the laws of evidence allow for admissibility of computer-generated documents.

As for (a), security devices using digital cryptology that make computer break-ins

---

100 Eg, Australia, Singapore, Malaysia, India. See also Carr, 'India joins the cyber-race: Information Technology Act 2000' (2000) 6(4) International Trade Law and Regulation 120.

101 See Chapter 3.

102 See Chapter 4.

near impossible, thereby reducing the chances of forgery or alterations to the data by a fraudster or a mischievous hacker, are technically feasible. Encryption of data is also possible. Of course, such technology in some countries[103] is treated as defence material, and hence regulated. Its free availability and use in some countries cause concern, since terrorists, drug barons and money launderers are likely to use it to cloak their activities. Leading Western governments would like to give government agencies extensive powers to intercept communications[104] and access computer-held information for purposes of national security and preserving the economic infrastructure. It raises policy issues, ranging from the acceptable level of tolerance to criminal activities that undermine the social and economic structure, the paternalistic role of states, to the rights of individuals (for instance, the right to privacy). Organisations such as the Organisation for Economic Co-operation and Development (OECD) and economic groupings such as the European Union (EU) are continuously considering policy issues with a view to arriving at a solution that makes electronic commerce secure without jeopardising the well-being of nations, societies and the individual.[105]

As for (b), Britain is one among many countries to introduce legislation on computer misuse – the Computer Misuse Act 1990. Legislation in this area came about when traditional criminal law could not cope with certain kinds of computer-related crime due to the intangible nature of the information held on computers.[106] This legislation carries criminal sanctions in the event of computer misuse. Its success in curbing computer misuse is debatable. Prosecutions are few, and yet the Audit Commission estimates annual losses caused by computer misuse at more than £2m. The failure may be due to difficulties in gathering evidence and limited police resources.[107] The Council of Europe, with the intention of harmonising the law on computer misuse, has drafted the International Convention on Cybercrime,[108] which it is hoped will have wide impact.

As for (c), international organisations such as the Council of Europe have recommended various measures that countries may take both nationally and internationally. Their success depends on the countries' (political) willingness to participate.[109]

---

103 Eg, the US.

104 See the Regulation of Investigatory Powers Act 2000 which gives extensive powers to authorities in the United Kingdom. See also Indian Information Technology Act 2000, Williams and Carr, 'Crime risk and computers' [2002] Electronic Communications LR 23; Carr and Williams, 'A step too far in controlling computers? The Singapore Computer Misuse (Amendment) Act 1998' [2000] International Journal of Law and Information Technology 48.

105 To cite a few: OECD, *Report on Background and Issues of Cryptography Policy; A European Initiative in Electronic Commerce*, COM (97) 157; Commission Green Paper, *Legal Protection of Encrypted Services in the Internal Market*, COM (96) 76, European Commission. See also Chapters 3 and 4 for further references.

106 See *R v Gold; R v Schifreen* [1988] AC 1063; *Cox v Riley* (1986) 83 Cr App 554.

107 See Carr and Williams, 'Regulating the e-commerce environment: enforcement measures and penalty levels in the computer misuse legislation of Britain, Malaysia and Singapore' (2000) 16(5) Computer Law and Security Report 295.

108 The text of the convention is available on www.coe.org. See also Chapter 4, pp 143–55; Carr and Williams, 'Criminalisation of new offences under the Council of Europe Convention on Cybercrime' (2002) 18(2) Computer Law and Security Report 91.

109 See Council of Europe, *Recommendation No R 95(13) Concerning Problems of Criminal Procedural Law Connected to Information Technology and Explanatory Memorandum*, text available at www.coe.org; United Nations, *Manual on the Prevention and Control of Computer related Crime*, 1994. See also Carr and Williams, 'Council of Europe on the Harmonisation of Criminal Procedural Law Relating to Information Technology (Recommendation No R95(13)) – some comments' [1998] JBL 468.

As for (d), rules of evidence in common law countries have been developed largely to handle the oral nature of the trial, resulting in the hearsay rule, whereby witnesses can testify on the basis of their own first-hand knowledge. Anything short of this requirement falls foul of the hearsay rule. In England, computer-generated evidence in civil matters is admissible due to recent legislation. Following the Law Commission's Report, *The Hearsay Rule in Civil Proceedings*,[110] the Civil Evidence Act was passed in 1995 which allows the admissibility of computer-generated evidence. There are no special rules about the reliability of the computer from which the document is generated for it to be admissible. Presumably, this is due to the difficulties in guaranteeing the non-corruptibility of computer systems. The course recommended by the Commission is one of weighing the evidence according to its reliability.[111]

Prior to the Civil Evidence Act 1995, under s 5 of the Civil Evidence Act 1968, a statement contained in a document produced by a computer was admissible as evidence of any fact stated therein of which direct oral evidence would be admissible, provided the conditions stipulated below were satisfied:

(a) the documents must have been prepared during a period over which the computer was regularly used to process information for the purposes of the activities regularly carried on over that period;

(b) information of the kind contained in the document, or from which it is derived, was, over that period, regularly supplied to the computer in the ordinary course of those activities;

(c) the computer was operating properly throughout that period; or if not, the reason for any malfunction was not such as to affect the accuracy of the document; and

(d) the information contained in the document is reproduced or is derived from information supplied to the computer in the ordinary course of the activities for which it was used.

The court also had to be satisfied that these conditions were fulfilled either by oral evidence or by a certificate signed by a person occupying a responsible position.

Though innovative at the time, s 5 lacked clarity: for instance, it was unclear whether s 5 of the Civil Evidence Act 1968 was a general rule relating to the admissibility of all computer-generated evidence, or whether it was an exception to the hearsay rule, due to the inclusion of this section under that part of the Act headed 'Hearsay Evidence'. If the heading was an operative part, s 5 was an exception to the hearsay rule. Conditions stipulated in s 5 also posed problems. Its emphasis on regularity of use of the particular computer from which the document was retrieved, rather than the reliability of the computer, excluded documents generated by a computer as a one-off task.

The UNCITRAL Model Law on Electronic Commerce,[112] on which many jurisdictions have based their legislation, allows for the admissibility of computer-generated evidence in its Art 9 which states:

---

110 Law Com No 216, 1993, HMSO.
111 Paragraph 4.43, *The Hearsay Rule in Civil Proceedings*. See also s 7(1) of the Electronic Communications Act 2000 which allows electronic signatures and authentication certificates to be admitted in legal proceedings.
112 See also UNCITRAL's draft for an International Convention on Electronic Transactions (Proposal Date 29 June–10 July 1998 – A/CN 9 WG IV/WP 77) available at www.uncitral.org.

(1) In any legal proceedings, nothing in the application of the rules of evidence shall apply so as to deny the admissibility of a data message in evidence:

    (a) on the sole ground that it is a data message; or

    (b) if it is the best evidence that the person adducing it could reasonably be expected to obtain, on the grounds that it is not in its original form.

(2) Information in the form of a data message shall be given due evidential weight. In assessing the evidential weight of a data message, regard shall be had to the reliability of the manner in which the data message was generated, stored or communicated, to the reliability of the manner in which its originator was identified, and to any other relevant factor.

Electronic bills of lading: the SEADOCS scheme, CMI Rules for Electronic Bills of Lading

In the mid-1980s, the International Association of Independent Tanker Owners (INTERTANKO), in association with Chase Manhattan Bank, experimented with an electronic system known as SEADOCS. Primarily devised to combat fraud, the bill of lading started life in a tangible form – that is, as a paper bill of lading. This was lodged with Chase Manhattan Bank, which functioned as a central registry. Acting as an agent for all parties, the bank transferred ownership in the goods on electronic notification. The system did not take off, since the participants were worried about the confidentiality of the information they divulged to the bank. The scheme was also economically unviable, due to insurance costs to cover the bank's liability. Further, questions were also raised about whether the bill of lading was truly electronic since it came into existence in a tangible form.

The CMI came up with a proposal where the carrier (instead of the bank) is responsible for effecting the transfer of the bill of lading. The CMI Rules for Electronic Bills of Lading (hereinafter CMI Rules),[113] like INCOTERMS 2000, need to be incorporated into the contract. From the very beginning, the document starts life in an intangible form. Once the carrier receives the goods from the shipper, the carrier sends a receipt message of the goods to the shipper (Article 4(a)) containing the usual details found in such receipts – the name of the shipper, the description of the goods including any reservation, the date and place of receipt, a reference to the terms of carriage, and the private key to be used (Articles 4(b)(i)–(v)). One of the omissions at this stage is the date and place of shipment that is included in a paper bill of lading. Article 4(c) makes provision for this by requiring that the receipt message be updated with these details as soon as the goods have been loaded. But the onus seems to be on the holder to demand the updating. So, what is the effect if such an updating takes place? According to Article 4(d), the description of the goods, including any reservation, the date and place of receipt, a reference to the terms of carriage and the date/place of shipment, 'shall have the same force and effect as if the receipt message were contained in a paper bill of lading'. In other words, the receipt function of the electronic bill is to be no different from a paper bill of lading.[114]

Once the shipper confirms the receipt message, he becomes the holder (Art

---

113   Text available in Carr and Kidner, *International Trade Law Statutes and Conventions*, 5th edn, 2008, Routledge-Cavendish.

114   See 'Bill of lading as a receipt', pp 174–8 above.

4(b)(v)).[115] By becoming holder, according to Art 7(a), the CMI Rules enable him to, as against the carrier:

(i) claim delivery of the goods;
(ii) nominate the consignee or substitute a nominated consignee for any other party, including itself;
(iii) transfer the Right of Control and transfer to another party;
(iv) instruct the carrier or any other subject concerning the goods, in accordance with terms and of the Contract of Carriage, as if he were the holder of a paper bill of lading.

It seems from the above that the holder of the private key has all the rights traditionally associated with a paper bill of lading, naming of a consignee, transferring it to another including by way of pledge, and claim delivery. In other words, it is seen as equivalent to a paper bill of lading. The private key, which plays a crucial role in imparting identity as well as identification, is defined in Art 1(f) as a 'technical appropriate form such as a combination of numbers and/or letters, which the parties may agree for securing the authenticity and integrity of a transmission'. The private key is unique to the holder and upon transfer the new holder is given a new private key (Art 8). The CMI Rules are technology neutral apart from indicating it must be letter/numbers or a combination. The parties are free to choose. Given the developments in relation to electronic signatures and their sophistication, the parties are likely to choose this rather than the well-known four-digit PIN codes since they are easy to hack into. As to what the consequences are for careless or reckless use in relation to these keys, the CMI Rules are silent apart from one provision which talks about misdelivery and the standard of care to be exercised by the carrier. According to Art 9, the carrier is obliged to notify the holder of the place and date of the intended delivery of the goods. Upon notification, the holder is expected to nominate a consignee and to give delivery instructions to the carrier with verification by the private key. If the holder has been careless with the private key as a result of which an entity other than the holder gives instructions to the carrier on which the carrier acts, then it seems the loss will fall on the holder, since according to Art 9(c) the 'carrier shall be under no liability for misdelivery if it can prove that it exercised care to ascertain that the party who claimed to be the consignee was in fact that party'. Equally, where the holder is unaware that the private key has been compromised, the carrier will escape liability if he can establish reasonable care on his part.[116] The burden, however, is on the carrier that he exercised reasonable care.[117]

The terms and conditions of carriage, however, unlike the majority of paper bills of lading, are not included in the receipt message. Article 4(b)(iv) requires that there is a reference to the terms of carriage in the receipt message and Art 5(a) provides that such a reference to the terms will be effective in incorporating those terms in the contract of carriage. This means that a consignee or transferee will be subject to the terms. It is difficult to see why the CMI Rules separate the terms from the receipt

115 Holder is defined in Art 1(g) as 'the party who is entitled to the rights described in Art 7(a) by virtue of its possession of a valid private key'.
116 The presentation rule is not as stringent here as at common law. See 'Delivery against bills of lading', pp 183–5 above.
117 Of course, the carrier may include clauses in his conditions of carriage that exempt him from liability for misdelivery even where he is negligent. It is debatable whether the courts in England would enforce such a clause. As it is, the CMI Rules have lessened common law presentation rules. See *Motis Exports Limited v Dampskibsselskabet AF 1912 Aktieselskabm Akteiselskabet Dampskibsselskabet Svendborg* and 'Delivery against bills of lading', pp 183–5 above.

message. Surely, the receipt message could easily include the standard terms unless of course they were worried by technical aspects such as hard disk space and preferred to simplify the process by replicating a short form bill of lading.[118]

Unlike a paper bill of lading, electronic bills of lading require a third party to effect a transfer. Under the CMI Rules, the carrier plays an important role in transferring the bill of lading. To effect a transfer, the shipper (transferor) has to inform the carrier of the details of the proposed new holder (transferee). Once the carrier has confirmed the notification message, the carrier will issue a new private key to the new holder. Once the holder has accepted the right of control and transfer, the carrier will then issue a private key to the transferee and cancel the private key issued to the shipper (Art 7(b)).

Some jurisdictions may require a contract of carriage to be in writing and signed. In the event of the parties adopting the CMI Rules, Art 11 ensures that they agree not to raise the defence that the contract is not in writing. Of course, at any moment prior to delivery, the holder can demand a paper bill of lading (Art 10(a)). The issue of a paper bill of lading will cancel the private key and terminate the EDI procedures under the CMI Rules but does not affect the rights, obligations or liabilities while performing under the CMI Rules nor the rights, obligations or liabilities under the contract of carriage (Art 10(d)). In other words, the change in medium – paperless to paper – in no way affects the rights, obligations and liabilities of the parties.

It must at this stage be noted that most bills of lading may attract the mandatory application of national law or international conventions such as the Hague-Visby Rules[119] or the Hamburg Rules.[120] Bills of lading incorporating the CMI Rules are subject to mandatorily applicable law according to Art 6 which states:

> The contract of carriage shall be subject to any international convention or national law which would have been compulsorily applicable if a paper bill of lading had been issued.

The success of the CMI Rules will depend on whether merchants are ready to relinquish their control over the bill of lading and entrust the carrier with information to effect a transfer. If they were unhappy in giving information to banks as in the SEADOCs scheme, why should they trust a carrier more than a bank? After all, banks do subscribe to codes of conduct and the duty of confidentiality is a core part of their obligations to their clients. The CMI Rules, however, have the advantage of being freely available to all. It does not require membership to a closed network. This brings us to the BOLERO Rules.

The EU set up a pilot project in the mid- to late-1990s, called the BOLERO project, to study the feasibility of electronic bills of lading. It resulted in the formation of BOLERO International Ltd.[121] It is a closed network and available to those who

---

118 In short form bills of lading, the carrier's standard terms and conditions are incorporated by reference, and the short form includes details such as names of shipper, consignee, and vessel, ports of loading and discharge, description of goods, marks and quantity. This form of bill was introduced to simplify and speed up the process of producing the document. SITPRO (Simplification of International Trade Procedures) in the United Kingdom have produced a standard short form bill. The forms are also available from SITPRO at www.sitpro.org.uk.

119 See Chapter 8, pp 268–73 below. The Hague-Visby Rules do not make provision for their applicability to electronic bills of lading. See also Chapter 9 on electronic transport records under Rotterdam Rules.

120 See Chapter 9.

121 Visit www.bolero.net for further details. Jointly owned by TT Club and SWIFT (an organisation that processes financial transfer for banks).

subscribe with BOLERO taking on the role of a trusted third party providing a platform for secure exchange of trade documents – transport documents such as bills of lading and documentary credits. The subscribers are subject to the BOLERO Rule Book[122] which provides the legal framework for paperless transactions. The BOLERO title registry plays a vital role in respect of bills of lading; it is a database of information relating to bills of lading which is centrally operated. Transfer is effected by a combination of notification, confirmation and authentication through digital signatures. It is not very clear how widely this system is used, though the BOLERO website indicates that major banks, shipping companies and traders are their members. This means that it might also be possible to meet the other functions of bill of lading such as financing the sale/purchase by way of pledge.

CONCLUSION

In this chapter, the many different functions of a bill of lading, ranging from a mere receipt to a contract of carriage and a document of title in international commerce, were described. The bill of lading as a contract of carriage of course defines the rights and duties of both the shipowner and the consignee or endorsee. The 19th century saw the insertion of terms in bills of lading that were extremely disadvantageous to the consignee or endorsee. Common law tried to protect the consignee by construing clauses limiting responsibility (for example, implied undertaking to provide a seaworthy ship), or excluding liability narrowly. Clearly worded clauses, however, were given effect, since it was not the job of the courts to intervene in the parties' contract. International organisations sought to protect the weaker party (cargo owner in this case) through the formulation of international conventions. The following three chapters (7, 8 and 9) examine the rights and responsibilities of the parties to a bill of lading at common law, under the Hague-Visby Rules (implemented by the United Kingdom with the Carriage of Goods by Sea Act 1971), and the Hamburg Rules. Chapter 9 also includes a brief overview of the recently adopted Rotterdam Rules.

FURTHER READING

Bennett, *The History and Present Position of the Bill of Lading as a Document of Title to Goods*, 1914, CUP.

Bools, *The Bill of Lading*, 1997, LLP.

Bradgate and White, 'The Carriage of Goods by Sea Act 1992' (1993) MLR 188.

Burden, 'EDI and bills of lading' [1992] Computer Law and Security Report 269.

Chandler, 'The electronic transmission of bills of lading' (1989) 20(4) JMLC 571.

Colinvaux (ed), *Carver's Carriage by Sea*, 2 vols, 13th edn, 1982, London: Stevens.

Curwen, 'The problems of transferring carriage rights: an equitable solution' [1992] JBL 245.

---

122 Available on www.bolero.net. See also the legal feasibility study prepared by Allen and Overy and Richards Butler, available at www.bolero.net.

Davies, 'Continuing dilemmas with passing of property in part of a bulk' [1991] JBL 111.

Faber, 'Shipping documents and electronic data interchange' [1993] Law, Computers and Artificial Intelligence 21.

Faber, 'Electronic bills of lading' [1996] LMCLQ 232.

Gaskell, Baatz and Asariotis, 'Bills of lading', in Yates (ed), *Contracts for the Carriage of Goods by Land, Sea and Air*, 1993, LLP.

Gliniecki and Ogada, 'The legal acceptance of electronic documents, writings, signatures and notices in international transport convention: a challenge in the age of global electronic commerce' (1992) 13 Northwestern Journal of International Law and Business 117.

Gronfors, 'The paperless transfer of transport information and legal functions', in Schmitthoff and Goode (eds), *International Carriage of Goods: Some Legal Problems and Possible Solutions*, 1988, Centre for Commercial Law Studies, Queen Mary College.

Humphreys and Higgs, 'Waybills: a case of common law laissez faire in European commerce' [1992] JBL 453.

Kelly, 'The CMI charts a course on the sea of electronic data interchange' [1992] Tulane Maritime LJ 349.

Kindred, 'When bits replace bills, what shall the law byte on? Legal consequences of automating carriage documentation', in Sharpe and Spicer (eds), *New Directions in Maritime Law*, 1984, Toronto: Carswell.

Kozolchyk, 'Evolution and present state of bill of lading from a banking law perspective' [1992] JMLC 161.

Kozolchyk, 'The paperless letter of credit and related documents of title' [1992] Law and Contemporary Problems 39.

Livermore and Krailerk, 'Electronic bills of lading' [1997] Journal of Maritime Law and Commerce 55.

Lloyd, 'The bill of lading – do we really need it?' [1989] LMCLQ 47.

Merges and Reynolds, 'Towards a computerized system for negotiating ocean bills of lading' (1986) 6 Journal of Law and Commerce 36.

Ritter, 'Defining international electronic commerce' (1992) 13 Northwestern Journal of International Law and Business 3.

Tetley, 'Waybills: modern contract of carriage of goods by sea' [1983] JMLC 501.

Urbach, 'The electronic presentation and transfer of shipping documents', in Goode (ed), *Electronic Banking: the Legal Implications*, 1985, The Institute of Bankers and Centre for Commercial Law Studies, Queen Mary College.

Walden and Savage, 'The legal problems of paperless transaction' [1989] JBL 102.

Williams, 'Waybills and short form documents: a lawyer's view' [1979] LMCLQ 297.

Wilson, *Carriage of Goods by Sea*, 6th edn, 2008, Pearson Longman.

CHAPTER 7

BILLS OF LADING AND COMMON LAW

INTRODUCTION

It is probable that a proportion of bills of lading issued in the UK is likely to be governed by the liability regime of the Hague-Visby Rules[1] – the product of an international convention to redress the imbalance caused by the extended use of, and tolerance towards, exclusion clauses operating in favour of shipowning interests.

Regardless, common law may still be relevant since not all types of bills of lading, or kinds of cargo carried under a transferable bill of lading, trigger the application of the Hague Rules or the Hague-Visby Rules.[2] Bills of lading issued for the carriage of live animals, deck cargo, bills of lading that are not documents of title (that is, bills of lading that are non-transferable),[3] and bills of lading issued for the carriage of goods by inland waterway are likely to attract the application of rules founded in common law.

Parties to such bills of lading are free to expressly incorporate the Hague-Visby Rules under ss 1(6)(a) and 1(6)(b) of the Carriage of Goods by Sea Act 1971.[4] In the absence of express incorporation of the Hague-Visby Rules, the terms of carriage are largely determined in England by common law – derived from custom and commercial usage – and general principles of contract law as applied to the terms as agreed by the parties.[5]

Common law implies a number of obligations on the part of both the shipowner (or carrier) and the shipper. The parties can lessen the liability imposed by these implied undertakings, or exclude them altogether with the aid of contractual stipulations. The stipulations need to be expressed in clear language, since lack of clarity will attract the application of the common law implied undertakings to the contract of carriage.[6]

IMPLIED OBLIGATIONS ON THE PART OF THE SHIPOWNER

The shipowner is under an implied obligation at common law to:

- provide a seaworthy ship;
- proceed with due dispatch;
- carry the cargo to the agreed destination without deviation; and
- use due care and skill in navigating the vessel and in carrying the goods.

---

1 See Chapter 8 for an account of the Hague-Visby Rules.
2 Of course, the parties may incorporate the Hague-Visby Rules with a clause paramount. See 'Scope of Application', Chapter 8, pp 268–73 below.
3 Eg, a bill of lading made out to a named consignee. See Chapter 8, pp 269–70, below on straight bills of lading.
4 See Chapter 8.
5 This applies equally to other Commonwealth countries such as India, Malaysia and Singapore. See Carr, 'Bills of lading – India', in Jackson (ed), *World Shipping Laws*, loose-leaf, 1990, Oceana.
6 See 'Seaworthiness', pp 208–12 below, below; also *The Galileo* [1914] P 9; *Nelson v Nelson* [1908] AC 16.

Seaworthiness

Common law places the shipowner under an implied warranty to supply a ship that is fit for its purposes. As Lord Blackburn said in *Steel v State Line*:[7]

> I take it . . . to be quite clear, both in England and in Scotland, that where there is a contract to carry goods in a ship, whether that contract is in the shape of a bill of lading, or any other form, there is a duty on the part of the person who furnishes or supplies that ship, or that ship's room, unless something is stipulated which prevents it, that the ship shall be fit for its purposes. That is generally expressed by saying that it shall be seaworthy . . . [at p 86].

The meaning of seaworthiness is a two-fold one. It refers to both the physical state of the ship and its fitness for receiving the cargo – that is, cargoworthiness.[8]

As for the ship's physical state, it must be fit for the purposes of the voyage to be undertaken. That is, the ship must be fit in design and structure, and must be suitably equipped to encounter the ordinary perils that are likely on the particular route to her destination at that time of the year.[9] The ship is also required to have a sufficient and competent crew for carrying out the intended voyage. So, where the captain and the chief officer are in a drunken state at the start of the voyage,[10] or the master or the crew is incompetent,[11] the ship would be deemed unseaworthy. She must also take a safe supply of bunkers (that is, fuel) for the intended voyage.[12]

The question of whether a ship is fit for the voyage or not is a question of fact and will vary from case to case. So, where the weather is expected to be exceptionally rough, the level of seaworthiness will be far higher than the level of seaworthiness for a voyage on calm seas. In other words, the question of seaworthiness is to be ascertained in terms of the surrounding circumstances.

The ship must be seaworthy at the time of sailing.[13] If the ship develops faults after the ship has sailed or during the process of getting out of the harbour, the undertaking of seaworthiness would have been satisfied. The ship is deemed to sail when she leaves the moorings with no intention of returning to the moorings.[14]

The ship must also be cargoworthy – that is, fit to carry the particular cargo safely. So, if the contract of carriage is for carriage of frozen meat, then the ship must have the

---

7   [1877] 3 AC 72.
8   *Rathbone v MacIver* [1903] 2 KB 378.
9   *Stanton v Richardson* (1874) LR 7 CP 421.
10   *Moore v Lunn* (1923) 38 TLR 649.
11   Eg, in *Standard Oil v Clan Line* [1924] AC 100, Lord Atkinson said:

> It is not disputed, I think, that a ship may be rendered unseaworthy by the inefficiency of the master who commands her. Does not that principle apply where the master's inefficiency consists, whatever his general efficiency may be, in his ignorance as how his ship may, owing to the peculiarities of her structure, behave in circumstances likely to be met with on an ordinary ocean voyage. There cannot be any difference in principle, I think, between disabling want of skill and disabling want of knowledge. Each equally renders the master unfit and unqualified to command, and therefore makes the ship he commands unseaworthy [at p 120].

> See also *Hong Kong Fir v Kawasaki Kisen Kaisha* [1962] 2 QB 21. See *Toepfer v Tossa Marine (The Derby)* [1985] 2 Lloyd's Rep 325 on the lack of documentation and seaworthiness.

12   *Fiumana Societa di Navigazione v Bunge* [1930] 2 KB 47.
13   *Stanton v Richardson* (1874) 9 CP 390.
14   *The Rona* (1884) 51 LT 28.

necessary refrigeration to carry the meat safely on the agreed voyage. Defective refrigerators will be a breach of the seaworthiness warranty.[15] If the holds need to be disinfected for the safe carriage of the cargo, failure to do so would be regarded as unseaworthiness.[16] Once again, the question of whether or not the ship is fit to carry the cargo is a question of fact.

The undertaking of cargoworthiness, however, needs to be distinguished from that of bad stowage. The distinction between the two may not always be that clear cut. In some instances, it is possible for bad stowage to appear to be an issue of cargoworthiness as the case of *Elder, Dempster v Pater Zochonis*[17] illustrates. The ship loaded a cargo of palm oil in casks which were stored at the bottom of the hold. Lacking 'tween decks', six tons of palm kernel were stowed on top of the casks. On arrival at Hull, it was found that much of the oil was lost or damaged due to pressure on the casks caused by the sacks stored directly above them. There was conclusive evidence in the log to show that damage to the casks happened *after they were loaded but before the ship set sail*. The bill of lading contained an exception clause which protected the shipowners from loss caused due to bad stowage. The plaintiffs argued that the lack of 'tween decks' was a breach of cargoworthiness. The defendants argued bad stowage. Both the Court of First Instance and the Court of Appeal decided that the absence of 'tween decks' was an issue of cargoworthiness. The decision was reversed in the House of Lords who concluded that the ship was structurally, at the time the casks were loaded, fit to receive and carry the cargo without injury. The presence of 'tween decks' was not necessary for the carriage of the casks and the damage was caused by bad stowage.

The House of Lords acknowledged the difficulties in distinguishing cargoworthiness from bad stowage and went on to say that in some situations bad stowage could amount to unseaworthiness – that is, where it affected the physical safety of the ship. So, for instance, if the casks had been stored in a manner that would have caused the ship to sink on sailing, there would have been a breach of the seaworthiness undertaking due to bad stowage.[18]

At this juncture, it would be natural to ask whether the warranty of seaworthiness in relation to cargo needs to be satisfied only at the commencement of loading or whether it extends to the time of sailing. According to *McFadden v Blue Star Line*,[19] it seems that the warranty must be fulfilled at the time of loading. Here, a sluice door was opened and improperly closed after the goods were loaded on to the ship but before she set sail. The goods were damaged as a consequence. The court came to the conclusion that there was no breach of seaworthiness since the event causing the damage took place after the goods were loaded on to the ship. The decision in *McFadden v Blue Star Line* was cited with approval in the House of Lords in *Elder, Dempster v Pater Zochonis*.[20] However, the judgment of Viscount Cave in the latter suggests that the warranty of seaworthiness for cargo 'extends to fitness for the cargo not only at the time of loading but also at the time of sailing'. In support, he cites *The Thorsa*.[21]

---

15 *Cargo per Maori King v Hughes* [1895] 2 QB 550.
16 *Tattersall v National SS Co* (1884) 12 QBD 297.
17 [1924] AC 522.
18 See, however, Lord Finlay's dissenting statement in respect of unseaworthiness.
19 [1905] 1 KB 697.
20 [1924] AC 522.
21 [1916] P 257.

However, it is difficult to find *dicta* for Lord Viscount's proposition in *The Thorsa*. In this case, cheese and chocolate were stowed together as a result of which the chocolate became tainted. On the question of breach of the cargoworthiness warranty, the court came to the conclusion that the cheese was stowed after the chocolate, which did not make the ship uncargoworthy as regards the cargo of chocolate. As Carver states, the *dicta* in *The Thorsa* seems to be inconsistent with Viscount Cave's interpretation in *Elder, Dempster v Pater Zochonis*. Besides, later judgments have not followed Viscount Cave's suggestion. For instance, in *Reed v Page*,[22] according to Scrutton LJ:

> ... the highest measure of liability as a cargo carrying adventure, that is, of 'cargowor-thiness', is when cargo is commenced to be loaded. It has been decided that if at this stage the ship is fit to receive her contract cargo, it is immaterial when she sails on her voyage, though fit as a ship to sail, she is unfit by reason of stowage to carry her cargo safely [at p 755].

A related question that arises in this context is if the warranty of physical safety of the ship attaches at the time of sailing and that of cargoworthiness at the time of loading, are there no intermediate warranties for the period after the goods have been loaded and the ship is waiting to set sail? In *Reed v Page*, an overloaded barge sank after loading but before being towed to her destination. According to Scrutton LJ, the highest measure of liability attaches at the time when the ship starts on her voyage. Nonetheless, there could be other stages when the warranty of seaworthiness as a ship was applicable – and that is, where the ship was waiting after loading to sail. In his opinion:

> ... the barge was unseaworthy as a barge from the time loading finished, unfit to lie in the river and unfit to be towed ... it seems ... clear that if an overloaded barge, sea-worthy in the calm waters of a dock, went out into the river to wait for a tug, there would be a renewed warranty of fitness to navigate and wait, which would be broken by overloading, rendering the barge to lie waiting in the river. In the present, when the loading was finished and the man in charge, apparently in the ordinary course of his business, left her unattended in the river waiting for a tug, and unfit in fact either to lie in the river or be towed, there was a new stage of the adventure, a new warranty of fitness for that stage, and a breach of that warranty ... [at p 757].

The undertaking to provide a seaworthy ship is an absolute obligation at common law. This means that the shipowner has to show that the ship is seaworthy *in fact*. He cannot escape liability simply by showing that he has taken every precaution to make the ship seaworthy. As Lord Blackburn stated in *Steel v State Line*:[23]

> ... in marine contracts, contracts for sea carriage, there is what is properly called a 'warranty' not merely that they should do their best to make the ship fit, but that the ship should really be fit [at p 86].

It seems that the absolute undertaking to provide a seaworthy ship is personal to the shipowner and he cannot escape liability by showing that he has taken care to dele-gate work to dependable skilled employees and reputable independent contractors. Of course, if the shipowner wishes to lessen his absolute liability, he can do so through express stipulations but these must be clearly and unambiguously expressed.

The test for ascertaining the seaworthiness of a ship is an objective one. The

---

22   [1927] 1 KB 743.
23   (1877) 3 App Cas 72.

question to ask is 'would a prudent owner have remedied the defect before sending the ship to sea had he been aware of the defect'?[24] If the answer is affirmative, the ship would be deemed unseaworthy.

The shipowner however is not expected to provide a ship that is perfect in every way. Lack of the latest or best appliances therefore would not affect the seaworthiness of the ship.[25] What is required is that the ship is fitted for the particular voyage, the particular cargo and the particular time of the year according to the degree of care exercised by an ordinary and prudent owner. In other words, the standard expected of the ship is relative to the existing state of knowledge and the standards prevailing at the material time.[26]

The burden of proof for establishing unseaworthiness rests on the party who asserts it. The party relying on unseaworthiness must plead it in sufficient detail. The unexplained sinking of a ship normally does not automatically raise the presumption that the ship was unseaworthy. However, in some circumstances, the facts may raise this presumption easily, in which case the burden shifts to the other party to show that the ship was in a seaworthy state at the time of sailing. In *Fiumana Societa Navigazione v Bunge*,[27] there was a fire in the coal bunkers as a result of which the cargo was damaged. No satisfactory explanation for the occurrence of the fire was given and in the circumstances this raised the inference that the fire was caused due to the unfitness of the bunker coal – a breach of the seaworthiness warranty. The cargo owner also has to show that it was the unseaworthiness that caused the damage or loss.[28]

In the event of damage or loss to the cargo due to unseaworthiness, it seems that the shipowner may be liable even where part of the damage could be attributed to other causes as long as seaworthiness is a cause or a real, actual or effective cause of the damage. That is to say, *novus actus interveniens* will not break the chain of causation and reduce seaworthiness from 'a cause that causes' (*causa causans*) to a cause which is 'merely an incident which precedes in the history or narrative of events, but as a cause is not in at the death, and hence is irrelevant' (*causa sine qua non*). In *Smith, Hogg v Black Sea and Baltic General Insurance*,[29] deck cargo was stored on deck in a manner that made the ship extremely unstable. During bunkering operations, the forepeak was emptied which increased her degree of list. As a consequence, she lay on her beams and the cargo was damaged. There was an exception clause in the contract that protected the owners for loss or damage caused due to the negligence of their employees. The defendants contended that the negligent act of the master in bunkering was the cause of the loss and relied on the exception clause. The court came to the conclusion that a cause of the loss was unseaworthiness. The alleged negligence of the master was proximate in time to the disaster and may have contributed to the disaster 'but the disaster would not have arisen *but for* the unseaworthiness'. In other words, the unseaworthiness was effective in bringing about the loss even though other events equally detrimental may have taken place between the moment of unseaworthiness and the moment of damage.

The undertaking of providing a seaworthy ship is regarded as an innominate

---

24   *McFadden v Blue Star Line* [1905] 1 KB 706.
25   *Virginia Co v Norfolk Co* (1912) 17 Com Cas 277.
26   *Bradley v Federal SN Co* (1927) 137 LT 266.
27   [1930] 2 KB 47.
28   *International Packers v Ocean Steamship* [1955] 2 Lloyd's Rep 218.
29   [1940] AC 997.

term. In the event of a breach, the remedy available to the injured party will depend on the seriousness of the breach. If the breach goes to the root of the contract such as to make further commercial performance of the contract impossible, the injured party can repudiate the contract and claim damages; however, if it does not frustrate the commercial purpose of the contract, the remedy available is damages.[30]

The shipowner is free to contract out of the implied undertaking of seaworthiness. The stipulation however needs to be express, clear and unambiguous.[31] A clause couched in general terms would be construed restrictively. For instance, phrases such as 'at ship's expense and shipper's risk' would be insufficient to exclude the implied obligation.[32] In construing the effectiveness of a clause, the courts, however, tend to look at the agreement as a whole.[33] A clearly worded clause exempting liability for unseaworthiness may therefore be rendered totally or partially ineffective when read in the context of the whole agreement. In *Elderslie SS Co v Borthwick*,[34] amongst others, the bill of lading contained the following clauses:

> Clause 1 – Neither the steamer nor her owners, nor her charterers, shall be accountable for the condition of goods shipped under this bill of lading, nor for any loss or damage thereto, whether arising from failure or breakdown of machinery, insulation, or other appliances, refrigerating or otherwise, or from any other cause whatsoever, whether arising from a defect existing at the commencement of the voyage or at the time of shipment of the goods or not.

> Clause 2 – ... whether or not any of the perils, causes or things above mentioned or the loss or injury arising therefrom, be occasioned by or arise from any act or omission, negligence, default of error in judgement of the master, pilot, ... crew, stevedores, or other persons whomsoever in the service of the owners or charterers ... *if reasonable means have been taken to provide against such defects and unseaworthiness* [emphasis added].

The court came to the conclusion that though cl 1 excluded unseaworthiness in clear language, the combined effect of cll 1 and 2 meant that the shipowner could exclude liability only if he could show that he had taken reasonable measures to provide against unseaworthiness.

Due dispatch

Common law implies that the voyage must be prosecuted with due dispatch, that is, the vessel will proceed on the voyage, load and discharge at the time agreed. In the absence of express agreement or agreement by implication, the law implies the performance of the voyage within a reasonable time. What is reasonable is inferred in relation to what can reasonably be expected from the carrier under the actual circumstances at the time of performance.[35]

This undertaking seems to be treated as an innominate term. The remedy available to the injured party on the breach of this term would therefore depend on the consequences of the breach. If the consequences of the breach are not so serious as to

---

30 *Hong Kong Fir Co v Kawasaki Kisen Kaisha* [1962] 2 QB 26.
31 See for a recent clause that was successful *Mitsubishi Corporation v Eastwind Transport Ltd (The Irbensky Proliv)* [2005] 1 Lloyd's Rep 383.
32 *The Galileo* [1914] P 9.
33 *Nelson v Nelson* [1908] AC 16.
34 [1905] AC 93.
35 *Hick v Raymond* [1893] AC 22.

go to the root of the contract, the injured party can claim damages only by way of compensation. However, if the consequences are so serious as to frustrate the contract of carriage, the injured party can repudiate the contract and claim damages. In *Freeman v Taylor*,[36] a ship was chartered to take cargo to the Cape of Good Hope and then proceed to Bombay with all convenient speed to load a cargo of cotton. The captain after discharging the goods at the Cape loaded a cargo of cattle and mules for discharge at Mauritius. The vessel was delayed by seven weeks. On arrival at Bombay, the charterer refused to load the cotton. The delay of seven weeks was regarded as sufficient to frustrate the commercial purpose of the contract.

Deviation

Under common law, the shipowner is under an implied obligation to carry the cargo to the agreed destination directly without any deviation. The shipowner is presumed to take the direct geographical and safe route to the port of discharge. Where he does not take the direct route to the port of destination, evidence may be adduced to show that the route that he took is the normal customary route. In *Reardon Smith Line v Black Sea and Baltic General Insurance*,[37] the ship deviated from the direct geographical route on a voyage from Poti (in the Black Sea) to Sparrow's Point (in the US) to Constanza to obtain cheap fuel. The defendants were able to show that their vessels invariably went to Constanza for fuel and that 25% of the vessels plying that route stopped at Constanza. The rule that the ship must not deviate is, however, not that strict, and common law does allow the ship to depart from the direct geographical route in the following circumstances:

- for saving human life; and
- for the prosecution of the voyage or for the safety of the adventure.

Deviation from the route defined in the contract is regarded as justified where it occurs for the purposes of saving human lives. This justification, however, is construed strictly and does not extend to the saving of property during the course of saving lives. In *Scaramanga v Stamp*,[38] The Olympias was carrying a cargo of wheat when she sighted *The Arion* in distress. Instead of taking the crew off the ship, *The Olympias* agreed to tow the Arion for £1,000. The weather was fine so there would have been no difficulty in taking the crew off *The Arion*. It was held that the saving of property during the course of saving life did not amount to a justifiable deviation. However, if saving property is an essential step for saving lives, the saving of property in these circumstances will not be regarded as unjustifiable deviation. So, if the crew cannot be lifted off the ship in distress due to extreme weather conditions, the towing of the vessel would be justifiable. The law relating to deviation was succinctly stated in *Scaramanga v Stamp*:

> ... deviation for the purpose of communicating with a ship in distress is allowable, inasmuch as the state of the vessel in distress may involve danger to life. On the other hand, deviation for the sole purpose of saving property is not thus privileged, but entails all the usual consequences of deviation. If, therefore, the lives of the persons on

---

36 (1831) 8 Bing 124. Note that the due dispatch obligation also applies to the approach voyage.
37 (1939) AC 562.
38 (1880) 5 CPD 295.

board a disabled ship can be saved without saving the ship, as by taking them off, deviation for the purposes of saving them will carry with it all the consequences of an unauthorised deviation. But where the preservation of life can only be effected through the concurrent saving of property, and the *bona fide* purpose of saving life forms part of the motive which leads to the deviation, the privilege will not be lost by reason of the purpose of saving property having formed a second motive for deviating [at p 304].

Of course, it is possible for the shipowner to extend justifiable deviation to cover deviation for the purposes of saving property through express clauses in the contract of carriage. Such liberty clauses, however, need to be clearly expressed if they are to be effective.

Common law imposes a duty on the shipowner to use all reasonable care to conclude the adventure satisfactorily and, to that end, allows the master to take necessary steps to protect the cargo and the ship from undue risks. So, where the ship sustains damage such that repairs are essential for continuing the adventure safely, he is allowed to put into port for repairs even if this results in a deviation from the contractual route.[39]

Deviation which is brought about due to the ship's unseaworthiness at the commencement of the voyage is justifiable on the reasoning that the introduction of a double standard – one dependent on the master's own culpable act and the other on the lack of it – would result in an increase in the dangers to which life and property are exposed to at sea. As the court explained in *Kish v Taylor*:

> Must the master of every ship be left in this dilemma that, whenever by his own culpable act, or a breach of contract by his owner, he finds his ship in a perilous position, he must continue on his voyage at all hazards, or only seek safety under the penalty of forfeiting the contract of affreightment? Nothing could ... tend more to increase the dangers to which life and property are exposed at sea than to hold that the law of England obliged the master to choose between such alternatives [at pp 618–19].

The shipowner is free to include express liberty to deviate clauses that increase the kinds of situations in which he can deviate. These clauses are construed in the light of the general principle that the object of the contract must not be defeated by the clause. As Lord Wright stated in *Foreman v Federal SN Co*, 'every deviation clause must be construed with reference to the contemplated adventure'.[40] Where the clause is couched in broad general terms and inserted primarily for the shipowner's benefit, the courts give the clause an extensively restricted interpretation. In *Glynn v Margetson*,[41] oranges were loaded at Malaga under a bill of lading which described the ship as 'now lying in the port of Malaga bound for Liverpool'. There was also a liberty clause which read:

> ... liberty to proceed to and stay at any port or ports in any rotation in the Mediterranean, Levant, Black Sea or Adriatic, or on the coasts of Africa, Spain, Portugal, France, Great Britain and Ireland for the purpose of delivering coals, cargo, or passengers, or for any other purpose whatsoever.

After loading the oranges, the ship went to a port on the north-eastern coast of Spain before proceeding on her voyage to Liverpool. The wide ambit of the clause however

---

39   *James Phelp and Co v Hill* [1892] 1 QB 605.
40   [1928] 2 KB 424, at p 431.
41   [1893] AC 351.

was ineffective in protecting the shipowner from damages for the decayed condition of the oranges since the clause was seen as frustrating the object of the described voyage. Similarly, in *Leduc v Ward*,[42] 'liberty to call at any ports in any order' was construed as imparting a limited right of calling only at those ports that would naturally and usually be ports of call in the voyage named. However, not all liberty clauses are ineffective. In *Connolly Shaw v Nordenfjeldske SS Co*,[43] lemons were shipped under a bill of lading from Palermo to Hull. The clause read: '... to proceed to ... any ports whatsoever ... although ... out of or beyond the route ...'

The ship deviated to Hull and the shipowner invoked the liberty clause. The court held that the ship had the right to deviate to Hull under the liberty clause provided the object of the contract, the carriage of perishable goods to London, was not frustrated. A suitably worded liberty clause in the right circumstances will protect the shipowner.

The implied obligation of not to deviate is regarded as a condition of the contract. This entitles the cargo owner to repudiate the contract and claim damages, or waive the deviation while reserving the right to damages. In the event of repudiation, the shipowner will be unable to rely on clauses such as exception clauses and freight clauses in the contract of carriage – a rather harsh result as far as the shipowner is concerned. The adverse effect of unjustifiable deviation was justified in *Thorley v Orchis SS Co*[44] on the reasoning that it is 'such a serious matter, and changes the character of the voyage so essentially, that a shipowner who has been guilty of a deviation cannot be considered as having performed his part of the bill of lading contract, but something fundamentally different, and therefore he cannot claim the benefit of stipulations in his favour contained in the bill of lading' (p 690). A further reason for regarding deviation as a matter of grave importance is that the shipper loses the benefit of insurance from the moment the vessel actually deviates.

Once the shipper has elected to repudiate the contract, the shipowner is relegated to the position of a common carrier. The general opinion is that, as a common carrier, he is entitled to the common law exceptions – act of God, act of Queen's enemies and inherent vice – provided he can show that the damage would have been caused by the excepted perils even if he had not deviated[45] and reasonable freight on a *quantum meruit* basis.[46]

Where the shipper decides to treat the contract as subsisting after hearing of the deviation, the shipowner will have the benefit of the terms of the contract. The waiver of the right to repudiate on the part of the cargo owner must be unequivocal, definite, clear, cogent and complete for it to be operative.[47] The waiver of a deviation by a charterer however does not affect the consignee of a bill of lading who has no notice of the deviation. In *Hain v Tate and Lyle*,[48] a ship was chartered to carry sugar from Cuban ports and a port in San Domingo to be nominated by the charterers. The ship loaded at the Cuban ports and proceeded to Queenstown. Owing to a communication problem, the master was not aware of the nomination of a port in San Domingo. Once

---

42   (1888) 20 QBD 475.
43   (1934) 50 TLR 418.
44   [1907] 1 KB 660.
45   *Morrison v Shaw, Savill* [1916] 2 KB 783.
46   *Hain v Tate and Lyle* (1936) 41 Com Cas 350, at pp 368–9.
47   *McCormick v National Motor Insurance* (1934) 40 Com Cas 76, at p 93.
48   (1936) 41 Com Cas 350.

the parties realised the mistake, the master was ordered to proceed to the nominated port. On leaving San Domingo, the ship stranded and part of the cargo was lost. The salvaged cargo was shipped on another vessel which was collected by the endorsees of the bill of lading who had no knowledge of the deviation. Upon learning of the deviation, Tate and Lyle, the endorsees, commenced an action to recover the deposit they had paid towards general average contributions. The House of Lords held that the consignees could rely on the deviation. The waiver of the deviation by the charterers did not affect their right to repudiate, since waiver could not take place in ignorance.

Where a ship deviates after the cargo is lost or damaged, it is unclear whether the carrier loses the benefit of the exception clauses with regard to the damage or loss that occurred before the deviation. In *Internationale Guano v MacAndrew*,[49] the judgment of Pickford J suggests that the shipowner cannot take advantage of the exclusion clauses in the contract even where the damage or loss occurred before the deviation. However, in *Hain v Tate and Lyle*,[50] there are *dicta* to suggest that the cargo owner can treat the contract at an end only from the date of deviation, which means that the exclusion clauses will be operative in respect of those damages that occurred before the deviation. The opinion expressed in *Hain v Tate and Lyle* is perhaps the better one, since it is difficult to see how rights that have accrued prior to a deviation can be displaced by that deviation.

The view that the shipowner loses the benefit of exclusion clauses in the contract of carriage is the subject of some debate since the decision in *Photo Production v Securicor*.[51] Even though Lord Wilberforce stated in *Photo Production* that deviation cases must be preserved as a body of authority *sui generis*, legal and academic opinion, however, seem to favour the view that the extent to which exclusion clauses apply to the contract of carriage upon deviation should be treated as a matter of construction.[52]

Negligence

There is an implied obligation in every contract of affreightment, according to Lord Mcnaghten in *The Xantho*,[53] that the shipowner will 'use due care and skill in navigating the vessel and carrying the goods' (at p 515). There is also a duty, according to Willes J in *Notara v Henderson*,[54] on the part of the master representing the shipowner 'to take reasonable care of the goods entrusted to him, not merely in doing what is necessary to preserve them on board the ship during the ordinary incidents of the voyage, but also in taking reasonable measures to check and arrest their loss, destruction or deterioration, by reason of accidents' (p 235).

The shipowner can exclude liability for damage or loss caused by negligence but these clauses, like the clauses exempting liability for deviation and unseaworthiness, need to be express, pertinent and apposite.

---

49   [1909] 2 KB 360.
50   The effect of fundamental breach on exclusion clauses was discussed in a number of cases prior to *Photo Production* (see below) and referred to in *Photo Production*.
51   [1980] AC 827.
52   See also Chapter 8, pp 243–6 below.
53   [1887] 12 AC 503.
54   (1872) LR 7 QB 225.

IMPLIED OBLIGATIONS ON THE PART OF THE SHIPPER

Common law implies an obligation on the shipper to inform the shipowner of the dangerous nature of the goods. Notification, however, is not required where the carrier or a member of the crew knows or ought to have been reasonably aware of the dangerous nature of the cargo. In *Brass v Maitland*,[55] the shipowner was expected to know of the dangerous character of chloride of lime since the cargo was described as bleaching powder.

The concept of dangerous goods has been widely construed. It not only includes intrinsically dangerous substances (for instance, radioactive materials, explosives, petroleum) but also what apparently is safe cargo which in appropriate circumstances may create a hazardous situation. The dangerousness of the cargo is determined in the light of the overall nature of the situation.[56] Goods are regarded as dangerous not only where they endanger the safety of the ship and the cargo but also where they detain the vessel. In *Mitchell, Cotts v Steel Bros and Co Ltd*,[57] a cargo of rice was held to be dangerous since the charterer knew of the need for permission from the British government in order to unload the cargo but did not inform the shipowner of this.

It is unclear whether or not the undertaking implied at common law is an absolute obligation. There is authority to support both views. In *Brass v Maitland*, bleaching powder containing chloride of lime was shipped in casks. The fumes from the powder escaped and corroded goods that had been stowed alongside the casks. The shipper had shipped the goods on acquiring them from a third party without inspecting the consignment. Lord Campbell and Wightman J were of the view that the shipper's liability is an absolute one, so that he is liable even where he is unaware of the dangerous nature of the goods. Crompton J, however, doubted the wisdom of this view; first, there was no authority to support the view that the undertaking not to ship dangerous goods was an absolute one on the part of the shipper and, secondly, though expedient, it had the unfortunate result of making an ignorant shipper liable. He felt that the warranty extended only to 'cases where the shipper has knowledge, or means of knowledge, of the dangerous nature of the goods when shipped or where he has been guilty of some negligence as shipper, as by shipping without communicating danger, which he had the means of knowing, and ought to have communicated' (p 57). The subsequent case of *Mitchell, Cotts v Steel Brothers*, however, suggests that the guarantee provided by the shipper is a guarantee that it is not dangerous to his knowledge and that he has taken reasonable care to assure himself of that fact. The much more recent case of *The Athanasia Comninos*[58] may have resolved the ambiguity to some extent. It supports the strict liability approach put forward in *Brass v Maitland*.

The shipowner has the burden of proving lack of notification regarding the dangerous nature of the goods.

---

55   (1856) 26 LJ QB 49.
56   *Ministry of Transport v Lamport and Holt* [1952] 2 Lloyd's Rep 371.
57   [1916] 1 KB 610.
58   [1990] 1 Lloyd's Rep 277.

SHIPOWNER'S IMMUNITIES

The shipowner is free to negotiate the terms of sea carriage. It is not unusual for bills of lading not governed by Carriage of Goods by Sea Act 1971 to include an extensive list of exception clauses that operate in the shipowner's favour. In the absence of express exemption clauses in a bill of lading, common law implies a number of exclusions that operate in favour of the shipowner. These common law exceptions are also available to common carriers;[59] hence, shipowners whose contracts have been repudiated can also take advantage of these exceptions provided they can show that the damage would have occurred even if they had not deviated. In *Morrison v Shaw Savill,*[60] the ship deviated from the contract route. It was sunk by an enemy ship. The carrier could not take advantage of the common law exception of act of the King's enemies since the carrier could not establish that the vessel would have sunk even if there had been no deviation.

COMMON LAW EXCEPTIONS

In the absence of express stipulations in the contract of carriage, common law implies the following exclusions:

- act of God;
- act of Queen's enemies; and
- inherent vice.

Act of God

The carrier is not liable for loss or damage where it is the result of natural causes independent of human intervention, and which could not be prevented by the exercise of foresight and reasonable care.[61]

Act of Queen's enemies

The carrier is not liable for loss or damage which has occurred due to acts committed by states or their subjects with whom the Sovereign is at war. This exception does not, however, cover acts perpetrated by pirates or robbers.[62]

Inherent vice

The carrier is not liable for loss or damage to goods where it is caused by defects that are inherent in the goods. Loss or damage includes wastage in bulk or weight.

---

59 A common carrier, unlike a private carrier, holds himself willing to carry goods for anyone for reward. *Tyly v Morrice* (1699) Carth 485; 90 ER 879; *Bennet v Peninsular and Orient Steamboat Co* (1848) 6 CB 775; (1848) 136 ER 1453; *Liver Alkali v Johnson* (1874) LR 9 Ex 338. See Lord Mansfield's judgment in *Forward v Pittard* (1785) 1 TR 27, at p 33. See also Chapter 13.

60 [1916] 2 KB 783.

61 *Nugent v Smith* (1876) 1 CPD 423.

62 *Russell v Niemann* (1864) 17 CB (NS) 163.

Inherent vice has been construed as the unfitness of the goods to withstand the ordinary incidents of the voyage despite the exercise of care required of the carrier.[63] So, where goods are damaged due to rust, evaporation or defective packing, they have been regarded as constituting inherent vice.

CONTRACTUAL EXCEPTIONS

The parties, as stated earlier, under English law are free to negotiate the terms of carriage. It is not unusual to find a long list of exemption clauses that relieve the shipowner of liability, for instance, in the event of negligence of the ship's crew, collision, strikes, perils of the sea and strikes. The exclusion clauses will be effective in protecting the shipowner only if they are clearly worded. Where the clauses are ambiguous, they are construed *contra proferentem* following the general principles of English contract law.[64] As for s 2 of the Unfair Contract Terms Act 1977 – which requires exclusion clauses to fulfil the requirements of reasonableness – para 2 of Sched 1 to the Act specifically states that ss 2–4 (excepting s 2(7)) do not extend to any contract of carriage of goods except in favour of a person dealing as a consumer. A party deals as a consumer where he neither makes the contract in the course of business nor holds himself out as doing so and the other party makes the contract in the course of business according to s 12(1)(a) and (b). It is therefore unlikely that the Unfair Contract Terms Act 1977 has a major impact on exclusion clauses in bills of lading.

Since the list of exception clauses is inexhaustible, it will not be possible to look at all of them. Therefore, only some of the more commonly found contractual exception clauses will be considered in this chapter.[65]

Perils of the sea

Where the contract expressly excludes liability for perils of the sea, the courts have interpreted it to refer to any damage that has been caused by storms, sea water, collision, standing or perils that are peculiar to the sea or to ship at sea and which could not have been avoided by the exercise of reasonable care.[66]

This exception does not protect the shipowner from damage or loss from events that are not peculiar to the sea or a ship at sea. So, where goods are destroyed due to rats on board a ship,[67] or due to cargo being dropped upon them during loading,[68] the shipowner will be unable to invoke this exception. Neither do perils of the sea extend to the inevitable action of the wind and the waves which results in wear and tear.[69]

---

63   *The Carcore* [1896] 65 LJ Ad 97.
64   See Cheshire, Fifoot and Furmston, *Law of Contract*, 2006, OUP, for an account of the construction of exclusion clauses in English contract law.
65   See *Scrutton on Charterparties*, 20th edn, 1996, Sweet & Maxwell for an extensive list of contractual exceptions.
66   *Canada Rice Mills v Union Marine* [1941] AC 55.
67   *Hamilton v Pandorf* (1887) 12 App Cas 518.
68   *Scott v Marten* [1916] 1 AC 304.
69   *The Xantho* (1887) 12 AC 503.

Arrest or restraint of princes

An exclusion clause in a bill of lading excluding liability for loss or damage due to arrest or restraint of princes, rulers and peoples has been interpreted to apply to a number of situations. It has been successfully invoked where the government of a country takes possession of the goods through embargo, arrests or blockades;[70] where there is a prohibition against importation of the goods;[71] or where the goods cannot be discharged due to quarantine restrictions. It does not, however, apply to situations where there is restriction imposed on sea routes for the safety of shipping or to any political disturbances.[72]

Hostilities and riots

Bills of lading normally contain an exclusion clause relieving the shipowner of liability in the event of damage caused to riots or other commotion. The reason for such a clause is that the common law exception of 'act of Queen's enemies' does not cover civil war, riots or other disturbances. The common law exception only extends to cover acts of war committed by states with whom the Sovereign is at war.

Strikes

It is common to find clauses exempting liability in the event of strikes. The word 'strike' was interpreted by Lord Denning in *The New Horizon*[73] and refers to a concerted stoppage of work by men done with a view to improving their wages or conditions. The strike exception clause not only covers direct loss but also losses caused due to the after-effects of a strike – for instance, where loading is delayed as a result of congestion due to a strike even though the strike had ended by the time the ship calls at the port of loading.[74]

Strike clauses in bills of lading have recently become more specific and range from clauses that place the entire risk on the shipper to those that attempt to spread the risks evenly between the carrier and the shipper.

The bill of lading may also contain a clause that allows the carrier to discharge goods for a strike-bound port at any safe and convenient port (known as the Caspiana clause). Where there is a Caspiana clause, the consignee will not be able to recover the cost of transhipping the goods to the original destination once the strike is over.[75]

---

70 *Geipel v Smith* (1872) LR 7 QB 404.
71 *Stringer v English and Scottish Marine Insurance Co* (1870) LR 5 QB 599.
72 *Nesbitt v Lushington* (1792) 4 TR 783.
73 [1975] 2 Lloyd's Rep 314, at p 317.
74 *Leonis v Rank (No 2)* (1908) 13 Com Cas 215.
75 *Renton v Palmyra Trading Corp* [1957] AC 149.

Latent defects

Where the bill of lading contains a clause excluding liability for a latent defect, it has been interpreted to mean a defect that could not be discovered on such an examination that a reasonably skilled man would make.[76]

This exception, however, does not qualify the implied or express undertaking of seaworthiness.[77] However, where the exclusion for latent defect is qualified by appropriate words, the clause may be successful in restricting the undertaking of seaworthiness. For instance, in *Cargo ex Lacoles*,[78] use of the phrase 'latent defect existing even at the time of shipment' was deemed sufficient to qualify the seaworthiness undertaking.

Fire

The shipowner may be able to claim statutory protection for loss or damage due to fire under s 186 of the Merchant Shipping Act 1995 (previously, s 18 of the Merchant Shipping Act 1979) if the ship is a UK ship and the goods are lost or damaged on board the ship.[79] So, a clause excluding liability for damage or loss due to fire is required in the contract of carriage if the ship is not a British ship. Where the ship is a British ship and the shipowner wants to exclude liability in case of fire not on board, a specific exclusion clause is needed.

As for the statutory exception, it is available even where the fire has been caused due to unseaworthiness as long as the fire occurred without the actual fault or privity of the owner.[80] The onus, however, is on the cargo owner to establish that the fire resulted from the carrier's personal act or omission, committed with intent to cause such loss, or recklessly, and with knowledge that such a loss would probably result.

OTHER TERMS IN BILLS OF LADING

Apart from terms considered above, the bill of lading normally contains terms relating to loading, freight and liens. In the absence of express terms, common law or statute may be relevant in determining the extent of the rights and liabilities of the parties to the contract of carriage.

Responsibility for loading

The general assumption at common law is that the operation of loading is one that is carried out by the shipowner and the shipper jointly, unless custom or express agreement dictates otherwise; in the absence of custom or express agreement, to bring the goods alongside the ship and lift them to the ship's rail and the shipowner is

---

76 *Dimitrios Ralhas* (1922) 13 Lloyd's Law Rep 363.
77 *Minister of Materials v World SS Co* [1952] 1 Lloyd's Rep 485.
78 (1887) 12 PD 187.
79 See 'Fire', Chapter 8, pp 248–50 below.
80 *Virginia Carolina Chemical v Norfolk and North American Steam Shipping* [1912] 1 KB 229.

under an obligation to stow the cargo properly,[81] and exercise the same skill in stowing and lashing as a properly qualified stevedore.[82] If the shipper plays an active role in the stowage of the cargo, he cannot complain of any apparent defects in stowage if he did not voice his reservations at the time.

The shipowner cannot escape liability where he has employed a stevedore unless it has been expressly agreed that he is not to be held responsible for any negligent stowage on the part of his employees or stevedores. Also he can extend this clause to protect his employees and stevedores from liability for negligent stowage as long as he makes it clear that he is contracting as agent on behalf of his employees and stevedores.[83] As for burden of proof that lies on the party who alleges lack of reasonable care in stowage, he must also show that the loss or damage to the cargo was a result of negligent stowage.

Freight

Freight is the consideration, or agreed amount, payable to the carrier for carrying cargo to and delivering it at its destination. It is calculated either on the basis of weight, number of packages or volume. The parties normally agree on when freight is earned and payable – for example, on loading, on sailing of ship, or on signing of bill of lading. Clause 11(a) of the Conlinebill (standard liner bill of lading approved by the Baltic and International Maritime Council – BIMCO) provides that 'pre-payable freight, whether actually paid or not, shall be considered as fully earned upon loading and non-returnable in any event'. The P&O Containers Ltd Bill of Lading for Combined Transport Shipment or Port to Port Shipment standard terms states, in cl 13(1), that 'freight shall be deemed fully earned on receipt of the goods by the carrier and shall be payable and non-returnable in any event'.

In the absence of agreement, at common law, freight is payable on delivery of goods at destination. Freight and delivery are concurrent conditions. In other words:

> ... the true test of the right to freight is the question whether the service in respect of which the freight was contracted to be paid has been substantially performed; and, according to the law of England, as a rule, freight is earned by the carriage and arrival of the goods ready to be delivered to the merchant, though they be in a damaged state when they arrive. If the shipowner fails to carry the goods to the destined port, the freight is not earned. If he carries part, but not the whole, no freight is payable in respect of the part not carried, and freight is payable in respect of the part carried unless ... carriage of the whole [is] a condition precedent in the earning of any freight.[84]

The above rule is inflexible, such that, where cargo fails to reach the destination through no fault of the cargo, freight is not payable. Natural circumstances such as ice preventing a vessel from reaching its destination will not displace the rule.[85] Similarly, where cargo is lost, or arrives in an unsatisfactory state. For instance, in *Asfar and Co v*

---

81 *Sandeman v Scurr* (1866) LR 2 QB 86.
82 *Anglo-African Co v Lamzed* (1866) LR 1 CP 226.
83 *New Zealand Shipping v Satterthwaite* [1975] AC 154. See Chapter 8, pp 254–8 below, also ss 1 and 6(5) of the Contracts (Rights of Third Parties) Act 1999.
84 *Dakin v Oxley* (1864) 15 CB (NS) 646, at p 660. See also *Black v Rose* (1864) 2 Moore PC (NS) 277; *Paynter v James* [1867] LR 2 CP 348; *Ritchie v Atkinson* (1808) 10 East 294.
85 *Metcalfe v Britannia Iron Work Co* (1877) 2 QBD 423.

at the risk of the charterer and the subsequent incidents and misfortunes of the voyages do not entitle him to transfer any of that risk back to the shipowner' (p 246). In other words, advance freight is seen as an agreement in respect of allocation of risks for the voyage to be undertaken and, once allocated, there can be no reallocation on the basis of events arising during the course of the voyage. The rule is said to have originated in the long voyages to India. According to Brett LJ, in *Allison v Bristol Marine Insurance Co*:

> I have drawn attention to all the cases, in order to show how uniform the view has been as to what construction is to be put upon shipping documents in the form of the present charterparty, and as to the uniform, though perhaps anomalous rule, that the money to be paid in advance of freight must be paid, though the goods are before payment lost by perils of the sea and cannot be recovered back after, if paid before the goods are lost by perils of the sea. Although I have said that this course of business may in theory be anomalous, I think its origin and existence are capable of reasonable explanation. It arose in the case of Indian voyages. The length of the voyage would keep the shipowner for too long a time out of money; and freight is much more difficult to pledge, as a security to third persons, than goods represented by a bill of lading. Therefore, the shipper agreed to make the advance on what he would ultimately have to pay and . . . took the risk in order to obviate a repayment, which disarranges business transactions [p 226].

Interestingly, bills of lading reinforce this common law rule expressly, as illustrated by cl 13(1) of the P&O Containers bill of lading terms cited earlier in this section.[96]

Where goods are shipped under a bill of lading, the shipper is normally regarded as liable for the freight. The shipper, however, can relieve himself of liability for freight in a number of ways:

(a) by informing the carrier at the time of contracting that he (the shipper) is contracting as an agent on behalf of another (for instance, where the shipper – that is, seller – may be acting as agent for the buyer under an FOB with additional services sale contract);

(b) by an express term in the contract of carriage; or

(c) by obtaining a freight collect bill of lading (for example, where the parties to a sale contract on CIF terms agree to the issue of a freight collect bill of lading placing the buyer under an obligation to pay on arrival of the goods).[97]

The shipper, however, is freed of liability where the carrier gives credit to the consignee, for instance, by accepting a bill of exchange drawn on the consignee for the sake of his own convenience.[98]

Once the bill of lading is endorsed, it creates enhanced rights in favour of the carrier as against the consignee and the endorsee. It does not, however, extinguish the shipper's liability to pay freight. The rights and liabilities of the various parties to the bill of lading are created and preserved by the Carriage of Goods by Sea Act 1992.[99] According to s 3(3), an endorsement of a bill of lading does not extinguish the shipper's liability for freight. It states:

---

96 See p 222 above.
97 *The Pantanassa* [1970] 1 Lloyd's Rep 153.
98 *Strong v Hart* (1827) 6 B&C 160; (1827) C&P 55
99 See Chapter 6, pp 189–94 above.

Blundell,[86] where dates, due to fermentation and contamination with sewage, were not satisfactory as dates, freight was not payable. As Lord Escher explained:

> There is a perfectly well known test which has for many years been applied to such cases as the present – that test is whether, as a matter of business, the nature of the thing has been altered. The nature of a thing is not necessarily altered because the thing itself has been damaged; wheat or rice may be damaged, but may still remain the things dealt with as wheat or rice in business. But if the nature of thing is altered, and it becomes for business purposes something else, so that it is not dealt with by business people as the thing which it originally was, the question for determination is whether . . . the original article of commerce, has become a total loss . . . If they were totally lost as dates, no freight in respect of them become due from the consignee to the person whom the bill of lading freight was payable . . . [at p 127].[87]

A question likely to arise is whether a carrier is entitled to the full freight on delivery of damaged goods (short of loss of identity of cargo). Put another way, can a cargo owner's claim in respect of damaged cargo be set off against freight? The rule in English law is that the cargo owner does not have a right to set off against freight and is traceable to *Sheels v Davies*.[88] It has received subsequent approval in *Dakin v Oxley and Meyer v Dresser*.[89] In a more recent decision, *Aries Tanker Corp v Total Transport Ltd (The Aries)*,[90] the House of Lords said that the rule against deduction from freight for damage to cargo in carriage by sea cases was a well settled common law rule. Often criticised as an arbitrary rule, it can be justified on policy grounds: to allow a right to set off against freight is to give the cargo owner the right to take the law into his own hands. And, in Lord Denning's opinion, a change in the established rule would also 'enable unscrupulous persons to make all sorts of unfounded allegations so as to avoid payment . . . even with the most scrupulous, it would lead to undesirable delay'.[91] So, in the event of goods arriving damaged, the cargo owner will have to bring a separate action or a cross claim. It must, however, be noted that a right to set off against freight can be expressly created by the parties in the carriage contract.[92]

In the event of deviation, it must be noted that the freight payable will be calculated on a *quantum meruit* basis.[93]

Where parties agree to pay freight in advance, it is not repayable if the carrier fails to deliver the cargo at the destination at common law.[94] It is difficult to understand why freight is not repayable, since there is a total failure of consideration. However, advance freight is not treated as a contractual obligation and the rule is explained in terms of risk. As Hobhouse J said, in *The Dominique*,[95] 'it is not . . . a contractual obligation to which rules of failure of consideration, or partial failure, apply in the same way as in other branches of the law of contract. Once earned, advance freight is

---

86 [1896] 1 QB 123.
87 See also *Duthie v Hilton* (1868) 4 CP 138; *Montedison v Icroma The Caspian Sea* [1980] 1 Lloyd's Rep 91.
88 (1814) 4 Camp 119; (1814) 6 Taunt 65.
89 (1864) 33 LJ Rep CP 289.
90 [1977] 1 Lloyd's Rep 334.
91 *The Brede* [1973] 2 Lloyd's Rep 333, at p 338.
92 *The Olympic Brilliance* [1982] 2 Lloyd's Rep 205.
93 *Hain v Tate and Lyle* (1936) 155 LT 177; (1936) 41 Com Cas 350, at pp 368–9; [1936] 2 All ER 597. For more on deviation, see pp 213–16 above and Chapter 8, pp 243–6 below.
94 *Allison v Bristol Marine Insurance Co* (1876) 1 App Cas 209.
95 [1987] 1 Lloyd's Rep 239.

This section, so far as it imposes liabilities under any contract on any person, shall be without prejudice to the liabilities under the contract of any person as an original party to the contract.

As for the endorsee or consignee, it seems he is liable for freight under s 3(1):

Where sub-s (1) of s 2 of this Act operates in relation to any document to which this Act applies and the person in whom rights are vested by virtue of that subsection:

(a) takes or demands delivery from the carrier of any of the goods to which the document relates;

(b) makes a claim under the contract of carriage against the carrier in respect of any of those goods; or

(c) is a person who, at a time before those rights were vested in him, took or demanded delivery from the carrier of any of those goods,

that person shall (by virtue of taking or demanding delivery or making the claim or, in a case falling within para (c) above, of having rights vested in him) become subject to the same liabilities under that contract as if he had been a party to that contract.

As regards the liability of pledgees, like banks who hold bills of lading for security purposes, they will not be liable unless they take or demand delivery of the cargo (s 3(1)).

Lien

At common law, the shipowner has the right to retain the cargo as security in certain circumstances. In other words, he has a lien over the goods. The circumstances in which he can exercise this right are:

(a) payment for freight, assuming payment and delivery are concurrent;[100]

(b) moneys spent in protecting the cargo; and

(c) general average contribution.

General average is a long established rule in maritime law and the foundation for it is to be found in the Code of Rhodes in the following terms: 'Concerning the Rhodian Law of Jettison. By the Rhodian Law, care is taken that if, for the sake of lightening the ship, a jettison of merchandise is made, that which is given for all shall be made good by a contribution of all.'[101] It requires those engaged in a maritime adventure whose properties have been saved to contribute to those whose cargo or freight is lost or sacrificed. General average refers to the loss incurred by all involved in the maritime adventure – this includes the cargo owner as well as the shipowner who may have incurred extraordinary expenditure to save the cargo and the adventure. A more 'modern' definition, regarded as authoritative, is provided by Lawrence J, in *Birkley v Presgrave*,[102] in the following terms:

All loss which arises in consequence of extraordinary sacrifices made or expenses incurred for the preservation of the ship and cargo come within general average and must be borne proportionately by all who are interested [at p 228].

---

100 On freight, see pp 222–5 above.
101 Waykins William J in *Pirie and Co v Middle Dock Co* (1881) 44 LT 426, at p 430.
102 (1801) 1 East 220.

This right of lien can be exercised only as long as the shipowner retains possession of the cargo. Once cargo is delivered, he loses the right of lien. Liens may also be created by express agreement for dead freight (damages payable to shipowner for not loading agreed amount of cargo),[103] or demurrage (liquidated damages agreed as payable between parties delayed in loading or unloading beyond the time agreed). No proof of loss will be required for payment of damages. Courts may intervene if the amount fixed in contract is 'extravagant and unconscionable',[104] for damages for detention and 'all charges whatsoever'.

Lien clauses are normally found in charterparties – that is, where a vessel is contracted for voyages or for a period of time from the shipowner. However, a bill of lading issued under a charterparty may contain a lien clause. Where a lien clause is found in the bill of lading, the shipowner cannot exercise, as against the bill of lading holder other than the charterer or his agent, a lien for freight payable under the charterparty in respect of the same or other goods, or for the difference, if any, between the bill of lading freight and the charterparty freight or for dead freight, or for demurrage at the port of loading. The only lien he can exercise against the bill of lading holder, who is not the charterer or his agent, is for the freight payable under the bill of lading on delivery.

However, where the lien clause in the bill of lading is sufficiently wide and clear to extend the shipowner's right, then he can exercise lien against the bill of lading holder other than the charterer or his agent for payment of charterparty freight, dead freight and demurrage.

CONCLUSION

The limited operation of the Hague Rules and the Hague-Visby Rules means that the policy objective of protecting the weaker party is not totally achieved. Freedom of contract still affects some kinds of bills of lading bringing in its wake uncertainty and unpredictability since different jurisdictions view exclusion clauses variously. To some extent, common law in England gives the cargo owner some protection. However, the common law implied undertakings are not mandatory, and can always be contracted out of. This means that the shipper, in some cases, still has to bear the burden of the excesses and inequities caused by a tolerant attitude to disclaimers. An acceptable solution to redress the imbalance thus caused would be to impose a minimum level of liability on the shipowner without making distinctions in the kinds of cargo carried or the types of transport documents for carriage by sea – for example, waybills, bills of lading – a solution adopted by the Convention on the Carriage of Goods by Sea, Hamburg, 1978.[105]

FURTHER READING

Boyd, Burrows and Foxton (eds), *Scrutton on Charterparties and Bills of Lading*, 20th edn, 1996, Sweet & Maxwell.

---

103 See *Cargo ex Argos* (1873) LR 5 CP 134; (1873) 28 LT 745.
104 *Dunlop Tyre Co v New Garage Ltd* [1915] AC 79, at p 86.
105 See Chapter 9.

Colinvaux (ed), *Carver's Carriage by Sea*, 2 vols, 13th edn, 1982, Stevens.

Tetley, *Marine Cargo Claims*, 4th edn, 2008, Blais.

Treitel and Reynolds, *Carver on Bills Lading*, 2nd edn, 2005, Sweet & Maxwell.

Wilson, *Carriage of Goods by Sea*, 6th edn, 2008, Longman.

CHAPTER 8

CARRIAGE OF GOODS BY SEA: BILLS OF LADING AND THE CARRIAGE OF GOODS BY SEA ACT 1971 (HAGUE-VISBY RULES)

INTRODUCTION

The bill of lading, as indicated in the previous chapter, plays an important role in most international sale transactions. Amongst others, the bill of lading is a contract of carriage between the carrier and the consignee[1] or endorsee. Terms contained in the bill of lading play a central part in determining the rights and liabilities of the parties to the contract. Most bills of lading issued today are subject to international conventions – the Hague Rules, the Hague-Visby Rules and the Hamburg Rules,[2] which impose on the carrier minimum responsibilities and liabilities that cannot be lessened with suitable clauses in the contract. The current legal regime relating to bills of lading, however, is a consequence of developments that started approximately 200 years ago.

At common law, the carrier was strictly liable for the safe transport of the cargo to its destination and delivery to the designated person.[3] The carrier could however disclaim this strict liability by inserting suitable clauses in the contract of carriage. The increase in ocean traffic in the 19th century increased the use of exemption clauses.[4] It was also an important era for English contract law due to the rise of the *laissez faire* philosophy which promoted unrestricted freedom in commercial agreements. The courts perceived their role simply as one of ensuring that the parties kept to the terms of their agreement and were reluctant to intervene in the contract between men. This tolerant attitude obviously benefited those in a better bargaining position.

In the context of contracts of carriage of goods by sea, the shipowner, the stronger of the contracting parties, inevitably inserted all embracing exclusion clauses. Carriers were exempted from liability for loss or damage from perils of the sea, decay, strikes, deviation to unseaworthy ships and their own negligence.[5] The exclusion clauses operated totally in the carrier's favour and the goods were carried entirely at the merchant's risk. Judges in Britain, following the tenor set by the *laissez faire* philosophy, were sympathetic to such clauses. And of course, Britain, a nation with huge maritime interests, had a lot to gain with the increase in the volume of ocean traffic.

---

1 In most cases, the consignee is likely to be the buyer. This does not preclude the seller to name himself as the consignee.

2 See Chapter 9. The text of all these conventions is available in Carr and Kidner, *International Trade Law Statutes and Conventions*, 5th edn, 2008, Routledge-Cavendish. They are also available on www.jus.uio.no/lm.

3 Ocean carriers were also strictly liable under Roman law to transport safely the goods in their custody. They were liable for loss or damage to goods caused by themselves or their employees but were not liable for shipwreck or damage caused by pirates that could not be resisted (*vis maior*). Strict liability was imposed on ocean carriers since they were presumed to be dishonest (*improbitas*). See *Justinian Digest* § 4.9.3.1; Berger, *Encyclopedic Dictionary of Roman Law under Receptum Nautae*, 1953, American Philosophical Society, at pp 668–69.

4 For an interesting overview of shipping policies from the 15th–20th centuries, see Sweeney, 'From Columbus to cooperation – trade and shipping policies from 1492 to 1992' (1989/1990) 12 Fordham International LJ 481.

5 See Colinvaux (ed), *Carver's Carriage by Sea*, 2 vols, 13th edn, 1982, Stevens (hereinafter '*Carver's Carriage by Sea*'), for a list of the various exclusion clauses found in bills of lading. See also *Tessler Bros Ltd v Italpacific Line* 494 F2d 438 (1974).

The liberal British attitude to disclaimers in bills of lading was not followed in other jurisdictions. The US Supreme Court, for instance, read exclusion clauses extremely restrictively and subjected them to a number of overriding obligations, such as the obligation to provide a seaworthy ship and to take due care of the cargo.[6] The US Congress, in response to approaches made by the shipping interests, addressed the inequities by enacting the Harter Act in 1893[7] which limited the shipowner's freedom of contract and sought to protect the cargo owner.[8] However, it was felt that an international convention was required to redress the imbalance caused by the *laissez faire* philosophy. To this end, the International Convention for the Unification of Certain Rules Relating to Bills of Lading, Brussels, 1924[9] (hereinafter 'Hague Rules') was drafted between 1921 and 1923 and signed by major trading nations in August 1924.[10] Many of the convention's provisions are modelled on provisions found in the Harter Act. The Hague Rules set a minimum level of liability that could not be contracted out of by the carriers. The United Kingdom implemented the Hague Rules with the Carriage of Goods by Sea Act 1924.[11]

Failings of the Hague Rules however surfaced over time as a consequence of litigation and developments in shipping technology. For instance, the defences and limitation of liability afforded by the Rules did not extend to the servants or agents of the carriers, and the calculation of limitation of liability in terms of packages or units was not sufficiently flexible to accommodate consolidation of cargo in containers.[12] This led to the drafting of the Brussels Protocol which revised the Hague Rules (hereinafter Hague-Visby Rules) in 1968. The Hague-Visby Rules were implemented in the

---

6   See Gilmore and Black, *The Law of Admiralty*, 1975, Foundation Press, at pp 140–1. Clauses excluding liability for negligence were viewed as unenforceable (see *Liverpool and Great Western Steam Co v Phoenix Insurance Co* 129 US 397 (1889)).

7   46 USC App (1988) §§ 190–96.

8   According to Kozolchyk, 'Evolution and present state of the ocean bill of lading from a banking perspective' (1992) 23(2) JMLC 161, the Harter Act 1893 is a precursor of consumer protection law. He also suggests the drafters of the Act did not regulate charterparties since they viewed the parties to such contracts as having equal bargaining strength. The view that parties to a charterparty are of equal bargaining strength is a legal myth and is dependent on market conditions. For instance, if international trade is buoyant, cargo owners are likely to be the weaker of the two parties until saturation point due to an expansion of the shipping sector. See Peck, 'Economic analysis of the allocation of liability for cargo damage: the case for the carrier, or is it?' (1998) 26 Transportation LJ 73.

9   The International Law Association (ILA) adopted the Rules, formulated by the Comité Maritime International (CMI), when it met at The Hague in September 1921. After further amendments, it was laid before the International Diplomatic Conference on Maritime Law at Brussels and was signed on 24 August 1924. The official text of the Convention is in French. See Sturley, *The Legislative History of the Carriage of Goods by Sea Act and the Travaux Préparatoires of the Hague Rules*, 1990, FB Rothman; Sturley, 'The history of COGSA and the Hague Rules' (1991) 22 JMLC 1; Knauth, *The American Law of Ocean Bills of Lading*, 1953 American Maritime Cases; Yancey, 'The carriage of goods: Hague, COGSA, Visby and Hamburg' (1983) 57 Tulane LR 1238.

10 For more on the creation of the CMI and the role of the CMI in formulating these Rules, see Griggs, 'Uniformity of maritime law – an international perspective' (1999) 73 Tulane LR 1551.

11 The US implemented this convention only in 1936 even though it was based on its Harter Act.

12 See *Owners of Cargo Lately on Board The River Gurara v Nigerian National Shipping Line Ltd* [1997] 1 Lloyd's Rep 225. The matter at issue was whether containers constituted package or unit under Art IV(5) of the Hague Rules. The court held that parcels loaded in a container were packages for the purposes of Art IV(5). What constituted relevant packages could not be based on the parties' agreement since a carrier could evade the minimum liability set by the Hague Rules by applying the agreed definition to containers. (The clause in the bill of lading which said that the container was to be regarded as package if goods were packed by shipper in the container was held to be void.) The plaintiff had the burden of proving the number of packages in the container with extrinsic evidence and liability to be calculated on that basis rather than by reference to the description in the bill of lading.

United Kingdom with the Carriage of Goods by Sea Act 1971 which repealed the earlier Act of 1924. The Hague-Visby Rules were not adopted by all the signatories to the Hague Rules with the result that both the Hague Rules and the Hague-Visby Rules exist side by side. The US, for instance, is not a party to the Hague-Visby Rules. This means that a bill of lading issued for goods sent from the US to the United Kingdom may, in some circumstances, be subject to the Hague Rules rather than the Hague-Visby Rules.

The implementing legislation, the Carriage of Goods by Sea Act 1971 to which the Hague-Visby Rules are attached as a schedule, provides in s 1(2) that the Rules shall have the *force of law*. In other words, the Rules must be treated as if they are a part of directly enacted statute. The consequence of this, according to *The Hollandia*,[13] is that the parties' intentions are overridden by the provisions of the Rules.

Since for the most part the Hague Rules are similar to the Hague-Visby Rules, all references are to Hague-Visby Rules in this chapter, though attention to the Hague Rules is drawn where required.

INTERPRETATION OF THE HAGUE-VISBY RULES IN THE ENGLISH COURTS

The Hague-Visby Rules, unlike some of the more recent international conventions (for example, Art 7 of the United Nations Convention on Contracts for the International Sale of Goods 1980[14] which states that 'in the interpretation of this convention, regard has to be had to its international character, and to the need to promote uniformity in its application and the observance of good faith in international trade') are silent regarding their interpretation.

English judges, however, are conscious of the international nature of the Hague-Visby Rules as well as other international conventions and periodically urge the need to seek uniformity in the law of all states adhering to the convention. The House of Lords in *Stag Line Ltd v Foscola, Mango and Co*[15] advocated the view that interpretation of the Hague Rules should not be rigidly controlled by domestic precedents of ante-cedent date but that the language of the convention must be construed on broad principles of general acceptation (at p 350). Recent decisions (eg, *The Rafaela S*) seem to be following the principles enunciated in *Stag Line*. This conscious need for harmon-isation is reflected in the interpretation of other transport conventions such as the Convention for the Unification of Certain Rules relating to International Carriage by Air, Warsaw, 1929.[16] For instance, *Lord Denning in Corocraft Ltd v Pan American Airways Inc*[17] said 'even if I disagreed, I would follow [decisions of other courts] in a manner which is of international concern. The courts of all countries should interpret [the Warsaw Convention] in the same way' (at p 655).

It is not uncommon for the courts to look to the decisions of courts in other jurisdictions as an aid to interpretation of the Hague-Visby Rules for purposes of

---

13   Aka *The Morviken* [1983] 1 Lloyd's Rep 1.
14   See Chapter 2 for further comments on Art 7.
15   [1932] AC 328. See also *The Rafaela S* [2004] QB 702.
16   See Chapters 10, p 335 below.
17   [1969] 1 QB 616.

achieving uniformity.[18] If any doubts regarding the wording in the Hague-Visby Rules arise, these will be resolved by looking at the French text.[19] Both the French and English texts are authentic. The more recent case of *Effort Shipping Co Ltd v Linden Management SA and Others (The Giannis K)*[20] indicates that the courts will be willing to consider not only the *travaux préparatoires*, but also the historical setting of the Hague Rules for the purposes of interpretation.

Regardless of the English courts' tolerant attitude and forward thinking in their commendable promotion of the international character of the Hague/Hague-Visby Rules, they are prone to conflicting interpretations across jurisdictions and seem to be influenced largely by domestic law and national concerns. For instance, perils of the sea, deck carriage, the nature of the seaworthiness obligation are all interpreted variously. The causes are diverse: ambiguous provisions;[21] lack of judicial expertise in interpreting international conventions;[22] differences in legal tradition as reflected in techniques of interpretation; and the influence of national/economic policies. The end result is uncertainty. With uncertainty comes greater risk which in the long run may undermine free trade vehemently supported and promoted by policy makers, national and international. One possible way to counteract this problem would be to give extensive definitions and also allow the courts to refer to the organisation responsible for drafting international conventions to provide guidance on interpretation. Alternatively, an international court of appeals for international disputes involving international conventions may bring about the required level of harmonisation and certainty.[23] However, not all would go along with such solutions on the grounds that they undermine a nation's sovereignty[24] and interests. As Tetley pertinently observes, '. . . the persistence of nationalism, even in the 21st century, also accounts for some problems in achieving greater harmony on maritime law matters within the community of nations. States do not easily surrender sovereignty in fields where they perceive that their 'vital interests' are, or could be, adversely affected by subscribing to new international regimes and standards'.[25] While it is easy to empathise with the primacy of national values and interests, it is debatable whether such a view can be sustained when the world is marching steadfastly towards a global

---

18   *Hellenic Steel Co v Svolomar Shipping Co Ltd (The Komninos S)* [1991] 1 Lloyd's Rep 370. See
      also *Owners of Cargo Lately on Board The River Gurara v Nigerian National Shipping Line Ltd* [1997]
      1 Lloyd's Rep 225, at pp 227–28; *The Rosa S* [1988] 2 Lloyd's Rep 574, at p 581.

19   *Pyrene v Scindia Navigation Ltd* [1954] 2 QB 402. See also *ibid The Komninos S*.

20   [1998] 2 WLR 206. See also 'Dangerous goods', pp 265–7.

21   In 'International uniform rules in national courts: the influence of domestic law in conflicts of
      interpretation' (1987) 27(4) Virginia Journal of International Law 729, at pp 797–98, Sturley is
      of the opinion that ambiguous provisions in the Hague Rules drive national courts to reconcile
      the uniform law with their own domestic legal doctrines, and since domestic legal doctrines
      are not the same, they give rise to conflicting interpretations.

22   The CMI has recently set up a database consisting of cases involving the Hague and the
      Hague-Visby Rules. This is likely to introduce some degree of uniformity of interpretation.
      Visit http://comitemaritime.org for further information. The database also includes cases
      interpreting the Hamburg Rules (see Chapter 9).

23   See Black, 'The Bremen, COGSA and the problem of conflicting interpretation' (1973) 6
      Vanderbilt Journal of Transnational Law 365.

24   See, eg, Krasner, *Sovereignty: Organized Hypocrisy*, 1999, Princeton UP for an interesting analysis of sovereignty.

25   'Uniformity of international private maritime law – the pros, cons and alternatives to international conventions – how to adopt an international convention' (2000) 24 Tulane Maritime
      LJ 775, at p 810.

community fuelled by the goal of economic prosperity through international trade.[26] Sovereignty, at best, is an excuse for not engaging in a meaningful discussion to resolve issues, be they legal, economic or social and seems to be of 'value for purposes of oratory and persuasion rather than of science and law'.[27]

CARRIER'S RESPONSIBILITIES AND LIABILITIES

Before considering the responsibilities of the carrier, it is essential to establish who is the 'carrier' for the purposes of the Hague-Visby Rules. Article I(a) defines carrier to *include* the owner or charterer who enters into a contract of carriage with the shipper. The identity of the carrier is a matter of utmost importance since the Hague-Visby Rules impose a time limit of one year within which the action should be brought. If the action is not brought within the time limit set by the Hague-Visby Rules, the cargo owner loses any claims he has for breach of contract against the carrier. The identity of the carrier is normally established on the basis of the bill of lading and other documents.[28]

Generally, where there is a voyage charterparty or time charterparty, the bills of lading are signed by the master on behalf of the shipowner. In these circumstances, the shipowner would be deemed the carrier who enters into the contract of carriage with the shipper.[29]

It is possible that the charterer may have an express agreement to sign the bill of lading on behalf of the shipowner as in cl 8[30] of the NYPE (New York Produce Exchange) 1981 and cl 30(a)[31] of NYPE 93 standard time charter form. Here, the shipowner would be regarded as the carrier for the purposes of the Hague-Visby Rules. Where the charterer signs the bill of lading as the shipowner's agent, of course, applying the laws of agency, the shipowner would be liable.

There may be situations where the charterer issues the bill of lading in his own name.[32] Here, the charterer will be regarded as the principal and hence liable on the

---

26   See the Preamble to the World Trade Organization (WTO) Agreement. See also Singer and Ansari, *Rich and Poor Countries*, 4th edn, 1988, Routledge.

27   See Fowler and Bunck, *Power and the Sovereign State*, 1995, Pennsylvania State UP.

28   See Davies, 'The elusive carrier: whom do I sue and how?' (1991) 19 ABLR 230; Tetley, 'Whom to sue – identity of the carrier', in Block *et al* (eds), *Liber Amicorum Lionel Tricot*, 1988, Kluwer; Tetley, 'Who may claim or sue for cargo loss or damage' (Pts I and II) (1986) 17 JMLC 153, at p 407.

29   See *The Khian Zephyr* [1982] 1 Lloyd's Rep 73, at p 75. See also *The Venezuela* [1980] 1 Lloyd's Rep 393.

30   Clause 8, in relevant part, reads:

    ... The captain (although appointed by the owners) shall be under the orders and direction of the charterers ... Charterers are to perform all cargo handling at their expense under the supervision of the captain, who is to sign bills of lading for cargo ... However, at charterers' option, the charterers or their agents may sign bills of lading on behalf of the captain ...

    See Pritchett, 'Charterer's authority to sign bills of lading under standard time charter terms' [1980] LMCLQ 21.

31   It reads:

    The master shall sign the bills of lading or waybills for cargo as presented in conformity with mate's or tally clerk's receipts. However, the charterers may sign bills of lading on behalf of the master, with the owner's prior written authority, always in conformity with mate's or tally clerk's receipts.

32   See 'Scope of Application', pp 268–73 below for incorporation of charterparty terms in bills of lading.

contract of carriage. The meaning of the word 'carrier' in Art I(a) was elaborated upon by Robert Goff J in *The Khian Zephyr*[33] in the following manner:

> ... the function of Art I(a) ... in providing that the word 'carrier' includes the owner or charterer who enters into a contract of carriage with a shipper, is to legislate for the fact that you may get a case – for example, under bills of lading – where the bills of lading are charterers' bills; and where there are charterers' bills, of course, the charterer is in a contractual relationship with the cargo owner and is responsible under the bills of lading to the cargo owners. In those circumstances, the effect of the definition in Art I(a) is to ensure that provisions which apply to the carrier under the Hague Rules shall likewise apply not only to the shipowner in whose ship the goods are physically being carried and through whose servants and agents, the master and crew of the ship he is physically in possession of the goods, but shall also apply to a charterer who has contracted as the other party to the bill of lading. That makes good sense, and provides a common sense explanation why the definition of 'carrier' should be so defined in Art I(a) as to include the owner or the charterer who enters into a contract of carriage with a shipper [at pp 75–76].

However, bills of lading issued in the charterer's name may contain a demise clause which seeks to transfer contractual liability to the shipowner. The English courts are tolerant towards such clauses. In *The Berkshire*,[34] the demise clause used in a bill of lading issued by the sub-charterer, which was effective in transferring liability, read as follows:

> If the ship is not owned or chartered by demise to the company or line by whom this bill of lading is issued (as may be the case notwithstanding anything that appears to the contrary), the bill of lading shall take effect as a contract with the owner or demise charterer as the case may be as principal made through the agency of the said company or line who act as agents and shall be under no personal liability whatsoever in respect thereof.

Use of demise clauses has come under considerable attack from academics since they create uncertainty regarding the identity of the party with whom the shipper is contracting – an undesirable result given the short time within which the cargo owner has to institute proceedings.[35] However, Brandon J in *The Berkshire*[36] did not foresee any problems in holding demise clauses as effective; he did not perceive them as extraordinary clauses at all but as entirely usual and ordinary clauses.

Where the charterer is a demise charterer, he would be liable since he has taken over complete possession of the ship and its management. The shipowner who has chartered the vessel has no control over the master. The master of the ship is the agent of the charterer and therefore bills of lading bind the charterer as principal.[37]

The difficulties in determining the party liable under the contract of carriage from the documentation are amply illustrated by *Homburg Houtimport BV v Argosin Pvt Ltd and Others (The Starsin)*.[38] *The Starsin* was time chartered to Continental Pacific Shipping Ltd (CPS). Liner bills of lading on CPS shipping forms were issued. Clause 1 defined 'carrier' as the party on whose behalf the bill of lading was signed and all bills

---

33   [1982] 1 Lloyd's Rep 73. See also *The Venezuela* [1980] 1 Lloyd's Rep 393.
34   [1974] 1 Lloyd's Rep 185.
35   *Tetley, Marine Cargo Claims*, 3rd edn, 1988, Blais, at p 248.
36   [1974] 1 Lloyd's Rep 185.
37   *Baumwoll Manufactur von Carl Scheibler v Furness* [1893] AC 8.
38   [2003] 1 Lloyd's Rep 571.

of lading were signed 'as agents' for CPS. The bill of lading contained further clauses relating to the party liable under the contract of carriage. Clause 33 relating to the identity of the carrier stated that the contract evidenced by the bill of lading was between the merchant and the owner of the vessel who was to be liable for any damages that arose out of the contract of carriage. Clause 35 stated that, 'if the vessel is not owned or chartered by demise to the company or line by whom this bill of lading is issued (as may be the case notwithstanding anything that appears to the contrary) this bill of lading shall take effect only as a contract of carriage with the owner'.

At the court of first instance the bills of lading were held to be charterer's bills. On appeal, however, cll 1(c), 33 and 35 were read together and by a majority the court concluded that the bills were shipowner's bills. Upon further appeal the House of Lords held that the carrier was plainly identified by the language on the face of the bill of lading which took priority. They also went on to say that the commercial community, including banks (that is Art 23 of Uniform Customs and Practice for Documentary Credits 1994), expected the identity to be given on the face of the bill of lading and not printed on the reverse.[39] The bills were therefore charterer's bills.

Duty to provide a seaworthy ship

The carrier under Art III(1) is under an obligation before and at the beginning of the voyage to exercise due diligence[40] to:

- make the ship seaworthy;
- properly man, equip and supply the ship; and
- make the holds, refrigerating and cool chambers, and all other parts of the ship in which the goods are carried fit and safe for their reception, carriage and preservation.

Seaworthiness relates to both the physical state of the ship and cargoworthiness as under common law.[41] For instance, a mechanically unsound ship or an incompetent crew can render the ship seaworthy,[42] so can stowing dangerous goods below deck in breach of international regulations.[43] The question of whether due diligence has been exercised is one of fact. In *The Amstelslot*,[44] where the vessel during the voyage suffered an engine breakdown due to failure of her reduction gear, the courts treated due diligence similarly to negligence. According to Lord Devlin:

> Lack of due diligence is negligence; what is at issue . . . is whether there was an error of judgment that amounted to professional negligence [at p 235].

---

39 See Chapter 15 for more letters of credit. Would it have made a difference if there was a printed clause on the face of the bill of lading referring to the terms and conditions on the reverse of the bill?

40 The due diligence standard as opposed to the absolute duty found in common law was adopted from the US Harter Act.

41 See Chapter 7, pp 208–12 above.

42 See *Rey Banano del Pacifico CA and Others v Transportes Navieros Ecuatorianos and Another (The Isla Fernandina)* [2000] 2 Lloyd's Rep 15 – a voyage charterparty incorporating the Hague Rules where the claimants were unsuccessful in establishing that the defendants had not exercised due diligence to properly man the ship. See also *The Star Sea* [1997] 1 Lloyd's Rep 360.

43 See *Northern Shipping Co v Deutsche Seereederei GmbH and Others (The Kapitan Sakharov)* [2000] 2 Lloyd's Rep 255.

44 [1963] 1 Lloyd's Rep 223.

The standard for ascertaining the exercise of due diligence is determined in terms of the actions of other skilled men in similar circumstances.[45] The question to be posed is 'would a prudent shipowner, if he had known of the defect, have sent the ship to sea in that condition?'.[46] It must be noted that the seaworthiness undertaking under the Hague-Visby Rules is not an absolute undertaking as at common law.[47] This is specifically reinforced by s 3 of the Carriage of Goods by Sea Act 1971 which states:

> ... there shall not be implied in any contract for the carriage of goods by sea to which the Rules apply by virtue of this Act any absolute undertaking by the carrier of the goods to provide a seaworthy ship.

Due diligence must be exercised by the shipowner 'before and at the beginning of the voyage' (Art III(1)). This phrase was considered in *Maxine Footwear Co Ltd v Canadian Government Marine Ltd*.[48] Shortly before the vessel was due to sail, an officer of the ship ordered and supervised the thawing of a frozen drain pipe with an oxyacetylene torch. This started a fire in the cork insulation of the ship and the master had to scuttle the ship. During the scuttling operation, the appellant's cargo was lost.

The respondent relied on the exception relating to fire in Art IV(2)(b) and argued that they were not liable for the lost goods since the fire did not result from their actual fault or privity. Further, on the construction of Art III(1), the obligation to exercise due diligence to make the ship seaworthy arose at the commencement of loading and at the commencement of the voyage. The Privy Council held that the interpretation of the word 'before' in the context of the absolute undertaking of seaworthiness under common law did not apply, and that the Hague Rules had to be construed in the light of their language. And from the words used in the Hague Rules, it was clear that the phrase 'before and at the beginning of the voyage' meant the period from at least the beginning of the loading until the ship started on her voyage. Therefore, the vessel was unseaworthy and the respondent was liable for the damage caused to the appellant's goods.

The obligation created by Art III(1) is an overriding obligation such that where the damage is caused by its non-fulfilment, the carrier will lose the immunities available to him under Art IV(2). Until recently, it was commonly held, at least by commenta-

---

45   *The Toledo* [1995] 1 Lloyd's Rep 40.

46   *MDC Ltd v NV Zeevaart Maatschappij 'Beursstraat'* [1962] 1 Lloyd's Rep 180; *Fyffes Group Ltd and Carribbean Gold Ltd v Reefer Express Lines Pty Ltd and Reefkrit Shipping Inc (The Kriti Rex)* [1996] 2 Lloyd's Rep 171; *UBC Chartering Ltd v Liepaya Shipping Co Ltd (The Liepaya)* [1999] 1 Lloyd's Rep 649.

47   See Chapter 7, pp 208–12 above.

48   [1959] AC 589. See also *A Meredith Jones and Co Ltd v Vangemar Shipping Co Ltd (The Apostolis)* [1997] 2 Lloyd's Rep 241. In this case, a cargo of cotton caught fire. The claimant was unable to prove that the welding (which was taking place on the ship) was the probable cause of the fire as opposed to a discarded cigarette end. Neither was there anything about the ship that rendered her unseaworthy. The holds were safe and the welding was not taking place to render her seaworthy. It was held that the shipowner could not be held to be in breach of the Art III(1) obligation on the basis that welding exposed the cargo to an ephemeral risk of ignition. *Maxine Footwear* was distinguished on the basis '. . . it was fire in the fabric of the vessel, namely the cork lining of the hold, which rendered her unseaworthy' (at p 245). But what if there had been more than an ephemeral risk of ignition? Would this have changed the decision in any way? Probably not. Should the welding work have been allowed to take place where there was a possibility of the cargo catching fire, however remote? Of course, the cargo owner of the destroyed cargo can always raise a breach of Art III(2). The obvious disadvantage is that Art III(2) is not an overriding obligation. Note also the fire exception available under the Merchant Shipping Act 1995 (see 'Fire', pp 248–50).

tors,[49] that breach of the seaworthiness obligation did not affect the rights imparted by Art IV(6). However, in *Mediterranean Freight Services Ltd v BP Oil International Ltd (The 'Fiona'))*,[50] a cargo of oil exploded as a result of contamination with residues of cargo previously carried. Since it was a breach of the seaworthiness obligation, an overriding obligation, the court held that the carrier could not rely on Art IV(6) which, along with others, imparted a right to an indemnity. Diamond J, while saying that he disagreed with Scrutton, expressed his views thus:

> Article IV(6) contains provisions some of which are in the nature of exceptions clauses and one of which confers on the carrier a right to an indemnity. The exceptions are very far reaching. If goods of an inflammable, explosive or dangerous nature are shipped and if they become a danger to the ship or cargo, then whether or not the carrier consented to the shipment and whether or not he had knowledge of their nature and character at the time of shipment, the carrier may land and destroy the goods without incurring liability to the shipper except in general average; see both the first and second paragraphs of the rule. It would be wholly contrary to the scheme of the rules and likewise inconsistent with equity and commercial common sense that a carrier should be entitled to destroy dangerous goods without compensation and without liability except to general average if the cause of the goods having to be destroyed was a breach by the carrier of his obligations as to seaworthiness. The exception in Art IV(6) is clearly in my judgment subject to the performance by the carrier of his overriding obligation set in Art III(1). So also in my judgment is the right to an indemnity conferred by the first paragraph of the rule [at p 286].[51]

Once the carrier has exercised due diligence to make the ship seaworthy before she sets sail, he is not in breach of Art III(1) should faults develop during the voyage or while calling at an intermediate port. The common law doctrine of stages (which requires that the ship is seaworthy at each stage) does not apply. In *Leesh River Tea Co v British India Steam Navigation Co*,[52] chests of tea were shipped aboard *The Chybassa* for carriage from Calcutta to London, Hull and Amsterdam via Port Sudan. While the vessel was in Port Sudan, the stevedores when unloading goods from the ship removed the brass cover plate from one of the ship's storm valves. As a result, water entered the hold and damaged the tea. The court found that the defendants were not in breach of the obligation imposed by Art III(1).

However, it is possible that faults that develop after the vessel has set sail are traceable to the unseaworthy state of the ship before she set sail. Where this is the case, the shipowner would be in breach of Art III(1).[53]

---

49 According to Boyd, Burrows and Foxton (eds), *Scrutton on Charterparties and Bills of Lading*, 20th edn, 1996, Sweet & Maxwell (hereinafter '*Scrutton on Charterparties*'), 'the shipowner can presumably exercise his rights under this rule (viz Art IV(6)) even if in breach of his obligations as to seaworthiness' (at p 453).

50 [1993] 1 Lloyd's Rep 257.

51 Also see 'Monetary unit for calculation', pp 260–1, on the relationship of Art III(1) and Art IV(5)(a).

52 [1966] 2 Lloyd's Rep 193.

53 In *The Subro Valour* [1995] 1 Lloyd's Rep 509, three possible causes for fire in the engine room were identified: discarded cigarette, ignition of flammable material on the exhaust, or ignition of wiring. On the basis of evidence, the fire was most likely to have been caused by damage to wiring as a result of shelving rubbing against it. In the absence of unexpected voyage conditions or any suggestion that the shelving was rubbing against the wiring after the voyage began, the court concluded that the wiring was in a vulnerable state before the ship set sail and the carriers were in breach of the seaworthiness obligation at the commencement of the voyage.

Responsibility of exercising due diligence to make the ship seaworthy is personal to the carrier even where the work has been delegated to a servant of the carrier or to a reputable independent contractor. In *The Muncaster Castle*,[54] cases of tinned ox tongues were shipped under bills of lading from Sydney to London. On discharge, the cases were found to be damaged by sea water. It was found that defective storm valve covers had let the sea water enter into the hold. The inspection covers had been removed for inspection shortly before the vessel started on her voyage. The covers had not been properly refitted by the fitter employed by the firm of ship repairers who had been instructed by the carrier to carry out the survey. The cargo owner alleged lack of due diligence to make the ship seaworthy on the part of the carrier. The carrier argued that, by employing a firm of reputable ship repairers to carry out the task, he had discharged his obligation of exercising due diligence to make the ship seaworthy. The court, however, came to the conclusion that no other solution was possible than to say that the shipowner's obligation of due diligence demands due diligence in the work of repair by whomsoever it may be done. In other words, Art III(1) requires due diligence not only in the acts of the shipowner, but also in the acts on the part of those to whom he may have committed the work of fitting the vessel for sea and this obligation of due diligence is personal to the shipowner.

A certificate issued by a Lloyd's surveyor will be inadequate to establish the seaworthy state of the ship if the defect is apparent on a reasonable inspection of the ship.[55] So, if the carriers are to escape liability, they must prove that due diligence has been exercised not only by themselves and by their servants but also by a Lloyd's registered shipping surveyor.[56] So, where the surveyor is negligent, the shipowner will be liable under the Hague-Visby Rules.

A cargo owner may wish to sue the classification society which employs the surveyor in tort for damages. Such an action will be unsuccessful under English law. In *Marc Rich and Co AG and Others v Bishop Rock Marine Co Ltd (The Nicholas H)*,[57] the English courts examined the issue of whether a classification society owes a duty of care to the cargo owners giving rise to liability in damages. In this case, the ship, carrying a cargo of zinc and lead from South America to Italy under bills of lading incorporating the Hague Rules, developed a crack in its hull. The surveyor employed by the vessel's classification society recommended permanent repair in dry dock. The owners, however, carried out temporary repairs and were able to convince the surveyor to change his recommendation. He agreed that the vessel could proceed on its voyage as long as the repairs carried out underwent further examination and attended to as soon as possible after the discharge of the cargo. Soon after the vessel set sail, the temporary repair work cracked and she sank a week later. The cargo owners, who received damages calculated in terms of tonnage limitation for the vessel from the shipowner, looked to the classification society for the balance of their loss. At the court of first instance, Hirst J had no difficulties in establishing a necessary close relationship between the parties and concluded that he did not see any reason based on public policy for denying a duty of care on the part of the classification

---

54   [1961] 1 Lloyd's Rep 57.
55   *The Amstelslot* [1963] 2 Lloyd's Rep 223.
56   It is debatable whether the obligation in respect of the ship is personal to the carrier under Art 5 of the Hamburg Rules (see Chapter 9).
57   [1995] 3 All ER 307.

society to the cargo owners.[58] The classification society appealed from the judgment of Hirst J. The Court of Appeal[59] concluded that the Hague Rules were an internationally accepted code that balanced the rights and duties existing between shipowners and shippers. To impose an identical or almost identical duty on the classification society without any of the internationally recognised balancing factors (available to shipowners under the Hague Rules) would be unfair. Allowing the appeal, Saville LJ said:

> The balance of rights and duties between the principal parties (cargo owners and shipowners) has been settled on an internationally acceptable basis and I can see no justice or good reason for altering this by imposing on the society a like duty to that owed by the shipowners, but without any of the checks and balances which exist in the present regime [at p 697].

On appeal to the House of Lords,[60] the majority agreed with the Court of Appeal in holding that there was no duty of care on the part of the classification society towards the cargo owner. According to Lord Steyn, to recognise such a duty would be unfair, unjust and unreasonable for a number of reasons. First, it would impose a greater burden on the shipowner who at the end of the day will have to bear the financial burden of the classification society's liability. This would tip the balance of the internationally recognised legal framework embodied in the Hague Rules. It was not as if the cargo owner was left without any remedy. He was protected, albeit limitedly, under the Rules and the tonnage limitation provisions. The cargo owner, if unhappy about the level of damages available under the existing system, could always take out adequate insurance to meet the shortfall. Secondly, classification societies act for the collective welfare. Imposing liability on them might well force the societies into taking a protective stance. There is a 'risk that classification societies might be unwilling from time to time to survey the very vessels which most urgently require independent examination' (at p 332).

It must be said that, while Lord Lloyd's dissenting judgment is well reasoned and extremely persuasive, against the backdrop of an international convention designed to promote an agreed framework for allocation of risks (however disagreeable it may be from a cargo owner's perspective), Lord Steyn's conclusion is the correct one.

What about defects that exist in the ship before the ship comes under the carrier's control? Presumably, the carrier will be held responsible for defects that existed when the ship came under his control if those defects would have been discoverable on a reasonable inspection. Where the defect was latent and could not have been reasonably discovered, the carrier would not be responsible.

As for burden of proof, Art IV(1) states that:

> ... neither the carrier nor the ship shall be liable for loss or damage rising or resulting from unseaworthiness unless caused by want of due diligence on the part of the carrier to make the ship seaworthy ... in accordance with the provisions of Art III(1). Whenever loss or damage has resulted from unseaworthiness, the burden of proving the exercise of due diligence shall be on the carrier or other person claiming exemption under this article.

---

58   See [1992] 2 Lloyd's Rep 481.
59   See [1994] 3 All ER 686.
60   [1995] 3 All ER 307. Lord Lloyd gave a dissenting judgment. He disagreed with the Court of Appeal's view that the existence of a contract of carriage between cargo owners and the shipowners militated against the liability of the surveyor in tort. Equally, he felt that the incorporation of the Hague Rules was an irrelevant factor (at p 317).

A reading of this article together with policy considerations would suggest that the onus to show that due diligence has been exercised should be on the carrier since he is the party with better access to facts relating to the ship's condition. The courts however have interpreted this provision differently. In *The Hellenic Dolphin*,[61] a cargo of asbestos shipped in good order and condition was destroyed as a result of ingress of sea water through an indent in the ship's plating. The defendant pleaded perils of the sea and the court found that he could avail himself of the exception since the plaintiffs failed to prove that the vessel was unseaworthy before the commencement of the voyage. This suggests that the onus is initially on the shipper to establish that the vessel was in an unseaworthy state, upon which the onus is cast on the carrier to disprove lack of due diligence.[62] This approach is open to criticism since it places the shipper under too onerous a burden which would, by and large, prove very difficult to displace.[63] On the other hand, it may be said to be fair given that the obligation to provide a seaworthy ship is an overriding obligation which deprives the carrier of the benefit of immunities available under Art IV where a breach is established.

Cargo management

The carrier is under an obligation to 'properly and carefully load, handle, stow, carry, keep, care for and discharge the goods carried' (Art III(2)).[64] The word 'carefully' has been construed as requiring reasonable care. As to whether the word 'properly' adds anything further to the standard of care has seen judicial discussion. In *Albacora SRL v Westcott & Laurance Line*,[65] the cargo consisted of wet salted fillets of fish for carriage from Glasgow to Genoa. The fish deteriorated due to bacterial action. The fish had been stored away from the boilers on instructions from the shipper. The cargo was not stored in refrigerated compartments. The courts had to consider whether the carrier had carried the goods 'properly' in accordance with Art III(2). The House of Lords came to the conclusion that the carrier had fulfilled the obligation required of him under Art III(2). 'Properly' means in accordance with a sound system, or in an appropriate manner in the light of all the knowledge that the carrier has or ought to have about the nature of the goods. It is tantamount to providing an efficient system and did not require the carrier to provide a system 'suited to all the weaknesses and idiosyncrasies of a particular cargo'.[66]

---

61 [1978] 2 Lloyd's Rep 336.
62 See *Eridania SPA and Others v Rudolf A Oetker and Others (The 'Fjord Wind')* [2000] 2 Lloyd's Rep 191; *Guinomar of Conarky v Samsung Fire & Marine Insurance (The Kamsar Voyager)* [2002] 2 Lloyd's Rep 57.
63 See Chapter 9 below. See also Ezeoke, 'Allocating onus of proof in sea cargo claims: the contest of conflicting principles' [2001] LMCLQ 261; Mankabady, 'The duty of care for the cargo' [1974] European Transport Law 2.
64 Normally, the master would be responsible for ensuring that the cargo is loaded properly and carefully, and cared for. Where the master is in breach, the carrier would be liable. See *Vinmar International Ltd and Another v Theresa Navigation SA* [2001] 2 Lloyd's Rep 1, at p 12.
65 [1966] 2 Lloyd's Rep 53.
66 As Lord Reid stated:
    The argument is that in this Article 'properly' means in the appropriate manner looking to the actual nature of the consignment, and that it is irrelevant that the shipowner and ship's officers neither knew nor could have discovered that special treatment was necessary.
    This construction of the word 'properly' leads to such an unreasonable result that I would not adopt it if the word can properly be construed in any other sense. The

Article III(2) is generally taken to impose a continuous obligation to take care from tackle to tackle on the presumption that the carrier has undertaken to load and discharge the goods. Where the duties of loading and discharge have been varied expressly by contract, the period of responsibility will run presumably from the time the goods have come under the charge of the carrier.[67]

The obligation relating to cargo management, like the seaworthiness obligation, is personal to the carrier and reliance on the advice of a competent surveyor is not adequate to lessen the liability of the carrier under the Hague-Visby Rules. In *International Packers v Ocean SS Co*,[68] the ship was carrying a cargo of tinned meat from Melbourne to Glasgow (via Freemantle). During the course of the voyage, sea water entered into the hold containing the cartons. The master of the ship sought advice from a surveyor. On the surveyor's advice, part of the cargo was sold and the remainder carried to the original destination. On arrival, it was found that the remaining cargo was also damaged due to dampness in the hold and the heating of wet canary seeds stored above the cartons of tinned meat. The cargo owners alleged breach of duty in failing to deal adequately with the cargo at Freemantle. The defendants denied negligence on the part of their officers or their surveyors and contended that, even if the surveyor gave negligently wrong advice, they were not liable for the acts of the surveyor. The court held, on the facts, that the surveyor had been negligent in formulating advice without insisting upon accurate data and this act of the surveyor was imputable to the owners so as to make them liable. Presumably, if the advice had not been negligent, then the shipowner would not have been liable for failure to take care of the cargo.[69]

The question of which party must prove or disprove the lack of proper care has not been consistently answered. The shipper's initial claim is generally based on showing that the goods have arrived damaged or have not arrived. According to *Gosse Millard v Canadian Government Merchant Marine*,[70] this initial claim sets up a *prima facie* liability of the carrier for breach of duty under Art III(2). If the carrier is to avoid liability, he must prove that he has taken proper care of the cargo and the loss is covered by one of the exceptions in Art IV(2). According to Wright J:

---

appellants argue that, because the article uses the word 'properly' as well as 'carefully', the word 'properly' must mean something more than carefully. Tautology is not unknown even in international conventions, but I think that 'properly' in this context has a meaning slightly different from 'carefully'.

In my opinion, the obligation is to adopt a system which is sound in light of all the knowledge which the carrier has or ought to have about the nature of the goods and, if that is right, then the respondents did adopt a sound system. They had no reason to suppose that the goods required any different treatment from that which the goods in fact received [at p 58].

67   According to *Jindal Iron and Steel Co v Islamic Solidarity Shipping Co* [2005] 1 Lloyd's Rep 55, Art III(2) does not place the shipowner under an obligation to provide the loading and discharge operations, but if he does provide these services he must perform them properly and carefully. See also *Compania Sud American Vapores v MS ER Hamburg Schiffahrtsgesellschaft MBH & Co KG* [2006] 2 Lloyd's Rep 66 wherein a clause stating responsibility for loading and stowing at charterer's expense under the supervision of the captain was held to place the responsibility on the charterer (see paras 41 and 42).

68   [1955] 2 Lloyd's Rep 218.

69   In *Balli Trading Ltd v Afalona Shipping Co Ltd (The Coral)* [1993] 1 Lloyd's Rep 1, the Court of Appeal seems to be making the (disturbing) suggestion that the carrier may not, in some circumstances, be liable for improper storage of cargo by stevedores. See Gaskell, 'Shipowner liability for cargo damage caused by stevedores' [1993] LMCLQ 171 for an excellent discussion of this case.

70   [1927] 2 KB 432.

... [the carrier] has to relieve himself of the *prima facie* breach of contract in not delivering the goods as received from the ship. I do not think that the terms of Art III put the
preliminary onus on the goods owner to give affirmative evidence that the carrier was
negligent. It is enough if the goods owner proves that the goods were not delivered or
were delivered damaged [at p 435].

The judgment in *Albacora SRL v Westcott and Laurance Line*, however, suggests that the
carrier can simply discharge his burden of proof by showing that the loss was covered
by one of the exceptions and that it is not necessary to disprove negligence.

Specific reference was made to the judgment in *Gosse Millard*, and Lord Pearce
doubted the correctness of the statement made by Wright J that an additional onus lies
on the defendant to show lack of negligence. This suggests that, if the carrier can show
that the cause of the loss falls within the Art IV exceptions, the burden of proof will
shift to the shipper to show negligence on the part of the carrier. Since *Albacora* is a
House of Lords' decision and is likely to be followed, this means that the shipper has
once again the extremely difficult task of showing negligence on the part of the carrier
without access to all the facts surrounding the loss.

Documentary responsibilities

The carrier is under an obligation *on demand* by the shipper to issue a bill of lading
which contains among other things the leading marks necessary for the identification
of the goods, the number of packages or pieces, the quantity or weight of the goods
and the apparent order and condition of the goods (Art III(3)). The right to demand
the issue of this document seems to exist in favour of the shipper and does not extend
to the consignee or the indorsee.

The statements made on the bill of lading are regarded as *prima facie* evidence of
the goods as described according to Art III(4). Proof to the contrary may be provided
by the carrier whilst the bill of lading is in the hands of the shipper. However, where
the bill has been transferred to a third party acting in good faith, the carrier cannot
submit proof to the contrary.

Where the quantity or leading marks acknowledged on the bill of lading based on
the information provided by the shipper later turn out to be false, Art III(5) implies
an indemnity to cover losses in favour of the carrier. This does not, however, extend to
statements regarding the condition of the goods.

The carrier is allowed to make some reservations on the bill of lading. According
to Art III(3), the carrier, master or agent is not bound to state or show in the bill of
lading any marks, number, quantity or weight when he has reasonable grounds that
the information regarding the above is not accurately represented or where he has no
reasonable means of checking them. It is fairly common for the carrier to qualify the
entries in relation to weight and quantity with phrases such as 'weight unknown'[71]
and 'quantity unknown'. Where such phrases are entered on the bill of lading, the bill
of lading does not provide *prima facie* evidence for the weight or the quantity shipped
against the carrier. As Longmore J explained in *Noble Resources Ltd v Cavalier Shipping
Corp (The Atlas)*:[72]

---

71   See *The Esmeralda* [1988] 1 Lloyd's Rep 206 (Australia, Sup Ct NSW); *The Atlas* [1996] 1 Lloyd's
      Rep 642; and *Agrosin Pte Ltd v Highway Shipping Co Ltd (The Mata K)* [1998] 2 Lloyd's Rep 614.
72   [1996] 1 Lloyd's Rep 642.

The words of Art III(4) '... such a bill of lading shall be *prima facie* evidence of the receipt by the carrier of the goods...' refer back to the words of Art III(3) '... the carrier ... shall ... issue to the shipper a bill of lading showing ... (b) either the number of package ... or the quantity, or weight ...'

Do the ... bills show the number of packages or weight (as furnished in writing by the shipper)? In one sense, it can be said they do, because the bills have figures which were in fact provided by the shipper in writing. But if the bills provide 'Weight ... number ... quantity unknown', it cannot be said that the bills 'show' that number or weight. They 'show' nothing at all because the shipowner is not prepared to say what the number of weight is. He can of course be required to show it under Art III(3) but, unless and until he does so, the provisions of Art III(4) as to *prima facie* evidence cannot come into effect [at p 646].

Duty to pursue the contract voyage

The carrier is under a general duty to proceed on the contract voyage. Deviation,[73] however, is justified in certain circumstances and therefore not deemed a breach of contract. Any deviation in saving or attempting to save life or property at sea, or any reasonable deviation, will not be an infringement or breach of the Hague-Visby Rules or of any contract of carriage, and the carrier will not be liable for the resulting loss or damage (Art IV(4)).[74] Deviation for the purposes of saving life is a mirror image of an instance of deviation justified at common law.[75] What is of interest is deviation for the purposes of saving property and reasonable deviation.

At first sight, it seems that deviation solely for the purpose of saving property will not be an infringement of the Hague-Visby Rules. It is not clear whether the carrier will be well within his rights under Art IV(4) to conduct salvaging operations or whether he will be allowed to salvage property only where he deviates to save life. If the former, it places the carrier in an extremely advantageous position. Indeed, it seems to provide an incentive to deviate purely for saving property – a highly profitable operation that may be conducted at the expense of the cargo owners since the carrier may be well aware that the goods could be lost during the operations or could arrive damaged. It is questionable whether this was intended by drafters of the Hague-Visby Rules given the policy reasons for the convention.

If Art IV(4) is construed as giving the carrier the liberty to deviate solely for the purposes of saving property regardless of the circumstances, the cargo owner will be unable to invoke Art IV(5)(e) which deprives the carrier from the benefit of the limitation of liability if it is proved that damage resulted from an act or omission of the carrier, done with the intent to cause damage or recklessly and with the knowledge that damage would probably result. The reason for this is that Art IV(5)(e) assumes that the carrier comes within one of the provisions which attracts the application of limitation of liability. But Art IV(4) is a provision that takes the carrier outside the parameters of liability which means that it does not come within the bounds of Art IV(5) at all, unless some limitation is placed on the extent to which the carrier can deviate to save property.

---

73 The doctrine of deviation at common law is often traced to *Davis v Garrett* (1830) 130 ER 1456. See also Dockray, 'Deviation: a doctrine all at sea?' [2000] LMCLQ 76 for an excellent comprehensive account of the historical background of the doctrine.

74 See Morgan, 'Unreasonable deviation under COGSA' (1977–78) 9 JMLC 481.

75 See Chapter 7, pp 213–15 above.

According to commentators,[76] a similar liberty to deviate clause in the US Harter Act of 1893 was construed as extending only to the necessity of the particular case. So, where a ship carries on a salvaging operation despite the presence of tugs that could render the same service, it would be regarded as going beyond the necessity of the particular case. As to how much reliance can be placed on the interpretation of similar phrases in the Harter Act, however, this is open to debate given the statements made about interpretation of the Rules in *Stag Line v Foscola, Mango and Co.*[77] Nonetheless, the historical context seems to contribute to imparting meaning to the provisions.[78]

The better approach would be to view Art IV(4) as justifying deviation for the purposes of saving property during the course of saving lives or deviation for the purposes of saving the adventure – for instance, where deviation is necessary to repair the ship or to unload unfit cargo that may affect other cargoes in the hold or the ship itself.

The concept of reasonable deviation is another source of uncertainty since it is not elucidated in the Hague-Visby Rules. There is some judicial opinion on what this concept might embody. In *Stag Line v Foscola, Mango and Co*, the vessel, on a voyage from Swansea to Constantinople, had on board two engineers to test and adjust fuel-saving apparatus. It deviated to St Ives in order that the engineers could disembark. The ship did not then return to the recognised route but remained very close to the coast, as a result of which she hit a rock. The House of Lords held that the deviation was not a reasonable deviation and attempted to define the concept. A number of different meanings were put forward by their Lordships but Lord Atkin provided a fuller opinion. He suggested that reasonable deviation should not be confined simply to the question of:

(a) deviation to avoid some imminent peril; or

(b) deviation in the joint interest of cargo owner or ship; or

(c) deviation as would be contemplated by both cargo owner and ship.

According to Lord Atkin's suggestion, deviation may be regarded as reasonable deviation even though it is made solely in the interests of the ship, or indeed in the direct interests of neither as, for instance, where the presence of a passenger or a member of the ship or crew is urgently required after the voyage had begun on a matter of national importance or where some person on board was a fugitive from justice and there were urgent reasons for his immediate presence. The question for determining reasonable deviation is:

> ... what departure from the contract voyage might a prudent person controlling the voyage at the time make and maintain, having in mind all the relevant circumstances existing at the time including the terms of the contract and the interests of all the parties concerned but without obligation to consider the interest of any as conclusive [at pp 343–44].

It is common for bills of lading to include clauses that allow the carrier to deviate from the contract voyage. Prior to *Stag Line v Foscola, Mango and Co*, it was unclear whether the combined operations of Art III(8) and Art IV(4) may render liberty to deviate

---

76 See, eg, *Carver's Carriage by Sea.*
77 [1932] AC 328. See 'Interpretation of the Hague-Visby Rules in the English Courts', pp 235–7 above.
78 See 'Dangerous goods', pp 265–7 below.

clauses ineffective. It is now well settled that express liberty to deviate clauses define the scope of the voyage and do not affect Hague-Visby Rules which define the terms on which the voyage is to be performed. The liberty to deviate clause is a misnomer in that it does not excuse a carrier were he to deviate; it defines the voyage permitted by the contract.

Unjustified deviation at common law was regarded as a fundamental breach of the contract and the carrier was, as a rule of law, deprived of the protection of the exclusion clauses on the principle that some breaches of contract are so contrary to the basic requirements of a particular contract that the benefit of any exclusion clause is lost to the party in breach. The justification for this draconian measure is the need to protect the cargo owner against loss of insurance cover since he is insured only for the contract voyage.[79] Where the voyage is different from the one contemplated, the cargo owner will not be covered and in these circumstances the law places the shipowner in the insurer's shoes.

In *Stag Line v Foscola, Mango and Co*, the House of Lords approached the effect of unjustifiable deviation on the contract in the time honoured way. The carrier therefore lost the benefit of the exemptions provided to him under the Hague Rules. However, since this decision, there has been the historic decision of *Photo Productions v Securicor*,[80] where the House of Lords categorically stated that the question whether, and to what extent, an exclusion clause is to be applied to a fundamental breach or to any breach of contract, is a matter of construction of the contract. Unfortunately, Lord Wilberforce also expressed the opinion that it may be preferable to preserve deviation cases as a body of authority *sui generis* with special rules derived from commercial and historical reasons.

There have been no cases on deviation since the *Photo Productions* case to put Lord Wilberforce's obiter statement to the test. However, in *The Antares*[81] and subsequently in *State Trading Corporation of India Ltd v M Golodetz Ltd*,[82] Lloyd LJ has expressed the view that deviation cases should be assimilated into the ordinary law of contract.

What would be the effect on deviation under the Hague-Visby Rules if Lloyd LJ's opinion was followed?[83] The question of whether the carrier can rely on the exception clauses contained in the Rules will become entirely a matter of construction of those clauses. The only impediment to accepting the 'matter of construction' approach would be the loss of insurance cover in the event of deviation.[84] But this is not an obstacle, since insurance policies with a 'held covered' clause are available for an extra premium. Such a policy would cover the cargo owner should there be a deviation. In any event, where the standard Institute Cargo Clauses (Clauses A, B or C)

---

79 Section 46(1) of the Marine Insurance Act 1906.
80 [1980] AC 827.
81 [1987] 1 Lloyd's Rep 424.
82 [1989] 2 Lloyd's Rep 277.
83 See Baughen, 'Does deviation still matter?' (1991) LMCLQ 70; Debattista, 'Fundamental breach and deviation in the carriage of goods by sea' [1989] JBL 22; Mills, 'The future of deviation on the law of carriage of goods' [1983] LMCLQ 587; Cashmore, 'The legal nature of the doctrine of deviation' [1989] JBL 492; Hubbard, 'Deviation in contracts of sea carriage: after the demise of fundamental breach' (1986) 16 Victoria University of Wellington LR 147. For a comparative article, see Sarpa, 'Deviation in the law of shipping: the United States, United Kingdom and Australia – a comparative study' (1976) 11 Journal of International Law and Economics 476. On Australian law, see Davies, 'Deviation is alive and well and living in New South Wales' (1991) 19 ABLR 379.
84 See Chapter 14, pp 448–9 below.

drafted by the Institute of London Underwriters to replace the Lloyd's SG Policy (Ships and Goods Policy) attached to the Marine Insurance Act 1906 as a model are used, cl 8.3 of all three sets of clauses provides:

> This insurance shall remain in force ... during delay beyond the control of the assured, any deviation, forced discharge, reshipment or transhipment and during any variation of the adventure arising from the exercise of a liberty granted to shipowners or charters under the contract of affreightment.

No extra premium is required of the assured under this clause.[85]

It seems, however, from *Daewoo Heavy Industries Ltd and Another v Klipriver Shipping Ltd and Another (The Kapitan Petko Voivoda)*[86] (albeit a case of unauthorised deck stowage and Art IV(5)) the court said the Hague Rules were an international convention and should be constructed on broad precedents of general acceptation. They were unwilling to import the principle of deviation into unauthorised deck stowage like the US courts since it was a peculiar creature of common law. If this reasoning reflects the current approach to international conventions and the consequences following from it, the English courts in the future will move away from the doctrine of fundamental breach in deviation cases.

CARRIER'S IMMUNITIES

The Hague-Visby Rules provide an extensive list of exceptions in favour of the carrier that reflect the exceptions commonly found in most contracts of affreightment. Hence, the interpretation of similarly worded exceptions under common law will be useful for an understanding of the extent of protection given by the Hague-Visby catalogue of exceptions. The carrier, however, under the Rules cannot increase the list of exceptions since they will be regarded as an attempt to lessen his liability and, therefore, void under Art III(8).[87]

Unseaworthiness

The carrier is not liable for loss or damage that is a consequence of unseaworthiness as long as he has exercised due diligence to make the ship seaworthy (Art IV(1)). However, the exercise of due diligence has been construed to be personal to the carrier whereby he is liable for the negligent acts of his servant, agent or independent contractor he may have employed to put the ship into a seaworthy state.[88] In these circumstances, this provision seems to give protection only against latent defects in the ship not discoverable on a reasonable inspection.

Negligence in navigation or management of the ship

The carrier is not liable for loss or damage to the goods as a result of the act, neglect or default of the master, mariner, pilot or the servants of the carrier in the navigation or

---

85   For more on Institute Cargo Clauses, see Chapter 14 pp 452–6 below.
86   [2003] EWCA Civ 451.
87   See 'Contracting Out', pp 280–3 below.
88   See 'Duty to provide a seaworthy ship', pp 235–40 above.

management of the ship (Art IV(2)(a)). The two limbs of this exception – fault in navigation and fault in management – have been difficult to interpret. Fault in the navigation of the ship has been construed as applying to situations where, due to the negligent act on the part of the master or crew, the vessel has been grounded or has collided with another vessel.[89]

More recently, the House of Lords had to consider whether the Art IV(2)(a) exception could be raised where a master did not comply with the charterer's order to proceed on the shortest route in *Whistler International Ltd v Kawasaki Kisen Kaisha (The Hill Harmony)*,[90] though the issue was decided in the context of a time charterparty, as a result of paramount clauses[91] in the charterparty. Art IV(2)(a) of the Hague Rules was incorporated into the charterparty. The judgment therefore is of relevance to bills of lading affected by the Hague-Visby Rules. In brief, the facts are as follows. Under a time charterparty[92] (7–9 months), the vessel performed two trans Pacific voyages: one from Vancouver to Yokkaichi and the other from Vancouver to Shiogama. The master instead of following the shortest route (due to bad weather he had experienced on that route on a previous voyage) as instructed by the charterer took the rhumb line route with the result that one voyage took six and a half days long and consumed 130 tons more fuel; the other three and one third days long with an increased consumption of 60 tons fuel. The charterer sought to recover loss of $89,800 from the owners. The arbitrators found for the claimants on the basis of breach of the duty to follow the charterer's order and failure to prosecute the voyage with utmost dispatch.[93] Both the Queen's Bench and the Court of Appeal on appeal held otherwise. Clarke J held that the dispute related to matters of navigation.[94] Similar reasoning was also followed in the Court of Appeal.[95] The House of Lords allowed the appeal on the grounds that there was a contractual duty to proceed with due dispatch and the choice of route in the absence of an overriding factor was a matter of employment rather than navigation. The planning of the voyage was not a matter of navigation. Lord Hobhouse expressed his views thus:

> The meaning of any language is affected by its context. This is true of the words 'employment' in a time charter and of the exception for negligence in the 'navigation' of the ship in a charterparty or contract of carriage. They reflect different aspects of the operation of the vessel. 'Employment' embraces the economic aspect – the exploitation

---

89   *The Xantho* [1887] 12 AC 503; *The Portland Trader* [1964] 2 Lloyd's Rep 443. See also Lee and Kim,' A carrier's liability for commercial default and default in navigation or management of the vessel' (2000) 12 Transportation LJ 205.

90   [2000] 1 AC 638.

91   On paramount clauses, see pp 271–2 below.

92   NYPE form with amendments.

93   Under cl 8 of the charterparty, the captain was to prosecute the voyages with the utmost dispatch and was, although appointed by the owners, to be under the orders and directions of the charterer as regards employment and agency.

94   He said:

> In my judgment, an order as to where the vessel was to go, as for example to port A or B to load or discharge or to port A or port B via port C to bunker, would be an order as to employment which the master would be bound to follow, subject of course (as all parties agreed) to his overriding responsibility for the safety of his ship. An order as to how to get from where the ship was to port A, B or C would not, however, be an order as to employment but an order as to navigation [[1999] QB 72, at p 81].

See also Davenport, 'Rhumb line or direct circle? – that is a question of navigation' [1998] LMCLQ 502.

95   See Potter LJ [2000] QB 241, at p 261.

of the earning potential of the vessel. 'Navigation' embraces matters of seamanship . . . What is clear is that to use the word 'navigation' in this context as if it includes everything which involves the vessel proceeding through the water is both mistaken and unhelpful . . . where seamanship is in question, choices as to the speed or steering of the vessel are matters of navigation, as will be the exercise of laying off a course on a chart. But it is erroneous to reason, as did Clarke J, from the fact that the master must choose how much of a safety margin he should leave between his course and a hazard or how and at what speed to proceed up a hazardous channel to the conclusion that all questions of what route to follow are questions of navigation [at pp 657–58].[96]

Interpretation of the phrase 'fault in management' also poses difficulties, since the difference between cargo damage due to events that are attributable to lack of proper care of that cargo and those that are attributable to fault in management of the ship may not always be apparent as illustrated by *Gosse Millard v Canadian Government Merchant Marine*.[97] The plaintiffs shipped a cargo of tinplates from Swansea to Vancouver. The ship went to Liverpool to load some more cargo and, whilst undocking, collided with a pier. She had to be dry docked for repairs. On arrival, the tinplates stored in hold 5 of the ship were found to have sustained serious damage caused by fresh water. The repairers had been careless in moving and replacing the tarpaulins covering hold 5 where repairs were carried out as a result of which rain water entered the hold. The cargo owners alleged breach of the duty to take care of the cargo under Art III(2) on the part of the carrier. The carrier relied on Art IV(2)(a).

In the opinion of the House of Lords, the negligent act in not replacing the tarpaulins was primarily a neglect of the cargo, and not a neglect of the ship which affected the cargo. The carrier was therefore liable. In other words, the distinction between care of cargo and management of ship is one between want of care of cargo and want of care of the vessel indirectly affecting the cargo. Or, as Greer LJ expressed it, 'if the negligence is not negligence towards the ship but only negligent failure to use the apparatus of the ship for the protection of the cargo, the ship is not . . . relieved' (at p 200).

Fire

The carrier, under Art IV(2)(b), is excluded from responsibility for loss or damage arising or resulting from fire unless caused by the actual fault or privity of the carrier.[98]

The courts have defined fire to mean a flame and not merely heat. So, mere heating, which has not arrived at the state of incandescence or ignition, is not regarded as fire, according to *Tempus Shipping Co v Louis Dreyfus*.[99]

In the event of loss or damage due to fire, if the operative cause is a failure to

---

96 Does it follow from Lord Hobhouse's statement that a master is obliged to enter a port even in the face of risk? The answer is 'no'. As Lord Hobhouse acknowledged, 'the master remains responsible for the safety of the vessel, her crew and cargo. If an order is given, compliance with which exposes the vessel to a risk which the owners have not agreed to bear, the master is entitled to refuse to obey it; indeed, as the safe port cases show, in extreme situations the master is under an obligation not to obey it' (at p 658).

97 (1927) 29 Lloyd's Rep 190.

98 See *Macieo Shipping Ltd v Clipper Shipping Lines Ltd (The MV Clipper Sao Luis)* [2000] 1 Lloyd's Rep 645.

99 [1930] 1 KB 699.

exercise due diligence to make the ship seaworthy on the part of the carrier, this exception will not be available to the carrier. In *Maxine Footwear Co Ltd v Canadian Merchant Marine*,[100] the carrier could not invoke Art IV(2)(b) when the cargo was lost due to a fire caused by oxyacetylene torches used for thawing frozen pipes.

If the fire is caused by the actual fault or privity of the carrier, he is not protected from liability under this exception. Whether there is actual fault or privity on the carrier's part is a question of fact. The question of establishing the actual fault or privity of the carrier becomes a difficult issue where the carrier is a public company. The reason for this is that the company acts through individuals, and not all negligent acts of the individuals working in a company need be necessarily the negligent act of the company. According to *Lennard's Carrying v Asiatic Petroleum*,[101] the negligent act of the individual will be ascribed to the company only where he stands in an extremely special relationship to the company – a relationship where it would be natural to say that the person acts and speaks as the company. In other words, to make the company liable, the negligent act must be the act of that individual who is the directing mind or the brain of the company. As Viscount Haldane expressed it:

> . . . the fault or privity is the fault or privity of somebody who is not merely a servant or agent for whom the company is liable upon the footing *respondeat superior*, but somebody for whom the company is liable because his action is the very action of the company itself. It is not enough that the fault should be the fault of a servant in order to exonerate the owner, the fault must also be one which is not the fault of the owner, or a fault to which the owner is privy [at p 713].

Where the carrier does not supervise the work of his employees adequately, then it seems, according to *The Marion*,[102] that it would be regarded as actual fault or privity of the carrier.

The carrier, in some circumstances, may be able to take advantage of the statutory provisions of s 186 of the Merchant Shipping Act 1995 (previously s 18 of the Merchant Shipping Act 1979) as a result of the combined operations of Art VIII of the Hague-Visby Rules and s 6(4) of the Carriage of Goods by Sea Act 1971. Section 186 of the Merchant Shipping Act 1995 provides that 'the owner of a United Kingdom ship shall not be liable for any loss or damage . . . where any property on board the ship is lost or damaged by reason of fire on board the ship'. 'Owner', for the purposes of this section, includes any part owner and any charterer, manager or operator of the ship.

At first sight, s 186 protection appears extensive. It must be pointed out, however, that this provision is operative only where the goods are destroyed *on board the ship*. So, where goods catch fire on shore or on a lighter while awaiting loading or discharging, then s 186 will be inoperative.

Another important point that must be noted about s 186 is that it protects the shipowner even where the fire has been caused due to the unseaworthiness of the vessel. It is, therefore, of greater advantage than the fire exception under Art IV(2) of the Rules, since the exceptions are not available to the carrier under the Rules where he has not exercised due diligence to make the ship seaworthy. Note that s 186 is available *only to UK ships*.

---

100 [1959] 2 Lloyd's Rep 105.
101 [1915] AC 705.
102 [1984] 2 All ER 243.

The carrier cannot rely on s 186 if 'it is proved that the loss resulted from his personal act or omission, committed with the intent to cause such loss, or recklessly and with knowledge that such loss would probably result'. The onus to establish this is on the cargo owner and this, in practice, may prove to be extremely difficult, since he does not have the opportunity to access all the facts surrounding the incident.

Perils of the sea

The carrier is not liable for loss or damage to the goods where it has occurred due to the perils, dangers and accidents of the sea or other navigable waters (Art IV(2)(c)). Common law has interpreted the phrase 'perils of the sea' to refer to any damage that has been caused by storms, sea water, collision, stranding and other perils that are peculiar to the sea or to a ship at sea which could not have been avoided by the exercise of reasonable care. This exception only refers to perils that are encountered at sea and not to those encountered on land or any other form of transport.[103] Article IV(2)(c), however, extends the perils exception to other navigable waters which would include rivers and other inland waters.[104]

Act of God

The carrier is not liable for loss or damage to the goods that has resulted from an act of God (Art IV(2)(d)). At common law, this has been interpreted to mean acts that are independent of human intervention that could not have been prevented by the exercise of foresight and reasonable precaution. In *Nugent v Smith*,[105] the death of a horse through injuries received in a storm was held to be an act of God which the carrier was unable to prevent by taking reasonable measures.

Act of war, public enemies and riots

The carrier is not liable for loss or damage on account of act of war (Art IV(2)(e)). War has been construed by common law to include a state of hostilities between states where diplomatic relations may not have been severed.[106] This exclusion is also probably wide enough to cover acts done in civil war.

---

103 *Hamilton Fraser and Co v Pandorf and Co* (1887) 12 App Cas 518.
104 An issue that has been discussed in relation to this exception in some Commonwealth jurisdictions is whether it could be raised when goods lost or damaged by the event constituting perils of the sea is reasonably foreseeable. In *Great China Metal Industries Co Ltd v Malaysian International Shipping Corp Berhad (The Bunga Seroja)* [1994] 1 Lloyd's Rep 455, the New South Wales Supreme Court, following the Anglo-Australian approach, held that 'damage to cargo ... occasioned by a storm which was "expectable" does not, of itself, exclude a finding that the damage was occasioned by perils of the sea' (at p 470). See also the following US and Canadian decisions: *Re Complaint of Tecomar SA (The Tuxpan)* (1991) 765 F Supp 1150 (SDNY); *JJ Gerber and Co v SS Sabine Howaldt* 437 F 2d 580 (2d Cir) (1971); *New Rotterdam Insurance Co v SS Loppersum* 215 F Supp 563 (1963) (SDNY); *Charles Goods Fellow Lumber Sales Ltd v Verrault* [1971] 1 Lloyd's Rep 185. According to the US-Canadian approach, 'perils of the sea' refers to events peculiar to the sea and are of 'an extraordinary nature or arise from irresistible force or overwhelming powers, and which cannot be guarded against by the ordinary exertions of human skill'.
105 (1876) 1 CPD 423.
106 *Kawasaki Kisen v Bantham SS Co* [1939] 2 KB 544.

The carrier is excluded from liability for loss or damage to the goods due to the act of public enemies (Art IV(2)(f)). This probably includes the acts of enemies of the state and perhaps those of terrorists and pirates.

The carrier is also not liable for loss or damage due to riots and civil commotions. This probably covers disturbances that do not amount to civil war Art IV(2)(k)).

Act of authorities and quarantine

The carrier is exempt from liability for loss or damage to the goods due to the arrest or restraint of princes or rulers or people or seizure under legal process (Art IV(2)(g)). Under common law, exclusion clauses worded similarly have been interpreted to apply to a number of situations. For instance, it has been construed to cover loss or damage where the government of a country takes possession of the goods through embargo, arrests or blockades; where there is a prohibition against the import of goods; and where goods cannot be discharged due to quarantine restrictions. The Hague-Visby Rules, however, specifically exclude liability for loss or damage to the goods caused due to quarantine restrictions (Art IV(2)(h)).

Act or omission of shipper

The carrier is relieved of liability where the cargo has been damaged or lost due to the act or omission of the shipper or owner of the goods, his agent or representative (Art IV(2)(i)). It is difficult to envisage what this exception covers since there are specific exceptions relating to loss or damage caused due to defective marking, defective packing or inherent vice of the goods.[107] It has been suggested that the exception could cover damage to the goods caused by improper stowage due to the misdescription of the goods provided by the shipper.[108]

Strikes and lock outs

The carrier is relieved of liability for loss or damage on account of strikes or lock outs or restraint of labour from whatever cause, whether partial or general (Art IV(2)(j)). The word 'strike' has been defined by Lord Denning as:

> ... a concerted stoppage of work done by men with a view to improving their wages or conditions, or giving vent to grievance, or making a protest about something or other, or supporting or sympathising with other workmen in such endeavour. It is distinct from a stoppage brought about by an external event such as bomb scare or by apprehension of danger.[109]

Bills of lading normally have clauses (known as the *Caspiana* clause)[110] that allow the carrier to discharge goods bound for a strike-bound port at any other safe and convenient port. The inclusion of such clauses in bill of lading governed by the Hague-Visby Rules are not construed as a lessening of the carrier's obligation towards cargo

---

107 See 'Wastage and inherent vice', p 252 below.
108 See *Carver's Carriage by Sea*, at para 537.
109 *The New Horizon* [1975] 2 Lloyd's Rep 314, at p 317.
110 Named after *Renton v Palmyra Trading Corp of Panama* [1957] AC 149.

management under Art III(2) and therefore void under Art III(8). Article III(2), as interpreted in *Renton v Palmyra*, applies only to the method of loading, carrying and discharging and not to the place of discharge.

Saving life or property and deviation

The carrier is not liable for loss or damage to the cargo while saving or attempting to save life or property at sea (Art IV(2)(l)). It is not clear whether this provision covers deviation to save life, or property at sea. Presumably, this exception refers to situations where the vessel while on the contract route is delayed in completing the voyage because of attempts to save life or property on board the carrier's ship itself or on other ships it may have encountered on course. Further under Art IV(4), the carrier is also not liable for loss or damage that is a result of reasonable deviation.[111]

Wastage and inherent vice

The carrier is also protected from liability for wastage in bulk or weight or any other loss or damage from inherent defect, quality or vice of the goods (Art IV(2)(m)). Inherent vice has been construed as the unfitness of the goods to withstand the ordinary incidents of the voyage despite the exercise of care required of the cargo.[112]

Defective packing and marking

The carrier is not liable for loss or damage that is a consequence of insufficiency of packing (Art IV(2)(n)). Goods are regarded as insufficiently packed if they cannot withstand the kind of handling that the goods are likely to undergo during the course of the voyage.[113] If the carrier however issues clean bills of lading, he cannot exclude liability for insufficient packing as against the consignee or indorsee acting in good faith.[114]

Where goods are lost or damaged due to insufficiency or inadequacy of marks, the carrier is protected by the Hague-Visby Rules (Art IV(2)(o)). However, where the bill of lading is transferred to a third party acting in good faith, the carrier will not be able to rely on this exception. If the marks acknowledged on the bill of lading turn out to be inaccurate, the carrier can claim indemnity from the shipper (Art III(5)).[115]

Latent defects

The carrier is not liable for loss or damage to the goods that is caused due to latent defects not discoverable by due diligence (Art IV(2)(p)). It is not clear what this

---

111 See 'Duty to pursue the contract voyage', pp 243–6 above.
112 *Albacora SRL v Westcott Laurance Line* [1966] 2 Lloyd's Rep 53. According to Lord Reid, 'whether there is an inherent defect or vice must depend on the kind of transit required by the contract. If this contract had required refrigeration, there would have been no inherent vice. But as it did not, there was inherent vice because the goods could not stand the treatment which the contract authorised or required' (at p 59).
113 *Silver v Ocean Steamship Co* [1930] 1 KB 416.
114 See also 'Documentary responsibilities', pp 242–3 above.
115 See 'Shipper's guarantee', pp 264–5 below.

exception might cover. If it refers to latent defects in the ship that seems to be already covered by Art IV(1).[116] It has been suggested that this exception bears a wider meaning and may protect the carrier where, for instance, damage is caused by a shore crane belonging to him due to a latent defect that would not have been discovered by the exercise of due diligence. This provision may also give an immunity additional to that specified in Art IV(1) in that it would cover defects that would not have been discovered by the exercise of due diligence in situations where the carrier could not show that he had in fact exercised due diligence.[117]

Catch-all exception

Neither the carrier nor the ship is liable for loss or damage that arises or results from any other cause arising without the actual fault or privity of the carrier, or without the fault or neglect of the agents or servants of the carrier (Art IV(2)(q)).

The opinion of commentators is that this provision cannot be given an *ejusdem generis* interpretation since the list of exceptions provided in Art IV(2) does not form a single genus.[118] It is therefore to be regarded as referring to circumstances not covered by Art IV(2)(a)-(p).

The carrier can take advantage of this provision only if it can be established that the loss or damage occurred without the actual fault or privity of the carrier *and* without the fault or neglect on the part of his servants or agents. This exception was successfully invoked in *Leesh River Tea Co v British India Steam Navigation*.[119] where cargo was damaged due to theft of a storm valve cover by stevedores employed by the carrier. The court came to the conclusion that the carrier was not responsible for the act of the stevedore, since the stevedore was not performing a duty for the shipowner when the theft took place. In other words, the act of the thief was the act of a stranger; it was not done in the course of employment.

The suggestion that a carrier could escape liability for an act that affects the cargo but where it is done outside the parameter of duties entrusted to the servant or the independent contractor is irrational, since it is reasonable to expect the carrier to be in control of the servants or independent contractors who are on the ship with his permission. Therefore, should he not be held responsible for all their acts – whether they are carried out in the course of discharging their duties for which they were employed or not?

The onus of disproving negligence or privity is on the person claiming the benefit of this exception. The burden is not discharged however where the cause is inexplicable. This however does not mean that the carrier has to establish the precise cause. It is sufficient if he can disprove negligence. In *Goodwin, Ferreira & Co v Lamport and Holt*,[120] a crate while being lowered onto a lighter broke open and damaged some other cargo in the vessel. The carrier was able to establish that he had adopted a sound system of work and therefore escaped liability.

---

116   See 'Unseaworthiness', p 246 above.
117   *Scrutton on Charterparties*, 20th edn, 1996, at p 445. See also *Corporacion Argentina de Productores v Royal Mail Lines Ltd* (1939) 64 Ll LRep 188, at p 192; *The Antigoni* [1991] 1 Lloyd's Rep 209.
118   *Scrutton on Charterparties*, 20th edn, 1996, at pp 445–6.
119   [1966] 2 Lloyd's Rep 193.
120   (1929) 34 Ll LR 192.

LIMITATION OF LIABILITY

The Hague-Visby Rules contain provisions in respect of the extent of liability and time limitation and the carrier is not allowed by the Rules to lower the liability limits or lessen the specified time limits.[121]

Liability for 'loss or damage'

Under the Hague-Visby Rules, the carrier is liable for loss or damage. It is not clear from the Rules whether the phrase 'loss or damage' which is used in a number of provisions[122] covers only the loss or damage to the goods carried or whether it includes loss or damage that the cargo owner suffers, for instance, as a result of late delivery of the cargo by the carrier. The phrase was construed in the context of Art III(8) as covering loss in connection with goods due to discharge at the wrong port and not restricted to actual loss or physical damage.[123] Likewise, the phrase in the context of Art IV(1) and IV(2) was construed as covering loss caused to the cargo owner as a result of late delivery or misdelivery on the reasoning that the Rules, in dealing with contractual liabilities, must have foreseen that contractual liabilities are not restricted purely to physical damage. Devlin J stated the position in *Anglo-Saxon v Adamastos Shipping Co*[124] thus:

> The last question asks whether the words 'loss or damage' in s 4(1) and (2) of the Act relate only to physical loss of or damage to goods. The words themselves are not qualified or limited by anything in the section. The Act is dealing with responsibilities and liabilities under contracts of carriage of goods by sea, and clearly such contractual liabilities are not limited to physical damage. A carrier may be liable for loss caused to the shipper by delay or misdelivery, even though the goods themselves are intact [at p 253].

Liability in contract and in tort and availability of limitation

The defences and limits of liability provided for in the Hague-Visby Rules according to Art IV *bis* (1) apply in an action for loss or damage to goods covered by a contract of carriage whether the action is founded in contract or in tort.[125] Defences and limits of liability in respect of loss or damage to goods as set out in the Hague-Visby Rules are available under Art IV *bis* (1) and (2) to the carrier and to the servant or agent of the carrier as long as the servant or agent is not an independent carrier.[126] So, where the carrier employs independent contractors like stevedores to load and discharge the goods from the ship, they cannot avail themselves of the extended protection available under these provisions.

Until recently, if independent contractors wanted to avail themselves of the immunities provided in the Rules, the carrier needed to expressly include clauses that

---

121 See 'Contracting out', pp 280–3 below.
122 Eg, Arts III(8), IV(1), IV(2), IV(4) and IV(5).
123 See *Renton v Palmyra* [1957] AC 149.
124 [1957] 2 QB 233.
125 This provision was introduced by the Brussels Protocol.
126 An amendment introduced by the Brussels Protocol.

extend the protection to them.[127] This express inclusion was to get round the privity rule in English law under which only parties to the contract could rely on the contractual terms.[128] The clauses are known as 'Himalaya' clauses – named after the ship in *Adler v Dickson*,[129] where a crew member was unable to invoke the exception clause contained in the contract between passenger and shipowner due to the common law doctrine of privity of contract. The courts regard Himalaya clauses as effective in protecting the stevedores. In *New Zealand Shipping Co Ltd v AM Satterthwaite and Co Ltd (The Eurymedon)*,[130] the bill of lading contained the following clause:

> It is hereby expressly agreed that no servant or agent of the carrier (including every independent contractor employed by the carrier) shall in any circumstances whatsoever be under any liability whatsoever to the shipper, consignee or owner of the goods or to any holder of the bill of lading for any loss or damage or delay of whatsoever kind arising or resulting directly or indirectly from any neglect or default on his part while acting in the course of or in connection with his employment and, without prejudice to the generality of the foregoing provisions in this clause, every exemption, limitation, condition and liberty herein contained and every right, exemption from liability, defence and immunity of whatsoever nature applicable to the carrier or to which the carrier is entitled hereunder shall also be available and shall extend to protect every such servant or agent of the carrier acting as aforesaid and, for the purpose of all the foregoing provisions of this clause, the carrier is or shall be deemed to be acting as agent or trustee on behalf of and for the benefit of all persons who might be his servants or agents from time to time (including independent contractors as aforesaid) and all such persons shall to this extent be or be deemed to be parties to the contract on or evidenced by this bill of lading.

The cargo was damaged during the unloading operations carried out by an independent firm of stevedores. When sued, the stevedores relied on the clauses excluding liability in the bill of lading. The Privy Council held that the bill of lading was a contract between the stevedores and the cargo owner that had been effected through the carrier who acted as the agent. Hence, the stevedores could rely on the exemption clauses contained in the contract of carriage. Technical points in the law of contract formation like consideration were dealt with swiftly on the basis that the law

---

127 *Adler v Dickson* [1954] 2 Lloyd's Rep 267. See also *Scruttons v Midland Silicones Ltd* [1962] AC 446. Both these cases establish the sanctity of the privity of contract doctrine in English law. However, the House of Lords in the latter indicated the circumstances in which a clause inserted in a contract may protect a third party. According to Lord Reid:

> I can see a possibility of success ... if [first] the bill of lading makes it clear that the stevedore is intended to be protected by the provisions in it which limit liability; [secondly] the bill of lading makes it clear that the carrier, in addition to contracting for these provisions on his own behalf, should apply to the stevedore; [thirdly] the carrier has authority from the stevedore to do that, or perhaps later ratification by the stevedore would suffice; and [fourthly] that any difficulties about consideration moving from the stevedore were overcome ... [at p 474].

128 Another means of protecting sub-contractors is to use circular indemnity causes whereby the cargo owner promises not to sue the sub-contractors and also promises to indemnify the carrier if it does (see *Nippon Yusen Kaisha v International Import and Export Co Ltd (The Elbe Maru)* [1978] 1 Lloyd's Rep 606). Typically, if a cargo owner sues a sub-contractor in breach of the circular indemnity clause, the carrier is likely to seek a stay of action or injunction from the courts.

129 [1954] 2 Lloyd's Rep 267.

130 [1975] AC 154.

must take a pragmatic approach to commercial transactions.[131] Subsequent cases like *Salmond and Spraggon (Australia) Pty Ltd v Port Jackson Stevedoring Pty Ltd*[132] and others have applied the approach taken in the *New Zealand Shipping* case and it is common to include Himalaya clauses in bills of lading. In *New Zealand Shipping*, Lord Wilberforce stated specifically that the principle was applicable to exemptions, limitations, defences and immunities contained in the bill of lading (at p 169). Does this mean that the stevedore will not be able to avail of other clauses in the contract – for instance, a jurisdiction clause?

This issue came up for consideration by the Privy Council in *The Mahkutai*.[133] The relevant clause read:

> Carrier means the PT Rejeki Sentosa Shipping Co and/or subsidiary companies on whose behalf the bill of lading has been signed . . .
>
> 4 Sub-contracting
>
> (i) The carrier shall be entitled to sub-contract on any terms the whole or any part of the carriage, loading, unloading, storing, warehousing . . .
>
> The merchant undertakes that no claim or allegation shall be made against any servant, agent or sub-contractor of the carrier, including but not limited to stevedores and terminal operators . . . every such servant, agent and sub-contractor shall have the benefit of all exceptions, limitations, provision, conditions and liberties herein benefiting the carrier as if such provisions were made expressly for their benefit . . .
>
> 19 Jurisdiction clause
>
> The contract evidenced by the bill of lading shall be governed by the law of Indonesia and any dispute arising hereunder shall be determined by the Indonesian courts according to that law to the exclusion of the jurisdiction of the courts of any other country.

The question at issue was whether the shipowner as sub-contractor could rely on the jurisdiction clause. Did the word 'provisions' in the Himalaya clause bring within it the jurisdiction clause? The Privy Council came to the conclusion that it could not, since a jurisdiction clause did not benefit only one party. It was not like an exception or limitation clause. It 'embodies a mutual agreement under which both parties agree with each other as to the relevant jurisdiction for the resolution of disputes' (at p 666).

---

131 Of course, if the Himalaya clause had been held to be ineffective, the cargo owner could avoid the exception clauses that operate to his disadvantage by suing the third party who is unprotected by the exception clauses. As Lord Goff observed in *The Mahkutai* [1996] AC 650:

> . . . recognition has been given to the undesirability, especially in a commercial context, of allowing plaintiffs to circumvent contractual exception clauses by suing in particular the servant or agent of the contracting party, thereby undermining the purpose of the exception, and so redistributing the contractual allocation of risk which is reflected in the freight rate and in the parties' respective insurance arrangements [at p 661].

Third party protection through contractual clauses has generated a great deal of academic discussion. See, eg, Reynolds, 'Himalaya clause resurgent' (1974) 90 LQR 301; Clarke, 'The reception of the *Eurymedon* decision in Australia, Canada and New Zealand' (1980) 29 ICLQ 132. See also *Glebe Island Terminals Pty Ltd v Continental Seagram Pty Ltd and Another (The Antwerpen)* [1994] 1 Lloyd's Rep 213. For a review of the American position on such clauses, see Zawitoski, 'Limitation of liability for stevedores and terminal operators under the carrier's bill of lading and COGSA' [1985] JMLC 337. For a German view, see Schmidt, 'The Himalaya clause under the law of the Federal Republic of Germany' [1984] European Transport Law 675.

132 [1981] 1 WLR 138. See also the following where the Himalaya clause was ineffective: *Raymond Burke Ltd v The Mersey Docks and Harbour Co* [1986] 1 Lloyd's Rep 155; *Lotus Cars Ltd and Others v Southampton Cargo Handling Plc and Other and Associated British Ports (The Rigoletto)* [2000] 2 Lloyd's Rep 532.

133 [1996] AC 650.

Could the word 'provision' in the clause have made a difference, given that it appeared in the centre of a series of words that share the same characteristic, imparting benefits as opposed to rights that entail correlative obligations on the cargo owner? The word 'provision' in their opinion was 'inserted with the purpose of ensuring that any other provision in the bill of lading which, although it did not strictly fall within the description "exceptions, limitations . . . conditions and liberties" nevetheless benefited the carrier in the same way in the sense that it was inserted in the bill of lading for the carrier's protection, should enure for the benefit of the servants, agents and subcontractors . . . It cannot therefore extend to . . . an exclusive jurisdiction clause, which is not of that character' (at p 666). Of course, it is possible to get round the decision in *The Mahkutai* by drafting a clause suitably worded to include the jurisdiction clause.

While clever drafting may widen the extent of protection offered to an independent contractor, the Himalaya clause is subject to the mandatory limitations imposed by the Hague-Visby Rules. So, in *The Starsin*[134] the court held that the Himalaya clause protected the owner to the same extent as the carrier was itself protected under its contract of c⁓rriage. A wider exemption available to the independent contractor would be void under Art III(8).

Reforms to the doctrine of privity as reflected by the Contracts (Right of Third Parties) Act 1999 mean that extensive clauses are not required in contracts for a stevedore to take advantage of the exemptions and limitations in the contract. The reform came about as a consequence of discontent with the doctrine of privity. Widely regarded as outdated,[135] the doctrine came under pressure not only from academics but also the judiciary. For instance, Steyn LJ in *Darlington BC v Wiltshier Northern Ltd*[136] expressed his discontent clearly:

> The case for recognising a contract for the benefit of a third party is simple and straightforward. The autonomy of the will of the parties should be respected. The law of contract should give effect to the reasonable expectations of contracting parties. Principle certainly requires that a burden should not be imposed on a third party without his consent. But there is no doctrinal, logical, or policy reason why the law should deny effectiveness to a contract for the benefit of a third party where that is the expressed intention of the parties. Moreover, often, the parties and particularly third parties organise their affairs on the faith of the contract. I will not struggle with the point further since nobody seriously asserts the contrary [at p 76].

The Law Commission, which started work on the reform of privity in 1990, published its final report *Privity of Contract: Contracts for the Benefit of Third Parties* in 1996,[137] which also included a draft Contracts (Rights of Third Parties) Bill. With further amendments, the Bill received the Royal Assent on 11 November 1999 and came into force on 11 May 2000.

Section 1(1)(a) of the Contracts (Rights of Third Parties) Act 1999[138] enables the

---

134 [2003] 1 Lloyd's Rep 57.
135 Countries with a common law background such as the US and New Zealand abolished the privity rule well before England.
136 [1995] 1 WLR 68.
137 Law Com No 242. For an analysis, see Burrows, 'Reforming privity of contract: Law Commission Report No 242' [1996] LMCLQ 467.
138 Available in Carr and Kidner, *International Trade Law Statutes and Conventions*, 5th edn, 2008 Routledge-Cavendish. Also available at www.hmso.gov.uk.

third party to enforce contractual terms, including exclusion clauses and limitation clauses (s 1(6)), where there is express provision that he may. There is no requirement that the third party be named according to s 1(3), so words such as 'independent contractors shall have the right to enforce the contract' will suffice. Section 1(1)(b) enables a third party to enforce the contractual terms where the contract purports to confer a benefit on that third party and there is no indication that the parties did not intend the term to be enforceable by the third party.[139] Section 6 of the Act lists the exceptions and, according to s 6(5):[140]

> Section 1 confers no rights on a third party in the case of:
>
> (a) a contract for the carriage of goods by sea; or
>
>   . . .
>
> except that a third party may in reliance on that section avail himself of an exclusion or limitation of liability in such a contract.

Definitions of contract for the carriage of goods by sea and bills of lading are dealt with in s 6(6) and (7):

>   . . .
>
> means a contract of carriage:
>
> (a) contained in or evidenced by a bill of lading, sea waybill or a corresponding electronic transaction; or
>
> (b) under or for the purposes of which there is given an undertaking which is contained in a ship's delivery order or a corresponding electronic transaction.
>
> (7) For the purposes of sub-s (6):
>
> (a) 'bill of lading', 'sea waybill' and 'ship's delivery order' have the same meaning as in the Carriage of Goods by Sea Act 1992; and
>
> (b) a corresponding electronic transaction is a transaction within s 1(5) of that Act which corresponds to the issue, indorsement, delivery or transfer of a bill of lading, sea waybill or ship's delivery order.

While the Act excludes bills of lading for obvious reasons – to avoid overlap with the Carriage of Goods by Sea Act 1992 – s 6(5) does specifically provide that a third party can avail of the exclusion and limitation of liability in such a contract. This means that s 1 would be available to a third party provided the conditions set out in s 1(1)(a) or (b) are met. Being limited to exclusion and limitation of liability, the issue of whether a third party can avail himself of a jurisdiction clause will need to be addressed specifically through an appropriately worded Himalaya clause in the contract.

---

139 Note that s 2 allows variation and rescission by the contracting parties. Broadly, it revolves around assent/reliance and, once the third party has communicated assent or reliance, the third party's entitlement cannot be varied without consent.

140 Note that this exclusion does not affect charterparties. For further analysis of the effect of the Act on carriage of goods by sea, see Treitel, 'The Contracts (Rights of Third Parties) Act 1999 and the law of carriage of goods by sea', in Rose (ed), *Lex Mercatoria (Essays on International Commercial Law in Honour of Francis Reynolds)*, 2000, LLP.

Calculation of liability

Package/unit/weight [141]

The amount of liability under Art IV(5)(a) is calculated in terms of package, unit or weight of the cargo and the shipper can invoke that calculation which yields a higher amount. The words 'package' and 'unit' have not attracted analysis in the English courts and the words are used interchangeably.

In calculating liability for damage under Art IV(5)(a) it seems reference will be made only to the physical damage as at the date of discharge. [142]

Container

If a container is used, the method for calculating the amount of liability is set out in Art IV(5)(c) which states:

> Where a container, pallet or similar article of transport is used to consolidate goods, the number of packages enumerated in the bill of lading as packed in such article of transport shall be deemed the number of packages or units concerned. Except as aforesaid, such article shall be considered the package or unit.

It is not clear, however, from this Article as to who shoulders the responsibility of entering the number of units in the container – the shipper or the carrier. In practice, the shipper packs the container and enters the number of packages in the container on the bill of lading. Presumably, where the shipper is the party responsible for the entry of details on the bill of lading, they need not be taken as conclusive evidence in the event of calculating damages, since under Art III(3) the carrier can make his reservations known on the bill of lading with phrases like 'said to contain'. [143] Carver suggests that it would be wise for the carrier to take such precautionary measures where he has

---

141 The Hague Rules 1924 do not have a special provision in respect of containers. For the US approach to containerisation and per package limitation, see, eg, Alexander, 'Containerisation, the per package limitation and the concept of fair opportunity' (1986) 11 Maritime Lawyer 123; Luciano, 'Much ado about packages: containers and the COGSA limitation of liability provision' (1982) 48 Brooklyn LR 721.

142 See *Serena Navigation Ltd v Dera Commercial Establishment and Another (The Limnos)* [2008] EWHC 1036 (Comm) at paras 37–44.

143 In *Owners of Cargo Lately Aboard the River Gurara v Nigerian National Shipping Line Ltd* [1997] 1 Lloyd's Rep 225, the bill of lading governed by the Hague 1924 stated that the container was said to contain eight cases inside the container. The court held that liability was to be calculated in terms of the number of packages in the container. However where the contents of the container were expressed in a manner that did not make clear whether the goods were packed separately, the container would be treated as the package. It seems that use of words such as 'said to contain' may not be sufficient. However, see *Ace Imports Ltd v Companhia de Navegacao Lloyd Brasileiro (The Esmeralda)* NSW Sup Ct, 12 Aug 1987, where the bill of lading stated that the container was said to contain 437 boxes and along the margin the words 'particulars furnished by shipper of goods'. There was also a clause on the bill of lading above the master's signature which read:

> Shipped on board the above vessel . . . weight, measure, . . . quantity, condition, contents . . . if mentioned in this bill of lading were furnished by the shippers and were not or could not be ascertained or checked by the master unless the contrary has been expressly acknowledged and agreed to. The signing of this bill of lading is not considered as such an agreement . . .

The court held that any inference about the number of packages in the container was rebutted by the terms of the bill of lading.

not had the opportunity to check the number of packages in the container.[144] On the other hand, the carrier could always cover the risk he undertakes in issuing a bill of lading with no reservations by charging additional freight.

Doubts have been raised by legal commentators about the flexibility of Art IV(5)(c) to handle novel methods of cargo transportation. For instance, Scrutton states that the provision does not make room for roll-on roll-off trucks.[145] However, as Carver states, it is difficult to understand why this uncertainty about Art IV(5)(c) exists at all given that it acknowledges the possibility of items of transport similar to containers that are used to consolidate the goods.[146] Further, given the judicial expertise at sleight of hand there should be no difficulty in applying Art IV(5)(c) suitably to novel methods of transport in the future.

Where containers are used for consolidation it seems that items as packaged will have to be indicated to qualify as units for the purposes of Art IV(5)(c). A reference to 200,945 pieces of posters and prints without any indication of how they were packaged was regarded as one unit for purposes of limitation.[147]

Monetary unit for calculation

The unit of account for calculation purposes is the SDR (Special Drawing Right) as defined by the International Monetary Fund (Art IV(5)(d)). The United Kingdom replaced the Poincaré Franc as drafted in the 1968 convention with the SDR since it is a party to the Brussels Protocol of 1979. The SDR is based on a basket of currencies and is not tied to the price of gold.

The limitation amounts prescribed by the Hague-Visby Rules are 666.67 units of account per package or unit or 2 units of account per kilo of the gross weight of the goods lost or damaged, whichever is the higher (Art IV(5)(a)). These amounts are to be converted into national currency on the basis of the value of the currency on a date to be determined by the law of the court seized of the case.

If the shipper declares the value of the goods and it is inserted in the bill of lading, then the limitation of liability under the Hague-Visby Rules can be broken. However, insertion of the value as declared by the shipper on the bill of lading is only *prima facie* evidence and is not binding or conclusive evidence on the carrier (Art IV(5)(f)). In practice, cargo owners rarely declare the full value of the cargo. The reason is a purely financial one, since the amount payable for an increase in freight charges is likely to be far greater than that of obtaining insurance cover.

A question likely to arise in the context of Art IV(5)(a)[148] is whether the carrier can rely on the limitation amount in the event of his breach of the overriding Art III(1)

---

144   *Carver's Carriage by Sea*, at para 557.
145   *Scrutton on Charterparties*, at p 451.
146   *Carver's Carriage by Sea*, at para 557.
147   *El Greco (Australia) Pty Ltd v Mediterranean Shipping Co* [2004] 2 Lloyd's Rep 537.
148   It reads:

Unless the nature and value of such goods have been declared by the shipper before shipment and inserted in the bill of lading, neither the carrier nor the ship shall *in any event* be or become liable for any loss or damage to or in connection with the goods in an amount exceeding . . . [emphasis added].

obligation.[149] It appears from *The Happy Ranger*[150] that the inclusion of the phrase 'in any event' would allow the carrier to limit his liability. Referring to two decisions, one in the US[151] and the other in Canada,[152] Tuckey LJ said:

> ... if the loss resulted from unseaworthiness ... caused by want of due diligence on the part of the carrier ... the exceptions from immunity are of no avail to the carrier but the limitation to liability in r 5 where the words 'in any event' are used applies ... I think the words 'in any event' mean what they say. They are unlimited in scope and I can see no reason for giving them anything other than their natural meaning ... [at p 364].

The carrier and shipper may agree to fix a higher maximum of liability but cannot reduce the maximum that is set by the Hague-Visby Rules (Art IV(5)(g)). Any clause that attempts to reduce the level of liability to a level below that set by Art IV(5)(a) will be null and void (Art III(8)).

Under the Hague Rules, the amount recoverable is 100 pounds sterling per package (Art IV(5)) and the monetary units are taken to be as gold value.[153]

Loss of limitation

Carrier

The carrier and the ship lose the benefit of the limitation provisions where it is proved that the damage resulted from an act or omission of the carrier done with intent to cause damage or recklessly and with knowledge that damage would probably result (Art IV(5)(e)).

The Hague-Visby Rules do not provide any guidelines on establishing recklessness. The courts may look to other conventions where similar phrases have attracted analysis for guidance. For instance, in *Goldman v Thai Airways*,[154] the concept of recklessness in the context of Art 25 of the Warsaw Convention as amended at The Hague in 1955 and implemented in the United Kingdom by the Carriage by Air Act 1961 was examined. The court there held that the test of recklessness was a subjective one and not an objective one in that the state of the pilot's mind was of paramount importance. The court did not see it fit to attribute to the pilot knowledge that another pilot may have possessed or which he himself should have possessed.

Servant/agent of carrier

The servant or the agent of the carrier will lose the benefit of both the limitation provisions and the defences available to him under Art IV *bis* (4) where it is proved

---

149 See *Maxine Footwear Co Ltd v Canadian Government Merchant Marine Ltd* [1959] 2 Lloyd's Rep 105 for effect of breach of Art III(1) on Art IV(2) and *The Kapitan Saharov* [2002] 2 Lloyd's Rep 255 for effect on Art IV(6).
150 [2002] 2 Lloyd's Rep 357.
151 *The John Weyerhaeuser* [1975] 2 Lloyd's Rep 439.
152 *Falconbridge Nickel Mines Ltd v Chimo Shipping Ltd* [1969] 2 Lloyd's Rep 277.
153 See *The Rosa S* [1988] 2 Lloyd's Rep 574, clarifying that the words of Art IX were intended to have the effect of expressing the sterling figure as a gold value figure (at p 578). Of course, as Justice Hobhouse stated in this case, the purpose of the gold value is to escape from the principle of nominalism (at p 579). See also *Feist v Societe Intercommunale Belge de Electricite* [1934] AC 161.
154 [1983] 1 WLR 1186. See Chapter 10, pp 345–6 below.

that the damage resulted from the act or omission of the servant or agent done with intent to cause damage or recklessly and with knowledge that damage would probably result.

Time limitation

The carrier and the ship shall in any event be discharged from all liability in respect of the goods unless suit is brought within one year of their delivery or of the date on which they would have been delivered (Art III(6)). This period, however, may be extended if the parties so agree after the cause of action has arisen.[155] It is not clear from the Hague-Visby Rules whether delivery is seen as occurring during or at the end of the discharge or when the goods are received by the consignee.[156]

The courts have construed this provision restrictively in favour of the defendant. If the action is not to be time barred, suit must be brought within one year in the jurisdiction in which the dispute is finally decided. In *Compania Columbiana de Seguros v Pacific SN Co*,[157] the plaintiff initiated the action in the US even though the bill of lading had provided for exclusive English jurisdiction. By the time the mistake was discovered, the one-year time limit had lapsed and the action was held to be time barred in the English court.

The word 'suit'[158] has been construed as including arbitration proceedings provided the bill of lading has an arbitration clause or the parties have agreed to go to arbitration after the cause of action has arisen. In *The Merak*,[159] the arbitration clause of the charterparty had been incorporated into the bill of lading and the court held that the time bar applied to the arbitration clause thus imported.

In the event of arbitration, s 12 of the Arbitration Act 1996[160] provides beneficial relief by allowing the court to extend time for beginning arbitral proceedings. The issue in the context of the Rules is whether the courts can extend the time using this provision despite the one-year time bar imposed by Art III(6). The Arbitration Act 1950 in s 27 gave a similar discretion to the courts to extend the time for beginning arbitral proceedings. In *Nea Agrex SA v Baltic Shipping Co Ltd and Intershipping (The*

---

155   Note that the parties cannot agree to reduce the period. However, where the claim is in relation to matters that fall outside the scope of the Rules, the parties are free to determine the time limit. See *The Ion* [1971] 1 Lloyd's Rep 541 and *The Zhi Jiang Kou* [1991] 1 Lloyd's Rep 493 (NSW, Australia).

156   See *Trafigura Beheer v Gold Stavraetos Maritime Inc (The Sonia)* [2003] 2 Lloyd's Rep 211, where time ran from actual discharge. The facts of the case are peculiar and may have influenced the decision.

157   [1963] 2 Lloyd's Rep 527.

158   An issue likely to arise (given the popularity of mediation as an alternative form of dispute resolution) is whether mediation will come within the ambit of 'suit' for the purposes of Art III(6). Since it covers arbitration, there is no reason why it should not. But, it is possible to argue the contrary, since mediation does not share the features of arbitration, eg, formality, enforceability, etc (see Chapter 20).

159   [1964] 2 Lloyd's Rep 527. See also *Nea Agrex SA v Baltic Shipping Co Ltd and Intershipping (The Agios Lazaros)* [1976] 2 Lloyd's Rep 47; *The Ion* [1971] 1 Lloyd's Rep 541. The position with respect to the application of time bar on arbitration clauses is different in the US. See *Son Shipping Co Inc v de Fosse and Tanghe* (1952) 1999 Fed Rep (2nd) 687.

160   Note that the Arbitration Act 1996 while giving freedom to the parties to agree when arbitral proceedings are to be regarded as commenced in s 14 lists the circumstances in which the arbitration is to be regarded as commenced. See *Seabridge Shipping AB v AC Orsleff S Eftf's A/S* [1999] 2 Lloyd's Rep 685 and *The Smaro* [1999] 1 Lloyd's Rep 225.

Agios Lazaros),[161] where the charterparty attracted the application of the Hague Rules through a clause paramount, the court was of the opinion that the discretion under s 27 would apply. According to Goff LJ:

> ... in my judgment, it is wrong to say either that the discretion under s 27, though applicable, can never be exercised otherwise than adversely to the applicant, which is illogical anyway, or even that it can only be exercised in exceptional circumstances. Moreover, although the importance of the factor that one is dealing with the time bar imported by the Hague Rules may make it rare, it is not a matter of principle that it should only rarely be exercised. At the end of the day in my judgment, the court must consider, having regard to all the facts and circumstances, whether the applicant has made out a case of 'undue hardship' which is the criterion laid down by the statute and whether it would be fair to extend the time.

> I would, therefore, allow the appeal and hold that the respondents were subject to the time in Art III(6), but on the cross notice I would hold that the plaintiffs commenced arbitration in due time and the claims are not barred and, although on this finding it is academic, I would also hold that s 27 of the Arbitration Act 1950 applies and that the discretion under that section is exercisable in accordance with the principles I have enunciated, and in this case, if contrary to my view arbitration was not effectively commenced by the letter . . . I would extend the time [at p 56].

What is the position then with regard to a bill of lading which attracts the mandatory application of the Hague-Visby Rules? It seems from *Kenya Railways v Antares Co Pte Ltd (The Antares) (Nos 1 and 2)*[162] that the courts will have no discretion to extend the time limit. Article III(6) excludes the operation of s 27.[163]

Where there is a breach of contract as in unauthorised deck stowage, the time limit as specified in the Hague-Visby Rules still applies, since s 1(2) of the Carriage of Goods by Sea Act 1971 provides that the Rules 'shall have the force of law' and Art III(6) states that the carrier shall *in any event* be discharged of all liability. Where there is unjustified deviation, the time limitation clause would be available for the same reasons. Of course, where the Hague-Visby Rules have been incorporated voluntarily by the parties, the question would be a matter of construction.

The Hague-Visby Rules allow the parties to extend the time limit after the cause of action has arisen, but there is no reason why an agreement to extend the time limit before the action has arisen will not be permitted. Presumably, the conduct of the parties, though not amounting to an express agreement, would also be regarded as sufficient for waiver of the provision of time limit specified under the Hague-Visby Rules.

Article III(6) has far-reaching consequences. Not only has it the effect of barring the claim but it also extinguishes it. In *Aries Tanker Corp v Total Transport Ltd (The Aries),*[164] cargo had been short delivered and the cargo owners made a deduction in the freight to cover the short delivery. The carrier sued two years after delivery for the balance of the freight and the cargo owner claimed the defence of set-off. The House of Lords held that the defence was inadmissible since any right on which it might have been initially based had been extinguished by the time lapse.

---

161   [1976] 2 Lloyd's Rep 47.
162   [1987] 1 Lloyd's Rep 424. See also *The Ion* [1971] 1 Lloyd's Rep 541, where an agreement between the parties for a three-month time limit for arbitration (in a charterparty) incorporated into a bill of lading was held invalid to the extent it was in conflict with the Rules.
163   See Lloyd LJ at p 428.
164   [1977] 1 Lloyd's Rep 334.

Given the consequences of Art III(6), it is important that the correct claimant and the correct defendant are sued in the competent jurisdiction within the stipulated period since the correct claimant or defendant cannot be joined once the period has expired.[165]

An action for indemnity however may be brought outside the 12 month period according to Art III(6) bis,[166] provided the action for indemnity is initiated within the normal limitation period of the courts seized of the case. In England, ss 2 and 5 of the Limitation Act 1980 bar the initiation of a claim in contract or tort respectively after the expiration of six years.

SHIPPER'S DUTIES AND IMMUNITIES

Delivery for loading

The Hague-Visby Rules are silent regarding the shipper's obligation to bring the goods alongside the ship for loading. According to Art 1(e), the carrier's responsibilities for the goods start from the time when the goods are loaded, which suggests that the shipper has to bring the goods alongside the ship. However, according to the judgment in *Pyrene v Scindia Navigation Ltd*,[167] the parties are free to determine the role each is going to play in the contract of carriage. Where such arrangements are made, the extent of the rights and obligations between the parties will be considered under the general principles of contract law.

Shipper's guarantee

The shipper is deemed to have guaranteed to the carrier at the time of shipment the accuracy of the marks, number, quantity and weight provided by him. Where the carrier incurs loss, damage and expenses as a consequence of the inaccuracies of the particulars, the carrier has a right of indemnity against the shipper (Art III(5)).[168]

There is, however, a problem with this provision. It does not specify whether the carrier has the right of indemnity as against the consignee or indorsee. Carver suggests that Art III(5) is carefully worded so as to make only the shipper liable since the guarantee is expressed as a recital of a collateral agreement that the shipper qua shipper has with the carrier. Therefore, the consignee or indorsee is not liable for the inaccuracies that are present.[169] Moreover, from a practical point of view, it may be possible to argue that the shipper after all is the person who has packed the goods and is therefore in a better position to guarantee the veracity of the statements made.

---

165 See *The Jay Bola* [1992] 1 Lloyd's Rep 62; *The Havhelt* [1993] 1 Lloyd's Rep 523. On amendment of cause of action, see *The Pionier* [1995] 1 Lloyd's Rep 223. See also *Fort Sterling Ltd and Another v South Atlantic Cargo Shipping NV and Others (The Finnrose)* [1994] 1 Lloyd's Rep 559.

166 There is no equivalent in the Hague Rules. See *Lauritzen Reefers v Ocean Reef Transport Ltd SA (The Bukhta Russkaya)* [1997] 1 Lloyd's Rep 744.

167 [1954] 2 QB 402.

168 See Jarvis, 'Expanding the carrier's right to claim indemnity under s 3(5) of COGSA for inaccurate bills of lading' (1986) 24 Duquesne Law Review 811.

169 *Carver's Carriage by Sea*, at para 521.

Where the carrier is aware that the statements made by the shipper are false, presumably, he will lose his right of indemnity.

Dangerous goods

Article IV(6) provides that, where goods of an inflammable, explosive, or dangerous nature are shipped without the consent of the carrier, the master or the agent of the carrier, then the carrier is at liberty any time before discharge to land them at any place or destroy or render the goods innocuous. In the event of such action on the part of the carrier, he is not liable to pay any compensation to the shipper. The shipper will be liable for all damages arising directly or indirectly as a result of such a shipment.

Where goods are shipped with the carrier's consent and knowledge, and the goods become a danger to other cargo or the ship, then the carrier is at liberty to land them at any place, destroy or render them innocuous. In the event of such an act, the carrier will be liable only in general average.

The Hague-Visby Rules do not make it clear whether the word 'dangerous' is restricted to goods that are physically dangerous. It is possible to argue that it is restricted to physically dangerous, applying the *ejusdem generis* rule of statutory interpretation.[170] A recent decision indicates that the word is not restricted to events that are 'physically dangerous'. In *Effort Shipping Co Ltd v Linden Management SA and Another*,[171] a cargo of processed nuts infested with a beetle of voracious appetite (Khapra beetle) was held to be dangerous for the purposes of Art IV(6). The shipper was held liable to the carrier for damages arising out of the need to destroy the cargo and fumigate the ship.

Further, Art IV(6) does not make it clear whether the consignee or the endorsee is liable to the carrier. It could be that it affects only the shipper, since he is the person in the best position to know the nature of the cargo shipped.

No fault

The shipper will not be held responsible for the loss or damage that is sustained by the carrier or the ship arising or resulting from any cause without the act, fault or neglect of the shipper, his agents or his servants (Art IV(3)).

Carver submits that this provision is not intended to relieve the shipper from liability for the guarantee he provides that the goods shipped are not dangerous under Art IV(6).[172] This suggestion is based on the belief that the guarantee is an absolute guarantee and the shipper is liable whether he knew the goods were dangerous or not. This view however seems to place the shipper under an unfair burden. Besides, there is no suggestion in Art IV(6) that the guarantee provided by the shipper applies in all eventualities. The better view therefore is that Art IV(3) will relieve the shipper of liability where goods the shipper reasonably believes to be safe subsequently become dangerous and cause damage.

A recent case, however, has put the above uncertainty to rest. The House of Lords

---

170   See *Carver's Carriage by Sea*, para 566.
171   [1998] 2 WLR 206.
172   *Carver's Carriage by Sea*, at paras 544 and 545.

in *Effort Shipping Co Ltd v Linden Management SA*[173] examined whether Art IV(3) qualified the liability imposed on the shipper by Art IV(6). Failing to find an answer in the *travaux préparatoires* of the Hague Rules, the House of Lords turned to the historical setting of the Hague Rules to find a solution. Since the approach taken in *Brass v Maitland*[174] was the prevalent view at the time the Hague Rules were drafted, Lord Steyn surmised that, if drafters had wished to adopt a position that ran counter to the widely accepted view of the time, they would have catered for this in Art IV(6). In the absence of any indication that the shipper's actual or constructive knowledge was relevant in Art IV(6), the provision was seen as free-standing, imposing strict liability on the shippers in relation to the shipment of dangerous goods, irrespective of fault or neglect on their part. According to Lord Steyn:

> ... the overall position is that the language of Art IV(6), read with Art IV(3), tends to suggest that Art IV(6) was intended to be a free-standing provision ... As against that there is the fact that the United States courts have interpreted Art IV(3) as qualifying Art IV(6). Given the desirability of uniform interpretation of the Hague Rules, the choice between the competing interests is finely balanced. But there is a contextual consideration which must also be weighed in the balance. It is permissible to take into account the legal position in the United Kingdom and in the United States regarding the shipment of dangerous cargo before the Hague Rules were approved. It is relevant as part of the contextual scene of the Hague Rules: *Riverstone Meat Co Pty Ltd v Lancashire Shipping Co Ltd*.[175] In *Brass v Maitland*, the majority held that under a contract of carriage there is a term implied by law that a shipper will not ship dangerous goods without notice to the carrier; the obligation is absolute. The same view prevailed in the Court of Appeal in *Bamfield v Goole and Sheffield Transport Co Ltd*[176] and in *Great Northern Rly Co v LEP Transport and Depository Ltd*.[177] This view was controversial. It was disputed in a string of minority judgments in *Brass v Maitland and in Bamfield v Goole and Sheffield Transport Co Ltd*; see, also, *Mitchell, Cotts and Co v Steel Bros and Co Ltd* (1916);[178] and Abbott's *Merchant Ships and Seamen*, 13th edn, 1892, p 522. Nevertheless, the law of England was as held by the majority in *Brass v Maitland*. That view probably would have been regarded as authoritative in most countries in what was then the British Empire. In 1861, a court in the United States (the Massachusetts District Court) adopted the majority holding in *Brass v Maitland* as a sound rule on the policy grounds, *viz*, that 'It throws the loss upon the party who generally has the best means of informing himself as to the character of article shipped' (*Pierce v Winsor*;[179] see also Parsons, *A Treatise on the Law of Shipping and the Law and Practice of Admiralty*, Vol 1, 1869, pp 265–66). That remained the legal position in the United States until the conferences that led to the adoption of the Hague Rules. The United States was then already a great maritime power. Its shipping law was a matter of great importance. The British Empire was in decline but, collectively, the trading countries under its umbrella controlled a considerable proportion of the ocean-going world trade. That means that, at the time of the drafting of the Hague Rules, the dominant theory in a very large part of the world was that shippers were under an absolute obligation not to ship dangerous goods. The circumstance must have been known to those who drafted and approved the Hague Rules. No doubt they also knew there was an alternative theory, namely, that the ship-

---

173   [1998] 2 WLR 206.
174   (1856) 26 LJ QB 49.
175   [1961] AC 807, at p 836, *per* Viscount Simonds.
176   [1910] 2 KB 94.
177   [1922] 2 KB 742.
178   [1916] 1 KB 610, at pp 613–14, *per* Atkin J.
179   (1861) 2 Sprague 35, at p 36.

per of dangerous goods ought only to be liable for want of due diligence in the shipment of dangerous goods. If this contextual scene is correctly described ... one is
entitled to pose the practical question: What would the framers of the Hague Rules have
done collectively had they been minded to adopt the step of reversing the dominant
theory of shippers; liability for the shipment of dangerous goods? There is really one
realistic answer: they would have expressly provided that shippers are only liable in
damages for the shipment of dangerous goods if they knew or ought to have known of
the dangerousness of the goods. In that event, the three parts of Art IV(6) would have
had to be recast to make clear that the shippers' actual or constructive knowledge was
irrelevant to the carriers' right to land dangerous cargo, but a condition precedent to the
liability of the shippers for damages in the second part. Moreover, if this idea had been
put forward for discussion, the *travaux préparatoires* would no doubt have reflected the
observations of carriers on such a fundamental change to their rights. The idea was
never put forward. The inference must be that the framers of the Hague Rules proceeded on what was at that time an unsurprising assumption that shippers would be
absolutely liable for the shipment of dangerous cargo.

In all these circumstances, I am constrained to conclude that, despite the decisions of the
United States courts, the best interpretation of the language of Art IV(6) read with
Art IV(3) seen against its contextual background, is that it created free-standing rights
and obligations in respect of the shipment of dangerous cargo [at pp 221–23].

Interestingly, Lord Cooke, while agreeing that the scope of the obligation created by
Art IV(6) is an absolute one, was unhappy with its description as a free-standing
obligation. He preferred to read Art IV(6) as an integral part of the Hague Rules and
apply the maxim *generalia specialibus non derogant* which would lead to the conclusion
that on a fair reading of the Rules in its entirety, Art IV(6) is to take priority over
Art IV(3) (at p 224).

Though this case was decided with regard to the Hague Rules, it applies equally
to Art IV(6) in the Hague-Visby Rules, which is identical to Art IV(6) of the Hague
Rules.

General average

The Hague-Visby Rules are silent regarding general average. Article V, however,
states that the Rules shall not prevent the insertion in a bill of lading of any lawful
provision regarding general average. So, the bill of lading can be made subject to both
the Hague-Visby Rules and the York-Antwerp Rules.

Status of terms not included in the Rules

The Hague-Visby Rules are not a complete code regulating all matters relating to the
contract of carriage by sea. They do not regulate, for instance, terms relating to freight,
liens and demurrage that are commonly found in bills of lading. Hence, common law
presumptions, English law of contract, and statutory rights and liabilities as specified
in the Bills of Lading Act 1855 (for bills of lading issued before 16 September 1992)
and Carriage of Goods by Sea Act 1992 (for bills of lading issued after 16 September
1992)[180] are equally relevant to a bill of lading governed by the Hague-Visby Rules.

---

180 See Chapter 6.

It is also normal for bills of lading to include arbitration clauses, choice of forum and choice of law clauses. Where arbitration clauses are included, it is well established that arbitration proceedings must be initiated within the one year time limit imposed by Art III(6) unless the parties agree otherwise.[181] Concerning choice of law and choice of jurisdiction clauses, the courts will recognise the parties' intentions unless the object of these clauses is to lessen the liability imposed by the Hague-Visby Rules or to avoid the operation of the Hague-Visby Rules altogether.[182]

SCOPE OF APPLICATION

Applicability of the Hague-Visby Rules to a contract of carriage is determined by a number of factors such as:

(a) the type of document covering the contract of carriage;

(b) the kind of carriage; and

(c) the kind of cargo.

Taking (a), the type of document covering the contract of carriage, the Hague-Visby Rules come into operation where the contract of carriage by sea is covered by a bill of lading or similar document of title (Art I(b)). The bill of lading or other similar document of title need not exist at the time of damage for the Hague-Visby Rules to apply. In *Pyrene Co Ltd v Scindia Navigation*,[183] one of the fire tenders was damaged while it was lifted aboard by the ship's tackle. At the time of the damage, there was no bill of lading though one was issued eventually. The damage to the fire tender was not noted on the document and the carrier, when sued, relied on the limitation of liability available under the Hague Rules. The plaintiff argued that since the damage to the tender occurred at a time when it was not 'covered by a bill of lading', the limits did not apply. The court held that, even though the bill of lading in fact was not in existence at the time of the damage, the parties had contemplated issuing a bill of lading in due course. In these circumstances, 'the contract is from its very creation "covered" by a bill of lading, and is, therefore, from its very inception a contract of carriage with the meaning of the Rules and to which the Rules apply' (at p 419).

Article I(b) states that the Hague-Visby Rules are applicable to documents of title that are similar to a bill of lading. At present, in British shipping practice, a document of title similar to a bill of lading is not issued. It is, however, possible that the custom of a trade may play a role in determining whether a particular document is a document of title. The creation of a document of title through mercantile custom is not unknown in English law. In *Lickbarrow v Mason*,[184] custom was admitted as establishing bills of lading as a document of title. And in the more recent case of *Kum v Wah Tat Bank Ltd*,[185] the court has acknowledged that in principle a document of title could be

---

181 See 'Time limitation', pp 262–4 above.

182 See 'Contracting out', pp 280–3 below.

183 [1954] 2 QB 402. See also *Harland and Wolff Ltd v Burns and Laird Lines Ltd* (1931) 40 LIL Rep 286. See Chapter 11, for the position relating to consignment notes in relation to international carriage by rail and the CIM Rules (Uniform Rules Concerning the Contract for the International Carriage of Goods by Rail).

184 (1794) 5 Term Rep 683.

185 [1971] 1 Lloyd's Rep 439.

created by custom of trade. To qualify, however, the custom must be sufficiently widely known such that enquiries by an outsider would reveal it. As Lord Devlin stated in *Kum v Wah Tat Bank Ltd*:

> In speaking of a custom of merchants, the law has not in mind merchants in the narrow sense of buyers and sellers of goods. A mercantile custom affects transactions either in a particular trade or in a particular place, such as a market or a port, and binds all those who participate in such transactions, whatever the nature of their callings. It is true that a document relating to goods carried by sea and said to be negotiated through banks could hardly be recognised as a document of title if the evidence did not show it to be treated as such by shipowners, shippers and bankers. But the limits of the custom, if it be established, are not to be defined by reference to categories of traders or professional men; if established, it binds everyone who does business in whatever capacity. To describe a custom as belonging to particular callings diverts attention from its true character which consists in its attachment to a trade or place.
>
> Universality, as a requirement of custom, raises not a question of law but a question of fact. There must be proof in the first place that the custom is generally accepted by those who habitually do business in the trade or market concerned. Moreover, the custom must be so generally known that an outsider who makes reasonable enquiries could not fail to be made aware of it. The size of the market or the extent of the trade affected is neither here nor there. It does not matter that the custom alleged in this case applies only to part of the shipping trade within the state of Singapore, so long as the part can be ascertained with certainty, as it can here, as the carriage of goods by sea between Sarawak and Singapore. A good and established custom . . . obtains the force of a law, and is, in effect, the common law within that place to which it extends . . . [at p 444].

Until recently it was thought that the Hague-Visby Rules did not apply to non-transferable shipping documents such as straight bills of lading[186] (since they lacked the quality of transferability). Straight bills of lading were seen as having the same status as mate's receipts, and delivery orders.[187] In *Macmillan Co Inc v Mediterranean Shipping Co Sa (The Rafaela S)*,[188] the cargo was shipped on a straight bill of lading. The carriage was from Durban to Felixstowe with the final destination specified as Boston. Upon discharge at Felixstowe the cargo was reshipped to Boston. The cargo was damaged on its way to Boston. Both carriages were on ships owned by the same carrier. No bill of lading was issued in respect of the voyage to Boston. The Court of Appeal concluded that there were two voyages and a straight bill of lading would have been issued had there been a demand for a fresh bill of lading. Since Felixstowe was the port of shipment the question was whether the straight bill of lading was

---

186 See *Henderson v The Comptoir D'Escompte* (1873) LR 5 PC 253 – a bill naming a consignee lacking the words 'or order or assigns' is not transferable. As Tuckey LJ acknowledged in *The Happy Ranger* [2002] 2 Lloyd's Rep 357, 'a "straight" bill has no English law definition, but the term derives, it appears, from earlier US legislation referring to "straight" bill as one in which the goods are consigned to a specific person as opposed to an "order" bill where the goods are consigned to the order of any one named in the bill or bearer' (at p 363). Note, however, that the Carriage of Goods by Sea Act uses the phrase "sea waybills" and is defined s 1(3). See also *The Chitral* [2000] 1 Lloyd's Rep 529; *The Rafaela S* [2004] QB 702.

187 See *Comalco Aluminium Ltd v Mogul Freight Services Pty Ltd (The Oceania Trader)* (1993) 21 ABLR 377; (1993) ALR 677, where the Australian court held that the consignment note issued by a freight forwarder attracted the application of the Hague Rules since it possessed the essential elements of a bill of lading. See also *Carrington Slipways Pty Ltd v Patrick Operations Pty Ltd (The Cape Comorin)* (1991) 24 NSWLR 745; Hetherington [1992] LMCLQ 32. Tetley (*Marine Cargo Claims*, 2008, Blais) is of the opinion that the scope of applicability of the Hague-Visby Rules to shipping documents is to be determined by Art VI since the overriding authority to Art VI is given by Art II.

188 [2004] QB 702.

subject to the Hague-Visby Rules. The straight bill of lading, even though it was drafted on a classic bill of lading form, was held to be a document of title for the purposes of Art I(b). A number of reasons were provided by Rix LJ in reaching this conclusion. Firstly, the focus of the Hague Rules was with the content of the contract of carriage and protection of the parties to the contract including third parties, not with transferability. A straight bill of lading, while not showing the succession of transfers associated with a classic bill of lading, is still capable of one transfer to the named consignee (a third party). So a named consignee under a straight bill of lading is within the purview of the Hague-Visby Rules.

Secondly, in practice, the straight bill of lading is used like a classic bill as a document against which payment is required thus marking the transfer of property. Thirdly, in practice, a straight bill of lading is required for the purpose of taking delivery of the cargo. In *The Rafaela S* there was an attestation clause requiring surrender of a bill of lading against delivery of the cargo.

Does this mean that in the absence of an attestation clause the straight bill of lading will not be treated as a document of title? If so, then it is likely to create confusion, bringing with it uncertainty. Rix LJ makes reference to this issue and is of the opinion that it should not be treated differently since it would be 'undesirable to have a different rule for different kinds of bills of lading'.[189]

For shipping documents other than a bill of lading (straight or classic) to attract the application of the Hague-Visby Rules, the documents must expressly state that the Hague-Visby Rules are to govern as if the receipt were a bill of lading.[190] However, where the Hague-Visby Rules are incorporated, it is possible to include them partially. In *The European Enterprise*,[191] para 3 of the consignment note provided *inter alia* that the goods were carried subject to the Hague-Visby Rules set out in the schedule to the Carriage of Goods by Sea Act 1971, except that the goods and the respective contents were to be regarded as one package or unit for the purposes of Art IV(5)(a) and that the carrier was entitled to limit his liability to 10,000 francs per package. The plaintiff argued that the clause reducing liability to an amount lower than that set by the Hague-Visby Rules was invalid since the Carriage of Goods by Sea Act 1971 had the force of law by virtue of s 1(6)(b). Construing the section literally, the court held that it imparted force of law to a voluntary incorporation of the Hague-Visby Rules into a contract only if the conditions laid down in that section were followed – that is, the consignment note must have expressly provided that 'the Rules are to govern as if the receipt were a bill of lading'. These words however were not included in the consignment note. Further, the defendant had incorporated the Hague-Visby Rules partially. In these circumstances, Steyn J felt that:

> ... it would be curious if a voluntary paramount clause, which reflected only a partial incorporation of the Hague-Visby Rules, had a result that a statutory binding character was given to all the Hague-Visby Rules, even where there was no primary contractual bond ... in enacting s 1(6)(b), the legislation did not intend to override the agreement of

---

189   At p 752. See *Carewins Development China Ltd v Bright Fortune Shipping Ltd* [2007] 3 HKLRD 396 (available also on http://legalref.judiciary.gov.hk) where the Hong Kong Court of Appeal considered *The Rafaela* in detail and concluded that the straight bill of lading has to be produced for the named consignee to obtain delivery.

190   Section 1(6)(b) of the Carriage of Goods by Sea Act 1971.

191   [1989] 2 Lloyd's Rep 185. See also Debattista, 'Sea waybills and the Carriage of Goods by Sea Act 1971' [1989] LMCLQ 403.

the parties when the parties had the freedom of choice whether or not to incorporate the rules into their contract.[192]

The Hague-Visby Rules do not apply to charterparties (Arts I(b) and V). However, it is fairly common for charterparties to voluntarily incorporate the Rules with a clause paramount.[193] Such paramount clauses, the purpose of which are to give the Rules contractual force, will be effective in incorporating the Rules even though the Rules were drafted with bills of lading in mind, as *Anglo-Saxon Petroleum Co v Adamasatos Shipping Co*[194] indicates. Incorporation of the Rules with a clause paramount makes the Rules prevail over any of the exceptions in the charterparty.[195]

Parties do not always indicate whether they wish the Hague Rules or the Hague-Visby Rules to apply in their paramount clause. This has been the subject of some judicial discussion in a number of cases. The matter is to be resolved, it seems, from what the term 'general paramount clause' means to shipping men. In *Nea Agrex SA v Baltic Shipping Co Ltd and Intershipping Charter Co (The Agios Lazaros)*,[196] the charter-party in cl 31 provided:

> . . . and also paramount clause are deemed to be incorporated to this charterparty.

The Court of Appeal, contrary to the position taken by the lower court,[197] reached the view that the paramount clause incorporated the Hague Rules. As Lord Denning said:

> What does 'paramount clause' or 'clause paramount' mean to shipping men? Primarily, it applies to bills of lading. In that context, its meaning is, I think, clear beyond question. It means a clause by which the Hague Rules are incorporated . . . we have to see what its meaning is in this charterparty . . . It brings the Hague Rules into the charterparty so as to render the voyage, or voyages, subject to the Hague Rules so far as applicable to . . . [at p 50].[198]

The above test was applied fairly recently in *Lauritzen Reefers v Ocean Reef Transport Ltd SA (The Bukhta Russkaya)*.[199] The relevant clause read:

> . . . in trades involving neither US nor Canadian ports, the general paramount clause to apply in lieu of the USA clause paramount.

The court on the basis of the construction of the contract concluded that the intention was to incorporate the Hague Rules in the contract.

Where a bill of lading clause states 'For all trades this B/L shall be subject to the 1924 Hague Rules . . . or, if compulsorily applicable, subject to the 1968 Protocol

---

192 [1989] 2 Lloyd's Rep 185, at p 191.

193 *Anglo-Saxon Petroleum Co v Adamastos Shipping Co* [1957] 1 Lloyd's Rep 271.

194 [1959] AC 133.

195 Note also that the courts may have to consider priority on the basis of whether a clause is printed, typed or handwritten. The order of priority is as follows: handwritten clauses prevail over typed and typed over printed. This is justified on the basis that the parties have given more consideration to the written or typed terms. See *Metalfer Corp v Pan Ocean Shipping Co Ltd* [1998] 2 Lloyd's Rep 632; *Seven Sea Transportation Ltd v Pacifico Union Marina Corp (The Satya Kailash and Oceanic Amity)* [1984] 1 Lloyd's Rep 558; *Bayoil SA v Seawind Tankers Corp (The Leonidas)* [2001] 1 Lloyd's Rep 533.

196 [1976] 2 Lloyd's Rep 47.

197 Donaldson J held that it was unclear what paramount clause was to be incorporated and must be struck out as meaningless as in *Nicolene v Simmonds* [1953] 1 Lloyd's Rep 189. See, however, *Hillas and Co Ltd v Arcos* (1932) 147 LT 503.

198 See also *Seabridge Shipping AB v AC Orsleff S Eftf's A/S* [1999] 2 Lloyd's Rep 685.

199 [1997] 2 Lloyd's Rep 744.

(Hague-Visby) or any compulsory legislation based on the Hague Rules and/or said Protocols' the phrase 'compulsorily applicable' will be construed as compulsorily applicable according to a particular system of law. In *Trafigura Beheer BV and Another v Mediterranean Shipping Co SA*[200] the carriage was for goods from Durban (South Africa) to Shanghai and contained the above paramount clause. It also contained an English law and jurisdiction clause. The judge at the lower court held that Hague-Visby Rules applied as a matter of contract. He construed the phrase 'compulsorily applicable' as including compulsory application at the port of shipment. On appeal, the Court came to a different conclusion. As a matter of contract the owners agreed to accept the Hague Rules unless they were made to accept the Hague-Visby Rules by the proper law of the contract. Since South Africa was not a contracting state, the Hague-Visby Rules were not compulsorily applicable. In the words of Longmore LJ:

> I, therefore, agree . . . that the scheme of the bill of lading in the present case is that the owners, as a matter of contract, accept Hague Rules 1924 obligations but only accept HVR obligations if they are forced to do so. They can only be forced to do so if the proper law of the contract compels it (or if the place where the cargo owners choose to sue them compels it). Neither law compels it on the facts of the present case and they are not contractually obliged further than the law compels [at para 16].

An issue that is likely to arise in the context of a clause paramount is whether the claims under the charterparty are subject to Art III(6) which provides that the carrier and the ship shall in any event be discharged from all liability in respect of the goods unless suit is brought within one year of their delivery or of the date on which they would have been delivered. In *Noranda Inc and Others v Barton Ltd and Another (Time Charter) (The Marinor)*,[201] the plaintiffs made a number of claims in respect of voyage 32: an amount by which the market price would have exceeded the actual price had the goods been sold uncontaminated; an amount in respect of the additional length of the voyage; and an amount in respect of additional port expenses. They also claimed for substitute tonnage which *The Marinor* could not carry due to its defective condition. The court had no hesitation in holding that Art III(6) applied to the amounts claimed in respect of voyage 32, since the liability in respect of the goods and the claims were sufficiently connected with the goods shipped. As for the substitute tonnage claim, Art III(6) did not apply since it was not in respect of the cargo but a claim in respect of loss of use of the vehicle. As Colman J said:

> . . . liability 'in respect of goods' (the words of Art III(6) is not to be construed in the context of a periodic time charter as meaning a liability arising from facts which would found a claim by a cargo owner under the Hague or Hague-Visby Rules in the context of a bill of lading contract but rather as meaning a liability based on facts involving a particular cargo or intended cargo and, in the absence of physical loss or damage, sufficiently closely involving that cargo for it to be said that the financial loss was referable to what was done with that cargo or was directly associated with it [at p 310].

It is also common practice to issue bills of lading under charterparties. Where bills of lading are so issued, they must comply with the terms of the Hague-Visby Rules.

---

200 [2007] EWCA Civ 794.
201 [1996] 1 Lloyd's Rep 301. In *Cargill International SA v CPN Tankers Ltd (The OT Sonja)* [1993] 2 Lloyd's Rep 435, where the time bar under Art III(6) operated in a claim for consequential financial loss and expense due to the state of the holds which had to be cleaned before loading of cargo could take place. See also *Interbulk Ltd v Ponte Deo Sospiri Shipping Co (The Standard Ardour)* [1988] 2 Lloyd's Rep 159.

Where goods are carried under a charterparty and bills of lading are issued to the charterer, as between the charterer and the shipowner, the terms of carriage are governed by the charterparty since the bill of lading in the hands of the charterer is a mere receipt. However, where a bill of lading is issued to a shipper other than the charterer, the bill of lading will be governed by the Hague-Visby Rules.

An interesting question that arises where a bill of lading is issued under a charterparty to a shipper is the status of the bill of lading in the hands of the charterer if it is subsequently endorsed to the charterer by the shipper. In *The President of India v Metcalfe Shipping*,[202] a bill of lading issued under a charterparty to a shipper was endorsed by the shipper to the charterer. The court held that the arbitration clause contained in the charterparty applied to the charterer despite the fact that the bill of lading endorsed to the charterer did not have an arbitration clause. It seems that the rights of the charterer against the carrier are always determined by the charterparty unless the terms of the charterparty include a supercession clause – a clause in the charterparty that states, as between the parties, the terms of the charterparty are to be superseded by the terms of the bill of lading given under it.

Incorporation of charterparty terms in bills of lading

Bills of lading issued under charterparties generally make reference to charterparty terms. Clauses importing terms of the charterparty into the bill of lading are viewed with tolerance by the courts, provided these are brought to the notice of the shipper and charterparty clauses are adequately incorporated into the bill of lading. Judicial interpretation of incorporation clauses, however, is very strict and a number of conditions need to be met for charterparty terms to be successfully included in a bill of lading as seen in *The Varenna*.[203] In this case, the bill of lading issued under a charterparty for the carriage of crude oil contained the following clause:

> cargo ... to be delivered ... to Petrofina SA upon payment of freight as per charterparty, all conditions and exceptions of which charterparty including the negligence clause are deemed to be incorporated in the bill of lading.

The charterparty provided *inter alia*:

> ... any dispute arising under this charter shall be settled in London by arbitration.

It was argued the arbitration clause in the charterparty had been successfully incorporated into the bill of lading with the phrase 'all conditions and exceptions'.[204] The court, however, came to the conclusion that it was not incorporated. For successful inclusion:

- Effective words of incorporation must be found in the bill of lading itself. Words that require reference to the charterparty to realise the intentions of the parties to the contract – namely, the charterer and the shipowner – will be inadequate. A general reference in the bill of lading to charterparty terms will be insufficient to allow the

---

202 [1970] 1 QB 289.
203 [1983] 2 Lloyd's Rep 592; see Park, 'Incorporation of charterparty terms into bill of lading contracts – a case rationalisation' (1986) 16 Victoria University of Wellington Law Review 77.
204 See McMahon, 'The Hague Rules and incorporation of charterparty arbitration clauses into bills of lading' [1970] JMLC 1, for a comparative account of the US and English interpretations.

court to discover from the charterparty as to what clauses were intended to be included in the charterparty.

... an incorporation cannot be achieved by agreement between the owners and the charterers. It can only be achieved by the agreement of the parties to the bill of lading contract and thus the operative words of incorporation must be found in the bill of lading [at p 594].

- Words of incorporation must be sufficiently descriptive to indicate the precise charterparty clause sought to be included in the bill of lading. Use of phrases like 'all conditions and exceptions in the charterparty' would be read literally and will be insufficient to incorporate the arbitration clause. In *The Varenna*, the phrase was construed as referring to only those conditions and exceptions that are appropriate to the carriage of and delivery of goods and not extensive enough to cover the arbitration clause.[205]

Use of wide clauses may be effective in including all the terms of a charterparty into a bill of lading. In *The Miramar*,[206] the phrase 'all terms of the charterparty' was regarded as sufficiently descriptive to incorporate all the terms (including the demurrage clause) of the charterparty. Once the charterparty terms are incorporated into a bill of lading, the courts read the contents of the clauses literally and are unwilling to engage in any verbal manipulation. Where the clauses of a charterparty are included *verbatim* into the bill of lading and the clause states that the charterer is liable as in *The Miramar*, the courts will not substitute the word 'charterer' with the words 'the bill of lading holder'.

Where terms of the charterparty have been incorporated in the bill of lading, they must not conflict with the terms of the bill of lading. In the event of any inconsistency, the terms of the bill of lading will preside. And where the charterparty terms lessen the liability of the carrier below that set by the Hague-Visby Rules, the courts will regard these clauses as null and void under Art III(8).[207]

The strict approach taken by the courts to clauses incorporating charterparty terms into the bill of lading is justifiable both on pragmatic and equitable grounds. If incorporation clauses are interpreted liberally, uncertainties in respect of the extent of liabilities undertaken would affect the attractiveness of the document as security, and will also impede the ease of transferability: two of the major functions of a bill of lading. Further, it would be unjust to hold the consignee/indorsee liable on terms that he has no way of knowing since he is not privy to the charterparty.

Kinds of carriage

The Hague-Visby Rules apply to every bill of lading where the carriage is between ports in two different states in the following circumstances:

205　The courts are continuing to adopt a strict approach to clauses incorporating charterparty terms into a bill of lading as indicated by the recent case *Siboti v BP France* [2003] 2 Lloyd's Rep 364. See also *The Epsilon Rosa* [2003] 2 Lloyd's Rep 509.

206　*Miramar Maritime Corp v Holburn Oil Trading Ltd* [1984] 2 Lloyd's Rep 129. See also *The Nai Matteini* [1988] 1 Lloyd's Rep 452; *Daval Aciers D'Usinor Et De Sacilor and Others (The Nerano)* [1994] 2 Lloyd's Rep 50.

207　See 'Contracting out', pp 280–3 below.

- where a bill of lading is issued in a contracting state;[208]
- where carriage is from a port in a contracting state;
- where the contract contained in or evidenced by the bill of lading specifies that the Hague-Visby Rules or the legislation of a state giving effect to them are to govern the contract.

Where a consignment is sent from a port in a non-contracting state to a contracting state, or a bill of lading is issued in a non-contracting state, the contract of carriage will not be subject to the Hague-Visby Rules, unless they are incorporated through a choice of law clause.

The ambit of the Hague-Visby Rules is extended by the implementing statute to apply to coastal trade.[209] Where goods, for instance, are sent from Southampton to Hull by sea, and the voyage is covered by a bill of lading, the Hague-Visby Rules will be applicable.

Kinds of cargo

The Hague-Visby Rules are applicable to all goods, wares, merchandise and articles of every kind except live animals and cargo which by the contract of carriage is stated as being carried on deck and is so carried (Art I(c)).

Live animals are excluded due to their peculiar characteristics – easy susceptibility to diseases, accidents and mortality, and stringent quarantine and health requirements. Since the Hague-Visby Rules do not apply to live animals, the carrier is at liberty to negotiate the terms of carriage. If he includes clauses exempting liability for damage or loss to the goods, he is not expected to make these clauses subject to the terms of reasonableness, as stipulated by s 2 of the Unfair Contract Terms Act 1977, unless the person he is contracting with is a consumer.[210]

If the parties so wish, the carriage of live animals can be made subject to the Hague-Visby Rules through express stipulation. This must be in the form stipulated by s 1(6)(a) and (b) of the Carriage of Goods by Sea Act 1971 if the rules are to have the force of law following the decision in *The European Enterprise*.[211] Where such a stipulation is made then, in the event of a clash between the terms of the Hague-Visby Rules

---

208 The emerging commercial practice of issuing switch bills (issuing a second set of original bills of lading where different information regarding supplier, origin, etc, is inserted) may cause problems in respect of the applicability. For instance, in *Noble Resources Ltd v Cavalier Shipping Corp (The Atlas)* [1996] 1 Lloyd's Rep 642, the original Russian bills of lading were switched with bills issued in Hong Kong. According to Longmore J, the original bills were governed by the Hague Rules and the switched bills governed by the Hague-Visby Rules. The practice of issuing switch bills poses legal problems and introduces a great deal of uncertainty regardless of whatever good commercial reasons (eg, not divulging the supplier's name) there might be. As Longmore J correctly observed: 'No doubt this provision for a second set of bills of lading to come into existence was agreed for not unreasonable commercial motives but it is a practice fraught with danger; not only does it give rise to obvious opportunities for fraud (which is not suggested in this case) but also, if it is intended that the bills of lading should constitute contracts of carriage with the actual owner of the ship (as opposed to the disponent owner), the greatest care has to be taken to ensure that the practice has the shipowner's authority' [at p 644].
209 Section 1(3) of the Carriage of Goods by Sea Act 1971.
210 Paragraph 2 of Sched 1 to the Unfair Contract Terms Act 1977 specifically states that ss 2–4 (excepting s 2(1)) do not extend to any contract for the carriage of goods by ship except in favour of a person dealing as a consumer.
211 [1989] 2 Lloyd's Rep 185.

and the express terms of the contract, the provisions of the contract will be overridden by those of the Hague-Visby Rules.

Deck cargo will fall outside the operation of the Hague-Visby Rules[212] provided the two requirements set out by Art I(c) are met:

- the cargo *must in fact* be stowed on deck; and
- the stowage of the cargo on deck *must be made explicit on the face of the bill of lading*.

In practice, bills of lading generally contain clauses whereby the carrier reserves the right to stow goods on deck since he would want to utilise the ship's space to the fullest. Clauses that give liberty to carry on deck however are regarded as giving the carrier only authority to carry on deck, but are ineffective in ousting the operation of the Hague-Visby Rules.[213] In *Svenska Traktor v Maritime Agencies*,[214] the bill of lading issued for the carriage of tractors from Southampton included the following clause:

> Steamer has liberty to carry goods on deck and shipowners will not be responsible for any loss, damage or claim arising therefrom.

The cargo was carried partly on and partly below deck. One of the tractors carried on deck was washed overboard during the journey. The carriers contended that the liberty clause in the bill of lading gave them authority to carry the goods on deck, and also took the contract outside the scope of the Hague Rules. They could therefore exclude liability. It was held that though the liberty clause gave them authority to carry on deck, it did not meet the requirements set out by Art I(c). To take the cargo outside the operation of the Hague Rules, the bill of lading must on the face of it specifically state that the goods are carried on deck. The literal rendering of Art I(c) is of course aimed at protecting the consignee/indorsee who relies on the bill of lading for full knowledge of the terms of the contract of carriage. As Pilcher J said:

> ... such a statement on the face of the bill of lading would serve as a notification and a warning to consignees and indorsees ... that the goods that they were to take were shipped as deck cargo. They would thus have full knowledge of the facts when accepting the documents and would know that the carriage was not subject to the Act [at p 300].

It is generally customary in the trade for containers and cargoes like timber and highly inflammable goods to be stowed on deck. Practices prevalent in the trade however will be ineffective in bringing the bill of lading outside the parameters of the Hague-Visby Rules unless stipulations laid down in Art I(c) are met.[215]

Where deck cargo meets the requirements of Art I(c), the parties are free to negotiate the terms of the contract of carriage. Clauses excluding liability will not be expected to meet the requirements of reasonableness stipulated by the Unfair Contract Terms Act 1977 according to para 2, Sched 1 to the Act. However, where the

---

212 If the Hague-Visby Rules do not apply, the carrier can exclude liability for loss or damage. He is at liberty to include clauses that exclude liability for the unseaworthy state of the ship. See *Transocean Liners Reederei GmbH v Euxine Shipping Co Ltd (The Imvros)* [1999] 1 Lloyd's Rep 848.

213 On American law, see Wooder, 'Deck cargo: old vices and new law' (1991) 22 JMLC 131; Bauer, 'Deck cargo: pitfalls to avoid under American law in clausing your bills of lading' (1991) 22 JMLC 287.

214 [1953] 2 QB 295.

215 For comparison with the Hamburg Rules, see Table 9.1, Chapter 9.

shipper, or the ultimate bill of lading holder, is a consumer, requirements of reason-ableness imposed by the Unfair Contract Terms Act 1977 need to be satisfied.

Where goods are stowed on deck on the basis of a liberty clause in the contract of carriage, deck stowage will not be construed as a breach of contract and the carrier will be able to rely on the immunities provided by the Hague-Visby Rules.

The important issue, however, is the availability of the immunities in the event of unauthorised deck stowage. This has seen some debate.[216] The general view is that unauthorised deck stowage should be regarded as a breach which would deprive the carrier of the protections provided by the Hague-Visby Rules. This view was followed by the American courts in *Encyclopaedia Brittanica v Hong Kong Producer*,[217] where the limitation of liability under the Hague Rules was lost due to unauthorised deck stow-age. A more extreme view is the suggestion that unauthorised deck stowage should be treated as a fundamental breach of the contract – that is, a breach of such a serious nature that the parties are no longer bound by any of the contract terms – which means that the carrier would naturally lose the benefit of the immunities available to him under the Hague-Visby Rules.

In the more recent case of *The Antares*,[218] none of the above views has been fol-lowed. In this case, the courts had to decide whether the owners could rely on the limitation period of one year under Art III(6) when there had been a breach of the contract of carriage as a result of unauthorised stowage. At first instance, it was held that the question of whether or not the breach was fundamental did not arise at all for consideration since the Hague-Visby Rules had the force of law which meant they had effect as if directly enacted by statute. Further, the Hague-Visby Rules had to be construed in the light of the language used therein and no distinction between fun-damental and non-fundamental breach was found. Therefore, the carrier could rely on Art III(6). On appeal, the decision of the lower court was upheld.

Subsequent to this decision, the English courts had to consider the effect of unauthorised deck stowage on the availability of limitation of liability to the carrier. In *The Chanda*,[219] part of an asphalt drying and mixing plant was stored on deck. The ship encountered rough weather resulting in damage to the electronic control units of the plant. The shipowner sought to limit his liability under the Hague-Visby Rules incorporated into the bill of lading with a paramount clause. Hirst J rejected the 'fundamental breach' approach on the basis that the matter was one of construction. In the circumstances, he concluded that the limitation of liability clause could hardly have been intended to protect the shipowner who, as a result of the breach, exposed the cargo to such palpable risks of damage.

The decision in *The Chanda* seems to be at odds with the decision in *The Antares*. However, according to Hirst J there is no real conflict between the two decisions since, in the latter, the one-year time limitation had statutory force by virtue of Carriage of Goods by Sea Act 1971, and the time-limitation clause did not undermine the purpose of the shipowner's obligation to stow below deck.

It must however be pointed out that both Art III(6) relating to time limitation and

---

216 Livermore, 'Deviation, deck cargo and fundamental breach' [1990] 2 Journal of Contract Law 241.
217 [1969] 2 Lloyd's Rep 536.
218 [1987] 1 Lloyd's Rep 424.
219 [1989] 1 Lloyd's Rep 494.

Art IV(5) on limitation of liability state that they are available to the carrier 'in any event' which suggests that the provisions are applicable even where there is a breach of contract. And this seems to have been taken into account by the court recently. In *Daewoo Heavy Industries Ltd and Another v Klipriver Shipping Ltd and Another (The Kapitan Petko Voivoda)*,[220] the Court of Appeal had an opportunity to examine the phrase 'in any event' in Art IV(5) where the bill of lading attracted the application of the Hague Rules, as enacted in Turkey, by virtue of a paramount clause. The goods from Korea to Turkey were carried on deck in breach of the contract of carriage. On the issue of whether the carrier could take advantage of Art IV(5) overruling *The Chanda* the court held that the most natural meaning of the words 'in any event' is 'in every case' – regardless of whether or not the breach is particularly serious; whether or not the cargo was stowed below deck. Does this mean that the list of exclusions provided under Art IV(2) will not be available to the carrier in the event of unauthorised deck stowage since the provision does not state that they will be applicable 'in any event'? It seems from the two English decisions that what is of fundamental importance is whether the Hague-Visby Rules are applicable by force of law. If they do apply, the immunities are available to the carrier regardless of whether or not there is a breach. However, where they are applicable due to contractual incorporation, the issue becomes one of construction.

Article VI of the Hague-Visby Rules stipulates that where particular goods are shipped, the parties are free to negotiate the terms of the contract. Particular goods are defined as shipments where the character, condition or circumstances of the goods carried justifies a special contract but excludes commercial shipments in the ordinary course of trade.[221] The kinds of cargo that may fall within this provision could be one-off shipments. However, in order for particular goods to fall outside the operation of the Hague-Visby Rules, it is essential that the contract of carriage is not covered by a document of title.

Where particular goods are carried and no negotiable document of title covers the contract of carriage, the parties are free to negotiate the terms of the contract. However, where the term negotiated relates to the seaworthiness of the ship, it should not be contrary to public policy. In England, there are no cases where a stipulation regarding the seaworthiness of a ship has been disallowed on grounds of public policy. It is difficult to state what this might be in the abstract but acts that affect the interests of the state, or the interests of society, humanity may be well within the realm of public policy. Much will depend on the circumstances of the case. For instance, it is possible, where the cargo carried is highly radioactive nuclear waste, exclusion of liability for the seaworthy state of the ship may be disallowed on the grounds it would be injurious to environmental protection, and the courts might insist that the undertaking of seaworthiness does not fall below that set by the Hague-Visby Rules.

Period of application

The Hague-Visby Rules apply to the contract of carriage under Art I(e) from the 'time when the goods are loaded to the time when they are discharged from the ship'. It is difficult to enunciate a general principle to determine at what point loading begins

---

220   [2003] EWCA Civ 451.
221   In *Harland and Wolff Ltd v Burns and Laird Lines Ltd* (1931) 40 LIL Rep 286.

and discharge finishes since varied methods of cargo handling are used depending on the kind of cargo carried. For instance, where cargo is packed in containers or packages, tackle may be used for getting the goods on board the ship. But if the cargo consists of grain, it may be fed directly into the holds through shutes. So, each operation will have to be examined in terms of the nature of the cargo, the custom of the port or trade. As Devlin LJ said in *Pyrene v Scindia Navigation*,[222] the Rules are not intended to impose universal rigidity in respect of loading and discharging operations. It also seems that the parties have the freedom to decide the role that each is going to play in the loading and discharging operations. Where the parties enter into specific agreements, these will not be construed as affecting the Hague-Visby Rules since they are seen as defining the terms of the voyage and not the scope of the contract service. Where tackle is used, the Rules apply from the moment the ship's tackle is hooked on at the port of loading until the moment that cargo is landed and the ship's tackle released at the port of discharge.

The goods carried by a ship may be transhipped during the course of the voyage. This transhipment may be necessitated by circumstances. For instance, the ship may be unable to continue with the voyage due to damage, or the carrier may want extra space on the ship to accommodate other cargo at an intermediate port and it is commercially convenient for him to tranship. It is therefore common for bills of lading to have clauses that give carriers the liberty to tranship. A particular question that arises when the carrier exercises his liberty to tranship is: will the Hague-Visby Rules govern the contract of carriage when the goods are lying by the dockside or transported by road to another port for transhipment? Or could the carrier escape liability, if goods are damaged or lost while they are awaiting transhipment, on the basis that the Hague-Visby Rules apply only when the goods are carried on sea?

In *Mayhew Foods v OCL*,[223] the contract was for the carriage of frozen chicken and turkey portions from Sussex to Jeddah. The cargo was to be transported by road to a port on the South coast of England from where it was to be sent to Jeddah. The bill of lading contained an extended liberty to tranship clause. The goods were shipped from Shoreham for Jeddah. At Le Havre, however, the carrier decided to exercise his liberty to tranship and discharged the container containing the frozen poultry pieces. The container remained at Le Havre for approximately five days. During this period, the contents of the container started decaying. The cargo was eventually found to be in a putrefied state due to inadequate refrigeration.

In an action brought by the shipper, the carrier sought to limit the amount of liability relying on a clause in the bill of lading which specified an upper limit of US$2 per kilo of gross weight of the goods lost or damaged. They relied on this contractual clause limiting amount of liability on the basis that the Hague-Visby Rules were inapplicable while the goods were at Le Havre awaiting transhipment since they applied only in relation to and in connection with the carriage of goods by sea in ships. In support, they cited the Canadian case of *Captain v Far Eastern Steamship Co.*[224] In this case, goods had been shipped from Madras to Vancouver. The parties had envisaged transhipment en route. The goods discharged at Singapore for transhipment were stored for three weeks during which the cargo suffered damage. The court

---

222 [1954] 2 QB 402, at p 418.
223 [1984] 1 Lloyd's Rep 317.
224 [1979] 1 Lloyd's Rep 595.

held that the Hague Rules did not apply during the period when the goods were stored in dock, since they did not relate to carriage of goods by water.

The court in *Mayhew Foods v OCL*, however, found for the plaintiffs on the reasoning that the rights and liabilities attach to the contract and that, in the present instance, was for carriage from Shoreham to Jeddah. The operations carried out during transhipment were in relation to and in connection with the carriage of goods by sea in ships. Hence, the carrier could not escape liability to which he would have been subject by carrying the goods to Le Havre and storing them there before transhipment.

The Canadian case cited by the defendants was distinguished on two counts: first, the parties to the contract of carriage were aware that transhipment was likely to take place and, secondly, separate bills of lading were issued for different legs of the journey.

Applying the general view propounded in *Pyrene v Scindia Navigation*, the operation of the Rules in the event of lighterage will depend on the particular contract of carriage and whether the carrier has contracted to perform the lightering operation as part of the discharging operation.

An issue of relevance in international trade is whether bills of lading including transhipment will be recognised as a valid tender for documentary credit purposes by banks. Where Uniform Customs and Practice for Documentary Credits (UCP) 500 govern the documentary credit, there should be no problems since Art 23[225] of the UCP allows banks to accept bills of lading involving transhipment, provided the letter of credit does not prohibit transhipment and excludes Art 23(d)(i) and (ii) of UCP.

CONTRACTING OUT

Since the Hague-Visby Rules apply only where a bill of lading is issued, is it possible for the carrier to opt out even where the carriage is from a contracting state to Hague-Visby Rules by issuing a notice that he does not issue bills of lading in a particular trade? As Steyn J correctly observed in *The European Transporter*,[226] shipowners, if they are in a strong enough position, could escape the application of the Rules by taking the step of issuing non-transferable documents. However, given the policy reasons behind the convention, the equitable solution would be to interpret the Rules as applying to all outward-bound voyages from the United Kingdom unless the shipper is not entitled to demand the issue of a bill of lading due to custom in a particular trade.[227]

Article III(8) of the Hague-Visby Rules renders null and void any 'clause, covenant or agreement which attempts to relieve or lessen that liability' which the carrier would otherwise have under the Hague-Visby Rules.[228] There are no clear guidelines to determine the dividing line between clauses that do and do not offend the Hague-Visby Rules. The status of such clauses has to be gathered on a case-by-case basis.

225　See also para 88 of International Standard Banking Practice (ISBP), 2003, ICC Publishing SA.
226　[1989] 2 Lloyd's Rep 185, at p 188.
227　See Wilson, *Carriage of Goods by Sea*, 6th edn, 2008, Pearson Longman.
228　On Art III(8) and the Himalaya clause see *The Starsin* [2003] 1 Lloyd's Rep 571.

Some guidance can be found in English judicial decisions.[229] In *Pyrene v Scindia Navigation Co*,[230] Devlin LJ stated that the object of the Hague Rules is to define the terms on which the service is to be performed and not the scope of such service. This has been used to justify some freedom of contract. Clauses defining, for instance, the extent of responsibility for loading and discharging of the goods would, according to Devlin LJ, be tolerated. Similarly, in *Renton v Palmyra*,[231] a clause giving liberty to deviate was construed by Hodgson LJ as defining the scope of the contract voyage and therefore not contrary to Art III(8). Presumably, where a liberty to deviate clause goes to the root of the contract, it would be possible to argue that the clause affects the terms of the carriage and therefore should be regarded as null and void.

However, the limited principle of freedom of contract allowed by the courts is curtailed when it is apparent that the carrier is seeking to limit his liabilities under the Hague-Visby Rules. A clause placing limitation on the amount to a level below that specified in Art IV(5)(a) would be rendered null and void.[232] Similarly, an attempt to lessen the obligation of due diligence to provide a seaworthy ship with a clause which states that a survey certificate should be deemed to be conclusive evidence of due diligence to make the ship seaworthy will be considered void.

Where the effect of a choice of jurisdiction clause is to oust the mandatory regime of the Hague-Visby Rules, the clause will once again be null and void. In *The Hollandia*,[233] machinery was shipped from Leith to the Dutch Antilles. The bill of lading included the following clauses:

> Law of application and jurisdiction: The law of the Netherlands in which the Hague-Visby Rules . . . are incorporated . . . shall apply to this contract.

> All actions under the present contract of carriage shall be brought before the Court of Amsterdam and no other court shall have jurisdiction with regard to such action.

The plaintiffs initiated action in the English courts. The carriers sought to have the action stayed on the basis that the choice of forum clause applied. The House of Lords however refused to stay proceedings on the reasoning that the Carriage of Goods by Sea Act 1971 had given the Hague-Visby Rules the force of law, and the bill of lading in this case was one to which the Hague-Visby Rules applied under Art X(a) and (b) since it was issued in a contracting state and the port of loading was in a contracting state. The foreign court chosen as the exclusive forum would apply a domestic substantive law which would result in limiting the carrier's liability to a sum far lower than that to which the plaintiff would be entitled if Art IV(5) of the Hague-Visby Rules applied, and this would clearly contravene Art III(8). Furthermore, the court felt that giving effect to jurisdiction clauses that had the effect of lessening the amount of liability to an amount lower than that imposed by the Rules would only encourage shipowners to choose courts of convenience – that is, courts that would not apply the Hague-Visby Rules.

---

229 *European Gas Turbines Ltd v MSAS Cargo International Inc* (2000) unreported, 26 May and Tettenborn, 'The defaulting carrier's liability in respect of undamaged goods' [2001] LMCLQ 203, at p 205.
230 [1954] 1 Lloyd's Rep 321.
231 [1956] 1 QB 462.
232 See *Owners of Cargo Lately Aboard the River Gurara v Nigeria National Shipping Lines Ltd* [1997] 1 Lloyd's Rep 225, where a clause defining package for the purposes of Art IV(5) of the Hague Rules was held to be null and void under Art III(8).
233 [1983] 1 Lloyd's Rep 1. See also *The Benarty* [1985] QB 325.

Though criticised for not giving primacy to the parties' intentions,[234] the decision in *The Hollandia* must be supported on policy grounds since the stated purpose of the Hague-Visby Rules when it was drafted was to prescribe an irreducible minimum of liabilities. And yet, it is this irreducible minimum that will be under jeopardy if effect is given to a choice of jurisdiction/law clause.

It seems from a recent decision that a jurisdiction clause will be effective provided the defendant gives an undertaking that he will not take advantage of the lower limit. In *Pirelli Cables Ltd and Others v United Thai Shipping Corp Ltd and Others*,[235] goods were carried from Southampton to Singapore and Bangkok under bills of lading. By virtue of Art X, the Hague Rules applied. The bill of lading contained a jurisdiction clause stating that disputes were to be determined in Thailand to the exclusion of the jurisdiction of any other country. Since Thailand was not a party to the Rules, the application of Thai legislation would result in lower limitation figures, and the claimants were entitled to disregard the jurisdiction clause and bring proceedings in England unless the defendant undertook he would not take advantage of the lower limit (at p 669).[236]

It seems that clauses that are repugnant to the Hague-Visby Rules will be valid where the bill of lading does not attract the automatic application of the Rules. In *The Komninos S*,[237] the plaintiff's cargo of steel coils was shipped at Thessaloniki for carriage to Ravenna and Ancona. On arrival at Ravenna, the coils were found corroded as a result of condensation of water due to lack of ventilation and failure to pump the bilges. The bill of lading contained exemption clauses as well as a clause stating that all disputes were to be referred to British courts. The issue that the court had to decide on was whether the words 'all disputes to be referred to British courts' amounted to a provision that the legislation of the United Kingdom giving effect to the Hague-Visby Rules should govern the contract. If the effect of the above words was that the Hague-Visby Rules applied to the bill of lading, the exemption clauses would be invalidated.

The court held that, since the bill of lading was not issued in a contracting state to the Hague-Visby Rules and in the absence of an express provision incorporating the Hague-Visby Rules in the bill of lading, the forum clause did not import the automatic application of the Hague-Visby Rules. So, the carrier was able to successfully rely on the exclusion clauses. The judgment, as Bingham LJ said, is one that 'gives effect, for better or for worse, to what the parties expressly agreed' (p 377).

The carrier is at liberty to surrender in part or in whole any of the rights and immunities allowed to him under the Hague-Visby Rules. He can also increase his responsibilities and liabilities under the Hague-Visby Rules. The surrender or the

---

234 See Jackson, 'The Hague-Visby Rules and forum, arbitration and choice of law clauses' [1980] LMCLQ 159; Schnarr, 'Foreign forum selection clauses under COGSA: the Supreme Court charts new waters in the *Sky Reefer* case' (1996) 74 Washington University Law Quarterly 867. See also *Indussa Corp v SS Ranborg* 377 F 2d 200 (1967) and *Vimar Seguros Y Reaseguros SA v M/V Sky Reefer* 515 US 528 (1995). Courts in the US until recently did not recognise foreign jurisdiction clauses for a number of reasons – practical and ideological: difficulties of litigating in a foreign forum; lessening of liability where COGSA or Hague Rules were not applied; and lack of assurance that the foreign forum will reach the same results as the US courts even if it applied the Hague Rules or COGSA. In *Sky Reefer*, a clause allowing arbitration in Japan was held to be valid. The Supreme Court in this case also went on to say that it would follow similar reasoning in respect of forum selection clauses. The reasoning was followed in *Effron v Sun Lines Cruises* 67 F 3d 7 (1995).

235 [2000] 1 Lloyd's Rep 663.

236 Also see *Baghlaf Al Zafer v Pakistan National Shipping Co* [1998] 2 Lloyd's Rep 229.

237 [1991] 1 Lloyd's Rep 370.

increase, however, has to be embodied in the bill of lading that is issued to the shipper (Art V). Where there is a surrender of rights and immunities and an increase of responsibilities and liabilities that are embodied in the bill of lading, they presumably apply as against the shipper who is not the charterer and against third parties, but not against the charterer. The reason for this is that the bill of lading in the hands of the charterer is merely a receipt and the terms of the contract between the charterer and the shipowner are to be found in the charterparty.[238]

THE FUTURE

Without doubt, the Hague and Hague-Visby Rules, with their stated purpose of protecting the cargo owner, were revolutionary and set a trend that would guide future developments. The emphasis on protecting the cargo owner found a new voice with the emergence of developing countries and the United Nations Conference on Trade and Development (UNCTAD) and their dissatisfaction (political and legal) with the Hague Rules saw the drafting of the United Nations Convention on the Carriage of Goods by Sea 1978 (Hamburg Rules) which introduced a broader scope of application and a simpler liability regime. The coming into force of this convention in 1992, however, has not displaced the Hague Rules and the Hague-Visby Rules. They still continue to apply to most contracts of carriage. The discontent with the current legal regime remains. The Comité Maritime International (CMI) along with the the United Nations Commission on International Trade Law (UNCITRAL) recently adopted a new convention[239] which is more far reaching than the existing conventions. As to whether legislators and politicians will discard the shackles of conservative attitudes and adopt this new convention, thus heralding a new era of uniformity, remains to be seen.

FURTHER READING

Asser, 'Golden limitations of liability in international transport conventions and the currency crisis' [1974] JMLC 645.

Baughen, 'Does deviation still matter?' [1991] LMCLQ 70.

Berlingieri (compiled by), *The Travaux Préparatoires of the International Convention for the Unification of Certain Rules of Law relating to Bills of Lading of 25 August 1924, the Hague Rules and the Protocols of 23 February 1968 and 21 December 1979, the Hague-Visby Rules, 1997*, Comité Maritime International.

Berlingieri, 'The Hague-Visby Rules and actions in tort' [1991] LQR 18.

Cashmore, 'The legal nature of the doctrine of deviation' [1989] JBL 492.

Clarke, 'The reception of the *Eurymedon* decision in Australia, Canada and New Zealand' [1980] ICLQ 132.

Colinvaux (ed), *Carver's Carriage by Sea*, 2 vols, 13th edn, 1982, Stevens.

---

238   See 'Scope of Application, pp 268–73, above.
239   See Chapter 9.

Davies, 'The elusive carrier: whom do I sue and how?' [1991] Australian Business LR 230.

Debattista, 'Fundamental breach and deviation in the carriage of goods by sea' [1989] JBL 22.

Debattista, 'Carriage Convention and their interpretation in English courts' [1997] JBL 130.

Hubbard, 'Deviation in contracts of sea carriage: after the demise of fundamental breach' [1986] Victoria University of Wellington LR 147.

Livermore, 'Deviation, deck cargo and fundamental breach' [1990] Journal of Contract Law 241.

Mendelsohn, 'Why the US did not ratify the Visby amendments' (1992) 23 JMLC 29.

Mills, 'The future of deviation in the law of carriage of goods' [1983] LMCLQ 587.

Morris, 'The scope of the Carriage by Sea Act 1971' [1979] LQR 59.

Munday, 'The uniform interpretation of international conventions' [1978] ICLQ 450.

Park, 'Incorporation of charterparty terms into bill of lading contracts – a case rationalisation' [1986] Victoria University of Wellington LR 177.

Powles, 'The Himalaya clause' [1979] LMCLQ 331.

Powles, 'Time limits and misdelivery (sea)' [1990] JBL 155.

Richardson, *The Hague and Hague-Visby Rules*, 4th edn, 1998, LLP.

Sturley, *The Legislative History of the Carriage of Goods by Sea Act and the Travaux Préparatoires of the Hague Rules*, 3 vols, 1990, FB Rothman.

Sturley, 'The history of COGSA and the Hague Rules' [1991] JMLC 1.

Sturley and Grover, '*Ad valorem* rates under Art 4(5) of the Hague Rules' [1992] JMLC 621.

Tetley, 'Identity of the carrier – the Hague Rules, Visby Rules, UNCITRAL' [1977] LMCLQ 519.

Tetley, *Marine Cargo Claims*, 4th edn, 2008, Blais.

Tetley, 'Who may claim or sue for cargo loss or damage', Pts I and II [1989] JMLC 153 and 407.

Tettenborn, 'Privity of contract: the Law Commission's proposals' [1992] LMCLQ 182.

Tobolewski, 'The special drawing right in liability conventions: an acceptable solution' [1979] LMCLQ 169.

Treitel, 'Bills of lading and third parties' [1986] LMCLQ 294.

Wilson, *Carriage of Goods by Sea*, 6th edn, 2008, Pearson Longman.

CHAPTER 9

THE HAMBURG RULES AND RECENT DEVELOPMENTS (THE ROTTERDAM RULES)

INTRODUCTION

During the late 1960s, the Hague Rules and the Hague-Visby Rules came under vehement attack from underdeveloped nations who believed that the 'operation of the "traditional maritime law" along with certain aspects of international trade law, impaired [their] balance of payments and ensured [their] continued poverty and perpetual underdevelopment in an industrial age'.[1] The United Nations Conference on Trade and Development (UNCTAD),[2] charged with the task of examining the operation of the Hague Rules and the commission of a working paper,[3] consulted interested parties ranging from shippers, shipowners, insurers and legal bodies from many countries, and concluded that there was a compelling need for a new carrier liability regime. A number of convincing objections in respect of the two existing conventions on carriage by sea were put forward. In brief:

- Lack of a uniform standard for burden of proof in both conventions. Where there was a reference to burden of proof, as in Art IV(1),[4] the courts tended to interpret it in favour of the carrier, thus placing the shipper under a burden difficult to displace due to a lack of access to facts.

- Two of the long list of exceptions found in Art IV(2) operate exclusively in favour of the shipowner. Article IV(2)(a) which allows the carrier to escape liability for the 'act, neglect or default of the master, mariner, pilot, or the servants of the carrier in the navigation or in the management of the ship' is objectionable on policy grounds, since it allows the carrier to escape for negligent acts that take place on his vessel, despite his control of the cargo and the vessel.[5] The other, Art IV(2)(q) – the catch-all exception – gives the carrier an opportunity to escape liability arising from events not covered by Art IV (2)(a)–(p).[6]

- The 'tackle-to-tackle' formula adopted by the Hague-Visby Rules does not address carriage involving lighterage and transhipment adequately.[7]

- Article IV(4) seems to permit the carrier to deviate solely for the purposes of saving property; if this was the intended effect, it imparts an unfair advantage to the carrier.

- Loss due to delay in delivery is not specifically covered by the Hague-Visby Rules, even though some jurisdictions tend to read Art IV(1) widely.[8]

- The one-year time limit for bringing actions is too short since, in practice, it takes

---

1 Yancey, 'The carriage of goods: Hague, COGSA, Visby and Hamburg' (1983) 57 Tulane LR 1238, at p 1257.

2 Established in 1964 under GA Res 1995, 19 UN GAOR Supp (No 15) at 1, UN Doc A/5815.

3 Report of the UNCTAD Secretariat on Bills of Lading UN Doc No E72 II D2 New York 1971.

4 See *The Hellenic Dolphin* [1978] 2 Lloyd's Rep 336.

5 See *Gosse Millerd v Canadian Government* (1927) 44 TLR 143, at p 151.

6 See *Leesh River Tea Co v British India Steam Navigation* [1966] 3 All ER 593.

7 See *Captain v Far Eastern Steamship Co* [1979] 1 Lloyd's Rep 595 and *Mayhew Foods v OCL* [1984] 1 Lloyd's Rep 317.

8 See *Anglo-Saxon v Adamastos Shipping Co* [1957] 1 Lloyd's Rep 79.

longer than a year to establish the identity of the party against whom suit must be brought.[9]

- Lack of provisions on jurisdiction and arbitration in the Hague Rules results in the inclusion of unfair jurisdiction and arbitration clauses in the bill of lading.
- Though Art III(8) renders null and void any clause that attempts to lessen or limit the liability of the carrier below that set by the Hague Rules, it does not deter the carrier from inserting such clauses.[10] For instance, there is no mechanism for compensating a cargo owner for legal costs should he test the validity of such clauses.

The results of the UNCTAD study were passed on to the United Nations Commission on International Trade Law (UNCITRAL)[11] who took on the task of drafting a new convention. The move to the UNCITRAL did not, however, dampen the political zeal[12] in the drafting of the Convention on the International Carriage of Goods by Sea 1978 (hereinafter 'Hamburg Rules'). In drafting the convention, UNCITRAL had the following aims:

... the removal of such uncertainties and ambiguities as exist and at establishing a balanced allocation of risks between the cargo owner and the carrier, with appropriate provisions concerning the burden of proof, in particular the following areas, among others should be considered for revision and simplification:

(a) responsibility for cargo for the entire period it is in the charge or control of the carrier or his agents;

(b) the scheme of responsibilities and liabilities, and rights and immunities incorporated in Arts III and IV of the convention as amended by the Protocol [Hague-Visby Rules] and their interaction, and including the elimination or modification of certain exceptions to carriers' liability;

(c) burden of proof;

(d) jurisdiction;

(e) responsibility for deck cargos, live animals and transhipments;

(f) extension of the period of limitation;

(g) definition under Art I of the convention;

(h) elimination of invalid clauses in bills of lading;

(i) deviation, seaworthiness and unit limitation of liability.[13]

The regime of carrier liability under the Hamburg Rules, in broad terms, is far more stringent than that of the Hague or the Hague-Visby Rules. The liability of the carrier is based on the principle of presumed fault or neglect which means that the onus is on him to show otherwise. The carrier does not have the benefit of a long list of exceptions including the negligence in navigation exception. Further, the Hamburg Rules are more of a self-contained code than the other two conventions since, among others,

---

9 Davies, 'The elusive carrier: who do I sue and how?' [1991] Australian Business LR 230; Selvig, 'Through-carriage and on-carriage of goods by sea' (1979) 27 American Journal of Comparative Law 369; Tetley, 'Who may claim or sue for cargo loss or damage?' [1986] JMLC 171.

10 See Shah, 'The revision of the Hague Rules – key issues', in Mankabady (ed), *The Hamburg Rules on the Carriage of Goods by Sea*, 1978, Sijthoff, at p 5.

11 Established in 1966 under GA Res 2205, 21 UN GAOR Supp (No 15) at 115, UN Doc A/7134.

12 See Frederick, 'Political participation and legal reform in international maritime rule making process: from the Hague Rules to the Hamburg Rules' (1991) 22(1) JMLC 81 for an interesting account of the role of politics in international maritime treaties.

13 TD/B/C 4 86; TD/B/C 5/ISL/8 Annex 1.

they include specific provisions on jurisdiction, the carrier's right to freight and demurrage.

Reaction to the Hamburg Rules can be neatly classified into those against[14] and those for,[15] and, needless to say, each camp had influential members. According to the anti-Hamburg Rules group, the convention, drafted largely under political pressure, did not reflect commercial practicalities and predicted increased insurance costs[16] and uncertainty by 'casting aside the results of half a century of expensive litigation and pave the way for another half century of legal debate on a new and different regime'.[17] It has also been suggested that the drafting of the Hamburg Rules, civilian in style, also contributed to its unpopularity.[18] As for those in favour, the Hamburg Rules promote a fair allocation of risks. And as for the argument that they 'will herald a period of uncertainty and confusion is . . . a little like refusing to update computer software because it takes a certain investment in time to learn the new program and derive the full benefits from the innovation'.[19]

Despite its cold reception from the shipowning countries, the Hamburg Rules came into force on 1 November 1992 under the impetus of developing nations.[20] This Convention now exists alongside the other two well established conventions: the Hague Rules and the Hague-Visby Rules. They are not yet part of English law, though it is likely that the English courts will be called upon to apply and interpret the Convention.[21] The parties may specifically incorporate the Hamburg Rules to a bill of lading or charterparty. Where the bill of lading attracts the mandatory application of

---

14 See Moore, 'The Hamburg Rules' (1978) 10(1) JMLC 1; Tetley, 'The Hamburg Rules – a commentary' [1979] LMCLQ 1.

15 Honnold, 'Ocean carriers and cargo; clarity and fairness – Hague or Hamburg?' (1993) 24(1) JMLC 75. Professor Honnold was a member of the United States delegation to the 1978 conference.

16 Chandler, in 'A comparison of "COGSA", the Hague/Visby Rules and the Hamburg Rules' (1984) 15 JMLC 233 writes '[the] Hamburg Rules were meant to cut overall shipping costs, particularly for the developing countries . . . they might well raise costs' (at p 237). A fairly recent study on the effects of the Hamburg Rules is that of Eun Sup Lee who conducted a survey on insurance in Korea. According to Lee, the traders felt that the increase in carrier liability would not change cargo insurance practices, and change in insurance premiums would at most be minimal. The carriers, on the other hand, felt that the Hamburg Rules would have a strong impact on their business terms and there would be a rise in the costs of liability of coverage. To meet these costs, instead of raising freight they would try to 'save by resorting to re-engineering, mark up reduction, and service reduction'. Eun Sup Lee on the basis of his study concludes that '. . . in the long term, the Hamburg Rules have the potential to induce a restructuring of insurance practices . . . [and] majority of carriers, however, will not be able to charge additional freight because of intensive competition in the industry. Freight levels will consequently not be directly affected by the Hamburg Rules in the short term': 'Analysis of the Hamburg Rules on marine cargo insurance and liability insurance' (1987) 4 ILSA Journal of International and Comparative Law 153.

17 See Waldron, 'The Hamburg Rules' [1991] JBL 305, at p 318, quoting BIMCO (Baltic and International Maritime Council) Bulletin produced in 1988.

18 Tetley, 'Mixed jurisdictions: common law v civil law (codified and uncodified)' (2000) 60 Louisiana LR 677, at p 704.

19 Nicoll, 'Do the Hamburg Rules suit a shipper-dominated economy?' (1993) 24(1) JMLC 151, at p 179.

20 The convention needed 20 signatories to become effective. These came from Barbados, Botswana, Burkina Faso, Chile, Egypt, Guinea, Hungary, Kenya, Lebanon, Lesotho, Malawi, Morocco, Nigeria, Romania, Senegal, Sierra Leone, Tanzania, Tunisia, Uganda and Zambia. Since 1992, Austria, Burundi, Cameroon, Republic of Congo, Czech Republic, Dominican Republic, Gambia, Georgia, Jordan Kazakhstan, Liberia, Paraguay, Saint Vincent and the Grenadines and the Syrian Arab Republic have become contracting states to the convention.

21 See *East-West Corp v DKBS 1912* [2002] 2 Lloyd's Rep 182.

the Hague-Visby Rules, the voluntary incorporation of the Hamburg Rules is unlikely to be regarded as void under Art III(8) of the Hague-Visby Rules since the liability scheme and liability amounts are favourable to the cargo interest.

It must also be pointed out that, in spite of the small number of ratifications, the Hamburg Rules have impacted indirectly on the maritime legislation of countries with noticeable shipowning interests. For instance, China,[22] Korea,[23] the Nordic countries[24] and Australia[25] have hybrid maritime legislation that reflects both the Hague Rules/Hague-Visby and Hamburg Rules. More recently, the US Maritime Law Association[26] has put forward proposals for a new Carriage of Goods by Sea Act that incorporates some of the Hamburg provisions. In light of these developments, it would be premature to dismiss the Hamburg Rules as unimportant.

What follows in this chapter is an overview of the main provisions in respect of carrier liability and immunities and shipper's responsibilities that are found in other sea carriage conventions along with an account of some of the innovative provisions. The chapter concludes with an overview of a new convention for sea carriage drafted by UNCITRAL and the Comité Maritime International (CMI).

INTERPRETATION OF THE CONVENTION

Before proceeding with an examination of the Hamburg Rules, a few words must be said about its interpretation since provisions of any international convention have to be interpreted in national courts. English courts recognise the international character of a convention and normally steer clear of principles and precedents found in domestic law.[27] A number of international conventions include provisions on their interpretation and the Hamburg Rules is one among these. Article 3 provides that 'in the interpretation and application of the provisions regard shall be had to its international character and to the need to promote uniformity'. The Hamburg Rules are available in Arabic, Chinese, English, French, Russian and Spanish,[28] all texts being equally authentic (Art 34(2)). Availability of authentic texts in six languages, other than for political reasons, may also be motivated by the need to promote uniformity. After all, if there were problems in understanding the text in one language, reference to the text in another language would aid to resolve the ambiguities. However, this is based on a number of debatable assumptions. For instance, it assumes that there is

---

22 Li, 'The Maritime Code of the People's Republic of China' [1993] LMCLQ 204; Xia Chen, 'Chinese law on carriage of goods by sea' (1999) 8 WTR Currents: International Trade LJ 89; Zhang Lixing, 'Recent maritime legislation and practice in the People's Republic of China' (1994) 6 University of San Francisco Maritime LJ 273.

23 Rok Sang Yu and Jongkwan Peck, 'The revised maritime section of the Korean Commercial Code' [1993] LMCLQ 403.

24 Tiberg and Beijer, 'The Nordic Maritime Code' [1995] LMCLQ 527. The Nordic countries have adopted a substantial portion of the Hamburg Rules on the basis that they were forward looking.

25 Hetherington, 'Australian hybrid cargo liability regime' [1999] LMCLQ 12.

26 See www.mlaus.org for further details. The latest version of the US bill on carriage of goods by sea is also available on http://tetley.law.mcgill.ca, along with Professor Tetley's comments on the proposed changes.

27 See Sturley, 'International uniform laws in national courts: the influence of domestic law in conflicts of interpretation' (1987) 27 Vanderbilt Journal of International Law 729 for a US viewpoint.

28 These are the official languages recognised by the United Nations.

parity between legal concepts, that an exact translation is possible and if so that the text is an exact translation.[29] The wisdom of giving equal status to texts in six different languages is highly questionable, since equivalence of concepts is not always achieved through equivalence in words. As Simmonds correctly observes, 'problems of interpretation will be exacerbated also by the fact that six language texts are equally authentic'.[30] He also notes that a cursory glance of the Spanish, French and English texts indicate problems may occur in a linguistic comparison.[31] Difficulties with multilingual treaties, however, are not insurmountable and the Vienna Convention on the Law of Treaties, 1969 in its Arts 31–33[32] provides some guidance on treaty interpretation. The general rule is that a treaty is to be interpreted in accordance with the ordinary meaning of the terms and according to its object and purpose. However, where on the application of the general rules terms are ambiguous or obscure, an acceptable degree of uniformity will be achieved if judges look to the interpretation of other jurisdictions. This of course requires decisions in different jurisdictions to be reported as and when available. UNCITRAL has established a system for gathering decisions on its texts through national reporters.[33]

SCOPE OF APPLICATION

The Hamburg Rules come into operation where:

- the contract for carriage is for carriage by sea; and
- an element of internationality is present in that the contract of affreightment is between two different states.

It is not, however, a necessary condition that the different states involved in the contract of carriage are all contracting states. It is sufficient if one of the operations involved in the handling of the goods takes place in a contracting state. So, if the port of loading is located in a contracting state (Art 2(1)(a)) or if the port of discharge is located in a contracting state (Art 2(1)(b)), the Hamburg Rules will be applicable. This means that both inward shipments and outward shipments from a contracting state are subject to the Hamburg Rules. For instance, where cargo is shipped from state X (a contracting state) to Y (a non-contracting state), the Rules will apply. Similarly, where cargo is shipped from state Y (a non-contracting state) to X (a contracting state), the Rules will be triggered. In *Compagnie Sénéglaise d'assurances et de réassurances CSA and 27 Other Companies v Roscoe Shipping Co, the Captain of the Ship 'World Appolo', and the*

---

29 See Shelton, 'Reconcilable differences? The interpretation of multilingual treaties' [1997] Hastings International and Comparative LR 611, at pp 621–2, for an illustration of how inconsistencies may be introduced and left in multilingual treaties deliberately by negotiators.
30 'The interpretation of the Hamburg Rules convention: a note on Art 3', in Mankabady (ed), *The Hamburg Rules on the Carriage of Goods by Sea*, 1978, Sijthoff, at p 118.
31 See also Peyrefitte, 'The period of coverage of maritime transport – comments on Art 4 of the Hamburg Rules', in Mankabady (ed), *The Hamburg Rules on the Carriage of Goods by Sea*, 1978, Sijthoff.
32 The text of this convention is available at www.un.org/law/ilc.
33 UNCITRAL Yearbook, Vol XIX, 1988, at pp 15, 16, 130–36. So far, the abstracts of well over 300 decisions pertaining to the United Nations Sales Convention, Model Law on Arbitration and the Hamburg Rules are available. The abstracts are also available on the web at www.uncitral.org. Jurisprudence on the interpretation of the Hamburg Rules is also available on the website of Comité Maritime International at www.comitemaritime.org.

Steaming Mutual Underwriting Association,[34] a contract of carriage from a port in Thailand to Daker in Senegal attracted the application of the Hamburg Rules since the port of discharge was situated in a state that had ratified the Rules.[35]

Application of the Hamburg Rules to inward- and outward-bound shipments is a major advance on the Hague-Visby Rules which apply only to outward shipments from a contracting state, unless the state implementing the Rules extends its operation to inward shipments.[36] Article 2(1)(b) is likely to establish Hamburg Rules in the international maritime scene in spite of its unpopularity amongst shipowning countries.

Article 2(1)(c) extends the applicability of the Hamburg Rules where an optional port situated in a contracting state and named in the contract of carriage becomes the actual port of discharge. Article 2(1)(d), like Art X(a) of the Hague-Visby Rules, provides for the applicability of the Hamburg Rules where the bill of lading or document evidencing the contract of carriage is issued in a contracting state.

An element of contact with a contracting state as specified in the above paragraphs is not always necessary to bring a contract of carriage within the ambit of the Convention. A contract may be subject to the Hamburg Rules where the parties expressly stipulate that the provisions of the Hamburg Rules, or the laws of a state giving effect to the Hamburg Rules are to govern the contract of carriage.[37]

Unlike the Hague-Visby Rules, the operation of the Hamburg Rules is not dependent on the issue of a bill of lading or a similar document of title. The provisions of the convention are applicable to all contracts of carriage. They therefore govern waybills, short sea notes and other contracts of carriage used in the trade (Art 2(1)).

Charterparties are excluded from the ambit of the Hamburg Rules except where bills of lading are issued pursuant to a charterparty (Art 2(3)). Accordingly, the convention is applicable only where: (1) the bill of lading is issued to the shipper who is not the charterer; or (2) where the bill of lading issued under a charterparty to the charterer is subsequently endorsed by him to a third party. In other words, the question of whether the Hamburg Rules apply to a bill of lading issued under a charterparty is to be determined in terms of the identity of the holder.

It is not clear whether the Rules will apply to a bill of lading which is issued by the charterer to a shipper and which is subsequently endorsed by him to the charterer. It could be argued that, since the charterer has acquired the bill of lading as an indorsee,

---

34 UNCITRAL A/CN.9/SER.C/ABSTRACTS 11, 2 December 1996 (Case 159) Commercial Court of Marseilles (France); 1996 Rev Scapel 51–55.

35 However, see *Ocean View Shipping Ltd and Others v Cargill International Antigua and Others* 1998 DMF 588 as cited at http://comitemaritime.org/jurisp/ju_hamburg.html. The cargo was carried from Burma to Guinea and proceedings were commenced at the Tribunal de Commerce of Paris who affirmed their jurisdiction on the basis that the bill of lading was issued in Paris. The Tribunal held that the bill of lading attracted the application of the Hamburg Rules since Guinea (place of discharge) was a party to the Rules. On appeal, the Cour d'Appel of Paris overturned the judgment on grounds that France had not ratified the Hamburg Rules. The fact that the port of discharge was located in a state party to the Hamburg Rules did not matter. See also *Brendani AB v Magazzini Genrali and Frigoriferi SpA* Core di Cassazione 14 February 2001, No 2155 (unreported but cited at http://comitemaritime.org/jurisp/ju_hamburg.html) where the Supreme Court held that even though the Italian Parliament had authorised the ratification of the Hamburg Rules (Law 25 January 1983 No 40) they could not be applied to the dispute since the ratification had never taken place.

36 The US, Japan and Belgium have extended the application of the Rules to inward shipments.

37 A similar provision is found in Art X(c) of the Hague-Visby Rules.

it should be subject to the Rules. A literal reading of Art 2(3), however, suggests that the bill of lading will be subject to the Rules only where the holder is not the charterer.

The Hamburg Rules also govern 'volume' or 'tonnage' contracts – that is, contracts of carriage where the carrier agrees to a future carriage of goods in a series of shipments during an agreed period (Art 2(4)). However, where such an agreement is in the form of a charterparty, they will be subject to Art 2(3).

The Hamburg Rules cover all kinds of cargo including live animals and deck cargo. There are however specific provisions relating to deck cargo (Art 9) and live animals (Art 5(5)). The carrier is entitled to carry the goods on deck only if such carriage is in accordance with an agreement with the shipper or with the usage of the particular trade or is required by statutory rules or regulations. Where the carrier and the shipper have agreed that the goods shall or may be carried on deck, the carrier must insert in the bill of lading or other document evidencing the contract of carriage by sea a statement to that effect. In other words, deck cargo will be regarded as normal cargo in the following situations (Art 9(1)):

- If there is usage to do so. Usage will depend on prevalent trade practices; for instance, containers are deck cargo due to current shipping practice.
- If there are statutory rules or regulations to that effect. This covers situations where statute may require certain kinds of cargo (for example, explosives, corrosive chemicals) to be carried on deck.
- If there is an agreement. Where there is an agreement, this must be inserted in the document relating to the carriage of goods by sea (Art 9(2)). This perhaps is the most problematic of the three situations circumscribed by Art 9(1), since the form the agreement must take is left unspecified. Does the agreement have to be express and appear on the face of the bill of lading or will a liberty clause allowing the carrier to carry the goods on deck qualify as sufficient to constitute an agreement for the purposes of this provision? It may be possible to argue that a liberty clause is an agreement since the Rules do not use the words 'express agreement' in relation to Art 9(1), whereas they do in relation to Art 9(4), which suggests that the drafters were aware of the conceptual distinction between agreement and express agreement.

Where goods are carried on deck in circumstances stipulated by Art 9(1), the carrier can take advantage of the limitation of liability set out in Art 6 of the Rules. The carrier, however, will lose this entitlement where:

- cargo is carried on deck in the absence of usage or agreement or statutory rules, and it can be shown by the claimant that 'loss, damage or delay in delivery resulted from an act or omission of the carrier done with the intent to cause such loss, damage or delay, or recklessly and with knowledge that such loss, damage or delay would probably result' (Art 8); or
- cargo is carried on deck contrary to an express agreement to carry below deck – deemed to be an act or omission within the meaning of Art 8 (Art 9(4)).

Historically, live animals were excluded due to their peculiar nature. There was no way of guaranteeing that the animals would be delivered in the condition they were received, that is, alive. The Hamburg Rules have deviated from the norm in making their carriage subject to them. The carrier however is not liable if he can show that he has complied with the instructions given by the shippers but the damage, loss or delay in delivery was caused by the special risks inherent in the kind of carriage (Art 5(5)). Presumably, special risks will be determined by the type of animal carried and the risks generally present in the transportation of live animals by sea. In the absence of a definition, there is some scope for interpretation of live animals – for instance, are viruses and bacteria live animals?

Carrier's responsibilities and liabilities

Definition of 'carrier'

The Hamburg Rules make a distinction between carrier and actual carrier. The distinction was introduced in order to simplify the process of identifying the party against whom proceedings are to be brought, so that the difficulties encountered by the claimant under the Hague-Visby Rules could be avoided.

A carrier is 'any person by whom or in whose name a contract of carriage of goods by sea is concluded with any shipper' (Art 1). This would include the shipowner, the charterer, the freight forwarder, or any transport operator who has entered into the contract of carriage. It is therefore not essential for the contracting carrier to be personally involved in the carrying of the cargo.

An actual carrier, on the other hand, is 'any person to whom the performance of the carriage of the goods or of part of the carriage has been entrusted by the carrier, and includes any other person to whom such performance has been entrusted' (Art 1).

Though the Rules draw a distinction between carrier and actual carrier for the purposes of liability, the contracting carrier remains liable for the entire voyage (Art 10). The carrier is therefore liable for the acts and omissions of the actual carrier and of his servants and agents acting within the scope of their employment in relation to the carriage.

This general rule, however, need not apply where there is through carriage. So, where transhipment is envisaged, the carrier can exclude liability for loss, damage or delay in delivery which takes place while the goods are in the charge of the actual carrier, provided this is explicitly stated in the document of carriage (Art 11(1)). The burden of proving that the loss, damage or delay in delivery was caused by an occurrence while the goods are in the hands of the actual carrier is on the carrier.

Period of responsibility

Article 4(1) states that:

> ... the responsibility of the carrier for the goods under this convention covers the period during which the carrier is in charge of the goods at the port of loading, during the carriage and at the port of discharge.

The precise moment of the applicability of the Rules is calculated not from the time the goods are placed on board ship but is determined from the time the carrier can exercise the right of control and supervision of the goods. The carrier is regarded as being in charge of the goods when he takes over from the shipper, or a person acting on his behalf or an authority or third party to whom the goods must be handed for shipment (Art 4(2)(a)). The carrier is regarded as having delivered the goods when he hands them over to the consignee[38] or places them at the disposal of the consignee in accordance with the contract, or by handing over the goods to an authority or third party to whom the goods must be handed over (Art 4(2)(b)).

The question of when the goods are taken over or delivered by the carrier will presumably be decided from the terms of the contract. However, it is not clear from Art 4(2) whether the carrier will be deemed to be *in charge* of the goods if the goods are handed to the carrier's agent. A similar provision found in Art 18(2) of the Warsaw Convention 1929 as amended by Hague Protocol 1955 – an international convention concerning carriage by air – was considered by the courts in *Swiss Bank Corp v Brinks Mat*.[39] It was held that the carrier was in charge of the goods when the goods were weighed and checked by the air carrier's handling agents.

The formula adopted by the Hamburg Rules should cause no problems in relation to lighterage operations since the question will be decided in terms of who was in charge of the goods. If an independent contractor is employed by the shipper, or servants or agents of the shipper are used to conduct the operation, this would suggest that the carrier took over the goods when they were loaded on the ship. On the other hand, if the lightering operations are conducted for the carrier either by his servants or agents, or independent contractors employed by him, the carrier would be responsible for the goods during the process.

As for transhipment, it seems that the Rules will apply to the period when the goods are awaiting transhipment, since Art 4 suggests that the carrier is responsible for the entire period – that is, from the time the goods are taken over to the time they are delivered to the relevant party at the port of discharge. In these circumstances, it would be common for a through bill of lading to be issued.

Where a through bill of lading is issued, the carrier is responsible throughout the carriage of goods by sea (Art 10), unless the contracting carrier excludes his liability under Art 11(1). This exemption is effective provided the actual carrier is named in the contract of carriage, and details are given in the contract of carriage of that part of the carriage to be undertaken by the actual carrier. Where these requirements are met, the actual carrier is responsible for the goods only when they are in his charge.

Documentary responsibilities

Once the carrier or the actual carrier takes charge of the goods, he must *on demand* by the shipper issue a bill of lading to the shipper (Art 14(1)). This right, however, does not extend to the consignee or indorsee of the bill of lading. The bill may be signed by the master and, where the master signs the document, he is deemed to have signed it on behalf of the carrier.

Where the shipper demands a 'shipped' bill of lading, the carrier is under an obligation to issue such a document (Art 15(2)). If the carrier has previously issued a

---

38   In *Compagnie Sénéglaise d'assurances et de réassurances CSA and 27 Other Companies v Roscoe Shipping Co, the Captain of the Ship 'World Appolo', and the Steaming Mutual Underwriting Association*, the Commercial Court of Marseille found that the carrier was deemed to have delivered for the purposes of Art 4(2)(b) when the hatches were opened and the stevedoring company appointed by the consignee began discharge operations: UNCITRAL A/CN 9/SER C/ ABSTRACTS 11, 2 December 1996 (Case 159).

39   [1986] QB 853.

bill of lading to the shipper, the shipper must surrender this document in return for the 'shipped' bill of lading.

Articles 15(1) and (2) list the particulars that need to be included in the bill of lading. These particulars relate to the cargo (for instance, general nature of the goods, dangerous character of cargo, apparent condition of the goods, number of packages, weight, leading marks necessary for identification of the cargo), the contracted voyage (for example, port of loading, port of discharge, date/period of delivery), the carriage contract (for example, number of original bills of lading, place of issue of the bill of lading) and the identity/obligations of the parties to the contract (for example, name of shipper, name of consignee, name and principal place of business of the carrier, consignee's obligation to pay freight and increased limit(s) of liability where agreed).

Where a 'shipped' bill of lading is issued, it must contain the following additional statements:

- that the goods are on board a named ship/ships (Art 15(2)); and
- the date or dates of loading (Art 15(2)(a)).

Failure on the part of the carrier to include some of the particulars required will not affect the legal character of the bill of lading as long as the requirements for a bill of lading laid down by Art 1(7) are met (Art 15(3)). According to Art 1(7), a bill of lading is 'a document which evidences a contract of carriage by sea and the taking over as the loading of goods by the carrier, and by which the carrier undertakes to deliver the goods against its surrender. A provision in the document that the goods are to be delivered to the order of a named person, or to order, or to bearer would constitute such an undertaking'.

The Hamburg Rules do not impose any penalties on the carrier for not including details listed in Art 15 unlike the Convention for the Unification for Certain Rules relating to International Carriage by Air Warsaw 1929. Under the latter where the carrier does not include details listed in its Art 8, the carrier loses the benefit of provisions excluding or limiting his liability available under the convention. However, the Hamburg Rules make available a compensation scheme where the cargo owner's loss is a result of the carrier's omission of a statement that the bill of lading or other document of carriage is subject to the Hamburg Rules which nullify any stipulation derogating from the Rules to the detriment of the shipper or the consignee (Art 23(3) and (4)).

The carrier has the right to enter reservations on the bill of lading relating to the general nature of the goods, the number of packages or pieces, or weight or quantity of the goods (Art 16(1)). He or any other person issuing the bill of lading can enter these reservations only where he has no reasonable means of checking the particulars or he knows or has reasonable grounds to believe that the particulars furnished are incorrect. So, where the shipper has enumerated the number of packages in a container that the carrier has no reasonable means of checking, reservations to this effect can be entered on the bill of lading with phrases such as 'said to contain'. In *'Carte' Société tuniso-européenne d'assurances et de réassurances v Sudcargos*,[40] the cargo consisting of domestic appliances for carriage from a French port to Rades in Tunisia was

---

40 1996 Rev Scapel, 40–42; UNCITRAL A/CN 9/SER C/ABSTRACTS 11, 2 December 1996, (Case 160).

packed by the shipper in a container and sealed with lead. The defendants were unable to inspect the contents of the container and therefore entered a reservation on the bill of lading to the effect that the carrier was not liable in respect of statements regarding the nature and number of packages on the bill of lading. On discharge, the consignee discovered that 57 cases were missing. The Tunis Court of First Instance, applying Art 16, held that the carrier was not liable since the consignee did not adduce proof of the number of packages and nature of the cargo handed to the carrier at the port of loading. Of course, the shipper could have taken steps to reduce the risk of bearing the loss by inserting the weight of the container at the time of loading. As Bovio correctly observes:

> [This] does not mean that, when a sealed container is delivered for international carriage by sea and the well known clause is stamped on the bill of lading by the carrier, the shipper is thereby to run the risks of pilferage at the loading pier, on board the vessel, during the voyage and the port of loading and at the port of discharge, so long as the carrier is in charge of the goods, because the carrier cannot be held to account for what is within the container. There is a simple precaution (not employed in this case) which is particularly suited to these kinds of goods (and other goods that are easily saleable by an unscrupulous party in possession). That precaution, which common sense and a reading of the cases would seem to dictate, is to ascertain beyond question the weight of the container at the time it is delivered for carriage. To that end, the carrier's agent at the port of loading would participate in the weighing operation or perform it himself; the same would occur immediately upon arrival at the port of discharge. If there were any discrepancy between the two weights, the carrier would be liable for it.[41]

As for noting the apparent condition of the goods on the bill of lading, the onus is on the carrier. Failure on the part of the carrier to do this would mean that the goods will be regarded as shipped in apparent good condition.

The statements made on the bill of lading are regarded as *prima facie* evidence of the taking over or the loading of the goods by the carrier (Art 16(3)(a)). However, proof to the contrary may be provided by the carrier. But, once the bill of lading is transferred to a third party, that is, a consignee or an indorsee, who has acted in good faith, proof to the contrary cannot be submitted by the carrier (Art 16(3)(b)).

It is not clear whether the carrier will be required to enter the details listed in Art 15(1) in respect of bills of lading. Where the carrier issues a document other than a bill of lading as a receipt of the goods received, Art 18 provides that 'such a document is *prima facie* evidence of the conclusion of the contract of carriage by sea and the taking over by the carrier of the goods therein described'. The provision does not state whether the carrier can insert reservations on such a document. Presumably, since it is a receipt for the goods, he will be able to insert suitable reservations regarding the condition of the goods, packaging, etc.

Carrier liability

The Hamburg Rules have adopted a different formula from that of the Hague-Visby Rules for determining carrier liability (see Table 9.1, pp 317–28). They introduce a uniform test of liability based on presumed fault. Carrier liability, based on presumed

---

41   Bovio, 'The first decisions applying the Hamburg Rules' [1997] LMCLQ 351, at p 358. See also *Bally Inc v MV Zim Container Service et al* (1994) AMC 2762 (2 Cir).

fault, is nothing new and is found in other international conventions on carriage of goods, such as the Convention on the Contract for the International Carriage of Goods by Road 1956[42] (Art 17(1) and (2)) and the Convention for the Unification of Certain Rules relating to International Carriage by Air 1929 (Arts 18(1) and 20).[43] Article 5(1) provides that:

> ... the carrier is liable for loss resulting from loss of or damage to the goods as well as from delay in delivery, if the occurrence which caused the loss, damage or delay took place while the goods were in his charge ... unless the carrier proves that he, his servants or agents took all measures that could reasonably be required to avoid the occurrence and its consequences.

The introduction of a standard basis of liability means that the level of responsibility that can be expected is not dependent on the kind of obligation undertaken. In other words, the question whether the breach was a breach of the seaworthiness obligation or cargo management obligation is not essential for the application of Art 5(1).

Article 5(1) requires the carrier to show that he took all measures that could reasonably be required to avoid the occurrence and its consequences. It is unclear whether the carrier will be required to show lack of negligence on his (including his servants or agents) part alone or whether it is personal to the carrier so that he is liable for the negligent work of an independent contractor. A literal reading of this provision suggests that the requirement of the duty of care is not personal to him, so that he can escape liability for the negligent workmanship of a contractor as long as he has exercised reasonable care in choosing that contractor.

Article 5(7) goes further than the provisions of the Hague-Visby Rules by providing for partial liability where there is joint causation. So, where there is loss, damage or delay in delivery partly due to the carrier's servants 'or agents' fault or neglect and partly due to another cause, the carrier is liable only to the extent that the loss, damage or delay in delivery is attributable to such fault or neglect. The onus however is on the carrier to prove the amount of loss, damage or delay in delivery that is not attributable thereto.

The above provision will be of help only where it is possible to distinguish the various causes of the damage and the extent to which each cause is directly responsible for the damage. In practice, it may not always be possible to measure the degree to which a particular cause is directly responsible for the end result.

The burden of proof requirement adopted in Art 5(1) in relation to carrier liability means that the onus is always on the carrier to show that the loss, damage or delay occurred despite all measures reasonably taken by him, his servants or agents to avoid the occurrence and its consequences. Only in the event of damage that has been caused by fire is the burden shifted to the claimant under Art 5(4) which states that the carrier is liable. So the carrier will be liable for loss or damage due to fire if the claimant can show that it arose from the fault or neglect on the part of the carrier, his servants or agents or resulted from the fault or neglect of the carrier, his servants or agents, in taking all measures that could reasonably be required to put out the fire and avoid or mitigate its consequences.

As apparent from Art 5(1) the carrier is liable for delay in delivery. But when does

---

42   Also known as CMR after its French title Convention Relative au Contrat de Transport International de Marchandises par Route.

43   See Chapters 10 and 12.

delay in delivery occur? The obvious answer would be to look at the contractual terms to determine the issue. Article 5(2) does this precisely by drawing attention to the express contractual terms. If there is agreement that delivery is to take place at Port X between the beginning and the end of October 2009 failure to deliver within this period would constitute delay in delivery. However, it is possible that parties may not have agreed on the delivery period. In this event, according to Art 5(2) the time of delivery is to be established by what a diligent carrier would regard as reasonable taking the circumstances into account. The formula adopted by the Hamburg Rules has been cited with approval in the Seoul District Court in the Republic of Korea even though it is not a signatory to this Convention. In *Song Dong Geun v Geumchun Maritime Shipping*[44] the shipper (seller) sold fabric to the buyer (the importers) which was sent by sea under a bill of lading. The importers claimed for delay in delivery of the fabric and the seller (plaintiff) brought an action against the carrier (defendant) stating that they should be responsible for the damages. In considering Art 788(1) of the Commercial Code of Korea the Court concluded that it did not provide a 'clear standard' by which to determine the issue of delay in delivery. However, it went on to state that Art 5(2) of the Hamburg Rules provided an 'internationally reasonable standard'.[45]

Carrier's exceptions

The Hamburg Rules, along with the carrier's duties in relation to seaworthiness and cargo management,[46] also drop the long list of exceptions, including the controversial navigation exception,[47] that are to be found in the Hague Rules. Article 5 makes reference to specific instances where the special provisions become relevant. As far as clauses such as 'perils of the sea', 'act of God' normally found in bills of lading are concerned, these will no doubt be raised where relevant by the carrier under Art 5 when trying to show that he took all measures required of him to avoid the occurrence and its consequences.

Live animals

Where live animals are carried, the carrier is not liable if he can show that he has complied with the special instructions given by the shippers but the damage, loss or delay in delivery was caused by the special risks inherent in the kind of cargo carried (Art 5(5)). In other words, this provision exempts liability for damage caused due to

---

44   28 August 2002. Abstract available on CLOUT database (A/CN.9/SER.C/ABSTRACTS/70) Case 745.

45   This case is interesting since it shows that courts in non-signatory countries are taking note of the Hamburg Rules.

46   See Arts III(1) and (2) of the Hague and Hague-Visby Rules.

47   The CMI during the conference stressed the importance of retaining the negligence in navigation exception on the grounds that it made economic sense to do so, since to remove it would result in an increase in insurance premium and hence freight charges. It was also suggested that retaining this exception would benefit those developing countries in the process of building maritime fleets. According to William Tetley, the error in navigation and management of the ship exception is a 'sacred cow' to shipowners, their associations and P&I clubs. Interestingly, this exception was included in the CMI/UNICITRAL Preliminary Draft Convention on Carriage of Goods by Sea, thus endorsing Tetley's observation. This however is not the case in the adopted version of the Rotterdam Rules. See pp 305–16 below.

inherent vice of the cargo carried as long as it can be established that the carrier complied with instructions given by the shipper relating to cargo management.

Deviation

Unlike the Hague-Visby Rules, the Hamburg Rules do not contain a specific provision solely devoted to deviation. Instead, the concept is alluded to under Art 5(6) as a specific instance whereby the carrier can escape liability. According to this provision:

> ... the carrier is not liable, except in general average, where loss, damage or delay in delivery resulted from measure to save life or from reasonable measures to save property at sea.

It is not clear from this provision whether the carrier can deviate solely for the purposes of saving property. However, the use of the phrase 'reasonable measures' in relation to saving property suggests that the carrier cannot escape liability where the measures he took are solely for the purposes of a highly lucrative salvage operation.

In the event of deviation, the carrier does not escape liability for all loss, damage or delay in delivery that occurs after the deviation. He escapes liability only for that loss, damage or delay in delivery that results from the measures taken. This suggests that any detrimental effect on the cargo interest prior to the measures taken, or not attributable to the measures taken, will be the responsibility of the carrier.

Fire

The carrier is liable for loss or damage to the goods or delay in delivery caused by fire if it can be proved by the claimant that the fire arose from fault or neglect on the part of the carrier, his servants or agents (Art 5(4)(a)(i)), or from the fault or neglect of the carrier, his servants or agents, in taking all measures that could reasonably be required to put out the fire and avoid or mitigate its effects (Art 5(4)(a)(ii)).

Electronic data interchange (EDI) and the Hamburg Rules

Despite their radicalism, it is surprising that the Hamburg Rules do not address the issue of electronic shipping documents. It is not the case that the wonders of computer technology were unknown at the time, since the Montreal Protocol No 4 drafted in 1975 in respect of carriage by air makes provisions for 'other means' for preserving records of carriage.[48] Though Art 2 of the Hamburg Rules does not make specific mention of electronic documents, Art 14(3) provides that the signature on the bill of lading may be in handwriting, printed in facsimile, perforated, stamped or in symbols, or made by any other mechanical or electronic means, if not inconsistent with the law of the country where the bill of lading is issued. This suggests that (even in the absence of specific reference to electronic transport documents) accommodating an electronic document would not be a major obstacle since electronic signatures are normally attached to electronic documents. The only restriction placed by the

---

48 Article III, Additional Protocol No 4 to Amend the Convention for the Unification of Certain Rules relating to International Carriage by Air, signed at Warsaw on 12 October 1929 as amended by Protocol done at The Hague on 28 September 1955.

convention is that the law of the country where the bill of lading is issued must recognise electronic signatures.[49]

Contracting out

Reducing liability

Any stipulation in a contract of carriage by sea or any document evidencing a contract of carriage by sea that derogates from the provisions of the Hamburg Rules is null and void to the extent of its derogation (Art 23(1)).

What is of interest from the cargo owner's point of view is the combined effect of Art 23(3) and (4). Article 23(3) provides that the bill of lading or other document evidencing the contract of carriage by sea must state that it is subject to the Hamburg Rules and that clauses derogating from the Rules are null and void. Obviously, the intention behind this provision is to make the cargo owner aware that the contract of carriage is governed by the provisions of the Rules and thus alert him to his rights. Under Art 23(4), the carrier is placed under an obligation to compensate the claimant where he incurs loss either: (a) as a result of the omission of the statement as required under Art 23(3); or (b) as a result of the insertion of stipulations that are null and void under Art 23(1). Further, the carrier is also required to pay compensation for costs incurred by the claimant for the purposes of exercising his rights provided such costs are allowed by the law of the state where the proceedings take place. The objective of Art 23(4) is to put the cargo owner in the position he would have been had he known about the applicability of the Rules or about the status of the 'rogue' clause.

Article 23(4) poses problems if read in conjunction with Art 20(1) which stipulates a two-year limitation period for bringing any action. The following examples illustrate the problems that could arise.

Example A: What if a cargo owner discovers two years after the goods have been delivered that the bill of lading contains a term that is null and void under Art 23(1) of the Rules and as a result of which he has suffered loss? Had he known of the nature of the term, he would have brought an action and not suffered the loss. In this event, will he be able to institute proceedings even though it is time barred under Art 20(1)?

Example B: What if a cargo owner discovers two years after delivery of the goods that the bill of lading should have stated that it was governed by the provisions of the Rules and that it contains a stipulation that would have been contrary to Art 23(1) of the Rules as a result of which he has suffered loss? Would he be time barred under Art 20(1)?

A literal reading of Art 20(1) suggests that any action, including an action for loss and compensation under Art 23(4), would be time barred. This conclusion is justifiable where the cargo owner knows that the bill of lading is covered by the Rules; however, it seems to go against the spirit of Art 23(4). The seriousness of the problem is more obvious in Example B where the claimant is completely unaware that the contract of carriage is governed by the Hamburg Rules.

The answer is perhaps to be found in the rationale of this provision, which is

---

49   For more on electronic signatures, see Chapter 4.

essentially one of curbing gross disregard of the rights of the cargo owner. If seen in this light, it could be argued that the time limitation specified in Art 20(1) should not apply where actions are founded on Art 23(4).

Increasing responsibility

The carrier is at liberty to increase his responsibilities and obligations (Art 23(2)). The carrier's special agreement with the shipper in respect of obligations not imposed by the convention, or waiver of rights conferred on him by the convention, affects the actual carrier only to the extent that he has agreed to them expressly and in writing (Art 10(3)). Regardless of whether or not there is agreement between the carrier and the actual carrier, the carrier remains bound by any of the obligations or waivers which are a consequence of a special agreement between him and the shipper.

The carrier by agreement with the shipper can exceed the limits of liability set out by Art 6(1) of the Hamburg Rules (Art 6(4)).

Carrier's rights

As stated earlier, the Hamburg Rules are more of a self-contained code in making specific provisions to clarify some of the rights that the carrier may have against the consignee under the contract of carriage.

Freight

The Hamburg Rules do not make any general statement regarding the shipper's duty to pay freight under the contract of carriage. Generally, where goods are shipped under a bill of lading, the shipper is normally regarded as liable for freight. However, where the consignee is responsible for paying the freight, this must be indicated on the bill of lading (Art 15(1)(k)). Where the bill of lading does not indicate that freight is payable by the consignee or the extent to which the consignee is responsible for the payment of freight, it will be regarded as *prima facie* evidence that no freight is payable by the consignee. Upon transference to a third party taking in good faith, the evidence will be regarded as conclusive and proof to the contrary by the carrier will be inadmissible (Art 16(4)).

Demurrage

It seems from Art 16(4) that any demurrage incurred at the port of loading and payable by the consignee must be stated on the bill of lading. Where such a statement does not appear on the bill of lading, it will be regarded as *prima facie* evidence that no demurrage is payable by the consignee. Where the bill of lading is transferred to a third party in good faith, proof to the carrier will be inadmissible (Art 16(4)).

General average

The Rules do not prevent the application of the provisions in the contract of carriage or any national laws on the adjustment of general average. However, if the carrier is liable to the consignee under the Rules, he cannot ask for contribution in general average from the consignee (Art 24(2)).

Liability limits

The carrier is liable for loss resulting from loss or damage to the cargo as well as delay in delivery (Art 5), that is, when the goods have not been delivered at the port of discharge within the time expressly agreed upon in the contract of carriage (Art 5(2)). In the absence of an express agreement, the time of delivery is that which would be reasonable to expect of a diligent carrier having regard to the circumstances of the case.

The defences and limits of liability in respect of loss or damage to the goods or delay in delivery, whether the action is founded in contract or tort, are available to: (a) the carrier; and (b) the servant or agent of the carrier as long as such servant or agent proves that he acted within the scope of his employment (Art 7(2)).

There is no reference in Art 7(2) of the Hamburg Rules to independent contractors who might be employed by the carrier, unlike Art IV(2) *bis* of the Hague-Visby Rules which specifically excludes them. It may be possible to argue that since the phrase 'servants or agents' is not qualified or limited by anything in that paragraph, it would extend to include independent contractors; moreover, it is common knowledge in the shipping trade that independent contractors are generally employed, for instance, for loading and unloading the cargo. It may however be advisable, due to lack of clarity, to include specific clauses in the contract of carriage extending the availability of the immunities under the Rules to independent contractors.

Liability amount

The amount of limitation set by the Hamburg Rules is far above that set by the Hague Rules or the Hague-Visby Rules. The Special Drawing Right is the unit of account used. The carrier's liability is limited to an amount equivalent to 835 units of account per package or other shipping unit, or 2.5 units of account per kilogram of gross weight of the goods lost or damaged, whichever is the higher (Art 6(1)(a)).[50]

The liability of the carrier where there is delay in delivery is two and a half times the freight payable for the goods. This amount must not be greater than the total freight payable under the contract of carriage of sea (Art 6(1)(b)).

Calculation of liability – package or shipping unit

The limitation of liability available under the Hamburg Rules is calculated in terms of package or shipping unit. Where packages are sent in a container or a pallet, the number of packages in the article of transport must be enumerated on the bill of lading or contract of carriage. Failure to do so would result in the container being treated as a shipping unit for the purposes of calculating the carrier's liability (Art

---

50   See Table 13.1, Chapter 13, for a comparison of the liability amounts with other carriage conventions.

6(2)(a)). If the article of transport provided by the shipper is lost or damaged, it will be regarded as a shipping unit for calculating the amount of liability (Art 6(2)(b)).

Loss of limits

The carrier loses the entitlement to limit liability provided by Art 6 if it is proved that the loss, damage or delay in delivery was a consequence of the act or omission of the carrier done with the intent to cause such loss, damage or delay or recklessly and with knowledge that such loss, damage or delay would probably result (Art 8(1)). The servant or agent of the carrier loses the benefit of limitation of liability if it is proved that the loss, damage or delay in delivery resulted from act or omission on his part done with the intent to cause such loss, damage or delay, or recklessly and with knowledge that such loss, damage or delay would probably result (Art 8(2)).

The Hamburg Rules do not make it clear whether the courts should apply an objective or a subjective test to establish recklessness. Guidance may, however, be sought from the interpretation of similarly worded provisions in other international conventions.

Limitation period

The Hamburg Rules impose a two-year limitation period for bringing any action relating to carriage of goods whether it is a judicial or an arbitration proceeding (Art 20(1)). The adoption of a two-year period is a response to the criticism raised against the relatively short period imposed by Art III(6) of the Hague-Visby Rules. The one-year period of the Hague-Visby Rules was regarded as placing the cargo owner under an extremely difficult position, since it may not always be possible, at a practical level, to establish the identity of the person against whom judicial proceedings are to be instituted.

It is arguable whether the two-year limitation period introduced by the Hamburg Rules is really necessary since the matter of establishing the identity of the party against whom proceedings are to brought under the Rules is easier.

Shipper's responsibilities

Accuracy of particulars

The shipper is deemed to have guaranteed to the carrier the accuracy of particulars provided by him regarding the general nature of the goods – that is, details about marks, number, weight and quantity that are inserted in the bill of lading. Where the details provided are inaccurate and as a result of which the carrier suffers loss, the shipper must indemnify him for the losses suffered. The shipper's duty to indemnify subsists even where the bill of lading is transferred to a consignee or indorsee (Art 17).

Dangerous goods

Where the shipment consists of dangerous goods, the shipper is under an obligation to inform the carrier or actual carrier of the dangerous nature of the goods and the precautions that need to be taken in relation to the goods. Further, he is required to mark or label these goods in a suitable manner (Art 13(1)) and, where a bill of lading is issued, the particulars about the dangerous nature of the goods must be included in the document.

The shipper is liable for any loss to the carrier where he has failed to furnish the required information and the carrier or actual carrier does not otherwise have knowledge of the dangerous character of the goods (Art 13(2)(a)). It would be easy to establish knowledge on the part of the carrier where the goods are obviously dangerous – for instance, where the cargo contracted for carriage is dynamite – or commonly known to be dangerous in the trade. Where dangerous cargo is carried without the carrier's knowledge, he can unload, destroy or render it innocuous depending on the circumstances without incurring liability to the shipper (Art 13(2)(b)).

Where the carrier consents to the carriage of dangerous goods, he may unload, destroy or render them innocuous if they become an actual danger to life or property. The Rules do not place him under an obligation to pay compensation, except where there is an obligation to pay general average, or where he is in breach of the provisions of Art 5 (Art 13(4)).

Presumably, the shipper will be liable to the carrier for freight and any other costs he incurs in dealing with the dangerous cargo.

Shipper's undertaking to indemnify carrier

In practice, shippers generally require clean bills of lading from the carrier even though he may have had no reasonable means of checking the accuracy of the information entered by the shipper in the bill of lading. A carrier may, however, agree to issue a bill of lading with no reservations on an understanding from the shipper that he will be indemnified should he suffer any losses as result of issuing such a bill. Such agreements are valid between the carrier and the shipper provided the carrier has no intention to defraud a third party (Art 17(3)). The shipper's agreement to indemnify the carrier for his losses however is void against any third party (Art 17(2)).

Choice of forum

Judicial proceedings

Unlike the Hague-Visby Rules, the Hamburg Rules provide for choice of forum. Judicial proceedings can be initiated, at the option of the claimant, in a court which is competent according to the law of the state and within its jurisdiction, where one of the following places are located:

- the principal place of business of the defendant (Art 21(1)(a)); or
- the place of habitual residence of the defendant in the absence of a principal place of the defendant (Art 21(1)(a)); or
- the place where the contract was made, provided the defendant has a place of business, branch or agency through which the contract was made (Art 21(1)(b)); or
- the port of loading (Art 21(1)(c)); or
- the port of discharge (Art 21(1)(c)); or
- the place designated by the parties to the contract of carriage (Art 21(1)(d)); or

- the courts of any port or place of a contracting state where the carrying vessel or vessel for that ownership may have been arrested in accordance with the rules of that state and of international law (Art 21(2)(a)).

The Hamburg Rules give a wide choice of fora to the claimant, and it is inevitable that his choice will be guided by what is convenient for him, and tactics – for example, whether the choice of forum is likely to cause discomfort in terms of time and money to the defendant.[51] An issue that is likely to arise in this context is whether the defendant can invoke the doctrine of *forum non conveniens* in order to stay proceedings in the jurisdiction chosen by the claimant. The answer to this will depend largely on the interpretation of the words 'institute proceedings'[52] in Art 21. The words seem to suggest that a court seised of a case can decline jurisdiction on the ground of *forum non conveniens*.

Article 21 seems to undermine the aims of the Rules – namely, uniformity, certainty and better protection of the cargo owner, considered by the drafters as the weaker party. The issue of staying proceedings is dependent on the procedural rules of a forum and the views on *forum non conveniens* are not uniform across different jurisdictions. For instance, the doctrine is a recent import into English law. Given the divergencies, the emphasis in Art 21 on institution of proceedings is open to exploitation by the parties to contract of carriage.

The Hamburg Rules preserve the parties' agreement to choose a forum as long as the agreement is made after a claim has arisen (Art 21(5)).

Arbitration

The parties may, by agreement that is evidenced in writing, provide that any dispute that arises in relation to the contract of carriage be referred to arbitration (Art 22(1)). The parties may agree to submit to arbitration subsequent to a claim arising under the contract of carriage by sea (Art 22(6)).

The Hamburg Rules once again give a wide range of choice of arbitration forum ranging from the place of business of the defendant, the habitual residence of the defendant, the port of loading or discharge to a place designated in the arbitration agreement.[53]

The Hamburg Rules do not give the freedom to the arbitrators or the arbitration panel to decide the issue by applying *lex mercatoria* or principles of equity (*ex aequo et bono*) since Art 22(4) states that 'the arbitrator or arbitration tribunal shall apply the rules of this convention'.

Hamburg Rules – the future

The shipowning interests, regardless of the incorporation of Hamburg provisions in their maritime code, such as China and Australia, are still reluctant to make the Hamburg Rules in their entirety a part of their law, which suggests that they are still

---

51 See Chapter 16.
52 See Chapter 10 for the confusion raised by the use of the word 'brought' in the Warsaw Convention 1929 relating to carriage by air.
53 See Art 22(3).

holding on to the past with an iron grip. Objections based on high insurance costs as a result of increase in liability amounts and the dropping of negligence in navigation exception, and uncertainty in litigation are still vehemently rehearsed. The political origins of the instrument have also played a dominant role in its dismissal as an undesirable convention. The mandatory application of the Hamburg Rules to out-ward and inward shipments is arguably the factor most likely to make the force of the Hamburg Rules felt but this will take time, since the impact of the nations who are contracting states on world trade is negligible. However, it must be pointed out that a number of countries who have not ratified the Hamburg Rules have nonetheless amended their maritime codes to reflect some of the provisions of their maritime code. Notable amongst these are China, Australia and Sweden. In the meantime, another convention affecting carriage of goods by sea (considered briefly in the fol-lowing section) has appeared on the maritime scene which may displace the existing conventions and may succeed in harmonising the law on sea carriage in a more satisfactory manner.

THE UN CONVENTION ON CONTRACTS FOR THE INTERNATIONAL CARRIAGE OF GOODS WHOLLY OR PARTLY BY SEA – THE ROTTERDAM RULES

The United Nations adopted the text of its new convention, the UN Convention on Contracts for the International Carriage of Goods Wholly or Partly by Sea, on 11 December 2008.[54] The Resolution adopted by the General Assembly also recom-mended that the rules embodied in the Convention be called the 'Rotterdam Rules'. The Convention is not yet open for signature but the ceremony for opening of the signatures will be held on 23 September 2009. The Convention requires twenty ratifi-cations, acceptances, approvals or accessions to come into force.[55] Once a state becomes a party to this Convention it will have to denounce the other conventions it may be a party to (eg, the Hague Rules, the Hague-Visby Rules or the Hamburg Rules).[56]

The initial initiative for this Convention is traceable to 1996.[57] The Commission, informed of the gaps in the existing international legal framework in respect of bills of lading and seaway bills, their relation to the rights and obligations of the seller, the buyer and the parties providing financing, and the uncertainties caused by the emer-gence of electronic communication, asked the Secretariat to solicit views and possible solutions from states and international organisations (both inter-governmental and non-governmental) representing parties with an interest in international carriage of goods by sea. An invitation was extended to the CMI who expressed their willingness to co-operate. In 1998, they were charged with the task of obtaining and analysing

---

54   Resolution adopted by the General Assembly, A/Res/63/122, 2 February 2009.
55   Art 94.
56   Art 89.
57   See paras 210–14 UN Document A/CN 9 WG III WP21. See Girvin, 'The 37th Comité Maritime International Conference: a report' [2001] LMCLQ 406, for a review of the developments that took place in respect of the draft international transport convention. See also Sturley, 'The proposed amendments to the Carriage of Goods by Sea Act' (1996) 18 Houston Journal of International Law 609; Sturley, 'The proposed amendments to the Carriage of Goods by Sea Act: an update' (2000–01) 13 University of San Francisco Maritime LJ 1.

views from interested parties. In 2000, in a transport law colloquium jointly held by the Secretariat of UNCITRAL and CMI, the Commission supported their continued co-operation and requested they produce a report identifying the issues on which further work by the Commission was required. The report, put before the Commission in 2001, resulted in the setting up of the Working Group on Transport Law. The Secretariat, charged with preparing possible draft solutions for consideration by the Working Group on Transport Law in April 2002, produced the Preliminary Draft Instrument on the Carriage of Goods by Sea. This underwent various amendments and the final version was adopted in 2008.

Scope of application

The Rotterdam Rules apply to contracts of carriage where the port of loading or place of acceptance and the port of discharge or the place of delivery are located in different states.[58] There is no requirement that both the places/ports are in contracting states. It is sufficient if one of the states is a contracting state thus creating the potential for the Rules to have wide applicability. 'Contract of carriage', compared with other sea transport conventions, is defined widely to include not only carriage by sea but also carriage by other modes of transport used in addition to the sea carriage.[59] In other words, the Rotterdam Rules bring door-to-door transport within its ambit. For instance, where the goods are carried partly by sea and partly by road and the port of delivery is in a contracting state then the Rotterdam Rules will be applicable. There are however a number of international conventions relating to carriage by other modes.[60] In order to avoid potential conflicts the Rotterdam Rules make way for network liability. So where a non-sea leg part of the carriage would have attracted the application of a mandatory international convention (had a separate contract for that leg of the journey been made between the carrier and the shipper) and if the loss, damage or delay was caused in that segment then the carrier's liability will be determined by the other international convention.[61] A similar approach to combined transport is also to be found in other transport conventions.[62]

Unlike the Hague-Visby Rules, the Rotterdam Rules do not require any specific document (ie a bill of lading or similar document to be issued) to trigger its applicability. It applies to all transport documents[63] such as waybills and negotiable transport documents such as bills of lading, although the Rules refrain from using the phrase 'bill of lading'. Instead it adopts the phrase 'negotiable transport document' defined in Art 1(16) as 'a transport document that indicates, by wording such as "to order" or "negotiable" or other appropriate wording recognised by the law applicable

---

58 Art 5(1).
59 Art 1(1).
60 For further on this see Chapters 10, 11, 12 and 13.
61 Art 26. This type of liability is often called network liability.
62 See Chapter 13.
63 It is defined in Art 1(14) as follows:
   . . . means a document issued under a contract of carriage by the carrier that:
   (a) evidences the carrier's or a performing party's receipt of goods under a contract of carriage; and
   (b) evidences or contains a contract of carriage.

to the document, that the goods have been consigned to the order of the shipper, to the order of the consignee, or the bearer, and is not explicitly stated as being "non-negotiable" or "not negotiable" '. As in the Hague-Visby and Hamburg Rules, charterparties are excluded from the Rotterdam Rules.[64]

The Rotterdam Rules recognise electronic versions of transport documents (negotiable and non-negotiable) and where such electronic transport records[65] are used Art 9 requires that procedures for methods of issuing and transferring the record, ensuring their integrity, method for the holder to demonstrate that he is the holder, and confirmation of delivery to holder are in place. Further details or indications of acceptable procedures are not provided which is disappointing since it may result in divergent approaches in different jurisdictions. The transport industry itself is likely to take steps in harmonising the procedures. The CMI Rules on Electronic Bills of Lading or the BOLERO Rules may provide the necessary framework.[66]

One of the noticeable features of the Rotterdam Rules is the adoption of some new terminology[67] and a move away from hitherto established terms, eg, 'bill of lading' and 'actual carrier' being the most obvious. The adoption of new phrases may be viewed with some caution by states considering ratification since it has the potential to cause uncertainties in interpretation. Nonetheless it has to be said that this move away from established terminology found in the context of sea carriage is justifiable since the Rotterdam Rules go beyond simply sea carriage to include the utilisation of another mode of transport.

The Rotterdam Rules are not applicable to gratuitous carriage since Art 1(1) specifies that the contract made by a carrier for carrying goods is to be against payment of freight. Goods for the purposes of the Rules are merchandise, wares and articles of all kinds and also include the packing and containers that are supplied by the shipper.[68]

The Rotterdam Rules apply to all types of cargo. But like the Hamburg Rules there are specific provisions in respect of deck cargo and live animals. The carrier is allowed to carry goods on deck where:

- required by statutory rules and regulation;
- they are carried in containers or vehicles and the decks are adequately fitted for carrying these containers and vehicles;

---

64 Art 6. Note that the Rotterdam Rules make a distinction between liner transportation and volume contract. Liner transportation, according to Art 1(3), refers to transportation service that is offered to the public through publication or similar means and includes transportation by ships operating on a regular schedule between specified ports in accordance with publicly available timetable of sailing dates. Volume contract, on the other hand, according to Art 1(2) means a contract of carriage that provides for carriage of a specified quantity of goods in a series of shipments during an agreed period of time.

65 Art 1(17) defines electronic transport record as information in one or more messages issued by electronic communication under a contract of carriage by a carrier, including information logically associated with the electronic transport record by attachments or otherwise linked to the electronic transport record contemporaneously with or subsequent to its issue by the carrier, so as to become part of the electronic transport record, that: (a) evidences the carrier's or a performing party's receipt of goods under a contract of carriage; and (b) evidences or contains a contract of carriage.

66 See Chapter 6.

67 See p 309 on 'performing party'.

68 Art 1(26).

- the shipper and carrier have agreed in their contract of carriage; or
- there is usage or practice to do so in a particular trade.[69]

In the event of permitted deck carriage the carrier is not liable for any loss or damage to the goods that are caused by the special risks that are inherent in the carriage of deck cargo. But where there is unauthorised deck carriage the carrier will lose his entitlement to the list of defences provided by Art 17 if the loss or damage to the goods have been caused as a result of deck carriage. To illustrate, if sacks of sand strapped to pallets are carried on deck, in the absence of usage or agreement, and are lost in heavy seas the carrier will not be entitled to raise, for instance, the defence of perils, dangers and accidents of the sea allowed under Art 17(3)(b).

In respect of live animals, Art 81 permits the exclusion or limitation of liability but this will be ineffective if the claimant proves that loss, damage or delay in delivery resulted from an act or omission of carrier or those who acted on his behalf 'done with the intent to cause such loss of or damage to the goods or such loss due to delay or done recklessly and with knowledge that such loss or damage or such loss due to delay would probably result'. The language used is largely similar to that found in Art 25 of Warsaw Convention as amended by the Hague Protocol and no doubt the jurisprudence that has developed in relation to that provision will be of some relevance.[70]

Carrier's responsibilities, liabilities and rights

As will become apparent from the following paragraphs, the framework adopted by the Rotterdam Rules is influenced by the existing sea carriage conventions, the Hague-Visby Rules and the Hamburg Rules, and other transport conventions such as the CIM Rules on rail transportation.[71] The result certainly is an odd mixture that may indeed act as a disincentive when it comes to the question of its ratification. It will be interesting to monitor over the next few years the reception of the Rotterdam Rules by the cargo owning interests and shipowning interests since, as will become more apparent below, the carrier seems to be placed under a fairly onerous burden even though a number of defences are available to him.

Definition of carrier

Like the Hamburg Rules, a distinction is drawn between a 'carrier' and an 'actual carrier', except the Rotterdam Rules use the phrase 'performing party' which is wider in ambit. A carrier is 'a person who enters into a contract of carriage with a shipper'.[72] This is designed to include a range of persons from the freight forwarder and charterer to the shipowner who signs the contract of carriage. A performing party, on the other hand, is one 'who performs or undertakes to perform any of the carrier's obligation with respect to the receipt, loading, handling, stowage, carriage, care, unloading

---

69   See Art 25 (1) (a)–(c).
70   See Chapter 10.
71   See Chapter 12 for further on the CIM Rules.
72   Art 1(2)(5).

or delivery of the goods directly or indirectly, at the carrier's request or under the carrier's supervision or control'.[73] This is designed to include a whole range of actors, from stevedores and providers of warehousing facilities to other transport operators. Performing party is classified further into a 'maritime performing party' and refers to a party who performs any of the carrier's obligations at the port of loading or at the port of discharge. For instance, a party who offers lightering services to the carrier would be regarded as a maritime performing party. It is also possible that an inland carrier might offer services exclusively within the port area, for instance where the goods have to be transported from a ship to a warehouse at the perimeters of the port. Such a carrier would also be regarded as a maritime performing party according to Art 1(2)(7).[74]

Responsibilities and liabilities of carrier and maritime performing party

The carrier is under an obligation to carry the goods to its destination and deliver them to the consignee.[75] The period of responsibility runs from the time the goods are received to the time they are delivered.[76] The question of when goods have been received or delivered will depend on the circumstances. Regulations at the place of delivery or place of receipt may determine when these events occur. So for instance, if the regulations require that the goods be collected for transportation from an authority then the carrier will assume responsibility from the moment he collects from that authority. In the absence of such regulations the parties may agree the precise time and location for receipt or delivery.[77]

Two positive obligations are imposed on the carrier by the Rotterdam Rules that are reminiscent of the carrier's obligations under the Hague-Visby Rules.[78] One is in relation to care of cargo, the other in relation to seaworthiness. As for care of cargo the carrier, during his period of responsibility, must properly and carefully receive, load, handle, stow, carry, keep and care for, unload and deliver the goods.[79] The obligation in respect of seaworthiness refers to both the physical safety of the ship and cargoworthiness, that is the state of the ship to carry the cargo. The carrier is required to exercise due diligence in making the ship[80] seaworthy, properly crew and equip it and ensure that the parts of the ship in which the goods are carried or containers[81] supplied by the ship are fit and safe for their reception, carriage and preservation.[82] This obligation to exercise due diligence, unlike the Hague-Visby Rules, is a continuous obligation – that is, the obligation runs from before, the beginning and *during* the voyage.[83] This is a major departure and likely to be perceived as heavily weighted

---

73   Art 1(2)(6).
74   For further on the liability of the carrier and the maritime performing party see below.
75   Art 11.
76   Art 12.
77   Ibid.
78   See Chapter 8.
79   Art 13(1).
80   'Ship' is defined in Art 1(25) as any vessel used to carry goods by sea.
81   'Container' is defined in Art 1(26) as any types of container, transportable tank or flat, swap-body, or any similar unit load used to consolidate goods, and any equipment ancillary to such unit load.
82   Art 14.
83   *Ibid.*

against the carrier. This continuous obligation will be reflected in higher insurance costs, thus resulting in higher freight rates. In light of the current economic downturn carriers in shipowning countries are highly likely to lobby strongly against the Rotterdam Rules. Higher insurance cost was a reason often advanced by ship-owning states against the Hamburg Rules.

As for the carrier's liability, the approach adopted may come across as a strange combination of the liability schemes found in the Hamburg Rules and the Hague-Visby Rules. Like the Hamburg Rules, the carrier is liable for loss or damage to the goods or delay in delivery during his period of responsibility. The onus is on the carrier to prove that the cause or one of the causes of the loss, damage, or delay is not attributable to his fault or the fault of the performing party, the ship's crew or master of employees, be they his or the performing party's.[84] But then Art 17(3) gives the carrier an opportunity to point to one of the events listed in it to relieve himself of liability. This is an alternative to proving absence of fault. The list contained in Art 17(3) largely resembles Art IV(2) of the Hague-Visby Rules but does not include the highly criticised negligence in navigation or management of ship and the catch-all exception found in Art IV(2). There are some innovative provisions as well, such as the one on reasonable measures to avoid damage to the environment. Equally some of the language used in the defences is couched in more modern language, for instance there is no reference to 'restraint of princes'. Instead it is 'interference by or impedi-ments created by government, public authorities, rulers . . .'.[85]

Like the Hamburg Rules, there is no specific provision on deviation. The long list of defences in Art 17(3) however provides for saving or attempting to save life at sea (Art 17(3)(l)) and reasonable measures to save or attempt to save property at sea (Art 17(3)(m)). The question of whether the defences or limitations provided by the Rotterdam Rules are available in the event of deviation is settled in favour of the carrier by Art 24 which provides:

> When pursuant to applicable law a deviation constitutes a breach of the carrier's obliga-tions, such deviation in itself shall not deprive the carrier or a maritime performing party of any defences or limitation of this Convention, except to the extent provided in article 61.[86]

Seaworthiness however is a fundamental obligation on the carrier's part in the Rotterdam Rules. So, in spite of the defences available to carrier, if the claimant proves that unseaworthiness, improper crewing, equipping and supplying of the ship, the lack of fitness of the containers or parts of the ship for the reception and carriage of the goods caused or contributed to the loss, damage or delay, the carrier will be liable unless he can show otherwise. The onus is then on the carrier to show, for instance, that he had exercised due diligence in providing a seaworthy ship or that it was not poor equipping of the ship that caused the loss.[87]

The carrier's liability includes the acts and omission of the performing party as well as the employees of the performing party.[88] The maritime performing party is also subject to the obligations and liabilities imposed on the carrier. In return however

---

84   Arts 17(1) and (2).
85   Art 17(2)(e).
86   See p 313 on loss of limitation of liability.
87   Art 17(5).
88   Arts 18(a) and (c)

he is entitled to the carrier's defences and limits of liability.[89] The maritime performing party only assumes these obligations provided he received the goods in a contracting state or delivered them in a contracting state or performed any of the obligations in respect of the goods in a contracting state and the occurrence that caused the loss, damage or delay took place:

- during the period between the arrival of the goods at the port of loading of the ship and their departure from the port of the discharge;
- while the maritime performing party of the goods had custody of the goods; or
- at any other time to the extent that it was participating in the performance of any of the activities contemplated by the contract of carriage.[90]

By way of illustration, a stevedore who loads in a non-contracting state would not be subject to the Rotterdam Rules' scheme of obligations and liabilities, whereas a stevedore loading in a contracting state who damages the goods in the process of loading (that is while the goods are in his custody) would be liable under the Rotterdam Rules.

The Rotterdam Rules also impart certain rights to the carrier. For instance, the shipper's[91] failure to provide information regarding dangerous goods, to furnish particulars that are accurate, to pack the goods properly and lash the contents of the container properly, as a result of which the carrier suffers loss or damage means that the shipper will be liable to the carrier.[92]

Documentary responsibilities

In the absence of agreement or custom, usage or practice of the trade the shipper is entitled to a non-negotiable transport document or electronic record or a negotiable transport document or electronic record.[93] Article 36 expects such documents to contain a number of particulars. These include the description of the goods, the leading marks for identification, number of packages, name and address of carrier,[94] date on which goods received for carriage or date on which date loaded or date of issue of transport record, apparent order and condition of goods (which are to be based on a reasonable external inspection of the packaged goods at the time goods delivered for carriage and any additional inspection conducted by the carrier or other performing party at the time the transport document is issued).[95]

The Rotterdam Rules require that the transport document issued is signed and

---

89 Art 19(1).
90 Art 19(2).
91 'Shipper' is defined in Art 1(8) as a person that enters into a contract of carriage with a carrier. There is a further classification introduced by the Rules and that is a 'documentary shipper' defined in Art 1(9) as a person, other than the shipper, that accepts to be named as the 'shipper' in the transport document or electronic transport record. This may become relevant, for instance, in extending right of control over the goods to persons other than the shipper. See p 315.
92 See Arts 27, 29, 30, 31 and 32.
93 Art 35.
94 In the absence of not including the identity of the carrier, Art 37 addresses the issue of how the carrier is to be identified. If the ship's name is indicated in the contract particulars then the registered owner of the ship will be presumed to be the owner. See Chapter 8.
95 See Art 36 for a full list of particulars. See also Art 31.

where an electronic transport record is issued the signature is to be an electronic signature.[96] The carrier has the opportunity to qualify the information included in the transport document or record, according to Art 40. So he can indicate that he does not assume responsibility for the accuracy of the information where he has actual knowledge or reasonable ground to believe that a material statement made in the document or record is false or misleading.[97] The particulars on the transport document/record are to be treated as *prima facie* evidence but proof to the contrary will be inadmissible if they are transferred to an endorsee or consignee acting in good faith.[98]

Shipper's liabilities

As made apparent in the section of carrier's liabilities and rights, the shipper has a number of obligations in respect of packing, providing particulars, informing the carrier of the dangerous nature of the goods and marking them suitably. Any loss or damage caused as a result of insufficiency or inaccuracy will result in the shipper becoming liable. The onus for proving loss or damage as a result of the breach of the obligations by the shipper is on the carrier.[99] If the shipper can establish that one of the cause or causes is not attributable to its fault then, according to Art 30(2), he will be relieved of all liability or part of the liability. The liability of the shipper includes the acts or omissions of his employees, agents and sub-contractors to whom the performance of any of the obligations has been entrusted. This however does not include the acts or omissions of the carrier or the performing party acting on behalf of the carrier to whom the shipper has entrusted the performance of his obligations.[100]

As stated earlier (see fn 92) the Rotterdam Rules recognise a documentary shipper. This documentary shipper is subject to the shipper's obligations and liabilities but can also avail of the rights and defences available to the shipper.

Contracting out

Any stipulation that indirectly or directly excludes or limits the obligations or liability of the carrier or the maritime performing party for breach of an obligation under the Rotterdam Rules is void.[101]

Liability limits

The amount of limitation set by the Rotterdam Rules is above that of the Hamburg Rules. The SDR is the unit of account and the carrier's liability is limited to an amount equivalent to 875 units of account per package or other shipping unit, or 3 units of account per kilogram of the gross weight.[102] Where the shipper has declared the value

---

96   Art 38. For more on electronic signature see Chapter 4.
97   Art 40(1).
98   See Art 41.
99   Art 30(1).
100 Art 34.
101 Art 79. Note that there are special rules for live animals and particular goods (Art 81) and volume contracts (Art 82).
102 Initially the Hague-Visby Rules liability amount was suggested but it met with a great deal of opposition.

of the goods or when a higher amount than the amount of limitation of liability has been agreed between the carrier and the shipper the liability amounts set by Art 59 do not apply.

Economic loss caused due to delay in delivery is recognised by the Rotterdam Rules and liability for such loss due to delay is limited to an amount equivalent to two and one-half times the freight payable on the goods delayed.[103]

The defences and limits set out in the Rotterdam Rules are available to the carrier as well as others such as the maritime performing party, the master, crew and employees of the maritime performing party and are applicable regardless of whether the action is founded in contract, tort or otherwise.[104]

Calculation of liability – package or shipping unit

Liability is calculated in terms of shipping unit or package and in this it is no different from the Hamburg Rules. So if goods are carried in containers, for instance, it is important to enumerate the number of units packed within the containers, otherwise the container will be treated as one unit.[105]

Loss of liability limits

The entitlement to limit liability is however lost in certain circumstances: for instance where the claimant proves that the loss resulting from a breach of the obligations under the Rules is attributable to a personal act or omission of the person (eg carrier, master or crew, performing party) claiming a right to limit done with the intent to cause such loss or recklessly and with knowledge that such loss would probably result.[106] This is equally the case where there is delay in delivery.[107]

Time limitation

The time for instituting an action, be it arbitral or judicial, is no different from the Hamburg Rules. It is two years[108] although the party against whom the claim is brought can extend the period during the running of the period with a declaration to the claimant. There is no limit placed on the number of times such an extension may be extended further.[109]

The period for the purposes of Art 62(1) commences from the day the carrier has delivered the goods. It is possible that the carrier may have delivered only part of the goods or has delivered no goods at all. In these circumstances the commencement is the last day on which the goods should have been delivered.[110] Where there is an

---

103   Art 60.
104   Art 4.
105   See Chapter 8 on calculating liability where containers are used.
106   Art 61(1).
107   Art 61(2). See Chapter 10 on interpretation of a similarly worded provision.
108   Art 62(1).
109   Art 63.
110   Art 62(2).

action for indemnity it can be instituted after the two year limit set by Art 62(1) but within the time allowed by the law applicable of the jurisdiction where the action is brought or within 'ninety days commencing from the day when the person instituting the action for indemnity has either settled the claim or has been served with the process in the action against itself'.[111] This provision is no different from the Hamburg Rules.[112]

Choice of forum

Like the Hamburg Rules the Rotterdam Rules provide for a choice of forum for both judicial and arbitral proceedings. For judicial proceedings, according to Art 66 an action against the carrier can be instituted in a court which is competent according to the law of the state and within its jurisdiction, where one of the following places are located:

- The domicile of the carrier; (Art 66(a))
- The place of receipt agreed in the contract of carriage; (Art 66(a))
- The place of delivery agreed in the contract of carriage; (Art 66(a))
- The port where the goods are initially loaded or the port where the goods are finally discharged from the ship; (Art 66(a)) or
- The competent court or courts designated by agreement between the shipper and the carrier (Art 66(b)).[113]

As for an action against the maritime contracting party the choice is more limited and restricted to the domicile of the maritime performing party or the ports where the goods are received/delivered by the maritime performing party or the port in which the maritime performing party performs its activities in relation to the goods.[114]

When it comes to arbitral proceedings there is a number of choices available and these include the place designated in the arbitration agreement, or the place of the domicile of the carrier, the place of receipt/delivery agreed in the contract of carriage or the port where goods are loaded/discharged from the ship.[115]

Innovative provisions

The Rotterdam Rules also focus on areas hitherto unaddressed by the other sea transport conventions. These relate to delivery, rights of control and transfer of rights and are contained in Chapters 9, 10 and 11 respectively. These provisions are considered in brief in this section.

Taking delivery first, the consignee is placed under an obligation to accept

---

111 Art 64(b).
112 See Art 20(5).
113 Note that the court chosen by agreement is to be regarded as exclusive jurisdiction only in volume contracts (Art 67). A party who is not a party to the volume contract is bound by an exclusive jurisdiction clause only if it is included in the transport document/record or he has notice or the court is one of the places designated in Art 66(a) or the law of the court seised recognises that he may be bound by the exclusive choice of court agreement.
114 Art 68.
115 Art 75(1)–(3). Note also the provisions in respect of volume contracts in Art 75(4).

delivery[116] and also acknowledge receipt of the goods if the carrier or performing party so require.[117] Failure to provide this receipt may result in non-delivery.[118] The delivery must be at the time and place agreed although the rules on how delivery is to be effected and to whom will depend on the type of transport document. So where a negotiable transport document has been issued, delivery will take place upon surrender of the negotiable transport document and the holder[119] of the document properly identifying itself.[120] Where the transport document is a non-negotiable transport document that requires surrender delivery can take place when the consignee properly identifies itself and against the surrender of the non-negotiable transport document.[121]

It is possible that goods remain undelivered due to a number of reasons: eg, where the consignee or holder of the transport document has not been able to meet the stipulations required for delivery[122] or the regulations at the port of discharge disallows the delivery of the goods to the consignee. In such circumstances Art 48 enables the carrier to take a number of actions in respect of the goods such as sell or destroy the goods or warehouse the goods at the risk of the person entitled to the goods provided he gives reasonable notice of the intended action.[123]

The Rotterdam Rules also impart some rights of control over the goods in limited circumstances and these include the right to replace the consignee by any other person, including the controlling party, or the right to obtain delivery at a scheduled port during the carrier's entire period of responsibility.[124] The controlling party is normally the shipper unless at the time of the conclusion of the carriage another person has been nominated by the shipper. The other persons for these purposes are the documentary shipper or the consignee. The right of control can however be transferred to another person but for it to become effective it has to be notified to the carrier. Certain formalities also need to be followed by the controlling party in order to exercise this right of control and these are to be found in Art 51(2)–(4). The right of control over the goods while they are in the carrier's hands is not an entirely new concept and is also found in non-sea transport conventions.[125]

Chapter 11 of the Rules focuses on how to effect the transfer of rights incorporated into a negotiable transport document/electronic record to another. It is no different from the processes found for transferring bills of lading in English law. For instance, according to Art 57(1) an order document can be transferred through endorsement to

---

116   Art 43.
117   Art 44.
118   *Ibid.*
119   Holder is defined in Art 1(10) as
   (a) A person that is in possession of a negotiable transport document; and (i) if the document is an order document, is identified in it as the shipper or the consignee, or is the person to which the document is duly endorsed; or (ii) if the document is a blank endorsed order document or bearer document, is the bearer thereof; or
   (b) The person to which a negotiable transport document has been issued or transferred in accordance with the procedures referred to in Article 9, paragraph 1.
120   Art 45(1).
121   Art 46, see also Art 45 for delivery when no negotiable transport document or negotiable electronic transport is issued.
122   See Arts 45, 46 and 47.
123   Art 48(1)–(3).
124   Art 50.
125   See Chapters 11 and 12.

a person or in blank. In the case of a negotiable electronic transport record the transfer will have to follow the procedures that have been put in place for electronic transport records.[126]

CONCLUSION

It is still too early to predict whether the Rotterdam Rules will meet with a warm reception from the shipowning interests since there are a number of provisions that are weighted against these interests – for instance, the continuing obligation to exercise due diligence in relation to the seaworthiness of the ship and the higher liability limits. Regardless, the Rotterdam Rules also have a number of positive features, for example, their applicability to electronic versions of transport documents and the inclusion of important incidents relating to carriage of goods such as delivery.

126   See Chapter 6 above.

Table 9.1 Material differences between the Hague regime (Hague and Hague-Visby Rules) and the Hamburg Rules

Specific issues	Hague Rules	Hague-Visby Rules	Hamburg Rules	Rotterdam Rules*
Entry into force	2 June 1931	23 June 1977 Modifications (slight) signed Brussels 21 December 1979	1 November 1992	
Applicability (documents)	• Bills of lading or similar document of title • Bills of lading issued pursuant to charterparty • Other documents (eg, waybills) if expressly incorporated (NB can apply to charterparties where there is express incorporation)	Same as Hague Rules	All types of contracts of carriage – eg: • waybills • short sea notes • bills of lading • bills of lading issued pursuant to charterparty (does not apply to charterparties, unless expressly incorporated)	All types of contracts of carriage – e.g: • waybills • negotiable transport document • electronic transport records Does not apply to charterparties
Applicability (voyages)	Applies to bills of lading where carriage is between ports in two different States if: • the bill of lading is issued in a Contracting State • carriage is from a port in a Contracting State • the contract contained in or evidenced by the bill of lading specifies Rules to govern the contract	Same as Hague Rules	Applies if: • outbound voyage is from a Contracting State • inbound voyage is to a Contracting State • an optional port situated in a Contracting State and named in the contract of carriage becomes the actual port of discharge	Applies if: • port of loading, or place of acceptance, or place of discharge or place of delivery located in a contracting state

Table 9.1 Continued

	• the contract contained in or evidenced by the bill of lading specifies that the laws of a state giving effect to the Rules are to govern the contract		• the bill of lading or document evidencing the contract of carriage is issued in a contracting state • the Rules are incorporated by the parties • there is provision that the laws of a state giving effect to the Rules are to govern the contract	
Applicability (cargo)	Does not apply to: • deck cargo 　○ where in fact stowed on deck, and 　○ made explicit on the face of the bill of lading • live animals • particular cargo	Same as Hague Rules	Applies to all types of cargo (including deck cargo and live animals). Cargo qualifies as deck cargo on the basis of: • usage • statutory rules • special agreement	Applies to all types of cargo (including deck cargo and live animals). Cargo qualifies as deck cargo on the basis of: • statutory requirement • goods in containers or vehicles and decks specifically fitted to carry these • usage, practice in trade • agreement (*Note*: carrier not liable for loss or damage or delay if caused by special risks inherent to such carriage)
Carrier's obligations in respect of ship, cargo and voyage	Must exercise due diligence to:	Same as Hague Rules		Must exercise due diligence before, at the beginning and *during* voyage to:

Specific issues	Hague Rules	Hague-Visby Rules	Hamburg Rules	Rotterdam Rules*
	• make the ship seaworthy • properly man, equip and supply the ship • make holds, refrigerating, etc, fit for reception, carriage and preservation of cargo Must properly and carefully: • load, handle, stow, carry, keep, care for and discharge goods Must pursue the contract voyage, unless deviation is: • to save life or property at sea • reasonable			• make and keep ship seaworthy; • properly crew, equip and supply ship and keep ship so crewed, equipped and supplied throughout voyage • make and keep holds and all other parts of ship in which goods carried and any containers supplied by the carrier in or upon which the goods are carried fit and safe for their reception, carriage and preservation
Carrier's documentary responsibilities	The carrier is to issue a bill of lading on demand by the shipper, showing: • leading marks • number of packages or pieces • quantity/weight of goods • apparent order and condition of goods	Same as Hague Rules	The carrier, on demand by the shipper, is to issue a bill of lading, showing details enumerated in Art 15. The document must state that the contract of carriage is governed by the Rules, which nullify any stipulations derogating from the Convention to the detriment of the shipper or consignee (see 'Carrier liability', below)	Shipper entitled to a non-negotiable transport document or electronic record or a negotiable transport record or electronic document. These documents to contain a number of particulars such as description of goods, name/address of carrier, apparent order and condition of goods

Table 9.1 Continued

Carrier's period of responsibility	From the time when goods are loaded to the time when they are discharged from the ship – interpreted as 'tackle to tackle'	Same as Hague Rules	From the time the carrier is in charge at the port of loading until the port of discharge	From the time when goods are received for carriage to the time when goods are delivered
Carrier liability	Liable for loss of or damage to cargo where he has not exercised his obligations in respect of seaworthiness, cargoworthiness and cargo management (see above). Note the long list of defences available to the carrier under Art IV NB: the responsibility in respect of seaworthiness (including cargoworthiness) is an overriding obligation, such that the carrier loses the benefit of immunities available under Art IV (see below)	Same as Hague Rules	• A uniform test of liability is adopted. The carrier is presumed to be at fault for loss of, damage to or delay in delivery of cargo unless he proves that he or his servants or agents took all measures that they could reasonably be required to in order to avoid the occurrence and its consequences. (See 'Carrier's defences immunities below.) • The carrier to compensate where a claimant has incurred loss as a result of the insertion of a clause in the contract deemed null and void, or as a result of the omission of a statement that carriage is subject to the Convention which nullifies any stipulation derogating from the Convention to the detriment of shipper or consignee	• Carrier presumed to be at fault for loss of damage or delay in delivery unless he proves that the causes of loss, damage or delay not attributable to his fault or of any person (master, crew of ship, performing party, employees of carrier or performing party, or any other person who performs or undertakes any of the carrier's obligations) Carrier allowed a number of defences (See Carrier's defences immunities below).

Specific issues	Hague Rules	Hague-Visby Rules	Hamburg Rules	Rotterdam Rules*
Burden of proof	No uniform burden, with the result that different jurisdictions have interpreted burden of proof variously	Same as Hague Rules	On the carrier, except in cases of loss, damage or delay in delivery due to fire, when the burden shifts to the claimant	On carrier
Carrier's defences/ immunities	A long list of immunities are allowed to the carrier, ranging from loss or damage caused due to any act, neglect or default of a master, mariner, pilot or the servants of the carrier in the navigation or management of the ship; act of God; riots and civil commotions; fire; to latent defects not discoverable by due diligence (see Art IV(2); also Art IV(1)).	Same as Hague Rules	No list of immunities comparable to the Hague Rules. However, there are a few specific provisions: • the carrier is not liable, except in general average, where loss, damage or delay in delivery is a result of measures to save life or from reasonable measures to save property at sea; • the carrier is not liable for loss, damage or delay in delivery caused by fire unless the claimant proves that the fire was a consequence of the carrier's, servant's, or agent's fault or neglect in taking all reasonable measures to put out the fire or mitigate its effects;	A list of defences provided. These are act of God; perils, dangers, and accidents of the sea or navigable waters; wars, hostilities, armed conflict, piracy, terrorisms, riots, civil commotions; quarantine restrictions; interference or impediments created by governments, public authorities, rulers, or people including detention, arrest or seizure (not attributable to carrier or performing party etc: see 'Carrier liability' above for full list); strikes, lock-outs; fire on the ship; latent defects not discoverable by due diligence; act or omission of the shipper, loading, handling, stowing or unloading

Table 9.1 Continued

performed by the shipper; wastage in bulk or weight, inherent defect, vice of the goods insufficient, defective packing by shipper; saving or attempting to save life at sea; reasonable measures to save or attempt to save property at sea; reasonable measures to avoid or attempt to avoid damage to the environment; sacrifice of goods for preserving human life or other property; measures taken in respect of dangerous goods (see Arts 15, 16, 17(2) and (3))

• In respect of live animals, exclusion or limitation of liability permitted unless claimant proves that loss, damage or delay resulted from an act/omission of carrier or others acting on his behalf, done with intent to cause such loss/damage or done recklessly and done with knowledge that such loss or damage would probably result

• in the case of live animals, the carrier is not liable if he can show that he complied with instructions given by the shippers, and the loss, damage or delay in delivery was caused by special risks inherent in the kind of cargo being carried

Specific issues	Hague Rules	Hague-Visby Rules	Hamburg Rules	Rotterdam Rules*
Shipper's responsibilities	• To guarantee the accuracy of marks, number, quantity and weight • To inform the carrier of any dangerous nature of the goods	Same as Hague Rules	• To guarantee the accuracy of marks, number, weight and quantity • To inform the carrier of any dangerous nature of the goods and to mark them in a suitable manner; particulars of the dangerous nature of the goods are to be included on the bill of lading	• To deliver goods ready for carriage and in such condition as to withstand journey • If obligations in respect of loading and stowing undertaken by shipper then these to be done properly and carefully • Packing of container or vehicle to be done properly and carefully • To provide information, instructions and documents in a timely manner • To inform carrier of dangerous nature or character of goods
Freight			The carrier can claim freight from the consignee where so indicated on the bill of lading	Carrier cannot assert right to freight against holder of transport document or consignee where contract particulars state 'freight prepaid'. This, however, does not apply where holder/consignee is shipper

Table 9.1 Continued

Demurrage			The carrier can claim demurrage incurred at the port of loading from consignee where so indicated on the bill of lading	• Shipper liable to carrier where loss or damage caused due to failure to inform carrier of dangerous nature of goods and carrier or performing party does not otherwise have knowledge; • Shipper liable where carrier suffers, loss or damage due to shipper's failure to label dangerous goods; • Shipper liable for inaccuracy/insufficiency of information; • Shipper's liability extends to the acts/omissions of his employees, agents and sub-contractors to whom performance of any obligation is entrusted
Carrier's right to indemnity, costs and damages	• The shipper is to indemnify for loss, damage and expenses incurred from inaccurate particulars. (It is unclear whether this right exists against a consignee or endorsee) • The shipper is to pay damages and expenses arising directly or indirectly from the shipment of dangerous cargo without the carrier's consent	Same as Hague Rules	• The shipper is to indemnify for loss suffered due to the inaccuracy of any particulars. Duty subsists even where the bill of lading is transferred to a consignee or endorsee • The shipper is liable for loss suffered by the carrier where the carrier is unaware of any dangerous nature of the cargo • There is an agreement between the shipper and carrier, void against any third party, to indemnify the carrier for any losses suffered from issuing a clean bill of lading	

Specific issues	Hague Rules	Hague-Visby Rules	Hamburg Rules	Rotterdam Rules*
Time limitation	One year after: • delivery of the goods; or • the date when the goods should have been delivered	Same as Hague Rules	Two years from: • the date of delivery; or • the last day when the goods should have been delivered	Two years from: • the date of delivery; or • the last day when goods should have been delivered • Party against whom claim brought may extend period
Liability amount	100 Pounds Sterling per package/unit for loss or damage	666.67 SDRs per package or unit, or 2 SDRs per kilogram of gross weight of goods lost or damaged	835 SDRs per package or unit, or 2.5 SDRs per kilogram of gross weight of goods lost or damaged	875 SDRs per package or unit or 3 SDRs per kilogram of gross weight

Availability of defences and B limitation	Available to the carrier. It is not stated whether defences available when an action is founded in contract or in tort	• Defences and limits of liability are available whether an action is founded in contract or in tort
		• Available to:
		  ○ the carrier
		  ○ the servant or agent of the carrier, provided the servant or agent is not an independent contractor
			• Defences and limits of liability are available whether an action is founded in contract or in tort
			• Available to:
			  ○ the carrier
			  ○ the servant or agent of the carrier, provided the servant or agent acted within the scope of employment
				• Defences and limits of liability are available whether an action is founded in contract, tort or otherwise
				• Available to
				  ○ the carrier or maritime performing party
				  ○ master, crew or any other person performing services on board ship
				  ○ employees of carrier or maritime performing party

Table 9.1 Continued

Loss of limitation		
• The carrier loses entitlement to limit liability where it is proved that the loss, damage or delay in delivery was a consequence of an act or omission of the carrier done with intent to cause such loss, damage or delay or recklessly and with knowledge that such loss, damage or delay would probably result. • The above applies to a servant or agent who is not an independent contractor	• The carrier loses benefit of limitation where it is proved that the damage occurred from an act or omission of the carrier done with intent to cause damage or recklessly and with knowledge that damage would probably result. • The above applies to a servant or agent who is not an independent contractor. • In case of deck cargo, the carrier loses limits where cargo is carried on deck contrary to express agreement or, in the absence of usage, agreement or statutory rules, and it can be shown that the loss, damage or delay occurred from an act or omission of the carrier done with intent to cause such loss, damage or delay or recklessly and with knowledge that such loss, damage or delay probably result	• Entitlement to benefit of limitation of liability is lost where it is proved that the loss, damage, or delay in delivery was a consequence of an act or omission of the carrier or others (performing party, master/crew of ship, employees of carrier/performing party, any other person who performs or undertakes to perform any of carrier's obligations) done with intent to cause loss/delay or recklessly and with knowledge that such loss/delay would probably result. • In case of unauthorised carriage of deck cargo carrier loses entitlement to defences provided in Art 17

Specific issues	Hague Rules	Hague-Visby Rules	Hamburg Rules	Rotterdam Rules*
Jurisdiction			At the option of the claimant, proceedings can be initiated in a competent court located in: • the defendant's principal place of business • the defendant's habitual place of residence, in the absence of a principal place of business • the place where the contract was made, provided the defendant has a place of business, branch or agency through which the contract was made • the port of loading • the port of discharge • the place designated by parties to the contract of carriage • the place where the carrying vessel or another vessel of the same ownership has been arrested	Proceedings against carrier can be instituted in a competent court at: • domicile of carrier • place of receipt agreed in contract of carriage • place of delivery agreed in contract of carriage • port where goods initially loaded • port where goods finally discharged from ship Shipper and carrier may designate competent court Proceedings against maritime performing party may be instituted at: • domicile of maritime performing party • port/ports where goods received/delivered by maritime performing party • port where maritime performing party performs activities in relation to the goods

Table 9.1 Continued

Arbitration		At the option of the claimant, the arbitration forum may be at: • the defendant's principal place of business • the defendant's place of habitual residence in the absence of a principal place of business • the place where the contract was made, provided the defendant has a place of business, branch or agency through which the contract was made • the port of loading • the port of discharge • the place designated in an arbitration clause	Arbitration forum may be at: • place designated in arbitration agreement • place of carrier's domicile • place of receipt/delivery agreed in contract of carriage • port where goods loaded/discharged from ship

* Note: The Rotterdam Rules have innovative provisions on rights of control, transfer of rights and delivery, see pp 314–16.

FURTHER READING

Astle, *The Hamburg Rules*, 1981, Fairplay.

Basanayake, 'Origins of the 1978 Hamburg Rules' (1979) 27 AJCL 353.

Bauer, 'Conflicting liability regimes: Hague-Visby v Hamburg Rules – a case by case analysis' (1993) 24 JMLC 53.

Bovan, 'The first decision applying the Hamburg Rules' [1997] LMCLQ 351.

Chandler, 'A comparison of the "COGSA", the Hague-Visby Rules and the Hamburg Rules' (1984) 15 JMLC 233.

Donovan, 'Why a new convention on carriage of goods by sea?' (1979) 4 Maritime Law 9.

Goldie, 'Effect of the shipowners' liability insurance' (1993) 24 JMLC 151.

Grönfors, 'The Hamburg Rules – failure or success?' [1978] JBL 334.

Hellawell, 'Allocation of risk between cargo owner and carrier' (1979) 27 American Journal of Comparative Law 357.

Herber, 'The UN Convention on the Carriage of Goods by Sea 1978: its future and the demands of developing countries' (1984) Yearbook of Maritime Law 81.

Jackson, 'The Hamburg Rules and conflict of laws', in Mankabady (ed), *The Hamburg Rules on the Carriage of Goods by Sea*, 1978, Sijthoff.

Maher and Maher, 'Marine transport, cargo risks, and the Hamburg Rules: rationalisation or imagery?' (1980) 84 Dickinson LR 183.

Makins, 'Uniformity of the law of carriage of goods by sea in the 1990s: The Hamburg Rules – a casualty' (1991) 8 MLAANZ Journal 34.

Mandelbaum, 'Creating uniform worldwide liability standards for sea carriage of goods under the Hague, COGSA, Visby and Hamburg Conventions' (1996) 23 Transportation LJ 471.

Mankabady (ed), *The Hamburg Rules on the Carriage of Goods by Sea*, 1978, Sijthoff.

O'Hare, 'Cargo dispute resolution and the Hamburg Rules' (1980) 29 ICLQ 219.

Pika, 'The Hamburg Rules fault concept and common carrier liability under US law' [1979] Virginia Journal of International Law 433.

Ramberg, 'The vanishing bill of lading and the "Hamburg Rules Carrier" ' (1979) 27 AJCL 391.

Sassoon and Cunningham, 'Unjustifiable deviation and Hamburg Rules', in Mankabady (ed), *The Hamburg Rules on the Carriage of Goods by Sea*, 1978, Sijthoff.

Selvig, 'The Hamburg Rules, the Hague Rules and Marine Insurance Practice' (1981) 12 JMLC 299.

Sturley, 'Changing liability rules and marine insurance: conflicting empirical arguments about Hague, Visby and Hamburg in a vacuum of empirical evidence' (1993) 24 JMLC 119.

Sweeney, 'UNCITRAL and the Hamburg Rules – the risk allocation problem in maritime transport of goods' (1991) 22 JMLC 51.

Tetley, 'Some general criticisms of the Rotterdam Rules' (2008) 14 The Journal of International Maritime Law 625.

CHAPTER 10

INTERNATIONAL CARRIAGE OF GOODS BY AIR

INTRODUCTION

The law relating to the international carriage by air of cargo, passengers and luggage is to be found in two distinct sources, (1) Montreal Convention 1999,[1] and (2) a network of legal instruments commonly known as the Warsaw system.[2] The Montreal Convention 1999 is largely a tidying up exercise of the fragmentation of law found in the Warsaw system, examined in the following section. It consolidates and modernises the Warsaw system where needed and reflects the liability scheme adopted by the Warsaw Convention as amended by the Hague Protocol as further amended by Montreal Additional Protocol No.4. A knowledge of the Warsaw system is therefore necessary in order to understand the liability scheme adopted by the Montreal Convention, besides providing guidance on how the provisions of this new Convention are likely to be interpreted by the courts. Further, it must be noted that not all parties to the various instruments found in the Warsaw system have as yet ratified the Montreal Convention. Hence a carriage by air from a state that has ratified the Montreal Convention to a state that is a party to the Warsaw Convention 1929 will be governed by the latter.[3] This chapter therefore starts with an examination of the Warsaw system.

THE WARSAW SYSTEM

The Warsaw system consists of the following legal instruments:

- Warsaw Convention 1929;[4]
- Warsaw Convention as amended by the Hague Protocol 1955;[5]
- Guadalajara Convention 1961;[6]

---

1   Unification of Certain Rules for International Carriage by Air, Montreal. Signed in Montreal in 28 May 1999. The signatories include the UK and the US. The UK ratified the Convention on 29 May 2004 and it came into force on 28 June 2004. The text of the Convention available at www.icao.int. See also the Carriage by Air Acts (Implementation of the Montreal Convention 1999) Order 2002. Currently 87 countries have ratified this Convention.
2   The texts of all the conventions and protocols commonly referred to as the Warsaw system are to be found in *International Trade Law Statutes and Conventions*, 5th edn, 2008, Routledge-Cavendish. They are also available at www.jus.uio.no.
3   See 'The Montreal Convention', pp 334–5 below.
4   Convention for the Unification of Certain Rules relating to International Carriage by Air, Warsaw, 1929.
5   Hague Protocol to amend the Convention for the Unification of Certain Rules relating to International Carriage by Air signed at Warsaw on 12 October 1929 (The Hague Protocol) 1955.
6   Convention supplementary to the Warsaw Convention for the Unification of Certain Rules relating to International Carriage by Air performed by a Person other than the Contracting Carrier (Guadalajara) 1961.

- Warsaw Convention as amended at The Hague and by the Guatemala Protocol 1971;[7]
- Montreal Additional Protocol No 1 1975;[8]
- Montreal Additional Protocol No 2 1975;[9]
- Montreal Additional Protocol No 3 1975;[10] and
- Montreal Additional Protocol No 4 1975.[11]

However, not all states who were parties to the Warsaw Convention 1929 ratified the Hague Protocol with the result that international carriage by air law is as complex, if not more, as the law of carriage of cargo by sea.[12] Other than the above, there are numerous inter-carrier agreements[13] – drawn up largely to satisfy the US' demand[14] for higher liability limits for passengers. These agreements are by no means amendments to the Warsaw Convention 1929, and are a matter of contract between the parties. Since they relate to carriage of passengers, they are beyond the scope of this chapter.

A brief outline of the focus of the various conventions and protocols are given below before examining topics such as documentation requirements, carrier liability, liability limits, and choice of forum.

Warsaw Convention 1929

(Hereinafter 'unamended version'.)

This convention was primarily drafted to avoid conflicts of laws through harmonisation, and protect an infant industry from excessive liability. The carriers sought to protect themselves from excessive liability through exclusion clauses in their contracts of carriage,[15] but the attitude of the courts to these clauses varied. For instance, the English courts were tolerant while the US courts were hostile.[16]

---

7   Protocol to amend the Convention for the Unification of Certain Rules relating to International Carriage by Air signed at Warsaw on 12 October 1929 as amended by the Protocol done at The Hague on 28 September 1955 and at Guatemala City on 8 March 1971.

8   Additional Protocol No 1 to amend the Convention for the Unification of Certain Rules relating to International Carriage by Air signed at Warsaw on 12 October 1929.

9   Additional Protocol No 2 to amend the Convention for the Unification of Certain Rules relating to International Carriage by Air signed at Warsaw on 12 October 1929 as amended by the Protocol done at The Hague on 28 September 1955.

10 Additional Protocol No 3 to amend the Convention for the Unification of Certain Rules relating to International Carriage by Air signed at Warsaw on 12 October 1929 as amended by the Protocols done at The Hague on 28 September 1955 and at Guatemala City on 8 March 1971.

11 Additional Protocol No 4 to amend the Convention for the Unification of Certain Rules relating to International Carriage by Air signed at Warsaw on 12 October 1929 as amended by the Protocol done at The Hague on 28 September 1955.

12 See Chapters 8 and 9.

13 Eg, the Montreal Intercarrier Agreement, 1966; IATA Intercarrier Agreement on Passenger Liability 1995. See also Fincher, 'Watching liability limits under the Warsaw Convention fly away and the IATA Initiative' (1997) 10 Transnational Law 309. For a European perspective, see Ortino and Jurgens, 'The IATA agreements and the European regulation: the latest attempts in the pursuit of a fair and uniform liability regime for international air transportation' [1999] Journal of Air Law and Commerce 377.

14 The US threatened to pull out of the Warsaw Convention if higher liability limits for passengers were not agreed.

15 The International Air Traffic Association, established in 1919, produced standard form contracts with suitable exclusion clauses for use by carriers.

16 See Chapter 8, pp 229–31 above, on the attitude of English courts towards exclusion clauses in bills of lading.

The Warsaw Convention, a product of a specialist committee established by the Conférence Internationale de Droit Privé Aérien, was given effect in English law by the Carriage of Air Act 1932 (now repealed by the Carriage of Air Act 1961). The Warsaw Convention 1929 is still a part of English law as a result of its reincorporation through the Carriage by Air Act (Application of Provisions) Order 1967.

Apart from introducing extensive documentation requirements, the convention creates a scheme of liability that places the burden of proof on the carrier. Briefly, fault on the part of the carrier is presumed on proof of damage. The onus is on the carrier to show that he, his servants or agents have taken all necessary measures to avoid the damage. In return for this onerous burden, the convention protects the carrier by limiting the amount of damages that can be awarded against him. The carrier however loses this benefit where the plaintiff establishes that damage was the result of wilful misconduct on the part of the carrier, his servants or agents.

Warsaw Convention as amended by the Hague Protocol 1955

(Hereinafter 'amended version'.)

Low limits of liability for death of passenger and the difficulty of interpreting the phrase 'wilful misconduct' in the Warsaw Convention 1929 led to the drafting of the Hague Protocol. The amended version is part of English law and was implemented by the Carriage by Air Act 1961.

Guadalajara Convention 1961

The unamended and amended versions do not make clear whether the actual carrier – that is, the one who actually carries but is not the contracting or successive carrier (mentioned in the Warsaw Convention) – is protected. The Guadalajara Convention therefore extends the protection of the Warsaw Convention to actual carriers. It is part of English law by virtue of the Carriage by Air (Supplementary Provisions) Act 1962.

Guatemala Protocol 1971

The Guatemala Protocol introduces major amendments to carrier liability and documentation in respect of carriage of passengers and their baggage. The convention is not yet in force.[17] The Carriage by Air and Road Act 1979 provides for the Protocol to be implemented into English law.

Montreal Additional Protocols Nos 1–3

The unit of account for calculation purposes in the amended and unamended versions of the convention is the Poincaré franc defined as 'consisting of 65½ milligrams of gold of millesimal fineness 900'.[18] However, due to the fluctuation of gold value, it

---

17 The table of the various conventions affecting air, their status and details of ratifications, can be obtained from ICAO's website at www.icao.org. ICAO stands for International Civil Aviation Organization.

18 Art 22(4) of the Warsaw Convention 1929 and Art 22(5) of the Warsaw Convention as amended at The Hague 1955.

was felt that the SDR (Special Drawing Right) based on a basket of currencies was a better unit for calculation purposes.[19] The Montreal Additional Protocols Nos 1, 2[20] and 3 express liability limits in terms of SDRs. Montreal Additional Protocol No 3 is not in force and relates to Guatemala Protocol. There is however provision in the Carriage by Air and Road Act 1979 to enable implementation of Protocol No 3 into English law.

Montreal Additional Protocol No 4

(Hereinafter Montreal4.)

Montreal4 introduces major changes to the liability scheme. It came into force on 14 June 1998 and is part of English law.[21]

Both the Warsaw Convention 1929 (the unamended version) and the Warsaw Convention 1929 as amended by the Hague Protocol 1955 (the amended version) exist side by side. Since for the most part they are similar, the emphasis in this chapter will be on the amended version. So reference to Warsaw Convention (or the convention) in this chapter will be to both versions unless otherwise indicated. Points of difference between the amended and unamended versions will be considered where relevant. Where required, attention is also drawn to amendments introduced to the Hague Protocol 1955 (amended version) as a result of the coming into force of Montreal4, so that a reader will be able to appraise the changes and improvements introduced over a period of seventy years. Though the convention applies to carriage by air of cargo, passengers and baggage, provisions relating to carriage of passengers or baggage will not be examined here since they are beyond the scope of this book.

Before proceeding, brief mention needs to be made of situations where an air carriage does not fall within the ambit since it does not meet the criteria of inter-national air carriage[22] as set out by the Warsaw regime. This situation is addressed in English law by the Carriage by Air Acts (Application of Provisions) Order 1967.[23] Often called non-Convention Rules, they apply to carriage that takes place from the United Kingdom or to the United Kingdom to a state or from a state not party to the conventions. It does not have any effect on a contract of carriage made and performed in a foreign state or between two foreign states.[24]

---

19 Bristow, 'Gold franc: replacement of unit of account' [1978] LMCLQ 31; Costabel, 'Gold values in carriage of goods conventions – an up-to-date review' [1979] LMCLQ 326; Kindelberger, 'The SDR as international money', in Kindelberger (ed), *International Money: A Collection of Essays*, 1981, Allen and Unwin.

20 Montreal Protocols 1 and 2 are part of English law. Both Protocols came into force on 15 February 1996. For further information on ratifications and accessions to the various instruments, visit www.icao.org who maintain a database. Also see Carriage by Air (Applica-tion of Provisions) Order 1967 (Fourth Amendment Order) SI 1998/1058; Carriage by Air and Road Act 1979 (Commencement No 2 Order) SI 1997/2565 regarding their implementation into English law.

21 Carriage by Road and Air Act 1979 provided for its implementation into English law once Montreal4 came into force; see also Carriage by Air Acts (Implementation of Protocol No 4 Order) SI 1999/1312; SI 1999/1737.

22 See 'Scope of Application of the Warsaw Convention (Unamend and Amended Versions)', pp 335–7; for the meaning of 'international air carriage'.

23 This Order was made under the Carriage by Air Act 1961. See also Warsaw Convention 1929 above.

24 See *Holmes v Bangladesh Biman Corp* [1989] 1 All ER 852; see Lord Bridge at pp 860–1 and Lord Griffiths at p 877.

APPROACH TO INTERPRETATION OF THE WARSAW CONVENTION IN THE ENGLISH COURTS

As already highlighted in Chapter 8, English courts have a tradition of taking a flexible attitude in interpreting international commercial conventions.[25] They generally do not follow precedents set in domestic law,[26] but construe the language of the convention on 'principles of general acceptation'. They are also willing to look, with caution, at the *travaux préparatories*[27] (where available), and the foreign language text where the English text is unclear. Their attitude to the interpretation of the Warsaw regime is no different. In *Fothergill v Monarch Airlines*,[28] the House of Lords adopted a flexible approach by looking to the object of the provision under consideration, and also turned to the French text for the purposes of interpretation.[29] They are also willing look to the decisions of other courts for purposes of interpretation. As Lord Denning observed in *Corocraft Ltd v Pan American Airways Inc*,[30] 'even if I disagreed, I would follow them in a matter which is of international concern. The courts of all the countries should interpret this convention in the same way' (at p 655).

SCOPE OF APPLICATION OF THE WARSAW CONVENTION (UNAMENDED AND AMENDED VERSIONS)

Both the amended and unamended versions apply to international carriage of cargo, passengers and luggage performed by aircraft for reward (Art 1(1)). In the absence of a definition of aircraft, presumably all airborne crafts, whether powered engines or not, such as aeroplanes, helicopters,[31] gas balloons and gliders come within their ambit. Though performance for reward is another requirement for applicability, Art 1(1) does not rule out gratuitous carriage altogether, since it states that the Warsaw Convention applies equally to gratuitous carriage by aircraft performed by an air transport undertaking.[32]

As for cargo, the convention does not exclude live animals like the Hague Rules or Hague-Visby Rules in respect of carriage by sea.[33] Presumably, there was no need to exclude live animals since journey times for air transport are much shorter than for sea transport. However, in the context of sea carriage, quarantine restrictions are often cited as reasons for excluding live animals from the ambit of the Hague and Hague-Visby Rules. That reason applies equally here. It is possible that, in order to promote an infant industry, the framers of the Warsaw Convention may well have

---

25 See Munday, 'The uniform interpretation of international conventions' (1978) 27 ICLQ 450.
26 See *Rustenburg Platinum Mines Ltd v South African Airways* [1977] 1 Lloyd's Rep 564, at pp 576–7; also [1979] 1 Lloyd's Rep 19, at p 23.
27 *Data Card Corp v Air Express International Corp* [1983] 2 All ER 639, at p 644.
28 [1981] 2 AC 251.
29 The Carriage by Air Act 1961 also provides in s 1(2) that, in the event of inconsistency between the English text and the French text, the latter, available in Part II of the Schedule to the Act, prevails.
30 [1969] 1 QB 616.
31 In *Barnes v Service Aérien Français* (Cour de Cass, 6 February 1996), carriage by helicopter qualified for the application of the Warsaw Convention.
32 This means that a passenger travelling on a free ticket obtained as a result of collecting air miles on a British Airways flight would be subject to the Warsaw regime.
33 See Chapter 8, pp 275–8 above.

included live animals within its scope. Carriage of mail and postal packages are however excluded, since these are normally subject to international postal conventions (Art 2(2)).[34]

International carriage is defined in Art 1(2) of the amended version as:

> ... any carriage in which, according to the agreement between the parties, the place of departure and the place of destination, whether or not there be a break in the carriage or a transshipment, are situated either within the territories of two High Contracting Parties or within the territory of a single High Contracting Party if there is an agreed stopping place within the territory of another state, even if that state is not a High Contracting Party. Carriage between two points without an agreed stopping place within the territory of another state is not international carriage for the purposes of the convention.

According to the above definition, an agreement to carry goods in the situations listed below will be international:

- Goods carried from a place of departure in state X to a place of destination in state Y where both states are parties to the amended version of the convention.
- Goods carried from a place of departure in state X to a place of destination in the same state with an agreed stopping place in state Z. Whether state Z is a party to the convention would not be relevant.[35]

Where one of the states is a party to the unamended version, and the other a party to the amended version, the amended version will not apply to the agreement.[36] For instance, an agreement to carry goods from London (a party to the Hague Protocol) to state Y (not a party to the Hague Protocol) will not be governed by the Warsaw Convention as amended by the Hague Protocol, since state Y is not a party to the amended version. However, since the unamended version is still a part of English law by virtue of Carriage by Air Acts (Application of Provisions) Order 1967, the contract of carriage will be subject to the Warsaw Convention 1929.

The emphasis in Art 1(2) is on agreement. So, where an aircraft crashes on take-off at the place of departure, or force lands within the state of departure,[37] the contract will be subject to the convention. Similarly, where the aircraft proceeds to the airport of destination without landing at the agreed stopping place, the contract will still be subject to the convention.

The voyage may be broken into stages and different carriers used for the different stages. Where the parties contemplate the carriage to be a single operation, the carriage will be regarded as international even though one stage of the carriage is performed within the same state (Art 1(3)). The successive air carrier will come within the ambit of the Warsaw Convention and will be responsible for the part of the carriage he performs (Art 30(1)).

However, for a carrier to be regarded as a successive carrier for the purposes of the Warsaw Convention, there must be prior agreement between the consignor and

---

34 Article 2(2). Note that the wording in the amended and unamended versions are different.

35 See *Grein v Imperial Airways Ltd* [1937] KB 50, where a ticket from London-Antwerp-London was held to be international, even though Belgium had not ratified the Warsaw Convention, 1929. See however the dissenting judgment of Greer LJ.

36 See *United International Stables Ltd v Pacific Western Airlines* (1969) 5 DLR (3d) 67 BCSC.

37 *Supernant v Air Canada* [1973] CA 107.

the contracting carrier to use a particular carrier as a successive carrier. Where a carrier is used for a part of the journey without prior consent from the consignor, it is questionable whether the actual carrier will come within the ambit of the unamended and amended versions of the convention. This ambiguity is resolved by the Guadalajara Convention 1961 (part of English law).[38] Article I(c) of the Guadalajara Convention defines actual carrier as:

> ... a person, other than the contracting carrier, who, by virtue of authority from the contracting carrier, performs the whole or part of the carriage ... but who is not with respect to such part a successive carrier within the meaning of the Warsaw Convention.

And according to Art II, the actual carrier is subject to the Warsaw Convention and is responsible for the part of the carriage he performs.

The situation with regard to international carriage in the unamended version (Art 1(2)) is no different apart from the slight difference in the wording of the provision.

Both versions of the Warsaw Convention make provisions regarding liability where combined transport is concerned – that is, where cargo is carried partly by aircraft and partly by other means of carriage such as sea or road.[39] In the event of combined transport, only part of the carriage performed by air is subject to the convention (Arts 31 and 18).

It is not uncommon for some of the operations prior to loading to involve other forms of transport. Where this takes place in the performance of the contract, it will be regarded as carriage by air (Art 18).

CONTRACTING OUT

Article 23 of the Warsaw Convention (unamended and amended versions) renders null and void any 'provision tending to relieve the carrier of liability or to fix a lower limit' which the carrier would otherwise have under the convention. The nullity of such a clause however does not affect the whole contract.

Article 32 renders null and void a choice of jurisdiction, or a choice of law clause that is agreed prior to the damage. Presumably, this is to avoid disadvantaging one of the parties. The emphasis on agreements reached before the damage in Art 32 suggests that parties are free to agree on jurisdiction, or choice of law after the damage. This would not be objectionable on policy grounds, since both parties will have the opportunity to assess the situation.

An agreement to submit the dispute to arbitration is allowed under the convention provided it relates to carriage of goods, and the arbitration conducted in one of the places specified in Art 28(1).

The carrier can increase his liability to a sum greater than that set by the convention, provided the consignor, when handing the package over to the carrier, has made a declaration of the value at delivery and, where required, paid the supplementary sum or surcharge (Art 22 of the unamended version; Art 22(a) of the amended version).

---

38 See Art 39 Montreal Convention.
39 For the application of the Convention on the International Carriage of Goods by Road 1956 to carriage involving air and road transportation, see *Quantum Corp Inc and Others v Plane Trucking Ltd and Another* [2002] 2 Lloyd's Rep 25 and Chapter 12.

The consignor's declaration on value at delivery other than the actual value of the goods may include profits expected on resale. Where the value includes over-optimistic profit figures, the carrier can rebut the presumption raised by the consignor's declaration.

DOCUMENTARY RESPONSIBILITIES

The documentary responsibilities are not uniform in the unamended and amended versions of the convention. The unamended version calls for a long list of particulars, whereas the amended version tries to keep it to a bare minimum. The approach adopted in the latter is also followed in Montreal4.

Amended version

The document used in carriage of cargo under the amended Warsaw Convention is called an air waybill. The consignor has the responsibility of making out three parts (Art 6(1)) of the air waybill and deliver it with the cargo to the carrier (Art 5(1)). The first part, marked 'for the carrier', requires the signature of the consignor. The second part, marked 'for the consignee', and signed by the consignor as well as the carrier, accompanies the cargo. The third part, signed by the carrier, is handed by him to the consignor after the acceptance of the cargo (Art 6(2)).

Where the carrier prepares the air waybill at the request of the consignor, he will have presumed to have done this as an agent for the consignor (Art 6(5)). The air waybill must include:

- the places of departure and destination (Art 8(a));
- if the places of departure and destination are within the territory of a single High Contracting Party, one or more agreed stopping places being within the territory of another state, an indication of at least one such stopping place (Art 8(b)); and
- a notice to the consignor to the effect that, if the carriage involves an ultimate destination or stop in a country other than the country of departure, the Warsaw Convention may be applicable and that the convention governs and in most cases limits the liability of carriers in respect of loss of or damage to cargo (Art 8(c)).

Though the convention requires only the above particulars to be entered on the air waybill, it is common for the air waybill to include information such as number of packages, weight, apparent condition of the cargo and nature of the cargo.

The air waybill is *prima facie* evidence of the conclusion of the contract, the terms of carriage and receipt of the goods (Art 11(1)). Where the waybill contains statements as to the weight and packing of the goods, these will be *prima facie* evidence and the carrier will be able to adduce evidence to the contrary. As for statements relating to contents of the package and the actual condition of the goods, these will not be regarded as evidence unless they are checked by the carrier and are stated to have been checked by the carrier. As for statements regarding the apparent condition of the goods, it seems it will be regarded as *prima facie* evidence, since Art 11(2) makes a distinction between condition and apparent condition of the goods.

Documentation is an important aspect of the convention with the result that, where goods are loaded without an air waybill with the consent of the carrier, the carrier loses the benefit of limitation of liability provided by Art 22(2).[40] Similarly, the benefit of Art 22(2) is not available to the carrier where the air waybill does not include a statement to the effect that the Warsaw Convention might apply.

Unamended version

Under the unamended version of the convention, the document used in carriage of cargo is called an air consignment note[41] and must include the following:

- the place of and date of its execution (Art 8(a));[42]
- the place of departure and of destination (Art 8(b));
- the agreed stopping places, provided that the carrier may reserve the right to alter the stopping places in cases of necessity, and that if he exercises that right the alteration shall not have the effect of depriving the carriage of its international character (Art 8(c));
- the name and address of the consignor (Art 8(d));
- the name and address of the first carrier (Art 8(e));
- the name and address of the consignee, if the case so requires (Art 8(f));
- the nature of the goods (Art 8(g));
- the number of packages, the method of packing and the particular marks or numbers upon them (Art 8(h));
- the weight, the quantity and the volume or dimensions of the goods (Art 8(i));
- the apparent condition of the goods and of the packing (Art 8(j));
- the freight, if it has been agreed upon, the date and place of payment, and the person who has to pay it (Art 8(k));
- if the goods are sent for payment on delivery, the price of the goods, and, if the case so requires, the amount of expenses incurred (Art 8(l));
- the amount of the value in accordance with Art 22(2) (Art 8(m));
- the number of parts of the air consignment note (Art 8(n));
- the document handed to the carrier to accompany the air consignment note (Art 8(o));
- the time fixed for the completion of carriage and a brief note of the route to be followed, if these matters have been agreed upon (Art 8(p)); and
- a statement that the carriage is subject to the rules relating to liability established by the Warsaw Convention (Art 8(q)).[43]

As under the amended version, non-compliance with the requirements of Art 8 of the unamended version of the convention has dire consequences for the carrier. Where the carrier *accepts* the goods without an air consignment note, or where the air consignment does not contain the first nine and the last particulars listed, the carrier

---

40   See *Fujitsu Ltd v Fed Express Corp* 247 F 3d 423 (2d Cir 2001).
41   There is no difference between an air consignment note and an air waybill. The former is a British expression and the latter an Americanism.
42   See also *Corocraft Ltd v Pan American Airways Inc* [1969] 1 QB 616.
43   A statement that the terms of carriage are based on the Warsaw Convention will not be sufficient (see *Westminster Bank Ltd v Imperial Airways Ltd* [1936] 2 All ER 890). See also *Samuel Montagu and Co Ltd v Swiss Air Transport* [1966] 1 All ER 814.

loses the benefit of provisions that exclude or limit his liability under the Warsaw Convention (Art 9).[44]

The unamended version is harsher than the amended version towards the carrier in that the benefit provided by the convention is lost as soon as he accepts the goods without the air consignment note. The amended version triggers the unavailability of the limitation provisions only where the goods are loaded with the carrier's consent without the air waybill. In most cases, the moment of loading will be later than the moment of acceptance. Moreover, under the amended version, the carrier loses only the benefit provided by Art 22(2) and does not lose any exclusions that he may be allowed under the convention.

As for the effect of statements regarding weight, condition of the goods, etc, the position is the same as under the amended convention.

Montreal4

The Montreal4 makes a few changes to the Hague Protocol on documentation require-ments for the carriage of cargo to reflect modern practices of preserving records of the carriage to be performed.

As for the contents of the air waybill, the first two requirements in respect of air waybills listed in the amended version are retained. The third requirement in Art 8 of the amended version is replaced with the requirement to indicate the weight of the consignment. Unlike the unamended and the amended versions, Montreal4 does not penalise the carrier if he loads or accepts the goods without an air waybill. The limitation provisions will therefore be available to the carrier even where he does not comply with document requirements imposed by Arts 5–8 of Montreal4.[45]

AIR WAYBILL AND NEGOTIABILITY

Unlike a bill of lading,[46] an air waybill is not a document of title. However, accord-ing to Art 15(3) of the amended version, an air waybill may be negotiable (that is, transferable). There is no practice of issuing a negotiable air waybill in Britain but, were it to become a custom in the trade, it would be recognised under English law.[47] The advantages of a negotiable air waybill are difficult to see. Negotiable bills of lading evolved due to the need to sell goods during long periods when they were on the high seas. Air transport, by nature, is speedy. Moreover, if the consignor wishes the goods to be delivered to another consignee, he has the right to instruct the carrier to do so under Art 12(1). In these circumstances, the purposes served by a negotiable air waybill are unclear. Article 15(3) may have been included to reflect established custom in some countries. It is also possible that banks involved in a letter of credit transaction might prefer the transport document to be in a negotiable format.

---

44   See also the US case *Intercargo Ins Co v China Airlines Ltd* 208 F 3d 64 (2d Cir 2000).
45   Article III amending Art 9. See also Arts 5 and 9 of the Montreal Convention.
46   See Chapter 6, pp 181–2 above, for further on bill of lading as a document of title.
47   *Lickbarrow v Mason* (1793) 102 ER 1191.

ELECTRONIC DATA INTERCHANGE (EDI) AND THE WARSAW REGIME

Given the ever increasing use of electronic data interchange and the discussion about electronic bills of lading,[48] an important issue is the applicability of the Warsaw regime to electronic equivalents of air consignment notes/air waybills. As for the unamended version, Art 6 requires that the consignor and carrier sign the air waybill. The signature of the carrier may be stamped and that of the consignor stamped or printed. If the convention had not listed the forms of acceptable signature, it would have been possible to argue that electronic signatures could have come within the ambit of the convention without further amendments. The situation in the amended version is no different. Montreal4 introduces changes to documentation relating to cargo and Art 5 states that any other means which would preserve a record of the carriage to be performed may be substituted with the consent of the consignor. The use of the phrase 'any other means' in Art 5(1) is sufficiently wide to accommodate electronic documentation. However, Art 6(3) still requires the signature to be printed or stamped which suggests that the air waybill must be in a tangible form unless the attachment of a digital signature could be construed as stamping. It seems therefore that the convention is perhaps not that flexible to allow the use of electronic documentation and suitable amendments are worthy of consideration.

CARRIER LIABILITY

Both under the unamended and amended versions of the Warsaw Convention, the carrier is *prima facie* liable for loss or damage to cargo (Art 18(1)) or damage occasioned by delay (Art 19),[49] unless he can show that he and his servants or his agents took 'all necessary measures to avoid the damage, or that it was impossible for him or them to take such measures' (Art 20). 'All necessary measures', if construed literally, does not provide the carrier with a defence, for if the carrier had taken all necessary measures there would have been no damage or loss. Case law, both in England and in other jurisdictions, has established that 'all necessary measures' should be construed as 'all reasonable measures' or 'all measures necessary in the eyes of the reasonable man'.[50] As for the word 'impossible', it has been said that it should not be construed as 'not reasonably possible' but as 'damage which was inevitable, or which no human precaution or foresight would have prevented'.[51]

Unlike the Hague and Hague-Visby Rules,[52] the Warsaw Convention does not provide a list of circumstances such as 'act of God' and 'act of war' which would exclude the carrier's liability. Presumably, these will be raised during the course of litigation to show that the carrier could not avoid the damage.

The carrier can also raise, under Art 21 of both versions of the Warsaw Conven-

---

48 See Chapter 6, pp 197–204 above; Chapter 4.
49 See *Panalpina International Transport v Densil Underwear* [1981] 1 Lloyd's Rep 187.
50 *Goldman v Thai Airways International Ltd* [1983] 1 All ER 693. This interpretation is also applied in other jurisdictions – see *United International Stable Ltd v Pacific Western Airlines Ltd* (1969) 5 DLR (3d) 67 BCSC.
51 *Swiss Bank Corp v Brink's Mat* [1986] 2 Lloyd's Rep 79, at p 96.
52 Article IV(2). See Chapter 8, pp 246–53 above.

tion, the defence of contributory negligence.[53] This has been successfully raised in respect of inadequate packaging as well as failing to follow the carrier's recommendation regarding care of cargo prior to loading.[54] Where successful, the carrier may be exonerated wholly or partly from his liability. The proof for establishing contributory negligence is on the defendant.[55]

The unamended version in Art 20(2) provides the carrier with one further defence – namely, the defence of negligent pilotage, or negligence in the handling of the aircraft. This defence is similar to the one allowed in Art IV(2)(a) of the Hague-Visby Rules, much criticised by the drafters of the Hamburg Rules.[56] It is surprising that this defence is included in a convention that revolves round a presumed fault liability framework. A possible explanation for including this defence could have been to protect the carrier from the as yet unknown effects of a relatively new technology. It is interesting that this defence was not included in the amended version.

Note, however, that Montreal4 amends the liability of the carrier extensively. First, the carrier is made strictly liable for loss or damage to cargo and the carrier cannot escape liability by showing that he took all necessary measures to avoid the loss or damage (Art IV amending Art 18). However, other than the defence of contributory negligence (Art VI amending Art 21), it lists the circumstances in which the carrier can escape liability for loss or damage to cargo in Art 18(3). These are:

- inherent defect, quality or vice of that cargo;
- defective packing of that cargo performed by a person other than the carrier, his servants or agents;
- an act of war or an armed conflict;
- an act of public authority carried out in connection with the entry, exit or transit of the cargo.

It is interesting that the list does not include the exception of act of God allowed to carriers under English common law.[57]

As regards damage due to delay, the carrier, under Montreal4, can still raise the defence of all necessary measures (Art V amending Art 20).[58]

Period of responsibility

Under both the amended and unamended versions of the Warsaw Convention, the carrier is liable for loss of cargo or damage to cargo if the event causing the loss or damage to the cargo took place during carriage by air (Art 18(1)). Carriage by air:

> ... comprises the period during which the baggage or cargo is in the charge of the carrier, whether in an aerodrome or on board an aircraft, or, in the case of a landing outside an aerodrome, in any place whatsoever [Art 18(2)].

---

53 *Rustenburg Platinum Mines v South African Airways* [1977] 1 Lloyd's Rep 564.
54 *AG World Exports v Arrow Air Inc* 22 Avi Cas 18, at p 221.
55 *Rustenburg Platinum Mines v South African Airways* [1977] 1 Lloyd's Rep 564.
56 See Chapter 9.
57 See Chapters 5 and 7. See also Arts 18 and 20, Montreal Convention 1999.
58 See Art 19, Montreal Convention 1999.

The precise moment when the carrier takes charge and relinquishes charge of the cargo will presumably depend on the terms of the contract. In *Swiss Bank Corp v Brink's Mat*,[59] of the three consignments of bank notes stolen, only two had been weighed and checked in by the handling agents of KLM. It was held that the airline was liable for only two consignments since formalities in relation to the third had not taken place. Had KLM's handling agents collected the goods from the consignor's premises, they would have been liable for all three, since the goods would be in their charge. The question of deciding whether the carrier is in charge of the goods will depend on the circumstances of each case.

Liability limits

Under Art 22(2) of the Warsaw Convention, the limit of liability for loss, damage or delay is 17 SDRs per kilogram.[60] Where part of the cargo is lost, damaged or delayed, the weight of the part determines the amount of liability according to Art 22(2)(b) of the amended Warsaw Convention. However, where the part lost, damaged or delayed affects the total value of the other packages, then the total weight will be taken into account in calculating the liability amount.

Article 22(2)(b) was examined fairly recently in *Applied Implant Technology Ltd and Others v Lufthansa Cargo AG and Others; Nippon Express UK Ltd v Lufthansa Cargo AG*.[61] The cargo consisted of a number of crates containing an ion implantation system which were carried from England to Japan via Germany. One of the parts (a beamline module) was damaged beyond repair. The absence of this part meant that the remainder of the parts could not function. The weight of the damaged part was 3,590 kg and the combined weight of all the parts was 11,675 kg. The issue before the court was whether liability was to be calculated in terms of the combined weight or the damaged part's weight. The defendant, in response to the claimant's argument that the remainder of the parts were affected due to the damage to the beamline module, said the impact on the remaining parts was not permanent since a replacement had been obtained swiftly. The court came to the conclusion that the limit of liability had to be assessed by 'reference to the state of affairs at the end of the carriage by air in which the damage was sustained'. Of course, the claimant may have obtained a part subsequently that eliminates their loss. In which event, according to David Steel J, 'it will be significant from the point of view of quantum but not limitation' (at p 49).[62]

It is inevitable that 'package' in Art 22(2)(b) raises questions about its meaning. Are separately packed items within a cardboard box packages or is the cardboard box a package for the purposes of Art 22(2)(b)? In *Electronic Discount Centre Ltd v Emirates Skycargo (A Body Incorporated in Accordance with the Laws of the United Arab Emirates)*,[63] the county court was asked to decide on the meaning of package in the first sentence

---

59 [1986] 2 Lloyd's Rep 79. See also *Rolls Royce Plc and Another v Heavylift Volga Dnepr Ltd and Another* [2000] 1 Lloyd's Rep 653.

60 The move to SDRs is as a result of the various Montreal Protocols coming into force – namely Montreal Protocols 1, 2 and 4. The liability limits for loss, damage or delay was previously expressed as 250 gold francs per kilogram.

61 [2000] 2 Lloyd's Rep 46.

62 See also *Vibra v Alitalia and Lufthansa* (1991) XVI Air Law 299. See also references to academic opinions cited in the case.

63 8 April 2002, unreported, but available on Westlaw under reference 2002 WL 498959 (CC).

of Art 22(2)(b).[64] The claimant lost a number of mobile phones, out of a total of 600 mobile phones, from three of the four cartons consigned to it by the defendant. Was liability limits to be calculated by reference to weight of the items lost or the weight of the cartons? The solution turned on the meaning of 'package or packages' in Art 22(2)(b). Did the phrase refer to the cartons or the items in the cartons? Judge Kenny, after taking on board the dictionary meaning of package along with authorities dealing with the question in the context of sea carriage,[65] concluded that the relevant time for determining the number of packages was at the time the parties concluded the contract. There was nothing in the air waybill to indicate that there were 600 separately packed items in the cartons. The cartons were therefore the packages for the purposes for calculating liability limits. Of course, as the judge pointed out, if the parties wished each item to be treated as a package, they could have entered 600 packages on the air waybill at the time of entering the contract.[66]

The unamended version does not contain Art 22(2)(b). However, in *Data Card Corp v Air Express International*,[67] the court held that, where part of the cargo was lost or damaged, the liability amount should be calculated by reference to the weight of the part lost. The issue of liability limits where the value of the other parts are affected as the result of the damaged or lost part is unclear.

Payment of interest

An interesting question that arises in relation to liability limits is whether interest payments are included within limits set by the Warsaw Convention or whether interest can be awarded over the limits set by the convention. The question was considered in *Swiss Bank v Brink's MAT Ltd* and Bingham J concluded that, on the wording of Art 22(4),[68] interest payments were included within the compensation limits set by the convention.

According to Bingham J:

> It seems . . . a matter of construction that the inclusion of that clause in Art 22 indicates that the awarding of costs or legal fees on top of the sum limited would not have been permissible under the convention but for that express provision. It is of course noticeable that there is no reference to interest either in Art 22(4) or elsewhere in that Article or in any other Article. It would seem to me that had those who framed the convention intended interest to be awarded in addition to the monetary limits and to be treated in the same way as court costs or legal expenses, it would have been the subject of special mention [at p 101].

---

64 It reads:
> In the case of loss, damage or delay of part of registered baggage or cargo, or of any object contained therein, the weight to be taken into consideration in determining the amount to which the carrier's liability is limited shall be only the total weight of the package or packages concerned.

65 *The River Gurara* [1997] 4 All E R 498; see also Chapter 8, pp 259–60 above.

66 See paras 35, 37 and 38 of Kenny J's judgment.

67 [1984] 1 WLR 198. This case was decided under the unamended version.

68 Art 22(4) reads:
> The limits prescribed in this Article shall not prevent the court from awarding, in accordance with its own law, in addition the whole or part of the court costs and of the other expenses of the litigation incurred by the plaintiff . . .

Loss of limits of liability

Amended version

Under the Warsaw Convention as amended by the Hague Protocol, the carrier loses the liability limits set by Art 22[69] where it is 'proved that damage resulted from an action or omission of the carrier, his servants, or agents, done with intent to cause damage, or recklessly and with knowledge that damage would probably result; provided that, in the case of such act or omission of a servant or agent, it is also proved that he was acting within the scope of his employment', according to Art 25.[70]

Article 25 was considered by the English courts in *Goldman v Thai Airways International Ltd*.[71] The pilot, in spite of being made aware of two areas of air turbulence on his route and the flight manual instructions, did not tell the passengers to fasten their seat belts. The aircraft hit an area of turbulence and the plaintiff was injured as a result of being thrown against the roof of the aeroplane. At first instance, the judge, applying the meaning attributed to the word 'reckless' in English criminal law,[72] concluded that the carrier was liable for injuries caused to the passenger. The Court of Appeal, however, applied a subjective test, and not the objective one applied in English criminal law cases in respect of recklessness. As Eveleigh LJ noted in *Goldman*, the doing of the act or omission is qualified not only by the word 'recklessly' but also by the phrase 'with knowledge that damage would probably result'. In these circumstances, he found it difficult to see how one could attribute to him knowledge which he should have possessed or another pilot should have possessed. The question therefore is whether the pilot's act is reckless and with knowledge that injury was likely.

There have been a few cases subsequent to *Goldman* where Art 25 has been considered.[73] Notable amongst these is *Nugent and Killick v Michael Goss Aviation Ltd and Others*.[74] The issue that the Court of Appeal had to consider was whether knowledge in Art 25 included imputed knowledge. The court had no hesitation in concluding on the basis of decided cases and the *travaux préparatoires* that actual knowledge was required and it was insufficient to show that a pilot by reason of his training ought to have knowledge that damage would probably result. According to Dyson J:

> I do not believe that those who drafted Art 25 intended that anything less than actual conscious knowledge would suffice. That is a mental state that is clear and simple to understand. Once one moves away from actual conscious knowledge, uncertainty is introduced, and difficulties of classification will arise. To use a metaphor, in common currency, a fact may be just below the surface of a person's mind, it may be deeply or not so deeply buried in its recesses. It may be just below the surface of his mind because he is distracted, or tired, or because he has forgotten it temporarily ... There will be circumstances in which a person has so completely forgotten a fact that it cannot

---

69   See *Antwerp United Diamond BVBA and Another v Air Europe* [1996] QB 317, where the court held that the limits imposed by Art 22 were subject to Art 25. So, a claimant could recover a sum in excess of the declaration of interest in the event of wilful misconduct.

70   Note the different wording of Art 25 in the unamended version, pp 346–7 below.

71   [1983] 3 All ER 673.

72   The leading cases on the meaning of 'reckless' in English criminal law are *Metropolitan Police Commissioner v Caldwell* [1981] All ER 961, at p 966; *R v Lawrence* [1981] 1 All ER 974, at p 981.

73   See, eg, *Gurtner v Beaton* [1993] 2 Lloyd's Rep 369; *Rolls Royce plc and Another v Heavylift-Volga Dnepr Ltd and Another* [2000] 1 Lloyd's Rep 653.

74   [2002] 2 Lloyd's Rep 222.

sensibly be said that he has actual knowledge of it at all, although he may well have imputed knowledge of it. If knowledge means more than actual conscious knowledge, then there will be argument as to where on the gradient between actual conscious knowledge and imputed knowledge a particular case comes. I do not believe that it was intended that it would be necessary to embark on subtle and difficult questions of this kind in order to determine whether a claimant could rely on Art 25. There in nothing in the language of Art 2 or the travaux préparatoires to indicate that it was intended to include some, and not all, categories of knowledge not present to the mind at the time of the act or the omission. Why should knowledge that has been temporarily forgotten be excluded? If a person fails to apply his mind to a fact because he has temporarily forgotten it, he has no more and no less actual knowledge of that fact at the time of his act or omission than a person who fails to apply his mind to it because he has been temporarily distracted [at pp 232–33].[75]

The subjective test also seems to be applied in other jurisdictions.[76] Of course, the consequence of a subjective test is that it would prove extremely difficult to break the liability limits.

Unamended version

According to Art 25 of the unamended version, the carrier cannot avail himself of the provisions that exclude or limit his liability, 'if the damage is caused by his wilful misconduct or by such default on his part as, in accordance with the law of the court seised of the case, is considered to be equivalent to wilful misconduct'. 'Wilful misconduct' in other contexts has been construed subjectively[77] by the English courts, so that the state of the mind of the person in question is taken into account. This interpretation was applied in relation to Art 25 by the English courts. In *Horabin v BOAC*,[78] wilful misconduct was construed as 'conduct to which the mind is a party, and it is wholly different in kind from negligence or carelessness however gross that negligence or carelessness may be, the will must be a party to the misconduct and not merely to the conduct of which the complaint is made' (at p 1019).[79] Barry J illustrated the difference between negligence and wilful misconduct thus:

You may think that that what was actually done matters less than the intention or state of mind of the person who did it. The same act may amount on one occasion to mere negligence and on another to wilful misconduct. Two men driving motor cars may both pass traffic lights after they have changed from yellow to red. In both cases, there are the same act, the same traffic lights, the same crossroads and the same motor cars. In the first case, the man may have been driving a little too fast. He may not have been keeping a proper look out, and he may not have seen the lights (although he ought to have seen them) until he was too close and was unable to stop, and therefore crossed the roads

---

75 Also see judgment of Auld LJ at pp 229–33 and Pill LJ at p 231.
76 See, eg, *Newell v Canadian Pacific Airlines Ltd* (1976) 74 DLR (3d) 574; *Tondriau v Air India* (1976) 11 Eur Tr L 907.
77 See *Forder v Great Western Rly* [1905] 2 KB 532.
78 [1952] 2 All ER 1016.
79 In *Rustenburg Platinum Mines Ltd v South African Airways* [1977] 1 Lloyd's Rep 564, Ackner J explained it thus:
　　... wilful misconduct goes far beyond negligence, even gross or culpable negligence, and involves a person doing or omitting to do that which is not only negligent but which he knows and appreciates is wrong, and is done or committed regardless of the consequences, not caring what the result of that carelessness may be [at p 569].

when the lights were against him. He was not intending to do anything wrong . . . to endanger the lives of anyone using the road, but he was careless . . . as a result, without intending to do anything wrong, he committed an act which was clearly an act of misconduct. The second driver is in a hurry. He knows all about lights, and he sees in plenty of time that they changing from yellow to red but he says to himself: 'Hardly any traffic comes out of this side road which I am about to cross. I will go on. I am not going to bother to stop'. He does not expect an accident to happen, but he knows that he is doing something wrong. He knows that he should stop, and he is able to stop, but he does not, and he commits exactly the same act as the other driver. But, in that frame of mind, no jury would have very much difficulty in coming to the conclusion that he had committed an act of wilful misconduct. Of course, he did not intend to kill anyone or to injure anyone coming out of the side road. He thought that in all probability nobody would be coming out of the side road. Nonetheless, he took a risk which he knew he ought not to take, and in those circumstances, he could be rightly found to have committed an act of wilful misconduct [at p 1020].

However, the approach to Art 25 is not uniform, and different jurisdictions tend to construe the phrase differently. For instance, the French courts apply the objective test.[80] Similarly, in the US, the carrier's state of mind is inferred from objective facts.[81] The intention related confusion in respect of Art 25 could be, as commentators suggest, the result of an inexact translation of the French word 'dol'.[82]

Montreal4

Montreal4 makes an important change to Art 25 of the amended version. It deletes the word 'cargo' from Art 25 which means that it will not be possible to break the liability limits as far as cargo is concerned. Since the carrier is strictly liable apart from the limited defences allowed by Art 18(3) under Montreal4, it was perhaps prudent to give him the protection of the liability limits set by the regime, at least as far as cargo carriage is concerned. It is always possible for the consignors/consignees to take out adequate insurance for eventualities such as recklessness on the part of the carrier. Passengers, as consumers, of course, fall into a different category altogether.

Availability of limitation to parties other than carrier

Liability limits specified in Art 22 in respect of loss or damage to the goods is available to the carrier's servants or agents under Art 25A(1) of the amended version provided they act within the scope of their employment. No reference is made to independent contractors, and it is difficult to see how they can be accommodated within this provision since they do not have an employment contract with the carrier. In order to include them, the phrase 'scope of employment' would need to be construed as 'scope of the contract'.[83]

---

80 For an excellent review of the different approaches, see Cheng, 'Wilful misconduct: from Warsaw to The Hague and Brussels to Paris' (1977) 12 Annals Air and Space Law 55; McGilchrist, 'Wilful misconduct and the Warsaw Convention' [1977] LMCLQ 539.

81 *Reiner v Alitalia Airlines* 9 Avi Cas 18,228 (SCNY 1966).

82 See Shawcross and Beaumont, *Air Law*, loose leaf, 1977. Butterworths; Palmer, *On Bailment*, 1991 Sweet & Maxwell.

83 Note that the use of a Himalaya clause will be effective in imparting the benefits to independent contractors. See Chapter 8, pp 254–8 below, on Himalaya clauses and also the impact of the Contracts (Right of Third Parties) Act 1999.

The servant or agent loses the benefit of Art 25A(1) if it is established that the 'damage resulted from an act or omission of the servant or damage done with intent to cause damage or recklessly and with knowledge that damage would probably result' (Art 25A(3)). Note, however, that Montreal4 amends Art 25A(3) and specifies its application to carriage of passengers and baggage.

CONSIGNOR'S RESPONSIBILITIES AND RIGHTS

The consignor is responsible for ensuring that the details entered on the waybill are correct under Art 10(1) of both versions of the convention. Where the carrier suffers damage as a result of the incorrect, irregular or incomplete particulars and statements, the consignor must indemnify the carrier under Art 10(2). There is no specific requirement in the Warsaw Convention that the consignor inform the carrier of dangerous goods. Article 10 seems wide enough to accommodate damage suffered as a result of carrying dangerous cargo.

However, under common law, the consignor impliedly warrants that the goods are fit to be carried. So, where the carrier suffers damage as a result of the nature of the goods, he can recover his losses from the consignor.[84]

The consignor is also required by Art 16(1) to 'furnish and attach to the air waybill such documents as are necessary to meet the formalities of customs, octroi or police before the cargo can be delivered to the consignee'. Where the carrier suffers damage as a result of absence of documents or insufficient or irregular documents or information, the consignor is liable. Where the consignor establishes that the damage was due to the fault of the carrier or his servants or agents, the consignor escapes liability. Presumably, the kind of situations contemplated by Art 16(1) is where the carrier loses the documents through carelessness and the carrier has to warehouse the cargo – in this event, the consignor will not be liable.

The Warsaw Convention gives the consignor a number of rights of control over the goods. According to Art 12(1), the consignor has the right to:

- withdraw the goods at the point of departure as well as at the destination;
- stop the goods in transit;[85]
- order the goods to be delivered at a stopping place;
- deliver the goods to someone other than the consignee named on the air waybill;
- have the goods returned.

In order to exercise these rights, he must produce his copy of the air waybill (Art 12(3)). From the consignee's viewpoint, the rights given by Art 12(1) may be acceptable where he has not paid for the goods. But, where the consignee has paid for the goods, it seems that he might have no right of action against the carrier for wrongful delivery against the carrier, since the carrier will be well within the ambit of Art 12 were he to deliver to someone other than the 'original' consignee, unless there is fraud and the carrier is aware of the fraud.

---

84 *Bamfield v Goole and Sheffield Transport Co* [1910] 2 KB 94; *Great Northern Rly v LEP Transport* [1922] 2 KB 742.

85 Right of stoppage in transit in English law is not unknown but this is available only where the seller is unpaid and the buyer is insolvent (ss 44–46 of the Sale of Goods Act 1979).

If the buyer is unhappy with the extreme powers of control granted by Art 12, he can protect himself by express agreement whereby the rights of control are granted to him and this express agreement must be included in the air waybill (Art 15(2)).

As for payment of freight, it seems that the consignor will be liable to pay to the consignor.[86]

CONSIGNEE'S RESPONSIBILITIES AND RIGHTS

On arrival at the destination, the consignee, by handing over his copy of the waybill, can demand delivery of the goods provided he pays the charges and complies with the delivery conditions set out in the waybill (Art 13(1)), as long as the consignor has not exercised his rights under Art 12(1). It is not clear what is meant by charges in the context of Art 13(1). Presumably, it refers to freight that may be payable on collection. However, where the arrangement is for the consignor to pay the freight, then he will be liable to the carrier.

PROCEEDINGS

Choice of forum

Both versions of the Warsaw Convention[87] contain a provision specifying the places where a plaintiff may bring an action for damages against the carrier. Article 28(1) states that the plaintiff has the option of bringing an action for damages in the territory of one of the High Contracting Parties, in a court having jurisdiction at one of the following places:

- where the carrier is ordinarily resident; or
- where the carrier has his principal place of business; or
- where the carrier has an establishment by which the contract has been made; or
- at the place of destination.

There are obvious advantages of having an exhaustive and clearly worded jurisdiction provision, since it reduces uncertainties about where to bring an action and also puts an end to forum shopping. Article 28(1), unfortunately, is not exhaustive and far from clear. The provision is inexhaustive since it only mentions action for damages against the carrier. An action for freight by the carrier against the consignor or the consignee, and an action for indemnity between carriers, for instance, would not fall within the ambit of Art 28(1).

Of the four options the plaintiff has for bringing an action, the place where the carrier has his principal place of business is the least difficult for interpretation

---

86 *Swiss Air Transport v Palmer* [1976] 2 Lloyd's Rep 604; *Panalpina International Transport v Densil Underwear* [1981] 1 Lloyd's Rep 197.

87 The Gautemala Protocol 1971 adds a further forum but this applies to action for damages resulting from death, injury or delay of a passenger, or the destruction, loss or delay of baggage.

purposes. The principal place of business is commonly understood to be the place where the major part of the executive work is carried on.[88]

The possibility of bringing an action where the carrier is ordinarily resident causes problems. The use of the phrase 'ordinarily resident' in Art 28 is surprising, since in English law this is generally applied to individuals and not to corporations. There are a few tax cases however where residence, as applied to companies, has been construed to mean the place where the 'central management and control actually abides'.[89] The phrase was considered in England[90] in *Rothmans of Pall Mall (Overseas) Ltd v Saudi Arabian Airlines Corp*.[91] The defendants carried a cargo of cigarettes from Amsterdam to Jeddah. The cargo was partly lost and partly damaged during transit, and the defendants were served with a writ at their London office. Both at first instance, and on appeal, it was held that the defendants were not ordinarily resident in England. The existence of a branch office was deemed insufficient. Mustill J suggested that 'ordinarily resident', if it applies to corporations at all,[92] could mean the place where the body is incorporated, or the place where the central management and control are found. The Court of Appeal, while agreeing with the decision, did not elaborate on the suggestions put forward by Mustill J.

As for the third option – that is, where the carrier has an establishment by which the contract has been made – normally, the air waybill will be issued where the cargo has been handed over to the carrier or his handling agents. Problems may arise where cargo is weighed and checked in by a cargo handler who is not the 'appointed agent' for the carrier. It is difficult to see how a one-off transaction will be sufficient to suggest the degree of permanence the word 'establishment' seems to imply. It must, however, be said that the US courts have been willing to state that the carrier has a place of business in the most tenuous of relationships by importing notions of agency.[93] This wide interpretation on the part of the US courts is (arguably) made possible since the American translation of the French text *'un établissement par le soin duquel le contrat a été conclu'* reads 'a place of business through which the contract has been made'.

The fourth option allows the action to be brought in the appropriate court at the place of destination. Generally, the place of the destination will be stated on the air waybill and there is no problem where the consignor does not change his mind about the destination. However, Art 12(1) gives the right to request carriage to another destination. Presumably, the action can be brought at the new destination since the purpose of the provision seems to be for the consignee's benefit.

A question that arises in relation to Art 28(1) is whether the options limit the claimant's choice of jurisdiction. What if the defendant were to put in an uncontested appearance in the jurisdiction chosen by the claimant which is not a forum specified in Art 28(1)? According to Art 32, an arrangement regarding jurisdiction made prior to the damage would be null and void. This emphasis on the timing of the agreement

---

88   See *Eck v United Arab Airlines Inc* [1966] 2 Lloyd's Rep 485.

89   *De Beers Consolidated Mines Ltd v Howe* [1906] AC 455, at p 458.

90   The US decisions are not of much use for interpretation purposes, since the American translation uses the word domicile (*domicile* in the French text). In French law, the domicile of a corporation is its seat and is not the same as the common law notion of domicile.

91   [1981] QB 368; [1980] 3 All ER 359.

92   Miller, *Liability in International Air Transport*, 1977, Kluwer, at pp 300–1.

93   *Eck v United Arab Airlines Inc* [1966] 2 Lloyd's Rep 485.

suggests that where an agreement regarding damage is reached after the event, or the defendant puts in an appearance, it will be acceptable. Policy arguments such as protection of the weaker party (for example, consumer or trader from a developing country) will not affect such a conclusion, since the claimant will inevitably be the person whose cargo has been lost or damaged.

As for rules of procedure, Art 28(2) states that these should be left to be determined by the law of the forum. If procedural matters are not part of the convention, would it be possible for a defendant to invoke the doctrine of *forum non conveniens* in order to stay proceedings in the jurisdiction chosen by the plaintiff? In *Milor SRL and Others v British Airways plc*,[94] the defendants carried four cartons of jewellery and gold, worth US$750,000, from Milan to Philadelphia. The cartons, stored in a bonded warehouse (also used by American Airlines) as general cargo on an open shelf, were stolen. The shippers, consignees and the forwarding agents brought an action for breach of contract in England, British Airways' principal place of business. The defendants sought to move the proceedings to the State of Pennsylvania in the US on the grounds that much of the evidence was situated at the place of the incident. According to the doctrine of *forum non conveniens* (a recent import into English private international law), a stay of action will be granted if the court is satisfied that another forum is more appropriate in the interests of justice.[95]

The defendants argued that though Art 28(1) gave the plaintiffs an option to bring an action in a court of their choice, the word 'brought' in that Article meant 'instituted' since Art 28(2) gave authority to the court seised of the case to decide on issues of procedure. The issue of granting a stay on the grounds of *forum non conveniens* was a procedural matter and therefore, under Art 28(2), the court had the discretion to grant a stay. In support of their interpretation, the defendants provided instances of judgments from the courts of other contracting states to the Warsaw Convention.[96]

The plaintiffs for their part argued that Art 28 of the Warsaw Convention was a self-contained and exclusive provision on jurisdiction which could not be derogated from, according to Art 32 which states:

> Any clause contained in the contract and all special agreements entered into before the damage occurred by which the parties purport to infringe the rules laid down by this schedule, whether by deciding the law to be applied, or by altering the rules to jurisdiction, shall be null and void. Nevertheless for the carriage of cargo arbitration clauses are allowed subject to this schedule, if the arbitration is to take place within one of the jurisdictions referred to in the first paragraph of Art 28.

If the court seised of the case were to have the discretion to stay proceedings on the ground of *forum non conveniens*, it would go against the substance of Art 32.

It was further claimed that the aim of Art 28 was to restrict forum shopping and harmonise the rules on jurisdiction among the contracting parties to the Warsaw Convention. If the Article were to be interpreted in a manner that imparted discretion to the courts seised of the case to stay proceedings, this would undermine the purpose of Art 28 and render meaningless the option given to the plaintiff by Art 28(1). It was

---

94   [1996] 3 All ER 537.
95   See Lord Goff's judgment in *Spiliada Maritime Corp v Consulex Ltd* [1987] AC 460.
96   *Air Crash Disaster Near New Orleans on 9 July 1982* 821 F 2d 1147 (a decision of the Federal Court of Appeal of the United States, 5th Cir); *Lu v Air China International Corp* 24 Avi Cas 17 (decision of the United States District of New York) and *Brinkerhoo Maritime Drilling Corp v PT Airfast Services Indonesia* 2 S&B Av R 125 (decision of the Singapore Court of Appeal).

also suggested that the ambiguity in the English text of Art 28 could be resolved by examining the French text and the *travaux préparatoires*.[97]

At the court of first instance,[98] Longmore J held that 'to construe the word "bring" in Art 28 as "initiate subject to a stay on the basis of a distinctly more appropriate forum elsewhere" [would be] too narrow an interpretation of that word' (at p 8B), and he did not regard Art 28 as unclear to warrant a reference to the French text. Accordingly, he held that it was inappropriate for the court to consider the question of *forum non conveniens*. On appeal, Phillips LJ also came to the conclusion that the court could not apply the doctrine of *forum non conveniens* where the contract of carriage was governed by the Warsaw Convention for the following reasons:

- Though the word 'bring' could, in appropriate circumstances, mean commencing an action (for example, Art 29(1)), the option granted by Art 28, however, would be of value to the plaintiff only if the forum of his choice could resolve the dispute. Besides, the French text of the convention used two words. Article 28 used the word 'portée' and Art 29 'intentée'. The latter conveyed the narrow meaning of initiated and the former, in its context, meant commenced and pursued.

- Article 28(2) did not restrict the right granted by Art 28(1), since an express provision of the convention could not be validly displaced by a rule of procedure of the court seised of the case. For instance, a one-year limitation period under the laws of a chosen forum could not be used to displace the two-year limitation period imparted by Art 29 of the convention. Similarly, a grant of stay would go against the rights expressly granted to the plaintiff by Art 28.

- The creation of a self-contained code on jurisdiction implied that the purpose of the convention was to harmonise the different national laws on jurisdiction.

- The doctrine of *forum non conveniens* was not that prevalent in common law jurisdictions and was unknown in civil law countries when the Warsaw Convention was drafted.

The decision reached by the Court of Appeal is a sensible one, since harmonisation and certainty – the primary aims of international conventions relating to trade – are recognised. Where a convention specifically provides for jurisdiction, the drafters clearly intend to restrict forum shopping and ensure an even greater degree of unity amongst the laws of different jurisdictions. In these circumstances, a decision which would have allowed the circumvention of a convention with a mandatory effect through the use of procedural rules of a forum would have undermined the framework of the convention and resulted in chaos. It is indeed unfortunate that the US courts have allowed such a possibility through their interpretation of the Warsaw Convention.

What is the position where a claim is brought not only against the carrier but also against the manufacturer of an aircraft in a jurisdiction other than those listed in Art 28? In *Deaville and Others v Aeroflot Russian International Airlines*,[99] an Aeroflot flight crashed en route from Moscow to Hong Kong as a result of one of the pilots allowing his 13-year-old daughter and 15-year-old son to take the controls of the

---

97   In *Fothergill v Monarch Airlines* [1981] 2 AC 152, the House of Lords said that reference can be made to the *travaux préparatoires* provided this was done with caution.

98   Transcript (No 1995 folio 1384, High Court of Justice, Queen's Bench Division) produced by V Wason & Associates.

99   [1997] 2 Lloyd's Rep 67.

aircraft. The plaintiffs, dependants and relatives, brought an action in France against Airbus Industrie (the manufacturer) and Aeroflot (the carrier).[100] They also initiated proceedings in England against Aeroflot[101] in case the case failed for want of jurisdiction in France. The defendants sought for a declaration that the plaintiffs' claim was governed by the Warsaw Conventions and France was not an Art 28 jurisdiction. They also sought an anti-suit injunction on the basis that proceeding in France contravened international law and was oppressive and unjust. The plaintiffs in turn applied to stay proceedings. Mr Geoffrey Brice QC, dismissed the defendants' application for a declaratory judgment and an anti-suit injunction. As for the declaratory judgment, he said it would go against the principles of comity and that the matter of interpretation and jurisdiction was for the French court. And as for the anti-suit injunction, he did 'not regard the plaintiff's attempt to establish jurisdiction in the French courts as vexatious, oppressive or unjust' bearing in mind that 'whatever order [the] court might make, the French court will be deciding its own jurisdiction over Aeroflot in any event'. He felt it was 'more appropriate for the French court to determine its own jurisdiction than for the English court to make an order against some claimants only to prevent them participating in those proceedings' (at p 74).

However, Mr Geoffrey Brice QC seems to be indicating that, from an English perspective, the only permissible jurisdictions allowed where a carrier is joined by the manufacturer are those listed in Art 28 when he says:

> The claims before this court fall full square within the Warsaw Convention, and that convention lays down obligatory rules as to the options open to a claimant regarding in which jurisdictions he may choose to bring his claim. These include a claim in the English courts, but not in the French courts. However, the convention is silent as to the position where the claim is brought not only against the carrier but also against the manufacturer. The claimants, relying upon what they perceive to be French domestic law, have brought their claims in France against both the carrier and the manufacturer. Following the reasoning in *Sidhu*,[102] in my judgment, on the construction of the Warsaw Convention as interpreted in English law, this is not permissible; the only jurisdictions in which a claim may be brought against the carrier are those specified in Art 28. There is nothing in the convention to suggest that this rule may be modified either under domestic law or otherwise so as to enable a claim to be brought in some jurisdiction not otherwise permissible under Art 28 on the ground that some other defendant (for example, the manufacturer) is being sued by the same claimant in some other jurisdiction [at p 72].

Arbitration

Parties are free to agree to submit disputes relating to carriage of goods either before or after the damage occurs. The arbitration however must be conducted at one of the fora specified in Art 28(1) (Art 32). Article 32 does not state whether the arbitration agreement must be in writing apart from saying that 'carriage of goods arbitration clauses are allowed'. The use of the word 'clauses', read in conjunction with the first sentence of the provision which uses the words 'clauses contained in the contract', tentatively suggests that the agreement to arbitrate may be required to be in writing.

---

100 Action commenced on 15 May 1996.
101 Issued a writ on 21 March 1996 but served on 4 November 1996.
102 *Sidhu v British Airways plc* [1997] 2 Lloyd's Rep 76.

By whom

The consignor and the consignee have a right of action against the carrier under the amended and unamended versions of the Warsaw Convention (Art 14). However, it is possible that a person other than the consignee (for instance, the owner of the goods) may wish to sue the carrier. According to Art 14, the consignor or the consignee can sue in the interest of another, but it is possible that they may not wish to sue in the interest of one who owns the goods.[103] Decisions in other jurisdictions suggest that the provisions dealing with title to sue restricts the parties who can bring an action against the air carrier.[104] However, the English courts have held that the convention's silence in respect of the cargo owner's right to sue should not be read as a removal of the rights which he would normally have.[105] In *Gatewhite Ltd v Iberia Lineas Aeraes de Espana SA*,[106] the plaintiff, named as 'notify party', but not as consignee, who was the owner of a cargo of chrysanthemums was regarded by the court as having title to sue and, according to Gatehouse J, there was nothing in the convention that excluded him from having the right to sue the carrier thus leaving to the forum to decide the issue. In his words:

> In my view, the owner of goods damaged or lost by the carrier is entitled to sue in his own name and there is nothing in the convention which deprives him of that right. As the convention does not expressly deal with the position by excluding the owner's right of action (though it could so easily have done so), the *lex fori*, as it seems, can fill the gap. While bearing in mind the need to guard against the parochial view of the common lawyer, I see no good reason why the civil lawyer's approach to the construction of the convention, based on the importance of contract, should be of overriding importance. The fact is that the convention is silent where it could easily have made simple and clear provision excluding the rights of the 'real party in interest', had that been the framers' intention.

> It would be a curious and unfortunate situation if the right to sue had to depend on the ability and willingness of the consignee alone to take action against the carrier, when the consignee may be (and no doubt frequently is) merely a customs clearing agent, a forwarding agent or the buyer's bank [at p 950].

The view expressed by Gatehouse J is sensible and without doubt injustice will result if the owner has to rely on their goodwill to bring an action against the carrier.

---

103   This point was also made by Prichard J in a New Zealand case (*Tasman Pulp and Paper Co Ltd v Brambles JB O'Loghlen Ltd* [1981] 2 NZLR 225) as follows:

> The effect is that the owner of the goods is put completely in the hands of a nominal consignee who, for a variety of reasons, may be incapable of or averse to instituting proceedings against an airline. The consignee may be a customs agent or forwarding agent who is insolvent or in liquidation. Or the consignee may be a bank, the directors of which might well refuse to embark on costly litigation on behalf of a customer – even though that customer offered to indemnify the bank for costs. And, finally, however willing and able he may be, the action may not be one which the consignee is empowered to bring – his right to sue being limited to the rights conferred on him by Article 13 [at p 235].

104   *Bart v British West Indian Airways Ltd* [1967] 1 Lloyd's Rep 239 (heard in the Guyana Court of Appeal); in *Manhattan Novelty Corp v Seaboard and Western Lines Inc* (1957) 5 Avi Cas 17229, (NYSC), the judge said that Arts 12, 13, 14, 15 and 30 are exclusive and the plaintiff has no right of action despite having a proprietary interest.

105   See *Gatewhite Ltd v Iberia Lineas Aeraes de Espana SA* [1989] 1 All ER 944, where the court considered judgments from other courts in arriving at their conclusion. See also *Tasman Pulp and Paper Co Ltd v Brambles JB O'Loghlen Ltd* [1981] 2 NZLR 225, where Prichard J said that the views expressed in *Bart v British West Indian Airways Ltd* and *Manhattan Novelty Corp v Seaboard and Western Lines Inc* were unreasonable.

106   [1989] 1 All ER 944.

In *Western Digital Corp and Others v British Airways plc*,[107] the Court of Appeal approved the approach taken in *Gatewhite*, and held that the owners of the consignment, not named as the consignee or the consignor or person entitled to delivery of the air waybill, had title, as principal, to sue. The court, after considering cases from a variety of jurisdictions (French, US, Guyana, New Zealand), and the wording of the provisions in the Warsaw Convention and approaching the issue from a pragmatic stance, concluded that it was sufficiently flexible to permit principals to have right of suit. According to Mance LJ:

> In the view I take, the convention's references to consignor and consignee should not therefore be read in an exclusive sense. The convention assumes, and to some extent (for example, in the context of Arts 13(3) and 30(3)) imposes, a particular contractual model. But that model also allows for flexibility, both in the identification of the consignor or consignee and, more importantly, in the identification of the principals of persons named in the air waybill as consignor or consignee.
>
> I adopt the view, taken by other courts which have considered this problem, that there are, in this respect, strong considerations of commercial sense in favour of an interpretation which recognises and gives effect to the underlying contractual structure, save in so far this is positively inconsistent with the Warsaw and Guadalajara Conventions . . .
>
> The interests of international uniformity no longer point towards a restriction of the right of suit to any named consignor, consignee or person entitled under Art 12(1). The new magnetic pole of jurisprudence draws quite strongly towards conclusions that there is no such general restriction in the convention, and that, at least under systems which recognise the rights of unnamed or even undisclosed principals, there is nothing in the conventions to prevent such principals of the named consignor or consignee intervening and suing (or being sued) in reliance on the relevant contract for carriage by air. As principals, they will necessarily be subject to any limitations on suit which the convention imposes on their consignor or consignee agents [at pp 765–68].

Time limitation

An action for damages will be time barred if it is not brought within two years (Art 29(1)).[108] Time starts to run from the date of arrival at the destination, or from the date on which the aircraft ought to have arrived, or from the date the carriage stopped. The method of calculating the time is left to the forum (Art 29(2)). In Britain, s 5(1) of the Carriage by Air Act 1961 extends the availability of the time limitation to carriers' agents and servants who have acted in the scope of their employment.

An action for freight or an action for indemnity between carriers is not affected by Art 29(1), since the provision restricts itself to action for damages.

THE MONTREAL CONVENTION

The Warsaw regime had been questioned for quite a while due to the complexity brought about by the co-existence of the Warsaw Convention 1929 and the Warsaw Convention as amended by the Hague Protocol 1955, along with the four Montreal

---

107   [2001] QB 733.
108   Note also Art 26, which specifies the time for submitting written complaints. See also *Western Digital Corp and Other v British Airways plc* [2001] QB 733.

Protocols. Attention to the shambles of the Warsaw system was continuously drawn by academic writers.[109] The dissatisfaction with the system emanating from industry, legal practitioners, academics and policy makers seems to have had some impact and, under the auspices of the International Air Transport Association (IATA), the convention, known as the Montreal Convention, was approved in 1999. As stated in the Introduction, the Montreal Convention does not introduce any dramatic changes to the liability scheme.[110] There is however one important change introduced in relation to cargo documentation by the Montreal Convention which reflects its modernisation aspect. Article 4(2) gives recognition to the use of electronic documentation by providing that 'any other means which preserves a record of the carriage to be performed may be substituted for the delivery of an air waybill'. Where an alternative to a tangible document is used, Art 4(2) allows the carrier when requested by the consignor to deliver 'a cargo receipt permitting identification of the consignment and access to the information contained in the record preserved by such other means'. Provisions in respect of jurisdiction, where cargo claims are involved, are no different from the Warsaw regime.

The liability limits are also dealt with sensitively. While the liability limits for cargo purposes are no different from the Warsaw regime (17 SDRs), there is provision in Art 24 of the Montreal Convention to review it periodically at five year intervals. This at least introduces a degree of realism into the instrument.

The Montreal Convention will apply to carriage by air where the place of departure and place of destination are situated in two contracting states. So carriage by air from the UK to Switzerland (both contracting states) will be subject to the Montreal Convention but a carriage from a contracting to a non-contracting state (eg from the UK to Ethiopia) will not attract its application. However, according to Art 1(2), a carriage within a single contracting state (a round trip originating in a contracting state) with an agreed stopping place in another state, even if it is a non-contracting state, will come within the ambit of the Montreal Convention.

The Montreal Convention has so far received well over eighty ratifications and there is no doubt that over time it will come to replace the Warsaw regime in its entirety. Nevertheless decisions under the Warsaw regime will continue to play a role in the future in aiding the interpretation of those provisions of the Montreal Convention that are similar, if not identical, to those found in the Warsaw system.

---

109 See Matte, 'The Warsaw system and the hesitation of the US Senate' (1983) 8 Annals Air and Space Law 151; Harakas, 'The Montreal Protocols in the United States 17 years later: the road to ratification or final defeat' (1992) 41 ZLW 354.

110 See Table 10.1 on carrier liability in relation to cargo under the different variations of the Warsaw Convention and the Montreal Convention.

Table 10.1: Carrier Liability in relation to Cargo under Warsaw Convention 1929 (WC1929), Warsaw Convention 1929 as amended by Hague Protocol 1955 (WC1955), Warsaw Convention 1929 as amended by Hague Protocol 1955 as amended by Montreal Protocol No 4 (MP4), and the Montreal Convention 1999

Issues	WC1929	WC1955	MP4	Montreal Convention 1999
Carrier liability	Carrier liable for destruction or loss of, damages to goods (Art 18 (1)), and damage occasioned by delay (Art 19)	Same as WC1929	No change to liability except change in defences (see below)	Same as MP4
Period of responsibility	Responsible for goods when in carrier's charge (Art 18(2)). This period does not extend to carriage by other modes of transport – eg, land, sea, river – unless undertaken in the performance of carriage by air as in loading and delivery (Art 18(3))	Same as WC1929	Effect of replacement Art 18 (see Arts 18(4) & 5) has same effect as Art 18(2) & (3) of WC1929 (see Art IV amending Art 18)	Responsible for cargo when carrier in charge of cargo (Art 1(3)). It does not extend, however, to carriage by land, sea or inland waterway unless done for the purpose of loading, delivery etc. However, where the carrier substitutes air carriage with another mode of carriage without the consent of the consignor the entire carriage would be treated as within the period of air carriage (Art 18(4))

Issues	WC1929	WC1955	MP4	Montreal Convention 1999
Defences	Not liable if he proves that he and his agents have taken all necessary measures to avoid damage or it was impossible for him/them to take such measures (Art 20(1)). Also not liable if he proves damage caused by negligent handling of aircraft or in navigation (Art 20(2))	Same as WC1929 except negligent navigation, management exception dropped (see Art 10)	Not liable in the event of inherent defect, quality or vice of the cargo; defective packing of the cargo performed by a party other than carrier, servants or agents; an act of war or armed conflict; or an act of public authority carried out in connection with the entry, exit or transit of cargo (Art IV amending Art 18). In the event of damage caused by delay, not liable if he can show that he took all necessary measures that could reasonably be required to avoid the damage or that it was impossible to take such measures (Art V amending Art 20)	Same as MP4 (see Arts 18 and 19)

Issues	WC1929	WC1955	MP4	Montreal Convention 1999
Liability limits	250 per kg unless there is a declaration of interest by consignor (Art 22). (Expressed as 17 SDRs in Montreal Protocol No 1 amending WC1929)	Same as WC1929 Expression in SDRs due to Montreal Protocol No 2	No change	Same as WC1955 as amended by Montreal Protocol. (Art 22(3)) Note, however, Montreal Convention allows for periodic review of liability limits (Art 24)
Breaking the limits	Limits broken in the event of damage caused by wilful misconduct or by default that is considered equivalent to wilful misconduct (Art 25)	Limits broken where damage resulted from an act or omission of the carrier, his servants or agents done with intent to cause damage or recklessly and with know-ledge that damage would probably result (see Art 13 amending Art 25)	Limits cannot be broken in the carriage of cargo (Art IX amending Art 25)	Same as MP4 (see Art 22(5))
Time limitation	Two years from date of arrival or from date when aircraft ought to have arrived (Art 29)	No change	No change	No change (see Art 35)

FURTHER READING

Batra, 'Modernization of the Warsaw system – Montreal 1999' (2000) 65 Journal of Air Law and Commerce 429.

Buff, 'Reforming the liability provisions of the Warsaw Convention: does the IATA Intercarrier Agreement eliminate the need to amend the Convention?' (1997) 20 Fordham International LJ 1768.

Caplan, 'The modernisation of the Warsaw Convention: the threat from ICAO' (1997) 5(9) International Insurance LR 267.

Christy, 'Changes in international air cargo: Montreal Protocol No 4 attains force of law' (1999) 5 ILSA Journal of International and Comparative Law 531.

Clarke and Yates, *Contracts of Carriage by Land and Air*, 2008, Informa.

Grant, 'The Unfair Terms in Consumer Contracts Regulations and the IATA General Conditions of Carriage – a United Kingdom consumer's perspective' [1998] JBL 123.

Jones, 'The US ratifies Montreal Protocol No 4: a commentary', available at www.forwarderlaw.com.

Mankiewicz, *The Liability Regime of the International Air Carrier*, 1981, Kluwer.

Mauritz, 'Current legal developments: the ICAO International Conference on Air Law, Montreal, May 1999' [1999] Air and Space Law 153.

Mendelsohn and Lieux, 'The Warsaw Convention Article 28: the doctrine of *forum non conveniens* and the foreign plaintiff' (2003) 68 Journal of Air Law and Commerce 75.

Miller, *Liability in International Air Transport*, 1977, Kluwer.

Palmer, *On Bailment*, 1991, Sweet & Maxwell (new edition expected September 2009).

Rueda, 'The Warsaw Convention and electronic ticketing' (2002) 67 Journal of Air Law and Commerce 401.

Shawcross and Beaumont, *Air Law*, loose leaf (3 vols) 1977, Lexis Nexis Butterworths.

Whalen, 'The new Warsaw Convention: the Montreal Convention' [2000] Air and Space Law 17.

CHAPTER 11

INTERNATIONAL CARRIAGE OF GOODS BY RAIL

INTRODUCTION

The law relating to international rail carriage is to be found in the Convention on International Carriage by Rail (COTIF). Harmonisation in respect of international rail carriage was achieved as far back as 1890 with the Convention internationale sur le transport de marchandises par chemin de fer. This Convention created an Administrative Union served by the Central Office for the International Carriage by Rail formed in 1893. Periodic amendments were made to the Convention at various revision conferences. At the eighth revision conference held in 1980, however, substantial reforms regarding the institutional provisions found in the original convention were undertaken leading to the creation of the Inter-governmental Organisation for the International Carriage by Rail (OTIF).[1] The aim of OTIF is to promote, improve and facilitate, in all respects international traffic by rail.[2] Part of its remit is to establish systems of uniform law including contract of international carriage of goods, dangerous goods and passengers by rail. The Uniform Rules Concerning the Contract for the International Carriage of Goods by Rail (CIM)[3] were attached as appendix B to COTIF 1980. COTIF 1980[4] underwent periodic revisions. However, in the mid 1990s the OTIF undertook a major programme to revise COTIF and Vilnius Protocol 1999[5] presented a new version of COTIF 1999.[6] The reason for this new version was to better reflect the developments in rail carriage brought about by privatisation and the changing market structures in rail transportation. As with COTIF 1980 the new version of the CIM Rules are attached as Appendix B to COTIF 1999.[7] The Vilnius Protocol came into force on 1 July 2006. The UK is a party to this Protocol and has implemented it.[8] All

---

1   The secretariat services for OTIF have been provided by the Secretary General since 2006. Previously it was served by a permanent secretariat, the Central Office for Carriage by Rail (Office Central des transports Internationaux (OCTI)), located at Berne.

2   Art 2(1).

3   Règles uniformes concernant le contrat de transport international ferrovaire des merchandises. The CIM Rules apply to over 240,000 km of railway lines and to complementary carriage of goods on shipping lines and inland waterways. Visit www.otif.org for further details on lines that are registered.

4   COTIF 1980 contained two appendices: (A) CIV Rules, Uniform Rules concerning contracts for the international carriage of passengers and (B) CIM Rules.

5   Protocol of 3 June 1999 for the Modification of the Convention concerning International Carriage by Rail 1980.

6   The text of COTIF 1999 is available at www.otif.org. One of the major changes brought about by the Vilnius Protocol is the introduction of English as a working language. The other working languages are French and German.

7   COTIF 1999 has 7 appendices: Appendix A – CIV Rules on contracts concerning international carriage of passengers by rail; Appendix C – RID Regulation concerning the international carriage of goods by air; Appendix D – CUV Uniform rules concerning contracts of use of vehicles in international rail traffic; Appendix E – CUI Uniform Rules concerning the contract of uniform rules for use of infrastructure in international rail traffic; Appendix F – APTU validation of technical standards and adoption of uniform technical prescriptions for railway material; Appendix G – ATMF Procedure for the technical admission of railway vehicles and other railway material used in international traffic.

8   The Railways (Convention on International Carriage by Rail) Regulation SI 2005 2092. Text available in Carr and Kidner, *International Trade Law Statutes and Conventions*, 5th edn, 2008,

references in this chapter will be to the CIM Rules as appended to COTIF 1999 unless otherwise indicated.

Before going on to examine the various aspects of the CIM Rules, from its applicability to the liability scheme, a few words on the principles guiding its drafting. The Explanatory Note to the CIM Rules makes it apparent that the aim was to achieve harmonisation with other conventions applicable to other modes of transport, especially the CMR. And in this the drafters of the CIM seem to have followed the example of the CMR whilst leaving themselves sufficient scope for adapting and improving some of the provisions suitably for the peculiarities of rail carriage.

INTERPRETATION OF THE CIM

There is no special provision regarding the interpretation of the convention. Though the text is available in German, English and French languages, the French text is to prevail (Art 45, COTIF 1999). In the event of ambiguity, the courts will look to the French text for guidance – a step commonly resorted to in other transport conventions, such as the Convention for the Unification of Certain Rules Relating to International Carriage by Air 1929.[9] OTIF does produce a bulletin[10] that reports decisions from various courts. This may also aid in achieving a uniform interpretation of the convention.

SCOPE OF APPLICATION

The CIM Rules come into operation where there is a contract for the carriage of goods[11] for reward[12] in the following situations:

- When the place for taking over the goods and place designated for delivery are located in two different member states (Art 2(1));
- When the place of taking over and place designated for delivery of goods are located in two different states, one of which is a member state and the parties agree that the contract is to be subject to the Rules (Art 2(2));
- When the international carriage subject to a single contract involves a road or inland waterway element as a supplement to carriage by rail (Art 2(3));[13]
- Where complementary services by sea or inland waterway are provided and these are included in the CIM list of maritime and inland waterway services (Art 2(4)).[14]

Routledge-Cavendish. So far 35 countries have ratified the Protocol. It required 27 for coming into force. The full list is available at www.otif.org.

9   See Chapter 10.

10 Unfortunately, OTIF does not maintain an easily accessible electronic database like UNCITRAL which reports decisions on the Convention on the International Sale of Goods (see Chapter 2).

11 It does not apply to other types of contracts such as charter contracts.

12 It does not apply to gratuitous carriage.

13 According to the *Explanatory Report on the Uniform Rules Concerning the Contract of Carriage by Rail (CIM)* the phrase 'as a supplement' is 'intended to express the idea that the principal subject-matter of the carriage is transfrontier carriage by *rail*'. (Emphasis in original.) See para 16.

14 See Art 24 COTIF 1999.

The CIM Rules however do not recognise as international carriage carriage that is performed between stations situated in the territory of neighbouring states, state X and state Y, where the station located in the neighbouring state Y is not operated by that state or entities from state Y but by entities belonging to state X. Such carriages will be subject to national law.

While a through consignment note covering the entire carriage was necessary for bringing the carriage within the ambit of CIM 1980, the CIM Rules do not impose such a requirement. Nonetheless, a consignment note does play an important role in the CIM Rules since it is viewed as providing documentary proof (even if refutable) of conclusion and the content of the contract of carriage and the taking over of the goods. Article 6(2) therefore requires that the contract of carriage be confirmed with a consignment note. The absence, irregularity or loss of the consignment note does not in anyway affect the validity of the contract of carriage or the applicability of the CIM Rules to the carriage contract.

Unlike CIM 1980,[15] the CIM Rules do not categorise cargo into those that are acceptable and those that are not and therefore are applicable to all kinds of cargo.

Status of carrier

In CIM 1980 the status of the carrier was broadly comparable to that of the common carrier at common law, thus reflecting the role of the railway as provider of public services.[16] The CIM Rules however do not impose such an obligation on the carrier and the agreement between the carrier and consignor is viewed as a consensual one. For purposes of clarity the different types of carriers are also defined in Art 3. 'Carrier' for the purposes of the CIM Rules refers to the contractual carrier (the carrier with whom the consignor has signed the contract of carriage) or a subsequent carrier who is liable on the basis of the contract (Art 3(a)). It does not however include a substitute carrier who is defined under a separate provision (Art 3(b)) as a carrier to whom the carrier referred to in Art 3(a) has entrusted in part or in whole the performance of the carriage by rail.

Combined transport

As stated earlier (see p 362) it is possible that complementary services by sea or inland waterway may be provided in transporting the goods by rail. Where such complementary services by water are included in the CIM list of maritime and inland waterways, the CIM Rules will also apply to the carriage not performed by rail. For instance where goods are unloaded and carried by ferry to their destination, the CIM Rules will apply to the entire voyage, provided that the service is included in the CIM list.

Where rail and sea transport are combined, Art 38(1) allows a state to include exceptions peculiar to sea carriage provided it is appropriately noted in the list of services. The exceptions allowed under Art 38(1) are:

---

15 See Arts 4 and 5(1).

16 A common carrier under common law is one who carries for all in return for a reward. The CIM 1980 did stipulate a number of conditions in Arts 3, 4 and 5. For further information see the 3rd edn of Carr, *International Trade Law*, 2005, Routledge-Cavendish, pp 359–60.

- fire, if the carrier proves that it was not caused by his act or fault, or that of the master, a mariner, pilot or the carrier's servants;
- perils, dangers and accidents of the sea or navigable waters;
- saving or attempting to save life or property at sea; and
- the loading of goods on the deck of the ship, if they are so loaded with the consent of the consignor in the consignment note and are not in wagons.

The exemptions listed in Art 38(1) seem to be modelled on exclusions allowed by the Hague Rules and Hague-Visby Rules.[17] The carrier will be able to rely on these exceptions only where he can show that the loss, damage or exceeding the transit period occurred in the course of the sea journey between the time the goods were loaded on board the ship and the time when they are unloaded from the ship (Art 38(2)). The CIM Rules do not specify the precise moment the goods are deemed to be on board the ship or discharged from the ship. Presumably, the tackle-to-tackle rule applied in the Hague Rules and Hague-Visby Rules[18] will be taken into account in the interpretation of Art 38(1). The exceptions allowed by Art 38(2)(a–d) do not, however, affect the liability limits set by the CIM Rules. However, the carrier will be unable to rely on the exemptions if the claimant proves that the loss, damage or exceeding the transit period is due to the fault of the carrier, the master, mariner, the pilot or the carrier's servants (Art 38(3)).

DOCUMENTARY RESPONSIBILITIES

The consignment note

As stated earlier (p 363) the contract of carriage must be confirmed with a consignment note Art 6(2)). The CIM Rules lay down a number of formalities in relation to the consignment note and also the particulars that need to be included in this document. While these formalities may seem too extensive and rigid the reason for this stems from the expectation that it will play an important evidentiary role in the event of a dispute between the consignor/consignee and the carrier as for instance where the goods arrive damaged or there is a shortfall in the quantity delivered.

As for the consignment note itself the CIM Rules do not recommend a model consignment note but leave it to the international associations and bodies to draft a suitable model consignment note. As for the formalities in respect of the consignment note it must be made out for each consignment unless there is a contrary agreement (Art 6(6)). Both carrier and the consignor are to sign it, although the signature need not be a handwritten signature. It can be replaced by a stamp, or an accounting machine entry or some other suitable means (Art 6(4)). Upon taking over the goods the carrier must certify that he has done so in the duplicate part of the consignment note which he must return to the consignor. The original travels with the consignment.

As for the contents of the consignment note Art 7(1) stipulates a mandatory list of particulars to be included as follows:

---

17 See Chapter 8.
18 See Chapter 8, pp 278–80 above.

- Place and date on which the consignment note is made out;
- Name and address of the consignor;
- Name and address of the carrier who has concluded the contract;
- Name and address of the person to whom the goods have been handed over if not the carrier with whom contract concluded;
- Place of delivery;
- Description of the goods and the method of packing;
- Where goods are dangerous the description provided for in the Regulation concerning the International Carriage of Dangerous Goods by Rail (RID);
- Number of packages and special marks or numbers necessary for identification of consignments less than full wagon loads;
- Number of wagon if full wagon load;
- If railway vehicle running on own wheels is handed over for carriage as goods the number of railway vehicle;
- In case of intermodal transport units,[19] the category, the number or other characteristics necessary for their identification;
- Gross mass or quantity of the goods expressed in other ways;
- Detailed list of documents required for customs required by customs or other administrative authorities which are attached to the note itself or held at the disposal of the carrier with a designated authority or body;
- Carriage costs including carriage charge, customs duties and other costs incurred from conclusion of contract until delivery paid or statement that they are payable by the consignee; and
- Statement that the carriage is subject to the CIM Rules.

Article 7(2) further lists the particulars that need to be included if the circumstances so require and these include:

- Particulars of the carrier who must deliver the goods in case goods are carried by successive carriers where he has consented to the entry on the consignment note;
- Costs to be paid by the consignor, if relevant;
- Amount of cash on delivery charge;
- Declaration of value of goods and amount representing special interest in delivery;
- Agreed transit period;
- Route agreed upon;
- List of documents such as customs documents and other relevant documents referred to in Art 7(1) handed over to the carrier;
- Entries concerning the number and description of seals affixed by the consignor.

The parties are also free to enter other particulars they regard as useful should they so wish.

Unlike CIM 1980, the consignor is not under an obligation to fill in the details on the consignment note. Presumably the contracting parties will have to come to some

---

19 Eg, containers, swap body (freight-carrying unit used for combined transportation of goods involving road and rail elements).

agreement on this issue. In most cases it is likely to be the consignor since he is in a better position to enter details on matters such as the name of the consignee, description of the goods and customs documents. Further, Art 8(3) presumes that the carrier, where requested by the consignor to make entries on the consignment note, makes the entries on behalf of the consignor. This seems to indicate that the expectation is that the consignor is expected to fill out the consignment note.

That the particulars on the consignment note are an important element in the CIM Rules is endorsed by Art 8. It seems the responsibility for ensuring the accuracy of statements on the consignment note rests largely with the consignor. Where the particulars are incorrect, irregular, incomplete or not made in the allocated space on the consignment note and the carrier sustains loss or damage as a result of this, the consignor will be liable. For instance, where the customs documents are incomplete any loss or damage suffered by the carrier has to be compensated by the consignor according to Art 8(1). Failure to make entries prescribed by RID makes the consignor responsible for all costs, loss or damage suffered by the carrier.

As for the inclusion of the statement that the carriage is subject to the CIM Rules on the consignment note, that responsibility lies with the carrier. If the carrier fails to include a statement to this effect then he will be responsible for any costs, losses or damage suffered by the person entitled (Art 8(3)). The reason for this is to ensure that the CIM Rules will govern the contract should the parties bring their dispute in the courts of a state which is not a party to the CIM Rules.[20]

Evidential value

The evidential value of the consignment note is addressed in Article 12 according to which it is to be regarded as *prima facie* evidence of (1) the conclusion of the contract, (2) the conditions of the contract of carriage and (3) the taking over of the goods by the carrier. As *prima facie* evidence it is rebuttable.

Since loading may be carried out by either the carrier or the consignor Art 12 distinguishes between loading carried out by the carrier and the consignor for the purposes ascribing evidential value to the consignment note. In the event of loading by the carrier statements regarding the condition of the goods and packaging, number of packages, weight, marks and numbers are regarded as *prima facie* evidence (Art 12(2)). In the case of loading by the consignor statements regarding condition,[21] packaging, marks etc will be regarded as *prima facie* evidence *only* if they have been examined by the carrier and recorded as such on the consignment note (Art 12(3)).

Reasoned reservations can be entered by the carrier, for instance, where he has been unable to check the accuracy of the statements entered on the consignment note by the carrier. In this event the consignment note will not be regarded as *prima facie* evidence.

Examination and verification

Given that Art 12(3) highlights the importance of verification by the carrier where goods are loaded by the consignor, do the CIM Rules impart any rights in respect of

---

20   See 'Scope of Application' above.
21   According to the Explanatory Report the phrase 'apparent good condition' was not included since damaged goods such as motor vehicles can also be transported (at p 23).

examination to the carrier? For instance, can he examine the consignment? Article 11(1) gives the right to examine at any time to ensure that the consignment corresponds with the entries. Where the examination is of the contents of the consignment it is expected that it will be carried out in front of the person entitled (presumably the consignor). If this is not possible then it must be conducted in the presence of two witnesses unless the laws of the State provide otherwise. The inclusion of independent witnesses is to maintain the evidential value of the consignment note. Any reservations can be noted on the consignment note which accompanies the goods. If the duplicate is still available then reservations are to be entered on that note too.[22]

Art 12(3) deals specifically with consignments loaded by the consignor. The consignor can require the carrier to examine the goods and the carrier is obliged to do so and verify the accuracy of the statements on the consignment note provided he has the appropriate means of conducting it. Any charges he incurs for the examination of the goods will be charged to the consignor and noted on the consignment note.

ELECTRONIC DATA INTERCHANGE (EDI) AND THE CIM RULES

While the CIM 1980[23] seemed to give limited recognition to electronic documents the position is much clearer in the CIM Rules. According to Art 6(9) '[t]he consignment note and its duplicate may be established in the form of electronic data registration which can be transformed into legible written symbols. The procedure used for the registration and treatment of data must be equivalent from the functional point of view, particularly as far as concerns the evidential value of the note represented by those data'. This means that an electronic consignment note should be treated no differently from a paper consignment note including its evidential value. The emphasis on evidential value obviously touches upon some of the perceived weakness of electronic data, its intangibility and susceptibility to corruption, and the reluctance in some jurisdictions to admit electronic documents as evidence. Nevertheless, as seen in Chapters 3 and 4, developments in the EU and UNCITRAL have brought about some harmonisation in treating electronic documents no differently from paper documents and their admissibility as evidence. Since consignment notes are not documents of titles under the CIM Rules,[24] none of the issues raised regarding transferability in the context of electronic bills of lading affect consignment notes.

CONTRACTING OUT

The parties are not free to contract out of the provisions of the CIM Rules unless otherwise provided in the Rules (Art 5). So a stipulation that directly or indirectly derogates from the Rules will be regarded as null and void. The CIM Rules do not indicate the kind of clauses that would be regarded as repugnant. However, it is more

---

22   The duplicate is normally given to the consignor.

23   See Art 8(4)(g) and Chapter 11 of 3rd edn of Carr, *International Trade Law*, 2005, Routledge-Cavendish.

24   Art 6(5). In some countries (eg, India) consignment notes are regarded as documents of title. See *CI and B Syndicate v Ramachandra* [1968] AIR 133; *Official Assignee of Madras v Mercantile Bank of India* [1935] AC 53. Where consignment notes are treated as documents of title, issues in respect of transferability of electronic consignment notes may arise, as in the case of electronic documents.

than likely that clauses lowering the carrier's maximum liability[25] or the time limitation for bringing an action[26] set by the CIM Rules, and a choice of forum other than those indicated in Art 46[27] will be regarded as derogations, hence null and void. Article 5 however does not stop the carrier from agreeing to assume greater liability and obligations.

CARRIER'S RESPONSIBILITIES AND LIABILITIES

Period of responsibility and liability for loss, damage or delay

The carrier is responsible for the goods from the time of taking over of the goods to the time of delivery (Art 23). The CIM Rules do not lay down the precise parameters of the taking over of or the delivery of the goods. No doubt this will be determined by a number of factors and the agreement between the parties which would indicate the places designated for taking over and delivery of goods and provisions that are in force at the delivery point. So, for instance, where the goods have to be handed over to the custom authorities or octroi[28] authorities at their warehouses that are not subject to the carrier's supervision this will be deemed to be equivalent to delivery to the consignee (see Art 17(2)(a)).

The carrier is also responsible for the acts of his servants and other persons whose services are used to perform the carriage as long as they are acting within the scope of their authority (Art 40).

The carrier is liable for loss or damage resulting from total or partial loss, or damage to the goods while they are in his charge as well as damage or loss resulting from exceeding the transit[29] period (Art 23(1)). The CIM Rules however provide two types of defences, general defences and defences specific to goods that fall within the special risks category. The general defences under Art 23(2) available to the carrier for escaping liability are:

- where the person entitled is at fault or has given orders that result in the loss or damage to the goods or exceeding of the transit period;
- inherent defect in the goods;[30] or
- circumstances which the carrier could not avoid and the consequences of which he was unable to prevent.[31]

---

25 See p 370.

26 See p 375.

27 See p 375.

28 Duty on goods.

29 The parties will normally agree the transit period. However in the absence of such an agreement Art 16 sets out the calculation of transit periods depending on whether the consignment is a wagon-load consignment or less than wagon-load consignment.

30 The CIM 1980 used the phrase 'inherent vice'. In the context of rail carriage *Blower v GW Railway* (1872) LR 7 CP 655, it was construed as 'some defect in the goods themselves which by its development tends to the injury or destruction of the thing carried' (at p 662).

31 Presumably, as where unexpected heavy snowfall renders the railway lines unusable. There is some debate on whether unavoidable circumstances is the same as *force majeure*. Art 17(2) of the CMR (see Chapter 12) allows a similar defence and this was interpreted in *Silber v Islander Trucking* [1985] 2 Lloyd's Rep 243. According to Mustill J the words 'could not avoid' in

The burden of proof in these cases rests with the carrier who has to show that he falls within one of the above exceptions (Art 25(1)).

Where the carrier carries goods that fall within the special risks category listed in the CIM Rules the presumption regarding the cause of loss or damage to the goods will operate in the carrier's favour.[32] The burden will then fall on the claimant to provide proof to the contrary. Under Art 23(3), the special risks are:

- carriage by open wagons pursuant to the General Conditions of Carriage or when the parties have agreed to such carriage and it has been entered on the consignment note;[33]
- absence or inadequacy of packaging in the case of goods which by their nature are liable to loss or damage when not packed or when not packed properly;
- loading of goods by consignor or unloading by consignee;[34]
- nature of certain goods that particularly expose them to total or partial loss or damage, especially through breakage, rust, interior and spontaneous decay, desiccation or wastage;
- irregular, incorrect or incomplete description or numbering of packages;
- carriage of live animals;
- carriage which, under the provisions applicable or under an agreement made between the consignor and the railway and entered on the consignment note, must be accompanied by an attendant, if the loss or damage results from any risk which risk the attendant was intended to avert.

A further defence is available to the railway for goods that are normally subject to wastage in transit by the sole fact of carriage. Article 31 lists the goods and the acceptable levels of wastage. Where the wastage exceeds the permissible limits, the railway will be liable.

It is likely that there might be a number of carriers involved in the carriage of the goods performed under a single contract. In this event, the successive carrier by taking over the goods with the consignment note becomes a party to the contract of carriage and as such is subject to its terms. Each successive carrier therefore assumes responsibility for the entire carriage over the entire route up to delivery (Art 26).[35] Where the carrier uses a substitute carrier[36] the carrier is not relieved of liability but the substitute carrier (Art 27 (2)) will be subject to all the provisions of the CIM Rules governing liability.[37] And the substitute carrier is equally subject to the loss of rights to invoke limits of liability. These provisions ensure that the claimant is not

---

Art 17(2) include the rider 'even with utmost care'. 'Utmost care' lies 'somewhere between, on the one hand, a requirement to take every conceivable precaution, however extreme, within the limits of the law and, on the other hand, a duty to do no more than act reasonably in accordance with prudent current practice' (at p 247).

32 Where however an abnormally large quantity or package has been lost when goods are carried on open wagons this presumption will not apply (Art 23(3)).

33 Goods in intermodal units or road vehicles carried on wagons will not be regarded as being carried on open wagons. Where consignor uses sheeting on open wagon the carrier will still assume the same liability as for carriage by open wagons.

34 Normally wagon load consignments are loaded by consignor.

35 A similar provision is found in the CMR which was interpreted by the English courts in *James Buchanan and Co Ltd v Babco Forwarding and Shipping UK Ltd* [1978] AC 141. See Chapter 12.

36 On the question of whom to sue in the event of damage, loss or delay see p 374 below.

37 On definition of substitute carrier see p 363 above.

disadvantaged in anyway should the carriage be performed by successive or substitute carrier. It is possible that the carrier may have waived certain of his rights by agreement. This waiver will not affect the substitute carrier unless he has agreed expressly and in writing to them.

Liability amount

The CIM Rules use a complex formula for the calculation of liability depending on whether the goods are lost or damaged. Where there is total loss or partial loss, the value of the goods is calculated on the basis of the commodity exchange quotation, or the market price in the absence of commodity exchange quotation (Art 30(1)). If the market price is unavailable, the value is determined from the price of goods of the equivalent kind and quality at the time and place of acceptance (Art 30(1)). The maximum liability of the railway is 17 Special Drawing Rights (SDRs) per kilogram of weight lost (Art 30(2)).

In addition to this, where goods are lost, the carrier is also under an obligation to repay carriage charges, customs duties and other charges that are incurred (Art 30(3)).[38]

Where goods are damaged, the compensation is the loss in the value of the goods. The amount is calculated by applying to the value derived, using the formula given in Art 30, the percentage of loss in value to the goods as a result of the damage at the place of destination (Art 32(1)). Where the entire cargo has lost value as a result of damage, the compensation cannot exceed the amount that would have been paid had the consignment been a total loss. Carriage charges and customs duties and other charges are also recoverable by the claimant in proportionate amounts (Art 32(4)). Where goods are lost or damaged as a result of the railway exceeding the transit period, then the carrier can claim four times the carriage charges (Art 33(1)).

The above limits apply only in the absence of a declaration of value (Art 35) or interest in delivery (Art 36). In these cases the compensation payable would be higher than the liability amount set by the CIM Rules.

The carrier, however, loses the benefit of the compensation limits if it is proved that the loss or damage results from an act or omission, which the carrier has committed either with intent to cause such loss or damage, or recklessly and with knowledge that such loss or damage would probably result under Art 36. This provision seems to be based on Art 25 of the Warsaw Convention as amended by the Hague Protocol. Words that import a mental element like 'recklessly' always cause difficulties in relation to the test to be applied. Should it be an objective or subjective test to determine whether the act or omission was reckless? As for the English courts, in the context of air carriage, the courts have applied a subjective test. Equally, knowledge in the context of Art 25 of the Warsaw Convention as amended was construed as not including imputed knowledge.[39]

---

38 Presumably the liability will relate only to his part of the carriage. See Explanatory Report p, 33.

39 See Chapter 10. Since the Explanatory Report to the CIM Rules state that one of the objectives was to achieve harmonisation with other transport conventions it is likely that reference to court decisions in respect of similar or related provisions will be made in the course of arguing the case in the court. As to how the courts will respond is another matter.

Documentary formalities

During the course of carriage from the forwarding point to the destination point, customs and other administrative formalities have to be completed in respect of the goods. These are the responsibility of the carrier though it may delegate these tasks to an agent.[40] If the carrier or the agent it has appointed is at fault for instance, if the documents are lost or misused, then it shall be liable to the consignor. However the responsibility for ensuring that the documents and information are correct rests with the consignor.

CARRIER'S RIGHTS

The CIM Rules give a number of rights to the carrier. Apart from its right to charges,[41] it also has the right to verify that the consignment corresponds with the particulars furnished in the consignment note by the consignor and any conditions for the carriage of certain types of goods are complied with (Art 11)).

Where circumstances prevent carriage, the carrier, under Art 20, has the freedom to decide whether to carry on with the carriage by using a route other than the one agreed upon or wait for instructions from the person entitled. Where carriage is impossible, the carrier must ask for instructions and if no instructions are forthcoming within a reasonable time he must take steps that seem to be in the best interests of the person entitled, for instance, where the carrier decides to sell perishable goods (Art 22(3)). Of course the carrier will have to place the proceeds of sale at the disposal of the person entitled (Art 22(4)). In the event of circumstances preventing delivery he must await instructions from the consignor or consignee depending on the circumstances (see Art 21). The carrier in the above circumstances is entitled to receive the costs he has incurred for requesting instruction, acting on the instruction, failure of requested instruction to reach him or reach him on time and acting in accordance with Art 20 as long as such costs were not caused by the carrier's fault. Charges applicable to the route followed can also be recovered and he will also be allowed the transit periods that are applicable to such routes (Art 23).

The carrier who has paid compensation also has a right of recourse against the carrier who has caused the loss or damage. Article 50 addresses the issue of this right of recourse in different scenarios, for instance, where it is difficult to establish when the loss or damage occurred or where one of the carriers become insolvent.[42]

CONSIGNOR'S RESPONSIBILITIES AND RIGHTS

Loading operations

The responsibility for loading may be the subject of an agreement between the consignor and the carrier, but in the absence of an agreement the carrier is responsible for loading packages and the consignor for wagon loads (Art 13).

---

40   See Art 15.
41   See 'Consignor's Responsibilities and Rights', pp 371–3 below.
42   See p 374, 'Against Whom'.

Responsibilities in respect of customs documents,[43] loading and packing of goods

All documents required by various authorities such as customs and other authorities are the responsibility of the consignor, and these must be attached to the consignment note or made available to the carrier (Art 15(1)). The consignor must ensure that the documents are complete, correct and regular. Where the carrier suffers loss or damage due to insufficient or irregular documents, the consignor will be liable (Art 15(2)).

The consignor also has the responsibility of packing the goods adequately and will be liable for losses or damage suffered by carrier unless the carrier knew or the defects were apparent when he took over but failed to make reservations. He must also comply with any packing or sheeting requirements of the customs or other administrative authorities. Where the consignor has not fulfilled these requirements, the carrier may take the necessary steps to ensure compliance. The consignor, however, will be liable for the costs incurred by the carrier (Art 15(8)).

Payment of charges

The consignor is responsible for charges of carriage, supplementary charges, customs duties and other charges that are incurred from the time of acceptance to the time of delivery depending on whether he has undertaken to do so (Art 10(1)). It is possible that the carrier and consignor may have agreed that the consignee is to pay the costs. Failure on the part to assert his rights in relation to the goods or take possession of the goods means the consignor remains liable (Art 10(2)).

The consignor may make the goods subject to cash on delivery when he hands over the goods to the carrier. This means that it is the carrier's duty to collect cash from the consignee before delivery. If the carrier delivers without collecting the payment, he will be liable to the consignor for the amount. Of course, it is always open to the carrier to sue the consignee for recovery (Art 17(6)).

Choice of route and transit

The parties to the carriage contract can agree on the transit period and the route. However in the absence of agreement Art 16 provides the maximum transit periods to be calculated taking into account the agreed route. If there is no agreed route then the calculations are to be based on the shortest route. The carrier however may fix additional transit periods where, for instance, there is a sea leg. This applies also to exceptional circumstances such as exceptional increase in traffic (Art 16). These additional transit periods however must appear in the General Conditions of Carriage.[44]

---

43   See also 'Documentary Responsibilities', pp 364–7 above.
44   Art 3(c) defines General Conditions of Carriage as 'the conditions of the carrier in the form of general conditions or tariffs legally in force in each Member State and which have become, by the conclusion of the contract of carriage, an integral part of it'. These General Conditions of Carriage are normally available on the rail operators' websites.

Modification of contract

The CIM Rules give the consignor a number of rights to modify the contract of carriage. According to Art 18(1) of the CIM Rules, the consignor may:

- discontinue the carriage of the goods;
- request delivery of goods to be delayed;
- request that the goods be delivered to a person other than the named consignee; or
- request goods to be delivered at a place other than the one named on the consignment note.

This right to modify the contract is extinguished however in the event the consignee has taken possession of the goods, or accepted the goods, or has exercised his right to modify the contract. This right cannot be exercised where modification is not possible, lawful and reasonable and does not interfere with the normal working of the carrier's undertaking or prejudice consignors and consignees or other consignments (Art 18(3)).

In order to modify the contract certain formalities must be met and the duplicate of the consignment note must be presented so that the modifications can be noted.

CONSIGNEE'S RESPONSIBILITIES AND RIGHTS

Charges and delivery

The consignee is responsible for charges to the railway depending on whether the consignor has undertaken to pay all the charges or not. Where the cargo is sent on 'cash on delivery' basis, the consignee must make the required payment to the railway at the destination point. Were the carrier to deliver without collection of cash on delivery he is liable to the consignor for the charges. He will have right of recourse against the consignee (Art 17(6)).

Once the goods arrive at the destination point, the consignee can require the carrier to hand over the consignment note and deliver the goods to him (Art 17(4)). The precise place or moment at which the goods are deemed to have been delivered will depend on the provisions in force at the destination or any agreement that the consignee and the carrier may have (Art 17(2)).

Modification of contract

The consignee has the right to modify the contract from the time the consignment note is drawn up unless the consignor indicates otherwise on the consignment note (Art 17(3)).

Once the consignee has taken possession of the goods or the consignment note, he cannot modify the contract. Where the 'new' consignee (that is, the person nominated by the consignee) has taken delivery of the goods, the consignee cannot modify the contract (Art 18(4)). The right to modify the contract does not extend to the person nominated by the consignee (Art 18(5)).

PROCEEDINGS

By whom

The CIM Rules contain specific provisions in respect of the parties entitled to bring an action against the carrier. An action for recovering of money paid to the carrier can be brought only by the person who has made the payment (Art 44(2)). An action in respect of cash on delivery payments can be brought only by the consignor (Art 44(4)). As for other claims arising from the contract of carriage, the consignor is entitled to bring the action provided the consignee has not entered the picture. Once the consignee takes possession of the consignment note, or accepts the goods, or requires the railway to hand over the consignment note and deliver the goods to him, or modifies the contract of carriage the consignor loses the right to bring an action against the carrier (Art 44(1)). Where the goods are delayed beyond 30 days from the expiry of the transit period, the consignee can sue the carrier in his own name (Art 17(3)).

The consignee also loses his right to bring an action where the person designated by him has accepted the goods or taken up the consignment note or asserted his rights (Art 44(2)). The consignment note plays a central role, since it must be produced for bringing an action. Where the consignor brings an action, the duplicate of the consignment note must be produced (Art 44(5)). If he is unable to do this, then an authorisation from the consignee is required. Where the consignee has refused to accept the goods, he must be able to show proof to this effect. Similarly, the consignee can bring an action on production of the consignment note. Where the consignee has modified the contract then presumably the 'new' consignee will acquire the right to sue the carrier, provided he has possession of the consignment note, accepted the goods, or required the carrier, on arrival at the destination, to hand over the consignment note and deliver the goods.

Against whom

The rules against whom the claimant can bring an action are laid out clearly in Art 45 of the CIM Rules. Where the action is for recovering sums paid, it can be brought against the carrier which has collected the sum. However, where a carrier who has collected the sum on behalf of another, the action can be brought against the carrier on whose behalf the money was collected Art 45(3). Where the action is in respect of cash on delivery, it can be brought only against the carrier who has taken over the goods at the place of consignment (Art 45(4)). All other actions can be brought either against the carrier that accepted the cargo, or the carrier that delivers the cargo, or the carrier on which the event giving rise to the action occurred. Where an action is brought against the successive carrier who is to deliver the goods, it is not necessary, as a precondition of the action, that the carrier has received the goods, or the consignment note (Art 43(2)).

Choice of forum

All other actions relating to the carriage contract[45] can be brought against the first carrier, the last carrier or the carrier who performed the part of the carriage during which the event (eg damage to the goods) took place (Art 45(1)). Where a successive carrier is to perform the delivery leg according to Art 45(2) an action may brought against him even if he is not in possession of the consignment note or the goods. It must also be noted that where the goods are accepted it will extinguish all rights of action be it for partial loss, damage or exceeding the transit period under Art 47(1). A number of exceptions however are allowed, for instance, where the loss or damage is not apparent but is revealed subsequent to acceptance of the goods by the person entitled.[46]

Unlike CIM 1980 which did not give any choice in respect of forum the CIM Rules adopt a more liberal approach. According to Art 46, the parties are free to bring their action in the court or tribunals of a State where the defendant has his domicile or habitual residence or his principal place of business, or branch or agency which concluded the contract of carriage. Alternatively they can choose the place of taking over the goods or the place designated for delivery is situated. In the absence of specific reference it is unclear from Art 44 whether the parties can elect for arbitration. However Art 28(2) of COTIF 1999 suggests that if a dispute is not settled amicably or brought before the ordinary courts or tribunals it may by agreement be referred to an arbitration tribunal. Articles 29–32 deal with the arbitration procedure and composition of the arbitration tribunal.

Time limitation

The period of limitation for an action in relation to the contract of carriage is one year. However, the limitation period is two years in the following matters:

- an action for recovery of cash on delivery collected from the consignee by the carrier;
- recovery of proceeds of sale effected from a sale effected by the carrier;
- where the loss or damage has resulted from an act or omission done with intent to cause such loss or damage, or recklessly and with knowledge that such loss or damage would probably result; or
- where a consignment originally consigned under the CIM Rules which is subsequently reconsigned before the loss or damage was ascertained, provided it is subject to the CIM Rules and the carrier remained in charge of them and it was reconsigned in the same condition as when it arrived at the place from which it was reconsigned.[47]

---

45   In all cases where the CIM Rules apply any action against the carrier (or his servants or others for whom he is liable) in regard to liability on whatever grounds will be subject to the conditions and limitations of the CIM Rules (Art 41). In other words this provision is intended to prevent extra-contractual proceedings. See Explanatory Report, p 39 for further on this.

46   See Art 47.

47   On reconsignment see Art 28.

CONCLUSION

While it is the case that the CIM Rules have limited impact when seen in a global context, it seems that OTIF will be playing a prominent role since it lists amongst its future tasks 'widening the scope of COTIF and harmonising with other transport legislation in order to make possible in the longer term through-carriage by rail under a single legal regime from the Atlantic to the Pacific; ongoing updating of the regulations concerning the carriage of dangerous goods' and 'participation in the preparation of other international conventions concerning rail transport within UNECE [United Nations Economic Commission for Europe] and UNIDROIT [International Institute for the Unification of Private Law]'.[48] Hopefully, this increased engagement with other organisations will increase the profile of rail transportation.

FURTHER READING

'Carriage of Goods by Rail', in Clarke and Yates (ed), *Contracts for the Carriage of Goods by Land, Sea and Air*, looseleaf, LLP.

---

48   See www.otif.org/html/e/pres_info_generales.php.

CHAPTER 12

INTERNATIONAL CARRIAGE OF GOODS BY ROAD

INTRODUCTION

The law relating to international carriage of goods by road was standardised in 1956 with the Convention on the International Carriage of Goods by Road (hereinafter 'CMR').[1] Largely modelled on the CIM Rules,[2] this convention was drafted by the United Nations Economic Commission for Europe (ECE) based in Geneva.[3] The parties to the CMR consist of both ECE and non-ECE member countries.[4] The United Kingdom acceded to this convention in 1967 which is attached as a schedule to the enabling Act – the Carriage of Goods by Road Act 1965. This Act, still in force, was amended in 1979 by the Carriage by Air and Road Act.

INTERPRETATION OF THE CMR BY THE ENGLISH COURTS

As already made clear, international conventions have to be interpreted in a tolerant manner if the stated aims of uniformity and certainty are to be achieved successfully. Fortunately, English courts have adopted a sensitive attitude when it comes to the interpretation of international conventions.[5] Interpretation of the CMR was considered in *James Buchanan and Co Ltd v Babco Forwarding and Shipping (UK) Ltd* by the Court of Appeal[6] and the House of Lords.[7] The point at issue was whether duty paid on a cargo of whisky stolen prior to export was recoverable from the defendant as 'another charge in respect of the carriage' under Art 23(4).[8] If construed literally, the defendant would have escaped liability. The House of Lords, however, followed the standard set in *Stag Line v Foscola, Mango and Co*.[9] Remembering the primary objective of international conventions is to bring about standardisation and uniformity, and to avoid forum shopping, the words were construed sensibly and

---

1   The abbreviation is from its French title Convention Relative Au Contrat de Transport International de Marchandises par Route.
2   See Chapter 11.
3   See for a general history, Donald, 'CMR – an outline and its history' [1975] LMCLQ 420. There is also an Inter-American Convention on International Carriage of Goods 1989. See Larsen, '1989 Inter-American Convention on international Carriage of Goods by Road' (1991) 39 AJCL 121. The text of this convention can be found on www.oas.org.
4   46 countries had acceded to or ratified the convention as of 12 September 2004. This information is based on the table available on the ECE website: www.unece.org. The contracting ECE member countries include Austria, Belgium, Denmark, Finland, France, Germany, Greece, Hungary, Italy, Latvia, Luxembourg and non ECE member countries include the Islamic Republic of Iran, Jordan and Tunisia. The majority of ratifications are from European states.
5   It seems that in other jurisdictions, eg, Greece, international conventions, until recently, were interpreted in a manner that was consistent with their civil code. See Murray, 'Wilful misconduct under the CMR' [1999] JBL 180.
6   [1977] QB 208. See Sacks and Harlow, 'Interpretation, European style' (1977) 40 MLR 578.
7   [1978] AC 141. See Munday, 'The uniform interpretation of international conventions' [1978] ICLQ 450.
8   See also *Tatton and Co Ltd v Ferrymasters Ltd* [1974] 1 Lloyd's Rep 203, where the Court of Appeal held that the cost of retransportation did not come within the ambit of the phrase 'other charges'.
9   See [1932] AC 328 and Chapter 8, pp 231–3 above.

liberally[10] in favour of the plaintiff. Where ambiguity persists despite the broad construction of words, the courts may look to the French text of the CMR according to the *obiter* statements made in *James Buchanan and Co Ltd v Babco Forwarding and Shipping Co Ltd*.[11] Both the English and French texts of the CMR are equally authentic (Art 51).[12] The English courts will also consider, with caution, official documentation (*travaux préparatoires*).[13] However, in relation to the CMR, only a commentary based on conference papers is available,[14] and it is debatable whether this has a status similar to that of official documentation. Other than the *travaux préparatoires*, the courts may also consider foreign decisions,[15] depending on the jurisdiction, the status of the court within the foreign jurisdiction, and the extent of reasoning available in the judgments. However, a note of caution must be added. These decisions may prove to be of little use in the absence of a consensus. As Lord Salmon said:

> If a corpus of law had grown up overseas which laid down the meaning of Art 23, our courts would no doubt follow it for the sake of uniformity which it is the object of the convention to establish. But no such corpus exists. The appellants have relied on a Dutch case, *British American Tobacco Co (Netherland) BV v Van Swieten BV*, decided in Amsterdam on 30 March 1977. The facts were very similar to those of the present case and a clear judgment was given in favour of the carriers. Unfortunately, I find myself quite unable to accept the reasons on which that judgment was based. There is a French case decided by the Court of Appeal in Paris on 30 March 1973 which seems to be similar to the present in which the interpretation of Art 23 contended for by the present respondents was accepted. Far from there being any uniform corpus of law relating to the convention . . . disharmony reigns, for 12 different interpretations have been produced by the courts of different member countries concerning the supposed meaning of the various Articles in the convention. Our courts are therefore thrown back on their own resources. We must rely on our own methods of interpretation . . .[16]

SCOPE OF APPLICATION

The CMR comes into operation when:

- there is a contract of carriage of goods by road for reward;
- the goods are carried on vehicles;
- the place of taking over and the place designated for delivery specified in the contract are situated in two different states; and
- the place of taking over or the place of delivery is a contracting state (Art 1(1)).

---

10 See *Stag Line v Foscola, Mango and Co* [1932] AC 328, at p 350; *James Buchanan and Co v Babco Forwarding and Shipping UK* [1977] QB 208, at p 213; *Gefco (UK) Ltd v Mason* [2000] 2 Lloyd's Rep 555, at p 562. See also Art 3(1) of the Vienna Convention on the Law of Treaties on the purposive approach.
11 See [1978] AC 141, at pp 152, 161 and 167.
12 Only the English text is attached as a schedule to the Carriage of Goods by Road Act 1965 and given force of law by s 1. See Palmer, *On Bailment*, 1991, Sweet & Maxwell, p 1114.
13 Stated in *Fothergill v Monarch Airlines* [1981] 2 AC 251 in relation to the Warsaw Convention. See Chapter 10, pp 328–9 above.
14 Loewe, 'Commentary on the Convention of 19 May 1956 on the Contract for the International Carriage of Goods by Road (CMR)' [1976] ETL 311.
15 *James Buchanan and Co v Babco Forwarding and Shipping UK* [1978] AC 141, at p 168.
16 *Ibid.*

The international element – that is, carriage from one country to another – is essential for the applicability of the CMR.[17] It is not, however, necessary that both the country where the goods are taken over and the country where the goods are delivered are parties to the convention. So, where goods are taken over in London and delivered in Cairo, the CMR will apply. Similarly, where goods are sent from Cairo to London, the CMR will come into operation. It must, however, be noted that the CMR's applicability is triggered by the contract. The actual arrival (or non-arrival, as the case may be)[18] at its international destination is an irrelevant factor. Contracts for gratuitous carriage of goods, even where international, will fall outside the scope of the CMR. The goods must be carried by vehicles which are defined as 'motor vehicles, articulated vehicles, trailer, and semi-trailers as defined by Art 4 of the Convention on Road Traffic dated 19 September 1949' (Art 1(2)).[19] The CMR applies only to carriage of goods. Goods however are not defined. It is possible that the courts might look to their domestic legislation for a definition.[20]

The wisdom of relying on a definition found in domestic legislation is debatable given the international dimension of the CMR and the need to promote uniformity. In the circumstances it might be preferable to construe goods as including items that are not excluded specifically by the CMR.[21] Under Art 1(4), funeral consignments, furniture removal,[22] and carriage performed under the terms of any international postal convention fall outside the scope of the CMR. As to whether 'goods' would include containers and packaging is unclear. Presumably, where containers[23] or packaging is part of the gross weight, compensation for containers would be allowed.

According to s 14(2) of the Carriage of Goods by Road Act 1965, the CMR affects the rights and liabilities of the sender,[24] the consignee, the carrier,[25] any successive carrier who becomes a party to the contract of carriage,[26] and any person for whom

---

17 See Pesce, 'The contract and carriage under the CMR', in Theunis (ed), *International Carriage of Goods by Road (CMR)*, 1987, LLP. Carriage from England to Jersey does not fall within the ambit of the CMR. See *Chloride Industrial Batteries Ltd v F and W Freight Ltd* [1989] 2 Lloyd's Rep 274. Note that under Art 1(5) contracting states are allowed to exclude the application of the CMR to frontier traffic. The Protocol excludes the application of the convention to traffic between United Kingdom and the Republic of Ireland.

18 See *James Buchanan and Co v Babco Forwarding and Shipping UK* [1978] AC 141, where the consignment did not arrive at Paris. Also see *Moto-Vespa v MAT* [1979] 1 Lloyd's Rep 175, where a domestic leg of the journey, as a result of fresh instructions, attracted the application of the CMR.

19 See Haak, *The Liability of the Carrier under the CMR*, 1986, Stichting Vervoeradres, pp 48–9.

20 As for England, the Sale of Goods Act 1979 defines goods in s 61(1). See Glass and Cashmore, *Introduction to the Law of Carriage*, 1989, Sweet & Maxwell, para 3.10.

21 Loewe, 'Commentary on the Convention of 19 May 1956 on the Contract for the International Carriage of Goods by Road (CMR)' [1976] ETL 311, para 25. See also Clarke, *International Carriage of Goods by Road: CMR*, 2003, LLP.

22 There is some doubt about the scope of this phrase. According to Clarke (see *International Carriage of Goods by Road: CMR*, 2003, LLP), the scope of removal is to be gathered from the French word *déménagement* which includes packing and other services provided by the carrier.

23 See *RB Antwerp 7.1.77* (1977) 22 ETL 420, where containers did not fall within the scope of the convention.

24 The sender could be acting as agent of the consignee – see *Moto-Vespa v MAT* [1979] 1 Lloyd's Rep 175.

25 These identities are not always fixed. For instance, a party could be a sender in some circumstances and for another a successive carrier. See *Gefco (UK) Ltd v Mason* [2000] 2 Lloyd's Rep 555, at p 565.

26 For the successive carrier to come within the ambit of the CMR, the successive carrier must perform under a single contract, namely, where a single consignment note is issued. See *Arctic Electronic Co UK Ltd v McGregor Sea and Air Services Ltd* [1985] 2 Lloyd's Rep 510. See also

the carrier is responsible under Art 3 of the convention – that is, his agents, servants and other person whose services he uses to perform the carriage. Questions have arisen as to whether a freight forwarder, not engaged in the carriage, comes within the ambit of the convention. In *Ulster-Swift Ltd v Taunton Meat Haulage Ltd*,[27] the court said that where a freight forwarder has signed the contract of carriage, the CMR will apply, unless of course the person signing the contract has acted as an agent. The question of whether an individual has signed as the principal or agent has to be gathered from the facts. Factors such as details on the invoice, charge structure,[28] and the extent of communication between the person signing the contract and the person for whom he purports to act may indicate whether the relationship is one of agent and principal or not.[29]

Combined transport

The CMR, with some hesitation,[30] can be said to be innovative in providing for combined transport. According to Art 2, where goods are carried on a vehicle that is loaded on to another mode of transport, such as a ship or an aircraft (that is, ro-ro[31] traffic), the convention applies to the entire voyage. In other words, where combined transport is used and the goods are unloaded for any reason (for example, for loading on to the other mode of transport, for purposes of convenience), the CMR will not apply. So far, so good. However, in some circumstances, the carrier may become subject to a different liability scheme, since Art 2 contains the following proviso:

> Provided that to the extent that it is proved any loss, damage or delay in delivery of the goods which occurs during the carriage by the other means of transport was not caused by an act or omission of the carrier by road, but by some event which could only have occurred in the course of and by reason of the carriage by that other means of transport, the liability of the carrier by road shall be determined not by this convention but in the manner in which the liability of the carrier by the other means of transport would have been determined if a contract for the carriage of the goods alone had been made by the sender with the carrier by the other means of transport in accordance with the conditions *prescribed by law* for the carriage of goods by that means of transport [emphasis added].

And this is where the problems begin. Article 2 talks of the road carrier being subject to conditions prescribed by law for the carriage by the other means of transport. Does

---

Coggins T/A PC Transport v LKW Walter IT AG [1999] 1 Lloyd's Rep 255; *ITT Schaub-Lorenz Vertriebgesellschaft mbH v Birkart Johann Internationale Spedition GmBH and Co KG* [1988] 1 Lloyd's Rep 487.

27   [1977] 1 Lloyd's Rep 346.

28   *See Aqualon UK Ltd v Vallana Shipping Corp* [1994] 1 Lloyd's Rep 669. See also Chapter 13, pp 401–2 below, for further on this issue.

29   See *Hair and Skin Trading Co Ltd v Norman Air Freight Carrier and World Transport Agencies Ltd* [1974] 1 Lloyd's Rep 443; *Tetroc v Cross Con* [1981] 1 Lloyd's Rep 192; *Electronska v Transped* [1986] 1 Lloyd's Rep 49; *Texas Instruments Ltd v Nasan (Europe) Ltd* [1991] 1 Lloyd's Rep 146.

30   Article 2 was inserted at the insistence of the UK delegation. See Theunis, 'The liability of a carrier by road in roll on, roll off traffic', in Theunis (ed), *International Carriage of Goods by Road (CMR)*, 1987, LLP. For an excellent analysis of Art 2, see Glass, 'Article 2 of the CMR Convention – an appraisal' [2000] JBL 562.

31   Stands for roll on, roll off.

this mean that the carrier will be subject to international conventions such as the Hague-Visby Rules when they are mandatorily applicable? The Hague-Visby Rules apply mandatorily only where a bill of lading or similar document of title is issued.[32] Consignment notes used in road transport however are not documents of title. Does this mean that the Hague-Visby Rules need to be contractually incorporated? Can contractual incorporation be said to be *prescribed by law*?[33] If not, will the courts apply their domestic law to the sea part of the journey? Or, will the entire journey be governed by the CMR for the sake of uniformity?

Article 2 was considered by the English courts in *Thermo Engineers v Ferry-masters*.[34] The case involved the carriage of a steam exchange heater from Aylesbury to Copenhagen with the sea voyage starting at Felixstowe subject to a bill of lading. The heater, carried on a trailer, hit the deck head during loading and was damaged. The court had to decide whether liability was to be calculated in terms of the Hague-Visby Rules. According to Neill J, the proviso to Art 2 applies only where the loss, damage or delay:

- occurs when carriage by the other means of transport starts;
- is not caused by an act or omission of the carrier; and
- is caused by an event that could only have occurred in the course of and by reason of the other mode of transport.

As for the first condition, the plaintiffs argued that the CMR was the relevant convention for the purposes of determining liability since the vehicle was moving when the damage occurred. This suggestion was declined by the judge who felt that there was force in the submission that the CMR was meant to fit in with other conventions. Applying *Pyrene v Scindia Navigation*,[35] he concluded that the Hague-Visby Rules applied when loading of the trailer onto ship began.[36] The issue of whether the trailer was moving or not was irrelevant. As regards the second condition, the carrier will be able to fulfil it only in exceptional circumstances[37] since Art 3 states that '. . . for the purposes of this convention the carrier shall be responsible for the acts and omissions of his agents and servants and of any other persons of whose services he makes use for the performance of the carriage, when such agents or servants or other persons are acting within the scope of their employment, as if such acts or omissions were his own'. Neill J, however, felt that, for the purposes of Art 2, Art 3 must be ignored since a reading of the two provisions together would make Art 2 meaningless. 'Carrier by road' in Art 2 included only the servants and agents of the road carrier himself.[38] As

---

32   See Chapter 8, pp 273–8 above, for recent developments regarding the applicability of the Hague Rules to waybills. See also Pejovic, 'Documents of title in carriage of goods by sea: present status and possible future directions' [2001] BL 461.

33   See the French decision *The Anna Oden* (Cass fr 5 July 1989, reported in [1990] ETL 221) discussed in De Wit, *Multimodal Transport*, 1995, LLP, at p 105, where the court held that the Hague-Visby Rules did not apply to the sea leg of the journey despite a clause incorporating the Rules. See also the Dutch decision (*The Gabriel Wehr*) discussed in *Multiple Transport* at pp 106–7.

34   [1981] 1 Lloyd's Rep 200.

35   [1954] 1 Lloyd's Rep 321.

36   [1981] 1 Lloyd's Rep 200, at p 204.

37   For instance, collision with another ship and where the other ship is at fault; detention by port authorities which could not have been reasonably foreseen.

38   [1981] 1 Lloyd's Rep 200, at p 205.

for the third condition, Neill J held that the collision with the bulkhead could only have taken place in the course of loading the ship.[39]

Article 2 of the CMR addresses issues related to roll on, roll off transportation – that is, where one mode of transport (for example, truck) is carried on another mode (for example, the ship). But what if there is a combination of mode where the goods are transported partly by another mode of transport such as air and then by road? Will the CMR be applicable to the road limb? This issue came up for consideration in *Quantum Corp Ltd v Plane Trucking Ltd*.[40] Goods were transported from Singapore to Dublin under an air waybill which stated that the goods would be transported by air to Paris and from Paris via Manchester by road. At first instance, the court concluded, looking at the entire movement of goods from Singapore to Dublin, that the contract was essentially a contract for carriage by air. The Warsaw Convention however did not apply to the road limb.[41] Equally, the CMR did not, since the goods had been taken over at Singapore by Air France and not at Paris. The road carriage was therefore subject to Air France's contract terms. Until this decision, it was commonly believed[42] that, where there is segmented transport, the CMR would apply to the road segment within the scope of Art 1. On appeal, however, the decision was overturned on the reasoning that, in the instant case, the contract as recorded was for two legs, one of which was to be performed by road, and Art 1(1) of the CMR was to be read as applying to the road carriage element of a mixed or multimodal contract providing for more than one means of carriage.[43]

CONTRACTING OUT

The parties are not free to contract out of the provisions of the CMR. Where a contract of carriage contains a term that directly or indirectly derogates from the terms of the convention, it will be null and void (Art 41(1)). The convention does not provide a list of the kind of clauses that would be regarded as repugnant, but Art 41(2) states that a clause shifting the burden of proof or a benefit of insurance in favour of the carrier will be null and void.[44] A general lien or a particular lien clause that is wider than the lien granted by Art 13(2) of the CMR will be regarded as null and void.[45] So also are clauses that attempt to remove the carrier's liability for loss, damage or delay that he would incur under Art 17 of the CMR.[46]

---

39 [1981] 1 Lloyd's Rep 200, at p 205. See *The Inchmaree, Thames and Marine Insurance Co v Hamilton, Fraser and Co* (1887) 12 App Cas 484, where 'perils of the sea' was construed as perils that could take place only at sea.

40 [2001] 2 Lloyd's Rep 133. See Clarke, 'A multimodal mix-up' [2002] BL 210 for an excellent critique of the decision from the Queen's Bench Division.

41 See on Chapter 10, pp 335–7 above, for further on combined transport and the Warsaw Convention.

42 See Theunis (ed), *International Carriage of Goods by Road (CMR)*, 1987, LLP, at p 246.

43 [2002] EWCA Civ 350; see paras 10, 56–59 and 65. See also Clarke, 'The line in law between land and sea' [2002] JBL 522.

44 See Chapters 8, 9, 10, 11 and 13 in relation to other carriage conventions.

45 See *T Comedy (UK) Ltd v Easy Managed Transport Ltd* [2007] EWHC 611 (Comm). In the court's view Art 13(2) 'creates a self contained code whereby the consignee has the *right* to require delivery of the goods on payment of the charges. A general lien would derogate from the consignees' right of delivery on payment of the charges, because the consignee could only obtain payment of additional sums due in respect of other carriages. So . . . a general lien is null and void under Art 41 of the CMR Convention' [at para 52].

46 *Datec Electronics Holdings Ltd v United Parcels Service Ltd* [2007] UKHL 23.

Though the convention limits the compensation payable by the carrier, he is free to agree to a higher liability amount with the sender. The sender can declare a value for the goods (Art 24) in excess of the limits laid down in the CMR (Art 23(3)), or he may fix the amount of special interest in delivery (Art 26(1)). The latter would be appropriate where the sender wishes to cover consequential loss (such as, loss of profit) as a result of loss, damage or delay in delivery of the goods. In both cases, the amount must be declared in the consignment note.[47] The sender may find that he has to pay a surcharge to the carrier.

DOCUMENTARY RESPONSIBILITIES

The consignment note plays an important role in the CMR. It must be in three original copies; the first to be handed to the sender, the second to accompany the goods, and the third to be retained by the carrier (Art 5(1)). The note must be signed by the sender and the carrier. Reference to local law will decide on the acceptability of stamping or printing of signatures (Art 5(1)).[48] According to Art 6(1), following particulars need to be included in the consignment note:

- the date of the consignment note;
- the place where the consignment note is made;
- name and address of the sender;
- name and address of the carrier;
- the place of taking over of the goods;
- the date of taking over;
- the place designated for delivery;
- the name and address of the consignee;
- common description of the goods and details about its packaging;
- generally recognised description of dangerous goods;
- number of packages, special marks and numbers;
- gross weight or other indication of quantity of goods;
- charges in respect of carriage (including supplementary charges, customs duties and other charges incurred from the time of taking over to the time of delivery);
- instructions in respect of customs and other formalities; and
- a statement that the carriage is subject to the provisions of the convention.

The consignment note, where applicable, must also contain the following information according to Art 6(2):

- a statement that transhipment is not allowed;
- charges that the sender agrees to pay;
- amount of 'cash on delivery' charges;
- declaration of value of the goods and amount representing special interest in delivery;

---

47   See 'Documentary Responsibilities', pp 383–5 below, and Art 6(2)(d).
48   See *Texas Instrument Ltd v Nasan (Europe) Ltd* [1991] 1 Lloyd's Rep 146.

- sender's instructions to carrier regarding insurance of the cargo;
- agreed time limit within which carriage to be carried out; and
- list of documents handed to the carrier.

There is no indication in the CMR as to who is responsible for filling in the particulars of the consignment note. Since the onus is cast on the sender for the accuracy and adequacy of details entered in Art 6(2) and in Art 6(1), such as name and address of sender, date and place of taking over the goods, description of goods and packaging and weight/quality of goods, there is strong indication that the convention expects the sender to complete much of the consignment note. Where the carrier incurs expenses, or suffers loss or damage as a result of inaccuracies or inadequate information, the sender will be liable to the carrier (Art 7(1)). It is possible that the carrier may be asked to fill in the details by the sender. Where this is undertaken by the carrier, he shall be presumed to have done so on behalf of the sender unless the contrary is proved (Art 7(2)).

As for the statement that the carriage is subject to the convention, it seems that the onus is on the carrier to ensure that this is included since its absence would make him liable for all expenses, loss and damage sustained by the person entitled to dispose of the goods (Art 7(3)).

The making of the consignment note is *prima facie* evidence of the making of the contract of carriage, its conditions and receipt of goods (Arts 4 and 9). The lack of a consignment note, its loss or irregularity, however, will not affect the existence or validity of the contract of carriage.[49] The contract of carriage will still be subject to the provisions of the CMR (Art 4). The lack of a consignment note, however, is likely to affect the rights of disposal that the sender and the consignee possess under the CMR due to the formalities in respect of the consignment laid down in Art 12(5). There is a similar problem where successive carriers are involved. According to Art 34, where a single contract is performed by successive carriers, the successive carriers become a party to the contract of carriage under the terms of the consignment note, by reason of acceptance of the goods and the consignment note (Art 34).[50] In the light of these formalities, it is questionable whether a carrier can be a successive carrier for the purposes of the CMR in the absence of a consignment note.[51] However, it seems that the carrier who omits to enter his name and address on the consignment note which travels with the goods will nonetheless be a successive carrier and subject to the CMR.[52]

Though the sender is responsible for inserting information about the number of packages, marks, and numbers, it is the carrier's duty to check the accuracy of these details (Art 8(1)(a)). The carrier, if he is unable to check the accuracy of these particulars, is free to make reservations together with reasons for his inability to check the

---

49   See *Gefco UK Ltd v Mason* [1998] 2 Lloyd's Rep 585.
50   The lack of a consignment note in *Sandeman Coprimar SA v Transits y Transportes Integrales SL, Bradford Cargo Terminal Ltd, Spain TIR Centro Transportes Internacionales SA, Interserve International Freight plc, Joda Freight* [2003] EWCA Civ 113 meant that all the links in the contractual chain could not be welded into a single contract. However, sub-bailment on CMR terms was found (see paras 64–66).
51   *Transcontainers Express Ltd v Custodian Security Ltd* [1988] 1 Lloyd's Rep 128. In some countries, Art 4 has been used to support the view that acceptance of a consignment note by the successive carrier is not essential for bringing him within the CMR. See also Clarke, *International Carriage of Goods by Road: CMR* 2003 LLP.
52   *SGS-ATES Componenti Elettronici v Grappa* [1978] 1 Lloyd's Rep 281.

details provided (Art 8(2)).[53] Where the sender expressly agrees with the reservations made on the consignment note, he will be unable to dispute them. The CMR does not indicate what would constitute an express agreement on the part of the sender. A verbal agreement (preferably in the presence of a third party) may suffice, though a written agreement would be far better for evidential purposes.[54] In the absence of endorsements, it will be presumed that the details on the consignment note are correct. However, the carrier will be able to adduce evidence to the contrary as against the sender and the consignee.[55]

The carrier is also responsible for checking the apparent condition of the goods and their packaging (Art 8(1)(b)). Once again, reservations together with reasons may be entered on the consignment note (Art 8(2)). Express agreement by the sender will be binding. As for apparent condition, presumably, it refers to the condition that is perceivable on a reasonable examination. Similarly, the packaging must be adequate to withstand the journey. In the absence of reservations, particulars entered on the consignment note will be presumed to be correct. The carrier will however be able to adduce evidence to the contrary.

Though the carrier is under an obligation to check certain particulars (Art 8(1)(a)), the CMR does not impose any liability on the carrier if he does not carry out his obligations. At most, the carrier will find it difficult to establish that the particulars on the consignment note were incorrect. Further, the sender will not be liable to the carrier for damage to persons, equipment or other goods, or for any expenses due to defective packing of the goods as provided for in Art 10.[56]

There is no requirement that the carrier check the gross weight, quantity or contents of the package. The sender can however ask the carrier to check these (Art 8(3)). Presumably, where the carrier has checked these and entered suitable statements on the consignment note, he will not be able to deny them. In evidential terms, it will be to the sender's benefit. The consignee may also be able to use the consignment note as security for raising credit.[57] The carrier is likely to incur expenses were he to carry out these checks. The provision therefore entitles the carrier to be reimbursed for these costs.

ELECTRONIC DATA INTERCHANGE (EDI) AND THE CMR

There is no provision regarding electronic documents in the CMR. It is doubtful whether an electronic equivalent of a consignment note will suffice for the purposes of the convention, since Art 5 requires the note to be signed and expects the signature to be either printed or stamped depending on the local law. Digital signatures could

---

53 The carrier may be unable to check marks, or numbers of packages, since he may not be able to physically get to them – eg, when they are packed in containers.
54 According to Loewe ('Commentary on the Convention of 19 May 1956 on the Contract for the International Carriage of Goods by Road (CMR)' [1976] ETL 311, at para 104), a signature on the consignment note will be insufficient to establish agreement with the carrier's reservations, since the sender has to sign it any way under Art 5(1). A signature against the reservation on the consignment note would be sufficient however.
55 Compare with Art III(4) of the Hague-Visby Rules – see Chapter 8 p 242 above.
56 Loewe, 'Commentary on the Convention of 19 May 1956 on the Contract for the International Carriage of Goods by Road (CMR)' [1976] ETL 311, at para 96.
57 A consignment note is not a document of title, even though the sender and the consignee have rights to modify the contract under the CMR. See 'Modification of contract' p 393 below.

hardly, in the strict sense, be construed as printing or stamping, though the acceptance of the United Nations Commission on International Trade Law (UNCITRAL) Model Law on Electronic Commerce[58] worldwide will ease the use of electronic documents including electronic signatures. In 2008 an Additional Protocol to the CMR concerning electronic consignment note was adopted which enables the use of electronic consignment note provided the authentication and integrity requirements are met.

CARRIER'S LIABILITIES AND RIGHTS

Roadworthy vehicle

There is no provision which specifically states that the carrier is to provide a roadworthy vehicle. The carrier's obligation to provide a non-defective vehicle however arises from Art 17(3) which states that the carrier cannot escape liability under the CMR by reason of the vehicle's defective condition in the performance of the carriage.[59] This responsibility is personal to him. So, even in the case of a hired vehicle, its defective condition arising from the wrongful act or neglect of the persons from whom he has rented the vehicle or their servants or agents will not lessen his liability.

Period of responsibility

The carrier is responsible for the goods from the time when he takes over the goods to the time of delivery (Art 17(1)). It seems from Loewe's commentary[60] that taking over[61] occurs when the carrier assumes control of the goods and delivery, when he relinquishes control by placing them at the consignee's disposal.

Liability for loss, damage and delay

The carrier is liable for both total and partial loss of goods, and for damage to the goods from the time he takes over the goods to the time of delivery. He is also liable in the event of delay in delivery (Art 17(1)). For the purposes of deciding whether there is delay in delivery, one has to look to the time limit the parties may have agreed. Where there is an agreed time limit, the carrier should deliver within that limit to avoid liability for delay (Art 19). In the absence of a time limit, delay occurs when it is not delivered within a reasonable time. However, where the goods are not delivered within 30 days of the agreed time limit or, in the absence of an agreed time limit, within 60 days from the time the carrier took charge of the goods, the goods will be treated as lost (Art 20(1)). So, for the purposes of calculating compensation, provisions relating to liability for loss are relevant.

---

58 See Chapter 3. Also see the Electronic Communications Act 2000.
59 *Walek and Co v Chapman and Ball* [1980] 2 Lloyd's Rep 279. See Glass, 'CMR and hire-trailers – a tilt too far' [1981] LMCLQ 384.
60 Loewe, 'Commentary on the Convention of 19 May 1956 on the Contract for the International Carriage of Goods by Road (CMR)' [1976] ETL 311.
61 A narrow interpretation could cause problems however – see *Quantum Corp Ltd v Plane Trucking Ltd* [2001] 2 Lloyd's Rep 133.

A number of defences are available to the carrier under the convention. Like the CIM Rules, the defences can be categorised as general defences and special risks defences. The burden of proof differs in the two categories since, in the latter, it is assumed that the sender (claimant) assumes the risk where special circumstances apply – for instance, where he has arranged for the loading of the goods.

The general defences are laid down in Art 17(2) according to which the carrier is relieved of liability where the loss, damage or delay is caused by:

(1) wrongful act or neglect of the claimant;

(2) the claimant's instructions given otherwise than as a result of a wrongful act or neglect of the carrier;

(3) inherent vice; and

(4) circumstances which the carrier could not avoid and the consequences of which he was unable to prevent.

The onus of proof in respect of the above defences rests with the carrier (Art 18(1)). Turning now to the first defence, presumably, it will cover situations where documentary responsibilities are not fulfilled adequately – for example, incomplete customs documents from the claimant. As for the second defence, it seems that it is not restricted to instructions in respect of disposal (Art 12), but extends to instructions such as care of cargo.[62] Both defences talk only of the wrongful act or neglect of the claimant. Does this mean that the carrier cannot raise this defence against a claimant who has not committed the wrongful or negligent act as in the case of a consignee who has not filled in the consignment note? The general opinion seems to be that it would be unjust if the carrier cannot raise this defence against a claimant who is not a party to the wrongful act.[63]

As for inherent vice, no definition is provided by the convention. However, it must be noted that inherent vice appears in other international carriage conventions and has been interpreted. No doubt, such interpretations will be relevant in the context of the CMR.[64]

As for the fourth defence, the issue is whether the carrier should have done everything in his power to avoid the circumstances, or is it sufficient that he took reasonable care? The scope of this defence was considered in *Michael Galley Footwear Ltd v Dominic Iaboni*.[65] In this case, cargo was lost when one of the unattended lorries was driven off by thieves while the drivers stopped for a meal at a cafe. The lorry was equipped with an alarm system but that had been dismantled by the thieves. The theft could have been prevented had the drivers parked the lorries in a secure car park, or taken turns in eating their meals. The first option was not available according to the defendants, since it would have resulted in exceeding the driving times permitted by

---

62 *BGH 27.10.78* (1979) Vers R 419; *Cass 23.2.82* (1983) 18 ETL 13.

63 Loewe, 'Commentary on the Convention of 19 May 1956 on the Contract for the International Carriage of Goods by Road (CMR)' [1976] ETL 311, at para 151; see also Glass and Cashmore, *Introduction to the Law of Carriage*, 1989, Sweet & Maxwell.

64 *Albacora SRL v Westcott and Laurance Line* [1966] 2 Lloyd's Rep 53. See Chapter 8, p 252 above. See *Ulster-Swift v Taunton Meat Haulage* [1975] 2 Lloyd's Rep 502, where the defence of inherent vice was raised when pork was found to be unfit for human consumption on arrival due to inadequate refrigeration. The defence was rejected since the pork had been allowed to get warm after the goods had been handed to the carrier. The refrigeration equipment was not seen as falling within Art 17(3) dealing with roadworthy vehicle.

65 [1982] 2 All ER 200.

the EEC (European Economic Community) regulations. However, the defendants for their part argued that they had exercised reasonable care by acting in a manner common to the trade. Though the court admitted that the carrier was not negligent, nonetheless, judgment was given for the plaintiff. The decision in this case suggests that the courts are looking for something more than reasonable care. The standard expected of the carrier was enunciated with clarity in *Silber v Islander Trucking*[66] by Mustill J who said that the words 'could not avoid' in Art 17(2) includes the rider 'even with utmost care'. 'Utmost care' lies 'somewhere between, on the one hand, a requirement to take every conceivable precaution, however extreme, within the limits of the law, and on the other hand a duty to do no more than act reasonably in accordance with prudent current practice' (at p 247). *Silber v Islander Trucking* suggests that, once the carrier has raised the defence, the carrier could indicate what the carrier could have done to avoid the loss, at which juncture it is open to the carrier to rebut them.

In addition, the claimant is also relieved of liability where dangerous goods have been sent without his knowledge (Art 22(2)). Besides these general defences, the convention relieves the carrier of liability when the loss or damage arises from special risks inherent in the following circumstances (Art 17(4)):

- use of open unsheeted vehicles, when their use has been expressly agreed and specified in the consignment note;
- the lack of, or defective condition of, packing in the case of goods, which by their nature are liable to wastage or to be damaged when not packed or when not properly packed;
- handling, loading, stowage or unloading of the goods by the sender, the consignee or persons acting on behalf of the sender or the consignee;
- the nature of certain kinds of goods which particularly exposes them to total or partial loss or to damage, especially through breakage, rust, decay, dessication, leakage, normal wastage, or the action of moth or vermin;
- insufficiency or inadequacy of marks or numbers on the packages;
- the carriage of livestock.

Where the carrier can establish that the loss or damage is a result of one or more of the above circumstances, there will be a presumption it was so caused (Art 18(2)). However, being a presumption, it is open to the claimant to show that it was not attributable partly or wholly to the specified risks. It seems that in relation to special risks defences, the burden of proof is something less than a balance of probabilities.[67]

The presumption provided by Art 18(2) does not apply if there is excessive shortage or loss of package where goods are carried on unsheeted open vehicles (Art 18(3)). Where goods are carried in refrigerated vehicles, the carrier can claim the special risk defence of the nature of goods (fourth in the list above) only if he can prove that all steps incumbent upon him in the circumstances with respect to the choice, maintenance and use of such equipment were taken and that he complied with any special instructions given to him (Art 18(4)). The extent of the carrier's duty in this respect however is not clear. Is it one of due diligence? Or is the duty strict? The courts by and

---

66 [1985] 2 Lloyd's Rep 243.
67 *Ulster-Swift v Taunton Meat Haulage* [1977] 1 Lloyd's Rep 346, at p 354.

large have tended to treat the carrier's duty as strict.[68] For instance, in *Ulster-Swift v Taunton Meat Haulage*,[69] the carrier was held liable since he was unable to show the cause of damage in the absence of inherent vice. However, it is possible that this standard may not be that strict after all as *Centrocoop Export-Import SA v Brit European Transport*[70] suggests. The carrier in this case was able to show that he had taken all steps incumbent on him by hiring the unit from a reputable hirer and subjecting it to inspection and regular maintenance.

Similarly, in relation to carriage of livestock, he has to prove that all steps normally incumbent on him in the circumstances were taken and that he complied with any special instructions issued to him (Art 18(5)).

Carrier liability and 'cash on delivery'

The carrier may be required to collect 'cash on delivery' charges. This obligation would normally be included in the consignment note (Art 6(2)(c)). Were the carrier to deliver the goods without collecting the charges, he will be liable to the sender. His compensation will not exceed the amount of such charge (Art 21). The CMR does not define cash. Presumably, the issue of whether a cheque or draft is sufficient may depend on domestic law. Practices in the trade may also contribute towards deciding whether a particular mode of payment would be acceptable or not.[71]

Liability amount

The CMR adopts a complex formula for calculating compensation payable by the carrier. In the event of total or partial loss, the amount payable is calculated by reference to the value of the goods at the place and time at which the goods were accepted for carriage (Art 23(1)). The value is determined from the commodity exchange price or the current market price (Art 23(2)). It is possible that the market price may vary depending on whether domestic market or export market is used as the yardstick. According to *James Buchanan v Babco Forwarding and Shipping Co (UK) Ltd*,[72] export market price is relevant for the purposes of arriving at the value. The use of export price has been criticised, since Art 23(1) states that compensation is to calculated by reference to the value of the goods at the place where the goods are accepted for carriage.[73] Where the commodity exchange value or the current market price is unavailable, the value is to be gathered from the normal value of the goods of the same kind or quality (Art 23(2)).[74] Compensation is limited to 8.33 Special Drawing Rights (SDRs) per kilogram or gross weight short.[75] This limit does not apply,

---

68   Chao, 'Carriage at controlled temperatures (Art 18(4))', in Theunis (ed), *International Carriage of Goods by Road (CMR)*, 1987, LLP.

69   [1977] 1 Lloyd's Rep 346.

70   [1984] 2 Lloyd's Rep 618.

71   Goode, *Payment Obligations in Commercial and Financial Transactions*, 1983, Sweet & Maxwell.

72   [1978] AC 141. See also Lord Wilberforce at p 182.

73   See Hardingham, 'Damages under CMR: the decision of the House of Lords' [1978] LMCLQ 51.

74   See *Fatme Ghandour v Circle International Ltd* (1999) unreported, 2 November, available on Westlaw database under identification no 1999 WL 1019554.

75   The unit for calculation purposes in the CMR is the gold franc. The replacement of the gold franc with SDRs was brought about by the Carriage by Air and Road Act 1979.

however, where the value of the goods (Art 24) or special interest in delivery (Art 26(1)) has been declared on the consignment note.

As for carriage charges, customs duties, and other charges in respect of carriage,[76] these are recoverable in full under Art 23(4).

In the event of damage, the carrier is liable for the amount by which the goods have diminished in value (Art 25(1)). The value is once again determined by reference to the commodity exchange price, the current market price or the normal value of the goods of the same kind or quality (Art 23(2)). In any event, compensation for damage to the entire consignment cannot be more than that payable for total loss (Art 25(2)(a)). A question that has come up for consideration in this context is whether substantial damage to goods should be treated as a case of constructive total loss thus attracting the application of Art 25 for the purposes of calculating liability. In *William Tatton v Ferrymasters*,[77] the cargo, valued at £32,700, was worth £9,000 after damage. Though the plaintiff argued that compensation ought to be calculated under Art 23 since it was a case of constructive total loss,[78] the court came to the conclusion that it was a case of damage.

In the event of delay, the claimant will be compensated up to the amount of carriage charges if he can show that damage has resulted from the delay (Art 23(5)). There is uncertainty as to the precise scope of 'damage' in this context. If the word refers to physical damage normally associated with the word, then that is recoverable under Art 25 anyway. The provision for damage in Art 23(5) appears meaningless. So, 'damage' in the context of Art 23(5) could only refer to economic loss, or damage to the claimant's pocket as Clarke suggests.[79] In *Gefco (UK) Ltd v Mason*,[80] the court indicated there was nothing in the CMR to prevent recovery of economic loss including loss of profits provided that was limited to the carriage. In the event of delay in delivery, a reservation in writing has to be sent within the time limit prescribed by Art 30(3) in order to obtain damages.

Availability of limitation

The defences and limits of liability provided by the CMR are available to the carrier where a claim arising under the contract of carriage is founded extra-contractually, for instance, in tort or bailment (Art 28(1)). The same applies to the carrier's agents, servants and those whose services he uses for the performance of the carriage, provided they act within the scope of their employment (Art 29(2)).

Loss of limitation of liability

The provisions relating to exclusion and limitation of liability provided by the CMR is lost where the damage is caused by the carrier's wilful misconduct or default on his

---

76   In *James Buchanan v Babco Forwarding and Shipping UK* [1978] AC 141, excise duty was regarded as another charge. Does Art 23(4) cover costs incurred in the preparation of invoices and other documents such as pre-inspection certificates, and certificate of quality? See [1978] AC 141, at p 158.

77   [1974] 1 Lloyd's Rep 203.

78   On constructive total loss, see Chapter 14, pp 451–2 below.

79   Clarke, *International Carriage of Goods by Road: CMR* 2003, LLP.

80   [2000] 2 Lloyd's Rep 555.

part, which according to the law of the court seised of the case, is regarded as equivalent to wilful misconduct (Art 29(1)). This is also the case where wilful misconduct or default is committed by the carrier's servants, or agents, or by any other persons whose services he makes use of in the performance of the carriage acting within the scope of their employment. This provision is modelled on Art 25 of the Warsaw Convention 1929 and, as Clarke says, it is odd that Art 25 was used at a time when it was under review.[81] For interpretation, case law developments in respect of Art 25[82] are pertinent and followed as suggested by *Jones v Bencher*.[83] Recent cases decided in the context of CMR reinforce the view that for there to be wilful misconduct either knowledge on the part of the carrier that his conduct was wrong or his reckless indifference to the rightness or wrongness of his conduct has to be established. In *TNT Global Spa and Another v Denfleet International Ltd and Another*[84] the driver fell asleep at the wheel as a result of which the lorry crashed and burst into flames resulting in the destruction of the cargo. From the evidence it transpired that the driver was conscious that he was sleepy but carried on driving. On appeal it was held that this of itself was insufficient to conclude that there was wilful misconduct. To quote Toulson, LJ:

> To establish wilful misconduct within the meaning of the CMR, it is not enough to show that the carrier was at fault in failing to take proper care of the goods and that the carrier's conduct was the product of a conscious decision. It has to be shown that the actor knew that his conduct was wrong or was recklessly indifferent whether it was right or wrong; and, as part of that requirement, he must have appreciated that his conduct created or might create additional risks to the goods.[85]

Carrier's rights

Other than the right to freight, charges, expenses incurred in following instructions, etc, the CMR gives the carrier rights to sell the goods, dispose of the goods, or unload them in specific circumstances. The carrier can sell or dispose of the goods without awaiting instructions, where:

- they are perishable; or
- their condition warrants such a course; or
- the storage expenses would be out of proportion to the value of the goods (Art 16(3)).[86]

Cargo that does not fall within the above can be sold if he has not received instructions to the contrary from the person entitled to dispose of the goods after a reasonable length of time (Art 16(3)). The CMR does not indicate whether the carrier is

---

81 See Chapter 10, pp 345–7. See also Clarke, *International Carriage of Goods by Road: CMR*, 2003, LLP.

82 See also *Laceys Footwear (Wholesale) Ltd v Bowler International Freight Ltd and Another* [1997] 2 Lloyd's Rep 369, at pp 374–5.

83 [1986] 1 Lloyd's Rep 54. See also *Texas Instruments v Nasan (Europe) Ltd* [1991] 1 Lloyd's Rep 146.

84 [2007] EWCA Civ 405. See also *Datex Electronics Holdings Ltd v United Parcels Service Ltd* [2007] UKHL 23.

85 At para 24.

86 This right is similar to the agency of necessity found in common law. See Fridman, *Law of Agency*, 1996, Butterworths.

under an obligation to request information. Presumably, he will since the sender will not be aware of the precise circumstances which necessitate sale during carriage.

The person entitled to dispose of the goods has the right to the proceeds of the sale subject to any charges incurred by the carrier. Where the expenses are in excess of the sale proceeds, the carrier can claim the difference (Art 16(4)).

The carrier is also given the right to act in the best interests of the person entitled to dispose of the goods where circumstances prevent the carrying out of the contract and instructions have not been received by him (Arts 14(1) and (2)).

SENDER'S RESPONSIBILITIES AND RIGHTS

Dangerous goods

The sender is under an obligation to inform the carrier of the dangerous nature of the goods and precautions that need to be taken in respect of those goods (Art 22(1)). Dangerous goods are not defined by the CMR. At common law, dangerous goods include not only goods that are intrinsically dangerous (for example, dynamite), but also cargo that may create a hazardous situation (for example, grain).[87] As to how far this common law definition could be relied on is debatable due to the CMR's international character. The definition of dangerous goods as goods that present an immediate risk in normal transport found in Loewe's commentary[88] is perhaps more reliable. Some guidance on dangerous substances may also be obtained from the European Agreement Concerning the Carriage of Dangerous Goods by Road, 1957. However, in the absence of an exhaustive list, it is unlikely that it includes all goods that would pose an immediate risk.

Where the carrier has not been informed of the nature of the goods, the carrier is free to unload the goods, destroy them, or render them harmless. He will not be liable for any compensation to the sender or consignee (Art 22(2)). Generally, the information about the dangerous nature of the goods would be entered on the consignment note (Art 6(1)(f)). However, where the note does not contain this information, the onus is on the sender or the consignee to show that the carrier was aware of the nature of the goods (Art 22(1)).

Packing

The sender is responsible for ensuring that the goods are adequately packed. If the goods are defectively packed, then the sender is liable to the carrier for damage to persons, equipment or other goods (Art 10). This applies only where the defective packing was not apparent to the carrier. However, where the defective packing is apparent and the carrier did not make any reservations, the risk lies with the carrier. It must be noted that the carrier is responsible for checking the packaging of the goods (Art 8(1)). Presumably, the issue of whether goods are adequately packed or not will depend on factors such as the nature of the goods, the length of the

---

87 *Ministry of Transport v Lamport and Holt* [1952] 2 Lloyd's Rep 371, at p 382.
88 Loewe, 'Commentary on the Convention of 19 May 1956 on the Contract for the International Carriage of Goods by Road (CMR)' [1976] ETL 311, at para 186.

journey, the packaging customarily used in the trade, the weather conditions and so on.

The CMR is silent on the party responsible for loading. Presumably, that will be a matter of agreement between the carrier and the sender. Where the sender has loaded the goods, it may be in the interests of the carrier to note this on the consignment note (Art 6(3)).

Customs formalities

Documents needed for customs, and other formalities at the frontier, are the responsibility of the sender. Any expenses caused as a result of inadequate documentation will be to the account of the sender (Art 11).

Choice of route

Unlike the CIM Rules, the CMR does not make any special provisions on the choice of route. At common law, the route to be followed is the usual route, which is the direct geographical route unless it is customary for the trade to use another route.[89] As to whether this applies to carriage governed by the CMR is debatable. Of course, the sender and the carrier may agree on a specific route. Alternatively, the carrier may have agreed to deliver the goods by a certain date which means that he will have to take a route that will make this possible.

Modification of contract

Like the CIM Rules,[90] the CMR allows the sender to modify the contract. According to Art 12(1), the sender can ask the carrier to:

- stop the goods in transit;
- change the place at which the delivery is to take place; or
- deliver the goods to a consignee other than the one indicated on the consignment note.

The carrier is obliged to carry out these instructions only if it is possible for him to do so – that is, the carrying out of the orders does not interfere with his normal working, or affect senders or consignees of other consignments (Art 12(5)(b)), or result in division of the consignment (Art 45(1)(c)). If the instructions cannot be carried out, the onus is on the carrier to inform the sender (Art 12(6)). Failure to do so will result in liability for loss or damage (Art 12(7)). The right to modify the contract on the sender's part subsists as long as the consignee has not demanded delivery (as provided for in Art 13(1)), or the second copy of the consignment note has not been handed to the consignee (Art 12(2)). It is also possible that the sender may have given the rights to modify the contract to the consignee by making a suitable entry on the consignment note (Art 12(3)). In this case, the sender will have no rights under Art 12(1). Modification of the contract, however, requires completion of certain formalities. The

---

89   *Reardon Smith Line v Black Sea and Baltic General Insurance* [1939] AC 562.
90   See Chapter 11.

first copy of the consignment note must contain the new instructions, and should be handed over to the carrier (Art 12(5)(a)). It seems that the formalities must be strictly followed, since carrying out of instructions without requiring the consignment note will make the carrier liable for any resulting loss or damage (Art 12(7)). Where the carrier incurs expenses, or suffers loss or damage as a result of carrying out his instructions, he has the right to be indemnified (Art 12(5)(a)).

CONSIGNEE'S RIGHTS AND RESPONSIBILITIES

The consignee has the right to demand delivery of the goods and the consignment note (second copy) on arrival of the cargo at its destination against a receipt (Art 13(1)). The CMR does not state whether the receipt needs to be signed. However, since the receipt is likely to be of evidential value, it would be in the carrier's best interests to require the consignee to sign and date the receipt on collection of the goods. There is no provision on the means of identification to be produced by the consignee. Presumably, this will depend on the practices in the trade.

Modification of contract

The consignee has the right to modify the contract where:

• the sender gives the right of disposal to the consignee (Art 12(3)); or
• the consignee obtains the second consignment note on arrival of the goods (Art 13(1)).

The formalities laid down for the modification of contract and the carrier's rights in respect of charges, refusal to carry out the instructions, etc, laid down in Art 12(5) apply equally to the consignee.[91] It must, however, be noted that any 'new' consignee named by the consignee will not have the right to modify the contract.

Freight and supplementary charges

The responsibility for paying freight and other charges to the carrier is generally a matter of agreement between the parties. However, the consignee, when he demands delivery of the cargo on arrival, may find he is liable to pay the charges to the carrier shown due on the consignment note. This applies even where the sender may have agreed to pay them. If there is a dispute, the carrier can refuse delivery until some form of security is furnished by the consignee (Art 13(2)).

PROCEEDINGS

By whom

There is no clear indication as to who is entitled to sue the carrier under the convention. Article 7(3) states that the carrier is answerable to the person entitled to dispose

---

91 See 'Carrier's Liabilities and Rights' and 'Sender's Responsibilities and Rights', pp 386–94 above.

of the goods for failure to omit to include the paramount clause as required by Art 6(1)(k). Article 13(1), on the other hand, gives the consignee the right to sue in the event of delay or loss of cargo.[92] It is not unsurprising that different jurisdictions have come to different solutions, guided by their national law, when it comes to the question of who has the right to sue the carrier under the CMR. Some jurisdictions favour the view that the party with the right of disposal has the right to sue the carrier.[93] But, in the view of some commentators, this view totally ignores the fact that Art 13(1) gives a right to the consignee (albeit limited) to sue when the goods are delayed or lost.[94] The alternative view, held in some jurisdictions, is that both the consignee and the sender have the right to sue the carrier, since Art 13(1) in giving the consignee the right to sue does not take away rights that others may have.[95] However, what if the owner of the goods is neither the sender nor the consignee? Presumably, in England, an action in bailment could be brought against the carrier.

Against whom

Article 36 lists the carriers against whom an action can be brought for loss, damage or delay. These are the first carrier, the last carrier, or the carrier who was performing the portion of carriage when the event causing the loss, damage or delay occurred. The words 'first carrier' suggests that the carrier must be the first to be physically involved in carrying the goods and excludes the carrier who has subcontracted the carriage. It has however been held that the first carrier is one who has contracted with the sender.[96] As for the last carrier, this should cause no problem where the goods are delivered. However, where the goods are lost, who is the last carrier? Is it the carrier who would have been the last carrier had the goods been passed on to him, or the successive carrier who lost the goods? There are different views on this. According to some, the last carrier should be the one who is meant to deliver the goods, even if he never accepted the goods or the consignment note, since the CMR is modelled on the CIM Rules (Art 55(3)),[97] and the consignee of the goods has a convenient defendant. The issue of a convenient defendant does not really make much sense, since Art 31 allows an action to be brought at the place of delivery. This means that the consignee will not have any problems in suing the first carrier, or any of the other carriers at the destination any way. The alternative suggestion that the last carrier is the successive carrier who loses the goods seems more acceptable, since he is in possession of the goods and the consignment note at the time of the loss.

The convention also provides for the apportionment of liability between successive carriers in Arts 37 In *Rosewood Trucking Ltd v Balaam* [2005][98] the court held that

---

92   *Texas Instruments Ltd v Nasan (Europe) Ltd* [1991] 1 Lloyd's Rep 146.

93   (Germany) OLG Karlsruhe, ULC 289. See also CIM Rules in Chapter 11.

94   See, eg, Glass and Cashmore, *Introduction to the Law of Carriage*, 1989, Sweet & Maxwell, also Cashmore, 'Who are consignors and consignees for the purposes of a contract of carriage?' [1990] JBL 377.

95   See Clarke, *International Carriage of Goods by Road: CMR*, 2003, LLP, for an excellent account of the views in different jurisdictions.

96   *Ulster-Swift v Taunton Meat Haulage* [1977] 1 Lloyd's Rep 346. The same view has been held in other jurisdictions – see, eg, *OGH* 4.6.87 (1988) 23 ETL 714.

97   See also Chapter 11.

98   EWCA Civ 1461.

for the purposes of Art 37 compensation paid by a carrier to another in compliance with his obligations under a sub-contract is not included. 'To allow the claimant to pass on that contractual liability would be doing something outside the scheme of the CMR, which is obviously intended to be self-contained' (at para 13). However, successive carriers can derogate from the provisions of rules for apportionment laid down in Arts 37 and 38 (Art 40).

Jurisdiction

The CMR allows the plaintiff to bring his action[99] in an appropriate court in the country where:

- the defendant is ordinarily resident (Art 31(1)(a));[100]
- the defendant has his principal place of business (Art 31(1)(a));
- the branch or agency through which the contract of carriage was made (Art 31(1)(a));
- the goods were taken over by the carrier (Art 31(1)(b)); or
- the place designated for delivery is situated (Art 31(1)(b)).

The parties are also free to agree to bring an action in a court or tribunal in a state which is a party to the convention (Art 31(1)). In this context, a number of interesting questions can be raised. For instance, where the parties agree that the jurisdiction of their choice is to be the exclusive jurisdiction, will this negate the options listed in Art 31(1)(a) and (b)? Will an agreement on jurisdiction between the sender and the carrier bind the consignee?

As for the first issue, it is unlikely that an exclusive jurisdiction clause will be tolerated, since there is nothing in the wording of Art 31 to support it. Indeed, Art 31 specifically states that the options listed in Art 31(1) are available *in addition* to the court designated by agreement between the parties. Further, a clause nominating a jurisdiction as exclusive is likely to be regarded as null and void (Art 41), since it derogates from the provisions of the CMR.

As for the second question, majority opinion is that the consignee will not be affected by any agreement that exists between the sender and the carrier due to lack of notice.[101] This view is in line with the general principles of contract law. However, the consignee would be bound where the agreement on jurisdiction appears on the consignment note or other document that has been accepted on delivery, or where the sender contracts with the carrier as agent of the consignee.

A procedural question likely to arise in the context of the convention is whether a court can decline jurisdiction on the basis of *forum non conveniens*. This is an issue

---

99 The issue of starting a new action where an action is pending before a court or tribunal is dealt with in Art 31(2). In *Andrea Merzario Ltd v Internationale Spedition Leitner Gesellschaft GMBH* [2001] 1 Lloyd's Rep 490, the Court of Appeal held for the purposes of Art 31(2) that proceedings will not be regarded as pending until they were served. See also Rüfner, 'Lis alibi pendens under CMR' [2001] LMCLQ 460. See also *Frans Maas Logistics UK Ltd v CDR Trucking BV* [1999] 2 Lloyd's Rep 179.

100 As for the meaning of the words 'ordinarily resident', see Chapter 10 pp 349–53 above.

101 Loewe, 'Commentary on the Convention of 19 May 1956 on the Contract for the International Carriage of Goods by Road (CMR)' [1976] ETL 311, at para 242. See also Messent and Glass, *Hill and Messent CMR, Contracts for the International Carriage of Goods by Road*, 2000, LLP; Clarke, *International Carriage of Goods by Road: CMR* 2003, LLP.

that has seen judicial discussion in the context of the Warsaw Convention.[102] The wording of Art 31(1) is similar to Art 28(1) of the Warsaw Convention and the question of whether the word 'brought' in the CMR refers simply to commencement or commenced and pursued remains open. It is likely that the word will be interpreted as the latter since it is an international convention meant to achieve uniformity.[103] Besides, it does not contain a provision on the rules of procedure (see Art 28(2) of the Warsaw Convention)[104] and therefore leaves no scope for arguing that it is up to the court where the proceedings have been initiated whether or not to grant stay of proceedings on the grounds of *forum non conveniens*.

Some indication of how the courts might approach the issue of *forum non conveniens* can be gathered from *Royal & Sun Alliance Insurance Plc and Another v MK Digital Fze (Cyprus Ltd) and Others*[105] (reversed by the Court of Appeal, CMR not applicable to contract). Nonetheless what was said in the High Court regarding the availability of *forum non conveniens* in relation to CMR is interesting. Referring to *Milor SRL v British Airways plc*[106] in the judge's view Art 31(1) was 'an exclusive code as to where proceedings "arising out of the carriage under this Convention" may be brought. The final words of that paragraph are "and in no other courts or tribunals". As with the Warsaw Convention . . . article 31(1) leaves no scope for a challenge to the jurisdiction on the grounds of *forum non conveniens*'.[107]

Arbitration

Under the CMR, the parties are free to agree to submit their dispute to arbitration as long as the clause in the contract imparting competence to the arbitration tribunal provides that the tribunal is to apply the CMR (Art 33). As to whether a choice of law clause that attracts the application of the CMR is sufficient to fulfil the requirements of Art 33 has seen judicial discussion. In *Bofors UVA v Skandia Transport*,[108] the arbitration clause read as follows:

> Disputes between the freight forwarder and the customer shall with the exclusion of ordinary courts of law be referred to arbitration in Stockholm according to the Swedish law on arbitrators and with the application of Swedish law.

The defendants applied for a stay of proceedings in the English courts. The plaintiffs submitted that the arbitration clause under consideration was void (under Art 41)[109] since, under Art 33, the clause must expressly provide that the tribunal should apply the CMR. For their part, the defendants argued that the goal of Art 33 is to guarantee the application of the CMR. An appropriate choice of law that would result in the

---

102 See Chapter 10, pp 349–53 above.

103 See Glass, 'CMR: putting practice into theory' [1984] LMCLQ 30. See also Clarke, *International Carriage of Goods: CMR*, 2003, LLP.

104 See Chapter 10, pp 349–53 above.

105 [2005] EWHC 1408 (Comm). For Court of Appeal decision see [2006] EWCA Civ 629.

106 [1996] QB 702. See also Chapter 10, pp 349–53.

107 Para 72.

108 [1982] 1 Lloyd's Rep 410.

109 See *Shell Chemicals UK Ltd v P and O Roadways Ltd* [1993] 1 Lloyd's Rep 114, where an indemnity clause in favour of the carrier in respect of the carrier's liability to owners other than the contracting party was held to go against Art 41. Cashmore, 'CMR. Delivery of wrong goods, rights of indemnity' [1993] JBL 498 for a critical discussion of this case.

application of the CMR would suffice. The court however found for the plaintiff on the basis the drafters would have worded the provision differently if indicators such as the proper law of the contract were acceptable.

Time limitation

The period of limitation for bringing an action under the CMR is one year (Art 32(1)), unless it is wilful misconduct in which case it is three years.[110] The limitation period applies to all actions, whether they be brought in contract or in tort, and applies to claims by and against carriers. According to Art 32(1), the limitation period is set to run:

- in the case of partial loss, damage or delay, from the date of delivery (Art 32(1)(a));
- in the case of total loss, from the 30th day after the expiry of the agreed time limit or where there is no agreed time limit from the 60th day from the date on which the goods were taken over by the carrier (Art 32(1)(b));
- in all other cases, on the expiry of a period of three months after the making of the contract of carriage (Art 32(1)(c)).

Despite its seeming clarity, much judicial discussion has centred around this provision, especially where goods have not been delivered to the consignee due to the extent of the damage. Should such a case be treated as attracting the application of Rule 1 above, since the goods are 'delivered' to the sender when they are returned? Or, does Rule 2 apply since the goods should be deemed to be lost, since they are not delivered to the consignee within the period specified by Art 20(1)?[111] Alternatively, is the situation covered by Rule 3, since it does not fall squarely within Rules 1 or 2? Or, is it a case of applying domestic law? Interestingly, all of the above have either been endorsed or adopted by the courts. In *Worldwide Carriers v Ardtran*,[112] the first three options were examined, and, according Parker J, all of them were acceptable, though he applied the second (that is, Art 32(1)(b)) to the case at hand.[113] As for the fourth, it was adopted in *Moto Vespa v MAT*.[114] Mocatta J felt that the circumstances of the case were not covered by Art 32(1)(a), (b) or (c), and applied domestic law, thus giving a six year limitation period. It must be said that the judgment in this case was not followed in any of the subsequent cases in England, and is unlikely to be followed. Of the available options, the third seems, by far, the most sensible. Article 32(1)(c) is envisaged to cover all situations that do not fall neatly within Art 32(1)(a) or (b). To strain the concept of delivery in a manner so that the return of goods to the sender fits within Art 32(1)(a) is questionable. Likewise, to treat the goods as lost, when their existence and location can be established, so that Art 32(1)(b) can be applied, seems to go against common sense. As to why all these forced readings are needed is surprising when Art 32(1)(c) provides a tidy solution.

---

110 See *Jones v Bencher* [1986] 1 Lloyd's Rep 54.
111 According to Art 20, if the goods have not been delivered within 30 days of the expiry of the agreed time limit, or within 60 days from the time the carrier took over the goods in the absence of an agreed time limit, they will be regarded as lost.
112 [1983] 1 All ER 692.
113 See also *ICI Fibres Ltd v MAT Transport Ltd* [1987] 1 Lloyd's Rep 354.
114 [1979] 1 Lloyd's Rep 175. See also Hardingham, 'Aspects of the limitation of actions under CMR' [1979] LMCLQ 362.

The limitation period applies to actions brought by the carrier as well. Actions by the carrier for freight, expenses incurred for carrying out instructions under Art 12 will fall within Art 32(1)(c).

The period of limitation is suspended where a written claim is sent to the carrier (Art 32(2)).[115] However, once the carrier rejects the claim and returns all the documents attached to the claim, the suspension will no longer apply.[116] Further claims on the same object will not operate to suspend the running of the period of limitation (Art 32(2)).

It would be possible for the parties to agree to extend the time limits imposed by the CMR after the claim has arisen. The question that is likely to pose a problem is whether an implicit agreement to extend the time limit will be acceptable. In some jurisdictions, it seems that this would be allowed.[117]

CMR – THE FUTURE

Like the other transport conventions,[118] the CMR is disappointing. It is inexhaustive and central concepts are left undefined with the result that courts often resort to domestic law. For instance, delivery, central to carriage of goods, is undefined; and liability for loss or damage to goods occurring prior to taking over and delivery is not dealt with in the CMR. Given these and other shortcomings raised, it is fair to question the usefulness of international conventions in standardising the law.[119] If an open-textured approach to drafting of conventions is the only way to attract states to become signatories to a convention, would it not be better to let harmonisation take place through uniform rules devised for the mercantile community by an international organisation it respects?

FURTHER READING

Clarke, *International Carriage of Goods by Road: CMR*, 2003, LLP.

Messent and Glass, *CMR Contracts for the International Carriage of Goods by Road*, 2000, LLP.

Theunis (ed), *International Carriage of Goods by Road (CMR)*, 1987, LLP.

---

115 It seems that the claim does not have to be formal or for that matter quantified in England. See *ICI Fibres Ltd v MAT Transport Ltd* [1987] 1 Lloyd's Rep 354; *William Tatton v MAT Ferrymasters* [1974] 1 Lloyd's Rep 203; *Moto Vespa v MAT* [1979] 1 Lloyd's Rep 175.

116 See *Microfine Minerals and Chemicals Ltd v Transferry Shipping Co Ltd* [1991] 2 Lloyd's Rep 630.

117 Wetter, 'The time-bar regulations in the CMR Convention' [1979] LMCLQ 504.

118 See Chapters 8, 9, 10, 11 and 13.

119 See Clarke, 'Doubts from the dark side – the case against codes' [2001] JBL 605, for some thought-provoking views.

CHAPTER 13

INTERNATIONAL MULTIMODAL TRANSPORT

INTRODUCTION

Use of containers for consolidation of cargo was one of the most important developments in the transport industry in the latter part of the last century.[1] They reduced losses caused by congestion, delay and pilferage at ports. Improvements in transport management through information technology, innovative ship and other vehicle building methods (for example, cellular ships, articulated lorries) also contributed to the emergence of multimodal[2] (also called combined or intermodal) transport[3] – door-to-door carriage using two or more modes of transport such as road/sea/road and road/rail/sea/road.[4] The growth of multimodal transport brought with it the evolution of single transport documents, such as through bill of lading and multimodal (combined) transport document, to cover the entire carriage of cargo from door-to-door. It also fuelled an expansion of freight forwarders who not only provided packing services, warehousing, customs clearance, etc, but also undertook transport arrangements across international frontiers involving several carriers. Not all freight forwarders, however, operated vessels;[5] some acted as either principal or agent of the consignor in arranging carriage, while others also carried goods part of the way on their vessels.

Unlike other forms of unimodal transport,[6] multimodal transport unregulated by an international convention brought with it legal chaos. Questions such as whom to sue (freight forwarder, contracting carrier, actual carrier) in the event of delay in delivery, loss or damage to goods, where to sue, time limits for initiating action, or the basis and extent of the forwarder's or carrier's liability take on a new urgency.

International attempts to bring order have received a mixed response. The United Nations Convention on International Multimodal Transport of Goods (hereinafter

---

1   For an interesting review of the growth of containerisation, see Graham and Hughes *Container-isation in the Eighties*, 1985, LLP. Note, however, that the concept of transportation of goods using containers was known as far back as 1801. See Section II ('The evolution of multimodal transportation') in Palmer and DeGiulio, 'Terminal operations and multimodal carriage: history and prognosis' (1989) 64 Tulane LR 281.

2   The concept of multimodal transport is perceived by the United Nations Conference on Trade and Development (UNCTAD) as door-to-door transport under the responsibility of a single transport operator. See Item 3, Fostering competitive multimodal transport services, 3rd session, 6–12 June 1995 (available at www.unctad.org) and seen by many as offering a safe and efficient means of transporting goods.

3   The United Nations Economic and Social Council (UNECE) defines multimodal transport as 'carriage of goods by two or more modes of transport'; intermodal transport as 'movement of goods in one and the same loading unit or road vehicle, which uses successively two or more modes of transport without handling the goods themselves in changing modes' and combined transport as 'intermodal transport where the major part of the European journey is by rail, inland waterways or sea and initial or final legs carried out by road are as short as possible' (TRANS/WP.24/2000/1 available at www.unece.org). However, UNCTAD seems to use these terms interchangeably in their documents.

4   See Palmer and DeGiulio, 'Terminal operations and multimodalism carriage: history and prognosis' (1989) 64 Tulane LR 281, for an interesting account of the evolution of multimodal transport.

5   Hence, some freight forwarders call themselves NVOC (non-vessel owning carrier).

6   Eg, the Warsaw Convention 1929, the Montreal Convention 1999 regulating air carriage, the Hague-Visby Rules 1968 regulating carriage of goods by sea. See Chapters 8 and 10. See also Table 13.1 for further details.

'MT Convention') signed at Geneva on 24 May 1980[7] has not attracted the thirty signatures/accessions to come into force because it is seen as overly consignor-friendly by the transport industry. Also, its association with the Hamburg Rules[8] may have been a major contributory factor for its unpopularity. According to a recent report based on the responses to questionnaires[9] from the UNCTAD Secretariat,[10] lack of sufficient ratifications to enable the MT Convention to come into force is attributable to a number of factors. Among them, lack of interest in the MT Convention from leading maritime countries, the large number of ratifications required for the MT Convention to enter into force, dissatisfaction with the liability scheme (namely, basis of liability, monetary limitation of liability and the principle of uniform liability) adopted by the MT Convention, lack of commitment by governments, and adoption of network system with regard to limitation of liability.[11]

The International Chamber of Commerce (ICC)'s Uniform Rules for a Combined Transport Document 1973 as amended in 1975[12] and the UNCTAD[13]/ICC Rules for Multimodal Transport Documents 1992[14] (hereinafter 'UNCTAD/ICC Rules') have had more success through their acceptance by transport operators. Transport documentation such as the International Federation of Freight Forwarders Associations (FIATA)[15] Negotiable Multimodal Transport Bill of Lading (hereinafter 'FIATA Bill') is modelled on the latter. Of course, like other rules drafted by the ICC (for example, the International Rules for the Interpretation of Trade Terms (INCOTERMS)),[16] the UNCTAD/ICC Rules have to be incorporated into a contract by the parties.

The lack of a uniform liability regime for multimodal transportation inevitably affects commerce due to uncertainty in respect of its legal infrastructure. As observed by the WTO:[17]

> The consequence of current arrangements is therefore a patchwork of regimes which fails to capitalize on modern IT-based communications systems and practices, which impedes the introduction of a single multimodal waybill/transport document, and which does not reflect fully the increased use of containerised transportation operating across different modes, making mode-specific liability arrangements inappropriate. In cases of loss or damage to goods, this creates uncertainty as to the time of loss. Damage,

---

7   UN Doc TD/MT/CONF/17(1981).
8   See Chapter 9.
9   The questionnaires were sent to all governments and industry as well as interested intergovernmental and non-governmental organisations and a number of experts on the subject. The report says that they received 109 replies but does not indicate how many questionnaires were sent out in total.
10 'Multimodal transport: the feasibility of an international legal instrument', UNCTAD/SDTE/TLB 2003/1 (13 January 2003).
11 UNCTAD/SDTE/TLB 2003/1 (13 January 2003), paras 22–26.
12 ICC Publication No 298. BIMCO (Baltic and International Maritime Council) produced a document called COMBICON which conformed with the 1975 ICC Rules.
13 United Nations Commission on Trade and Development.
14 ICC Publication No 481. The Rules, adopted by the ICC Executive Board on 11 June 1991, came into effect on 1 January 1992. Text available at www.unctad.org.
15 International Federation of Freight Forwarders Association. Further details about the organisation is obtainable by visiting their website www.fiata.com.
16 See Chapter 1, pp 49–51 above.
17 World Trading Organization.

uncertainty as to mode and identity of the carrier; and uncertainty as to the applicable legal regime for liability and its effects.[18]

The United Kingdom does not have specific legislation regulating multimodal transport.[19] To the extent it is regulated, it is based on general contract law, law of bailment, the law of tort and the voluntary incorporation of UNCTAD/ICC Rules or Standard Trading Conditions by members of the British International Freight Association[20] (BIFA) in their contracts.

This chapter concentrates on legal problems encountered by the cargo interest (consignor/consignee)[21] using a freight forwarder and available solutions in English law,[22] unification through use of BIFA's Standard Trading Conditions,[23] existing provisions for combined transport in the international unimodal transport conventions implemented by the United Kingdom and the future of the United Nations Convention on International Multimodal Transport of Goods. Relevant problems faced by freight forwarders *vis à vis* carriers and sub-carriers will also be highlighted.

FREIGHT FORWARDER – AGENT OR PRINCIPAL?

The freight forwarder,[24] as stated earlier, assumes a number of different roles. Where he takes on the role of arranging transport, his capacity is important in sorting out the liability of the various parties involved in multimodal transport. Ideally, the transport document issued by the forwarder should expressly indicate capacity: that is, whether he is acting as agent[25] for the consignor or as principal. In practice, this is rarely the case.[26] The question is resolved by looking to other factors such as:

---

18   G/C/W 133, 2 December 1998, 'Issues relating to the physical movement of consignments (transport and transit) and payment, insurance and other financial questions affecting cross-border trade in goods'.

19   A number of countries world wide have enacted legislation to address multimodal transport, eg, India. See Carr, 'International multimodal transportation of goods: the Indian response' (2000) 3(1) International Trade Law Quarterly 1. See also UNCTAD/SDTE/TLB/2, 25 June 2001, 'Implementation of multimodal transport rules', for illustrations of multimodal legislation in various parts of the world. The Asean (Association of Southeast Asian Nations) recently adopted in 2005 the Asean Framework Agreement on Multimodal Transport. Text available on www.asean.org.

20   BIFA is the United Kingdom body representing international freight services and the only source for obtaining FIATA bills in the UK. It also provides expert determination service as an alternative form of dispute resolution. Further information is available on www.bifa.org.

21   In English law, the person who has property in the goods is *prima facie* the party with whom the contract is made (see *Mullinson v Carver* (1843) LT (OS) 59). In a sale contract, this would normally be the buyer, though complications may arise as where seller retains property in the goods, etc. See Chapter 1, pp 24–6 above.

22   Applies also to Wales.

23   All references to the BIFA Standard Trading Conditions are to 2000 version unless otherwise indicated. Reproduced in Carr and Kidner, *International Trade Law Statutes and Conventions* 5th edn, 2008, Routledge-Cavendish.

24   Freight forwarders some times call themselves also by other names, eg, road transport operator, air cargo agent and multimodal transport operator.

25   See *Victoria Fur Traders v Rodline* [1981] 1 Lloyd's Rep 570. In this case, cl 6 of the way bill was held to be incorporated as a result of past course of dealings and British Airways were acting as agents for the plaintiffs.

26   See cl 4(A) of the BIFA Standard Trading Conditions, which in itself is insufficient to establish whether the forwarder acted as an agent or as principal.

- The type of transport document. For instance, a forwarder's house bill of lading[27] referring to the groupage bill of lading issued by the carrier may indicate the forwarder's intention to act as principal.

- The charges. An inclusive price[28] as opposed to freight charges plus commission may indicate that the forwarder is acting as principal. This presumption may be displaced by contract terms.[29]

- The language used by the consignor and forwarder. For instance, did the consignor request the forwarder to carry or to make transport arrangements?

- The extent and frequency of communication between the consignor and the forwarder. Regular updates on developments in transport arrangements to the consignor may suggest that the forwarder is acting in the capacity of agent. Under BIFA Standard Trading Conditions, a forwarder's failure to produce evidence of any contract entered into as agent on demand by the consignor changes his capacity to that of principal (cl 6(B)).

- Past course of dealings between forwarder and consignor.

- The usual capacity of the forwarder. Does the forwarder normally provide the services as agent or principal?[30]

In the event of the forwarder acting as agent, the consignor is in a direct contractual relationship with the carrier(s) performing the different segment(s) of the multimodal transport operation. The issue of whom to sue in the event of loss or damage is dependent on the kind of transport document issued by the contracting carrier:

- The contracting carrier may issue a FIATA Bill or a multimodal transport document that incorporates the UNCTAD/ICC Rules 1992. In this event, the claimant (cargo owner) will be able to sue the contracting carrier (multimodal transport operator) for loss of, or damage to, goods while they are in his charge – that is, from the moment of collection to delivery.

- The contracting carrier may issue a through bill of lading.[31] The situation here is

---

27 House bills of lading are normally issued where there is groupage of cargo – ie, where cargo of a compatible nature is consolidated into a container load and the carrier issues a groupage bill of lading to the forwarder. Groupage is popular since it helps reduce transportation costs, insurance costs and theft. It must be noted that house bills of lading are merely regarded as a receipt of cargo. They are not negotiable like shipped bills of lading. See also Hetherington, 'Freight forwarders and house bills of lading: *The Cape Comorin*' (1992) 1 LMCLQ 32.

28 See *Colley v Brewer's Wharf and Transport* (1921) 9 Lloyd's Law Rep 5. See also *Aqualon (UK) Ltd v Vallana Shipping Corp* [1994] 1 Lloyd's Rep 669, where the stamping of consignment note by the second defendant Nilsson International BV with the words 'as agents only' was held to be insufficient to treat them as an agent. There was nothing in the relationship or dealings between Aqualon and Nilsson that prevented Aqualon from treating Nilsson as a CMR (Convention on the International Carriage of Goods by Road 1956) carrier (at p 677). For more on the CMR, see Chapter 12.

29 For instance, cl 5(B) of the BIFA Standard Trading Conditions 1989 stated: 'The offer and acceptance of an inclusive price for the accomplishment of any service or services shall not itself determine whether any such service is or services are to be arranged by the company acting as agent or to be provided by company acting as a contracting principal.'

30 See *Marston Excelsior Ltd v Arbuckle, Smith and Co* [1971] 1 Lloyd's Rep 70; [1971] 2 Lloyd's Rep 306 (CA); *Jones v European and General Express Co* (1920) 25 Com Cas 296 and *Troy v Eastern Co of Warehouses* (1921) 37 TLR 428. The phrase forwarding agent is normally not understood as a carrier as established in *Jones v European and General Express Co*. Correspondence may indicate otherwise, even the addition of an extra percentage to a quotation. It is a matter to be established taking into account all the circumstances.

31 A through bill of lading was initially invented to cover sea voyage involving transhipment. However, it was modified to include goods by two or more different modes of transport. A

complex. The issue of whether the contracting carrier assumes responsibility for the entire voyage or only for the portion he has performed is determined by looking to the terms of the through bill of lading. Normally, the contracting carrier will assume responsibility only for his part of the carriage and acts as an agent either for the sender or for the on-carriers.[32] In the event of damage to, or loss of, goods, the claimant needs to sue the carrier responsible for the loss or damage. This may prove difficult especially where a container is used. The document given by the carrier would only show the condition of the container when received, not the condition of the goods in the container. If expert opinion shows that the damage was caused by incursion of sea water, for instance, this would show that damage occurred during the sea leg. In most cases, however, it may not be possible to localise the cause of the damage. The problems are compounded where the damage is gradual – for example, from slow leaks. The terms and conditions of each carrier will be relevant to establish the extent of carrier liability. There is the problem of deciding the venue for judicial proceedings. The claimant may have to sue the carrier in a foreign jurisdiction. He will also have to ensure that he sues the carriers within the time limits set by the liability regime applicable to the particular transport segment.[33]

It must be noted that the consignor cannot sue the freight forwarder acting as agent for loss or damage to goods, though he can be sued for not exercising due care and skill in carrying out his duties as agent.[34],[35]

Where the forwarder acts as principal, the consignor can sue him for loss of, or damage to, the goods.[36] English law, until recently, adhered (strictly) to the principle of privity[37] of contract (that is, the principle that only parties to the contract can sue on the contract), thus leaving the cargo owner unable to sue third parties (carriers with whom the forwarder has contracted for carriage).[38] This doctrine has been relaxed as a result of the Contracts (Rights of Third Parties) Act 1999. As stated in Chapter 8, s 1 enables a third party to enforce contractual terms where there is express provision that he may do so, or where the contract purports to confer a benefit on a third party.

---

distinction is also drawn in the context of sea carriage between a 'pure ocean through bill of lading' and an 'ocean through bill of lading' (see Tetley, *Marine Cargo Claims*). In a pure ocean through bill of lading, the sea carrier issuing the through bill takes responsibility for the entire carriage. In the case of the ocean bill of lading, the first carrier acts as an agent of the shipper *vis à vis* successive carriers. Hence each carrier is responsible for that segment when he is in possession of the goods.

32 This view is also put forward in Faber *et al, Multimodal Transport Avoiding Legal Problems*, Practical Guides Series, 1997, LLP, at p 1.

33 See Table 13.3.

34 See 'Responsibilities and liabilities of an agent', pp 407–8 below.

35 Clause 5(C) of the BIFA Standard Trading Conditions 1989 provided that a company acting as agent secures services for carriage, handling, packing, etc 'by establishing contracts with third parties so that direct contractual relationships are established between customer and such third parties'.

36 If the forwarder is found liable, he will try and recover his losses from the carrier responsible for the damage. As to whether he is successful or not will depend on the contract terms between himself and the carrier. It is therefore important that these terms at the very least reflect the terms of contract with the cargo owner.

37 See also 'Liability in contract and in tort and availability of limitation', Chapter 8, pp 254–8 above.

38 On Carriage of Goods by Sea Act 1992 and through bills of lading, combined transport documents, etc, see Chapter 6.

However, the exceptions contained in s 6, for our purposes, are relevant. According to s 6(5), s 1 confers no rights on a third party in the case of:

(a) a contract for the carriage of carriage of goods by sea; or

(b) a contract for the carriage of goods by rail, road or for the carriage of cargo by air, which is subject to the rules of the appropriate international transport convention

except that a third party may in reliance on that section avail himself of an exclusion or limitation of liability in such a contract.[39]

This means that the cargo owner will be unable to sue a third party since most carriages are bound to be subject to an international convention dependant on the mode.[40] However, common law allows actions in tort and in bailment. Bailment is peculiar to common law; it is *sui generis* and exists independently of contract or tort.[41] The law of bailment allows the owner of the goods or a person who has a right to possession to bring an action in bailment against third parties with whom no contractual relationship exists.

Bailment comes into existence when X is knowingly and willingly in possession of goods belonging to Y.[42] X is the bailee and Y the bailor – that is, one who leaves the goods in possession of X. It is likely that bailment will be for reward, though gratuitous bailment[43] is recognised.

In the carriage context, the carrier (or forwarder) is the bailee and, as a bailee, is required to carry the goods safely and deliver them in the condition he received them.[44] Where the forwarder as principal subcontracts the carriage to a third party, the forwarder is the intermediate bailee, the third party the sub-bailee. A cargo owner who sues the sub-bailee in bailment will have to face the question of whether the sub-bailee can rely on any of the terms of sub-bailment. It seems from the cases that, in authorising the forwarder to making sub-bailments, the bailor is bound by the sub-bailment terms.[45] In most cases, the consignor in appointing the forwarder to act as principal would have given permission impliedly or expressly to arrange sub-bailment on terms.

It must be pointed out that bailment can aid the forwarder who can show that he has a title in possession. He can sue third parties with whom the carrier may have contracted. In other words, if the carrier with whom the forwarder has contracted (as principal) sub-contracts the carriage to another carrier (sub-carrier), then the forwarder can sue the sub-carrier in bailment.[46]

It would be convenient at this juncture to introduce another feature of English

---

39 See Chapter 8, pp 254–8 above, on how this might help stevedores.

40 Of course, where an international convention is not triggered, s 1 of the Contracts (Rights of Third Parties) Act 1999 will be applicable.

41 See *History and Sources of the Common Law: Tort and Contract*, 1949, Stevens. See also *The Kapetan Marcos (No 2)* [1987] 2 Lloyd's Rep 321.

42 See Palmer, *On Bailment*, 1991, Sweet & Maxwell, for a thorough discussion.

43 As when A lends his bicycle to B.

44 *Travers v Cooper* [1915] 1 KB 73.

45 See *Morris v CW Martin and Sons Ltd* [1966] 1 QB 716. See also *The Pioneer Container* [1994] 1 Lloyd's Rep 593. Note that this is a Privy Council decision. *The Pioneer Container* applied in *Spectra International v Hayesoak Ltd* [1997] 1 Lloyd's Rep 153. There was an appeal to the Court of Appeal on the question of limitation ([1998] 1 Lloyd's Rep 162). Note it seems it is not necessary to have physical charge of the goods to create a bailment. The giving of instructions may be sufficient.

46 *Transcontainer Express v Custodian Security* [1988] 1 Lloyd's Rep 128.

law.[47] Common law makes a distinction between private carriers and common carriers. In contrast to a private carrier, a common carrier gives the impression that he will carry goods for anyone in return for a reward.[48] In other words, a common carrier does not reserve the right to refuse to carry.[49] A common carrier is a bailee like the private carrier; however, as a common carrier, his liability is strict. That is, he is liable for loss or damage to goods even where he is not negligent.[50] He can, however, take advantage of the defences allowed him by common law: act of God,[51] act of Queen's enemies, inherent vice and consignor/consignee's fault.[52] Given the differences in liability it is important to establish whether the forwarder, contracting carrier or the sub-carrier is a private carrier or common carrier.[53] It is possible for a common carrier to exclude his liability at common law.[54]

Responsibilities and liabilities of an agent[55]

As an agent,[56] the forwarder will be expected to act in accordance within the express or implied authority given to him.[57] He must also exercise reasonable skill and care in the performance of his duties.[58] The question of whether the agent has exercised reasonable skill and care in performing his obligations will depend on the instructions

---

47   The common law notions are also found in other jurisdictions as a result of Britain's colonial influence – eg, Commonwealth countries such as Canada, Australia, New Zealand and India.
48   *Tyly v Morrice* (1699) Cath 485. In *Colley v Brewers' Wharf and Transport Ltd* (1921) 9 LlL Rep 5, the court explained the distinction between a common carrier and a carrier thus:
      . . . in order to make a common carrier, it should be shown that he held himself out to carry for all persons, either over definite routes or given areas, for given prices; or that he is ready to carry at reasonable prices. Where the evidence is that he only carries when it is convenient to him to carry, when his lighters and carts are not occupied . . . that man is not a common carrier. He is a cartage contractor . . . being a cartage contractor, he does not come under the responsibility of a common carrier [at p 6].
49   A common carrier can be sued in tort for unreasonable refusal to carry. See *Jackson v Rogers* (1683) 2 Show 327; *Crouch v London North Western Railway (No 2)* (1854) 14 CB 255. However, note that a common carrier can limit the class of goods he is prepared to carry (*Chitty on Contracts*, 23rd edn, vol 2, para 482 as cited in *Siohn v Hagland Transport* [1976] 2 Lloyd's Rep 483).
50   *Siohn v Hagland Transport* [1976] 2 Lloyd's Rep 483.
51   *Nugent v Smith* (1876) 1 CPD 423.
52   *Berkeley v Watling* (1827) 7 A&E 382.
53   Clause 34 of the Institute of Freight Forwarders Ltd Standard Trading Conditions 1984 states that '. . . the company is not a common carrier and deals on the basis of these Conditions only . . .'. As to whether such clauses are effective in making a carrier a private carrier is debatable since the issue is one to be decided on an objective basis – eg, whether the company offers to carry for any one or not. Interestingly, the BIFA Standard Trading Conditions do not include a similar clause.
54   Most contracts of carriage however are subject to terms of the contract or mandatorily applicable laws.
55   The Council Directive on the Co-ordination of the Laws of the Member States Relating to Self-Employed Commercial Agents Directive 86/653/EEC, OJ L382/17 (31.12.1986) was given effect in the United Kingdom by the UK Commercial Agents (Council Directive) Regulations 1993, SI 1993 No 3053. The freight forwarder who acts in the capacity of agent for arranging transportation will not come within the ambit of this Regulation (Reg 2(1)).
56   See Fridman, *Law of Agency*, 1996, Butterworths, for a comprehensive account of the English law of agency. The book also draws comparisons with Commonwealth cases.
57   *Cunliffe Owen v Teather and Greenwood* [1967] 3 All ER 561.
58   There is no implied term however to guard against fraud. The implied term is to exercise reasonable care. See *Pringle of Scotland Ltd v Continental Express Ltd* [1962] 2 Lloyd's Rep 80.

provided by the principal[59] and the skills of an agent in his position. If no instructions are provided the agent must act in the best interests of his principal.[60] Unclear instructions can be interpreted reasonably by the agent.[61] The agent, as forwarder, will be expected to appoint persons who are capable and competent to perform the tasks.[62]

In English law, an agent also has fiduciary duties towards his principal since the relationship is seen as one of trust. In other words, there must be no conflict between the agent's personal interests and his obligations to the principal.[63]

Where the forwarder has acted negligently, the principal will be able to sue him for damages. In the event of fraud, the principal can sue him for fraud and conspiracy or sue to recover the profit made by him.[64]

Agent's rights

As an agent, the forwarder is not liable (personally) to the carrier for freight charges, customs duties, etc, unless there is an established custom.[65] The agent has the right to be indemnified for the expenses he incurs in carrying out his principal's instructions.[66] The agreed remuneration must be paid by the principal to the agent. Where he is not paid, the agent can sue the principal for the sum due. He also has a lien over the goods – he can retain possession of goods in respect of which outstanding debts due to him arise.[67]

UNIFICATION EFFORTS BY THE INDUSTRY

BIFA has made a major contribution to standardising the terms of multimodal carriage by drafting the Standard Trading Conditions for use by its members.[68] These set out the responsibilities and liabilities of the company (defined in cl 1 as 'the BIFA member trading under these Conditions') and the customer (defined in cl 1 as 'any person at whose request or on whose behalf the company undertakes any business or provides advice, information or services') who warrants that he is either the 'owner or the authorised agent of the owner' (cl 3). Owner is defined by cl 1 as 'owner of the goods transport unit and any other person who is or may become interested in them'. The definitions are sufficiently wide to bring freight forwarders and consignors/consignees within their ambit. BIFA has also

---

59   *Bertram v Godfray* (1830) 1 Knapp 381; *World Transport v Royte* [1957] 1 Lloyd's Rep 381.

60   *Harrods Ltd v Lemon* [1931] KB 157.

61   *Ireland v Livingston* (1872) LR 5 HL 395.

62   *Gillete Industries v Martin* [1966] 1 Lloyd's Rep 554.

63   *McPherson v Watt* (1877) 3 App Cas 254; *De Bussche v Alt* (1878) 8 Ch D 286; *Boardman v Phipps* [1967] 2 AC 461.

64   *T Mahesan v Malaysia Government Officers' Co-operative Housing Society Ltd* [1979] AC 374.

65   In *Anglo Overseas Transport Ltd v Titan Industrial Corp Ltd* [1959] 2 Lloyd's Rep 152, custom in the London freight market was relevant to make the forwarding agents personally liable to the ship's agents.

66   See *PSA Transport Ltd v Newton Landsdowne and Co Ltd* [1956] 1 Lloyd's Rep 121.

67   See *Fraser v Equitorial Shipping Co Ltd and Equitorial Lines Ltd* [1979] 1 Lloyd's Rep 103.

68   BIFA requires that organisations meet certain requirements before they are considered for membership. These include adequate liability insurance and adoption of Standard Trading Conditions.

endorsed the FIATA Bill which incorporates the UNCTAD/ICC Rules. The terms of this transport document where issued upon agreement will substitute for the Conditions.

Of the freight forwarders operating in the United Kingdom, members of BIFA are responsible for handling 80% of the overall business.[69] This suggests that a large proportion of goods that are transported are governed by the Conditions. Forwarders who are not members of BIFA use their own terms which, by and large, are not as favourable as the Conditions. The transport document may stipulate that only the carrier with custody of the goods at the time of loss or damage is responsible for the loss or damage. The difficulties in establishing when or where the loss or damage occurred or whom or where to sue may leave the claimant shouldering the losses.

BIFA Standard Trading Conditions

Historical background

The current Standard Trading Conditions 2005[70] (hereinafter 'Conditions') replaced the Standard Trading Conditions 1989 and 2000a[71] and 2000b which replaced Institute of Freight Forwarders Conditions 1984 (hereinafter 'IFF 1984'). The Conditions are largely derived from IFF 1984 though there are some differences by way of arrangement and expression of terms and number of clauses.[72]

Applicability of the conditions

The Conditions, for use by members, need to be incorporated into the contract. Express incorporation is the ideal method. However, they may be incorporated impliedly or otherwise. Reference to the Conditions during the course of negotiations, past course of dealings between the company and the customer, etc, will be relevant. On incorporation, the terms determine the rights, responsibilities and liabilities of the various parties unless the contract attracts the application of mandatory provisions. In this event, the Conditions' contradictory provisions will be replaced by the provisions of the mandatory law to the extent of the derogation (cl 2(B)). To illustrate, where the road part of a multimodal transport operation attracts the application of the CMR, and it is established that damage to the goods occurred on the road segment, the forwarder will be liable to the maximum of 8.33 Special Drawing Rights (SDRs) per kg instead of the 2 SDRs per kg set by the Conditions.[73]

---

69 BIFA, *The International Freight Guide*, 1997, LLP, at p 2.

70 Available at www.bifa.org.

71 Clause 21(c) of the 2000a version had to be amended; reference to the Late Payments Act in the clause had to be dropped as a result of a court decision. See BIFA Link Issue 148, January 2003, p 6.

72 The IFF 1984 had 44 clauses and was categorised in a more obvious fashion. Eg, it had sections entitled 'Company as forwarding agent', 'Company contracting as principal', making it user-friendly. The Conditions bunch the different capacities of the company under the heading 'The company'. There are also a number of clauses in the IFF 1984 which are not found in the Conditions – eg, cl 34 which states the company is not a common carrier and cl 36(a)–(d).

73 See Table 13.1 for the maximum liability limits expressed in SDRs by the various unimodal international carriage of goods conventions and Table 13.2 for the various conditions and conventions relating to multimodal transport.

The Conditions will also be superseded where a FIATA Bill is issued. The terms of the FIATA Bill are considered in the latter part of this chapter.

Responsibility and liability of the forwarder

The forwarder in his capacity of *principal* is responsible for the goods from the time of taking charge of them to the time of delivery.[74] In other words, he remains responsible for the goods while they are in his control. Delivery is not defined in the Conditions.[75] A reading of cl 10(A) indicates that delivery will be deemed to have taken place as and when they are placed at the disposal of the customer.

The forwarder is required to perform his duties with a reasonable degree of care, diligence, skill and judgment (cl 23). In other words, he should not be negligent in performing his duties in relation to the goods from the point of receipt to the point of delivery. He is responsible for loss of or damage to the goods unless occasioned by an event that could not be avoided and the consequences of which could not be prevented by the exercise of reasonable diligence (cl 24(B)).[76] The forwarder is not liable for loss or damage caused by specific events – strikes, lock-outs, stoppage or restraint of labour – which he is unable to avoid by the exercise of reasonable diligence (cl 24(A)).[77] The Conditions are no different from the UNCTAD/ICC Rules (r 5.1) in respect of the forwarder's basis of liability. He is presumed to be at fault in the event of loss or damage and the burden is cast on him to show that it could not be avoided despite the exercise of reasonable diligence. The standard of care required by the forwarder is expressed as one of 'reasonable diligence'. Lack of reasonable diligence is likely to be treated as negligence,[78] and the standard for ascertaining the exercise of reasonable diligence will be determined by looking to the actions of skilled men in similar circumstances.

The forwarder's maximum liability under the Conditions is 2 SDRs per kilogram.[79] Where the claim involves errors or omissions, maximum liability is set at 75,000 SDRs. In the event of delay in delivery, the compensation payable is set at twice the charges for the relevant transaction. The Conditions allow the parties to agree to a higher limit but this may require the payment of additional charges. The forwarder will be liable for the higher amount only if it has been agreed in writing (cl 26(D)).

Assessment of compensation is to be made by reference to the value of the goods when they were shipped or should have been shipped. The formula adopted by the Conditions is different from the formula adopted in the UNCTAD/ICC Rules (r 5.5.1), where assessment is made by reference to the value of the goods at the place and time where they are delivered or where they should have been delivered according to the transport document. Of course, the difference in approach to calculation of

---

74 This is no different from r 4 of the UNCTAD/ICC Rules.
75 Compare with r 2.8 of the UNCTAD/ICC Rules. See also cl 12.1 of the FIATA Bill.
76 This is similar to cl 36(f) of the IFF 1984.
77 Compare with cl 36 (a)–(e) of the IFF 1984, which lists the circumstances where the forwarder is relieved of liability. They include insufficiency of packing, inherent vice, strikes, lock-out and omission of the customer.
78 The Hague-Visby Rules use the phrase 'due diligence' in Art III(1). Lord Devlin in *The Amsteslot* [1963] 1 Lloyd's Rep 223 treated the issue as one of ascertaining negligence on the part of the carrier.
79 This corresponds with the liability set in the Hague-Visby Rules. See Table 13.1 for a comparison with other unimodal international carriage of goods conventions. See also Table 13.2.

compensation can be seen as exhibiting bias one way or another. Compensation calculated in terms of value of goods from place of shipment favours the forwarder since he is likely to have a better idea of value of the goods at the place of shipment as opposed to the place of delivery,

It must be noted that where the forwarder has acted in the capacity of agent, general principles of agency outlined earlier in this chapter are relevant. The consignor/consignee will have to claim for his losses or damage from the actual carrier or contracting carrier. The forwarder as agent however is liable for negligence on his part in carrying out the principal's actions or for acting outside the scope of his authority. He will also be liable for breach of his fiduciary duties. The Conditions however do impart wide powers in respect of the choice of routes, and procedure to be followed in the performance of any service provided, to the forwarder (cl 4B).

Forwarder's rights

The contract will normally specify the charges to be paid by the consignor to the forwarder. The Conditions require the customer to pay all sums as and when they are due in cash or as otherwise agreed (cl 21(A)). Where this is not paid, the Conditions create a general lien (cl 8(A)) on goods and documents in its possession. In other words, the forwarder can hold on to the goods and documents till the sums due are paid by the customer or owner. The forwarder has the right to sell the goods on 28 days' notice in writing (cl 8(A)(ii)).

It must be noted that, at common law, a common carrier also has a lien for freight.[80] There is some dispute as to whether a private carrier has this right.[81] Whether a forwarder is a common carrier or not will depend on the circumstances. If the forwarder offers to carry the goods for reward to all and does not reserve the right to refuse, he will be deemed a common carrier.[82]

It is customary for carriers to pay freight forwarders commissions and other allowances. Since the legality of receiving of such allowances is questionable, the Conditions allow the freight forwarder to retain brokerages, commissions, allowances and other remunerations customarily paid (cl 9).

Right of sale is also imparted under the Conditions in a number of situations – that is: (1) where the cargo has perished or is in danger of perishing and likely to cause damage to third parties or contravene regulations (cl 8(B)); and (2) where goods are not collected or the person supposed to take delivery is not traceable (cl 10(B)(i)).

The Conditions also contain a number of indemnity clauses to protect the forwarder, ranging from liability, costs, expenses, etc, arising as a result of following the customer's instructions (cl 20(A)), general average costs (cl 20(D)) to claims, 'costs and demands whatsoever and by whomsoever made or preferred in excess of the liability of the company under the terms of these Conditions regardless of whether such claims, costs and demands arise from or in connection with the negligence or breach of duty of the company, its servants, sub-contractors or agents' (cl 20(C)).

---

80 *Skinner v Upshaw* (1702) 2 Ld Raym 752.
81 See *Electric Supply Stores v Gaywood* (1909) LT 855; *United States Steel Products v Great Western Railway* [1916] AC 189.
82 *Belfast Ropework Co v Bushell* [1918] 1 KB 210. See also *Tyly v Morrice* (1699) Carth 485.

Responsibility and liability of the consignor

The consignor is responsible for providing accurate and adequate descriptions of the goods and must pack the goods adequately, mark and label them properly. Where loss, damage or delay has occurred as a result of the consignor's fault, the forwarder will not be liable and the consignor will be required to indemnify the forwarder (cl 20).[83]

Time limit, jurisdiction and applicable law

Where the Conditions apply, the cargo owner must institute proceedings within nine months of the event giving rise to a cause of action.[84] The cargo owner is also required to make his claim in writing to the forwarder within 14 days of the date on which the cargo owner became aware of the event giving rise to the claim, unless he can show that it was not possible for him to do so within the time limit.[85]

Under the Conditions, English courts will have exclusive jurisdiction and the applicable law will be that of England (cl 28).

FIATA NEGOTIABLE MULTIMODAL BILL OF LADING

As stated earlier, the parties may agree to issue a FIATA Bill.[86] In this event, the terms of the FIATA Bill replace the Conditions.

A legal issue likely to arise is whether a negotiable multimodal bill of lading is recognised as such – that is, as a document of title – in English law. Common law recognises only a shipped bill of lading as a document of title.[87] However, a document of title may be created by mercantile custom at common law.[88] It would therefore be possible for a multimodal bill of lading to be recognised as a document of title through customary use in the trade.[89] A likely problem that might be encountered in imparting negotiable quality to a multimodal transport document is that cargo in most cases would only be received for shipment at the time of issue. In other words, it would be no more than a received for shipment bill of lading which is not recognised as a document of title at common law. It would of course be feasible for a received for shipment document to be converted to a shipped document through appropriate notation. It must be noted that a bill of lading is only transferable, not negotiable in

---

83 See Table 13.3 for further on MTO liability.
84 Clause 27(B).
85 Clause 27(A).
86 Reproduced in the Appendices. Note that BIMCO has also devised negotiable multimodal bill called MULTIDOC 95 which is also modelled on the UNCTAD/ICC Rules. See Appendix 6.
87 A received for shipment bill of lading is not recognised as a document of title at common law. Where a non-negotiable bill of lading is used, the consignee needs to produce the bill of lading to obtain delivery from the carrier. This is not the case with a waybill. See Chapters 6 and 8, above.
88 *Kum v Wah Tat Bank* [1971] 1 Lloyd's Rep 439.
89 However, the English courts draw a distinction between custom and practice. See *Sucre Export SA v Northern Shipping Ltd (The Sormovskiy 3068)* [1994] 2 Lloyd's Rep 266 and Chapter 6. The recognition of the Multimodal Transport Document in the Uniform Customs and Practice for Documentary Credits 600 (UCP 600) may (arguably) be used to establish custom.

the legal sense of the term in English law. In other words, on transfer, the transferee does not get a better title than the transferor.[90]

The FIATA Bill, modelled on the UNCTAD/ICC Rules, is outlined in brief below.

Applicability of FIATA Bill terms

The provisions of the FIATA Bill apply when parties agree to contract on these terms. The terms assume that the freight forwarder (defined as multimodal transport operator who issues the bill, is named on the face of the document and assumes liability for the multimodal transport contract as a carrier) is the principal. They govern carriage of all types of cargo, including live animals. They apply equally where one mode of transport is used to carry the cargo.

Responsibilities, liabilities and rights of the freight forwarder

The freight forwarder is responsible for the cargo from the moment he takes them in his charge to the time of delivery. He does, however, have the right to choose the method of transportation, the route and the procedure of handling and storage of the goods. The basis of his liability is one of presumed fault, that is, he is liable for loss of or damage to or delay in delivery while the goods are in his charge unless the freight forwarder[91] 'proves that no fault or neglect of his own, his servants or agents or any other person referred to in cl 2.2 has caused or contributed to such loss, damage or delay'.

However, where there is carriage by sea or inland waters, the forwarder is allowed two more defences:

- act, neglect, or default of the master, mariner, pilot or the servants of the carrier in the navigation or in the management of the ship;
- fire, unless caused by the actual fault or privity of the carrier, however, always provided that whenever loss or damage has resulted from unseaworthiness of the ship, the freight forwarder can prove that due diligence has been exercised to make the ship seaworthy at the commencement of the voyage.

The two-tier liability scheme imparts importance to localisation of damage. This is enhanced by the maximum amounts that the freight forwarder is liable for – 2 SDRs per kg of gross weight or 666.67 units per package where there is a water (sea, inland waters) trajectory according to the contract and 8.33 SDRs per kg of gross weight in its absence.

The terms also provide that they apply only to the extent they are not contrary to the mandatory provisions of national law or international conventions which may be applicable to the contract. This is likely to cover situations where a unimodal carrier takes on the mantle of a multimodal transport operator to avoid mandatory provisions.

The protection given to the freight forwarder is extended to his servants, agents and other persons (including any independent contractor) whose services he may

---

90   See Tettenborn, 'Transferable and negotiable documents of title – a redefinition?' [1991] 4 LMCLQ 538.
91   The FIATA Bill throughout uses the phrase 'freight forwarder'.

have used in performing the contract. The defences and limits of liability are available regardless of whether the action is founded in contract or in tort. Clauses purporting to extend immunities to parties (including sub-contractors) whose services the forwarder may use are effective in English law.[92]

The terms of the FIATA Bill are available regardless of whether the action is brought in contract or in tort against the freight forwarder.

The FIATA Bill also lists a number of rights in favour of the freight forwarder: right to freight and charges, lien on goods and cargo and general average.

Consignor's responsibilities

The consignor is responsible for the accurate description, marks, quantity, weight, etc, of the goods and the consignor remains liable to the freight forwarder for any loss or damage he may have suffered even though the document is transferred to the consignee. Consignor is defined as the person who enters into the contract with the freight forwarder and consignee as the person entitled to receive the goods from the freight forwarder.

Time limit

An action would be time barred if it is not brought within nine months after the delivery of the goods or the date when the goods should have been delivered or the date when the goods could be treated as lost.[93]

Both the FIATA Bill and UNCTAD/ICC Rules[94] work within the parameters of a network framework in that there are different provisions in respect of extent of liability – that is, whether or not the carriage involves a sea or inland waterways segment. This issue of kind of mode also affects the maximum amount of the carrier's liability. (Of course, it is always open to the parties to agree expressly to a higher limit.) All this is subject to the proviso that mandatory laws, be they domestic or international, do not enter into the picture.

Provision for combined transport in unimodal conventions

Some of the unimodal conventions that have been implemented by the United Kingdom have special provisions for combined transport. The 1955 Hague Protocol amending the Convention for the Unification of Certain Rules Relating to the International Carriage by Air 1929 provides, in Art 31, that where part of the combined carriage is performed by air, the Convention is to apply to air carriage that comes within the ambit of Art 1. Similarly, CIM also makes provision for combined transport and Art 38 of the CIM Rules provides some special defences where sea and rail transport are combined.

---

92 *New Zealand Shipping v AM Satterthwaite and Co Ltd (The Eurymedon)* [1975] AC 154. See also Chapter 8.

93 See Table 13.3.

94 See Table 13.4 for a comparative framework of carrier liability under the UNCTAD/ICC Rules and the United Nations Multimodal Convention 1980.

The CMR also addresses the issue of combined transport. Its provisions are innovative. According to Art 2, where goods are carried on a vehicle that is loaded on to another mode of transport such as a ship or an aircraft (that is, ro-ro traffic), the convention applies to the entire voyage. Where goods are unloaded from the vehicle for any reason (for example, for loading on to the other mode of transport, for purposes of convenience), the application of the CMR to the entire voyage is broken. In some circumstances, however, the road carrier may find himself within a different liability scheme as a result of the proviso to Art 2 which states:

> Provided that to the extent that it is proved any loss, damage or delay in delivery of the goods which occurs during the carriage by the other means of transport was not caused by an act or omission of the carrier by road, but by some event which could only have occurred in the course of and by reason of the carriage by that other means of transport, the liability of the carrier by road shall be determined not by this convention but in the manner in which the liability of the carrier by the other means of transport would have been determined if a contract for the carriage of the goods alone had been made by the sender with the carrier by the other means of transport in accordance with the conditions prescribed by law for the carriage of goods by that means of transport.

This proviso, as seen in the previous chapter, raises many questions and its consideration by the English courts in *Thermo Engineers v Ferrymasters*[95] highlights some of the difficulties. In contrast to the CIM, under the CMR, different liability limits apply where the location of the loss or damage is ascertained.

The United Nations Convention on International Multimodal Transport 1980 – its future

The formulation of standard terms such as the BIFA Standard Trading Conditions and the FIATA Bill for use by freight forwarders has brought about some harmonisation and certainty in the area of multimodal transport. Standard terms, however, apply only when incorporated in the carriage contract. The ideal solution for cargo interests would be a mandatory regime. Modelled on the Hamburg Rules[96] (United Nations Convention on the Carriage of Goods by Sea 1978), the United Nations Multimodal Convention 1980 (hereinafter 'Multimodal Convention'), were it to come into force, would create a regime of minimum liability which cannot be derogated from unless of benefit to cargo interests. It was hoped that the convention would come into force once the Hamburg Rules came into force. Those hopes have receded with the passage of time. And the recent report from UNCTAD reinforces the view that we may have to visit the harmonisation of multimodal transport afresh. It is unlikely that the United Kingdom will ratify the Hamburg Rules or the Multimodal Convention in the near future. It might be persuaded to do so if countries with shipping interests or EU member states[97] were to ratify it.

It is not as if the United Kingdom is unaware of the need to harmonise the law in respect of international multimodal transport. For instance, Diana Tribe in 1994

---

95 [1981] 1 Lloyd's Rep 200.
96 Selvig, 'The influence of the Hamburg Rules on the work for a convention on international multimodal transport', in *Speakers' Papers for the Bill of Lading Conference*, 1978, LLP.
97 See Chapter 2, pp 57–9 above, on the implementation of the Vienna Convention 1980 in the United Kingdom.

(then Law Commissioner) is cited as voicing her dissatisfaction with the multimodal transport regime thus:

> The multimodal industry is investing heavily in improving its services. It is a very sophisticated industry but the same cannot be said of its legal infrastructure. There is a large number of transport conventions which are potentially applicable to any contract ... enormous sums, which would be better applied commercially, are spent in legal disputes ... The best way forward would be the abolition of all individual conventions and introduce one which would govern all transport contracts, by whatever means of transport and whether unimodal or multimodal. This may see legal expenditure in the short term while precedents are established for the construction of such a convention, but in the long term it would obviate many of the current problems and save costs [cited in fn 6 UNCTAD Doc UNCTAD/SDTE/TLB2, 25 June 2001].

It must be said that the views expressed are idealistic and it is unforseeable that the various interests are likely to agree to even drafting a text for a single convention to replace the existing transport conventions. While the observation that the long term (economic) benefits ought to be the motivating feature in the drafting of a convention is correct, sadly, humanity tends to think in terms of short term benefits. Until there is a change in human perceptions and attitudes, and perhaps a shift in calculation of economic benefits, the drafting of a single convention remains a dream. But then, occasionally dreams do invade reality.

The Multimodal Convention is designed to introduce a uniform liability scheme. The liability of the multimodal transport operator is therefore not dependant on establishing during which mode of transport the loss or damage occurred. It adopts a simple scheme: the multimodal transport operator is responsible for loss, damage or delay in delivery while the goods are in his control – that is, from the time he takes them in his charge to the time of delivery (Art 14). The basis of the multimodal transport operator's liability is one of presumed fault or neglect. To escape liability, the burden is on him to show that he, his servants, agents, or any other person of whose services he makes use for the performance of the multimodal transport contract (Art 15) took all measures that could reasonably be required to avoid the occurrence and its consequences (Art 16).

The above simplicity in respect of liability does not mean that the Multimodal Convention is the perfect solution to a complex situation. It has its fair share of problems, some of which are highlighted here.[98] It adopts a complex network scheme for compensation by drawing a distinction between multimodal transport involving a sea trajectory and multimodal transport not involving a sea trajectory. So, where there is sea carriage, liability amount is limited to 920 SDRs per package or other shipping unit or 2.75 SDRs per kilogram of gross weight of goods lost or damaged (Art 18(1)). In the absence of a sea limb, liability is set at the maximum of 8.33 SDRs per kilogram of gross weight of goods lost or damaged (Art 18(3)). However, where loss or damage occurs on a mode of transport where application of a mandatory national law or international convention would provide a higher limit of liability than that set in Art 18 of the Multimodal Convention, the multimodal transport operator's liability amount will be calculated by reference to the international convention (Art 19)[99] or

---

98 For an interesting, thorough and extensive account of the legal problems faced in multimodal transport, see De Wit, *Multimodal Transport*, 1995, LLP. See also Diamond, 'Liability of the carrier in multimodal transport', in Schmitthoff and Goode (eds), *International Carriage of Goods: Some Legal Problems and Possible Solutions*, 1988, Centre for Commercial Law Studies.

99 See Table 13.1.

mandatory national law. The 'limited "network" system of compensation'[100] means that the issue of where the damage or loss occurred is still pertinent if not for the basis of liability, then for calculation of liability amounts.

The Multimodal Convention also innocently assumes that transport documents clearly state whether the freight forwarder acts in the capacity of principal to bring him within the definition of multimodal transport operator provided in Art 1(2). This is likely to produce expensive and, not to say, time-consuming litigation to ascertain the forwarder's capacity.

Another surprising feature of the convention is the lack of a precise definition of international multimodal transport. Article 1(1) defines it as:

> ... the carriage of goods by at least two different modes of transport on the basis of a multimodal transport contract from a place in one country at which the goods are taken in charge by the multimodal transport operator to a place designated for delivery situated in a different country. The operations of pick up and delivery of goods carried out in the performance of a unimodal transport contract, as defined in such contract, shall not be considered as international multimodal transport.

No attempt has been made to define mode of transport. Is mode of transport restricted to the vehicle (for example, plane, ship), the medium (for example, air, sea) or does it include both? The definition also excludes operations of pick-up and delivery of goods in the performance of a unimodal transport; it does not specify the acceptable extent of these operations. For instance, will a road-leg/sea-leg/road-leg operation be regarded as a multimodal carriage, or are the road legs simply operations of pick-up and delivery? Will the issue be decided by looking at how the road legs are described in the documents, or will factors such as the time taken to complete the different legs and calculation of charges be relevant to ascertain whether the particular carriage contract is a unimodal transport contract or not?

Regardless of these ambiguities, the Multimodal Convention, if adopted, will herald a new era of predictability. This is no bad thing. To some extent, this has been achieved by use of UNCTAD/ICC Rules in standard terms devised by freight association for use by their members. This may arguably be true of the United Kingdom and other member states of the European Community, such as Germany and Holland, but the same is not true of the developing countries who are playing an increasingly important role in the global marketplace. Against this backdrop, the Multimodal Convention introduces a regime which will protect the cargo interests by giving a minimum level of legal protection.

CONCLUSION

A comparison of the carrier liability framework of the UNCTAD/ICC Rules and the Multimodal Convention (see Table 13.4) indicates there is much that is common. It is indeed odd why there is reluctance on the part of nations to adopt the Multimodal Convention when the UNCTAD/ICC Rules are heralded as a great success. At best, it is political antipathy towards a document drafted by an international organisation which openly promotes the interests of developing countries and least developed nations.

---

100   Glass and Cashmore, *Introduction to the Law of Carriage*, 1989, Sweet & Maxwell, p 265.

It seems that the law of multimodal transportation is an area that is likely to see further debate (if not significant developments in the form of a revised Multimodal Convention or new convention) in the near future.[101]

---

101   See UNCTAD Doc UNCTAD/SDTE/TLLB/2003/1 (13 January 2003), at para 116.

Table 13.1: Liability limits expressed in SDRs in various unimodal conventions

Convention	Mode	Entry into force	SDR/kg	SDR/unit
Hague-Visby Rules[A]	Sea	23/6/1977	2	666.67
Hamburg Rules[B]	Sea	2/11/1992	2.5	835
Warsaw Convention[C] .... Montreal Protocol No 4[D] .... Montreal Convention[E]	Air	.... 14/6/1998 .... 4/11/2003	17	
CMR (as amended)[F]	Road	28/12/1980	8.33	
COTIF/CIM 1999[G]	Rail	1/7/2006	17	

A International Convention for the Unification of Certain Rules of Law Relating to Bills of Lading 1924, known as the Hague Rules). Amended by Brussels Protocol signed at Visby in 1968 which came to be called the Hague-Visby Rules. The United Kingdom implemented the Hague-Visby Rules with the Carriage of Goods by Sea Act 1971. (The Hague Rules liability is limited to £100 per package or unit.)

B United Nations Convention on the Carriage of Goods by Sea 1978. Not ratified by the United Kingdom.

C Convention for the Unification of Certain Rules Relating to International Carriage by Air 1929. Amended by the Hague Protocol in 1955. The United Kingdom implemented the Hague Protocol with the Carriage by Air Act 1961. (The limits in the Warsaw Convention as amended by the Hague Protocol is set at 250 gold francs per kilogram.)

D The Montreal Protocol No 4 is part of United Kingdom law. See Carriage By Air and Road Act 1979, Carriage by Air Acts (Implementation of Protocol No 4 Order) SI 1999/1312, 1999/1737. Unfication of Certain Rules for International Carriage 1999. See carriage by Air Acts (Implementation of the Montreal Convention 1999) Order 2 SI 2002/263.

E Unification of Certain Rules for International Carriage by Air 1999. Implemented by the UK. See Carriage by Air Act (Implementation of the Montreal Convention 1999) Order 2001.

F Convention on Contract for the International Carriage of Goods by Road was implemented by Carriage of Goods by Road Act 1965. This Act, still in force, was amended in 1979 by the Carriage by Air and Road Act 1979.

G This was given effect by The Railways (Convention on International Carriage by Rail) Regulation SI 2005/2092.

Table 13.2: Maximum liability limits in standard contracts on multimodal transport, the United Nations Multimodal Convention and UNCTAD/ICC Rules

Multimodal Terms/Convention	SDR/kg	SDR/package
BIFA Standard Trading Conditions	2	
Localised damage which attracts mandatory law	Higher limit of mandatory law applies◆	
UNCTAD/ICC Rules		
Sea/Inland Waterways Trajectory	2	666.67
No Sea/Inland Waterways Trajectory	8.33	
Localised damage which attracts mandatory law	Higher limit of mandatory law applies◆	
FIATA FBL Multimodal Negotiable Bill of Lading		
Sea/Inland Waterways Trajectory	2	666.67
No Sea/Inland Waterways Trajectory	8.33	
Localised damage which attracts mandatory law	Higher limit of mandatory law applies◆	
Multimodal Convention[A]		
Sea/Inland Waterways Trajectory	2.75	920
No Sea Carriage/Inland Waterways Trajectory	8.33	
Localised damage which attracts mandatory law	Higher limit of mandatory law applies◆	

A United Nations Convention on International Multimodal Transport of Goods. Not ratified by the United Kingdom. Convention not yet in force.
◆ See Table 13.1

Table 13.3: Time limitation in the various carriage conventions, Multimodal standard terms and UNCTAD/ICC Rules

Convention/rules/standard terms	Time limit
Hague/Hague-Visby Rules	One year (after delivery of goods or date when goods should have been delivered)
Hamburg Rules	Two years (from date of delivery or from last day when goods should have been delivered)
Warsaw Convention	Two years (from day of arrival at destination or from date on which aircraft ought to have arrived or from date on which carriage stopped)
Montreal Convention	Same as the Warsaw Convention
CMR	One year (from date of delivery). Three years in the case of wilful misconduct
COTIF/CIM 1999	One year. Two years in special circumstances – eg, recovery of cash on delivery payment collected by carrier
Multimodal Convention	Two years after delivery of goods or on date when goods should have been delivered. If notification not given within 6 months after date of delivery or date when they should have been delivered time-barred after 6 months
BIFA Standard Trading Conditions	9 months from date of event or occurrence alleged to give rise to an action
UNCTAD/ICC Rules	9 months after delivery of goods or date when goods should have been delivered or goods deemed lost applying formula provided in Rules 5.2[+] and 5.3[++]
FIATA Bill	9 months after delivery of goods or date when goods should have been delivered or goods deemed lost applying provisions in Clauses 6.3[#] and 6.4[##]

[+] Rule 5.2 states:
Delay in delivery occurs when the goods have not been delivered within the time expressly agreed upon or, in the absence of such agreement, within the time which, it would be reasonable to require of a diligent MTO, having regard to the circumstances of the case.
[++] Rule 5.2 states:
If the goods have not been delivered within 90 consecutive days following the date of delivery determined according to Rules 5.2, the claimant may, in the absence of evidence to the contrary treat the goods as lost.
[#] Clause 6.3 states:
Arrival times are not guaranteed by the freight forwarder. However, delay in delivery occurs when the goods have not been delivered within the time limit expressly agreed upon or, in the absence of such agreement, within the time which, it would be reasonable to require of a diligent freight forwarder, having regard to the circumstances of the case.
[##] Clause 6.4 states:
If the goods have not been delivered within ninety consecutive days following the date of delivery determined according to Rules 5.2, the claimant may, in the absence of evidence to the contrary treat the goods as lost.

Table 13.4: Comparison of MTO Liability Framework under the Multimodal Convention and UNCTAD/ICC Rules

Issues	UNCTAD/ICC Rules	Multimodal Convention
Definition of multimodal transport	Single contract for carriage by at least two modes of transport (Rule 2.1)	Carriage by at least two modes of transport on the basis of a multimodal transport contract. Operation of pick-up and delivery of goods under a unimodal contract not multimodal carriage (Art 1(1)).
When applicable	Incorporation by contract (Rule 1) Note: Mandatory provisions however supersede Rules (Rule 13)	Place of taking in charge of goods or place of delivery in contracting state (Art 2) Note: Convention mandatorily applicable. Consignor however has right to choose between multimodal transport or segmented transport (Art 3)
Period of responsibility	From time of taking charge through to delivery (Rule 4.1)	From time goods in charge of multimodal transport operator (MTO) to time of delivery (Art 14(1))
MTO responsibility	Responsible for acts/omissions of servants/agent acting within the scope of their employment or any other person engaged for the performance of the contract (Rule 4.2)	Responsible for acts/omissions of servants/agent acting within the scope of their employment or any other person engaged for the performance of the contract (Art 15)
Basis of liability	Presumed to be at fault where goods lost, damaged or there is delay in delivery while goods in his charge unless he can prove that those he is responsible for took all measures that could reasonably be required to avoid the occurrence and its consequences (Rule 5.1)	Presumed to be at fault where goods lost, damaged or there is delay in delivery while goods in his charge unless he can prove that those he is responsible for took all measures that could reasonably be required to avoid the occurrence and its consequences (Art 16(1)) Note: burden of proof on MTO
When delay in delivery	When not delivered within time expressly agreed upon. Where no express agreement then reasonable time required of a diligent MTO taking surrounding circumstances (Rule 5.2)	When not delivered within time expressly agreed upon. Where no express agreement then reasonable time required of a diligent MTO taking surrounding circumstances (Art 16(2))

Issues	UNCTAD/ICC Rules	Multimodal Convention
Concurrent causes		Where another cause alongwith MTO's fault/neglect causes loss/ damage/delay in delivery them MTO liable only to the extent that the loss is attributable to such cause (Art 17). Note: burden of proof on MTO
Consequential loss	In the event of consequential loss from delay in delivery or consequential loss other than loss or damage to the goods liability limited to an amount not exceeding equivalent of freight	
Special exemptions	Not responsible where damage during sea carriage caused by • Act, neglect or default of the master, mariner, pilot or servants of the carrier in the navigation or management of ship • Fire unless caused by actual fault or privity of the carrier Where unseaworthiness cause of damage MTO to show that he has exercised due diligence to make ship seaworthy (Rule 5.4)	
Non-contractual liability	Rules applicable regardless of whether claim founded in contract or in tort (Rule 11)	Defences and limits of liability available equally for actions founded in tort or otherwise (Art 20(1))
Availability of defences and liability limits to third parties	Available to Agent/ Servant or Other Person used to perform multimodal transport contract (Rule 12)	Available if Agent/Servant acted within scope of employment or if Other Person acted within performance of the contract (Art 20(2))
Liability limits	See Table 13.2	See Table 13.2

Issues	UNCTAD/ICC Rules	Multimodal Convention
Loss of liability limits	Liability limits lost in the event of personal act/ omission of MTO done with intent to cause such loss, damage or delay in delivery or reckless and with knowledge that such loss, damage or delay would probably result (Rule 7)	Liability limits lost in the event of act/omission of MTO done with intent to cause such loss, damage or delay in delivery or reckless and with knowledge that such loss, damage or delay would probably result. Burden of proof on claimant (Art 21)
Documentation		Detailed list on information to be included in multimodal transport document. Includes names of consignor, consignees, place of delivery, place of taking in charge of goods (Art 8)
Evidential status	In the absence of reservations such as 'shipper's weight, load, count', shipper packed container' multimodal transport document prima facie evidence of taking in charge of goods; if transferred to third party conclusive evidence (Rule 3)	Multimodal transport document prima facie evidence of taking in charge of goods; if transferred to third party conclusive evidence (Art 10). Note: Reservations allowed concerning general nature, leading marks, number of packets or pieces, weight or quantity of goods (Art 9)
Electronic documentation	Allows replacement of multimodal transport document with an electronic equivalent insofar as applicable law permits	Seems to allow electronic documentation since signature defined to include signature in electronic form (Art 5)
Jurisdiction		• Principal place/habitual residence of defendant • Place where multimodal transport contract concluded provided defendant has place of business, branch or agency through which contract made • Place of taking over goods for international multimodal transport or place of delivery • Other place designated in the multimodal transport contract and evidenced in the multimodal transport document (Art 26)

Issues	UNCTAD/ICC Rules	Multimodal Convention
Arbitration		• Principal place/habitual residence of defendant • Place where multimodal transport contract concluded provided defendant has place of business, branch or agency through which contract made • Place of taking over goods for international multimodal transport or place of delivery • Other place designated in arbitration clause or arbitration agreement (Art 27)
Time limitation	See Table 13.3	See Table 13.3

FURTHER READING

Coffey, 'Multimodalism and the American carrier' (1989) 64 Tulane LR 569.

De Wit, *Multimodal Transport*, 1995, LLP.

Driscoll, 'The Convention on International Multimodal Transport: a status report' (1978) 9 JMLC 441.

Driscoll and Larsen, 'The Convention on International Multimodal Transport of Goods' (1982) 57 Tulane LR 193.

Herber, 'The European legal experience with multimodalism' (1989) 64 Tulane LR 611.

Knebel and Blocker, 'United States statutory regulation of multimodalism' (1989) 64 Tulane LR 543.

Mankabady, 'The multimodal transportation of goods: a challenge to Unimodal Transport Convention' (1983) 32(1) ICLQ 123.

Nasser, 'The Multimodal Convention' (1988) 19(2) JMLC 231.

Palmer and DeGiulio, 'Terminal operators and multimodal carriage: history and prognosis' (1989) 64 Tulane LR 281.

Sorkin, 'Limited liability in multimodal transport and the effect of deregulation' (1989) 13 Tulane Maritime LJ 285.

PART IV

FINANCING AND INSURANCE

OVERVIEW

The seller and buyer, once they have agreed on the specifications, quantity, price and mode of delivery of the goods, have to arrange insurance to cover the hazards likely to be encountered during the transportation of goods from the seller's country to the buyer's country. As to who arranges for insurance during transportation will depend on the terms of the contract. As gathered from Chapter 1 on standard trade terms where the goods, for instance, have been sold on cost, insurance, freight (CIF) terms, the seller obtains insurance. Where the sale, for instance, is on free on board (FOB) terms, the buyer is likely to take out insurance if he wishes to protect himself against loss or damage to goods in the course of transportation. Chapter 14 illustrates, using marine insurance, the general principles underlying insurance contracts.

Other than insurance, the mode of payment for the merchandise sold is another important event in any international sale contract. While it is the case that payment can be made by cash or through a bill of exchange, the most popular method is through letters of credit, described as the life blood of commerce. Chapter 15, besides providing a brief account of bills of exchange, examines the obligations of the various parties to a letter of credit arrangement against the backdrop of English common law and the current version of the Uniform Customs and Practices for Documentary Credit 600 (UCP 600) drafted by the International Chamber of Commerce (ICC). There is also a brief section on the recently adopted Electronic Transmission Supplement Uniform Customs and Practices for Documents Credits (eUCP) which enables the use of electronic letters of credit. The chapter concludes with a section on other means of minimising the risk of non-payment.

CHAPTER 14

MARINE INSURANCE

INTRODUCTION

In international sales, goods are normally insured against the hazards they are likely to encounter during the voyage from the seller's country to the buyer's country. In the event of loss or damage to cargo due to perils of the voyage, the insured will be able, depending on the terms of the insurance policy, to recover his losses from the underwriter or insurer. In other words, under an insurance contract, the insurer undertakes to indemnify the insured (assured) against future losses/damage to goods caused by specific circumstances, such as fire, earthquakes and theft. The question of what type of insurance needs to be obtained to cover the cargo – for example, marine insurance, air cargo insurance – depends on the mode of transport agreed by the parties in the contract of sale. Where parties have concluded their contracts on cost, insurance and freight (CIF) and free on board (FOB) terms,[1] goods will be transported by sea and will therefore be covered by a marine insurance contract. The question of who is responsible for effecting the insurance is dependent on the contract terms. A CIF contract requires the seller, at his expense, to obtain insurance cover for the voyage and tender the policy to the buyer (or the advising/confirming bank where the parties have agreed on a letter of credit arrangement),[2] along with the bill of lading. In an FOB contract, there is no legal requirement to obtain insurance cover on the part of the buyer or the seller. The buyer, however, would be well advised to obtain insurance if he wishes to cover himself against losses or damage while the goods are on the high seas. It is not unusual for a buyer in an FOB contract to request the seller to arrange insurance cover on the understanding that the buyer will reimburse the costs incurred. Such contracts are known as FOB with additional services contracts.[3]

Insurance of goods during their transit from the exporting country to the importing country is an important incident in an international sale transaction. This chapter, therefore, focuses on cargo insurance, with the emphasis on marine insurance contracts, since much of the cargo is still transported by sea. The general principles applicable to marine insurance contracts, the circumstances in which risk does not attach, the undertakings (warranties) of the insured and the liabilities of the insurer in a marine insurance policy are topics for consideration. It must be noted that the principles applied to marine insurance contracts are relevant to other types of non-marine insurance contracts – that is, where the insurance contract covers carriage by other modes of transport, such as air or road.[4]

---

1 See Chapter 1 for further on standard trade terms such as CIF and FOB.
2 See Chapter 15 for further on letters of credit arrangements.
3 See Chapter 1, p 46 above.
4 The liabilities of the parties under the various types – unimodal and multimodal – transport contracts are discussed in Part III.

SCOPE AND NATURE OF MARINE INSURANCE CONTRACTS

The law relating to marine insurance is contained in the Marine Insurance Act 1906.[5] A marine insurance contract, according to s 1 of the Marine Insurance Act (hereinafter 'MIA'), 'is a contract whereby the insurer undertakes to indemnify the assured, in a manner and to the extent agreed, against marine losses, that is to say, the losses incident to marine adventure'. There is a marine adventure, according to s 3(2), 'where any ship, goods, or other movables are exposed to maritime perils', that is, 'perils, consequent on or incidental to the navigation of the sea, that is to say, perils of the sea, fire, war perils, pirates, rovers, thieves, captures, seizures,[6] restraints and detainments of princes and peoples, jettison, barratry, and any other perils, either of the like kind or which may be designated by the policy'.

The perils listed in s 3(2) are by no means exhaustive. It is therefore possible to insure against other perils if the peril insured against is consequent on or incidental to the navigation of the sea.[7] Moreover, under s 2(1) of the Act, it is possible to insure against mixed land and sea risks.[8]

Until 1982, the insurance market used the SG policy (Ship and Goods policy) as the standard contract. This has now been replaced by Institute Cargo Clauses (A), (B) and (C), and these are considered below. Some of the terms found in these three sets of clauses modify provisions relating to, for instance, availability of cover during deviation and the extent of causal connection (doctrine of proximate causation) in the MIA. The Institute Cargo Clauses (A), (B) and (C) are widely used and, therefore, as much a part of marine insurance law as the statute.

Obtaining marine insurance cover

As for the mechanics of obtaining insurance cover, the interested party will normally instruct an insurance broker (regarded as the assured's agent) and provide him with details about the cargo, the voyage, date of shipment, name of vessel and also state other requirements, such as the amount of cover, the kind of cover, for example, Institute Cargo Clauses (A), (B) or (C), and other terms, for example, Institute Strike Clauses or Institute War Clauses.[9]

The broker will put all this information on a document known as a slip,[10] and take it to the underwriters. Where an underwriter is willing to accept the risk, he will 'write a line' on the slip. He may underwrite the entire risk or only part of the risk, in which case he will write the percentage of risk he is willing to underwrite. The first

---

5   See Carr and Kidner, *International Trade Law Statutes and Conventions*, 5th edn, 2008, Routledge-Cavendish.

6   See *Cory v Burr* (1883) 8 App Cas 393.

7   See Mustill LJ in *Continental Illinois National Bank and Trading Co of Chicago v Bathurst (The Captain Panagos DP)* [1985] 1 Lloyd's Rep 625, at pp 630–1.

8   *Renton (GH) and Co Ltd v Black Sea and Baltic General Insurance Co Ltd* [1941] 1 KB 206; 1 All ER 149; *Cousins (H) and Co Ltd v D and C Carriers Ltd* [1971] 1 All ER 55.

9   The text of these cargo clauses are reproduced in Carr and Kidner, *International Trade Law Statutes and Conventions*, 5th edn, 2008, Routledge-Cavendish.

10 For an excellent article on the character of the slip, see Bennett, 'The role of the slip in marine insurance law' [1994] LMCLQ 94.

underwriter is usually known as the lead underwriter.[11] The broker will then have to approach other underwriters until the entire risk is covered. Even after obtaining sufficient 'lines' to cover the entire risk, the broker may decide to approach other underwriters, in order to spread the risk more evenly. This may result in the slip being oversubscribed. In such an event, the 'lines' will be adjusted appropriately.

The 'writing of a line' by the underwriter gives rise to a binding contract between the underwriter and the insured. As Kerr LJ said, in *General Re-insurance Corp v Försäkringsaktiebolaget Fennia Patria*:[12]

> ... each line written on a slip gives rise to a binding contract *pro tanto* between the underwriter and the insured or reinsured for whom the broker is acting when he presents the slip. The underwriter is therefore bound by his line, subject only to the contingency that it may fall to be written down on 'closing' to some extent if the slip turns out to have been over-subscribed [at p 867].[13]

Once the entire risk is covered, the insured will receive a cover note from the broker.[14] The cover note will be a closed cover where the insured has provided all the details pertaining to the subject matter. Where the information is incomplete, the cover note will be an open cover note[15] and the insured has to provide further details. As for the insurance policy, it is normally issued and signed subsequently.

It normally takes time for the policy to be issued and it is not uncommon for a seller, in order to 'facilitate business',[16] when required to tender documents, as in a CIF contract or in a letter of credit arrangement, to tender cover notes, certificate of insurance or a letter of insurance.[17] The tender of such alternatives, however, is not regarded as valid tender in English law.[18] However, the International Chamber of Commerce (ICC) has relaxed the rules where INCOTERMS 2000[19] (in relation to standard terms) or the UCP[20] 600 relating to letters of credit) are incorporated.

INCOTERMS 2000 addresses the issue of insurance in two terms – CIF and CIP (cost and insurance paid to). In both these cases, cl A3(b) states:

---

11   Subsequent underwriters are normally also subject to the same terms as the lead underwriter. It is not uncommon to find the notation 'tba L/U', which stands for 'terms to be agreed with lead underwriter'. See *Jaglom v Excess Insurance Co Ltd* [1972] 1 QB 250; *American Airlines Inc v Hope* [1973] 1 Lloyd's Rep 233.

12   [1983] QB 856.

13   See also *Ionides v Pacific Fire and Marine Insurance Co* (1871) 6 QB 674.

14   Note, however, that the broker is not placed under a duty to forward the cover note or inform the assured of the terms of cover as soon as possible. See *United Mills Agencies Ltd v RE Harvey Bray and Co* (1952) 1 TLR 149. Under English law of agency, agents are expected to act with reasonable care – see *Beales and South Devon Rly Co* (1864) 3 H&C 337. The duty may be somewhat different in the case of car insurance – see *Osman v J Ralph Moss Ltd* [1970] 1 Lloyd's Rep 313.

15   Not to be confused with open cover on which see 'Floating policy and open over', p 436–7 below.

16   See Bailhache J in *Wilson, Holgate and Co Ltd v Belgian Grain and Produce Co Ltd* [1920] 2 KB 1, at p 8.

17   The letter of insurance is a letter from the seller stating that the goods have been insured.

18   See *Diamond Alkali Export Corp v Fl Bourgeois* [1921] 3 KB 443; see Chapter 1, pp 19–20 above. See also Bailhache J in *Wilson, Holgate and Co Ltd v Belgian Grain and Produce Co Ltd* [1920] 2 KB 1, at p 7. He had no difficulty in accepting American insurance certificates as equivalent to a policy, since the terms of the policy are normally included in the certificate.

19   International Rules for the Interpretation of Trade Terms. See Chapter 1, above, for further on INCOTERMS.

20   Uniform Customs and Practices relating to Documentary Credits. See also Chapter 15.

The seller must obtain at his own expense cargo insurance as agreed in the contract such that the buyer, or any other person having insurable interest in the goods, shall be entitled to claim directly from the insurer and provide the buyer with the insurance policy or other evidence of insurance cover.

Given that other evidence of insurance cover is allowable, the suggestion seems to be that certificate of insurance or cover notes will be acceptable.

Article 28, which focuses on insurance document and coverage, states:

a. An insurance document, such as an insurance policy, an insurance certificate or a declaration under an open cover, must appear to be issued and signed by an insurance company, an underwriter or their agents or their proxies. Any signature by an agent or proxy must indicate whether the agent or proxy has signed for or on behalf if the insurance company or underwriter.

b. . . .

c. Cover notes will not accepted

d. An insurance policy is acceptable in lieu of an insurance certificate or a declaration under an open cover.

e-j. . . .

It seems from the above that tender of insurance certificates (provided it is signed by an insurance company, underwriters, agents or proxies) will be treated as good tender unless the credit stipulates otherwise. Cover notes are specifically excluded and therefore will not be regarded as good tender.

Payment of premium

Premium is payable against the issue of the policy unless the parties have made other arrangements, according to s 52 of the MIA:

Unless otherwise agreed, the duty of the assured or his agent to pay the premium and the duty of the insurer to issue the policy to the assured or his agent, are concurrent conditions, and the insurer is not bound to issue the policy until payment or tender of the premium.

The insurer normally looks to the broker, even though he is the agent of the assured, for payment of the premium, and the broker, according to s 53(1), 'is directly responsible to the insurer for the premium'. The origin of this peculiar rule is traceable to a time when underwriters preferred to deal with brokers they could trust.

The assured, of course, is under an obligation to pay the premium to the broker. Where the assured fails to pay the premium, the broker has a lien on the policy until the premium due to him from the assured is paid (s 53(2)).

The onus is on the assured to ensure that premiums are paid as agreed on time. Of course, it is open as between the insurer and the assured to agree otherwise.[21]

---

21 See *Betty Weldon v GRE Linked Life Assurance Ltd and Paragon Finance plc* [2000] 2 All ER (Comm) 914.

Different kinds of policies

Voyage policy and time policy

A voyage policy, as the name suggests, is a policy for a particular voyage. In other words, the subject matter is insured for a voyage, for instance, from Istanbul to Southampton. Voyage policies are commonly used in international sale transactions. A time policy,[22] on the other hand, is a policy that insures the subject matter for a fixed time – for example, where the ship, *Benedict*, is insured for two years, commencing at noon on 16 June 2004. Normally, hulls are insured under time policies. It is also possible to have a mixed policy,[23] where the policy covers a particular voyage and runs for a specified period – for example, where a vessel is insured for a voyage from Singapore to Portsmouth and for 30 days after her arrival at Portsmouth. All these different types of policies are recognised by s 25(1) of the MIA.

In practice, however, it is common for pre- and post-shipment risks to be covered. All three sets of Institute Cargo Clauses – that is, (A), (B) and (C) – in cl 8 provide for cover from the moment the cargo leaves the warehouse or storage depot at the place named in the policy for commencement of the transit[24] until they are delivered,[25] as agreed, to the consignee/final warehouse/place of storage at the port of destination (cl 8.1.1), or the warehouse or storage place at the port of destination or prior to port of destination (cl 8.1.2). Where delivery to the consignee, or warehouse/storage place has not taken place, cover continues for a period of 60 days from the time the goods are discharged overside of the oversea vessel at the final port of discharge (cl 8.1.3). The 60 days' cover operates in favour of the assured where the cargo is delayed for some reason after discharge – for example, delay in customs formalities or other import formalities. Where cargo, during the 60-day period post-discharge, is forwarded to a destination not specified in the insurance, cover will cease when transit to the other destination commences (cl 8.2).

Valued policy and unvalued policy

A valued policy is one where the agreed value of the subject matter is specified (s 27(2) of the MIA). The value agreed between the insurer and the assured does not, however, necessarily reflect the actual or real value of the goods. For instance, the agreed value may be far less than the actual value of the goods, or the agreed value may be far greater than the actual value of the goods. Valued policies are generally used in international sales, since the buyer can include the anticipated profits with the value of the goods in the agreed value. Where the agreed value is in excess of the real value, it would be advisable for the assured to disclose this to the insurer. Failure to do so may be regarded as a non-disclosure of a material fact, especially where the 'discrepancy between the insured value and the actual value is of such a nature to change

---

22 *Compania Maritima San Basilio SA v Oceanus Mutual Underwriting Association (Bermuda) Ltd* [1977] QB 49.

23 See *The Al Jubail IV* [1982] 2 Lloyd's Rep 637.

24 See *Crow's Transport Ltd v Phoenix Assurance Co Ltd* [1965] 1 Lloyd's Rep 139; *Overseas Commodities Ltd v Style* [1958] 1 Lloyd's Rep 546.

25 See *Reinhart v Joshua Hoyle and Sons Ltd* [1961] 1 Lloyd's Rep 346.

the nature of risk from a business risk to a speculative risk'.[26] Where a material fact is not disclosed, the contract can be avoided by the aggrieved party.[27]

By contrast, in an unvalued policy, in the absence of express provision, the value of the subject matter is left to be calculated by applying the rules set out in s 16 of the MIA. According to s 16(3), 'in insurance on goods or merchandise, the insurable value is the prime cost of the property insured, plus the expenses of and incidental to shipping and the charges of insurance upon the whole'. The prime cost is the true value of the goods at the commencement of the risk. The true value, according to *Berger and Light Diffusers Pty Ltd v Pollock*,[28] is not necessarily the original cost, but the commercial value of the goods – the onus being on the insured to provide evidence (such as receipts, invoices, etc) to establish the insurable value of the goods. In the words of Kerr J:

> ... the words 'prime cost' require qualification. Where the assured is not the manu-facturer and has bought the goods some time before the insured adventure commenced, their original cost may not give any reliable guidance to their value at the relevant time. Although their cost is no doubt a matter to be borne in mind, the function of the court in such cases is to assess what the true value was at the commencement of the adventure: see *Williams v Atlantic Assurance Co Ltd*,[29] in particular, per Scrutton LJ, p 92, and Greer LJ, pp 102 and 103. The latter passage and the judgment of Slesser LJ, p 107, also show that a false undervaluation for Customs' purposes is not by itself determinative of the court's assessment of the insurable value. If there is no evidence on which the court can form any view then the plaintiff will recover nothing or only nominal damages: *Tanner v Bennett*.[30] Similarly, the plaintiff may fail entirely if, on the evidence as a whole, the court cannot ascertain what the true value was. This was the conclusion of Scrutton LJ, in *Williams v Atlantic Insurance*. The onus of establishing the insurable value and the other ingredients necessary to establish his claim always rests on the plaintiff. The court must look at the whole of the evidence and then arrive at the conclusion if it can. It is natural that the insurable value is often referred to as the market value, but it is not necessary that there should be a market in the goods in the ordinary sense. The value to the plaintiff may be sufficient, provided that it is not a purely subjective or senti-mental value. Perhaps 'commercial value' is the best description of what the court must seek to determine [at p 455].

It must be noted that, in an unvalued policy, the profit margin will not be included. As a consequence, unvalued policies are not in common use. Merchants prefer valued policies, due to the scope for including the profit margin.

Floating policy and open cover

In a floating policy, the insurance is described in general terms. A floating policy is useful where several consignments of cargo are sent over a period and the insurer does not have all the details, such as the names of the vessels on which the consign-ments are to be shipped and the dates of the shipments at the time of taking out the policy. The names of the ships, dates of shipments, and the values of the shipments

---

26   See Bailhache J in *Mathie v The Argonaut Marine Insurance Co Ltd* (1924) 18 LlL Rep 118.
27   See 'A contract of utmost good faith', pp 437–42 below.
28   [1973] 2 Lloyd's Rep 442. Also see *Kyzuna Investments Ltd v Ocean Marine Mutual Insurance Association* [2000] 1 Lloyd's Rep 505.
29   [1933] 1 KB 81.
30   (1825) Ry&M 182.

will be declared by the assured as and when the goods are shipped.[31] On declaration of the values,[32] the amount of cover available on the floating policy will be reduced by that amount, and when the declared values add up to the original amount, the policy will be run off or written off. Section 29 of the MIA defines a floating policy thus:

> Where goods are shipped under a floating policy, a certificate of insurance will be issued in respect of the goods shipped where evidence of insurance is required.

This may cause problems where the goods have been shipped on CIF terms. Under English law, a certificate is not recognised as a good substitution for an insurance policy.[33] The parties may agree to tender a certificate of insurance instead of an insurance policy, in which case the tender will be a good tender.[34]

The problem with floating policies is that, once the amount is exhausted, cover ceases immediately and the assured might suddenly find that some of the cargo is not covered. Issue of a further floating policy is required for the assured to remain under cover. To minimise inconvenience (for example, continuous monitoring of declarations to ascertain whether the agreed amount is exhausted), the practice emerged of providing cover where a further floating policy was not taken out. This arrangement came to be known as open cover. Open cover is similar to a floating policy, in that the insurer agrees to insure the goods of the assured. However, unlike the floating policy, the open cover is not a policy. It is simply an arrangement where the insurer undertakes to issue policies, floating or specific, when required by the assured. Open cover is extremely popular in the insurance market, due to its flexibility, and is said to have replaced floating policies.[35]

PRINCIPLES OF MARINE INSURANCE LAW

A contract of utmost good faith

It is a long established principle that all insurance contracts, including marine insurance contracts, are contracts of utmost good faith (*uberrimae fidei*).[36] This means that the insurer[37] and the assured are placed under an obligation to disclose information that is likely to affect the judgment of the other.

This requirement of utmost good faith in insurance contracts is an exception to the

---

31   There may be a contractual clause of when the insured should declare shipments to the insurer. Such clauses are read strictly, so a breach would result in the assured losing his right to recover for losses under the policy. See *Union Insurance Society Canton Ltd v George Wills and Co* [1916] 1 AC 281.

32   Where the insured declares value after the loss, according to s 29(4), the policy will be treated as an unvalued policy, which means that the value of the goods will be calculated on the basis of the rules contained in s 16(3). See 'Valued policy and unvalued policy', pp 435–6 above.

33   See *Diamond Alkali Export Corp v Fl Bourgeois* [1921] 3 KB 443; see Chapter 1, p 19 above.

34   See *Burstall v Grimsdale* (1906) 11 Com Cas 280; also see Chapter 1, pp 17–20.

35   There is also another type of policy known as a blanket policy, where the insured does not have to make declarations of his shipments. It is an attractive alternative since it cuts down on administration.

36   Lord Clyde in *Manifest Shipping Co Ltd v Uni-Polaris Insurance Co and La Réunion Européene (The Star Sea)* [2001] 1 Lloyd's Rep 389 observed that he was unable to trace the origins of the concept of *uberrimae fidei*. See also Lord Hobhouse at pp 398–9.

37   On whether the insurer's mutual obligation of good faith limits his right of avoidance. See *Drake Insurance plc v Provident Insurance plc* [2004] QB 601, p 626 ff.

general principles of English contract law, which does not impose a duty on the contracting parties to reveal information that is likely to affect the other's judgment. Insurance contracts are treated as an exception to the rule, since the insurer relies solely on information provided by the assured to decide whether or not to provide insurance cover and for fixing the premium. As Lord Mansfield observed in *Carter v Boehm*:[38]

> The special facts upon which the contingent chance is to be computed lie most commonly in the knowledge of the insured only; the underwriter trusts his representation and proceeds upon confidence that he does not keep back any circumstance in his knowledge to mislead the underwriter into a belief that the circumstance does not exist and to induce him to estimate the risk as if it did not exist. The keeping back of such circumstances is a fraud, and therefore the policy is void[able]. Although the suppression should happen through mistake without any fraudulent intention, yet still the underwriter has been deceived, and the policy is void[able] because the risk run is really different from the risk understood and intended to be run at the time of the agreement. The policy would be equally void[able] against the underwriter if he concealed anything within his own knowledge as, for example, if he insured a ship on a voyage, and he privately knew that she had already arrived, and in such circumstances he would be liable to return the premium paid. Good faith forbids either party, by concealing what he privately knows, to draw the other party into a bargain owing to his ignorance of that fact, and his believing the contrary [at p 1909].

Where utmost good faith has not been observed by either of the parties to an insurance contract, the contract can be avoided if the aggrieved party so wishes. This principle of utmost good faith is enshrined in s 17 of the MIA, which provides:

> A contract of marine insurance is a contract based upon the utmost good faith, and, if the utmost good faith be not observed by either party, the contract may be avoided by the other party.

The assured must disclose all material circumstances known to him before the conclusion of the contract (s 18(1)). The assured is 'deemed to know every circumstance which, in the ordinary course of business, ought to be known by him'. This means that knowledge that his agents or servants possess will be imputed to the assured, even though the assured is not personally aware of the circumstances since he has not been informed of them by his agent or servant.[39]

A circumstance is material if it 'would influence the judgment of a prudent insurer in fixing the premium, or determining whether he will take the risk' (s 18(2)). The extent to which a circumstance must influence the prudent insurer's judgment has been much debated since *Container Transport International Inc and Reliance Group Inc v Oceanus Mutual Underwriting Association (Bermuda) Ltd*.[40] In this case, the court concluded that a fact is material if it would have had an impact on the formation of the prudent insurer's opinion – that is, if the prudent insurer would have wished to be aware of it. There was no need to prove that the prudent insurer would have written the risk on different terms or charged a higher premium had he known of the undisclosed circumstance. According to Kerr LJ:

> The word 'judgment' – to quote the *Oxford English Dictionary* to which we were referred – is used in the sense of 'the formation of an opinion'. To prove the materiality of an

---

38   (1766) 3 Burr 1905.
39   *Republic of Bolivia v Indemnity Mutual Insurance Co Ltd* (1908) 14 Com Cas 156.
40   [1984] 1 Lloyd's Rep 476.

undisclosed circumstance, the insurer must satisfy the court on a balance of probability – by evidence or from the nature of the undisclosed circumstance itself – that the judgment in this sense, of a prudent insurer would have been influenced if the circumstance in question had been disclosed. The word 'influenced' means that the disclosure is one which would have had an impact on the formation of his opinion and his decision making process in relation to the matters covered by s 18(2) [at p 492].

The judgment in *Container Transport International* was widely criticised, since it places the insured under the onerous burden of having to reveal endless information of the insured's past. The insured cannot point to the particular insurer's failure to request certain information as a defence, since the standard is an objective one – that is, that of the prudent insurer. In *Pan Atlantic v Pine Top*[41] (a non-marine insurance case), the Court of Appeal, acknowledging the criticisms of the decision in *Container Transport International*, took the view that a fact is material only if the prudent insurer would have regarded the non-disclosure as increasing the risk. There is, however, no need to prove that he would have a taken a different decision. As Steyn LJ said:

> ... I would rule that, as the law now stands, the question is whether the prudent insurer would view the undisclosed material as probably tending to increase the risk. That does not mean that it is necessary to prove that the underwriter would have taken a different decision about the acceptance of the risk. After all, there may be many commercial reasons for still writing the risk on the same terms [at p 506].

On appeal, the House of Lords, by a majority of 3 to 2, upheld *Container Transport International* – namely, for the purposes of s 18(2), a circumstance is material if it would have had an effect on the mind of a prudent insurer in assessing the risk.[42] However, to avoid the contract for non-disclosure, the undisclosed material circumstance must have induced the (particular) insurer into making the contract. In other words, the test for establishing whether the undisclosed fact is material is objective, whereas the test for avoiding the contract for non-disclosure is a subjective one.[43] The introduction of this subjective test means that an insurer will be unable to avoid a contract simply on the grounds that a prudent insurer would have wished to be aware of the undisclosed circumstance. As expressed by Lord Mustill:

> Before embarking on this long analysis, I suggested that the questions in issue were short. I propose the following short answers. (1) A circumstance may be material even though a full and accurate disclosure would not have had a decisive effect on the prudent underwriter's decision whether to accept the risk and if so at what premium. But (2) if the misrepresentation or non-disclosure of a material fact did not in fact induce the making of the contract (in the sense in which that expression is used in the general law of misrepresentation), the underwriter is not entitled to rely on it as a ground for avoiding the contract.

> These propositions do not go as far as several critics of the *CTI* [*Container Transport International*] case would wish, but they maintain the integrity of the principle that insurance requires utmost good faith ... [at p 618].

---

41   [1994] 3 All ER 581; [1993] Lloyd's Rep 496. See also *New Hampshire Insurance Co v Oil Refineries Ltd* [2002] 1 Lloyd's Rep 462.

42   [1994] 3 All ER 581, at p 607.

43   The attribute of materiality of a given circumstance has to be tested at the time of the placing of the risk and by reference to the impact which it would have on the mind of a prudent insurer. See *The Grecia Express* [2002] 2 Lloyd's Rep 88 at pp 131–2, *Peter Malcolm Brotherton and Others v Asegurdaro Colseguros SA and 1 Other* [2003] EWHC 1741 (Comm).

Though *Pine Top* has curtailed the harshness of the *Container Transport International* decision by introducing an actual inducement test for the purposes of avoiding the contract on grounds of non-disclosure of material circumstances, the onus seems to be on the insured to show that the underwriter was not induced into making the contract due to the non-disclosure of a material fact. This, in practice, may be difficult to establish. The insured may have to examine past practices of the insurer in relation to similar risks and establish whether he was or was not induced by the non-disclosure of the material circumstances. Such information may not always be readily available or, where available, may not be easily forthcoming. Past course of dealings between the insurer and the assured to cover similar risks may make the task much easier. In most cases, the insurer is likely to say that there was actual inducement. The problems are compounded where more than one insurer has underwritten the risk as in a slip. It also seems that, where the undisclosed fact is objectively material, the presumption of inducement is easily raised.[44]

In *Assicurazioni Generali Spa v Arab Insurance Group (BSC)* [2002] EWCA Civ 1642 Clarke LJ enunciated the relevant principles of inducement succinctly as follows:

(i) In order to be entitled to avoid a contract of insurance or reinsurance, an insurer or reinsurer must prove on the balance of probabilities that he was induced to enter into the contract by a material non-disclosure or by a material misrepresentation.

(ii) There is no presumption of law that an insurer is induced to enter in the contract by a material non-disclosure or misrepresentation.[45]

(iii) The facts may, however, be such that it is to be inferred that the particular insurer or reinsurer was so induced even in the absence from evidence from him.

(iv) In order to prove inducement the insurer or reinsurer must show that the non-disclosure or misrepresentation was an effective cause of his entering into the contract on the terms on which he did. He must therefore show at least that, but for the relevant non-disclosure or misrepresentation, he would not have entered into the contract on those terms. On the other hand, he does not have to show that it was the sole effective cause of his doing so [at para 62].

Since the 'drastic remedy'[46] for non-disclosure is avoidance, no doubt, the principle of utmost good faith as applied has come under vehement criticisms[47] from all quarters – the most extreme being that it should be abolished altogether. This suggestion was put forward in *Mutual and Federal Insurance Co Ltd v Transport Industries Insurance Co Ltd.*[48] This may be possible where contract law generally embodies the principle of

---

44 See Longmore, 'An Insurance Contracts Act for a new century?' [2001] LMCLQ 356. It must be said that there are interesting issues as between leading underwriters and subsequent under-writers. If a subsequent underwriter is aware of dubious practices on the part of the insured in the past, should he alert the leading underwriter to this? In *Peter Malcolm Brotherton and Others v Asegurdaro Colseguros SA and 1 Other* [2003] EWHC 1741 (Comm) the following market was entitled to avoid the policy since the lead underwriter was entitled to avoid the policy. The overwhelming evidence indicated that the following market wrote the risk on the basis that there had been a fair presentation to the lead underwriter and this was commercially sensible (at para 44).

45 This question of presumption is a source of some dissatisfaction. It seems that this presump-tion will operate, where a number of underwriters are involved, in favour of the absent underwriter as *St Paul's Fire and Marine Insurance v McConnell Dowell Construction Ltd* [1995] 2 Lloyd's Rep 116.

46 See Staughton LJ in *Kausar v Eagle Star* [1997] CLC 129, at p 133.

47 See Longmore, 'An Insurance Contracts Act for a new century?' [2001] LMCLQ 356 for various suggestions for reform and brief account of reforms in Australia.

48 1985 1 SA 419.

good faith as in Roman law. English law lacks such an underlying principle. This may well change once the Principles of European Contract Law[49] exercise more influence on the development of English contract law.

There is also the associated issue of whether this requirement of utmost good faith continues once the contract is concluded. In other words, does it subsist post-contract?[50] The matter was more recently considered by the House of Lords in *Manifest Shipping Co Ltd v Uni-Polaris Insurance Co and La Réunion Européene (The Star Sea)*.[51] While the court acknowledged that good faith subsisted post-contract, it was not an absolute, and the degree varied according to circumstances. In the words of Lord Clyde:

> In my view, the idea of good faith in the context of insurance contracts reflects the degrees of openness required of the parties in the various stages of their relationship. It is not an absolute. The substance of the obligation which is entailed can vary according to the context in which the matter comes to be judged. It is reasonable to expect a very high degree of openness at the stage of the formation of the contract, but there is no justification for requiring that degree necessarily to continue once the contract has been made [at p 392].

The duty of good faith, however, does not extend to litigation: '. . . once the parties are in litigation, it is the procedural rules which govern the extent of disclosure' (at p 407).

It is very difficult to say beforehand which circumstance will be regarded as material and which not. It really is a question of fact to be decided by the surrounding circumstances, attitudes of the underwriters and so on. Nonetheless, decided cases do provide a few rough indications. For instance, excessive valuation of the goods,[52] low priced end of stock goods,[53] contracts with stevedores at below market rates,[54] proven dishonesty,[55] and facing charges of fraud, even if unfounded,[56] are likely to be regarded as material facts. Suspicions and rumours may affect materiality.[57]

In *Strive Shipping Corp v Hellenic Mutual War Risks Association (The Grecia Express)*,[58] the defendants (insurers) were suspicious concerning the loss of vessels in which the assured had an interest on a number of previous occasions. They argued there was fraudulent conduct on the part of the insured and the sinking of the ships should have been disclosed. They were material and affected the magnitude of the risk. The court found for the claimant since the facts and evidence examined by the court did not lend support to the allegation of scuttling. As to the standard of proof it seems that the insurer has to prove on a balance of probabilities that the assured acted fraudulently.[59]

---

49 See Chapter 2, p 95 above.
50 See *Cory v Patton* (1872) LR 7 QB 304; *Lishman v Northern Maritime Insurance Co* (1875) LR 10 CP 179.
51 [2001] 1 Lloyd's Rep 389. For facts of the case, see 'Warranties on the Part of the Insured – Implied and Express', pp 446–8 below.
52 See *Ionides v Pender* (1874) LR 9 QB 531.
53 See *Liberian Insurance Agency Inc v Mosse* [1977] 2 Lloyd's Rep 560.
54 See *Tate v Hyslop* (1885) 15 QBD 368.
55 See *Cleland v London General Insurance Co* (1935) 51 LlLR 156.
56 See *North Shipping Ltd v Sphere Drake Insurance plc* [2006] EWCA Civ 378.
57 It seems that the worth of rumours has to be decided in terms of their provenance. The better the provenance they cannot be dismissed as idle gossip. See *Brotherton v Asegurdaro* [2003] EWHC 1741 (Comm), para 33.
58 [2002] 2 Lloyd's Rep 82.
59 See p 98 ff.

As for the burden of proving lack of utmost good faith, that is on the party alleging it.

Where the contract is not made in utmost good faith and the insurer elects to avoid it, the premium paid must be returned, unless there is fraud on the part of the insured according s 84(3)(b).

According to s 18(3), an insured, unless asked, is not required to disclose the following:

(a) any circumstance which diminishes the risk;

(b) any circumstance which is known or presumed to be known to the insurers,[60]

(c) any circumstance as to which information is waived by the insurer;[61] and

(d) any circumstance which it is superfluous to disclose by reason of an implied or express warranty.[62]

The requirement of utmost good faith also applies to material representations made during negotiations. So, where a material representation – that is, a representation that influences the judgment of a prudent insurer in fixing the premium, or determining whether he will take the risk – is untrue, the insurer can elect to avoid the contract (s 20(1)). However, the insurer can avoid the contract if the misrepresentation did in fact induce the making of the contract.[63]

Insurable interest

Another established principle of marine insurance law – a consequence of the marine insurance contract being a contract of indemnity – is that the person for whose benefit the insurance policy is effected has or expects to acquire an insurable interest in the property.[64] Section 5 of the MIA defines insurable interest as:

(1) Subject to the provisions of this Act, every person has an insurable interest who is interested in a marine adventure.

(2) In particular, a person is interested in a marine adventure where he stands in any legal or equitable relation to the adventure to any insurable property at risk therein, in consequence of which, he may benefit by the safety or due arrival of insurable property, or may be prejudiced by its loss, or by damage thereto, or by the detention thereof, or may incur liability in respect thereof.

The MIA, in ss 6–16, also lists a number of specific interests that are regarded as insurable interests. Accordingly, amongst others, buyers,[65] consignees, those who have advanced money on the goods, shipowners, charterers, bailees[66] and insurers have an insurable interest.

The Institute Cargo Clauses (A), (B) and (C) reflect this requirement of insurable

60 See *Brotherton v Asegurdaro* [2003] EWHC 1741 (Comm).
61 See *Wise Underwriting Agency Ltd v Grupo National Provincial SA* [2004] 2 Lloyd's Rep 483.
62 On warranties, see pp 446–8 below.
63 See *Pan Atlantic v Pine Top* [1994] 3 All ER 581, at p 618.
64 See *Lucena v Craufurd* (1806) 2 B&PNR 269.
65 On insurable interest of an FOB buyer, see *John Gillanders Inglis v William Ravenhill Stock* (1885) 10 App Cas 263. In FOB contracts, risk passes when goods pass the ship's rail. See also *Karlshamns Oljefabriker v Eastport Navigation Co, The Elafi* [1981] 2 Lloyd's Rep 679.
66 See *Tomlinson v Hepburn* [1966] AC 451.

interest in their cl 11.1, which states that, 'in order to recover under this insurance, the assured must have an insurable interest in the subject matter insured'.

Where there is some doubt about whether the assured's interest comes within the ambit of s 5 of the Act, insurers may issue ppi policies.[67] A policy proof of interest (ppi) policy is one where the policy is taken to be sufficient proof of the assured's interest and the assured does not have to prove the nature of his interest in the subject matter. Such policies are regarded as wagering or gaming contracts (s 4(2)) and are therefore void under s 4(1). Therefore, they cannot be legally enforced. Despite this, ppi policies are in common use. These policies are binding in honour only and, if the insurer decides not to pay the insured on the policy, the latter cannot enforce it in a court of law. This also means that, where an insurer has paid out on a ppi policy, he cannot claim under subrogation. In *John Edwards Co Ltd v Motor Union Insurance Co*,[68] the defendants had paid out for the total loss of a vessel under a ppi policy to the plaintiffs. The plaintiffs subsequently recovered damages from the owners of the vessel responsible for the collision. In an action for declaration that the defendants were not entitled to the recovered sums, the court held that rights of subrogation could arise only where there is a contract of indemnity. As MacCardie J said:

> [A contract destitute of all legal effect between the parties] cannot operate as if it were a valid bargain carrying with it the legal and equitable remedies and the body of jural remedies which ordinarily flow from an insurance contract. Legal proceedings to enforce subrogative rights cannot be based on a document which is stricken with sterility by Act of Parliament [at p 256].

Subrogation and double insurance

It is a well established principle in insurance law that once the insurer settles the assured's claim, he is subrogated to all the rights and remedies of the assured in relation to the subject matter. That is, the insurer takes the place of the insured, and can exercise any rights and remedies the insured has in respect of the loss for which the insurer has paid out. In other words, as Lord Cairns, the Lord Chancellor, stated in *Simpson v Thomson*:[69]

> ... [suborgation is founded] on the well known principle of law that, where one person has agreed to indemnify another, he will, on making good the indemnity, be entitled to succeed to all the ways and means by which the person indemnified might have protected himself against or reimbursed him for the loss. It is on this principle that the underwriters of a ship that has been lost are entitled to the ship *in specie* if they can find and recover it; and it is on the same principle that they can assert any right which the owner of the ship might have asserted against a wrongdoer for damage for the act which has caused the loss [at p 284].[70]

This principle applies (equally) to marine insurance contracts (s 79).

Under the doctrine of subrogation,[71] the insurer will be entitled to recover only

---

67 *Cheshire and Co v Thompson* (1919) 24 Com Cas 198.
68 [1922] 2 KB 249.
69 (1877) 3 App Cas 279.
70 See also *Burnard v Radocanchi* (1888) 7 App Cas 333.
71 On the difference between subrogation and assignment, see *Colonia Versicherung AG v Amoco Oil Co* [1997] 1 Lloyd's Rep 261, at pp 270–1. On assignment, see 'Assignment', p 445 below.

what he has paid out. *Yorkshire Insurance v Nisbet Shipping*[72] exhibits this well. In this case, a ship insured by the plaintiffs sank as a result of a collision. The insurers paid out the insured sum of £72,000 to the assured. The shipowners were successful in their proceedings against the tortfeasors in Canada and received damages that produced a sum of £127,000 as a result of devaluation. The shipowners returned the sum of £72,000 to the insurers and retained the balance. The insurers brought an action against the assured for the balance. The court held the assured could retain the balance and the insurer was not entitled to the windfall.

The doctrine of subrogation has to be distinguished from proprietary rights that the insurer acquires on abandonment after total loss is paid. The case of *AG v Glen Line Ltd*[73] provides a good illustration. The vessel, in this case, was seized due to the outbreak of war. The insurers paid for total loss and the ship was abandoned to the insurers. Once hostilities ceased, the ship was sold for an amount greater that that paid to the shipowner by the insurers. The shipowners (that is, the assured) also received compensation from the German government for the loss of use of their vessel. The issues for consideration were:

(a) Did the insurers have a right to retain the excess they received from the sale of the ship?

(b) Did the insurers have a claim on the compensation received by the assured?

The court held that profits made on the sale of the subject matter belonged to the insurer since he had acquired proprietary rights upon abandonment. As for the compensation, that was paid to the owners for the loss of profits and was not related to the loss of the ship itself. The insurer had no rights to the compensation. Lord Atkin elucidated the distinction between proprietary rights and subrogation thus:

> But a right to sue a wrongdoer for a wrongful act which causes a loss which gives rise to an abandonment appears to be something quite different from the proprietary rights incidental to the ship which passes on abandonment.
>
> If one treats the insurer by analogy as a purchaser after the marine peril had taken effect, it is plain that the sale by itself would not pass the right to sue which would remain in the vendor. The fact is that confusion is often caused by not distinguishing the legal rights given by abandonment (s 63) from the rights of suborgation (s 79). No one doubts that the underwriter on hull damaged by collision and abandoned as a constructive total loss is entitled to the benefit of the rights of the assured to sue the wrongdoer for the damage to the hull. But he derives his right from the provisions of s 79, whereby he is subrogated to 'all rights and remedies of the assured in and in respect of the subject matter', very different words from 'all proprietary rights incidental thereto' and it is to be noted that in respect of abandonment the rights exist on a valid abandonment, whereas in respect of subrogation they only arise on payment; and that subrogation will only give the insurer rights up to 20 shillings in the £ on what he has paid [at pp 13–14].

The origins of the doctrine of subrogation is uncertain. Some of the judges regard it as a creation of common law.[74] Others regard it as a creation of equity with conviction.[75]

Regardless of its origins, it must be pointed out that subrogation ensures that the insured is not overcompensated – that is, does not make a profit out of his loss, which

---

72 [1962] 2 QB 330.
73 (1930) 46 TLR 451.
74 *Yorkshire Insurance Co v Nisbet Shipping* [1962] 2 QB 330, at p 339.
75 *Napier v Hunter* [1993] 2 WLR 42, at pp 57–60.

leads us as a matter of course to double insurance. It is possible that the cargo is insured with two insurers – for example, where the cargo is insured by the shipper as well as the consignee. Double insurance is explained by s 32(1) as:

> Where two or more policies are effected by or on behalf of the assured on the same adventure and interest or any part thereof, and the sums insured exceed the indemnity allowed by this Act, the assured is said to be over-insured by double insurance.

Where there is double insurance, in the event of loss, the assured cannot recover the loss twice. Where one of the insurers pays out on the loss, he is entitled to look to the other insurer for contribution. The rules relating to double insurance and right of contribution[76] are set out in s 32(2) and s 80 of the MIA.

Assignment

In international sales, goods frequently change hands while they are still in transit. Just as it is important for bills of lading to be made out to order to enable transfer,[77] it is also important for the marine insurance policy[78] to be assignable so that the buyer is covered in the event of loss or damage to the goods due to perils of the voyage. Assignment of the policy does not follow passing of property as a matter of course (s 15). Section 50(1) of the MIA allows assignment of the policy as long as the policy does not expressly forbid assignment. Marine policies covering cargo normally do not carry a clause prohibiting assignment, for to do so would impede international trade.

The Institute Cargo Clauses (A), (B) and (C) prevent the passing of the insurance policy to bailees or carriers in cl 15. The object of this clause is to stop bailees or carriers from contracting out of liability by inserting a clause in the contract of carriage which gives them the benefit of the insurance cover. Of course, such a clause would be void under the Hague-Visby Rules and the Hamburg Rules, since it would lessen the liability of the carrier under these conventions.[79]

Endorsement is the method normally used to effect assignment,[80] recognised by s 50(3). Section 50(3) also allows for the possibility of assignment through other customary means. Mere delivery of the policy to the purported assignee is, however, insufficient to establish assignment. An intention to transfer the rights under the policy also must be shown.[81]

A policy can be assigned before or after the loss. However, an assignment after loss is possible only as long as the implied or express agreement to assign is made when the assignor has an interest in the subject matter (s 51). *North of England Pure Oil*

---

76 The following cases address various issues relating to contribution: *Commercial Union Assurance Co Ltd v Hayden* [1977] QB 804; *Legal and General Assurance Society Ltd v Drake Insurance Co Ltd* [1992] QB 887; *Eagle Star Insurance Co Ltd v Provincial Insurance plc* [1994] 1 AC 130.

77 See Chapter 6, pp 181–2 above.

78 An insurance policy however is not a negotiable instrument like a bill of exchange. See pp 466–70 below on bills of exchange.

79 See Chapters 8 and 9.

80 Note that, on assignment, according to s 50(2) 'the defendant is entitled to make any defence arising out of the contract which he would have been entitled to make if the action had been brought in the name of person by or on behalf of whom the policy was effected'.

81 *Baker v Adams* (1910) 15 Com Cas 227. In CIF contracts, it is customary to assign by tendering the document.

Cake Co v Archangel Maritime Bank and Insurance Co Ltd[82] provides an illustration. In this case, the cargo was insured with the defendants from Istanbul to London. The insurance included the risk of lighterage. The original assured sold the goods to the plaintiffs while they were in transit. According to the sale contract, the plaintiffs were required to pay for the goods 14 days from delivery. The cargo was unloaded on to the plaintiffs' lighters. Some of the cargo was lost when one of the lighters sank. The original assured assigned the policy after the loss and the plaintiffs tried to recover their loss from the insurers. There was, however, no agreement to assign the policy to the plaintiffs in the sold note and nor could an intention to assign be inferred from the sold note. In the circumstances, the court held that the defendants were not liable for the loss of the cargo, since the interest of the assured had ceased on delivery of the goods to the plaintiffs' lighters and the assignment had taken place after the loss.

WARRANTIES ON THE PART OF THE INSURED – IMPLIED AND EXPRESS

A number of warranties are implied into the insurance contract by ss 39–40 of the MIA. Warranties are undertakings on the part of the insured that some particular thing shall or shall not be done, or that some condition will be fulfilled, or that a particular state of affairs does or does not exist (s 33(1)) and are construed strictly. Where there is a breach of a warranty, the insurer is not liable as from the date of the breach.

Implied warranties (seaworthiness, legality)

In every voyage policy, it is implied that the ship is seaworthy for the particular voyage – that is, that she is reasonably fit to encounter the ordinary perils of the sea (s 39(1) and (4)). Where the voyage policy relates to a voyage to be performed in stages and requires special equipment or preparation for a particular voyage, the ship must be seaworthy at the commencement of each stage and for the purposes of that stage (s 39(3)). Where the policy covers risks while the ship is in port, the ship must be reasonably fit to encounter the ordinary perils of the port. Where the policy is a voyage policy on goods, according to s 40(2), it is implied that the ship is not only seaworthy as a ship, but also reasonably fit to carry the goods to their destination.[83] Warranties, implied or express, require strict compliance. This means that, where there is a breach of warranty, the insurer will not be liable on the policy as from the date of the breach (s 33(3)).

In other words, the fulfilment of the warranty is a condition precedent to the liability of the insurer.[84]

The implied warranty of seaworthiness places the cargo owner in an onerous position, since he has no way of knowing whether the ship can withstand the perils of the journey, is in a fit state of repair, is manned properly and so on. In these

---

82 (1875) LR 10 QB 249.

83 As in common law, the undertaking of seaworthiness covers both the physical state of the ship and the cargoworthiness of the ship. See Chapter 7, pp 208–12 above.

84 See Lord Goff in *Bank of Nova Scotia v Hellenic Mutual War Risks Association (The Good Luck)* [1992] 1 AC 233, at pp 262–3. See also *Agapitos v Agnew (The Aegeon No 2)* [2002] EWHC 1558 (Comm).

circumstances, it is common to insert a clause excluding the implied warranties of seaworthiness. Such a clause is found in the Institute Cargo Clauses. Clause 5.2 states:

> The underwriters waive any breach of the implied warranties of seaworthiness of the ship and fitness of the ship to carry the subject matter insured to destination unless the assured or their servants are privy to such unseaworthiness or unfitness.

The issue of whether the assured was privy raises some interesting questions about state of knowledge of the assured. Can knowledge be imputed on the basis that any reasonable person, where the facts are plainly staring him in his face, would have known of the unseaworthiness? In other words, can we ascribe the assured with knowledge that they should have had? In *Manifest Shipping Co Ltd v Uni-Polaris Insurance Co and La Réunion Européene (The Star Sea)*,[85] *The Star Sea* was on a voyage from Nicaragua to Zeebrugge. She left on 27 May 1990, and on 29 May 1990 a fire broke out accidentally started by an engineer using an oxyacetylene torch in the engine workshop. The crew tried to extinguish the fire for two and a half hours after which the master decided to use the carbon dioxide (CO_2) extinguishing system kept in store outside the engine room, holding four banks of bottles. Their use was ineffective and the fire continued to burn even though the crew thought the fire was extinguished. The damage to the ship was to an extent so as to make the loss a constructive total loss.[86] The insurers of *The Star Sea*, owned by the Kollakis family, insured under a time policy, said they were not liable, since the ship had been sent to sea in an unseaworthy state with the privity of the assured. The CO_2 system was discharged by pulling a lever but, because of poor maintenance, the levers on two of the banks broke leaving only two banks operational. The judge in the lower court had found that the master was incompetent in that he was ignorant of what was required to use the system successfully. The issue that the court had to consider was whether the assured were privy to the unseaworthy state of the ship on the basis of 'blind-eye knowledge',[87] since it was accepted that they did not have actual knowledge of the unseaworthiness. The insurers, in support of the privity argument, drew on what had happened in the past on two other vessels, *The Centaurus* and the *The Kastora*, which were part of the fleet owned by the Kollakis family. Both these ships were manned by Korean crew. There was fire aboard both these ships. In the case of the first ship, the CO_2 system was used and, in the second, the system's use was ineffective since the dampers did not have adequate sealing. As a result of these fires, the Korean crew of *The Star Sea* was replaced with a Greek crew. Regardless, Tuckey J found that the steps that had been taken were incompletely inadequate – for instance, no steps had been taken to ensure that the master was competent in using the CO_2 system – and came to the conclusion that there was blind-eye knowledge on the part of the assured.

---

85 [2001] 1 Lloyds's Rep 389.

86 See pp 451–2 below for the meaning of constructive total loss.

87 Expression used by Lord Denning in *The Eurasthenes* [1976] 2 Lloyd's Rep 171 and explained in the following manner:

> To disentitle the shipowner, he must, I think, have knowledge not only of the facts constituting the unseaworthiness, but also knowledge that those facts rendered the ship unseaworthy, that is, not reasonably fit to encounter the ordinary perils of the seas. And, when I speak of knowledge, I mean not only positive knowledge but also the sort of knowledge expressed in the phrase 'turning a blind eye'. If a man, suspicious of the truth, turns a blind eye to it, and refrains from inquiry – so that he should not know it for certain – then he is to be regarded as knowing the truth. This 'turning a blind eye' is far more blameworthy than mere negligence. Negligence in not knowing the truth is not equivalent to knowledge of it [at p 179].

On appeal, however the finding of the judge was reversed. As Lord Justice Legatt said 'an allegation that they ought to know [is] not an allegation that they suspected or realised but did not make further enquiries'.[88] The test to be used therefore is a subjective one. On appeal, the House of Lords agreed with the Court of Appeal.

There is also an implied undertaking that the adventure insured is a legal one. Where the adventure is illegal, the policy will be unenforceable. For instance, where goods are exported contrary to existing regulation, the policy will be unenforceable for illegality.[89] It is possible that an adventure which is legal to start with becomes illegal due to a change in the circumstances – for instance, declaration of war. Where the assured abandons the adventure (that is, acts in a lawful manner), the assured will be covered.[90]

Express warranties

Other than warranties that are implied into the insurance contract, it is normal for policies to include express warranties, such as a warranty that the ship will sail before a certain date, a warranty that the ship will not carry certain types of cargo, and so on. Express warranties must be included in, or written on, the policy. However, where they are contained in a document other than the policy, then that document must be incorporated by reference in the policy (s 35(2)).

As with implied warranties, where there is a breach of an express warranty, the insurer is discharged from liability as from the date of the breach (s 33(3)).

DEVIATION

Under the MIA, it is expected that the vessel will proceed on the voyage on the usual or customary course, or the course specifically designated for the voyage (s 46). Where the vessel deviates from the voyage contemplated, without any lawful excuse, the insured loses cover from the moment of deviation.[91]

Deviation in the following circumstances is excused by s 49(1)(a)–(g):

(a) where authorised by any special term in the policy;

(b) where caused by circumstances beyond the control of the master and his employer;

(c) where reasonably necessary in order to comply with an express or implied warranty;

(d) where reasonably necessary for the safety of the ship or subject matter insured;

(e) for the purpose of saving human life, or aiding a ship in distress where human life may be in danger;

(f) where reasonably necessary for the purpose of obtaining medical or surgical aid for any person on board the ship;

---

88 [1997] 1 Lloyd's Rep 360, at p 377.
89 *Parkin v Dick* (1809) 11 East 502.
90 *Sanday v British and Foreign Marine Insurance Co Ltd* [1915] 2 KB 781.
91 On the drastic effect of deviation on exclusion clauses in carriage contracts, see Chapter 7, pp 213–16 above, and 8, pp 243–6 above.

(g) where caused by the barratrous conduct of master or crew, if barratry is a peril insured against.

It is common practice for insurance contracts to specify that cover does not cease on deviation. Clause 8.3 of Institute Cargo Clauses (A), (B) and (C) provides that the 'insurance shall remain in force during delay beyond the control of the assured, any deviation, forced discharge, reshipment or transhipment and during any variation of the adventure arising from the exercise of a liberty granted to shipowners or charterers under the contract of affreightment'. As is obvious, cl 8.3 covers situations other than deviation. So, where, for instance, during repairs, the goods are warehoused, the cargo will continue to be covered. Where the events listed in cl 8.3 occur, the insured has no obligation to give notice to the insurer and no extra premium is payable.

Clause 8 must not be confused with cl 10 (found in all three sets of Institute Cargo Clauses), which provides that 'where, after attachment of this insurance, the destination is changed by the assured, *held covered at a premium and on conditions to be arranged on conditions subject to prompt notice being given to the underwriters*' (emphasis added). This clause does not apply to deviation but applies where there is a voluntary change of the voyage by the insured – for instance, where the assured changes the destination from Mumbai (destination on policy) to Chennai subsequent to commencement of risk.

For the goods to be covered in the event of a change of destination, the insured is under an obligation to give prompt notice as expressly stated in cl 10.

LIABILITY OF INSURER

Doctrine of proximate causation

According to s 55(1) of the MIA, 'the insurer is liable for any loss proximately caused by a peril insured against' unless the policy provides otherwise. In other words, one should look to the proximate cause and not the remote cause to establish the liability of the insured on the policy (*causa proxima non remota spectatur*).

Until the decision in *Leyland Shipping Co v Norwich Union Fire Insurance Soc (The Ikaria),*[92] there was a tendency to treat the cause closest in time to the loss as the proximate cause.[93] In *Leyland Shipping*, a ship was torpedoed by a German boat near Le Havre. The ship managed to reach Le Havre where she put into harbour. As a result of a swell caused by a gale, the ship was moved to an outer harbour where she sank. The House of Lords held that the torpedoing of the ship was the real and efficient cause of the event. The proximity in time of the gales (perils of the sea) to the loss was totally irrelevant. According to Lord Shaw:

> To treat *proxima causa* as the cause which is nearest in time is out of the question. Causes are spoken as if they were as distinct from one another as beads in a row or links in a chain, but – if this metaphysical topic has to be referred to – it is not wholly so. The chain of causation is a handy expression, but the figure is inadequate. Causation is not a chain, but a net. At each point, influences, forces, events, precedents and simultaneous, meet, and the radiation from each point extends infinitely. At the point where these various

---

92 [1918] AC 350. See also *Brownsville Holdings v Adamjee Insurance* [2000] 2 Lloyd's Rep 458.
93 See *Pink v Fleming* (1890) 25 QB 396.

influences meet, it is for the judgment as upon a matter of fact to declare which of the causes thus joined at the point of effect was the proximate and which was the remote cause.

To treat proximate cause as if it was the cause which is proximate in time is, as I have said, out of the question. The cause which is truly proximate is that which is proximate in efficiency. That efficiency may have been preserved although other causes may meantime have sprung up which have not yet destroyed it, or truly impaired it, and it may culminate in a result of which it still remains the efficient cause to which the event can be ascribed [at p 369].

It must be stressed that the courts are not engaging in a philosophical discourse when discussing the meaning of proximate cause or efficient cause, as Lord Shaw pointed out in *Leyland Shipping*. When the courts look at the issue of causation, they are doing so in common sense terms.[94]

Section 55(2) lists the circumstances in which an insurer will not be held liable. Unless the policy provides otherwise, the insurer is not liable for loss that is proximately caused by: (1) delay, even though the delay is caused by a peril insured against; (2) ordinary wear and tear, ordinary leakage and breakage, inherent vice or nature of the subject matter; and (3) rats or vermin. Section 55(2)(a) provides that the insurer is also not liable for a loss that is attributable to the wilful misconduct of the assured. He is, however, liable for any loss that is proximately caused by a peril insured against, even though it would not have occurred but for the negligence, unless the terms of the policy provide otherwise.

Where the loss is attributable to a number of proximate causes, and one of them is excepted, the insurer is not liable for the loss.[95]

It is for the insured to make out a *prima facie* case that a loss was proximately caused by a peril insured against.[96] The burden then shifts to the insurer to show that the loss falls within one of the exceptions listed in the policy.

The requirement that the cause of loss be proximate for the purposes of liability is not an absolute requirement – the parties may agree otherwise. Where Institute Cargo Clauses (B) and (C) are used, it is enough to show that loss or damage to goods was reasonably attributable to perils listed in cl 1.[97]

Types of losses

Under s 56(1) of the MIA, a loss can be a total loss or a partial loss. The question of whether the insured is covered for a total loss or a partial loss will depend on the terms of the policy. The Institute Cargo Clauses (A), (B) and (C) cover the insured for partial as well as total loss, except for cl 1.3 of Institute Cargo Clause (B), which covers the insured only for total loss of any package lost overboard or dropped whilst loading or unloading from the vessel or craft.[98]

---

94 *Yorkshire Dales Steamship Co Ltd v Minister of War Transport* [1942] AC 691, at p 706.
95 *Wayne Tank and Pump Co Ltd v Employers Liability Association Corp Ltd* [1973] 2 Lloyd's Rep 237; *Lloyd Instruments Ltd v Northern Star Insurance Co Ltd (The Miss Jay Jay)* [1985] 1 Lloyd's Rep 264; [1987] 1 Lloyd's Rep 32.
96 See *Cobb and Jenkins v Volga Insurance Co of Petrograd* (1920) 4 LlL Rep 178.
97 See Table 14.1.
98 See Table 14.1.

Total loss

According to s 56(2), a total loss can be an actual total loss or a constructive total loss.

Actual total loss

Under s 57(1), a claim for actual total loss arises: (a) where the entire subject matter is destroyed – for example, where the cargo is destroyed by fire; (b) where the subject matter is destroyed to an extent that it ceases to be a thing of the kind insured – for example, where a cargo of dates was found unfit for human consumption when it was retrieved from a ship that sank, as in *Asfar v Blundell*;[99] and (c) where the insured is irretrievably deprived of the subject matter – for example, where a vessel is captured and there is no likelihood of it being returned.[100] Goods may also be presumed to be a total loss where a vessel concerned in the adventure goes missing for a reasonable period of time (s 58).

An obliteration of marks, due to a peril insured against which renders the goods unidentifiable, will not give rise to a claim for actual total loss. It will give rise only to a claim for partial total loss (s 56(5)).

Where the insurer pays for total loss, he becomes entitled to take over the interest of the assured in whatever may remain of the subject matter (s 79). In practice, insurers hardly ever take over what remains of the subject matter and may come to some arrangement with the insured.

Constructive total loss

According to s 60(1), there is a constructive total loss: (a) where it is reasonable to abandon the subject matter insured, since actual total loss seems to be unavoidable; or (b) where the cost of preserving the subject matter insured from actual total loss is far in excess of the value of the subject matter.

Where the owner is deprived of goods, there is constructive total loss only if it is unlikely that he will recover them, or the cost of recovering them would exceed the value of the goods when recovered (s 60(2)(i)). The meaning of 'unlikely' was examined in *Polurrian SS Co Ltd v Young*,[101] where a vessel from Newport to Constantinople (Istanbul) was captured by the Greeks during the war between the Turks and the Greeks. According to Pickford J, 'unlikely' did not mean 'unlikely that it could ever be recovered' but 'unlikely that it could be recovered within a reasonable time'.[102] Where there is damage to the cargo, there is constructive total loss if the cost of making good the damage and forwarding it to its destination exceeds its value on arrival (s 60(2)(iii)).[103]

The three sets of Institute Cargo Clauses – (A), (B) and (C) – in cl 13 provide that 'no claim for constructive loss shall be recoverable . . . unless the subject matter insured

---

99   [1896] 1 QB 123.
100 See also *Roux v Salvador* (1836) 3 Bing NC 266.
101 [1915] 1 KB 922.
102 [1915] 1 KB 922 (CA), at p 938, affirming Pickford J. See also *The Bamburi* [1982] 1 Lloyd's Rep 312.
103 See *Vacuum Oil Co v Union Insurance Society of Canton* (1926) 25 LIL Rep 546.

is reasonably abandoned either on account of its actual total loss appearing to be unavoidable or because the cost of recovering, reconditioning and forwarding the subject matter to the destination to which it is insured would exceed its value on arrival'. Though worded differently, the effect of this clause is the same as that of s 60, in that the constructive total loss is determined in terms of the value of the goods on arrival.

Where there is constructive total loss, the insured has a couple of options. Either he can treat the constructive total loss as a partial loss, or he can treat the loss as an actual total loss. If he decides to do the latter, he must abandon the subject matter to the insurer (s 61) and give notice of abandonment to the insurer (s 62(1)). The notice must be given clearly in writing, or orally, or partly in writing and partly by word of mouth (s 62(2)).[104] The acceptance of the notice of abandonment can be either express or implied but silence on the part of the insurer does not constitute an acceptance (s 62(4)). In the event of a valid abandonment, the insurer is entitled to take over the interest of the assured in whatever may remain of the subject matter (s 63).[105]

Partial loss

According to s 56(1), a loss that is not a total loss is a partial loss. So, for instance, where 20 crates of a cargo of 100 crates of whisky are lost, there is a partial loss.

INSTITUTE CARGO CLAUSES (A), (B) AND (C)

Historical background

Throughout this chapter, references have been made to the Institute Cargo Clauses (A), (B) and (C).[106] These three sets of Institute Cargo Clauses, in wide use in the insurance industry, are standard terms and were introduced in 1982. Prior to the Institute Cargo Clauses, the insurance market used a standard form SG policy, attached as a schedule to the Marine Insurance Act 1906. The acronym 'SG' stood for ships and goods. The SG policy, apart from using archaic language, was issued for insurance on ship, as well as goods and freight. The SG policy was criticised by the judiciary for its lack of clarity, simplicity and certainty.[107]

In 1978, the United Nations Conference on Trade and Development (UNCTAD) had also published a report[108] that echoed the criticisms of the SG policy as antiquated and unclear. In response to these criticisms, the Institute of London Underwriters[109]

---

104 In some circumstances, a notice of abandonment can be excused. See 62(7) and *Kastor Naviga-tion Co Ltd v AGF MAT* [2004] 2 Lloyd's Rep 119. A right to claim for constructive total loss is not lost where the vessel becomes an actual total loss.
105 See 'Subrogation and double insurance', p 443 above.
106 For a comparative table of the extent of cover under these three sets of Institute Cargo Clauses, see Table 14.1.
107 See *Shell International Petroleum Co Ltd v Gibbs (The Salem)* [1982] 1 QB 948; *Merten v Vestey Bros Ltd* [1920] AC 307, at pp 314–15.
108 *Marine Insurance – Legal and Documentary Aspects of the Marine Insurance Contract*, UNCTAD Document TD/B/C14/ISL/270.
109 It was founded in 1884 consisting of insurance companies involved in marine insurance as members.

and the Lloyds Underwriters Association[110] set up a working party to see how best the criticisms raised by the report could be addressed. The working party recommended the replacement of the SG policy with a new user-friendly form and cargo clauses. A new form (often called the MAR Policy, from Lloyd's Marine Policy) was introduced. The Companies Marine Policy of the Institute of London Underwriters is similar to the MAR Policy, except that they use the word 'Company' instead of 'Underwriter'. The MAR Policy validates the existence of the contract, since s 22 of the MIA states:

> Subject to the provisions of any statute, a contract of marine insurance is inadmissible in evidence unless it is embodied in a marine policy in accordance with this Act. The policy may be executed and issued either at the time when the contract is concluded or afterwards.

The MAR Policy lists the information to be provided:

(a) the policy number;

(b) the name of the assured (required by s 23(1));

(c) the vessel;

(d) the voyage or period of insurance;

(e) the subject matter insured;

(f) the agreed value (if there is any);

(g) the amount insured;

(h) clauses, endorsements, special conditions and warranties; and

(i) the underwriters' (companies') proportions.

Under s 24(1) of the MIA, the marine policy needs to be signed by or on behalf of the insurer. Where a company or corporation is the insurer, a corporate seal will be sufficient. Provision for the signature is made on the top page of the policy. The terms of insurance are set out in the Institute Cargo Clauses (A), (B) and (C), to be used with the MAR Policy form.

Institute Cargo Clauses (A)

The Institute Cargo Clauses (A) provide the widest cover. They cover all risks of loss or damage to the subject matter insured (cl 1), excepting loss or damage caused by:

(a) wilful misconduct of the assured (cl 4.1);[111]

(b) ordinary leakage,[112] ordinary loss in weight or volume, or ordinary wear and tear[113] (cl 4.2);

(c) insufficiency or unsuitability of packing (cl 4.3);[114]

(d) inherent vice (cl 4.4);[115]

---

110 It represents Lloyd's marine underwriters.
111 See Chapter 10, pp 346–7 above, on the meaning of wilful misconduct in relation to the Warsaw Convention. See also *Lewis v Great Western Railway Co* (1877) 3 QB 195.
112 See *Monchy v Phoenix Insurance Co of Hartford* (1929) 34 LIL Rep 201.
113 See *ED Sasson and Co Ltd v Yorkshire Insurance Co* (1923) 16 LIL Rep 129.
114 See *Berk and Co v Style* [1956] 1 QB 180.
115 See *Soya GmNH Mainz Kommanditgesellschaft v White* [1982] 1 Lloyd's Rep 122; *Mayban General Assurance Bhd, Ami Insurans Bhd, Malaysian National Insurance v Alstom Power Plants Ltd* [2004] EWHC 1038 (Comm).

(e) delay, even though the delay was caused by a risk insured against (cl 4.5);

(f) insolvency and financial default of managers, charterers or operators of vessel (cl 4.6);

(g) use of any weapon of war employing atomic or nuclear fission and/or fusion or other like reaction or radioactive force or matter (cl 4.7);

(h) unseaworthiness of vessel or craft (cl 5.1);

(i) unfitness of vessel, craft, container, or liftvan for the safe carriage of the subject matter insured (cl 5.1);

(j) war,[116] civil war, revolution, rebellion, insurrection, or civil strife arising therefrom, or any hostile act by or against a belligerent power (cl 6);

(k) capture, seizure, arrest or restraint, or detainment (piracy excepted), or the consequences from such events (cl 6);

(l) derelict mines, torpedoes or bombs, or other derelict weapons of war (cl 6);

(m) strikers, locked out workmen, or persons taking part in labour disturbances, riots or civil commotions (cl 7);

(n) strikes, lock-outs, labour disturbances, riots or civil commotion (cl 7);

(o) any terrorist or any person acting from a political motive (cl 7).

Some of the above exceptions are also found in the Marine Insurance Act 1906 (for example, wilful misconduct (s 55(2)(a)), delay (s 55(2)(b)), wear and tear (s 55(2)(c)) and inherent vice (s 55(2)(c)).

The phrase 'all risks' has been judicially interpreted to include losses that occur fortuitously. In *British and Foreign Marine Insurance Co Ltd v Gaunt*,[117] a cargo of wool arrived damaged due to wetting. Lord Sumner expounded the ambit of 'all risks' thus:

> 'All risks' has the same effect as if all insurable risks were separately enumerated: for example, it includes the risk that when it happens to be raining the men who ought to use the tarpaulins to protect the wool may happen to be neglecting their duty. This concurrence is fortuitous; it is also the cause of the loss of the wetting. It appears to be what happened. For wool to get wet in the rain is a casualty, though not a grave one; it is not a thing intended but is accidental; it is something that injures the wool from without; it does not develop from within. It would not happen at all if the men employed attended to their duty.
>
> There are, of course, limits to 'all risks'. They are risks and risks insured against. Accordingly, the expression does not cover inherent vice or mere wear and tear . . . It covers a risk, not a certainty; it is something which happens from without, not the natural behaviour of that subject matter, being what it is, in the circumstances in which it is carried.

As for burden of proof, it is on the claimant (the insured) to show that the loss or damage was fortuitous. There is no requirement on his part to show the exact cause of the loss. As expressed by Lord Sumner:

> . . . the quasi-universality of the description does affect the onus of proof in one way. The claimant insured against and averring a loss by fire must prove loss by fire, which involves proving that it is not something else. When he avers loss by some risk coming within 'all risks', as used in this policy, he need only give evidence reasonably showing

---

116 See *Kawasaki Kisen Kabushiki Kaisha of Kobe v Bantham Steamship Co Ltd* [1939] 2 KB 544 on the meaning of war.

117 [1921] 2 AC 41.

that the loss was due to a casualty, not to a certainty or inherent vice or to wear and tear. That is easily done. I do not think he has to go further and pick out one of the multitude of risks covered, so as to show exactly how his loss was caused. If he did so, he would not bring it any the more within the policy [at pp 57–58].

It must be noted that Institute Cargo Clauses (A) specifically exclude loss or damage due to wear and tear as well as inherent vice, mentioned as excluded in an 'all risks' policy by Lord Summer above.

Other than 'all risks', Institute Cargo Clauses (A) cover the assured for general average and salvage charges (cl 2), and collision liability (cl 3). The assured may become liable in the event of collision as a result of a 'both-to-blame collision' clause in the contract of carriage. It may come about as follows. Generally, where there is a collision and both ships are to blame, each is liable according to the degree of fault. It is customary for contracts of carriage to exclude liability for loss or damage caused by collision. Since the cargo owner cannot look to the carrier (even though the ship that is carrying the cargo is to blame for the collision) due to the exclusion, the issue is whether he can look to the other ship for full compensation. Under US law, this is possible. Once the non-carrying ship has compensated the cargo interest in full, they will include the sum paid to the cargo owner as part of the damages against the carrying vessel in proportion to the degree of fault. This means that, despite the exclusion clause in the contract of carriage between the cargo owner and (cargo carry-ing) shipowner, the latter becomes liable for loss or damage to cargo due to collision, albeit indirectly. In order to protect himself against this, the cargo carrying shipowner will normally include another clause (a both-to-blame collision clause) in the carriage contract, requiring the cargo owner to reimburse him with the sum paid to the other ship for collision damage to cargo. The end result is that the cargo owner bears some of the loss. Clause 3 is therefore designed to protect the cargo owner. (The both-to-blame collision clause has been held to be invalid in respect of bills of lading[118] where the clause was held to be valid in charterparties.) Clauses 2 and 3 are also found in Institute Cargo Clauses (B) and (C).

Institute Cargo Clauses (B) and (C), unlike Institute Cargo Clauses (A), list the risks covered. The risks covered by Cargo Clauses (B) and Cargo Clauses (C) are, for the most part, identical. The differences are highlighted below. As for exclusions, they are identical for all three sets of Clauses, apart from one in cl 4, namely exclusion of deliberate damage or deliberate destruction of cargo by wrongful act of person or persons, which is not included in Clauses (A).[119]

Institute Cargo Clauses (B)

The risks covered in Institute Cargo Clauses (B) can be grouped into two categories based on the strength of the causal connection. Clause 1.1 provides cover for loss or damage to goods which is reasonably attributable to:

(a) fire or explosion (cl 1.1.1);

(b) the vessel or craft being stranded, ground, sunk or capsized (cl 1.1.2);

(c) overturning or derailment of land conveyance (cl 1.1.3);

---

118   See *United States of American v Atlantic Mutual Insurance Co* [1952] AMC 659, at p 661; *American Union Transport Inc v United States of America* [1976] AMC 1480, at p 1482.
119   See Table 14.2.

(d) collision or contact of vessel, craft, or conveyance with any external object other than water (cl 1.1.4);

(e) discharge of cargo at a port of distress (cl 1.1.5);

(f) earthquake, volcanic eruption, or lightning (cl 1.1.6).

Clause 1.2 provides cover where loss or damage to the goods is caused by:

(g) general average sacrifice (cl 1.2.1);

(h) jettison or washing overboard (cl 1.2.2);

(i) entry of sea, lake, or river water into vessel, craft, hold, conveyance, container, liftvan, or place of storage (cl 1.2.3).

Clause 1.3 provides cover for total loss of any package washed overboard or dropped whilst loading on to, or unloading from, the vessel or craft.

Under cll 1.2 and 1.3, the causal requirement is one of proximate causation.[120]

Institute Cargo Clauses (C)

Under this set of Cargo Clauses, cover available under cll 1.1.6, 1.2.3 and 1.3 of Institute Cargo Clauses (B) above is not available. Further, cover under cl 2.2 of Institute Cargo Clauses (C) is restricted to jettison, and does not extend to washing overboard as in Institute Cargo Clauses (B).

The Institute Cargo Clauses (A), (B) and (C), as stated earlier, do not include war risks or strike risks.

Should the cargo interest wish to obtain cover for war or strikes, specialised trade terms such as Institute War Clauses (Cargo) and Institute Strikes Clauses (Cargo) are available.[121]

CONCLUSION

So far, the obligations and liabilities of the parties to a bill of lading and marine insurance policy – the two documents that play a central role in CIF contracts – have been considered. Nothing, however, has been said about the ways in which the buyer pays the seller for the goods. Chapter 1 mentioned in passing that payment normally takes place against the tender of documents. The following chapter, therefore, deals with the different payment mechanisms and focuses on letters of credit – the most popular method of payment in international sales since they are widely perceived as a secure method of payment due to the involvement of a bank – a reliable third party.

---

120 See 'Doctrine of proximate causation', pp 449–50 above.
121 See Carr and Kidner, *International Trade Law Statutes and Conventions*, 5th edn, 2008, Routledge-Cavendish for the text of these Institute Clauses.

Table 14.1 Risks covered under Institute Cargo Clauses (A), (B) and (C)

	EXTENT OF COVER	
Institute Cargo Clauses (A) 'All risks' of loss of or damage to the subject matter insured. (Doctrine of proximate causation applies)	**Institute Cargo Clauses (B)** Loss or damage *reasonably attributable* to: • fire or explosion • the vessel or craft being stranded, grounded, sunk or capsized • overturning or derailment of land conveyance • collision or contact of the vessel, craft or conveyance with any external object other than water • discharge of cargo at port of distress • earthquake, volcanic eruption or lightning Loss or damage to the subject matter caused by: • general average sacrifice • jettison • entry of sea, lake or river water into vessel, craft, hold, conveyance, container liftvan, or place of storage (Doctrine of proximate causation applies) Total loss • of any package lost overboard or dropped during loading or unloading from vessel or craft (Doctrine of proximate causation applies)	**Institute Cargo Clauses (C)** Loss or damage *reasonably attributable* to: • fire or explosion • vessel or craft being stranded, grounded, sunk or capsized • overturning or derailment of land conveyance • collision or contact of the vessel craft, or conveyance with any external object other than water • discharge of cargo at port of distress Loss or damage to the subject matter caused by: • general average sacrifice • jettison (Doctrine of proximate causation applies)
• Covers general average and salvage charges • Covers assured against such proportion of liability under contract of affreightment 'both-to-blame collison' clause	• Covers general average and salvage charges • Covers assured against such proportion of liability under contract of affreightment 'both-to-blame collision' clause	• Covers general average and salvage charges • Covers assured against such proportion of liability under contract of affreightment 'both-to-blame collision' clause

Table 14.2 Risks excluded under Institute Cargo Clauses (A), (B) and (C)

	EXCLUSIONS	
Institute Cargo Clauses (A) (Clause 4 exclusions) Cover does not extend to: • loss, damage, or expense attributable to wilful misconduct of the assured • ordinary leakage, ordinary loss in weight or volume, or ordinary wear and tear of the subject matter insured • loss, damage, or expense caused by insufficiency or unsuitability of packing of the insured subject matter • loss, damage, or expense, inherent vice or nature of insured subject matter • loss, damage, or expense proximately caused by delay, even where the delay is caused by a risk insured against • loss, damage, or expense arising from insolvency or financial default of the owners, managers, charterers or operators of the vessel • loss, damage, or expense arising from the use of any weapon of war employing atomic or nuclear fission and/or fusion or other like reaction or radioactive force or matter	**Institute Cargo Clauses (B)** (Clause 4 exclusions) Cover does not extend to: • loss, damage, or expense attributable to wilful misconduct of the assured • ordinary leakage, ordinary loss in weightor volume, or ordinary wear and tear of the subject matter insured • loss, damage, or expense caused by insufficiency or unsuitability of packing of the insured subject matter • loss, damage, or expense, inherent vice or nature of insured subject matter • loss, damage, or expense proximately caused by delay, even where the delay is caused by a risk insured against • loss, damage, or expense arising from insolvency or financial default of the owners, managers, charterers or operators of the vessel • loss, damage, or expense arising from the use of any weapon of war employing atomic or nuclear fission and/or fusion or other like reaction or radioactive force or matter • deliberate damage to or deliberate destruction of the subject matter insured or any part thereof by the wrongful act of any person or persons	**Institute Cargo Clauses (C)** (Clause 4 exclusions) Cover does not extend to: • loss, damage, or expense attributable to wilful misconduct of the assured • ordinary leakage, ordinary loss in weight or volume, or ordinary wear and tear of the subject matter insured • loss, damage, or expense caused by insufficiency or unsuitability of packing of the insured subject matter • loss, damage, or expense, inherent vice or nature of insured subject matter • loss, damage, or expense proximately caused by delay, even where the delay is caused by a risk insured against • loss, damage, or expense arising from insolvency or financial default of the owners, managers, charterers or operators of the vessel • loss, damage, or expense arising from the use of any weapon of war employing atomic or nuclear fission and/or fusion or other like reaction or radioactive force or matter • deliberate damage to or deliberate destruction of the subject matter insured or any part thereof by the wrongful act of any person or persons

(Clause 5 exclusions)

Cover does not extend to:

- loss, damage, or expense arising from unseaworthiness of vessel or craft where the assured or their servants are privy to such unseaworthiness at the time the subject matter is loaded
- loss, damage, or expense arising from unfitness of vessel, craft, conveyance, container, or liftvan for the safe carriage of the subject matter insured where the assured or their servants are privy to such unfitness at the time the subject matter is loaded

Note: under cl 5.2, the underwriter waives the implied warranties of seaworthiness of the ship and fitness of the ship to carry the subject matter insured to the destination where the assured or their servants are not privy to such unfitness or unseaworthiness. (The waiver of fitness extends only to the ship, not to the conveyance, container, etc)

(Clause 6 exclusions)

Cover does not extend to loss, damage, or expense caused by:

- war, civil war, revolution, rebellion, insurrection, or civil strife arising therefrom, or any hostile act by or against a belligerent power

(Clause 5 exclusions)

Cover does not extend to:

- loss, damage, or expense arising from unseaworthiness of vessel or craft where the assured or their servants are privy to such unseaworthiness at the time the subject matter is loaded
- loss, damage, or expense arising from unfitness of vessel, craft, conveyance, container, or liftvan for the safe carriage of the subject matter insured where the assured or their servants are privy to such unfitness at the time the subject matter is loaded

Note: under cl 5.2, the underwriter waives the implied warranties of seaworthiness of the ship and fitness of the ship to carry the subject matter insured to the destination where the assured or their servants are not privy to such unfitness or unseaworthiness. (The waiver of fitness extends only to the ship, not to the conveyance, container, etc)

(Clause 6 exclusions)

Cover does not extend to loss, damage, or expense caused by:

- war, civil war, revolution, rebellion, insurrection, or civil strife arising therefrom, or any hostile act by or against a belligerent power

Clause 5 exclusions)

Cover does not extend to:

- loss, damage, or expense arising from unseaworthiness of vessel or craft where the assured or their servants are privy to such unseaworthiness at the time the subject matter is loaded
- loss, damage, or expense arising from unfitness of vessel, craft, conveyance, container, or liftvan for the safe carriage of the subject matter insured where the assured or their servants are privy to such unfitness at the time the subject matter is loaded

Note: under cl 5.2, the underwriter waives the implied warranties of seaworthiness of the ship and fitness of the ship to carry the subject matter insured to the destination where the assured or their servants are not privy to such unfitness or unseaworthiness. (The waiver of fitness extends only to the ship, not to the conveyance, container, etc)

(Clause 6 exclusions)

Cover does not extend to loss, damage, or expense caused by:

- war, civil war, revolution, rebellion, insurrection, or civil strife arising therefrom, or any hostile act by or against a belligerent power
- capture, seizure, arrest, restraint or detainment, and consequences thereof or any attempt thereat

	EXCLUSIONS	
• capture, seizure, arrest, restraint or detainment, and consequences thereof or any attempt thereat • derelict mines, torpedoes, bombs or other derelict weapons of war (Clause 7 exclusions) Cover does not extend to loss, damage or expense: • caused by strikers, locked-out workmen, or persons taking part in labour disturbances, riots or civil commotions • resulting from strikes, lock-outs, labour disturbances, riots or civil commotions caused by any terrorist or any person acting from a political motive	• capture, seizure, arrest, restraint or detainment, and consequences thereof or any attempt thereat • derelict mines, torpedoes, bombs or other derelict weapons of war (Clause 7 exclusions) Cover does not extend to loss, damage or expense: • caused by strikers, locked out workmen, or persons taking part in labour disturbances, riots or civil commotions • resulting from strikes, lock-outs, labour disturbances, riots or civil commotions caused by any terrorist or any person acting from a political motive	• derelict mines, torpedoes, bombs or other derelict weapons of war (Clause 7 exclusions) Cover does not extend to loss, damage or expense: • caused by strikers, locked out workmen, or persons taking part in labour disturbances, riots or civil commotions • resulting from strikes, lock-outs, labour disturbances, riots or civil commotions caused by any terrorist or any person acting from a political motive

FURTHER READING

Bennett, 'The role of the slip in marine insurance law' [1994] LMCLQ 94.

Bennett, *The Law of Marine Insurance*, 2006, OUP.

Brooke, 'Materiality in insurance contracts' [1985] LMCLQ 437.

Clarke, *Law of Insurance Contracts*, 5th edn 2006, Informa Maritime and Transport.

Clarke, 'Recession: inducement and good faith' [2004] CLJ 1.

Condon, 'The making of the marine insurance contract: a comparison of English and US law' [1986] LMCLQ 484.

Diamond, 'The law of insurance – has it a future?' [1986] LMCLQ 25.

Forte, 'The materiality test in insurance' [1993] LMCLQ 557.

George, 'The new Institute Cargo Clauses' [1986] LMCLQ 438.

Hasson, 'Subrogation in insurance law – a critical evaluation' (1985) 5 OJLS 416.

Hodges, *Cases and Materials on Marine Insurance Law*, 1999, Cavendish Publishing.

Koh, 'Insurable risks and the new Institute Cargo Clauses' [1988] JMLC 287.

Lloyd-Bostock, 'The ordinary man and the psychology of attributing causes and responsibility' (1979) 42 MLR 143.

McGee, 'The proposer's duty of utmost good faith after *Pine Top*' (1995) 4 Insurance Law and Practice 95.

McKellar, 'Marine insurance – an ancient art that meets modern demands' [1986] Victoria University of Wellington LR 16.

Merkin, *Marine Insurance Legislation*, 3rd edn 2005, Informa Professional.

Mustill, 'Fault and marine losses' [1988] LMCLQ 310.

O'May, 'The new marine policy and Institute Clauses' [1985] LMCLQ 191.

O'May, 'Marine insurance law: can the lawyers be trusted?' [1987] LMCLQ 29.

Schoenbaum, 'The duty of utmost good faith in marine insurance law: a comparative analysis of American and English law' (1998) 29 JMLC 1.

Soyer, *Warranties in Marine Insurance*, 2nd edn, 2005, Cavendish Publishing.

Stone, 'The proper law of a marine insurance policy' [1984] LMCLQ 438.

CHAPTER 15

LETTERS OF CREDIT

INTRODUCTION

In international sales, because of the long periods during which the cargo is in transit and the location of the seller and the buyer in different countries, problems arise when it comes to payment, since a simultaneous exchange of goods for money is not possible. The seller (exporter) cannot deliver goods to the buyer (importer) with one hand, and take money from the buyer with the other. Ideally, the exporter would prefer to be paid for the goods as soon as they are put on board the ship. Financially, it is best if capital tied in the goods is released at the earliest opportunity, so that uncertainty about whether payment will be received on arrival at the destination is removed. Insolvency of the importer by the time goods reach their destination, or inability to raise sufficient funds to pay for them, does not concern the exporter. Of course, the seller could sell the goods at the port of destination if he still retains property in the goods, but then takes on the risk of unfamiliar conditions of a foreign market. Equally troubled about tying capital to cargo in transit, the buyer would wish to delay payment until arrival. Payment on arrival would also enable him to ascertain that he has not received sub-standard goods.

Payment can be effected in a number of ways. The degree of risk, be it from the seller's perspective or the buyer's, is dependent on the mode of payment. Which method is used is guided by factors such as the bargaining strengths of the parties to the sale contract, the economic climate in the importing and exporting countries, the political stability of the countries affecting the sale transaction, and the degree of trust and confidence of each party in the other. Payment may be effected by:

(a) open account;
(b) bill of exchange;
(c) documentary bill; and
(d) letter of credit (also known as documentary credit).

This chapter examines the first three modes of payment briefly to assess their relative strengths and weaknesses before focusing on letters of credit (also known as documentary credits or commercial credits),[1] the most frequently used mode of payment.

OPEN ACCOUNT

Parties to a sale contract may agree to payment by cash on order. This type of arrangement exposes the buyer to maximum risk, since he parts with the cash before delivery. The parties may agree to payment on sight of documents ('sight payment'). On presentation of documents,[2] the buyer remits money to the buyer, using telegraphic transfer or mail transfer. Such arrangements are extremely risky from the

---

1   See also 'Standby letters of credit', pp 503–7 below.
2   Typically, transport documents such as a bill of lading or certificate of quality. See also Chapters 1, pp 15–16 above, and 6, pp 174–85 above.

exporter's point of view, and are used only when he has confidence in the financial standing of the importer. This may have been established through past dealings with the importer. Typically, this arrangement is used in transactions between a parent and its subsidiaries.

Where the exporter is unsure about the financial health of the importer, he could arrange for payment in cash against documents, or on delivery. This way, he protects himself from the financial disasters of the importer. In rail and road transport, it is common for the rail or road carrier (transport operator) to undertake the task of collecting cash on delivery (COD) of goods at destination.[3]

Cash on delivery can also be used where the buyer collects goods from the seller's premises, as in 'ex works' contracts.[4]

BILLS OF EXCHANGE

The parties may agree to effect payment by bill of exchange. A bill of exchange (also known as a draft), along with others (for example, cheques or share warrants), belongs to a class of documents called negotiable instruments. A negotiable instrument, which evidences an obligation to pay money by one party to another, has the following characteristics. First, it is transferable by delivery and, with the transfer, rights embodied in it are transferred, such that the transferee can enforce them in his own name. (No notice to the obligor, or assignment, is necessary.) Secondly, where the transferee takes it in good faith and for value, he takes it free of any defects of title of the transferor.[5]

The bill of exchange is an autonomous contract and is not affected by breach in the underlying contract that resulted in the creation of a bill of exchange. Because of these characteristics, bills of exchange are treated as cash.[6]

The law relating to bills of exchange in English law is to be found in the Bills of Exchange Act 1882 (hereinafter 'BEA'). Section 3(1) defines a bill of exchange as 'an unconditional order in writing, addressed by one person to another, signed by the person giving it, requiring the person to whom it is addressed to pay on demand or at a fixed or determinable future time a sum certain in money to or to the order of a specified person, or bearer'.[7] A bill of exchange will look something like this:

Suppose that Smokey Sprays Ltd (S) has sold sprayers worth £1,000 to Benedict Noble (B). S (drawer) will draw a bill of exchange on B (drawee). It will be drawn in favour of a payee (to whom money is payable). It is not necessary that the payee is a third party. It could, for instance, be drawn in favour of the drawer (see Figure 15.1), or the bearer (see a Figure 15.2). As to when money is payable will depend on the terms of the bill. Where it is payable on demand, or at sight (known as sight bills), money is payable on presentation. Where money is payable at a fixed or determinable time in the future (known as time bills), the buyer gets credit until the due date. The

---

3 See for example CIM Rules (Uniform Rules Concerning the Contract for the International Carriage of Goods by Rail) (Chapter 11) in relation to rail and The Convention on the International Carriage of Goods by Road 1956 (CMR) (Chapter 12) in relation to road.

4 See Chapter 1, p 6 above.

5 *Crouch v Credit Foncier of England* (1873) LR 8 QB 374, at p 382.

6 *Nova (Jersey) Knit Ltd v Kammgarn Spinnerei GmbH* [1977] 2 All ER 463, at p 470.

7 See also *Hamilton v Spottiswoode* (1894) 4 Ex 200; *Korea Exchange Bank v Debenhams* [1979] 1 Lloyd's Rep 548.

Figure 15.1:   Illustration of an order bill of exchange

Exeter
1 March 2009
30 days after date pay to our order the sum of one thousand pounds, value received.
£1,000
Smokey Sprays Ltd
To: Benedict Noble Ltd,
Mollies Lane,
New York.

Figure 15.2:   Illustration of a bearer bill of exchange

Exeter
1 March 2009
30 days after date pay to bearer the sum of one thousand pounds, value received.
£1,000
Smokey Sprays Ltd
To: Benedict Noble Ltd,
Mollies Lane,
New York.

seller, for his part, will be able to realise money by selling the bill of exchange at a discount.[8] A time bill will be sent to the drawee for acceptance, who, if willing, will enter the words 'accepted' and sign it. On acceptance, the drawee will become the acceptor. It is not necessary that the bill is accepted by the drawee prior to negotiation (that is, transfer by delivery), if bearer bill (s 31(2)), or by endorsement and delivery, if order bill (s 31(3)). The rights of the party to whom the bill is negotiated (holder) will depend on his status as holder. All holders are *prima facie* presumed to be holders in due course (s 30(1)), unless it is admitted or proved that the acceptance, issue or negotiation of the bill is affected by fraud, duress or illegality (s 30(2)). In this case, the holder has the burden of proving, according to s 30(2) of the BEA, that, subsequent to the alleged fraud or illegality, value has in good faith been given for the bill. A holder in due course takes the bill of exchange free of any defects, and will be able to enforce payment against all parties liable on the bill (namely, indorsers, drawer and drawee). Any personal defences that may exist between the parties do not affect the holder in due course (s 38(2)). However, the holder in due course must meet the conditions laid down in s 29(1) of the BEA:

A holder in due course is a holder who has taken a bill, complete and regular on the face of it, under the following conditions, namely:

(a) that he became the holder of it before it was overdue, and without notice that it had been previously dishonoured, if such was the fact;

---

8   *Jade International Steel Stahl und Eisen GmbH and Co KG v Robert Nichols (Steels) Ltd* [1978] QB 917.

(b) that he took the bill in good faith and for value, and that at the time the bill was negotiated to him he had no notice of any defect in the title of the person who negotiated it.

A bill will be regarded as regular if there is nothing on the bill to arouse suspicion. In *Arab Bank Ltd v Ross*,[9] the payee, Fathi and Faysal Nabulsy Company, discounted the bills to the bank. The backs of the bills were indorsed 'Fathy and Faysal Nabulsy'. The word 'Company' was omitted. The issue was whether the bank could claim against Ross as holders in due course. The court held that the bank was not a holder in due course, since the bill was irregular on its face. It did not set out the indorser's name in full. According to Lord Denning LJ:

> The first question in this case is whether the Arab Bank Ltd were holders in due course ... that depends on whether, at the time they took it, it was 'complete and regular on the face of it' within s 29 of the Bills of Exchange Act 1882. Strangely enough, no one doubts the 'face' of a bill includes the back of it. I say 'strangely enough', because people so often insist on the literal interpretation of Acts of Parliament, whereas here everyone agrees that the literal interpretation must be ignored because the meaning is obvious ... looking at the bill, front and back, without the aid of outside evidence, it must be complete and regular in itself.
>
> Regularity is a different thing from validity. The Act itself makes a careful distinction between them. On the one hand, an indorsement which is quite invalid may be regular on the face of it. Thus, the indorsement may be forged or unauthorised and, therefore, invalid under s 24 of the Act, but nevertheless there may be nothing about it to give rise to any suspicion. The bill is then quite regular on the face of it. Conversely, an indorsement which is quite irregular may nevertheless be valid. Thus, by a misnomer, a payee may be described on the face of the bill by the wrong name, nevertheless, if it is quite plain that the drawer intended him as payee, then an indorsement on the back by the payee in his own true name is valid and sufficient to pass the property in the bill ... but the difference between front and back makes the indorsement irregular unless the payee adds also the misnomer by which he was described in the front of the bill [at p 226].

A drawer and payee cannot be holder in due course for the simple reason that s 29 requires the bill of exchange be negotiated to the holder. However, a drawer or payee can become a holder in due course, in circumstances prescribed by s 29(3), which provides:

> A holder (whether for value or not), who derives his title to a bill of exchange through a holder in due course, and who is not himself a party to any fraud or illegality affecting it, has all the rights of the holder in due course as regards the acceptor and all parties to the bill prior to the holder.

For instance, where the seller, S (the drawer/payee), indorses the bill to I1, I1 indorses it to I2, and I2 indorses it to S, S will be a holder in due course under s 29(3). This issue was considered in *Jade International Steel Stahl und Eisen GmbH and Co KG v Robert Nichols (Steels) Ltd*.[10] Jade International sold steel to the defendants and drew a bill of exchange on the buyers. The sellers discounted the bill to Sparkasse, a German bank. They discounted it to another German bank, and they in turn to Midland Bank. Midland presented the bill to the buyers who accepted it, but subsequently dishonoured it. Midland Bank exercised its right of recourse against the German

---

9 [1952] 2 QB 216.
10 [1978] QB 917.

bank, which, for its part, exercised its right of recourse against Sparkasse. It eventually reached Jade International, who brought an action against the buyers. The question before the court was whether the sellers as drawers/payees had become holders in due course under s 29(3) of the BEA. In a unanimous decision, the Court of Appeal found that Jade International had lost their capacity as drawer on discounting the bill and acquired the capacity of holder in due course when the bill was delivered to them as a result of Sparkasse's right of recourse.

As is obvious from the above paragraphs, a bill of exchange offers the seller the opportunity to realise cash, and the buyer obtains credit under a time bill. However, as Jade International exhibits, a buyer (drawee) may dishonour a bill that he has accepted – that is, not pay the money when the bill is presented for payment on the due date. Though the primary liability lies with the drawee, the drawer becomes liable on recourse, provided notice of dishonour has been given by a holder or indorser. So, the seller might find himself holding the short straw where the buyer does not honour his obligations under the bill of exchange.

Mention needs to be made of the United Nations Convention on International Bills of Exchange and International Promissory Notes (hereinafter 'UNCITRAL Convention') adopted in 1988.[11] This convention is not yet in force. It requires 10 states to take action to come into force. So far, it has received five ratifications/accessions.[12] The intention, as with any international convention, is to harmonise the law relating to bills of exchange and in doing so introduces new concepts.[13] Currently, legislation in most countries follows either the Anglo-American system (reflected by the United Kingdom BEA) or the Geneva system[14] adopted by countries with a civil law system. There are some differences between these two systems, for instance, in relation to forgeries and the distinction between different types of holders.[15]

The UNCITRAL Convention is primarily aimed at international bills of exchange which is defined in its Art 2(1). For attracting the application of the UNCITRAL Convention, Art 1(1) requires that the bill of exchange be headed 'International bill of exchange (UNCITRAL Convention)' as well as included in the text. Were this convention to come into force, it inevitably introduces a third system that could affect a bill of exchange provided the factors set out in Arts 1 and 2 are met. Unless there is a widespread willingness to adopt the UNCITRAL Convention, all it produces is disharmony and uncertainty.

DOCUMENTARY BILL

The parties may agree to effect payment through documentary bills. Here, the seller (drawer) draws a bill of exchange on the buyer (drawee) and attaches this to the bill of lading. The advantage for the seller is that, on acceptance of the bill of exchange by the

---

11   The text of this convention is available at www.uncitral.org. Also reproduced in Carr and Kidner, *International Trade Law Statutes and Conventions*, 5th edn, 2008, Routledge-Cavendish.

12   According to information available at www.uncitral.org.

13   Eg, the notion of a protected holder. See Arts 5(g) and 29.

14   See Convention Providing a Uniform Law for Bills of Exchange and Promissory Notes 1930. Text reproduced in Carr and Kidner, *International Trade Law Statutes and Conventions*, 5th edn, 2008, Routledge-Cavendish.

15   See Odeke, 'The United Nations Convention on International Bills of Exchange and Promissory Notes' [1992] JBL 281.

buyer, money can be obtained by the seller, before the maturity date of the bill of exchange, by selling it at a discount (discounting) to a bank. As for the buyer, he obtains credit until the bill of exchange's maturity date. A major disadvantage for the seller, however, with a documentary bill, is that the buyer may not honour the bill of exchange, in which case, the party to whom the seller discounted the bill of exchange would have recourse to him. In the event of dishonour of the bill of exchange by the buyer, the property remains with the seller and the buyer is required to return the bill of lading to the seller according to s 19(3) of the Sale of Goods Act 1979.

If the buyer retains the bill of lading, he will be liable in conversion to the seller. Were he to collect the goods and sell them on to a third party, he will be liable to the seller again in conversion. The third party, as long as he has acted in good faith, may avail himself of the statutory protection under s 25 of the Sale of Goods Act 1979 or s 9 of the Factors Act 1889. Since a documentary bill arrangement is open to abuse, it is common practice to use a bank for the presentation of documents and collection of payment. Acting on instructions from the seller, the seller's bank (the remitting bank) will arrange for a bank in the buyer's country (the collecting bank) to deliver documents against acceptance of bill of exchange (D/A), or against payment (D/P).[16] Where a collecting bank releases the documents without obtaining an acceptance or payment, the seller can sue the collecting bank. Lack of privity of contract will not be an issue, since the remitting bank acts as the seller's agent.[17] Practices in relation to collection arrangements have been standardised by the ICC in its Uniform Rules for Collections (URC). The latest version of the URC[18] was formulated in 1995, and came into force on 1 January 1996. The revision was necessitated by developments in the use of information technology and changing banking practices. As with other ICC rules, such as INCOTERMS,[19] they need to be specifically incorporated in the contract.[20]

LETTERS OF CREDIT

Letters of credit (also known as documentary credits or commercial credits) are better alternatives to a documentary bill. Depending on the type of credit, they offer the seller (beneficiary of a credit arrangement) greater security.[21] Their popularity in international commerce has led judges to describe them as 'the life blood of international commerce'.[22] Their origins have been traced to various ancient cultures such as that of Rome, Egypt and China. It is difficult to point with certainty to the culture

---

16   See Art 2(a) of the International Chamber of Commerce (ICC) Uniform Rules for Collection (Brochure No 522), 1996, ICC.

17   See *Calico Printers Association Ltd v Barclays Bank* (1930) 36 Com Case 197. A bank may decide to release the documents to the buyer under a trust receipt which evidences the bank's ownership. The buyer as trustee is under an obligation to maintain the goods or the sale proceeds distinct from his assets so that they are identifiable. The buyer, in other words, holds them ready for repossession. See also *Lloyd's Bank v Bank of American National Trust and Saving Association* [1937] 2 KB 631; *Midland Bank Ltd v Eastcheap Dried Fruit Co* [1921] 1 Lloyd's Rep 359.

18   ICC Brochure No 522, 1995, ICC.

19   See Chapter 1, pp 49–51 above.

20   See Chapter 1, pp 49–51 above, and also 'Letters of credit', pp 471–504 below.

21   See 'Letters of credit: their nature and advantages', p 470–1 below.

22   *United City Merchants (Investments) Ltd v Royal Bank of Canada (The American Accord)* [1982] 2 QB 208, at p 222; *Harbottle (RD) (Mercantile) Ltd v National Westminster Bank Ltd* [1978] QB 146, at p 155.

responsible for introducing this mechanism in some form or another.[23] In modern times, reference to letters of credit in England can be found in *Pillans v Van Mierop*.[24] Regardless of their origins, merchants across the world embraced and continue to embrace them whole-heartedly, and much of the law governing letters of credit is grounded in custom and mercantile practice.[25]

Law relating to letters of credit

No attempt was made to harmonise the law on letters of credit through international conventions. A near global unification, however, has been achieved through the efforts of the ICC, which is responsible for the Uniform Customs and Practice of Documentary Credits (hereinafter 'UCP'). An eminent academic, Professor RM Goode, describes it as the 'most successful harmonising measure in the history of inter-national commerce'.[26] The unification is, as Professor EP Ellinger (a leading expert on letters of credit) observes, a consequence of necessity and use of banks as agents in international trade.[27] The UCP was by no means an overnight success. The first set of rules drafted by the ICC in 1929 was not well received, with adoptions from only France and Belgium. A new version of the UCP, formulated in 1933, met with moder-ate success, with 40 countries adopting it. The United Kingdom and the Common-wealth countries were not among them. The 1951 version, despite adoption in 80 countries (including the US) was received unfavourably in both the United Kingdom and the Commonwealth. A much revised version in 1962 (addressing the concerns of the United Kingdom) gained acceptance in the United Kingdom. Further revisions were produced in 1974 and 1983 to refine some of the provisions and introduce rules to reflect new modes of transport and emerging practices amongst the mercantile community. Though the 1983 version was used in over 170 countries, the ICC felt the need to undertake yet another revision in the 1990s and that resulted in the 1994 version (UCP 500). However, the UCP 500, over time, came to be seen as complicated and prone to ambiguity which resulted in many presentations being rejected due to minor discrepancies thus raising doubts about the role of letters of credit as a secure method of payment. So the ICC set to work again on the UCP in the early part of this decade, which culminated in the UCP 2007 version (Publication No. 600).[28] The 2007 version is leaner than the UCP 500 and is more user-friendly. Consisting of thirty nine articles the UCP 600 applies only to irrevocable letters of credit. Besides undertaking a tidying up exercise it also contains new articles on definitions and interpretation thus providing for more clarity. For instance, Art 3 states how words such as 'on or about', 'prompt', 'immediately', 'to', and 'until' often found in documents are to be inter-preted for the purposes of the UCP 600, thus cutting down on the chances of

---

23 See De Rooy, *Documentary Credits*, 1984, Kluwer, for an excellent, comprehensive account on the evolution of letters of credit.

24 (1763) 3 Burr 1663, at p 1668.

25 Many disputes relating to letters of credit are referred to arbitration. The International Center for Letter of Credit Arbitration (ICLOCA) offers specialist arbitration in this area and their rules are modelled on the UNCITRAL Arbitration Rules. For more on ICLOCA visit www.iiblp.org. See also Chapters 19 and 20.

26 See Goode, *Commercial Law*, 2004, Butterworths.

27 See Ellinger, *Documentary Letters of Credit: A Comparative Study*, 1970, University of Singapore Press.

28 This publication is available for purchase from the International chamber of Commerce www.iccwbo.org.

uncertainty brought about by a variety of interpretations. The UCP 600 also contains other new articles, for example, advising credits and amendments (Art 9), the effect of nomination (Art 12) and dealing with originals and copies (Art 17). A number of articles found in UCP 500 have also been deleted (Art 5 on instructions to issue and amend, Art 6 on revocable credits, Art 8 on revocation of credits, Art 12 on incomplete instructions, Art 15 on complying presentation and Art 38 on other documents). In the following sections all references to UCP are to UCP 600 unless otherwise indicated.

The UCP 600, like INCOTERMS 2000,[29] does not have the force of law in England. This means that the UCP needs to be specifically incorporated. In the absence of incorporation, it will not apply. This, for the most part, will not affect the rights and liabilities of the parties greatly under the credit, since English courts do take mercantile customs and practices into account. Moreover, the rules of the UCP largely reflect those of common law, apart from a few differences. For instance, under Art 18(c) of the UCP, 'the description of the good services or performance in the commercial invoice must correspond exactly with that appearing in the credit'. There is, however, no corresponding requirement at common law since, it seems, a commercial invoice need not contain a description of the goods.[30] The UCP also allows certain tolerances in quantity, credit amount and unit price in Art 30, which is not the case in common law.[31] Since the UCP does not have the force of law in England, it will apply subject to any express terms. If an express term in the contract contradicts the UCP terms, the former prevails. As Mustill J stated in *Royal Bank of Scotland plc v Cassa di Risparmio delle Provincie Lombard*:[32]

> ... it must be recognised that [the UCP] terms do not constitute a statutory code. As their title makes clear, they contain a formulation of customs and practices, which the parties to a letter of credit can incorporate into their contracts by reference. If it is found that the parties have explicitly agreed such a term, then the search need go no further, since any contrary provision in UCP must yield to the parties' expressed intention.

The UCP, it must be added, is not comprehensive. It does not, for instance, address the effect of fraud or illegality on the documentary credit arrangement. The sections that follow will, therefore, take into account both the UCP provisions and common law, as relevant, when examining the nature and characteristics of documentary credits, the different types of credits, and obligations of the various parties involved in the transaction.

In 2007, the ICC also issued the International Standard Banking Practice (hereinafter 'ISBP'),[33] which explains in detail how the UCP 600 is to be applied. It provides a list of items that document examiners need to check.

Letters of credit: their nature and advantages

Under a documentary credit, the buyer (applicant) agrees to pay the seller (beneficiary) using a reliable paymaster – generally, a reputable bank in the seller's country

---

29 See Chapter 1.
30 *Ireland v Livingstone* (1871) 27 LT 79; see also Chapter 1.
31 See 'Doctrine of strict compliance', pp 479–82 below.
32 (1992) *Financial Times*, 21 January.
33 Publication No 681, ICC Publishing. The 2002 version of ISBP was a supplement to UCP 500.

– who pays against the presentation of stipulated documents that comply with the terms of the credit. The UCP defines documentary credit in Art 2 as:

> ... any arrangement, however named or described, that is irrevocable and thereby constitutes a definite undertaking of the issuing bank (the bank that issues a credit at the request of an applicant or on its own behalf) to honour[34] a complying presentation.

The documentary credit arrangement is advantageous to both seller and buyer. The seller has the assurance that he will be paid by a bank – a reliable and solvent paymaster – in his own country as soon as he presents the stipulated documents to it. If necessary, he will also be able to use the documentary credit arrangement (using special transferable or back-to-back credit) to obtain goods from the manufacturer.[35] Localisation of the financial transaction, as in a confirmed letter of credit, will enable the seller to sue the bank in his own country should it, for instance, refuse to honour the credit on presentation of the documents specified in the contract of sale.[36] The buyer can raise funds from the bank on the strength of the documents, thus alleviating the need to have sufficient funds to pay the seller.[37]

Stages in a documentary credit transaction

A documentary credit transaction involves a number of stages:

Stage 1

The parties to the contract of sale agree to settle by documentary credit.[38]

Stage 2

The buyer (applicant) applies to his bank (issuing bank) to open a credit in favour of the seller (beneficiary). The applicant will give details of the documents required, such as transport documents, invoices, insurance policies, certificate of quality and certificate of origin to the bank.[39] The instructions will also include the time and place for presenting documents.

Given the different methods for transport documents in use, the UCP makes provisions for the acceptability of these different transport documents. Articles 20, 21, and 22 deal with the marine bill of lading, non-negotiable sea waybill[40] and charterparty bill of lading. Whilst the UCP recognises these other types of

---

34 Honour according to Art 2 means:
   a. to pay at sight if the credit is available by sight payment;
   b. to incur a deferred payment undertaking and pay at maturity if the credit is available by deferred payment;
   c. to accept a bill of exchange ('draft') drawn by the beneficiary and pay at maturity if the credit is available by acceptance.
35 See 'Back-to-back credits', p 488 below.
36 See 'Confirmed credit', pp 486–8 below.
37 See *Soproma SpA v Marine and Animal By-Products Corp* [1966] 1 Lloyd's Rep 367, at p 385.
38 Dependant on the terms of the contract, the provision for the opening of letter of credit may operate as a condition precedent to the obligation of the seller to load the cargo. See *Kronos Worldwide Ltd v Sempra Oil Trading SARL* [2004] 1 Lloyd's Rep 260.
39 See *Commercial Banking Co of Sydney Ltd v Jalsard Pty Ltd* [1973] AC 279; *European Asian Bank AG v Punjab and Sind Bank (No 2)* [1983] 1 WLR 642. See also *Bayerische Vereinsbank Aktiengesellschaft v National Bank of Pakistan* [1997] 1 Lloyd's Rep 59.
40 Ie, a straight bill of lading. For more on bills of lading, see Chapter 6.

transport documents in relation to sea carriage, it does not follow that these will be acceptable substitutes where the letter of credit calls for a bill of lading. The UCP also enables the acceptability of air transport document (Art 23), multimodal transport document (Art 19), road and rail documents (Art 24) provided the documents contain the stipulated information[41] and meets the conditions as stipulated in the credit.

In relation to insurance, the banks will not accept cover notes (Art 28(c))[42] An insurance document containing references to exclusion clauses will be acceptable (Art 28(i)).

Stage 3

The issuing bank[43] (also sometimes called the opening bank) will generally instruct a correspondent bank in the beneficiary's country to advise the buyer of the opening of the documentary credit. (Note, however, that the issuing bank may advise the beneficiary directly, though this is rare.) The correspondent/advising bank[44] would normally, though not necessarily, be the seller's bank. The instruction from the issuing bank to the advising bank will generally be worded as follows:

> Please advise the terms of this credit to the beneficiary (seller) without engagement on your part. Please honour presentation of documents and debit our account with you in settlement.[45]

The choice of bank in the exporter's country will depend on the issuing bank's banking network. However, it is not unknown for a seller to insist on a particular bank to act as the advising bank in the sale contract. For instance, American companies often insist that importing countries with nationalised banks use only major international banks (preferably US or English) as issuing banks and advising banks. Hostility towards nationalised banks is fuelled by lack of confidence about the solvency of such banks, fear of state intervention, and possible claim of immunity from suit, in the event of litigation, on the grounds of being an arm of the state.[46] Nationalised banks are commonly found in developing countries such as India. The issue of which banks to use needs to be resolved when agreeing to documentary credit for effecting payment. If the documentary type is of a type called a confirmed credit,[47] the correspondent bank will add its own confirmation to the credit.

---

41 Eg, the name of the carrier, place of destination and shipment, and indication that goods have been shipped on board at the port of loading stated in the credit. See, eg, Art 20(a)(i)–(vi).
42 In UCP 500 cover notes were acceptable provided the letter of credit authorised it.
43 The issuing bank is defined in Art 2, UCP as 'The bank that issues a credit at the request of an applicant or on its own behalf'.
44 Advising bank is defined in Art 2, UCP, as 'the bank that advises the credit at the request of the issuing bank'. There is a contractual relationship between the issuing bank and the advising bank/confirming bank. If a confirming bank does not receive reimbursement, it can obtain damages. See *Bayerische Vereinsbank Aktiengesellschaft v National Bank of Pakistan* [1997] 1 Lloyd's Rep 59. See also the interesting case of *Standard Chartered Bank v Pakistan National Shipping Corp (Nos 2 and 4)* [2003] 1 Lloyd's Rep 227 and Todd, 'Outlawing dishonest international traders' [2000] LMCLQ 394.
45 Clause used by National Westminster Bank plc – *Documentary Credits Service Booklet*.
46 See *Trendtex Trading Corp v Central Bank of Nigeria* [1977] QB 529.
47 See 'Confirmed credit', pp 486–8 below.

Stage 4

The advising/confirming bank will inform the beneficiary of the opening of the credit. Where the credit is a confirmed one, it is likely to contain a clause worded as follows:

> We are requested to add our confirmation to this credit and we hereby undertake to pay you the face amount of your bills of exchange (drafts) drawn within the credit terms and provided such bills of exchange bear the number and date of the credit and that the letter of credit and all amendments thereto are attached.[48]

As gathered from the reading of the above clause, important rights in favour of the beneficiary flow from the adding of the confirmation by a bank. These are considered later in this chapter.

Stage 5

The seller will ship the goods, provided the letter of credit conforms with what was agreed in the sale contract. The seller, however, may decide to ship goods even where the terms of the credit do not conform with the terms agreed in the contract of sale. The seller's behaviour may constitute a waiver or variation. This will depend on the circumstances.[49]

Stage 6

On shipment, the seller will obtain the transport documents (for example, bill of lading, consignment note) and other documentation as required under the credit, such as certificate of quality and certificate of origin, and present them to the advising or confirming bank. The banks normally expect clean transport documents. A clean transport document is defined in Art 27 as a document which 'bears no clause or notation which expressly declares a defective condition of the goods the packaging'. According to Art 27 however the word 'clean' need not appear on the transport document even if a credit has a requirement for that transport document to be 'clean on board'. Of course, it is open to the parties to stipulate the notations or clauses that may be accepted.

Stage 7

The bank will effect payment, provided the documents conform. Payment will depend on what has been agreed in the credit. The agreement may be for:

(a) payment at sight;

(b) deferred payment;

(c) acceptance credit (also known as usance credit or term credit); or

(d) negotiation credit.

Where payment at sight is agreed, the seller will receive cash on presentation of conforming documents. In a deferred payment situation, payment in cash will take place at a future time as agreed by the parties – for example, '30 days after sight', '60 days after shipment'. In an acceptance credit, the bank will accept bills

---

48 Clause used by National Westminster Bank plc – *Documentary Credits Service Booklet*.
49 See 'Waiver and variation', p 493–4 below.

of exchange drawn on it by the seller. The bill of exchange could call for immediate payment (payment at sight) or payment on a fixed date or determinable future date (time bill). In most cases, it is likely to be a time bill. Once the bill of exchange is accepted and returned to the seller, he will be able to sell it at a discount. In the case of a negotiation credit, the bank will agree to negotiate the bill of exchange drawn on the issuing bank or the buyer. Whether negotiation[50] is restricted to the advising bank, the confirming bank, or is freely negotiable with any bank in the exporter's country, will depend on the terms of the agreement. A negotiating bank will normally have recourse to the seller if the issuing bank does not reimburse the negotiating bank due to discrepancies in the documents. A confirming bank will negotiate without recourse, provided documents conform with the terms of the credit.

Stage 8

The advising bank or the confirming bank will forward the documents to, and will be reimbursed by, the issuing bank, who, in turn, will pass the documents on to the buyer and collect payment.

The above stages can be diagramatically expressed in the following manner (Figure 15.3):

Characteristics of letters of credit – autonomy and strict compliance

Fundamental to letters of credit are two characteristics which establish their importance in international commerce. These are:

(a) the autonomy of letters of credit;

(b) the doctrine of strict compliance.

Autonomy of letters of credit

According to the principle of autonomy, the undertaking of the issuing bank or confirming bank to pay against the documents is seen as a primary obligation. Any dispute that may exist between seller and buyer in respect of the contract of sale which brought the documentary credit into existence will not affect the credit. The obligations of the banks (issuing bank and confirming bank) are in respect of the documents, not in respect of the goods. As long as the documents are in order, the banks cannot get out of their obligations by pointing to incidents such as shipment of defective goods. This principle of autonomy, which secures payment of price against documents, is well established in law. As Jenkins LJ said, in *Hamzeh Malas and Sons v British Imex Industries Ltd*:[51]

---

50 Negotiation is defined in Art 2 of UCP as 'the purchase by the nominated bank of drafts (drawn on a bank other than the nominated bank) and/or documents under a complying presentation, by advancing or agreeing to advance funds to the beneficiary on or before the banking day on which reimbursement is due to the nominated bank'. Nominated bank is defined as 'The bank with which the credit is available or any bank in the case of credit available with any bank'. See also Arts 7(c) and 8(c) UCP on reimbursement to nominated bank upon negotiation by nominated bank.

51 [1958] 2 QB 127.

Figure 15.3: Stages in a typical documentary credit arrangement

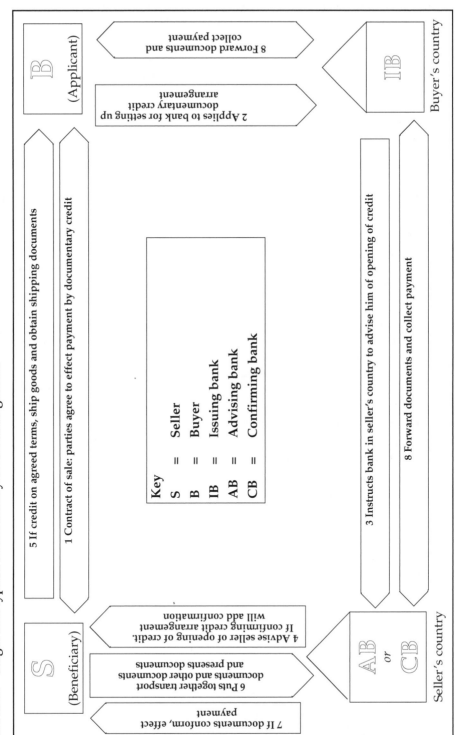

S (Beneficiary)

B (Applicant)

IB

AB or CB

Seller's country

Buyer's country

Key
S = Seller
B = Buyer
IB = Issuing bank
AB = Advising bank
CB = Confirming bank

1 Contract of sale: parties agree to effect payment by documentary credit

2 Applies to bank for setting up documentary credit arrangement

3 Instructs bank in seller's country to advise him of opening of credit

4 Advise seller of opening of credit. If confirming credit arrangement will add confirmation

5 If credit on agreed terms, ship goods and obtain shipping documents

6 Puts together transport documents and other documents and presents documents

7 If documents conform, effect payment

8 Forward documents and collect payment

8 Forward documents and collect payment

We have been referred to a number of authorities, and it seems to be plain enough that the opening of a confirmed letter of credit constitutes a bargain between the banker and the vendor of the goods, which imposes upon the banker an absolute obligation to pay, irrespective of any dispute there may be between the parties as to whether the goods are up to contract or not ... A vendor of goods selling against a confirmed letter of credit is selling under the assurance that nothing will prevent him from receiving the price. That is of no mean advantage when goods manufactured in one country are being sold in another. It is, furthermore, to be observed that vendors are often reselling goods bought from third parties. When they are doing that, and when they are being paid by a confirmed letter of credit, their practice is ... to finance the payments necessary to be made to their suppliers against the letter of credit. That system of financing these operations, as I see it, would break down completely if a dispute as between the vendor and the purchaser was to have the effect of 'freezing', if I may use that expression, the sum in respect of which the letter of credit was opened [at p 129].[52]

The separation of the letter of credit transaction from the sale transaction, regarded as sacrosanct, is enshrined in Arts 4 and 5 of the UCP as follows:

Credits v contracts

4 (a) A credit, by its nature, is a separate transaction from the sale or other contract on which it may be based. Banks are in no way concerned with or bound by such contract, even if any reference whatsoever to it is included in the credit. Consequently, the undertaking of a bank to honour, to negotiate or to fulfil any other obligation under the credit, is not subject to claims or defences by the applicant resulting from his relationships with the issuing bank or the beneficiary.

A beneficiary can in no case avail himself of the contractual relationships existing between the banks or between the applicant and the issuing bank.

(b) An issuing bank should discourage any attempt by the applicant to include as an integral part of the credit, copies of the underlying contract, proforma invoice and the like.

Documents v goods, services or performance

5   Banks deal with documents, and not with goods, services or performance to which the documents may relate.

Buyers often seek an injunction to stop the bank from paying where goods do not match the contract description, but courts are unwilling to grant such injunctions. *Discount Records Ltd v Barclays Bank Ltd*[53] illustrates this. On delivery of the cargo, the buyer discovered that some of the boxes (which should have contained records) were empty, while others contained cassettes rather than records. The buyer sought an injunction to stop the bank from paying the seller. It was refused by the court. According to Megarry J, the banker's obligation to pay under the credit was separate from the contract of sale, and the court could intervene only if a sufficiently grave cause was shown. To allow buyers to intervene in the payment arrangements between the issuing bank and the seller (beneficiary) where the goods do not match the contract description would seriously affect international trade, since the seller enters into the contract of sale with a documentary credit arrangement in the belief that he will be

---

52 See also *United City Merchants (Investments) Ltd v Royal Bank of Canada* [1983] 1 AC 168, at pp 182–3; *Tukan Timber Ltd v Barclays Bank plc* [1987] 1 Lloyd's Rep 171, at p 174. The autonomy of the letter of credit was recently reasserted *Montrod Ltd v Grundkotter Fleischvertriebs GmBH, Standard Chartered Bank* [2001] EWCA Civ 1954. See also *Solo Industries UK Ltd v Canara Bank* [2001] 2 Lloyd's Rep 57.

53 [1975] 1 Lloyd's Rep 444.

paid under an irrevocable credit and may rely on the provision of the credit to purchase goods from manufacturers, or manufacture the goods himself. If courts were to intervene, certainty of payment normally associated with commercial credits is seriously affected.

Payment by the bank, however, does not affect the buyer's rights under the contract of sale. The buyer can always sue the seller for breach of contract in the event of receiving no goods, or sub-standard goods.

The sanctity of the separation of a letter of credit from the underlying sale contract is also illustrated by *Power Curber International Ltd v National Bank of Kuwait*,[54] where the English courts enforced payment by the bank despite an order from a Kuwaiti court forbidding payment. In this case, Power Curber, an American company, sold machinery to a firm in Kuwait. An irrevocable letter of credit was issued by the National Bank of Kuwait, who instructed the Bank of America to advise the sellers of the credit. On delivery, the buyers raised a counterclaim against the sellers, and obtained a provisional attachment order from the courts in Kuwait, restraining the bank from paying the seller on the credit. The bank, which had a registered office in London, was sued by the sellers in the English courts. At first instance, and in the Court of Appeal, it was held that the order obtained in Kuwait did not affect the bank's obligation to pay the seller on the credit, since the bank is not concerned with any dispute that arises from the contract of sale. As Lord Denning MR said:

> ... it is vital that every bank which issues a letter of credit should honour its obligations. The bank is in no way concerned with any dispute that the buyer may have with the seller. The buyer may say that the goods are not up to contract. Nevertheless, the bank must honour its obligations. The buyer may say that he has a cross-claim in a large amount. Still, the bank must honour its obligations. No set-off or counterclaim is allowed to detract from it ... a letter of credit is given by a bank to the seller with the very intention of avoiding anything in the nature of a set-off or counterclaim [at p 1241].

The principle of autonomy favours the banks (be it an issuing bank or confirming bank) and the seller. Banks are not placed under an obligation to ensure that the cargo corresponds to the contract description. Risk is on the buyer, because he cannot involve the issuing bank to police the seller's activities in the exporting country. The principle of autonomy places the buyer at the beneficiary's mercy.

It is always open to the issuing bank to agree to get involved in the underlying sale contract – to ensure the actual performance of the underlying contract. A reference to the sale contract with statements such as 'Documents evidencing shipment in accordance with Contract No BEN/CT/321 dated 12/7/98 must be presented', found normally in letters of credit, is not indicative of consent on the part of the banker. This view is preserved in Art 4(a) of the UCP when it states that reference to the contract of sale in the credit does not destroy the separation of the credit transaction from the sale transaction. Clearer words are needed for incorporation of the underlying contract into the letter of credit.[55] It is questionable whether the wide wording – 'any reference whatsoever to it' – in Art 4(a) of the UCP will nullify an express term to incorporate the contract of sale in the letter of credit under English law. As stated in *Royal Bank of Scotland plc v Cassa di Risparmio delle Provincie Lombard*,[56] the UCP must yield to the

---

54   [1981] 1 WLR 1233.

55   For an American decision on this point, see *NMC Enterprises Inc v Columbia Broadcasting System Inc* 14 UCC Rep 1427 (1974 NYSC).

56   (1992) *Financial Times*, 21 January.

parties' expressed intention. In practice, it would be extremely rare to find a bank willing to get involved beyond the level of payment against documents.

The principle of autonomy is affected in the event of illegality in the underlying transaction or fraud. The fraud defence is examined below.[57] As for illegality, there is precedent to say that no obligation exists to pay on a letter of credit issued contrary to exchange control regulations. In *United City Merchants (Investments) Ltd v Royal Bank of Canada (The American Accord)*,[58] English sellers contracted for the sale of a manufacturing plant to Peruvian buyers. The sellers quoted double the genuine purchase price, at the request of the buyer, with the intention that the sellers, on obtaining payment, would transfer the excess amount to a bank account in the US. In other words, the intention was to exchange Peruvian currency for US dollars using the contract of sale and the documentary credit. This was contrary to the exchange regulations of Peru. Article VIII, s 2(b) of the Bretton Woods Agreement, to which England was a party, provided:

> Exchange contracts which involve the currency of any member and which are contrary to exchange regulations of that member maintained or imposed consistently with this agreement shall be unenforceable in the territories of any member . . .

The House of Lords concluded that the transaction in respect of the excess amounted to an exchange contract and was unenforceable, since it contravened the Bretton Woods Agreement. In Lord Diplock's view:

> . . . if in the course of the hearing of an action the court becomes aware that the contract on which a party is suing is one that this country has accepted an international obligation to treat as unenforceable, the court must take the point itself, even though the defendant has not pleaded it, and must refuse to lend its aid to enforce the contract. But this does not have the effect of making an exchange contract that is contrary to the exchange control regulations of a Member State other than the United Kingdom into a contract that is 'illegal' under English law or render acts undertaken in this country in performance of such a contract unlawful . . . it is [simply] unenforceable and nothing more [at pp 188–89].

As is obvious from Lord Diplock's judgment, the transaction was seen as unenforceable, not illegal under English law. The illegality of the underlying contract will also, according to a recent case, affect the payment undertaking in letters of credit.[59] In *Mahonia Ltd v JP Morgan Chase Bank and Another*[60] the underlying swaps transactions were illegal under US law. While acknowledging the impregnability of letters of credit the court went on to say that as a matter of public policy they would not permit the process to be used to obtain the benefit of an unlawful act. According to Colman J:

> It would, however, be wrong in principle to invest letters of credit with a rigid inflexibility in the face of strong countervailing public policy considerations. If a beneficiary should as a matter of public policy (*ex turpi causa*) be precluded from utilizing a letter of credit to benefit from his own fraud and it is hard to see why he should be permitted to use the courts to enforce part of an underlying transaction which would have been unenforceable on grounds of illegality if no letter of credit had been involved, however serious the material illegality involved. To prevent him doing so in an appropriately

---

57   See 'The Fraud exception', pp 500–2.
58   [1983] 1 AC 168.
59   See *Group Josi Re v Walbrook Insurance Co Ltd* [1996] 1 Lloyd's Rep 345, at pp 362–3.
60   [2003] EWHC 1927 (Comm).

serious case such as one involving international crime could hardly be seen as a threat to the lifeblood of international commerce [at para 68].

Many interesting questions can be asked in this context. Is a bank under a duty to look into the underlying contract of sale before agreeing to issuing or confirming a credit? Is the bank expected to have expert knowledge of descriptions used in a particular trade, scientific descriptions of chemicals, etc? If a bank is suspicious about the underlying transaction, should it make further enquiries? How vigilant should the bank be?

Doctrine of strict compliance

As stated earlier,[61] the beneficiary will present documents to the issuing, advising or confirming bank as appropriate. Acceptance or rejection of the documents by the bank is dependent on whether the documents conform on their face to the terms of the credit. If, on their face, they are in strict conformity with the terms of the credit, the bank will accept the documents. If they are not, they will reject the documents. This is commonly referred to as the doctrine of strict compliance.

The tender of documents that are similar is not acceptable under the doctrine of strict compliance. As Lord Summer said in *Equitable Trust Co of New York v Dawson Partners Ltd*,[62] '. . . there is no room for documents which are almost the same, or which will do just as well' (at p 52). The strict application of the doctrine is well illustrated by *Moralice (London) Ltd v ED and F Man*[63] and *JH Rayner and Co Ltd v Hambros Bank Ltd*.[64] In the former case, the credit stipulated a bill of lading for 5,000 bags. The bank's rejection of the tendered bill, which referred to 4,997 bags, was allowed. According to McNair J, *de minimis non curat lex* could not be applied. In the latter case, the credit referred to a shipment of 'Coromandel groundnuts'. The bill of lading tendered by the seller referred to 'machine-shelled groundnut kernels'. This was understood in the trade to be the same as 'Coromandel groundnuts'. The bank, however, rejected the documents and the Court of Appeal held that it was right to do so. According to Mackinnon LJ:

> The words in that bill of lading clearly are not the same as those required by the letter of credit. The whole case of the plaintiffs is, in the words of Lord Summer, that 'they are almost the same, or they will do just as well'. The bank, if they had accepted that proposition, would have done so at their own risk. I think on pure principle that the bank were entitled to refuse to accept this sight draft on the ground that the documents tendered, the bill of lading in particular, did not comply precisely with the terms of the letter of credit which they have issued [at p 40].

He also went on to say that the bank was not expected to know the customary terms of the trade. A reasonable view, since the bank is an expert in finance and not in a particular trade. In other words, the bank trades in documents, not in goods. This sentiment is also expressed in the UCP by Art 5, when it states that parties to a documentary credit 'deal with documents, and not with goods, services or performance to which the documents may relate'.

---

61   See Stage 7 under 'Stages in a documentary credit transaction', p 473 above.
62   (1927) 27 LlL Rep 49.
63   [1954] 2 Lloyd's Rep 526.
64   [1943] 1 KB 37, at pp 40–1, *per* McKinnon LJ.

Since the bank is not imputed with knowledge of trade practices, this means that the documents must meet the specific requirements of the credit, however trivial they might appear. In *Seaconsar v Far East Ltd v Bank Makazi Jomhouri Islami Iran*,[65] the credit required that each document tendered should list the letter of credit number, and the name of the buyer. However, these were omitted on one of the documents, and the bank rejected the tender. The seller argued that the omission of the credit number and name of buyer was of a trivial nature. The court held that the bank was entitled to reject the documents; the credit number and the name of the buyer could not be treated as trivial, since they were specifically required.

The harshness of the doctrine of strict compliance is eased by the UCP. Though Art 18(c) requires that the 'description of the goods in a commercial invoice must correspond with the credit', other documents, according to Art 14(e) however, may [describe] the goods in general terms not conflicting with the description of the goods in the credit. The UCP also allows various tolerances in credit amount, weight and value of the goods under Art 30:

(a) The words 'about' or 'approximately', used in connection with the amount of the credit or the quantity or the unit price stated in the credit, are to be construed as allowing a tolerance not to exceed 10% more or 10% less than the amount or the quantity or the unit price to which they refer.

(b) A tolerance not to exceed 5% more or 5% less than the quantity of the goods is allowed, provided the credit does not state the quantity in terms of a stipulated number of packing units or individual items and the total amount of the drawings does not exceed the amount of the credit.

(c) Even when partial shipments are not allowed, a tolerance not to exceed 5% less than the amount of the credit is allowed, provided that the quantity of the goods, if stated in the credit, is shipped in full and a unit price, if stated in the credit, is not reduced or that sub-Art 30(b) is not applicable. This tolerance does not apply when the credit stipulates a specific tolerance or uses the expressions referred to in sub-Art 30(a).

It is not uncommon for copies of documents to be tendered rather than the originals. While the common law rule is that only originals are acceptable, Art 20(b) of the UCP 500 seemed to relax this rule somewhat and allow documents which were not originals or did not appear to be originals since it stated that unless otherwise stipulated in the credit, banks would also accept as an original document(s) a document(s) produced or appearing to have been produced:

(i) by reprographic, automated or computerised systems;

(ii) as carbon copies;

provided that it is marked as an original and, where necessary, appears to be signed.

Article 20(b), however, created uncertainties and resulted in a number of cases in the English courts. In *Glencore International AG v Bank of China*,[66] the dispute was over photocopies of a certificate that had been printed with a laser printer. The laser printed document and the photocopies were indistinguishable. One of the photocopies was signed by the beneficiary and tendered. The documents were rejected by

---

65 [1993] 1 Lloyd's Rep 236; [1994] 1 Lloyd's Rep 1.
66 [1996] 1 Lloyd's Rep 135.

the issuing bank. Two arguments were put forward in the litigation. One, that the signature on the document made it an original and took it outside the purview of Art 20(b); two, if the document was caught by Art 20(b), then the signature was sufficient to mark the document as an original. Both at first instance and on appeal, the arguments were rejected. According to Sir Thomas Bingham MR, 'a signature on a copy does not make it an original; it makes it an authenticated copy; and Art 20(b) does not treat a signature as a substitute for marking as "original", merely as an additional requirement' (at p 153). The documents needed to be marked 'original' to meet the conditions set out in Art 20(b). The court perceived Art 20(b) as a clear provision intended to clarify any doubts there might be about documents produced by modern technology. According to Sir Thomas Bingham MR:

> ... there is abundant room to debate what, in the context of modern technology, is an original. A handwritten or typed document plainly is, but other documents can also plausibly be said to be so. Article 20(b) is, as it seems to us, designed to circumvent this argument by providing a clear rule to apply in the case of documents produced by reprographic, automated or computerized systems. The sub-Article requires documents produced in a certain way (whether 'original' or not) to be treated in a certain way. It is understandable that those framing these should have wished to relieve issuing bankers of the need to make difficult and fallible judgments on the technical means by which documents were produced. The beneficiary's certificates in this case may, in one sense, have been originals: but it is plain on the evidence that they were produced by one or other of the listed means and so were subject to the rule [at p 153].

The scope of Art 20(b) was considered yet again in *Kredietbank Antwerp v Midland Bank plc*.[67] The dispute was over an insurance contract produced with a word processor on headed, watermarked, high quality paper. The contract was signed with a blue pen and stapled to a form containing standard terms. The issue was whether the conditions stipulated in Art 20(b) applied to documents produced by computerised systems. The defendants (the issuing bank who rejected the documents) argued that it did and, since it was not marked 'original', it did not meet the stipulations laid down in Art 20(b). The plaintiffs for their part suggested that Art 20(b) did not apply to obvious originals – the use of the word 'also' in Art 20(b) lending support for this view. Further, they said that, even if the document under examination fell within Art 20(b), the documents tendered indicated that it was an original. While exhibiting sympathy with this suggestion, the court of first instance held that the document fell within the purview of Art 20(b). According to Diamond J, the requirement that the document be marked 'original' would be satisfied 'if it's a necessary implication from the terms and marks in the bill of lading, or ... the set of documents, that the document or documents are originals' (at p 183). In the case under discussion, the document met the requirements since it was produced on original headed paper; it also stated that it had been issued both in the original and duplicate (the duplicate being the photocopy of the document on the headed and watermarked paper), and the photocopied document accompanied the document on the headed, watermarked paper. On appeal, the court concluded that the document was not caught by Art 20(b) but was clearly an original. In the words of Evans LJ:

> ... there is nothing in Art 20(b) which entitles the bank to reject an original document which previously was a valid tender under the credit. A document which is

---

67 [1998] Lloyd's Rep Bank 173; [1999] Lloyd's Rep Bank 219 (CA).

clearly the original, in the sense that it contains the relevant contract, and which is not itself a copy of some other document, is certainly an original for the purposes . . . [at p 227].

Further, the use of the word 'also' in Art 20(b) indicated that the intention of the drafters was to extend the types of documents that would be acceptable. Article 20(b) was not meant to apply to documents that were originals but to those that were copies of an original document.

Subsequent to these decisions, the ICC (Commission on Banking Technique and Practice) in 1999 published guidelines for the purposes of interpreting Art 20(b).[68] They list a wide range of documents as originals that fall outside the ambit of Art 20(b): written/typed/perforated documents; documents carrying a hand/facsimile signature; documents on original headed paper (original stationery); documents that state they are originals unless the statements do not appear to apply to the document tendered. Statements such as 'duplicate original', 'third of three' would also indicate that the document is an original in its own right. Article 20(b) applies to documents that are produced by a telefax machine, any document that appears to be a photocopy lacking marking,[69] and a document that states that it is a true copy of another document or that another document is the sole original.[70]

The UCP 600 addresses what is acceptable as original for its purposes in much clearer terms than the earlier version of UCP. Art 17 provides:

(a) At least one original of each document stipulated in the credit must be presented.

(b) A bank shall treat as an original any document bearing an apparently original signature, mark, stamp, or label of the issuer of the document, unless the document itself indicates that it is not an original.

(c) Unless a document indicates otherwise, a bank will also accept a document as original if it:
  (i) appears to be written, typed, perforated or stamped by the document issuer's hand; or
  (ii) appears to be on the document issuer's original stationery; or
  (iii) states that it is original, unless the statement appears not to apply to the document presented.

(d) If a credit requires presentation of copies of documents, presentation of either originals or copies is permitted.

(e) If a credit requires presentation of multiple documents by using terms such as 'in duplicate', 'in two fold' or 'in two copies', this will be satisfied by the presentation of at least one original and the remaining number in copies, except when the document itself indicates otherwise.

It must be noted that the doctrine of strict compliance applies not only between the seller and the bank, but also between the buyer and the issuing bank,[71] and between the issuing bank and the confirming bank.[72]

---

68 See 1999 Documentary Credits Insight. Also reproduced in UCP 500 and eUCP Publication No 500/2, 2002 ICC. Note: The ICC also published four position papers in respect of Arts 9(d)(iii), 18(b)(ii), 13(c) and Arts 23 and 24 of UCP 500. These are not relevant to UCP 600.

69 A photocopy on original stationery will be treated as an original.

70 For an excellent critique of these proposals, see Bennett, 'Original sins under the UCP' [2001] LMCLQ 88.

71 See *Equitable Trust Co of New York v Dawson Partners Ltd* (1927) 27 LlL Rep 49.

72 See *Bank Melli Iran v Barclays Bank DCO* [1951] 2 Lloyd's Rep 367.

Ambiguous instructions from buyer and linkage of documents

It is extremely important that clear instructions are given by the buyer, since ambiguity will mitigate the doctrine of strict compliance. Where instructions are ambiguous, and the bank has construed them reasonably, there would be no breach of contract. In *Midland Bank Ltd v Seymour*,[73] instructions were given on the bank's application form. Under 'Description, quantity and price', the buyer entered 'Hong Kong duck feathers – 85% clean; 12 bales each weighing about 190 lb; 5 s per lb'. The bill of lading did not contain the entire description, though an entire description was possible when all the documents tendered were read together. The bank accepted the documents. The buyer, when sued for reimbursement by the issuing bank, put forward the defence that the documents tendered did not conform to the credit, since the bill of lading did not give a description, quantity and price of the goods. The court held that the buyer had not clearly stated that the bill of lading should contain all these details, and the bank had adopted a reasonable meaning.

In linking the documents, the banks, however, must ensure that there is consistency between the documents, in that there must be unequivocal reference to the same goods in all the documents. In *Banque de l'Indochine et de Suez SA v JH Rayner (Mincing Lane) Ltd*,[74] the contract was for the sale of sugar. The credit required certificates of origin, EUR 1 certificates, and a full set of clean bills of lading. According to the bills of lading, shipment had taken place on board *Markhor* but, according to one of the certificates of origin, goods were on board *MV Markhor* or substitute. The court came to the conclusion that it was unclear whether the bill of lading and the certificate of origin were referring to the same parcel of sugar, since *MV Markhor* or substitute could be a different vessel. In other words, there was no consistency between the documents.

Types of letters of credit

Letters of credits are categorised into revocable and irrevocable credits, irrevocable confirmed and irrevocable unconfirmed credits. There are also a number of variants such as transferable credits, back-to-back credits, revolving credits, red clause credits and green clause credits. In this section, the nature and differences between revocable and irrevocable credits, and confirmed and unconfirmed credits will be examined, before moving on to the special forms.

Revocable credit

Unlike UCP 500, UCP 600 does not recognise revocable credits and therefore will not apply to such credits. Parties who use revocable credits will have to make them

---

73 [1955] 2 Lloyd's Rep 147. In *Credit Agricole Indosuez v Muslim Commercial Bank Ltd* [2000] 1 Lloyd's Rep 273, cl 9 of the letter of credit stated that 'original documents along with eight copies each of invoice, package list, weight and measurement list, Bill of Lading and certification of origin should be sent to us by courier . . .'. Credit Agricole did not send the weight and measurement list or the certificate of origin and the tender was rejected by the Muslim Bank. The Court of Appeal held that Credit Agricole was entitled to payment since it was unclear whether cl 9 was stating that the documents referred to were stipulated documents essential for the operation of the credit. It did not as required by Art 5(b) state precisely that the weight and measurement list and certificate of origin were documents against which payment was to be made. See also *Commercial Banking Co of Sydney Ltd v Jalsard Pty Ltd* [1973] AC 279 at p 286.

74 [1983] QB 711; *Baumwoll Manufactur von Carl Scheibler v Furness* [1893] AC 8.

subject to the UCP 500. Article 8(a) of the UCP 500 defines a revocable credit as a credit which:

> ... may be amended or cancelled by the issuing bank at any moment and without prior notice to the beneficiary.

In practice, banks normally inform the beneficiary of the withdrawal of credit. Desirable and businesslike though this may be, banks are not legally obliged to give prior notice to the seller. The common law rule is no different. In *Cape Asbestos Co Ltd v Lloyds Bank Ltd*,[75] Lloyds Bank advised the sellers that they had opened a credit in their favour, and expressly stated 'This is merely an advice for the opening of the above mentioned credit, and is not a confirmation of the same'. The sellers initially shipped 17 tons of the cargo, for which they were paid under the credit by the bank. Subsequent to the payment for the 17 tons, Lloyds Bank was instructed by the buyer's bank that the credit was cancelled. Lloyds Bank, however, failed to inform the beneficiary of the cancellation of the credit. The sellers shipped the remaining cargo. On presentation of documents, the bank refused to pay. The sellers brought an action against the bank, claiming that the bank had a duty to inform the seller of the revocation. The court held the bank had no legal duty. According to Bailhache J:

> ... the crucial question is whether the defendants are under any legal duty to inform the plaintiffs when the credit is withdrawn of the fact of its withdrawal. It is clear from the evidence that it is the practice of the defendants to inform persons to whom credits of this kind are given of the withdrawal of the credit, and that they would have done so in this instance but that, under pressure of business, they forgot to do so. What has to be considered, however, is not the practice of the defendants, but whether any legal duty is laid upon them to give notice. It is to be observed that the letter of 14 June 1920, from the defendants to the plaintiffs, announced the opening of a revocable and not of a confirmed credit. A letter in that form intimates to the person in whose favour the credit was opened that he might find that the credit is revoked at any time. That being the representation by the defendants to the plaintiffs, are the defendants under any legal duty to give notice to the plaintiffs when the credit is revoked? ... there is no legal obligation on the defendants to give notice in the circumstances. In a case of this kind, the wise course for the seller to take before making a shipment of the goods would certainly be to inquire of the bank whether or not the credit had been withdrawn. The practice of the defendants to give notice in such cases is a most prudent, reasonable and businesslike practice, and I hope that nothing I have said in this case leads banks to alter that practice; but at the same time, it does not seem to be based upon any legal obligation or duty. It has been said that the defendants regard the giving of notice as an act of courtesy which they always perform except when, as in this case, it is unfortunately forgotten. That is the true view of the proceeding. It is an act of courtesy which it is very desirable should be performed, but it is not founded upon any legal obligation [at p 275].

Bailhache J's suggestion that it might be prudent for the seller to inquire whether the credit is withdrawn, or not, before making the shipment, is of interest. Whether this course of action will aid the seller, since the credit can be revoked at any time prior to acceptance of the tendered documents, is questionable. It could well be that the credit is revoked after the seller's inquiry, and before the tender of documents.

In terms of risk, from the seller's viewpoint, without doubt, revocable credits offer the least security for obtaining payment from a bank, since the issuing bank does not undertake to pay on tender of stipulated documents. Coupled with this is the rule that there is no obligation on the part of the bank to inform the beneficiary of revocation of the credit. Revocable credits are uncommon unless the sale transaction is, for instance, between sister companies, or between a parent and a subsidiary, since the bank charges for servicing revocable credits are far lower than those for irrevocable letters of credit. Economic conditions (for example, recession) might fuel their use in the future.

The credit can be revoked either by the buyer (applicant), or the issuing bank on its own initiative, to protect itself should the buyer get into financial difficulties. A likely question is: at what moment does a revocable credit become irrevocable? Until when can a bank revoke the credit? It depends on the stage reached in the transaction. Until, and also on, presentation of documents, the bank will be well within its rights to revoke the credit. Once documents are accepted, it will not be able to revoke the credit. At the moment of acceptance, the credit stops being a revocable credit. Article 8(a) of the UCP 500 states that the credit can be cancelled at any moment – this is meaningless, unless the words 'prior to acceptance' are inserted in this provision.

Due to the gap in time before transmission and receipt of instructions, it is possible that the advising bank receives instructions from the issuing bank to cancel or amend the credit after it has paid the seller. In these circumstances, the issuing bank will have to reimburse the advising bank under Art 8(b) of UCP 500.

Realising the beneficiary's exposure to great risk, common law and the UCP 1994 require that the revocable or irrevocable nature of a documentary credit should be clearly spelt out. In the absence of a statement to this effect, the credit will be regarded as irrevocable (Art 6(b) and (c)).[76]

Irrevocable unconfirmed credit

According to Arts 2 and 7(a) of the UCP, the issuing bank assumes the legal responsibility of paying the beneficiary should he present the documents in accordance with the credit. Once the credit has been communicated to the seller, it cannot be amended or cancelled without the agreement of the issuing bank, confirming bank (if any) and the seller (beneficiary), according to Art 10(a) of the UCP. The common law position is no different.

Payment will normally be arranged in the buyer's country through an advising bank. (Appointment of an advising bank in the beneficiary's country is not necessary. The issuing bank can advise the opening of the credit directly, though this is unusual.) The advising bank acts as an agent of the issuing bank, and does not give an independent undertaking to pay the seller. The undertaking comes from the issuing bank. As apparent, a number of contractual undertakings are found in this type of credit. They are:

(a) between seller and buyer as a result of the contract of sale;

(b) between buyer and issuing banks, as a result of arrangements made for opening the credit;

(c) between issuing bank and advising bank; and

(d) between issuing bank and seller.

---

76 Note, however, that in the 1983 version of the UCP, the absence of a statement in respect of the credit's revocable or irrevocable nature rendered it revocable – Art 7(c).

The undertakings found in an irrevocable credit can be diagrammatically represented as shown below (Figure 15.4).

In terms of risk, the beneficiary is in a far better position, since the credit cannot be withdrawn or cancelled as under a revocable credit. The disadvantage with an unconfirmed irrevocable credit is that, should the issuing bank reject the documents, litigation will take place in a foreign jurisdiction. The contractual undertakings between seller and buyer, buyer and issuing bank, and issuing and advising bank present no problems at the conceptual level since offer, acceptance and consideration are present in these undertakings. What is difficult to see is how there could be a contractual link between issuing bank and seller (and, in the case of a confirmed credit, between seller and confirming bank),[77] since no consideration seems to be present. Various explanations have been put forward to resolve this lack of fit between letters of credit and traditional concepts of contract law.[78] The view that is most appealing to date is to treat the letter of credit as an exception to the doctrine of consideration. An issue with irrevocable credits is the moment at which it becomes irrevocable. Does it become irrevocable on notification of the credit to the seller? Or, does it become irrevocable when the seller acts upon the undertaking given by the bank? Existing case law is not of much help. Support can be found for both views. *Urquhart Lindsay and Co v Eastern Bank Ltd*[79] backs the latter and *Dexters Ltd v Schenkers Ltd*[80] the former. The view propounded in *Urquhart Lindsay and Co v Eastern Bank Ltd* may fulfil the requirements of conventional contract law, but brings with it uncertainty. From a commercial viewpoint, *Dexters Ltd v Schenkers Ltd*, incapable of accommodation in contract theory, imparts certainty; and men of commerce desire certainty. The sensible direction is to treat documentary credit as an exception to the doctrine of consideration – adopted, for instance, by the US.[81]

Confirmed credit

A confirmed[82] credit is always irrevocable. Where the letter of credit is a confirmed credit,[83] the seller also receives an undertaking from the confirming bank (situated in his country), in addition to that of the issuing bank, that he will be paid on presentation of the stipulated documents. In other words, in a confirmed credit, there 'is a direct undertaking by the banker that the seller, if he presents the documents as required in the required time, will receive payment'.[84] The UCP also takes the same approach to confirmed irrevocable credits according to Arts 2 and Art 8(a).[85]

---

77 See 'Confirmed credit' pp 486–8 below.

78 See Sarna, *Letters of Credit*, 1989, Carswell; Gutteridge and Megrah, *Law of Bankers' Commercial Credits*, 2001, Europa.

79 [1922] 1 KB 318, at pp 321–2.

80 (1923) 14 LlL Rep 586, at p 588.

81 See Arts 5–105 of the Uniform Commercial Code.

82 On ambiguity in the act of confirmation, see *Wahbe Tamari and Sons Ltd v Calprogeca-Soceidada Geral de Fibras* [1969] 2 Lloyd's Rep 18.

83 This is not to be confused with a credit where the confirmation is silent. For further on this, see Lloyd, 'Sounds of silence: emerging problems of undisclosed confirmation' (1990) 56 Brooklyn LR 139.

84 See *Ian Stach Ltd v Baker Bosley Ltd* [1958] 2 QB 130.

85 Art 2 defines Confirmation as 'a definite undertaking of the confirming bank, in addition to that of the issuing bank, to honour or negotiate a complying presentation'. And according to Art 8(a):

Figure 15.4: Contractual undertakings in an irrevocable documentary credit

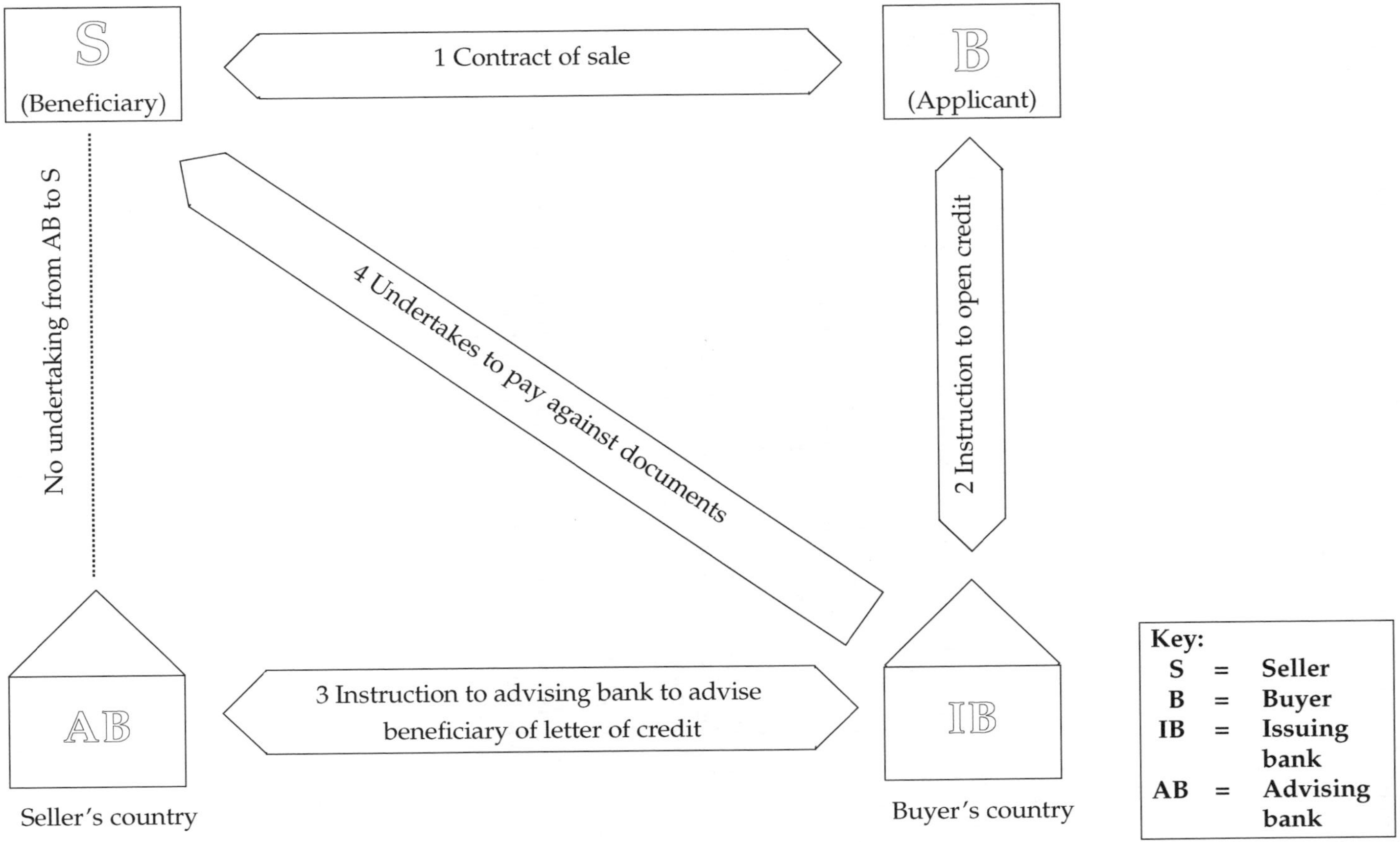

| B (Applicant) |
| IB |
| S (Beneficiary) |
| AB |

2 Instruction to open credit

1 Contract of sale

4 Undertakes to pay against documents

3 Instruction to advising bank to advise beneficiary of letter of credit

No undertaking from AB to S

Buyer's country

Seller's country

Key:
S = Seller
B = Buyer
IB = Issuing bank
AB = Advising bank

A confirmed credit gives maximum security to the seller; if the confirming bank is a reputable bank, he is certain of receiving payment. Moreover, should the seller wish to initiate proceedings for non-payment under the credit arrangement, he will be able to do so in his own jurisdiction. In a confirmed credit, other than the four contractual undertakings listed under irrevocable credits,[86] there is a fifth contractual undertaking – that is, between confirming banks and seller. The undertakings between the various parties are diagramatically represented below (Figure 15.5):

Back-to-back credits

This type of credit is mainly used where the seller is a 'middleman', for instance, where the seller (S) in the UK buys goods from the manufacturer (X) in Australia, and sells them to the buyer (B) in Kenya. In a back-to-back credit arrangement, S will use the credit opened in his favour by B (Credit 1) as security for opening a credit in favour of X (Credit 2). On presentation of documents that conform by X, S's bank will pay X. S will be asked to replace X's invoice in the letter of credit with his (that is, S's) invoice. The documents will be presented to B's bank for payment. Since the documents presented to B by S are the documents presented by X to S, it is important to ensure that the documents required by B and those provided by X match. Where X's documents do not tally with the documents that B requested in his credit arrangement, B's bank may reject the documents. S's bank may find that payment is effected under Credit 2, but that payment under Credit 1 does not take place. Further, if S were to become insolvent, S's bank may find itself in deep waters unless it has taken sufficient precautions to protect its interests. Because of the complexities with documentation, the resulting administration costs and risk, banks are extremely reluctant to use back-to-back credits.

Transferable credits

A better alternative to a back-to-back credit for a 'middleman' seller is a transferable credit. Article 38(b) of the UCP recognises transferable credit.

The transferable credit operates in the following way. Suppose S (first beneficiary) in London sells 1,000 lifeboats to the buyer (B) in Malaysia. S is not a manufacturer of lifeboats and has to purchase them from the manufacturer (X) in Cardiff. S could

---

'Provided that the stipulated documents are presented to the confirming bank or to any other nominated bank and that they constitute a complying presentation, the confirming bank must:

(i) honour, if the credit is available by
    (a) sight payment, deferred payment or acceptance with the confirming bank;
    (b) sight payment with another nominated bank and that nominated bank does not pay;
    (c) deferred payment with another nominated bank and that nominated bank does not incur its deferred payment undertaking or, having incurred its deferred payment undertaking, does not pay at maturity;
    (d) acceptance with another nominated bank and that nominated bank does not accept a draft drawn on it or, having accepted a draft drawn on it, does not pay at maturity;
    (e) negotiation with another nominated bank and that nominated bank does not negotiate'.

86   See 'Irrevocable unconfirmed credit', pp 485–6 above.

Figure 15.5: Contractual undertakings in an irrevocable confirmed documentary credit

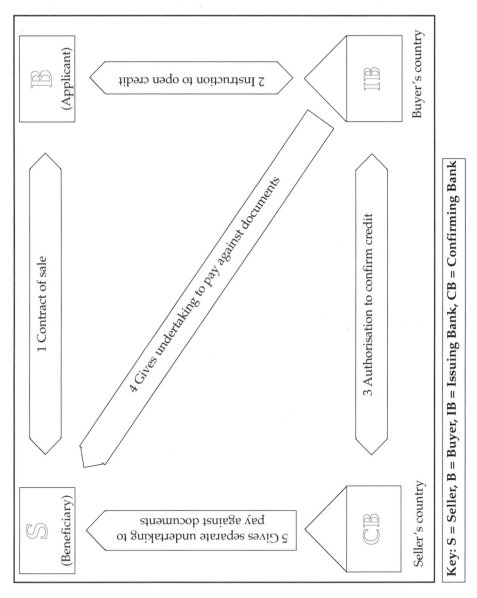

use the transferable credit mechanism to pay X by transferring rights and duties in respect of the documents to X who, as second beneficiary, will be paid from the credit set up by B. In other words, under a transferable credit, the first beneficiary (S) arranges for the transfer of the whole or part of the credit to the second beneficiary (X). A transferable credit arrangement is set up where the parties agree, and it is expressly agreed to by the issuing bank.[87] Articles 38(a) and (b) of the UCP provide:

---

87   See also *Bank Negara Indonesia 1946 v Lariza Singapore Pte Ltd* [1988] AC 583.

(a) A bank is under no obligation to transfer a credit except to the extent and in the manner expressly consented to by that bank.

(b) Transferable credit means a credit that specifically states it is 'transferable'. A transferable credit may be made available in whole or in part to another beneficiary ('second beneficiary') at the request of the beneficiary ('first beneficiary').

Transferring bank means a nominated bank that transfers the credit or, in a credit available with any bank, a bank that is specifically authorized by the issuing bank to transfer and that transfers the credit. An issuing bank may be a transferring bank.

Transferred credit means a credit that has been made available by the transferring bank to a second beneficiary.

In practice, a transfer form will be attached when the credit to the value of, say, £50,000 is advised to S (first beneficiary). S, who completes the form, will request that the credit for £40,000 be transferred to X (second beneficiary). X will be advised of the credit and will show S as the buyer. On presentation of documents by X, X's invoice will be substituted with S's invoice and presented to B. S. will be paid £10,000 and X £40,000. Article 38(h) of the UCP allows for the substitution of documents.

In practice, by and large, there is likely to be a substitution of the invoice.[88] It may be that the first beneficiary fails to supply it. In these circumstances, the UCP allows the transferring bank to deliver documents received from the second beneficiary (Art 38(i)).

A transferable credit is transferable only once, unless it is indicated otherwise. In other words, the second beneficiary cannot transfer the credit (Art 38(d)).

It must, however, be stated at this juncture that a letter of credit is not a negotiable instrument like a bill of exchange. It is unfortunate that Lord Denning, when talking about the autonomous character of a letter of credit in *Power Curber International Ltd v National Bank of Kuwait SAK*,[89] went on to say that a letter of credit is like a bill of exchange. It must be said that a letter of credit is not like a bill of exchange, for the following reasons:

(a) it is non-negotiable;

(b) it is not possible to be holder in due course of a letter of credit;[90] and

(c) a letter of credit is not as good as cash, since the opening of a letter of credit in most cases is a conditional payment.[91]

Revolving credits

Used in relation to transactions conducted on a regular basis between seller and buyer, this type of credit revolves around an agreed value or time. Where the credit revolves around a value agreed between the parties, once payment has been made against documents, the value of the credit will be automatically reinstated.

---

88 In *Jackson v Royal Bank of Scotland* [2005] UKHL 3 the transferring bank inadvertently sent the second beneficiary's invoice to the applicant. This meant that the mark-up on the goods on the part of the first beneficiary was revealed to the applicant. The bank was held liable for breach of confidentiality.

89 [1981] 3 All ER 607.

90 See 'Bills of exchange', pp 464–7 above.

91 See 'Obligations of the bank(s) to the seller', pp 497–500 below.

For instance, if the revolving credit is for the value of £50,000, on payment of £30,000 against documents to the beneficiary, the credit will be topped up to £50,000.

Red clause credits and green clause credits (also known as anticipatory credits)

Red clause credits first came to be used in the wool trade in New Zealand, Australia and South Africa. They are also said to have been used in trade with China. These credits allow the seller to draw on the documentary credit in advance of shipment. The advances are made against the warehouseman's receipt, even though the beneficiary is able to deal with the goods. This type of credit came to be known as the red clause credit, since the clause is printed in red ink. Though its origins are in the wool trade, its use is not restricted to it.[92] Since the seller under this credit can deal with the goods, it is used when there is a high degree of trust between the parties to the contract.[93] The typical clause is likely to read as follows:

> Under the credit, advance payment of up to — % of the credit amount is allowed prior to shipment against beneficiaries' receipt accompanied by signed declaration stating that shipping documents prescribed under this credit will be delivered in good order and within the validity of this credit. The advance must be deducted from payment to beneficiaries against prescribed documents.

Green clause credits came to be used in the coffee trade in Zaire and operate in the same way as red clause credits. The only difference is that in this type of credit, the goods are stored in the name of the bank.

The opening of a letter of credit

Arrangements for opening a documentary credit are made by the buyer. He also gives instructions about the documents that need to be tendered by the seller. Opening of a letter of credit is generally regarded as a condition precedent to the delivery of the goods by the seller. This means that the seller is not under an obligation to perform his side of the bargain till the letter of credit is opened.[94] However, it is possible that the parties may have agreed to the opening of the credit as a condition precedent of the contract of sale itself. In such a situation, where no letter of credit is provided, there will be no contract between the parties. As Denning LJ observed, in *Trans Trust SPRL v Danubian Trading Co Ltd*:[95]

> ... sometimes [the opening of a letter of credit] is a condition precedent to the formation of a contract, that is, it is a condition which must be fulfilled before any contract is concluded at all. In those cases, the stipulation 'subject to the opening of a letter of credit' is rather like a stipulation 'subject to contract' ... In other cases, a contract is concluded and the stipulation for a credit is a condition which is an essential term of the contract. In those cases, the provision of the credit is a condition precedent, not to the formation of the contract, but to the obligation of the seller to deliver the goods. If the buyer fails to provide the credit, the seller can treat himself as discharged from

---

92 *Tukan Timber Ltd v Barclays Bank plc* [1987] 1 Lloyd's Rep 171.
93 *South African Reserve Bank v Samuel and Co* (1931) 40 LlL Rep 291.
94 *Garcia v Page* (1936) 55 LlL Rep 391.
95 [1952] 1 Lloyd's Rep 348.

any further performance of the contract and can sue the buyer for damages for not providing the credit [at p 355].

It must, however, be said that the opening of the letter of credit as a condition of the contract of sale is extremely rare.

The credit opened by the buyer must conform with the terms agreed by the parties in the sale contract. So, if the parties have agreed to an irrevocable confirmed contract, the opening of a revocable credit will not do. However, were the buyer to open a credit that does not conform with the terms agreed, he can cure the defect provided it can be done before the credit is required.

When must the credit be opened?

The contract of sale may stipulate a fixed date for opening the letter of credit. In this case, it must be opened[96] by that date. Where the sale contract provides that the credit should be opened 'immediately', according to *Garcia v Page*,[97] it must be opened 'within such time as is required for a person of reasonable diligence to get the credit established' (at p 392). Where the contract does not expressly provide a date for opening the credit, but stipulates a shipment period, the credit should be opened before the entire shipment period. In *Pavia and Co SpA v Thurmann-Neilsen*,[98] a CIF contract of sale provided for shipment from 1 February to 30 April 1949. Payment was to be by confirmed irrevocable credit. The contract was silent on the date for opening the credit. The buyers opened the credit on 22 April. The seller sought damages for breach of contract caused by delay in opening the credit. The buyers argued that they saw no reason as to why the credit should be opened prior to the shipment period, since the credit was just a way of paying the seller on the tender of documents. The court, however, came to the conclusion that the object of the credit is to assure the seller, prior to shipment, that he will be paid upon shipment. The buyers were, therefore, in breach of contract. As Denning LJ said:

> ... the question in this case is this: in a contract which provides for payment by confirmed credit, when must the buyer open the credit? In the absence of an express stipulation, I think the credit must be made available to the seller at the beginning of the shipment period. The reason is because the seller is entitled, before he ships the goods, to be assured that, on shipment, he will get paid. The seller is not bound to tell the buyer the precise date when he is going to ship: and whenever he does ship the goods, he must be able to draw on the credit. He may ship on the very first day of the shipment period. If, therefore, the buyer is to fulfil his obligations he must make the credit available at the very first date when the goods may be lawfully shipped in accordance with the contract [at p 157].

Where there is a fixed date for shipment, the buyer must open the credit at a reasonable time before shipment date.[99] What is reasonable will depend upon the circumstances of each case.[100]

---

96 On the meaning of 'opened', see *Bunge Corp v Vegetable Vitamin Foods (Pte) Ltd* [1985] 1 Lloyd's Rep 613.

97 (1936) 55 LlL Rep 391.

98 [1952] 1 Lloyd's Rep 153.

99 See *Plasticmoda SpA v Davidsons (Manchester) Ltd* [1952] 2 Lloyd's Rep 527.

100 See *Etablissements Chainbaux SARL v Harbormaster Ltd* [1955] 1 Lloyd's Rep 303.

Failure to open a letter of credit

Where the buyer fails to open a credit as stipulated by the sale contract,[101] the seller can sue the buyer for damages. The damages awarded in such a situation are not restricted by s 50(3) of the Sale of Goods Act 1979, according to which, the amount of damages awarded is the difference between the contract price and the market price. The damages awarded would include the profit the seller would have made had the contract been successfully completed, subject to the rule of remoteness of damage.[102] In *Trans Trust SPRL v Danubian Trading Co Ltd*,[103] the contract was for the purchase of steel. The buyers did not open the letter of credit on time, and the seller claimed lost profits as damages. The buyers argued that only nominal damages were payable, since the sellers could have sold the steel at a profit in a market that was rising. The court viewed the credit arrangement as not simply a mode of paying the seller, but a mechanism which provided the seller with security and the opportunity of raising credit for the purchase of materials he may need to fulfil the sale contract. The foreseeable loss of profits could therefore be recovered. As Denning LJ said:

> ... this argument reminds me of the argument we heard in *Pavia and Co v Thurmann-Nielsen*. It treats the obligation to provide a credit as the same thing as the obligation to pay the price. That is, I think, a mistake. A banker's confirmed credit is a different thing from payment. It is an assurance in advance that the seller will be paid. It is even more than that. It is a chose in action which is of immediate benefit to the seller. The seller may be relying on it to obtain the goods himself. If it is not provided, the seller may be prevented from obtaining the goods at all. The damages will not in fact be nominal ... His loss will be the profit which he would have made if the credit had been provided [at p 356].

Waiver and variation

Even though the buyer fails to open a credit, or the terms of the credit do not conform to the terms agreed by the parties in the sale contract, the seller may decide to ship the goods. The question of whether the seller's action is a waiver or a variation seems to depend on whether the term in the contract is for the benefit of the seller, or whether it is of benefit to both the seller and the buyer – that is, where there is consideration. Where it is the former, the seller's act will be regarded as a waiver and, where it is the latter, it will be regarded as a variation.

If the seller has waived a requirement, he can reinstate the requirement upon giving the buyer reasonable notice. In *Panoustos v Raymond Hadley Corp of New York*,[104] the contract was for a number of shipments of flour. The buyers agreed to open a confirmed letter of credit, but opened an unconfirmed credit instead. The sellers, aware of this defect, made a few shipments on unconfirmed letters of credit, but repudiated the contract when an unconfirmed credit was provided for a later

---

101 The opening of a letter of credit may be a condition precedent for the loading of the goods. See *Kronos Worldwide Ltd v Sempra Oil Trading SARL* [2004] 1 Lloyd's Rep 260.
102 See *Hadley v Baxendale* (1854) 23 LJ Ex 179.
103 *Trans Trust SPRL v Danubian Trading Co Ltd* 1 Lloyd's Rep 337. See also *Ian Stach Ltd v Baker Bosly Ltd* [1958] 2 QB 130, at p 145.
104 (1917) 117 LT 330.

shipment. The court held that the seller could not revoke the waiver without giving the buyer reasonable notice.

Where there is a variation, the seller will be unable unilaterally to reinstate the terms initially agreed upon by the parties. In *WJ Alan and Co Ltd v El Nasr Export and Import Co*,[105] under the terms, payment was to take place in Kenyan shillings under a letter of credit. The credit that was opened, however, stated that payment was to be in sterling. The seller, who did not object at first, did so as soon as the sterling was devalued, and claimed damages for the difference between the two currencies. The Court of Appeal, by a majority, held that the contractual term had been varied, since it was supported by consideration – the fluctuations in the currency were of benefit to both the seller and the buyer.

Tender of documents by seller (beneficiary)

Once the seller is advised about the opening of the credit, he must arrange ship-ment and tender the documents.[106] He is under an obligation to tender the stipu-lated documents to the bank. The seller cannot waive the requirement of tendering the documents to a bank, and tender them directly to the buyer, and demand payment from the buyer directly. In *Soproma SpA v Marine and Animal By-Products Corp*,[107] the seller made a tender to the bank, which was validly rejected. The seller re-tendered the documents to the buyer, who rejected them. The seller sued the buyer. The court held that the second tender was invalid, since it was tendered to the buyer; to allow otherwise would go against the express terms of the contract. As McNair J said:

> . . . it seems to me to be quite inconsistent with the express terms of a contract such as this to hold that the sellers have an alternative right to obtain payment from the buyers by presenting the documents direct to the buyers. Assuming that a letter of credit has been opened by the buyers for the opening of which the buyer would nor-mally be required to provide the bank either with cash or some form of authority, could the seller at his option disregard the contractual letter of credit and present the docu-ments direct to the buyer? As it seems to me, the answer must plainly be in the negative [at p 386].

The restriction against approaching the buyer for payment under the letter of credit does not apply where the bank, for instance, goes insolvent. Where the bank is unable to pay the seller because of insolvency, the seller can go directly to the buyer for payment. The seller is able to approach the buyer in such circumstances, since pay-ment by letter of credit is regarded as a conditional payment of the price. As Lord Denning stated *obiter*, in *WJ Alan and Co Ltd v El Nasr Export and Import Co*:

> I am of the opinion that in the ordinary way, when the contract of sale stipulates for payment to be made by confirmed irrevocable letter of credit, then, when the letter of credit is issued and accepted by the seller, it operates as conditional payment.
>
> It is analogous to the case where, under a contract of sale, the buyer gives a bill of exchange or a cheque for the price. It is presumed to be given, not as absolute payment,

---

105 [1972] 2 QB 189.

106 See Stage 5 under 'Stages in a documentary credit transaction', p 573 above.

107 [1966] 1 Lloyd's Rep 367. See also *Ficom SA v Soceidad Cadex Limitada* [1980] 2 Lloyd's Rep 118; *Shamsher Jute Mills Ltd v Sethia (London) Ltd* [1987] 1 Lloyd's Rep 388.

nor as collateral security, but as conditional payment. If the letter of credit is honoured by the bank when the documents are presented to it, the debt is discharged. If it is not honoured, the debt is not discharged: and the seller has a remedy in damages against both the bank and the buyer [at p 212].

However, it is possible that the parties have agreed that payment by letter of credit is an absolute payment. They may do so expressly or impliedly. A stipulation by the seller that the credit should be opened by a particular bank may lead to the inference that the letter of credit is an absolute payment.[108] The agreement on a particular bank by the parties should not, however, lead to the conclusion that the letter of credit is an absolute payment – it is just one factor amongst others.[109]

Treating the letter of credit as a conditional payment may, in some circumstances, leave one of the innocent parties bearing the loss, as *Ng Chee Chong, Ng Weng Chong, Ng Cheng and Ng Yew (a firm trading as Maran Road Saw Mill) v Austin Taylor and Co Ltd*[110] well illustrates. The defendants acted as the plaintiffs' agents for the sale of timber in the United Kingdom and the Continent. Payment for the goods was made by irrevocable letters of credit. The letters of credit provided that drafts were to be negotiable by the Bangkok Bank in Kuala Lumpur (Malaysia) at the sight rate. Interest was to be claimed from Sale and Co (the merchant bankers used by the defendants) when the documents were presented for acceptance. The arrangement went through the following stages:

(a) the plaintiffs took the shipment documents and the bill of exchange (drawn by them on Sale and Co) to the Bangkok Bank;

(b) Bangkok Bank took the shipment documents and bill of exchange from the plaintiffs and passed the shipment documents to Sale and Co in return for their acceptance of the bill of exchange;

(c) Sale and Co passed the shipment documents to the defendants upon payment or against a trust letter, that is, a letter where the defendant undertook to hold the documents and the goods and proceeds for the bank (trust letters, also known as trust receipts, are fairly common in international commerce, since a buyer will normally raise money against the documents from the bank to pay the seller from whom he has bought the goods, and sell the goods on to third parties and use the proceeds of the sale to repay the bank. It is normal for banks to insist, when they release the goods, that the goods be warehoused in their name so that they can retain the goods until payment);

(d) the defendants would release the shipping documents to the buyer on payment.

The above arrangement worked well until Sale and Co became insolvent. The buyer had paid for the goods and the seller had deposited the sums with Sale and Co. Sale and Co failed to honour the bills of exchange when the Bangkok Bank presented them for payment. The bills of exchange were protested and the Bangkok Bank sought recourse to the plaintiffs as the drawers of the bills of exchange.[111] The plaintiffs reimbursed the Bangkok Bank and looked to the defendants (their agents) for payment on the basis of the agency agreement. The defendants argued that they had

---

108 See *WJ Alan and Co Ltd v El Nasr Export and Import Co* [1972] 2 QB 189, at p 220.
109 *Man, ED and F Ltd v Nigerian Sweets and Confectionery Co Ltd* [1977] 2 Lloyd's Rep 50.
110 [1975] 1 Lloyd's Rep 156.
111 See s 55(1) of the BEA 1882.

discharged their contractual obligation by opening the irrevocable letter of credit, on the basis of the clause in the agency contract, which provided.

> ... in consideration of our [the defendants] paying by letter of credit 100% of the invoice value of the goods shipped less our commission ... you [the plaintiffs] agree in the event of a dispute arising under such contract that cannot be decided amicably that we [the defendants] have the power, and that you hereby authorise us, to appoint the arbitrator on your behalf in such dispute. Further, we may take this letter as your authority to use and to pursue in your name for the recovery of any monies due from the buyers in respect of goods shipped under this contract.

Ackner J, after due consideration of the above clause, reached the conclusion that the defendants had 'promised to pay by letter of credit, not to provide by a letter of credit a source of payment which did not pay' (at p 158). The fact that the letter of credit was opened by the plaintiffs' agents made no difference to the commonly held view that the letter of credit is a conditional payment. No implied or express agreement that the plaintiffs were to look to a particular banker to the exclusion of the agent existed. He agreed that the submissions made by the plaintiffs' counsel were correct in that:

> ... a letter of credit operates as a conditional payment and not as absolute payment [and] is based on the analogy of a case of contract of sale where the buyer gives a bill of exchange or a cheque for the price. This is presumed to be given, not as absolute payment nor as collateral security, but as conditional payment. If this view, with which I respectfully agree is correct in relation to contracts of sale where payment is to be made by letter of credit, I can see no reason why it does not equally apply to a contract of agency in which the agent is to make the payment due to his principal by letter of credit. Of course, the very nature of any detailed instructions which a principal may give his agent as to the mode and method of payment of the money held by the agent to the principal's use, may well rebut the presumption that there is nothing in the genesis and aim of this transaction, viewed objectively, or in any other relevant circumstance which can properly be said to have this effect [at p 159].

The defendants were therefore held liable – in effect, they had to pay twice. For the letter of credit mechanism to work effectively – that is, to reduce the risk of the innocent party to a near negligible level of risk – it is essential to employ a *reliable and solvent paymaster*. The buyer can also protect himself against the possibility of the paymaster's insolvency by providing that the letter of credit is an absolute payment. Such a provision needs to be clearly stated. A buyer's disclosure that it is a small business and that payment was to be by unconfirmed letter of credit does not raise the inference that the buyer is not liable to the seller for the price where no payment under the letter of credit takes place.[112]

Obligations of the bank(s) to the seller

Upon presentation of the documents by the seller,[113] the advising/issuing or confirming bank (depending on the type of credit) must examine the documents to ensure that they comply on their face with the terms of the credit and decide whether to

---

112 See *Chloride Batteries SA Asia Pte Ltd v BPS International plc* (1996) unreported, 21 March, available on LEXIS.

113 See Stage 6, 'Stages in a documentary credit transaction', p 473 above.

accept or reject the documents.[114] Article 14(a) of the UCP sets out the standard of examination of documents as follows:

> A nominated bank acting on its nomination, a confirming bank, if any, and the issuing bank must examine a presentation to determine, on the basis of the documents alone, whether or not the documents appear on their face to constitute a complying presentation.

The wording adopted by UCP in Art 14(a) is different from that of Art 13(a) of the UCP 500 which stated:

> (a) Banks must examine all documents stipulated in the credit with reasonable care, to ascertain whether or not they appear, on their face, to be in compliance with the terms and conditions of the credit. Compliance of the stipulated documents on their face with the terms and conditions of the credit, shall be determined by international standard banking practice as reflected in these Articles. Documents which appear on their face to be inconsistent with one another will be considered as not appearing on their face to be in compliance with the terms and conditions of the credit.

It is apparent from the above that if the bank were to exercise reasonable care then this position was no different from that adopted in common law. The bank is to conduct a visual examination and exercise reasonable care.[115] There is some debate that UCP 600 does away with reasonable care and introduces a strict liability on the bank, though practitioners in England seem to think that it is 'unlikely to affect what was in any event a restatement of the common law position',[116] though it could be argued that the absence of the phrase 'reasonable care' introduces strict liability.

The UCP gives each bank a maximum of five days for examining the documents. Article 14(b) provides:

> A nominated bank acting on its nomination, a confirming bank, if any, and the issuing bank shall each have a maximum of five banking days[117] following the day of presentation to determine if a presentation is complying. This period is not curtailed or otherwise affected by the occurrence on or after the date of presentation of any expiry date or last day for presentation.

It seems from the above provision that the bank is obliged to pay as soon as it has checked that the documents comply, since Art 15 provides as follows:

> (a) When an issuing bank determines that a presentation is complying, it must honour.
> (b) When a confirming bank determines that a presentation is complying, it must honour or negotiate and forward the documents to the issuing bank.
> (c) When a nominated bank determines that a presentation is complying and honours or negotiates, it must forward the documents to the confirming bank or issuing bank.

---

114 See Stage 7, 'Stages in a documentary credit transaction', p 473 above. See also ISBP on the practice adopted in relation to the documentation such as the invoice and transportation documentation in its various guises such as bills of lading, multimodal transport documents and consignment notes.

115 *Gian Singh and Co Ltd v Banque de l'Indochine* [1974] 1 WLR 1234.

116 Isaacs and Barnett, 'International Trade Finance – Letters of credit, UCP and Examination of Documents' 2007 JIBLR 660, at p 662.

117 Banking day is defined in Art 2 as 'a day on which a bank is regularly open at the place at which an act subject to these rules is to be performed'.

Does this mean that a bank may be liable to the beneficiary if it does not honour after an examination completed on the second banking day but nonetheless takes advantage of the maximum five banking days available to it under Art 14(b))? Is the combined operation of Arts 14 and 15 likely to result in litigation? Will reasonable practice of banks be taken into account?

Banks, in England, normally take three days, though the size of the bank and its expertise may be relevant.[118] Where documents do not conform, the bank is free to consult the applicant, but must not send them to the applicant for examination. Consultation with the applicant, however, will not extend the time allowed for examination. Article 16(b) states:

> When the issuing bank determines that a presentation does not comply, it may in its sole judgment approach the applicant for a waiver of the discrepancies. This does not, however, extend the period mentioned in sub-Art 14(b).

In the event of rejection of the documents by the bank, the bank must inform beneficiary of the reasons for rejection. Under the UCP, the beneficiary is to be notified, at the very latest, by the end of the five days allowed for examination of documents.

Articles 16(c) and (d) provide as follows:

(c) When a nominated bank acting on its nomination, a confirming bank, if any, or the issuing bank decides to refuse to honour or negotiate, it must give a single notice to that effect to the presenter.

  The notice must state:

  (i) that the bank is refusing to honour or negotiate; and

  (ii) each discrepancy in respect of which the bank refuses to honour or negotiate; and

  (iii) (a) that the bank is holding the documents pending further instructions from the presenter; or

      (b) that the issuing bank is holding the documents until it receives a waiver from the applicant and agrees to accept it, or receives further instructions from the presenter prior to agreeing to accept a waiver; or

      (c) that the bank is returning the documents; or

      (d) that the bank is acting in accordance with instructions previously received from the presenter.

(d) The notice required in sub-article 16 (c) must be given by telecommunication or, if that is not possible, by other expeditious means no later than the close of the fifth banking day following the day of presentation.

A number of possibilities are open to the seller when he learns of the rejection. He could rectify the defects, and re-tender the documents, provided he can do so within the expiry period. Article 6(d) of the UCP requires that:

(i) A credit must state an expiry date for presentation. An expiry date stated for honour or negotiation will be deemed to be an expiry date for presentation.

(ii) The place of the bank with which the credit is available is the place for presentation. The place for presentation under a credit available with any bank is that of any bank. A place for presentation other than that of the issuing bank is in addition to the place of the issuing bank.

---

118   See *Bankers Trust Ltd v State Bank of India* [1991] 2 Lloyd's Rep 443.

The seller may also contact the buyer and inform him of the reasons for rejection and he may agree to instruct the bank to accept the documents as they stand. The seller may also be able to persuade the confirming bank to pay him on the non-conforming documents by agreeing to indemnify the bank for any loss or damage the bank suffers as a result of the lack of conformity of the tendered documents with the credit terms. Alternatively, the bank may agree to make payment 'under reserve'. There is no generally accepted meaning of 'payment under reserve'. So one has to look to what the parties had in mind. Did they agree that the seller would repay the confirming bank should the issuing bank reject the documents? In *Banque de l'Indochine et de Suez SA v JH Rayner (Mincing Lane) Ltd*,[119] it was held that the confirming bank could demand repayment of the money paid 'under reserve' to the seller, since the issuing bank had rejected the documents. According to Kerr LJ:

> What the parties meant, I think, was that payment was to be made under reserve in the sense that the beneficiary would be bound to repay the money on demand if the issuing bank should reject the documents, whether on its own initiative or on the buyer's instructions. I would regard this as a binding agreement between the confirming bank and the beneficiary by way of a compromise to resolve the impasse created by the uncertainty of their respective legal obligations and rights [at p 733].

The judgment of Sir John Donaldson Mr is extremely instructive. The arrangement must be viewed from the commercial point of view. He imputed a dialogue between the beneficiary and the bank on the following lines:

Merchant: 'These documents are sufficient to satisfy the terms of the letter of credit and certainly will be accepted by my buyer. I am entitled to the money and need it.'

Bank: 'If we thought that the documents satisfied the terms of the letter of credit, we would pay you at once. However, we do not think that they do and we cannot risk paying you and not being paid ourselves. We are not sure that your buyer will authorise payment, but can, of course, ask.'

Merchant: 'But that will take time and meanwhile I shall have a cash flow problem.'

Bank: 'Well, the alternative is for you to sue us and that will also take time.'

Merchant: 'What about your paying me without prejudice to whether I am entitled to payment and then your seeing what is the reaction of your correspondent bank and our buyer?'

Bank: 'That is all right, but if we are told that we should not have paid, how do we get our money back?'

Merchant: 'You sue me.'

Bank: 'Oh no, that would leave us out of our money for a substantial time. Furthermore, it would involve us in facing in two directions. We should not only have to sue you, but also to sue the issuing bank in order to cover the possibility that you might be right. We cannot afford to pay on those terms.'

Merchant: 'All right. I am quite confident that the issuing bank and my buyer will be content that you should pay, particularly since the documents are, in fact, in order. You pay me, and if the issuing bank refuses to reimburse you for the same reason that you are unwilling to pay, I will repay you on demand and then sue you. But I do not think that this will happen.'

Bank: 'We agree. Here is the money "under reserve" ' [at pp 727–78].

Given the uncertainty, it would be wise for the parties to agree to payment under reserve only while stating what is meant by it.

The fraud exception

The bank's obligation to pay on documents that appear to conform on their face is curtailed in the event of fraud. The first English case which considered fraud as an exception to the principle of autonomy was *Discount Records Ltd v Barclays Bank Ltd*,[120] where the buyers, alleging fraud, sought an injunction to stop the bank from paying the sellers on the credit. Mere allegation of fraud was insufficient to issue an injunction. Similarly, information that would lead a reasonable banker to infer fraud is insufficient.[121] According to the courts, the fraud must be proven. The subsequent case of *United City Merchants (Investments) Ltd v Royal Bank of Canada (The American Accord)*[122] considered the circumstances in which the fraud exception[123] could be successfully raised. Shipment under the contract terms was to take place by 15 December 1976. The cargo was shipped on 16 December 1976, and the bill of lading backdated by the loading brokers. The sellers, however, were unaware of the loading brokers' fraud. The bank, having discovered the fraud, refused to pay the seller, who brought an action against the bank for non-payment against the documents. The question before the court was whether the bank could refuse to pay against documents that appeared to be in order on their face, but where goods had not been shipped as stipulated in the sale contract. The House of Lords held that, unless the seller was fraudulent, or was privy to the fraud, the bank could not refuse payment. Of course, where the seller is himself fraudulent, or has knowledge of the fraud, policy considerations would fully justify depriving the seller from benefiting from his fraud. As Lord Diplock said:

> ... to this general statement of principle as to the contractual obligations of the confirming bank to the seller, there is one established exception: that is, where the seller, for the purpose of drawing on the credit, fraudulently presents to the confirming bank documents that contain, expressly or by implication, material representations of fact that to his knowledge are untrue ... The exception of fraud on the part of the beneficiary seeking to avail himself of the credit is a clear application of the maxim *ex turpi causa non oritur actio* or, if plain English is to be preferred, 'fraud unravels all'. The courts will not allow their process to be used by a dishonest person to carry out a fraud [at p 183].

This decision clearly protects the beneficiary who, with no knowledge of fraud, buys

---

120 [1975] 1 Lloyd's Rep 444.
121 See *The Society of Lloyd's v Canadian Imperial Bank of Commerce and Others* [1993] 2 Lloyd's Rep 579.
122 [1983] 1 AC 168. See also *Banco Santander SA v Bayfern Ltd* [2000] 1 All ER (Comm) 776. In this case the confirming bank discounted its deferred payment undertaking before the maturity fraud in the documents was discovered. It was held by the Court of Appeal that the issuing bank did not have to reimburse the confirming bank, thus placing the risk on the bank that discounted. This unfairness has been rectified by Arts 7(c) and 8(c) since they establish an undertaking to reimburse on maturity, thus placing the risk on the issuing bank. See also *The Society of Lloyd's v Canadian Imperial Bank of Commerce and Others* [1993] 2 Lloyd's Rep 579.
123 The fraud exception is traceable to the American case *Sztejn v Henry Schroder Banking Corp* (1941) 31 NYS 2d 631. See *Edward Owen Engineering Ltd v Barclays Bank International Ltd* [1978] 1 QB 159, at p 169. Note that this case dealt with performance bonds. On more about performance bonds, see 'Performance Bonds/Guarantees and Standby Letters of Credit', pp 503–6 below. See also *Solo Industries UK Ltd v Canara Bank* [2001] 2 Lloyd's Rep 57.

goods afloat and sells them to the buyer.[124] However, the risk of paying for valueless documents is on the buyer. The narrow ambit of the fraud exception is generally justified on grounds of commercial efficacy. In other words, the fraud exception is construed restrictively in order to maintain the efficiency of documentary credit as an instrument for financing international commerce – a view expressed unambiguously by *Kerr J in RD Harbottle (Mercantile) Ltd v National Westminster Bank*,[125] as follows:

> It is only in exceptional cases that the courts will interfere with the machinery of irrevocable obligations assumed by banks. They are the life blood of international commerce. Such obligations are regarded as collateral to the underlying rights and obligations between the merchants at either end of the banking chain. Except possibly in clear cases of fraud of which the banks have notice, the courts will leave the merchants to settle their disputes under the contracts by litigation or arbitration as available to them or stipulated in the contracts. The courts are not concerned with their difficulties to enforce such claims: these are the risks which the merchants take . . . The machinery and commitments of banks are on a different level. They must allow to be honoured, free from interference by the courts. Otherwise trust in international commerce could be irreparably damaged [at p 870].

There is truth in the observation that trust in the documents is essential for preserving commerce to flourish. Documentary fraud is on the increase.[126] In these circumstances, in policy terms, would it not be better to consolidate the trust placed in letters of credit by reassessing the narrow fraud exception?[127] The current attitude is to the detriment of the buyer, even where the bank, or the buyer, has strong grounds for suspecting foul play. The burden is cast on the party alleging fraud[128] – a burden difficult to discharge in the majority of cases. The present rule makes investigators of buyers and banks. (There are not many cases where fraud has been established.)[129]

One avenue open to the buyer to protect himself is a performance guarantee from the seller that is issued by a reputable bank.[130]

---

124 See Chapter 1.

125 *Harbottle (RD) (Mercantile) Ltd v National Westminster Bank Ltd* [1977] 2 All ER 862.

126 For instance, loss through fraud involving letters of credit is estimated to be around US$1 bn per annum. See www.bolero.net.

127 In the US, the fraud exception as expressed in the *Sztejn* case has been variously interpreted. The fraud rule was expressed in *Sztejn* as applying to situations where the 'seller has intentionally failed to ship any goods ordered by the buyer . . .' (at pp 634–5). The use of the word 'intentionally' has resulted in a myriad of suggestions: from intentional fraud, egregious fraud, equitable fraud to no clear statement on degree of fraud required. See *New York Life Insurance Co v Hartford National Bank and Trust Co* 378 A 2d 562 (Conn 1977); *NMC Enterprises v Columbia Broadcasting System, Inc* 14 UCC Rep Ser 1427 (NY Sup Ct 1974); *United Bank Ltd v Cambridge Sporting Goods Corp* 392 NYS 2d 265 (NY 1976); *Dynamics Corp of America v Citizens and Southern National Bank* 356 F Supp 991 (ND Ga 1973). See also Xiang and Buckley, 'A comparative analysis of the standard of fraud required under the fraud rules in letter of credit law' (2003) 13 Duke Journal of Comparative and International Law 293.

The Uniform Commercial Code in Art 5, s 109 adopts the following fraud standard for letters of credit:

> If . . . required document is forged or materially fraudulent, or honor of the presentation would result in a material fraud by the beneficiary on the issuer or applicant . . . the issuer, acting in good faith, may honor or dishonour the presentation.

128 Uncorroborated statements are insufficient. Strong corroborative evidence in the form of contemporary documents is required. See *United Trading Corp SA and Murray Clayton Ltd v Allied Arab Bank Ltd* [1985] 2 Lloyd's Rep 554.

129 See *Rafsanjan Pistachio Producers Co-operative v Bank Leumi (UK) plc* [1992] 1 Lloyd's Rep 513. See also *Themehelp Ltd v West and Others* [1996] QB 84.

130 See 'Performance bonds/Guarantees and standby letters of credit', pp 503–6 below.

Information technology (IT) and letters of credit

As with other trade documents (for example, the bill of lading), a question that inevitably arises is whether there is scope for electronic letters of credit. The issue of a paperless letter of credit has been considered by various academics since the IT revolution.[131] In 2002, the ICC produced a supplement to the UCP – the eUCP Version 1– and this has been replaced with Version 1.1 (hereinafter 'eUCP').[132] The eUCP enables electronic presentation and caters for the recognition of electronic documents. Signature in the digital context is addressed and the meaning of an original in the electronic environment is clarified. The requirement of presenting one or more originals or copies is satisfied by an electronic record according to Art e8, and an electronic record is defined in Art e3(b)(i) as:

- Data created, generated, sent, communicated, received or stored by electronic means;
- That is capable of being authenticated as to the apparent identity of the sender and the apparent source of the data contained in it, and as to whether it has remained complete and unaltered; and
- Is capable of being examined for compliance with the terms and conditions of the eUCP credit.

The eUCP takes a technology-neutral approach so that an electronic signature is defined in Art e3(b)(ii) as 'a data process attached to or logically associated with an electronic record and executed or adopted by a person in order to identify that person and to indicate that person's authentication of the electronic record'.

Recognising that electronic data are prone to corruption, Art e11 addresses the issue of a bank's procedure in relation to corrupted electronic records.

As with the UCP, the eUCP has to be specifically incorporated. It is a supplement to the UCP, so the UCP will continue to apply equally to the electronic presentation (Art e1).[133] While most commercial lawyers are skeptical about the use of electronic documentary credits or, for that matter, electronic bills of lading, it must be said that this skepticism is unwarranted. Legal frameworks exist[134] alongside technical means to make paperless document transactions a vital and necessary part of the international commercial arena. The recognition of negotiable and non-negotiable transport records is also made possible by the recently adopted Rotterdam Rules.[135]

---

131 See for instance, Kozolchyk, 'The paperless letter of credit and related documents of title' (1992) 55 Law and Contemporary Problems 39.
132 UCP 500 and eUCP Publication No 500/2 ICC. It came into force as of 1 April 2002.
133 Note that the presentation of documents could consist of a combination of electronic records and paper documents.
134 See Chapters 3 and 4 on electronic commerce, and Chapter 6, on the BOLERO project.
135 See Chapter 9.

PERFORMANCE BONDS/GUARANTEES AND STANDBY LETTERS OF CREDIT

Performance bonds/guarantees

These are usually used to secure the performance of the seller under a sale contract. In other words, performance bonds, also frequently termed performance guarantees, provide security in the event of non-performance of the contract. The way performance bonds work is provided by *Edward Owen Engineering Ltd v Barclays Bank International Ltd*.[136] Edward Owen (S) contracted with the buyer (B) in Libya to supply and erect glasshouses. Payment was to be effected under a confirmed letter of credit and S was to provide a performance bond of 10% of the contract value. S instructed the defendants to provide the bond against their counter-guarantee. The defendants instructed Umma Bank in Libya – the bond payable 'on demand without proof or conditions'. Since B failed to open the letter of credit, S refused to supply the items. B nonetheless claimed from Umma Bank under the performance bond and Umma Bank, in turn, claimed from Barclays Bank International. S was granted an interim injunction to restrain the defendants from paying. On appeal, the Court of Appeal held that an injunction could not be granted. The performance bond was seen as similar to a documentary credit – that is, the undertaking of the bank was independent of the underlying contract. The bank, therefore, had to honour its obligations if the terms of the bond were satisfied. According to Lord Denning:

> A performance bond is a new creature so far as we are concerned. It has many similarities to a letter of credit, with which of course we are very familiar. It has long been established that, when a letter of credit is issued and confirmed by a bank, the bank must pay it if the documents are in order and the terms of the credit are satisfied. Any dispute between buyer and seller must be settled between themselves . . .
>
> . . . these performance guarantees are virtually promissory notes payable on demand. So long as the Libyan customers make an honest demand, the banks are bound to pay: and the banks will rarely, if ever, be in a position to know whether the demand is honest or not. At any rate, they will not be able to prove it to be dishonest. So they will have to pay.
>
> All this leads to the conclusion that the performance guarantee stands on a similar footing to a letter of credit. A bank which gives a performance guarantee must honour the guarantee according to its terms. It is not concerned in the least with the relations between the supplier and the customer; nor with the question whether the supplier is in default or not. The bank must pay according to its guarantee, on demand, if so stipulated, without proof or conditions. The only exception is when there is a clear fraud of which the bank has notice [at pp 169–71].

In *Edward Owen Engineering Ltd v Barclays Bank International Ltd*, the bond was payable on demand without proof or conditions. If a party wishes to protect himself, he can do so by imposing conditions such as a certificate signed by an independent third party.[137]

---

136 [1978] QB 159.
137 For instance, in *Gur Corp v Trust Bank of Africa Ltd* ((1986) unreported, 28 October – see LEXIS), the performance guarantee was payable on production of a certificate signed by a certified quantity surveyor.

The ICC has formulated a set of rules for use with performance guarantees. The 1978 version entitled Uniform Rules for Contract Guarantees has been replaced with the Uniform Rules for Demand Guarantees (URDG) in 1992 (Brochure 458). Like the UCP, these rules apply only if incorporated. The term 'demand guarantee' used in URDG includes the two types of performance bonds mentioned above. Article 2 of the URDG defines demand guarantee as:

(a) ... any guarantee, bond or other payment undertaking, however named or described, by a bank, insurance company or other body or person (hereinafter referred to as 'guarantor') given in writing for the payment of money on presentation in conformity with the terms of the undertaking is a written demand for payment and such other document(s) (for example, a certificate by an architect or engineer, a judgment or an arbitral award) as may be specified in the guarantee, such undertaking being given:

(i) at the request or on the instructions and under liability of a party (hereinafter called the 'principal'); or

(ii) at the request or on the instructions and under the liability of a bank, insurance company or any other body or person (hereinafter the 'instructing party') acting on the instructions of a principal to another party (hereinafter the 'beneficiary').

The URDG reiterates in Art 2(b) the views found in the cases mentioned above – that is, that the guarantee is autonomous, and the banks are in no way concerned with the underlying contract.

Because guarantees are payable on demand by the beneficiary, they are open to abuse in that a beneficiary can demand payment even when there has been no breach by the principal (the party who has requested the issue of a guarantee). In order to give some protection, Art 20 of URDG provides that any demand for payment under the guarantee be accompanied by a written statement stating that '(i) the principal is in breach of his obligation(s) under the underlying contract(s) ... and (ii) the respect in which the principal is in breach'. As to how effective this will be in curtailing abuse is open to doubt, since the statement is required only of the beneficiary. On receiving the statement, the guarantor (bank) is required to transmit, without delay, the message to the principal (Art 21), thus alerting the principal and enabling him to take action should he wish to.

Standby letters of credit

At this juncture, it would be convenient to introduce an arrangement known as standby letters of credit. Though termed letters of credit, standby letters of credit have more in common with performance bonds/guarantees that call for payment against documents. Under a standby letter of credit, the agreement is to pay the beneficiary against documents in the event of default by the applicant. Standby letters of credit were designed in the USA to circumvent rules that prevent a bank from giving guarantees. Standby letters of credit are widely used in construction industries though their use is not unknown in other contexts, such as supporting a reinsurance obligation and an obligation to repay money. As Professor Goode observes, standby credits, in practice, are now used as a 'general purpose financial tool ... to support financial as well as non-financial undertakings and domestic as well as international transactions, and to secure credit enhancement of public issues of securities, which if underpinned by a standby credit issued by a first class bank may attract a higher credit rating from agencies . . .'.[138] The difference between a standby credit and performance guarantee, it seems, is in business practice not in law.

Though the UCP is applicable to standby letters of credit if the parties so wish, the rules are not satisfactory since they were primarily devised for letters of credit.[139] In 1998, the ICC adopted a set of rules known as the International Standby Practices[140] (hereinafter 'ISP 98'), initially formulated by the US Institute for International Banking Law and Practice, which reflects 'accepted practices, custom and usage'[141] relating to standby letters of credit. As with the UCP, the ISP 98 needs to be incorporated by the parties. The ISP 98 deals with various obligations such as the undertaking to honour by issuer, presentation of documents as required by the standby, examination of the documents for compliance and the various standby document types and the transfer and assignment of drawing rights. Though the ISP 98 has a number of similarities with the UCP, it goes beyond the UCP in a number of respects. First, the ISP 98 is more extensive in its drafting and tries to clarify concepts that could cause uncertainties – for instance, the meaning of the words 'original' and 'copies' which raised substantial doubts in the context of Art 20(b) of the UCP 500.[142] The ISP 98 in r 4.15(c) states:[143]

(i)   A presented document is deemed to be an 'original' unless it appears on its face to have been reproduced from an original.
(ii) A document which appears to have been reproduced from an original is deemed to be an original if the signature or authentication appears to be original.

Secondly, it caters specifically for standby letters of credit. For instance, it allows for more than one transfer (r 6.02),[144] partial drawing (r 3.08), syndication (r 10.01) and participation (r 10.02). Like the UCP, the ISP 98 is silent on issues such as fraud. However, unlike the UCP, it specifically states that the ISP Rules do not define or otherwise provide for defences to honour based on fraud, abuse or similar matters (r 1.05(g)).

Alongside the UCP and ISP 98, there is another instrument that could well apply to a standby letter of credit. This is the United Nations Convention on Independent Guarantees and Standby Letters of Credit 1995 (hereinafter 'Standby Convention').[145] The Standby Convention's aim is to provide a harmonised set of rules for the use of standby letters of credit and independent guarantees (performance/demand

---

138   *Commercial Law*, 2004, Butterworths, at p 1018. See also Kozolchyk, 'The emerging law of standby letters of credit and bank guarantees' (1982) 24 Arizona LR 319; Ryan, 'Letters of credit supporting debt for borrowed money: the standby as backup' [1983] 100 Banking LJ 404.
139   Note the UCP itself acknowledges the limited applicability of its rules to standby letters of credit in Art 1 which states:
       The . . . (UCP) are rules that apply to any documentary credit . . . (including to the extent to which they may be applicable, any standby letter of credit) when the text of the credit expressly indicates that it is subject to these rules.
140   ICC. Also visit www.ISP98.com. The ISP 98 came into effect on 1 January 1999.
141   See *International Standby Practices (ISP 98)*, 1998, ICC, Preface.
142   See *Glencore International AG v Bank of China* [1996] 1 Lloyd's Rep 135; see also 'Doctrine of strict compliance', pp 481–5 above.
143   See also r 4.15(a) and (b). 'Signature' is defined in r 1.09.
144   See also 'Transferable credits', pp 488–90 above, and Art of the UCP.
145   The text of this convention is available at www.uncitral.org. It is also reproduced in Carr and Kidner, *International Trade Law Statutes and Conventions*, 5th edn, 2008, Routledge-Cavendish. It came into force on 1 January 2000.

guarantees) and ensures the independence of independent undertakings through the principles it sets out. It is consistent with the solutions found in rules of practice[146] such as the UCP and URDG. It also supplements them by dealing with areas not currently dealt with in the UCP or for that matter ISP 98. The scope of application of the Standby Convention is set out in Art 1. It applies to an international undertaking where the place of the guarantor/issuer[147] is in a contracting state, or the private international law leads to the application of the law of a contracting state. It is open for the parties to exclude the application of the Standby Convention. The word 'undertaking' introduced in the Standby Convention is defined in Art 2(1) thus:

> For the purposes of this Convention, an undertaking is an independent commitment, known in international commercial law as independent guarantee or standby letter of credit, given by a bank or other institution or person ('guarantor/issuer') to pay to the beneficiary a certain or determinable amount upon simple demand or upon demand accompanied by other documents, in conformity with the terms and any documentary conditions of the undertaking, indicating, or from which it is to be inferred, that payment is due because of default in the performance of an obligation, or because of another contingency, or for money borrowed or advanced, or on account of any mature indebtedness undertaking by the principal/applicant or another person.

The internationality of the undertaking is determined on the basis of place of business. According to Art 4(1): '. . . an undertaking is international if the places of business, as specified in the undertaking, of any two of the following persons are in different states: guarantor/issuer, beneficiary, principal/applicant, instructing party, confirmer'. What is innovative about the Standby Convention is its attempt to address fraud. As seen earlier, fraud, which poses a significant problem, is construed very restrictively with the result that, in the absence of actual fraud, the victim is the buyer. Fraud affects performance guarantees and standby letters of credit and the approach of the English courts in relation to fraud in these types of undertakings is no different from the approach adopted in relation to documentary credits.[148] There is, however, no harmonised approach to fraud across jurisdictions.[149] The various ICC rules (for example, UCP, ISP 98) are of no use in this thorny area. Article 19(1) of the Standby Convention does not use the word 'fraud' as such, but lists the circumstances in which the guarantor can withhold payment. So, where it is manifest and clear:

(a) any document is not genuine or has been falsified;

(b) no payment is due on the basis asserted in the demand and the supporting documents; or

---

146   The ICC endorsed the Standby Convention on 21 June 1999. It must be added that the Standby Convention was not drafted in isolation; full recognition was given to the ICC rules in this area. It is meant to work alongside rules of practice such as the UCP and URDG.

147   Ie, the bank, person or institution giving the independent guarantee.

148   See *Balfour Beatty Civil Engineering Ltd v Technical and General Guarantee Ltd* [2000] 68 Con LR 108; *Themehelp Ltd v West and Others* [1996] QB 84; *Czarnikow-Rionda Sugar Trading Inc v Standard Bank London* [1999] 1 All ER (Comm) 890. Note that the principles when obtaining an injunction are the same regardless of whether it is sought against the bank or the beneficiary (see *Group Jose, Re v Walbrook Insurance Co Ltd* [1996] Lloyd's Rep 345).

149   Another emerging exception to autonomy is unconscionability in some jurisdictions – see *Bocotra Construction Pte Ltd v Attorney General (No 2)* (1995) 2 SLR 733; *Dauphin Offshore Engineering and Trading Pte Ltd v The Private Office of HRH Sheikh Sultan bin Khalifa bin Zayed Al Nayhan* (2000) 1 SLR 657 from Singapore. Unconscionability seems to be broadly defined as lack of *bona fides*.

(c) judging by the types and purpose of the undertaking, the demand has no conceivable basis,[150]

the guarantor/issuer acting in good faith will be well within his rights to withhold payment as against the beneficiary.

Article 19(1) does not impose an obligation on the guarantor/issuer to withhold payment. He has the discretion to do so. The Standby Convention takes this approach in order to preserve the commercial reliability of undertakings as independent from the underlying transactions.[151] It must also be pointed out that the Standby Convention recognises that the investigation of the underlying transactions are to be left to the courts and Art 19(3) affirms the entitlement of the principal/applicant to provisional court measures in accordance with Art 20.

It is difficult to predict whether the Standby Convention will be accepted widely. Nonetheless, it must be said that it is well worth a serious consideration given its bold attempt to harmonise the controversial area of fraud.

OTHER MEANS OF MINIMISING RISK OF NON-PAYMENT

Undoubtedly, the letter of credit is a popular means of obtaining payment from the buyer. Despite its popularity, it does present a few risks in obtaining payment – for instance, where the buyer or indeed the bank becomes insolvent. There are other mechanisms available which may afford some protection to the seller. Insurance is one obvious answer. Private insurers provide credit insurance where consumer goods and other materials are sold on credit terms of six months or less.[152] For longer-term credit, in the United Kingdom, a government department known as the Exports Credits Guarantee Department[153] offers an export insurance policy against the risk of not getting paid in circumstances such as buyer's insolvency, default, and lack of foreign exchange.

Another popular method available to the seller that imparts the highest level of protection is the use of a factor – a third party to whom the seller assigns[154] his receivable (right to payment of monies from the buyer) without recourse.[155] The factor, obviously, offers these services at a charge since he takes on the task and risk of collecting the payment from the buyer. The factoring agreement can also be conducted on a recourse basis.[156] Generally, the factor offers what is known as 'full-service

---

150 See Art 19(2) for types of situations in which a demand has no conceivable basis.

151 See paras 45–49 of the Explanatory Note to the Standby Convention (available at www.uncitral.org).

152 The British Insurance and Investment Brokers' Association provide information on credit insurance. Visit www.biba.org for further information.

153 Visit www.ecgd.gov.uk for further information about this organisation. They also provide other services – such as providing guarantees for loans to foreign buyers wishing to purchase from the United Kingdom.

154 The seller might disclose or not disclose the factoring arrangement to the buyer. The former is normally termed disclosed factoring, and the latter undisclosed factoring. Assignment in the event of disclosed factoring is a legal assignment and subject to the Law of Property Act 1925 (s 136), and in the latter equitable assignment.

155 Where the seller sends goods that do not conform to the contract description, the factor will be able to claim the monies back from the seller even though the factoring was on a without-recourse basis.

156 For further information on this, see www.factors.org.uk.

factoring' whereby he undertakes all credit management and collection work – that is, takes on the responsibility of the sales ledger.[157] The alternative to full-service factoring is invoice discounting where the operation of the sales ledger remains with the seller but cash is made available against invoices submitted by the seller.[158]

In 1988, an international convention called the UNIDROIT Convention on International Factoring was adopted in Ottawa (hereinafter 'Factoring Convention').[159] The convention's aim, as with other international conventions, is to harmonise the laws in respect of international factoring. It addresses factoring agreements arising from international contracts for the sale of goods. Internationality is determined, as in the Convention on the International Sale of Goods 1980,[160] on the basis of place of business being in different states (Art 2(1)). And a factoring contract is defined in Art 1(2) as concluded between the supplier and the factor pursuant to which:

(a) the supplier may or will assign to the factors receivables arising from contracts of sale of goods made between the supplier and his customers (debtors) other than those for the sale of goods[161] bought primarily for their personal, family or household use;

(b) the factor is to perform at least two of the following functions:

   – finance for the supplier, including loans and advance payments;

   – maintenance of accounts (ledgering) relating to receivables;

   – collection of receivables;

   – protection against default in payment by debtors;

(c) notice of the assignment of the receivables is to be given to debtors.

It must, however, be pointed out that the parties have the freedom to opt out of the application of the Factoring Convention to their contract (Art 3).

A question commonly posed is what happens if the sale contract contains a clause prohibiting assignment? Would this be effective? The Factoring Convention in Art 6(1) provides that the assignment of a receivable by the supplier shall be effective notwithstanding a clause prohibiting assignment. However, this does not override any obligation of good faith that the supplier has to the debtor or any liability that the supplier has to the debtor in respect of an assignment made in breach of the terms of the contract of sale of goods according to Art 6(3).

---

157 Factoring is widely used in the UK. Visit www.factorscan.co.uk for details on the factored volume in the UK, both domestic and international.

158 See Salinger, *Factoring: The Law and Practice of Invoice Finance*, 1999, Sweet & Maxwell for a full and excellent account of factoring.

159 It came into force on 1 May 1995. The text of this convention can be found on www.unidroit.org. It is also reproduced in Carr and Kidner, *International Trade Law Statutes and Conventions*, 5th edn, 2008, Routledge-Cavendish. See also Goode, 'Conclusion of the leasing and factoring conventions, Pt 2' [1988] JBL 510.

160 See Chapter 2 for further on this convention. The Factoring Convention was intended to supplement the Vienna Convention. See also Ferrari, 'General principles and international uniform commercial law conventions: a study of the 1980 Vienna Sales Convention and the 1988 UNIDROIT Conventions' (1997) 2(3) Uniform LR 293; Ferrari, 'International factoring and leasing and UNIDROIT Principles' (1999) 19(3) European Journal of Law Reform 217; Sommer, 'Factoring, international factoring networks and the FCI Code of International Factoring Customs' [1998] Uniform LR 685; Alexander, 'Towards unification and predictability: the International Factoring Convention' [1989] Columbia Journal of Transnational Law 589. Also visit www.unidroit.org which provides a useful bibliography of useful articles on this the Factoring Convention.

161 Goods include services and supply of services (Art 1(3)).

More recently, the UNCITRAL has adopted a new convention[162] entitled United Nations Convention on the Assignment of Receivables in International Trade (hereinafter 'Receivables Convention') which is wider in ambit than the Factoring Convention since it is not restricted to factoring agreements. According to Art 45, five states have to ratify, accede, approve or accept the Receivables Convention for it to come into force.[163]

The Receivables Convention is intended to create certainty and transparency whilst taking into account the interests of debtors. The Receivables Convention applies to assignments of international receivables and to international assignments of receivables if the assignor at the time of the conclusion of the contract is located in a contracting state (Art 1(1)(a)).[164] Internationality is established on the basis of the location of the debtor and the assignor. According to Art 3, 'a receivable is international if, at the time of the conclusion of the original contract, the assignor and the debtor are located in different states; and an assignment is international if at the time of conclusion of the contract of assignment the assignor and the assignee are located in different states'. Combining Arts 1 and 3, it seems that where a receivable is international it will attract the application of the Receivables Convention even if the assignment is domestic. Equally, where the receivable is domestic it will attract the application of the Receivables Convention if the assignment is international.[165]

The meanings of 'assignment' and 'receivables' can be gathered from Art 2(1). Assignment is 'the transfer from one person ("assignor") to another person ("assignee") of all or part of an undivided interest in the assignor's contractual right to payment of a monetary sum ("receivable") from a third person ("the debtor"). The creation of rights in receivables as security for indebtedness or other obligation is deemed to be a transfer'. Given the wide definition, it is clear that the Receivables Convention will apply to factoring. This is also endorsed by UNCITRAL's commentary on the draft convention[166] on receivables.[167]

The Receivables Convention appears comprehensive in addressing a number of issues relating to assignment such as notification to debtor (Art 13), debtor protection (Arts 15–20), and the law applicable to competing claims (Art 22) and priority (Art 30). It also provides alternative models of priority rules in the Annex for the contracting state to adopt. In the absence of adopting one of the suggested models, the national law will be relevant for deciding priority in relation to the receivables that

---

162 Adopted on 12 December 2001. The text of this convention can be found on www.uncitral.org.

163 So far, Luxembourg, Madagascar and the US have signed this convention. Liberia has acceded to the Convention.

164 Note that subsequent assignment will also come within the ambit of the Receivables Convention provided any of the prior assignment in respect of the same receivable attracts the application of the convention (see Art (1)(1)(b)).

165 See UN Doc A/CN 9/489, para 15; available at www.uncitral.org.

166 The wording of Art 2(1) in the adopted Receivables Convention is the same as that of the draft convention.

167 See para 7 (UN Doc A/CN 9/489). Also note that Art 4 excludes the application of the Receivable Convention to an individual for his or her personal, family or household purposes. For further on the draft conventions, see Bazinas, 'Lowering the cost of credit: the promise in the future UNCITRAL Convention on Assignment of Receivables in International Trade' (2001) 9 Tulane Journal of International and Comparative Law 259.

have been assigned.[168] However, the Receivables Convention does not affect all matters relating to an assignment – for instance, the validity of an assignment agreement.[169] This will be determined according to the applicable law.

The Receivables Convention is equally applicable to another risk-minimising practice that is commonly found in the financing of international sale of goods known as 'forfaiting'.[170] In a forfaiting arrangement, the forfaiter purchases bills of exchange which evidences the buyer's obligation without recourse to the seller (the exporter). However, the forfaiter will require security from a bank which is normally given, after the bill of exchange has been accepted, in the form of an *aval* [171] (a signature) on the back of the bill of exchange. The avaliser (that is, the bank) backs the bill of exchange, thus assuring payment on the bill of exchange.[172]

Given that only five states need to take action for the Receivables Convention to come into force, there is a high likelihood for it to come into force. This of course raises the all-important issue of its effect on the Factoring Convention. Article 38(1) of the Receivables Convention addresses the issue of conflict with other international agreements by stating that the 'convention does not prevail over any international agreement that has already been or may be entered into and that specifically governs a transaction otherwise governed by this convention'. However, there is a proviso to Art 38(1) which is important from the Factoring Convention perspective. Article 38(2) provides that 'notwithstanding para 1 . . . this convention prevails over the UNID-ROIT Convention on International Factoring ("the Ottawa Convention"). To the extent that this convention does not apply to the rights and obligations of a debtor, it does not preclude the application of the Ottawa Convention with respect to the rights and obligations of that debtor'. Of course, this is in the event of the factoring agreement coming within the ambit of the Receivables Convention.

CONCLUSION

Letters of credit are a useful payment mechanism in international trade and are extremely popular and rightly deserve to be called 'the life blood of international commerce'. However, in certain circumstances, such as fraud and insolvency of the bank, the documentary credit method may not provide absolute assurance to the

---

168 For a fuller account of the framework of the Receivables Convention, see Sigman and Smith, 'Toward facilitating cross-border secured financing and securitization: an analysis of the United Nations Convention on the Assignment of Receivables in International Trade' (2002) 57 Business Lawyer 727.

169 See UN Doc A/CN 9/489, para 25.

170 See UN Doc A/CN 9/489, para 8.

171 Normally, the phrase '*bon pour aval*' is used. The United Nations Convention on International Bills of Exchange and International Promissory Notes 1988 addresses the issue of guaranteeing payment of payment instruments in its Art 46. See also Arts 30–32 of the Convention Providing a Uniform Law for Bills of Exchange and Promissory Notes, Geneva 1930. This convention is reproduced in Carr and Kidner, *International Trade Law Statutes and Conventions*, 5th edn, 2008, Routledge-Cavendish. The framework embodied in this convention is often referred to as the Geneva system and is followed in most civil law countries such as France and Switzerland.

172 No special provision in the Bills of Exchange Act 1882, though *avals* are recognised in the United Kingdom. *See G&H Montage GmBH v Irvani* [1988] 1 Lloyd's Rep 460; [1990] 1 WLR 667. See also *Gerald MacDonald and Co v Nash and Co* [1924] AC 625; *Steele v M'Kinlay* (1880) 5 App Cas 754.

seller that he will get paid. It is possible for him to increase his protection through other mechanisms such as performance guarantees and factoring, dealt with in the last two sections of this chapter. The law in relation to the variety of protective mechanisms available have been harmonised to some extent through rules formulated by the ICC and international conventions,[173] thus imparting some degree of certainty.

FURTHER READING

Arkins, 'Snow white v frost white: the cold war in banking law' (2000) 15 Journal of International Banking Law 30.

Arora, 'The legal position of banks in performance bond cases' [1981] LMCLQ 264.

Arora, 'The dilemma of an issuing bank: to accept or reject documents under a letter of credit' [1984] LMCLQ 81.

Bennett, 'Bank-to-bank reimbursements under documentary credits: the Uniform Rules' [1998] LMCLQ 114.

Bennett, 'Performance bonds and the principle of autonomy' [1994] JBL 574.

Bennett, 'Documentary credits: a reasonable time for what?' [1997] LMCLQ 169.

Bennett, 'Strict compliance under UCP 500' [1997] LMCLQ 7.

Bennett, 'Original sins under the UCP' [2001] LMCLQ 88.

Buckley, 'Potential pitfalls with letters of credit' (1996) 70 ALJ 217.

Chatterjee, 'Letters of credit transactions and discrepant documents: an analysis of the judicial guidelines developed by the English courts' (1996) 12 Journal of International Banking Law 510.

Creed, 'The governing law of letter of credit transactions' (2001) 16 Journal of International Banking Law 41.

Davidson, 'The evolution of letters of credit transactions' [1995] Butterworths Journal of International Banking and Financial Law 128.

Dolan, 'Standby letters of credit and fraud' [1985] Cardozo LR 1.

Dolan, 'Strict compliance with letters of credit: striking a fair balance' [1985] Banking LJ 18.

Ellinger, 'The tender of fraudulent documents under documentary letters of credit' (1965) 7(1) Malaya LR 24.

Ellinger, 'Documentary credits and fraudulent documents', in Kee and Chan (eds), *Current Problems of International Trade Financing*, 2nd edn, 1990, National University of Singapore.

Ellinger, 'The uniform customs and practice for documentary credits – the 1993 revision' [1994] LMCLQ 377.

Gao, *The Fraud Rule in Letters of Credit: A Comparative Study*, 2002, Kluwer.

---

173 It must, however, be remembered that not all of the conventions are in force.

Goode, 'The new ICC Uniform Rules for demand guarantees' [1992] LMCLQ 190.

Goode, 'Abstract payment undertakings and the rules of international chamber of commerce' (1995) 35 St Louis ULJ 725.

Goode, *Commercial Law*, 3rd edn, 2004, Butterworths.

Guest, *Chalmers and Guest on Bills of Exchange, Cheques and Promissory Notes*, 16th edn, 2005, Sweet & Maxwell.

International Chamber of Commerce, *Commercial Crime Bureau, Special Report: Prime Bank Instrument Frauds*, 1994, ICC Commercial Crime Bureau.

Jack, *Documentary Credits*, 2009 (new publication expected)

Kee, 'The fraud rule in letters of credit transactions', in Kee and Chan (eds), *Current Problems of International Trade Financing*, 2nd edn, 1990, National University of Singapore.

King, *Gutteridge and Megrah's, Law of Banker's Commercial Credits*, 2001, Europa.

Kozolchyk, 'Bank guarantees and letters of credit: time for a return to the fold' (1989) 11 University of Pennsylvania Journal of International Business Law 1.

Kozolchyk, 'Strict compliance the reasonable document checker' (1990) 56 Brooklyn LR 48.

Kozolchyk, 'The paperless letter of credit and related documents of title' (1992) 55 Law and Contemporary Problems 39.

Maduegbuna, 'The effects of electronic banking techniques on the use of paper based payment mechanisms in international trade' [1994] JBL 338.

Mann, *The Legal Aspect of Money*, 5th edn, 1997, Clarendon.

McGuinness, *The Law of Guarantee: A Treatise on Guarantee, Indemnity and the Standby Letter of Credit*, 1996, Carswell.

Ortego and Krinick, 'Letters of credit: benefits and drawbacks of the independence principle' [1998] 115 Banking LJ 487.

Postan, 'Credit in medieval trade' (1927) 1 Economic History Review 234.

Usher, 'The origin of the bill of exchange' (1914) 22 Journal of Political Economy 566.

Wunnicke Wunnicke & Taylor *Standby and Commercial Letters of Credit*, (Looseleaf) Last update 2008, Wolters Kluwer.

PART V

DISPUTE RESOLUTION

OVERVIEW

It is inevitable that the many contractual relationships between seller and buyer, seller and issuing bank, buyer and issuing bank, and seller and shipowner that arise in the course of an international sales transaction will become sources of dispute. At some stage, the parties need to decide on the means of resolving the dispute. Should they go to the courts – the mechanism provided by the state – to settle the issue? Or should they look to other methods, such as arbitration or conciliation? The decision is one to be made in the light of the advantages and disadvantages of the different methods, their suitability for the particular business relationship, and the legal, economic and commercial backgrounds of the parties to the dispute. Litigation operating around well-settled legal rules and principles, procedural rules, and the abundance of precedents is the obvious choice. Acrimony created during the course of litigation, however, may not suit parties intending to consolidate or maintain a long-term commercial relationship. In an international commercial context, uncertainties about procedural rules and substantive laws of different states may also make it unattractive.

Unification of law relating to international sales and transportation of cargo has been achieved to a limited extent through international conventions such as the Vienna Convention, the Hague-Visby Rules, the Hamburg Rules, and rules such as the International Rules for the Interpretation of Trade Terms (INCOTERMS) and the Uniform Customs and Practice for Documentary Credits 500 (UCP), devised by international organisations. However, such harmonisation is piecemeal, since not all states have adopted the international conventions, or promote the use of standardised rules. Protection against nasty surprises may be sought by inserting clauses on jurisdiction (the forum for instituting proceedings) and choice of law (the law applicable to the contract; for example, English law or French law). But the insertion of choice of jurisdiction and choice of law clauses is not always effective in achieving the parties' wishes. It is possible that the forum might take the view that it is not the appropriate forum, or it may not apply the law chosen by the parties on grounds of public policy. In an uncertain climate, other forms of dispute resolution, such as arbitration, which impart a greater degree of control to the parties over procedural rules and legal principles – for example, law merchant (*lex mercatoria*) or equitable principles (*ex aequo et bono*), to be used for deciding the issue – may be attractive. The decision, at the end of the day, is a pragmatic one. It depends on the circumstances of the case, what the parties perceive as offering the best solution in the light of the merits and demerits of the different methods available, and which method best serves their needs.

The chapters in this Part deal with the different forms of dispute resolution: litigation, arbitration and mediation. Chapter 16 addresses the civil jurisdiction of the English courts, now governed primarily by EC Regulation 44/2001. Chapter 17 deals with the rules applicable by English courts for determining the substantive law applicable to a contract, now contained in EC Regulation 593/2008, which has replaced the Rome Convention 1980 and applies to contracts concluded after 17 December 2009. Chapter 18 considers the recognition in England of foreign judgments – both European judgments under Regulation 44/2001 and other judgments under the common law, the Administration of Justice Act 1920 and the Foreign Judgments (Reciprocal Enforcement) Act 1933. Lastly, Chapters 19 and 20 consider arbitration and mediation as alternative forms of dispute resolution.

Arbitration, as a form of dispute resolution, became popular after the Second World War. Chapter 19 considers the advantages and disadvantages of arbitration, and examines the various rules for international arbitration, the (English) Arbitration Act 1996 inspired by the United Nations Commission on International Trade Law (UNCITRAL)'s Model Law on Arbitration, and the recognition and enforcement of foreign arbitral awards under the New York Convention 1958.

The last decade of the 20th century saw the emergence of mediation as an effective medium for resolving commercial disputes. Chapter 20 examines some of its features, along with the associated issues of this new technique.

CHAPTER 16

CIVIL JURISDICTION

INTRODUCTION

The jurisdiction of the English courts to entertain civil proceedings is now governed primarily by EC Regulation 44/2001 on Jurisdiction and the Recognition and Enforcement of Judgments in Civil and Commercial Matters, which is commonly known as the Brussels I Regulation.[1] The Regulation entered into force on 1 March 2002 in 14 of the 15 states which were then EC member states (the exception being Denmark), on 1 May 2004 for the 10 states which joined the Community on the date, on 1 January 2007 for Bulgaria and Romania, and on 1 July 2007 for Denmark. The Regulation largely replaces the Brussels Convention of 27 September 1968 on Jurisdiction and the Enforcement of Judgments in Civil and Commercial Matters (as amended).[2] Although the Regulation deliberately departs from the Convention in a few important respects, much of the substantial case law of the European Court on the interpretation of the Convention remains applicable to the corresponding provisions of the Regulation.[3] The traditional English law applies only interstitially, where the Regulation remits jurisdiction to the law of the forum country. Such remission occurs, however, in most cases where the defendant is not domiciled in any EC member state (nor, in view of the Lugano Convention,[4] in Switzerland, Norway or Iceland).

The Regulation consists of a Preamble, followed by 76 Articles arranged in eight Chapters, and six Annexes.[5] The core is contained in Chapter II (Arts 2–31) on direct jurisdiction, and Chapter III (Arts 32–56) on the recognition and enforcement of judgments. Chapter II lays down the rules applicable by a court of a member state, when seised of an action on the merits, for the purpose of deciding its own jurisdiction to entertain the action. In order to strengthen the legal protection of persons established in the Community, it establishes a general rule that a defendant domiciled in a member state must be sued in that state, and harmonises the exceptional cases in which a defendant domiciled in one member state can be sued in another member state. Chapter III seeks to establish the 'free movement of judgments', by strictly limiting the grounds on which a judgment given in one member state can

---

1   [2001] OJ L12/1.

2   For the fifth and final version of the Brussels Convention, see [1998] OJ C27/1.

3   Guidance on the interpretation of the Regulation may also be drawn from the various reports on the Convention. See the Jenard Report [1979] OJ C59/1; the Schlosser Report [1979] OJ C59/71; the Evrigenis and Kerameus Report [1986] OJ C298/1; the Jenard and Möller Report [1990] OJ C189/57; and the Cruz, Real and Jenard Report [1990] OJ C189/35.

4   The Lugano Convention of 16 September 1988 on Jurisdiction and the Enforcement of Judgments in Civil and Commercial Matters [1988] OJ L3 19/9. This was designed in substance to extend the Brussels Convention to the EFTA countries. It continues to govern English jurisdiction where the defendant is domiciled in Switzerland, Norway or Iceland, and its provisions on exclusive jurisdiction, jurisdiction clauses and simultaneous actions continue to apply where they exclude English jurisdiction in favour of that of those countries; see Art 54B of the Lugano Convention. A revised Lugano Convention, designed to reflect the Brussels I Regulation, was signed on behalf of the European Community on 30 October 2007, but has not yet entered into force; see EC Council Decision 2007/712, [2007] OJ L339/1.

5   The Annexes contain lists of national legislation, rules, courts and procedures, and standard forms for use in connection with enforcement.

be refused recognition or enforcement in another member state, and establishing a swift procedure for obtaining a declaration of enforceability or a decision establishing recognition. In view of the harmonisation of direct jurisdiction achieved by Chapter II, a court in which recognition or enforcement is sought under Chapter III is prevented in most cases from reviewing the jurisdiction of the original court.

Chapter I (Art 1) defines the material scope of the Regulation. It applies to civil or commercial matters, as distinct from criminal, revenue, customs, administrative or other public matters.[6] But certain matters are excluded, such as individual status, matrimonial property (as distinct from familial maintenance),[7] succession on death,[8] insolvent liquidation[9] and arbitration.[10]

In Chapter II, the basic rules on the existence of direct jurisdiction are specified by Arts 2–4. Where the defendant is domiciled in a member state, Art 2 confers jurisdiction over actions against him on the courts of that state, and Art 3 deprives the courts of the other member states of jurisdiction to entertain actions against him. Where the defendant is not domiciled in any of the member states, the jurisdiction of the courts of each member state is referred to the law of that state. These basic rules are subject to exceptions defined by the remaining provisions of Chapter II.

Articles 5 and 6 derogate from Art 3 by specifying a number of cases in which they confer jurisdiction on courts of one member state over a defendant domiciled in another member state. In such a case, the plaintiff has the choice of suing at the

---

6   Thus the Regulation does not apply to a dispute between a private person and a public authority which arises out of acts done by the public authority in the exercise of its powers as such, nor where the relevant legal relationship between a public authority and a private person involves the exercise by the state of powers going beyond those existing under the rules applicable to relations between private persons. See Case 29/76: *LTU v Eurocontrol* [1976] ECR 1541; Case 814/79: *Netherlands v Rüffer* [1980] ECR 3807; Case C-172/91: *Sonntag v Waidmann* [1993] ECR I-1963; Case C-167/00: *VKI v Henkel* [2002] ECR I-8111; Case C-271/00: *Gemeente Steenbergen v Baten* [2002] ECR I-10489; Case C-266/01: *Tiard* [2003] ECR I-4867; Case C-433/01: *Freistaat Bayern v Blijdenstein* [2004] ECR I-981; Case C-265/02: *Frahuil v Assitalia* [2004] ECR I-1543; Case C-292/05: *Lechouritou v Germany* [2007] ECR I-1519; and *Re Senator Hanseatische Verwaltungsgesellschaft* [1996] 2 BCLC 562 (Scott V-C), affirmed on other issues [1996] 4 All ER 933 (CA). Cf *QRS v Frandsen* [1999] 3 All ER 289 (CA), a decision now discredited by subsequent rulings of the European Court.

7   See Case 143/78: *De Cavel v De Cavel (No 1)* [1979] ECR 1055; Case 120/79: *De Cavel v De Cavel (No 2)* [1980] ECR 731; Case 25/81: *CHW v GJH* [1982] ECR 1189; Case 143/78: *Van den Boogaard v Laumen* [1979] ECR 1055; *Fournier v Fournier* [1998] 2 FLR 990 (CA); *Cartwright v Cartwright* [2002] 2 FLR 610 (CA); *Prazic v Prazic* [2006] 2 FLR 1128 (CA); *Moore v Moore* [2007] EWCA Civ 361 (CA); and *DT v FL* [2007] ILPr 56 (Irish High Court). See also EC Regulation 2201/2003 concerning Jurisdiction and the Recognition and Enforcement of Judgments in Matrimonial Matters and the Matters of Parental Responsibility [2003] OJ L338/1; and EC Regulation 4/2009 on Jurisdiction, Applicable Law, Recognition and Enforcement of Decisions and Co-operation in Matters relating to Maintenance Obligations [2009] OJ L7/1. Regulation 4/2009 is designed to replace the Brussels I Regulation in relation to maintenance. It is expected to become applicable on 18 June 2011.

8   See *Re Hayward* [1997] Ch 45.

9   See Case 133/78: *Gourdain v Nadler* [1979] ECR 733; *Ashurst v Pollard* [2001] Ch 595 (CA); *Re Leyland DAF Ltd* [1994] 2 BCLC 106 (CA); *Re Hayward* [1997] Ch 45; *QRS v Frandsen* [1999] 3 All ER 289 (CA); *UBS v Omni Holding* [2000] 1 WLR 916; *Re Cover Europe Ltd* [2002] BPIR 931; *Grupo Torras v Al-Sabah* [1995] 1 Lloyd's Rep 374 (Mance J), affirmed without consideration of the insolvency aspect, [1996] 1 Lloyd's Rep 7 (CA); and Case C-267/97: *Coursier v Fortis Bank* [1999] ECR I-2543. See also EC Regulation 1346/2000 on Insolvency Proceedings [2000] OJ L160/1.

10 See Case C-190/89: *Marc Rich v Impianti* [1991] ECR I-3855; Case C-391/95: *Van Uden v Deco-Line* [1998] ECR I-7091; Case C-185/07: *Allianz v West Tankers*, 10 February 2009; *The Ivan Zagubanski* [2002] 1 Lloyd's Rep 106; and *The Hari Bhum* [2004] 1 Lloyd's Rep 206. See also Case C-116/02: *Gasser v MISAT* [2003] ECR I-14693; and Case C-159/02: *Turner v Grovit* [2004] ECR I-3565.

defendant's domicile in accordance with Art 2, or in another member state in accordance with Arts 5 or 6. The bases of jurisdiction used by Art 5 involve a connection between the cause of action and the territory of the court on which jurisdiction is conferred – for example, as the place of performance of a contractual obligation; as the place where a tortious event occurred; or as the location of a secondary establishment involved. The bases used by Art 6 involve a connection between the claim and another claim pending in the same court. It deals with co-defendants, third party proceedings and counterclaims. Article 7 deals with admiralty limitation actions. None of these provisions applies where the defendant is not domiciled in any of the member states.

Articles 8–21 lay down particular jurisdictional rules for insurance, consumer and employment contracts. They are based on the assumption that the policyholder, consumer or employee is in a weaker bargaining position than the insurer, supplier or employer, and thus merits special protection. Accordingly, a policyholder, consumer or employee is given a choice of places at which to sue, while actions by the insurer, supplier or employer must be brought at the defendant's domicile, and contrary agreements, concluded before the dispute has arisen, are rendered invalid. But all these provisions apply only where the defendant is domiciled in a member state, or where the defendant insurer, supplier or employer has a secondary establishment in a member state and the dispute has arisen from the operations of that establishment.

Article 22 provides for exclusive jurisdiction over certain disputes on account of their subject matter. Thus exclusive jurisdiction over disputes concerning proprietary rights[11] to or tenancies[12] of land is conferred on the courts of the member state in which the land is situated; over certain disputes governed by company law, on the courts of the corporate seat;[13] over disputes concerning the validity of entries in public registers, on the courts of the country where the register is kept;[14] over disputes concerning the registration or validity of patents, trade marks, designs, or similar registrable rights, on the courts of the country of registration;[15] and over proceedings

---

11 See Case 115/88: *Reichert v Dresdner Bank (No 1)* [1990] ECR I-27; Case C-294/92: *Webb v Webb* [1994] ECR I-1717; Case C-292/93: *Lieber v Goebel* [1994] ECR I-2535; Case C-518/99: *Gaillard v Chekili* [2001] ECR I-2771; Case C-343/04: *Land Oberösterreich v ČEZ* [2006] ECR I-4557; *Lightning v Lightning Electrical Contractors* (1998) unreported, 23 April (CA); *Ashurst v Pollard* [2001] Ch 595 (CA); *Re Hayward* [1997] Ch 45; *Union de Credit Pour Le Batiment*, 22 January 1999 (CA); *Griggs v Evans* [2004] EWHC 1088 (Ch); and *Prazic v Prazic* [2006] 2 FLR 1128 (CA).

12 See Case 73/77: *Sanders v Van der Putte* [1977] ECR 2383; Case 241/83: *Rösler v Rottwinkel* [1985] ECR 99; Case C-280/90: *Hacker v Euro-Relais* [1992] ECR I-1111; Case C-8/98: *Dansommer v Götz* [2000] ECR I-393; Case 158/87: *Scherrens v Maenhout* [1988] ECR 3791; Case C-73/04: *Klein v Rhodos Management* [2005] ECR I-8667; and *Jarrett v Barclays Bank* [1997] 2 All ER 484 (CA).

13 See Case 34/82: *Peters v ZNAV* [1983] ECR 987; Case C-214/89: *Powell Duffryn v Petereit* [1992] ECR I-1745; Case C-372/07: *Hassett v The Medical Defence Union*, 2 October 2008; *Grupo Torras v Al-Sabah* [1996] 1 Lloyd's Rep 7 (CA); and *Speed Investments v Formula One Holdings* [2005] 1 BCLC 455 (CA).

14 See *Re Hayward* [1997] Ch 45.

15 See Case 288/82: *Duijnstee v Goderbauer* [1983] ECR 3663; Case C-539/03: *Roche Nederland v Primus* [2006] ECR I-6535; Case C-4/03: *GAT v Lamellen* [2006] ECR I-6509; *Napp Laboratories v Pfizer* [1993] FSR 150; *Coin Controls v Suzo International* [1997] 3 All ER 45; *Fort Dodge v Akzo* [1998] FSR 222 (CA); *Prudential Assurance Co Ltd v Prudential Insurance Co of America* [2003] 1 WLR 2295 (CA); and *Griggs v Evans* [2004] EWHC 1088 (Ch). Certain EC regulations which create Community-wide intellectual property rights (Regulation 40/94 on Community Trade Marks [1994] OJ L11/1; Regulation 2100/94 on Community Plant Variety Rights [1994] OJ L227/1; and Regulation 6/2002 on Community Designs [2002] OJ L3/1) contain provisions on jurisdiction which override Regulation 44/2001. On Regulation 40/94, see *Prudential Assurance Co Ltd v Prudential Insurance Co of America* [2003] 1 WLR 2295 (CA).

concerned with the enforcement of judgments, on the courts of the country of enforcement.[16] This provision is overriding: it applies regardless of domicile, agreement or appearance; and even where the defendant is not domiciled in any of the member states.

Articles 23 and 24 provide for submission by agreement or appearance. Article 23 enables parties by an express and sufficiently formal agreement to choose a court of a member state which will have (usually exclusive) jurisdiction to determine disputes concerning a particular legal relationship. This freedom is restricted by Arts 13–14, 17 and 21 in relation to insurance, consumer and employment contracts, and by Art 22 in relation to disputes which are subject to exclusive jurisdiction on account of their subject matter. By Art 24, a court before which the defendant enters an appearance without contesting its jurisdiction becomes competent, unless the dispute falls within Art 22.

The foregoing provisions of Chapter II define the connecting factors on which the existence of jurisdiction depends. They are followed by a group of provisions concerned with the exercise of jurisdiction. Articles 25 and 26(1) require a court to decline jurisdiction of its own motion where it is rendered incompetent by Art 3 or 22. Article 26(2)–(4) requires a court to stay its proceedings until appropriate steps have been taken to notify a defendant who is domiciled in another member state. Articles 27–30 deal with the situation where similar or related proceedings are pending in courts of different member states. They require or permit the court subsequently seised to decline jurisdiction or stay its proceedings in favour of the court first seised. Lastly, Art 31 enables a court to grant provisional relief even if it lacks jurisdiction to determine the substance of the dispute.

Chapter III provides for the recognition and enforcement in each member state of judgments given by the courts of the other member states. The obligation to recognise is subject to very limited exceptions relating to public policy, insufficient service or irreconcilability with another judgment. Only in exceptional cases is the court addressed permitted to review the jurisdiction of the original court, and it is never allowed to review the substance or merits of the judgment. A judgment which qualifies for recognition also qualifies for enforcement, provided that it is enforceable in the original country. The procedure for obtaining a declaration of enforceability is elaborated in detail, and the same procedure may be used to obtain a decision establishing recognition, though recognition may in any event be invoked incidentally whenever it is relevant. Chapter IV (Arts 57–58) provides for the enforcement in a member state of authentic instruments drawn up or registered, and court settlements approved, in other member states.

Chapter V (Arts 59–65) lays down rules for the determination of domicile for the purpose of the Regulation. Whether an individual is domiciled in a member state is governed by the law of that state, but corporate domicile is given a substantive definition referring alternatively to the registered office, actual headquarters or principal place of business. Chapter V of the Regulation also contains a miscellany of minor supplementary or exceptional provisions. Chapter VI (Art 66) contains transitional provisions. Chapter VII (Arts 67–72) deals with the relationship between the

---

16 See Case 220/84: *AS-Autoteile Service v Mahle* [1985] ECR 2267; and Case C-261/90: *Reichert v Dresdner Bank (No 2)* [1992] ECR I-2149. Article 22(5) prevents an English court from enforcing a judgment by garnishment of a debt situated in another member state; see *Kuwait Oil Tanker Co v Qabazard* [2004] 1 AC 300.

Regulation and international conventions[17] or other EC legislation.[18] Chapter VIII (Arts 73–76) deals with matters such as entry into force, amendment and texts.

THE DEFENDANT'S DOMICILE

The principal connecting factor used by Chapter II of Regulation 44/2001 is the defendant's domicile at the institution of the proceedings. The basic rules on direct jurisdiction are laid down by Arts 2–4. Where the defendant is domiciled in a member state, Art 2 confers jurisdiction on the courts of that state, and Art 3 deprives the courts of the other member states of jurisdiction. Where the defendant is not domiciled in any member state, Art 4 remits the jurisdiction of the courts of each member state to the law of that state. These basic rules are subject to the exceptions specified in the remaining provisions of Chapter II.

The rationale of the general rule in favour of the defendant's domicile was considered in *Handte v TMCS*,[19] where the European Court explained that the rule reflects the purpose of strengthening the legal protection of persons established within the Community, and rests on an assumption that normally it is in the courts of his domicile that a defendant can most easily conduct his defence. Moreover, as the European Court ruled in *Group Josi v UGIC*,[20] the claimant's domicile is immaterial except where a provision of the Regulation explicitly refers to it (as do certain provisions on familial maintenance, insurance and consumer contracts). Although the Regulation is not explicit on the point, it is settled that the crucial date for determining the defendant's domicile is that of the institution of the proceedings – in England the issue (rather than the service) of the claim form.[21]

The effect of Art 2 of the Regulation (taken with supplementary United Kingdom legislation)[22] is, with minor exceptions, to confer jurisdiction on the English courts whenever the defendant is domiciled in England.[23] By Art 59(1) of the Regulation, in order to determine whether an individual is domiciled in the forum state, the court

---

17 On specialised conventions, see Art 71 of the Regulation. These include the Brussels Convention on Certain Rules concerning Civil Jurisdiction in Matters of Collision (1952); the Brussels Convention relating to the Arrest of Seagoing Ships (1952); and the Geneva Convention on Carriage by Road (1956)). See also Case C-406/92: *The Maciej Rataj* [1994] ECR I-5439; and *Merzario v Leitner* [2001] 1 Lloyd's Rep 490 (CA).

18 See Art 67 of the Regulation. Other relevant legislation includes Art 6 of Directive 96/71 on the Posting of Workers in the Framework of the Provision of Services [1997] OJ L18/1; and Regulation 40/94 on the Community Trade Mark [1994] OJ L11/1.

19 Case C-26/91: [1992] ECR I-3967.

20 Case C-412/98: [2000] ECR I-5925.

21 See *Canada Trust v Stolzenberg (No 2)* [2002] 1 AC 1; *Petrotrade v Smith* [1998] 2 All ER 346; and *Grupo Torras v Al-Sabah* [1995] 1 Lloyd's Rep 374 (Mance J).

22 See s 16 and Sched 4 to the Civil Jurisdiction and Judgments Act 1982 (hereinafter the '1982 Act'), as amended by the Civil Jurisdiction and Judgments Order 2001 (SI 2001/3929). These provisions allocate jurisdiction between the courts for the various parts of the United Kingdom (England and Wales; Scotland; Northern Ireland; and Gibraltar) where the defendant is domiciled in the United Kingdom.

23 The English courts also have a discretionary jurisdiction over a defendant individual who is not domiciled in any EC member state or Lugano Convention country but who is present in England at the time of service, however brief his visit, and even if the dispute has no other connection with England. See Part 6 of the Civil Procedure Rules (CPR) 1998; *Maharanee of Baroda v Wildenstein* [1972] 2 QB 283 (CA); *Barclays Bank of Swaziland v Hahn* [1989] 1 WLR 506 (HL); and *Chellaram v Chellaram (No 2)* [2002] 3 All ER 17 (Lawrence Collins J).

applies its own law.[24] By para 9 of Sched 1 to the Civil Jurisdiction and Judgments Order 2001, for this purpose an individual is domiciled in England if he is resident in England and the nature and circumstances of his residence indicate that he has a substantial connection with England (or with the United Kingdom as a whole but not with any particular part); and there is a rebuttable presumption that an individual who has been resident in England for the last three months or more has a substantial connection therewith.

Perhaps surprisingly, these provisions seem to have created little difficulty. In *Bank of Dubai v Abbas*,[25] Saville LJ emphasised that for this purpose 'residence' requires a settled or usual place of abode with a substantial degree of permanence or continuity, and that the presumption of substantial connection from three months' residence provides no guidance as to whether the person has become resident. Moreover the significance of the existing duration of a person's stay in England varies according to the circumstances of the case. Thus a person who comes to England to retire and who buys a house for that purpose and moves into it, selling all his foreign possessions and cutting all his foreign ties, probably becomes resident here immediately; but in other circumstances it may be necessary to balance the length of time that the person has been here with his connections abroad. Somewhat similarly, Sheriff Palmer in *Daniel v Foster*[26] and Mance J in *Grupo Torras v Al-Sabah*[27] equated 'residence' in the present context with 'ordinary residence', as defined by Lord Scarman in *Shah v Barnet London Borough Council*.[28] Thus an individual can have more than one domicile at a given time; and it is enough to make a person domiciled in a part of the United Kingdom that he has a place of business or a dwelling place therein which he frequently visits (perhaps for short periods) on a continuing basis, even though his main residence is in another part of the United Kingdom or abroad. But one who visits England for a few days, during which he is arrested and then released on bail on conditions preventing his leaving the country, and who then remains in England for the next few weeks because he is so prevented from leaving, will not have acquired an English domicile.[29] Nor is a person domiciled in England if he spends the majority of his time in Russia, even though he owns a house in England which he uses for infrequent, intermittent and fleeting visits, amounting to fewer than 30 nights each year.[30]

By Art 60(1) of the Regulation, a company or other legal person, or association of natural or legal persons, is domiciled at the place where it has any of the following connections: (a) its statutory seat; or (b) its central administration; or (c) its principal place of business. Article 60(2) adds that, for British and Irish purposes, 'statutory seat' means the registered office; or, where there is no such office anywhere, the place of incorporation; or, where there is no such place anywhere, the place under the law of which the formation took place.

---

24 By Art 59(2), where an individual is not domiciled in the forum state, then, in order to determine whether he is domiciled in another member state, the court must apply the law of that other member state. See *Haji-Ioannou v Frangos* [1999] 2 Lloyd's Rep 337 (CA), applying Art 51 of the Greek Civil Code, whereby for business purposes an individual is domiciled at his place of business.
25 [1997] ILPr 308 (CA).
26 [1989] SCLR 378.
27 [1995] 1 Lloyd's Rep 374.
28 [1983] 2 AC 309.
29 See *Petrotrade v Smith* [1998] 2 All ER 346.
30 See *Cherney v Deripaska* [2007] 2 All ER (Comm) 785.

The concept of central administration was clarified by the Court of Appeal in *The Rewia*,[31] which involved a one-ship company which was incorporated and had its registered office in Liberia, but whose directors were resident in Germany and held their meetings there, and whose ship was managed by agents in Hong Kong. The Court of Appeal held that the company was domiciled for the purposes of the Brussels Convention both in Liberia, as the place of its incorporation and registered office, and in Germany, as the place of its central management and control. Although in practice the company's agents in Hong Kong had a free hand in the day-to-day management of the vessel, their activities were subject to the control of the directors in Hamburg, which was the centre from which instructions were given when necessary and where ultimate control was exercised. Although there may be considerable overlap between the concepts of central administration and principal place of business,[32] it seems likely that under the Regulation the company would also be regarded as domiciled in Hong Kong, as its principal place of business, since its commercial activities were mainly carried out there. In any event it is clear that a merely electronic presence in the form of a web-server does not constitute a domicile.[33]

The rule conferring jurisdiction over an English defendant on the English courts is subject to very limited exceptions. It applies even if the dispute has no other connection with England. Three exceptions are specified by the Regulation:

(a) where, by reason of its subject matter (such as proprietary rights in land), the dispute falls within the exclusive jurisdiction of the courts of another member state (such as the state in which the land is situated) under Art 22;

(b) where an agreement between the parties confers exclusive jurisdiction on a designated court of another member state under Art 23; and

(c) where a simultaneously pending proceeding in a court of another member state has priority under Arts 27–30.[34]

Moreover, the doctrine of reflex effect, endorsed by the European Court in *Coreck Maritime v Handelsveem*,[35] enables each member state to extend these exceptions so as to respect similar connections with a non-member state.

But there is no general exception permitting the English courts to continue to invoke the traditional English doctrine of *forum non conveniens* (sometimes known as the *Spiliada* doctrine),[36] so as to arm themselves with a discretion to decline jurisdiction over an English defendant in favour of a court of a non-member state whenever

31 [1991] 2 Lloyd's Rep 325.

32 See also *King v Crown Energy* [2003] EWHC 163 (Comm); and *Royal & Sun Alliance Insurance v MK Digital* [2006] 2 Lloyd's Rep 110 (CA).

33 See also Directive 2000/31 on Electronic Commerce [2000] OJ L178/1.

34 There are three similar exceptions in favour of the courts of Switzerland, Norway and Iceland under Arts 16, 17 and 21–23 of the Lugano Convention. There is also an exception, similar to the first exception, in favour of the courts of another part of the United Kingdom under r 11 of Sched 4 to the 1982 Act.

35 Case C-387/98: [2000] ECR I-9337, at para 19, citing the Schlosser Report [1979] OJ C59/71, at para 176. Cf *Ace Insurance v Zurich Insurance*, [2001] 1 Lloyd's Rep 618 (CA). See also *Berisford v New Hampshire Insurance Co* [1990] QB 631; *Arkwright v Bryanston* [1990] 2 QB 649; the decision of the French Court of Cassation in *Europa Carton v Cifal* (1978) unreported, 19 December; Droz, *Compétence Judiciaire et Effets des Jugements dans le Marché Commun*, 1972, at paras 165–68, 216–18, and 329–30; and Gaudemet-Tallon, *Les Conventions de Bruxelles et de Lugano*, 1996, Montchrestien, at paras 75, 84, 111 and 281.

36 See *The Spiliada* [1987] 1 AC 460.

they consider it to be a more appropriate or suitable forum for the trial of the action in the light of the interests of all the parties and the ends of justice. For, as the Schlosser Report emphasises, the Regulation is based on the principle, generally accepted in the laws of the Continental European countries, that a competent court, properly seised of an action, is bound to determine the substantive dispute.[37] Moreover, the other member states, whose courts are deprived of jurisdiction by the Regulation, are entitled to expect an English decision on the merits which their courts can recognise under Chapter III. Unfortunately, for well over a decade a perverse line of decisions of the English Court of Appeal, commencing with *Re Harrods (Buenos Aires) Ltd*,[38] strenuously denied this obvious reality. Eventually the matter was definitively resolved by the ruling of the European Court in *Owusu v Jackson*[39] that the Regulation precludes a court of a member state from declining the jurisdiction conferred on it by Art 2 on the ground that a court of a non-member state would be a more appropriate forum for the trial of the action, even if the jurisdiction of no other member state is in issue and the proceedings have no connection with any other member state. On the other hand, since Art 2 is indifferent to the allocation of jurisdiction between the courts for different parts of the member state in which the defendant is domiciled, it is clear that the English courts retain power to decline jurisdiction over an English defendant in favour of the Scottish, Northern Irish or Gibraltar courts.[40]

By Art 5(5) of the Regulation, the English courts have jurisdiction over a defendant who is domiciled in another member state but has a secondary establishment in England, as regards disputes arising out of the operations of the English establishment.[41] A secondary establishment has been defined by the European Court as an effective place of business, which has the appearance of a permanent extension of a parent body, has a management, and is materially equipped to negotiate business with third parties, so that the latter, although knowing that there will if necessary be a legal link with the parent body whose head office is abroad, do not have to deal directly with the parent body but may transact business at the extension.[42] Thus a merely electronic presence in the form of a web-server does not constitute an establishment;[43] in the case of a contract concluded electronically through the

---

37   [1979] OJ C59/71, paras 76–81. See also the decision of the French Court of Cassation in *Grimal v Ameliorair* (1997) unreported, 30 April; and Gaudemet-Tallon, *Les Conventions de Bruxelles et de Lugano*, at paras 66 and 75.

38   [1992] Ch 72. See also *The Po* [1991] 2 Lloyd's Rep 206; *The Nile Rhapsody* [1994] 1 Lloyd's Rep 382; *Nike v Parker* (1994) unreported, 31 October; *Connelly v RTZ* [1996] QB 361; *Sarrio v Kuwait Investment Authority* [1997] 1 Lloyd's Rep 113; *Lubbe v Cape plc (No 1)* [1999] ILPr 113 and *Lubbe v Cape plc (No 2)* [2000] 1 Lloyd's Rep 139; *Re Polly Peck International* [1998] 3 All ER 812; and *Ace Insurance v Zurich Insurance* [2001] 1 Lloyd's Rep 618. Two of these decisions were reversed by the House of Lords, on the ground that if the discretion existed, it should be exercised in favour of the claimant: see *Connelly v RTZ* [1997] 4 All ER 335, and *Lubbe v Cape plc* [2000] 1 WLR 1545. Cf *Milor v British Airways* [1996] 3 All ER 537 (CA), on the Warsaw Convention on carriage by air.

39   Case C-281/02, [2005] ECR I-1383.

40   See s 49 of the 1982 Act; *Cumming v Scottish Daily Record* [1995] EMLR 538; and *Lennon v Scottish Daily Record* [2004] EMLR 18.

41   The same connection creates jurisdiction where the defendant is domiciled in Switzerland, Norway, Iceland, Scotland, Northern Ireland or Gibraltar; see Art 5(5) of the Lugano Convention, and r 3(e) of Sched 4 to the 1982 Act (as amended).

42   See Case 33/78: *Somafer v Saar-Ferngas* [1978] ECR 2183; and Case C-439/93: *Lloyd's Register of Shipping v Campenon Bernard* [1995] ECR I-961.

43   See also Directive 2000/31 on Electronic Commerce [2000] OJ L178/1.

defendant's website, its relevant establishment will be its office from which the website is maintained. Moreover, an essential characteristic of a secondary establishment is that it must be subject to the direction and control of the parent body, so that an independently owned, exclusive distributor of a manufacturer's products is not a secondary establishment of the manufacturer.[44] Similarly, an independent commercial agent does not constitute a secondary establishment of an undertaking which he represents if he merely negotiates business, he is basically free to arrange his own work and decide what proportion of his time to devote to the interests of the undertaking represented, he cannot be prevented by that undertaking from also representing its competitors, and he merely transmits orders to the undertaking without being involved in either their terms or their execution.[45] On the other hand, one company within a corporate group will be regarded as a secondary establishment of another company in the same group if it acts as such by negotiating and concluding transactions in the name and on behalf of the other company, at least if the companies have similar names and a common management.[46] As regards operations, Art 5(5) extends to any contractual obligations entered into by the secondary establishment in the name of its parent body, regardless of where and by what establishment they are to be performed.[47] It also extends to claims in respect of tortious acts authorised by the secondary establishment, regardless of where they are committed.[48]

Where the defendant is not domiciled in any EC member state or Lugano Convention country but it has a secondary establishment in England, the English courts have jurisdiction even if the dispute has no connection with the English establishment,[49] but they may in discretion decline jurisdiction in favour of a court elsewhere.

SUBMISSION BY APPEARANCE

Article 24 of the Regulation[50] confers jurisdiction, additional to that derived from other provisions, on a court of a member state before which the defendant enters an appearance without contesting its jurisdiction, unless another court has exclusive jurisdiction by virtue of subject matter under Art 22. This applies regardless of the domiciles of the parties,[51] and even if the parties had previously concluded an agreement designating some other court as exclusively competent in accordance with Art 23.[52]

A defendant may, without submitting to the jurisdiction, simultaneously raise defences as to both jurisdiction and merits, provided that his challenge to the

---

44   See Case 14/76: *De Bloos v Bouyer* [1976] ECR 1497.
45   See Case 139/80: *Blanckaert and Willems v Trost* [1981] ECR 819. See also *per* Darmon AG in Case C-89/91: *Shearson Lehman Hutton v TVB* [1993] ECR I-139.
46   Case 218/86: *Schotte v Parfums Rothschild* [1987] ECR 4905. See also *Latchin v General Mediterranean Holidays* [2002] CLC 330 (Andrew Smith J).
47   See Case C-439/93: *Lloyd's Register of Shipping v Campenon Bernard* [1995] ECR I-961.
48   See *Anton Durbeck v Den Norske Bank* [2003] QB 1160 (CA).
49   See Art 4 of the Regulation; the Companies Act 1985 (as amended), ss 694A and 695; the Civil Procedure Rules 1998, Part 6; *Saab v Saudi American Bank* [1999] 1 WLR 1861 (CA); and *Sea Assets Ltd v PT Garuda Indonesia* [2000] 4 All ER 371.
50   See similarly Art 18 of the Lugano Convention, and r 13 of Sched 4 to the 1982 Act (as amended).
51   See Case C-412/98: *Group Josi v UGIC* [2000] ECR I-5925, at paras 44–45.
52   See Case 150/80: *Elefanten Schuh v Jacqmain* [1981] ECR 1671.

jurisdiction is made no later than the submissions which, under the procedural law of the court seised, are regarded as the first defence addressed to the court.[53] Moreover a defendant who enters an unqualified appearance accepts the jurisdiction of the court to entertain only the case which has been formulated against him by the plaintiff at that stage, and not some wider case which the claimant may subsequently try to advance.[54] But there will be submission by appearance if the defendant, after unsuccessfully contesting the jurisdiction up to the court of last resort, then proceeds to file a defence on the merits;[55] or if the defendant, without expressly reserving his right to dispute jurisdiction, makes an application for discovery of documents relevant to the merits.[56] On the other hand, as the European Court explained in *Mietz v Intership Yachting Sneek*,[57] the defendant's appearance before a court dealing with interim measures in the context of fast procedures intended to grant provisional or protective measures in case of urgency, and without prejudicing the examination of the substance, cannot by itself suffice to confer on that court unlimited jurisdiction to order any provisional or protective measure which the court might consider appropriate if it had jurisdiction as to the substance of the matter.

ORDINARY CONTRACTS

For present purposes, 'ordinary contract' refers to any contract other than those excluded from or subjected to special rules by the Regulation (contracts relating to matrimonial property or succession on death; insurance, consumer and employment contracts; and tenancies of land).[58]

Article 5(1) of the Regulation confers jurisdiction on the English courts, in matters relating to an ordinary contract, where the defendant is domiciled in another member state and the place of performance of the obligation in question is in England. In full it provides:

A person domiciled in a member state may, in another member state, be sued:

(a) in matters relating to a contract, in the courts for the place of performance of the obligation in question;

(b) for the purpose of this provision and unless otherwise agreed, the place of performance of the obligation in question shall be:

    – in the case of the sale of goods, the place in a member state where, under the contract, the goods were delivered or should have been delivered,

    – in the case of the provision of services, the place in a member state where, under the contract, the services were provided or should have been provided;

(c) if sub-paragraph (b) does not apply then sub-paragraph (a) applies.

---

53 Case 150/80: *Elefanten Schuh v Jacqmain* [1981] ECR 1671; Case 27/81: *Rohr v Ossberger* [1981] ECR 2431; Case 25/81: *CHW v GJH* [1982] ECR 1189; and Case 201/82: *Gerling v Treasury Administration* [1983] ECR 2503. For procedure in England, see the CPR 1998, r 11; *Hewden Stuart v Gottwald* (1992) unreported, 13 May (CA); and *IBS v APM* [2003] All ER (D) 105 (Apr).

54 See *Murray v Times Newspapers* (1997) unreported, 29 July (Irish Supreme Court).

55 See *Marc Rich v Impianti (No 2)* [1992] 1 Lloyd's Rep 624 (CA).

56 See *Caltex v Metro* [1999] 2 Lloyd's Rep 724.

57 Case C-99/96:, [1999] ECR I-2277.

58 See Arts 1(2)(a) 8–21 and 22(1).

In this respect, the Regulation departs significantly from the Brussels and Lugano Conventions, by adding sub-paras (b) and (c) to a provision formerly consisting only of sub-para (a),[59] and thus altering the meaning of 'the obligation in question'.

But the concept of contractual matters appears to be unchanged. Thus Art 5(1) extends to a relationship (such as that between members of an association) that involves close links of the same kind as those between the parties to a contract.[60] But it does not apply to a situation in which there is no obligation freely assumed by one party towards another, as where:

- a sub-buyer of goods sues a manufacturer who is not the direct seller to the sub-buyer, complaining of defects in the goods or their unsuitability for their intended purpose;[61] or

- the action is brought by a consignee of goods carried under a bill of lading contract, and allegedly damaged in the course of such carriage, not against the issuer of the bill of lading, but against the actual carrier;[62] or

- the action is founded on the defendant's liability for the unjustified breaking off of pre-contractual negotiations, contrary to a legal rule requiring the parties to act in good faith in negotiations with a view to the formation of a contract;[63] or

- the action is brought by a consumer protection organisation for the purpose of preventing a trader from using unfair terms in transactions with private individuals;[64] or

- a guarantor who has paid customs duties under a guarantee obtained by a forwarding agent seeks, by way of subrogation to the rights of the customs authorities, to recover the sum from the goods owner, if the goods owner was not a party to, and did not authorise the conclusion of, the contract of guarantee.[65]

Jurisdiction under Art 5(1) is not excluded merely because the defendant disputes facts relevant to its existence, but the plaintiff must satisfy the court that the existence of such facts is strongly arguable.[66]

As regards 'the obligation in question', in a series of decisions under the Brussels Convention the European Court had established that this referred to the contractual

---

59 Article 5(1) of the Lugano Convention continues to apply where the defendant is domiciled in Switzerland, Norway or Iceland. Where the defendant is domiciled in another part of the United Kingdom, English jurisdiction continues to be governed by a rule echoing Art 5(1) of the Brussels Convention rather than of the Regulation; see r 3(a) of Sched 4 to the Civil Jurisdiction and Judgments Act 1982, as amended by SI 2001/3929.

60 See Case 34/82: *Peters v ZNAV* [1983] ECR 987.

61 See Case C-26/91: *Handte v TMCS* [1992] ECR I-3967. Cf *Atlas Shipping Agency v Suisse Atlantique* [1995] 2 Lloyd's Rep 188 (Rix J), permitting a broker to sue on a promise by the buyer, contained in a contract for the sale of a ship, to pay the broker's commission, the promise being made to the seller but treated under English law as held by the seller on trust for the broker.

62 See Case C-51/97: *Réunion Européenne v Spliethoff's Bevrachtingskantoor* [1998] ECR I-6511.

63 See Case C-334/00: *Tacconi v Wagner* [2002] ECR I-7357.

64 See Case C-167/00: *VKI v Henkel* [2002] ECR I-8111.

65 See Case C-265/02: *Frahuil v Assitalia* [2004] ECR I-1543.

66 See Case 38/81: *Effer v Kantner* [1982] ECR 825; Case 73/77: *Sanders v Van der Putte* [1977] ECR 2383; Case C-68/93: *Shevill v Presse Alliance* [1995] ECR I-415; *Seaconsar v Bank Markazi* [1994] 1 AC 438; *Boss Group v Boss France* [1997] 1 WLR 351 (CA); *Canada Trust v Stolzenberg (No 2)* [2002] 1 AC 1; *Chellaram v Chellaram (No 2)* [2002] 3 All ER 17 (Lawrence Collins J); *Bank of Tokyo-Mitsubishi v Baskan Gida* [2004] ILPr 26 (Lawrence Collins J); and *Bols Distilleries v Superior Yacht Services* [2007] 1 Lloyd's Rep 683 (PC).

obligation on which the plaintiff's action was based;[67] or, where he made claims based on a number of obligations under the same contract, to the principal (or most important) contractual obligation among those on which such claims were based.[68] The court had specifically rejected arguments that any obligation under the relevant contract would do; or that reference should be made to the obligation which was characteristic of the contract; or that jurisdiction should belong to the court with whose territory the dispute had its closest connection. Thus where a buyer of goods sued the seller, complaining of defects in the quality or fitness of the goods supplied, the relevant place was where the goods in question were delivered to the buyer.[69] On the other hand, where a seller or supplier sued for the price of goods delivered or services supplied, the relevant obligation was that of the buyer or recipient to pay the price, and the place where the goods or services were delivered or supplied was in itself irrelevant.[70] But Art 5(1) did not apply where the place of performance of the obligation on which the claim was based was indeterminate, because the contractual obligation at issue consisted in a negative undertaking without any geographical limitation and therefore having multiple places of performance, as in the case of an obligation not to participate in a competing bid for a concession.[71]

This case law is now to a large extent replaced by Art 5(1)(b). In the case of the sale of goods, the relevant place is now the place in a member state where, under the contract, the goods were or should have been delivered. No doubt delivery refers to

---

67 See Case 14/76: *De Bloos v Bouyer* [1976] ECR 1497; Case 266/85: *Shenavai v Kreischer* [1987] ECR 239; Case C-288/92: *Custom Made v Stawa* [1994] ECR I-2913; and Case C-420/97: *Leathertex v Bodetex* [1999] ECR I-6747. Where the claimant sought a declaration that he was not bound to perform a contract because of the defendant's breach of a particular term of the contract, that term was the obligation in question, and not the claimant's obligation to perform the contract: see *AIG Group v The Ethniki* [2000] 2 All ER 566 (CA).

68 See Case 266/85: *Shenavai v Kreischer* [1987] ECR 239; and Case C-420/97: *Leathertex v Bodetex* [1999] ECR I-6747, which ruled that where the claimant's claims were based on several obligations which were of equal importance, the court was competent to entertain only those claims which were based on obligations whose places of performance were within its territory. See also *Union Transport v Continental Lines* [1992] 1 WLR 15 (HL); *Source v TUV Rheinland Holding* [1998] QB 54 (CA); and *Raiffeisen Zentralbank v National Bank of Greece* [1999] 1 Lloyd's Rep 408.

69 See *Thompson Hayward v Sirena* [1988] ECC 319 (French Court of Cassation); *Re a Consignment of Italian Wine* [1988] ECC 159 (German Supreme Court); *Hewden Stuart v Gottwald* (1992) unreported, 13 May (CA); *Viskase v Paul Kiefal* [1999] 3 All ER 362 (CA); and *MBM Fabri-Clad v Eisen und Huttenwerke Thale* [2000] ILPr 505 (CA). See also *The Sea Maas* [1999] 2 Lloyd's Rep 281, on claims for damage to or loss of cargo under a bill of lading contract; and *Royal & Sun Alliance Insurance v MK Digital* [2006] 2 Lloyd's Rep 110 (CA). On exclusive distribution contracts, see *Knauer v Callens* [1978] I Pas Belge 871; *Audi-NSU v Adelin Petit* (1979) 94 Journal des Tribunaux 625; *Hacker Kuchen v Bosma* [1993] ECC 55; *Medway Packaging v Meurer Maschinen* [1990] 2 Lloyd's Rep 112 (CA); and *Boss Group v Boss France* [1997] 1 WLR 351 (CA).

70 See Case 56/79: *Zelger v Salinitri (No 1)* [1980] ECR 89; Case 266/85: *Shenavai v Kreischer* [1987] ECR 239; and Case C-288/92: *Custom Made v Stawa* [1994] ECR I-2913. See also *Mercury Publicity v Loerke* [1993] ILPR 142 (CA), which involved a claim for money due under a contract of commercial agency; *Chailease Finance Corp v Credit Agricole Indosuez* [2000] 1 Lloyd's Rep 348 (CA), holding that where a beneficiary sued an issuing bank for payment under a letter of credit, it was the place of payment, and not that of presentation of the documents, which constituted the relevant place of performance, and that if the letter of credit entitled the beneficiary to choose the place of payment, by notifying the bank at the time of presentation, Art 5(1) enabled the beneficiary to sue at the place thus notified; and *Tavoulareas v Tsavliris* [2006] 1 All ER (Comm) 109, holding that, in the case of a loan which is governed by English law and is repayable on demand, Art 5(1) confers jurisdiction over a claim for repayment on the court for the creditor's residence at the time of the demand.

71 See Case C-256/00: *Besix v WABAG* [2002] ECR I-1699. Cf *Kenburn Waste Management v Bergmann* [2002] ILPr 33 (CA), holding that, in the case of a negative obligation to produce a result in a particular country (eg, not to communicate threats of patent litigation to persons there), the place of performance would be in the country where the result was to be achieved.

the transfer of possession of the goods by the seller to the buyer or to an agent for the buyer, and the point at which such a transfer occurs must be determined in the light of all of the terms of the contract of sale. It is however clear that the effect of Art 5(1)(b) is that in the majority of transnational sales of goods the seller will be able to sue in his own country, whether he is suing for the price, for damages for non-acceptance, or for a negative declaration that he has complied with the contract and thus is not liable to return the price received or to pay damages. On the other hand, the buyer will usually be unable to sue in his own country. This can be seen when we examine ordinary examples of the four main types of transnational sale. In the case of a sale ex-works, delivery takes place at the seller's factory. Similarly in the case of an FOB sale, delivery takes place at the port of loading, which is usually in the seller's country.[72] In the case of a CIF sale, delivery of the relevant documents (especially the bill of lading) presumably amounts to symbolic or constructive delivery of the goods, so the relevant place will be where the documents were or should have been tendered, rather than where the goods were located at the time of the tender; and at least where English law applies, the documents should be tendered, unless otherwise agreed, at the buyer 's residence.[73] But a contrary agreement will often exist, especially where the contract provides for payment by means of a documentary credit, usually involving tender at and payment by a bank located in the seller's country. It is only in the case of an arrival contract that Art 5(1)(b) will usually confer jurisdiction on the courts of the buyer's country.[74] The merits of such results are difficult to discern.

So far the European Court has merely ruled, in *Color Drack v LEXX International*,[75] that, as regards the sale of goods, Art 5(1)(b) is applicable where there are several places of delivery within a single member state. In such a case, the court having jurisdiction to hear all claims based on the contract of sale is that for the principal place of delivery, which must be determined on the basis of economic criteria. If the principal place of delivery cannot be ascertained, the plaintiff may sue the defendant in the court for the place of delivery of its choice. But the European Court was careful to emphasise that this ruling applies solely to the case where there are several places of delivery within a single member state, and is without prejudice to the situation where there are several places of delivery in a number of member states.

The reference in Art 5(1)(b) to the place of service provision may raise difficulties where the provision involves transborder activity. One example would be a contract for the carriage of goods or passengers between different countries. Another would be a contract for the provision of code or data, to be downloaded from a website via the internet. At least three types of solution may seem plausible at first glance. One solution would be that any place at which at least a substantial part of the service provision under the contract took, or should have taken, place will qualify for jurisdiction. Thus, in the case of carriage, jurisdiction would exist at the place of loading or boarding and also at the place of destination, and perhaps also at any place en route. In the case of a contract for downloading, it would exist at the location of the server and also at that of the receiving computer, and perhaps also at any place en route.

---

72 See *Scottish and Newcastle International Ltd v Othon Ghalanos Ltd* [2008] 2 All ER 768 (HL).
73 See *Johnson v Taylor* [1920] AC 144; and *The Albazero* [1974] 2 All ER 906 (Brandon J), reversed on other grounds [1977] AC 774.
74 For an example of an arrival contract, in the context of Art 5(1) of the Brussels Convention, see *MBM Fabri-Clad v Eisen und Huttenwerke Thale* [2000] ILPr 505 (CA).
75 Case C-386/05: [2007] ECR I-3699.

Since the wording of Art 5(1)(b) clearly envisages a single place whose courts are to be rendered competent, there is little doubt that this first solution must be ruled out.

A second solution would be to focus exclusively on the principal place of the service provision. This would presumably be the place of destination, where the carriage terminated or was to terminate, or the download was or was to be received. This solution accords with that proposed under the Brussels Convention by Colomer AG, but rejected by the court, in *Groupe Concorde v 'The Suhadiwarno Panjan'*.[76] It also benefits analogistically from the court's ruling in *Shenavai v Kreischer*,[77] in favour of the place of performance of the principal obligation among those on which the plaintiff's claims are based. Moreover, it has the merit of a substantial measure of practicability, especially as a supplier under an electronic commercial contract will normally have only himself to blame if he is ignorant of his customer's location. Against this solution is the wording of the provision. It would have been simple to insert 'principally' before 'provided', and the failure to do so could be taken as indicating a contrary intention.

A third solution would be to apply Art 5(1)(b) only where the whole of the service provision took, or should have taken, place in a single country, so that contracts requiring the provision of services by acts performed in more than one country will be governed by Art 5(1)(a) and (c). The result would be to restore the Brussels Convention approach, referring to the obligation on which the plaintiff's sole or principal claim is based. This solution accords analogistically with the European Court's ruling under the Brussels Convention in *Besix v WABAG*,[78] that no court is competent under Art 5(1) where the place of performance is indeterminate or multiple. It also gains support from the wording of the provision, read in the most literal manner. On this basis, in the case of goods damaged or lost in the course of carriage under a bill of lading contract, the complexities examined in *The Sea Maas*[79] will continue to delight us. In the case of a contract for access to or downloading of data or code, much may depend on the precise terms of the contract in question and on the manner in which the plaintiff frames his claim, though his case for jurisdiction will have to be strongly arguable.[80] In some cases, the customer may complain that the code or data supplied were in some way defective – the code would not run, or did not provide the facilities promised; the data were inaccurate, or were not updated as frequently as promised.

---

76   Case C-440/97: [1999] ECR I-6307.

77   Case 266/85: [1987] ECR 239.

78   Case C-256/00: [2002] ECR I-1699.

79   [1999] 2 Lloyd's Rep 281. There Rix J considered that everything depended on the nature of the bill holder's claim. If the shipowner had misdelivered the goods at the destination, the place of performance of the obligation in question would be the port of discharge. If the ship were seaworthy, but the alleged failure of due diligence was some lack of care during the voyage (such as failure to tighten the lashing as needed, or to maintain appropriate reefer temperatures), the relevant obligation would be to carry and care for the goods with due diligence, and its place of performance might be the high seas, so that there would be no special jurisdiction under Art 5(1). But if the fundamental matter of complaint was that the shipowner never provided a seaworthy vessel, the relevant place would be the port of loading. Cf the view of Colomer AG (rejected by the Court) in Case C-440/97: *Groupe Concorde v 'The Suhadiwarno Panjan'* [1999] ECR I-6307, that in the case of a bill of lading contract, the port of destination as specified in the bill should be regarded as the place of performance of all obligations under the contract.

80   See Case 38/81: *Effer v Kantner* [1982] ECR 825; Case 73/77: *Sanders v Van der Putte* [1977] ECR 2383; Case C-68/93: *Shevill v Presse Alliance* [1995] ECR I-415; *Seaconsar v Bank Markazi* [1994] 1 AC 438; *Boss Group v Boss France* [1997] 1 WLR 351 (CA); *Canada Trust v Stolzenberg (No 2)* [2002] 1 AC 1; and *Bols Distilleries v Superior Yacht Services* [2007] 1 Lloyd's Rep 683 (PC).

In other cases, his claim may be that he was unable to access the code or data as promised – the defendant's server rejected the password issued, or was too frequently unavailable. In either type of case, one will have to ask whether the obligation (as asserted by the claimant and accepted as strongly arguable by the court) required an act to be performed by the defendant at the location of the server, or a result to be achieved at the plaintiff's office or residence. Since the answer may differ under various laws, the question will have to resolved in accordance with the law which governs the contract under the Rome Convention 1980 or the Rome I Regulation.[81] The merits of such complexity seem elusive. All things considered, it is submitted that the second solution (focusing exclusively on the principal place of the service provision) is to be preferred.

Another difficulty arises from the reference in Art 5(1)(b) of the Brussels I Regulation to a contrary agreement, which will apparently exclude Art 5(1)(b). It seems that the effect of such an agreement (that the place of delivery or service provision shall not be regarded as the place of performance) will be to eliminate the operation of Art 5(1)(b) and restore the operation of the Brussels Convention approach, in accordance with Art 5(1)(a) and (c).

The effect of Art 5(1)(a) and (c) of the Regulation is to preserve the Brussels Convention approach, referring to the place of performance of the obligation on which the sole claim or principal claim made by the plaintiff is based, in cases where the new rules specified by Art 5(1)(b) of the Regulation, referring to the place of delivery or service provision, do not apply. There appear to be at least four such situations. First, where the contract is not for the sale of goods or the provision of services; but (for example) for the sale of land or corporate securities (shares or bonds), or for the exchange of goods (guns for butter), or for the licensing of an intellectual property right,[82] or for a loan of money, repayable on demand.[83] Secondly, where the place of delivery or service provision is not located in a member state but in an external country, or outside any national territory (such as on the high seas). Thirdly, where the place of delivery or service provision is multiple or indeterminate, as where goods have to be delivered or services provided at a frontier, or where one party has an option to choose the place of delivery or service provision and has not done so, or (on one view) where the service provision involves acts performed or to be performed in more than one country. Fourthly, where the parties have agreed to exclude the operation of Art 5(1)(b) and have not also made a valid agreement on exclusive jurisdiction in accordance with Art 23, so as to exclude Art 5(1) altogether.

Probably (in both the Regulation and the Brussels Convention) Art 5(1) is confined to actions which are based on a contractual obligation, in the normal sense of a promise which constitutes a valid term of a binding contract (or equivalent transaction) so that its non-performance is actionable as a breach of contract. Thus a claimant can invoke Art 5(1) only where he bases his claim on an allegation that the defendant has committed or threatened to commit one or more breaches of a valid contract between them. But it does not matter whether he seeks damages for breach, specific

---

81 See Case 12/76: *Tessili v Dunlop* [1976] ECR 1473; and Case C-440/97: *Groupe Concorde v 'The Suhadiwarno Panjan'* [1999] ECR I-6307. On the Rome Convention 1980 and the Rome I Regulation, see Chapter 17 below.
82 See Case C-533/07: *Falco and Rabitsch v Weller-Lindhorst*; 23 April 2009.
83 See *Tavoulareas v Tsavliris* [2006] 1 All ER (Comm) 109.

performance, restoration of benefits for which (owing to the defendant's breach) the consideration has failed, or a declaration that by reason of the defendant's breach the plaintiff is released from his obligations under the contract. In contrast, Art 5(1) is not available to a claimant who seeks restitution of money paid under a contract which is indisputably void *ab initio* on account of the defendant's incapacity to enter into the contract;[84] nor to a claimant who seeks a negative declaration that, contrary to the defendant's assertion, no exclusive distribution contract exists between the parties.[85] Nor is Art 5(1) available to a claimant who complains of the defendant's misconduct in pre-contractual negotiations, whether by way of misrepresentation or non-disclosure, or of breaking off negotiations unexpectedly and in bad faith, and whether he seeks rescission or damages.[86]

Once the relevant contractual obligation has been identified, the place of its performance must be determined, and in this respect the Regulation does not seem to have altered the position. In *Tessili v Dunlop*[87] and *Groupe Concorde v 'The Suhadiwarno Panjan'*,[88] the European Court ruled that this concept does not have an independent meaning. Rather, the place of performance must be determined in accordance with the substantive law which is applicable to the obligation under the conflict rules of the forum country. Usually, the relevant substantive law will be the proper law of the contract, determined under Arts 3 and 4 of the Rome Convention 1980 or the Rome I Regulation.[89] Moreover, as the European Court ruled in *Zelger v Salinitri (No 1)*,[90] the same substantive law also governs the formal requirements applicable to an express agreement as to the place of performance. Those laid down by Art 23, on agreements as to jurisdiction, do not apply to an agreement specifying a place of performance. Thus an entirely informal agreement on the place of performance of an obligation will be effective under Art 5(1) if the applicable substantive law imposes no formal requirements. However, in *MSG v Les Gravieres Rhénanes*,[91] the European Court made

---

84   See *Kleinwort Benson v City of Glasgow DC* [1999] AC 153.

85   The contrary was held in *Boss Group v Boss France* [1997] 1 WLR 351 (CA), but the decision seems irreconcilable with the subsequent ruling of the House in *Kleinwort Benson v City of Glasgow District Council* [1999] AC 153.

86   See Case C-334/00: *Tacconi v Wagner* [2002] ECR I-7357, where the European Court held that an action founded on the defendant's liability for the unjustified breaking off of pre-contractual negotiations, contrary to a legal rule requiring the parties to act in good faith in negotiations with a view to the formation of a contract, is not within Art 5(1), since there is no obligation freely assumed by one party towards another. It explained (rather puzzlingly) that, while Art 5(1) does not require a contract to have been concluded, it is nevertheless essential to identify an obligation, since jurisdiction is determined by the place of performance of the obligation in question. See also *Dunhill v Diffusion Internationale de Maroquinerie de Prestige* [2002] ILPr 13 (on damages for fraudulent or negligent misrepresentation). The decision of the House of Lords in *Agnew v Länsförsäkringsbolagens* [2001] 1 AC 223, accepting jurisdiction under Art 5(1) of the Lugano Convention over an action brought by a reinsurer seeking avoidance of the reinsurance contract for breach of the duty to make a fair presentation of the risk by giving full disclosure and avoiding misrepresentation in the negotiations, conducted in England, leading to the conclusion of the contract, seems impossible to reconcile with the subsequent decision of the European Court in *Tacconi v Wagner*.

87   Case 12/76: [1976] ECR 1473.

88   Case C-440/97: [1999] ECR I-6307. See also *per* Alber AG in Case C-256/00: *Besix v WABAG* [2002] ECR I-1699.

89   See Case C-440/97: *Groupe Concorde v 'The Suhadiwarno Panjan'* [1999] ECR I-6307; and *Raiffeisen Zentralbank v National Bank of Greece* [1999] 1 Lloyd's Rep 408. On the Rome Convention 1980 and the Rome I Regulation, see Chapter 17 below.

90   Case 56/79: [1980] ECR 89.

91   Case C-106/95: [1997] ECR I-911. See also *Gotz v Noge* (1996) unreported, 27 February (French Court of Cassation).

clear that this approach applies only to a genuine agreement, designed to determine the place of actual performance. A fictitious agreement, purporting to specify the place of performance but in reality designed only to establish jurisdiction, is not effective under Art 5(1) but must be treated as an agreement on jurisdiction governed by Art 23.

Where the defendant is not domiciled in any EC member state or Lugano Convention country, the English courts may in their discretion assume jurisdiction over a claim which relates to a contract in each of the following cases: where the contract was made in England; or where the contract was made by or through an agent trading or residing in England; or where the contract is governed by English law; or where the claim is in respect of a breach of contract committed in England.[92]

TORT CLAIMS

By Art 5(3) of the Regulation, the English courts have jurisdiction to entertain an action in tort against a defendant domiciled in another member state if the harmful event occurred or may occur in England.[93] It is enough that either the wrongful conduct or the initial injury occurred in England,[94] but it is not enough that the claimant suffered in England loss consequential on an initial injury sustained elsewhere (whether by the claimant himself or by an associated person, such as a sister company).[95]

In the context of defamation by newspaper article, the European Court ruled in *Shevill v Presse Alliance*[96] that the place of the wrongful conduct is that of the publisher's establishment from which the libel was issued and put into circulation, and the courts for that place have jurisdiction to award damages for all the harm caused anywhere by the defamation. In addition, by enabling the claimant to sue at the place of injury, Art 5(3) confers jurisdiction on the courts of any member state in which the newspaper was distributed and where the victim claims to have suffered injury to his reputation, but such jurisdiction is limited to the harm caused in the forum state. The same principles apply to a television broadcast.[97] No doubt they also extend to

---

92 See the Civil Procedure Rules 1998 (as amended), r 6.36; and Practice Direction B, para 3.1(6)–(7).

93 See, similarly, Art 5(3) of the Lugano Convention; Case C-167/00: *VKI v Henkel* [2002] ECR I-8111; and r 3(c) of Sched 4 to the Civil Jurisdiction and Judgments Act 1982 (as amended). Where the defendant is not domiciled in any EC Member State or Lugano Convention country, the English courts have a similar but discretionary jurisdiction under r 6.36 of the Civil Procedure Rules 1998 (as amended) and Practice Direction B, para 3.1(2) and (9).

94 See Case 21/76: *Bier v Mines de Potasse d'Alsace* [1976] ECR 1735; and Case C-343/04: *Land Oberösterreich v ČEZ* [2006] ECR I-4557. .

95 See Case 220/88: *Dumez v Hessische Landesbank* [1990] ECR I-49; Case C-364/93: *Marinari v Lloyd's Bank* [1995] ECR I-2719; Case C-51/97: *Réunion Européenne v Spliethoff's Bevrachtingskantoor* [1998] ECR I-6511; Case C-168/02: *Kronhofer v Maier* [2004] ECR I-6009. Cf Case C-18/02: *DFDS Torline v SEKO* [2004] ECR I-1417, where, in the context of an action in Denmark seeking to establish the illegality of a notice of industrial action ('blacking') given by a Swedish trade union acting in the interests of the Polish crew of a Danish ship operating between Sweden and England, the European Court ruled that the nationality or flag of the ship is decisive only if the national court reaches the conclusion that the damage arose on board the ship.

96 Case C-68/93: [1995] ECR I-415. See also *Berezovsky v Michaels* [2000] 1 WLR 1004 (HL), applying the same principles to an American defendant under the predecessor of r 6.36 of the Civil Procedure Rules 1998 (as amended) and Practice Direction B, para 3.1(9).

97 See *Ewins v Carlton Television* [1997] 2 ILRM 223.

publication by means of a webpage on the Internet. In such a case, the relevant establishment of the website operator will be its domicile or branch from which the website is maintained by its staff, for a merely electronic presence in the form of a website does not constitute an establishment.[98]

As regards the tort of inducing breach of contract, jurisdiction exists at the place where the most important breaches induced occurred and the plaintiff suffered direct financial loss, even though the defendant's acts of inducement took place elsewhere.[99] But as regards the tortious interference with a contract of carriage of goods by the arrest of the carrying vessel, the place of the relevant conduct is that where the arrest takes place, rather than that where the decision to arrest is made.[100]

With regard to liability for false statements made by the defendant and relied on by the claimant, jurisdiction exists at the place where the statement was issued by the defendant (as the place of the wrongful act), and also at the place where goods were delivered or money was paid as a result of the plaintiff's reliance on the statement (as the place of injury), but not at the place where the statement was merely received by the claimant and he acted in reliance on it by taking decisions or giving instructions leading to the delivery or payment.[101]

As regards the tortious conversion of goods by their detention and use, Art 5(3) confers jurisdiction on the court for the place of the detention and use, and not on the court for the place at which the claimant suffered consequential loss because (for example) the detention of master tapes prevented his exploitation there of his copyright in the sound recordings embodied in the tapes.[102] As regards the fraudulent conversion of corporate funds by an officer of the company, where the officer diverts funds received from a customer abroad into his own bank account, the place where his bank account is kept counts as the place of injury, even if the funds are transferred from the customer's account in another country; and where the officer removes funds from a corporate bank account into his own bank account, the place where the corporate bank account is kept counts as the place of conduct, even if the funds are transferred to the officer's own account in another country.[103]

As regards passing off, jurisdiction over a manufacturer of deceptively packaged goods exists at the place where he manufactured the goods and delivered them for export, as that of the wrongful conduct, and also at the place where the goods were subsequently sold to a deceived public, as the place of injury; but not elsewhere, such as at the claimant's domicile, where he ultimately suffered loss by receiving fewer

---

98 See Directive 2000/31 on Electronic Commerce [2000] OJ L178/1, recital 19 and Art 2(c). See also, on defamation by web publication, *Dow Jones v Gutnick* (2002) 194 ALR 433, and *King v Lewis* [2004] EWCA Civ 1329.

99 See *Metall und Rohstoff v Donaldson Lufkin and Jenrette* [1990] QB 391 (CA), decided under the predecessor of r 6.36 of the Civil Procedure Rules 1998 (as amended) and Practice Direction B, para 3.1(9).

100 See *Anton Durbeck v Den Norske Bank* [2002] EWCA Civ 1173; partly reversed on other grounds [2003] QB 1160 (CA).

101 See *Domicrest v Swiss Bank Corp* [1999] QB 548; *Dunhill v Diffusion Internationale de Maroquinerie de Prestige* [2002] ILPr 13; *Raiffeisen Zentralbank v National Bank of Greece* [1999] 1 Lloyd's Rep 408; *ABCI v Banque Franco-Tunisienne* [2003] 2 Lloyd's Rep 146 (CA); and *Bank of Tokyo-Mitsubishi v Baskan Gida* [2004] ILPr 26.

102 See *Mazur Media Ltd v Mazur Media Gmbh* [2004] EWHC 1566 (Ch) (Lawrence Collins J). See also *Bank of Tokyo-Mitsubishi v Baskan Gida* [2004] ILPr 26 (Lawrence Collins J), at para 218.

103 See *Cronos Containers v Palatin* [2003] 2 Lloyd's Rep 489 (Morison J).

orders.[104] In respect of actions for infringement of a specific intellectual property right, such as a patent, a copyright or a registered trade mark, Art 5(3) confers jurisdiction at the place where the infringing act was committed, even over a defendant who authorised the infringement by an act committed elsewhere.[105]

It is now clear that Art 5(3) extends beyond tort[106] to cover other liabilities which are not contractual matters within the scope of Art 5(1), such as restitutionary obligations which are unconnected with any contract, or which arise from the invalidity of a contract, and claims arising from misconduct in negotiations leading or designed to lead to the conclusion of a contract. This has been established by decisions of the European Court applying Art 5(3): in *Kalfelis v Schröder*,[107] to a restitutionary claim arising from the invalidity of a contract; in *Tacconi v Wagner*,[108] to an action founded on pre-contractual liability for damage caused by the unjustified breaking off of negotiations with a view to the formation of a contract, in breach of a rule requiring parties to act in good faith in such negotiations; and in *VKI v Henkel*,[109] to an action brought by a consumer protection organisation for the purpose of preventing a trader from using unfair terms in contracts with private individuals. Its ruling in *Reichert v Dresdner Bank (No 2)*,[110] refusing to apply Art 5(3) to an application by a creditor for the setting aside of a transfer of property by his debtor on the ground that it was made in fraud of the creditor's rights, must be understood as based on the proprietary, as distinct from obligational, character of the claim. It seems clear from the line of European Court rulings that, as regards Art 5(3), the decisions of the House of Lords in both *Kleinwort Benson*[111] and *Agnew*[112] must now be recognised as erroneous.

It is also clear that Art 5(3) extends to equitable wrongs (in so far as the claim is not based on a breach of contract or of an express or statutory trust),[113] such as the misuse of confidential information, or dishonest assistance in a breach of trust, or knowing

---

104 See *Modus Vivendi v Sanmex* [1996] FSR 790; and *Mecklermedia v DC Congress* [1998] Ch 40.

105 See *ABKCO v Music Collection* [1995] RPC 657 (CA); and *IBS v APM* [2003] All ER (D) 105 (Apr).

106 See also Case C-18/02: *DFDS Torline v SEKO* [2004] ECR I-1417, which involved an action in Denmark seeking to establish the illegality of a notice of industrial action ('blacking') given by a Swedish trade union acting in the interests of the Polish crew of a Danish ship operating between Sweden and England. The European Court ruled that Art 5(3) extends to an action concerning the legality of industrial action, in respect of which, under the law of the member state concerned, exclusive jurisdiction belongs to a court other than the court which has jurisdiction to try the claims for compensation for the damage caused by the industrial action.

107 Case 189/87: [1988] ECR 5565.

108 Case C-334/00: [2002] ECR I-7357.

109 Case C-167/00: [2002] ECR I-8111.

110 Case C-261/90: [1992] ECR I-2149.

111 *Kleinwort Benson v City of Glasgow District Council* [1999] AC 153.

112 *Agnew v Länsförsäkringsbolagens* [2001] 1 AC 223.

113 Article 5(6) confers jurisdiction over a defendant domiciled in another member state, when he is sued as settlor, trustee or beneficiary of a trust created by the operation of a statute, or by a written instrument, or created orally and evidenced in writing, on the courts of the member state in which the trust is domiciled. For this purpose, by Art 60(3), the court seised applies its own law to determine the domicile of a trust; and, by Art 12 of the Civil Jurisdiction and Judgments Order 2001, a trust is domiciled in England if English law is the law with which the trust has its closest and most real connection. As Lawrence Collins J ruled in *Chellaram v Chellaram (No 2)* [2002] 3 All ER 17, this test must be applied as of the date when the proceedings are instituted, and in the light of the Hague Convention on the Law Applicable to Trusts and on their Recognition 1985 and the Recognition of Trusts Act 1987. It is thought that claims falling within Art 5(6) are excluded from Art 5(3).

receipt of trust property.[114] Moreover, where a claimant is entitled to frame his claim alternatively in contract and tort, his claim in tort falls within Art 5(3).[115]

ANCILLARY JURISDICTION

The Regulation recognises the desirability, in the interests of the sound administration of justice and of reducing the risk of conflicting judgments, for related disputes to be decided together in a single proceeding. Article 6 gives positive effect to this principle, by providing for ancillary jurisdiction over co-defendants, third parties and counterclaims, and by enabling a court exercising exclusive jurisdiction over a right *in rem* in land to entertain a related contractual claim against the same defendant, even if the court would not have had jurisdiction to entertain the additional claim in its own right. The principle is also given negative effect by Arts 27–30, which endeavour to prevent simultaneous actions in different member states in respect of similar or related disputes by requiring or encouraging the court subsequently seised to decline jurisdiction, or at least stay its proceedings, in favour of the court first seised. But the Regulation does not ensure that in all cases a court properly seised of one claim will also be competent to entertain a related claim by the same claimant against the same defendant,[116] and it is possible for contracting parties to exclude the operation of Art 6 between themselves by means of a clearly worded agreement on jurisdiction complying with Art 23.[117]

Co-defendants

By Art 6(1), a person domiciled in a member state may be sued, where he is one of a number of defendants, in the courts for the place where any one of them is domiciled, provided that the claims are so closely connected that it is expedient to hear and determine them together to avoid the risk of irreconcilable judgments resulting from separate proceedings.[118] The relevant date for ascertaining whether one of the defendants is domiciled in England, so as to enable the joinder of a co-defendant domiciled in another member state, is that of the issue of the claim form initiating the proceedings against the allegedly English defendant, and not that of service on him, nor that of the subsequent joinder of the foreign defendant.[119] Article 6(1) extends to a counterclaim, so as to enable a defendant who counterclaims against an English plaintiff

---

114 See *Kitechnology v Unicor* [1995] FSR 765 (CA); *Casio Computer v Sayo* [2001] ILPr 43 (CA); and *Dexter v Harley* (2001) *The Times,* 2 April. See also, as regards defendants not domiciled in any EC member state or Lugano Convention country, r 6.36 of the Civil Procedure Rules 1998 (as amended) and Practice Direction B, para 3.1(15) and (16).

115 See Case 189/87: *Kalfelis v Schröder* [1988] ECR 5565, and *Raiffeisen Zentralbank v National Bank of Greece* [1999] 1 Lloyd's Rep 408, where Tuckey J recognised that the contrary view, adopted in *Source v TUV Rheinland Holding* [1998] QB 54 (CA), was impliedly overruled by *Kleinwort Benson v City of Glasgow District Council* [1999] AC 153. Cf *Rayner v Davies* [2002] 1 All ER (Comm) 620 (Morison J).

116 See Case 189/87: *Kalfelis v Schröder* [1988] ECR 5565; Case 150/80: *Elefanten Schuh v Jacqmain* [1981] ECR 1671; Case C-51/97: *Réunion Européenne v Spliethoff's Bevrachtingskantoor* [1998] ECR I-6511; and Case C-420/97: *Leathertex v Bodetex* [1999] ECR I-6747.

117 See Case 23/78: *Meeth v Glacetal* [1978] ECR 2133; and *Hough v P&O Containers* [1999] QB 834.

118 See to similar effect Art 6(1) of the Lugano Convention, and r 5(a) of Sched 4 to the 1982 Act (as amended).

119 See *Canada Trust v Stolzenberg (No 2)* [2002] 1 AC 1; and *Petrotrade v Smith* [1998] 2 All ER 346.

to join a foreign co-defendant to the counterclaim, and even to claims by a third party (joined by a defendant) against English and foreign plaintiffs, or against an English defendant (who joined the third party) and a foreign plaintiff.[120] But there is no provision enabling joinder of a co-defendant as such, if he is domiciled in another member state, in an action against another defendant who is domiciled in a non-member state.[121]

As regards the sufficiency of the connection between the claims against the English and foreign defendants, it has been accepted in England that a broad approach must be applied in the determination of the risk of irreconcilable decisions, so as to include inconsistent findings of fact, rather than one based on close analysis of the respective claims; and that there need only be a risk, rather than a certainty, of irreconcilable decisions.[122] However in *Roche Nederland BV v Primus*[123] the European Court left open whether it is sufficient under Art 6(1) that there is a risk of conflicting decisions (as is sufficient under Art 28), or whether there must be a risk of decisions which give rise to mutually exclusive legal consequences (as is required under Art 34). It ruled that even if a risk of contradictory decisions would satisfy Art 6(1), it is not enough that there is a divergence in the outcome of the dispute. The divergence must also arise in the context of the same situation of law and fact. No such divergence arose in the case of claims for infringement of a European patent, granted for several member states, against several defendants, domiciled in different member states, each being sued for an infringement committed in the state of its domicile.

Article 6(1) has been used to enable an English purchaser of a French horse, who was suing his English agent who had acted in the purchase, to join as a co-defendant a German veterinary surgeon who had been engaged to examine and report on the condition of the horse, the claims against both defendants being for negligence in advising in favour of the purchase.[124] Joinder has also been allowed where the English and foreign defendants were both alleged to have assisted dishonestly in breaches of fiduciary duty at different stages in the operation of a fraudulent scheme to mis-appropriate a sum belonging to the plaintiff;[125] and where claims against an English individual and a foreign company related to similar contracts negotiated together by the individual with the claimant, one on his own behalf and the other on behalf of the company.[126]

As well as a sufficient connection between the claims against the English and foreign defendants, it had been held in England and Ireland that it is necessary under Art 6(1) that the claim against the local defendant should be plausible, or seriously arguable, and not made solely for the purpose of enabling the foreign defendant to be

120 See *Aiglon v Gau Shan* [1993] 1 Lloyds Rep 164; *SCOR v Eras* (No 2) [1995] 2 All ER 278; and Gaudemet-Tallon, *Les Conventions de Bruxelles et de Lugano*, 1996, Montchrestien, at para 223.
121 See Case C-51/97: *Réunion Européenne v Spliethoff's Bevrachtingskantoor* [1998] ECR I-6511.
122 See *Bank of Tokyo-Mitsubishi v Baskan Gida* [2004] ILPr 26, at paras 188 and 216.
123 Case C-539/03: [2006] ECR I-6535.
124 See *Gascoine v Pyrah* [1994] ILPr 82 (CA).
125 See *Casio Computer v Sayo* [2001] EWCA Civ 661 (CA). Cf *The Xing Su Hai* [1995] 2 Lloyd's Rep 15, refusing to allow joinder where the claim against the English defendant was merely for disclosure of information about the location of assets of the foreign defendants; and *Messier Dowty v Sabena* [2000] 1 WLR 2040 (CA), refusing to allow joinder where the plaintiff's claim was for declarations of non-liability, and the foreign defendant had made no claim against the plaintiff.
126 See *Latchin v General Mediterranean Holidays* [2002] CLC 330.

joined.[127] But the European Court has now (rather surprisingly) established that there is no such requirement. Joinder under Article 6(1) is possible even if the action against the local defendant is regarded under a national provision as inadmissible from the time when it is brought, for example by reason of insolvency proceedings, and even if the claims are brought with the sole object of ousting the jurisdiction of the courts of the member state where one of the defendants is domiciled.[128]

In *Réunion Européenne v Spliethoff's Bevrachtingskantoor*,[129] the European Court puzzlingly suggested that there is no sufficient connection between claims by the same plaintiff against two defendants in respect of the same loss, if one of the claims is contractual and the other is based on tort. The correctness of this remarkable suggestion was the principal question referred by the Court of Appeal in *Watson v First Choice Holidays*,[130] where an English tourist, who had suffered personal injuries during a holiday in Spain, brought an action in contract against the English organiser of the package holiday, and sought to join a claim in tort against a Spanish sub-contractor in respect of the same injuries. Unfortunately, the reference was eventually abandoned, presumably because the parties had settled the claim. Subsequently the dictum was rejected by Cooke J in *Andrew Weir Shipping Ltd v Wartsila UK Ltd*.[131] It was also rejected in Ireland.[132] Eventually the dictum was overruled by the European Court in *Freeport v Arnoldsson*.[133]

Where the co-defendant whose joinder as such is sought is not domiciled in any EC member state or Lugano Convention country, the English court has discretion to join him if he is a necessary or proper party to a claim which is made against another person who has been or will be served, and which involves a real issue which it is reasonable for the court to try.[134]

Third parties

By Art 6(2), a person domiciled in a member state may also be sued as a third party in third party proceedings, in the court seised of the original proceedings, unless these were instituted solely with the object of removing him from the jurisdiction of the court which would be competent in his case.[135]

In *Hagen v Zeehaghe*,[136] the European Court made clear that this power of a

---

127 See *The Rewia* [1991] 2 Lloyd's Rep 325 (CA); *The Xing Su Hai* [1995] 2 Lloyd's Rep 15; *Holding Oil v Marc Rich* (1996) unreported, 27 February (CA); *Messier Dowty v Sabena* [2000] 1 WLR 2040 (CA); *Bank of Tokyo-Mitsubishi v Baskan Gida* [2004] ILPr 26, at para 217; and *Andrew Weir Shipping Ltd v Wartsila UK Ltd* [2004] EWHC 1284 (Comm).

128 See Case C-103/05: *Reisch Montage v Kiesel Baumaschinen* [2006] ECR I-6827; and Case C-98/06: *Freeport v Arnoldsson*, [2007] ECR I-8319.

129 Case C-51/97: [1998] ECR I-6511, at para 50.

130 [2001] 2 Lloyd's Rep 339.

131 [2004] EWHC 1284 (Comm).

132 See *Daly v Irish Group Travel* [2003] ILPr 38.

133 Case C-98/06: [2007] ECR I-8319.

134 See r 6.36 of the Civil Procedure Rules 1998 (as amended), and Practice Direction B, para 3.1(3).

135 See to similar effect Art 6(2) of the Lugano Convention, and rule 5(b) of Sched 4 to the 1982 Act (as amended). For English jurisdiction over a third party who is not domiciled in any EC member state or Lugano Convention country, see the Civil Procedure Rules Part 20 and r 6.36, and Practice Direction B, para 3.1(4).

136 Case 365/88: [1990] ECR I-1845.

defendant to join a third party applies regardless of the basis of the court's jurisdiction over the defendant, which could be based, as in that case, on Art 5(1), or presumably, on any other provision of Chapter II, including Arts 4 or 24.[137] It also ruled that the procedural admissibility of a third party proceeding in non-territorial respects is governed by the law of the court seised, provided that the effectiveness of the community legislation is not impaired, but that leave to join a third party cannot be refused on the ground that the third party resides or is domiciled in another member state. Thus, as Rix J recognised in *Caltex v Metro*,[138] Art 6(2) requires there to be a proper connection between claim and third party claim such as would be recognised by the forum's own third party statute (in England, Part 20 of the Civil Procedure Rules 1998); but it is not permissible to exercise a *forum non conveniens* discretion in relation to Art 6(2).

As regards the proviso to Art 6(2), in *Hough v P&O Containers*,[139] Rix J explained that this is confined to situations where the claimant and the defendant are effectively in collusion to bring a claim against a third party in an otherwise incompetent forum; or where, even without collusion, the claimant has no good reason to sue the defendant but is hoping that by doing so the defendant will, with the aid of Art 6(2), bring the third party to such a forum.

An application for the costs of litigation, made under s 51 of the Supreme Court Act 1981 against a non-party to the litigation (such as a controlling shareholder of a claimant company), amounts to a third party proceeding within the scope of Art 6(2).[140]

Counterclaims

By Art 6(3), a person domiciled in a member state may also be sued, on a counterclaim arising from the same contract or facts on which the original claim was based, in the court in which the original claim is pending.[141] Probably the reference to the same contract or facts is to be construed broadly, in the light of the definition of related actions provided by Art 28(3), and thus includes a case where the claimant sues for the price of goods supplied and the defendant counterclaims for damages for infringement or repudiation of an exclusive distribution contract pursuant to which the contract of sale sued on by the claimant was entered into.[142] In any event Art 6(3) is confined to a cross-claim made by a person sued, and does not extend to a claim made by a sister company of the defendant.[143] It is also limited to a counterclaim against the

---

137 See *Veenbrink v BIAO* (1992) unreported, 14 May (French Court of Cassation), permitting the use of Art 6(2) where jurisdiction over the main action was governed by Art 4; and Gaudemet-Tallon, *Les Conventions de Bruxelles et de Lugano*, 1996, Montchrestien, at para 226.

138 [1999] 2 Lloyd's Rep 724.

139 [1999] QB 834.

140 See *The Ikarian Reefer* [2000] 1 WLR 603 (CA).

141 See to similar effect Art 6(3) of the Lugano Convention, and r 5(c) of Sched 4 to the 1982 Act (as amended). For English jurisdiction over a counterclaim against a plaintiff who is not domiciled in any EC member state or Lugano Convention country, see Part 20 of the CPR 1998, and *Factories Insurance v Anglo-Scottish Insurance* (1913) 29 TLR 312.

142 See *Gianotti v Montuori* (1994) unreported, 18 February (French Court of Cassation); and Gaudemet-Tallon, *Les Conventions de Bruxelles et de Lugano*, 1996, Montchrestien, at para 229. Cf *per* Léger AG in Case C-341/93: *Danvaern v Otterbeck* [1995] ECR I-2053; and *Dollfus Mieg v CDW International* [2004] ILPr 12.

143 See *Dollfus Mieg v CDW International* [2004] ILPr 12.

original claimant; it does not provide for jurisdiction over an additional party joined by counterclaim.[144]

In the context of monetary claims, the European Court in *Danvaern v Otterbeck*[145] confined Art 6(3) to a true counterclaim, as distinct from a purely defensive set-off. It applies where the defendant, by a separate claim made in the same proceedings, seeks a judgment ordering the plaintiff to pay him a debt, possibly of an amount exceeding that claimed by the plaintiff, even if the plaintiff's claim is dismissed. In contrast the admissibility of a purely defensive set-off, invoked solely for the purpose of wholly or partially extinguishing the plaintiff's claim, is governed not by Art 6(3) but by the law of the court seised.

JURISDICTION CLAUSES

Article 23 of the Regulation authorises parties to existing or potential disputes to enter into an agreement designating the court or courts which will be competent to determine such disputes.[146] Such agreements are generally referred to as 'jurisdiction clauses'. Article 23 is a complex provision, which regulates both the formal and essential validity of jurisdiction clauses and their effects. In general, it gives exclusive effect to a valid jurisdiction clause. Article 23 provides:

1   If the parties, one or more of whom is domiciled in a member state,[147] have agreed that a court or the courts of a member state are to have jurisdiction to settle any disputes which have arisen or which may arise in connection with a particular legal relationship,[148] that court or those courts shall have jurisdiction. Such jurisdiction shall be exclusive unless the parties have agreed otherwise.[149] Such an agreement conferring jurisdiction shall be either:

---

144   See *Bank of Tokyo-Mitsubishi v Baskan Gida* [2004] ILPr 26, at para 189.
145   Case C-341/93: [1995] ECR I-2053.
146   See also Art 17 of the Lugano Convention; r 12 of Sched 4 to the 1982 Act (as amended); and the Civil Procedure Rules Part 20 and r 6.36, and Practice Direction B, para 3.1(6). Article 23 of the Regulation differs in minor respects from Art 17 of the Brussels and Lugano Conventions. A Convention on Choice of Court Agreements was adopted at the Hague Conference on Private International Law on 30 June 2005. Although the Hague Convention 2005 has not yet entered into force, on 26 February 2009 the EC Council adopted Decision 2009/397, authorising its signature on behalf of the European Community, and it was signed accordingly on 1 April 2009; see [2009] OJ L133/1.
147   In Case C-412/98: *Group Josi v UGIC* [2000] ECR I-5925, the European Court emphasised that it is sufficient under this provision that either the plaintiff or the defendant is domiciled in a member state, even if the other party is not domiciled within the member states. Probably the provision applies if any of the parties to the agreement on jurisdiction was domiciled in a member state either at the time when the agreement was concluded, or at the time of the institution of the action in which the agreement is relied on.
148   The relationship between a company and its shareholders as such is sufficiently particular for this purpose; see Case C-214/89: *Powell Duffryn v Petereit* [1992] ECR I-1745.
149   A court whose jurisdiction is excluded by a clause has the same powers as the court whose jurisdiction is chosen by the clause to determine its validity under Art 23; see *per* Léger AG in Case C-159/97: *Castelletti v Trumpy* [1999] ECR I-1597. In England the burden lies on a defendant who relies on a foreign exclusive jurisdiction clause to show a good arguable case for its existence and validity; see *Bank of Tokyo-Mitsubishi v Baskan Gida* [2004] ILPr 26, at para 194. See also, as to the effect of the slightly different provisions on exclusivity contained in the Brussels and Lugano Conventions, Case 23/78: *Meeth v Glacetal* [1978] ECR 2133; Case 22/85: *Anterist v Crédit Lyonnais* [1986] ECR 1951; *Kurz v Stella Musical* [1992] Ch 196; *Kitechnology v Unicor* [1995] FSR 765 (CA); *Lafi v Meriden* [2000] 2 Lloyd's Rep 51; *Mercury Communications v Communication Telesystems International* [1999] 2 All ER (Comm) 33; and *Insured Financial Structures v Elektrocieplownia Tychy* [2003] QB 1260 (CA). On non-exclusivity under the Regulation, see *Evialis v Siat* [2003] 2 Lloyd's Rep 377.

(a) in writing or evidenced in writing; or

(b) in a form which accords with practices which the parties have established between themselves; or

(c) in international trade or commerce, in a form which accords with a usage of which the parties are or ought to have been aware and which in such trade or commerce is widely known to, and regularly observed by, parties to contracts of the type involved in the particular trade or commerce concerned.

2 Any communication by electronic means which provides a durable record of the agreement shall be equivalent to 'writing'.[150]

3 Where such an agreement is concluded by parties, none of whom is domiciled in a member state, the courts of other member states shall have no jurisdiction over their disputes unless the court or courts chosen have declined jurisdiction.[151]

4 The court or courts of a member state on which a trust instrument has conferred jurisdiction shall have exclusive jurisdiction in any proceedings brought against a settlor, trustee or beneficiary, if relations between these persons or their rights or obligations under the trust are involved.[152]

5 Agreements or provisions of a trust instrument conferring jurisdiction shall have no legal force if they are contrary to Articles 13, 17 or 21, or if the courts whose jurisdiction they purport to exclude have exclusive jurisdiction by virtue of Article 22.[153]

As regards formal validity, the reference in Art 23(1)(a) to an agreement made or evidenced in writing normally requires writing signed by both parties, containing or incorporating by reference a jurisdiction clause; but it is also sufficient if an oral contract contains a specific reference to jurisdiction and its conclusion is followed by the issue of a confirmatory document by one party to the other, and the failure of the recipient to object within a reasonable time.[154] Moreover, as the European Court recognised in *MSG v Les Gravieres Rhénanes*[155] and *Castelletti v Trumpy*,[156] a confirmatory document which does not satisfy Art 23(1)(a) will now be effective under Art 23(1)(c) if it accords with a usage regularly observed in the relevant branch of international commerce. The European Court accepted that such a usage may exist where one of the parties to the contract has remained silent in the face of a commercial letter of confirmation from the other party containing a pre-printed jurisdiction clause, or

---

150 This does not in itself address the need for a signature, or the sufficiency of an electronic signature, but Art 5 of Directive 1999/93 [2000] OJ L13/12, and in England s 7 of the Electronic Communications Act 2000, may apply. See also Chapter 4 for further on electronic signatures.

151 In this situation, the chosen courts must determine the existence and exercise of their jurisdiction in accordance with their own law, as provided for by Art 4. Where the English High Court is chosen, it will in its discretion accept jurisdiction unless the defendant establishes strong grounds showing that it would be unjust to do so: see the Civil Procedure Rules Part 20 and r 6.36, and Practice Direction B, para 3.1(6); *The Chaparral* [1968] 2 Lloyd's Rep 158; and *Sinochem v Mobil* [2000] 1 Lloyd's Rep 670.

152 On trusts, see also Art 5(6).

153 Articles 13, 17 and 21 apply to insurance, consumer and employment contracts. Article 22 deals with exclusive jurisdiction by reason of subject matter (eg, of the situs over proprietary rights in land). The Regulation prevents a member state from imposing additional restrictions relating to the subject matter in respect of which a jurisdiction clause is permitted; see Case 25/79: *Sanicentral v Collin* [1979] ECR 3423.

154 See Case 24/76: *Estasis Salotti v RÜWA* [1976] ECR 1831; Case 25/76: *Segoura v Bonakdarian* [1976] ECR 1851; Case 71/83: *Tilly Russ v Haven* [1984] ECR 2417; Case 221/84: *Berghoefer v ASA* [1985] ECR 2699; and Case 313/85: *Iveco Fiat v Van Hool* [1986] ECR 3337. See also *AIG Group v The Ethniki* [2000] 2 All ER 566 (CA); *Siboti v BP France* [2003] 2 Lloyd's Rep 364; and *Bols Distilleries v Superior Yacht Services* [2007] 1 Lloyd's Rep 683 (PC).

155 Case C-106/95: [1997] ECR I-911.

156 Case C-159/97: [1999] ECR I-1597.

where one of the parties has repeatedly paid without objection invoices issued by the other party containing such a clause, or where a jurisdiction clause is included among the clauses printed on the back of a bill of lading, the front of which has been signed by the parties. Moreover, compliance with a relevant usage will establish the existence of an agreement on jurisdiction, as well as its formal validity. The crucial issue relates to the existence of a usage, and this must be determined not by reference to the law of a member state, nor in relation to international trade or commerce in general, but under a Community standard and in relation to the branch of international trade or commerce in which the parties to the contract operate. Such a usage exists where a certain course of conduct is generally and regularly followed by operators in the relevant branch when concluding contracts of a particular type, and the relevant branch must be identified in terms of both substance and location. Actual or presumptive awareness will be established whenever, in the branch of trade or commerce in which the parties operate, a particular course of conduct is generally and regularly followed in the conclusion of a particular type of contract, so that it may be regarded as an established usage.[157]

Although in general an agreement on jurisdiction operates only between the parties thereto, the European Court has recognised two exceptions. First, where a substantive contract (for example, of insurance) is concluded wholly or partly for the benefit of a third party, and it contains a jurisdiction clause which is also designed to benefit the third party and which is validly agreed to by the contracting parties in accordance with Art 23, the third party may take advantage of the clause, even though he himself has not agreed to it in a manner contemplated by Art 23.[158] Secondly, a jurisdiction clause which was contained in a substantive contract and was validly agreed to by the original contracting parties also operates in favour of and against a third person who, under the national law applicable under the conflict rules of the court seised, has succeeded to the rights and obligations of one of the parties under the contract (such as a subsequent holder of a bill of lading).[159] More generally, in *Glencore v Metro*,[160] Moore-Bick J held that an assignee of a contractual debt is bound by a jurisdiction clause contained in the contract from which the debt arises and agreed between the original parties in accordance with the requirements of Art 23; and in *The Kribi*,[161] Aikens J held that, as against a carrier under a bill of lading contract, a cargo insurer is in the same position as its insured.

In *Elefanten Schuh v Jacqmain*,[162] the European Court ruled that the formal requirements specified by Art 23 are exhaustive. Thus, it is not open to a member state to

---

157 See also as to the effectiveness between a company and its shareholders of a jurisdiction clause contained in the corporate constitution, Case C-214/89: *Powell Duffryn v Petereit* [1992] ECR I-1745.

158 See Case 201/82: *Gerling v Treasury Administration* [1983] ECR 2503; and *per* Léger AG in Case C-159/97: *Castelletti v Trumpy* [1999] ECR I-1597. See also *Firswood v Petra Bank* (1995) unreported, 13 December (CA); and Gaudemet-Tallon, *Les Conventions de Bruxelles et de Lugano*, 1996, Montchrestien, at para 141.

159 See Case 71/83: *Tilly Russ v Haven* [1984] ECR 2417; Case C-159/97: *Castelletti v Trumpy* [1999] ECR I-1597; and Case C-387/98: *Coreck Maritime v Handelsveem* [2000] ECR I-9337. Under English conflict rules, succession to a bill of lading contract is governed by the proper law of the contract; see *The Kribi* [2001] 1 Lloyd's Rep 76.

160 [1999] 2 Lloyd's Rep 632. See also *Bank of Tokyo-Mitsubishi v Baskan Gida* [2004] ILPr 26, at para 191.

161 [2001] 1 Lloyd's Rep 76.

162 See Case 150/80: [1981] ECR 1671.

require additional formalities, such as that a jurisdiction clause be expressed in a particular language. This approach was confirmed in *Castelletti v Trumpy*,[163] where the court ruled that in the context of the provision permitting a form according with international commercial usages, the acceptability of the language used (in this case, the English language for a bill of lading between an Argentinian shipper and a Danish shipowner in respect of the carriage of goods from Argentina to Italy) depends on whether its use accords with such usages. Presumably, however, if a party abusively chose to use a language which he knew the other would not understand, there would be no 'agreement', under an independent Community standard, within the meaning of Art 23.[164] Somewhat similarly, the French Court of Cassation has ruled a jurisdiction clause invalid under Art 23 because it was printed in characters so small as to be unreadable.[165]

Article 23 does not require any objective connection between the parties or the subject matter of the dispute and the territory of the court chosen.[166] Thus, it permits parties to choose a 'neutral' forum; for example, the choice of an English court by a French seller and a German buyer of goods to be manufactured and delivered in France and paid for in Germany. Probably Art 23 applies even if, at the date of the agreement on jurisdiction, the relevant relationship is otherwise connected exclusively with a single member state.

As the European Court explained in *Coreck Maritime v Handelsveem*,[167] Art 23 does not require a jurisdiction clause to be formulated in such a way that the competent court can be determined on its wording alone. It is sufficient that the clause states the objective factors on the basis of which the parties have agreed to choose a court or the courts to which they wish to submit disputes. Such factors must be sufficiently precise to enable the court seised to ascertain whether it has jurisdiction, but they may, where appropriate, be determined by the particular circumstances of the case. Thus it is permissible to choose, in a bill of lading contract, the courts of 'the country where the carrier has his principal place of business'.

As regards the possible invalidity of a jurisdiction clause by reason of lack of consent, owing to such factors as fraud, mistake or improper pressure, the European Court ruled in *Benincasa v Dentalkit*[168] that for reasons of legal certainty, even where a jurisdiction clause is contained in a substantive contract, its validity must be distinguished from that of the substantive contract and its operation cannot be affected by allegations that the substantive contract is invalid, even for lack of consent, under the national law applicable under the conflict rules of the court seised. This leaves open the situation where it is alleged that there is lack of consent to the jurisdiction clause itself, by reason of fraud, error or pressure relating specifically to that clause, as

---

163 Case C-159/97: [1999] ECR I-1597.
164 See *per* Lenz AG in Case C-288/92: *Custom Made v Stawa* [1994] ECR I-2913; and Gaudemet-Tallon, *Les Conventions de Bruxelles et de Lugano*, 1996, Montchrestien, para 124.
165 See *Pavan v Richard* (1996) unreported, 27 February.
166 See Case 56/79: *Zelger v Salinitri (No 1)* [1980] ECR 89; and Case C-159/97: *Castelletti v Trumpy* [1999] ECR I-1597, where the court also emphasised that it is not open to a court excluded by the clause to disregard it on the ground that the chosen court would apply different substantive rules in determining the merits of the dispute from those which would have been applied by the court excluded. In that case an English court was chosen in a bill of lading for the carriage of goods by a Danish shipowner from Argentina to Italy.
167 Case C-387/98: [2000] ECR I-9337.
168 Case C-269/95: [1997] ECR I-3767.

where the clause refers to the court for the place where one party's head office is located and that party misleads the other about such location. In such a case, the analogy of *Tessili v Dunlop*[169] suggests that the issue should be governed by the law applicable under the conflict rules of the court seised.[170]

Article 23 envisages a choice of 'a court or the courts' of a member state. It is advisable to choose a specific court, such as the English High Court, and thus pre-empt any problem of finding the territorially appropriate court within the chosen state. It is clear that the chosen court need not otherwise have *territorial* competence, though the parties cannot override the member state's rules allocating competence over categories of subject matter between different types of court; for instance, by attempting to confer jurisdiction over a commercial contract on a British employment tribunal.[171] If the parties merely choose the courts in general of a specified member state, it will be for the law of that state to determine which of its courts shall be competent. It is submitted that in such a case the chosen state is bound to provide at least one competent court; and if it lacks any applicable rule for selecting that court or courts, all its courts become territorially competent.[172] In any event, in the context of an international maritime contract between foreign parties, the Court of Appeal has construed a clause specifying 'British Courts' as referring to the English High Court.[173]

Since Art 23 is based on the principle of party autonomy, it does not prevent parties who have concluded an agreement on jurisdiction from subsequently conclud-ing a further agreement varying or rescinding the earlier agreement.[174] Similarly, as the European Court ruled in *Elefanten Schuh v Jacqmain*[175] and *Spitzley v Sommer Exploitation*,[176] Art 24 (on submission by appearance)[177] prevails over Art 23, so that a court seised of an action or counterclaim in breach of a valid agreement on jurisdiction becomes competent if the defendant thereto enters an appearance without contesting its jurisdiction.

Although the mandatory effect of Art 23(1) was recognised in *Kitechnology v Unicor*,[178] in subsequent decisions English courts asserted a discretion to disregard an English jurisdiction clause in favour of a supposedly more appropriate forum in a non-member state, even where a party is domiciled in a member state.[179] As in the case of Art 2,[180] such an approach misunderstands the nature and purpose of the

---

169 Case 12/76: [1976] ECR 1473. The validity of jurisdiction clauses is excluded from the scope of the Rome Convention 1980 by Art 1(2)(d), and from the Rome I Regulation by Art 1(2)(e). On these measures, see Chapter 17 below.

170 Cf *per* Slynn AG in Case 150/80: *Elefanten Schuh v Jacqmain* [1981] ECR 1671.

171 See the Jenard Report [1979] OJ C59/1, at p 38.

172 See Gaudemet-Tallon, *Les Conventions de Bruxelles et de Lugano*, 1996, Montchrestien, at para 133. Cf the Jenard Report, [1979] OJ C59/1, at p 37.

173 See *The Komninos S* [1991] 1 Lloyd's Rep 370.

174 See *Sinochem v Mobil* [2000] 1 Lloyd's Rep 670.

175 Case 150/80: [1981] ECR 1671.

176 Case 48/84: [1985] ECR 787.

177 See pp 525–6 above.

178 [1995] FSR 765 (CA).

179 See *Eli Lilly v Novo Nordisk* [2000] ILPr 73 (CA); *Mercury Communications v Communication Telesystems International* [1999] 2 All ER (Comm) 33; and *Sinochem v Mobil* [2000] 1 Lloyd's Rep 670. See also *Ace Insurance v Zurich Insurance* [2001] 1 Lloyd's Rep 618 (CA).

180 See pp 521–5 above.

Regulation and has been rendered obsolete by the decision of the European Court in *Owusu v Jackson.*[181]

Although the wording of Art 23 refers only to agreements which choose courts of member states, in *Coreck Maritime v Handelsveem,*[182] the European Court accepted that Art 23 gives rise to an implied 'reflex effect' which, derogating from the generally mandatory character of Chapter II of the Regulation, enables a member state to permit its courts to decline jurisdiction so as to respect a jurisdiction clause which would have been valid and effective under Art 23 but for its choosing a court of a non-member state. The Court explained that Art 23 does not apply to clauses designating a court in a third country, but that a court of a member state must, if it is seised notwithstanding such a jurisdiction clause, assess the validity of the clause by reference to the law, including the conflict rules, of its own country.[183]

INSURANCE, CONSUMER AND EMPLOYMENT CONTRACTS

In order to protect the party who is expected to be economically weaker and less experienced in legal matters than the other party to the contract,[184] Chapter II of the Regulation lays down special rules on jurisdiction in respect of insurance contracts,[185] consumer contracts,[186] and contracts of employment.[187] Accordingly these provisions offer the weaker party (the policyholder, consumer, or employee) a wide choice of fora in which to sue the stronger party (the insurer, supplier, or employer), while limiting those in which the stronger party can sue the weaker party and in many cases invalidating contrary agreements. Moreover, in the case of insurance and consumer contracts (though not of employment contracts), the protective policy is reinforced by Art 35, which prevents the recognition and enforcement of judgments under Chapter III where the original court accepted jurisdiction in contravention of the protective provisions.

In general the protective provisions apply only when the defendant is domiciled in a member state. Otherwise jurisdiction in respect of these contracts is usually remitted by Art 4 to the law of the forum state in the same way as for ordinary contracts, and in such cases English law treats insurance, consumer and employment contracts in the same way as ordinary contracts. But, by Arts 9(2), 15(2) and 18(2), where an insurer, a supplier under a consumer contract, or an employer is not (under the normal rules) domiciled in any member state, but he has a secondary establishment in a member state, and the dispute arises from the operations of the secondary establishment, the insurer, supplier or employer is treated as domiciled in the state in which the secondary establishment is situated.

181　Case C-281/02: [2005] ECR I-1383.
182　Case C-387/98: [2000] ECR I-9337, citing the Schlosser Report [1979] OJ C59/71, at para 176.
183　See also *Ace Insurance v Zurich Insurance* [2001] 1 Lloyd's Rep 618 (CA), respecting an American jurisdiction clause and declining jurisdiction over a Swiss defendant in favour of a Texas court; a questionable decision, in view of the court's interpretation of the clause as non-exclusive.
184　See Case C-89/91: *Shearson Lehman Hutton v TVB* [1993] ECR I-139, at para 18; and recital 13 to the Regulation.
185　Chapter II, Section 3, Arts 8–14.
186　Chapter II, Section 4, Arts 15–17.
187　Chapter II, Section 5, Arts 18–21.

The protective provisions do not affect a number of important provisions of Chapter II, which apply in the normal way to the protected contracts. Thus an action based on a protected contract can always be brought in the courts of the member state in which the defendant is domiciled, and in such cases the Regulation retains its normal indifference to the allocation of jurisdiction between the courts for the various areas of that state.[188] Similarly, it remains possible to sue at the location of the defendant's secondary establishment from whose operations the dispute arose;[189] or to make a counterclaim based on the same contract in the court seised of the original action;[190] and submission by appearance remains effective to found jurisdiction.[191] Again, Arts 26–31 of the Regulation (on the consideration of jurisdiction by the court seised of its own motion, on service of the defendant, on simultaneously pending actions, and on provisional measures) remain applicable.

Insurance

No explicit definition of insurance is provided but, as in the case of consumer contracts,[192] the concept is likely to be given an independent meaning by the European Court. In any event it is clear that all types of insurance (as generally understood) are covered, and that the protective provisions are not confined to insurance taken out for domestic or private purposes.[193] But they do not extend to reinsurance, except in relation to direct claims by an insured under the primary insurance against a reinsurer.[194]

The Regulation offers to a policyholder, or other insured or beneficiary, a wide choice of fora in which to bring an action against an insurer domiciled in a member state. A similar choice is extended by Art 11(2) to a third party victim of a tort covered by liability insurance, where he brings a direct action against the insurer, if such a direct action is permissible under the law governing the issue according to the conflict rules of the court seised.[195] In accordance with the general principle in favour of the defendant's country, the Regulation confers jurisdiction on the courts of the member state in which the defendant insurer is domiciled,[196] and on the courts for the place (in another member state) at which the defendant insurer has a secondary establishment from the operations of which the dispute has arisen.[197] But, radically departing from the normal approach to jurisdiction, Art 9(1)(b) enables an insurer domiciled in a

---

188   See Arts 9(1)(a), 12(1), 16(1)–(2), 19(1) and 20(1). In the United Kingdom, insurance is treated for the purpose of such allocation in the same way as ordinary contracts, since Sched 4 to the 1982 Act deliberately omits any specific provision for insurance.

189   See Arts 5(5), 8, 15(1) and 18.

190   See Arts 6(3), 12(2), 16(3) and 20(2).

191   See Arts 13(1), 17(1), 21(1) and 24.

192   See Case C-89/91: *Shearson Lehman Hutton v TVB* [1993] ECR I-139.

193   See *New Hampshire Insurance Co v Strabag Bau* [1992] 1 Lloyd's Rep 361 (CA).

194   See Case C-412/98: *Group Josi v UGIC* [2000] ECR I-5925.

195   Under traditional English law the admissibility of such a direct action was governed by the proper law of the insurance contract; see *The Hari Bhum* [2004] 1 Lloyd's Rep 206. But now Art 18 of the Rome II Regulation (EC Regulation 864/2007, [2007] OJ L199/40; considered in Chapter 17 below) enables a tort victim to bring his claim directly against the tortfeasor's liability insurer, if either the law applicable to the tort or the law applicable to the insurance contract so provides.

196   See Art 9(1)(a).

197   See Arts 5(5) and 8.

member state to be sued in another member state by a policyholder or other insured or beneficiary or even a third-party victim at the place of the claimant's domicile.[198]

The jurisdiction normally conferred by Art 5(1) on the courts for the place of performance of the obligation in question is excluded by Art 8. But in the case of liability insurance, or insurance of land, or where land and moveable property are covered by the same insurance policy and adversely affected by the same contingency, Art 10 confers jurisdiction on the courts for the place (in a member state other than that of the defendant insurer's domicile) at which the harmful event occurred. It seems clear that in the case of insurance of land, or of land and moveables together, the damage to the land (and perhaps moveables) constitutes the relevant 'harmful event', so that jurisdiction is conferred on the courts of the situs. In the case of liability insurance, the concept is presumably the same as under Art 5(3).[199]

As regards ancillary jurisdiction, Art 6(1)[200] is excluded by Art 8, but Art 9(1)(c) confers jurisdiction over a defendant co-insurer on a court of a member state (other than the defendant co-insurer's domicile) in which proceedings are pending against the leading insurer. It does not appear to matter on what basis jurisdiction over the leading insurer was obtained. Thus an English co-insurer could be joined as a co-defendant in a French action against an American leading insurer, in which jurisdiction was founded on the plaintiff's French nationality under Art 4 of the Regulation and Art 14 of the French Civil Code. Similarly, Art 6(2)[201] is excluded, but Art 11(1) permits third party proceedings against a liability insurer in a court (of a member state other than the defendant insurer's domicile) in which proceedings brought by a victim against an insured are pending; and Art 12(2) enables the making of a counterclaim in a court (of a member state other than the defendant insurer's domicile) in which an action arising from the same policy is pending. As regards submission, Art 13(2) ensures that an insurer can be sued in a court of a member state which has been chosen by an agreement on jurisdiction which complies with Art 23, and Arts 13(1) and 24 that a court of a member state will become competent if the defendant insurer enters an appearance without contesting its jurisdiction.

In accordance with its protective purpose, the Regulation severely restricts jurisdiction to entertain an action brought by an insurer against a policyholder or other insured or beneficiary who is domiciled in a member state.[202] In general the action must be brought in the courts of the member state in which the defendant is domiciled; or in another member state, in the courts for the place at which the defendant has a secondary establishment from the operations of which the dispute has arisen.[203]

---

198 See Case C-463/06: *FBTO Schadeverzekeringen v Odenbreit*, [2007] ECR I-11321.
199 On Art 5(3), see pp 533–6 above.
200 On Art 6(1), see pp 536–8 above.
201 On Art 6(2), see pp 538–9 above.
202 The restrictions extend to actions by the insurer against persons other than a policyholder, insured or beneficiary, if the insurer's claim against them arises from the insurance, such as persons who have conspired with the policyholder to defraud the insurer, and apply even if the plaintiff insurer is not domiciled in any member state; see *Jordan v Baltic Insurance Group* [1999] 2 AC 127. But an application for the costs of litigation, made under s 51 of the Supreme Court Act 1981 against a non-party to the litigation (such as a controlling shareholder of a plaintiff company), does not fall within the scope of the protective provisions, even where the litigation in question relates to insurance and the costs are sought against the controlling shareholder of a plaintiff corporate policyholder; see *The Ikarian Reefer* [2000] 1 WLR 603 (CA).
203 See Arts 5(5), 8 and 12(1).

But Art 12(2) enables the making of a counterclaim in a court in which an action arising from the same policy is pending;[204] Art 11(3) enables a liability insurer to join a policyholder or other insured as a third party in a direct action brought by a victim; and submission by appearance remains effective.[205]

To ensure the effectiveness of the protective policy, Art 13 invalidates any agreement on jurisdiction which departs from the protective provisions, except in five specified cases. The invalidation probably extends to clauses choosing a court of a non-member state, but not to arbitration clauses.[206] The first exception permits an agreement on jurisdiction which is entered into after the dispute has arisen. The second allows an agreement in so far as it enables the policyholder, an insured or a beneficiary to sue in additional courts. The third exception permits an agreement which is concluded between a policyholder and an insurer who at its conclusion are domiciled or habitually resident in the same member state, and which has the effect of conferring jurisdiction on the courts of that state, to the exclusion of the courts for the place of a possible harmful event elsewhere (or of a subsequently acquired domicile elsewhere), unless such an agreement is contrary to the law of the chosen state. But in view of the general requirement of privity applicable under Art 23, such an agreement will not be effective against a third party victim who brings a direct action against a liability insurer.[207] The fourth exception permits an agreement which is concluded with a policyholder who is not domiciled (presumably at the conclusion of the agreement)[208] in any member state, except in so far as the insurance is compulsory under the law of a member state, or the insurance relates to land situated in a member state.[209]

It is in respect of the fifth exception that the Regulation has made one of its most important departures from the Brussels and Lugano Conventions. Previously, the fifth exception concerned insurance of most maritime or aviation risks, other than personal injury to passengers and loss of or damage to their baggage. Now it has been extended by Arts 13(5) and 14(5) to cover any insurance of a large risk, as defined by EC Directives 73/239, 88/357 and 90/618. The effect is to permit a jurisdiction clause contained in an insurance contract in most cases where the policyholder is acting in the course of a large or medium-sized business.[210]

Consumer contracts

Section 4 (Arts 15–17) of Chapter II of the Regulation lays down protective rules in respect of certain consumer contracts, which are elaborately defined and may conveniently be referred to as protected consumer contracts. In the case of such a

---

204 But Art 12(2) only permits a counterclaim against the original plaintiff, and not against additional co-defendants to the counterclaim, such as persons alleged to have conspired with the policyholder to defraud the insurer; see *Jordan v Baltic Insurance Group* [1999] 2 AC 127.
205 See Arts 13(1) and 24.
206 See Arts 1(2)(d) and 66; and Art II of the New York Convention of 10 June 1958 on the Recognition and Enforcement of Foreign Arbitral Awards.
207 See Gaudemet-Tallon, *Les Conventions de Bruxelles et de Lugano*, 1996, Montchrestien, at para 254.
208 *Ibid*, at para 256.
209 On compulsory insurance, see the Schlosser Report [1979] OJ C59/71, at para 138.
210 The definition of large risks is examined in detail in Chapter 17 below.

contract, the consumer may sue the supplier in the courts of the member state where the supplier is domiciled. The consumer also has the option of suing the supplier, in another member state, at the location of the supplier's secondary establishment from whose operations the dispute arises, or at the consumer's own domicile.[211] On the other hand, the supplier must sue the consumer in the member state where the consumer is domiciled.[212] In addition, Art 17 invalidates a jurisdiction clause in respect of such a contract, with three exceptions corresponding to the first three exceptions applicable to insurance.[213] Whichever party is claimant or defendant, the Regulation permits the making of a counterclaim based on the same contract in the court seised of the original action, and submission by appearance remains effective to found jurisdiction.[214]

Viewed generically, a consumer contract might be defined as a contract entered into by an individual, not acting in the course of a business, whereby he acquires goods or services, for his own private consumption, from a supplier acting in the course of a business, or whereby he obtains credit in connection with such an acquisition of goods or services. But the Regulation departs in various ways from this generic definition.

Article 15(1) of the Regulation refers to 'a contract concluded by a person, the consumer, for a purpose which can be regarded as being outside his trade or profession'. But, unlike the Brussels Convention, the Regulation does not confine the scope of the protective provisions to contracts for the supply of goods or services, or of credit in connection with the sale of goods.

As regards the character of the acquirer, the European Court has emphasised, in rulings on the Brussels Convention, that Section 4 is confined to cases where the contract was entered into by a private final consumer, not engaged in trade or professional activities,[215] and it is clear that the same applies to Section 4 of the Regulation. It also seems clear that under the Regulation, as under the Brussels Convention, the acquirer must be an individual, as distinct from a corporate entity,[216] and that Section 4 does not apply where a person acquiring goods or services holds himself out as contracting for business purposes to a person who contracts in good faith on that basis.[217]

The problem of a person acting for mixed business and non-business purposes was addressed by the European Court in *Gruber v Bay Wa*,[218] which involved a contract concluded by a farmer for the purchase of roofing tiles for a farmhouse which was occupied by him partly in a private capacity as a family dwelling and partly for

---

211 See Arts 5(5), 15(1) and 16(1).
212 See Art 16(2).
213 On these exceptions, see p 548 above. Despite the third exception, a clause in a contract between parties domiciled in the same country, choosing the court for the place of the supplier's domicile, may be rendered invalid by Directive 93/13 on Unfair Terms in Consumer Contracts; see Case C-240/98: *Océano Grupo Editorial v Murciano Quintero* [2000] ECR I-4941.
214 See Arts 6(3), 16(3), 17(1) and 24.
215 See Case C-89/91: *Shearson Lehman Hutton v TVB* [1993] ECR I-139; Case C-269/95: *Benincasa v Dentalkit* [1997] ECR I-3767; Case C-167/00: *VKI v Henkel* [2002] ECR I-8111; and Case 150/77: *Bertrand v Ott* [1978] 1431.
216 See Case C-269/95: *Benincasa v Dentalkit* [1997] ECR I-3767; and Art 6(1) of the Rome I Regulation.
217 See Case C-460/01: *Gruber v Bay Wa* [2005] ECR I-439.
218 Case C-464/01: [2005] ECR I-439.

farming purposes to house livestock and fodder. The European Court ruled that a person who concludes a contract partly for business purposes and partly for non-business purposes does not count as a consumer unless his business purpose is of negligible importance in relation to the transaction. Moreover, in the case of a contract for mixed purposes it is for the alleged consumer to establish that the business purpose is of negligible importance. In determining whether the contract in question was concluded to a more than negligible extent for business purposes, the court seised must refer primarily to the objective facts as a whole, rather than confining itself to matters known to the supplier at the time of conclusion of the contract. But there is an exception where the alleged consumer so conducted himself as to create the impression in the supplier that he was acting for business purposes. This would be the case, for example, where an individual, in ordering goods which are capable of business use, uses notepaper with a business letter-head, has the goods delivered to his business address, or refers to the possibility of reclaiming value-added tax. In such circumstances Section 4 would not apply even if in reality the contract did not have a more than negligible business purpose, for the consumer would be regarded as having renounced its protection in view of the impression he had created in the supplier, acting in good faith.

Under the Brussels Convention the European Court had also insisted that the contract must be concluded for the purpose of satisfying the acquirer's own needs in terms of private consumption.[219] The requirement appeared to exclude a contract entered into for purposes of investment or financial speculation, such as purchase of corporate shares or commodity futures. On the other hand, a contract for the provision of credit designed to enable the borrower to obtain goods or services for his private consumption was within Section 4. Now, however, in *Ilsinger v Dreschers*[220] the European Court has ruled that under the Regulation there is no requirement that the contract must be concluded for the purpose of satisfying the acquirer's own needs in terms of private consumption. Subject to the specific exclusion of certain transport contracts,[221] Section 4 of the Regulation extends to all contracts, whatever their purpose, if they have been concluded by a consumer with a professional and fall within the latter's commercial or professional activities. It follows that Section 4 of the Regulation extends not only to contracts for financial services such as banking, but also to contracts entered into for purposes of investment or financial speculation, including contracts for the acquisition of financial instruments or transferable securities (such as corporate shares, corporate or public bonds, units in an investment fund, commodity futures, or other derivative instruments). It also seems clear that under the Regulation Section 4 extends to cases where an individual purchases land for non-business purposes.

A series of cases in the European Court have dealt with claims brought under consumer protection legislation by a consumer against a supplier for a prize promised by the supplier as a marketing device with a view to inducing the consumer to place an order for goods or services. Under the Brussels Convention it was held that Section

---

219 See Case C-269/95: *Benincasa v Dentalkit* [1997] ECR I-3767.

220 Case C-180/06, 14 May 2009. See especially at paras 48–50.

221 Article 15(3) of the Regulation excludes from Section 4 a contract of transport, other than a contract which, for an inclusive price, provides for a combination of travel and accommodation. But it seems likely that this exclusion will be constructed restrictively, so that a contract for a combination of transport and admission to a cultural or sporting event may fall within the Section. It is clear that insurance contracts are always governed by Section 3, to the exclusion of Section 4.

4 extended to a claim for a prize promised upon the placing of an order for goods,[222] but did not apply where the prize was not made conditional on the placing of an order for goods or services, but only on a request for payment of the prize, and no order was placed.[223] In contrast, the European Court has ruled in *Ilsinger v Dreschers*[224] that in this context Section 4 of the Regulation has a wider operation.

In *Ilsinger* the European Court addressed the situation where a consumer seeks, in accordance with protective legislation, an order requiring a mail-order company to pay a prize which the consumer has apparently won, after the company, with the aim of encouraging the consumer to conclude a contract, had sent a letter addressed to him personally giving the impression that he would be awarded a prize if he requested payment by returning the 'prize claim certificate' attached to the letter, but without the award of the prize depending on an order for goods offered for sale by the company. The European Court ruled that such an action brought by the consumer falls within Section 4 of the Regulation where either the professional vendor has undertaken in law to pay the prize to the consumer, or the consumer has in fact placed an order with the professional vendor. The Court explained that Section 4 of the Regulation is not limited to situations in which the parties have assumed reciprocal obligations, but that the Section does require that the action relates to a contract which has been concluded between a consumer and a professional. For this purpose a contract may exist where one of the parties merely indicates its acceptance, without assuming any legal obligation to the other party, but it is necessary that the latter party should assume such a legal obligation by submitting a firm offer which is sufficiently clear and precise with regard to its object and scope as to give rise to a link of a contractual nature. In the context of a prize notification, the mail-order company must have expressed clearly its intention to be bound by a legal commitment, if it is accepted by the other party, by declaring itself to be unconditionally willing to pay the prize at issue to consumers who so request. Accordingly Section 4 of the Regulation cannot apply if the professional did not undertake contractually to pay the prize promised to the consumer who requests its payment, unless the misleading prize notification was followed by the conclusion of a contract by the consumer with the mail-order company evidenced by an order placed with the latter.

As regards the character of the supplier, Section 4 of the Regulation (like Section 4 of the Brussels Convention) clearly requires that the other party to a consumer contract, the supplier, must be acting in the course of a trade or profession. This has been confirmed by the European Court in rulings on the Brussels Convention,[225] and is made explicit by Article 15(1)(c) of the Regulation.

In addition, Art 15(1) requires that the contract must be either (a) a contract for the sale of goods on instalment credit terms;[226] or (b) a contract for a loan repayable by

---

222 See Case C-96/00: *Gabriel* [2002] ECR I-6367.
223 See Case C-27/02: *Engler v Janus Versand* [2005] ECR I-481; also holding that such a claim counted as a contractual matter within Article 5(1).
224 Case C-180/06, 14th May 2009.
225 See Case C-96/00: *Gabriel* [2002] ECR-I-6367, at para 39; and Case C-27/02: *Engler v Janus Versand* [2005] ECR I-481, at para 34. See also the Giuliano and Lagarde Report on the Rome Convention 1980, [1980] OJ C282/1 at p 23; and Article 6(1) of the Rome I Regulation.
226 This case is confined to situations where the seller has granted credit to the buyer, in the sense that the seller has transferred possession of the goods to the buyer before the buyer has paid the full price, and does not apply where the full price had to be paid before transfer of possession, even it was payable in several instalments; see Case C-99/96: *Mietz v Intership Yachting Sneek* [1999] ECR I-2277.

instalments, or for any other form of credit, made to finance the sale of goods; or (c) a contract which is concluded with a person who pursues commercial or professional activities in the member state of the consumer's domicile or, by any means, directs such activities to that member state or to several states including that member state, and which falls within the scope of such activities.

Article 15(1)(c) replaces Art 13(1)(3) of the Brussels and Lugano Conventions, which referred to any other contract for the supply of goods or a contract for the supply of services, where the conclusion of the contract was preceded by a specific invitation addressed to the consumer, or by advertising, in the state of his domicile, and the consumer took in that state the steps necessary for the conclusion of the contract on his part.[227] The intention is to emphasise that contracts concluded through the Internet are included, but probably this was already largely achieved by the earlier provisions. Under the Regulation, there is no doubt that, in the ordinary case of a consumer ordering goods or services electronically from a website maintained by the supplier, the supplier is by means of the website directing commercial activities to all countries, including the member state of the consumer's domicile, from which the page is accessible, and that the order falls within the scope of such activities. The only noticeable difference seems to be that the new, but not the old, definition would be satisfied where the consumer was not in his own country when he accessed the site and placed the order; for example, if an English domiciliary placed the order from an Internet café while on holiday in France. Since the location of the terminal used by the consumer has no real significance in relation to electronic transactions, this very minor change seems well justified. Moreover, the risk of unfair surprise to the trader is largely eliminated once it is recognised that the Regulation should be construed as respecting the principles of predictability[228] and good faith.[229] Accordingly, a consumer who misleads the supplier as to the location of the consumer's domicile, as by entering on the order form an address (perhaps of a relative or friend) in a different country, will be estopped from relying on his actual domicile so as to satisfy the definition if the trader would have rejected the order (probably by setting his software in advance to do so) had he known the consumer's true domicile.

Employment contracts

Articles 18–21 of the Regulation lay down protective rules in respect of individual contracts of employment.[230] The nature of such contracts was addressed by the European Court in *Shenavai v Kreischer*,[231] where it emphasised that such contracts create a lasting bond which brings the worker to some extent within the organisational

---

227 On Art 13(1)(3) of the Brussels and Lugano Conventions, see Case C-96/00: *Gabriel* [2002] ECR I6367; *per* Jacobs AG in Case C-464/01: *Gruber v BayWa* [2005] ECR I-439; and *Rayner v Davies* [2003] 1 All ER (Comm) 394 (CA).

228 See Case C-26/91: *Handte v TMCS* [1992] ECR I-3967; and Case C-51/97: *Réunion Européenne v Spliethoff's Bevrachtingskantoor* [1998] ECR I-6511.

229 See Case 25/76: *Segoura v Bonakdarian* [1976] ECR 1851; and Case C-464/01: *Gruber v Bay Wa* [2005] ECR I-439.

230 These provisions modify and replace Art 5(1), second sentence, and Art 17(6) of the Brussels Convention.

231 See Case 266/85: [1987] ECR 239.

framework of the employer's business, and that they are linked to the place where the activities are pursued, which determines the application of mandatory rules and collective agreements. Thus the concept is confined to cases involving a personal relationship of master and servant, and does not extend to contracts for professional services, such as those of an architect or lawyer, engaged as an independent contractor to carry out a particular task. *A fortiori* it does not include a commercial contract whereby a company obtains exclusive rights to canvass in its country for advertising in a foreign newspaper.[232] It has been held in England that Arts 18–21 are confined to claims based on a contract of employment, and do not extend to a claim by an employer against an employee in tort for conspiracy to interfere unlawfully with a commercial contract between the employer and a supplier.[233]

Article 19 gives the employee a choice of courts in which to sue an employer who is domiciled in a member state. He may sue in the courts of the member state where the defendant employer is domiciled; or (in another member state) in the courts for the place where the employee habitually carries out his work, or for the last place where he did so; or, if the employee does not or did not habitually carry out his work in any one country, in the courts for the place where the business which engaged the employee is or was situated. In addition he may sue under Art 5(5) (in a member state other than the employer's domicile) in the courts for the place where a secondary establishment of the employer, from whose operations the dispute arises, is located. In contrast, Art 20(1) confines actions brought by an employer to the courts of the member state in which the employee is domiciled.[234] Article 21 invalidates jurisdiction clauses, except ones which are entered into after the dispute has arisen, or which allow the employee to bring proceedings in additional courts. The ordinary rules on counterclaims and submission by appearance remain applicable in employment cases,[235] but not the rule specified by Art 6(1) enabling joinder of co-defendants. Thus an employee who is jointly employed by two employers who are domiciled in different member states cannot utilise Art 6(1) so as to sue both employers at the domicile of one of them.[236]

The concept of the place of habitual work has been clarified by the European Court in *Mulox v Geels*[237] and *Rutten v Cross Medical*.[238] Where the employee carries out his work in more than one country, the concept refers to the place where the employee has established the effective centre of his working activities, at or from which he performs the essential part of his duties to his employer. Thus, for example, a sales manager will habitually work at the office where he organises his work, even though he makes frequent business trips to other countries. But where, as in *Weber v Universal Ogden Services*,[239] there is no such permanent centre of activities (for example, because the employee worked for the employer as a cook, first on mining vessels or installa-

---

232 See *Mercury Publicity v Loerke* [1993] ILPr 142 (CA).
233 See *Swithenbank Foods Ltd v Bowers* [2002] 2 All ER (Comm) 974.
234 This departs from the Brussels and Lugano Conventions, under which the employer could sue the employee at the place of habitual work. The Lugano Convention also permits the employer to sue an employee without any habitual place of work at the location of the employer's establishment through which the employee was engaged.
235 See Arts 6(3), 20(2) and 24.
236 See Case C-462/06: *Glaxosmithkline v Rouard*, [2008] ECR I-3965.
237 Case C-125/92: [1993] ECR I-4075.
238 Case C-383/95: [1997] ECR I-57.
239 Case C-37/00: [2002] ECR I-2013.

tions in the Dutch continental shelf area, and later on a floating crane in Danish territorial waters), the whole of the duration of the employment relationship must be taken into account. The relevant place will normally the place where the employee has worked the longest; but by way of exception, weight will be given to the most recent period of work where the employee, after having worked for a certain time in one place, then takes up his work activities on a permanent basis in a different place.

The position where an employee is recruited by one company to work temporarily for an associated company abroad, and then to return to work for the initial employer in their home country, arose in *Pugliese v Finmeccanica*,[240] which involved an Italian who had been recruited by Aeritalia to work initially for Eurofighter in Germany for at least three years, and who now sought to sue Aeritalia in Germany. The European Court ruled that, in a dispute between an employee and first employer, the place where the employee performs his obligations to a second employer can be regarded as the place where he habitually carries out his work when the first employer, with respect to whom the employee's contractual obligations are suspended, has, at the time of the conclusion of the second contract of employment, an interest in the performance of the service by the employee to the second employer in a place decided on by the latter. The existence of such an interest must be determined on a comprehensive basis, taking into consideration all the circumstances of the case. Relevant factors may include the fact that the conclusion of the second contract was envisaged when the first was being concluded; the fact that the first contract was amended on account of the conclusion of the second contract; the fact that there is an organisational or economic link between the two employers; the fact that there is an agreement between the two employers providing a framework for the co-existence of the two contracts; the fact that the first employer retains management powers in respect of the employee; and the fact that the first employer is able to decide the duration of the employee's work for the second employer.

SIMULTANEOUS ACTIONS

Chapter II of the Regulation frequently gives a plaintiff a choice of member states in which to sue. Hence, in order to reduce the risk of irreconcilable judgments being given by courts of different member states, and also to increase co-ordination in the exercise of judicial functions within the Community so as to promote litigational economy and avoid waste, Section 9 (Arts 27–30) of Chapter II regulates the problem of proceedings simultaneously pending in courts of different member states[241] in respect of similar or related disputes.[242] These provisions are based primarily on a simple test of chronological priority, under which the court subsequently seised is required or invited to defer to the court first seised, rather than on a judicial evaluation of the relative appropriateness or convenience of the two fora. In the case

---

240 Case C-437/00: [2003] ECR I-3573.
241 If both actions are instituted in the same member state, the problem is impliedly remitted to the law of that state, and in the United Kingdom s 49 of the 1982 Act leaves the matter to be dealt with under the principle of *forum non conveniens*.
242 Section 9 does not apply where the first proceeding is confined to an investigative measure, designed to preserve evidence or establish facts relevant to liability to be determined in separate, subsequent, substantive proceedings; see *Miles Platts v Townroe* [2003] 1 All ER (Comm) 561 (CA).

of similar actions, Art 27 imposes on the court subsequently seised a mandatory obligation to decline jurisdiction in favour of the court first seised.[243] In the case of dissimilar but related actions, Art 28 gives the second court a discretion to stay its proceedings, or in certain circumstances to decline jurisdiction, in favour of the first court. But in no case do these provisions authorise the first court to give way to the second court.[244]

Articles 27–30 apply regardless of the domicile of the parties to the actions, and even if the defendant in either or both of the actions is not domiciled in any of the member states.[245] They remain applicable in cases where the existence of jurisdiction is governed by a specialised convention within the scope of Art 71 (such as the 1952 Convention on the Arrest of Seagoing Ships) but the specialised convention contains no provision dealing with simultaneous actions.[246]

Article 30 now establishes that for these purposes a court is seised at the time when it issues the document instituting the proceedings (in England, the claim form).[247]

As regards similar actions, Art 27 provides that where proceedings involving the same cause of action and between the same parties are brought in the courts of different member states, a court subsequently seised shall of its own motion stay its proceedings until such time as the jurisdiction of the court first seised is established; and where the jurisdiction of the court first seised is established, a court subsequently seised shall decline jurisdiction in favour of the court first seised.[248] As the European Court emphasised in *Overseas Union Insurance v New Hampshire Insurance*,[249] Art 27 does not permit the second court, even where the jurisdiction of the first court is contested, itself to examine the jurisdiction of the first court, except possibly where the question is whether the second court has exclusive

---

243 Article 27 must be applied even if the second court considers that proceedings in the first country are excessively slow; see Case C-116/02: *Gasser v MISAT* [2003] ECR I-14693.

244 See *Cronos Containers v Palatin* [2003] 2 Lloyd's Rep 489. But where Art 4 remits the jurisdiction of the first court to its own law, because the defendant is not domiciled in any member state, such remission includes any power conferred by the relevant national law to decline jurisdiction on grounds such as *forum non conveniens*.

245 See Case C-351/89: *Overseas Union Insurance v New Hampshire Insurance* [1991] ECR I-3317.

246 Case C-406/92: *The Maciej Rataj* [1994] ECR I-5439.

247 Formerly, the relevant time was usually that of service on the relevant defendant. See Case 129/83: *Zelger v Salinitri (No 2)* [1984] ECR 2397; *Dresser v Falcongate* [1992] QB 502; *Neste Chemicals v DK Line* [1994] 3 All ER 180; *Grupo Torras v Al-Sabah* [1996] 1 Lloyd's Rep 7; *Fox v Taher* [1997] ILPr 441; *Glencore v Metro* [1999] 2 Lloyd's Rep 632; *Molins v GD* [2000] 2 Lloyd's Rep 234; *Tavoulareas v Tsavliris* [2004] EWCA Civ 48; and *Phillips v Symes* [2008] UKHL 1. It seems that Art 30 applies to the determination of the time of seisin of both courts, whenever the action brought before the court which is considering the question of concurrent actions was instituted after the commencement date of the Regulation for its state, even if the action in a court of another member state was instituted at an earlier date; see *Tavoulareas v Tsavliris* [2006] 1 All ER (Comm) 109.

248 By Art 29, this applies even where the actions come within the exclusive jurisdiction of several courts. The duty to stay under Art 27(1) applies where an appeal is pending in the country of the court first seised against a decision of that court, where in favour of or against its jurisdiction; see *William Grant v Marie-Brizard* [1996] SCLR 987, and *Moore v Moore* [2007] EWCA Civ 361 (CA). But Art 27 does not apply where the proceedings in the first court have proceeded to judgment, or have been discontinued, between the time when the proceedings were brought in the second court, and the time when the second court determines whether it should decline jurisdiction; Art 27 applies where there are concurrent proceedings at the time when the second court makes its determination. See *Tavoulareas v Tsavliris (No 2)* [2006] 1 All ER (Comm) 130.

249 Case C-406/89: [1991] ECR I-3317.

jurisdiction by virtue of subject matter under Art 22.[250] Nothing in that decision lent any substantial support to the view that Art 27 did not apply where, as a result of an agreement on jurisdiction between the parties, Art 23 confers exclusive jurisdiction on the second court. Eventually in *Gasser v MISAT*[251] the European Court has given a clear and unqualified ruling that under Art 27 a court second seised whose jurisdiction has been claimed under an agreement conferring jurisdiction under Art 23 must nevertheless stay proceedings until the court first seised has declared that it has no jurisdiction, thus overruling an indefensible line of English case law[252] giving priority to Art 23 over Art 27.

The concept of the same cause of action has been construed widely. In *Gubisch v Palumbo*,[253] the European Court ruled that Art 27 applies where one party to a contract brings an action before a court of one member state for the rescission or discharge of the contract whilst an action by the other party to enforce the same contract is pending before a court of another member state. It explained that both actions were based on the same contractual relationship, one being aimed at giving effect to the contract and the other at depriving it of any effect. Thus the question whether the contract was binding lay at the heart of both actions. The subsequent action for rescission or discharge of the contract could be regarded simply as a defence against the first action, brought in the form of independent proceedings before a court of another member state. While the two actions must have the same subject matter, this does not mean that the two claims must be entirely identical. Similarly in *The Maciej Rataj*,[254] which involved damage to cargo carried under bill of lading contracts, the European Court ruled that an action seeking to have the defendant shipowner held liable for causing loss and ordered to pay damages had the same cause of action and the same object as earlier proceedings brought by the shipowner seeking a declaration that he was not liable for that loss. It explained that the actions had the same cause, being based on the same facts and the same legal rule, and the same object, since the issue of liability was central to both actions and the reversal in the position of the parties (as claimant and defendant) was immaterial.[255] On the other hand, as the European Court ruled in *Ganter v Basch*,[256] for this purpose account must be taken only of the claims of the

---

250   This exception was applied by the English Court of Appeal in *Speed Investments Ltd v Formula One Holdings Ltd* [2005] 1 BCLC 455 (CA) in the context of corporate matters governed by Art 22(2). For a transitional exception, see Case C-163/95: *Von Horn v Cinnamond* [1997] ECR I-5451.

251   Case C-116/02: [2003] ECR I-14693. See also *Evialis v Siat* [2003] 2 Lloyd's Rep 377; and *Bank of Tokyo-Mitsubishi v Baskan Gida* [2004] ILPr 26.

252   See *Continental Bank v Aeakos* [1994] 1 WLR 588 (CA); *Kloeckner v Gatoil* [1990] 1 Lloyd's Rep 177; *IP Metal v Ruote (No 2)* [1994] 2 Lloyd's Rep 560 (CA); *Toepfer v Molino Boschi* [1996] 1 Lloyd's Rep 510; *Toepfer v Cargill* [1997] 2 Lloyd's Rep 98; *Bank of Scotland v Banque Nationale de Paris* 1996 SLT 103; *Glencore v Metro* [1999] 2 Lloyd's Rep 632; and *The Kribi* [2001] 1 Lloyd's Rep 76. Cf *Toepfer v Cargill* [1998] 1 Lloyd's Rep 379 (CA); and *Evialis v Siat* [2003] 2 Lloyd's Rep 377.

253   Case 144/86: [1987] ECR 4861. Cf *J P Morgan Europe Ltd v Primacom AG* [2005] EWHC 508 (Comm), where Cooke J held that Art 27 does not apply, even where the dispute is between the same parties and relates to the same contract, if the first action is concerned exclusively with one obligation under the contract, and the second is concerned with other obligations under the contract; for example, in the case of a loan, where the first action is brought by the debtor and seeks only the invalidation of the contractual provision concerning the interest payable, while the second action is brought by the creditor and seeks enforcement of contractual provisions preventing the debtor from selling assets without the creditor's consent and requiring the debtor to provide financial information to the creditor.

254   Case C-406/92: [1994] ECR I-5439.

255   See also *William Grant v Marie-Brizard* 1996 SCLR 987; and *The Linda* [1988] 1 Lloyd's Rep 175.

256   Case C-111/01: [2003] ECR I-4207.

respective claimants, to the exclusion of defence submissions, including ones alleging set-off, raised by a defendant. But an interpleader proceeding by a debtor is probably not similar to an ordinary contractual claim for the debt.[257]

On the other hand, the concept of the same parties has been construed narrowly. In *The Maciej Rataj*,[258] the European Court ruled that where some, but not all, of the parties to the second action are the same as the parties to the first action, Art 27 requires the second court seised to decline jurisdiction only to the extent to which the parties to the second proceedings are also parties to the first action. It does not prevent the second proceedings from continuing between the other parties. The consequent undesirable fragmentation of proceedings may in some cases be mitigated by Art 28, on related actions. The European Court also ruled that an action *in rem* against a ship must be treated for the purpose of Art 27 as an action against the shipowner or other person interested in the ship against whom the plaintiff would wish to proceed *in personam* if he entered an appearance.[259] In *Drouot Assurances v Consolidated Metallurgical Industries*,[260] the European Court accepted that the requirement under Art 27 that the parties to both actions must be the same does not eliminate all possibility of identification by virtue of privity (for example, between an insurer and its insured), but it emphasised that such identification is possible only when, with regard to the subject matter of both actions, the interests of the persons in question are identical and indissociable. Such identification may be possible between a company in solvent liquidation and its liquidator, as regards a claim by a creditor of the company.[261]

Article 28 applies to actions which are dissimilar but related. It provides that where related actions are pending in the courts of different member states, a court subsequently seised may stay its proceedings, and may also, where the actions are pending at first instance, on the application of one of the parties, decline jurisdiction if the court first seised has jurisdiction over the actions in question and its law permits the consolidation thereof.[262] By Art 28(3), actions are deemed to be related where they are so closely connected that it is expedient to hear and determine them together to avoid the risk of irreconcilable judgments resulting from separate proceedings.

The concept of related actions has been construed broadly. In *The Maciej Rataj*,[263] the European Court ruled that actions brought in different member states against the same shipowner by owners of different parts of a bulk cargo, shipped under separate but identical contracts between the relevant cargo owner and the shipowner, seeking

---

257   See *Glencore v Shell* [1999] 2 Lloyd's Rep 692. Cf *Glencore v Metro* [1999] 2 Lloyd's Rep 632.

258   Case C-406/92: [1994] ECR I-5439.

259   But an admiralty limitation action brought by a shipowner and an action for damages brought against the shipowner by an injured party are not similar actions within Art 27, but related actions within Art 28. See Case 39/02: *Maersk Olie & Gas v de Haan & de Boer* [2004] ECR I-9657.

260   Case C-351/96: [1998] ECR I-3075.

261   See *Re Cover Europe Ltd* [2002] BPIR 931. See also *Mecklermedia v DC Congress* [1998] Ch 40, where Jacob J refused to treat a licensor of intellectual property and his licensee as the same party for the purposes of Art 27; and *Turner v Grovit* [1999] 1 WLR 794 (CA), involving sister companies in the same group.

262   It is the law of the country whose court is first seised (not that of the country subsequently seised) which must permit consolidation; see *William Grant v Marie-Brizard* 1996 SCLR 987, and *Sarrio v Kuwait Investment Authority* [1999] AC 32.

263   Case C-406/92: [1994] ECR I-5439.

damages for contamination alleged to have occurred during the voyage, fell within Art 28. The Court explained that Art 28 covers all cases where separate trial and judgment would involve a risk of conflicting decisions, even if the judgments could be separately enforced and their legal consequences would not be mutually exclusive. Similarly, in *Sarrio v Kuwait Investment Authority*,[264] the House of Lords declined jurisdiction under Art 28 over an English action in tort seeking damages for negligent misstatements by the defendant which had induced the plaintiff to enter into a contract with the defendant's subsidiary, in favour of an earlier Spanish action seeking to hold the defendant liable on the same contract by piercing the corporate veil.[265] Although in *Réunion Européenne v Spliethoff's Bevrachtingskantoor*[266] the European Court puzzlingly suggested that there is no sufficient connection between claims by the same plaintiff against two defendants in respect of the same loss, if one of the claims is contractual and the other is based on tort, this dictum was subsequently abandoned in *Freeport v Arnoldsson*.[267] But there is no sufficient connection between claims for infringement of a European patent, granted for several member states, against several defendants, domiciled in different member states, each being sued for an infringement committed in the state of its domicile.[268]

The solution to the problem of related actions adopted by Art 28 is to confer discretionary powers on the second court. That court is authorised by Art 28(1) to stay its own proceedings, so as to enable it to have the benefit of the first court's judgment before it reaches its own decision. It is also authorised, by Art 28(2), to decline jurisdiction altogether, in order to enable the whole matter to be determined by the first court. A third choice remains available, in that the second court may, after due consideration, refuse both to stay its proceedings and to decline jurisdiction in favour of the first court. The second court will then proceed to determine its action, without waiting for the first court to determine the first action. In that event, there may be a rush to judgment, since the first judgment on the merits, given by either of the courts, will qualify for recognition by the other court under Chapter III of the Regulation, for Chapter III makes no exception to the obligation to grant recognition and enforcement to judgments given in other member states on account of the pendency of related proceedings in a court of the state addressed.[269]

The English courts have traditionally claimed a discretionary power to restrain a party by injunction from commencing or continuing to prosecute proceedings in a foreign court, on the ground that the continuance of the foreign proceedings would be oppressive,[270] or that the foreign action has been brought in breach of an agreement for English exclusive jurisdiction or arbitration. They continued for many years to assert such a power even in respect of proceedings in another member state within the

---

264 [1999] AC 32.
265 See also *D v P* [1998] 2 FLR 25; and *Prazic v Prazic* [2006] 2 FLR 1128 (CA).
266 Case C-51/97: [1998] ECR I-6511.
267 Case C-98/06: [2007] ECR I-8319.
268 See Case C-539/03: *Roche Nederland BV v Primus* [2006] ECR I-6535.
269 See *Brasserie du Pecheur v Kreissparkasse Main-Spessart* (1996) unreported, 14 May (French Court of Cassation). For English discussion of the exercise of the discretion conferred by Art 28, see *per* Mance J in *Grupo Torras v Al-Sabah* [1995] 1 Lloyd's Rep 374, and *Sarrio v Kuwait Investment Authority* [1996] 1 Lloyd's Rep 650; *per* Rimer J in *Trustor v Barclays Bank* (2000) *The Times*, 22 November; *per* Lawrence Collins J in *Bank of Tokyo-Mitsubishi v Baskan Gida* [2004] ILPr 26, at para 228; and *per* Cooke J in *J P Morgan Europe Ltd v Primacom AG* [2005] EWHC 508 (Comm).
270 See *SNIA v Lee Kui Jak* [1987] AC 871, and *Airbus Industrie v Patel* [1999] 1 AC 119.

scope of the Brussels Convention,[271] despite the implausibility of the arguments that this was compatible with the Brussels Convention. But in *Turner v Grovit*[272] the European Court gave a clear, emphatic and unqualified ruling that the Brussels Convention and the Regulation preclude the grant of an injunction whereby a court of a member state prohibits a party to proceedings pending before it from commencing or continuing legal proceedings before a court of another member state; and that this is so even where that party is acting in bad faith with a view to frustrating existing proceedings. It has further ruled in *Allianz v West Tankers*[273] that it is incompatible with the Regulation for a court of a member state to make an order to restrain a person from commencing or continuing proceedings before the courts of another member state on the ground that such proceedings would be contrary to an arbitration agreement.

INTERIM RELIEF

Article 31 of the Regulation enables application to be made to the courts of a member state for such provisional, including protective, measures as may be available under the law of that state, even if under the Regulation the courts of another member state have jurisdiction as to the substance of the matter. This provision confers an additional jurisdiction, limited to provisional measures. In any event, as the European Court made clear in *Van Uden v Deco-Line*[274] and confirmed in *Mietz v Intership Yachting Sneek*,[275] a court which has substantive jurisdiction under Arts 2 and 5–24 also has jurisdiction to order any provisional or protective measures which may prove necessary.[276] Article 31 applies whether the substantive action has already been commenced or is to be commenced subsequently, and extends to cases where the substantive proceedings are to be conducted before arbitrators.[277]

The principle which underlies Art 31 is that the courts of each member state should be willing to assist the courts of another member state by providing such interim relief as would be available if its own courts were seised of the substantive proceedings.[278] The type of interim relief most commonly granted under Art 31 will be an order freezing assets which belong to the defendant and which are located in the territory of the granting court, so as to prevent their disappearance before the merits of the claimant's claim have been determined by a court of another member state, and thus to ensure their availability to meet an eventual judgment for the claimant on the

---

271 See, as regards English jurisdiction or arbitration clauses, *Continental Bank v Aeakos* [1994] 1 WLR 588 (CA); *The Angelic Grace* [1995] 1 Lloyd's Rep 87 (CA); *Ultisol v Bouygues* [1996] 2 Lloyd's Rep 140; *Toepfer v Cargill* [1997] 2 Lloyd's Rep 98; *Donohue v Armco* [2000] 1 Lloyd's Rep 579 (CA); and *The Kribi* [2001] 1 Lloyd's Rep 76. As regards oppression, see *Turner v Grovit* [1999] 1 WLR 794 (CA).

272 Case C-159/02: [2004] ECR I-3565; on a reference from the House of Lords [2002] 1 WLR 107.

273 Case C-185/07: 10 February 2009; on a reference from the House of Lords [2007] UKHL 4.

274 Case C-391/95: [1998] ECR I-7091.

275 Case C-99/96: [1999] ECR I-2277.

276 This applies even where the court has stayed its substantive proceedings under Art 27(1), while awaiting a decision on jurisdiction from a previously seised court of another member state; but not where the court has declined jurisdiction under Art 27(2) in favour of the court first seised. See *J P Morgan Europe Ltd v Primacom AG* [2005] EWHC 508 (Comm).

277 Case C-391/95: *Van Uden v Deco-Line* [1998] ECR I-7091.

278 See *per* Millett LJ in *Credit Suisse v Cuoghi* [1998] QB 818 (CA).

merits which will be given in another member state if his claim succeeds. In *Reichert v Dresdner Bank (No 2)*[279] and *St Paul Dairy Industries v Unibel Exser*[280] the European Court emphasised that Art 31 is intended to avoid losses to the parties resulting from the long delays inherent in international proceedings, and is confined to measures which are intended to preserve a factual or legal situation so as to safeguard rights whose recognition is sought elsewhere from the court having substantive jurisdiction. Thus it does not extend to an application by a creditor for the revocation of a fraudulent transfer of property by his debtor, since the purpose of such an application is to vary the legal situation of the debtor's assets and of the transferee; nor to an application for a measure ordering the hearing of a witness before substantive proceedings are initiated, for the purpose of enabling the applicant to decide whether to bring a case, to determine whether it would be well founded, and to assess the relevance of evidence which might be adduced.

In *Van Uden v Deco-Line*[281] and *Mietz v Intership Yachting Sneek*,[282] the European Court ruled that the granting of provisional measures under Art 31 is conditional on the existence of a real connecting link between the subject matter of the measures sought and the territory of the forum state. Thus interim payment of a contractual consideration does not constitute a provisional measure within Art 31 unless repayment to the defendant of the sum awarded is guaranteed if the claimant is unsuccessful as regards the substance of his claim,[283] and unless in addition the measure sought relates only to specific assets of the defendant located or to be located within the territory of the forum state. In *Mietz* the European Court also emphasised the importance of ensuring that enforcement under Chapter III in another member state of provisional or protective measures allegedly founded on jurisdiction under Art 31, but which go beyond the limits of that jurisdiction, does not result in circumvention of the rules on substantive jurisdiction set out in Chapter II. For the jurisdiction recognised by Art 31 constitutes, within the context of the Regulation, a special regime. Thus enforcement under Chapter III must be refused where: (a) the judgment was delivered at the end of proceedings which were not, by their very nature, proceedings as to substance but summary proceedings for the granting of interim measures; (b) the measure ordered (such as unconditional interim payment) is not a provisional or protective measure permissible under Art 31; and (c) the original court either expressly indicated in its judgment that it based its jurisdiction on Art 31, or was silent as to the basis of its jurisdiction.

Under s 25 of the Civil Jurisdiction and Judgments Act 1982 and the Civil Jurisdiction and Judgments Act 1982 (Interim Relief) Order 1997,[284] the English High Court now has power to grant interim relief in aid of any substantive proceedings in a foreign court. It is immaterial whether or not the foreign proceedings have already been commenced; whether the foreign court is a court of another part of the United Kingdom, or of another EC member state or Lugano Convention country, or of some other country; and whether or not the subject matter of the foreign proceedings falls

---

279   Case C-261/90: [1992] ECR I-2149.
280   Case C-104/03: [2005] ECR I-3481.
281   Case C-391/95: [1998] ECR I-7091.
282   Case C-99/96: [1999] ECR I-2277. See also *Comet Group v Unika Computer* [2004] ILPr 1.
283   Similarly an order in divorce proceedings for maintenance pending suit is not a provisional measure within the scope of Art 31; see *Wermuth v Wermuth* [2003] 1 WLR 942 (CA).
284   SI 1997/302.

within the scope of the Regulation or the Lugano Convention.[285] In addition, where an English court declines jurisdiction over an admiralty action *in rem* in favour of arbitration or a foreign court, it will normally retain the property arrested or require the provision of equivalent security for the satisfaction of the eventual award or judgment in the same way as if the merits were to be determined in the English action *in rem*.[286]

CONCLUSION

This chapter has addressed the direct jurisdiction of the English courts in civil and commercial matters, and has focused on the Brussels I Regulation. The Regulation also deals with the recognition and enforcement of judgments, and this aspect is considered in Chapter 18. Meanwhile, Chapter 17 focuses on choice of law in respect of contracts under the Rome I Regulation, and in respect of torts and restitutionary obligations under the Rome II Regulation.

FURTHER READING

Collins *et al* (eds), *Dicey, Morris and Collins on the Conflict of Laws*, 14th edn, 2006, Sweet & Maxwell.

Stone, *EU Private International Law*, 2006, Edward Elgar.

---

285 On the exercise of this power, see *Credit Suisse v Cuoghi* [1998] QB 818 (CA), and *Motorola Credit Corp v Uzan* [2004] 1 WLR 113 (CA). For service abroad of an English application for interim relief in support of foreign proceedings, see Civil Procedure Rules 1998 (as amended), r 6.36, and Practice Direction B, para 3.1(5). For similar English powers to grant interim relief in support of English or foreign arbitration proceedings, see the Arbitration Act 1996, ss 2(3) and 44.

286 See s 26 of the 1982 Act, and *The Bazias 3* [1993] QB 673 (CA).

CHAPTER 17

CHOICE OF LAW

INTRODUCTION

In English litigation relating to contracts, choice of the applicable substantive law is now governed largely by EC Regulation 593/2008 on the Law Applicable to Contractual Obligations, which is usually referred to as the Rome I Regulation.[1] By Art 24(1) the Regulation replaces the Rome Convention 1980,[2] which was given the force of law in the United Kingdom by the Contracts (Applicable Law) Act 1990. The Regulation applies to contracts concluded after its entry into application on 17 December 2009, and the Convention remains applicable in the United Kingdom to contracts concluded between 1 April 1991 and 16 December 2009.[3] In most respects the Regulation closely resembles the Convention, and in general, case law decided under the Convention remains reliable in relation to corresponding provisions of the Regulation.[4] In this Chapter we shall focus on the Regulation, but important departures from the Convention will be noted.[5]

By Art 1(1) the Rome I Regulation applies, in situations involving a conflict of laws, to contractual obligations in civil and commercial matters, but it does not apply, in particular, to revenue, customs or administrative matters.[6] By Art 2, any law specified by the Regulation must be applied whether or not it is the law of a member state. Article 22(1) adds that where a state (such as the United Kingdom) comprises several territorial units, each of which has its own rules of law in respect of contractual obligations, each territorial unit (such as England and Wales; Scotland; and Northern Ireland) is to be considered as a country for the purposes of identifying the law applicable under the Regulation.[7] Thus, from an English viewpoint, the Regulation is equally applicable whether the foreign connection is with another EC country (such as France), or with a country external to the European Community (such as the USA), or even with another part of the United Kingdom (such as Scotland).

---

1 For its text, see [2008] OJ L177/6. With regard to the belated acceptance of the Regulation by the United Kingdom, see EC Commission Decision 2009/26 [2009] OJ L10/22. The Regulation applies in all of the member states except Denmark.

2 EC Convention, opened for signature at Rome on 19 June 1980, on the Law Applicable to Contractual Obligations. For its text, see [1998] OJ C27/34, or Sched 1 to the Contracts (Applicable Law) Act 1990.

3 See Arts 28 and 29 of the Regulation, and Art 17 of the Convention.

4 The case law on the Rome Convention consists mainly of decisions given by national courts, since it was not until August 2004 that the European Court gained power under the Brussels Protocols, signed on 19 December 1988, to give preliminary rulings on the interpretation of the Rome Convention; see [1989] OJ L48, or Sched 3 to the 1990 Act. Guidance on the interpretation of the Rome Convention, and thus of the Rome I Regulation, may also be drawn from the Giuliano and Lagarde Report; see [1980] OJ C282, and s 3(3)(a) of the 1990 Act.

5 In the final section of this Chapter, we shall briefly examine the rules on choice of law in respect of torts and restitutionary obligations, laid down by EC Regulation 864/2007, which is commonly referred to as the Rome II Regulation. For its text, see [2007] OJ L199/40.

6 This is subject to the exclusions of certain types of contract, term or issue specified in Art 1(2)–(3).

7 Although Art 22(2) permits a state within which different territorial units have their own rules of law in respect of contractual obligations not to apply the Regulation to conflicts solely between the laws of such units, the United Kingdom has chosen not to utilise this permission; see s 2(3) of the 1990 Act.

Moreover, it is clear from Art 3(3) that the Regulation applies even where the only foreign element arises from a choice of law agreed to by the parties and the situation is otherwise exclusively connected with a single country, as where a contract concluded in England between English residents and requiring all performances to take place in England contains a clause choosing French law as governing the contract.

The Rome I Regulation does not contain a definition of 'contractual obligations'. But in view of Recital 7, it seems clear that the concept of a contractual obligation, for the purpose of the Regulation, must be given an independent meaning, defined by Community law in the light of the purposes of the Regulation and of the general trend which emerges from the laws of the member states viewed as a whole, rather than as being remitted to the law of the country whose court is seised, and that the concept must have essentially the same meaning as in Art 5(1) of the Brussels I Regulation, as referring to obligations freely assumed by one party towards another.[8] In any event, the concept should not be restricted by technical rules of the internal *lex fori*, such as the English rule requiring consideration, which are designed to regulate the validity, rather than define the nature, of a contract.[9]

The material scope of the Rome I Regulation is, however, restricted to a limited extent by Art 1(2)–(3), which excludes certain types of transaction, certain terms and certain issues from the ambit of the Regulation, thus remitting them (in the absence of other EC legislation) to the traditional conflict rules of the court seised.

As regards types of transaction, the Regulation has almost entirely eliminated an important exclusion formerly made by Art 1(3) and (4) of the Convention, which had referred to contracts of insurance (other than reinsurance) covering risks situated within the European Community.[10] In contrast Art 1(2)(j) of the Regulation makes a very minor exclusion from its scope in respect of insurance contracts whereby an insurer who is not established in a member state provides death, unemployment or sickness benefits in connection with particular employers or trades. Another exclusion, made by Art 1(2)(d), concerns obligations arising under bills of exchange, cheques or promissory notes, or under other negotiable instruments in so far as the obligations arise from the negotiable character of the instrument.[11] A further exclusion, made by Art 1(2)(h), concerns the constitution of trusts and the relationship between settlors, trustees and beneficiaries. Another exclusion, made by Art 1(2)(b) and (c), covers obligations arising out of family or comparable relationships, including maintenance obligations, or from matrimonial or comparable property regimes, or wills and succession. This exclusion, taken with the exclusion made by Art 1(2)(a) of questions of individual status or capacity, seems designed to cover all contracts which fall within the sphere of family law.[12]

Whatever the type of contract, Art 1(2)(e) excludes the validity and interpretation

---

8   See Case C-26/91: *Handte v TMCS* [1992] ECR I-3967; and Case C-51/97: *Réunion Européenne v Spliethoff's Bevrachtingskantoor* [1998] ECR I-6511.

9   See *Re Bonacina* [1912] 2 Ch 394.

10   Instead the matter had been regulated by EC Directive 88/357 (as amended) in the case of non-life insurance, and EC Directive 2002/83 in the case of life insurance. See [1988] OJ L172, [1992] OJ L228, and [2002] OJ L345.

11   Negotiable instruments are subject to special conflict rules both in the United Kingdom (under the Bills of Exchange Act 1882, s 72) and in Continental countries (under the Geneva Conventions of 7 June 1930 and 19 March 1931 for the Settlement of Certain Conflicts of Laws in Connection with (respectively) Bills of Exchange or Cheques).

12   See Giuliano and Lagarde [1980] OJ C282, at p 10.

of arbitration or jurisdiction clauses from the scope of the Rome I Regulation.[13] But the exclusion does not extend to the substantive contract containing an arbitration or jurisdiction clause, and it does not prevent such a clause from being taken into account in determining the law which governs the substantive contract under Arts 3 and 4 of the Regulation.[14]

Other exclusions by Art 1(2) encompass particular issues, rather than types of transaction or clause. They relate to:

- individual status or capacity (Art 1(2)(a));
- questions governed by company law, such as the creation (by registration or otherwise), legal capacity, internal organisation or winding up of companies and other bodies, and the personal liability of officers and members as such for the obligations of a company or body (Art 1(2)(f));
- the question whether an agent is able to bind a principal, or an organ to bind a company or other body, to a third party (Art 1(2)(g));[15]
- obligations arising out of dealings prior to the conclusion of a contract (Art 1(2)(i));[16] and
- evidence and procedure (Art 1(3)).

In view of the last-mentioned exclusion, there is no reason to suppose that the Regulation requires any change to the English rule that the possible applicability of foreign law must be ignored unless a party invokes a foreign rule by appropriate pleading and proof.

By Art 23, the Rome I Regulation gives way to other Community legislation which, in relation to particular matters, lays down conflict rules relating to contractual obligations. Accordingly, the Regulation gives way to Directive 93/13 on unfair terms in consumer contracts;[17] to Directives 94/47, 97/7, 1999/44 and 2002/65, which deal with various other aspects of consumer protection;[18] and to Directive 96/71 on the posting of workers in the framework of the provision of services.[19] Similarly, the Regulation gives way to Arts 17 and 18 of Directive 86/653, on self-employed commercial agents, which guarantee certain rights to commercial agents after the termination of agency contracts. As the European Court ruled in *Ingmar v Eaton Leonard*,[20] these provisions must be applied where the commercial agent carried on his activity in a member state, even if the principal is established in a non-member country and a clause of the contract stipulates that the contract is to be governed by the law of that country. But Art 23 of the Regulation makes an exception for Art 7, which deals with insurance and replaces the relevant provisions of Directives 88/357 and 2002/83.

---

13   See *Akai v People's Insurance* [1998] 1 Lloyd's Rep 90 (Thomas J).

14   See Giuliano and Lagarde [1980] OJ C282, at p 12.

15   But see *Marubeni v Mongolian Government* [2002] 2 All ER (Comm) 873, where Aikens J accepted, on the basis of Dicey Rule 228, that ostensible authority, usual authority and ratification are governed by the putative proper law of the main contract, itself determined under the Rome I Regulation.

16   But such obligations are subjected to the actual or putative proper law of the contract by Art 12(1) of the Rome II Regulation.

17   [1993] OJ L95/29. See especially Art 6(2).

18   See at pp 592–3 below.

19   [1997] OJ L18/1. See recital 11 to the Directive.

20   Case C-381/98: [2000] ECR I-9305.

By Art 25, the Rome I Regulation does not prejudice the application of international conventions to which one or more member states were parties when the Regulation was adopted, and which lay down conflict rules relating to contractual obligations. From an English perspective, Art 25 saves the operation of the (United Kingdom) Carriage of Goods by Sea Act 1971, which makes the Hague-Visby Rules applicable to shipments from either the United Kingdom or another contracting state, with the result that in the case of such a shipment they override a choice of a foreign proper law.[21] It also saves the operation of Art VIII(2)(b) of the International Monetary Fund Agreement signed at Bretton Woods in 1944, by which exchange contracts which involve the currency of an International Monetary Fund (IMF) member state and which contravene exchange control regulations of that state, maintained or imposed consistently with the IMF Agreement, are rendered unenforceable in other member states. This provision is implemented in the United Kingdom by the Bretton Woods Agreements Act 1945 and Order 1946.[22] Since the breakdown of the system of fixed parities in the early 1970s, Art VIII(2)(b) has been construed narrowly. Thus a contract is an 'exchange contract' only when it provides for the exchange of one currency for another and not (for example) for the sale of goods, or in so far as it is a monetary transaction in disguise.[23]

Under the Rome I Regulation, most issues relating to a contract are governed by a single law, which the Regulation refers to as the law governing or applicable to the contract but which may more conveniently be referred to by the traditional English term, 'the proper law of the contract'. The proper law is determined under the rules laid down by Arts 3 and 4, which refer to an express or a clearly demonstrated implied choice by the parties, or, in default of any such choice, to the country most closely connected, usually presumed to be the residence of the characteristic performer. By Art 20, only the internal law of country referred to, and not its conflict rules, is applied.[24] Special rules designed to protect the weaker party are laid down for certain types of contract (contracts for the carriage of passengers, consumer contracts, insurance contracts, and employment contracts) by Arts 5–8. Savings for the public policy or overriding interest of the *lex fori* are made by Arts 9 and 21. The extent to which the proper law is applicable to, or to some extent displaced in relation to, particular issues is clarified by Arts 10–12 and 18.

THE PROPER LAW – EXPRESS CHOICE

Under the Rome I Regulation, as under the traditional English law,[25] the proper law of a contract is determined primarily by reference to any express agreement on choice of law concluded by the parties to the contract. Only in the absence of any – or any valid – express choice is reference made, secondarily, to implied choice or closest connection. Thus, Art 3(1) of the Regulation specifies that a contract is governed by

---

21 See *The Hollandia* [1983] 1 AC 565. See Chapter 8.
22 SR&O 1946/36.
23 See *Wilson Smithett and Cope v Terruzzi* [1976] QB 683; and *United City Merchants v Royal Bank of Canada* [1983] 1 AC 168.
24 An exception is made by Art 7 in the case of insurance.
25 See *R v International Trustee* [1937] AC 500; *Vita Food Products v Unus Shipping* [1939] AC 277; *Co Tunisienne de Navigation v Co d'Armement Maritime* [1971] AC 572; and *Amin Rasheed v Kuwait Insurance Co* [1984] 1 AC 50.

the law chosen by the parties, and that the choice may be made expressly by the terms of the contract.[26] Since no requirement of writing or other formality is required for an express choice of law, an oral agreement on the applicable law, concluded in the negotiations leading to the conclusion of a substantive contract in writing, will be effective.[27]

Any express choice of law will usually be made by a clause contained in the contract as concluded, but Art 3(2) permits an express choice to be agreed on after the conclusion of the contract (so as to replace the proper law resulting from a previous express or implied choice, or from the closest connection), though such a subsequent choice will not prejudice the formal validity of the contract, nor adversely affect the rights of third parties (such as guarantors or beneficiaries). Probably a subsequent choice will normally have retroactive effect, unless a contrary intention is indicated.[28] It also seems consistent with the policy of the Regulation to accept an express choice agreed on before the contract, so that, for example, a long term distribution agreement could effectively provide that particular contracts of sale subsequently concluded between the same parties pursuant to the agreement should be governed by a specified law, unless the particular contract should otherwise provide.

A very minor restriction on the effect of an express choice is imposed by Art 3(3), which specifies that where all other elements relevant to the situation at the time of the choice are located in a country other than the country whose law has been chosen, the choice of the parties shall not prejudice the application of provisions of the law of that other country which cannot be derogated from by agreement; and Recital 15 indicates that this applies even if the choice of law is accompanied by a choice of court or tribunal.[29] Thus where parties resident in France negotiate and contract in France for performance exclusively in France, but include a clause providing for English jurisdiction and English law, the English court will have to give effect to all mandatory rules contained in French law; but subject to that proviso the choice of English law will be effective. (It may be doubted whether a case caught by Art 3(3) will arise more often than a solar eclipse visible in Colchester.)

Thus in *Caterpillar Financial Services v SNC Passion*[30] Cooke J explained that the terms of Art 3(1) give the parties a freedom to choose the law applicable to the agreement which they are making. Article 3(3) provides an exception to this in the case where the agreement is entirely domestic in content so that the choice of a foreign law is designed to circumvent the mandatory rules of the country which alone is concerned with the transaction. If, however, there are other elements, outside the choice

---

26 In full, Art 3(1) provides: 'A contract shall be governed by the law chosen by the parties. The choice shall be made expressly or clearly demonstrated by the terms of the contract or the circumstances of the case. By their choice the parties can select the law applicable to the whole or to part only of the contract.' By Art 3(5), the existence and validity of the consent of the parties as to the choice of the applicable law must be determined in accordance with the same provisions (Arts 10, 11 and 13) as apply to their consent to other terms.

27 See *Oakley v Ultra Vehicle Design Ltd* [2005] EWHC 872 (Ch) (Lloyd LJ).

28 See Mayer and Heuzé, *Droit International Privé*, 9th edn, 2007, Montchrestien, at para 716.

29 In addition, Art 3(4), a new provision, specifies that where all other elements relevant to the situation at the time of the choice are located in one or more EC member states, the parties' choice of the law of an external country shall not prejudice the application of provisions of Community law, where appropriate as implemented in the forum state, which cannot be derogated from by agreement.

30 [2004] 2 Lloyd's Rep 99.

of law and jurisdiction clause, relevant to the situation at the time of concluding the agreement, which are connected with other countries, the agreement is not a domestic agreement of concern only to one country, and Art 3(3) does not apply. Moreover, Art 3(3) refers to elements relevant to the situation, which is wider than elements relevant to the contract, and much wider than elements relevant to the mandatory rules of any one country. Accordingly he held that Art 3(3) did not make French mandatory rules applicable to a contract of loan between an American lender and a French borrower, whereby finance was provided for the construction of a vessel in Singapore, and which contained a clause choosing English law as the proper law.

The very limited scope of the exception specified by Art 3(3) reinforces the clear intention of Art 3(1) that otherwise an express choice should be effective. The Regulation requires an express choice to be respected even if the chosen law has no other connection with the contract, and even if the choice was made for the purpose of avoiding mandatory rules contained in the law of the country which is most closely connected with the contract and which would in the absence of express or implied choice have been the proper law under Art 4. The rationale for freedom to choose an unconnected law is commercial convenience: the rules of the chosen law may be well developed and familiar to the parties, while those of all the connected laws may be obscure or a matter for speculation; or it may be convenient to use the same law for associated transactions (such as a chain of sales of the same goods), even though the connection with the other transactions is not immediately apparent from the contract.[31] Moreover, it would have been senseless to introduce the French doctrine of evasion of law in a context where the primary choice of law rule is based on intention, and the test of closest connection has only a supplementary role, to provide a solution where no intention is apparent. On the other hand, an expressly chosen law will apply even where its effect is to invalidate the contract.[32]

It is clear from Arts 1, 4 and 22 of the Rome I Regulation, and was accepted by the Court of Appeal in *Shamil Bank of Bahrain v Beximco Pharmaceuticals*,[33] that the proper law, whether chosen by the parties or determined by reference to closest connection, must be the law of a country, in the sense of a territory having its own legal rules on contracts. It cannot be general principles of law recognised by civilised nations, or the International Institute for the Unification of Private Law (UNIDROIT) Principles of International Commercial Contracts,[34] or Islamic law (in a generic sense, independently of its operation in any particular country). It must be borne in mind, however, that the Rome I Regulation and the other conflict rules applicable by English courts are not necessarily applicable in arbitrations which have their seat in England, for

---

31 See *Vita Food Products v Unus Shipping* [1939] AC 277, where the Privy Council (on appeal from Nova Scotia) upheld an express choice of English law in a bill of lading contract for the carriage of herrings from Newfoundland to New York in a Nova Scotian ship. Lord Wright specifically rejected an argument that, since the transaction allegedly had no connection with English law, the choice could not seriously be taken, and emphasised that connection with English law was not as a matter of principle essential. See also *OT Africa Line v Magic Sportswear Corp* [2005] 2 Lloyd's Rep 170 (CA).

32 See *Fraser v Buckle* [1996] 1 IR 1, where the Irish Supreme Court gave effect to an express choice of English law in a contract between English heir locators and an Irish resident, under which the heir locators pursued the client's claim to an inheritance in New Jersey in return for a share in the proceeds. But the contract was void for champerty under English, Irish and New Jersey laws.

33 [2004] 2 Lloyd's Rep 1 (CA).

34 See www.unidroit.org.

the Arbitration Act 1996 enables parties to empower an English arbitrator to decide disputes in accordance with non-legal considerations.[35]

Similarly, it seems clear that parties are limited, in choosing the proper law, to the laws of countries which exist at the time of the choice, but that they cannot limit their choice to the content of a law as it exists at the time of contracting or some other specified date, and must accept subsequent changes in its substantive rules which the chosen law makes applicable to existing contracts, except in so far as such retroactive effects may infringe a stringent public policy of the forum.[36] Moreover, since Art 3 refers to a choice *by the parties*, it seems probable that the parties cannot confer on one of them a unilateral power subsequently to designate the proper law (whether directly or indirectly, for example by fixing the location of a relevant factor, such as the seat of an arbitration proceeding).[37] But there seems no reason why parties should not be able to subject the identity of the proper law to the resolution of a contingency over which none of the parties has control.[38]

Perhaps the greatest practical problem in connection with express choice concerns clauses the meaning of which is less than clear. An example of this is *Co Tunisienne de Navigation v Co d'Armement Maritime*,[39] which involved a tonnage contract between a French shipowner and a Tunisian shipper for the carriage of oil between two Tunisian ports. The contract permitted the carrier to use ships owned, controlled or chartered by him, but the contract was expressed on a standard form designed for a voyage charter-party, and contained a clause choosing the law of the flag of the vessel carrying the goods. In the House of Lords, the majority, which included Lord Diplock, relying on a finding that the parties contemplated that the carrier would, at least primarily, use his own ships, which all flew the French flag, managed to construe the choice of law clause as referring to the law of the flag of the vessels owned by the carrier, and thus to French law. The minority, which included Lord Wilberforce, felt unable to interpret or rewrite the clause in this way, and concluded that it was void for uncertainty. It is now clear from the decision of the Court of Appeal in *Centrax v Citibank*[40] that, even under the Rome I Regulation, the English courts will apply English principles of contractual interpretation in determining the meaning (or lack of any discernible meaning) of an ambiguous choice of law clause. If a choice of law clause is void for uncertainty, probably it is nonetheless effective to eliminate the possibility of an implied choice, so that the test of closest connection under Art 4 will then become operative.

---

35 By s 46 of the 1996 Act, an arbitral tribunal seated in England will decide a dispute: (a) in accordance with the internal law chosen by the parties as applicable to the substance of the dispute; or (b) if the parties so agree, in accordance with such other considerations as are agreed by them or determined by the tribunal. If there is no such choice or agreement, the tribunal will apply the law determined by the conflict rules which it considers applicable.

36 See *R v International Trustee* [1937] AC 500, where the House of Lords gave effect to American legislation adopted in 1933, invalidating gold clauses contained in contracts concluded in 1917; Dicey, Morris and Collins, 14th edn, at para 32–082; and Mayer and Heuzé, *Droit International Privé*, 9th edn, 2007, Montchrestien, at para 708.

37 See *The Armar* [1981] 1 WLR 207 (CA); *The Iran Vojdan* [1984] 2 Lloyd's Rep 380 (Bingham J); *The Stolt Marmaro* [1985] 2 Lloyd's Rep 428 (CA); *The Star Texas* [1993] 2 Lloyd's Rep 445 (CA); *Sonatrach Petroleum Corp v Ferrell International Ltd* [2002] 1 All ER (Comm) 627 (Colman J); and Dicey, Morris and Collins, 14th edn, at para 32–086. Cf *Du Pont de Nemours v Agnew* [1987] 2 Lloyd's Rep 585 (CA); *King v Brandywine Reinsurance Co* [2004] Lloyd's Rep. IR 554 (Colman J), reversed [2005] 1 Lloyd's Rep 655 (CA); and Dicey, Morris and Collins, at para 32–087.

38 See *The Mariannina* [1983] 1 Lloyd's Rep 12 (CA); *CGU International Insurance v Szabo* [2002] 1 All ER (Comm) 83 (Toulson J); and Dicey, Morris and Collins, 14th edn, at para 32–087.

39 [1971] AC 572.

40 [1999] 1 All ER (Comm) 557 (CA).

The last sentence of Art 3(1) specifies that 'By their choice the parties can select the law applicable to the whole or to part only of the contract'. Thus it is, perhaps regrettably, open to the parties to choose different proper laws for different parts of a contract. But it seems proper to require that the parts should be logically severable because they relate to distinct transactions. Thus where a contract provides both for a sale of goods and the supply of technical assistance, severance will be possible between the sale and the assistance. On the other hand, severance by reference to issues or terms (for example, as between the validity and effect of exclusion clauses, and all other issues relating to the contract) should not be permitted.[41] In any event there must be a single law which governs issues such as frustration which affect the contract as a whole.[42]

That severance is usually inadvisable is apparent from the decision of the Court of Appeal in *Centrax v Citibank*,[43] which involved a contract for electronic payment services. The clause read:

> This Agreement and all documents, agreements and instruments related to this Agreement shall be governed by and interpreted according to the laws of the state of New York, United States of America, provided that any action or dispute between the parties regarding any Payment Instrument shall be governed by and interpreted according to the laws of the country or state in which the Drawee of such Payment Instrument is located.

The customer sued the bank, complaining that the bank had wrongfully debited the customer's account in respect of cheques forged by an employee of the customer. The bank was based in New York, but the cheques were drawn on its London branch, and the customer sought to invoke the (English) Unfair Contract Terms Act 1977 so as to invalidate terms of the contract on which the bank was relying in defence. A divided Court of Appeal applied English principles of construction to the choice of law clause, and concluded that where, as in the present action, the dispute raised the interpretation or effect of the contract and went beyond the validity and effect of the payment instrument, the law of New York was to be applied.

Moreover, as the Court of Appeal recognised in *Shamil Bank of Bahrain v Beximco Pharmaceuticals*,[44] it is not open to parties to designate two different laws as governing the whole contract. Thus where a financing agreement specified that 'Subject to the principles of Glorious Sharia'a, this agreement shall be governed by and construed in accordance with the law of England', the reference to Islamic law was construed as merely decorative and therefore ignored.

THE PROPER LAW – IMPLIED CHOICE

In the absence of an express choice, Art 3 of the Rome I Regulation directs the court to consider next whether an implied choice of law by the parties can be discovered. It is sufficient under Art 3(1) that the parties' choice, though not expressed in the contract, is 'clearly demonstrated by the terms of the contract or the circumstances of the case'.

---

41 See Mayer and Heuzé, *Droit International Privé*, 9th edn, 2007, Montchrestien, at para 710.
42 See *Centrax v Citibank* [1999] 1 All ER (Comm) 557 (CA); and Dicey, Morris and Collins, 14th edn, at paras 32–050 to 32–053.
43 [1999] 1 All ER (Comm) 557 (CA).
44 [2004] 2 Lloyd's Rep 1 (CA).

The Regulation agrees with the traditional English law in its post-war phase[45] in adopting a fairly restrictive approach to the discovery of an implied choice. Some factor which supplies a clear indication in favour of a particular law, as being evidently much more suitable to achieve the purposes of the parties in entering into the contract, is necessary. Otherwise the court should accept that no choice, express or implied, has been made by the parties, and should proceed to apply the default rules laid down by Art 4.

The factors which may amount to a clear indication, warranting the recognition of an implied choice, cannot be definitively listed, but it is in principle unlikely that a sufficiently strong indication will have escaped attention up to the present date. English case law prior to the Rome Convention indicates that the clearest possible indication arises where, as matters stand at the time of contracting, one connected law upholds the validity of the contract and all its terms, while another connected law would have total or partial invalidating effect.[46] In such circumstances a choice of the validating law is necessary to give effect to the contract as concluded. A similar situation arises where one connected law is familiar with the type of contract, and contains well-established detailed rules for interpreting and supplementing its express terms, while the content of another connected law in relation to such contracts, as matters stand at the time of contracting, is a matter for the broadest speculation.[47] In such circumstances, a choice of the adequately developed law is necessary to give sufficient certainty to the contract. Although these factors of validation or adequate supplementary content have not been considered by English courts since the entry into force of the Rome Convention, there is no reason to suppose that the Convention or the Regulation has altered the position in these respects.

Another factor amounting to a clear indication of an implied choice of law by the parties is the inclusion in the contract of a jurisdiction clause, specifying the court that will be competent to hear disputes relating to the contract. Thus Recital 12 to the Regulation explains that an agreement between the parties to confer on one or more courts or tribunals of a member state exclusive jurisdiction to determine disputes under the contract should be one of the factors to be taken into account in determining whether a choice of law has been clearly demonstrated. More generally, a jurisdiction clause will normally imply a choice of the substantive law of the country whose court is chosen.[48] The same will apply to an arbitration clause if the arbitral tribunal designated is one which, as is generally known, will usually apply a particular substantive law.[49]

---

45   See especially *Bonython v Australia* [1951] AC 201; *Re United Railways of Havana* [1961] AC 1007; and *Amin Rasheed v Kuwait Insurance Co* [1984] 1 AC 50.

46   See *Peninsular Line v Shand* (1865) 16 ER 103; *Re Missouri Steamship Co* (1889) 42 ChD 321; *Hamlyn v Talisker Distillery* [1894] AC 202; *Spurrier v La Cloche* [1902] AC 445; *Sayers v International Drilling* [1971] 3 All ER 163; *Coast Lines v Hudig and Veder* [1972] 2 QB 34; and *Co Tunisienne de Navigation v Co d'Armement Maritime* [1971] AC 572, per Lord Wilberforce at p 598.

47   See *Amin Rasheed v Kuwait Insurance Co* [1984] 1 AC 50.

48   See *The Komninos S* [1991] 1 Lloyd's Rep 370, decided under the traditional English law before the Rome Convention; and *Marubeni v Mongolian Government* [2002] 2 All ER (Comm) 873 (Aikens J), decided under the Convention. See also *King v Brandywine Reinsurance Co* [2005] 1 Lloyd's Rep 655 (CA).

49   See *Co Tunisienne de Navigation v Co d'Armement Maritime* [1971] AC 572, decided before the Rome Convention; and *Egon Oldendorff v Libera Corp* [1995] 2 Lloyd's Rep 64 (Mance J) and [1996] 1 Lloyd's Rep 380 (Clarke J), confirming that the Convention has not altered the position. See also *King v Brandywine Reinsurance Co* [2005] 1 Lloyd's Rep 655 (CA). But no implication as to the proper law can be drawn from a clause under which the place of arbitration is to be chosen by one of the parties; see *The Star Texas* [1993] 2 Lloyd's Rep 445 (CA).

The rationale is that dispute resolution is simplified if the chosen forum applies the law with which it is most familiar, and (where relevant) that a choice of a neutral forum (in a country where neither party is resident) is designed also to render applicable a neutral law. But a forum clause will be outweighed by the factor of validity where the law of the chosen forum would invalidate a contract which would be valid under another connected law.[50] In some circumstances, the use of a standard form not containing a forum clause may be an important indication in favour of an implied choice of the law of the country of origin of the form, at least if one of the parties is resident in that country and the other contracts through a broker there.[51]

Another factor capable of amounting to a clear indication of an implied choice arises from the connection between several related contracts. Where, as a matter of commercial reality, related contracts need to be governed by the same law if their purpose is to be achieved, an implied choice to that effect may be discovered. This is most obviously the case with regard to a guarantee in the strictest sense, whereby the intention is that the guarantor should assume a secondary obligation identical to the primary obligation of the main debtor. Thus the guarantee obligation will be governed by the law which governs the obligation guaranteed.[52] Somewhat similarly, all obligations arising from a letter of credit (between the beneficiary and the issuing bank; between the beneficiary and the correspondent bank; and between the two banks) will normally be governed by a single law, that of the country in which the banking establishment through which the letter is payable is situated.[53] On the same basis, a counter-undertaking given by one bank will be governed by the law which governs the performance bond given by another bank at the former's request.[54] Similarly the need for a single law to govern a group insurance policy, under which worldwide cover is provided to a parent company and its subsidiaries, may indicate an implied choice of the law of the country in which both the insurer and the leading policyholder were resident and the contract was negotiated and concluded.[55] Moreover, weight may sometimes be attached to the fact that a contract is one of a group of similar contracts between one party (for example, as employer or principal) and numerous others (for example, as employees or agents), with the result that all such contracts may be governed by the law of the residence of the party common to all the similar contracts.[56]

---

50 See *Co Tunisienne de Navigation v Co d'Armement Maritime* [1971] AC 572, *per* Lord Wilberforce at p 598.

51 See *Tiernan v Magen Insurance* [2000] ILPr 517 (Longmore J); *Tonicstar v American Home Assurance* [2004] EWHC 1234 (Comm) (Morison J); *Munchener Ruckverischerungs Gesellschaft v Commonwealth Insurance Co* [2004] EWHC 914 (Comm) (Morison J); and *Tryg Baltica v Boston Compania De Seguros* [2004] EWHC 1186 (Comm) (Cooke J), in all of which the implied choice accorded with the result of applying the presumption in favour of the reinsurer's residence under Art 4. See also *Miller v Whitworth* [1970] AC 583.

52 See *Bank of Scotland v Butcher* [1998] EWCA Civ 1306 (CA), holding that a guarantee by an English and a Scottish director of a Scottish company of the company's liabilities to a Scottish bank was governed by Scots law. See also *Broken Hill Pty v Xenakis* [1982] 2 Lloyd's Rep 304.

53 See *Attock Cement v Romanian Bank for Foreign Trade* [1989] 1 WLR 1147 (CA); *Bank of Baroda v Vysya Bank* [1994] 2 Lloyd's Rep 87 (Mance J); *BCCHK v Sonali Bank* [1995] 1 Lloyd's Rep 22 (Cresswell J); and *Marconi Communications v Pt Pan Indonesia Bank* [2005] EWCA Civ 422 (CA), affirming [2004] 1 Lloyd's Rep 594 (David Steel J). Although this case law relies on Art 4(5) of the Convention, now Art 4(3) of the Regulation, to achieve the necessary unity, it is submitted that the use of implied choice under Art 3 would be more appropriate.

54 See *Wahda Bank v Arab Bank* [1996] 1 Lloyd's Rep 470 (CA).

55 See *American Motorists Insurance v Cellstar* [2003] ILPr 22 (CA).

56 See *Sayers v International Drilling* [1971] 3 All ER 163 (CA); and *Mercury Publicity v Loerke* ILPR 142 (CA).

The relation between connected contracts must not, however, be given a weight beyond the needs of the commercial situation. Thus a letter of credit or a performance bond will not be affected by the law governing the underlying supply contract.[57] Similarly in the case of reinsurance, although the risk covered will usually be the same as that covered by the primary insurance contract, the law governing the reinsurance contract will not be influenced by that chosen in or otherwise governing the primary insurance contract.[58]

In any event, as the Court of Appeal recognised in *Samcrete v Land Rover*,[59] a choice otherwise implied may be negated by the negotiations leading to the contract, as where a guarantor deletes from the form proffered by the other party a clause expressly choosing the same law as governs the main contract under which the obligation guaranteed arises.

THE PROPER LAW – CLOSEST CONNECTION

In the absence of any valid express or implied choice by the parties, the proper law of a contract is in most cases determined in accordance with the default rules laid down by Arts 4 and 5 of the Rome I Regulation. Article 4 of the Regulation provides:

1. To the extent that the law applicable to the contract has not been chosen in accordance with Article 3 and without prejudice to Articles 5 to 8, the law governing the contract shall be determined as follows:

   (a) a contract for the sale of goods shall be governed by the law of the country where the seller has his habitual residence;

   (b) a contract for the provision of services shall be governed by the law of the country where the service provider has his habitual residence;

   (c) a contract relating to a right in rem in immovable property or to a tenancy of immovable property shall be governed by the law of the country where the property is situated;

   (d) notwithstanding point (c), a tenancy of immovable property concluded for temporary private use for a period of no more than six consecutive months shall be governed by the law of the country where the landlord has his habitual residence, provided that the tenant is a natural person and has his habitual residence in the same country;

   (e) a franchise contract shall be governed by the law of the country where the franchisee has his habitual residence;

   (f) a distribution contract shall be governed by the law of the country where the distributor has his habitual residence;

   (g) a contract for the sale of goods by auction shall be governed by the law of the country where the auction takes place, if such a place can be determined;

   (h) a contract concluded within a multilateral system which brings together or facilitates the bringing together of multiple third-party buying and selling

---

57 See the cases cited in fns 53 and 54 above. See also *Raiffeisen Zentralbank v National Bank of Greece* [1999] 1 Lloyd's Rep 408 (Tuckey J), where a bank-to-bank agreement for the further financing of a shipbuilding project was regarded an autonomous agreement independent of the surrounding transactions.

58 See *Gan Insurance v Tai Ping Insurance* [1999] Lloyd's Rep 472 (CA). See similarly *Dornoch Ltd v Mauritius Union Assurance Co Ltd* [2006] 2 Lloyd's Rep 475 (CA), dealing with associated reinsurance contracts.

59 [2001] EWCA Civ 2019.

interests in financial instruments, as defined by Article 4(1), point (17) of Directive 2004/39/EC, in accordance with non-discretionary rules and governed by a single law, shall be governed by that law.

2. Where the contract is not covered by paragraph 1 or where the elements of the contract would be covered by more than one of points (a) to (h) of paragraph 1, the contract shall be governed by the law of the country where the party required to effect the characteristic performance of the contract has his habitual residence.

3. Where it is clear from all the circumstances of the case that the contract is manifestly more closely connected with a country other than that indicated in paragraphs 1 or 2, the law of that other country shall apply.

4. Where the law applicable cannot be determined pursuant to paragraphs 1 or 2, the contract shall be governed by the law of the country with which it is most closely connected.

Article 4 of the Regulation is supplemented by Article 5, which deals with contracts of carriage. As regards the carriage of goods,[60] Art 5(1) and (3) of the Regulation provides:

1. To the extent that the law applicable to a contract for the carriage of goods has not been chosen in accordance with Article 3, the law applicable shall be the law of the country of habitual residence of the carrier, provided that the place of receipt or the place of delivery or the habitual residence of the consignor is also situated in that country. If those requirements are not met, the law of the country where the place of delivery as agreed by the parties is situated shall apply.

3. Where it is clear from all the circumstances of the case that the contract, in the absence of a choice of law, is manifestly more closely connected with a country other than that indicated in paragraphs 1 or 2, the law of that other country shall apply.

Articles 4 and 5 of the Regulation must be read in conjunction with Art 19, which provides:

1. For the purposes of this Regulation, the habitual residence of companies and other bodies, corporate or unincorporated, shall be the place of central administration.

    The habitual residence of a natural person acting in the course of his business activity shall be his principal place of business.

2. Where the contract is concluded in the course of the operations of a branch, agency or any other establishment, or if, under the contract, performance is the responsibility of such a branch, agency or establishment, the place where the branch, agency or any other establishment is located shall be treated as the place of habitual residence.

3. For the purposes of determining the habitual residence, the relevant point in time shall be the time of the conclusion of the contract.

In these provisions the Regulation departs substantially from Art 4 of the Rome Convention, which provided:

1   To the extent that the law applicable to the contract has not been chosen in accordance with Article 3, the contract shall be governed by the law of the country with which it is most closely connected. Nevertheless, a severable part of the contract which has a closer connection with another country may by way of exception be governed by the law of that other country.

2   Subject to the provisions of paragraph 5 of this Article, it shall be presumed that the contract is most closely connected with the country where the party who is to effect the performance which is characteristic of the contract has, at the time of conclusion

---

60   On Art 5(2), which deals with contracts for the carriage of passengers, see p 593 below.

of the contract, his habitual residence, or, in the case of a body corporate or unincorporate, its central administration. However, if the contract is entered into in the course of that party's trade or profession, that country shall be the country in which the principal place of business is situated or, where under the terms of the contract the performance is to be effected through a place of business other than the principal place of business, the country in which that other place of business is situated.

3   Notwithstanding the provisions of paragraph 2 of this Article, to the extent that the subject matter of the contract is a right in immovable property or a right to use immovable property it shall be presumed that the contract is most closely connected with the country where the immovable property is situated.

4   A contract for the carriage of goods shall not be subject to the presumption in paragraph 2. In such a contract if the country in which, at the time the contract is concluded, the carrier has his principal place of business is also the country in which the place of loading or the place of discharge or the principal place of business of the consignor is situated, it shall be presumed that the contract is most closely connected with that country. In applying this paragraph single voyage charter-parties and other contracts the main purpose of which is the carriage of goods shall be treated as contracts for the carriage of goods.

5   Paragraph 2 shall not apply if the characteristic performance cannot be determined, and the presumptions in paragraphs 2, 3 and 4 shall be disregarded if it appears from the circumstances as a whole that the contract is more closely connected with another country.

It is evident that in this respect the provisions of the Regulation have been drafted much more elaborately than those of the Convention. But the differences are essentially in matters of detail. Both the Regulation and the Convention provide in substance for a rebuttable presumption, in most cases in favour of the residence of the characteristic performer, which may be displaced by establishing a closer connection with another country.[61] The Regulation differs from the Convention in specifying in more detail which party is to be treated as the characteristic performer in respect of various types of contract; in strengthening the presumption by requiring for rebuttal that a manifestly closer connection must be clearly shown; and by eliminating the possibility of severance in the context of the default rules.[62]

The main effect of Art 4 of the Rome I Regulation is to provide in most cases[63] for a rebuttable presumption in favour of the law of the characteristic performer's

---

61   See *Samcrete v Land Rover* [2001] EWCA Civ 2019, where under the Convention Potter LJ adopted a two-stage approach to the application of Art 4: first, to identify the characteristic performance of the contract and the country of the party who is to effect it; and, secondly, to ascertain what factors, if any, might lead the court to disregard the presumption under Art 4(5), the burden of proof in that respect lying upon the party who asserts that the presumption in Art 4(2) should be disregarded.

62   On the limited availability of severance under Art 4 of the Rome Convention, see *Bank of Scotland v Butcher* [1998] EWCA Civ 1306 (CA), and *CGU International Insurance v Szabo* [2002] Lloyd's Rep IR 196 (Toulson J).

63   Exceptional cases, to which the presumption in favour of the law of the characteristic performer's residence does not apply, are: certain contracts involving land, for which Art 4(1)(c) provides a presumption in favour of the lex situs; auction sales, for which Art 4(1)(g) provides a presumption in favour of the location of the auction; contracts concluded within a market in financial instruments, for which Art 4(1)(h) provides a presumption in favour of the law which governs the relevant market; contracts of carriage of goods, for which Art 5(1) provides a more limited presumption in favour of the carrier's residence; contracts for the carriage of passengers, for which Art 5(2) provides a limited presumption in favour of the passenger's residence; certain consumer contracts, which are governed by Art 6; certain insurance contracts covering mass risks, for which Art 7(3) provides a presumption in favour of the location of the risk; and contracts of employment, which are governed by Art 8.

residence, which may be displaced by establishing clearly a manifestly closer connection with another country. Thus Art 4(2) refers to the law of the country where the party required to effect the characteristic performance of the contract has his habitual residence, and the function of Art 4(1)(a)–(b) and (e)–(f) is to indicate the party who counts as the characteristic performer in certain types of contract. These sub-paragraphs identify the characteristic performer as: (a) the seller, in the case of a contract for the sale of goods (other than by auction); (b) the service provider, in the case of a contract for the provision of services; (e) the franchisee, in the case of a franchise contract; and (f) the distributor, in the case of a distribution contract.[64] Similarly Art 7(2) identifies the characteristic performer as the insurer, in the case of an insurance contract covering a large risk. More generally, it is clear from the Giuliano and Lagarde Report[65] that it is the supply of goods or services, rather than the receipt of or payment for them, which constitutes the characteristic performance of a contract for the supply of goods or services in return for payment, so that the presumption amounts to a preference for the law of the seller or other supplier's country.

The reference by Art 4(1)(b) of the Regulation to the service provider's residence confirms a line of English decisions under the Convention which have referred a contract for a bank account to the law of the country in which the branch at which the account is kept is situated, since the characteristic performance, repayment of the sum deposited, is to be effected through that branch;[66] a contract whereby an insurance broker is instructed to arrange insurance to the law of the country in which the broker carries on business;[67] a contract under which an architect is to design a building to the law of the architect's residence;[68] and a reinsurance contract to the law of the reinsurer's residence.[69] On the other hand Art 4(1)(b) of the Regulation appears to overrule some English decisions under the Convention which have ruled that, in the case of a unilateral contract for services (such as a promise to pay a fee and/or expenses if certain services are rendered, without a reciprocal promise to provide the services), it is the party who promises to pay, and not the service provider, who counts as the characteristic performer.[70]

Another English ruling under the Convention which appears to remain applicable

---

64 Cf *Print Concept v GEW* [2001] ECC 36 (CA). The Regulation does not contain any specific provision identifying the characteristic performer in the case of a contract relating to intellectual or industrial property rights. In Case C-533/07: *Falco and Rabitsch v Weller-Lindhorst*, 23 April 2009, Trstenjak AG opined that a contract for the licensing of an intellectual property right (such as a copyright) does not count as a contract for the provision of services within Art 4(1)(b) of the Rome I Regulation, and the European Court ultimately ruled that such a contract does not count as a contract for the provision of services for the purpose of Art 5(1)(b) of the Brussels I Regulation.

65 [1980] OJ C282, at p 20.

66 See *Sierra Leone Telecommunications v Barclays Bank* [1998] 2 All ER 821 (Cresswell J). See also *Raiffeisen Zentralbank v National Bank of Greece* [1999] 1 Lloyd's Rep 408 (Tuckey J), which involved an agreement between banks whereby, in order to enable one bank to provide additional finance for a shipbuilding project, the other bank undertook to divert to the bank providing the additional finance the stage payments which it was already bound to make to the building purchaser. It was held that the obligation to divert the payments constituted the characteristic obligation, so that Art 4(2) of the Convention pointed to the law of the residence of the bank which undertook to divert.

67 See *HIB v Guardian Insurance* [1997] 1 Lloyd's Rep 412 (Longmore J).

68 See *Latchin v General Mediterranean Holidays* [2002] CLC 330 (Andrew Smith J).

69 See *Gan Insurance v Tai Ping Insurance* [1999] Lloyd's Rep 472 (CA); and *Tonicstar v American Home Assurance* [2004] EWHC 1234 (Comm) (Morison J).

70 See *Ark Therapeutics v True North Capital* [2006] 1 All ER (Comm) 138 (Nigel Teare QC); and *Armstrong International v Deutsche Bank Securities* [2003] All ER (D) 195 (Jul) (Judge Reid QC).

under the Regulation is that, in the case of a contract whereby money is invested in a company, whether by the issue of shares or by way of loan, the characteristic performance is the issue of the shares or the repayment of the loan.[71] As to loans in general, it has been held in England that it is the borrower who counts as the characteristic performer,[72] but in Scotland that it is the lender who counts as the characteristic performer.[73] A further possibility is to look to the residence of the lender where it is a bank or similar institution, on the basis that lending then counts as a financial service, but to the residence of the borrower in other cases, on the ground that repayment of the principal money is then the characteristic performance.

Unlike the Convention, the Regulation does not provide for severance between parts of a contract in the absence of an express or implied choice by the parties. Instead, by Art 4(2) of the Regulation, where the elements of the contract would be covered by more than one of the sub-paragraphs of Art 4(1), the contract is governed by the law of the characteristic performer's habitual residence. Recital 19 explains that in the case of a contract consisting of a bundle of rights and obligations capable of being categorised as falling within more than one of the specified types of contract, the characteristic performance of the contract should be determined having regard to its centre of gravity. Thus where, for example, the contract provides for the sale of goods by A to B for a price in cash, and also for the provision of services by B to A for a monetary consideration, one must (if possible) identify the characteristic performer by reference to the centre of gravity of the contract.

As regards the concept of habitual residence, while Art 19 of the Rome I Regulation defines the concept in the case of a company and of an individual acting in the course of his own business, no definition is offered in respect of an individual who is not acting in the course of his own business. As regards companies, the primary reference by Art 19(1) to the place of central administration contrasts with the Rome Convention, where Art 4(2) referred mainly to the principal place of business. Thus the Regulation appears to connect a company primarily with the place where the board of directors (or equivalent managerial organ) usually meets, rather than the place from which its most important and numerous trading transactions with third parties are negotiated.[74]

No doubt the reference in Art 19(2) of the Rome I Regulation to a branch, agency or other establishment must be construed as equivalent to a secondary establishment under Art 5(5) of the Brussels I Regulation,[75] and as not including a merely electronic presence in the form of a web-server.[76] Article 19(2) of the Rome I Regulation follows Art 4(2) of the Rome Convention in referring to the location of the secondary establishment in cases where, under the contract, performance is the responsibility of the establishment. To satisfy this proviso, the contract must expressly or impliedly require that the performance should be effected through the establishment. It is not enough that the parties expected the contract to be performed through the

---

71 See *Mirchandani v Somaia* [2001] WL 239782 (Morritt V-C). But see Art 4(1)(h) of the Regulation, on contracts concluded within a multilateral market in financial securities.

72 See *Tavoulareas v Tsavliris* [2006] 1 All ER (Comm) 109 (Andrew Smith J).

73 See *Atlantic Telecom GmbH* [2004] SLT 1031 (Lord Brodie in the Outer House of the Court of Session).

74 See *The Rewia* [1991] 2 Lloyd's Rep 325 (CA); *Latchin v General Mediterranean Holidays* [2002] CLC 330 (Andrew Smith J); *King v Crown Energy* [2003] ILPr 28 (Chambers QC); and *Royal & Sun Alliance Insurance v MK Digital* [2006] 2 Lloyd's Rep 110 (CA).

75 See pp 524–5 above.

76 See Directive 2000/31 on Electronic Commerce, [2000] OJ L178/1, Recital 19 and Art 2(c).

establishment, if there was no contractual requirement to that effect.[77] But Art 19(2) of the Regulation departs from Art 4(2) of the Convention is offering an alternative condition, so as to refer to the location of the secondary establishment in cases where the contract is concluded in the course of the operations of the establishment. It is uncertain what solution is envisaged where, for example, the company has its central administration in New York, but it has a branch in London by which the contract was concluded, and another branch in Paris from which performance of the contract is required. Article 19(3) of the Regulation specifies that, for the purposes of determining the habitual residence, the relevant point in time is that of the conclusion of the contract. This echoes Art 4(2) of the Convention, and accords with the traditional English rule that connections which come into existence after the conclusion of the contract are irrelevant except in support of a (rarely successful) argument that there was a subsequent implied agreement to vary the proper law.[78]

Article 4(4) of the Regulation recognises that there are cases where the characteristic performance cannot be determined, and thus there is no applicable presumption. In such cases Article 4(4) subjects the contract to the law of the country with which it is most closely connected.[79] Recital 21 adds that, in order to determine the country of closest connection, account should be taken, inter alia, of whether the contract in question has a very close relationship with another contract or contracts. Article 4(4) clearly applies to a contract to exchange guns for butter, or hotel accommodation for advertising; or, as Mann J held in *Apple Corps v Apple Computer*,[80] an agreement for the worldwide division of the use of a trade mark in terms of fields of use (computers and sound recordings). It probably also applies to a contract for the sale and lease-back of equipment. Other cases in which the characteristic performance may be unclear are contracts between authors and publishers, and contracts for corporate acquisitions.[81]

Perhaps the most problematic issue in determining the proper law under the Rome I Regulation concerns the strength of the presumption laid down by Art 4 in favour of the law of the characteristic performer's residence. Article 4(3) of the Regulation specifies that where it is clear from all the circumstances of the case that the contract is manifestly more closely connected with a country other than that indicated in Art 4(1) or (2), the law of that other country shall apply. Recital 20 describes this as an escape clause, and adds that for this purpose account should be taken, inter alia, of whether the contract in question has a very close relationship with another contract or contracts. The new formulation seems designed to strengthen the presumption, in comparison with Art 4(5) of the Rome Convention, which merely required for rebuttal that it should be apparent from the circumstances as a whole that the contract was more closely connected with another country. However, the Recital may be taken to endorse the English decisions displacing the presumption in order to

---

77 See *Ennstone Building Products v Stanger* [2002] 1 WLR 3059 (CA). See also *Iran Continental Shelf Oil Co v IRI International Corp* [2002] EWCA Civ 1024 (CA). Cf *Soc Ammerlaan Agro Projecten v Soc Les Serres de Cosquerou*, decided by the French Court of Cassation on 2 March 1999.

78 See *Co Tunisienne de Navigation v Co d'Armement Maritime* [1971] AC 572; and *Marconi Communications v Pan Indonesia Bank* [2005] EWCA Civ 422 (CA).

79 See also per Bot AG in pending Case C-133/08: *Intercontainer Interfrigo v Balkenende Oosthuizen*; opinion of 19 May 2009.

80 [2004] ILPr 34.

81 See Juenger (1997) 45 AJCL 195.

ensure that all of the contracts arising from the issue of a letter of credit are governed by the law of the country in which the banking establishment through which the letter is payable is situated.[82]

On the strength of the presumption, some clarification had emerged from English and Scottish decisions under the Convention. First, the reference in Art 4(5) to a closer connection had to be understood in terms of geographical location only, rather than party intention. Thus the relevant factors were the parties' residences and the places of performance of the various obligations under the contract.[83] Secondly, the presumption in Art 4(2) could be most easily rebutted in cases where the place of performance differed from the place of business of the party whose performance was characteristic of the contract.[84] Thirdly, after some confusion, a consensus had emerged that for the presumption in favour of the characteristic performer's residence to be displaced, it had to be *clearly* shown that the contract had a closer connection with some other country.[85] But, despite such clarification, some uncertainty remained as to what combination of factors would clearly establish a closer connection. Since the Regulation has now increased the strength of the presumption, earlier English decisions in which it was displaced may no longer be entirely reliable.

Since it is obvious that the place of the characteristic performance may differ from the residence of the characteristic performer, and evident that Art 4 deliberately prefers the residence to the place of performance, some further factor must be necessary to displace the presumption. As regards a contract for the sale of goods, in *Grant v Brizard*,[86] Lord Hamilton held that the fact that the contract was concluded in the context of a long term agreement for the exclusive distribution of such goods in the buyer's country was not enough to displace the presumption in favour of the law of the seller's country. On the other hand, in *Ferguson Shipbuilders v Voith Hydro*,[87] Lord Penrose found it sufficient under the Convention that the sale was of a component, to be delivered and then incorporated into a larger machine in the buyer's country. In that case, a German company had manufactured in Germany and delivered in Scotland propeller systems for incorporation in ships under construction by a Scottish shipbuilding company in Scotland.

In the context of services, under the Convention preference was ultimately accorded to the place of performance in *Definitely Maybe v Marek Lieberberg*,[88] where

---

82 See *Attock Cement v Romanian Bank for Foreign Trade* [1989] 1 WLR 1147 (CA); *Bank of Baroda v Vysya Bank* [1994] 2 Lloyd's Rep 87 (Mance J); *BCCHK v Sonali Bank* [1995] 1 Lloyd's Rep 22 (Cresswell J); and *Marconi Communications v Pt Pan Indonesia Bank* [2005] EWCA Civ 422 (CA), affirming [2004] 1 Lloyd's Rep 594 (David Steel J).

83 See *per* Hobhouse LJ in *Credit Lyonnais v New Hampshire Insurance Co* [1997] 2 Lloyd's Rep 1 (CA); and *per* Potter LJ in *Samcrete v Land Rover;* [2001] EWCA Civ 2019.

84 See *per* Mance J in *Bank of Baroda v Vysya Bank* [1994] 2 Lloyd's Rep 87; and *per* Potter LJ in *Samcrete v Land Rover* [2001] EWCA Civ 2019.

85 See *Definitely Maybe v Marek Lieberberg* [2001] 1 WLR 1745 (Morison J); *Samcrete v Land Rover* [2001] EWCA Civ 2019; *Ennstone Building Products v Stanger* [2002] 1 WLR 3059 (CA); *Iran Continental Shelf Oil Co v IRI International Corp* [2002] EWCA Civ 1024; *Caledonia Subsea v Microperi* [2003] SC 70 (Inner House), affirming [2001] SCLR 634 (Lord Hamilton); *Waldwiese Stiftung v Lewis* [2004] EWHC 2589 (Ch) (Mann J); *Ophthalmic Innovations International (UK) Ltd v Ophthalmic Innovations International Inc* [2004] EWHC 2948 (Ch) (Lawrence Collins J); *Marconi Communications v Pan Indonesia Bank* [2005] EWCA Civ 422 (CA); and Dicey, Morris and Collins, 14th edn, 2006, at para 32–125. Cf *Credit Lyonnais v New Hampshire Insurance Co* [1997] 2 Lloyd's Rep 1 (CA).

86 (1998) unreported, 19 January.

87 [2000] SLT 229.

88 [2001] 1 WLR 1745.

an English company had contracted to provide a band to perform at concerts in Germany organised by a German company. In concluding that overall the contract had a closer connection with Germany than with England, Morison J emphasised that Germany was the place of performance by both parties, where the band was to perform and the organiser was to make arrangements and provide facilities for the performance (such as marketing, promotion, security and equipment). On the other hand, the presumption was ultimately adhered to in *Caledonia Subsea v Micoperi*,[89] which involved a contract for diving services to be provided by a Scottish company to an Italian company in connection with the 'post trenching' of a pipeline in Egyptian waters. The place of the characteristic performance was substantially, but not exclusively, in Egypt, where the actual diving operations took place, but preparatory and supervisory activities took place elsewhere, including in Scotland. Lord Hamilton, whose decision was subsequently affirmed by the Inner House, explained that the effecting of the characteristic performance was significantly related to the country where the performer had its principal place of business, and the multinational character of the operations tended to favour the certainty of the presumptive country, not least where the alternative was the country of neither contracting party. The presumption was also adhered to in *Latchin v General Mediterranean Holidays*,[90] where the contract was negotiated in England between parties resident in England, although it was for the design of a building to be erected in Morocco; and in *Ennstone Building Products v Stanger*,[91] where the contract was between English companies for advice on a problem concerning a building in Scotland, and the advice was to be received in England.

The place of performance has also been preferred under the Convention in situations where, as in *Kenburn Waste Management v Bergmann*,[92] the characteristic obligation was a negative obligation to achieve a result in a given country. Thus the Court of Appeal (affirming Pumfrey J) displaced the presumption and subjected to English law an agreement by the German owner of a European patent not to make threats of infringement actions against the English customers of an English manufacturer of competing products. As Pumfrey J had noted, the contract had no objective connection with the patentee's German residence as such at all.

In *Samcrete v Land Rover*,[93] an Egyptian parent company had guaranteed the liability of its subsidiary to pay for products supplied by an English company under a distribution contract expressly governed by English law, but the negotiations leading to the guarantee negated any implied choice of the law governing it. The Court of Appeal accepted that, for the purpose of Art 4, in the case of a guarantee, the characteristic obligation is the guarantor's obligation to pay as promised. But ultimately it found that a closer connection with England was clearly demonstrated, so that the presumption was displaced and English law applied. England was not only the residence of the supplier/payee, but also the place of payment and the place of delivery of the products supplied.

Lastly, it is worth noting that Arts 3 and 4 present no particular problems for commercial contracts which are concluded by electronic means. They avoid tiresome analysis of the place of performance (or indeed the place of contracting) by focusing instead on the residence of the characteristic performer.

---

89   [2003] SC 70 (Inner House), affirming [2001] SCLR 634 (Lord Hamilton).
90   [2002] CLC 330 (Andrew Smith J).
91   [2002] 1 WLR 3059 (CA).
92   [2002] ILPr 33 (CA), affirming [2002] FSR 44.
93   [2001] EWCA Civ 2019.

PARTICULAR ISSUES

The Rome I Regulation takes pains to make clear that most types of issue relating to a contract are governed by the proper law. Thus, by Art 10(1), the existence and validity of a contract, or of any term of a contract, must be determined by the law which would govern it under the Regulation if the contract or term were valid, and Art 11 makes it sufficient for a contract to satisfy the formal requirements of the proper law. By Art 12(1), the proper law governs 'in particular: (a) interpretation;[94] (b) performance; (c) within the limits of the powers conferred on the court by its procedural law, the consequences of a total or partial breach of obligations, including the assessment of damages in so far as it is governed by rules of law; (d) the various ways of extinguishing obligations, and prescription and limitation of actions; and (e) the consequences of nullity of the contract'. In addition, by Art 18(1), the proper law applies to the extent that, in matters of contractual obligations, it contains rules which raise presumptions of law or determine the burden of proof. But the Regulation does specify a number of exceptions, by which an issue may be affected by a law other than the proper law.

Article 10(1) subjects questions of essential validity or formation to the actual or putative proper law; the putative proper law being the law which would be the proper law if the contract or term in question were valid. This applies to such questions as whether a contract has validly incorporated another document by reference, and whether an incomplete agreement has subsequently been completed by a further agreement.[95] It also applies to whether a person has become a party to an existing contract between others; for example, as the holder of a bill of lading.[96] As regards essential validity, the control of the proper law is subject to the provisions of Arts 9 and 21 on public policy and overriding interests.[97]

As regards formation, an exception is made by Art 10(2), by which a party may rely upon the law of his habitual residence to establish that he did not consent, if it appears from the circumstances that it would not be reasonable to determine the effect of his conduct in accordance with the actual or putative proper law. This would probably apply where an English resident ignores an offer (or counteroffer) received from abroad and governed by a foreign law under which silence is treated as consent. But in general, Art 10(2) will be applied with caution, as in *Egon Oldendorff v Libera Corp*,[98] where Mance J explained that in evaluating such a defence, the court should adopt a dispassionate, internationally-minded approach, and the onus is on the party invoking Art 10(2) to bring himself within its provisions. He ultimately rejected the defendant's argument invoking Japanese law, on the ground that it required one to ignore a London arbitration clause, contrary to ordinary commercial expectations,

---

94   Thus where two agreements are governed by the same proper law, it is for that law to determine, as a matter of interpretation, whether they should be treated as a single agreement; see *Carnoustie v ITWF* [2002] 2 All ER (Comm) 657.

95   See *Egon Oldendorff v Libera Corp* [1995] 2 Lloyd's Rep 64 (Mance J); and *The Atlantic Emperor (No 1)* [1989] 1 Lloyd's Rep 548 (CA). Cf *The Heidberg* [1994] 2 Lloyd's Rep 287 (Diamond QC); and *Dornoch Ltd v Mauritius Union Assurance Co Ltd* [2006] 2 Lloyd's Rep 475 (CA).

96   See *The Ythan* [2006] 1 All ER 367 (Aikens J).

97   See pp 584–9 below.

98   [1995] 2 Lloyd's Rep 64. See also *Welex v Rosa Maritime* [2002] Lloyd's Rep 701 (David Steel J), affirmed without reference to this point [2003] 2 Lloyd's Rep 509 (CA); *Morin v Bonhams & Brooks* [2003] 2 All ER (Comm) 36 (Hirst QC), affirmed without reference to this point [2004] 1 Lloyd's Rep 702 (CA); and *Horn Linie v Panamericana Formas E Impresos* [2006] EWHC 373 (Comm) (Morison J).

and despite every indication that the defendant had actually considered and accepted the clause, and that the clause was precisely the sort of clause which would be expected in an international charter agreement.

As regards formalities, Art 11 lays down a rule of alternative reference reflecting a policy of validation. By Art 11(1), a contract concluded between persons who, or whose agents, are in the same country at the time of its conclusion is formally valid if it satisfies the formal requirements of its proper law, or those of the law of the country where it is concluded. By Art 11(2), a contract concluded between persons who, or whose agents, are in different countries at the time of its conclusion is formally valid if it satisfies the formal requirements of its proper law, or those of the law of either of the countries where one of the parties or agents is present at the time of conclusion, or those of the law of the country where one of the parties is habitually resident at that time.[99] In addition, Art 18(2) enables a contract to be proved by any mode of proof which is recognised by the law of the forum or by any law which is applicable to its formal validity under Art 11 and under which the contract is formally valid, provided that such mode of proof can be administered by the forum. This effectively overrides the traditional English approach to the Statute of Frauds 1677, which was extended by means of procedural characterisation to contracts made abroad and governed by foreign law. By way of exception, Art 11(5) of the Regulation subjects a contract whose subject-matter is a right *in rem* in immovable property or a tenancy of immovable property to certain formal requirements of the law of the country where the property is situated. The formal requirements in question are ones which, under the *lex situs*, cannot be derogated from by agreement and are imposed irrespective of where the contract is concluded and of its proper law. Probably such mandatory requirements include those imposed by s 2 of the Law of Property (Miscellaneous Provisions) Act 1989, under which a contract for the sale or other disposition of an interest in land can only be made in writing.

The capacity of both individuals and companies to contract is excluded from the scope of the Rome I Regulation by Art 1(2)(a) and (f), with the exception that Art 13 (reflecting French case law)[100] insists that, in the case of a contract concluded between persons who are in the same country, an individual who would have capacity under the law of that country may not invoke his incapacity resulting from the law of another country unless the other party to the contract was aware of the incapacity at the time of the conclusion of the contract, or was not unaware of the incapacity as a result of negligence. Thus, subject to Art 13, English courts continue to determine a person's capacity to contract in accordance with the traditional English conflict rules. Under these it is probably sufficient in the case of ordinary contracts[101] that an individual has capacity either under the proper law of the contract (now ascertained under Arts 3 and 4 of the Regulation, and with full account taken of even an express choice by the parties),[102] or under the law of his domicile. But a company must have

---

99   The third alternative, referring to habitual residence, was added by the Regulation.

100 See *De Lizardi v Chaise*, Sirey 61.1.305 (1861), a decision of the Chambre des Requêtes of the Court of Cassation.

101 There is a special rule for marriage settlements, where each party's capacity is governed by the law of his or her domicile (see *Re Cooke's Trusts* (1887) 56 LT 737; *Cooper v Cooper* (1888) 13 App Cas 88; and *Viditz v O'Hagan* [1900] 2 Ch 87), and for contracts for the disposition of land, where capacity is governed by the *lex situs* (see *Bank of Africa v Cohen* [1909] 2 Ch 129).

102 See *Male v Roberts* (1800) 3 Esp 163; *McFeetridge v Stewarts and Lloyds* 1913 SC 773; *Charron v Montreal Trust* (1958) 15 DLR (2d) 240; and especially *Bodley Head v Flegon* [1972] 1 WLR 680. Cf Dicey, Morris and Collins, 14th edn, 2006, Rule 209(1).

capacity both under the proper law of the contract and under the law of the country of its incorporation.[103]

Article 12(1)(b) of the Rome I Regulation expressly includes performance among the issues governed by the proper law, but Art 12(2) adds a minor exception that, in relation to the manner of performance and the steps to be taken in the event of defective performance, regard must be had to the law of the country in which performance takes place. This seems to reflect Lord Wright's remark in *Mount Albert BC v Australasian Assurance Soc*[104] that the law of the place of performance may regulate the minor details of performance, but not so as to affect the substance of the obligation. It no doubt applies to such questions as what are normal business hours within which delivery should be effected under a contract of sale.[105] It also ensures that a sea carrier may comply with a requirement under the law of the country of discharge that the bill of lading should after presentation be returned to the customs agent, marked if necessary to show that delivery has been made.[106]

By Art 12(1)(c), the proper law governs, within the limits of the powers conferred on the court by its procedural law, the consequences of a total or partial breach of obligations, including the assessment of damages in so far as it is governed by rules of law. This cautious formulation ensures that English courts will not be required to follow a foreign proper law to the length of making available non-monetary remedies, such as orders for specific performance, in circumstances where English law would limit the plaintiff to monetary remedies; for example, because specific performance would necessitate continuing judicial supervision.[107] On the other hand, the Regulation seems to encourage the application of the proper law to the greatest extent practicable in connection with the assessment of damages – not only to questions of remoteness of damage, admissible heads of damage, and mitigation of loss, but even to mere quantification, in so far as the proper law supplies a rule sufficiently definite that a court elsewhere can apply it with reasonable accuracy. Moreover, as the Court of Appeal ruled in *Lesotho Highlands Development Authority v Impregilo*,[108] the proper law must be applied in determining the currency in which a monetary judgment should be given, and also whether the claimant is entitled to interest on unpaid sums, whether by virtue of a contractual term or of a rule of law; but if the rate of interest is not fixed by a contractual term, it must be determined in accordance with the *lex fori*.

By Art 12(1)(d), the Regulation specifies that the proper law governs prescription and limitation of actions. This substantive characterisation of time limits for bringing actions was anticipated by the Foreign Limitation Periods Act 1984,[109] which, however, invokes public policy to restrict its effect. Section 2 declares it inconsistent with public policy to apply a foreign rule on time limitation if to do so would cause

---

103 See *Carse v Coppen* [1951] SLT 145; *Kutchera v Buckingham International Holdings Ltd* [1988] IR 61; *Continental Enterprises Ltd v Shandong Zhucheng Foreign Trade Group Co* [2005] EWHC 92 (Comm) (David Steel J); and Dicey, Morris and Collins, 14th edn, 2006, Rule 162.

104 [1938] AC 224.

105 See Dicey, Morris and Collins, 14th edn, 2006, at para 32–199.

106 See *East West Corp v DKBS 1912* [2002] 2 Lloyd's Rep 182 (Thomas J). This point was not dealt with when the decision was affirmed on appeal [2003] 2 All ER 700 (CA).

107 See Dicey, Morris and Collins, 14th edn, 2006, at para 32–203.

108 [2003] 2 Lloyd's Rep 497 (CA), affirming [2003] 1 All ER (Comm) 22 (Morison J). The decision of the Court of Appeal was reversed by the House of Lords on other grounds (relating to the limits of judicial supervision of an arbitral award), [2006] 1 AC 221.

109 The 1984 Act largely implemented Law Commission, *Classification of Limitation in Private International Law*, Report No 114, 1982, HMSO. See also Stone, [1985] 4 LMCLQ 497.

undue hardship to one of the parties,[110] and also requires any foreign rule under which time does not run while a party is absent from a given country to be disregarded. In addition, s 1(3) insists in all cases on the English rule that it is the issue of the claim form, rather than (for example) its service, which constitutes the commencement of English proceedings for limitation purposes. As regards undue hardship, English courts have disregarded a foreign one-year period for personal injury actions, where the claimant had been long hospitalised and had been led by the defendant to believe that her claim would be met by its insurers;[111] or a limitation period contained in a law which the parties did not realise was the proper law of the relevant contract.[112] But a foreign one-year period for an industrial disease claim, which ran from the date at which the plaintiff obtained knowledge of the injury, and within which the plaintiff was in fact able to obtain relevant legal advice, has been respected.[113]

Article 12(1)(e) of the Rome I Regulation provides for the application of the proper law to the consequences of nullity of the contract. Under the Rome Convention the United Kingdom had made a reservation under Art 22 excluding the application of Art 10(1)(e) (which corresponds to Art 12(1)(e) of the Regulation) in this country.[114] The reservation seemed, however, to be illusory, since the decision of the House of Lords in *The Evia Luck*[115] indicated that the same rule existed in traditional English law. Their Lordships applied English law as the expressly chosen proper law of a contract entered into under economic pressure between foreigners abroad, to establish not only the illegitimacy of the economic pressure and the resulting invalidity of the contract, but also the existence of a consequential restitutionary right to money paid under the contract. In any event no reservation is possible under the Rome I Regulation. Moreover similar rules, subjecting restitutionary claims arising out of unjust enrichment, and non-contractual obligations arising out of dealings prior to the conclusion of a contract, to the law governing the related contract, are laid down by Arts 10 and 12 of the Rome II Regulation on the Law Applicable to Non-Contractual Obligations.[116]

ENGLISH PUBLIC POLICY AND OVERRIDING MANDATORY RULES

The Rome I Regulation derogates from its main rule, referring most contractual issues to the proper law, by making important exceptions in favour of the public policy or overriding interests of the forum country. Article 21 contains a traditional proviso permitting the forum to insist on respect for its own stringent public policy. It specified that the application of a provision of the law of any country specified by the

---

110 But s 2 of the 1984 Act does not enable an otherwise applicable *English* limitation rule to be disregarded by reference to public policy or undue hardship; see *Chagos Islanders v Attorney General* [2003] EWHC 2222 (QB) (Ouseley J), affirmed on other grounds [2004] EWCA Civ 997.
111 See *Jones v Trollope Colls* (1990) *The Times*, 26 January (CA).
112 See *The Komninos S* [1991] 1 Lloyd's Rep 370 (CA).
113 See *Durham v T&N* (1996) unreported, 1 May (CA).
114 See the 1990 Act, s 2(2). A similar reservation had been made by Italy.
115 [1992] 2 AC 152. Cf. *Baring Brothers v Cunninghame DC* [1996] WL 1093491 (Lord Penrose in the Outer House of the Court of Session).
116 EC Regulation 864/2007 [2007] OJ L199/40.

Regulation may be refused if such application is manifestly incompatible with the public policy of the forum. Article 9(2) specifies that nothing in the Regulation restricts the application of the overriding mandatory provisions of the law of the forum.

The public policy proviso specified by Art 21 of the Regulation refers primarily to the rare cases where the relevant foreign rule (as applied to the substantive facts) departs so radically from English concepts of fundamental justice that its application would be intolerably offensive to the English judicial conscience, even where all the connecting factors (except as to the forum seised) are with the country of the rule.[117] It applies, for example, where the foreign proper law would uphold the validity of a contract which was entered into under what English law regards as illegitimate non-economic pressure.[118] It would also be contrary to public policy, within Art 21 of the Regulation, to enforce a contract which infringed the competition rules laid down by Art 81 of the EC Treaty.[119] In addition, Art 21 appears to preserve the traditional English rule which insists on the invariable application of the English substantive rules as to the effect on existing contracts of the outbreak of a war to which the United Kingdom is a party.[120]

Article 21 of the Regulation also appears to maintain the operation of the traditional English rules which are designed to prevent the English courts from encouraging or requiring parties to perform acts abroad whose performance would contravene the criminal law of the country where the performance would take place. It is true that the problem of performances which are prohibited at the place of performance is also addressed by Art 9(3) of the Regulation, which specifies that effect may be given to the overriding mandatory provisions of the law of the country where the obligations arising out of the contract have to be or have been performed, in so far as those overriding mandatory provisions render the performance of the contract unlawful; and that in considering whether to give effect to those provisions, regard must be had to their nature and purpose and to the consequences of their application or non-application.[121] But there seems no reason why Art 21 cannot now be invoked in this context. In any event it seems probable that the English courts will continue to apply their traditional rules in this matter, whether they invoke Art 21 or Art 9(3) as the basis for doing so.

The first of these traditional rules applies where the parties' actual common intention at the time of contracting was that the contract should be performed by means of an act done in defiance of a known criminal prohibition imposed by the law of the country where the act was intended to be performed.[122] In such circumstances, the

---

117   See *per* Simon P in *Cheni v Cheni* [1965] P 85.
118   See *Kaufman v Gerson* [1904] 1 KB 591 (CA), which involved a threat to prosecute the promissor's husband for embezzlement, and *Royal Boskalis v Mountain* [1997] 2 All ER 929 (CA), which involved a threat by the Iraqi Government to detain the contractor's equipment and personnel in Iraq as the first Gulf War became imminent.
119   See Case C-126/97: *Eco Swiss China Time v Benetton International* [1999] ECR I-3055.
120   See *Ertel Bieber v Rio Tinto* [1918] AC 260.
121   Article 9(3) of the Regulation differs substantially from its predecessor, Art 7(1) of the Rome Convention. Moreover several member states, including the United Kingdom, had made reservations excluding the operation of Art 7(1) of the Convention by their courts. No reservation is possible in relation to Art 9(3) of the Regulation.
122   See *Foster v Driscoll* [1929] 1 KB 470 (CA), which involved a conspiracy to ship whisky into the US during 'prohibition'; *Regazzoni v Sethia* [1958] AC 301 (HL), where a contract expressed in the documents as a sale cif Genoa was in fact intended to be performed by exporting the goods from India in breach of an Indian prohibition on exports destined ultimately for South Africa; and *Royal Boskalis v Mountain* [1997] 2 All ER 929 (CA), which involved

entire contract will be regarded as illegal and unenforceable in England, even if the unlawful intention is concealed by the documentation and revealed only by oral testimony, and even if the contract is governed by a foreign proper law which takes a different view of its validity. An analogous result will be reached where the guilty intention to perform in defiance of a known prohibition was possessed by one, but not the other, of the parties. The guilty party will then be unable to enforce the contract at all, but (unless performance would inevitably require breach of the prohibition in the country where it was imposed, in which case a variation on the second rule would apply) the innocent party will be able to do so.[123]

The second rule relating to criminal prohibitions applies where there was no such guilty intention but, unknown to the parties, there in fact existed at the time of contracting, or there came into force between the time of contracting and the time for performance, in a country where the contract necessarily required an act of performance to be done, a criminal prohibition against the doing of that act. In such a case, if the contract is governed by English law, and the illegality is supervening, then at least the obligation, the performance of which is prohibited, will be *pro tanto* frustrated and discharged. Such a situation arose in *Ralli v Naviera*,[124] which involved a charterparty governed by English law for a voyage from India to Spain. The contract provided for payment of freight in Spain on arrival, but during the voyage a Spanish decree came into force prohibiting payment or receipt of freight at a rate exceeding a statutory limit, which was lower than the agreed rate. The Court of Appeal held that, under English law as the proper law, the supervening Spanish decree had the effect of frustrating the obligation to pay the contractual freight in so far as it exceeded the statutory limit. Probably a similar result would have followed if the prohibition had existed at the time of contracting but had not come to the knowledge of the parties until after the voyage had commenced. If, however, the prohibition had become known to the parties before any substantial performance (such as the commencement of the loading) had been carried out, it would seem proper to regard the entire contract as frustrated.

But if the proper law were that of a third country, it is probable that in cases of 'innocent' illegality, the English courts would respect a rule of the foreign proper law which substituted for the prohibited obligation a similar obligation to be performed in a different country where its performance was not prohibited. An example would be the *Ralli* situation, with the variation that the proper law was German, and German law substituted an obligation to pay the excess freight in Hamburg or London. On the other hand, if a foreign proper law were to insist on maintaining the obligation to perform in the original country, in defiance of the prohibition there, that would produce a situation contrary to stringent English public policy, and English law would insist on discharging the obligation as if the contract were governed by English law.

For the second rule (on innocent illegality) to apply, the prohibited act must be an act of performance, an act which the contract necessarily requires to be done by way of its performance. It is not enough that the prohibited act is merely a preliminary

---

a contract governed by Iraqi law and intended to be performed by acts to be carried out in the Netherlands and Switzerland in breach of Dutch and Swiss prohibitions imposed in implementation of United Nations' financial sanctions against Iraq in consequence of its invasion of Kuwait.

123 See *Royal Boskalis v Mountain* [1999] QB 674 (CA).
124 [1920] 2 KB 287.

or preparatory step which a party may need to take in order to reach a position from which he can carry out the contractually required performance.[125] Thus, a promise governed by English law to pay money in London will not normally be affected by the parties' awareness that the payer's assets are all located in Ruritania, and that the remission of funds from Ruritania to enable the payment to be made is prohibited by Ruritanian law unless the consent of the Ruritanian central bank is obtained. Unless it is clearly shown that the parties intended that if necessary the funds should be 'smuggled out' without such consent, there will be a valid contract, under which the payer effectively gives an absolute warranty that he will succeed in obtaining the necessary consent.

Article 9(2) of the Rome I Regulation, by specifying that nothing in the Regulation shall restrict the application of the overriding mandatory provisions of the law of the forum, goes beyond the traditionally limited concept of the forum's stringent public policy and effectively permits the law of the forum to define and effectuate its own overriding interests in invalidating contracts governed by foreign law. The concept of interest analysis, which was isolated by Brainerd Currie,[126] is essentially that a country may be said to have an interest in the application to a transnational situation of a rule contained in its internal law, if a policy or purpose which the substantive rule is designed to promote or achieve would be furthered to a substantial extent by the application of the substantive rule in the determination of the case in question, in view of the factual connections between the parties, acts and events involved in the case and the country in question. Where the law of the forum contains an invalidating substantive rule, Art 9(2) gives a broad permission to that law (by legislation or judicial decision) to define its own interests in the application of that substantive rule, to weigh them against other choice-influencing considerations, such as the general policies favouring party expectations and the convenient conduct of international trade which underlie the proper law doctrine, and ultimately to determine the circumstances in which the forum's invalidating interest will be given overriding effect. The breadth of the permission is reduced, but probably only slightly, by Art 9(1) of the Regulation, which defines overriding mandatory provisions as provisions the respect for which is regarded as crucial by a country for safeguarding its public interests, such as its political, social or economic organisation, to such an extent that they are applicable to any situation falling within their scope, irrespective of the law otherwise applicable to the contract under the Regulation.[127] In any event the forum is no doubt expected to proceed with caution before asserting an overriding interest, so as to avoid undermining the harmonising effect of the proper law doctrine as laid down by Arts 3 and 4. Thus the intervention of the law of the forum under Art 9(2) should be exceptional.

Before the Rome Convention, English and similar laws had sometimes given overriding effect to mandatory rules of the law of the forum designed to protect weaker parties, such as a consumer habitually resident and acting in the forum country,[128] but it is probable that the protection of consumers and employees should now be effected

---

125 See *Kleinwort v Ungarische Baumwolle* [1939] 2 KB 678 (CA); *Bodley Head v Flegon* [1972] 1 WLR 680; *Toprak v Finagrain* [1979] 2 Lloyd's Rep 98; and *Libyan Arab Foreign Bank v Bankers Trust* [1988] 1 Lloyd's Rep 259.

126 See his *Selected Essays on the Conflict of Laws*, 1963, Duke University Press.

127 Art 9(1) is a new provision introduced by the Regulation.

128 See *English v Donnelly* [1958] SC 494.

under the specific provisions of the Regulation designed for that purpose, to the exclusion of Art 9(2).[129] On the other hand, it seems acceptable for a forum to invoke Art 9(2) so as to apply its own mandatory rules for the protection of weaker parties other than consumers and employees; for example, in favour of small businesses. Moreover mandatory rules with overriding effect, analogous to that provided for by Art 9(2), may arise from Community legislation. Thus in *Ingmar v Eaton Leonard*,[130] the European Court ruled that Arts 17 and 18 of Directive 86/653, which guarantee certain rights to commercial agents after the termination of agency contracts, must be applied where the commercial agent carried on his activity in a member state, even if the principal is established in a non-member country and a clause of the contract stipulates that the contract is to be governed by the law of the non-member country.

English and similar laws have also sometimes asserted overriding interests based on more general purposes, and such decisions now illustrate the operation of Art 9(2) of the Rome I Regulation. Thus the forum rule against champerty (invalidating a contract by which a person who has no legitimate interest in a dispute agrees to finance litigation in return for a share of the proceeds) has been insisted on whenever the litigation to be financed is to take place in a court of the forum country.[131] The forum rule against unreasonable restraint of trade has been applied whenever the contract prejudiced trade which would take place in the forum country;[132] and a forum provision against tie-in clauses in patent licences has been applied to any licence under a forum patent.[133] Forum exchange control legislation has been applied to borrowings anywhere by a forum national or resident;[134] and forum legislation restricting credit in the interests of currency stability has been applied to all contracts concluded in the forum country.[135]

There is no provision in the Rome I Regulation which closely resembles Art 7(1) of the Rome Convention, which provided:

> When applying under this Convention the law of a country, effect may be given to the mandatory rules of the law of another country with which the situation has a close connection, if and in so far as, under the law of the latter country, those rules must be applied whatever the law applicable to the contract. In considering whether to give effect to these mandatory rules, regard shall be had to their nature and purpose and to the consequences of their application or non-application.

By virtue of a reservation made by the United Kingdom under Art 22(1)(a) of the Convention, and by s 2(2) of the 1990 Act, Art 7(1) was not applicable in the United Kingdom. Similar reservations were made by Ireland, Germany, Luxembourg, and Portugal. In countries where it applied, Art 7(1) of the Convention might have been expected to lead to respect for an overriding interest asserted by another country which closely resembled an overriding interest which the forum would have asserted in converse circumstances. The effect of its exclusion in the United Kingdom was illustrated by the decision of Thomas J in *Akai v People's Insurance*,[136] upholding in

---

129 See pp 589–97 below.
130 Case C-381/98: [2000] ECR I-9305.
131 See *Grell v Levy* (1864) 143 ER 1052, and *Re Trepca Mines* [1963] Ch 199.
132 See *Rousillon v Rousillon* (1880) 14 ChD 351.
133 See *Chiron v Murex* [1993] FSR 567 (CA).
134 See *Boissevain v Weil* [1950] AC 327.
135 See *Kay's Leasing v Fletcher* (1964) 116 CLR 124.
136 [1998] 1 Lloyd's Rep 90.

accordance with the expressly chosen English law a commercial insurance contract between an Australian policyholder and a Singapore insurer, and disregarding the invalidation of certain terms by protective Australian legislation which had been held applicable by the Australian High Court. Similarly, in *Shell v Coral Oil*,[137] which involved a contract for exclusive distribution of oil products in the Lebanon, Moore-Bick J gave effect to an express choice of English law, so as to deprive the distributor of the protection of mandatory rules of Lebanese law.

Under the Regulation a much more limited respect is offered to overriding mandatory rules of a country which is neither the forum country nor the country of the proper law. Article 9(3) permits effect to be given to the overriding mandatory provisions of the law of the country where the obligations arising out of the contract have to be or have been performed, in so far as those overriding mandatory provisions render the performance of the contract unlawful; and adds that in considering whether to give effect to those provisions, regard must be had to their nature and purpose and to the consequences of their application or non-application. This provision is confined to prohibitions on performance imposed by the law of the place of performance, and in the English context appears to add nothing to the traditional English rules on this problem which fall within the scope of the public policy proviso.

CERTAIN PARTICULAR TYPES OF CONTRACT

With a view to protecting weaker parties, special choice of law rules for certain types of contract are laid down by Arts 5–8 of the Rome I Regulation. These apply to consumer contracts, contracts for the carriage of passengers, employment contracts, and insurance contracts.

Consumer contracts

Article 6 of the Rome I Regulation lays down special conflict rules for certain consumer contracts. The contracts which satisfy the elaborate definition specified by Art 6 may conveniently be referred to as protected consumer contracts. By Art 6(1), in the absence of an express or implied choice of law by the parties, a protected consumer contract is governed by the law of the consumer's habitual residence. By Art 6(2), in the case of a protected consumer contract, an express or implied choice of law by the parties remains possible, but the chosen law operates subject to any rules for the protection of the consumer as a weaker party which are contained in the law of his habitual residence and which under that law cannot be derogated from by agreement. By Art 11(4), the formal validity of a protected consumer contract is governed exclusively by the law of the consumer's habitual residence.

With regard to the definition of a protected consumer contract, to which Art 6 applies, the Rome I Regulation departs from the Rome Convention and adopts a definition similar in many respects to that used by Art 15 of the Brussels I Regulation. As regards substantive elements, Art 6(1) of the Rome I Regulation refers to 'a contract concluded by a natural person for a purpose which can be regarded as being outside his trade or profession (the consumer) with another person acting in the

---

exercise of his trade or profession (the professional)'. This contrasts with the reference in Art 5(1) of the Rome Convention to 'a contract the object of which is the supply of goods or services to a person ('the consumer') for a purpose which can be regarded as being outside his trade or profession, or a contract for the provision of credit for that object'. Thus definition provided by the Rome I Regulation explicitly requires that the consumer must be an individual, rather than a corporate entity, and also makes explicit the requirement, which was implied in the definition used by the Rome Convention,[138] that the supplier must be, or at least appear to the consumer to be, acting in the course of his trade or profession. Under both definitions the purchaser must not be acting for business purposes; or, where he is acting partly for business purposes and partly for non-business purposes, his business purpose must be of negligible importance in relation to the transaction; and in any event he must not have so conducted himself as to create the impression in the supplier that he was acting for business purposes.[139]

Unlike the definition used by the Rome Convention, the definition specified by the Rome I Regulation makes no reference to the supply of goods or services. Thus a sale of land is no longer excluded by the primary definition. But Art 6(4)(c) of the Regulation provides a specific exclusion for a contract relating to a right in rem in immovable property or a tenancy of immovable property, other than a contract relating to the right to use immovable properties on a timeshare basis within the meaning of EC Directive 94/47. Thus contracts for the sale or letting of land, other than on a timeshare basis, do not count as protected consumer contracts, within the scope of Art 6 of the Regulation.

Exclusions from the scope of Art 6 of the Regulation are made by Art 6(4)(a) in respect of a contract for the supply of services, where the services are to be supplied to the consumer exclusively in a country other than that of his habitual residence; and by Art 6(4)(b) in respect of a contract of carriage, other than a contract relating to package travel within the meaning of EC Directive 90/314. These exclusions substantially accord with those previously made by Art 5(4) and (5) of the Rome Convention. It is also clear that Art 6 of the Regulation does not apply to insurance contracts, since the opening phrase of Art 6(1) gives priority to Art 7.

Since, unlike the definition used by the Rome Convention, Art 6(1) of the Rome I Regulation makes no reference to the supply of goods or services, a sale of financial instruments or securities is no longer excluded by the primary definition. But as regards financial instruments, transferable securities, and units in collective investment undertakings, complicated exclusions from Art 6 of the Regulation are provided by Art 6(4)(d) and (e). The exclusion by Article 6(1)(d) refers to rights and obligations which constitute a financial instrument, and rights and obligations constituting the terms and conditions governing the issuance or offer to the public and public takeover bids of transferable securities, and the subscription and redemption of units in collective investment undertakings, in so far as these activities do not constitute provision of a financial service. A further exclusion by Art 6(4)(e), along with Art 4(1)(h), refers to contracts concluded within a multilateral system which brings together or facilitates the bringing together of multiple third-party buying and selling interests in financial instruments, as defined by Art 4(1)(17) of EC Directive 2004/39, in accordance

---

138   See the Giuliano and Lagarde Report, at p 23; and Case 96/00: *Gabriel* [2002] ECR I-6367.
139   See Case C-464/01: *Gruber v Bay Wa* [2005] ECR I-439.

with non-discretionary rules and governed by a single law. These exclusions are further explained by Recitals 18, 26 and 28–31. In particular, Recital 26 indicates that, subject to these exclusions, financial services such as investment services, and contracts for the sale of units in collective investment undertakings, may fall within Art 6 of the Regulation.

Like the Rome Convention, the Rome I Regulation insists on imposing a territorial requirement for the application of the consumer-protective provisions, designed to ensure that the consumer is guaranteed the protection offered by the law of his country of habitual residence only in cases where the contract or the supplier has a sufficient connection with that country. But the Rome I Regulation has redefined the necessary territorial connection so as to accord with that used in the Brussels I Regulation. The Rome Convention had utilised a territorial requirement similar to that used by the Brussels Convention. In the Rome I Regulation, the territorial requirement is specified by Art 6(1), which insists that the professional must either (a) pursue his commercial or professional activities in the country where the consumer has his habitual residence, or (b) by any means, direct such activities to that country or to several countries including that country, and (in either case) that the contract must fall within the scope of such activities. In this connection Recital 24 explains that the mere fact that an Internet site is accessible is not sufficient to make Art 6 applicable, but it is a relevant factor that an Internet site solicits the conclusion of distance contracts and that a contract has actually been concluded at a distance, by whatever means.[140]

Perhaps the most disappointing feature of the Rome I Regulation is its failure to offer any protection to the 'mobile' consumer, who contracts abroad in circumstances where it would be unreasonable to subject the supplier to the law of the consumer's residence; for example, where an English visitor to France purchases goods at a shop in Paris. Under the Regulation (as under the Convention), the contract is governed by Arts 3 and 4 in the same way as a commercial contract. This is emphasised by Art 6(3) of the Regulation, which specifies that if the territorial requirement is not fulfilled, the law applicable to a contract between a consumer and a professional must be determined pursuant to Arts 3 and 4. Such a result is deeply unsatisfying. It means that the English visitor, buying at a shop in Paris, is vulnerable to an express choice of the law of Haiti. Admittedly Art 3(4) of the Regulation ensures that in such a case the consumer will still benefit from the substantive rules of consumer protection laid down by various EC Directives. But beyond that he could be deprived of protection which exists under both English and French laws. It is submitted that a far superior solution would have been to give the mobile consumer, despite any choice of law by the parties, the benefit of the mandatory rules for the protection of consumers as weaker parties which are contained in the law of the *supplier's* habitual residence.

In view of the particular and detailed provisions of Art 6 of the Rome I Regulation,

---

140 The new requirement of activities by the supplier in or directed to the consumer's country replaces the three alternative requirements formerly specified by Art 5(2) of the Rome Convention. The first alternative was that the conclusion of the contract was preceded by a specific invitation addressed to the consumer in the country of his habitual residence or by advertising there, and that he had taken in that country all the steps necessary on his part for the conclusion of the contract. The second alternative was that the supplier or his agent had received the consumer's order in that country. The third alternative was that the contract was for the sale of goods and the consumer had travelled from that country to another country and given his order there, his journey having been arranged by the seller for the purpose of inducing the consumer to buy. On these requirements, see Case 96/00: *Gabriel* [2002] ECR I-6367.

it is thought that Art 9(2) cannot be invoked for the purpose of consumer protection.[141] For Art 6 appears to be intended to deal exhaustively with the protection of consumers as weaker parties, even if its failure to protect the mobile consumer may give rise to doubt as to the adequacy of the protection achieved. On the other hand, there is no reason why Art 9(2) should not be invoked for the purpose of applying to a consumer contract mandatory rules, the aim of which is to protect the supplier (as by imposing a penal rate of interest where payment is delayed) or the general public interest (as by insisting on a minimum deposit, with a view to restricting credit in the interests of currency stability).

It also seems probable that Art 6 of the Regulation has the effect of eliminating self-limiting rules, such as those specified in the United Kingdom by ss 26 and 27(1) of the Unfair Contract Terms Act 1977, which prevent the controls on exemption clauses imposed by the 1977 Act from operating in the case of an international supply contract (as defined by s 26), or in cases where the proper law of the contract is the law of a part of the United Kingdom by choice of the parties but the closest connection is with a country outside the United Kingdom. For Art 6 is designed to establish a definitive solution to the protection of a consumer as a weaker party, overriding any national legislation dealing with choice of law or with the transnational operation of protective rules; and the continued operation of ss 26 or 27(1) in relation to a protected consumer contract could have the effect of denying the application of British mandatory rules designed to protect weaker parties in a manner inconsistent with the objectives of Art 6.

The harmonisation at Community level of various aspects of substantive law in respect of consumer contracts has been achieved by a series of Directives, and these also contain provisions affecting choice of law. The operation of the Directives is not affected by the Rome I Regulation, since Art 23 specifies that the Regulation does not prejudice the application of provisions of Community law which, in relation to particular matters, lay down conflict rules relating to contractual obligations. Under Directive 93/13, on unfair terms in consumer contracts,[142] unfair terms used in a contract concluded with a consumer by a seller or supplier are rendered not binding on the consumer, but the contract continues to bind the parties upon the rest of its terms, if it is capable of continuing in existence without the unfair terms. The Directive contains a choice of law provision in Art 6(2),[143] which requires member states to ensure that a consumer does not lose the protection granted by the Directive through a choice of the law of a country outside the European Economic Area as the proper law, if the contract has a close connection with the territory of the member states. This ensures that the protection provided by the Directive will be available in certain cases to which Art 6 of the Rome I Regulation does not apply because the connections referred to in Art 6 of the Regulation are not located in a single member state. For example, where an English consumer purchases goods from a French supplier who is

---

141   See the decision of the German Supreme Court in *Grand Canaries* [1997] NJW 1697, refusing to apply Art 7(2) of the Rome Convention in favour of the purchaser of a timehare, because the territorial requirements specified in Art 5(2) of the Convention were not satisfied. Cf. the Giuliano & Lagarde Report, at p 28; and Knofel, *Mandatory Rules and Choice of Law: A Comparative Approach to Article 7(2) of the Rome Convention* [1999] JBL 239. See also *Moquin v Deutsche Bank* (2000) Revue Critique de Droit International Privé 29 (French Court of Cassation).

142   [1993] OJ L95/29. This was transposed in the United Kingdom by the Unfair Terms in Consumer Contracts Regulations 1994 (SI 1994/3159).

143   This was transposed in the United Kingdom by SI 1994/3159, reg 7.

not pursuing activities in or directing activities to England, and there is an express choice of Swiss law.[144]

Provisions corresponding to Art 6(2) of Directive 93/13 are contained in Art 12(2) of Directive 97/7,[145] on the protection of consumers in respect of distance contracts; Art 7(2) of Directive 1999/44,[146] on certain aspects of the sale of consumer goods and associated guarantees; and Art 12(2) of Directive 2002/65,[147] on the distance marketing of consumer financial services. But Art 9 of Directive 94/47,[148] on the protection of purchasers in respect of certain aspects of contracts relating to the purchase of the right to use immovable properties on a timeshare basis, requires member states to ensure that, whatever the law applicable may be, the purchaser is not deprived of the protection afforded by the Directive, if the immovable property concerned is situated within the territory of a member state.

Contracts for the carriage of passengers

Articles 5(2) and (3) of the Rome I Regulation apply to contracts for the carriage of passengers. These provisions are new. Under the Rome Convention contracts for the carriage of passengers were treated as ordinary contracts, governed by Arts 3 and 4. In the case of a contract for the carriage of passengers, Art 5(2) of the Regulation permits the parties to choose the proper law in accordance with Art 3, but restricts the range of laws which are available to be chosen. The parties may choose between the laws of the following countries: the passenger's habitual residence; the carrier's habitual residence; the carrier's place of central administration; the place of departure; and the place of destination. In the absence of such a choice, Art 5(2) provides a presumption in favour of the law of the passenger's habitual residence, provided that either the place of departure or the place of destination is situated in that country. Otherwise there is a presumption in favour of the law of the carrier's habitual residence. But Art 5(3) provides for rebuttal of these presumptions where it is clear from all the circumstances of the case that the contract is manifestly more closely connected with a country other than that indicated by the presumptions. In that case the law of the manifestly more closely connected country applies. Recital 32 explains that, owing to the particular nature of contracts of carriage, specific provisions should ensure an adequate level of protection of passengers, and accordingly that Art 6, on protected consumer contracts, should not apply to such contracts.

Employment contracts

Again in the interest of protecting weaker parties, Art 8 of the Rome I Regulation makes special provision for individual contracts of employment. No express definition is offered, but it is thought that the concept of an employment contract should be given an autonomous Community meaning, inspired by the decisions of the European Court under the Brussels Convention and the Brussels I Regulation. Thus the contract

---

144 In Case C-70/03: *Commission v Spain* [2004] ECR I-7999, the European Court confirmed that Art 6(2) of the Directive has a wider scope than Art 5 of the Rome Convention.
145 [1997] OJ L144/19.
146 [1999] OJ L171/12.
147 [2002] OJ L271/16.
148 [1994] OJ L280/83.

must create a lasting bond which brings the worker to some extent within the organisational framework of the employer's business, so that the concept does not extend to a contract for professional services, such as those of an architect or lawyer, engaged as an independent contractor to carry out a particular task.[149]

Article 8(2)–(4) of the Rome I Regulation determines the proper law of an employment contract in the absence of a choice of law made by the parties in accordance with Art 3. The primary rule, laid down by Art 8(2), is that the proper law is that of the country in or from which the employee habitually carries out his work in performance of the contract; and the country of habitual work remains unchanged even if the employee is temporarily employed in another country. Recital 36 adds that work carried out in another country should be regarded as temporary if the employee is expected to resume working in the country of origin after carrying out his tasks abroad. But if there is no ascertainable country of habitual work, Art 8(3) refers instead to the law of the country in which the place of business through which the employee was engaged is situated.[150] Ultimately both of these rules are reduced to rebuttable presumptions by Art 8(4), which operates where it appears from the circumstances as a whole that the contract is more closely connected with a country other than that indicated in Art 8(2) or (3), and subjects the contract to the law of that other country.

The reference in Art 8(2) to the country *in which or, failing that, from which* the employee habitually carries out his work in performance of the contract is evidently designed to adopt the approach followed by the European Court under the Brussels Convention and the Brussels I Regulation. Thus in cases where the employee carries out his work in more than one country, reference must be made to the place where the employee has established the effective centre of his working activities, at or from which he performs the essential part of his duties towards his employer. For example, a sales manager will habitually work at the office where he organises his work, even though he makes frequent business trips to other countries.[151] But where there is no such permanent centre of activities (for example, because the man worked for the employer as a cook, first on mining vessels or installations in the Dutch continental shelf area, and later on a floating crane in Danish territorial waters), the whole of the duration of the employment relationship must be taken into account. The relevant place will normally be the place where the employee has worked the longest; but, by way of exception, weight will be given to the most recent period of work where the employee, after having worked for a certain time in one place, then takes up his work activities on a permanent basis in a different place.[152]

Recital 36 to the Rome I Regulation indicates that the conclusion of a new contract of employment with the original employer or an employer belonging to the same group of companies as the original employer should not preclude the employee from being regarded as carrying out his work in another country temporarily. This too reflects the approach followed by the European Court under the Brussels Convention and the Brussels I Regulation. Thus in *Pugliese v Finmeccanica*,[153] which involved an Italian employee who had been recruited by Aeritalia, an Italian company, to work

---

149   See Case 266/85: *Shenavai v Kreischer* [1987] ECR 239.
150   See *Booth v Phillips* [2004] 1 WLR 3292 (Teare QC), applying Art 8(3) in the case of a man employed as chief engineer on a sea-going vessel.
151   See Case C-125/92: *Mulox v Geels* [1993] ECR I-4075; and Case C-383/95: *Rutten v Cross Medical* [1997] ECR I-57.
152   Case C-37/00: *Weber v Universal Ogden Services* [2002] ECR I-2013.
153   Case C-437/00: [2003] ECR I-3573.

initially for Eurofighter in Germany for at least three years, the European Court ruled that, in a dispute between an employee and a first employer, the place where the employee performs his obligations to a second employer can be regarded as the place where he habitually carries out his work for the first employer, with respect to whom the employee's contractual obligations are suspended, when the first employer has, at the time of the conclusion of the second contract of employment, an interest in the performance of the service by the employee to the second employer in a place decided on by the latter. The existence of such an interest must be determined on a comprehensive basis, taking into consideration all the circumstances of the case. The relevant factors may include the facts that the conclusion of the second contract was envisaged when the first was being concluded; that the first contract was amended on account of the conclusion of the second contract; that there is an organisational or economic link between the two employers; that there is an agreement between the two employers providing a framework for the co-existence of the two contracts; that the first employer retains management powers in respect of the employee; and that the first employer is able to decide the duration of the employee's work for the second employer.

The rationale for the final reference in Art 6(2) to the closest connection is less than clear. Possibly the purpose is concealed discrimination: where the employee habitually works in an EC country, the presumption will prevail; but where an employee, habitually resident in an EC country, is recruited to work outside the Community for an employer resident in an EC country, the law of the EC country to which both parties belong, or, where they belong to different EC countries, that of the EC country to which the employer belongs, will prevail.[154] In any event, for the applicable presumption to be rebutted, a closer connection elsewhere must be clearly demonstrated, and rebuttal is very unlikely if the place of habitual work and the location of the engaging establishment are in the same country.[155]

By Art 8(1) of the Regulation, an express or implied choice of law by the parties in accordance with Art 3 is effective in determining the proper law of an employment contract, but such a choice operates subject to the rules for the protection of the employee as a weaker party which are contained in the law which in the absence of choice would have been applicable under Art 8(2)–(4), and which under that law cannot be derogated from by agreement.[156] The mandatory rules referred to by Art 8(1) are confined to ones whose purpose is to protect employees as weaker parties. The reference does not extend to mandatory rules which are designed to protect employers (for example, by ensuring that they have a right to dismiss, or to make deductions from pay, in certain circumstances); nor to ones which pursue a general public interest (for example, by prohibiting, or subjecting to a licensing scheme, the carrying out of certain economic activities thought likely to endanger the environment). In view of the specific and apparently exhaustive character of Art 8, it is thought that Art 9 cannot be used for the purpose of providing further protection to the employee as a weaker party, though it can be used for the purpose of applying mandatory formal requirements to contracts of employment.[157]

---

154   For an analogous decision, see *Nunez v Hunter Fan Co* 920 FSupp 716 (SD Texas, 1996).
155   See *Base Metal Trading Ltd v Shamurin* [2004] 1 All ER (Comm) 159 (Tomlinson J); affirmed [2005] 1 All ER (Comm) 17 (CA).
156   See *Gasalho v Tap Air Portugal*, decided by the French Court of Cassation on 17 October 2000.
157   See the Giuliano and Lagarde Report [1980] OJ C282, at p 32.

The Giuliano and Lagarde Report indicates that the mandatory rules envisaged by Art 8 are not confined to provisions relating to the contract of employment itself, but extend to provisions concerning industrial safety and hygiene; and that Art 8 extends to void contracts and *de facto* employment relationships.[158] Despite this, in *Base Metal Trading Ltd v Shamurin*[159] the English Court of Appeal firmly rejected the argument that the predecessor of Art 8 extended to claims in tort between an employer and an employee arising from things done in the performance of the contract of employment. It was accepted, however, that in such circumstances the fact that the contract of employment is governed by the law of a given country is an important connection with that country for the purpose of determining the country with which the tort has the most significant connection, and whose law may thus be applicable to the tort, by displacement of the general rule in favour of the law of the country in which the events constituting the tort occurred, under the exception then specified by s 12 of the Private International Law (Miscellaneous Provisions) Act 1995.[160] No doubt the same approach will be adopted by the English courts in the context of Art 8 of the Rome I Regulation and Art 4(3) of the Rome II Regulation, which has now replaced s 12 of the 1995 Act.

In any event it seems clear that, in view of its purpose, Art 8 extends to claims for unfair dismissal or in respect of unlawful discrimination in relation to employment, despite the statutory character of such rights, and that it overrides any self-limiting territorial rule contained in legislation which creates such claims, such as a restriction to cases where the employee's work is performed in the country in question. Thus the Regulation requires that the country whose law governs, or whose mandatory rules for the protection of employees have overriding effect in respect of, a contract of employment under Art 8 should admit any claim for unfair dismissal, or in respect of unlawful discrimination in relation to employment, which it would (apart from the Regulation) have admitted if the case had been connected exclusively with its own territory. Unfortunately this obvious point has not yet been accepted in England.[161]

An important exception to the rules laid down by Art 8 of the Rome I Regulation is made by Directive 96/71 on the posting of workers in the framework of the provision of services.[162] The Directive applies where an undertaking, in the framework of the transnational provision of services, posts a worker for a limited period to a member state other than the state in which he normally works. Three types of posting are covered. The first is where the undertaking posts workers to the territory of a member state on its own account and under its own direction, under a contract concluded between the undertaking and a service recipient operating in the receiving state; for example, where a Polish undertaking posts Polish workers to Germany, in the

---

158 [1980] OJ C282, at pp 25–6.

159 [2005] 1 All ER (Comm) 17 (CA); affirming [2004] 1 All ER (Comm) 159 (Tomlinson J). See also [2002] CLC 322 (Moore-Bick J).

160 See also *Johnson v Coventry Churchill* [1992] 3 All ER 14 (Kay QC); and *Glencore v Metro* [2001] 1 Lloyd's Rep 284 (Moore-Bick J).

161 On unfair dismissal, see *Lawson v Serco* [2006] 1 All ER 823 (HL); and *Bleuse v MBT Transport* [2008] IRLR 264 (Elias J in the EAT). On discrimination, see s 1 of the Equal Pay Act 1970 (as amended); ss 6 and 10 of the Sex Discrimination Act 1975 (as amended); ss 4 and 8 of the Race Relations Act 1976 (as amended); ss 4(6) and 68 of the Disability Discrimination Act 1995; and *Williams v University of Nottingham* [2007] IRLR 660 (Wilkie J in the EAT).

162 [1997] OJ L18/1. By virtue of Recital 34 and Art 23 of the Rome I Regulation, since the Directive lays down conflict rules relating to a particular matter, the Directive prevails over the Regulation.

framework of a construction sub-contract concluded between the Polish undertaking and a German main contractor.[163] The second is where the undertaking posts workers to an establishment or an undertaking owned by the same group in the receiving state. The third is where the undertaking is a temporary employment undertaking or placement agency, and it hires out a worker to a user undertaking established in or operating in the receiving state. In any event there must be an employment relationship between the undertaking making the posting and the worker during the period of posting. Where it applies, the Directive requires the member states to ensure that, regardless of the law otherwise applicable to the employment relationship, a posting undertaking guarantees to workers posted to their territory the minimum terms and conditions of employment relating to certain matters (such as minimum rates of pay) which are mandatorily applicable in the member state where the work is carried out. Thus, insofar as the Directive applies, the worker receives the benefit of protective rules contained in the law of the country where he temporarily, but not habitually, works.

Insurance contracts

Subject to a very minor exclusion,[164] the Rome I Regulation applies to all types of insurance contract. The Regulation applies both to life insurance and to non-life insurance, and also to reinsurance. It applies to large risks and to mass risks. It applies regardless of whether or not the insurer or the policyholder is resident or established, or the risk is located, within the Community. In contrast the Rome Convention had excluded from its scope contracts of insurance (other than reinsurance) covering risks situated within the European Community,[165] and choice of law for such contracts had been regulated by Art 7 of EC Directive 88/357 (as amended by Art 27 of Directive 92/49) and Art 32 of EC Directive 2002/83.[166] As Art 23 makes clear, the Rome I Regulation replaces the choice of law provisions contained in the Directives on insurance. But the change is more of form than substance, since Art 7 of the Regulation to a large extent echoes the relevant provisions of the Directives.

In the Regulation, Art 7(2) lays down specific rules for determining the proper law of an insurance contract covering a large risk, whether the risk is situated in Europe or elsewhere. Article 7(3) lays down specific rules for determining the proper law of an insurance contract covering a mass risk which is situated within the European Community. Article 7(4) provides additional rules for insurance contracts covering risks for which a member state imposes an obligation to take out insurance. But the Regulation treats an insurance contract covering a mass risk which is situated outside the European Community in the same way as an 'ordinary' or non-insurance contract. Similarly the Regulation treats any reinsurance contract as an 'ordinary' or

---

163 See Case C-346/06: *Rüffert v Land Niedersachsen*, 3 April 2008.
164 The exclusion, specified by Art 1(2)(j), is confined to insurance contracts which arise out of operations carried out by organisations which are not established within the Community, and of which the object is to provide benefits for employed or self-employed persons belonging to an undertaking or group of undertakings, or to a trade or group of trades, in the event of death or survival, or of discontinuance or curtailment of activity, or of sickness related to work or accidents at work.
165 See Art 1(3)–(4) of the Convention.
166 See [1988] OJ L172, [1992] OJ L228, and [2002] OJ L345. The Directives had been transposed in the United Kingdom by the Financial Services and Markets Act 2000 (Law Applicable to Contracts of Insurance) Regulations SI 2001/2635, made under the Financial Services and Markets Act 2000.

non-insurance contract, regardless of whether it covers a large risk or a mass risk, and of where the risk is situated.

Article 7(2) of the Rome I Regulation adopts the distinction between large risks and mass risks drawn by Art 5(d) and the Annex of Directive 73/239, as amended by Art 5 of Directive 88/357 and Art 2 of Directive 90/618.[167] Under the definition of large risks provided by Directive 73/239 as amended, many transport risks are regarded as large risks, regardless of the policy-holder's business character or size. This applies to damage to or loss of ships, aircraft, or railway rolling stock; damage to or loss of goods in transit or baggage, irrespective of the form of transport; and liability arising out of the use of ships or aircraft, including carrier's liability. Risks relating to credit or suretyship are regarded as large risks if the policy-holder is engaged in and the risks relate to a business activity, whether the business is large, medium-sized or small. A wide variety of risks are regarded as large risks if the policy-holder is engaged in and the risks relate to a large or medium-sized business activity. For a policy-holder's business activity to be regarded as large or medium-sized, two of the following three conditions must be fulfilled in respect of the policy-holder or the group to which it belongs: that the balance-sheet total exceeds €6.2 million; that the net turnover exceeds €12.8 million; and that the average number of employees during the financial year exceeds 250. The risks which are regarded as large if the policy-holder's business activity is regarded as large or medium-sized include damage to or loss of most types of property (including motor vehicles) by various causes (including fire, storm and theft); financial losses of various kinds; and various liabilities, including ones arising out of the use of motor vehicles. The only kinds of non-life risk which can never be regarded as large are accident and sickness benefits (including benefits for industrial injury or occupational disease, or for injury to passengers), and legal expenses. Life risks cannot be regarded as large. Risks other than large risks may be referred to as mass risks.

Article 7(2) of the Rome I Regulation specifies the rules for determining the proper law of an insurance contract covering a large risk. By Art 7(1), these rules apply regardless of whether the risk covered is situated within the European Community, but do not apply to reinsurance contracts. The primary rule specified by Art 7(2) subjects an insurance contract covering a large risk to the law expressly or impliedly chosen by the parties in accordance with Art 3. This accords with the solution formerly adopted for insurance of risks situated outside the European Community by Art 3 of the Rome Convention, and for insurance of large risks situated within the European Community by Art 7(1)(f) of Directive 88/357 as amended by Art 27 of Directive 92/49. In the absence of a choice by the parties, Art 7(2) of the Rome I Regulation provides for an insurance contract covering a large risk a rebuttable presumption in favour of the law of the country where the insurer has his habitual residence. But this presumption will be rebutted where it is clear from all the circumstances of the case that the contract is manifestly more closely connected with another country, and the law of that other country will then apply. These default rules closely resemble those formerly adopted for insurance of risks situated outside the European Community by Art 4 of the Rome Convention. They differ, however, from those formerly adopted for insurance of risks situated within the European Community by Art 7(1)(h) of Directive 88/357, where the rebuttable presumption was in favour of the law of the member state in which the risk is situated. Where an insurance contract

---

167   See [1973] OJ L 228, [1988] OJ L172, and [1990] OJ L330.

covers a large risk for which a member state imposes an obligation to take out insurance, the additional rules specified by Article 7(4) apply.

Article 7(3) of the Rome I Regulation specifies the rules for determining the proper law of an insurance contract covering a mass risk. By Art 7(1), these rules are confined to cases where the risk covered is situated within the European Community, and they do not apply to reinsurance contracts. Under the Regulation an insurance contract covering a mass risk which is situated outside the European Community is subject to the same rules as an 'ordinary' or non-insurance contract. Recital 33 explains that where an insurance contract covering a mass risk covers more than one risk, at least one of which is situated in a member state and at least one of which is situated in an external country, the special rules on insurance contracts in the Regulation should apply only to the risk or risks situated in the member states. Thus in such a case one must split the contract for choice of law purposes into at least two contracts, one covering the European risks and the other the non-European risks. Such an approach had been strenuously resisted (admittedly in the context of large risks) by the English courts in the period before the adoption of the Regulation.[168]

By Art 7(6), the Rome I Regulation adopts the rules laid down by Art 2(d) of Directive 88/357 and Art 1(1)(g) of Directive 2002/83 as to where a risk is situated. The general rule is that, where the policy-holder is an individual, the risk is located in the country where he has his habitual residence; or, where the policy-holder is a legal person, the risk is located in the country where its establishment to which the contract relates is situated. For this purpose, where one member of a corporate group takes out an insurance policy covering other companies in the group, another company in the group for whose activities insurance cover is obtained counts as an establishment of the policy-holder who obtains the insurance cover.[169] But there are three exceptions. In the case of insurance of buildings, or of buildings and their contents under the same policy, the risk is located in the country where the property is situated. In the case of insurance of vehicles of any type, the risk is located in the country of registration. In the case of policies of a duration of four months or less, covering travel or holiday risks, the risk is located in the country where the policy-holder took out the policy.

In the case of an insurance contract covering a mass risk situated within the European Community, Art 7(3) of the Rome I Regulation allows the parties a limited freedom to make an express or implied choice of the proper law in accordance with Art 3. By Art 7(3)(i), the law chosen must be one of the following: (a) the law of a member state where the risk is situated at the time of conclusion of the contract; (b) the law of the country where the policy-holder has his habitual residence;[170] (c) in the case of life assurance, the law of the member state of which the policy-holder is a national; (d) for insurance contracts covering risks limited to events occurring in a single member state other than the member state where the risk is situated, the law of the member state in which the events are to occur; and (e) where the policy-holder pursues a business activity, and the insurance contract covers two or more risks which relate to such activities and are situated in different member states, the law of

---

168 See *American Motorists Insurance v Cellstar* [2002] 2 Lloyd's Rep 216 (David Steel J) and [2003] ILPr 22 (CA); *Travelers Casualty v Sun Life* [2004] Lloyd's Rep IR 846 (Jonathan Hirst QC); and *CGU International Insurance v Astrazeneca Insurance* [2005] EWHC 2755 (Comm) (Cresswell J).

169 See Case C-191/99: *Kvaerner v Staatssecretaris van Financiën* [2001] ECR I-4447; and *American Motorists Insurance v Cellstar* [2003] ILPr 22 (CA).

170 See *American Motorists Insurance v Cellstar* [2003] ILPr 22 (CA).

any of those member states, or the law of the country of habitual residence of the policyholder.[171] In certain cases Art 7(3)(ii) extends the range of choice by reference to the conflict rules of a member state whose internal law may be chosen under Article 7(3)(i). It enables parties to choose another law where this is permissible under the conflict rules of the member state in which the risk is situated, or in which the policyholder has his habitual residence, or in which is located one of the risks relating to a business activity of the policyholder.[172] This constitutes an exception to the exclusion of *renvoi* by Art 20 of the Regulation. Where an insurance contract covers a risk for which a member state imposes an obligation to take out insurance, the additional rules specified by Art 7(4) apply.

Article 7(3)(iii) of the Regulation provides a default rule, applicable to an insurance contract covering a mass risk situated within the European Community, where no valid express or implied choice of law has been made by the parties. The contract is then governed by the law of the member state in which the risk is situated at the time of conclusion of the contract. This is a firm rule, without any exception in favour of a manifestly closer connection.[173] By Art 7(5), for this purpose, where the contract covers risks situated in more than one member state, the contract must be treated as constituting several contracts, each relating to only one member state.[174] Where an insurance contract covers a risk for which a member state imposes an obligation to take out insurance, the additional rules specified by Art 7(4) apply.

Article 7(4) of the Regulation specifies some additional rules which apply to insurance contracts covering risks for which a member state imposes an obligation to take out insurance. By Art 7(4)(a), an insurance contract will not satisfy the obligation to take out insurance unless it complies with the specific provisions relating to that insurance laid down by the member state which imposes the obligation. Moreover, where the law of the member state in which the risk is situated and the law of the member state imposing the obligation to take out insurance contradict each other, the latter will prevail.[175] It is far from clear when a difference will amount to a contradiction for the purpose of this provision. By Art 7(4)(b), by way of derogation

---

171 Art 7(3)(i) of the Regulation broadly follows Art 7(1)(a)–(c) and (e) of Directive 88/357 and Art 32 of Directive 2002/83. But the Regulation refers to a corporate policyholder's habitual residence, determined in accordance with Art 19, rather than its central administration as such.

172 Art 7(3)(ii) of the Regulation broadly follows Art 7(1)(a) and (d) of Directive 88/357 and Art 32 of Directive 2002/83. See also *American Motorists Insurance v Cellstar* [2003] ILPr 22 (CA), and *Evialis v Siat* [2003] 2 Lloyd's Rep 377 (Andrew Smith J).

173 This contrasts with Art 7(1)(h) of Directive 88/357, under which, if no valid choice had been made by the parties, the contract was governed by the law of the country, from amongst those from which choice was permissible, with which it was most closely connected. The contract was rebuttably presumed to be most closely connected with the member state in which the risk was situated. See *Credit Lyonnais v New Hampshire Insurance* [1997] 2 Lloyd's Rep 1, where the Court of Appeal adhered to the presumption, and applied English law, that of the corporate policyholder's secondary establishment to which the contract related, rather than French law, that of the policyholder's central administration.

174 This contrasts with Art 7(1)(h) of Directive 88/357, under which a severable part of the contract which had a closer connection with another country, amongst those from which choice was permissible, could by way of exception be governed by the law of that other country.

175 In contrast Art 7(2)(ii) of Directive 88/357 merely *permitted* a member state to stipulate in its law that the mandatory rules of the law of the member state in which the risk was situated or of a member state imposing an obligation to take out insurance could be applied if and in so far as, under the law of those states, those rules had to be applied whatever the law applicable to the contract.

from Art 7(2) and (3), a member state may lay down that the insurance contract shall be governed by the law of the member state which imposes the obligation to take out insurance. The United Kingdom has not made use of a similar permission formerly offered by Art 8(4)(c) of Directive 88/357. By Art 7(5), for these purposes, where the contract covers risks situated in more than one member state, the contract must be considered as constituting several contracts each relating to only one member state.

TORTS AND RESTITUTIONARY OBLIGATIONS

The Rome I Regulation (on contractual obligations) is complemented by the Rome II Regulation, which deals with choice of law in respect of torts and restititutionary obligations.[176] The Rome II Regulation became applicable on 11 January 2009, and applies to events giving rise to damage or equivalent consequences which occur after that date.[177]

By Art 1(1), the Rome II Regulation applies, in situations involving a conflict of laws, to non-contractual obligations in civil and commercial matters; but not, in particular, to revenue, customs or administrative matters, nor to the liability of the state for acts and omissions in the exercise of state authority (*acta iure imperii*). Recital 9 explains that claims arising out of *acta iure imperii* include claims against officials who act on behalf of the state, and liability for acts of public authorities, including liability of publicly appointed office-holders. Recital 11 adds that, since the concept of a non-contractual obligation varies from one member state to another, for the purposes of the Regulation 'non-contractual obligation' should be understood as an autonomous concept. Various exclusions from the scope of the Rome II Regulation are specified by Art 1(2) and (3). Many of these resemble exclusions from the Rome I Regulation,[178] but there are further exclusions in respect of obligations arising out of nuclear damage, and of obligations arising out of violations of privacy and rights relating to personality, including defamation.[179] By Art 3, any law specified by the Rome II Regulation must be applied, whether or not it is the law of a member state. Renvoi is excluded by Art 24, which declares that the application of the law of any country specified by the Regulation means the application of the rules of law in force in that country other than its rules of private international law.

Chapter II (Articles 4–9) of the Rome II Regulation deals with choice of law in respect of torts. It seems clear that the concept of a tort refers to an act which is wrongful, other than by reason of its being a breach of contract or trust, and which therefore gives rise to liability to pay compensation for loss arising therefrom. The main rule, which applies to most types of tort, is laid down by Art 4. The combined effect of Art 4(1) and (2) is to establish a general rule whose operation depends on the existence or otherwise of an habitual residence common to the parties at the time

---

176 EC Regulation 864/2007 on the Law Applicable to Non-contractual Obligations [2007] OJ L199/40. It applies in all the member states except Denmark. In the United Kingdom it replaces the choice-of-law rules for torts laid down by Part III of the Private International Law (Miscellaneous Provisions) Act 1995.

177 See Arts 2, 31 and 32.

178 These relate to family matters, negotiable instruments, company law, trusts, and evidence and procedure.

179 See Art 1(2)(f) and (g).

when the injury occurs.[180] If both parties were habitually resident in the same country, the tort is governed by the law of that country. If no such common habitual residence existed, the tort is governed by the law of the country in which the direct injury occurred. The reference is to the place of the direct injury, rather than the place of the wrongful conduct or the place of any consequential loss. Then Art 4(3) provides an exception which applies where it is clear from all the circumstances of the case that the tort is manifestly more closely connected with a country other than that indicated in Art 4(1) or (2); in that case the law of the country of the manifestly closer connection applies. Art 4(3) also specifies that a manifestly closer connection may be based in particular on a pre-existing relationship between the parties, such as a contract, which is closely connected with the tort in question.

A minor qualification to these rules is made by Art 17, which specifies that, in assessing the conduct of the person claimed to be liable, account must be taken, as a matter of fact and insofar as is appropriate, of the rules of safety and conduct which were in force at the place and time of the event giving rise to the liability.[181] Other exemptions are specified by Art 14, which (subject to some safeguards) enables parties to make an agreement choosing the law applicable to a tort claim between them, and by Arts 16 and 26, which make savings for the stringent public policy and the overriding mandatory rules of the law of the forum.

Particular rules for certain torts are laid down by Arts 5–9 of the Rome II Regulation. The relevant torts are product liability; unfair competition; restriction of competition; infringement of intellectual property; environmental damage; and industrial action. As regards product liability, Art 5 establishes a cascade of five choice of law rules, to be applied in order. If both the victim and the defendant were habitually resident in the same country at the time when the injury occurred, the applicable law is that of the common habitual residence. Otherwise the applicable law is that of the country in which the victim was habitually resident when the injury occurred, if the product was marketed in that country, and unless the defendant could not reasonably have foreseen the marketing of the product, or a product of the same type, in that country. Otherwise the applicable law is that of the country in which the product was acquired, if the product was marketed in that country, and unless the defendant could not reasonably have foreseen the marketing of the product, or a product of the same type, in that country. Otherwise the applicable law is that of the country in which the injury occurred, if the product was marketed in that country, and unless the defendant could not reasonably have foreseen the marketing of the product, or a product of the same type, in that country. Otherwise the applicable law is that of the country in which the defendant was habitually resident. But, by way of

---

180 By Art 23(1), as regards a company or other body, corporate or unincorporated, its place of central administration must be treated as its habitual residence; but where the event giving rise to the damage occurs, or the damage arises, in the course of operation of a branch, agency or other establishment, the location of that establishment must be treated as its habitual residence. By Art 23(2), as regards an individual acting in the course of a business activity on his own account, his principal place of business must be treated as his habitual residence.

181 As an obvious example of the operation of Art 17, one may envisage a claim between persons habitually resident in England, arising from a road accident in France. Although under Art 4 liability will be governed by English law, as that of the common habitual residence, in determining whether a driver has acted with reasonable care, as his duty under English law requires, one must take account of the French rule of the road which specifies that normally the correct course is to keep to the right, rather than (as in England) to the left, side of the road.

exception to the five foregoing rules, where it is clear from all the circumstances of the case that the tort is manifestly more closely connected with a country other than the country whose law would be applicable under those rules, the law of that other country applies.[182]

As regards torts arising out of an act of unfair competition, Art 6(1) applies the law of the country where competitive relations or the collective interests of consumers are, or are likely to be, affected. But where an act of unfair competition affects exclusively the interests of a specific competitor, Art 6(2) subjects the claim to the main rules laid down by Art 4. As regards torts arising out of a restriction of competition, Article 6(3) applies the law of the country where the market is, or is likely to be, affected. As regards infringements of intellectual property rights, Art 8 applies the law of the country in which the act of infringement was committed. As regards torts arising out of environmental damage, Art 7 effectively creates a rule of alternative reference, in favour of the law of the place of direct injury, or the law of the place of the defendant's conduct, whichever is more favourable to the plaintiff. As regards industrial action (such as strike action or lock-out), Art 9 applies law of the country where the action is to be, or has been, taken; subject to an exception in favour of the law of a common habitual residence, where this exists.

Articles 15 and 22(1) of the Rome II Regulation ensure that a wide range of issues are subjected to the law which is applicable to a tort by virtue of Arts 4–9. These include the admissibility and assessment of damages, since Art 15(c) refers to the existence, the nature and the assessment of damage or the remedy claimed. Thus the law which governs the tort must be applied to all issues concerning the assessment of the damages to be awarded, including mere quantification, except insofar as the proper law lacks any rule on the issue which is sufficiently definite to enable a court elsewhere to apply it with reasonable confidence and accuracy.[183] As regards the availability to a tort victim of a direct action against the tortfeasor's liability insurer, Art 18 admits such a claim where either the law applicable to the tort or the law applicable to the insurance contract so provides; but the option is limited to the admissibility of the direct action, for the scope of the insurer's obligations is determined by the law governing the insurance contract.[184]

The Rome II Regulation also deals with restitutionary obligations. These differ from torts in that a restitutionary obligation may arise without there being any wrongful act on the part of the defendant, and that a restitutionary obligation is designed to restore or transfer to the claimant a benefit which has been obtained by the defendant, rather than to compensate the claimant for an injury or loss which has been suffered by the claimant. Article 10 of the Regulation applies to non-contractual obligations arising out of unjust enrichment. Article 10(1) and (4) apply to cases where the restitutionary obligation concerns a relationship existing between the parties, such as one arising out of a contract or a tort, which is closely connected with the unjust enrichment. In such cases Art 10(1) provides a rebuttable presumption which subjects

---

182 On Art 5, see Stone, *Product Liability under the Rome II Regulation*, in Ahern & Binchy (eds), *The Rome II Regulation on the Law Applicable to Non-Contractual Obligations*, Martinus Nijhoff, 2009, pp 175–97.

183 This accords with the approach adopted by the Court of Appeal, but ultimately rejected by the House of Lords, in *Harding v Wealands* [2005] 1 All ER 415 (CA), reversed [2006] UKHL 32.

184 Art 18 is more favourable to the victim than the current English rule, which probably refers the admissibility of a direct action to the proper law of the insurance contract. See *The Hari Bhum* [2005] 1 Lloyd's Rep 67 (CA), affirming [2004] 1 Lloyd's Rep 206 (Moore-Bick J).

the restitutionary claim to the law which governs the existing relationship; but Art 10(4) provides an exception, which applies where it is clear from all the circumstances of the case that the obligation arising out of unjust enrichment is manifestly more closely connected with another country, and subjects the claim to the law of the country with which it is manifestly more closely connected.

In stand-alone cases, where there is no existing relationship between the parties from which the applicable law can be derived, Art 10(2) and (3) create a presumption subjecting an obligation arising out of unjust enrichment to the law of the country in which both parties had their habitual residence when the event giving rise to unjust enrichment occurred, if such a common residence existed; or in the absence of such a common residence, to the law of the country in which the unjust enrichment took place. This evidently refers to the country in which the immediate benefit was received. But Art 10(4) applies where it is clear from all the circumstances of the case that the restitutionary obligation is manifestly more closely connected with another country than that indicated in Art 10(2) and (3), and subjects the claim to the law of the country with which the obligation is manifestly more closely connected.

Article 11 deals with non-contractual obligations arising out of acts performed without due authority in connection with the affairs of another person. It resembles Art 10, except that in stand-alone cases where there is no common habitual residence Art 11(3) refers to the law of the country in which the unauthorised act was performed, instead of the law of the country in which the unjust enrichment took place.

Article 12 of the Rome II Regulation applies to non-contractual obligations arising out of dealings prior to the conclusion of a contract, regardless of whether the contract was actually concluded or not. It appears to apply whether the claim is restitutionary or tortious in character. Thus it applies to a tortious claim for damages which is based on the wrongful breaking off of negotiations, or on non-disclosure of material facts (for example, in the context of insurance), or on misrepresentation (whether fraudulent, negligent, or wholly innocent). Article 12(1) lays down the primary rule, which subjects the claim to the law which applies to the contract, or which would have been applicable to the contract if it had been entered into. This reference to the actual or putative proper law of the relevant contract is not subject to displacement by reference to a closer connection with another country. But since the actual or putative proper law of the contract cannot always be determined, for example where the negotiations broke down because of disagreement about a proposed choice-of-law clause, Art 12(2) provides for such cases a supplementary rule which is similar to the main rule for tort cases specified by Art 4. Thus Art 12(2)(a) and (b), read with Art 2(1), provide a rebuttable presumption in favour of the law of the country in which both parties were habitually resident when the event giving rise to the damage or equivalent consequence occurred; or in the absence of such a common residence, in favour of the law of the country in which the direct damage or equivalent consequence occurred. By Art 12(2)(c), this presumption is displaced where it is clear from all the circumstances of the case that the non-contractual obligation is manifestly more closely connected with another country, in favour of the law of the country which is manifestly more closely connected with the obligation.

CONCLUSION

We have now examined two of the three types of issue addressed by private international law. In the next chapter we shall turn to the third, which relates to the recognition and enforcement of foreign judgments.

FURTHER READING

Collins *et al* (eds), *Dicey, Morris and Collins on the Conflict of Laws*, 14th edn, 2006, Sweet & Maxwell.

Stone, *EU Private International Law*, 2006, Edward Elgar.

CHAPTER 18

FOREIGN JUDGMENTS

INTRODUCTION

Disputes arising in international trade may be determined by foreign courts or arbitral tribunals. The question therefore arises as to the circumstances in which the English courts will recognise or enforce a foreign judgment or arbitral award. Recognition implies that the judgment or award is treated as conclusive of some matter which it determined. Enforcement implies that the judgment or award ordered something to be done (such as the payment of a sum of money, or the actual performance of a contract) or not to be done (as in the case of an injunction prohibiting the commission of a breach of contract or a tort), and that steps of an official nature are taken with a view to ensuring that the order is complied with.

A variety of regimes apply to the recognition and enforcement in England of foreign judgments and awards. In the case of European judgments, the matter is governed mainly by EC Regulation 44/2001 on Jurisdiction and the Recognition and Enforcement of Judgments in Civil and Commercial Matters,[1] which is commonly known as the Brussels I Regulation and applies to judgments from other EC member states.[2] In the case of non-European judgments ('external judgments'), it is governed by the common law, the Administration of Justice Act 1920, and the Foreign Judgments (Reciprocal Enforcement) Act 1933. In the case of foreign arbitral awards, it is governed mainly by the New York Convention of 10 June 1958 on the Recognition and Enforcement of Foreign Arbitral Awards, now transposed by the Arbitration Act 1996.[3]

EUROPEAN JUDGMENTS

Chapter III (Arts 32–56) of the Brussels I Regulation governs the recognition and enforcement of judgments[4] between the EC member states. As well as defining the

---

1   [2001] OJ L12/1.
2   For the extension of the Brussels I Regulation to Denmark, see EC Council Decisions 2005/790 and 2006/325; [2005] OJ L299/61 and [2006] OJ L120/22. Judgments from Switzerland, Norway or Iceland are governed by the Lugano Convention of 16 September 1988 on Jurisdiction and the Enforcement of Judgments in Civil and Commercial Matters, [1988] OJ L319/9, which provides a regime broadly similar to the Brussels I Regulation. A revised Lugano Convention, signed on behalf of the European Community on 30 October 2007, has not yet entered into force; see EC Council Decision 2007/712 [2007] OJ L339. As regards judgments from other parts of the United Kingdom, see Pt II of the Civil Jurisdiction and Judgments Act 1982.
3   For this purpose, 'judgment' refers to a decision emanating from a judicial body of a member state deciding on its own authority the issues between the parties. Thus, the concept excludes a court settlement, falling within Chapter IV of the Regulation, even if it was reached in a court of a member state and brought legal proceedings to an end, since such settlements are essentially contractual in that their terms depend primarily on the parties' intention. See Case C-414/92: *Solo Kleinmotoren v Boch* [1994] ECR I-2237. On the other hand, the concept extends to an admiralty judgment ordering the creation of a limitation fund; see Case C-39/02: *Mærsk Olie & Gas v de Haan & de Boer* [2004] ECR I-9657. Chapter IV (Arts 57–58) provides for the enforcement of court settlements and authentic instruments from other member states. But it does not extend to an acknowledgment of indebtedness whose authenticity has not been established by a public authority or other authority empowered for that purpose by the state of origin; see Case C-260/97: *Unibank v Christensen* [1999] ECR I3715.
4   On the enforcement of foreign awards under the New York Convention, see Chapter 19 below.

substantive conditions for granting recognition or enforcement, the Regulation (in Arts 38–56) creates a unified procedure for obtaining a decision authorising enforcement. The unified procedure involves an ex parte application to a court of the state addressed, on which a prompt decision must be given. The decision on the initial application is subject to an appeal inter partes, and the decision on the appeal to a single further appeal on a point of law. The unified procedure leads to a decision granting (or refusing) a declaration of enforceability (or an order authorising registration for enforcement), and once this is obtained the measures of actual enforcement are governed mainly by the law of the state addressed. An ex parte decision in favour of enforcement enables the applicant to take protective measures against the respondent's property, but definitive enforcement is delayed until the appeal inter partes has become time barred or has been disposed of.

The same substantive conditions apply to both recognition and enforcement, except that for enforcement there is an additional requirement that the judgment should be enforceable in the original country.[5] The unified procedure for obtaining a declaration of enforceability (or an order authorising registration for enforcement) laid down by Arts 38–56 is exclusive.[6] The same procedure can also be used to obtain a decision establishing recognition, but recognition can also be sought incidentally in any proceedings where it is relevant.[7] In principle recognition entails that the judgment must be given the same effects in the state addressed as it has in the state of origin.[8] In the case of uncontested claims, a more radical solution has been adopted by EC Regulation 805/2004, creating a European Enforcement Order for Uncontested Claims,[9] which applies from 21 October 2005.

Chapter III of the Brussels I Regulation is confined to judgments which are principally concerned with matters which fall within the scope of the Regulation as defined by Art 1, and it gives way to existing specialised conventions in accordance with Art 71.[10] By Art 66, Chapter III applies to judgments given after the entry into force of

---

5   See Arts 34–36, 38 and 45(2). See also Case C-267/97: *Coursier v Fortis Bank* [1999] ECR I-2543, where the European Court ruled, rather surprisingly, that it is enough that the judgment is, in formal terms, enforceable in character, as where it bears a formal order for enforcement, even if it can no longer be enforced in the original country because of some subsequent development, such as payment of the debt or the debtor's bankruptcy. The effects of an insolvency judgment are to be determined by the court of the state addressed, hearing the debtor's appeal against the declaration of enforceability (or order authorising registration for enforcement), in accordance with its own rules of private international law, or since June 2002 with EC Regulation 1346/2000 on Insolvency Proceedings [2000] OJ L160/1.

6   See Case 42/76: *De Wolf v Cox* [1976] ECR 1759. See also s 34 of the Civil Jurisdiction and Judgments Act 1982.

7   See Art 33.

8   See Case 145/86: *Hoffmann v Krieg* [1988] ECR 645; the Jenard Report [1979] OJ C59/1, at p 43; and *The Tjaskemolen (No 2)* [1997] 2 Lloyd's Rep 476.

9   [2004] OJ L143/15. Chapter II of Regulation 805/2004 enables a court of a member state which has given a judgment on an uncontested claim to issue a certificate, certifying the judgment as a European Enforcement Order, provided that the minimum procedural standards laid down by Chapter III thereof have been satisfied. The certificate then renders the judgment enforceable in the other member states, without the need for a declaration of enforceability to be obtained from a court of the state addressed, as would be required under Regulation 44/2001. Under Chapter IV of Regulation 805/2004, enforcement procedures, including measures of actual execution, remain governed by the law of the state addressed, which must treat a certified judgment in the same way as a local judgment. With minimal exceptions any challenge to the judgment or the certificate must be made in the state of origin.

10 See Chapter 16. Moreover, Chapter III does not apply to the recognition or enforcement in a member state of a judgment given in another member state if the judgment is principally concerned with the recognition or enforcement of a judgment given in a non-member country; see Case C-129/92: *Owens Bank v Bracco* [1994] ECR I-117.

the Regulation for both the member state of origin and the member state addressed, subject to a minor transitional proviso for cases where the original action was instituted before the entry into force of the Regulation and of the Brussels or Lugano Conventions between the states in question.[11]

To be enforceable (as distinct from recognisable) abroad under Chapter III of the Regulation, the judgment must be enforceable in the state of origin, but it is unnecessary that the judgment should award a sum of money. It could, for example, order the specific performance of a contract.[12] There is no requirement that the judgment should in any sense be final in the original country.[13] On the contrary, Chapter III applies even if the judgment is subject to any form of appeal or review there, whether in a higher court or in the court which gave the judgment. Instead, the problem of appealable judgments is regulated by Arts 37 and 46, which enable the court addressed to stay its proceedings or require the applicant for enforcement to give security where an ordinary appeal is pending or admissible in the original country. Thus, in general, judgments on preliminary issues and interim orders, as well as judgments given at the conclusion of a trial, have to be recognised and enforced under Chapter III.[14] But Chapter III does not extend to interim orders which are not intended to govern the legal relationships of the parties, but to arrange the further conduct of the proceedings, such as orders for the taking of evidence;[15] nor to orders for provisional or protective measures (for example, freezing assets) which are made without the defendant having been summoned to appear and are intended to be enforced without prior service.[16]

As regards the conditions for recognition and enforcement, the basic principle, laid down by Arts 33 and 38, is that a judgment to which Chapter III applies must be recognised and enforced in the other member states. This is reinforced by Arts 36 and 45(2), which emphasise that in no circumstances may the court addressed review the substance or merits of the judgment, and by Art 35(3), which in most cases prevents the court addressed from reviewing the jurisdiction of the original court. A very limited range of exceptions, in which recognition and enforcement must be refused, are specified by Arts 34, 35 and 45(1). The specified exceptions are exhaustive,[17] but in these cases the Regulation insists that recognition and enforcement must be denied, regardless of the traditional law of the state addressed.[18]

The prohibition against reviewing the substance of the judgment excludes the traditional English rules preventing recognition of a judgment obtained by fraud,

---

11 Chapter III of the Brussels I Regulation does not apply at all if the judgment was given before the entry into force of the Regulation for both of the states involved. The recognition and enforcement of such judgments remains governed by the Brussels Convention or the Lugano Convention, if otherwise applicable. See *T v L* [2008] IESC 48 (Irish Supreme Court).

12 See Art 38; the Schlosser Report [1979] OJ C59/1, at p 132; and *EMI v Watterbach* [1992] 1 QB 115.

13 See Case C-183/90: *Van Dalfsen v Van Loon* [1991] ECR I-4743; Jenard [1979] OJ C59/1, at p 43; and Schlosser [1979] OJ C59/1, at p 126. But, by Art 49, a judgment which orders a periodic payment by way of penalty is enforceable in the other member states only if the amount of the payment has been finally determined by the courts of the original country.

14 See *The Heidberg* [1994] 2 Lloyd's Rep 287 (Diamond QC in the Queen's Bench Division); and *The Tjaskemolen (No 2)* [1997] 2 Lloyd's Rep 476 (Clarke J).

15 See Schlosser [1979] OJ C59/1, at pp 126–7.

16 Case 125/79: *Denilauler v Couchet Frères* [1980] ECR 1553; Case C-474/93: *Hengst v Campese* [1995] ECR I-2113; *EMI v Watterbach* [1992] 1 QB 115; and *Normaco v Lundman* (1999) *The Times* 6 January.

17 See *Guittienne v SNCI* (1996) unreported, 6 March (French Court of Cassation).

18 See Gaudemet-Tallon, *Les Conventions de Bruxelles et de Lugano*, 1996, Montchrestien, at paras 381–83.

under which the party alleging fraud could rely on evidence which he placed or could have placed before the foreign court.[19] Under the Regulation the remedy for fraud must normally be sought in the original country. It is acceptable for the court addressed to invoke the public policy proviso specified by Art 34(1) against recognition on account of fraud only in the rare situation where there is cogent newly discovered evidence, such as would enable the reopening of a judgment obtained in the country addressed, but the law of the original country denies any possibility of proceedings to reopen the judgment.[20]

The prohibition against reviewing the jurisdiction of the original court is subject to three minor exceptions. The first exception, laid down by Art 35(1), is where the dispute falls within the scope of Arts 8–14, 15–17 or 22, which deal respectively with insurance, protected consumer contracts, and exclusive jurisdiction by virtue of subject matter, and the original court assumed jurisdiction contrary to those provisions. The rationale is to prevent the policies of protecting policy-holders and consumers, and respecting the interests of the state of exclusive jurisdiction, from being undermined. But the significance of this exception is greatly reduced by the supplementary rule, laid down by Art 35(2), that for this purpose the court addressed is bound by the findings of fact on which the original court based its jurisdiction. Moreover in *Apostolides v Orams* [21] the European Court ruled that Art 35(1) does not enable a court of a member state to refuse recognition or enforcement of a judgment given by the courts of another member state concerning land situated in an area of the latter state over which its government does not exercise effective control. Nonetheless, the Court of Appeal has ruled that an important effect of Art 35(1), taken with Art 22(4), is to prevent a decision given in one member state on the validity of a local patent or trade mark from giving rise to an estoppel binding in proceedings concerning the validity, or the validity and infringement, or possibly the infringement alone, of another patent or trade mark in another member state.[22]

The second exception, laid down by Arts 35(1) and 72, is designed to offer some protection to persons domiciled or habitually resident outside the member states from judgments given on excessive jurisdictional bases under Art 4. It preserves the operation of agreements entered into prior to the entry into force of the Regulation pursuant to Art 59 of the Brussels Convention, by which a member state gave an undertaking to a third country not to recognise judgments given in other member states against defendants domiciled or habitually resident in the third country in cases where Art 4 applied and the judgment could be founded only on a ground of jurisdiction specified in Art 3(2). Such agreements exist between the United Kingdom and Canada[23] and Australia.[24]

---

19 See *Abouloff v Oppenheimer* (1882) 10 QBD 295; *Vadala v Lawes* (1890) 25 QBD 310; the Administration of Justice Act 1920, s 9(2)(d); the Foreign Judgments (Reciprocal Enforcement) Act 1933, s 4(1)(a)(iv); *Syal v Heyward* [1948] 2 KB 443; and *Owens Bank v Bracco* [1992] 2 AC 443.

20 See *Interdesco v Nullifire* [1992] 1 Lloyd's Rep 180; and *SISRO v Ampersand Software* [1994] ILPr 55 (CA).

21 Case C-420/07: 28 April 2009.

22 See *Prudential Assurance Co Ltd v Prudential Insurance Co of America* [2003] 1 WLR 2295 (CA).

23 See the Ottawa Convention of 24 April 1984, providing for the Reciprocal Recognition and Enforcement of Judgments in Civil and Commercial Matters; and the Reciprocal Enforcement of Foreign Judgments (Canada) Order 1987 SI 1987/468 (as amended).

24 See the Canberra Agreement of 23 August 1990, providing for the Reciprocal Recognition and Enforcement of Judgments in Civil and Commercial Matters; and the Reciprocal Enforcement of Foreign Judgments (Australia) Order 1994 SI 1994/1901.

The third exception, laid down by Art 66, applies where at the institution of the action leading to the judgment neither the Regulation nor the Brussels and Lugano Conventions were in force between the state of origin and the state addressed.

A fourth case of jurisdictional review, relating to Art 31, has emerged from the European Court's decision in *Mietz v Intership Yachting Sneek*.[25] The European Court emphasised the importance of ensuring that enforcement under Chapter III of provisional or protective measures allegedly founded on the jurisdiction laid down in Art 31, but which go beyond the limits of that jurisdiction, does not result in circumvention of the rules on jurisdiction as to the substance set out in Chapter II. Thus it ruled that enforcement under Chapter III must be refused where the following conditions are satisfied: the judgment was delivered at the end of proceedings which were not, by their very nature, proceedings as to substance but summary proceedings for the granting of interim measures; the measure ordered (such as an unconditional interim payment) is not a provisional or protective measure permissible under Art 31; and the original court had either expressly indicated in its judgment that it had based its jurisdiction on Art 31, or had been silent as to the basis of its jurisdiction.

Apart from the minor cases of permissible jurisdictional review, the substantive grounds for refusal of recognition and enforcement are laid down by Art 34. By Arts 34(1) and 45(1), a judgment is not to be recognised or enforced under Chapter III if its recognition is manifestly contrary to public policy in the state addressed. But Art 35(3) of the Regulation specifically forbids the use of public policy to extend jurisdictional review, and in *Krombach v Bamberski*[26] the European Court ruled that this applies even where the original court wrongly founded its jurisdiction, in regard to a defendant domiciled in the state addressed, on a rule which utilises nationality. Moreover in *Hoffmann v Krieg*[27] and *Hendrikman v Magenta Druck & Verlag*[28] the European Court emphasised that the public policy proviso should operate only in exceptional cases, and that recourse to it is in any event precluded when the issue is dealt with by a specific provision, such as Art 34(2) on timely notification of the defendant, or Art 34(3) on irreconcilability with a local judgment.

More generally, in *Krombach v Bamberski*,[29] the European Court emphasised that while the member states in principle remain free to determine according to their own conceptions what public policy requires, the limits of the concept are a matter of interpretation of the Regulation, for determination by the European Court. Thus, in view of Arts 36 and 45(2), the court addressed cannot refuse recognition solely on the ground that there is a discrepancy between the legal rule applied by the court of the state of origin and that which would have been applied by the court of the state addressed if it had been seised of the dispute. Nor can the court addressed review the accuracy of the findings of law or fact made by the court of origin. Recourse to public policy can be envisaged only where recognition or enforcement of the judgment would be at variance to an unacceptable degree with the legal order of the state addressed in as much as it infringes a fundamental principle. The infringement would have to constitute a manifest breach of a rule of law regarded as essential in the legal order of the state addressed, or of a right recognised as being fundamental within that

---

25 Case C-99/96: [1999] ECR I-2277. See also *Comet Group v Unika Computer* [2004] ILPr 1.
26 Case C-7/98: [2000] ECR I-1935.
27 Case 145/86: [1988] ECR 645.
28 Case C-78/95: [1996] ECR I-4943.
29 Case C-7/98: [2000] ECR I-1935.

legal order. The European Court applied these principles in *Renault v Maxicar*,[30] where it ruled that public policy could not be invoked on the ground that the original judgment involved an error of Community law; for example, as to the legitimacy under Arts 28–30 or 82 of the EC Treaty of a design right in spare parts. Somewhat similarly, the European Court of Human Rights has accepted that a court requested to enforce a foreign judgment need only carry out a limited review of the judgment's compatibility with the European Convention on Human Rights.[31]

One situation in which the public policy proviso may properly be invoked is where, despite proper notification of the institution of the original action (satisfying Art 34(2)), the respondent was in some other way denied a reasonable opportunity to present his case. This was accepted by the European Court in *Krombach v Bamberski*,[32] where a French court, hearing a prosecution for manslaughter and an ancillary civil claim by relatives of the victim, had ordered the accused to appear in person; and on his failure to do so, had refused to hear his defence counsel. The European Court ruled that a court of a member state is entitled to hold that a refusal to hear the defence of an accused person who is not present at the hearing constitutes a manifest breach of a fundamental right, and therefore to deny recognition under Art 34(1), despite the fact that Art 61 was inapplicable because of the intentional character of the offence.[33] Similarly in *Maronier v Larmer*[34] the Court of Appeal refused on grounds of public policy to enforce a Dutch judgment given in proceedings which had been reactivated after 12 years without the defendant's knowledge, and without his becoming aware of the reactivation until after the time for appealing against the judgment had expired.

In *Gambazzi v DaimlerChrysler*,[35] which involved the enforcement in Italy of an English default judgment, given after the English court had made an order debarring the defendant from participating in the proceedings because of his failure to comply with a disclosure order requiring him to provide information about his assets and to produce documents relevant to the claim, the European Court accepted that, under Art 34(1), the court addressed may take into account, with regard to public policy, the fact that the original court had ruled on the applicant's claims without hearing the defendant, who had entered appearance before it but who had been excluded from the proceedings by order on the ground that he had not complied with the obligations imposed by an order made earlier in the same proceedings. But it insisted that in this scenario refusal of recognition and enforcement would be justified only where the

---

30 Case C-38/98: [2000] ECR I-2973. Cf Case C-126/97: *Eco Swiss China Time v Benetton* [1999] ECR I-3055, involving a domestic arbitration award.
31 See Application No 48198/99: *Lindberg v Sweden*, 15 January 2004.
32 Case C-7/98: [2000] ECR I-1935.
33 By Art 61, without prejudice to more favourable provisions of national laws, where a person domiciled in a member state is prosecuted in a criminal court of another member state of which he is not a national for an offence which was not intentionally committed, he may be defended by persons qualified to do so, even if he does not appear in person. But the court seised may order appearance in person; and then, in the case of failure to appear, a civil judgment given without his having had the opportunity to arrange for his defence need not be recognised or enforced in the other member states. In Case 157/80: *Rinkau* [1981] ECR 1391, the European Court ruled that this provision extends to any offence whose definition does not require the existence of intent by the accused to commit the punishable act or omission, but that it is confined to criminal proceedings in which the accused's civil liability, arising from the elements of the offence for which he is being prosecuted, is in question or on which such liability might subsequently be based.
34 [2003] QB 620 (CA). See also *Citibank v Rafidian Bank* [2003] ILPr 49.
35 Case C-394/07: 2 April 2009.

court addressed reaches the conclusion, after a comprehensive assessment of the proceedings and in the light of all the circumstances, that the exclusion measure constituted a manifest and disproportionate infringement of the defendant's right to be heard.

By Arts 34(2) and 45(1), recognition and enforcement of a judgment must be refused where it was given in default of appearance, and the defendant was not served with the document which instituted the proceedings or with an equivalent document in sufficient time and in such a way as to enable him to arrange for his defence, unless the defendant failed to commence proceedings to challenge the judgment when it was possible for him to do so. This protection at the stage of recognition or enforcement is in addition to that conferred in the original action by Art 26, and applies regardless of the defendant's domicile.[36] But a defendant is deemed to have appeared where, in connection with a claim for compensation joined to criminal proceedings, he answered at the trial through counsel of his own choice to the criminal charges, but did not express a view on the civil claim on which oral argument was also submitted in the presence of his counsel.[37] On the other hand, there is no sufficient appearance where someone purporting to represent the defendant, but in fact acting without his authority, appeared before the original court.[38] A judgment which was originally given in default of appearance is regarded as a default judgment, despite the fact that the defendant subsequently lodged an objection against the judgment which was rejected by a court of the state of origin as inadmissible because it was out of time, or that the defendant unsuccessfully appealed against the judgment on the sole ground that the original court lacked jurisdiction.[39] The relevant instituting document is the document or documents whose service enables the claimant, under the law of the state of origin, to obtain, in default of appropriate action taken by the defendant, a decision capable of being recognised or enforced under the Regulation.[40]

Under Art 34(2), both the manner and the time of service are now subjected exclusively to a Community standard. Thus in *ASML v Semiconductor Industry Services*[41] the European Court recognised that under the Regulation a mere formal irregularity in service, which does not adversely affect the rights of defence, is not sufficient to prevent recognition and enforcement.[42] In exceptional circumstances, service in accordance with the law of the state of origin may be inadequate for the

---

36   See Case 166/80: *Klomps v Michel* [1981] ECR 1593; Case 228/81: *Pendy Plastic Products v Pluspunkt* [1982] ECR 2723; and Case 49/84: *Debaecker v Bouwman* [1985] ECR 1779.
37   See Case C-172/91: *Sonntag v Waidmann* [1993] ECR I-1963.
38   See Case C-78/95: *Hendrikman v Magenta Druck & Verlag* [1996] ECR I-4943.
39   See Case 166/80: *Klomps v Michel* [1981] ECR 1593; and Case C-39/02: *Mærsk Olie & Gas v de Haan & de Boer* [2004] ECR I-9657. See also *Tavoulareas v Tsavliris* [2006] EWHC 414 (Comm), where Tomlinson J held that a judgment counted as a default judgment where the only participation by the defendant had been to join in a request for an agreed adjournment, while at the same time protesting that the court lacked jurisdiction, and the judgment was expressed by the court rendering it to be given in default of appearance.
40   See Case 166/80: *Klomps v Michel* [1981] ECR 1593; and Case C-474/93: *Hengst v Campese* [1995] ECR I-2113. See also on admiralty limitation orders, Case C-39/02: *Mærsk Olie & Gas v de Haan & de Boer* [2004] ECR I-9657.
41   Case C-283/05: [2006] ECR I-12041. Cf *Tavoulareas v Tsavliris* [2006] EWHC 414 (Comm), where Tomlinson J held that an effective notification of the foreign instituting document through the defendant's English solicitors was insufficient.
42   Cf the rulings under the Brussels Convention in Case 166/80: *Klomps v Michel* [1981] ECR 1593; Case C-305/88: *Lancray v Peters* [1990] ECR I-2725; Case C-123/91: *Minalmet v Brandeis* [1992] ECR I-5661; and Case C-522/03: *Scania v Rockinger* [2005] ECR I-8639.

purposes of enabling the defendant to take steps to arrange for his defence, and account may be taken of exceptional circumstances which arose after service (such as the claimant's discovering the defendant's new address before obtaining a default judgment).[43] But service effected at the defendant's business address or home, where in the ordinary course it should come to his attention, will suffice, provided that the time between the date of service and the entry of the default judgment should have been sufficient for him to arrange for his defence, and a period of five weeks in which to enter a notice of appearance will normally be adequate.[44]

Departing from the Brussels Convention, Art 34(2) of the Regulation prevents the court addressed from refusing recognition and enforcement by reason of insufficient service of the instituting document if the defendant failed to commence proceedings to challenge the judgment in the state of origin when it was possible for him to do so. In *ASML v Semiconductor Industry Services*,[45] the European Court construed this proviso as meaning that it is 'possible' for a defendant to bring proceedings to challenge a default judgment against him only if he was in fact acquainted with its contents, because it was served on him in sufficient time to enable him to arrange for his defence before the courts of the state of origin. It explained that the necessary service of the default judgment need not comply with all the relevant formalities, but it must be effected in sufficient time and in such a way as to enable the defendant to arrange for his defence. Moreover the proviso does not prevent an objection to recognition and enforcement where the defendant commences proceedings to challenge the judgment in the state of origin after the application for recognition or enforcement is made, but before the court addressed considers whether to recognise or enforce the judgment.[46] But in *Apostolides v Orams*[47] the European Court ruled that recognition or enforcement of a default judgment cannot be refused under Art 34(2) where the defendant was able to and did in fact commence proceedings in the original country to challenge the default judgment; and those proceedings enabled him to argue that he had not been served with the instituting document in sufficient time and in such a way as to enable him to arrange for his defence; but his application to set aside the default judgment failed on the ground that he had failed to show any arguable defence on the merits.

Lastly, Arts 34(3)–(4) and 45(1) of the Regulation deal with irreconcilability between judgments. Recognition and enforcement must be refused if the judgment is irreconcilable with another judgment which was given in a dispute between the same parties in the state addressed. Recognition and enforcement must also be refused if the judgment is irreconcilable with an earlier judgment which was given in another member state or in an external country, which involved the same cause of action and was between the same parties, and which fulfils the conditions necessary for recognition in the state addressed. For this purpose, judgments are irreconcilable with each other where they entail mutually exclusive legal consequences.[48] Moreover, as the

---

43   See Case 166/80: *Klomps v Michel* [1981] ECR 1593; and Case 49/84: *Debaecker v Bouwman* [1985] ECR 1779.

44   See *TSN v Jurgens* [2002] 1 WLR 2459 (CA). See also *Lacoste v Keely Group* [1999] 1 ILRM 510.

45   Case C-283/05: [2006] ECR I-12041.

46   See *Tavoulareas v Tsavliris* [2006] EWHC 414 (Comm) (Tomlinson J).

47   Case C-420/07: 28 April 2009.

48   See Case 145/86: *Hoffmann v Krieg* [1988] ECR 645. Cf. Case C-406/92: *The Maciej Rataj* [1994] ECR I-5439, on Art 28; and Case C-539/03: *Roche Nederland BV v Primus* [2006] ECR I-6535. See also *T v L* [2008] IESC 48, where the Irish Supreme Court refused under Art 34(3) to recognise a Dutch maintenance order, made ancillarily to a Dutch divorce decree, as being irreconcilable with an Irish decision refusing to recognise the divorce.

European Court ruled in *Italian Leather v WECO Polstermöbel*,[49] these provisions extend to provisional measures (such as an interim injunction prohibiting the infringement of a trade mark), and a foreign judgment granting such an injunction is irreconcilable with a local judgment between the same parties refusing to grant such an injunction, even if the conflicting effects of the two judgments are due to differences in the procedural requirements for the grant of such relief laid down by the national laws in the relevant countries. The European Court also emphasised that these provisions have a mandatory character, so that once the court addressed finds that the relevant irreconcilability exists, it is bound to refuse to recognise the foreign judgment. But the irreconcilability must be with an actual judgment, and not merely with a court settlement falling within Chapter IV of the Regulation,[50] nor merely with a pending action, in favour of which the foreign court should have declined jurisdiction under Art 27.[51]

EXTERNAL JUDGMENTS

There are three distinct regimes which govern the enforcement in the United Kingdom of judgments given in a foreign country which is neither an EC member state nor a party to the Lugano Convention. The three regimes are provided for respectively by the common law; the Administration of Justice Act 1920; and the Foreign Judgments (Reciprocal Enforcement) Act 1933. The 1920 and 1933 Acts apply to judgments given in a country to which, on account of reciprocity, the Act in question has been applied by Order in Council,[52] while the common law applies to judgments from countries (such as the United States) to which these Acts have not been applied. The three regimes are substantially similar to each other, but radically different from the regime now applicable to European judgments.[53]

The common law regime involves the bringing of an ordinary action in an English court, pleading the foreign judgment and seeking the entry of a similar English judgment, while the statutory regimes involve an application to an English court for an order that the foreign judgment be registered for enforcement, but this distinction is formal and of little importance. As regards judgments within its scope, in general each regime is exclusive not only of enforcement of the judgment under the other regimes, but also of an English action based on the original claim.[54] To qualify for enforcement in England under any of the regimes, the judgment must be enforceable

---

49 Case C-80/00: [2002] ECR I-4995.
50 See Case C-414/92: *Solo Kleinmotoren v Boch* [1994] ECR I-2237.
51 See *Brasserie du Pecheur v Kreissparkasse Main-Spessart* (1996) unreported, 14 May (French Court of Cassation); Gaudemet-Tallon, *Les Conventions de Bruxelles et de Lugano*, 1996, Montchrestien, at para 369; and *Tavoulareas v Tsavliris* [2006] EWHC 414 (Comm) (Tomlinson J).
52 The 1920 Act applies to judgments from numerous Commonwealth countries. The 1933 Act applies to judgments from (among others) Australia, Canada, India, Pakistan and Israel. The 1933 Act also applies to judgments given in pursuance of certain international conventions dealing with particular matters (such as carriage by rail or road) in any country other than the United Kingdom which is a party to the relevant convention. But s 1(2A) of the 1933 Act (as amended) excludes from enforcement thereunder a judgment for the enforcement of a judgment given in a third country.
53 On European judgments, see at pp 607–15 above.
54 See the 1933 Act, s 6; the Civil Jurisdiction and Judgments Act 1982, s 34; *The Sylt* [1991] 1 Lloyd's Rep 240; and *Republic of India v India Steamship Co Ltd* [1993] AC 410. Cf s 9(5) of the 1920 Act.

in the original country[55] and must award a definite sum of money (rather than, for example, ordering the specific performance of a contract).[56] The judgment must not be for payment of a fine or tax.[57] It may, however, be a judgment given by a criminal court in ancillary civil proceedings, awarding compensation to a victim who has intervened in a prosecution to claim damages,[58] or even a judgment awarding exemplary damages in respect of a civil claim.[59]

As regards mere recognition without enforcement, external judgments are governed by the common law and s 34 of the Civil Jurisdiction and Judgments Act 1982, even if the original court is one to which, as regards enforcement, the 1920 Act or the 1933 Act applies.[60] Section 34 eliminates a former restriction on the effects of recognition, whereby recognition did not prevent a person entitled under an unsatisfied but enforceable money judgment from suing in England on the original claim. In effect it extends to foreign judgments the doctrine of merger, whereby a plaintiff's cause of action merges in a judgment in his favour and ceases to have any separate existence.[61] Accordingly, an external personal judgment against a shipowner will prevent a subsequent English action in rem against the ship in respect of the same claim.[62]

The three regimes differ, however, in their requirements concerning the finality of the judgment in the original country. At one extreme, a judgment cannot be registered for enforcement under the 1920 Act if the respondent satisfies the English court that an appeal is pending in the original country, or that he is entitled and intends to appeal there.[63] Less demandingly, to qualify for recognition or enforcement at common law, a judgment must be final in the original court, in the sense that it constitutes *res judicata* in the court by which it was given and cannot be reviewed by means of any proceedings in that court,[64] but even this requirement may be inapplicable to a default judgment,[65] or where only the amount of damages awarded by the judgment is open to adjustment.[66] On the other hand, the pendency or possibility of an appeal to a higher court in the original country does not prevent recognition or enforcement at common law, though a judgment will not be enforceable here if enforcement in the original country has been stayed pending appeal.[67]

---

55 See *Colt Industries v Sarlie (No 2)* [1966] 1 WLR 1287; s 9(1) of the 1920 Act; and s 2(1)(b) of the 1933 Act. A dubious exception seems to permit enforcement at common law despite a stay of execution in the original country on account of the judgment debtor's bankruptcy; see *Berliner Industriebank v Jost* [1971] 2 All ER 1513.

56 See *Sadler v Robins* (1801) 1 Camp 253; *Beatty v Beatty* [1924] 1 KB 807; ss 9(1) and (3) and 12(1) of the 1920 Act; and ss 1(2) and 2 of the 1933 Act.

57 See *Huntington v Attrill* [1893] AC 150; *Rossano v Manufacturers' Life* [1963] 2 QB 352; ss 9(2)(f) and 12(1) of the 1920 Act; and s 1(2)(b) of the 1933 Act.

58 See *Raulin v Fischer* [1911] 2 KB 83; and ss 2(5) and 11(1) of the 1933 Act.

59 See *General Textiles v Sun and Sand Agencies* [1978] 1 QB 279.

60 In the case of judgments to which the 1933 Act applies, s 8 makes some provision for mere recognition, but probably does not alter the results otherwise reached under the common law.

61 See *Republic of India v India Steamship Co Ltd* [1993] AC 410. Cf *Black v Yates* [1992] 1 QB 526.

62 See *The Sylt* [1991] 1 Lloyd's Rep 240.

63 See s 9(2)(e).

64 See *Nouvion v Freeman* (1889) 15 App Cas 1; *Harrop v Harrop* [1920] 3 KB 386; *Beatty v Beatty* [1924] 1 KB 807; and *Cartwright v Cartwright* [2002] 2 FLR 610 (CA).

65 See *Vanquelin v Bouard* (1863) 143 ER 817, p 828.

66 See *Lewis v Eliades* [2003] 1 All ER (Comm) 850.

67 See *Colt Industries v Sarlie (No 2)* [1966] 1 WLR 1287.

At first sight, the 1933 Act seems to follow the common law, since s 1(2)(a) (as amended by the 1982 Act) explicitly requires finality in the original country, except in the case of judgments for an interim payment. But other provisions of the 1933 Act appear to deprive the requirement of finality of all content. For s 1(3) specifies that a judgment counts as final even if in the original country an appeal against it is pending or still admissible; and s 11(1) defines 'appeal' as including any proceeding by way of discharging or setting aside a judgment, or an application for a new trial or a stay of execution, apparently including an application for review made to the very court which gave the judgment. Thus, it seems that in all cases the possibility that the judgment may be set aside or varied in the original country falls to be dealt with under s 5, whereby, on application by the respondent, the English court has a discretion to set aside the registration on the ground that an appeal in the original country is pending, or is admissible and intended, or to adjourn the respondent's application for a period reasonably sufficient to enable the applicant to take the necessary steps to have the foreign appeal disposed of, and also to impose appropriate terms. The English court remains free, however, to permit immediate and unconditional enforcement despite the pendency of a foreign appeal, and is likely to do so where it considers that the respondent is engaged in unmeritorious procedural manoeuvrings for purposes of delay.[68]

Under all three regimes, the English court will review the jurisdiction of the original court under the English rules of indirect jurisdiction, and will refuse recognition and enforcement if the foreign court lacked competence under those rules. Other available grounds for refusal are that the judgment was obtained by fraud; that the defendant abroad was not properly notified of the foreign proceedings; and that enforcement would contravene a stringent English public policy.

The general rule under all three regimes is that the English court cannot review the substance or merits of the foreign decision. It is not open to the English court to consider whether the original court made some error in determining the underlying dispute, whether the error alleged is of fact or of law (and whether of English or foreign law, and of substantive or conflict law).[69] But there is a major exception for judgments obtained by fraud, under which the English court will review the merits of the underlying dispute in order to ascertain the existence of fraud, even where the party alleging fraud relies on evidence which he placed or could have placed before the foreign court,[70] unless the claim that the judgment had been obtained by fraud has been rejected in a subsequent action in the foreign country.[71]

Under the three regimes, a personal judgment will not be recognised or enforced unless the original court is regarded as having had jurisdiction over the respondent (the person against whom the judgment is invoked) under the relevant English rules of indirect jurisdiction. The burden of establishing the existence of such indirect jurisdiction lies on the party seeking recognition or enforcement.[72] The rules of

---

68   See *General Textiles v Sun and Sand Agencies* [1978] 1 QB 279.
69   See *Godard v Gray* (1870) LR 6 QB 139; *Henderson v Henderson* (1844) 115 ER 111; *Ellis v McHenry* (1871) LR 6 CP 228; s 9(2) and (3) of the 1920 Act; and ss 2(1)–(2) and 4(1) of the 1933 Act.
70   See *Abouloff v Oppenheimer* (1882) 10 QBD 295; *Vadala v Lawes* (1890) 25 QBD 310; s 9(2)(d) of the 1920 Act; s 4(1)(a)(iv) of the 1933 Act; *Syal v Heyward* [1948] 2 KB 443; *Jet Holdings v Patel* [1990] 1 QB 335; and *Owens Bank v Bracco* [1992] 2 AC 443.
71   See *House of Spring Gardens v Waite* [1991] 1 QB 241.
72   See *Adams v Cape Industries* [1990] Ch 433.

indirect jurisdiction differ, but only slightly, between the common law, the 1920 Act and the 1933 Act. Under all three systems, the only connections giving rise to indirect jurisdiction over a person are his residence (in varying senses) in the original country at the institution of the action there; or his submission to the jurisdiction of the original court, either by express agreement to such jurisdiction, or by appearance in the original action.[73] It is not enough that some or all of the acts and events which gave rise to the cause of action occurred in the original country, and that an equivalent connection with England would have conferred direct jurisdiction on the English courts.[74]

As regards a respondent individual, under the common law the requirement of residence refers simply to his physical presence in person in the original country, however transiently, at the institution of the action there.[75] It is not enough that he was carrying on business there through an agent.[76] But under the 1920 Act, s 9(2)(b) makes it necessary and sufficient either that he was ordinarily resident in the original country, or that he was carrying on business there. Under the 1933 Act, it is probable that s 4(2)(a)(iv), which merely speaks of his residence, should be understood as referring simply to his physical presence in person, however transiently, so as to accord with the common law. However, s 4(2)(a)(v) makes it alternatively sufficient that he had an office or place of business in the original country, provided that the action was in respect of a transaction effected through or at that office or place.

Where the respondent is a corporation, the requirement of residence in the original country for the purposes of the common law (and the 1920 Act) was elucidated by the Court of Appeal in *Adams v Cape Industries*.[77] The court explained that residence requires that the corporation should have been carrying on business (or, in the case of a non-trading corporation, other corporate activities) in the original country at a definite and reasonably permanent place. Thus, a corporation is resident in a country if it has a fixed place of business of its own there (whether as owner, lessee or licensee) and for more than a minimal period of time has carried on its own business from such premises by its servants or agents. But a corporation may be resident in a country even though it has no fixed place of business of its own there, if an agent acting on its behalf has for more than a minimal period of time been carrying on the corporation's business (as opposed to his own business) at or from some fixed place of business in the country. To determine whether the business carried on by an agent should be regarded as his own business or as that of the corporation necessitates an investigation both of the activities and functions of the agent and of the relationship between him and the corporation. Many matters are relevant in this investigation, but no single one is conclusive. It is of great importance whether the agent has authority to enter into contracts on behalf of the corporation without submitting them to the corporation for approval; and the fact that a representative never makes contracts in the name of the corporation or otherwise in such manner

---

73 See *Schibsby v Westenholz* (1870) LR 6 QB 155; *Singh v Rajah of Faridkote* [1894] AC 670; *Emanuel v Symon* [1908] 1 KB 302; *Adams v Cape Industries* [1990] Ch 433; s 9(2)(a)–(b) of the 1920 Act; ss 4(1)(a)(ii), 4(2)(a), and 11(2) of the 1933 Act; and ss 32 and 33 of the 1982 Act.

74 See *Turnbull v Walker* (1892) 67 LT 767; *Re Trepca Mines* [1960] 1 WLR 1273; and *Sidmetal v Titan* [1966] 1 QB 828. Cf *Morguard v De Savoye* (1990) 76 DLR 4th 256 (Canadian Supreme Court).

75 See *Carrick v Hancock* (1895) 12 TLR 59; and *Adams v Cape Industries* [1990] Ch 433.

76 See *Blohn v Desser* [1962] 2 QB 116.

77 [1990] Ch 433. See also *Littauer Glove v Millington* (1928) 44 TLR 746; *Jabbour v Custodian of Israeli Absentee Property* [1954] 1 WLR 139; *Sfeir v National Ins Co of New Zealand* [1964] 1 Lloyd's Rep 330; *Vogel v Kohnstamm* [1973] 1 QB 133; and s 9(2)(b) of the 1920 Act.

as to bind it is a powerful factor pointing away from the residence of the corporation. The same principles apply where a parent company is alleged to have carried on business through the agency of a subsidiary company. Even though they may constitute a single economic unit, each of the companies in a group is a separate legal entity, and there is no presumption that a subsidiary is carrying on the business of its parent as its agent. A parent company is entitled to arrange the affairs of its group in such a way that the business carried on in a particular country is the business of its subsidiary and not its own, and the court will not 'pierce the corporate veil' merely because the parent's purpose was to reduce its own exposure to the jurisdiction of the foreign court.

In the instant case, the Court of Appeal concluded that an English parent company was not resident in Illinois through a subsidiary incorporated and carrying on business there, mainly because, although the main function of the subsidiary was to assist in the marketing in the US of asbestos sold by its sister companies, and for such services it was remunerated by way of commission on sales, paid to it by the sister companies, it had no general authority to bind the parent to any contractual obligations, and it never in fact, even with prior authority from the parent, effected any transaction in such a manner that the parent thereby became subject to contractual obligations to any person.

In contrast, for the purposes of the 1933 Act, s 4(2)(a)(iv) and (v) require that a respondent company should have had, in the original country, either its principal place of business, or a secondary office or place of business through or at which the transaction involved in the original action was effected.

In any event, by s 32 of the 1982 Act, residence does not create indirect jurisdiction over an individual or a company under any of the three regimes, if the original action was brought in defiance of a valid agreement for arbitration or for the exclusive jurisdiction of the courts of another country, unless the agreement was incapable of being performed for reasons not attributable to the claimant's fault. For this purpose the English court is not bound by findings of the original court.

Under all three regimes, indirect jurisdiction over a non-resident may arise from his submission, by agreement[78] or appearance. As regards submission by agreement, an agreement on jurisdiction must be explicit and can never be implied.[79] But an explicit agreement on jurisdiction may take the form of a clause contained in a standard form contract, such as the articles of association of a company,[80] or it may be constituted by an informal expression of consent to accept the jurisdiction.[81] It may contemplate exclusive or non-exclusive jurisdiction, and it may refer to the courts in general of a specified country, or to a particular court, and in the latter case it will not confer jurisdiction on other courts of the same country.[82]

As regards submission by appearance, it is enough that the respondent appeared as plaintiff or counterclaimant in the original proceedings.[83] Thus a plaintiff in a

---

78 See *Emanuel v Symon* [1908] 1 KB 302; *Feyerick v Hubbard* (1902) 71 LJ KB 509; s 9(2)(b) of the 1920 Act; and s 4(2)(a)(iii) of the 1933 Act.

79 See *Singh v Rajah of Faridkote* [1984] AC 670; *Emanuel v Symon* [1908] 1 KB 302; and *Vogel v Kohnstamm* [1973] 1 QB 133.

80 See *Copin v Adamson* (1874) LR 9 Ex 345; (1875) 1 ExD 17.

81 See *General Textiles v Sun and Sand Agencies* [1978] 1 QB 279.

82 *Ibid.*

83 See *Emanuel v Symon* [1908] 1 KB 302; the 1920 Act, s 9(2)(b); and the 1933 Act, s 4(2)(a)(ii).

foreign action is regarded as submitting to the jurisdiction of the original court not only as regards his own claim, but also in respect of any counterclaim which the original court permits to be made against him in the same proceedings by a person whom he has sued. Similarly, a defendant who counterclaims is regarded as submitting to the jurisdiction of the original court in respect of the plaintiff's claim against him as well as his own counterclaim against the plaintiff.

There is also submission by appearance on the part of a defendant in a foreign action who voluntarily appears in the original action without counterclaiming,[84] and the appearance may be either at first instance or on appeal.[85] However, s 33(1) of the 1982 Act requires that to found indirect jurisdiction under any of the three regimes the appearance must be on the merits, and not for the limited purposes of contesting the jurisdiction of the original court, or requesting it to decline jurisdiction in favour of arbitration or of adjudication in another country, or of protecting or obtaining the release of property seized or threatened with seizure in the foreign proceedings. Probably the reference to seizure of property should be construed as confined to seizure before judgment for the purpose of founding jurisdiction or providing security, as distinct from seizure after judgment in execution.[86]

Under all three regimes, the recognition and enforcement in England of an external judgment is subject to a proviso that recognition of the judgment must not be contrary to English public policy.[87] The proviso may apply where the English court considers that recognition of the judgment would be unconscionable because of the outrageous character of the substantive rule applied by the original court; for example, where the foreign judgment upheld and enforced a contract to pay a fee to an assassin for carrying out an assassination. It was once held that a maintenance order against the father of a non-marital child, lasting beyond the child's minority, fell into this category.[88]

Another situation in which public policy may be invoked is where, despite proper notification of the institution of the original action, the respondent was in some other way denied a reasonable opportunity to present his case, or was otherwise prejudiced by the use by the foreign court (perhaps in breach of its own law) of a procedure which is considered seriously unfair by English standards.[89] Thus in *Adams v Cape Industries*,[90] the Court of Appeal refused to enforce at common law an American judgment, given against a defaulting defendant in a personal injury action brought by numerous plaintiffs, because the American court, in unexpected breach of its own procedural law, had assessed damages without receiving evidence of the particular injuries sustained by the individual plaintiffs. It had instead fixed an average amount for all the plaintiffs, and left it to their counsel to distribute the total award so arrived at between them. An argument that the defendant should have applied to the American court to have the judgment set aside on the ground of this procedural irregularity, an application which would have succeeded if made timeously, rather than raising the objection in England when enforcement here was sought, was

---

84   See *Emanuel v Symon* [1908] 1 KB 302; s 9(2)(b) of the 1920 Act; and s 4(2)(a)(i) of the 1933 Act.
85   See *General Textiles v Sun and Sand Agencies* [1978] 1 QB 279.
86   Cf *De Cosse Brissac v Rathbone* (1861) 158 ER 123; *Voinet v Barrett* (1885) 55 LJ QB 39; and *Guiard v De Clermont* [1914] 3 KB 145.
87   See *Re Macartney* [1921] 1 Ch 522; the 1920 Act, s 9(1) and (2)(f); and the 1933 Act, s 4(1)(a)(v).
88   See *Re Macartney* [1921] 1 Ch 522.
89   See *Jacobson v Frachon* (1927) 44 TLR 103; and *Adams v Cape Industries* [1990] Ch 433.
90   [1990] Ch 433.

rejected on the ground that the defendant had not been aware of the method of assessment used until enforcement in England was threatened. Slade LJ conceded, however, that if a foreign law were to provide for the plaintiff to serve a notice specifying a sum claimed as damages, and then for a default judgment to be entered for that sum without proof or judicial assessment, such a procedure would usually be considered unobjectionable, provided that, after due allowance had been made for differences between the foreign law and English law in levels of award and in substantive law, the amount of the actual award was not irrational. He further held, perhaps surprisingly, that even if the only procedural impropriety related to the assessment of damages, the judgment creditor could not invoke the foreign judgment for the purpose merely of establishing liability, so as to obtain an English judgment under which damages would be assessed by the English court.

A crystallisation of English public policy is found in s 5 of the Protection of Trading Interests Act 1980, which prevents the enforcement at common law or under the 1920 or 1933 Acts of a judgment for multiple damages. Even the unmultiplied element of the damages awarded, representing the actual loss sustained, is rendered unenforceable in England; but severance is possible where the sum awarded by the judgment comprises an identifiable sum awarded as multiple damages in respect of one claim, and another identifiable sum awarded as ordinary damages in respect of another claim.[91] Section 6 goes further by enabling, in certain circumstances, a person who has satisfied, or suffered enforcement abroad of, an external judgment for multiple damages, to sue in England for recoupment of the multiple element paid or enforced.[92] But there appears to be no English policy against the enforcement of foreign judgments awarding exemplary or aggravated damages (for example, where the defendant has perversely refused to meet a clearly justified claim), if no multiplication is involved,[93] unless perhaps the amount awarded is entirely irrational.[94]

All three regimes make an exception preventing recognition of judgments given in default against a defendant who was not adequately notified of the original action. In the context of recognition at common law, Atkin LJ said in *Jacobson v Frachon*[95] that the foreign court must have given notice to the litigant that it was about to proceed to determine his rights, and must also have afforded him an opportunity of substantially presenting his case. It may be, however, that service in a form authorised by an agreement between the parties will always satisfy the common law.[96] Under the 1920 Act, s 9(2)(c) prevents enforcement if the judgment debtor, being the defendant in the original proceedings, was not duly served with the process of the original court and did not appear. Under the 1933 Act, s 4(1)(a)(iii) prevents registration if the English court is satisfied that the judgment debtor, being the defendant in the original court, did not receive notice of the proceedings there in sufficient time to enable him to defend them and did not appear, even if process was duly served on him in accordance with the law of the original country.

Lastly, a judgment may be refused recognition because it is irreconcilable with

---

91   See *Lewis v Eliades* [2004] 1 All ER (Comm) 545 (CA), affirming [2003] 1 All ER (Comm) 850.
92   See also s 7, which provides for the reciprocal enforcement of foreign 'recoupment' judgments.
93   See *General Textiles v Sun and Sand Agencies* [1978] 1 QB 279.
94   See *Adams v Cape Industries* [1990] Ch 433.
95   (1927) 138 LT 386 at 392.
96   See *Copin v Adamson* (1874) LR 9 Ex 345; (1875) 1 ExD 17.

another judgment. Thus, under all three regimes, an external judgment will be refused recognition in so far as it is irreconcilable with an English judgment, regardless of the order in time in which the judgments were given.[97] Where the irreconcilable judgments are from different foreign countries, s 4(1)(b) of the 1933 Act gives preference to the earlier judgment by permitting the court addressed to set aside the registration of a judgment if it is satisfied that the matter in dispute in the proceedings in the original court had previously to the date of the judgment in the original court been the subject of a final judgment by a competent court. The position at common law, and under the 1920 Act, was for a long time obscure, but eventually in *Showlag v Mansour*[98] the analogy of the 1933 Act prevailed. There the Privy Council, on appeal from Jersey, faced with a conflict between an earlier English and a later Egyptian judgment, held that where there were two competing foreign judgments, each of which had been pronounced by a competent court and each of which was final and otherwise unimpeachable, then the earlier in time had to be recognised to the exclusion of the later, unless there were circumstances connected with the obtaining of the second judgment which made it unfair for the party relying on the first judgment to do so.

CONCLUSION

This chapter has examined the respect which is accorded in England to foreign judgments. The recognition and enforcement in England of foreign arbitral awards is among the matters considered in the next chapter.

FURTHER READING

Collins *et al* (eds), *Dicey, Morris and Collins on the Conflict of Laws*, 14th edn, 2006, Sweet & Maxwell, Chapters 14 and 15.

Stone, *EU Private International Law*, 2006, Edward Elgar.

---

97 See *Vervaeke v Smith* [1983] 1 AC 145; *Man v Haryanto* [1991] 1 Lloyd's Rep 429; s 9(1) of the 1920 Act; and s 4(1)(a)(v) and (b) of the 1933 Act.

98 [1995] 1 AC 431.

CHAPTER 19

ARBITRATION

INTRODUCTION

Since the Second World War, arbitration has proved an extremely popular method of resolving disputes. Arbitration, arguably, could be said to be the first step towards privatisation of justice, in that it is an alternative to resolution through national (state) courts. As such, parties opting for arbitration have greater control over matters such as the appointment of arbitrators, the language of the arbitration, and the place of arbitration, Equally, the principles to be applied to issues under consideration need not be tied to a national law, such as English law or French law. The issue could be decided on equitable principles (*ex aequo et bono*) or law merchant (*lex mercatoria*).[1] The characteristics of arbitration, including those that contribute to its continued popularity, are highlighted below. While listing the characteristics, some of the issues that have generated some discussion are also considered.

CHARACTERISTICS

First, in contrast to litigation, arbitration is the product of consent between the parties. The parties can make this agreement[2] either before or after the dispute has arisen. Generally, arbitration agreements are expressed in writing. Section 5 of the Arbitration Act 1996, for instance, requires the arbitration agreement[3] to be in writing,[4] though there is no requirement that it be signed.[5] The modern practice of electronic exchange of information, of course, raises the issue of whether an electronic document will suffice for the purposes of this section. Section 5(6) states that 'references in this Part [Part I] to anything being written or in writing include its being recorded by any means'. Presumably this will be construed to include electronic (paperless) documents.

---

1   Lando, '*Lex mercatoria* in international commercial arbitration' (1985) 34 ICLQ 747.

2   The agreement may also bind third parties who claim through the contracting parties. See *Astra SA Insurance and Reinsurance Co v Yasuda Fire and Marine Insurance Co* [1999] CLC 950.

3   Section 6(1) defines arbitration agreement as 'an agreement to submit to arbitration present or future disputes (whether they are contractual or not)'.

4   The Arbitration Act 1975 (the predecessor to the Arbitration Act 1996) in s 7(1) stated that an arbitration agreement means 'an agreement in writing (including an agreement contained in an exchange of letters or telegrams) to submit to arbitration present or future differences capable of settlement by arbitration'. This section has generated some discussion. According to O'Connor LJ in *Zambia Steel and Building Supplies Ltd v James Clark and Eaton Ltd* [1986] 2 Lloyd's Rep 225, p 232: '... for an agreement to be a written agreement to arbitrate it is unnecessary for the whole of the contract, including the arbitration agreement to be contained in the same document. It is sufficient that the arbitration agreement is itself in writing; indeed it is sufficient if there is a document which recognises the existence of an arbitration agreement between the parties'. See also *Abdullah M Fahem and Co v Mareb Yemen Insurance Co and Tomen (UK) Ltd* [1997] 2 Lloyd's Rep 738.

5   An oral agreement to arbitrate is recognised at common law. This is preserved by s 81 ('Saving for certain matters governed by common law'), which provides: '(1) Nothing in this Part shall be construed as excluding the operation of any rule of law consistent with the provisions of this Part [Part I], in particular, any rules of law as to ... (b) the effect of an oral arbitration agreement ...'

The arbitration agreement need not be expressed in a specific manner that includes the word 'arbitrate' or its variants. Of course, clear expression of the intention of the parties' agreement to submit a dispute to arbitration would help. The International Chamber of Commerce (ICC), which offers institutional arbitration and is a popular venue for international commercial arbitration, has devised rules for the conduct of arbitration and recommends the following clause should parties wish to submit to ICC arbitration:

> All disputes arising out of or in connection with the present contract shall be finally settled under the Rules of Arbitration of the International Chamber of Commerce by one or more arbitrators appointed in accordance with the said Rules.[6]

Similarly, the London Court of International Arbitration (LCIA) recommends the following clauses:[7]

> *For Future Disputes:*
>
> Any dispute arising out of or in connection with this contract, including any question regarding its existence, validity or termination, shall be referred to and finally resolved by arbitration under the LCIA Rules, which Rules are deemed to be incorporated by reference into this clause.
>
> The number of arbitrators shall be *[one/three]*.
>
> The seat, or legal place, of arbitration shall be *[City and/or Country]*.
>
> The language to be used in the arbitral proceedings shall be [   ].
>
> The governing law of the contract shall be the substantive law of [   ].
>
> *For Existing Disputes:*
>
> A dispute having arisen between the parties concerning [   ], the parties hereby agree that the dispute shall be referred to and finally resolved by arbitration under the LCIA Rules.
>
> The number of arbitrators shall be *[one/three]*.
>
> The seat, or legal place, of arbitration shall be *[City and/or Country]*.
>
> The language to be used in the arbitral proceedings shall be [   ].
>
> The governing law of the contract *[is/shall be]* the substantive law of [   ].

The Arbitration Act 1996 does not make any recommendations as to choice of words or clauses and leaves it to the parties to express their intention to submit their dispute to arbitration with a suitable choice of words. The issue of whether a contractual clause is an arbitration agreement is a matter of construction, as *David Wilson Homes Ltd v Survey Services Ltd*[8] indicates. The Court of Appeal had to decide whether the clause under examination was an arbitration agreement within s 6[9] of the Arbitration Act 1996. The clause read:

> ... any dispute or difference arising hereunder between the Assured and the Insurers shall be referred to the Queen's Counsel of the English Bar to be mutually agreed between the Insurers and the Assured or in the event of disagreement by the Chairman of the Bar Council.

---

6   *ICC Rules of Arbitration*, p 3. Available at www.iccwbo.org.
7   Available on www.lcia-arbitration.com.
8   [2001] EWCA Civ 34.
9   Section 6(1) reads: '... an "arbitration agreement" means an agreement to submit to arbitration present or future disputes (whether contractual or not)'.

The court concluded that the absence of the words 'arbitration' or 'arbitrator' did not make it a non-binding alternative dispute resolution (ADR) clause (*per* Simon Brown LJ, at para 22). The reference to Queen's Counsel indicated that the inquiry was to be a judicial inquiry, since 'that is what Queen's Counsel are normally expected to do when matters are referred to them, and all the more so if the formality of the position is such that, if there is disagreement as to the identity of the Queen's Counsel, he is to be appointed by the Chairman of the Bar' (*per* Longmore LJ, at para 14).

The arbitration agreement also determines whether the particular dispute is within the purview of arbitration or not. The issue is one of construction, the parties' intentions to be gathered from the expression. Clauses such as 'all disputes arising out of the contract or in connection with it' have been construed to include extra contractual claims.[10] Without question, the drafting skills of the lawyer are crucial to ensure that the intentions are adequately expressed and conveyed in the arbitration clause. As Jacobs observes:

> The law reports are replete with cases, both in regard to international and domestic arbitration clauses, interpreting them and giving meaning to phrases chosen by the draft persons, drawn sometimes entirely at random from an old precedent or the database of a word processor, without any thought being given to its probable meaning, or whether or not what it provides is what one or more of the parties intends to be arbitrated.
>
> The fault might lie with standard form contracts . . . where the balance of the document is attractive but the Arbitration Clause receives scant attention from the lawyers involved at the contract negotiation stage, and this fact comes back to haunt one or more of the parties with a substantial involvement in costs and delays in bringing the dispute to a speedy conclusion. In this manner, arbitration which should be speedy and relatively cost-effective, may sometimes get a bad name.[11]

Separability, that is, the treatment of arbitration as a distinct agreement, is another feature. This feature is recognised by s 7 of the Arbitration Act 1996,[12] which provides:

> Unless otherwise agreed by the parties, an arbitration agreement which forms or was intended to form part of another agreement (whether or not in writing) shall not be regarded as invalid, non-existent or ineffective because that other agreement is invalid, or did not come into existence or has become ineffective, and it shall for that purposes be treated as distinct agreement.

That the arbitration clause, when included in a contract, is to be treated as a distinct agreement was confirmed by the House of Lords in *Fiona Trust Holding Co v Privalov*.[13] The allegations of bribery in respect of the procurement of the eight charterparties did not affect the validity of the arbitration agreement (see para 7).

A second characteristic of arbitration is that the parties to the arbitration agreement have the freedom to choose the arbitrators, which means that the dispute is decided

---

10   See *Ashville Investments Ltd v Elmer Contractors* [1988] 2 Lloyd's Rep 73; *Ethiopian Oilseeds and Pulses Export Corp v Rio del Mar Foods Inc* [1990] 1 Lloyd's Rep 86; *El Nasharty v J Sainsbury plc* [2004] 1 Lloyd's Rep 309. See also *Fiona Trust & Holding Co v Privalov* [2008] 1 Lloyds Rep 254 (para 13).

11   'The jurisidiction of the International Commercial Arbitration Tribunal', a paper delivered to the London Court of International Arbitration Group, Sydney, 15 April 1997.

12   See *Harbour Assurance Co UK Ltd v Kansa General Insurance Co Ltd* [1992] 1 Lloyd's Rep 812; *Kalmneft JSC v Glencore International AG* [2002] 1 All ER 76; and *LG Caltex Gas Co Ltd v China National Petroleum Corp* [2001] BLR 235.

13   [2008] 1 Lloyd's Rep 254.

by people with specialised knowledge of a particular trade and commercial practice. This common framework of reference boosts the confidence and trust of businessmen in the proceedings and the resulting award, which is especially important in international commerce where parties come from different legal cultures. To have people of their own kind on the panel should disputes arise contributes to the willingness of businesses to engage in international trade.

While the parties have the freedom to choose the arbitrators, the courts have the power, under s 24 of the Arbitration Act 1996, to remove an arbitrator on application by a party to the arbitration tribunal, among other things, for lack of qualifications as required by the arbitration agreement[14] and justifiable doubts as to his impartiality.[15]

The parties are also free to formulate the procedures that are to be applied to the arbitration. In the absence of an agreement, s 33 of the Arbitration Act 1996[16] (if applicable) lays down the general duty of the tribunal to act impartially, giving each party a reasonable opportunity for putting his case and dealing with that of his opponent,[17] and to adopt suitable, but not slow or expensive, procedures for a fair means for the resolution of the matters falling to be determined. The parties are also free to agree on the procedure to be followed where the procedure to appoint an arbitration tribunal has failed. In the absence of an agreement the courts have the power to make appointments or revoke appointments under s 18[18] of the Arbitration Act 1996.

Thirdly, parties are free to choose institutional arbitration, such as arbitration in the ICC or LCIA. These institutions have devised procedures designed with the mercantile community in mind, thus contributing to the parties' confidence in the system.

Fourthly, parties have control over where and when arbitration takes place. This could contribute to the lowering of costs, since parties may not have to incur expenses for travel, accommodation and the renting of premises.

Fifthly, parties can keep the nature of their dispute private, since arbitrations are not conducted in public.[19] Arbitrations are (arguably) deemed confidential,[20] in that information disclosed in an arbitration cannot be disclosed to a third party. In other words, the confidentiality obligation is perceived to apply internally and externally. (It must be noted that privacy is lost should the parties decide to take their dispute to the courts.) The views on disclosure of the documents prepared for an arbitration to third parties vary. Some jurisdictions view confidentiality as distinct

---

14   See Arts 11 and 12 of the *ICC Rules on Arbitration* on challenge and replacement of arbitrators.

15   See *AT&T Corp v Saudi Cable Co* [2000] 1 Lloyd's Rep 22; *Rustal Trading Ltd v Gill and Dufus* [2000] 1 Lloyd's Rep 14.

16   There is a similar rule in the *ICC Rules of Arbitration*, which in Art 15(2) provides: 'In all cases, the Arbitration tribunal shall act fairly and impartially and ensure that each party has a reasonable opportunity to present its case.'

17   See 'Challenging arbitral awards', pp 638–42 below.

18   See *R Durtnell and Sons Ltd v The Secretary of State for Trade and Industry* [2001] 1 Lloyd's Rep 275.

19   Challenge of an arbitral award under s 68 of the Arbitration Act 1996 can be heard in private or in public according to Rule 62.10 of the Civil Procedure Rules. It does not follow on the basis of a private hearing that the judgment would *not be* public unless it raised highly sensitive issues, for instance in the political or commercial realm. See *Department of Economic Policy and Development of the City of Moscow v Banker's Trust Co Industrial Bank* [2004] 2 Lloyd's Rep 179.

20   See Smit, 'Confidentiality in arbitration' (1995) 11(3) Arbitration International 337.

from privacy, and doubt the view that privacy embodies confidentiality. For instance, in an Australian decision, *Esso Australia Resources Limited v Plowman*,[21] the High Court was of the opinion that a third party (not party to the arbitration) could discover information provided in an arbitration. Though the private nature of a hearing was an integral part of an arbitration, confidentiality was not, on the grounds that:

(a) witnesses were not subject to the confidentiality obligation;

(b) court proceedings relating to arbitration procedure would bring the information deemed confidential into the public sphere;

(c) disclosure of awards to third parties such as shareholders and insurers was commonplace.[22]

As for England, there seems to be no problem in maintaining the confidentiality of arbitral proceedings. In *Hassneh Insurance Co of Israel Ltd v Mew*,[23] the court had no hesitation in saying that documents prepared for an arbitration hearing could not be disclosed to a third party on the grounds that such disclosure would be equivalent to opening the doors of the arbitration room to a third party. According to Colman J:

> ... if the parties to an English law contract refer their disputes to arbitration they are entitled to assume at the least that the hearing will be conducted in private. That assumption arises from a practice which has been universal in London for hundreds of years and, I believe, undisputed. It is a practice which represents an important advantage of arbitration over the Courts as a means of dispute resolution. The informality attaching to a hearing held in private and the candour to which it may give rise is an essential ingredient of arbitration, so essential that if privacy were denied by an officious bystander, I have no doubt that, in the case of practically every arbitration agreement, both the parties would object.
>
> If it be correct that there is at least an implied term in every agreement to arbitrate that the hearing shall be held in private, the requirement of privacy must in principle extend to documents which are created for the purpose of that hearing ... The disclosure to a third party of such documents would be almost equivalent to opening the door of the arbitration room to that third party [at pp 246–47].

Does it follow that this duty of confidentiality is absolute and no exceptions are allowed? Even at the cost of injustice? It may, for instance, be necessary in some circumstances to submit documents deemed confidential to a court in order to protect an arbitrating party against a third party. The courts have acknowledged that there are indeed exceptions to this rule. These, as listed in a more recent case, *Ali Shipping Corp v Shipyard Trogir*,[24] are:

(a) disclosure by express or implied consent of the parties;

(b) order of disclosure by the court for the purposes of a later court action;

(c) disclosure where it is reasonably necessary for the protection of the legitimate interests of an arbitrating party; and

---

21 (1995) 128 ALR 291; (1995) 183 CLR 10.

22 See also *United States v Panhandle Eastern Corp* 118 FRD 346 (D Del 1988); *Samuels v Mitchell* 155 FRD 195 (ND Cal 1994).

23 [1993] 2 Lloyd's Rep 243.

24 [1998] 1 Lloyd's Rep 643, p 651; see also *Insurance Co v Lloyd's Syndicate* [1995] 1 Lloyd's Rep 272; *The 'Hamtun' and 'St John'* [1999] 1 Lloyd's Rep 883.

(d) disclosure for reasons of public interest[25] (interests of justice).[26]

In *Ali Shipping*, where the issue was whether confidential documents from an arbitration between the plaintiffs and the yard could be disclosed in a second arbitration between the yard and the buyers, the court came to the conclusion that convenience and good sense were insufficient to satisfy the test of reasonable necessity.[27]

The finality of arbitration awards means that time and money are not wasted on appeals through various courts (in England, the Court of Appeal and House of Lords) as in litigation. Judicial review of arbitral awards is possible on points of law, but the courts are economical in giving leave to appeal.[28]

The cost and speed of arbitration are often cited as advantages. This may not always be the case. Arbitrators with specialist expertise and experience – for example, in the construction industry or computer industry – are expensive. A dispute involving complex issues is likely to prolong arbitration and inflate costs if the arbitrators' fees are calculated on a daily basis. Despite popular belief, arbitrations are not necessarily speedy. Arbitrations involving intricate issues may last as long as court proceedings. Moreover, in an arbitration agreement, parties may need to resort to court proceedings where an issue of law needs clarification,[29] or where the issue involves a third party who is not subject to the arbitration agreement. Also, poor drafting of the arbitration clause that requires clarification may increase the costs and slow down the arbitral process.

The anational character of arbitration is often said to be an appealing feature since parties agree to apply *lex mercatoria* or equitable principles (*ex aequo et bono*).[30] On the other hand, recourse will be had to national law where there are gaps in the ICC's[31] or United Nations Commission on International Trade Law's (UNCITRAL) rules on arbitration. Moreover, courts, used for enforcing an arbitral award, may refuse to enforce the award in some circumstances. Similarly, the award may, in some circumstances, be subject to judicial review.

Lastly, arbitral awards need to be enforceable if arbitration is to play a meaningful role in the dispute resolution process. In international commerce, the issue is whether an award made in England is enforceable abroad, and whether an award made abroad is enforceable in England. A number of international conventions make the

---

25 The public interest exception was recognised in *London and Leeds Estates Ltd v Paribas (No 2)* [1995] 2 EG134.

26 Potter LJ, however, preferred the use of the phrase 'interests of justice' to 'public interest' in 'order to avoid the suggestion that use of the latter phrase is to be read as extending to the wide issues of public interest contested in the *Esso Australia* case': *Ali Shipping Corp v Shipyard Trogir* [1998] 1 Lloyd's Rep 643, at p 652.

27 *Ali Shipping Corp v Shipyard Trogir* [1998] 1 Lloyd's Rep 643, at p 654.

28 *Pioneer Shipping Ltd and Others v BTP Tioxide Ltd (The Nema)* [1981] 2 All ER 1030; see 'Challenging arbitral awards', pp 638–42 below.

29 Section 45(1) of the Arbitration Act 1996 provides that: '. . . unless otherwise agreed by the parties, the court may on the application of a party to arbitral proceedings (upon notice to the other parties) determine any question of law arising in the course of the proceedings which the court is satisfied substantially affects the rights of one or more of the parties'.

30 Carbonneau (ed), *Lex Mercatoria and Arbitration*, 1990, Transnational Jurist; Paulsson, 'Delocalisation of international commercial arbitration: when and why it matters' (1983) 32 ICLQ 53.

31 For instance, Art 15(1) of the *ICC Rules on Arbitration* provides: 'The proceedings before the Arbitral Tribunal shall be governed by these Rules, and, where these Rules are silent by any rules which the parties or, failing them, the Arbitral Tribunal may settle on, whether or not reference is thereby made to the rules of procedure of a national law to be applied to the arbitration.'

recognition and enforcement process relatively simple. Important among these conventions is the New York Convention on Recognition and Enforcement of Arbitral Awards,[32] adhered to by well over 100 states.

ARBITRATION IN INTERNATIONAL COMMERCIAL CONTRACTS

Arbitration clauses are most common in international commerical contracts, and arbitration is expected to play more of a central role as a result of globalisation.[33] Parties may opt for institutional arbitration offered by national or international institutions, or *ad hoc* arbitration.

Institutional arbitration

The American Arbitration Association (AAA)[34] and the Nederland Arbitrage Instituut (NAI) are perhaps the better known national institutions offering services in the area of commercial arbitration. At the international level, the ICC and the LCIA have a well established worldwide reputation. Recently established arbitration institutions, such as the Australian Centre for International Commercial Arbitration (ACICA)[35] and the Australian Commercial Disputes Centre (ACDC), are also emerging as serious contenders in the provision of arbitration services in the Asia-Pacific region. Organisations such as Grain and Feed Association (GAFTA),[36] Federation of Oils, Seeds and Fats Associations (FOSFA)[37] and the London Maritime Arbitration Associations also provide arbitration facilities for commodities' trade and maritime disputes.

Use of institutional arbitration offers a number of advantages:

(a) *Set procedural rules.* For example, the AAA, LCIA and ICC have specific rules to address procedural issues such as the appointment of arbitrators and the language of the arbitration in the absence of any indication by the parties. The ICC, for instance, on 8 April 1997, adopted a revised version of *Rules of Arbitration* which came into effect on 1 January 1998.[38] The new rules introduce a number of changes: for example, according to Art 1, disputes of both national and international character may now be held under the auspices of the ICC; parties may, under Art 32, modify the time limits set by the rules while preserving the ICC court's power to extend deadlines on its own initiative where appropriate. The arbitral tribunal, under Art 22, must declare the proceedings closed once parties have had a reasonable opportunity to present their cases. On such a declaration,

---

32 See 'Foreign arbitral awards', pp 644–8 below.
33 See Wetter, 'The internationalization of international arbitration: looking ahead to the next 10 years' (1995) 11(2) Arbitration International 117.
34 www.adr.org.
35 www.acica.com.au.
36 www.gafta.com.
37 www.fosfa.org.
38 A new edition was produced in 2001. Apart from correcting typographical and grammatical errors in the first edition, and for the sake of consistency with the French version of the Rules, in the second sentence of Art 2(9) of Appendix III the words 'are expected' have been replaced by 'have a duty'. The text of this document is available on www.iccwbo.org.

further information can be submitted only at the request of the tribunal, or with the authority of the tribunal. The new rules obviously have been devised to reflect flexibility and reduce delay.

(b) *Handling administrative matters.* For example, assistance with establishing dates, time, venue.

(c) *Wide-ranging experience.* For example, the ICC has offered international commercial arbitration services for over 75 years.[39]

(d) *Scrutiny of arbitral awards.* For example, where the ICC Arbitration Rules apply, the tribunal is required to submit to the International Court of Arbitration of the ICC the award in draft form for its approval. The court may lay down modifications as to the form of the award, and may also draw its attention to points of substance without affecting the tribunal's liberty of decision (Art 27).

(e) Some institutions (for example, the ICC) fix arbitrators' remuneration and administrative costs within a scale providing the parties with a general idea about the likely cost of the arbitration. For instance, according to the *ICC Rules of Arbitration 1998*, where the sum in dispute is not in excess of $US50,000, administrative costs are fixed at $US2,500 and the arbitrator's fee between the minimum of $US2,500 and a maximum of 17% (that is, $US8,500). The actual amount payable to the arbitrator will be arrived at by taking into account the complexity of the dispute, the time spent, the rapidity of the proceedings and the diligence of the arbitrator according to Art 2 of Appendix III to the *ICC Rules of Arbitration*.

Brief mention must also be made of another important institution that provides arbitration and conciliation facilities – the International Centre for Settlement of Investment Disputes (ICSID).[40] Brought into existence as a result of the convention on the Settlement of Investment Disputes between States and Nationals of Other States 1965,[41] its focus, as can be gathered from the title of the convention, is investment disputes between states and foreign investors from contracting states. While having close links with the World Bank, it is an autonomous organisation with its headquarters in Washington DC.

The march of globalisation has inevitably seen an increase in the number of cases submitted to the ICSID. As with other types of arbitration, parties' submission to the ICSID arbitration is voluntary. As for recognition and enforcement of ICSID arbitral awards, contracting states are required under the convention to recognise and enforce such awards. Given the nature of the focus of ICSID, it does not impinge on commercial contracts for the sale of goods between two parties, and hence an examination of ICSID arbitration rules is beyond the scope of this book.

Ad hoc arbitration

Unlike institutional arbitration, no administration costs are payable in an *ad hoc* arbitration (that is, non-institutional arbitration), thus making it an attractive option.

---

39   According to the *ICC International Court of Arbitration Bulletin* (Vol 7(1):3), in 1995, the ICC received in excess of 400 new requests for arbitration to be held in more than 30 countries.

40   Visit www.worldbank.org/icsid for further information and documentation.

41   The convention came into force on 14 October 1966; and as of September 2004, 154 states are contracting parties to the convention. It was implemented in the United Kingdom by the Arbitration (International Investment Disputes) Act 1966.

However, this type of arbitration does not provide the advantages found in institutional arbitration. In the absence of institution drafted rules, parties need to draft their own procedural rules or fall back on the arbitration rules found in the national law of the seat of arbitration (if available). In the case of England, this is the Arbitration Act 1996. English arbitration law is well established, since London has a long history of 'being the hub of international commerce, a clearing house for the financial, legal and other concomitants of world trade'.[42] Parties are free, however, to incorporate rules designed by institutions, such as those of the ICC, though these may not always meet the requirements of the parties. A better alternative would be to adopt the arbitration rules devised by UNCITRAL, which does not provide arbitration services but whose rules provide certain safeguards in the event of a stalemate. For instance, if the parties are unable to reach agreement on the appointment of an arbitrator, Art 6(2) of the UNCITRAL Arbitration Rules provides that:

> . . . if within 30 days after receipt by a party of a proposal made in accordance with para 1 the parties have not reached agreement on the choice of a sole arbitrator, the sole arbitrator shall be appointed by the appointing authority agreed upon by the parties. If no appointing authority has been agreed upon by the parties, or if the appointing authority agreed upon refuses to act or fails to appoint the arbitrator within 60 days of the receipt of a party's request therefor, either party may request the Secretary General of the Permanent Court of Arbitration at The Hague to designate an appointing authority.

ARBITRATION UNDER ENGLISH LAW

The law relating to arbitration, until fairly recently (that is, with the enactment of the Arbitration Act 1996), was dispersed amongst three statutes – the Arbitration Act 1950, the Arbitration Act 1975, and the Arbitration Act 1979. The Arbitration Act 1950 was the main statute containing procedural rules relating to, for instance, the appointment of arbitrators, appointment of umpires and the removal of arbitrators. The Arbitration Act 1975 gave effect to the United Nations Convention on the Enforcement of Foreign Arbitral Awards 1958, and the Act of 1979 addressed judicial review of the arbitral award.

Impetus for the new legislation on arbitration came from the Departmental Advisory Committee that studied UNCITRAL's Model Law on International Commercial Arbitration 1985[43] with a view to adopting it into English law. While rejecting the suitability of adopting the Model Law, the Committee proposed that a new Act should be enacted that was 'user-friendly' and accessible to those familiar with the Model Law. This was to ensure that London still maintained its international reputation as an arbitration centre. As Saville LJ observed:

---

42 Sir Laurence Street in Tackaberry (ed), *International Commercial Arbitration for Today and Tomorrow*, 1991, p 226.

43 The Model Law was designed to harmonise arbitral procedure rules for the facilitation of international commerce. See Sanders, 'Unity and diversity in the adoption of the Model Law' (1995) 11 Arbitration International 1; Hotzmann and Neuhaus, *A Guide to the UNCITRAL Model Law on International Commercial Arbitration*, 1989, Kluwer; Broches, *Commentary on the UNCITRAL Model Law on International Commercial Arbitration*, 1990, Kluwer. Visit www.uncitral.org, which maintains a database of cases decided in countries that have adopted the Model Law. See also Steyn, 'England's response to the UNCITRAL Model Law on Arbitration' (1994) 10(1) Arbitration International 1.

User unfriendliness is a serious problem. London is still the leading world centre for arbitration. Far more often than not, in international trade and commerce, the only connection the parties have with this country is their agreement to arbitrate disputes here. It is in the interests of this country to promote our expertise in this field and to encourage parties to use arbitration here. The direct and indirect benefits are very large indeed, not just in the form of direct foreign exchange earnings (though these are very substantial), but as a significant selling point for City services generally.

There are, however, plenty of competitors, ready, willing and anxious to attract arbitrations to their jurisdictions so as to reap these benefits for themselves. Many countries have already adopted the Model Law or otherwise brought their arbitration procedures up to date. We cannot just sit on our existing reputation. The world moves on and to survive we must move with it. The fact is that 10 years have passed since the Model Law without this country improving its statutory framework with regard to arbitration. This is not a good advertisement for us; indeed it is calculated to make us very much second best in the world at large unless we can do something very quickly.[44]

In 1994, the Department of Trade and Industry published a Bill in its consultative paper, which, with amendments, received the Royal Assent in 1996 and came into force on 31 January 1997. The object of the Arbitration Act 1996 is to give greater autonomy to the parties and to aid a fair resolution of the disputes without unnecessary delay or expense. The general principles on which this legislation is based (as expressed in s 1) are:

(a) to obtain the fair resolution of disputes by an impartial tribunal without unnecessary delay or expense;

(b) to impart freedom to the parties to agree on how their disputes are resolved, subject only to those safeguards necessary in the public interest; and

(c) to restrict the extent of intervention by courts to matters specified in the Act.

The Arbitration Act 1996 is triggered when the seat of the arbitration is in England and Wales or Northern Ireland (s 2(1)). The seat of the arbitration is defined in s 3(1) as the juridical seat of the arbitration which has been designated:

(a) by the parties to the arbitration agreement; or

(b) by any arbitral or other institution or other person vested by the parties with powers in this regard; or

(c) by the arbitral tribunal if so authorised by the parties, or determined, in the absence of any such designation, having regard to the parties' agreement and all relevant circumstances.

The existence of a seat is central to arbitration under English law; it does not recognise the concept of an arbitration which has no seat.[45] Floating arbitration (that is, an arbitration that has no attachment to the law of a state or territory) is not recognised under English law.[46] In most cases, the venue (that is, physical location) of the arbitration tribunal and the seat of the arbitration will coincide. However, where proceedings take place in more than one location, or move to another location, the seat will

---

44 'The Denning Lecture 1995: Arbitration and the Courts' (1995) 61 Arbitration 159.

45 Departmental Advisory Committee on Arbitration Law, *Report on the Arbitration Bill*, 1996, HMSO, para 27.

46 See Mayer, 'The trend towards delocalisation in the last 100 years', in Hunter, Marriot and Veeder (eds), *The Internationalization of International Arbitration*, 1995, Graham & Trotman.

have to be established. Where neither the parties to the arbitration agreement nor any arbitral or other institutions have designated the seat of the arbitration, the task of establishing a seat taking into account *all the relevant circumstances* can be complex, as *Dubai Islamic Bank Pjsc v Paymentech Merchant Services Inc*[47] illustrates. The dispute between the plaintiff (a bank based in Dubai) and the respondent (credit card payment processing centre based in Texas, US) concerned the liability of the bank under a Visa card transaction. The two parties went through the Visa arbitration stages as provided for by the Visa regulations. The final stage (stage three) was the appeal process, to be dealt with by the Visa International Board acting as the appeal authority. The bank appealed against the decision given in favour of Paymentech to the International Board, which dismissed the appeal in a meeting that took place on 9 May 1999 in London. The bank then appealed against the appeal award, seeking relief under ss 67, 68 and 69 of the Arbitration Act 1996.[48] The primary issue for the court was whether the seat of the arbitration was in England and Wales. The bank argued that the seat was in England on the basis of the Visa International Board meeting in London. Other than this, the connections to England were: the original agreement concluded in England between the bank and Visa; the point of contact between the bank and Visa through the Visa centre based at Basingstoke; and the request for authorisation which would have originated from Basingstoke. Construing *all relevant circumstances* to mean taking into account any 'connections with one or more particular countries that could be identified in relation to (i) the parties; (ii) the dispute which will be the subject of the arbitration; (iii) the proposed procedures in the arbitration, including (if known) the place of interlocutory and final hearings; and (iv) the issue of awards',[49] the court held that the seat was not in England. A number of factors contributed to this conclusion: Visa was based in California; the worldwide payment card scheme headquarters were in California; the Visa regulations contemplated the appeal process as being handled in California; and the notification of the appeal process result was to be handled by the Visa headquarters in California. As for the hearing in London, it was purely accidental, since it was not within the contemplation of the parties that the appeal process would necessarily be heard in London.

The Arbitration Act 1996 empowers the parties to an arbitration with control over the proceedings. In keeping with this, the parties' freedom is wide ranging. It covers agreement on the number of arbitrators to form the tribunal, the procedure for appointment of arbitrators, the consequences on failure of the appointment procedure, the consequences of the resignation of an arbitrator, the filling of vacancies created by the resignation or death of an arbitrator, and the competence of the tribunal to rule on its own jurisdiction.[50] The Act lists, in Sched I, mandatory provisions from which the parties cannot agree to derogate. These, according to para 4(1) of Sched I, are:

(a) the stay of legal proceedings (ss 9–11);

(b) the power of the court to extend time limits (s 12);

---

47 [2001] 1 Lloyd's Rep 65.
48 See 'Challenging arbitral awards', pp 638–42 below.
49 [2001] 1 Lloyd's Rep 65, at p 74.
50 See ss 15–18, 27 and 30. See *R Durtnell and Sons Ltd v The Secretary of State for Trade and Industry* [2001] 1 Lloyd's Rep 275.

(c) the application of the Limitation Acts – that is, the Limitation Act 1980 and the Foreign Limitation Periods Act 1984 (s 13);

(d) the power of the court to remove an arbitrator (s 24);

(e) the effect of the death of an arbitrator (s 26(1));

(f) the liability of the parties for arbitrators' fees and expenses (s 28);

(g) the immunity of the arbitrator (s 29);

(h) objection to the substantive jurisdiction of the tribunal (s 31);

(i) determination of preliminary points of jurisdiction (s 32);

(j) the general duty of the tribunal (s 33);

(k) items to be treated as expenses of arbitrators (s 37(2));

(l) the general duty of the parties (s 40);

(m) securing the attendance of witnesses (s 43);

(n) the power to withhold the award in case of non-payment (s 56);

(o) the effectiveness of agreement of payment of costs in any event (s 60);

(p) enforcement of the award (s 66);

(q) challenging the award: substantive jurisdiction and serious irregularity (ss 67 and 68),[51] supplementary provisions, effect of order of court so far as relating to those sections (ss 70 and 71);

(r) saving for rights of persons who take no part in the proceedings (s 72);

(s) loss of the right to object (s 73);

(t) immunity of arbitral institutions (s 74); and

(u) a charge to secure payment of solicitors' costs (s 75).

Other than severability,[52] another important feature of the Arbitration Act 1996 is the recognition of the doctrine of *Kompetenz-Kompetenz* – that is, the power of the tribunal to rule on its own substantive jurisdiction. Unless agreed otherwise by the parties, s 30 enables the tribunal to rule on its own jurisdiction in respect of a number of matters – for example, the validity of an arbitration agreement,[53] the question of the proper constitution of the tribunal – and to determine what matters have been submitted to arbitration in accordance with the arbitration agreement. Of course, the jurisdiction of the arbitrator can be challenged under s 67 of the Arbitration Act 1996, provided the right to object is not lost under s 73.[54]

---

51 See *Paterson Farms Inc v C&M Farming Ltd* [2004] 1 Lloyd's Rep 603 on the issue of arbitrator's jurisdiction to award damages for 'parent losses' on the basis of 'group of companies' doctrine.

52 See 'Characteristics', pp 623–9 above; s 7 of the Arbitration Act 1996.

53 See *LG Caltex Gas Co Ltd v China National Petroleum Corp* [2001] 2 All ER (Comm) 97, confirming that s 30 gives the power to the arbitrator to rule on his own jurisdiction in the absence of agreement to the contrary. See also Goodwin, '*Ad hoc* agreements and the Arbitration Act 1996: the *LG Caltex* case' (2002) International Arbitration LR 15. See also *Kalmneft JSC v Glencore International AG* [2002] 1 All ER 76, where the court decided that even in the event of an overlap of facts relating to jurisdiction and substantive issues, the arbitrator could rule on his jurisdiction as a preliminary matter since it was efficient in terms of cost and time. See also *People's Insurance Company of China, Hebei Branch (2) China National Feeding Stuff Import/Export Corp v Vysanthi Shipping Co Ltd (The 'Joanna V')* [2003] 2 Lloyd's Rep 617.

54 See 'Challenging arbitral awards', pp 638–42 below.

Applicable substantive law

One of the issues that needs to be tackled in a non-domestic arbitration is what law the tribunal must apply to the contract.[55] According to s 46 of the Arbitration Act 1996:

(1) The tribunal shall decide the dispute:

    (a) in accordance with the law chosen by the parties as applicable to the substance of the dispute; or

    (b) if the parties so agree, in accordance with such other considerations as are agreed by them or determined by the tribunal.

(2) . . .

(3) If or to the extent that there is no such choice or agreement, the tribunal shall apply the law determined by the conflict of laws rules which it considers applicable.

From the above provisions, it is clear that the tribunal will apply the law chosen by the parties. There is no problem where parties have expressly chosen the law of a state to apply to the substance of the dispute. It is much less clear, however, whether s 46(1)(a) also admits of implied choice. Prior to the 1996 Act, a London arbitration clause was regarded by the English courts as a very strong indication of an implied choice of English law as the proper law of the contract, and the advent of the Rome Convention 1980 had not altered the position.[56] Unfortunately, the 1996 Act leaves it unclear whether such an implication remains operative under s 46(1)(a), or whether the existence of such an implied choice is to be remitted to the conflict rules which the arbitrator considers applicable under s 46(3). Probably the former law remains unchanged on this point, in view of the ambiguous wording of s 46 and the absence of a weakening of the widespread commercial expectations that a London arbitration clause normally implies a choice of English substantive law.

What if the parties have agreed to apply either 'internationally accepted principles of law governing contractual relations' or *lex mercatoria* (merchant law), or have authorised the arbitrator to decide the issues *ex aequo et bono* – that is, to be guided by notions of justice and fairness? (Where the choice is *ex aequo et bono*, the arbitrator takes a lenient view of legal rules, but cannot totally disregard them.) Are awards decided under these conditions acceptable and enforceable? It seems from the decided cases that there would be no problems where internationally accepted principles of law governing contractual relations are applied. In *Deutsche Schachtbau-und Tiefbohrgesells-chaft mbH v Ras al-Khaima National Oil Co*,[57] the enforcement under the New York Convention[58] of an award decided on the basis of such principles was allowed. The situation with *lex mercatoria* (a transnational system of law) may be different, but the wording of s 46(1) is wide enough to accommodate it. Commercial law in England has always taken mercantile custom into account, so why not the law merchant?

As for the arbitrator deciding *ex aequo et bono*, decisions before the 1996 Act were often hostile. In *Orion Compania Española de Sefuros v Belfort Maatschappij voor Algemene Verzekgringeen*,[59] according to Megaw J:

---

55 See Chukwumerije, 'Applicable substantive law in international commercial arbitration' (1994) Anglo-Am LR 265.

56 See Chapters 16 and 17.

57 [1987] 3 WLR 1023 (CA).

58 See 'Foreign arbitral awards', pp 644–8 below.

59 [1962] 2 Lloyd's Rep 257.

... in the conduct of arbitrations, arbitrators must in general apply a fixed and recognisable system of law, which primarily and normally would be the law of England, and that they cannot be allowed to apply some different criterion such as the view of the individual arbitrator in abstract justice or equitable principles [at p 264].

But other cases, such as *Eagle Star Insurance v Yuval Insurance Co*[60] and *Home and Overseas Insurance v Mentor Insurance*,[61] support resort to equitable principles. Moreover, s 46(1)(b) states that the arbitration tribunal can decide the issue in accordance with other considerations, and these must surely include equitable principles. Further, it must be remembered that one of the reasons for drafting the new legislation was to maintain London as a centre for arbitration in the face of competition from countries that have adopted the UNCITRAL Model Law on International Commercial Arbitration. Support for the view that the Model Law should be taken into account when interpreting the Arbitration Act 1996 can be found in a number of cases, such as *Jitendra Bhailbhai Patel v Dilesh R Patel*,[62] where the court said that 'the terms of the UNCITRAL Model Law on International Commercial Arbitration should be taken into account because it is clear that those responsible for drafting the Act had the provisions in mind when doing so' (at p 325). The Model Law allows for the possibility of arbitrators deciding *ex aequo et bono* or as *amiables compositeurs*, under Art 28(3) which states: 'The arbitral tribunal shall decide *ex aequo et bono* or as *amiable compositeur* only if the parties have expressly authorised it to do so.'

Absent choice, under s 46(3), the tribunal will determine the law applicable to the contract on the basis of the conflicts of law rules which it regards as appropriate. As stated earlier, the common law rules on determining the proper law of the contract have been largely supplanted by the Contracts (Applicable Law) Act 1990.[63] Although Art 1(2) of the Rome Convention specifically excludes arbitration agreements from its scope, it is clear that this relates only to the validity and interpretation of the arbitration clause itself, and to its potential effect in preventing judicial litigation. The Convention remains applicable in determining the proper law of a contract which contains an arbitration clause, and the arbitration clause must be taken into account under the Convention in determining the proper law of the contract by reference to implied choice or closest connection.[64] However, as we have seen, it is possible to read s 46(1)(a) as confined to an express choice of law, so that s 46(3) would leave the significance of an arbitration clause in determining the proper law to the conflict rules considered applicable by the arbitrator. On that basis the Rome Convention might not apply, and less weight might be given to a London arbitration clause if the parties are from New York and New South Wales, and the conflict rules of those jurisdictions agree, for example, that where the seller must deliver the goods in his own country, a clause specifying arbitration elsewhere is of little importance in determining the proper law.

Where arbitration is conducted under the *ICC Arbitration Rules*, the parties have a wide choice. According to Art 17(1), the parties are free to determine the rules of law

---

60   [1978] 1 Lloyd's Rep 357.
61   [1989] 1 Lloyd's Rep 473. See also *Channel Tunnel Group v Balfour Beatty* [1993] AC 334.
62   [1999] 3 WLR 322. See also *Westacre Investments Inc v Jugoimport-SPDR Holding Co Ltd* [1998] 4 All ER 570; Shackleton, 'English arbitration and international practice' (2002) 5(2) International Arbitration LR 67.
63   For Rome I which will come into effect in the UK in December 2009, see Chapter 17.
64   See Art 1(2) Rome I. For further on Rome I see Chapter 17.

to be applied to the merits of the dispute. The emphasis on rules of law suggests that the parties need not choose the law of a state but may agree for a body of law such as *lex mercatoria* (law merchant) to be applied. In the absence of agreement, the arbitral tribunal will apply rules that it determines are appropriate. Even where the parties have agreed to the application of a national law, the tribunal will take account of the contract provisions and the relevant trade usages (Art 17(2)). If the parties agree, Art 17(3) allows the arbitral tribunal to assume the powers of *amiables compositeurs*, or to decide *ex aequo et bono*.

Similar provisions on the law applicable to the dispute are also found in the UNCITRAL Arbitration Rules. Article 33 of these Rules provides that:

(1) The arbitration tribunal shall apply the law designated by the parties as applicable to the substance of the dispute. Failing such designation, the arbitral tribunal shall apply the law determined by the conflict of laws rules which it considers applicable.

(2) The arbitral tribunal shall decide as *amiable compositeur* or *ex aequo et bono* only if the parties have expressly authorised the arbitral tribunal to do so and if the law applicable to the arbitral procedure permits such arbitration.

(3) In all cases, the arbitral tribunal shall decide in accordance with the terms of the contract and shall take into account the usages of the trade applicable to the transaction.

Stay of court proceedings

It is possible that, despite an arbitration agreement, one of the parties initiates court proceedings. The question, in these circumstances, is whether the party who wishes to proceed to arbitration can stop the proceedings that have been initiated in court. According to s 9(1) of the Arbitration Act 1996, a party may, on notice to the other party, apply to the court for a grant of stay. The court will grant a stay of court proceedings unless:

(a) the arbitration agreement is null and void; or

(b) the arbitration agreement is inoperative; or

(c) the arbitration agreement is incapable of being performed (s 9(4)).[65]

An application for a stay, according to s 9(3), 'may not be made by a person before taking the appropriate procedural step (if any) to acknowledge the legal proceedings against or after he has taken any step in those proceedings to answer the substantive claim'. What constitutes an appropriate procedural step for the purposes of s 9(3) was examined in *Capital Trust Investment Ltd v Radio Design AB and Others*.[66] The defendant (Radio Design) made an application for a stay in December 1999; and in February 2000, the application was amended to refer expressly to s 9 and to make the assertion that it had not taken any step in the action, such as filing a defence to answer the substantial claim. In May 2000, before the hearing of the application, a further application notice was issued by the defendant in which it stated that an application

---

65 See *Halki Shipping Corp v Sopex Oils Ltd* [1998] 1 Lloyd's Rep 465; *Ahmad Al-Naimi v Islamis Press Agency Inc* [2000] 1 Lloyd's Rep 522. See also *Atlanska Plovidba v Consignaciones Asturianas SA (The Lapad)* [2004] 2 Lloyd's Rep 219.

66 [2002] EWCA Civ 135.

for stay had been made and 'in the event its application for a stay was unsuccessful [Radio Design] applies for a summary judgment against the claimant' (at paras 58 and 59). The court, taking into consideration case law[67] decided before the Arbitration Act 1996 and citing statements from commentaries on the 1996 Act approved in an earlier decision,[68] concluded that the application for the summary judgment, which stood only in the event that the application for a stay was not successful, was not an appropriate procedural step. In other words, the application did not 'express the willingness of Radio Design to go along with a determination of the courts instead of arbitration'; instead it was 'specifically seeking a stay' (at para 60).

Challenging arbitral awards

By giving the parties greater control over the arbitration process, the role of the court is substantially reduced by the Arbitration Act 1996. Nonetheless, it is possible to challenge the arbitral award on a point of law, for serious irregularity and for failure of substantive jurisdiction.

Point of law

The Arbitration Act 1996 draws a distinction between reasoned awards (that is, where the arbitrator provides reasons for his awards) and awards lacking reasons. Where parties have agreed to dispense with reasons, it is an agreement to exclude the court's jurisdiction over review of an arbitration award (s 69(1)). Reasoned awards may, on notice to the other parties and the tribunal, be reviewed by the courts on a question of law. In other words, questions on principles of law, such as whether there is frustration,[69] or whether certain terms can be implied into a contract,[70] may be reviewed by the courts.

Under s 69(2), an appeal to the court may be brought:

(a) with the consent of all the other parties to the proceedings; or

(b) with the leave of the court.

According to s 69(3), leave will be granted only where the court is satisfied that:

(a) the determination of the question of law concerned could substantially affect the rights of one or more parties to the arbitration agreement;

(b) the question is one which the tribunal was asked to determine;

(c) on the basis of the finding of fact in the award, the decision of the tribunal on the question is obviously wrong; or

(d) the question is one of general public importance and the decision of the tribunal is open to doubt; and

---

67   See *Kuwait Airways Corp v Iraq Airways Corp* [1994] 1 Lloyd's Rep 276.

68   *Per* Otton LJ in *Jitendra Bhailbhai Patel v Dilesh R Patel* [2000] QB 551, p. 558.

69   *Pioneer Shipping Ltd and Others v BTP Tioxide Ltd (The Nema)* [1981] 2 All ER 1030. See *The Agios Dimitrios* [2005] 1 Lloyd's Rep 23 at p 25 where the approach to s 69 appeal on question of law was no different from *The Nema*.

70   *Islamic Republic of Iran Shipping Lines v The Royal Bank of Scotland (The Anna Ch)* [1987] 1 Lloyd's Rep 226.

(e) despite the agreement to resolve the matter by arbitration, it is just and proper in all the circumstances for the court to determine the question.

Further, the right to appeal is subject to the provisions contained in s 73 and s 70(2). According to s 70(2), the applicant has first to exhaust any available arbitral process or review, or any available recourse for correction of an award or additional award, under s 57. Under s 73, a party will lose his right to object if he continues to take part in the arbitral proceedings without making his objections known within the stipulated time. The appeal must be brought within 28 days of the date of the award, according to s 70(3). In the event of arbitral process of review of the award, the 28 days is counted from the date when the party was notified of the result of the process.

The provisions in respect of granting leave to appeal are restrictive and reflect the sentiments expressed in the leading case, *Pioneer Shipping Ltd and Others v BTP Tioxide Ltd (The Nema)*,[71] decided under the old legislation (the Arbitration Act 1979). The judicial expressions in this case are still relevant; and as David Steel J observed, the limitations expounded in *The Nema* and reaffirmed in *The Antaios* (see p 640 below) were given statutory form in s 69 of the Arbitration Act 1996.[72] In *The Nema*, the House of Lords said that the courts should be economical in giving leave to appeal. In their guidelines, their Lordships drew a distinction between a one-off clause (for example, an individually negotiated clause) and standard terms, and suggested that in the former, leave should not normally be given, unless the judge is convinced that the decision of the arbitrator was obviously wrong. As for the latter, leave must be given more freely, since the term under consideration could affect like transactions amongst other parties. As Lord Diplock said:

> . . . where . . . the question of law involved is the construction of a one-off clause the application of which to the particular facts of the case is an issue in the arbitration, leave should not normally be given unless it is apparent to the judge, on a mere perusal of the reasoned award itself without the benefit of the adversarial argument, that the meaning ascribed to the clause by the arbitrator is obviously wrong; but if on such perusal it appears to the judge that it is possible that argument might persuade, despite impression to the contrary, that the arbitrator might be right, he should not grant leave; the parties should be left to accept, for better or worse, the decision of the tribunal that they had chosen to decide the matter in the first instance . . .

> . . . less strict criteria are, in my view, appropriate where questions of construction of contracts in standard terms are concerned. That there should be a high degree of legal certainty as it is practicable to obtain as to how such terms apply on the occurrence of events of a kind that is not unlikely may reproduce themselves in transactions between other parties engaged in the same trade is a public interest that is recognised by the 1979 Act, particularly in s 4. So, if the decision of the question of construction in the circumstances of a particular case would add significantly to the clarity and certainty of English commercial law it would be proper to give leave in a case sufficiently substantial to escape the ban imposed by the first part of s 1(4), bearing in mind always that a superabundance of citable judicial decisions arising out of slightly different facts is calculated to hinder rather than to promote clarity in settled principles of commercial law. But leave should not be given, even in such a case, unless the judge considered that a strong *prima facie* case had been made out that the arbitrator had been wrong in his construction; and when the events to which the standard clause fell to be applied in the particular arbitration were themselves one off events stricter criteria should be applied

---

71 [1981] 2 All ER 1030.
72 *Mousaka Inc v Golden Seagull Maritime Inc and Another* [2001] 2 Lloyd's Rep 657.

on the same lines as those that I have suggested as appropriate to one-off clauses [at pp 1039–40].

The guidelines set out in *The Nema* were not meant to be rigid, and the courts may adapt them to suit the circumstances. As Lord Diplock stated in *The Antaios*:[73]

> From the general guidelines stated in *The Nema*, I see, as yet, no reason for departing. Like all guidelines on how judicial discretion should be exercised they are not intended to be all-embracing or immutable, but subject to adaptation to match changes in practices when these occur or to refinement to meet problems of kinds that were not foreseen, and are not covered by, what was said by this House in *The Nema* [at p 200].

Where a point of European Community law needs to be referred to the European Court of Justice, leave to appeal will be given more readily. Only tribunals or courts (and not arbitrators) can refer the matter to the Court under Art 177 of the EC Treaty.[74]

As stated in s 69(1), it is possible to appeal on a question of law.[75] But which law? According to s 82(1), 'question of law' means 'for a court in England and Wales, a question of the law of England and Wales'. In *Reliance Industry Ltd v Enron Oil and Gas India Ltd*,[76] the court had to decide whether the application by the arbitrators, with the agreement of the parties, of principles of construction under English law which were the same as the principles of construction under Indian law (the proper law of the contract agreed to by the parties) was an application of English law for the purposes of s 69. Aikens J concluded that the arbitrator had applied the proper law of the contract, which according to the agreement was Indian law. It was purely incidental that the principles of construction were the same in English law and in Indian law. He illustrated his point thus:

> The point can be tested by imagining a contract governed by a foreign law and, as in the present case, before the arbitrators (sitting in London), the foreign law and English law were agreed to be the same. Imagine that the arbitrators issued their award applying the foreign law as agreed. Both parties agreed that, on the facts as found, the legal result must be as the arbitrators had determined. Then imagine the House of Lords subsequently declared that English law was different. But the advice of experts was that the foreign law remained as the English law had previously been declared. In that case leave to appeal under s 69 of the 1996 Act on a question of law could not be given. There would be 'no question of the law of England and Wales arising out of [the] award in the proceedings' because the award had stated accurately and applied correctly the foreign law that governed the contracts [at p 650].[77]

The court does not give reasons for its refusal to grant leave to appeal and there is no requirement that it does. Given the all-pervasive applicability of the Human Rights

---

73 [1985] AC 191.

74 *Bulk Oil (Zug) AG v Sun International Ltd (No 1)* [1983] 2 Lloyd's Rep 587; Case 102/81: *Nordsee Deutsche Hochseefischerei GmbH v Reederei Mond Hochseefischerei Nordstern AG and Co KG* [1982] ECR 1095, p 1111.

75 See *BR Cantrell, EP Cantrell v Wright & Fuller Ltd* [2003] EWCA Civ 1565.

76 [2002] 1 Lloyd's Rep 645. In *Sanghi Polyesters Ltd (India) v The International Investor (KCFC) Kuwait* [2000] 1 Lloyd's Rep 480, the applicable law was English law 'except to the extent it may conflict with Shari'a law, which shall prevail'. The court held that in deciding the extent to which the Shari'a law applied to various contracts the arbitrator was not applying English law.

77 Of course, s 46 on rules applicable to the substance of the dispute is itself part of English law. Thus appeal is possible on the ground that the arbitrator misconstrued or misapplied s 46, and therefore applied the wrong law or other principles.

Act 1998,[78] does the refusal to give reasons contravene the right to a fair hearing guaranteed by Art 6[79] of the European Convention on Human Rights 1950 (ECHR)? In *Mousaka Inc v Golden Seagull Maritime Inc and Another*,[80] the applicants sought permission to appeal pursuant to s 69 of the Arbitration Act 1996. Permission for leave to appeal was refused on grounds that the questions raised were not of public importance, and neither were the arbitrators' decisions obviously wrong or open to serious doubt. Full reasons for the refusal were sought by the applicants on the grounds that there was a duty on the courts to give reasons for their decisions, that it was inconsistent with Art 6 of the ECHR, and on principles of fairness and natural justice.

David Steel J drew attention to Lord Diplock's judgment in *The Antaios*, where he stated clearly:

> ... save in exceptional cases in which he does give leave to appeal to the Court of Appeal under 1(6)A) [of the Arbitration Act 1979] a judge ought not normally to give reasons for a grant or refusal under s 1(3)(b) of leave to appeal to the High Court from an arbitral award ... It has been the practice of this House at the close of the short oral argument ᴜₙ the petition, to say no more than that the petition is allowed or refused as the case may be. Save in very exceptional circumstances which I am unable at present to foresee, I can see no good reason why a commercial judge ... should do more than that ...[81]

After an examination of the Strasbourg jurisprudence in respect of Art 6, David Steel J concluded that 'where there are legitimate restraints on a right of appeal, such as the need for it to be a matter of general importance, it is sufficient for the Court to refer to these limitations' (at p 662). Further, in agreeing to arbitrate, the parties had opted for privacy and finality and had renounced the application of Art 6 of the ECHR. This limitation had a legitimate purpose and it was not disproportionate to that purpose.

What seem to have influenced the judge are the aims of the arbitral process – to provide an efficient system of dispute resolution which exudes confidence, privacy and finality. To elaborate on the refusal might well give the parties an opportunity to read reasons into the elaboration, thus leaving room for doubting the arbitrators' decision and the standing of arbitration as a reliable form of dispute resolution in the long run.[82]

Where an arbitration is subject to the *ICC Arbitration Rules*, Art 28(6) provides an exclusion clause, which reads:

---

78 An Act giving effect to rights and freedoms guaranteed under the European Convention on Human Rights 1950 (Convention for the Protection of Human Rights and Fundamental Freedoms).

79 Article 6(1) provides: 'In the determination of his civil rights and obligations or of any criminal charge against him, everyone is entitled to a fair and public hearing within a reasonable time by an independent and impartial tribunal established by law. Judgment shall be pronounced publicly but the press and public may be excluded from all or part of the trial in the interest of morals, public order or national security in a democratic society, where the interests of juveniles or the protection of the private life of the parties so require, or to the extent strictly necessary in the opinion of the court in special circumstances where publicity would prejudice the interests of justice.'

80 [2001] 2 Lloyd's Rep 657.

81 [1984] 2 Lloyd's Rep 235.

82 See also Ambrose, 'Arbitration and the Human Rights Act' [2000] LMCLQ 468 for an interesting account of the effect of the Human Rights Act 1998 on commercial arbitration.

Every award shall be binding on the parties. By submitting the dispute to arbitration under these Rules, the parties undertake to carry out any award without delay and to have waived their right to any form of recourse insofar as such waiver can be validly made.

A differently worded provision waiving the right of appeal, expressed in Art 24(2)[83] of the *ICC Rules for Arbitration 1988*, was recognised by the English courts as an advance exclusion agreement in *Arab African Energy Corp Ltd v Olieprodukten Nederland BV*.[84] No doubt the same approach will be taken to Art 28(6), above.

Serious irregularity

Challenging an arbitral award on grounds of serious irregularity is allowed by s 68[85] (subject to ss 73, 70(2) and 70(3))[86] of the Arbitration Act 1996. Events that will be regarded as comprising serious irregularity are listed in this section to include, among others: failure by the tribunal to comply with its general duty[87] (such as acting fairly and impartially as between the parties, and giving the parties a reasonable opportunity of putting their case and dealing with that of their opponent);[88] failure to deal with all issues put before it; the obtaining of an award through fraud; and failure to conduct the proceedings in accordance with the procedure agreed by the parties.[89]

Substantive jurisdiction

Section 67 makes room for the award to be challenged on the grounds that the arbitrators did not have substantive jurisdiction. Questions such as the validity of the arbitration agreement, the applicability of the arbitration agreement to parties not named in the agreement,[90] and the constitution of the tribunal will come within substantive jurisdiction. Like ss 68 and 69, this section is also subject to the provisions of ss 70(2), 70(3) and 73.[91]

---

83 It read: 'By submitting the dispute to arbitration by the International Chamber of Commerce, the parties shall be deemed to have undertaken to carry out the resulting award without delay and to have waived their right to any form of appeal insofar as such waiver can validly be made.'

84 [1983] 2 Lloyd's Rep 419.

85 The power of review by Court under s 68 is mandatory and cannot be excluded. See *Al Hadha Trading Co v Tradigrain SA and Others* [2002] 2 Lloyd's Rep 512.

86 See 'Point of law', pp 638–42 above.

87 See s 33; also 'Characteristics' pp 623–9 above.

88 See *Flotamentos Maritimos SA v Effohn International BV* [1997] 2 Lloyd's Rep 301; *Pacol Ltd v Joint Stock Co Rossakhor* [2000] 1 Lloyd's Rep 109; *Margulead Ltd v Exide Technologies* [2004] EWHC 1019 (Comm); *Petroships Pte Ltd of Singapore v Petec Trading & Investment Corp of Vietnam (The Petro Ranger)* [2001] 2 Lloyd's Rep 348.

89 See s 68(2) for a complete list. See for instance *Margulead Ltd v Exide Technologies* [2004] 2 All ER (Comm) 727; *World Trade Corporation Ltd v Czarnikow Sugar Ltd* [2004] 2 All ER (Comm) 813 and *Van der Giessen-De-Noord Shipbuilding Division BV v Imtech Marine & Offshore BV* [2008] EWHC 2904 (Comm) where arbitral awards were challenged under s 68.

90 See *Peterson Farms Inc v C&M Farming Ltd* [2004] 1 Lloyd's Rep 603. See also *Nisshin Shipping Co Ltd v Cleaves and Co Ltd and Others* [2004] 1 Lloyd's Rep 38, where shipbrokers (not party to a charterparty that contained an arbitration clause) were entitled to refer to arbitration by virtue of ss 1 and 8 of the Contracts (Rights of Third Parties) Act 1999.

91 See 'Point of law', pp 638–42 above.

Other than the powers imparted to the court as a result of an arbitral award being challenged, the court, it must be remembered, also has a number of other powers. These include the granting of interim orders, the enforcement of pre-emptory orders of the tribunals and securing the attendance of witnesses.[92]

Equally, to ensure that the tribunal can carry on its task of resolving the dispute smoothly, it is vested with powers including deciding on procedural and evidential matters subject to rights of the parties, the appointment of experts, and ordering security for costs and making provisional awards.[93] The tribunal also has the power to dismiss a claim in the event of a party's default; such circumstances are listed in s 41[94] of the Arbitration Act 1996.

Recent trends: arbitration online[95]

Before proceeding to recognition and enforcement of arbitral awards, a few words must be included about providing arbitration online. The late 1990s, as is well known and documented, witnessed the electronic commerce explosion widely predicted to be a vital contributor to global economic growth. Along with other legal issues, such as recognition of digital signatures and electronic bills of lading, providing arbitration online (that is, conducting all processes relating to an arbitration such as submission to the arbitration tribunal, hearings and award electronically) caught the imagination of information technology lawyers and the net community. As a result, projects such as the Virtual Magistrate project and the Global Arbitration and Mediation Association (GAMA) came into existence during 1996–97. The former was a pilot project for providing arbitration entirely online for disputes 'involving users of online systems, for those who claim to be harmed by wrongful messages, postings, or files, and system operators to the extent that complaints or demands are directed at system operators'. The Cyberspace Law Institute (CLI) and the National Center for Automated Information Research (NCAIR) were the main partners in the project, though the AAA was to provide help with the selection of arbitrators (called magistrates). The purpose behind the project was to provide a cheap, speedy and readily accessible remedy for the disputes. Unfortunately, post 1996–97,[96] nothing is available on the web to indicate the results of the project. The web address provided for the Virtual Magistrate project[97] does not elicit a response from the server. As for GAMA, it is reported as offering international commercial arbitration on the Internet.[98] A visit to their site provides a database of arbitrators and forums/organisations for

---

92 Sections 42 and 43. See also ss 18, 44 and 45. See *Hiscox Underwriting Ltd v Dickson Manchester and Co Ltd* [2004] EWHC 479 (Comm).

93 See, eg, ss 34, 37, 38 and 39.

94 For instance, in the event of failure to attend upon receiving due notice.

95 Also known as virtual arbitration, cyber arbitration.

96 See http://w2.eff.org/Legal/Arbitration/virtual_magistrate.announce; www.vmag.org/ docs/concept.html; www.umass.edu/dispute/ncair/gellman.htm; www.loundy.com/ CDLB/Virtual-Magistrate.html; http://mantles.sbs.umass.edu/vmag/disres.html. See also www.net-arb.org

97 http://vmag.law.vill.edu:8080/.

98 See Schneider and Kuner, 'Dispute resolution in international electronic commerce' (1997) 14 Journal of International Arbitration 1.

arbitration. This suggests that these attempts at online arbitration have not been successful.[99]

Other websites offering online arbitration have been set up recently and it is difficult, in the absence of statistics, to assess their success.[100] Nonetheless, the concept of online arbitration raises interesting legal issues that will have to be resolved before it becomes a realistic possibility. The purpose of locating a seat, as we saw earlier, is to identify the law of state that will apply to the arbitral process.[101] The Internet, with its global character, is not tied to notions of territory or nations, raising difficult questions about the seat of the virtual arbitration. Various solutions, such as the location of the arbitrator or the server, have been put forward, but these are not satisfactory. For instance, the arbitrators could be located in different places and the location of the arbitrator could change during the period of the hearing. Similarly, the server location solution is based on a naïve understanding of the way information networks operate.[102] Lack of security on the Internet also raises problems about privacy and confidentiality, although to some extent these can be resolved through sophisticated encryption systems. Further, there are problems with enforceability since the New York Convention on the Recognition and Enforcement of Foreign Arbitral Awards 1958 (examined below) requires that an authenticated original award or a certified copy is produced. It is debatable whether an award made in paperless form is an authenticated original award.

FOREIGN ARBITRAL AWARDS

As with foreign judgments, there are several regimes which govern the recognition and enforcement in England of foreign arbitral awards.[103] We shall, however, focus on the regime provided for by the New York Convention of 10 June 1958 on the Recognition and Enforcement of Foreign Arbitral Awards (hereinafter the 'Convention'), which was negotiated within the framework of the United Nations and has been ratified or acceded to by a large number of countries with a wide variety of political and legal traditions, including all 27 EC member states. The Convention is now transposed by Pt III (ss 100–04) of the Arbitration Act 1996.

The scope of the New York Convention is defined by Art I. The primary rule is that it applies to the recognition and enforcement of arbitral awards made in a state

---

99 WIPO (World Intellectual Property Organization), in respect of domain name disputes, offers online procedures for filling a case and submissions, and normally resolves most cases within two months from the date of filing. No in-person hearings are conducted except in extraordinary cases, and costs are low. Visit www.wipo.int.

100 See Schultz, Kaufmann-Kohler *et al, Online Dispute Resolution: The State of the Art and the Issues*, 2001, University of Geneva, available www.online-adr.org, for a complete list of organisations offering arbitration online.

101 *Dubai Islamic Bank Pjsc v Paymentech Merchant Services Inc* [2001] 1 Lloyd's Rep 65.

102 See Arsic, 'International commercial arbitration on the Internet: has the future come too early?' (1997) 14 Journal of International Arbitration, 210, p 209.

103 On the common law regime, see Collins *et al* (eds), *Dicey, Morris and Collins on the Conflict of Laws*, 14th edn, 2006 and 2nd Supp, 2008, Sweet & Maxwell, r 59–60. Where there is a foreign judgment authorising enforcement of an award, it is possible to seek enforcement in England under the Administration of Justice Act 1920, the Foreign Judgments (Reciprocal Enforcement) Act 1933, or Pt II of the Civil Jurisdiction and Judgments Act 1982; see *Dicey, Morris and Collins* r 64. But Art 1(2)(d) of EC Regulation 44/2001 prevents the recognition or enforcement thereunder of a European judgment authorising enforcement of an award.

other than the state where recognition or enforcement of the award is sought, and also to awards which are not considered as domestic awards in the state where recognition or enforcement is sought. But a contracting state is permitted to make a reservation restricting its application of the Convention to awards made in other contracting states, and such reservations have been made by many states, including the United Kingdom. Another reservation permissible to a contracting state confines its application of the Convention to disputes arising from legal relationships, whether contractual or not, which are regarded as commercial under its law, and such reservations have been made by many states (including France, Denmark and Greece), but not by the United Kingdom.[104] Article I also makes it clear that it is immaterial whether the parties are individuals or corporate bodies, and whether the arbitrator was appointed for the particular dispute or was a permanent arbitral body to which the parties submitted.

Under the 1996 Act, the Convention applies in England to awards made in an arbitration, the seat of which is in another contracting state.[105] The seat of an arbitration is defined by s 3 as its juridical seat, designated by the parties to the arbitration agreement, or by any arbitral or other institution or person vested by the parties with powers in that regard, or by the arbitral tribunal if so authorised by the parties, or determined, in the absence of any such designation, in the light of the parties' agreement and all the relevant circumstances. The English internal law on arbitration, laid down in Pt I of the Act, is in general restricted by s 2 to cases where the seat of the arbitration is in England or Northern Ireland; and s 53 specifies that, unless otherwise agreed by the parties, where the seat of the arbitration is in England or Northern Ireland, any award in the proceedings shall be treated as made there, regardless of where it was signed, despatched or delivered to any of the parties. Similarly, s 100(2) specifies that for the purpose of the provisions implementing the New York Convention, an award is treated as made at the seat of the arbitration, regardless of where it was signed, despatched or delivered to any of the parties.

Article III of the New York Convention requires each contracting state to recognise arbitral awards within its scope as binding and to enforce them, under the conditions laid down in Arts IV–VI. In general, the state addressed applies its own rules of procedure; and in England, s 101 enables a recognised award to be relied on by way of defence, set off or otherwise, and provides for enforcement by leave of the court in the same manner as an English judgment. By Art IV and s 102, a party seeking recognition or enforcement must produce the duly authenticated original award or a duly certified copy of it; the original arbitration agreement or a duly certified copy of it; and, where appropriate, certified translations.

The substantive exceptions to recognition and enforcement are exhaustively defined by Arts V and VI, which are echoed by s 103. In broad terms, they relate to the invalidity or inadequate scope of the arbitration agreement, procedural deficiencies in the arbitration proceedings, the invalidity of the award in the country of origin, the non-arbitrability of the subject matter, and the public policy of the state addressed.

---

104 For the difficulties which may arise if such a reservation is made by a state – such as India – whose law contains no clear distinction between commercial and non-commercial matters, see *Indian Organic Chemicals v Chemtex Fibres* (1978) 65 All India Reporter, Bombay Section, 108.

105 Cf *Hiscox v Outhwaite* [1992] 1 AC 562, decided under the Arbitration Act 1975.

The wording of Art V makes it clear that, except for non-arbitrability and public policy (which may be raised by the court addressed of its own motion), the burden of establishing the existence of a ground for refusal of recognition and enforcement rests on the party opposing recognition ('the respondent'). The only burden which rests on the applicant for recognition or enforcement is to produce the documents specified in Art IV, and to satisfy the court, by reference to these documents or otherwise, that the award falls within the scope of the convention as defined by Art I. If the applicant fulfils these requirements, the court is bound to recognise and enforce the award, unless the respondent establishes the existence of a ground for refusal under Art V, or the court of its own motion invokes Art V(2) on non-arbitrability of subject matter and public policy. Article V also makes it clear that where a ground for refusal is established, the court is not bound to refuse recognition and enforcement but has a discretion. Thus it may accord recognition and enforcement, despite the establishment of a ground for refusal, where the right to rely on the ground has been lost by another agreement or estoppel. But in most circumstances the English courts will refuse recognition and enforcement if one of the specified grounds is established.[106]

Article II of the Convention envisages an arbitration agreement in writing, and specifies that it may be contained in a substantive contract or may be a separate agreement, and that it may be signed by the parties or contained in an exchange of letters or telegrams. In England, ss 5 and 100 provide a very wide definition of an agreement in writing. It is enough that the agreement is made in writing, even if it is not signed by the parties, or that it is made by exchange of communications in writing, or that it is evidenced in writing. It is also sufficient for the parties to agree otherwise than in writing by reference to terms which are in writing, or for an agreement made otherwise than in writing to be recorded by one of the parties, or by a third party, with the authority of the parties to the agreement. Moreover, an exchange of written submissions in arbitral or legal proceedings in which the existence of an agreement otherwise than in writing is alleged by one party against another party and not denied by the other party in his response, constitutes as between those parties an agreement in writing to the effect alleged. Lastly, 'writing' includes recording by any means; thus, for example, email messages are included.

Article IV and s 102 require an applicant for recognition or enforcement of an award to produce a copy of the arbitration agreement. Hence, in the absence of a written agreement complying with Art II and ss 5 and 100, the application will fail *in limine*.

By Art V(1)(a) and s 103(2)(a), the court addressed may refuse recognition of an award if the respondent establishes that a party to the arbitration agreement was under some incapacity under the law applicable to him (according to the conflict rules of the state addressed).[107] By Art V(1)(a) and s 103(2)(b), it may also do so if the respondent establishes that the arbitration agreement was not valid under the law to which the parties subjected it or, failing any indication thereon, under the law of the seat of the arbitration. The law so ascertained will govern the essential validity of the arbitration agreement in relation to issues such as misrepresentation, mistake or improper pressure. But in view of Arts II and V(2)(a), it seems clear that Art V(1)(a) does not extend to questions concerning arbitrability of subject matter, and that for

---

106 *Kanoria v Guinness* [2006] I Lloyd's Rep 701.
107 For the English choice of law rules on capacity to contract, see Chapter 17.

the purposes of Art V(1)(a) any national rule which discriminates against arbitration agreements concluded before the dispute arose must be ignored.

By Art V(1)(c) and s 103(2)(d) and (4), the court addressed may refuse recognition of an award if the respondent establishes that the award deals with a difference not contemplated by or not falling within the terms of the submission to arbitration, or that it contains decisions on matters beyond the scope of the submission to arbitration. But severable decisions on matters submitted to arbitration may be recognised and enforced. In interpreting the arbitration agreement to determine its scope, the court addressed will no doubt apply the law which governs its essential validity under Art V(1)(a).

Article V(1)(b) and s 103(2)(c) enable the court addressed to refuse recognition of an award where the respondent establishes that he was not given proper notice of the appointment of the arbitrator or of the arbitration proceedings, or was otherwise unable to present his case. The court addressed will no doubt have regard to what is acceptable under its own law of civil procedure and the treaties (especially those on recognition of foreign judgments) to which its state is a party. Thus service in a manner which complies with the law of the seat of the arbitration will not automatically satisfy these requirements. For there to be inability to present one's case, the party must have been prevented from doing so by events beyond his control, and not merely have failed, for reasons within his control, to take advantage of an opportunity to present his case; but a party is unable to present his case if he is never informed of the case that he is called upon to meet.[108]

By Art V(1)(d) and s 103(2)(e), the court addressed may refuse recognition of an award where the respondent establishes that the composition of the arbitral authority, or the arbitral procedure, was not in accordance with the agreement of the parties or, failing such agreement, with the law of the seat of the arbitration. The court addressed must consider first the terms of the arbitration agreement, and only where they are silent should it refer to the law of the seat. It should not consider the validity of the agreed terms under any law, but should treat them as valid, leaving any attack on their validity to the courts of the country of origin. The need for Art V(1)(d) seems questionable, since a party dissatisfied with the arbitral proceedings can always attack the award in its country of origin in accordance with the law of that country, and Arts V(1)(e) and VI offer him derivative protection, ancillary to an attack in the country of origin, in other contracting states.

By Art V(1)(e) and s 103(2)(f), the court addressed may refuse recognition where the respondent establishes that the award has not yet become binding on the parties, or that it has been set aside or suspended by a competent authority of the country of the seat. This is supplemented by Art VI and s 103(5), which apply where an application for setting aside or suspension has been made to such an authority. In such a case, the court addressed may, if it considers proper, adjourn its decision on the recognition or enforcement of the award, and may also, on application by the party claiming recognition or enforcement, order the respondent to give security. Where the court grants such an adjournment it may also allow partial enforcement in respect of a sum indisputably due.[109]

---

108 *Minmetals v Ferco Steel* [1999] 1 All ER (Comm) 315; and *Kanoria v Guinness* [2006] 1 Lloyd's Rep 701 (CA).

109 See *IPCO (Nigeria) Ltd v Nigerian National Petroleum Corporation (No 2)* [2008] 2 Lloyd's Rep 59.

The meaning of 'binding', for the purposes of Art V(1)(e), is obscure. The expression replaces a requirement of the Geneva Convention 1927 that the award should be 'final', and appears to be intended to overrule decisions given in some countries, not including the United Kingdom,[110] by which 'finality' could only be proved by producing a decision of a court of the relevant country authorising enforcement of the award. Probably an award should be considered 'binding' unless it is proved that in the country of the seat it would be treated as non-existent, in the sense that it would be ignored in all judicial proceedings, without the need for a judgment setting it aside.

Article V(2) and s 103(3) enable the court addressed to refuse recognition where it finds, whether at the invitation of a party or of its own motion, either that the subject matter of the difference is not capable of settlement by arbitration under its own law, or that the recognition or enforcement of the award would be contrary to its own public policy. Article II makes it clear that a country can consider a matter as non-arbitrable, for the purposes of the Convention, only if it will not accept the validity of an agreement for arbitration in respect of the matter, even if the agreement is made after the dispute has arisen.

The public policy proviso in the New York Convention will no doubt have a limited operation, similar to that of the corresponding proviso in relation to the recognition of foreign judgments (see pp 619–21 above). Thus, even before the Arbitration Act 1996, the Court of Appeal held in *Deutsche Schachtbau-und Tiefbohrgesellschaft mbH v Ras Al Khaimah National Oil Co*[111] that it was not contrary to English public policy to enforce a Swiss award given under an ICC arbitration clause, using as the proper law 'internationally accepted principles of law governing contractual relations', even though at that time an English arbitrator had to apply the law of the country which would have been applied by the English court. Where a foreign award is challenged on the ground of illegality in the underlying transaction, the English court is likely to uphold the award unless the illegality is apparent from the face of the award.[112] Moreover a challenge on the ground of fraud in obtaining the award must be based on cogent evidence which was not available at the time of the arbitral hearing.[113] But, as the European Court ruled in *Eco Swiss China Time v Benetton*,[114] it would be contrary to public policy, within the New York Convention, to enforce an award which had upheld a contract which infringed the competition rules laid down by Art 81 of the EC Treaty.

CONCLUSION

Without doubt, arbitration has a great many advantages to recommend it as a workable alternative to litigation. Nonetheless, it can prove to be a costly and time consuming exercise. This has seen the emergence of other dispute resolution mechanisms, notably mediation, considered in the next chapter.

---

110 See *Union Nationale des Coopératives Agricoles v Catterall* [1959] 2 QB 44.

111 [1990] AC 295; reversed by HL on other grounds.

112 See *Soleimany v Soleimany* [1999] QB 785 (CA); *Westacre Investments v Jugoimport-SDPR* [1999] 2 Lloyd's Rep 65 (CA); *Omnium v Hilmarton* [1999] 2 Lloyd's Rep 222; and *R v V* (2008) 119 ConLR 73.

113 See *Westacre Investments v Jugoimport-SDPR* [1999] 2 Lloyd's Rep 65 (CA). See also *Gater Assets v Naftogaz (No 2)* [2008] 1 Lloyd's Rep 479.

114 Case C-126/97: [1999] ECR I-3055. Cf Case C-38/98: *Renault v Maxicar* [2000] ECR I-2973.

FURTHER READING

Collins (ed), *Dicey, Morris and Collins on the Conflict of Laws*, 14th edn, 2006 and 2nd supp, 2008, Sweet & Maxwell.

Hill, *International Commercial Disputes in English Counts*, 3rd edn, 2005, Hart Publishing.

Huleatt-James and Gould, *International Commercial Arbitration: A Handbook*, 1996, LLP.

Lew, Mistelis & Kröll, *Comparative International Commercial Arbitration*, 2003, Kluwer.

Merkin, *Arbitration Law*, 2004, Informa.

Mustill and Boyd, *The Law and Practice of Commercial Arbitration in England*, 1989, Butterworths.

Redfern, Hunter *et al*, *Law and Practice of International Commercial Arbitration*, 2004, Sweet & Maxwell.

Sanders, *Quo Vadis Arbitration? Sixty Years of Arbitration Practice, A Comparative Study*, 1999, Kluwer.

Sarcevic, *Essays on International Commercial Arbitration*, 1989, Graham & Trotman.

CHAPTER 20

MEDIATION (CONCILIATION): AN ALTERNATIVE FORM OF DISPUTE RESOLUTION

INTRODUCTION

There are, besides arbitration, other types of alternative dispute resolution (ADR)[1] that are binding on the parties, such as expert determination and ombudsman schemes. In expert determination, a third party, an expert chosen by the parties, is used to consider the particular matter raised by the parties. The decision of the expert is normally binding. Expert determination clauses are often found in construction contracts[2] and information technology contracts. Cost-effective and quick, the use of ombudsmen is another popular alternative frequently used worldwide for complaints by individuals against particular sectors such as insurance[3] and banking. In contrast to these, a non-binding type of ADR[4] that has caused a stir on the domestic and international commercial scene is mediation, or conciliation, as a mode of dispute resolution.[5]

Use of a third (neutral) party to aid the contracting parties to iron out their differences and arrive at an amicable solution is the distinctive feature of mediation. Though the terms 'mediation' and 'conciliation' are used interchangeably here, there is some suggestion that in mediation the third party plays an evaluative role (that is, by expressing his opinion), whereas in conciliation the role is a facilitative one (that is, the third party does not advise parties of his own opinion).[6] This distinction is by no

---

1 Also sometimes known as appropriate dispute resolution.

2 For instance, in *Channel Tunnel Group v Balfour Beatty Ltd* [1993] AC 334, the contract included an expert determination clause. Clause 67(1) of the contract provided:

> If any dispute or difference shall arise between the Employer and the Contractor during the progress of the Works . . . such dispute or difference shall at the instance of either the Employer or the Contractor in the first place be referred in writing to and be settled by a Panel of three persons (acting as independent experts but not as arbitrators) who shall . . . state their decision in writing . . . to the Employer and Contractor.

The expert determination clause was perceived by the House of Lords as 'nearly an immediately effective agreement to arbitrate, albeit not quite' (p 353). The expert determination clause was part of a two-stage procedure the parties had agreed for resolving disputes. The first port of call was a panel of experts. If either of the parties was dissatisfied with the decision of the experts they could, upon notice, refer the dispute to arbitration. The court held they had the power pursuant to its inherent jurisdiction to grant a stay of an action brought before it in breach of an agreed method of resolving disputes by some other method. They agreed they ought to grant a stay in the present case. See Lord Mustill at p 353.

3 See www.theiob.org.uk. Ombudsman schemes are commonly used in other jurisdictions.

4 Frank Sander, Roger Fisher and William Ury are widely acknowledged as the founders of ADR. However, see Menkel-Meadow, 'Mothers and fathers of invention: the intellectual founders of ADR' (2000) 16 Ohio State Journal on Dispute Resolution 1.

5 Other well-known types of ADR are early neutral evaluation (ENE), and mini-trial (aka executive tribunal) and Med-arb. In ENE, the parties present their cases in an adversarial manner which is evaluated by a neutral third party, and the parties negotiate on the basis of this evaluation. Mini-trial is conducted with a panel comprising a third party and a senior executive from each side with no connection to the dispute. After hearing the submissions, the senior executives negotiate for a settlement. In Med-arb, a hybrid of mediation and arbitration, parties start with mediation to try to find a mutually acceptable solution. In the event of failure, the mediator takes on the guise of arbitrator to issue a binding decision.

6 See International Labour Organization, *ILO Study on Conciliation and Arbitration Procedure*, 1989, ILO.

means well settled, neither is it widely accepted. For instance, an American writer[7] describes the processes thus:

> While differing somewhat in language and detail, most modern definitions of mediation contain two common elements: (1) third party facilitation of dispute settlement, and (2) lack of third party power to determine the resolution of the dispute. In other words, the principle of self-determination is paramount. The disputants, not the third party intervener, maintain the exclusive power to decide on a resolution of their dispute ... [at p 508].
>
> The process of 'conciliation' has yet to achieve a stable meaning, and is often used interchangeably with mediation. In earlier usage, conciliation usually referred to a process that emphasised facilitation of communications among disputants without third party recommendations, as contrasted with mediation, which allowed for more activist third party intervention. Ironically, this understanding (mainly in the labor field) appears to have been reversed in international dispute resolution, where a conciliator is regarded as a third party who makes a non-binding recommendation to resolve a dispute. In any event, in most contexts today, conciliation and mediation are considered synonymous, and both may involve activist intervention by the third party [at p 513].

The Centre for Effective Dispute Resolution (CEDR),[8] a major provider of commercial mediation in England, adopts the term 'mediation' to refer to both evaluative and facilitative mediation,[9] even though it promotes facilitative mediation.[10]

Since the mediation process does not share the trappings of the judicial or arbitral process (for example, handing down of awards or judgments, the adjudicative role of the arbitrator or judge), it is not acrimonious in nature. It helps focus the parties' minds on the nature of the differences, to try to see if they can come to some agreeable arrangement, thus preserving their business relationship. This positive aspect of mediation has contributed to its enthusiastic reception by businessmen, academics and practitioners alike. As The Rt Hon Lord Goff of Chieveley colourfully observed:

> ... cost and delay have been identified as two of the principal enemies of justice in the modern world; and, since time is money, it is really cost that we are talking about. But, in addition, formal arbitration has become to some extent afflicted by arthritis, the disease which, as time passes by, seems to attack nearly all institutions as it does nearly all human beings. ADR [alternative dispute resolution, that is, conciliation and mediation] is seen as the one means of escaping from the inflexible processes towards which substantial arbitrations seem to gravitate. ADR, if effective, may produce not only a less expensive but, also, a less traumatic resolution of disputes – especially important where the parties may wish to continue to do business together in the future.[11]

---

7   Weckstein, 'Praise of party empowerment – and of mediator activism' (1997) 33 Williamette LR 501.

8   Based in London, the CEDR has played an important role in raising the profile of commercial mediation in commercial disputes in England. More details on this organisation are available on www.cedr.com.

9   There is some debate about the relative merits of facilitative mediation and evaluative mediation. See, eg, Love, 'The top 10 reasons why mediators should not evaluate' (1997) 24 Florida State University LR 937.

10 It promotes facilitative mediation in the courses it offers. See Richbell, *The CEDR Mediator Handbook: Effective Resolution of Commercial Disputes*, 2004, CEDR; Mackie *et al*, *The ADR Practice Guide: Commercial Dispute Resolution*, 2007, Tottel.

11 Tackaberry (ed), *International Commercial Arbitration for Today and Tomorrow*, 1991, Euro Conferences, p 41.

Mediation, however, has its fair share of criticisms. For instance, it has been said that prejudice, power imbalance and bigotry are rife in mediation, and that most mediations go against the grain of rule of law.[12] It is also said that mediator neutrality is a myth, and that the sex[13] and ethnic backgrounds of the mediator and of the participants affect the outcomes.[14] While it may be the case that exhibition of raw emotion and the making of inflammatory statements by the parties in the course of mediation (for instance, during their opening statements, or when the parties have been brought together by the mediator for further discussion and problem solving) may not conform to the familiar trappings of legal discourse, in most cases, parties are aware of and informed by the framework of available legal solutions. In most cases involving commercial disputes, parties are accompanied by their legal advisers. Moreover, the advantage of mediation is its flexibility; its ability to arrive at a solution acceptable to both parties even if it does not strictly adhere to positive law. Informality and unusual turns of phrase in some mediations should not lead to the belief that 'anything goes'. As for the view that sex and ethnicity contribute to the outcome, the premise is based on a limited number of case studies; and like all empirical surveys, the framework, the interpretation and the results are open to debate.

Mediation, by and large, is voluntary.[15] Consent is required to initiate mediation, and parties also have to agree to settle the dispute. Apart from preserving the commercial relationship of the contracting parties, the costs of conciliation are not as high as those of arbitration or litigation. On the downside, conciliation does not always reach settlement since parties are free to walk away from the conciliatory process at any stage. They can turn to litigation or arbitration after carrying on with the conciliatory process for a fair while, thus doing away with one of the advantages that conciliation offers – reduction in costs. Further, it may be tactically disadvantageous to enter the conciliation stage, should the parties go to trial, since many of the reasons and arguments are likely to have been rehearsed during the conciliatory process.

The core features of mediation, associated issues and solutions are the subject matter of this chapter. But before proceeding with this task, a brief account of international developments and developments in England in respect of mediation is provided.

INTERNATIONAL DEVELOPMENTS

The two international organisations, the United Nations Commission on International Trade Law (UNCITRAL) and the International Chamber of Commerce (ICC), which have played an important role in the promotion of arbitration, have drawn

---

12 Delgado *et al*, 'Fairness and formality: minimizing the risk of prejudice in alternative dispute resolution' (1985) Wisconsin LR 1359.

13 For a feminist perspective on mediation, see Evans, 'Women and mediation: toward a formulation of an interdisciplinary empirical model to determine equity in dispute resolution' (2001) 17 Ohio State Journal on Dispute Resolution 145; McCabe, 'A forum for women's voices: mediation through a feminist jurisprudential lens' (2001) 21 Northern Illinois University LR 459; see also Grillo, 'The mediation alternative: process dangers for women' (1991) 100 Yale LJ 1545, who observes that mediation is not a feminist alternative.

14 Hermann *et al*, *The Metrocourt Project Final Report*, 1993, University of New Mexico Center for the Study and Resolution of Disputes.

15 A number of jurisdictions, such as the US, have been considering making mediation mandatory in some types of disputes, eg, employment.

up conciliation[16] rules, thus providing a framework. The ICC ADR Rules (hereinafter 'ADR Rules'),[17] which came into effect on 1 July 2001,[18] cover issues such as commencement of ADR proceedings, selection of a neutral (that is, mediator), fees and costs, and contain safeguards such as confidentiality and neutral immunity.[19] The ADR Rules leave it open to the parties to choose the ADR technique that most suits their needs for resolving the dispute amicably. In the absence of agreement, mediation is the technique to be adopted. Similar provisions on various aspects such as appointment and confidentiality are also found in the UNCITRAL Conciliation Rules (hereinafter 'UNCITRAL Rules').[20] The UNCITRAL Rules are, however, more detailed than the ADR Rules. For instance, Arts 3 and 4 cover the issue of appointment of conciliators extensively. Presumably, this was felt necessary, since UNCITRAL does not provide the type of services offered by the ICC in the appointment of conciliators. There are also provisions on the stages that the conciliator has to follow during the process, in Art 5. Further, there is an attempt to introduce finality to the settlement agreement reached by the parties, in that Art 13(3) provides 'that the parties by signing the settlement agreement put an end to the dispute and are bound by the agreement'. However, the parties are not bound by this provision if they use the UNCITRAL Rules, since they are free to exclude or vary the Rules at any time, according to Art 1(2). For instance, they could agree that the agreement is a 'gentleman's agreement' or binding 'in honour' only. Or they may make the agreement subject to conditions. For instance, Buyer B, claiming losses of £1 million for defective goods supplied by seller S, may settle for £100,000 provided S pays the amount within seven days of signing the agreement. The settlement agreement could read: 'S promises to pay B £100,000 within seven working days of the signature of this agreement. If he does so, the dispute is settled and B shall not raise the complaint in any manner or forum. If S does not pay as aforesaid, B shall be free to pursue any legal remedy as if this agreement has not been concluded.'

A recent development on the international scene that is likely to have a global impact emanates from UNCITRAL. With harmonisation in mind, it adopted the Model Law on International Commercial Conciliation (hereinafter 'Conciliation Law') in 2003.[21] Various versions of the draft are available on its website.[22] It covers the most obvious matters pertaining to mediation: appointment of a neutral party; conduct of conciliation; communication between conciliator and parties; admissibility of evidence in other proceedings; and enforceability of settlement.[23] The Conciliation Law applies to international commercial conciliation,[24] though parties may expressly agree

---

16 Of interest are the ICC figures on requests for conciliation. For instance, between 1993 and 1998, a conciliator was appointed only in 10 cases. Whether these figures say something negative about the usefulness of conciliation as a dispute resolution mechanism is debatable, since factors such as lack of information about the availability of such mechanisms, and cultural inhibitions, may be relevant.

17 ICC Publication 809. Text available at www.iccwbo.org.

18 This replaces the ICC Rules of Optional Conciliation 1988.

19 See Arts 2, 3, 4 and 7.

20 Available on www.uncitral.org.

21 So far legislation based on the Model Law has been enacted in Canada, Croatia, Hungary, Nicaragua and Slovenia.

22 See Doc A/CN.9/WG.II/WP.115, available at www.uncitral.org.

23 See Arts 7, 8, 9, 13 and 17.

24 According to Art 3, the factors required for internationality are:

    (a) if the parties to an agreement to conciliate have, at the time of conciliation of that agreement, their places of business in different States; or

to apply the provisions to domestic commercial conciliation (Art 1). Conciliation is defined in Art 1(3) as follows:

> For the purposes of this Law, 'conciliation' means a process, whether referred to by the expression conciliation, mediation or an expression of similar import, whereby parties request a third person, or persons ('the conciliator') to assist them in their attempt to reach an amicable settlement of their dispute arising out of relating to a contract or other legal relationship. The conciliator does not have the authority to impose upon the parties a solution to the dispute.

The definition does not promote a particular technique – facilitative or evaluative – and is sufficiently broad to accommodate the variety of techniques currently in use. Presumably, instead of imposing a certain technique, it was felt best to follow the current global trend and leave it to the market forces to decide the most appropriate one.

International organisations such as BIMCO[25] (which play an active role in drafting standard forms in respect of sea transportation[26]) have also responded to the arrival of mediation on the dispute resolution horizon with a mediation clause incorporated into the standard dispute resolution clause.[27] While BIMCO highlights the key benefits[28] of mediation, the clause is drafted with the intention that it will be used to mediate parts of a large dispute during an arbitration process. The arbitration process, it seems, will continue alongside mediation. The motivation behind this approach was to ensure that parties did not use mediation as a delaying tactic.[29]

(b) one of the following places is situated outside the state in which the parties have their place of business:
  (i) the place of conciliation; or
  (ii) any place where a substantial part of the obligations of the commercial relationship is to be performed or the place with which the subject matter of the dispute is most closely connected.
'Place of business' is not defined. Presumably, the interpretation of place of business in the context of the Vienna Convention on the International Sale of Goods 1980 would be relevant. See Chapter 2, pp 63–4 above.

25 Baltic and International Maritime Council.

26 Eg, GENCON for voyage charterparty.

27 BIMCO Standard Dispute Resolution Clause provides:
  (a) This Contract shall be governed by and construed in accordance with English law and any dispute arising out of or in connection with this Contract shall be referred to arbitration in London in accordance with the Arbitration Act 1996 or any statutory modification or re-enactment thereof save to the extent necessary to give effect to the provisions of this Clause.
  . . .
  (d) Notwithstanding (a), (b) or (c) above, the parties may agree at any time to refer to mediation any difference and/or dispute arising out of or in connection with this Contract. In the case of a dispute in respect of which arbitration has been commenced under (a), (b) or (c) above, the following shall apply:
    (i) Either party may at any time and from time to time elect to refer the dispute or part of the dispute to mediation by service on the other party of a written notice (the 'Mediation Notice') calling on the other party to agree to mediation.
    (ii) . . .
    (iii) If the other party does not agree to mediate, that fact may be brought to the attention of the Tribunal and may be taken into account by the Tribunal when allocating the costs of the arbitration as between the parties.
    (iv) The mediation shall not affect the right of either party to seek such relief or take such steps as it considers necessary to protect its interest.
    (v) Either party may advise the Tribunal that they have agreed to mediation. The arbitration procedure shall continue during the conduct of the mediation but the Tribunal may take the mediation timetable into account when setting the timetable for steps in the arbitration.

28 Speed, cost, confidentiality, control (in that the decisions are made by the parties) and rights (in that the rights of the parties are not affected by mediation).

29 See 'BIMCO: Standard Dispute Resolution Clause', press release dated April 2002, available at www.bimco.org.

DEVELOPMENTS IN ENGLAND

Before proceeding to discuss the features of mediation, a few words must be said about developments in respect of ADR in general in England. The Woolf Report on *Access to Justice*[30] played a pivotal role in raising the profile of ADR in England – so much so that solicitors and barristers are currently training to be commercial mediators. This, of course, does not mean that only those engaged in the legal profession are best qualified to offer mediation services. As in arbitration, individuals with special expertise in the industry, such as IT professionals and civil engineers, also play a central role in the provision of mediation services. Indeed, it is debatable whether lawyers are best placed to offer mediation, especially of the facilitative kind, since they bring with them their adversarial experience, not best suited to a technique founded on the principle of co-operation.[31] In the absence of empirical research, the debate at best revolves around conjectures, prejudice and bias.

Encouragement of the use of ADR in the Woolf Report has found its way into the Civil Procedure Rules 1998 (in force since 26 April 1999). Prior to these Rules, the Commercial Court had already started recommending the use of ADR in its *Practice Note*.[32] The Civil Procedure Rules have made co-operation and ADR part of the fabric of case management,[33] and promote encouraging the parties 'to co-operate with each other in the conduct of the proceedings' and 'to use an alternative dispute procedures if the court considers that to be appropriate and facilitating the use of such procedure' (r 1.4(2) a and e). The Commercial Court has also produced its own Guide[34] which endorses what was said in its *Practice Note*. Rule G 1.4 of the Guide provides that in all cases 'legal representatives should consider with their clients and the other parties concerned the possibility of attempting to resolve the dispute or particular issues by ADR'. The judge may, 'if he considers appropriate, adjourn a case for a specified period of time to encourage and enable the parties to use ADR', according to r G 1.7. The Guide also, in r G 1.8, allows the judge to make an ADR order.[35]

---

30 See also Lord Chancellor's Department, *Access to Justice: The Interim Report*, 1995, HMSO.

31 Menkel-Meadow, 'Pursuing settlement in an adversary culture: a tale of innovation co-opted or "the law of ADR" ' (1991) 19 Florida, State University LR 1; Menkel-Meadow, 'When dispute resolution begets disputes of its own' (1997) 44 UCLA LR 871; Nolan-Haley, 'Lawyers, non-lawyers and mediation' (2002) Harvard Negotiation LR 235.

32 [1994] 1 All ER 34. See *Practice Note* [1995] 1 All ER 385.

33 As part of case management, counsel are asked in the pre-trial checklist whether they have discussed the possibility of ADR with their clients. Recently in the United Kingdom, a survey was conducted on the use of mediation in the construction industry. The report concluded that lawyers are utilising mediation for construction disputes and a significant number of construction lawyers were found to hold positive attitudes towards the benefits of using ADR in terms of savings in legal and management costs, the speed of achieving settlement and satisfaction with using the process. However, the findings indicate that solicitors and barristers in the survey experience higher settlement rates for commercial than construction mediation'. Brooker, 'Construction lawyers' attitudes and experience with ADR' (2002) 18(2) Construction LJ 97, p 116.

34 Available at www.courtservice.gov.uk.

35 See *Halsey v Milton Keynes General NHS Trust* [2004] EWCA Civ 576; *Shirayana Shokusan Co Ltd v Danovo Ltd* [2003] EWHC 3006 (Ch). See *Dunnett v Railtrack* [2002] 1 WLR 2434 for using cost sanctions for refusal to pursue ADR. See also *Cable & Wireless PLC v IBM UK Ltd* [2002] EWHC 2059 (Comm); and *Burchall v Bullard* [2005] EWCA Civ 358.

FEATURES AND ASSOCIATED ISSUES

Before parties decide to opt for mediation, they need to consider its core features and their legal consequences – for instance, enforceability of the mediation clause and the settlement agreement, and the degree to which the information they divulge during mediation is likely to remain confidential. In an international context, different jurisdictions are likely to deal with these aspects differently, and parties need to be aware of the lack of predictability in these areas. To some extent, parties can cushion themselves against surprises with suitable choice of law and choice of jurisdiction clauses.[36] Harmonisation may, as in other areas of international commerce, hold the key.

Mediation agreement

As stated at p 653 above, mediation in most cases is a creature created by agreement between the parties. The UNCITRAL Rules, for instance, recommend the following model clause:

> Where, in the event of a dispute arising out of or relating to this contract, the parties wish to seek an amicable settlement of that dispute by conciliation, the conciliation shall take place in accordance with the UNCITRAL Conciliation Rules as at present in force.

The ADR Rules, on the other hand, set out a number of different Model Laws reflecting a variety of possibilities, ranging from optional ADR[37] and an obligation to consider ADR to an obligation to submit to ADR followed by ICC arbitration,[38] as required.

In an ideal world, parties would abide by their agreement. But what if one of the parties initiates proceedings? Could a party be stopped from taking a dispute to court in spite of a mediation clause in the contract? In other words, is an ADR clause enforceable? The answer depends on whether the clause is seen as an agreement to negotiate, or as participation in a structured process involving a neutral party as a mediator.

As for English law, it is well settled that an agreement to negotiate is unenforceable on grounds of uncertainty. Formulated in the well known Court of Appeal decision in *Courtney and Fairburn Ltd v Tolaini Brothers (Hotels) Ltd*,[39] the principle was

---

36   For instance, the CEDR recommends the following clause for international contracts: 'The mediation will take place in . . . and the language of the mediation will be . . . The Mediation Agreement . . . shall be governed by, and construed and take effect in accordance with . . . law. The courts of . . . shall have exclusive jurisdiction to settle any claim, dispute or matter of difference which may arise out of or in connection with, the mediation.'

37   This clause reads: 'The parties may at any time, without prejudice to any other proceedings, seek to settle any dispute arising out of or in connection with the present contract in accordance with the ICC ADR Rules.'

38   This clause reads: 'In the event of any dispute arising out of or in connection with the present contract, the parties agree to submit the matter to settlement proceedings under the ICC ADR rules. If the dispute has not been settled pursuant to the said Rules within 45 days following the filing of a Request for ADR or within such other period as the parties may agree in writing, such dispute shall be finally settled under the Rules of Arbitration of the ICC by one or more arbitrations appointed in accordance with the said Rules of Arbitration.'

39   [1975] 1 All ER 716. Lord Denning MR enunciated the unenforceability of an agreement to negotiate thus: 'If the law does not recognise a contract to enter into a contract (when there is a fundamental term yet to be agreed), it seems to me it cannot recognise a contract to negotiate. The reason is because it is too uncertain to have any binding force . . . It seems to me that a contract to negotiate, like a contract to enter into a contract, is not a contract known to law . . . I think we must apply the general principle that, when there is a fundamental matter left undecided and to be the subject of negotiation, there is no contract.'

affirmed by the House of Lords in a more recent case. *Walford v Miles*[40] concerned a lock-out agreement, where the vendor of a business agreed with the would-be purchaser not to negotiate for the sale of the business with third parties during the course of the negotiation. It did not specify how long the vendors were locked out from negotiating with a third party. The vendor decided to sell to a third party and an action for breach of the lock-out agreement was brought by the would-be purchaser. In the Court of Appeal, Bingham LJ, dissenting, said that a lock-out agreement, in the absence of a specified time, should be binding for a reasonable time, thus imposing a duty on the parties to negotiate in good faith. After due consideration of the views in the dissenting judgment, Lord Ackner concluded that the agreement was unenforceable due to uncertainty. He said:

> The agreement alleged in para 5 of the unamended statement of claim contains the essential characteristics of a basic valid lock-out agreement, save one. It does not specify for how long it is to last. Bingham LJ sought to cure this deficiency by holding that the obligation should continue to bind them for 'such time as is reasonable in all the circumstances' ...
>
> However, as Bingham LJ recognised, such a duty, if it existed, would indirectly impose upon the respondents a duty to negotiate in good faith. Such a duty, for the reasons I have given above, cannot be imposed. That it should have been thought necessary to assert such a duty helps to explain the reason behind the amendment to para 5 and the insistence of Mr Naughton that without the implied term the agreement, as originally pleaded, was unworkable – unworkable because there was no way of determining for how long the respondents were locked out from negotiating with any third party.
>
> Thus, even if, despite the way in which the Walford's case is pleaded and argued, the severance favoured by Bingham LJ was permissible, the resultant agreement suffered from the same defect ... as the agreement contended for in the amended statement of claim, namely that it too lacked the necessary certainty, and was thus unenforceable [at p 462].

Recently, in *Halifax Financial Services v Intuitive Systems Ltd*,[41] the court considered the issue of enforceability of an ADR clause. The clause in question was a stepped clause.[42] Clause 33 (headed 'Disputes') provided:

> 33.1 In the event of any dispute arising between the Parties in connection with this agreement, senior representatives of the Parties will, within 10 Business Days of a written notice from either Party to the other, meet in good faith and attempt to resolve the dispute without recourse to legal proceedings.
>
> 33.2 If the dispute is not resolved as a result of such meeting, either Party may, at such meeting (or within 10 Business Days from its conclusion) propose to the other in writing that structured negotiations be entered into with the assistance of a neutral adviser or mediator ('Neutral Adviser').
>
> 33.3–33.5 ...
>
> 33.6 If the Parties accept the Neutral Adviser's recommendations or otherwise reach agreement on the resolution of the dispute, such agreement will be recorded in writing

---

40 [1992] 1 All ER 453.

41 [1999] 1 All ER (Comm) 303.

42 Aka a tiered clause, by which the parties agree to enter the next step of the dispute resolution process, as specified in their agreement, if the previous step fails to resolve the dispute. The parties could agree to start with negotiation, proceed to mediation if the negotiation fails, and if the mediation fails to arbitration, and so on.

and, once it is signed by their duly authorised representatives, will be binding on the Parties.

33.7 Failing agreement, either of the Parties may invite the Neutral Adviser to provide a non-binding but informative opinion in writing.

33.8 If the Parties fail to reach agreement in the structured negotiations within 45 Business Days of the Neutral Adviser being appointed then any dispute between them may be referred to the Court unless within a further period of 25 Business Days the Parties agree to arbitration in accordance with the procedure set out below.

33.9 Any dispute between the Halifax and Intuitive in connection with this Agreement that cannot be resolved by the above procedure will be referred to and determined by a sole arbitrator ('the Arbitrator'), the arbitration to be held in London or any other place nominated by the Arbitrator.

It was argued on behalf of the defendant that cl 33 was similar to a *Scott v Avery* clause;[43] it was a condition precedent and hence a defence to the action. Clause 33, looked at as a whole, according to McKinnon J, could not be construed as suggesting that the contractual procedure had to be complied with before issuing proceedings. The parties did not bind themselves to any method of determining any dispute between them, unlike in *Cott UK Ltd v FE Barber Ltd*[44] where an ADR clause was seen (applying the *Channel Tunnel* principle)[45] as determinative to order a stay. The relevant clause provided that disputes were to be referred to a person who 'shall act as an expert and not as an arbiter and his decision shall be binding on the parties'.[46]

The Conciliation Law (see pp 654–5 above) addresses the issue of resorting to arbitral or judicial proceedings in Art 13 as follows:

Where the parties have agreed to conciliate and have expressly undertaken not to initiate during a specified period of time or until a specified event has occurred arbitral or judicial proceedings with respect to an existing or future dispute, such an undertaking shall be given effect by the arbitral tribunal or court until the terms of the undertaking have been complied with, except to the extent necessary for a party, in its opinion, to preserve its rights. Initiation of such proceedings is not of itself to be regarded as a waiver of the agreement to conciliate or as a termination of the conciliation proceedings.

It seems according to the above article that a party can apply for stay of arbitral or judicial proceedings while the conciliation process is taking place or where there is an express provision stating that they will not initiate arbitral/judicial proceedings for a specific period. This is similar to a *Scott v Avery* clause. Presumably, where one party notifies another party of its intention to enter into conciliation on the basis of their agreement, it will be construed widely as conciliation proceedings. However, Art 13 leaves the door open for the party to initiate judicial or arbitral proceedings even during conciliation proceedings, that is, to obtain interim measures on the basis that this is necessary for preserving its rights.[47]

It is expected that the Conciliation Law will have a wide impact of the kind witnessed by the UNCITRAL Model Law on Arbitration. It is nevertheless

---

43 A clause where parties agree that no action will be brought until an arbitration award is made. Named after *Scott v Avery* (1856) 10 ER 1121.

44 [1997] 3 All ER 540.

45 *Channel Tunnel Group v Balfour Beatty Ltd* [1993] AC 334.

46 See also *Cable & Wireless v IBM* [2002] EWHC 2059 Comm Ct where a contractual reference to CEDR and CEDR procedure was seen as not wanting in certainty.

47 See para 42, Doc A/CN 9/WG II/WP 115.

questionable whether Art 13 will further the cause of mediation. Mediation, as stated earlier, is well received in the international commercial dispute arena since it empowers businesses to resolve their disputes according to their needs. The current unpredictability regarding the enforceability of a mediation clause, however, is a source of discontent. UNCITRAL could have grabbed this opportunity to impart some degree of certainty.

Confidentiality and mediator immunity

One of the benefits often highlighted by the proponents of mediation is confidentiality. Confidentiality pervades the whole process, from the caucus meetings[48] to the settlement stage. Indeed, one of the opening statements in a mediation concerns the obligation to keep anything said by the parties in a common meeting or a caucus meeting confidential unless otherwise agreed. The imposition of confidentiality has obvious advantages – it opens the door for frank and open discussions between the mediator and each of the parties in their private meetings with the mediator, as well as between the parties during the course of the mediation including the settlement stage (where achieved). Given the widely assumed sensitivity of commercial information on the part of businessmen, parties would naturally prefer not to reveal their frank discussions to the public at large should the dispute end in litigation. As one US court[49] observed:

> If participants cannot rely on the confidential treatment of everything that transpires during [mediation] sessions, then counsel of necessity will feel constrained to conduct themselves in a cautious, tightlipped, non-committal manner more suitable to poker players in a high-stakes game than to adversaries attempting to arrive at a just resolution of a civil dispute. The atmosphere if allowed to exist would surely destroy . . . [its] effectiveness [at p 930].

Of course, it is debatable whether businesses primarily motivated by financial self-interest take advantage of full and frank discussion. The far reach of the duty of confidentiality, for instance, is indicated by Art 13 of the UNCITRAL Rules which states:

> The conciliator and the parties must keep confidential all matters relating to the conciliation proceedings. Confidentiality extends also to the settlement agreement, except where its disclosure is necessary for purposes of implementation and enforcement.

The ADR Rules, similarly (in Art 7) provide:

> In the absence of any agreement of the parties to the contrary and unless prohibited by applicable law, the ADR proceedings, including their outcome, are private and confidential. Any settlement agreement between the parties shall similarly be kept confidential except that a part shall have the right to disclose it to the extent that such disclosure is required by applicable law or necessary for purposes of its implementation or enforcement.

It is unclear from the above, however, whether this duty extends to witnesses and experts who may have played (albeit limited) roles during the mediation process. By

---

48   Private meetings between the mediator and each party.
49   *Lake Utopia Paper Ltd v Connelly Containers Inc* 608 F2d 928 (2d Cir 1997).

contrast, the CEDR Model Mediation Procedure and Agreement is more extensive. Paragraph 16 states:

> Every person involved in the mediation will keep confidential and not use for any collateral or ulterior purpose:
>
> - the fact that the mediation is to take place or has taken place, other than to inform a court dealing with any litigation of that fact; and
>
> - all information (whether given orally, in writing or otherwise) arising out of, or in connection with, the mediation including the fact of any settlement and its terms.

The Conciliation Law, while endorsing this general principle, interestingly does not use the word 'confidential'[50] in Art 10, though the explanatory remarks on the draft provision do state that it is designed to 'encourage frank and candid discussion in conciliation by prohibiting the use of information listed in its para (1) in any later proceedings'.[51]

The degree to which these confidentiality agreements may be upheld varies from jurisdiction to jurisdiction[52] and dependent on the circumstances. In England, for instance, courts have been willing, in the context of arbitration, to say that documents prepared for an arbitration hearing could not be disclosed to a third party,[53] subject of course to some exceptions such as where it is reasonably necessary in the interests of justice.[54]

A confidentiality agreement is likely to be challenged on a number of grounds. For instance, where one of the parties alleges that signature on the settlement agreement was obtained by fraud or duress, or indeed that there was no settlement agreement since the person who signed did not have any authority. The court, in these circumstances, will inevitably (in the interests of justice) have to encroach on matters deemed confidential. The Conciliation Law unfortunately fails to tackle the confidentiality aspect head-on by indicating the acceptable threshold – for instance, in the interest of national security and public interest – thus introducing a degree of uncertainty in international commercial mediation.

As part of the obligation of confidentiality, mediation agreements also grant a right of immunity to the mediators, since expecting mediators to testify would impair their impartiality. The mediation agreement may even extend this immunity to any members of the institution that offer the mediation services. For instance, the CEDR Mediation Procedure in para 19 provides:

> None of the parties to the mediation agreement will call the mediator or CEDR (or any employee, consultant, officer or representative of CEDR) as a witness, consultant or arbitrator or expert in any litigation or other proceedings whatsoever. The mediator will not voluntarily act in any such capacity without written agreement of all the parties.

It must be added that this contractually agreed right of immunity is not absolute, and

---

50 Note, however, that Art 8 (headed 'Disclosure of Information') deals with confidentiality in a limited context as between the participants in the conciliation process.

51 UN Doc A/CN 9/487, para 140.

52 In some US states, eg, Illinois, there are statutes that protect confidentiality in mediation agreements. See Kentra, *Confidentiality in ADR*, 2001, Illinois Institute for Continuing Legal Education (published in co-operation with the Center for Analysis of Alternative Dispute Resolution).

53 *Hassneh Insurance Co of Israel Ltd v Mew* [1993] 2 Lloyd's Rep 243.

54 *Ali Shipping Corp v Shipyard Trogir* [1998] 1 Lloyd's Rep 643.

it is possible that a court may in some extreme cases compel a mediator to give evidence in the public interest – for instance, information relating to unlawful conduct such as money laundering. The matter is one of balancing mediation confidentiality against public interest.[55] Given the importance of ADR in case management, in most civil disputes, it is unlikely that a court will require the mediator to divulge confidential information.

A related question is whether a mediator is under an obligation to report unlawful conduct that becomes apparent during the course of discussions with the parties. In English law, it seems that there is no obligation to do so in respect of civil matters. The issue for the mediator is an ethical one.

Settlement agreement and enforceability

While it is possible for the settlement agreement to be oral, it is normally reduced to a written document signed by the parties concerned. Short of want of authority, duress or fraud, a written agreement would prevent the parties from claiming that a settlement was not agreed and would give a clear indication of the terms. A statement to the effect that the settlement agreement is binding would also aid enforceability. The UNCITRAL Conciliation Rules reflect this arrangement in Art 13(2) and (3) as follows:

(2) If the parties reach agreement on a settlement of the dispute, they draw up and sign a written settlement agreement. If requested by the parties, the conciliator draws up, or assists the parties in drawing up, the settlement agreement.

(3) The parties by signing the settlement agreement put an end to the dispute and are bound by the agreement.[56]

The settlement agreement is a contract, and English law requires that it meets the usual criteria (such as certainty) required of contracts.[57] Parties can get around the uncertainty aspect of enforceability by converting the settlement agreement to a consent award.[58] They can ask the mediator to take on the role of arbitrator and issue a consent award which reflects the agreed terms of settlement. The advantage of opting for such a conversion, in an international context, is ease of recognition and enforcement across borders.[59]

Enforceability of settlement agreements is covered in the Conciliation Law in Art 14. The draft put forward four variants A, B, C and D for consideration. The variant that was widely preferred[60] during negotiations was B, which states that 'if the parties reach agreement on a settlement of the dispute, the agreement is binding and enforceable as a contract'. Open ended in character, it does not require the settlement

---

55 See the Australian case *Esso Australia Resources Ltd v Plowman* (1995) 128 ALR 291 for a different viewpoint.

56 The CEDR Model Mediation Procedure in cl 13 states that 'any settlement reached in the mediation will not be legally binding until it has been reduced to writing and signed by, or on behalf of the parties'.

57 For a US perspective, see Payne, 'Enforceability of mediated agreements' (1986) 1 Ohio State Journal on Dispute Resolution 385.

58 Where litigation has been initiated, parties may seek a stay by using a consent order (aka *Tomlin* order) whereby the court disposes of the claim on the basis that a settlement has been agreed.

59 See the New York Convention on Recognition and Enforcement of Foreign Arbitral Awards 1958 which is adhered to by well over 100 parties.

60 A/CN 0/WG II/WP 115, para 47.

agreement to be in writing or signed. Neither does it add much to ensuring enforceability, since it would be possible to challenge an agreement on grounds of uncertainty, for instance, under the applicable law (eg, English law). In contrast, variant D was perhaps the better solution providing that 'if the parties reach agreement on a settlement of the dispute and the conciliator or the panel of conciliators have signed the settlement agreement, that agreement is binding as an arbitral award'. If this variant had been accepted, further details – such as recognition and enforcement of foreign settlement agreements, and the grounds for refusal of recognition – would have required further work to facilitate movement of settlement agreements across borders. The Model Law on International Commercial Arbitration could have provided a template for these purposes.[61] Variant D was widely criticised for sharing the trappings of formality and undermining the flexibility that many proponents of mediation perceive to be its positive characteristic. Admittedly, flexibility, a commendable virtue, has to be weighed against certainty, and more so in an international context. If settlement agreements are treated as contracts with scope for challenge, thus bringing with them unpredictability, the very benefits that mediation offers (such as low cost and speed) would be lost.

Before concluding, a few words on the other variants. Variant A[62] simply provided that a signed settlement agreement is binding and enforceable. It does not state how such agreements may become enforceable and leaves it to the state to specify the provisions for enforceability, thus introducing an element of unpredictability. And it is this variant that has been adopted in the final text, namely in Art 14. Variant C is similar to the solution suggested earlier in this section, that is, appointing an arbitral tribunal post-mediation so that the settlement can be recorded in the form of an arbitral award. The objections raised earlier apply equally here.

MEDIATION ONLINE

As with arbitration, the provision of online mediation has been the subject of discussion since the late 1990s.[63] A number of private organisations[64] offer online dispute resolution[65] which includes mediation besides negotiation and arbitration. In a legal context, mediation is perhaps more conducive to the electronic medium than arbitration, since issues such as juridical seat are not relevant. This does not mean that online mediation is free of legal obstacles. Questions about the recognition of an electronic contract such as an electronic settlement agreement may arise. However, given the legislative changes taking place internationally to accommodate electronic contracts,

---

61   *Ibid*, para 49.
62   It reads: 'If the parties reach agreement on a settlement of the dispute and the parties and the conciliator or the panel of conciliators have signed the settlement agreement, that agreement is binding and enforceable [the enacting state inserts provisions specifying provisions for the enforceability of such agreements].'
63   See, eg, Cona, 'Application of online systems in alternative dispute resolution' (1997) 45 Buffalo LR 975; Donahey, 'Current developments in online dispute resolution' (1999) Journal of International Arbitration 115.
64   For a complete list, see Schultz, Kaufmann-Kohler *et al*, *Online Dispute Resolution: The State of the Art and the Issues*, 2001, University of Geneva, available at www.online-adr.org.
65   See http://onlineresolution.com.

as a result of instruments such as the UNCITRAL Model Law on Electronic Commerce, it should not be a major obstacle.[66]

In the absence of statistics on the web sites, the success of cyber mediation can be assessed only on the basis of empirical research. On the down side, lack of face to face contact in real space and the associated non-verbal communication techniques that play an important role in mediation may prove a major handicap. Current technology in the form of video conferencing (where available) does not not seem to be sufficiently sophisticated for the effective use of non-verbal communication.

Despite these apparent shortcomings, it seems that legislators are taking online mediation seriously, albeit for consumer disputes in the context of e-commerce.[67] The EU E-Commerce Directive on Electronic Commerce,[68] for instance, makes provision for dispute settlement using electronic means. Recitals 51 and 52 state:

> Each Member State should be required, where necessary, to amend any legislation which is liable to hamper the use of schemes for the out-of-court settlement of disputes through electronic channels; the result of this amendment must be to make the functioning of such schemes genuinely and effectively possible in law and in practice, even across borders.

> The effective exercise of the freedoms of the internal market make it necessary to guarantee victims effective access to means of settling disputes ... Member States should examine the need to provide access to judicial procedures by appropriate electronic means.

Art 17(1) provides: 'Member States shall ensure that ... their legislation does not hamper the use of out-of-court schemes, available under national law, for dispute settlement, including appropriate electronic means.'

RECENT DEVELOPMENTS – THE EU DIRECTIVE

With harmonisation in mind, the Directorate-General for Justice and Home Affairs initiated a preliminary draft proposal for a directive on certain aspects of mediation in civil and commercial matters.[69] After subsequent amendments Directive 2008/52/EC on certain aspects of mediation in civil and commercial matters (Directive) was adopted.[70] Its purpose is to promote the use of mediation in cross border disputes while providing a predictable framework for the key aspects of mediation and ensuring the quality of mediation. Member states are required to comply with the Directive by 21 May 2011.[71] According to Art 1(2) the Directive will apply to cross border disputes in civil and commercial matters but will not apply to revenue, customs or administrative matters or to the liability of the states for acts or omissions

---

66 See Chapters 3 and 4.

67 See *Recommendations of the OECD Council Concerning Guidelines for Consumer Protection in the Context of Electronic Commerce*, December 1999, available at www.oecd.org.

68 Directive 2000/31/EC of 8 June 2000 on Certain Legal Aspects of Information Society Services in Particular Electronic Commerce [2000] OJ L178/1.

69 Available at http://europa.eu.int. See also Green Paper on Alternative Dispute Resolution in Civil and Commercial Law (COM (2002) 196 available at http://europa.eu.int).

70 OJ L 136/3 24.5.2008.

71 In the case of Art 10, dealing with information on competent courts and authorities to receive requests for the enforceability of agreements resulting from mediation, the date of compliance is 21 November 2010.

in the exercise of State authority. The cross border element is established by looking at the domicile or habitual residence of the parties. According to Art 2(1) a cross border dispute is one where at least one of the parties is domiciled or habitually resident in a member state other than that of any other parties at the time when the mediation is agreed, or where mediation is ordered by the court, or an obligation to use mediation arises under national law or an invitation to use mediation to settle the dispute is made by a court.

The Directive does not apply to the different types of ADR (eg Med-arb) that are to be found. It is restricted to mediation and Art 3(a) defines mediation as follows:

> Mediation means a structured process, however named or referred to, whereby two or more parties to a dispute attempt by themselves, on a voluntary basis, to reach an agreement or settlement of their dispute with the assistance of a mediator. This process may be initiated by the parties or suggested or ordered by a court or prescribed by the law of a Member State.

The above definition does not prescribe any specific type of mediation and hence will, presumably, depend on what the parties choose.

Confidentiality, as stated earlier, is regarded as a central core of mediation and this aspect is addressed in Art 7. Article 7 expects confidentiality to be respected and requires member states to ensure that mediators and those involved in the administration of the mediation process are not compelled to give evidence in civil and commercial judicial proceedings and arbitration regarding information that arises out of or in connection with a mediation process. However this is subject to the following exceptions:

- where the parties agree otherwise (Art 7(1));
- overriding public policy of the Member State, such as protection of the best interests of children or to prevent physical or psychological harm of a person (Art 7(1)(a)) or
- where disclosure is necessary to implement or enforce the agreement (Art 7(1)(b)).

The enforceability of the mediation settlement is addressed in Art 6 and this provision requires member states to ensure that a written settlement be enforceable by a court. But this is subject to a number of exceptions, (1) where the content of the agreement is contrary to the law of the member state where the request is made, or (2) where the law of the member state does not provide for its enforceability.

Since ensuring the quality of mediation is one of the of objectives of the Directive, Art 4 expects states to encourage the adoption of and adherence to voluntary codes of conduct[72] and other quality control mechanisms. Initial and further training is another aspect addressed by the Article.

The EU initiative has seen some controversy. A number of organisations such as the Swedish Chamber of Commerce, Council of the Bars and Law Societies of the European Union (CCBE) and the Scottish Parliament, Justice 1 Committee were consulted on the draft proposal. The Swedish Chamber of Commerce saw no specific European need for an European directive on the issue of mediation since the need is addressed by the Conciliation Law. The CCBE on the other hand supported the EU initiative and made a number of suggestions for the improvement of the

---

72   For an example of a code of conduct visit www.cedr.com.

proposal.[73] The Scottish Parliament Justice 1 Committee's response to the Draft Proposal was lukewarm and it was felt that regulation may stifle the growth of mediation in Scotland, which was still very much in its infancy compared to England or Europe.[74]

While it is understandable that regulation is seen as a growth inhibitor,[75] and may in some circumstances actually result in stifling growth it is debatable whether it would in the context of mediation. For mediation to be conducted successfully it needs to be carried out within a framework. The EU Directive provides just such a framework.

As for the view that the Conciliation Law is sufficient for the purposes of harmonisation, it must be said that the Conciliation Law is not exhaustive and does not impact on the level of certainty in respect of enforceability of settlement agreements. At the very least the Directive has the opportunity to rectify this drawback in a suitable manner that makes mediation an attractive alternative.

There has been another major development in respect of disputes emanating from the ICC. This is the Dispute Board Rules[76] which came into force on 1 September 2004. Dispute Boards are designed to deal with disputes as they arise and are set up at the outset of a contract and remain in place throughout the duration of the contract.

These are ideal for mid or long-term contracts. The Dispute Board Rules cover a number of matters from definitions of the different types of dispute boards (Arts 4–6), appointment of members (Art 7) and their obligations (Arts 8–10) to operation and powers of the dispute board (Arts 14–15).

The Dispute Board must not be confused with mediation or conciliation that are meant to deal with disputes on a 'one-off' basis. However, like settlement agreements the determinations of the dispute board are not enforceable at law but may be contractually binding.

CONCLUSION

There is no denying the attractiveness of settling a dispute through co-operation instead of conflict. In a commercial context, leaving the parties to settle their differences before turning to the state legal machinery should cause no great inconvenience since businesses, at least in the developed countries, are used to self-regulation. Mediation, however, will work only where parties enter into it in good faith and intend to abide by their agreement. Without the spirit of co-operation, use of mediation is simply part of the armour in what may prove to be a long and hard battle for resolving a dispute. Some of the unpredictable aspects of mediation that may be a cause for concern could be dealt with through harmonisation. The UNCITRAL Conciliation Law has the potential to generate some degree of predictability. Whether it has done enough is highly debatable.

---

73 See *Preliminary CCBE Comments on the Preliminary Draft Proposal for a Directive on Certain Aspects of Mediation in Civil and Commercial Matters*, available at: www.ccbe.org.
74 See JI/52/04/22/6 (2 June 2004) Justice 1 Committee 'European Justice and Home Affairs Scrutiny'.
75 See Chapter 3, on the regulation/self-regulation debate in relation to electronic commerce.
76 Available at www.iccwbo.org.

FURTHER READING

Brooker and Lavers, 'Issues in the development of ADR for commercial and construction disputes' (2000) 19 CJQ 353.

Brooker and Lavers, 'Commercial and construction ADR: lawyers' attitudes and experience' (2001) 20 CJQ 327.

Brooker and Lavers, 'Commercial lawyers' attitudes and experience with mediation' 2002 (4) Web JCLI, http://webjcli.ncl.ac.uk/2002/issue4/brooker4.html.

Deason, 'Predictable mediation confidentiality in the US federal system' (2002) 17 Ohio State Journal on Dispute Resolution 239.

Genn, 'Court-based ADR initiatives for non-family civil disputes: the Commercial Court and the Court of Appeal', 2002, Lord Chancellor's Department Research Series No 1/02.

Katsch and Rifkin, *Online Dispute Resolution: Resolving Conflicts in Cyberspace*, 2001, Jossey Bass.

McAdoo and Welsh, 'Does ADR really have a place on the lawyer's philosophical map?' (1999) 18 Hamline Journal of Public Law and Policy 376.

Renfrew, 'The American experience with dispute resolution in all its forms' (1997) 16 CJQ 145.

Rosenberg, 'Keeping the lid on confidentiality: mediation privilege and conflict of law' (1994) 10 Ohio State Journal on Dispute Resolution 157.

Teitz, 'Providing legal services for the middle class in cyberspace: the promise and challenge of online dispute resolution' (2001) 70 Fordham LR 985.

Thornburg, 'Going private: technology, due process, and internet dispute resolution' (2000) 34 University of California Davis LR 151.

PART VI

CORRUPTION

OVERVIEW

Corrupt practices in the form of bribes and kickbacks (part of an income paid to a person having influence over the size and/or payment of the income by some illegal arrangement) are common phenomena in the world of international business. Such practices result in market distortions and increase the financial costs of doing business, thus undermining business performance. Businesses engaging in corrupt practices also expose themselves to reputational risks that seriously undermine their attractiveness as a business partner.

Realising the harmful effects of corruption, both in economic and social terms, regional and international organisations such as the Organisation for Economic Cooperation and Development (OECD) and the United Nations (UN), among others, have adopted anti-corruption conventions both in the business and wider context. Chapter 21 examines the conventions drafted by the OECD and the UN with a view to seeing how far these conventions can play a role in reducing corruption and considers the mechanisms that the private sector can adopt to improve their business integrity.

CHAPTER 21

FIGHTING CORRUPTION IN INTERNATIONAL BUSINESS

INTRODUCTION

The media often carry news items of alleged transnational corruption involving huge corporations and public officials in the host country. In 2002, for instance, Thames Water, Britain's biggest water company, was asked to renegotiate a contract to operate an $891 million[1] Turkish water plant due to alleged irregularities in the commissioning of the plant. A number of Turkish Government officials were also investigated for misconduct in approving a government guarantee for the project. Wide publicity of such cases however has not seen a reduction in allegations of grand corruption.[2] In 2005 the British Serious Fraud Office (SFO) started investigating[3] an electricity trading enterprise, EFT, headquartered in London, for alleged corruption in the Balkans as a result of special audits commissioned by the UN's[4] High Representative in Bosnia. The allegation was that kickbacks[5] may have been solicited by officials of a state owned power company to write advantageous electricity-swap contracts with private companies and that US[6] government aid of $11 million, for providing electricity to war-torn states in the region, was diverted to offshore accounts.[7] And more recently, the SFO's decision to drop the investigation of the highly publicised allegations of bribery of BAE's arms deals with Saudi Arabia is another instance.[8]

The impetus for international measures to combat corruption of foreign public officials came from the United States which had passed the Foreign Corrupt Practices Act (FCPA) in 1977 in the wake of the Lockheed scandal[9] and a report from its Securities and Exchange Commission (SEC) in 1976.[10] This report found that more

---

1   All references to $ are to US dollars unless otherwise indicated.
2   For some recent allegations see Simensen, 'Volkert Arrested over VW Bribery Scandal' *Financial Times,* 21 November 2006; Leigh and Evans, 'BAE Secret Millions Linked to Arms Broker' *The Guardian,* 29 November 2006. See also 'Siemens Bribery Probe could Sink Nokia Merger', 9 December 2006 available at http://uk.news.yahoo.com.
3   This was made possible due to clarification of UK law relating to the bribery of foreign public officials by UK nationals or companies as a result of the Anti-Terrorism, Crime and Security Act 2001 which came into force on 14 February 2002.
4   United Nations.
5   Part of an income paid to a person having influence over the size or payment of the income – especially by some illegal arrangement.
6   United States of America.
7   See Leigh and Evans, 'Fraud Office looks into British energy firm's role in Balkans Company' *The Guardian,* 26 February 2005; Leigh and Evans, 'Firm loses fight to block corruption inquiry' *The Guardian,* 23 July 2005.
8   See for example Leigh and Evans, 'National interest halts arms corruption inquiry' *The Guardian,* 15 December 2006. See pp 680 below.
9   The US company, Lockheed, had made illegal payments to government officials in various countries (including Japan, Netherlands, Italy) to secure contracts for the sale of aeroplanes. The Lockheed scandal in Japan resulted in the prosecution of various officials including Kakuei Tanaka (Prime Minister in office from 1972–74). In the Netherlands Prince Bernhardt resigned when inquiries into allegations that he had received $1 million from Lockheed were initiated. For more on this see Markkovits and Silverstein, *The Politics of Scandal,* 1998, Holmes & Meier; Mitchell, *Political Bribery in Japan,* 1996, University of Hawaii Press.
10 Committee on Banking and Urban Affairs, *Report of the Securities and Exchange Commission on Questionable and Illegal Corporate Payments and Practices* (1976).

than 400 US based companies had made illegal payments of well over $300 million[11] to foreign government officials and political parties to ensure the facilitation of trade. It also revealed that questionable or illegal foreign payments to foreign public officials and foreign politicians were a widespread phenomenon in the US corporate sector and included companies from the chemical, aerospace, pharmaceutical and oil and gas sectors.[12]

Lowering standards of business engagement by adopting corrupt practices of course does no good to anyone, the business sector, the economy, the country or the citizens in the long run. In the economic context, it distorts the market, increases financial costs and risks, and substantially lowers economic efficiency and market integrity. As the report to the House of Representatives correctly observed: such activities 'cast a shadow on all . . . companies. The exposure . . . can damage a company's image, lead to costly lawsuits, cause the cancellation of contracts, and result in the appropriation of valuable assets overseas'.[13]

Not much happened by way of international legislative initiatives between the 1970s and 1990s, but the mid-1990s suddenly witnessed a flurry of activity once the connection of corruption to socio-economic conditions and development was established.[14] International bodies were willing to openly raise the problem and its debilitating effects on the economy, development and the quality of life for millions of people around the world in an open forum and think of ways to combat such practices rather than treating corruption as a taboo subject.[15] Tackling corruption has now taken centre stage on the policy making agenda of influential international economic institutions such as the World Bank[16] and the International Monetary Fund. Coupled

---

11   According to a recent report from the US Association of Certified Fraud Examiners the problem of corruption is still a major issue in the United States. They estimate that corruption and fraud claim more than $700 million a year in the US.

12   Openness to international trade is often seen as a contributor to high levels of corruption especially in countries where there are complex bureaucratic structures. See Hors, 'Fighting Corruption on Customs Administration: What can we Learn from Recent Experiences' Technical Paper 175, 2001, OECD. Also see Krugman, 'Growing World Trade: Causes and Consequences' 1975 *Brookings Papers on Economic Activity*.

13   House of Representative, 95th Congress 1st Session, Report No 95–640.

14   See Alatas, *Corruption, Its Nature, Causes and Functions*, 1990, Brookfield; Mbaku, 'Africa after more than Thirty Years of Independence: Still Poor and Deprived' (1994) 11 Journal of Third World Studies 13, Gould and Mukendi, 'Bureaucratic Corruption in Africa: Causes, consequences and Remedies' (1989) 12 International Journal of Public Administration 427; *Eliminating World Poverty: Making Globalisation Work for the Poor* Cmnd 5006 (2000) London: HMSO; Rose-Ackermann, 'The Economics of Corruption' (1975) 4 Journal of Public Economics 187; Gray and Kaufmann, 'Corruption and Development' (1998) 35 Finance and Development 7, Tanzi, 'Corruption Around the World: Causes, Consequences, Scope and Cures' (1998) 45 IMF Staff Papers 559.

15   Of course, it is possible to view this unwillingness to do anything substantial pre-1990s cynically as a means of protecting Western economic interests. Equally the current frenzy towards adopting anti-corruption measures can be viewed as a means of protecting Western economic interests by ensuring that industries from newly emerging economies such as China and India do not obtain a competitive advantage in the global market as a result of engaging in corrupt practices. As it is, low labour costs in manufacturing industries in these countries are, to some extent, affecting the competitiveness of Western economic interests.

16   According to the World Bank, the cost of corruption globally stands around $1,000 billion. While the World Bank regularly raised concerns regarding corruption with its donees it was only in 1996 that it announced its commitment to 'fighting the cancer of corruption'. At the Ninth International Anti-Corruption Conference Mr Wolfensohn of the World Bank made their serious concerns known:

     So far as our institution is concerned there is nothing more important than the issue of corruption . . . At the core of the incidence of poverty is the issue of equity, at the core of

with the pioneering work of the civil society organisation Transparency International (TI)[17] this has further quickened the pace of policy makers to combat corruption. Often described as a cancer affecting development and poverty reduction globally, regional and international institutions have worked over the last decade to produce suitable legislative instruments in the form of conventions for adoption by countries. The result is a plethora of regional and international criminal law conventions against corruption indicated by the list below:

(i)   Organisation of American States Inter-American Convention Against Corruption 1996 (OAS Convention);[18]

(ii)   Organisation for Economic Cooperation and Development Convention on Combating Bribery of Foreign Public officials in International Business Transactions 1997 (OECD Convention);[19]

(iii) Convention drawn up on the basis of Article K.3 (2) (c) of the Treaty on European Union on the Fight Against Corruption involving Officials of the European Union Communities or Officials of Member States of the European Union 1999 (EU Convention);[20]

(iv)   Council of Europe Criminal Law Convention on Corruption 1999 (COE Convention);[21]

(v)   Southern African Development Protocol Against Corruption 2001 (SADC Protocol);[22]

(vi)   Economic Community of West African States Protocol on the Fight Against Corruption 2001 (ECOWAS Convention);[23]

(vii) African Union Convention on Preventing and Combating Corruption 2003 (AU Convention);[24] and

(viii) United Nations Convention Against Corruption, 2003 (UN Convention).[25]

---

the issue of equity is the issue of corruption. Corruption has to be dealt with by a combination of forces within the country . . . the best we could do was to try and assist in the building of the coalitions and in the forging of that interest in the issue of corruption and inequity, and get it out there.

See www.worldbank.org. The World Bank describes its approach as a multi-pronged approach. See *Helping Countries Combat Corruption: Progress at the World Bank since 1997*, 2000, Washington: World Bank. It has become commonplace for donor agencies to make loans subject to conditions – these require donee states to undertake legal reform (for instance, adopting anti-corruption legislation, money laundering legislation), setting up of anti-corruption agencies, reforming public procurement procedures and reforming public administration systems.

17   TI publishes a Corruption Perception Index, based on surveys where information is provided by country experts. More information on TI and their corruption indices are available at www.transparency.org.

18   Came into force on 6 March 1997.

19   Came into force on 15 February 1999.

20   Still in the process of receiving ratifications. See also Council Framework Decision 2003.568/ JHA of 22 July 2003 on combating corruption in the private sector (OJ L 192 of 31.07.2003). According to Art 249 of the EC Treaty as amended by the Treaty of Amsterdam a decision is binding in its entirety upon those to whom it is addressed.

21   Came into force on 1 July 2002.

22   Not yet in force.

23   Not yet in force

24   Came into force on 5 August 2006.

25   Came into force on 14 December 2005.

It is not the intention here to examine all these conventions. The discussion will be limited to the OECD Convention since it deals with bribery in the context of international business transactions and the UN Convention since it is an international convention with over 100 ratifications and is thus likely to be a major influence in harmonising anti-corruption laws across states.[26] However, attention will occasionally be drawn, as and when pertinent, to other conventions for the purposes of comparison.

However, before proceeding with an examination of the two conventions the following brief section on defining corruption indicates the difficulties in formulating a definition.

DEFINING CORRUPTION

Corruption is a complex concept that is affected by linguistic usage, ethical perspectives and cultural nuances. Taking linguistic usage first, as the following illustrations indicate, the word 'corruption' is used in a variety of contexts from perceived degradation of values in society and deep-seated changes in a person's character in the pursuit of goals, to irregular practices that undermine the sense of justice and fair play. It is common for older generations to talk of the corruption of the young, for instance, by new aesthetic styles, be they in fashion, music, dance or other art forms. The reference here is not only to changes at the surface level, but also to changes taking place at the deeper level to the value systems of the youth that may not correspond with those of the older generation or meet with their approval. The older generation perceives such changes as undesirable and of a degenerative kind. The response by the older generation to the rock and roll style of popular music in the 1950s provides just such an illustration. We also talk of corruption of a person's character, where his or her character takes a turn for the worse, for instance, where X, perceived as honest by his friends, betrays their confidences to a newspaper in return for a few minutes of fame. The word 'corruption' is also used in the context of institutions, as in institutional corruption where, for instance, the institution does not follow the processes that might have been set up to ensure impartiality, transparency and equality of opportunity in respect of staff promotions. Equally, systems are said to be corrupt, for instance where steps initiated for making an appointment within an organisation do not follow open and objective standards as where an individual is appointed purely on the basis of references from 'important people' without taking into account the quality of responses of the applicant at the interview.

Corruption has an ethical dimension as well. Acceptance of a gift with no economic value (eg, a small bag of sweets) by a teacher from a student a few weeks before the exams could raise questions with an ethical content such as 'What is the student's

---

26 Much of this chapter has been derived from a number of my published papers: Carr, 'Strategic Improvements in the Fight Against Corruption in International Business Transactions' (2006) JBL 375; Carr, 'Fighting Corruption Through Regional and International Conventions' (2007) 15(2) European Journal of Crime, Criminal Law and Criminal Justice 121; Carr, 'Corruption in Africa: Is the African Union on Combating Corruption the Answer?' (2007) JBL 111; Carr and Outhwaite, 'The OECD Anti-Bribery Convention Ten Years On, (2008) 5(1) MJIEL 3; Carr, 'The UN Nations Convention on Corruption: Making a Real Difference to the Quality of Life of Millions?' (2006) 3(3) MJIEL 3.

intention?', 'Is the gift likely to affect the teacher's impartiality when marking the student's exam script?', 'Was the teacher acting morally in accepting the gift?', even though the giving and acceptance of the gift is not illegal. One could equally question the dispositions and motivations of an individual who suddenly turns benevolent in helping his elderly neighbour who is thinking of selling his house.

The issue of corruption is also affected by cultural nuances. An act perceived with suspicion and one that raises questions of ethical standards in one culture may not in another. The act of giving a small gift by a student to a teacher may be part of a cultural pattern, symbolic of thanksgiving. For instance, teachers in the Hindu tradition are revered and it is common practice for students to give little gifts to their teachers as tokens of appreciation for the knowledge imparted to them. This tradition can be traced back to Vedic times. The intention is not to affect the teacher's judgment, since culturally the teacher has a duty and is expected to be impartial and not engage in favouritism.

Regardless of these complexities, attempts have been made to provide a general definition of corruption. As the few definitions given below indicate, however, they rotate around economic or other gains made by an individual in a position of power as a result of that individual's role within an organisation or institution. For Kennedy:

> corruption is a code word for 'rent-seeking' – using power to extract a higher price than that which would be possible in an arm's-length or freely competitive bargain – and for practices which privilege locals,[27]

while Nye defines corruption as:

> behavior which deviates from the formal duties of a public role because of private-regarding (personal, close family, private clique) pecuniary or status gains, or violates rules against the exercise of certain types of private-regarding influence. This includes such behavior as bribery (use of a reward to pervert the judgment of a person in a position of trust); nepotism (bestowal of patronage by reason of ascriptive relationship rather than merit); and misappropriation (illegal appropriation of public resources for private-regarding uses).[28]

Given the multi-layered and multi-perspective character of corruption, it is easy to see why the anti-corruption conventions have not attempted a general definition of corruption. The purpose of these conventions is harmonisation of the law and it would be short-sighted if a proposed convention were to fall at the first hurdle of deriving a definition. Further, note must also be taken of the policies driving a convention. In the case of an anti-corruption convention, the purpose is to combat and prevent corrupt behaviour that harms or affects the socio-economic climate and development of a country. *A priori* this restricts the types of acts and contexts that an anti-corruption convention is likely to engage with. In the absence of economic detriment, it is unlikely to be concerned with issues of emerging youth culture or the motivations of a student in giving a low value gift to a teacher.

---

27 'The International Anti-Corruption Campaign' (1999) 14 Connecticut Journal of International Law 455.

28 'Corruption and Political Development: A Cost-Benefit Analysis' (1967) 61 American Political Science Review 419.

THE OECD CONVENTION[29]

The OECD Convention is one of the earliest of the anti-corruption conventions and to a large extent is influenced by the framework of the FCPA. It targets the classic case of corruption, bribery. Article 1(1) requires the contracting states to make it a criminal offence for 'any person intentionally to offer, promise or give any undue pecuniary or other advantage whether directly or through intermediaries, to a foreign public official, for that official or for a third party, in order that the official act or refrain from acting in relation to the performance of official duties, in order to obtain or retain business or other improper advantage in the conduct of international business'. This provision is worded sufficiently widely to include the acts of inter-mediaries, such as agents or brokers who may be used for offering/giving bribes or where the bribe is received by a third party such as a friend or relative of the public official's.

The Commentaries to the OECD Convention however draw a distinction between facilitation payments and bribes and according to para 9 '[s]mall "facilitation" pay-ments do not constitute payments made "to obtain or retain business or other improper advantage" . . . and accordingly, are also not an offence'. The expectation is that companies would use good governance within companies to discourage the use of facilitation payments.[30] This is an unfortunate omission and the OECD has come under constant criticism from civil society organisations such as the TI for introducing this distinction. To some extent the distinction between a facilitation payment and a bribe is not that clear cut, though the common explanation given for facilitation pay-ments is that in some countries a distinction is drawn between 'bribes' and 'facilitation payments', and that the latter is more like tips.[31] Companies normally explain them away as conforming to local practices and a way of doing business by following the

---

29 In the UK the anti-corruption law was spread across two sources, common law and a number of statutes, the Public Bodies Corrupt Act 1889, the Prevention of Corruption Act 1906 and the Prevention of Corruption Act 1916. Ratification of the OECD Convention resulted in s108 of the Anti-Terrorism, Crime and Security Act 2001 introducing the foreign element into the common law offence of bribery and, amended s 1 of the Prevention of Corruption Act 1906, s 4(2) of the Prevention of Corruption Act 1916, and s 7 of the Public Bodies Corrupt Act 1889. In March 2003, as a result of dissatisfaction expressed by the Law Commission with the complex and obscure state of corruption law, the Home Office published a draft Corruption Bill, hereinafter 'the Bill') intended to provide a comprehensive statute on corruption and repeal the common law offence of bribery, the Public Bodies Corrupt Act 1889, parts of the Prevention of Corruption Act 1906 and s 4(2) of the Prevention of Corruption Act 1916. The Bill included a definition of 'what acting corruptly actually means' and based its analysis on a conception of corruption as a lack of loyalty between principal and agent. For instance, cl 3 stated that 'a person commits an offence if he performs his functions as an agent corruptly', and the meaning of agent is provided in cl 11. The Bill created in its first three clauses three offences – corruptly conferring an advantage, corruptly obtaining an advantage, and perform-ing functions corruptly. See Cmnd 5777 (2003), text available at www.hmso.gov.uk. Also see Hansard Debates (HL) July 16, 2004, col 1554. The Bill was criticised by an All Party Commit-tee of both Houses. A consultation process was commenced in December 2005. For more on the principal-agent model see Groenendijk, 'A Principal Agent Model of Corruption' (1997) 27 Crime, Law and Social Change 207. In May 2006, Hugh Bayley, MP introduced a new Corrup-tion Bill (Bill 185 (2005–2006) London: HMSO) under the ten minute rule. Transparency Inter-national played a substantial role in the drafting of this bill. For more on this see www.transparency.org.uk. The Law Commission in 2007 published a consultation paper *Reforming Paper* (consultation Paper No 185) and the Final Report *Reforming Bribery* was pub-lished in November 2008 (Law Com No 313). Earlier in 2009 The Bribery Bill 2009 was laid before Parliament.
30 See pp 695 below.
31 Bayart, *The State in Africa: The Politics of the Belly*, 1993, Longman.

local norms. The value of the facilitation payments and the expectations arising from such payments may say a great deal about whether it is a bribe or not, but this by no means is conclusive. Regardless of these cultural justifications it must be said that it would have been better for the OECD Convention not to have allowed such a distinction.

The OECD Convention focuses on the supply side of bribery, that is the offering or promising by the bribe giver, which is also known as active bribery. It does not focus on the demand or soliciting of bribes by the bribe taker, which is known as passive bribery. Presumably this restrictive focus was to avoid potential problems of jurisdiction over a foreign public official.

Only bribery of foreign public officials in the context of international business transactions is the concern of the OECD Convention. 'International business transactions' is left undefined though the Preamble states as follows:

> Considering that bribery is a widespread phenomenon in international business transactions, including trade and investment . . .

This means transactions such as sales of goods, services, investment contracts, countertrade agreements, concession agreements, as long as there is an international dimension to them will be construed as international business transactions.

A foreign public official, defined in Art 1(4), is sufficiently wide to include civil servants, the judiciary, Members of Parliament and those working in public undertakings.

Liability of legal persons

The OECD Convention expects contracting states to put in place measures in accordance with its legal principles as to the liability of legal persons. According to this requirement companies will be liable for bribing a foreign public official. As to whether Art 2 will achieve its intended purpose is highly debatable since the approach to establish fault on the part of the legal persons is not uniform even across common law jurisdictions. Since companies do not have the two characteristics possessed by natural persons (mind and body) attributing fault to them was difficult. *Lennard's Carrying Co Ltd v Asiatic Petroleum Co*[32] resolved these difficulties by proposing the 'directing mind' principle which seeks the active and directing will of the company 'in the person of somebody who for some purposes may be called an agent, but who is really the directing mind and will of the corporation, the very ego and centre or the personality of the corporation'.[33] Among the common law jurisdictions that have adopted this principle the approach ranges from the narrow (the UK)[34] to the more expansive (eg, Canada)[35] where the directing mind is found further down the command chain. By contrast, the United States does not focus on the mental element and instead finds the company liable for the acts of its employees, be they

---

32   [1915] AC 502.
33   At 713.
34   *Tesco Supermarkets v Natrass* [1972] AC 153 where it was held that a manager could not be a directing mind.
35   *Canadian Dredge & Dock Ltd v The Queen* (1985) 19 CCC (3d) 1 SCC.

directors or managers, as long as they act within the scope of their employment.[36] There is a lot to commend in the US approach, since modern methods of company management means that decisions are dispersed across the organisation and at different levels.

Sanctions

The OECD Convention does not provide any guidelines on levels or types of sanctions but leaves it open to the states to adopt effective, proportionate and dissuasive criminal penalties in Art 3. This applies equally to legal persons unless criminal responsibility against legal persons is not possible in the state concerned, in which case it needs to adopt effective, proportionate and dissuasive non-criminal sanctions – including monetary sanctions. Article 3 also requires parties to have provisions on seizure and confiscation of the proceeds in place.

Enforcement

Article 5 of the OECD Convention recognises prosecutorial discretion of the national regime. However the article goes on to state that 'they shall be influenced by considerations of national economic interest, the potential effect upon relations with another State or the identity of the natural or legal persons involved'. At first glance, it seems to be an unproblematic provision but it has been the subject of some discussion as a result of the SFO's decision to drop the investigation into the alleged false accounting by BAE in its arms deals with Saudi Arabia. The need to safeguard national was given as the reason to discontinue the investigation and the SFO stated that 'no weight had been given to the commercial interests or national economic interests'.[37] This dropping of the investigation caused a huge uproar, national and international. Amongst those shocked at the UK decision were the OECD, TI, other non-governmental organisations such as Campaign Against Arms Trade and Corner House. The question was 'Did Art 5 exclude national security'? The answer that reverberated from these organisations was that it did not. According to them in ratifying an international convention a state agrees to meet its international legal obligation by complying with that convention and the UK was not meeting this fundamental obligation. It is however highly debatable whether Art 5 does include national security.[38] Under international law a state can invoke 'necessity' as a defence. It is recognised in customary international law.[39] While necessity was associated with self-preservation historically, in modern times this concept has been construed widely to include essential interest of a state. Recent cases in the International Court of Justice suggest that necessity as a defence can be raised in other situations for instance ecological threat, as in *Gabcikova-Nagymoros*.[40] This wider conception of necessity is also

---

36   See Wells, *Corporations and Criminal Liability*, 1993, Clarendon Press.
37   SFO Press Statement, December 14, 2006, available www.sfo.gov.uk.
38   For opposing points of view see Rose-Ackerman and Billa 'Treaties and National Security' Yale and Economics Research Paper 351 and Carr & Outhwaite 'The OECD Convention Ten Years On' 2008 5(1) MJIEL 3.
39   See *Gabcikova-Nagymoros* ICJ Reports 1997 (25 September 2007).
40   Ibid.

embodied in Art 25 of the International Law Commission's[41] Articles on Responsibility of States for Wrongful Acts[42] which states:

1. Necessity may not be invoked by a State as a ground for precluding the wrongfulness of an act not in conformity with an international obligation of that State unless the act:

   (a) Is the only way for the State to safeguard an essential interest[43] against a grave and imminent peril; and

   (b) Does not seriously impair an essential interest of the State or States towards which the obligation exists, or of the international community as a whole.

2. In any case, necessity may not be invoked by a State as a ground for precluding wrongfulness if:

   (a) The international obligation in question excludes the possibility of invoking necessity; or

   (b) The State has contributed to the situation of necessity.[44]

Article 5, as it stands is certainly unsatisfactory and it is time that the OECD revisited this provision. This is all the more important since the Convention seems to have made a major impact in changing the laws in contracting states due to the peer review monitoring system that is carried out in two stages, Phase I and Phase II, whereby the laws and practices in each contracting state are examined with a view to seeing what further action needs to be taken by the ratifying state for effective implementation and enforcement of the OECD Convention.[45]

Other provisions

A number of related issues that could expose or prevent corruption are also included. Article 8 on accounting requires parties to have laws and regulations that bring about meaningful harmonisation with international accounting and auditing standards. It also prohibits the use of off-the-books accounts, recording of non-existent expenditures which are normally used in practice to hide illegal payments and receipts. Suitable sanctions for falsification and omissions are also a part of the requirement under Art 8.

Money laundering is another aspect that is addressed in Art 7. States that have made bribery of a public official a predicate offence for the application of its money laundering legislation are required to extend it to apply to bribery of a foreign public official.

The success of the OECD Convention, or for that matter any convention, is dependant on successful implementation. In this, it excels in having an enviable

---

41 This Commission was established by the United Nations General Assembly in 1948 (G.A.Res.174(II) of 21 November 1997. Its mandate is to encourage the codification of international law. One of its well known treaties is the Vienna Convention on the Law of Treaties (1969).

42 For an extensive commentary see Crawford. *The International Law Commission's Articles on State Responsibility: Introduction, Text and Commentaries* (Cambridge University Press: Cambridge, 2002).

43 No definition of essential interest is provided. See Addendum to the Eighth Report on State Responsibility by Robert Ago for examples of essential interest (UN Doc. A/CN.4/SER.A/1980/Add.1 (Part 2), para. 15).

44 Responsibility of States for Internationally Wrongful Acts, text adopted by the Commission at its fifty-third session, 2001.

45 See p 692 below.

monitoring system in place. Regardless, it is clear that this Convention suffers from a number of shortcomings. Among them, the confusion caused by the distinction between facilitation payments and bribes, lack of clarity in Art 5 and the lack of guidelines to establish fault on the part of legal persons.

THE UN CONVENTION[46]

The UN Convention has often been described by organisations such as TI as a comprehensive document. The Convention lends itself easily to this description since (1) it creates an extensive list of corruption and corruption-related offences; (2) it addresses the difficult issue of asset recovery by devoting an entire chapter (Chapter V) to it; (3) it vigorously promotes international co-operation, technical assistance and information exchange; and (4) it includes novel provisions on preventive measures.

Offences

The UN Convention targets specific acts of corruption and related offences and casts its net widely. The language of the UN Convention varies from the mandatory to the discretionary, from 'shall adopt' to 'shall consider adopting' thus indicating that the States Parties (SPs) in some cases have a degree of flexibility. This linguistic usage is also found in the creation of offences and on the basis of this distinction the offences are set out under what I call for convenience sake 'List A' and 'List B': the former covering offences of a mandatory character, the latter offences that include an element of choice.

List A

The most common form of corruption is bribery, involving a mutual exchange between X (the bribe giver) and Y (the bribe taker) where Y does or refrains from doing something in return for an undue advantage from X. The advantage promised to Y directly or indirectly in this mutual exchange situation need not always be of a monetary kind; neither need it be directed at Y. It can be one of kind, for instance, hospital treatment for an elderly relative or luxury holidays to be enjoyed by third parties. Article 15 focuses on passive and active bribery of domestic public officials[47] and requires SPs to adopt legislative measures to make them criminal offences when

---

46 This Convention came into being as a result of discussions in the UN Commission on Crime Prevention and Criminal Justice (see E/CN.15/1998/11). The UN Convention against Transnational Organised Crime in Arts 8 and 9 requires basic anti-corruption measures but it was felt that corruption required a separate convention. After due consideration by the Ad Hoc Committee work on the anti-corruption convention was started. The Convention consists of eight chapters, Chapter I (General Provisions); Chapter II (Preventive Measures); Chapter III (Criminalisation and Law Enforcement); Chapter IV (International Co-operation); Chapter V (Asset Recovery); Chapter VI (Technical Assistance and Information Exchange); Chapter VII (Mechanisms for Implementation) and Chapter VIII (Final Provisions). The text of the Convention is available at www.un.org.

47 'Public official' is widely construed to include any person holding a legislative, executive and administrative or judicial official of a state party. They can be elected or appointed, permanent or temporary post-holders, paid or unpaid members. It also includes those who perform a public function in a public agency or public enterprise, and also those defined as a 'public official' in the domestic law of the state party (Art 2(a)).

committed intentionally. Article 16 extends the bribery offence to active bribery of a foreign public official and officials of public international organisations when committed intentionally. In drafting these offences it adopts to some extent the language found in other anti-corruption conventions.

The next offence to fall within this list is embezzlement, misappropriation or diversion of property by a public official.[48] Existing laws on theft in many SPs are likely to cover this type of behaviour but it was felt that this should be specifically included within the list of corruption offences for a number of reasons: first, theft has a broad meaning and second, in some jurisdictions it may refer only to theft of tangibles. The kinds of activities that seem to be contemplated by Art 17 are use of government funds for improvements to personal real estates, unauthorised withdrawals from government accounts or false expense claims.[49]

Laundering of proceeds of crime also seems to fall within List A and SPs are required to establish as criminal offences the conversion, concealment, disposition, movement or ownership of property when committed intentionally and knowing that such property is proceeds of crime.[50]

Obstruction of justice is another offence created by the UN Convention. Under Art 25, SPs have to make the use of physical force, intimidation against members of the public, judicial and enforcement officers, or interference in the giving of testimony an offence when committed intentionally.[51] This is an unusual provision in a corruption convention but its inclusion is to strengthen the investigation and prosecution processes when a case of corruption is alleged.

Participatory act in any capacity such as that of an instigator, accomplice or assistant are also made a criminal offence.[52] Since companies participate in illegal activities Art 26 expects SPs to adopt measures to establish the liability of legal persons. The liability of these legal persons may be criminal, civil or administrative. Liability of the legal person does not however affect the liability of natural persons.

Intention as is to be expected forms the backbone for the committing of an offence under the UN Convention. It is the first anti-corruption convention to indicate how intentionality is to be construed thus doing away with potential debates on whether the subjective or objective test is to be applied. According to Art 28 'knowledge, intent or purpose required as an element of offence established in accordance with the Convention may be inferred from objective factual circumstances'.

List B

The UN Convention includes bribery in the private sector but under the discretionary list. Its exclusion from List A is a surprise given that (1) multi-national corporations now are as powerful in economic terms as some of the small nation states, and (2) many developing countries have privatised the provision of utilities such as

---

48   Art 17.
49   The Toolkit produced by UNODC (United Nations Office on Drugs and Crime) cites as an example the use of World Bank-funded vehicles for taking children of public officials to schools. See Part I *Legislative Guide for the Implementation of the United Nations Convention against Corruption* available at www.unodc.org.
50   Art 27.
51   Art 25.
52   Art 27.

electricity and water which were normally provided by the public sector. Europe argued strongly for including the private sector but faced major resistance from the United States who did not want to see the private sector included in the UN Convention at all on the basis that 'many practices viewed as corrupt in the government aren't improper in business'.[53] In the end, by way of compromise, the UN Convention requires SPs to consider adoption of legislative measures that may be necessary to establish as criminal offences, passive and active bribery and embezzlement of property when committed intentionally in the private sector. This leaves it open to the SPs to act as they see fit.[54]

A striking inclusion within List B is passive bribery of foreign public officials or an official of a public international organisation in Art 16(b). While it is easy to see how it might be applied to an official working with an international organisation, for instance an official of UNESCO located within the state that has implemented Art 16(b), it is difficult to see how it could extend to the act of a foreign public official located in another state unless the said act takes place within the implementing state.

Abuse of functions[55] by a public official is another offence introduced by the UN Convention. It moves away from the idea of mutual exchange present in the offence of bribery and refers to intentionally acting or omitting to act in violation of the law for the purpose of obtaining an undue advantage for himself or a third party. The emphasis of this provision is on the quality of the act of the public official and the consequences that flow from it. So if an official were to gain information from perusing sensitive and privileged documents and contrary to confidentiality laws uses the information to obtain some advantage for himself or a third party then an offence would be committed under this section as long as it is committed intentionally. Though somewhat differently worded the AU Convention also contains a provision that is intended to have the same result.[56]

Another offence included within this list is that of illicit enrichment which has proved highly controversial in the context of other conventions, in particular the OAS Convention and the AU Convention. For instance, the United States in respect of an illicit enrichment (Art IX) offence in the OAS Convention said it was contrary to the legal principles of the US legal system since it reversed the burden of proof. Article 20 of the UN Convention also seems to place the obligation on the public official to give a reasonable explanation for substantial increase of his assets. The UN Convention however does go on to state that this provision is subject to the constitution and the fundamental principles of the SP's legal system. This offence does give one major advantage to inexperienced investigation authorities however. In placing the onus on the accused all that the authorities have to show is a substantial increase in the wealth of the public official under scrutiny. The illicit enrichment offence certainly has been implemented by the South American states that have ratified the OAS Convention, many of whom lack the expertise and availability of personnel required for complex investigations.

---

53   Dabis, 'US Battles Europe to Narrow a Treaty Banning Corruption' The Wall Street Journal, 17 June 2003. The argument was that in many cultures the giving of expensive gifts to those working within the private sector would not be seen as a 'bribe'.
54   Arts 21 and 22.
55   Art 19.
56   See Art 4(c).

Trading in influence, be it passive or active, is made a criminal offence under Art 20. This offence is also to be found in other conventions (eg, the AU Convention). It is intended to cover situations where for instance a public official or a person offers his services to influence the decision making process in return for an undue advantage. It does not matter whether the supposed influence leads to the intended result or not for the purposes of this offence. There is reason to believe that such phenomena are fairly common in the corridors of power in many developing countries.

Lastly, an attempt to commit an offence and preparation for an offence established under the Convention[57] appears in the discretionary list, whereas participation appears as a mandatory offence. The reason for this may lie in differences between national laws.

What is also striking about the UN Convention is that it replicates the general approach to be found in the other anti-corruption conventions preceding it and restricts itself to improper behaviour that affects the decision-making processes and involves economic gain in the context of (a) private sector to the public sector as for instance when an individual or a company engages in corrupt behaviour with a public official and (2) private sector to private sector as for instance when a sales person of one company bribes a procurement manager of another company. However, improper exchanges where there is an effect on the decision-making process are to be found in other contexts and are likely to be viewed as corrupt though not corrupt under any of the anti-corruption conventions. For instance within the public sector public officials may engage in some form of illicit exchange which does not involve economic or monetary gain for the officials concerned or a third party but may have long term benefits for the department in which the public official works.[58] For instance a request from a senior public official from the police department to a senior official of the auditing and statistics department to massage the crime figures with the intention of receiving more resources is likely to be perceived as corruption. It results in public deceit but also deceit of various state actors involved in policy-making processes such as resource allocation and so on. Since this type of behaviour lacks personal advantage of an economic nature it is not caught by the anti-corruption conventions.

Investigation and other procedural aspects

The UN Convention, like the other anti-corruption conventions, is highly likely to suffer from an enforcement deficit. Part of the reason for this is the covert nature of the crime along with the difficulties associated in the investigation of such crimes. Successful investigation and prosecution are dependent on information provided by affected individuals or others who work alongside corrupt individuals. People are unlikely to come forward as informers or witnesses if they are likely to face external pressures such as intimidation and threats. Provision is made in Art 33 of the UN Convention which requires SPs to ensure that there are appropriate measures to provide protection against any unjustified treatment for a person who reports in good faith and on reasonable grounds to the competent authorities. Such informants, often

---

57   Art 27(2) and (3).
58   See Chibnall and Sanders, 'World Apart: Notes on the Social Reality of Corruption' (1977) 2 British Journal of Sociology 138.

termed whistleblowers,[59] are the subject of legal protection in many countries.[60] The purpose of such legislation is to ensure that whistleblowers are protected from reprisals at their workplace and that such protection will enable disclosure of information. The ambit of the legislation varies from country to country. While some restrict protection of whistleblowers to the public sector,[61] others have included both the public and private sector within the scope of such protection.[62] There are also variations amongst national legislations on who is protected (eg, a public official, an employee), what disclosures qualify for protection (eg, breach of health and safety regulations, breach of environmental regulations, criminal offences committed or about to be committed), to whom they should be reported (eg, ombudsman, Auditor General, employer at the first instance), and the level of belief on the whistleblower's part in respect of the illegal activity (eg, reasonable grounds of belief or strong reasons for suspicion), and how the whistleblower is to be protected from reprisals (eg, relief from liability, anonymous reporting). As to how effective such legislation is in encouraging people with information to come forward is highly debatable. There are no available comparative statistics relating to numbers of complaints about malpractices involving whistleblowers within different sectors to assess the success of the legislation. There is however plenty of statistical evidence to suggest that whistleblowers are simply victimised by their employers.[63]

The whistleblowers' legislation as currently adopted by jurisdictions is devoted to protecting informers from within an entity who expose malpractices within their place of employment. Informers who fall outside of this class also need to be protected, for instance a concerned individual who reports on the corrupt activities of his neighbour. Article 33 also has these types of informers[64] within its sight.

---

59 They alert their employers and other authorities regarding illegal activities within an institution such as corruption, fraud, false/irregular accounting practices, environmental violations, health and safety violations. There are a variety of definitions in respect of whistle-blowing: see Jubb 'Whistleblowing: A Restrictive Definition and Interpretation' (1999) 12(1) Journal of Business Ethics 77. See also Rothschild and Miethe, 'Whistleblower Disclosures and Management Retaliation' (1999) 26 (1) Work and Occupation 107.

60 US Sarbanes-Oxley Act 2002, the UK Public Interest Disclosure Act 1998. The ICC has also produced Guidelines on Whistleblowing (available at www.iccwbo.org).

61 Eg, Australia – see Protected Disclosures Act 1994 (NSW) as amended 1998.

62 Eg, South Africa (Protected Disclosures Acts 2000), UK (Public Interest Disclosure Act 1998), New Zealand (Protected Disclosures Act 2000).

63 See for example Glazer, 'Ten Whistleblowers and How They Fared' (1983) 13 Hasting Ctr Rpt 33. See also Westin, Kurtz and Robbins (eds) *Whistle-blowing: Loyalty and Dissent in the Corporation*, 1981, McGraw-Hill; Bucy, 'Information as a Commodity in the Regulatory World' (2002) 39(4) Houston Law Review 944.

64 Investigation authorities also recruit and use informers (also known as 'informants', 'police sources') but there is limited research on their background and their motivations in imparting information to the police. The available research (See Rose, *In the Name of the Law*, 1996, Vantage Press; Greer, *Supergrasses: A Study in the Anti-Terrorist Law Enforcement in Northern Ireland*, 1995, Clarendon Press; See Billingsley, Nemitz and Bean, *Informers*, 2001, Willan Publishing; see Martin, 'The Police Role in Wrongful Convictions: An International Comparative Study' in Westervelt and Humphreys (eds), *Wrongfully Convicted: When Justice Fails*, 2001, Rutgers University Press.) This largely 'secretive' policing activity suggests that most of the informers are in some way connected to the criminal fraternity directly or indirectly though there are the few who are not. Their motivations vary. Some are tempted by the police reward whilst others may divulge information in return for immunity or for a reduction in sentence or for the purposes of protecting loved ones from getting involved with the criminal fraternity. Revenge is also cited as a reason for providing police with information. And there are those who are driven by moral principles and act for the greater good. In most cases there is some sort of exchange between the informer and the informed, be it of money, leniency in sentencing or some other favour. It is indeed very difficult to gauge the success of this mechanism in the context of corruption. Regardless of various mechanisms that the police may have

Protection of experts and witnesses is addressed in Art 32 which requires SPs to take appropriate measures for their physical protection including relocation and non-disclosure of their identity. In reality many of the developing countries will not have the necessary resources to follow through these guarantees as expressed in legislative instruments. And in countries where corruption is endemic at best such provisions are likely to be nothing more than window dressing.

Investigation is also made more difficult when documents, key witnesses, and other materials are spread across jurisdictions. This is particularly so when trans-national corruption is involved. Even where there is no transnational element it is likely that corruptly obtained assets may have been sent abroad. The UN Convention seeks to promote co-operation both at the domestic and international levels and in Art 38 dealing with co-operation at the domestic level it is expected that public authorities and public officials co-operate with the enforcement authorities by provid-ing the necessary information that is requested. Article 38(a) also expects public authorities to act as informers where there are reasonable grounds to believe that offences under Arts 15, 21 and 23[65] have been committed.

Chapter IV headed 'International Co-operation' is devoted to co-operation at the international level and includes co-operation between law enforcement agencies on a number of matters such as establishing the identity, whereabouts and activities of persons suspected of involvement in corrupt activities; information on the movement of proceeds of crime or property that has been derived from the commission of offences listed in the UN Convention; to provide information requested for investiga-tive purposes, and to facilitate effective co-ordination between competent authorities. There are also provisions on extradition.[66] As to how far the inclusion of extradition will enable extradition in practice is open to scrutiny since SPs may enter reservations in respect of extradition.[67]

Mutual legal assistance is also covered extensively and can be requested in a number of matters such as the taking of statements, effective service of judicial docu-ments, and executing searches and seizures and freezing. It also lists the formalities to be followed in requesting mutual legal assistance and circumstances in which it may be refused. The UN Convention expects SPs to establish a special body[68] dedicated to combating corruption. The setting up of a specialised unit in management terms is attractive since it creates a group of personnel with expert knowledge of the relevant techniques for combating and preventing corruption.

Asset recovery

The most radical section in the UN Convention contains provisions on asset recovery. While conventions such as the AU Convention and the OAS Convention provide for seizure and freezing of assets they do not address the controversial and difficult issue

---

in place in accessing information from 'good' sources the reliability of such information is debatable and may result in miscarriages of justice.

65 Article 15 deals with active and passive bribery of domestic public official, Art 21 with bribery in the private sector, Art 23 with laundering of proceeds of crime,

66 Art 44.

67 See Cobain, Parfitt and Watt, 'Yard's poison murder investigators face huge extradition obstacle as they arrive in Moscow' *The Guardian*, 5 December 2006.

68 Arts 5 and 36.

of asset recovery. The UN Convention is therefore unique in going beyond seizure and freezing of assets[69] to include repatriation of assets obtained through corrupt activity. The whole of Chapter V (Arts 51–59) is devoted to asset recovery and Art 51 provides that 'the return of assets . . . is a fundamental principle[70] of this Convention, and States Parties shall afford one another the widest measure of cooperation and assistance in this regard'. Chapter V received the enthusiastic support of developing countries, many of whom have been gradually stripped of their national wealth by despotic regimes over time.[71] Much has been said and reported about the excesses of the leaders and politicians of developing countries[72] and the 'illegal export' of national wealth and their investments abroad in bonds, stocks and real estate. In a few cases states have had some success in recovering at least part of the stolen wealth located in other jurisdictions.[73]

Asset recovery however is beset with a number of problems. Much of the illicit gains are likely to be located in developed countries and laws in relation to freezing and confiscation orders are fairly complex and procedurally rigorous in these countries. Many of the developing countries, victims of 'national asset escape', lack the financial capacity and legal techniques and expertise required to engage in the investigation and prosecution for recovery of assets. Recovery of ill-gotten assets largely depends on the seriousness and commitment with which international co-operation, both at the investigative and legal level, is carried out. Developed countries also need to do a great deal in ensuring that they do not provide 'safe havens' to individuals engaged in corrupt activities. That there is a political will to do this at least seemed to emerge from the G8[74] countries' summit held at St Petersburg in July 2006.[75] The Leaders of G8 said 'we will work with all the international financial centres and . . . private sectors to deny safe haven to illicitly acquired assets by individuals engaged in high level corruption. . . . we reiterate our commitment to take concrete steps to ensure that financial markets are protected from criminal abuse, including bribery and corruption, by pressing all financial centres to attain and implement the highest international standards of transparency and exchange of information'.[76] While such public expressions impart a level of confidence the important question is whether it will make a real difference on the ground. It may in the present climate since there is a perceived degree of association between corruption and a threat to

---

69 On freezing, seizure and confiscation see Art 31.

70 However, it seems that this phrase does not have legal consequences on the provisions contained in Chapter V. See UN Doc A/58/422/Add.1, October 7, 2003 at 8. Available at www.unodc.org.

71 See The Nyanga Declaration on the Recovery and Repatriation of Africa's Wealth, 4 March 2001 (available www.legacy.transparency.org); The Nairobi Declaration, 7 April 2006 (available www.globalpolicy.org).

72 See Unzicker, 'From Corruption to Cooperation: Globalisation Brings a Multilateral Agreement Against Foreign Bribery' (2000) 7 Indiana Journal of Global Legal Studies 655.

73 For instance, the return of millions of dollars deposited by the Abacha military regime to Nigeria (www.ejpd.admin.ch); see also the Switzerland-Peruvian case, and the Marcos case (www.u4.no).

74 Group of Eight.

75 http://en.g8russia.ru.

76 See Donnelly, 'Rethinking Security' 2000 (48:3) NATO Review 32. Web edition available at www.nato.int. According to Donnelly 'corruption is a security threat in its own right, as well as a contributory factor to governmental failings . . . [It] is the single most serious threat to the viability of several countries' (at 32).

security.[77] With the current concerns about security there is reason to believe that movement of funds, including corruptly obtained funds, across jurisdictions through financial institutions will be under close scrutiny.

The language of Chapter V leans towards the mandatory and Art 52 focuses on the prevention and detection of transfers of proceeds of crime. It requires SPs to take steps in accordance with its domestic law to ensure that financial institutions in their countries identify customers and the beneficial owners of funds deposited into high value accounts. Without doubt, this will introduce a further layer of bureaucracy in some countries. And more so in developing countries where many of the banks are state-owned and are already subject to burdensome bureaucracy and where the decision-making at times is dispersed across different sections of the bank. While measures in relation to identification are important it may have the opposite unintended effect. After all, is it not excessive bureaucracy that provides the breeding ground for corrupt activities in developing countries? It seems the UN Convention in its attempt to tackle grand corruption unwittingly may be creating an opportunity for petty corruption and harassment of customers by lowly paid bank staff.

Article 52 further requires 'enhanced scrutiny of accounts sought or maintained by or on behalf of individuals who are, or have been, entrusted with public functions and their family members and close associates'. The intention here is one of detection but it is questionable whether this will work in practice in countries where corruption is endemic. The UN Convention addresses corruption in specific contexts, namely private to public and private to private. It does not address corruption within the public sector as between departments, for instance, where the Ministry of Finance requests a state-owned bank to relax scrutiny of the bank account of one of their civil servants. While nothing is openly agreed there may be an expectation that compliance with the request may result in favourable treatment when it comes to allocation of resources to state-owned banks.

Article 52 also addresses the issue of introducing financial disclosure schemes for public officials including declaration of any interest in a financial account in a foreign country. It is expected that SPs will introduce sanctions for non-compliance with these provisions.

Articles 53–57 deal with issues relating to confiscation, seizure, international co-operation and mutual assistance for the purposes of confiscation and the return and disposal of such assets. Article 53 is an important provision and requires SPs to take measures that will permit another state to initiate civil action in its courts to establish title to or ownership of property acquired through corrupt activities.

As a preventive and combating measure, Art 58, in a mandatory tone, requires SPs to establish a financial intelligence unit to be responsible for receiving, analysing and disseminating to the competent authorities reports of spurious financial transactions. In theory it sounds attractive to have an especially dedicated unit since it has the potential to increase the chances for detection and subsequent prosecution. However, the question is how it will work in practice. Most of the countries that have ratified the UN Convention fall within the group of developing and least developed countries and many of these are resource strapped and currently engaged in a variety of local issues ranging from civil unrest, sectarian conflict, high levels of illiteracy, and

---

77   It seems national security may be used as a tool to stop corruption related investigations. See 'National Interests Halts Arms Corruption Inquiry' The Guardian, 15 December 2006.

poverty to high incidence of malaria, TB and AIDS amongst their citizens. In real terms, intelligence units require funds, high levels of staffing and access to modern investigation techniques such as sophisticated information technology that have the potential to compile, hold and access databases, and relate information held in these databases in an effective manner for the purposes of analysis. Lacking funds and skills it is highly debatable whether these countries can cope with the requirements of Art 52. Funds and skills training are essential, followed by further financial injection for sustaining such units. International agencies such as the World Bank may be a source of finance, but would it be a realistic expectation that they will be able to provide sustained support for such activities? Various agencies (eg, UNODC,[78] FATF[79]) have organised workshops on asset recovery. Without extensive details and statistics however it is unclear how far these have resulted in initiation of actions and requests for cross-border co-operation. The UN Conference of the States Parties to the United Nations Convention on Corruption, which took place in Amman during 10–14 December 2006, considered the issue of asset recovery and the background paper suggested the creation of a centre forming the backbone of expertise for activities conducted under the five pillars described as: (a) needs assessment; (b) legal advisory services; (c) strategic planning and case-management support; (d) capacity-building and training; and (e) partnership-building and information-sharing. As the background paper correctly observed 'asset recovery may become the litmus test of the effectiveness of the Convention as a practical tool for fighting corruption. Building a comprehensive programme should be one of the top priorities of the Conference of the States Parties. That entails careful thinking about the components of such a programme and a readiness to make the necessary resources available'.[80] But where are these resources going to come from? One possible way to move this forward would be to explore the possibility of a public–private partnership where multi-nationals and international financial institutions could provide the technology and other resources as part of their corporate social responsibility agenda.[81] The Working Group set up on asset recovery is continuing with its explorations and deliberations and hopefully a clearer picture may emerge at UN Conference of the States Parties to the United Nations Convention on Corruption scheduled for November 2009.

Sanctions

One would expect a convention that creates a long list of corruption and corruption-related offences to provide an equally exhaustive list of sanctions. Other than stating

---

78 They have produced a guidance document for implementation of the UN Convention. See *Legislative Guide for the Implementation of the United Nations Convention against Corruption* available at www.unodc.org.

79 Financial Action Task Force on Money Laundering which has produced *Forty Recommendations to Counter Money Laundering* available at www.fatf.gafi.org.

80 CAC/COSP/2006/6 – Item 2 of the Provisional Agenda (CAC/COSP/2006/1) Consideration of ways and means to achieve the objectives of the Conference of the States Parties in accordance with Art 63, paras 1 and 4–7, of the United Nations Convention against Corruption, at 8.

81 The UN in 2004 added 'the promotion and adoption of initiatives to counter all forms of corruption, including extortion and bribery' as Principle 10 in its Global Compact, thus bringing corruption within the fold of corporate social responsibility. The Global Compact is a network to support the participation of the private sector and other social actors to advance responsible corporate citizenship and universal social and environmental standards.

that the level of sanctions should take into account the gravity of the offence,[82] the UN Convention is silent on the type of sanction, be it fines or loss of liberty, to be used. In this its approach is similar to those of other conventions that have included provisions on sanctions.[83]

Gravity is a complex concept and can be construed in a number of ways; for instance the gravity of the act itself or the gravity of the consequences that flow from the act. The following illustrations will help in clarifying the point.

(1) O (a public official) accepts a bribe of $100,000 from a drugs company (C) for planning permission to build a much needed hospital in a remote part of the country. C is well known internationally for using hospital patients for testing new drugs without obtaining consent from them. Indeed C has recently been prosecuted in a neighbouring country for experimenting on unknowing hospital patients.

(2) O takes a bribe of $150,000 from a well-known philanthropist (P) to build a much needed hospital in a remote part of the country.

(3) O accepts a bribe of $10 from an individual (I) for a telephone connection.

In all of the above O has committed the offence as set out in Art 15 and all the acts can be said to be grave since they are criminal. Does this mean that O is to be treated in the same manner in all of the above cases when it comes to sanctions, or is the value of the bribe relevant? If the value is relevant then (2) on the gravity scale comes out as the highest compared with (1) and (3). However, if consequences are important then (1) is extremely grave due to the testing of drugs on unknowing patients.

Leaving the interpretation of gravity to SPs will, no doubt, undermine the intended harmonisation of law on corruption expected of this Convention. To some extent this reluctance on the part of the Convention to enter the arena of criminal justice is understandable. Sentencing policies and guidelines vary across jurisdictions and it would have been foolhardy to even attempt to harmonise this area since it would have affected the 'saleability' of the Convention.

Investigation and prosecution of public officials poses special problems since public officials in most jurisdictions enjoy immunities that protect them from investigation and prosecution. Article 30(2) addresses the issue of immunities in discretionary language which suggests the matter is to be left to the SPs, even though it states that there should be 'an appropriate balance between any immunities or jurisdictional privileges accorded to its public official for the performance of their functions and the possibility, when necessary, of effectively investigating, prosecuting and adjudicating offences established in accordance with this Convention'. That domestic law is prioritised is again reiterated in Art 30(9) which states that '[n]othing contained in this Convention shall affect the principle that the description of the offences established in accordance with this Convention and of the applicable legal defences or other legal principles controlling the lawfulness of conduct is reserved to the domestic law of a State Party and that such offences shall be prosecuted and punished in accordance with that law'. This means that many of the offences created may not have the intended effect if immunities and privileges are raised as a defence. If the UN Convention is to have a real impact it is important that SPs consider the possibility of prosecuting an official once he has left office.

---

82 Art 30(1).
83 See for example the OECD Convention.

Implementation

As stated earlier the success of a convention is to be measured not just by the number of ratifications but also its effective implementation. Chapter VIII deals with issues relating to implementation and their review. According to Art 63 the review of the UN Convention is to be carried out through a Conference of the States Parties to the Convention. Such a Conference took place in December 2006. There is another scheduled for November 2009. The Background Paper[84] on implementation suggests that the implementation review process may start with an initial self-assessment on the part of the SPs to identify the weaknesses, strengths and vulnerabilities in their systems with a view to reviewing these further and to providing suitable help and guidance in meeting specific goals as identified.

That follow-up action is important after ratification is recognised by almost all of the anti-corruption conventions (see the OECD Convention, the AU Convention). There are available follow-up models that can provide some useful insights to how this mechanism can be fine tuned. The model adopted for the OECD Convention appears to be working quite well. The OECD's model[85] of systematic monitoring provides a useful framework. Consisting of two phases, Phase I assesses the conformity of a State Party's anti-bribery laws with the OECD Convention. In Phase II there is a one week long on-site meeting with actors from a variety of backgrounds: the government, trade councils, development agencies, businesses, and civil society. A number of Phase II reports have been published.[86] These Phase II reports are extremely detailed and exhaustive and exhibit the rigour with which the teams have followed up the issue of implementation of the OECD Convention through amendments to the national legislation, correlating the success rate with statistical data gathered by criminal agencies, public awareness, sanctions, jurisdiction and international co-operation. The examination of the legislation and other mechanisms for enforcing the legislation are thorough and recommendations robust as the reports exhibit.[87] Of course, in making recommendations there is always the danger that an SP fails to act on them though pressure from other SPs may have a greater impact.

Criminal law, its limitations and preventive measures

The creation of offences along with tough sanctions is normally expected to act as an effective deterrent. While this may be the case to some extent it would be an

---

84 CAC/COSP/2006/5, 15 November 2006.

85 Art 12 of the OECD Convention contains a provision on monitoring and follow-up and according to Art 12 the Parties are required to co-operate in 'carrying out a programme of systematic follow-up to monitor and promote the full implementation' [of the OECD Convention] and this is to be done in the 'framework of the OECD Working Group on Bribery in International Business Transactions'.

86 These Reports are available on the OECD website www.oecd.org. The Reports on the UK are highly critical and it seems the Government may be slowly moving towards responding to some of the criticism. See the Law Commission's Final Report *Reforming Bribery* 2008 (Law Com No 313).

87 Despite expectations, for example, that Sweden would have a sophisticated system for preventing and combating corruption, the Report recommends that awareness of the offence of bribery be raised amongst companies, and the Export Credit Guarantees Board, and encourages the Swedish defence industry to develop strong anti-corruption measures. Recommendations are also made in respect of amendments to their Anti-Corruption Regulation of 2001 and effective prosecution and sanctioning of bribery of foreign public officials.

over-optimistic expectation on the part of policy-makers that criminal legislation has the intended effect on human behaviour. Experience also shows otherwise. Criminal law, in most countries, creates a wide variety of offences along with tough sanctions. They cover a wide spectrum ranging from offences against the person and property to fraud. Existence of these offences by no means eradicates or reduces violent behaviour or fraudulent activities in society. To curb criminal activity, it is important to also have other mechanisms in place that will work effectively alongside criminal law. In respect of corruption, the UN Convention takes a progressive attitude by requiring SPs to put in place, maintain, and co-ordinate effective anti-corruption policies. The stance it adopts is of a holistic nature and it expects the engagement of the public sector, the private sector, the financial sector, and the judiciary in the prevention of corruption. Transparency, integrity and accountability are the principles it projects in the mandatory requirements it places on SPs.

Taking the public sector first, Art 7(a) advocates adoption of procedures in the hiring, retention, promotion and retirement of civil servants, the obvious aim is to reduce the incidence of cronyism and nepotism prevalent in the appointment and promotion of public officials. A number of studies on the causes of corruption have cited low wages as a reason for the high incidence of corruption in the public sector. This may be true certainly at the lower levels of public sector employment. With this in sight a provision requiring SPs to promote adequate remuneration subject to their levels of economic development is also included.[88] Whether this will see a significant rise in wages is debatable since many of the developing countries do not have the public funds to meet the wage demands. This shortfall is partly attributable in many cases to evasion of taxes on the part of high income groups and companies. Unless these areas are tightened it may take some time for developing countries to meet this requirement.

The public sector measures are further strengthened by Art 8 through the establishment of codes of conduct for the correct, honourable and proper performance of public functions. Many countries probably have such codes of conduct in place. As to how seriously these are followed is another matter. Monitoring and introduction of internal disciplinary actions may be one way of ensuring compliance and in a discretionary tone Art 8(6) suggests that SPs consider disciplinary and other measures for those who violate the standards or codes of conduct.

Specific provisions on the measures to be taken in respect of activities such as public procurement and management of public finances, which are known to present fertile opportunities for corrupt activities are also included. Article 9 indicates the steps that SPs need to adopt to ensure transparency and objectivity in public procurement contracts, thus limiting the scope for corrupt activities. SPs are expected to ensure that information about tenders is publicly distributed, and that the conditions of participation and criteria for selection are clear. Where rules of procedure are not followed, the provisions also make room for an effective system of appeal.

Any anti-corruption drive needs to ensure that the judiciary and prosecution services are above corruption. Mindful of the problem of corruption in this sector in many countries[89] the UN Convention requires SPs to take measures to strengthen the

---

88 Art 7(c).
89 On corruption in the judiciary see for instance *Tanzania: Corruption in the Police, Judiciary, Revenue and Land Services* available at www.ciet.org.

integrity of, and prevent opportunities for corruption among, members of these services.[90] It suggests once again codes of conduct in this context but these are likely to work only if effective measures for their monitoring are put in place.

Moving on to the private sector, anti-corruption measures are addressed through enhanced accounting and auditing standards along with effective, proportionate and dissuasive civil, administrative and criminal penalties for failure to comply. Codes of conduct are also seen as a means of strengthening the integrity and proper performance of business activities by the actors in the private sector.[91] And, as in the OECD Convention, SPs are required to disallow tax deductability of expenses that constitute bribes, as well as other expenses incurred in furtherance of corrupt conduct.

Since financial institutions play a major role in depositing and transferring illicitly obtained funds across borders, Art 14 requires SPs to take adequate measures to prevent money laundering by instituting a comprehensive regulatory and supervisory regime for banks and other financial institutions, including the keeping of meticulous records and the taking of adequate measures to check customer identification and reporting suspicious transactions. Since many money transfers are carried out electronically and the identity of the originator may not always be clear, the UN Convention requires that such information should be clearly included and maintained through the payment chain.

All of the above preventive measures make a constructive and important contribution to combating corruption. There is one major weakness however. While adoption of codes of conduct is easy, integrity can be assured only if they are followed assiduously. Without effective monitoring it means another set of rules will be broken with impunity, especially in developing countries that lack resources. Against this potentially gloomy backdrop the UN Convention seems to have taken the right approach by requiring SPs to bring in other stakeholders such as citizens, community based organisations, non-governmental organisations and activists within the preventive measures. The UN sees a greater role for the public in the decision-making processes within a state and for the state to put in place measures for greater access to information. It even goes as far as indicating that the detrimental effects of corruption and non-tolerance of corruption should be part of the school and university curricula.[92] Once again it is possible to criticise this as nothing more than an expression of ideals since many of the countries that have ratified the UN Convention suffer from high rates of illiteracy, and in countries that lack a democratic structure it is unlikely that they will adopt the trappings of democracy such as access to information and citizen participation in decision-making. A nihilistic picture can be painted of any convention. However, what has to be kept in mind is that it will take time to introduce changes and by no means is the UN Convention meant to be a quick-fix solution to a problem that has plagued humanity for centuries.

BUSINESS CODES OF CONDUCT

It must be reiterated that while the anti-corruption conventions would bring about much needed harmonisation provided they are implemented, it does not follow that

---

90   Art 11.
91   Art 12.
92   Art 13.

they will be effective in combating corruption since the laws will need to be enforced. And as stated earlier, enforcement deficit is likely to be a major hindrance to lowering the incidence of corruption. One way to give further weight to the fight against corruption, at least in the business context, is for businesses to adopt codes of conduct in respect of corruption – for instance, in relation to payment/acceptance of bribes. The International Chamber of Commerce (ICC) Rules of Conduct to Combat Extortion and Bribery (RCCEB) may provide a framework. It adopted these Rules in 1977 in response to the scandals that erupted in the mid-1970s and the US Security Exchange Commission survey, mentioned in the Introduction. The RCCEB,[93] amended further in 2005, are rules of good commercial practice and have no direct legal effect. It is intended to be a method of self-regulation by business against the legal backdrop of national anti-corruption laws. It promotes the prohibition of bribery and extortion, be it direct or indirect or through the use of agents or other intermediaries. The phrase 'agents and intermediaries' is construed widely to include sales agents, customs agents, lawyers and consultants. The distinction drawn between bribery and facilitation payments by the OECD Convention leaves room for facilitation payments to be used as a conduit by businesses for illicit purposes. The RCCEB takes a robust approach by requiring businesses to refrain from making such payments unless a managerial review indicates that they cannot be eliminated totally. In this event businesses are expected to ensure that it is limited to small payments to low level officials for routine actions. Businesses engaging in charitable contributions and sponsorships are expected to behave responsibly and not use them as a means of disguising bribery. As part of this responsibility they must act in accordance with national laws and make public disclosures where required. There is also the expectation that businesses will adopt codes of conduct which are also applicable to controlled subsidiaries (foreign and domestic) that provide guidance and training in identifying and avoiding bribery or extortion, include protection from retaliation to those wishing to seek advice or make reports of corrupt activities and disciplinary procedures to sanction misconduct. The RCCEB also address aspects of accounting and auditing and impose duties on those with ultimate responsibility for the business (eg, directors) to ensure that the Rules of Conduct are complied with and to sanction violations and take corrective actions. Appropriate public disclosure of the enforcement of business anti-corruption policies or codes is also expected. The ICC has also published *Fighting Corruption: Corporate Practices Manual* which is a practical toolkit providing guidance on how to comply with the Rules of Conduct.

TI, a civil society organisation devoted to fighting corruption, has also developed codes of conduct in partnership with other stakeholders including multinational companies. The Business Principles for Countering Bribery (BPCB) were adopted in 2002 and followed by a special edition devoted to small and medium enterprises in 2008. Like the RCCEB the BPCB's aim is that businesses will adopt values and practices to counter bribery and other manifestations of corruption. There are also global initiatives for fostering ethical business 'The Partnership against Corruption Principles on Countering Bribery' from the World Global Forum and the UN Global Compact which in its Tenth Principle states that 'businesses should work against corruption in all its forms, including extortion and bribery'.

---

93   Text available at www.iccwbo.org.

CONCLUSION

The coming into force of the OECD Convention and the UN Convention is a clear sign that the international community of policy-makers and lawmakers recognise the negative socio-economic impact of corruption and the need to find a solution. This recognition is important but a solution through legal regulation of itself is insufficient to achieve the objective of lowering corrupt practices thus making a noticeable impact on poverty globally. Legal regulation is always prone to enforcement deficit for a number of reasons ranging from lack of investigative expertise and mutual co-operation to political apathy. Without the political will of SPs, the willingness of civil society and the business community to take ownership of the problem, the conventions will remain just an interesting attempt to promote a global solution to a global problem.

FURTHER READING

Nicholls, Daniel, Polaine and Hatchard, *Corruption and the Misuse of Public Office*, 2006, OUP.

Rose-Ackerman, *Corruption: A Study in Political Economy*, 1978, Academic Press.

APPENDIX 1

GENCON (AS REVISED 1922 AND 1976)[1]

1. Shipbroker	RECOMMENDED THE BALTIC AND INTERNATIONAL MARITIME CONFERENCE UNIFORM GENERAL CHARTER (AS REVISED 1922 and 1976) INCLUDING "F.I.O." ALTERNATIVE, ETC. (To be used for trades for which no approved form is in force) CODE NAME: "GENCON" Part I
	2. Place and date
3. Owners/Place of business (Cl. 1)	4. Charterers/Place of business (Cl. 1)
5. Vessel's name (Cl. 1)	6. GRT/NRT (Cl. 1)
7. Deadweight cargo carrying capacity in tons (abt.) (Cl. 1)	8. Present position (Cl. 1)
9. Expected ready to load (abt.) (Cl. 1)	
10. Loading port or place (Cl. 1)	11. Discharging port or place (Cl. 1)
12. Cargo (also state quantity and margin in Owners' option, if agreed; if full and complete cargo not agreed state "part cargo") (Cl. 1)	
13. Freight rate (also state if payable on delivered or intaken quantity) (Cl. 1)	14. Freight payment (state currency and method of payment; also beneficiary and bank account) (Cl. 4)
15. Loading and discharging costs (state alternative (a) or (b) of Cl. 5; also indicate if vessel is gearless)	16. Laytime (if separate laytime for load. and disch. is agreed, fill in a) and b). If total laytime for load. and disch., fill in c) only) (Cl. 6)
	a) Laytime for loading
17. Shippers (state name and address) (Cl. 6)	b) Laytime for discharging
	c) Total laytime for loading and discharging
18. Demurrage rate (loading and discharging) (Cl. 7)	19. Cancelling date (Cl. 10)
20. Brokerage commission and to whom payable (Cl. 14)	
21. Additional clauses covering special provisions, if agreed.	

It is mutually agreed that this Contract shall be performed subject to the conditions contained in this Charter which shall include Part I as well as Part II. In the event of a conflict of conditions, the provisions of Part I shall prevail over those of Part II to the extent of such conflict.

Signature (Owners)	Signature (Charterers)

Printed and sold by Fr. G. Knudtzon Ltd., 55, Toldbodgade, Copenhagen, by authority of The Baltic and International Maritime Conference (BIMCO), Copenhagen.

1 Acknowledgment: the author and publisher thank the Baltic and International Maritime Council (BIMCO) for permission to reproduce 'GENCON' Charter (as revised 1922 and 1976).

PART II

"Gencon" Charter (As Revised 1922 and 1976)

Including "F.I.O." Alternative, etc.

1. It is agreed between the party mentioned in Box 3 as Owners of the steamer or motor-vessel named in Box 5, of the gross/nett Register tons indicated in Box 6 and carrying about the number of tons of deadweight cargo stated in Box 7, now in position as stated in Box 8 and expected ready to load under this Charter about the date indicated in Box 9, and the party mentioned as Charterers in Box 4 that:
The said vessel shall proceed to the loading port or place stated in Box 10 or so near thereto as she may safely get and lie always afloat, and there load a full and complete cargo (if shipment of deck cargo agreed same to be at Charterers' risk) as stated in Box 12 (Charterers to provide all mats and/or wood for dunnage and any separations required, the Owners allowing the use of any dunnage wood on board if required) which the Charterers bind themselves to ship, and being so loaded the vessel shall proceed to the discharging port or place stated in Box 11 as ordered on signing Bills of Lading or so near thereto as she may safely get and lie always afloat and there deliver the cargo on being paid freight on delivered or intaken quantity as indicated in Box 13 at the rate stated in Box 13.

2. **Owners' Responsibility Clause**
Owners are to be responsible for loss of or damage to the goods or for delay in delivery of the goods only in case the loss, damage or delay has been caused by the improper or negligent stowage of the goods (unless stowage performed by shippers/Charterers or their stevedores or servants) or by personal want of due diligence on the part of the Owners or their Manager to make the vessel in all respects seaworthy and to secure that she is properly manned, equipped and supplied or by the personal act or default of the Owners or their Manager.
And the Owners are responsible for no loss or damage or delay arising from any other cause whatsoever, even from the neglect or default of the Captain or crew or some other person employed by the Owners on board or ashore for whose acts they would, but for this clause, be responsible, or from unseaworthiness of the vessel on loading or commencement of the voyage or at any time whatsoever. Damage caused by contact with or leakage, smell or evaporation from other goods or by the inflammable or explosive nature or insufficient package of other goods not to be considered as caused by improper or negligent stowage, even if in fact so caused.

3. **Deviation Clause**
The vessel has liberty to call at any port or ports in any order, for any purpose, to sail without pilots, to tow and/or assist vessels in all situations, and also to deviate for the purpose of saving life and/or property.

4. **Payment of Freight**
The freight to be paid in the manner prescribed in Box 14 in cash without discount on delivery of the cargo at mean rate of exchange ruling on day or days of payment, the receivers of the cargo being bound to pay freight on account during delivery, if required by Captain or Owners.
Cash for vessel's ordinary disbursements at port of loading to be advanced by Charterers if required at highest current rate of exchange, subject to two per cent. to cover insurance and other expenses.

5. **Loading/Discharging Costs**
*(a) *Gross Terms*
The cargo to be brought alongside in such a manner as to enable vessel to take the goods with her own tackle. Charterers to procure and pay the necessary men on shore or on board the lighters to do the work there, vessel only heaving the cargo on board.
If the loading takes place by elevator, cargo to be put free in vessel's holds, Owners only paying trimming expenses.
Any pieces and/or packages of cargo over two tons weight, shall be loaded, stowed and discharged by Charterers at their risk and expense.
The cargo to be received by Merchants at their risk and expense alongside the vessel not beyond the reach of her tackle.
*(b) *F.i.o. and free stowed/trimmed*
The cargo shall be brought into the holds, loaded, stowed and/or trimmed and taken from the holds and discharged by the Charterers or their Agents, free of any risk, liability and expense whatsoever to the Owners.
The Owners shall provide winches, motive power and winchmen from the Crew if requested and permitted; if not, the Charterers shall provide and pay for winchmen from shore and/or cranes, if any. (This provision shall not apply if vessel is gearless and stated as such in Box 15).
* *indicate alternative (a) or (b), as agreed, in Box 15.*

6. **Laytime**
*(a) *Separate laytime for loading and discharging*
The cargo shall be loaded within the number of running hours as indicated in Box 16, weather permitting, Sundays and holidays excepted, unless used, in which event time actually used shall count.
The cargo shall be discharged within the number of running hours as indicated in Box 16, weather permitting, Sundays and holidays excepted, unless used, in which event time actually used shall count.
*(b) *Total laytime for loading and discharging*
The cargo shall be loaded and discharged within the number of total running hours as indicated in Box 16, weather permitting, Sundays and holidays excepted, unless used, in which event time actually used shall count.
(c) Commencement of laytime (loading and discharging)
Laytime for loading and discharging shall commence at 1 p.m. if notice of readiness is given before noon, and at 6 a.m. next working day if notice given during office hours after noon. Notice at loading port to be given to the Shippers named in Box 17.
Time actually used before commencement of laytime shall count.
Time lost in waiting for berth to count as loading or discharging time, as the case may be.
* *indicate alternative (a) or (b) as agreed, in Box 16.*

7. **Demurrage**
Ten running days on demurrage at the rate stated in Box 18 per day or pro rata for any part of a day, payable day by day, to be allowed Merchants altogether at ports of loading and discharging.

8. **Lien Clause**
Owners shall have a lien on the cargo for freight, dead-freight, demurrage and damages for detention. Charterers shall remain responsible for dead-freight and demurrage (including damages for detention), incurred at port of loading. Charterers shall also remain responsible for freight and demurrage (including damages for detention) incurred at port of discharge, but only to such extent as the Owners have been unable to obtain payment thereof by exercising the lien on the cargo.

9. **Bills of Lading**
The Captain to sign Bills of Lading at such rate of freight as presented without prejudice to this Charterparty, but should the freight by Bills of Lading amount to less than the total chartered freight the difference to be paid to the Captain in cash on signing Bills of Lading.

10. **Cancelling Clause**
Should the vessel not be ready to load (whether in berth or not) on or before the date indicated in Box 19, Charterers have the option of cancelling this contract, such option to be declared, if demanded, at least 48 hours before vessel's expected arrival at port of loading. Should the vessel be delayed on account of average or otherwise, Charterers to be informed as soon as possible, and if the vessel is delayed for more than 10 days after the day she is stated to be expected ready to load, Charterers have the option of cancelling this contract, unless a cancelling date has been agreed upon.

11. **General Average**
General average to be settled according to York-Antwerp Rules, 1974. Proprietors of cargo to pay the cargo's share in the general expenses even if same have been necessitated through neglect or default of the Owners' servants (see clause 2).

12. **Indemnity**
Indemnity for non-performance of this Charterparty, proved damages, not exceeding estimated amount of freight.

13. **Agency**
In every case the Owners shall appoint his own Broker or Agent both at the port of loading and the port of discharge.

14. **Brokerage**
A brokerage commission at the rate stated in Box 20 on the freight earned is due to the party mentioned in Box 20.
In case of non-execution at least ⅓ of the brokerage on the estimated amount of freight and dead-freight to be paid by the Owners to the Brokers as indemnity for the latter's expenses and work. In case of more voyages the amount of indemnity to be mutually agreed.

15. **GENERAL STRIKE CLAUSE**
Neither Charterers nor Owners shall be responsible for the consequences of any strikes or lock-outs preventing or delaying the fulfilment of any obligations under this contract.
If there is a strike or lock-out affecting the loading of the cargo, or any part of it, when vessel is ready to proceed from her last port or at any time during the voyage to the port or ports of loading or after her arrival there, Captain or Owners may ask Charterers to declare, that they agree to reckon the laydays as if there were no strike or lock-out. Unless Charterers have given such declaration in writing (by telegram, if necessary) within 24 hours, Owners shall have the option of cancelling this contract. If part cargo has already been loaded, Owners must proceed with same, (freight payable on loaded quantity only) having liberty to complete with other cargo on the way for their own account.
If there is a strike or lock-out affecting the discharge of the cargo on or after vessel's arrival at or off port of discharge and same has not been settled within 48 hours, Receivers shall have the option of keeping vessel waiting until such strike or lock-out is at an end against paying half demurrage after expiration of the time provided for discharging, or of ordering the vessel to a safe port where she can safely discharge without risk of being detained by strike or lock-out. Such orders to be given within 48 hours after Captain or Owners have given notice to Charterers of the strike or lock-out affecting the discharge. On delivery of the cargo at such port, all conditions of this Charterparty and of the Bill of Lading shall apply and vessel shall receive the same freight as if she had discharged at the original port of destination, except that if the distance of the substituted port exceeds 100 nautical miles, the freight on the cargo delivered at the substituted port to be increased in proportion.

16. **War Risks ("Voywar 1950")**
(1) In these clauses "War Risks" shall include any blockade or any action which is announced as a blockade by any Government or by any belligerent or by any organized body, sabotage, piracy, and any actual or threatened war, hostilities, warlike operations, civil war, civil commotion, or revolution.
(2) If at any time before the Vessel commences loading, it appears that performance of the contract will subject the Vessel or her Master and crew or her cargo to war risks at any stage of the adventure, the Owners shall be entitled by letter or telegram despatched to the Charterers, to cancel this Charter.
(3) The Master shall not be required to load cargo or to continue loading or to proceed on or to sign Bill(s) of Lading for any adventure on which or any port at which it appears that the Vessel, her Master and crew or her cargo will be subjected to war risks. In the event of the exercise by the Master of his right under this Clause after part or full cargo has been loaded, the Master shall be at liberty either to discharge such cargo at the loading port or to proceed therewith. In the latter case the Vessel shall have liberty to carry other cargo for Owners' benefit and accordingly to proceed to and load or discharge such other cargo at any other port or ports whatsoever, backwards or forwards, although in a contrary direction to or out of or beyond the ordinary route. In the event of the Master electing to proceed with part cargo under this Clause freight shall in any case be payable on the quantity delivered.
(4) If at the time the Master elects to proceed with part or full cargo under Clause 3, or after the Vessel has left the loading port, or the

PART II
"Gencon" Charter (As Revised 1922 and 1976)
Including "F.I.O." Alternative, etc.

last of the loading ports, if more than one, it appears that further 205
performance of the contract will subject the Vessel, her Master and 206
crew or her cargo, to war risks, the cargo shall be discharged, or if 207
the discharge has been commenced shall be completed, at any safe 208
port in vicinity of the port of discharge as may be ordered by the 209
Charterers. If no such orders shall be received from the Charterers 210
within 43 hours after the Owners have despatched a request by 211
telegram to the Charterers for the nomination of a substitute discharg- 212
ing port, the Owners shall be at liberty to discharge the cargo at 213
any safe port which they may, in their discretion, decide on and such 214
discharge shall be deemed to be due fulfilment of the contract of 215
affreightment, in the event of cargo being discharged at any such 216
other port, the Owners shall be entitled to freight as if the discharge 217
had been effected at the port or ports named in the Bill(s) of Lading 218
or to which the Vessel may have been ordered pursuant thereto. 219

(5) (a) The Vessel shall have liberty to comply with any directions 220
or recommendations as to loading, departure, arrival, routes, ports 221
of call, stoppages, destination, zones, waters, discharge, delivery or 222
in any other wise whatsoever (including any direction or recom- 223
mendation not to go to the port of destination or to delay proceeding 224
thereto or to proceed to some other port) given by any Government or 225
by any belligerent or by any organized body engaged in civil war, 226
hostilities or warlike operations or by any person or body acting or 227
purporting to act as or with the authority of any Government or 228
belligerent or of any such organized body or by any committee or 229
person having under the terms of the war risks insurance on the 230
Vessel, the right to give any such directions or recommendations. If, 231
by reason of or in compliance with any such direction or recom- 232
mendation, anything is done or is not done, such shall not be deemed 233
a deviation. 234

(b) If, by reason of or in compliance with any such directions or re- 235
commendations, the Vessel does not proceed to the port or ports 236
named in the Bill(s) of Lading or to which she may have been 237
ordered pursuant thereto, the Vessel may proceed to any port as 238
directed or recommended or to any safe port which the Owners in 239
their discretion may decide on and there discharge the cargo. Such 240
discharge shall be deemed to be due fulfilment of the contract of 241
affreightment and the Owners shall be entitled to freight as if 242
discharge had been effected at the port or ports named in the Bill(s) 243
of Lading or to which the Vessel may have been ordered pursuant 244
thereto. 245

(6) All extra expenses (including insurance costs) involved in discharg- 246
ing cargo at the loading port or in reaching or discharging the cargo 247
at any port as provided in Clauses 4 and 5 (b) hereof shall be paid 248
by the Charterers and/or cargo owners, and the Owners shall have 249
a lien on the cargo for all moneys due under these Clauses. 250

17. GENERAL ICE CLAUSE 251
Port of loading 252

(a) In the event of the loading port being inaccessible by reason of 253
ice when vessel is ready to proceed from her last port or at any 254
time during the voyage or on vessel's arrival or in case frost sets in 255
after vessel's arrival, the Captain for fear of being frozen in is at 256
liberty to leave without cargo, and this Charter shall be null and 257
void. 258

(b) If during loading the Captain, for fear of vessel being frozen in, 259
deems it advisable to leave, he has liberty to do so with what cargo 260
he has on board and to proceed to any other port or ports with 261
option of completing cargo for Owners' benefit for any port or ports 262
including port of discharge. Any part cargo thus loaded under this 263
Charter to be forwarded to destination at vessel's expense but 264
against payment of freight, provided that no extra expenses be 265
thereby caused to the Receivers, freight being paid on quantity 266
delivered (in proportion if lumpsum), all other conditions as per 267
Charter. 268

(c) In case of more than one loading port, and if one or more of 269
the ports are closed by ice, the Captain or Owners to be at liberty 270
either to load the part cargo at the open port and fillup elsewhere 271
for their own account as under section (b) or to declare the Charter 272
null and void unless Charterers agree to load full cargo at the open 273
port. 274

(d) This Ice Clause not to apply in the Spring. 275

Port of discharge 276

(a) Should ice (except in the Spring) prevent vessel from reaching 277
port of discharge Receivers shall have the option of keeping vessel 278
waiting until the re-opening of navigation and paying demurrage, or 279
of ordering the vessel to a safe and immediately accessible port 280
where she can safely discharge without risk of detention by ice. 281
Such orders to be given within 48 hours after Captain or Owners 282
have given notice to Charterers of the impossibility of reaching port 283
of destination. 284

(b) If during discharging the Captain for fear of vessel being frozen 285
in deems it advisable to leave, he has liberty to do so with what 286
cargo he has on board and to proceed to the nearest accessible 287
port where she can safely discharge. 288

(c) On delivery of the cargo at such port, all conditions of the Bill 289
of Lading shall apply and vessel shall receive the same freight as 290
if she had discharged at the original port of destination, except that if 291
the distance of the substituted port exceeds 100 nautical miles, the 292
freight on the cargo delivered at the substituted port to be increased 293
in proportion. 294

APPENDIX 2

GENCON (AS REVISED 1922, 1976 AND 1994)[1]

1. Shipbroker	RECOMMENDED THE BALTIC AND INTERNATIONAL MARITIME COUNCIL UNIFORM GENERAL CHARTER (AS REVISED 1922, 1976 and 1994) (To be used for trades for which no specially approved form is in force) CODE NAME: "GENCON" <div align="right">Part I</div>	
	2. Place and date	
3. Owners/Place of business (Cl. 1)	4. Charterers/Place of business (Cl. 1)	
5. Vessel's name (Cl. 1)	6. GT/NT (Cl. 1)	
7. DWT all told on summer load line in metric tons (abt.) (Cl. 1)	8. Present position (Cl. 1)	
9. Expected ready to load (abt.) (Cl. 1)		
10. Loading port or place (Cl. 1)	11. Discharging port or place (Cl. 1)	
12. Cargo (also state quantity and margin in Owners' option, if agreed; if full and complete cargo not agreed state "part cargo") (Cl. 1)		
13. Freight rate (also state whether freight prepaid or payable on delivery) (Cl. 4)	14. Freight payment (state currency and method of payment; also beneficiary and bank account) (Cl. 4)	
15. State if vessel's cargo handling gear shall not be used (Cl. 5)	16. Laytime (if separate laytime for load. and disch. is agreed, fill in a) and b). If total laytime for load. and disch., fill in c) only) (Cl. 6)	
17. Shippers/Place of business (Cl. 6)	a) Laytime for loading	
18. Agents (loading) (Cl. 6)	b) Laytime for discharging	
19. Agents (discharging) (Cl. 6)	c) Total laytime for loading and discharging	
20. Demurrage rate and manner payable (loading and discharging) (Cl. 7)	21. Cancelling date (Cl. 9)	
	22. General Average to be adjusted at (Cl. 12)	
23. Freight Tax (state if for the Owners' account) (Cl. 13 (c))	24. Brokerage commission and to whom payable (Cl. 15)	
25. Law and Arbitration (state 19 (a), 19 (b) or 19 (c) of Cl. 19; if 19 (c) agreed also state Place of Arbitration) (if not filled in 19 (a) shall apply) (Cl. 19)		
(a) State maximum amount for small claims/shortened arbitration (Cl. 19)	26. Additional clauses covering special provisions, if agreed	

It is mutually agreed that this Contract shall be performed subject to the conditions contained in this Charter Party which shall include Part I as well as Part II. In the event of a conflict of conditions, the provisions of Part I shall prevail over those of Part II to the extent of such conflict.

Signature (Owners)	Signature (Charterers)

1 Acknowledgment: the author and publisher thank the Baltic and International Maritime Council (BIMCO) for permission to reproduce 'GENCON' Charter (as revised 1922, 1976 and 1994).

PART II
"Gencon" Charter (As Revised 1922, 1976 and 1994)

1. It is agreed between the party mentioned in Box 3 as the Owners of the Vessel named in Box 5, of the GT/NT indicated in Box 6 and carrying about the number of metric tons of deadweight capacity all told on summer loadline stated in Box 7, now in position as stated in Box 8 and expected ready to load under this Charter Party about the date indicated in Box 9, and the party mentioned as the Charterers in Box 4 that:
The said Vessel shall, as soon as her prior commitments have been completed, proceed to the loading port(s) or place(s) stated in Box 10 or so near thereto as she may safely get and lie always afloat, and there load a full and complete cargo (if shipment of deck cargo agreed same to be at the Charterers' risk and responsibility) as stated in Box 12, which the Charterers bind themselves to ship, and being so loaded the Vessel shall proceed to the discharging port(s) or place(s) stated in Box 11 as ordered on signing Bills of Lading, or so near thereto as she may safely get and lie always afloat, and there deliver the cargo.

2. Owners' Responsibility Clause
The Owners are to be responsible for loss of or damage to the goods or for delay in delivery of the goods only in case the loss, damage or delay has been caused by personal want of due diligence on the part of the Owners or their Manager to make the Vessel in all respects seaworthy and to secure that she is properly manned, equipped and supplied, or by the personal act or default of the Owners or their Manager.
And the Owners are not responsible for loss, damage or delay arising from any other cause whatsoever, even from the neglect or default of the Master or crew or some other person employed by the Owners on board or ashore for whose acts they would, but for this Clause, be responsible, or from unseaworthiness of the Vessel on loading or commencement of the voyage or at any time whatsoever.

3. Deviation Clause
The Vessel has liberty to call at any port or ports in any order, for any purpose, to sail without pilots, to tow and/or assist Vessels in all situations, and also to deviate for the purpose of saving life and/or property.

4. Payment of Freight
(a) The freight at the rate stated in Box 13 shall be paid in cash calculated on the intaken quantity of cargo.
(b) *Prepaid.* If according to Box 13 freight is to be paid on shipment, it shall be deemed earned and non-returnable, Vessel and/or cargo lost or not lost.
Neither the Owners nor their agents shall be required to sign or endorse bills of lading showing freight prepaid unless the freight due to the Owners has actually been paid.
(c) *On delivery.* If according to Box 13 freight, or part thereof, is payable at destination it shall not be deemed earned until the cargo is thus delivered. Notwithstanding the provisions under (a), if freight or part thereof is payable on delivery of the cargo the Charterers shall have the option of paying the freight on delivered weight/quantity provided such option is declared before breaking bulk and the weight/quantity can be ascertained by official weighing machine, joint draft survey or tally.
Cash for Vessel's ordinary disbursements at the port of loading to be advanced by the Charterers, if required, at highest current rate of exchange, subject to two (2) per cent to cover insurance and other expenses.

5. Loading/Discharging
(a) Costs/Risks
The cargo shall be brought into the holds, loaded, stowed and/or trimmed, tallied, lashed and/or secured and taken from the holds and discharged by the Charterers, free of any risk, liability and expense whatsoever to the Owners. The Charterers shall provide and lay all dunnage material as required for the proper stowage and protection of the cargo on board, the Owners allowing the use of all dunnage available on board. The Charterers shall be responsible for and pay the cost of removing their dunnage after discharge of the cargo under this Charter Party and time to count until dunnage has been removed.
(b) Cargo Handling Gear
Unless the Vessel is gearless or unless it has been agreed between the parties that the Vessel's gear shall not be used and stated as such in Box 15, the Owners shall throughout the duration of loading/discharging give free use of the Vessel's cargo handling gear and of sufficient motive power to operate all such cargo handling gear. All such equipment to be in good working order. Unless caused by negligence of the stevedores, time lost by breakdown of the Vessel's cargo handling gear or motive power - pro rata the total number of cranes/winches required at that time for the loading/discharging of cargo under this Charter Party - shall not count as laytime or time on demurrage. On request the Owners shall provide free of charge cranemen/winchmen from the crew to operate the Vessel's cargo handling gear, unless local regulations prohibit this, in which latter event shore labourers shall be for the account of the Charterers. Cranemen/winchmen shall be under the Charterers' risk and responsibility and as stevedores to be deemed as their servants but shall

always work under the supervision of the Master.
(c) Stevedore Damage
The Charterers shall be responsible for damage (beyond ordinary wear and tear) to any part of the Vessel caused by Stevedores. Such damage shall be notified as soon as reasonably possible by the Master to the Charterers or their agents and to their Stevedores, failing which the Charterers shall not be held responsible. The Master shall endeavour to obtain the Stevedores' written acknowledgement of liability.
The Charterers are obliged to repair any stevedore damage prior to completion of the voyage, but must repair stevedore damage affecting the Vessel's seaworthiness or class before the Vessel sails from the port where such damage was caused or found. All additional expenses incurred shall be for the account of the Charterers and any time lost shall be for the account of and shall be paid to the Owners by the Charterers at the demurrage rate.

6. Laytime
* *(a) Separate laytime for loading and discharging*
The cargo shall be loaded within the number of running days/hours as indicated in Box 16, weather permitting, Sundays and holidays excepted, unless used, in which event time used shall count.
The cargo shall be discharged within the number of running days/hours as indicated in Box 16, weather permitting, Sundays and holidays excepted, unless used, in which event time used shall count.
* *(b) Total laytime for loading and discharging*
The cargo shall be loaded and discharged within the number of total running days/hours as indicated in Box 16, weather permitting, Sundays and holidays excepted, unless used, in which event time used shall count.
(c) Commencement of laytime (loading and discharging)
Laytime for loading and discharging shall commence at 13.00 hours, if notice of readiness is given up to and including 12.00 hours, and at 06.00 hours next working day if notice given during office hours after 12.00 hours. Notice of readiness at loading port to be given to the Shippers named in Box 17 or if not named, to the Charterers or their agents named in Box 18. Notice of readiness at the discharging port to be given to the Receivers or, if not known, to the Charterers or their agents named in Box 19.
If the loading/discharging berth or no available on the Vessel's arrival at or off the port of loading/discharging, the Vessel shall be entitled to give notice of readiness within ordinary office hours on arrival there, whether in free pratique or not, whether customs cleared or not. Laytime or time on demurrage shall then count as if she were in berth and in all respects ready for loading/ discharging provided that the Master warrants that she is in fact ready in all respects. Time used in moving from the place of waiting to the loading/ discharging berth shall not count as laytime.
If, after inspection, the Vessel is found not to be ready in all respects to load/ discharge time lost after the discovery thereof until the Vessel is again ready to load/discharge shall not count as laytime.
Time used before commencement of laytime shall count.
* *Indicate alternative (a) or (b) as agreed, in Box 16.*

7. Demurrage
Demurrage at the loading and discharging port is payable by the Charterers at the rate stated in Box 20 in the manner stated in Box 20 per day or pro rata for any part of a day. Demurrage shall fall due day by day and shall be payable upon receipt of the Owners' invoice.
In the event the demurrage is not paid in accordance with the above, the Owners shall give the Charterers 96 running hours written notice to rectify the failure. If the demurrage is not paid at the expiration of this time limit and if the vessel is in or at the loading port, the Owners are entitled at any time to terminate the Charter Party and claim damages for any losses caused thereby.

8. Lien Clause
The Owners shall have a lien on the cargo and on all sub-freights payable in respect of the cargo, for freight, deadfreight, demurrage, claims for damages and for all other amounts due under this Charter Party including costs of recovering same.

9. Cancelling Clause
(a) Should the Vessel not be ready to load (whether in berth or not) on the cancelling date indicated in Box 21, the Charterers shall have the option of cancelling this Charter Party.
(b) Should the Owners anticipate that, despite the exercise of due diligence, the Vessel will not be ready to load by the cancelling date, they shall notify the Charterers thereof without delay stating the expected date of the Vessel's readiness to load and asking whether the Charterers will exercise their option of cancelling the Charter Party, or agree to a new cancelling date.
Such option must be declared by the Charterers within 48 running hours after the receipt of the Owners' notice. If the Charterers do not exercise their option of cancelling, then this Charter Party shall be deemed to be amended such that

PART II
"Gencon" Charter (As Revised 1922, 1976 and 1994)

the seventh day after the new readiness date stated in the Owners' notification 149
to the Charterers shall be the new cancelling date. 150
The provisions of sub-clause (b) of this Clause shall operate only once, and in 151
case of the Vessel's further delay, the Charterers shall have the option of 152
cancelling the Charter Party as per sub-clause (a) of this Clause. 153

10. Bills of Lading 154
Bills of Lading shall be presented and signed by the Master as per the 155
"Congenbill" Bill of Lading form, Edition 1994, without prejudice to this Charter 156
Party, or by the Owners' agents provided written authority has been given by 157
Owners to the agents, a copy of which is to be furnished to the Charterers. The 158
Charterers shall indemnify the Owners against all consequences or liabilities 159
that may arise from the signing of bills of lading as presented to the extent that 160
the terms or contents of such bills of lading impose or result in the imposition of 161
more onerous liabilities upon the Owners than those assumed by the Owners 162
under this Charter Party. 163

11. Both-to-Blame Collision Clause 164
If the Vessel comes into collision with another vessel as a result of the 165
negligence of the other vessel and any act, neglect or default of the Master, 166
Mariner, Pilot or the servants of the Owners in the navigation or in the 167
management of the Vessel, the owners of the cargo carried hereunder will 168
indemnify the Owners against all loss or liability to the other or non-carrying 169
vessel or her owners in so far as such loss or liability represents loss of, or 170
damage to, or any claim whatsoever of the owners of said cargo, paid or 171
payable by the other or non-carrying vessel or her owners to the owners of said 172
cargo and set-off, recouped or recovered by the other or non-carrying vessel 173
or her owners as part of their claim against the carrying Vessel or the Owners. 174
The foregoing provisions shall also apply where the owners, operators or those 175
in charge of any vessel or vessels or objects other than, or in addition to, the 176
colliding vessels or objects are at fault in respect of a collision or contact. 177

12. General Average and New Jason Clause 178
General Average shall be adjusted in London unless otherwise agreed in Box 179
22 according to York-Antwerp Rules 1994 and any subsequent modification 180
thereof. Proprietors of cargo to pay the cargo's share in the general expenses 181
even if same have been necessitated through neglect or default of the Owners' 182
servants (see Clause 2). 183
If General Average is to be adjusted in accordance with the law and practice of 184
the United States of America, the following Clause shall apply: "In the event of 185
accident, danger, damage or disaster before or after the commencement of the 186
voyage, resulting from any cause whatsoever, whether due to negligence or 187
not, for which, or for the consequence of which, the Owners are not 188
responsible, by statute, contract or otherwise, the cargo shippers, consignees 189
or the owners of the cargo shall contribute with the Owners in General Average 190
to the payment of any sacrifices, losses or expenses of a General Average 191
nature that may be made or incurred and shall pay salvage and special charges 192
incurred in respect of the cargo. If a salving vessel is owned or operated by the 193
Owners, salvage shall be paid for as fully as if the said salving vessel or vessels 194
belonged to strangers. Such deposit as the Owners, or their agents, may deem 195
sufficient to cover the estimated contribution of the goods and any salvage and 196
special charges thereon shall, if required, be made by the cargo, shippers, 197
consignees or owners of the goods to the Owners before delivery.". 198

13. Taxes and Dues Clause 199
(a) *On Vessel* -The Owners shall pay all dues, charges and taxes customarily 200
levied on the Vessel, howsoever the amount thereof may be assessed. 201
(b) *On cargo* -The Charterers shall pay all dues, charges, duties and taxes 202
customarily levied on the cargo, howsoever the amount thereof may be 203
assessed. 204
(c) *On freight* -Unless otherwise agreed in Box 23, taxes levied on the freight 205
shall be for the Charterers' account. 206

14. Agency 207
In every case the Owners shall appoint their own Agent both at the port of 208
loading and the port of discharge. 209

15. Brokerage 210
A brokerage commission at the rate stated in Box 24 on the freight, dead-freight 211
and demurrage earned is due to the party mentioned in Box 24. 212
In case of non-execution 1/3 of the brokerage on the estimated amount of 213
freight to be paid by the party responsible for such non-execution to the 214
Brokers as indemnity for the latter's expenses and work. In case of more 215
voyages the amount of indemnity to be agreed. 216

16. General Strike Clause 217
(a) If there is a strike or lock-out affecting or preventing the actual loading of the 218
cargo, or any part of it, when the Vessel is ready to proceed from her last port or 219

at any time during the voyage to the port or ports of loading or after her arrival 220
there, the Master or the Owners may ask the Charterers to declare, that they 221
agree to reckon the laydays as if there were no strike or lock-out. Unless the 222
Charterers have given such declaration in writing (by telegram, if necessary) 223
within 24 hours, the Owners shall have the option of cancelling this Charter 224
Party. If part cargo has already been loaded, the Owners must proceed with 225
same, (freight payable on loaded quantity only) having liberty to complete with 226
other cargo on the way for their own account. 227
(b) If there is a strike or lock-out affecting or preventing the actual discharging 228
of the cargo on or after the Vessel's arrival at or off port of discharge and same 229
has not been settled within 48 hours, the Charterers shall have the option of 230
keeping the Vessel waiting until such strike or lock-out is at an end against 231
paying half demurrage after expiration of the time provided for discharging 232
until the strike or lock-out terminates and thereafter full demurrage shall be 233
payable until the completion of discharging, or of ordering the Vessel to a safe 234
port where she can safely discharge without risk of being detained by strike or 235
lock-out. Such orders to be given within 48 hours after the Master or the 236
Owners have given notice to the Charterers of the strike or lock-out affecting 237
the discharge. On delivery of the cargo at such port, all conditions of this 238
Charter Party and of the Bill of Lading shall apply and the Vessel shall receive 239
the same freight as if she had discharged at the original port of destination, 240
except that if the distance to the substituted port exceeds 100 nautical miles, 241
the freight on the cargo delivered at the substituted port to be increased in 242
proportion. 243
(c) Except for the obligations described above, neither the Charterers nor the 244
Owners shall be responsible for the consequences of any strikes or lock-outs 245
preventing or affecting the actual loading or discharging of the cargo. 246

17. War Risks ("Voywar 1993") 247
(1) For the purpose of this Clause, the words: 248
  (a) The "Owners" shall include the shipowners, bareboat charterers, 249
  disponent owners, managers or other operators who are charged with the 250
  management of the Vessel, and the Master; and 251
  (b) "War Risks" shall include any war (whether actual or threatened), act of 252
  war, civil war, hostilities, revolution, rebellion, civil commotion, warlike 253
  operations, the laying of mines (whether actual or reported), acts of piracy, 254
  acts of terrorists, acts of hostility or malicious damage, blockades 255
  (whether imposed against all Vessels or imposed selectively against 256
  Vessels of certain flags or ownership, or against certain cargoes or crews 257
  or otherwise howsoever), by any person, body, terrorist or political group, 258
  or the Government of any state whatsoever, which, in the reasonable 259
  judgement of the Master and/or the Owners, may be dangerous or are 260
  likely to be or to become dangerous to the Vessel, her cargo, crew or other 261
  persons on board the Vessel. 262
(2) If at any time before the Vessel commences loading, it appears that, in the 263
  reasonable judgement of the Master and/or the Owners, performance of 264
  the Contract of Carriage, or any part of it, may expose, or is likely to expose, 265
  the Vessel, her cargo, crew or other persons on board the Vessel to War 266
  Risks, the Owners may give notice to the Charterers cancelling this 267
  Contract of Carriage, or may refuse to perform such part of it as may 268
  expose, or may be likely to expose, the Vessel, her cargo, crew or other 269
  persons on board the Vessel to War Risks; provided always that if this 270
  Contract of Carriage provides that loading or discharging is to take place 271
  within a range of ports, and at the port or ports nominated by the Charterers 272
  the Vessel, her cargo, crew, or other persons onboard the Vessel may be 273
  exposed, or may be likely to be exposed, to War Risks, the Owners shall 274
  first require the Charterers to nominate any other safe port which lies 275
  within the range for loading or discharging, and may only cancel this 276
  Contract of Carriage if the Charterers shall not have nominated such safe 277
  port or ports within 48 hours of receipt of notice of such requirement. 278
(3) The Owners shall not be required to continue to load cargo for any voyage, 279
  or to sign Bills of Lading for any port or place, or to proceed or continue on 280
  any voyage, or on any part thereof, or to proceed through any canal or 281
  waterway, or to proceed to or remain at any port or place whatsoever, 282
  where it appears, either after the loading of the cargo commences, or at 283
  any stage of the voyage thereafter before the discharge of the cargo is 284
  completed, that, in the reasonable judgement of the Master and/or the 285
  Owners, the Vessel, her cargo (or any part thereof), crew or other persons 286
  on board the Vessel (or any one or more of them) may be, or are likely to be, 287
  exposed to War Risks. If it should so appear, the Owners may by notice 288
  request the Charterers to nominate a safe port for the discharge of the 289
  cargo or any part thereof, and if within 48 hours of the receipt of such 290
  notice, the Charterers shall not have nominated such a port, the Owners 291
  may discharge the cargo at any safe port of their choice (including the port 292
  of loading) in complete fulfilment of the Contract of Carriage. The Owners 293
  shall be entitled to recover from the Charterers the extra expenses of such 294
  discharge and, if the discharge takes place at any port other than the 295
  loading port, to receive the full freight as though the cargo had been 296

PART II
"Gencon" Charter (As Revised 1922, 1976 and 1994)

carried to the discharging port and if the extra distance exceeds 100 miles, 297
to additional freight which shall be the same percentage of the freight 298
contracted for as the percentage which the extra distance represents to 299
the distance of the normal and customary route, the Owners having a lien 300
on the cargo for such expenses and freight. 301

(4) If at any stage of the voyage after the loading of the cargo commences, it 302
appears that, in the reasonable judgement of the Master and/or the 303
Owners, the Vessel, her cargo, crew or other persons on board the Vessel 304
may be, or are likely to be, exposed to War Risks on any part of the route 305
(including any canal or waterway) which is normally and customarily used 306
in a voyage of the nature contracted for, and there is another longer route 307
to the discharging port, the Owners shall give notice to the Charterers that 308
this route will be taken. In this event the Owners shall be entitled, if the total 309
extra distance exceeds 100 miles, to additional freight which shall be the 310
same percentage of the freight contracted for as the percentage which the 311
extra distance represents to the distance of the normal and customary 312
route. 313

(5) The Vessel shall have liberty:- 314
(a) to comply with all orders, directions, recommendations or advice as to 315
departure, arrival, routes, sailing in convoy, ports of call, stoppages, 316
destinations, discharge of cargo, delivery or in any way whatsoever which 317
are given by the Government of the Nation under whose flag the Vessel 318
sails, or other Government to whose laws the Owners are subject, or any 319
other Government which so requires, or any body or group acting with the 320
power to compel compliance with their orders or directions; 321
(b) to comply with the orders, directions or recommendations of any war 322
risks underwriters who have the authority to give the same under the terms 323
of the war risks insurance; 324
(c) to comply with the terms of any resolution of the Security Council of the 325
United Nations, any directives of the European Community, the effective 326
orders of any other Supranational body which has the right to issue and 327
give the same, and with national laws aimed at enforcing the same to which 328
the Owners are subject, and to obey the orders and directions of those who 329
are charged with their enforcement; 330
(d) to discharge at any other port any cargo or part thereof which may 331
render the Vessel liable to confiscation as a contraband carrier; 332
(e) to call at any other port to change the crew or any part thereof or other 333
persons on board the Vessel when there is reason to believe that they may 334
be subject to internment, imprisonment or other sanctions; 335
(f) where cargo has not been loaded or has been discharged by the 336
Owners under any provisions of this Clause, to load other cargo for the 337
Owners' own benefit and carry it to any other port or ports whatsoever, 338
whether backwards or forwards or in a contrary direction to the ordinary or 339
customary route. 340

(6) If in compliance with any of the provisions of sub-clauses (2) to (5) of this 341
Clause anything is done or not done, such shall not be deemed to be a 342
deviation, but shall be considered as due fulfilment of the Contract of 343
Carriage. 344

18. General Ice Clause
Port of loading 346
(a) In the event of the loading port being inaccessible by reason of ice when the 347
Vessel is ready to proceed from her last port or at any time during the voyage or 348
on the Vessel's arrival or in case frost sets in after the Vessel's arrival, the 349
Master for fear of being frozen in is at liberty to leave without cargo, and this 350
Charter Party shall be null and void. 351
(b) If during loading the Master, for fear of the Vessel being frozen in, deems it 352
advisable to leave, he has liberty to do so with what cargo he has on board and 353
to proceed to any other port or ports with option of completing cargo for the 354
Owners' benefit for any port or ports including port of discharge. Any part 355
cargo thus loaded under this Charter Party to be forwarded to destination at the 356
Vessel's expense but against payment of freight, provided that no extra 357
expenses be thereby caused to the Charterers, freight being paid on quantity 358
delivered (in proportion if lumpsum), all other conditions as per this Charter 359
Party. 360
(c) In case of more than one loading port, and if one or more of the ports are 361
closed by ice, the Master or the Owners to be at liberty either to load the part 362
cargo at the open port and fill up elsewhere for their own account as under 363
section (b) or to declare the Charter Party null and void unless the Charterers 364
agree to load full cargo at the open port. 365

Port of discharge 366
(a) Should ice prevent the Vessel from reaching port of discharge the 367
Charterers shall have the option of keeping the Vessel waiting until the re- 368
opening of navigation and paying demurrage or of ordering the Vessel to a safe 369
and immediately accessible port where she can safely discharge without risk of 370
detention by ice. Such orders to be given within 48 hours after the Master or the 371
Owners have given notice to the Charterers of the impossibility of reaching port 372

of destination. 373
(b) If during discharging the Master for fear of the Vessel being frozen in deems 374
it advisable to leave, he has liberty to do so with what cargo he has on board and 375
to proceed to the nearest accessible port where she can safely discharge. 376
(c) On delivery of the cargo at such port, all conditions of the Bill of Lading shall 377
apply and the Vessel shall receive the same freight as if she had discharged at 378
the original port of destination, except that if the distance of the substituted port 379
exceeds 100 nautical miles, the freight on the cargo delivered at the substituted 380
port to be increased in proportion. 381

19. Law and Arbitration
* (a) This Charter Party shall be governed by and construed in accordance with 383
English law and any dispute arising out of this Charter Party shall be referred to 384
arbitration in London in accordance with the Arbitration Acts 1950 and 1979 or 385
any statutory modification or re-enactment thereof for the time being in force. 386
Unless the parties agree upon a sole arbitrator, one arbitrator shall be 387
appointed by each party and the arbitrators so appointed shall appoint a third 388
arbitrator, the decision of the three-man tribunal thus constituted or any two of 389
them, shall be final. On the receipt by one party of the nomination in writing of 390
the other party's arbitrator, that party shall appoint their arbitrator within 391
fourteen days, failing which the decision of the single arbitrator appointed shall 392
be final. 393
For disputes where the total amount claimed by either party does not exceed 394
the amount stated in Box 25** the arbitration shall be conducted in accordance 395
with the Small Claims Procedure of the London Maritime Arbitrators 396
Association. 397

* (b) This Charter Party shall be governed by and construed in accordance with 398
Title 9 of the United States Code and the Maritime Law of the United States and 399
should any dispute arise out of this Charter Party, the matter in dispute shall be 400
referred to three persons at New York, one to be appointed by each of the 401
parties hereto, and the third by the two so chosen; their decision or that of any 402
two of them shall be final, and for purpose of enforcing any award, this 403
agreement may be made a rule of the Court. The proceedings shall be 404
conducted in accordance with the rules of the Society of Maritime Arbitrators, 405
Inc.. 406
For disputes where the total amount claimed by either party does not exceed 407
the amount stated in Box 25** the arbitration shall be conducted in accordance 408
with the Shortened Arbitration Procedure of the Society of Maritime Arbitrators, 409
Inc.. 410

* (c) Any dispute arising out of this Charter Party shall be referred to arbitration at 411
the place indicated in Box 25, subject to the procedures applicable there. The 412
laws of the place indicated in Box 25 shall govern this Charter Party. 413
(d) If Box 25 in Part 1 is not filled in, sub-clause (a) of this Clause shall apply. 414
* (a), (b) and (c) are alternatives; indicate alternative agreed in Box 25. 415
** Where no figure is supplied in Box 25 in Part 1, this provision only shall be void but 416
the other provisions of this Clause shall have full force and remain in effect. 417

APPENDIX 3

NYPE 93[1]

TIME CHARTER©

New York Produce Exchange Form
Issued by the Association of Ship Brokers and Agents (U.S.A.), Inc.

November 6th, 1913 - Amended October 20th, 1921; August 6th, 1931; October 3rd, 1946;
Revised June 12th, 1981; September 14th 1993.

THIS CHARTER PARTY, made and concluded in   1
this   day of   19   2

Between   3
                                                                                         4
Owners of the Vessel described below, and   5
                                                                                         6
                                                                                         7
Charterers.   8

Description of Vessel   9

Name   Flag   Built   (year).   10
Port and number of Registry   11
Classed   in   12
Deadweight   long*/metric* tons (cargo and bunkers, including freshwater and   13
stores not exceeding   long*/metric* tons) on a salt water draft of   14
on summer freeboard.   15

Capacity   cubic feet grain   cubic feet bale space.   16
Tonnage   GT/GRT.   17
Speed about   knots, fully laden, in good weather conditions up to and including maximum   18
Force   on the Beaufort wind scale, on a consumption of about   long*/metric*   19
tons of   20

* Delete as appropriate.   21
For further description see Appendix "A" (if applicable)   22

1. **Duration**   23

The Owners agree to let and the Charterers agree to hire the Vessel from the time of delivery for a period   24
of   25
                                                                                         26
                                                                                         27
                                        within below mentioned trading limits.   28

2. **Delivery**   29

The Vessel shall be placed at the disposal of the Charterers at   30
                                                                                         31
                                                                                         32
                                                The Vessel on her delivery   33
shall be ready to receive cargo with clean-swept holds and tight, staunch, strong and in every way fitted   34
for ordinary cargo service, having water ballast and with sufficient power to operate all cargo-handling gear   35
simultaneously.   36

The Owners shall give the Charterers not less than   days notice of expected date of   37

---

1   Acknowledgment: the author and publisher thank the Association of Ship Brokers and Agents
     (USA) Inc for permission to reproduce NYPE 93.

delivery.   38

3. On-Off Hire Survey   39

Prior to delivery and redelivery the parties shall, unless otherwise agreed, each appoint surveyors, for their   40
respective accounts, who shall not later than at first loading port/last discharging port respectively, conduct   41
joint on-hire/off-hire surveys, for the purpose of ascertaining quantity of bunkers on board and the condition   42
of the Vessel. A single report shall be prepared on each occasion and signed by each surveyor, without   43
prejudice to his right to file a separate report setting forth items upon which the surveyors cannot agree.   44
If either party fails to have a representative attend the survey and sign the joint survey report, such party   45
shall nevertheless be bound for all purposes by the findings in any report prepared by the other party.   46
On-hire survey shall be on Charterers' time and off-hire survey on Owners' time.   47

4. Dangerous Cargo/Cargo Exclusions   48

(a) The Vessel shall be employed in carrying lawful merchandise excluding any goods of a dangerous,   49
injurious, flammable or corrosive nature unless carried in accordance with the requirements or   50
recommendations of the competent authorities of the country of the Vessel's registry and of ports of   51
shipment and discharge and of any intermediate countries or ports through whose waters the Vessel must   52
pass. Without prejudice to the generality of the foregoing, in addition the following are specifically   53
excluded: livestock of any description, arms, ammunition, explosives, nuclear and radioactive materials,   54
                                                                                                                       55
                                                                                                                       56
                                                                                                                       57
                                                                                                                       58
                                                                                                                       59
                                                                                                                       60
                                                                                                                       61
                                                                                                                       62
                                                                                                                       63
                                                                                                                       64

(b) If IMO-classified cargo is agreed to be carried, the amount of such cargo shall be limited to   65
                           tons and the Charterers shall provide the Master with any evidence he may   66
reasonably require to show that the cargo is packaged, labelled, loaded and stowed in accordance with IMO   67
regulations, failing which the Master is entitled to refuse such cargo or, if already loaded, to unload it at   68
the Charterers' risk and expense.   69

5. Trading Limits   70

The Vessel shall be employed in such lawful trades between safe ports and safe places   71
within   72
                                                                                              excluding   73
                                                                                                                       74
                                                                                                                       75
                                                  as the Charterers shall direct.   76

6. Owners to Provide   77

The Owners shall provide and pay for the insurance of the Vessel, except as otherwise provided, and for   78
all provisions, cabin, deck, engine-room and other necessary stores, including boiler water; shall pay for   79
wages, consular shipping and discharging fees of the crew and charges for port services pertaining to the   80
crew; shall maintain the Vessel's class and keep her in a thoroughly efficient state in hull, machinery and   81
equipment for and during the service, and have a full complement of officers and crew.   82

7. Charterers to Provide   83

The Charterers, while the Vessel is on hire, shall provide and pay for all the bunkers except as otherwise   84
agreed; shall pay for port charges (including compulsory watchmen and cargo watchmen and compulsory   85
garbage disposal), all communication expenses pertaining to the Charterers' business at cost, pilotages,   86

towages, agencies, commissions, consular charges (except those pertaining to individual crew members   87
or flag of the Vessel), and all other usual expenses except those stated in Clause 6, but when the Vessel   88
puts into a port for causes for which the Vessel is responsible (other than by stress of weather), then all   89
such charges incurred shall be paid by the Owners. Fumigations ordered because of illness of the crew   90
shall be for the Owners' account. Fumigations ordered because of cargoes carried or ports visited while   91
the Vessel is employed under this Charter Party shall be for the Charterers' account. All other fumigations   92
shall be for the Charterers' account after the Vessel has been on charter for a continuous period of six   93
months or more.   94

The Charterers shall provide and pay for necessary dunnage and also any extra fittings requisite for a   95
special trade or unusual cargo, but the Owners shall allow them the use of any dunnage already aboard   96
the Vessel. Prior to redelivery the Charterers shall remove their dunnage and fittings at their cost and in   97
their time.   98

99

8. Performance of Voyages

(a) The Master shall perform the voyages with due despatch, and shall render all customary assistance   100
with the Vessel's crew. The Master shall be conversant with the English language and (although   101
appointed by the Owners) shall be under the orders and directions of the Charterers as regards   102
employment and agency; and the Charterers shall perform all cargo handling, including but not limited to   103
loading, stowing, trimming, lashing, securing, dunnaging, unlashing, discharging, and tallying, at their risk   104
and expense, under the supervision of the Master.   105

(b) If the Charterers shall have reasonable cause to be dissatisfied with the conduct of the Master or   106
officers, the Owners shall, on receiving particulars of the complaint, investigate the same, and, if   107
necessary, make a change in the appointments.   108

109

9. Bunkers

(a) The Charterers on delivery, and the Owners on redelivery, shall take over and pay for all fuel and   110
diesel oil remaining on board the Vessel as hereunder. The Vessel shall be delivered with: 111
                                   long*/metric* tons of fuel oil at the price of   per ton;   112
                        tons of diesel oil at the price of   per ton. The vessel shall   113
be redelivered with: tons of fuel oil at the price of   per ton;   114
                            tons of diesel oil at the price of   per ton.   115

116

Same tons apply throughout this clause.

(b) The Charterers shall supply bunkers of a quality suitable for burning in the Vessel's engines   117
and auxiliaries and which conform to the specification(s) as set out in Appendix A.   118

The Owners reserve their right to make a claim against the Charterers for any damage to the main engines   119
or the auxiliaries caused by the use of unsuitable fuels or fuels not complying with the agreed   120
specification(s). Additionally, if bunker fuels supplied do not conform with the mutually agreed   121
specification(s) or otherwise prove unsuitable for burning in the Vessel's engines or auxiliaries, the Owners   122
shall not be held responsible for any reduction in the Vessel's speed performance and/or increased bunker   123
consumption, nor for any time lost and any other consequences.   124

125

10. Rate of Hire/Redelivery Areas and Notices
The Charterers shall pay for the use and hire of the said Vessel at the rate of $ 126
U.S. currency, daily, **or** $ U.S. currency per ton on the Vessel's total deadweight   127
carrying capacity, including bunkers and stores, on   summer freeboard, per 30 days,   128
commencing on and from the day of her delivery, as aforesaid, and at and after the same rate for any part   129
of a month; hire shall continue until the hour of the day of her redelivery in like good order and condition,   130
ordinary wear and tear excepted, to the Owners (unless Vessel lost) at   131
132
133
                                     unless otherwise mutually agreed.   134

The Charterers shall give the Owners not less than   days notice of the Vessel's 135
expected date and probable port of redelivery.   136

For the purpose of hire calculations, the times of delivery, redelivery or termination of charter shall be 137
adjusted to GMT.   138

11. **Hire Payment**   139

(a) *Payment*   140

Payment of Hire shall be made so as to be received by the Owners or their designated payee in 141
, viz   142
                                                                                                                        143
                                                                                                                        144
                                                                                               in   145
currency, or in United States Currency, in funds available to the 146
Owners on the due date, 15 days in advance, and for the last month or part of same the approximate 147
amount of hire, and should same not cover the actual time, hire shall be paid for the balance day by day 148
as it becomes due, if so required by the Owners. Failing the punctual and regular payment of the hire, 149
or on any fundamental breach whatsoever of this Charter Party, the Owners shall be at liberty to 150
withdraw the Vessel from the service of the Charterers without prejudice to any claims they (the Owners) 151
may otherwise have on the Charterers.   152

At any time after the expiry of the grace period provided in Sub-clause 11 (b) hereunder and while the 153
hire is outstanding, the Owners shall, without prejudice to the liberty to withdraw, be entitled to withhold 154
the performance of any and all of their obligations hereunder and shall have no responsibility whatsoever 155
for any consequences thereof, in respect of which the Charterers hereby indemnify the Owners, and hire 156
shall continue to accrue and any extra expenses resulting from such withholding shall be for the 157
Charterers' account.   158

(b) *Grace Period*   159

Where there is failure to make punctual and regular payment of hire due to oversight, negligence, errors 160
or omissions on the part of the Charterers or their bankers, the Charterers shall be given by the Owners 161
                  clear banking days (as recognized at the agreed place of payment) written notice to rectify the 162
failure, and when so rectified within those   days following the Owners' notice, the payment shall 163
stand as regular and punctual.   164

Failure by the Charterers to pay the hire within   days of their receiving the Owners' notice as 165
provided herein, shall entitle the Owners to withdraw as set forth in Sub-clause 11 (a) above. 166

(c) *Last Hire Payment*   167

Should the Vessel be on her voyage towards port of redelivery at the time the last and/or the penultimate 168
payment of hire is/are due, said payment(s) is/are to be made for such length of time as the Owners and 169
the Charterers may agree upon as being the estimated time necessary to complete the voyage, and taking 170
into account bunkers actually on board, to be taken over by the Owners and estimated disbursements for 171
the Owners' account before redelivery. Should same not cover the actual time, hire is to be paid for the 172
balance, day by day, as it becomes due. When the Vessel has been redelivered, any difference is to be 173
refunded by the Owners or paid by the Charterers, as the case may be. 174

(d) *Cash Advances*   175

Cash for the Vessel's ordinary disbursements at any port may be advanced by the Charterers, as required 176
by the Owners, subject to 2½ percent commission and such advances shall be deducted from the hire. 177
The Charterers, however, shall in no way be responsible for the application of such advances. 178

12. **Berths**   179

The Vessel shall be loaded and discharged in any safe dock or at any safe berth or safe place that 180
Charterers or their agents may direct, provided the Vessel can safely enter, lie and depart always afloat 181
at any time of tide. 182

13. Spaces Available
183

(a) The whole reach of the Vessel's holds, decks, and other cargo spaces (not more than she can 184
reasonably and safely stow and carry), also accommodations for supercargo, if carried, shall be at the 185
Charterers' disposal, reserving only proper and sufficient space for the Vessel's officers, crew, tackle, 186
apparel, furniture, provisions, stores and fuel. 187

(b) In the event of deck cargo being carried, the Owners are to be and are hereby indemnified by the 188
Charterers for any loss and/or damage and/or liability of whatsoever nature caused to the Vessel as a 189
result of the carriage of deck cargo and which would not have arisen had deck cargo not been loaded. 190

14. Supercargo and Meals
191

The Charterers are entitled to appoint a supercargo, who shall accompany the Vessel at the Charterers' 192
risk and see that voyages are performed with due despatch. He is to be furnished with free 193
accommodation and same fare as provided for the Master's table, the Charterers paying at the rate of 194
                                        per day. The Owners shall victual pilots and customs officers, and also, when 195
authorized by the Charterers or their agents, shall victual tally clerks, stevedore's foreman, etc., 196
Charterers paying at the rate of   per meal for all such victualling. 197

15. Sailing Orders and Logs
198

The Charterers shall furnish the Master from time to time with all requisite instructions and sailing 199
directions, in writing, in the English language, and the Master shall keep full and correct deck and engine 200
logs of the voyage or voyages, which are to be patent to the Charterers or their agents, and furnish the 201
Charterers, their agents or supercargo, when required, with a true copy of such deck and engine logs, 202
showing the course of the Vessel, distance run and the consumption of bunkers. Any log extracts 203
required by the Charterers shall be in the English language. 204

16. Delivery/Cancelling
205

If required by the Charterers, time shall not commence before   and should the 206
Vessel not be ready for delivery on or before   but not later than   hours, 207
the Charterers shall have the option of cancelling this Charter Party. 208

Extension of Cancelling
209

If the Owners warrant that, despite the exercise of due diligence by them, the Vessel will not be ready 210
for delivery by the cancelling date, and provided the Owners are able to state with reasonable certainty 211
the date on which the Vessel will be ready, they may, at the earliest seven days before the Vessel is 212
expected to sail for the port or place of delivery, require the Charterers to declare whether or not they will 213
cancel the Charter Party. Should the Charterers elect not to cancel, or should they fail to reply within two 214
days or by the cancelling date, whichever shall first occur, then the seventh day after the expected date 215
of readiness for delivery as notified by the Owners shall replace the original cancelling date. Should the 216
Vessel be further delayed, the Owners shall be entitled to require further declarations of the Charterers in 217
accordance with this Clause. 218

17. Off Hire
219

In the event of loss of time from deficiency and/or default and/or strike of officers or crew, or deficiency 220
of stores, fire, breakdown of, or damages to hull, machinery or equipment, grounding, detention by the 221
arrest of the Vessel, (unless such arrest is caused by events for which the Charterers, their servants, 222
agents or subcontractors are responsible), or detention by average accidents to the Vessel or cargo unless 223
resulting from inherent vice, quality or defect of the cargo, drydocking for the purpose of examination or 224
painting bottom, or by any other similar cause preventing the full working of the Vessel, the payment of 225

hire and overtime, if any, shall cease for the time thereby lost. Should the Vessel deviate or put back 226
during a voyage, contrary to the orders or directions of the Charterers, for any reason other than accident 227
to the cargo or where permitted in lines 257 to 258 hereunder, the hire is to be suspended from the time 228
of her deviating or putting back until she is again in the same or equidistant position from the destination 229
and the voyage resumed therefrom. All bunkers used by the Vessel while off hire shall be for the Owners' 230
account. In the event of the Vessel being driven into port or to anchorage through stress of weather, 231
trading to shallow harbors or to rivers or ports with bars, any detention of the Vessel and/or expenses 232
resulting from such detention shall be for the Charterers' account. If upon the voyage the speed be 233
reduced by defect in, or breakdown of, any part of her hull, machinery or equipment, the time so lost, and 234
the cost of any extra bunkers consumed in consequence thereof, and all extra proven expenses may be 235
deducted from the hire. 236

18. **Sublet** 237

Unless otherwise agreed, the Charterers shall have the liberty to sublet the Vessel for all or any part of 238
the time covered by this Charter Party, but the Charterers remain responsible for the fulfillment of this 239
Charter Party. 240

19. **Drydocking** 241

The Vessel was last drydocked 242

*(a) The Owners shall have the option to place the Vessel in drydock during the currency of this Charter 243
at a convenient time and place, to be mutually agreed upon between the Owners and the Charterers, for 244
bottom cleaning and painting and/or repair as required by class or dictated by circumstances. 245

*(b) Except in case of emergency no drydocking shall take place during the currency of this Charter 246
Party. 247

* *Delete as appropriate* 248

20. **Total Loss** 249

Should the Vessel be lost, money paid in advance and not earned (reckoning from the date of loss or 250
being last heard of) shall be returned to the Charterers at once. 251

21. **Exceptions** 252

The act of God, enemies, fire, restraint of princes, rulers and people, and all dangers and accidents of the 253
seas, rivers, machinery, boilers, and navigation, and errors of navigation throughout this Charter, always 254
mutually excepted. 255

22. **Liberties** 256

The Vessel shall have the liberty to sail with or without pilots, to tow and to be towed, to assist vessels 257
in distress, and to deviate for the purpose of saving life and property. 258

23. **Liens** 259

The Owners shall have a lien upon all cargoes and all sub-freights and/or sub-hire for any amounts due 260
under this Charter Party, including general average contributions, and the Charterers shall have a lien on 261
the Vessel for all monies paid in advance and not earned, and any overpaid hire or excess deposit to be 262
returned at once. 263

The Charterers will not directly or indirectly suffer, nor permit to be continued, any lien or encumbrance, 264
which might have priority over the title and interest of the Owners in the Vessel. The Charterers 265
undertake that during the period of this Charter Party, they will not procure any supplies or necessaries 266
or services, including any port expenses and bunkers, on the credit of the Owners or in the Owners' time. 267

24. <u>Salvage</u> 268

All derelicts and salvage shall be for the Owners' and the Charterers' equal benefit after deducting 269
Owners' and Charterers' expenses and crew's proportion. 270

25. <u>General Average</u> 271

General average shall be adjusted according to York-Antwerp Rules 1974, as amended 1990, or any 272
subsequent modification thereof, in   and settled in 273
currency. 274

The Charterers shall procure that all bills of lading issued during the currency of the Charter Party will 275
contain a provision to the effect that general average shall be adjusted according to York-Antwerp Rules 276
1974, as amended 1990, or any subsequent modification thereof and will include the "New Jason 277
Clause" as per Clause 31. 278

Time charter hire shall not contribute to general average. 279

26. <u>Navigation</u> 280

Nothing herein stated is to be construed as a demise of the Vessel to the Time Charterers. The Owners 281
shall remain responsible for the navigation of the Vessel, acts of pilots and tug boats, insurance, crew, 282
and all other matters, same as when trading for their own account. 283

27. <u>Cargo Claims</u> 284

Cargo claims as between the Owners and the Charterers shall be settled in accordance with the Inter-Club 285
New York Produce Exchange Agreement of February 1970, as amended May, 1984, or any subsequent 286
modification or replacement thereof. 287

28. <u>Cargo Gear and Lights</u> 288

The Owners shall maintain the cargo handling gear of the Vessel which is as follows: 289
290
291
292

providing gear (for all derricks or cranes) capable of lifting capacity as described. The Owners shall also 293
provide on the Vessel for night work lights as on board, but all additional lights over those on board shall 294
be at the Charterers' expense. The Charterers shall have the use of any gear on board the Vessel. If 295
required by the Charterers, the Vessel shall work night and day and all cargo handling gear shall be at the 296
Charterers' disposal during loading and discharging. In the event of disabled cargo handling gear, or 297
insufficient power to operate the same, the Vessel is to be considered to be off hire to the extent that 298
time is actually lost to the Charterers and the Owners to pay stevedore stand-by charges occasioned 299
thereby, unless such disablement or insufficiency of power is caused by the Charterers' stevedores. If 300
required by the Charterers, the Owners shall bear the cost of hiring shore gear in lieu thereof, in which 301
case the Vessel shall remain on hire. 302

29. <u>Crew Overtime</u> 303

In lieu of any overtime payments to officers and crew for work ordered by the Charterers or their agents, 304
the Charterers shall pay the Owners, concurrently with the hire   per month 305
or pro rata. 306

30. <u>Bills of Lading</u> 307

(a) The Master shall sign the bills of lading or waybills for cargo as presented in conformity with mates 308
or tally clerk's receipts. However, the Charterers may sign bills of lading or waybills on behalf of the 309
Master, with the Owner's prior written authority, always in conformity with mates or tally clerk's receipts. 310

(b) All bills of lading or waybills shall be without prejudice to this Charter Party and the Charterers shall   311
indemnify the Owners against all consequences or liabilities which may arise from any inconsistency   312
between this Charter Party and any bills of lading or waybills signed by the Charterers or by the Master   313
at their request.   314

(c) Bills of lading covering deck cargo shall be claused: "Shipped on deck at Charterers', Shippers' and   315
Receivers' risk, expense and responsibility, without liability on the part of the Vessel, or her Owners for   316
any loss, damage, expense or delay howsoever caused."   317

31. Protective Clauses   318

This Charter Party is subject to the following clauses all of which are also to be included in all bills of lading   319
or waybills issued hereunder: 320

(a) CLAUSE PARAMOUNT   321
"This bill of lading shall have effect subject to the provisions of the Carriage of Goods by Sea Act of the   322
United States, the Hague Rules, or the Hague-Visby Rules, as applicable, or such other similar national   323
legislation as may mandatorily apply by virtue of origin or destination of the bills of lading, which shall   324
be deemed to be incorporated herein and nothing herein contained shall be deemed a surrender by the   325
carrier of any of its rights or immunities or an increase of any of its responsibilities or liabilities under said   326
applicable Act. If any term of this bill of lading be repugnant to said applicable Act to any extent, such   327
term shall be void to that extent, but no further."   328

and   329

(b) BOTH-TO-BLAME COLLISION CLAUSE   330
"If the ship comes into collision with another ship as a result of the negligence of the other ship and any   331
act, neglect or default of the master, mariner, pilot or the servants of the carrier in the navigation or in   332
the management of the ship, the owners of the goods carried hereunder will indemnify the carrier against   333
all loss or liability to the other or non-carrying ship or her owners insofar as such loss or liability represents   334
loss of, or damage to, or any claim whatsoever of the owners of said goods, paid or payable by the other   335
or non-carrying ship or her owners to the owners of said goods and set off, recouped or recovered by the   336
other or non-carrying ship or her owners as part of their claim against the carrying ship or carrier.   337

The foregoing provisions shall also apply where the owners, operators or those in charge of any ships or   338
objects other than, or in addition to, the colliding ships or objects are at fault in respect to a collision or   339
contact."   340

and   341

(c) NEW JASON CLAUSE   342
"In the event of accident, danger, damage or disaster before or after the commencement of the voyage   343
resulting from any cause whatsoever, whether due to negligence or not, for which, or for the   344
consequences of which, the carrier is not responsible, by statute, contract, or otherwise, the goods,   345
shippers, consignees, or owners of the goods shall contribute with the carrier in general average to the   346
payment of any sacrifices, losses, or expenses of a general average nature that may be made or incurred,   347
and shall pay salvage and special charges incurred in respect of the goods.   348

If a salving ship is owned or operated by the carrier, salvage shall be paid for as fully as if salving ship   349
or ships belonged to strangers. Such deposit as the carrier or his agents may deem sufficient to cover   350
the estimated contribution of the goods and any salvage and special charges thereon shall, if required,   351
be made by the goods, shippers, consignees or owners of the goods to the carrier before delivery."   352

and   353

(d) U.S. TRADE - DRUG CLAUSE   354
"In pursuance of the provisions of the U.S. Anti Drug Abuse Act 1986 or any re-enactment thereof, the   355
Charterers warrant to exercise the highest degree of care and diligence in preventing unmanifested   356
narcotic drugs and marijuana to be loaded or concealed on board the Vessel.   357

Non-compliance with the provisions of this clause shall amount to breach of warranty for consequences 358
of which the Charterers shall be liable and shall hold the Owners, the Master and the crew of the Vessel 359
harmless and shall keep them indemnified against all claims whatsoever which may arise and be made 360
against them individually or jointly. Furthermore, all time lost and all expenses incurred, including fines, 361
as a result of the Charterers' breach of the provisions of this clause shall be for the Charterer's account 362
and the Vessel shall remain on hire. 363

Should the Vessel be arrested as a result of the Charterers' non-compliance with the provisions of this 364
clause, the Charterers shall at their expense take all reasonable steps to secure that within a reasonable 365
time the Vessel is released and at their expense put up the bails to secure release of the Vessel. 366

The Owners shall remain responsible for all time lost and all expenses incurred, including fines, in the 367
event that unmanifested narcotic drugs and marijuana are found in the possession or effects of the 368
Vessel's personnel." 369

and 370

(e) WAR CLAUSES 371
"(i) No contraband of war shall be shipped. The Vessel shall not be required, without the consent of the 372
Owners, which shall not be unreasonably withheld, to enter any port or zone which is involved in a state 373
of war, warlike operations, or hostilities, civil strife, insurrection or piracy whether there be a declaration 374
of war or not, where the Vessel, cargo or crew might reasonably be expected to be subject to capture, 375
seizure or arrest, or to a hostile act by a belligerent power (the term "power" meaning any de jure or de 376
facto authority or any purported governmental organization maintaining naval, military or air forces). 377

(ii) If such consent is given by the Owners, the Charterers will pay the provable additional cost of insuring 378
the Vessel against hull war risks in an amount equal to the value under her ordinary hull policy but not 379
exceeding a valuation of   In addition, the Owners may purchase and the 380
Charterers will pay for war risk insurance on ancillary risks such as loss of hire, freight disbursements, 381
total loss, blocking and trapping, etc. If such insurance is not obtainable commercially or through a 382
government program, the Vessel shall not be required to enter or remain at any such port or zone. 383

(iii) In the event of the existence of the conditions described in (i) subsequent to the date of this Charter, 384
or while the Vessel is on hire under this Charter, the Charterers shall, in respect of voyages to any such 385
port or zone assume the provable additional cost of wages and insurance properly incurred in connection 386
with master, officers and crew as a consequence of such war, warlike operations or hostilities. 387

(iv) Any war bonus to officers and crew due to the Vessel's trading or cargo carried shall be for the 388
Charterers' account." 389

32. **War Cancellation** 390

In the event of the outbreak of war (whether there be a declaration of war or not) between any two or 391
more of the following countries: 392
393
394
395
either the Owners or the Charterers may cancel this Charter Party. Whereupon, the Charterers shall 396
redeliver the Vessel to the Owners in accordance with Clause 10; if she has cargo on board, after 397
discharge thereof at destination, or, if debarred under this Clause from reaching or entering it, at a near 398
open and safe port as directed by the Owners; or, if she has no cargo on board, at the port at which she 399
then is; or, if at sea, at a near open and safe port as directed by the Owners. In all cases hire shall 400
continue to be paid in accordance with Clause 11 and except as aforesaid all other provisions of this 401
Charter Party shall apply until redelivery. 402

33. **Ice** 403

The Vessel shall not be required to enter or remain in any icebound port or area, nor any port or area 404

where lights or lightships have been or are about to be withdrawn by reason of ice, nor where there is 405
risk that in the ordinary course of things the Vessel will not be able on account of ice to safely enter and 406
remain in the port or area or to get out after having completed loading or discharging. Subject to the 407
Owners' prior approval the Vessel is to follow ice-breakers when reasonably required with regard to her 408
size, construction and ice class.   409

34. Requisition   410

Should the Vessel be requisitioned by the government of the Vessel's flag during the period of this Charter 411
Party, the Vessel shall be deemed to be off hire during the period of such requisition, and any hire paid 412
by the said government in respect of such requisition period shall be retained by the Owners. The period 413
during which the Vessel is on requisition to the said government shall count as part of the period provided 414
for in this Charter Party.   415
If the period of requisition exceeds   months, either party shall have the option 416
of cancelling this Charter Party and no consequential claim may be made by either party.   417

35. Stevedore Damage   418

Notwithstanding anything contained herein to the contrary, the Charterers shall pay for any and all 419
damage to the Vessel caused by stevedores provided the Master has notified the Charterers and/or their 420
agents in writing as soon as practical but not later than 48 hours after any damage is discovered. Such 421
notice to specify the damage in detail and to invite Charterers to appoint a surveyor to assess the extent 422
of such damage.   423

(a) In case of any and all damage(s) affecting the Vessel's seaworthiness and/or the safety of the crew 424
and/or affecting the trading capabilities of the Vessel, the Charterers shall immediately arrange for repairs 425
of such damage(s) at their expense and the Vessel is to remain on hire until such repairs are completed 426
and if required passed by the Vessel's classification society.   427

(b) Any and all damage(s) not described under point (a) above shall be repaired at the Charterers' option, 428
before or after redelivery concurrently with the Owners' work. In such case no hire and/or expenses will 429
be paid to the Owners except and insofar as the time and/or the expenses required for the repairs for 430
which the Charterers are responsible, exceed the time and/or expenses necessary to carry out the 431
Owners' work.   432

36. Cleaning of Holds   433

The Charterers shall provide and pay extra for sweeping and/or washing and/or cleaning of holds between 434
voyages and/or between cargoes provided such work can be undertaken by the crew and is permitted by 435
local regulations, at the rate of   per hold.   436

In connection with any such operation, the Owners shall not be responsible if the Vessel's holds are not 437
accepted or passed by the port or any other authority. The Charterers shall have the option to re-deliver 438
the Vessel with unclean/upswept holds against a lumpsum payment of   in lieu of cleaning. 439

37. Taxes   440

Charterers to pay all local, State, National taxes and/or dues assessed on the Vessel or the Owners 441
resulting from the Charterers' orders herein, whether assessed during or after the currency of this Charter 442
Party including any taxes and/or dues on cargo and/or freights and/or sub-freights and/or hire (excluding 443
taxes levied by the country of the flag of the Vessel or the Owners).   444

38. Charterers' Colors   445

The Charterers shall have the privilege of flying their own house flag and painting the Vessel with their 446
own markings. The Vessel shall be repainted in the Owners' colors before termination of the Charter 447
Party. Cost and time of painting, maintaining and repainting those changes effected by the Charterers 448
shall be for the Charterers' account.   449

39. Laid up Returns   450

The Charterers shall have the benefit of any return insurance premium receivable by the Owners from their   451
underwriters as and when received from underwriters by reason of the Vessel being in port for a minimum   452
period of 30 days if on full hire for this period or pro rata for the time actually on hire.   453

40. Documentation   454

The Owners shall provide any documentation relating to the Vessel that may be required to permit the   455
Vessel to trade within the agreed trade limits, including, but not limited to certificates of financial   456
responsibility for oil pollution, provided such oil pollution certificates are obtainable from the Owners'   457
P & I club, valid international tonnage certificate, Suez and Panama tonnage certificates, valid certificate   458
of registry and certificates relating to the strength and/or serviceability of the Vessel's gear.   459

41. Stowaways   460

(a) (i) The Charterers warrant to exercise due care and diligence in preventing stowaways in gaining   461
access to the Vessel by means of secreting away in the goods and/or containers shipped by the   462
Charterers.   463

(ii) If, despite the exercise of due care and diligence by the Charterers, stowaways have gained   464
access to the Vessel by means of secreting away in the goods and/or containers shipped by the   465
Charterers, this shall amount to breach of charter for the consequences of which the Charterers   466
shall be liable and shall hold the Owners harmless and shall keep them indemnified against all   467
claims whatsoever which may arise and be made against them. Furthermore, all time lost and all   468
expenses whatsoever and howsoever incurred, including fines, shall be for the Charterers' account   469
and the Vessel shall remain on hire.   470

(iii) Should the Vessel be arrested as a result of the Charterers' breach of charter according to   471
sub-clause (a)(ii) above, the Charterers shall take all reasonable steps to secure that, within a   472
reasonable time, the Vessel is released and at their expense put up bail to secure release of the   473
Vessel.   474

(b) (i) If, despite the exercise of due care and diligence by the Owners, stowaways have gained   475
access to the Vessel by means other than secreting away in the goods and/or containers shipped   476
by the Charterers, all time lost and all expenses whatsoever and howsoever incurred, including   477
fines, shall be for the Owners' account and the Vessel shall be off hire.   478

(ii) Should the Vessel be arrested as a result of stowaways having gained access to the Vessel   479
by means other than secreting away in the goods and/or containers shipped by the Charterers,   480
the Owners shall take all reasonable steps to secure that, within a reasonable time, the Vessel   481
is released and at their expense put up bail to secure release of the Vessel.   482

42. Smuggling   483

In the event of smuggling by the Master, Officers and/or crew, the Owners shall bear the cost of any   484
fines, taxes, or imposts levied and the Vessel shall be off hire for any time lost as a result thereof.   485

43. Commissions   486

A commission of   percent is payable by the Vessel and the Owners to   487
                                                                                                               488
                                                                                                               489
                                                                                                               490
on hire earned and paid under this Charter, and also upon any continuation or extension of this Charter.   491

44. Address Commission   492

An address commission of   percent is payable to   493

494
495
on hire earned and paid under this Charter.   496

45. Arbitration   497

(a) NEW YORK   498
All disputes arising out of this contract shall be arbitrated at New York in the following manner, and   499
subject to U.S. Law: 500

One Arbitrator is to be appointed by each of the parties hereto and a third by the two so chosen. Their   501
decision or that of any two of them shall be final, and for the purpose of enforcing any award, this   502
agreement may be made a rule of the court. The Arbitrators shall be commercial men, conversant with   503
shipping matters. Such Arbitration is to be conducted in accordance with the rules of the Society of   504
Maritime Arbitrators Inc.   505

For disputes where the total amount claimed by either party does not exceed US $ **   506
the arbitration shall be conducted in accordance with the Shortened Arbitration Procedure of the Society   507
of Maritime Arbitrators Inc.   508

(b) LONDON   509
All disputes arising out of this contract shall be arbitrated at London and, unless the parties agree   510
forthwith on a single Arbitrator, be referred to the final arbitrament of two Arbitrators carrying on business   511
in London who shall be members of the Baltic Mercantile & Shipping Exchange and engaged in Shipping,   512
one to be appointed by each of the parties, with power to such Arbitrators to appoint an Umpire. No   513
award shall be questioned or invalidated on the ground that any of the Arbitrators is not qualified as   514
above, unless objection to his action be taken before the award is made. Any dispute arising hereunder   515
shall be governed by English Law.   516

For disputes where the total amount claimed by either party does not exceed US $ **   517
the arbitration shall be conducted in accordance with the Small Claims Procedure of the London Maritime   518
Arbitrators Association.   519

*Delete para (a) or (b) as appropriate   520

** Where no figure is supplied in the blank space this provision only shall be void but the other provisions   521
of this clause shall have full force and remain in effect.   522

If mutually agreed, clauses   to   , both inclusive, as attached hereto are fully   523
incorporated in this Charter Party.   524

APPENDIX "A"   525

526
To Charter Party dated
Between   Owners   527
and   Charterers   528
529
Further details of the Vessel: 530

APPENDIX 4

CONGENBILL[1]

BILL OF LADING

TO BE USED WITH CHARTER-PARTIES
CODE NAME: "CONGENBILL"
EDITION 1994
ADOPTED BY
THE BALTIC AND INTERNATIONAL MARITIME COUNCIL (BIMCO)

Conditions of Carriage

(1) All terms and conditions, liberties and exceptions of the Charter Party, dated as overleaf, including the Law and Arbitration Clause, are herewith incorporated.

(2) **General Paramount Clause.**
(a) The Hague Rules contained in the International Convention for the Unification of certain rules relating to Bills of Lading, dated Brussels the 25th August 1924 as enacted in the country of shipment, shall apply to this Bill of Lading. When no such enactment is in force in the country of shipment, the corresponding legislation of the country of destination shall apply, but in respect of shipments to which no such enactments are compulsorily applicable, the terms of the said Convention shall apply.

(b) Trades where Hague-Visby Rules apply.
In trades where the International Brussels Convention 1924 as amended by the Protocol signed at Brussels on February 23rd 1968 - the Hague-Visby Rules - apply compulsorily, the provisions of the respective legislation shall apply to this Bill of Lading.

(c) The Carrier shall in no case be responsible for loss of or damage to the cargo, howsoever arising prior to loading into and after discharge from the Vessel or while the cargo is in the charge of another Carrier, nor in respect of deck cargo or live animals.

(3) **General Average.**
General Average shall be adjusted, stated and settled according to York-Antwerp Rules 1994, or any subsequent modification thereof, in London unless another place is agreed in the Charter Party.
Cargo's contribution to General Average shall be paid to the Carrier even when such average is the result of a fault, neglect or error of the Master, Pilot or Crew. The Charterers, Shippers and Consignees expressly renounce the Belgian Commercial Code, Part II, Art. 148.

(4) **New Jason Clause.**
In the event of accident, danger, damage or disaster before or after the commencement of the voyage, resulting from any cause whatsoever, whether due to negligence or not, for which, or for the consequence of which, the Carrier is not responsible, by statute, contract or otherwise, the cargo, shippers, consignees or the owners of the cargo shall contribute with the Carrier in General Average to the payment of any sacrifices, losses or expenses of a General Average nature that may be made or incurred and shall pay salvage and special charges incurred in respect of the cargo. If a salving vessel is owned or operated by the Carrier, salvage shall be paid for as fully as if the said salving vessel or vessels belonged to strangers. Such deposit as the Carrier, or his agents, may deem sufficient to cover the estimated contribution of the goods and any salvage and special charges thereon shall, if required, be made by the cargo, shippers, consignees or owners of the goods to the Carrier before delivery.

(5) **Both-to-Blame Collision Clause.**
If the Vessel comes into collision with another vessel as a result of the negligence of the other vessel and any act, neglect or default of the Master, Mariner, Pilot or the servants of the Carrier in the navigation or in the management of the Vessel, the owners of the cargo carried hereunder will indemnify the Carrier against all loss or liability to the other or non-carrying vessel or her owners in so far as such loss or liability represents loss of, or damage to, or any claim whatsoever of the owners of said cargo, paid or payable by the other or non-carrying vessel or her owners to the owners of said cargo and set-off, recouped or recovered by the other or non-carrying vessel or her owners as part of their claim against the carrying Vessel or the Carrier.
The foregoing provisions shall also apply where the owners, operators or those in charge of any vessel or vessels or objects other than, or in addition to, the colliding vessels or objects are at fault in respect of a collision or contact.

For particulars of cargo, freight, destination, etc., see overleaf.

---

1 Acknowledgment: the author and publisher thank the Baltic and International Maritime Council (BIMCO) for permission to reproduce CONGENBILL.

CODE NAME: "CONGENBILL". EDITION 1994

Shipper

BILL OF LADING
TO BE USED WITH CHARTER-PARTIES

B/L No.

Reference No.

Page 2

Consignee

Notify address

Draft Copy

Vessel	Port of loading

Port of discharge

Shipper's description of goods   Gross weight

Draft Copy

(of which   on deck at Shipper's risk; the Carrier not

being responsible for loss or damage howsoever arising)

Freight payable as per
CHARTER-PARTY dated

FREIGHT ADVANCE.
Received on account of freight:

Time used for loading   days   hours.

SHIPPED at the Port of Loading in apparent good order and
condition on board the Vessel for carriage to the Port
of Discharge or so near thereto as she may safely get the goods specified above.

Weight, measure, quality, quantity, condition, contents and value unknown.

IN WITNESS whereof the Master or Agent of the said Vessel has signed
the number of Bills of Lading indicated below all of this tenor and date,
any one of which being accomplished the others shall be void.

FOR CONDITIONS OF CARRIAGE SEE OVERLEAF

Freight payable at	Place and date of issue
Number of original Bs/L	Signature

APPENDIX 5

GENWAYBILL[1]

CODE NAME: "GENWAYBILL"			
Shipper		**NON-NEGOTIABLE**	GSWB No.
		GENERAL SEA WAYBILL	Reference No.
		Issued by The Baltic and International Maritime Council (BIMCO), subject to the CMI Uniform Rules for Sea Waybills	
		Revised 1995	
Consignee (not to order)			
Notify party/address			
Vessel	Port of loading		
Port of discharge			

Particulars declared by the Shipper

Description of cargo	Marks and Nos.	Number and kind of packages	Gross weight (kg)	Measurement (cbm)

(of which .... on deck at Shipper's risk; the Carrier not being responsible for loss or damage howsoever arising)

Issued pursuant to Voyage Charter Party indicated hereunder	SHIPPED on board the cargo specified above, according to Shipper's declaration in apparent good order and condition - unless otherwise stated herein - weight, measure, marks, numbers, quality, contents and value unknown, for delivery at the port of discharge or so near thereto as the Vessel may safely get, always afloat.
	The cargo shipped under this Waybill will be delivered to the Party named as Consignee or its authorised agent, on production of proof of identity without any documentary formalities.
Charter Party (Code name, place and date of issue)	Should the Shipper require delivery of the cargo to a party other than the Consignee stated in this Waybill, then written instructions must be given to the Carrier or his agent. The Shipper shall, however, be entitled to transfer right of control of the cargo to the Consignee, the exercise of such option to be noted on this Waybill and to be made no later than the receipt of the cargo by the Carrier. The Carrier shall exercise due care ensuring that delivery is made to the proper party. However, in case of incorrect delivery, the Carrier will accept no responsibility unless due to fault or neglect on his part.
	FOR CONDITIONS OF CARRIAGE SEE OVERLEAF.
	Freight payable at | Place and date of issue
Freight payable in accordance therewith.	| Signed for .... as Carrier
	| by ....
	| As agent(s) only to the Carrier

Printed by the BIMCO Charter Party Editor

---

1   Acknowledgment: the author and publisher thank the Baltic and International Maritime Council (BIMCO) for permission to reproduce Genwaybill.

THE BALTIC AND INTERNATIONAL MARITIME COUNCIL (BIMC
NON-NEGOTIABLE
GENERAL SEA WAYBILL

CODE NAME: "GENWAYBILL"

Conditions of Carriage.

(1) All the terms, conditions, liberties, clauses and exceptions of the Voyage Charter Party, as dated overleaf, including the Law and Arbitration Clause, shall be deemed to be incorporated in this Waybill and shall govern the transportation of the cargo described on the front page of this Waybill. In addition, the provisions set out below shall apply to this Waybill.

(2) Paramount Clause
(a) This Waybill is a non-negotiable document. It is not a bill of lading and no bill of lading will be issued. However, it is agreed that the Hague Rules contained in the International Convention for the Unification of certain rules relating to Bills of Lading, dated Brussels the 25th August 1924 as enacted in the country of shipment shall apply to this Waybill. When no such enactment is in force in the country of shipment, the corresponding legislation of the country of destination shall apply, but in respect of shipments to which no such enactments are compulsorily applicable, the terms of the said Convention shall apply in exactly the same way.

(b) *Trades where Hague-Visby Rules apply.*
In trades where the International Brussels Convention 1924 as amended by the Protocol signed at Brussels on February 23rd 1968 - the Hague-Visby Rules - apply compulsorily, the provisions of the respective legislation shall also apply to this Waybill.

(c) The Carrier shall in no case be responsible for loss of or damage to cargo howsoever arising prior to loading into and after discharge from the Vessel or while the goods are in the charge of another Carrier nor in respect of deck cargo and live animals.

(d) It is agreed that whenever the Brussels Convention and the Brussels Protocol or statutes incorporating same use the words "Bill of Lading" they shall be read and interpreted as meaning "Waybill".

(3) General Average
General Average shall be adjusted, stated and settled according to York-Antwerp Rules 1994 or any modification thereof at the place (if any) agreed in the Voyage Charter Party, as dated overleaf, otherwise in London.

Cargo's contribution to General Average shall be paid to the Carrier even when such average is the result of a fault, neglect or error of the Master, Pilot or Crew.

If the adjustment of General Average or the liability for any collision in which the Vessel is involved while performing the carriage under the terms of the Voyage Charter Party, as dated overleaf, which govern the transportation of the cargo described on the front page of this Waybill, falls to be determined in accordance with the law and practice of the United States of America, the following clauses shall apply:

New Jason Clause
In the event of accident, danger, damage or disaster before or after the commencement of the voyage, resulting from any cause whatsoever, whether due to negligence or not, for which or for the consequence of which, the Carrier is not responsible, by Statute, contract or otherwise, the cargo, shippers, consignees or owners of the cargo shall contribute with the Carrier in general average to the payment of any sacrifices, losses or expenses of a general average nature that may be made or incurred and shall pay salvage and special charges incurred in respect of the cargo.
If a salving vessel is owned or operated by the Carrier, salvage shall be paid for as fully as if the said salving vessel or vessels belonged to strangers. Such deposit as the Carrier, or his agent, may deem sufficient to cover the estimated contribution of the cargo and any salvage and special charges thereon shall, if required, be made by the cargo, shippers, consignees or owners of the cargo to the Carrier before delivery.

Both-to-Blame Collision Clause
If the Vessel comes into collision with another vessel as a result of the negligence of the other vessel and any act, neglect or default of the Master, Mariner, Pilot or the Servants of the Carrier in the navigation or in the management of the Vessel, the owners of the cargo carried hereunder will indemnify the Carrier against all loss or liability to the other or non-carrying vessel or her owners in so far as such loss or liability represents loss of, or damage to, or any claim whatsoever of the owners of the said cargo, paid or payable by the other or non-carrying vessel or her owners to the owners of the said cargo and set-off, recouped or recovered by the other or non-carrying vessel or her owners as part of their claim against the carrying vessel or the Carrier.
The foregoing provisions shall also apply where the owners, operators or those in charge of any vessel or vessels or objects other than, or in addition to, the colliding vessels or objects are at fault in respect of a collision or contact. ·

For particulars of cargo, freight,
destination, etc., see overleaf.

APPENDIX 6

MULTIDOC 95[1]

Code Name: "MULTIDOC 95"

Consignor

MT Doc. No.

Reference No.

Negotiable

MULTIMODAL TRANSPORT BILL OF LADING

Issued by The Baltic and International Maritime Council (BIMCO), subject to the UNCTAD/ICC Rules for Multimodal Transport Documents (ICC Publication No. 481).

Issued 1995

Consigned to order of

Notify party/address

Place of receipt

Ocean Vessel	Port of loading
Port of discharge	Place of delivery
Marks and Nos.	Quantity and description of goods	Gross weight, kg, Measurement, m³

Particulars above declared by Consignor

Freight and charges

RECEIVED the goods in apparent good order and condition, as far as ascertained by reasonable means of checking, as specified above unless otherwise stated.
The MTO, in accordance with and to the extent of the provisions contained in this MT Bill of Lading, and with liberty to sub-contract, undertakes to perform and/or in his own name to procure performance of the multimodal transport and the delivery of the goods, including all services related thereto, from the place and time of taking the goods in charge to the place and time of delivery and accepts responsibility for such transport and such services.
One of the MT Bills of Lading must be surrendered duly endorsed in exchange for the goods or delivery order.
IN WITNESS whereof MT Bill(s) of Lading has/have been signed in the number indicated below, one of which being accomplished the other(s) to be void.

Consignor's declared value of	Freight payable at	Place and date of issue
subject to payment of above extra charge. **Note:** The Merchant's attention is called to the fact that according to Clauses 10 to 12 of this MT Bill of Lading, the liability of the MTO is, in most cases, limited in respect of loss of or damage to the goods.	Number of original MT Bills of Lading	Signed for the Multimodal Transport Operator (MTO) .... as Carrier by .... As agent(s) only to the MTO

Copyright, published by
The Baltic and International Maritime Council
(BIMCO), Copenhagen, 1995

Printed by the BIMCO Charter Party Editor

p.t.o.

---

1   Acknowledgment: the author and publisher thank the Baltic and International Maritime Council (BIMCO) for permission to reproduce MULTIDOC 95.

MULTIMODAL TRANSPORT BILL OF LADING

CODE NAME: "MULTIDOC 95"

I. GENERAL PROVISIONS

1. Applicability

The provisions of this Contract shall apply irrespective of whether there is a unimodal or a Multimodal Transport Contract involving one or several modes of transport.

2. Definitions

"Multimodal Transport Contract" means a single Contract for the carriage of Goods by at least two different modes of transport.

"Multimodal Transport Bill of Lading" (MT Bill of Lading) means this document evidencing a Multimodal Transport Contract and which can be replaced by electronic data interchange messages insofar as permitted by applicable law and is issued in a negotiable form.

"Multimodal Transport Operators" (MTO) means the person named on the face hereof who concludes a Multimodal Transport Contract and assumes responsibility for the performance thereof as a Carrier.

"Carrier" means the person who actually performs or undertakes to perform the carriage, or part thereof, whether he is identical with the Multimodal Transport Operator or not.

"Merchant" includes the Shipper, the Receiver, the Consignor, the Consignee, the holder of this MT Bill of Lading and the owner of the Goods.

"Consignor" means the person who concludes the Multimodal Transport Contract with the Multimodal Transport Operator.

"Consignee" means the person entitled to receive the Goods from the Multimodal Transport Operator.

"Taken in charge" means that the Goods have been handed over to and accepted for carriage by the MTO.

"Delivery" means

(i) the handing over of the Goods to the Consignee; or

(ii) the placing of the Goods at the disposal of the Consignee in accordance with the Multimodal Transport Contract or with the law or usage of the particular trade applicable at the place of delivery; or

(iii) the handing over of the Goods to an authority or other third party to whom, pursuant to the law or regulations applicable at the place of delivery, the Goods must be handed over.

"Special Drawing Rights" (SDR) means the unit of account as defined by the International Monetary Fund.

"Goods" means any property including live animals as well as containers, pallets or similar articles of transport or packaging not supplied by the MTO, irrespective of whether such property is to be or is carried on or under deck.

3. MTO's Tariff

The terms of the MTO's applicable tariff at the date of shipment are incorporated herein. Copies of the relevant provisions of the applicable tariff are available from the MTO upon request. In the case of inconsistency between this MT Bill of Lading and the applicable tariff, this MT Bill of Lading shall prevail.

4. Time Bar

The MTO shall, unless otherwise expressly agreed, be discharged of all liability under this MT Bill of Lading unless suit is brought within nine months after:

(i) the Delivery of the Goods; or

(ii) the date when the Goods should have been delivered; or

(iii) the date when, in accordance with sub-clause 10 (e) failure to deliver the Goods would give the Consignee the right to treat the Goods as lost.

5. Law and Jurisdiction

Disputes arising under this MT Bill of Lading shall be determined by the courts and in accordance with the law at the place where the MTO has his principal place of business.

II. PERFORMANCE OF THE CONTRACT

6. Methods and Routes of Transportation

(a) The MTO is entitled to perform the transport in any reasonable manner and by any reasonable means, methods and routes.

(b) In accordance herewith, for instance, in the event of carriage by sea, vessels may sail with or without pilots, undergo repairs, adjust equipment, drydock and tow vessels in all situations.

7. Optional Stowage

(a) Goods may be stowed by the MTO by means of containers, trailers, transportable tanks, flats, pallets, or similar articles of transport used to consolidate Goods.

(b) Containers, trailers, transportable tanks and covered flats, whether stowed by the MTO or received by him in a stowed condition, may be carried on or under deck without notice to the Merchant.

8. Delivery of the Goods to the Consignee

The MTO undertakes to perform or to procure the performance of all acts necessary to ensure Delivery of the Goods:

(i) when the MT Bill of Lading has been issued in a negotiable form "to bearer", to the person surrendering one original of the document; or

(ii) when the MT Bill of Lading has been issued in a negotiable form "to order", to the person surrendering one original of the document duly endorsed; or

(iii) when the MT Bill of Lading has been issued in a negotiable form to a named person, to that person upon proof of his identity and surrender of one original document; if such document has been transferred "to order" or in blank, the provisions of (ii) above apply.

9. Hindrances, etc. Affecting Performance

(a) The MTO shall use reasonable endeavours to complete the transport and to deliver the Goods at the place designated for Delivery.

(b) If at any time the performance of the Contract as evidenced by this MT Bill of Lading is or will be affected by any hindrance, risk, delay, difficulty or disadvantage of whatsoever kind and if by virtue of sub-clause 9 (a) the MTO has no duty to complete the performance of the Contract, the MTO (whether or not the transport is commenced) may elect to

(i) treat the performance of this Contract as terminated and place the Goods at the Merchant's disposal at any place which the MTO shall deem safe and convenient; or

(ii) deliver the Goods at the place designated for Delivery.

(c) If the Goods are not taken Delivery of by the Merchant within a reasonable time after the MTO has called upon him to take Delivery, the MTO shall be at liberty to put the Goods in safe custody on behalf of the Merchant at the latter's risk and expense.

(d) In any event the MTO shall be entitled to full freight for Goods received for transportation and additional compensation for extra costs resulting from the circumstances referred to above.

III. LIABILITY OF THE MTO

10. Basis of Liability

(a) The responsibility of the MTO for the Goods under this Contract covers the period from the time the MTO has taken the Goods into his charge to the time of their Delivery.

(b) Subject to the defences set forth in Clauses 11 and 12, the MTO shall be liable for loss of or damage to the Goods as well as for delay in Delivery, if the occurrence which caused the loss, damage or delay in Delivery took place while the Goods were in his charge as defined in sub-clause 10 (a), unless the MTO proves that no fault or neglect of his own, his servants or agents or any other person referred to in sub-clause 10 (c) has caused or contributed to the loss damage or delay in Delivery.

However, the MTO shall only be liable for loss following from delay in Delivery if the Consignor has made a written declaration of interest in timely Delivery which has been accepted in writing by the MTO.

(c) The MTO shall be responsible for the acts and omissions of his servants or agents, when any such servant or agent is acting within the scope of his employment, or of any other person of whose services he makes use for the performance of the Contract, as if such acts and omissions were his own.

(d) Delay in Delivery occurs when the Goods have not been delivered within the time expressly agreed upon or, in the absence of such agreement, within the time which it would be reasonable to require of a diligent MTO, having regard to the circumstances of the case.

(e) If the Goods have not been delivered within ninety (90) consecutive days following the date of Delivery determined according to Clause 10 (d) above, the claimant may, in the absence of evidence to the contrary, treat the Goods as lost.

11. Defences for Carriage by Sea or Inland Waterways

Notwithstanding the provisions of Clause 10 (b), the MTO shall not be responsible for loss, damage or delay in Delivery with respect to Goods carried by sea or inland waterways when such loss, damage or delay during such carriage results from:

(i) act, neglect or default of the master, mariner, pilot or the servants of the Carrier in the navigation or in the management of the vessel;

(ii) fire, unless caused by the actual fault or privity of the Carrier;

(iii) the causes listed in the Hague-Visby Rules article 4.2 (c) to (p);

however, always provided that whenever loss or damage has resulted from unseaworthiness of the vessel, the MTO can prove that due diligence has been exercised to make the vessel seaworthy at the commencement of the voyage.

12. Limitation of Liability

(a) Unless the nature and value of the Goods have been declared by the Consignor before the Goods have been taken in charge by the MTO and inserted in the MT Bill of Lading, the MTO shall in no event be or become liable for any loss of or damage to the Goods in an amount exceeding:

(i) when the Carriage of Goods by Sea Act of the United States of America, 1936 (US COGSA) applies USD 500 per package or customary freight unit; or

(ii) when any other law applies, the equivalent of 666.67 SDR per package or unit or two SDR per kilogramme of gross weight of the Goods lost or damaged, whichever is the higher.

(b) Where a container, pallet or similar article of transport is loaded with more than one package or unit, the packages or other shipping units enumerated in the MT Bill of Lading as packed in such article of transport are deemed packages or shipping units. Except as aforesaid, such article of transport shall be considered the package or unit.

(c) Notwithstanding the above-mentioned provisions, if the Multimodal Transport does not, according to the Contract, include carriage of Goods by sea or by inland waterways, the liability of the MTO shall be limited to an amount not exceeding 8.33 SDR per kilogramme of gross weight of the Goods lost or damaged.

(d) In any case, when the loss of or damage to the Goods occurred during one particular stage of the Multimodal Transport, in respect of which an applicable international convention or mandatory national law would have provided another limit of liability if a separate contract of carriage had been made for that particular stage of transport, then the limit of the MTO's liability for such loss or damage shall be determined by reference to the provisions of such convention or mandatory national law.

(e) If the MTO is liable in respect of loss following from delay in Delivery, or consequential loss or damage other than loss of or damage to the Goods, the liability of the MTO shall be limited to an amount not exceeding the equivalent of the freight under the Multimodal Transport Contract for the Multimodal Transport.

(f) The aggregate liability of the MTO shall not exceed the limits of liability for total loss of the Goods.

(g) The MTO is not entitled to the benefit of the limitation of liability if it is proved that the loss, damage or delay in Delivery resulted from a personal act or omission of the MTO done with the intent to cause such loss, damage or delay, or recklessly and with knowledge that such loss, damage or delay would probably result.

13. Assessment of Compensation

(a) Assessment of compensation for loss of or damage to the Goods shall be made by reference to the value of such Goods at the place and time they are delivered to the Consignee or at the place and time when, in accordance with the Multimodal Transport Contract, they should have been so delivered.

(b) The value of the Goods shall be determined according to the current commodity exchange price or, if there is no such price, according to the current market price or, if there is no commodity exchange price or current market price, by reference to the normal value of Goods of the same kind and quality.

14. Notice of loss of or Damage to the Goods

(a) Unless notice of loss of or damage to the Goods, specifying the general nature of such loss or damage, is given in writing by the Consignee to the MTO when the Goods are handed over to the Consignee, such handing over is prima facie evidence of the Delivery by the MTO of the Goods as described in the MT Bill of Lading.

(b) Where the loss or damage is not apparent, the same prima facie effect shall apply if notice in writing is not given within six consecutive days after the day when the Goods were handed over to the Consignee.

15. Defences and Limits for the MTO, Servants, etc.

(a) The provisions of this Contract apply to all claims against the MTO relating to the performance of the Multimodal Transport Contract, whether the claim be founded in contract or in tort.

(b) The Merchant undertakes that no claim shall be made against any servant, agent or other persons whose services the MTO has used in order to perform the Multimodal Transport Contract and if any claim should nevertheless be made, to indemnify the MTO against all consequences thereof.

(c) However, the provisions of this Contract apply whenever claims relating to the performance of the Multimodal Transport Contract are made against any servant, agent or other person whose services the MTO has used in order to perform the Multimodal Transport Contract, whether such claims are founded in contract or in tort. In entering into this Contract, the MTO, to the extent of such provisions, does so not only on his own behalf but also as agent or trustee for such persons. The aggregate liability of the MTO and such persons shall not exceed the limits in Clause 12.

IV. DESCRIPTION OF GOODS

16. MTO's Responsibility

The information in the MT Bill of Lading shall be prima facie evidence of the taking in charge by the MTO of the Goods as described by such information unless a contrary indication, such as "shipper's weight, load and counts", "shipper-packed container" or similar expressions, have been made in the printed text or superimposed on the document. Proof to the contrary shall not be admissible when the MT Bill of Lading has been transferred, or the equivalent electronic data interchange message has been transmitted to and acknowledged by the Consignee who in good faith has relied and acted thereon.

17. Consignor's Responsibility

(a) The Consignor shall be deemed to have guaranteed to the MTO the accuracy, at the time the Goods were taken in charge by the MTO, of all particulars relating to the general nature of the Goods, their marks, number, weight, volume and quantity and, if applicable, to the dangerous character of the Goods as furnished by him or on his behalf for insertion in the MT Bill of Lading.

(b) The Consignor shall indemnify the MTO for any loss or expense caused by inaccuracies in or inadequacies of the particulars referred to above.

(c) The right of the MTO to such indemnity shall in no way limit his liability under the Multimodal Transport Contract to any person other than the Consignor.

(d) The Consignor shall remain liable even if the MT Bill of Lading has been transferred by him.

18. Return of Containers

(a) Containers, pallets or similar articles of transport supplied by or on behalf of the MTO shall be returned to the MTO in the same order and condition as when handed over to the Merchant, normal wear and tear excepted, with interiors clean and within the time prescribed in the MTO's tariff or elsewhere.

(b) (i) The Consignor shall be liable for any loss of, damage to, or delay, including demurrage, of such articles, incurred during the period between handing over to the Consignor and return to the MTO for carriage.

(ii) The Consignor and the Consignee shall be jointly and severally liable for any loss of, damage to, or delay, including demurrage, of such articles, incurred during the period between handing over to the Consignee and return to the MTO.

19. Dangerous Goods

(a) The Consignor shall comply with all internationally recognised requirements and all rules which apply according to national law or by reason of international convention, relating to the carriage of Goods of a dangerous nature, and shall in any event inform the MTO in writing of the exact nature of the danger before Goods of a dangerous nature are taken in charge by the MTO and indicate to him, if need be, the precautions to be taken.

(b) If the Consignor fails to provide such information and the MTO is unaware of the dangerous nature of the Goods and the necessary precautions to be taken and if, at any time, they are deemed to be a hazard to life or property, they may at any place be unloaded, destroyed or rendered harmless, as circumstances may require, without compensation and the Consignor shall be liable for all loss, damage, delay or expenses arising out of their being taken in charge, or their carriage, or of any service incidental thereto.

The burden of proving that the MTO knew the exact nature of the danger constituted by the carriage of the said Goods shall rest upon the person entitled to the Goods.

(c) If any Goods shipped with the knowledge of the MTO as to their dangerous nature shall become a danger to the vessel or cargo, they may in like manner be landed at any place or destroyed or rendered innocuous by the MTO without liability on the part of the MTO except to General Average, if any.

20. Consignor-packed Containers, etc.

(a) If a container has not been filled, packed or stowed by the MTO, the MTO shall not be liable for any loss of or damage to its contents and the Consignor shall indemnify any loss or expense incurred by the MTO if such loss, damage or expense has been caused by:

(i) negligent filling, packing or stowing of the container;

(ii) the contents being unsuitable for carriage in container; or

(iii) the unsuitability or defective condition of the container unless the container has been supplied by the MTO and the unsuitability or defective condition would not have been apparent upon reasonable inspection at or prior to the time when the container was filled, packed or stowed.

(b) The provisions of sub-clause (a) of this Clause also apply with respect to trailers, transportable tanks, flats and pallets which have not been filled, packed or stowed by the MTO.

(c) The MTO does not accept liability for damage due to the unsuitability or defective condition of reefer equipment or trailers supplied by the Merchant.

V. FREIGHT AND LIEN

21. Freight

(a) Freight shall be deemed earned when the Goods have been taken into charge by the MTO and shall be paid in any event.

(b) The Merchant's attention is drawn to the stipulations concerning currency in which the freight and charges are to be paid, rate of exchange, devaluation and other contingencies relative to freight and charges in the relevant tariff conditions. If no such stipulation as to devaluation exists or is applicable the following provision shall apply:

If the currency in which freight and charges are quoted is devalued or revalued between the date of the freight agreement and the date when the freight and charges are paid, then all freight and charges shall be automatically and immediately changed in proportion to the extent of the devaluation or revaluation of the said currency. When the MTO has consented to payment in other currency than the above mentioned currency, then all freight and charges shall - subject to the preceding paragraph - be paid at the highest selling rate of exchange for banker's sight draft current on the day when such freight and charges are paid. If the banks are closed on the day when the freight is paid the rate to be used will be the one in force on the last day the banks were open.

(c) For the purpose of verifying the freght basis the MTO reserves the right to have the contents of containers, trailers or similar articles of transport inspected in order to ascertain the weight, measurement, value, or nature of the Goods. If on such inspection it is found that the declaration is not correct, it is agreed that a sum equal either to five times the difference between the correct freight and the freight charges or to double the correct freight less the freight charges, whichever sum is the smaller, shall be payable as liquidated damages to the MTO notwithstanding any other sum having been stated on this MT Bill of Lading as the freight payable.

(d) All dues, taxes and charges levied on the Goods and other expenses in connection therewith shall be paid by the Merchant.

22. Lien

The MTO shall have a lien on the Goods for any amount due under this Contract and for the costs of recovering the same, and may enforce such lien in any reasonable manner, including sale or disposal of the Goods.

VI. MISCELLANEOUS PROVISIONS

23. General Average

(a) General Average shall be adjusted at any port or place at the MTO's option, and to be settled according to the York-Antwerp Rules 1994, or any modification thereof, this covering all Goods, whether carried on or under deck. The New Jason Clause as approved by BIMCO to be considered as incorporated herein.

(b) Such security including a cash deposit as the MTO may deem sufficient to cover the estimated contribution of the Goods and any salvage and special charges thereon, shall, if required, be submitted to the MTO prior to Delivery of the Goods.

24. Both-to-Blame Collision Clause

The Both-to-Blame Collision Clause as adopted by BIMCO shall be considered incorporated herein.

25. U.S. Trade

In case the Contract evidenced by this MT Bill of Lading is subject to U.S COGSA, then the Provisions stated in said Act shall govern before loading and after discharge and throughout

APPENDIX 7

NEGOTIABLE FIATA MULTIMODAL TRANSPORT BILL OF LADING[1]

Consignor	**FBL** FBL No. Customs Reference/Status **G B** **BIFA** Shipper's Reference ↶ Forwarder's Reference
Consigned to order of	NEGOTIABLE FIATA MULTIMODAL TRANSPORT BILL OF LADING Issued subject to UNCTAD/ICC Rules for Multimodal Transport Documents (ICC Publication 481) **ICC**
Notify address	

Container Number	Place of receipt
Ocean Vessel	Port of loading
Port of discharge	Place of delivery

Marks and numbers	Number and kind of packages:	Description of goods	Gross weight	Measurement

COPY FOR INFORMATION ONLY

according to the declaration of the consignor

Declaration of interest of the consignor in timely delivery (Clause 6.2.)	Declared value for ad valorem rate according to the declaration of the consignor (Clauses 7 and 8)

The goods and instructions are accepted and dealt with subject to the Standard Conditions printed overleaf.

Taken in charge in apparent good order and condition, unless otherwise noted herein, at the place of receipt for transport and delivery as mentioned above.

One of these Multimodal Transport Bills of Lading must be surrendered duly endorsed in exchange for goods. In Witness whereof the original Multimodal Transport Bills of Lading all this tenor and date have been signed in the number stated below, one of which being accomplished the other(s) to be void.

Freight amount	Freight payable at	Place and date of issue
Cargo Insurance through the undersigned ☐ not covered ☐ covered according to attached policy	Number of Original FBL's	Stamp and signature
For delivery of goods please apply to		
		As Carrier

1   Acknowledgment: the author and publisher thank the BIFA for permission to reproduce Negotiable FIATA Multimodal Transport Bill of Lading.

Standard Conditions (1992) governing the FIATA MULTIMODAL TRANSPORT BILL OF LADING

Definitions

- «Freight Forwarder» means the Multimodal Transport Operator who issues this FBL and is named on the face of it and assumes liability for the performance of the multimodal transport contract as a carrier.
- «Merchant» means and includes the Shipper, the Consignor, the Consignee, the Holder of this FBL, the Receiver and the Owner of the Goods.
- «Consignor» means the person who concludes the multimodal transport contract with the Freight Forwarder.
- «Consignee» means the person entitled to receive the goods from the Freight Forwarder.
- «Taken in charge» means that the goods have been handed over to and accepted for carriage by the Freight Forwarder at the place of receipt evidenced in this FBL.
- «Goods» means any property including live animals as well as containers, pallets or similar articles of transport or packaging not supplied by the Freight Forwarder, irrespective of whether such property is to be or is carried on or under deck.

1. **Applicability**
Notwithstanding the heading «FIATA Multimodal Transport Bill of Lading (FBL)» these conditions shall also apply if only one mode of transport is used.

2. **Issuance of this FBL**

2.1. By issuance of this FBL the Freight Forwarder
a) undertakes to perform and/or in his own name to procure the performance of the entire transport, from the place at which the goods are taken in charge (place of receipt evidenced in this FBL) to the place of delivery designated in this FBL;
b) assumes liability as set out in these conditions.

2.2. Subject to the conditions of this FBL the Freight Forwarder shall be responsible for the acts and omissions of his servants or agents acting within the scope of their employment, or any other person of whose services he makes use for the performance of the contract evidenced by this FBL, as if such acts and omissions were his own.

3. **Negotiability and title to the goods**

3.1. This FBL is issued in a negotiable form unless it is marked «non negotiable». It shall constitute title to the goods and the holder, by endorsement of this FBL, shall be entitled to receive or to transfer the goods herein mentioned.

3.2. The information in this FBL shall be prima facie evidence of the taking in charge by the Freight Forwarder of the goods as described by such information unless a contrary indication, such as «shipper's weight, load and count», «shipper-packed container» or similar expressions, has been made in the printed text or superimposed on this FBL. However, proof to the contrary shall not be admissible when the FBL has been transferred to the consignee for valuable consideration who in good faith has relied and acted thereon.

4. **Dangerous Goods and Indemnity**

4.1. The Merchant shall comply with rules which are mandatory according to the national law or by reason of International Convention, relating to the carriage of goods of a dangerous nature, and shall in any case inform the Freight Forwarder in writing of the exact nature of the danger, before goods of a dangerous nature are taken in charge by the Freight Forwarder and indicate to him, if need be, the precautions to be taken.

4.2. If the Merchant fails to provide such information and the Freight Forwarder is unaware of the dangerous nature of the goods and the necessary precautions to be taken and if, at any time, they are deemed to be a hazard to life or property, they may at any place be unloaded, destroyed or rendered harmless, as circumstances may require, without compensation. The Merchant shall indemnify the Freight Forwarder against all loss, damage, liability, or expense arising out of their being taken in charge, or their carriage, or of any service incidental thereto.
The burden of proving that the Freight Forwarder knew the exact nature of the danger constituted by the carriage of the said goods shall rest on the Merchant.

4.3. If any goods shall become a danger to life or property, they may in like manner be unloaded or landed at any place or destroyed or rendered harmless. If such danger was not caused by the fault and neglect of the Freight Forwarder he shall have no liability and the Merchant shall indemnify him against all loss, damage, liability and expense arising therefrom.

5. **Description of Goods and Merchant's Packing and Inspection**

5.1. The Consignor shall be deemed to have guaranteed to the Freight Forwarder the accuracy, at the time the goods were taken in charge by the Freight Forwarder, of all particulars relating to the general nature of the goods, their marks, number, weight, volume and quantity and, if applicable, to the dangerous character of the goods, as furnished by him or on his behalf for insertion on the FBL.
The Consignor shall indemnify the Freight Forwarder against all loss, damage and expense resulting from any inaccuracy or inadequacy of such particulars.
The Consignor shall remain liable even if the FBL has been transferred by him.
The right of the Freight Forwarder to such an indemnity shall in no way limit his liability under this FBL to any person other than the Consignor.

5.2. The Freight Forwarder shall not be liable for any loss, damage or expense caused by defective or insufficient packing of goods or by inadequate loading or packing within containers or other transport units when such loading or packing has been performed by the Merchant or on his behalf by a person other than the Freight Forwarder, or by the defect or unsuitability of the containers or other transport units supplied by the Merchant, or if supplied by the Freight Forwarder if a defect or unsuitability of the container or other transport unit would have been apparent upon reasonable inspection by the Merchant. The Merchant shall indemnify the Freight Forwarder against all loss, damage, liability and expense so caused.

6. **Freight Forwarder's Liability**

6.1. The responsibility of the Freight Forwarder for the goods under these conditions covers the period from the time the Freight Forwarder has taken the goods in his charge to the time of their delivery.

6.2. The Freight Forwarder shall be liable for loss of or damage to the goods as well as for delay in delivery if the occurrence which caused the loss, damage or delay in delivery took place while the goods were in his charge as defined in Clause 2.1 a, unless the Freight Forwarder proves that no fault or neglect of his own, his servants or agents or any other person referred to in Clause 2.2. has caused or contributed to such loss, damage or delay. However, the Freight Forwarder shall only be liable for loss following from delay in delivery if the Consignor has made a declaration of interest in timely delivery which has been accepted by the Freight Forwarder and stated in this FBL.

6.3. Arrival times are not guaranteed by the Freight Forwarder. However, delay in delivery occurs when the goods have not been delivered within the time expressly agreed upon or, in the absence of such agreement, within the time which would be reasonable to require of a diligent Freight Forwarder, having regard to the circumstances of the case.

6.4. If the goods have not been delivered within ninety consecutive days following such date of delivery as determined in Clause 6.3., the claimant may, in the absence of evidence to the contrary, treat the goods as lost.

6.5. When the Freight Forwarder establishes that, in the circumstances of the case, the loss or damage could be attributed to one or more causes or events, specified in a – e of the present clause, it shall be presumed that it was so caused, always provided, however, that the claimant shall be entitled to prove that the loss or damage was not, in fact, caused wholly or partly by one or more of such causes or events:
a) an act or omission of the Merchant, or person other than the Freight Forwarder acting on behalf of the Merchant or from whom the Freight Forwarder took the goods in charge;
b) insufficiency or defective condition of the packaging or marks and/or numbers;
c) handling, loading, stowage or unloading of the goods by the Merchant or any person acting on behalf of the Merchant;
d) inherent vice of the goods;
e) strike, lockout, stoppage or restraint of labour.

6.6. **Defences for carriage by sea or inland waterways**
Notwithstanding Clauses 6.2., 6.3. and 6.4. the Freight Forwarder shall not be liable for loss, damage or delay in delivery with respect to goods carried by sea or inland waterways when such loss, damage or delay during such carriage has been caused by:
a) act, neglect, or default of the master, mariner, pilot or the servants of the carrier in the navigation or in the management of the ship,
b) fire, unless caused by the actual fault or privity of the carrier, however, always provided that whenever loss or damage has resulted from unseaworthiness of the ship, the Freight Forwarder can prove that due diligence has been exercised to make the ship seaworthy at the commencement of the voyage.

7. **Paramount Clauses**

7.1. These conditions shall only take effect to the extent that they are not contrary to the mandatory provisions of International Conventions or national law applicable to the contract evidenced by this FBL.

7.2. The Hague Rules contained in the International Convention for the unification of certain rules relating to Bills of Lading, dated Brussels 25th August 1924, or in those countries where they are already in force the Hague-Visby Rules contained in the Protocol of Brussels, dated 23rd February 1968, as enacted in the Country of Shipment, shall apply to all carriage of goods by sea and also to the carriage of goods by inland waterways, and such provisions shall apply to all goods whether carried on deck or under deck.

7.3. The Carriage of Goods by Sea Act of the United States of America (COGSA) shall apply to the carriage of goods by sea, whether on deck or under deck, if compulsorily applicable to this FBL or would be applicable but for the goods being carried on deck in accordance with a statement on this FBL.

8. **Limitation of Freight Forwarder's Liability**

8.1. Assessment of compensation for loss of or damage to the goods shall be made by reference to the value of such goods at the place and time they are delivered to the consignee or at the place and time when, in accordance with this FBL, they should have been so delivered.

8.2. The value of the goods shall be determined according to the current commodity exchange price or, if there is no such price, according to the current market price or, if there are no such prices, by reference to the normal value of goods of the same name and quality.

8.3. Subject to the provisions of subclauses 8.4. to 8.9. inclusive, the Freight Forwarder shall in no event be or become liable for any loss of or damage to the goods in an amount exceeding the equivalent of 666.67 SDR per package or unit or 2 SDR per kilogramme of gross weight of the goods lost or damaged, whichever is the higher, unless the nature and value of the goods shall have been declared by the Consignor and accepted by the Freight Forwarder before the goods have been taken in his charge, or the ad valorem freight rate paid, and such value is stated in the FBL by him, then such declared value shall be the limit.

8.4. Where a container, pallet or similar article of transport is loaded with more than one package or unit, the packages or other shipping units enumerated in the FBL as packed in such article of transport are deemed packages or shipping units. Except as aforesaid, such article of transport shall be considered the package or unit.

8.5. Notwithstanding the above mentioned provisions, if the multimodal transport does not, according to the contract, include carriage of goods by sea or by inland waterways, the liability of the Freight Forwarder shall be limited to an amount not exceeding 8.33 SDR per kilogramme of gross weight of the goods lost or damaged.

8.6. a) When the loss of or damage to the goods occurred during one particular stage of the multimodal transport, in respect of which an applicable international convention or mandatory national law would have provided another limit of liability if a separate contract of carriage had been made for that particular stage of transport, then the limit of the Freight Forwarder's liability for such loss or damage shall be determined by reference to the provisions of such convention or mandatory national law.
b) Unless the nature and value of the goods shall have been declared by the Merchant and inserted in this FBL, and the ad valorem freight rate paid, the liability of the Freight Forwarder under COGSA, where applicable, shall not exceed US$ 500 per package or, in the case of goods not shipped in packages, per customary freight unit.

8.7. If the Freight Forwarder is liable in respect of loss following from delay in delivery, or consequential loss or damage other than loss of or damage to the goods, the liability of the Freight Forwarder shall be limited to an amount not exceeding the equivalent of twice the freight under the multimodal contract for the multimodal transport under this FBL.

8.8. The aggregate liability of Freight Forwarder shall not exceed the limits of liability for total loss of the goods.

8.9. The Freight Forwarder is not entitled to the benefit of the limitation of liability if it is proved that the loss, damage or delay in delivery resulted from a personal act or omission of the Freight Forwarder done with the intent to cause such loss, damage or delay, or recklessly and with knowledge that such loss, damage or delay would probably result.

9. **Applicability to Actions in Tort**
These conditions apply to all claims against the Freight Forwarder relating to the performance of the contract evidenced by this FBL, whether the claim be founded in contract or in tort.

10. **Liability of Servants and other Persons**

10.1. These conditions apply whenever claims relating to the performance of the contract evidenced by this FBL are made against any servant, agent or other person (including any independent contractor) whose services have been used in order to perform the contract, whether such claims are founded in contract or in tort, and the aggregate liability of the Freight Forwarder and of such servants, agents or other persons shall not exceed the limits in clause 8.

10.2. In entering into this contract as evidenced by this FBL, the Freight Forwarder, to the extent of these provisions, does not only act on his own behalf, but also as agent or trustee for such persons, and such persons shall to this extent be or be deemed to be parties to this contract.

10.3. However, if it is proved that the loss of or such loss or damage to the goods resulted from a personal act or omission of such a person referred to in Clause 10.1., done with intent to cause damage, or recklessly and with knowledge that damage would probably result, such person shall not be entitled to benefit of limitation of liability provided for in Clause 8.

10.4. The aggregate of the amounts recoverable from the Freight Forwarder and the persons referred to in Clauses 2.2. and 10.1. shall not exceed the limits provided for in these conditions.

11. **Method and Route of Transportation**
Without notice to the Merchant, the Freight Forwarder has the liberty to carry the goods on or under deck and to choose or substitute the means, route and procedure to be followed in the handling, stowage, storage and transportation of the goods.

12. **Delivery**

12.1. Goods shall be deemed to be delivered when they have been handed over or placed at the disposal of the Consignee or his agent in accordance with this FBL, or when the goods have been handed over to any authority or other party to whom, pursuant to the law or regulation applicable at the place of delivery, the goods must be handed over, or such other place at which the Freight Forwarder is entitled to call upon the Merchant to take delivery.

12.2. The Freight Forwarder shall also be entitled to store the goods at the sole risk of the Merchant, and the Freight Forwarder's liability shall cease, and the cost of such storage shall be paid, upon demand, by the Merchant to the Freight Forwarder.

12.3. If at any time the carriage unter this FBL is or is likely to be affected by any hindrance or risk of any kind (including the condition of the goods) not arising from any fault or neglect of the Freight Forwarder or a person referred to in Clause 2.2. and which cannot be avoided by the exercise of reasonable endeavours the Freight Forwarder may:
abandon the carriage of the goods under this FBL and, where reasonably possible, place the goods or any part of them at the Merchant's disposal at any place which the Freight Forwarder may deem safe and convenient, whereupon delivery shall be deemed to have been made, and the responsibility of the Freight Forwarder in respect of such goods shall cease.
In any event, the Freight Forwarder shall be entitled to full freight under this FBL and the Merchant shall pay any additional costs resulting from the above mentioned circumstances.

13. **Freight and Charges**

13.1. Freight shall be paid in cash, without any reduction or deferment on account of any claim, counterclaim or set-off, whether prepaid or payable at destination.
Freight shall be considered as earned by the Freight Forwarder at the moment when the goods have been taken in his charge, and not to be returned in any event.

13.2. Freight and all other amounts mentioned in this FBL are to be paid in the currency named in this FBL or, at the Freight Forwarder's option, in the currency of the country of dispatch or destination at the highest rate of exchange for bankers sight bills current for prepaid freight on the day of dispatch and for freight payable at destination on the day when the Merchant is notified on arrival of the goods there or on the date of withdrawal of the delivery order, whichever rate is the higher, or at the option of the Freight Forwarder on the date of this FBL.

13.3. All dues, taxes and charges or other expenses in connection with the goods shall be paid by the Merchant.
Where equipment is supplied by the Freight Forwarder, the Merchant shall pay all demurrage and charges which are not due to a fault or neglect of the Freight Forwarder.

13.4. The Merchant shall reimburse the Freight Forwarder in proportion to the amount of freight for any costs for deviation or delay or any other increase of costs of whatever nature caused by war, warlike operations, epidemics, strikes, government directions or force majeure.

13.5. The Merchant warrants the correctness of the declaration of contents, insurance, weight, measurements or value of the goods but the Freight Forwarder has the liberty to have the contents inspected and the weight, measurements or value verified. If on such inspection it is found that the declaration is not correct it is agreed that a sum equal either to five times the difference between the correct figure and the freight charged, or to double the correct freight less the freight charged, whichever sum is the smaller, shall be payable as liquidated damages to the Freight Forwarder for his inspection costs and losses of freight on other goods notwithstanding any other sum having been stated on this FBL as freight payable.

13.6. Despite the acceptance by the Freight Forwarder of instructions to collect freight, charges or other expenses from any other person in respect of the transport under this FBL, the Merchant shall remain responsible for such monies on receipt of evidence of demand and the absence of payment for whatever reason.

14. **Lien**
The Freight Forwarder shall have a lien on the goods and any documents relating thereto for any amount due at any time to the Freight Forwarder from the Merchant including storage fees and the cost of recovering same, and may enforce such lien in any reasonable manner which he may think fit.

15. **General Average**
The Merchant shall indemnify the Freight Forwarder in respect of any claims of a General Average nature which may be made on him and shall provide such security as may be required by the Freight Forwarder in this connection.

16. **Notice**

16.1. Unless notice of loss of or damage to the goods, specifying the general nature of such loss or damage, is given in writing by the consignee to the Freight Forwarder when the goods are delivered to the consignee in accordance with clause 12, such handing over is prima facie evidence of the delivery by the Freight Forwarder of the goods as described in this FBL.

16.2. Where the loss or damage is not apparent, the same prima facie effect shall apply if notice in writing is not given within 6 consecutive days after the day when the goods were delivered to the consignee in accordance with clause 12.

17. **Time bar**
The Freight Forwarder shall, unless otherwise expressly agreed, be discharged of all liability under these conditions unless suit is brought within 9 months after the delivery of the goods, or the date when the goods should have been delivered, or the date when in accordance with clause 6.4. failure to deliver the goods would give the consignee the right to treat the goods as lost.

18. **Partial Invalidity**
If any clause or a part thereof is held to be invalid, the validity of this FBL and the remaining clauses or a part thereof shall not be affected.

19. **Jurisdiction and applicable law**
Actions against the Freight Forwarder may be instituted only in the place where the Freight Forwarder has his place of business as stated on the reverse of this FBL and shall be decided according to the law of the country in which that place of business is situated.

The ICC logo denotes that this document has been deemed by the ICC to be in conformity with the UNCTAD/ICC Rules for Multimodal Transport Documents. The ICC logo does not imply ICC endorsement of the document nor does it in any way make the ICC party to any possible legal action resulting from the use of this document.

INDEX